CW01209402

MOUNT GRACE PRIORY

EXCAVATIONS OF 1957–1992

MOUNT GRACE PRIORY

Excavations of 1957–1992

by

Glyn Coppack and Laurence Keen

With contributions by

Colin Hayfield, Andrew Saunders, Jackie Hall, Mark Dinnin,
Andrew Jones, Brian Irvine and Kevin Leahy

OXBOW | books
Oxford & Philadelphia

Published in the United Kingdom in 2019 by
OXBOW BOOKS
The Old Music Hall, 106–108 Cowley Road, Oxford, OX4 1JE

and in the United States by
OXBOW BOOKS
1950 Lawrence Road, Havertown, PA 19083

© Historic England. Historic England thanks Oxbow Books for publishing this volume on their behalf.

Hardcover Edition: ISBN 978-1-78925-314-6
Digital Edition: ISBN 978-1-78925-315-3

A CIP record for this book is available from the British Library

Library of Congress Control Number: 2019945301

All rights reserved. No part of this book may be reproduced or transmitted in any form or by any means, electronic or mechanical including photocopying, recording or by any information storage and retrieval system, without permission from the publisher in writing.

Printed in the United Kingdom by Short Run Press

Typeset in India for Casemate Publishing Services. www.casematepublishingservices.com

For a complete list of Oxbow titles, please contact:

UNITED KINGDOM
Oxbow Books
Telephone (01865) 241249
Email: oxbow@oxbowbooks.com
www.oxbowbooks.com

UNITED STATES OF AMERICA
Oxbow Books
Telephone (610) 853-9131, Fax (610) 853-9146
Email: queries@casemateacademic.com
www.casemateacademic.com/oxbow

Oxbow Books is part of the Casemate Group

This volume has been funded by Historic England (formerly English Heritage)

Historic England

Front cover: The church at Mount Grace seen from the south-west (G. Coppack).
Back cover: The charterhouse of Witham (after RCHM(E)).

Contents

List of figures   vii
List of tables   xi
Summary   xiii
Foreign language summaries   xiv
Preface   xvii

CHAPTER 1: MOUNT GRACE PRIORY AND THE CARTHUSIAN ORDER   1
1.1 Origins of the Carthusian Order   1
1.2 Spread of the Carthusian Order   2
1.3 Carthusian Life   3
1.4 Layout of Carthusian Monasteries   4
1.5 The Carthusians in England   6

CHAPTER 2: HISTORY AND TOPOGRAPHY OF MOUNT GRACE PRIORY   27
2.1 History of the Charterhouse   27
2.2 The Estates, Demesnes and Site of Mount Grace Priory   32
2.3 Priory Community and the Local People   37
2.4 Suppression and Later History of Mount Grace   43

CHAPTER 3: THE SITE OF MOUNT GRACE PRIORY AND ITS ARCHAEOLOGICAL HISTORY   47
3.1 Site of the Priory   47
3.2 Previous Archaeological Excavation at Mount Grace Priory   51

CHAPTER 4: THE ARCHAEOLOGY OF THE GREAT CLOISTER   59
4.1 Note on Finds Numbering and Context Numbers   59
4.2 The Monks' Cells   60

CHAPTER 5: THE ARCHAEOLOGY OF THE INNER COURT   165
5.1 The South-west Cloister Range   165
5.2. The Guest House and Kitchen Ranges   215
5.3 The Cells of the Lesser Cloister   244
5.4 The South Range of the Inner Court   250

CHAPTER 6: THE BUILDINGS AND INFRASTRUCTURE OF MOUNT GRACE PRIORY AND THEIR DEVELOPMENT   255
6.1 The Development of the Priory Buildings 1398–1539   260
6.2 Water Supply and Drainage   293
6.3 The Development of the Guest-house Range 1540–1901   301

Chapter 7: The Cultural Collections		307
7.1	The Setting of the Site Evidenced by Insect Remains, *by Mark Dinnin*	307
7.2	Pottery, *by Colin Hayfield*	311
7.3	Coins and Jettons, *by Kevin Leahy*	324
7.4	The Ceramic Floor Tiles, *by Laurence Keen, with contributions by D F Williams and Sarah Paynter*	326
7.5	Fish Remains from the Kitchen and South-west Cloister Range, *by Brian Irving and Andrew Jones*	333
7.6	Small Finds, *by Laurence Keen*	341
7.7	Architectural Detail, *by Jackie Hall and Glyn Coppack*	349
7.8	Window Glass, *by Glyn Coppack*	352
Chapter 8: The Significance of the Mount Grace Project		357
8.1	Mount Grace Priory and its Significance	357
8.2	Future Research	402
Bibliography		405
Index		413

List of figures

Figure 1.1 The early 9th-century plan of St Gall Abbey.
Figure 1.2 The English charterhouses with the dates of their foundation.
Figure 1.3 The charterhouse of Witham (after RCHM(E)).
Figure 1.4 The charterhouse of Hinton (after Fletcher, with additions).
Figure 1.5 The earthworks of Hinton charterhouse (after RCHM(E)).
Figure 1.6 The charterhouse of Beauvale (after Hill and Gill 1908).
Figure 1.7 The earthworks of Beauvale charterhouse (after RCHM(E))
Figure 1.8 The charterhouse of London (after Grimes 1968, and Barber and Thomas 2002).
Figure 1.9 The charterhouse of Coventry (after Soden and RCHM(E), with additions).
Figure 1.10 The charterhouse of Axholme (after RCHM(E)).
Figure 1.11 The charterhouse of Mount Grace (after RCHM(E), with additions).
Figure 1.12 The charterhouse of Sheen (after Cloake 1990, with additions).
Figure 2.1 The foundation charter of Mount Grace Priory. This is the copy owned by the de Ingleby family and is now in the West Yorkshire Archives (Cat. no. Wyl230/25). The copies belonging to de Holand and the charterhouse are lost.
Figure 2.2 The national estates of Mount Grace.
Figure 2.3 The northern, local estates of Mount Grace, from the *Valor Ecclesiasticus* and Ministers' Accounts.
Figure 2.4 Plan of the estate of Mount Grace, 1768 (North Yorks County Record Office).
Figure 3.1 The precinct of Mount Grace Priory.
Figure 3.2 a) Plan of Mount Grace by William Riley, 1882. b) Plan of Mount Grace by William St John Hope, 1896.
Figure 3.3 Location plan of excavations at Mount Grace since 1957.
Figure 4.1 The sacrist's cell.
Figure 4.2 Cell 1.
Figure 4.3 Cell 1: cloister door, bearing the arms of Archbishop Scrope on the label stops (G. Coppack).
Figure 4.4 Cell 2.
Figure 4.5 Cell 2: section through the precinct wall and latrine pentice.
Figure 4.6 Cell 2: east end of the latrine pentice as excavated, showing the latrine pit and evidence for the later pentice wall, scale imperial (A. Saunders).
Figure 4.7 Cell 2: sockets cut into the cloister wall at the north end of the garden pentice (G. Coppack).
Figure 4.8 Cell 2: Finds Group 1 (pottery 1:4; wood 1:4).
Figure 4.9 Cell 3.
Figure 4.10 Cell 3: the cloister door and hatch (G. Coppack).
Figure 4.11 Cell 3: the interior showing the evidence for two phases of flooring in the north wall (G. Coppack).
Figure 4.12 Cell 3: axonometric reconstruction of the latrine.
Figure 4.13 Cell 3: Finds Group 2 (pottery 1:4; wood 1:4).
Figure 4.14 Cell 4.
Figure 4.15 Cell 4: the cloister door and hatch (G. Coppack).
Figure 4.16 Cell 4: corbelled fireplace in the south wall (Gg. Coppack).

Figure 4.17 Cell 4: the garden pentice door and the robbed location of the tap niche (G. Coppack).
Figure 4.18 Cell 4: Finds Group 3 (pottery 1:4).
Figure 4.19 Cell 5.
Figure 4.20 Cell 5: cloister door and hatch (G. Coppack).
Figure 4.21 Cell 5: garden pentice door (G. Coppack).
Figure 4.22 Cell 5: Finds Group 4 (pottery 1:4).
Figure 4.23 Cell 6.
Figure 4.24 Cell 6: cloister door and hatch (G. Coppack).
Figure 4.25 Cell 6: Finds Group 5 (pottery 1:4).
Figure 4.26 Cell 7.
Figure 4.27 Cell 7: latrine pentice door (G. Coppack).
Figure 4.28 Cell 7: sockets for the turning stair in the south-west angle (G. Coppack).
Figure 4.29 Cell 7: axonometric reconstruction of the latrine.
Figure 4.30 Cell 7: Finds Group 6 (pottery 1:4).
Figure 4.31 Cell 8: features in and on the great cloister terrace.
Figure 4.32 Cell 9: the spring chamber in the garden, showing the outlet in its east wall (R. Williams).
Figure 4.33 Cell 8: Finds Group 7 (pottery 1:4).
Figure 4.34 Cell 8: Period Two garden walls and Period Three cell and garden layout.
Figure 4.35 Elevations of Cell 8 showing the extent of medieval masonry within the rebuilt cell and evidence for its original form.
Figure 4.36 Cell 8: the round-headed window in the east wall in about 1890, before its repair by Bell (Canon J. C. Atkinson c. 1890).
Figure 4.37 Cell 8: the reconstructed latrine pentice (G. Coppack).
Figure 4.38 Cell 8: the reconstructed garden pentice (G. Coppack).
Figure 4.39 Cell 8: the 15th-century garden as excavated (G. Coppack).
Figure 4.40 Cell 8: Finds Group 9 (pottery 1:4; iron 1:4).
Figure 4.41 Cell 8: the early 16th-century garden and cloister alley.
Figure 4.42 Cell 8: the early 16th-century garden as excavated (G. Coppack).
Figure 4.43 Cell 8: Finds Group 10 (pottery 1:4; copper alloy 1:2).
Figure 4.44 Cell 8: Finds Group 11 (pottery 1:4).
Figure 4.45 Cell 8: Finds Group 11 continued (pottery 1:4, copper alloy 1:2).
Figure 4.46 Cell 8: Finds Group 12 (pottery 1:4; iron 1:4; copper alloy 1:2).
Figure 4.47 Cell 8: post-Suppression features.
Figure 4.48 Cell 8: architectural detail from demolition deposits (1:10).
Figure 4.49 Cell 9.
Figure 4.50 Cell 9: the garden as excavated, looking north (L. J. Keen).
Figure 4.51 Cell 9: Finds Group 13 (pottery 1:4, pipe clay 1:2; copper alloy 1:2; lead 1:2).
Figure 4.52 Cell 10.
Figure 4.53 Cell 10: as excavated, from the north-west (L. J. Barfoot).
Figure 4.54 Cell 10: the garden pentice as excavated, seen from the east, with the cill of the garden door and bridge over the eavesdrip gulley below the far scale pole (L. J. Barfoot).
Figure 4.55 Cell 10: the latrine pentice and living room as excavated (L. J. Barfoot).

Figure 4.56 The latrine pentice looking north and showing the wall plate socket and the mortar flashing of the pentice roof above the door to the latrine (L. J. Barfoot).
Figure 4.57 Cell 10: the northern part of the garden as excavated, seen from the west (L. J. Barfoot).
Figure 4.58 Cell 10: Finds Group 14 (pottery 1:4, copper alloy 1:2).
Figure 4.59 Cell 10: Finds Group 14 continued (lead 1:2; stone 1:2).
Figure 4.60 Cell 10: the pardon indulgence (L. J. Barfoot).
Figure 4.61 Cell 10: stone mortar (1:4).
Figure 4.62 Cell 10: architectural detail from demolition deposits (1:10).
Figure 4.63 Cell 11.
Figure 4.64 Cell 11: west–east section.
Figure 4.65 Cell 11: as excavated, seen from the north-west (L. J. Barfoot).
Figure 4.66 Cell 11: evidence for the turning stair in the north-east corner of the cell (L. J. Barfoot).
Figure 4.67 Cell 11: garden pentice as excavated, looking south (L. J. Barfoot).
Figure 4.68 Cell 11: Finds Group 15 (pottery 1:4; iron 1:4; copper alloy 1:2).
Figure 4.69 Cell 11: Finds Group 15 continued (lead 1:2; glass 1:2; stone 1:2).
Figure 4.70 Cell 11: architectural detail from demolition contexts (1:10).
Figure 4.71 Cell 12.
Figure 4.72 Cell 12: as excavated, looking east, showing the survival of the cloister wall with evidence for the stair, internal tap niche, cross-joist and fixings at first-floor level (L. J. Barfoot).
Figure 4.73 Cell 12: latrine and latrine pentice as excavated, looking east (L. J. Barfoot).
Figure 4.74 Cell 12: east–west section of precinct wall and latrine drain.
Figure 4.75 Cell 12: Finds Group 16 (pottery 1:4; copper alloy 1:2; stone 1:2; shell 1:2).
Figure 4.75 Finds Group 16: ceramics and small finds.
Figure 4.76 Cell 12: architectural detail from demolition contexts (1:10).
Figure 4.77 Cell 13 and adjacent cloister alley.
Figure 4.78 Cell 13: evidence for the floor joists in the living room, seen from the east (L. J. Barfoot).
Figure 4.79 Cell 13: latrine and latrine pentice as excavated, looking east (L. J. Keen).
Figure 4.80 Cell 13: latrine, latrine drain and precinct wall as excavated (L. J. Keen).
Figure 4.81 Cell 13: east–west section of the precinct wall and latrine drain.
Figure 4.82 Cell 13: Finds Group 17 (pottery 1:4; iron 1:4; copper alloy 1:2; lead 1:2; shell 1:2).
Figure 4.83 Cell 14.
Figure 4.84 Cell 14 and its garden pentice as excavated, looking north (L. J. Keen).
Figure 4.85 Cell 14: latrine pentice and latrine as excavated, looking west (L. J. Keen).
Figure 4.86 Cell 14: tank and sluice at the south-east corner of the cell (L. J. Keen).
Figure 4.87 Cell 14: Finds Group 18 (iron 1:4; copper alloy 1:2; lead 1:2).
Figure 4.88 Cell 15 and the 'prison' building.
Figure 4.89 Cell 15: Finds Group 19 (copper alloy 1:2; lead 1:2; stone 1:2).
Figure 4.90 Interior elevations of the 'prison' and adjacent buildings.
Figure 4.91 Prison block as excavated, looking south (L. J. Keen).
Figure 4.92 Water tower as excavated.
Figure 4.93 Water tower as excavated, seen from the north (G. Coppack).
Figure 4.94 Water tower: section A–B.
Figure 4.95 Water tower: architectural fragments from the ground storey (1:10).
Figure 4.96 Water tower: reconstruction of the ground storey (S. Hayfield).
Figure 4.97 Water tower: architectural detail (1:10) and lead pipes (1:2).
Figure 4.98 Water tower: Finds Groups 20 and 21 (pottery 1:4).
Figure 4.99 Cell 23: architectural detail (1:10).

Figure 5.1 The south-west cloister range seen from the south-west before excavation (G. Coppack).
Figure 5.2 Pre-monastic features below the south-west cloister range.
Figure 5.3 Pre-monastic features below the eastern half of the south-west cloister range as excavated, seen from the north (G. Coppack).
Figure 5.4 Finds Group 22 from the south-west cloister range (pottery 1:4).
Figure 5.5 Finds Group 23 from the south-west cloister range (pottery 1:4).
Figure 5.6 Finds Group 24 from the south-west cloister range (pottery 1:4)
Figure 5.7 Finds Group 25 from the south-west cloister range (pottery 1:4).
Figure 5.8 Finds Group 26 from the south-west cloister range (pottery 1:4).
Figure 5.9 The south-west cloister range and 'prison', construction and sub-floor features.
Figure 5.10 The south-west cloister range and 'prison', later features of Periods Two to Four.
Figure 5.11 Plan of the south-west cloister range and 'prison' as built in Period One.
Figure 5.12 Finds Group 27 from the south-west cloister range (pottery 12:4; copper alloy 1:2; lead 1:2).
Figure 5.13 Jambs and cill (partly in situ) in the west wall of the Period One south-west cloister range (1: 10).
Figure 5.14 Architectural detail from the Period One south-west cloister range (1:10).
Figure 5.15 Window fragments from the Period One south-west cloister range (1:10).
Figure 5.16 Plan of the south-west cloister range and 'prison' as rebuilt in Period Two (original work is shown in black).
Figure 5.17 The Period Two fireplace in the prior's cell.
Figure 5.18 The yards to the south of the south-west cloister range as excavated.
Figure 5.19 Finds Group 28 from the south-west cloister range (pottery 1:4; iron 1:4; bone 1:2).
Figure 5.20 Architectural detail from the Period Two south-west cloister range (1:10).
Figure 5.21 Plan of the south-west cloister range as rebuilt in Period Three.
Figure 5.22 The Period Three prior's cell as excavated, seen from the west (G. Coppack).
Figure 5.23 The Period Three paving in the eastern room of the first prior's cell, with sockets for a fitted bench and drainage channel, seen from the north (T. Gledhill).
Figure 5.24 The widening of the south wall of the prior's cell in Period Three.
Figure 5.25 Finds Group 29 from the south-west cloister range (pottery 1:4; lead 1:2).
Figure 5.26 Architectural detail from the Period Three south-west cloister range (1:10).
Figure 5.27 The western half of the south-west cloister range showing its appearance in Period Four, seen from the south (G. Coppack).
Figure 5.28 Finds Group 30 from the south-west cloister range (pottery 1:4; iron 1:4, copper alloy 1:2).
Figure 5.29 Finds Group 31 from the south-west cloister range (pottery 1:4; copper alloy 1:2, lead 1:2).
Figure 5.30 Finds Group 32 from the south-west cloister range (pottery 1:4; copper alloy 1:2, lead 1:2).
Figure 5.31 Finds Group 33 from the south-west cloister range (pottery 1:4).
Figure 5.32 Finds Group 33 from the south-west cloister range continued (iron 1:4; copper alloy 1:2, lead 1:2; bone 1:2).
Figure 5.33 Stone object from the period four south-west cloister range (1:10).
Figure 5.34 The south-west cloister range and 'prison', post-medieval features.

LIST OF FIGURES

Figure 5.35 The 17th-century garden overlying the western half of the south-west cloister range, seen from the south (G. Coppack).
Figure 5.36 Finds Group 34 from the south-west cloister range (pottery 1:4).
Figure 5.37 Finds Group 35 from the south-west cloister range (pottery 1:4).
Figure 5.38 Finds Group 35 from the south-west cloister range continued (iron 1:4; copper alloy 1:2; lead 1:2; bone 1:2; jet 1:2).
Figure 5.39 Architectural detail from demolition contexts in the south-west cloister range (1:10).
Figure 5.40 The kitchen area and 'refectory' as excavated and interpreted by Hope.
Figure 5.41 The Period One kitchen.
Figure 5.42 Finds Group 36 from the kitchen (pottery 1:4).
Figure 5.43 Architectural detail from the area of the Period One kitchen (1:10).
Figure 5.44 The Period Two kitchen as excavated.
Figure 5.45 The Period Two kitchen and its offices as excavated, seen from the east (T. Gledhill).
Figure 5.46 Elevation drawings of the north and west walls of the kitchen cross-wing.
Figure 5.47 Finds Group 37 from the kitchen (pottery 1:4; copper alloy 1:2, lead 1:2).
Figure 5.48 Finds Group 38 from the kitchen (pottery 1:4; iron 1:4).
Figure 5.49 The Period Three kitchen as excavated.
Figure 5.50 The hearth of the Period Three kitchen, seen from the north. The hollows worn by a metal tripod cauldron can be seen at its south-west corner (T. Gledhill).
Figure 5.51 Stair base [1395] seen from the west. The socket for the timber stair string is on the left (J. Hall).
Figure 5.52 Finds Group 39 from the kitchen (pottery 1:4; copper alloy 1:2).
Figure 5.53 Finds Group 40 from the kitchen (pottery 1:4; copper alloy 1:2).
Figure 5.54 The Period Four kitchen as excavated.
Figure 5.55 The Period Four kitchen and its offices as excavated, seen from the east (T. Gledhill).
Figure 5.56 Finds Group 41 from the kitchen (pottery 1:4).
Figure 5.57 Finds Group 42 from the kitchen (pottery 1:4; lead 1:2).
Figure 5.58 The kitchen area in the 17th century and later as excavated.
Figure 5.59 Finds Group 43 from the kitchen (pottery 1:4; copper alloy 1:2; lead 1:2).
Figure 5.60 Finds Group 44 from the kitchen (pottery 1:4; copper alloy 1:2).
Figure 5.61 Finds Group 45 from the kitchen (pottery 1:4).
Figure 5.62 Finds Group 45 from the kitchen continued (iron 1:4; copper alloy 1:2; lead 1:2)
Figure 5.63 Cell 16.
Figure 5.64 Architectural detail from cell 16 (scale 1:10).
Figure 5.65 Cell 18.
Figure 5.66 Cell 18 latrine.
Figure 5.67 Finds Group 46 from Cell 20 (pottery 1:4).
Figure 5.68 Cell 21.
Figure 5.69 The stables in the south range of the inner court as excavated.
Figure 5.70 Sections of the stable, granary and kiln house in the south range of the inner court.
Figure 5.71 The granary and kiln house in the south range of the inner court as excavated.
Figure 6.1 Phase plan of the priory buildings.
Figure 6.2 Masons' marks of Period One.
Figure 6.3 Masons' marks of Period Two.
Figure 6.4 Masons' marks of Period Three.
Figure 6.5 The guest-house range, medieval phases only.
Figure 6.6 Axonometric reconstruction of the kitchen cross-wing and related buildings as it was developed in Period Four.
Figure 6.7 The guest house and meat kitchen chimney on the 1890s before its repair, showing the scars of the kitchen roof (Canon J. C. Atkinson).
Figure 6.8 Axonometric cut-away drawing of the kitchen chimney (J. Dobie after S. Coll).
Figure 6.9 Axonometric reconstruction of the kitchen cross-wing showing the form of the roof.
Figure 6.10 The church at Mount Grace seen from the south-west (G. Coppack).
Figure 6.11 The church at Mount Grace, showing masonry of all four phases of development.
Figure 6.12 Development plans of the church at Mount Grace.
Figure 6.13 Plinth details of the Period One church and its Period Three burial chavpels.
Figure 6.14 The monks' choir before 1900, showing the ghost of the wooden barrel vault evidenced by whiteliming of the walls that no longer survives (Canon J. C. Atkinson).
Figure 6.15 Period One window from the south wall of the nave (1:10) (G. Coppack, J. Hall and S. Hayfield).
Figure 6.16 Possible reconstruction of the Period Two east window of the church (1:20) (J. Hall and S. Hayfield).
Figure 6.17 Alternate reconstruction of the Period Two east window of the church (1:20) (J. Hall and S. Hayfield).
Figure 6.18 Window tracery from the south and north burial chapels (1:10).
Figure 6.19 Windows from the east burial chapel (1:10).
Figure 6.20 Piscinas from the east burial chapel (1:10).
Figure 6.21 Other architectural detail derived from the church (1:10).
Figure 6.22 Other architectural detail derived from the church (1:10).
Figure 6.23 Details of the cloister roof fixings on the south and north walls of the great cloister.
Figure 6.24 The Period Two cloister arcade (G. Coppack, J. Hall and S. Hayfield).
Figure 6.25 Architectural detail from the Period Two cloister (1:10).
Figure 6.26 The Period Three cloister arcade (G. Coppack, J. Hall and S. Hayfield).
Figure 6.27 Door to the Period One prior's cell in the south-west cloister range (G. Coppack).
Figure 6.28 The south-west cloister range as originally built in Period One (G. Coppack and S. Hayfield).
Figure 6.29 The south-west cloister range as modified in Periods Two to Four (G. Coppack and S. Hayfield).
Figure 6.30 The south wall of the great cloister with (from left to right) the church entry, the door to Cell 23, the lavatorium, the door to Cell 22, the door to the later prior's cell and the base of his oriel window (G. Coppack).
Figure 6.31 Axonometric reconstruction of Cells 22 and 23.
Figure 6.32 The oratory of Cell 22 in the west wall of the Period Three north burial chapel of the church (G. Coppack).
Figure 6.33 The interior of Cell 23 (at first-floor level and above) (G. Coppack).
Figure 6.34 Architectural detail from the chapter house (1:10).
Figure 6.35 A 'typical' cell in the great cloister at Mount Grace.
Figure 6.36 Windows from the cells of the great cloister (1:10).
Figure 6.37 Windows from the cells of the great cloister (1:20).
Figure 6.38 Chimney base from the great cloister cells (1:10).
Figure 6.39 Chimney base from the great cloister cells (1:10).
Figure 6.40 Chimney shafts and caps from the great cloister cells (1:10).
Figure 6.41 Gable crosses from the great cloister cells (1:10).
Figure 6.42 Gable cross bases from the great cloister cells (1:10).
Figure 6.43 Gable cross bases from the great cloister cells (1:10).
Figure 6.44 Gable coping from the great cloister cells (1:10).
Figure 6.45 Axonometric reconstruction of the 'prison' and associated rooms.
Figure 6.46 Architectural detail from the little cloister.
Figure 6.47 The surface drainage of the priory site (a) before the priory was built and (b) as it was modified to serve the needs of the house.

LIST OF FIGURES

Figure 6.48 The southern well house (St John's Well) as it was in 1900 (Canon J. C. Atkinson).
Figure 6.49 The northern well house.
Figure 6.50 The central well house.
Figure 6.51 The tap niche in Cell 6 (G. Coppack).
Figure 6.52 The lavatorium in the great cloister (G. Coppack).
Figure 6.53 Plan of Mount Grace Priory showing all recorded evidence for water management.
Figure 6.54 Plan and section of the water mill in the outer court.
Figure 6.55 The Lascelles house as it appeared in the late 1890s before its repair and extension by Sir Lowthian Bell.
Figure 6.56 Ground- and first-floor plans of the house of 1652 built in the shell of the guest-house range.
Figure 7.1 Schematic section of the peat column from the water-tower excavation.
Figure 7.2 Floor tiles from Mount Grace and Sawley (1:3).
Figure 7.3 Location of floor tiles at Mount Grace.
Figure 7.4 Layout design for early Perpendicular screenwork from Mount Grace (scale 1:5).
Figure 7.5 Unlocated architectural detail (1:10).
Figure 7.6 Unlocated architectural detail (1:10).
Figure 7.7 Unlocated architectural detail (1:10).
Figure 7.8 Unlocated architectural detail (1:10).
Figure 7.9 Window glass from Mount Grace, Groups 1–4 (1:2).
Figure 7.10 Window glass from Mount Grace, Group 4 continued (1:2).
Figure 8.1 The extent of the village of Bordelby that preceded the priory. The shaded areas represent those parts of the site that have produced pottery from the 12th to late 13th century.
Figure 8.2 The development of Mount Grace Priory: $c.$1412; $c.$1430; $c.$1470; $c.$1530.
Figure 8.3 The church at Witham (from Campbell 1771).
Figure 8.4 The church, chapter house and lesser cloister at Hinton (after Fletcher 1958–9).
Figure 8.5 The church, chapter house and lesser cloister at Beauvale (after Hill and Gill 1908).
Figure 8.6 The church, chapter house and lesser cloister at London (after Knowles and Grimes 1954).
Figure 8.7 The church at Coventry (after Soden 1995).
Figure 8.8 The charterhouse of Nieuwlicht in the Netherlands, $c.$1725.
Figure 8.8A Plan of Nieuwlicht church showing burials (after Hundertmark and den Hartog).
Figure 8.9 Reconstruction of the church at Mount Grace based on the surviving fabric and detached architectural detail (G. Coppack and S. Hayfield).
Figure 8.10 The east window of Catterick church (G. Coppack).
Figure 8.11 The east window of Burneston church (G. Coppack).
Figure 8.12 The tower of the Greyfriars' church at Richmond from the west (G. Coppack).
Figure 8.13 Comparative cell plans from English charterhouses. Hinton, Cell 11 (after Fletcher 1958–9); Witham (after Burrow and Burrow 1990); Beauvale, Cell 3 (after Hill and Gill 1908); Coventry, Cell 3 (after Soden 1995); and Mount Grace, Cell 4.
Figure 8.14 Reconstructed cell plan at the charterhouse of Delft in Holland (after Vos 1975).
Figure 8.15 Cell 4 at the charterhouse of Notre-Dame-de-la-Verne, Var, France (J.-L. Mordefroid).
Figure 8.16 Comparative plans of prior's cells. A: Hinton; B: Mount Grace, the early cell; C: Mount Grace, the later cell; D: Coventry.
Figure 8.17 The development of the kitchen and its offices at Mount Grace from $c.$1420 to $c.$1530.
Figure 8.18 Comparative plans of refectories. A: Hinton; B: Coventry; C: Mount Grace $c.$1400; D: Mount Grace $c.$1430.

List of tables

Table 0.1 Charterhouse remains
Table 1.1 Charterhouses of England
Table 1.2 Carthusian communities derived from pension lists at the suppression, 1539–40
Table 2.1 Mount Grace, Total estates from the Valor Ecclesiasticus and Ministers' Accounts, 1534/5 and 1540
Table 2.2 The demesnes of Mount Grace Priory Taken mostly from the 1540 grant to Sir James Strangways
Table 2.3 Priors of Mount Grace
Table 2.4 Pension list of Mount Grace, 1539
Table 4.1 Cell 2, Finds Group 1: Ceramics
Table 4.2 Cell 3, Finds Group 2: Ceramics
Table 4.3 Cell 4, Finds Group 3: Cell and Garden
Table 4.4 Cell 4, Finds Group 3: Latrine
Table 4.5 Cell 5, Finds Group 4: Ceramics
Table 4.6 Cell 6, Finds Group 5: Ceramics
Table 4.7 Cell 7, Finds Group 6: Ceramics
Table 4.8 Cell 8, Finds Group 7: Ceramics
Table 4.9 Cell 8, Finds Group 8: Ceramics
Table 4.10 Cell 8, Finds Group 9: Ceramics
Table 4.11 Cell 8, Finds Group 10: Ceramics
Table 4.12 Cell 8, Finds Group 11: Ceramics
Table 4.13 Cell 8, Finds Group 12: Ceramics
Table 4.14 Cell 9, Finds Group 13: Ceramics
Table 4.15 Cell 10, Finds Group 14: Ceramics
Table 4.16 Cell 11, Finds Group 15: Ceramics
Table 4.17 Cell 12, Finds Group 16: Ceramics
Table 4.18 Cell 13, Finds Group 17: Ceramics
Table 4.19 Cell 14, Finds Group 18: Ceramics
Table 4.20 Cell 15, Finds Group 19: Ceramics
Table 4.21 Cell 2, Finds Group 20: Ceramics
Table 4.22 Water Tower, Finds Group 21: Ceramics
Table 5.1 South-west cloister range, Finds Group 22: Ceramics
Table 5.2 South-west cloister range, Finds Group 23: Ceramics
Table 5.3 South-west cloister range, Finds Group 24: Ceramics
Table 5.4 South-west cloister range, Finds Group 25: Ceramics
Table 5.5 South-west cloister range, Finds Group 26: Ceramics
Table 5.6 South-west cloister range, Finds Group 27: Ceramics
Table 5.7 South-west cloister range, Finds Group 28: Ceramics
Table 5.8 South-west cloister range, Finds Group 29: Ceramics
Table 5.9 South-west cloister range, Finds Group 30: Ceramics
Table 5.10 South-west cloister range, Finds Group 31: Ceramics
Table 5.11 Cloister range, Finds Group 32: Ceramics
Table 5.12 Cloister range, Finds Group 33: Ceramics
Table 5.13 Cloister range, Finds Group 34: Ceramics
Table 5.14 Cloister range, Finds Group 35: Ceramics
Table 5.15 Finds Group 36: Ceramics
Table 5.16 Finds Group 37: Ceramics
Table 5.17 Finds Group 38: Ceramics
Table 5.18 Kitchen, Finds Group 39: Ceramics
Table 5.19 Kitchen, Finds Group 40: Ceramics
Table 5.20 Kitchen, Finds Group 41: Ceramics
Table 5.21 Kitchen, Finds Group 42: Ceramics
Table 5.22 Kitchen, Finds Group 43: Ceramics
Table 5.23 Kitchen, Finds Group 44: Ceramics
Table 5.24 Kitchen, Finds Group 45: Ceramics
Table 5.25 Kitchen, Finds Group 46: Ceramics
Table 6.1 Masons' marks on fabric of Periods One, Two and Three
Table 7.1 Coleoptera recovered from Sample 1
Table 7.2 Numbers of stratified pre-priory vessels by fabric and by form (Finds Groups 22–6)
Table 7.3 The number of vessels in each fabric by area
Table 7.4 The number of identifiable pottery vessels from monastic contexts
Table 7.5 Composition of the tile glazes and slips, as determined by XRF analysis (all values as wt %, normalized)
Table 7.6 Quantities of fish bone recovered from kitchen deposits
Table 7.7 Numbers of fish bones from the samples studied in detail
Table 7.8 Identified fish species from the kitchen area by context and phase
Table 7.9 Other foodstuffs
Table 8.1 Dimensions of first-phase Carthusian churches

Summary

Mount Grace Priory was the eighth of only nine successful Carthusian monasteries established in England between 1178/9 and 1415 and is by far the best preserved. It was originally excavated for the Yorkshire Archaeological Society between 1896 and 1900 under the direction of Sir William St John Hope and has since been accepted as the type-site for its order in England and beyond.

In state guardianship since 1954, the site has been the subject of three campaigns of research excavation in 1957, 1968–74 and 1985–92, which have revealed its development and established its significance. A major study of the standing ruins, which comprise some 35% to 40% of the house at its greatest extent in 1538, was undertaken in 1987–8, providing for the first time a proper framework for the archaeological study.

Nine of the 18 monks' cells around the great cloister have been excavated to modern standards, three including the whole of the garden area, together with sample areas of the north, west and south alleys of the great cloister, and the water tower, which occupied the centre of the cloister garth. In addition, the interface between the great cloister and the inner court was excavated to examine the prior's cell, refectory and kitchens, and a sample area of the inner court was also examined, enabling the processes by which food was stored, prepared, cooked and distributed to be fully understood. The architectural study of unexcavated buildings, in particular the church and the earliest of the monks' cells, enabled these buildings to be properly understood and seen in the context of those that had benefited from modern excavation.

For the first time in a Carthusian context anywhere, the process of construction from initial foundation to maturity has been established, with the identification of a primary phase of both stone and timber buildings and three subsequent phases of development that relate the known history of the charterhouse and its endowments and to the evidence of archaeology. The peculiar nature of Carthusian life, where every member of the community lived in a separate house or cell with its own garden, has enabled the study of cultural collections that are associated with individuals, something that is rarely possible in other monasteries. The cultural collections at Mount Grace indicate the varied trades the monks practised, including the production of books, and the high social status of the community in the 140 years preceding the suppression of the house. Although the Carthusians espoused poverty and were known as 'Christ's Poor Men', the material culture of the monastery was that of the upper levels of society from which the religious and their principal patrons were drawn.

Excavation and a study of the surviving fabric have enabled the placing of Carthusian monasticism in its proper context in England and Western Europe at a time when the monastic church generally was undergoing significant change. For the first time it is now possible to see the influence of the Carthusians and their strict living on other regular orders, and to understand the context of the renaissance in monastic life that marked the 15th and early 16th centuries.

(Glyn Coppack)

Samenvatting

De priorij van Mount Grace was het achtste van slechts negen succesvolle Kartuizer kloosters die tussen 1178/9 en 1415 in Engeland zijn gesticht en is van alle het best bewaard gebleven. De eerste opgravingen, onder leiding van Sir William St John Hope voor de *Yorkshire Archaeological Society*, vonden plaats tussen 1896 en 1900. Sindsdien wordt de vindplaats als een representatief voorbeeld van de orde beschouwd, zowel in Engeland als daarbuiten.

Sinds 1954 heeft de vindplaats de status van rijksmonument, en is in 1957, 1968–74, en 1985–92 onderworpen geweest aan drie grootschalige archeologische onderzoekscampagnes die haar ontwikkeling onthulden en haar betekenis vaststelden. Een belangrijk onderzoek naar de nog bestaande ruïnes, die 35 tot 40% van het klooster behelzen dat op zijn grootst was in 1538, is uitgevoerd in 1987–88 en leverde voor het eerst een geschikt stramien voor het archeologisch onderzoek op.

Negen van de 18 cellen voor monniken rond de grote pandhof, waarvan drie met de bijbehorende tuinen, zijn volgens de moderne criteria opgegraven; zo ook delen van de noordelijke, westelijke en zuidelijke gangen van de grote pandhof, en de watertoren die zich in het midden van de pandhof bevond. Tevens is het gedeelte tussen de grote pandhof en de voorhof opgegraven om de cel van de prior, de refter en de keukens te onderzoeken en een deel van de voorhof om de processen van opslag, bereiding, koken en verdeling van voedsel volledig te kunnen begrijpen.

Voor het eerst is het proces van bouwen, vanaf de feitelijke stichting tot de volle wasdom, binnen een Kartuizer context vastgesteld, met de identificatie van de eerste fase waarin zowel stenen als houten gebouwen voorkomen en de drie daaropvolgende fasen van ontwikkeling die in verband kunnen worden gebracht met de bekende geschiedenis van het huis, de schenkingen en de archeologisch gegevens. De specifieke aard van het Kartuizer leven, waarbij ieder lid van de gemeenschap in een eigen huisje of cel met bijbehorende tuin leefde, heeft het mogelijk gemaakt de verzamelingen van vondstmateriaal die in verband kunnen worden gebracht met individuen te bestuderen, iets dat nauwelijks mogelijk is in andere kloosters. Het vondstmateriaal van Mount Grace toont de diverse ambachten die de monniken bedreven, waaronder het produceren van boeken, en de hoge sociale status van de gemeenschap in de 140 jaar voorafgaand aan de opheffing van het huis aan. Hoewel de Kartuizers armoede omarmden en bekend stonden als 'de arme mannen van Christus', is de materiële cultuur van het klooster er een van de hogere klassen van de samenleving waaruit de monniken en hun belangrijkste weldoeners voortkwamen.

De opgravingen en het onderzoek naar de overblijfselen hebben het mogelijk gemaakt het Kartuizer kloosterleven in zijn juiste context te plaatsen, zowel in Engeland als in West Europa, in een periode waarin de kerk in het algemeen belangrijke veranderingen onderging. Voor het eerst is het nu mogelijk om de invloed van de Kartuizers en hun strikte levenswijze op andere reguliere orden te zien en de context van de opleving van het monastieke leven kenmerkend voor de vijftiende en vroege zestiende eeuw te begrijpen.

(Caroline den Hartog)

Zusammenfassung

Die Priorei Mount Grace war die achte von lediglich neun erfolgreichen Kartäuserklöstern, die zwischen 1178/9 und 1415 in England gegründet wurden; sie ist die bei Weitem besterhaltene. Ausgrabungen fanden dort erstmals zwischen 1896 und 1900 unter der Leitung von Sir William St. John Hope für die Yorkshire Archaeological Society statt. Seitdem gilt die Priorei als Referenzfundort für ihren Orden in England und darüber hinaus.

Auf dem seit 1954 unter staatlicher Verwaltung stehenden Fundplatz wurden in den Jahren 1957, 1968–74 und 1985–92 drei Forschungsgrabungen durchgeführt, die die Klärung seiner Entwicklungsgeschichte zum Ziel hatten und seine Bedeutung für die Forschung begründet haben. Eine umfangreiche Untersuchung der oberirdisch sichtbaren Baureste, die etwa 35 bis 40% des Hauses zur Zeit seiner größten Ausdehnung im Jahre 1538 ausmachten, wurde 1987–88 durchgeführt und lieferte erstmals einen geeigneten Rahmen für die Einordnung der archäologischen Untersuchungen.

Von den 18 um den großen Kreuzgang gelegenen Mönchszellen wurden neun nach modernen Maßstäben ausgegraben, drei davon einschließlich der gesamten Gartenflächen. Des Weiteren wurden Testschnitte in der Nord-, West- und Südgalerie des großen Kreuzgangs sowie dem Wasserturm angelegt, der das Zentrum des Kreuzgangs einnahm. Darüber hinaus wurde die Schnittstelle zwischen dem großen Kreuzgang und dem Innenhof ausgegraben, um die Zelle des Priors, das Refektorium und die Küchen zu untersuchen. Auch im Innenhof wurde ein Testschnitt angelegt, sodass die Abläufe der Lebensmittellagerung und -zubereitung, des Kochens und der Essensausgabe vollständig verstanden werden konnten. Die architektonische Untersuchung von nicht ausgegrabenen Gebäuden, insbesondere der Kirche und der ältesten Mönchszellen, ermöglichte ein umfassende Dokumentation dieser Bauten und erlaubte es, sie im Kontext mit den im Rahmen der modernen Ausgrabungen untersuchten Gebäude richtig einzuordnen.

Erstmals ließ sich hier für ein kartäusisches Ordenshaus der Bauprozess von der Gründung bis zur Blüte nachvollziehen. Es gelang die Identifizierung einer Primärphase mit Stein- und Holzgebäuden sowie drei nachfolgenden Entwicklungsphasen, die die historisch bekannten Quellen zur Kartause und ihrer Ausstattung mit den archäologischen Ergebnissen verbinden. Die Eigenart des kartäusischen Lebens, bei dem jedes Mitglied der Gemeinschaft in einem separaten Haus oder einer Zelle mit eigenem Garten lebte, ermöglichte das Studium kultureller Quellen, die sich einzelnen Individuen zuordnen lassen, was in anderen Klöstern selten möglich ist. Die vielfältigen Handwerke, die die Mönche ausübten, u. a. die Herstellung von Büchern, sowie der hohe soziale Status der Gemeinschaft in den 140 Jahren vor der Auflösung des Hauses, lässt sich anhand der kulturellen Sammlungen von Mount Grace nachvollziehen. Obwohl die Kartäuser Armut gelobten und als "Arme Männer Christi" bekannt waren, reflektierte die materielle Kultur des Klosters die der höheren Gesellschaftsschichten, aus denen sich die Ordensleute und ihre Hauptpatrone rekrutierten.

Die Ausgrabungen und die Untersuchungen der obertägig erhaltenen Baustruktur haben eine Einordnung des Kartäuser-Mönchtums in seinem eigentlichen Umfeld in England und Westeuropa zu einer Zeit ermöglicht, als sich das klösterliche Leben im Allgemeinen stark veränderte. Erstmals ist es nun möglich, den Einfluss der Kartäuser und ihres strengen Lebens auf andere reguläre Orden zu sehen und die Zusammenhänge der Renaissance im Klosterleben zu verstehen, die das fünfzehnte und frühe sechzehnte Jahrhundert prägten.

Übersetzung: Jörn Schuster
(ARCHÆOLOGICALsmallFINDS)

Résumé

Le prieuré du mont Grace était le huitième de seulement neuf monastères cartusiens prospères établis en Angleterre entre 1178/9 et 1415 et est, de loin, le mieux préservé. Il fut fouillé originellement pour la société archéoligique du Yorkshire entre 1896 et 1900 sous la direction de Sir William St John Hope et a été depuis reconnu comme le site-type de cet ordre en Angleterre et au delà.

Sous la tutelle de l'état depuis 1954 , le site a fait l'objet de trois campagnes de fouilles de recherches, en 1957, 1968–74 et 1985–92, qui ont révélé son développement et établi, son importance. Une étude majeure de ses ruines debout, qui comprennent quelques 35 à 40% de la maison à son extension maximale en 1538, fut entreprise en 1987-8produisant pour la première fois un véritable cadre pour les études archéologiques.

Neuf des des 18 cellules monastiques autour du grand cloître furent fouillées selon les critères modernes trois comprennent la totalité de la surface du jardin ainsi que des aires échantillon des allées nord, ouest, et sud du grand cloître et e chsteau d'eau qui occupait le centre de la cour du cloître. De plus, l'interface entre le grand cloître et la cour intérieure fut excavé pour examiner la cellule du prieur, le réfectoire et les cuisines et une aire échantillon de la cour intérieure fut aussi examinée, nous permettant de comprendre exactement les procédés par lesquels lles aliments étaient conservés, préparés, cuits et distribués. Les études architecturales des bâtiments non excavés, en particulier l'église, et les plus anciennes des cellules mmonastiques nous ont permis de comprendre parfaitement ces bâtiments et de les voir dans le contexte de ceux qui avaient bénéficié de fouilles modernes.

Pour la première fois, dans un contexte cartusien, où que ce soit, le procédé de construction depuis les premières fondations jusqu'à son achèvement a été établi avec l'identification d'une phase primaire de bâtiments à la fois en bois et en pierre et trois phases ultérieures d'aménagement qui relient l'histoire de la chartreuse et de ses dotations telle qu'on la connait e aux témoignages de l'archéologie. La nature particulière de la vie des Chartreux dans laquelle chaque membre de la communauté habitait une maison ou cellule individuelle avec son propre jardin a permis l'étude de collections culturelles qui étaient associées à des individus particuliers, chose qui est rarement possible dans les autres monastères. Les collections culturelles du Mont Grace révèlent les différents travaux effectués par les moines, y compris la fabrication de livres et leur statut social élevé pendant les 140 ans qui ont précédé la suppression de la maison. Bien que les Chartreux faisaient voeu de pauvreté et étaient connus sous le nom de pauvres hommes du Christ, la culture matérielle du monastère était celle des couches supérieures de la société d'où venaient les religieux et leurs bénéfacteurs. Des fouilles et une étude du bâti survivant ont permis de replacer le monachisme cartusien dans son contexte en Angleterre et en Europe de l'ouest à une époque où l'église monacale en général subissait d'importantes modifications. Pour la première fois il est maintenant possible de voir l'influence des Chartreux et de leur strict style de vie sur d'autres ordres réguliers et de comprendre le contexte de la renaissance de la vie monastique qui a marqué le quinzième et le début du seizième siècle.

Traduction: Annie Pritchard

Preface

NOTE All dates follow new style where the month is known, unless forming part of a quotation, in which case they follow the original text. In England until the Calendar Act of 1752 the year began on 25 March (Lady Day). So, for example, the foundation licence of Mount Grace was granted in February 1397 (old style), but February 1398 (new style).

Mount Grace Priory was a monastery of the Carthusian Order and the last monastery to be established in Yorkshire before the Reformation, when the Act of Supremacy of 1534 made Henry VIII 'supreme head on earth under God of the Church of England'. There were 834 monasteries in England and Wales at the time of the Act. Only nine of these houses were of the Carthusian Order and by 1540 they had been suppressed. One, the royal house of Sheen, was revived in 1555, but was again suppressed, by Elizabeth I, in July 1559.

The Charterhouses of England

Mount Grace Priory was founded by Thomas de Holand, Duke of Surrey and nephew of Richard II, in 1398 and suppressed in 1539. It is the best preserved of the Carthusian houses in England and the only one accessible to the public. It is perhaps typical of the charterhouses (as Carthusian monasteries are styled) established in England, from the first foundation at Witham in 1178/9 to the last, royal foundation of Sheen in 1414 (see also Chapter 1.5). The significance of Mount Grace Priory in England can be gauged from its comparison with the other houses of the order, summarised in Table 0.1.

Charterhouse Remains

Standing Masonry

Only five Carthusian sites in England retain standing masonry. At Hinton, this is restricted to the chapter house, a small part of the church, the prior's house and what may have been the refectory. At Beauvale, a gatehouse and the western part of the church, which has been recently conserved, survive, together with the prior's house against the south-west corner of the church. At London, a low tower on the north side of the church, some sections of the great cloister wall, a conduit house and a gatehouse survive; and at Coventry the refectory and prior's house survive, together with part of the south wall of the church and the precinct wall.

Table 0.1 Charterhouse remains

Site	Foundation	Standing fabric	Earthworks	Post-medieval house	Excavation
Witham	1178/9	N	Y	Y (demolished)	Y
Hinton (house transferred from Hatherop)	1227 (Hatherop 1222)	Y	Y	Y	Y
Beauvale	1343	Y	Y	Y (fragments)	Y
London	1370	Y	Y	Y	Y
Hull	1377	Y	Y	Y (demolished)	N
Coventry	1381	Y	Y	Y	Y
Axholme	1397	N	Y	Y (demolished)	Y
Mount Grace	1398	Y	Y	Y	Y
Sheen	1414	N	N	Y (demolished)	N

In comparison, Mount Grace retains substantial ruins: much of its church, the remains of 19 cells for choir monks, which range from low walling to full height, the remains of six cells for lay brothers (see Chapter 1.1), the prior's cell, the refectory, kitchen, guest-house ranges and gatehouse, in addition to a range of stables and granaries in the inner court and a mill in the outer court.

Earthworks

Six sites retain earthworks. At Coventry these are only slight and damaged by excavation. At Witham the earthworks, although extensive, were severely modified during the creation of a garden associated with a post-medieval mansion that incorporated the church, and later by the construction of the Great Western Railway. At Hinton, the great cloister is still defined by clear earthworks, although the northern half of the site is levelled and maintained as lawns for the surviving house. At Beauvale, the whole site is defined by clear and well-preserved earthworks, which do not appear to have been seriously modified by post-medieval development. At Axholme, the whole site is defined by earthworks, although it is clear that they have been modified by the creation of gardens associated with the two mansions built on the site in the early post-medieval period.

Mount Grace retains only two areas of earthworks: the inner court and the whole of the outer court. Some of the outer court has been modified by post-Suppression development, but the damage is limited to an area adjacent to the 17th-century and later house.

Post-medieval Houses

All the English charterhouses were developed as major houses after the Suppression. At Witham, Axholme and Sheen these important houses, which incorporated medieval fabric, were demolished (Witham from 1762, Axholme probably by the end of the Civil War, and Sheen not much beyond it in any substance). Beauvale retains a fragment of a late 14th-century house and at Coventry the prior's house and the refectory were converted into a house that remains in use. At London there are substantial remains of a house that incorporates medieval fabric. At Witham, a late 16th-century house occupies the north range of the inner court and both incorporates and reuses medieval fabric.

At Mount Grace, the north-west range of the inner court was converted into a house from 1616 and gardens developed to the west. It was extended in 1900–1. This house, which incorporated substantial medieval fabric, remains.

First Excavations at Mount Grace: 1896–1900

Mount Grace first came to scholarly attention in the last quarter of the 19th century because of the interests of its then owner, William Brown. Brown was an amateur historian of some distinction who, in addition to researching the history of Mount Grace, edited the cartulary of nearby Gisborough Priory for the Surtees Society and published a number of papers on monastic subjects in the *Yorkshire Archaeological Journal*. Through the Yorkshire Archaeological Society he invited Sir William St John Hope, Assistant Secretary of the Society of Antiquaries of London and the leading authority on monasteries in Europe, to undertake a series of excavations intended to reveal the plan of the monastery.

Hope's excavations were conducted between 1896 and 1900. He was at the time undertaking a typological study of monasteries in England (his study extends from 1870 to 1913 or later), which ultimately included four Benedictine, two Cluniac, six Cistercian, one Gilbertine, six Premonstratensian, one Templar and two Carthusian monasteries, as well as a house of Augustinian nuns and two houses of friars. His magisterial article in 1905 in the *Yorkshire Archaeological Journal*, 'Architectural Description of Mount Grace Charterhouse', remains the classic study of a Carthusian charterhouse to this day and established the house as the type site for the order in England and beyond.

Mount Grace Passes into State Guardianship

Mount Grace Priory remained in private ownership until 1953, when it passed to the Government in lieu of death duties and was transferred to the ownership of the National Trust. The converted guest house and its gardens were leased to a tenant, Kitty Cooper-Abbs, and the rest of the monastic site and its ruins were, in 1955, placed by the Trust in

PREFACE

the guardianship of the Minister for Public Buildings and Works. The site was opened to the public in June of that year and a lengthy campaign of conservation was begun.

In 1981 the Trust placed the guest-house range and its garden in the guardianship of the Secretary of State for the Environment, and that building was repaired and similarly made accessible to the public from 1987. English Heritage has managed the site on behalf of the Government since 1984, while the Trust retains ownership of the site.

Roughly 75 per cent of the site is in State guardianship, the remainder lies largely below permanent pasture in the area of the outer court on land owned by Mount Lodge Farm. The greater part of the site is a Scheduled Ancient Monument (County Monument: North Yorkshire 10, Heritage List list no. 1013019) and the whole priory, including the roofed guest-house range, is listed Grade I (Heritage List list no. 1315123). The site lies just outside the western boundary of the North York Moors National Park at National Grid Reference SE 453982.

Second Excavations at Mount Grace: 1957

Since Hope completed his excavation in 1900, there was no further recorded archaeological research until after the site passed into State care. In 1957 Andrew Saunders was commissioned by the Ministry of Works to re-excavate part of Cell 2 (as numbered, and previously excavated, by Hope) after conservation work that year found the cell to be multi-phase and so not as simple as Hope had assumed. In spite of the results of Saunders's excavation, the decision was taken to continue conservation without further excavation, and the church and Cells 1 to 7 were stripped of debris and laid out for public display under the general supervision of Roy Gilyard-Beer (d.1984).

Laurence Keen's Campaign: 1969–74

In 1968, however, this decision was reversed. Tree cover had prevented Hope from examining the west side of the great cloister and Laurence Keen was commissioned by John Weaver of the Ministry of Works to excavate Cells 9 to 15 before those unexamined cells were conserved and displayed. His excavation of two cell gardens in their totality was one of the first instances of garden excavation in Britain and the first anywhere in a monastic context. Additionally, he was asked to examine the south range of the inner court, assisted by David Sherlock. That phase of work was completed in 1974.

Glyn Coppack's Campaign: 1985–92

The creation of English Heritage in 1984 altered dramatically the way in which ancient monuments were presented to the public. In particular, the educational and interpretative aspects of monument display were enhanced to make sites more easily understood. At Mount Grace this was demonstrated by the decision to complete the rebuilding of Cell 8 (a project which had originally been considered in the early 1960s).

Cell 8 had been partially reconstructed after Hope's excavation, to interpret Carthusian monastic life, but to complete as accurate a reconstruction as possible required the excavation of the cell's garden, and in 1985 English Heritage instructed then Inspector of Ancient Monuments Glyn Coppack (later Principal Inspector of Properties in Care) to undertake this work. It was intended as a limited exercise to complete Keen's research programme; however, the excavations revealed a complex series of developments in both the cell and its garden, suggesting once again that Hope's interpretation of the site had been too simplistic and that further work was needed to resolve problems of interpretation.

In 1987 a five-year programme of archaeological research was commissioned by English Heritage to complete the interpretation and display of the site, again directed by Coppack. This was to include (for the first time) the analysis of standing buildings and study of the collection of detached architectural fragments collected by Hope, by the Ministry of Works and its successor bodies, and by Keen. It was also to include the recording and analysis of the converted guest house of the 17th century and later.

Research Design

All campaigns of excavation have contributed to the elucidation of the development of Mount Grace, though none conducted before 1985 was done so according to a specific research design, because the concept of a research design was not formalised before the development of MAP2 (*Management of Archaeological Projects*, 2nd edition, 1991). Keen did, however, set himself specific research objectives relating to the construction and development of the Carthusian cell, its use by individual monks, and the development of cell gardens. Keen's work, and Coppack's in close succession, demonstrated at Mount Grace the medieval archaeology techniques as developing from the 1960s to the early 1990s.

The 1985 research design was simple: to excavate the garden of Cell 8 to natural deposits, so as to provide the necessary evidence to interpret and to reconstruct and display the garden. During the course of excavation it was decided additionally to excavate the cloister alley on the south side of the cell to elucidate development recorded within the garden. This piece of work was initially intended to stand alone.

In 1986–7 it became apparent that further work was required to complete the interpretation and display of the site and that substantial repairs were required to conserve the guest-house range. The original research strategy was consequently considerably expanded and developed. In summary, this proposed the following objectives:

- examination of pre-monastic levels and their relationship with the earliest Carthusian buildings
- study of the structural development of the site, both in terms of the surviving ruins and detached architectural elements, to provide a framework within which previous archaeology could be more properly understood
- integration of earlier research on Mount Grace and other Carthusian houses within a general study of this, the best-preserved Carthusian monastery in Britain, to illustrate late medieval monastic life in a period of change leading up to the Reformation
- study of the complex water supply and drainage system
- re-excavation of a representative sample (the south-west cloister range and kitchen) of the communal and service ranges to reunite the roofed buildings of the guest-house range with the ruined elements of the great cloister and so aid overall interpretation of the site.

The result of this work, which was on a scale not yet seen at any other Carthusian site in Europe at the time, has been to rewrite the story of Mount Grace Priory and to identify it as one of the most important monastic sites in Europe. Few monastic sites have had the benefit of such large-scale archaeological research. Where Hope had identified Mount Grace as the type site of the order in England, its significance can now be seen to be far greater: it is typical of later medieval charterhouses across Christendom.

The only comparable site in Europe is the charterhouse of Nieuwlicht at Utrecht in the Netherlands, which first appeared in the archaeological record in 1922, when the site was developed for housing. In 2001, and again from 2007 to 2011, substantial excavation was carried out under rescue conditions at the Marnixlaan (to the north of Utrecht city centre) and adjacent land was further redeveloped. The work produced evidence of a charterhouse of the same size and date as Mount Grace Priory, together with extensive cultural collections. Recently, two significant reports by Caroline Den Hartog have become publicly available on the municipality website (Hartog 2013 and 2016). It is possible, however, to make some comparison based on the site itself and its extensive late medieval documentation, which is accessible in the Utrechtse Archiev, part of the provincial archives.

Acknowledgements

Campaign of Laurence Keen

The four seasons that comprised the campaign of excavation directed by Keen took place from 1–18 September 1969, 22 March–19 April 1970, 16 August–11 September 1971, and 5 July–4 August 1974. He is grateful to Sylvia Leek (1969), the late Christina Colyer (1970), Robert Bradley (1971) and David Thackray (1974), who acted as Assistant Supervisors, and to the late Richard Hall (1970–1), Nigel Cooper (1971), C. J. Arnold (1974), R. Raper (1974) and Helen Nicholson (1974), who were Site Assistants. Most of the photography in the first three seasons was undertaken by James Barfoot.

A particular debt of gratitude is owed to the many excavators who came to work as volunteers: Caroline Atkins, Lynne Ballin, Jennifer Barlow, Robin Barlow, Joy Barningham, Richard Barrett, David Bennett, Sue Bennett,

PREFACE

John Black, Susan Black, Jane Bowden, Colin Bradshaw, Judith Brown, Rosemary Brown, David Chapman, Jean Clayton, Nigel Cooper, Marie Daniels, Susan Daniels, Loretta Dawson, Jennifer Deadman, John Deadman, Andrew de Lewandowicz, Karen Done, Bernard Downing, Neil Edbrooke, Ian Edelman, Simon Fraser, Kathryn Gee, Sara Gibbons, Heather Gibson, David Goodfellow, Jill Gregory, Michael Griffin, Simon Gudgeon, Richard Hall, Mathew Hallett, Colin Hazlehurst, Jonathan Hauxwell, Patricia Hendley, Patrick Holdsworth, Ann Holt, Martin Hoyle, Bruce Induni, John Inman, John Johnson, Susan Johnson, Dilwyn Jones, Elspeth King, John Lade, Rosamund Lade, Marianne Martin, Nicky Marskell, Nigel Maslin, Christopher Mayes, Stephen McCombe, Robert McMillan, J. B. Murray, Helen Nicholson, Martin O'Connell, Katherine Pafford, Hugh Penfold, Andrew Pinder, Susan Pitt, Sue Porter, Margaret Powell, Helen Reed, Philip Reynolds, Peter Richards, David Rimmer, Margaret Rogers, Peter Rollings, Nick Rowley, Brian Schofield, K. Simpson, Diana Stacey, Sally Stevenson, Sheila Stones, Hilary Taylor, the Thompson family, Barbara Thompson, Simon Timms, Alice Waite, Joyce Wallis, Sandra Walster, Michael Ward, Philip Watson and John Wilcox.

Throughout the excavations constant support was provided by the site's full-time works team and by Trevor Lancelot at the English Heritage office in York. The work was commissioned and encouraged by four Inspectors of Ancient Monuments: John Weaver, Michael Thompson, Stuart Rigold and (Principal Insepctor for England) Oswin Craster, all of whom visited the excavations regularly and provided much useful advice. Three other Inspectors – John Hurst, Roy Gilyard-Beer and Andrew Saunders – also took a particular interest. For allowing camping on their farm during the works thanks are due to Mr and Mrs Simpson, then of Mount Lodge, Staddlebridge.

On completion of Keen's campaign in 1974, a post-excavation programme was started immediately with the assistance of David Thackray. The finds were sorted and, where necessary, conserved and record drawings made. The late Jean le Patourel carried out research on the pottery and produced a report. Further work was delayed by Keen's appointment in 1975 as County Archaeological Officer for Dorset and by delays in the drawing of surviving elevations of the cells. However, it was clear that with the death of Miss Cooper-Abbs (the tenant of the National Trust who lived in the guest house and whose use of the grounds made excavation impossible), further archaeological work to the west of the church, which had long been thought to be desirable, would be possible. Despite the fact that it would have been possible to publish the results of Keen's work separately, the importance of the site as a whole led Keen and Coppack to agree that, rather than publish the results of Keen's campaign, it was academically advisable to work towards the combined publication of both campaigns of archaeological work. This decision accounts for the late appearance of the results of Laurence Keen's work.

Campaign of Glyn Coppack

In 1985, Glyn Coppack's co-director, who had day-to-day responsibility for the excavation team, was Dave Greenhalf, who was himself assisted by Rich Williams and Jerry Thorp. Planning was the responsibility of Jan Tulley, and finds administration Judith Roebuck.

Without the continuous support of the English Heritage direct works team, and particularly Tom Rudd and Willie Howden, who devised ingenious methods of dealing with the problems of spoil dispersal and recovery in one of the wettest summers on record at Mount Grace, the excavation of Cell 8 might easily have become an unpleasant chore. Technical support was provided throughout the excavation and after by Goff Hutchinson, area superintendent and one-time Mount Grace charge-hand, whose fund of stories about the conservation of the site and unrecorded discoveries made in the course of it directly led to the research strategy that controlled the excavation between 1987 and 1992.

The return to the site in 1987, though Coppack was initially reluctant because of other commitments, was the result of the request of Christopher Young, the then English Heritage Director for the North of England, who wanted to see the conservation of the site completed on the back of a major research campaign with which the conservation and display of the site was running in parallel. In this the late Francis Golding and Roy Swanston, successively Directors of Properties in Care at English Heritage, consistently supported him. Professional support came from John Weaver, until 1986 Inspector for the site, and from the late John Hurst, then Assistant Chief Inspector of Ancient Monuments. Both Martin Stancliffe, consultant architect for the completion of conservation at Mount Grace, and Derrick Willey, the superintendent of works who succeeded Goff Hutchinson in 1988, provided technical support. Tom Rudd and Willie Howden continued to provide almost daily assistance with the excavation, throughout the project, and with remarkably good grace as it was work they undertook over and above their regular duties. In this, Derrick Willey, who sometimes intentionally failed to notice what was going on, abetted them.

From 1989 to 1992, Caroline Atkins (who had worked for Keen in 1974) took over as co-director, and the quality of both the excavation and record over this period is very much a tribute to her. In this she was ably assisted by a growing number of area supervisors: Roz Nichol, Tom Gledhill, Trevor Carbin, Mick Cressey, Steve Page, Rich Williams, Jackie Hall, Darren Pullen, Nessie Pearson, Simon Johnson, Kevin Booth and Peter Richardson. Planning was the responsibility of Darren Pullen up to 1990, Jan Tulley (back temporarily from Australia) in 1991 and Nessie Pearson and Simon Ware in 1992. Finds administration was done throughout by Denny Coppack, assisted full time in 1991 and 1992 by Jonathan Brace.

Without the full-time assistance of Ba Weld (and Sharon Harvey in 1991), nobody would have been paid, fed or provided with a constant supply of tea and coffee, and the co-directors would not have been spared the miseries of site administration. A noticeable trend was the number of area supervisors who started out as diggers and were trained on the job, in spite of difficult working conditions (always too wet or too dry). The excavation was marked by so remarkably high a rate of returning diggers that over the five years the team effectively became an extended family.

Architectural analysis was supported by Steve Coll, who initially came to record the guest-house range, but who went on to provide a foil against which the development of the whole site could be tested, and by Jackie Hall, who undertook the study of loose architectural fragments before getting dragged into the project on a more permanent basis. Simon Hayfield undertook the publication drawing of all the loose architectural material, but found himself additionally providing those drawings that nobody else wanted to do because of their complexity. Post-excavation analysis was supported throughout by Colin Hayfield, who took on responsibility for all of the pottery from the site, including that from Keen's excavations and site clearance, and then found himself generally managing the post-excavation process. Scientific backup was provided by Glynis Edwards, Marjorie Hutchinson, Barry Knight and the late Colin Slack on the finds, and Allan Hall and Andrew Jones on food waste, with Kate Foley, then Head of the Ancient Monuments Laboratory, helping to cut corners and red tape to ensure prompt action. All the small finds were drawn by the late Jim Thorn, Margaret Tremayne, Claire Thorne and Judith Dobie, who also provided many of the plans and all of the elevation drawings for Glyn Coppack.

Production of this Report

This report is effectively the product of many people, though the structure used makes it difficult to identify them in the text. Colin Hayfield provided all the pottery analysis, descriptions and drawings, and was responsible for the identification and construction of the individual Finds Groups. Laurence Keen provided the small find descriptions used in all the Finds Groups as well as providing the analysis in Chapter 7 that bears his name, and undertook the study of the ceramic floor tiles. Similarly, Jackie Hall provided all the descriptions of the architectural fragments, as well as many of the ideas expressed in Chapters 6 and 8, and collaborated on the overview of the architectural collection in Chapter 7. Other contributors are identified in the text.

In the preparation of his specifically authored parts of this volume Keen owes a special debt of gratitude to Bernard Barr, then of York Minster Library, for draft texts on the indulgence stone and the inscribed lead strips. These were exhibited at Mount Grace in an exhibition held in the summer of 1970 at the instigation of Miss Kitty Cooper-Abbs. Throughout Keen's work Miss Cooper-Abbs was a source of much information and encouragement and an inspiring host to the volunteers when atrocious weather prevented work being undertaken.

PREFACE

Many people have helped in the preparation of the description and analysis of the finds. Special thanks are due to: Arthur MacGregor of the Ashmolean Museum; John Cherry, then of the British Museum; Andy Elkerton of the Mary Rose Trust; and the late Geoff Egan, then of the Museum of London Specialist Services. David Williams undertook the thin-sectioning of ceramic floor tiles and Sarah Paynter analysed the glazes. At the Yorkshire Museum, the late Elizabeth Hartley kindly allowed further study of the floor tiles in her care, and at the Scarborough Museum, Jane Davies gave much help in facilitating examination of the floor tiles in the collections there.

Coppack is indebted to both Mick Aston and Carol Rowntree for their help in the understanding of Carthusian monastic life, to Philip Dixon who helped him understand the buildings, to the late Richard K. Morris, who commented on a number of the architectural problems, and to Laurence Keen, who was always happy to share his ideas and long-standing knowledge of the site. Caroline den Hartog and Hein Hundertmark of Utrecht, Birgit Dukers of Roermond, and Harry van Royen, then of Koksijde, kindly provided material for comparison on charterhouses in the Netherlands and Belgium.

Completion of the post-excavation project was managed by Caroline Atkins and monitored by the late Sarah Jennings, both of whom made a complex job much easier than it could have been. The text was read by Ron Shoesmith at an early stage, and greatly improved by his comments. Any mistakes that remain are the responsibility of the main authors.

This report was originally delivered to English Heritage in 2005 after the revision of an earlier draft that was reviewed very positively by the late Professor Mick Aston, who suggested the inclusion of further background material on the Carthusian Order and on the pre-monastic archaeology of the site, and the provision of a glossary to make the narrative less 'technical'. Unavoidable delays in publication of so large a report inevitably meant that the national and international context of the project had changed and this particularly required the updating of Chapter 8 as a great deal of new understanding has developed, particularly of the site's significance, and it was collectively decided to incorporate any revisions into the editorial process to avoid further delay. Regrettably, it has not proved possible to make amendments to the individual finds reports, which were up to date in 2005, but all other aspects have been updated to 2018. The glossary has disappeared and, in common with the house style of the English Heritage Red Guides, explanations are given sparingly in the text.

The production of this report owes everything to its editors, Katherine Davey and Dr Sarah Harrison, who have made the process considerably easier than it might have been and achieved a degree of consistency in what is a multi-authored publication.

Glyn Coppack and Laurence Keen

Glyn Coppack dedicates his parts of this study to the memory of Roy Gilyard-Beer, his pupil-master in monastic studies, to Philip Rahtz who first introduced him to archaeology and to Mick Aston who shared his fascination with the Carthusians.

Laurence Keen dedicates his contribution to the memory of Miss Kathleen Cooper-Abbs, who supported him and his team throughout his excavations at Mount Grace.

Chapter 1: Mount Grace Priory and the Carthusian Order

Of the 834 religious houses that existed in England and Wales when Henry VIII was made head of the Church in England in 1534, only nine houses belonged to the Carthusian Order. Of those, Mount Grace Priory is the best preserved and the only one currently open to the public. Since 1953 it had been owned by the National Trust and since 1955 in the care of the State. Its ruins have been conserved for public display and subjected to the largest-scale excavation and analysis of any medieval Carthusian monastery.

Since the initial study at Mount Grace by William Brown and Sir William St John Hope at the end of the 19th century, and their published findings (Brown 1882; Hope 1905), its plan has been taken to typify the Carthusians' eremitic approach to monastic life. The priory was, however, a late medieval foundation, indeed the last monastic house to be founded (in 1398) in Yorkshire before the Suppression. Its buildings and their contents, therefore, reflect some 300 years of development within the order itself and of architectural and cultural development in England. Being both very well preserved and in the hands of the State, and therefore available for study, Mount Grace is the most intensively studied of all Carthusian monasteries in Europe, and provides exceptional evidence for its conception, development and occupation, throwing considerable light on late medieval Carthusian life, the form and location of the buildings, and in particular on the lives of individual monks.

In order to assess the contribution that Mount Grace might make to Carthusian, as well as general, monastic studies, the site should be seen in the context of the Carthusian Order itself and of the English province of the order.

1.1 Origins of the Carthusian Order

In the 3rd century many informal communities of Christian ascetics grew up in the deserts of Egypt, the most significant of which were followers of St Pachomius (d.348) and St Anthony of Egypt (d.356). These 'desert fathers' became the model for Christian monasticism, and it is from the Greek word for desert (*eremos*), that the word eremite (hermit), derives. Later monks developed and formalised rules for monastic living, notably St Augustine of Hippo (d.430) and of St Benedict of Nursia (d.*c*.547), which defined communal, rather than eremitic, living, and later gave rise to various monastic orders.

The Carthusian order began in 1084 when St Bruno Hartenfaust, a canon and later chancellor of the collegiate church of Rheims in northern France, rejected what he considered to be a corrupt church, and with a group of like-minded friends decided to withdraw from the world. He sought the advice of St Robert of Molesme, a Benedictine abbot experimenting with reform and the future founder of the Cistercian Order, but decided instead to follow the eremitic example of St Anthony of Egypt, and of Sts Jerome (d.420), and John Cassian (d.435). Bruno left Robert and, with six friends, sought the advice and assistance of St Hugh de Chateau-Neuf, Bishop of Grenoble, who provided a site for a monastery in the valley of the Chartreuse in the mountains of Dauphiné in Haute Savoie (now Isère, France), in 1084. Here Bruno developed an ideal that others were to evolve into the Carthusian order.

The austerity practised by the monks who joined the community at the Grande Chartreuse by the first quarter of the 12th century brought them the name of 'Christ's Poor Men'. Early accounts of life there tell of a small stone church, simple timber cells bereft of paintings, tapestries or other decorations, and monks clad in hair shirts and unbleached white habits leading a silent, austere and meditative life, and spending most of their days alone in their cells.

Early monastic communities contained very few ordained priests before the late 12th century, and all members performed the necessary manual labour of the house. Though the Rule of St Benedict defined the three elements of the monastic day as *Opus Dei* (the round of offices in the church), *Lectio Divina* (spiritual reading and meditation) and *Opus Manuum* (manual work), this last had largely disappeared by the 11th century, and the manual labour of the house was done by paid servants (*laici*) and lay brothers (*conversi*).

In the 6th century St Benedict had used the word *conversi*, which means 'converts', to identify men who had come late to the monastic life, but by the late 11th and 12th centuries it signified a member of the community who had taken a monastic vow as a servant. The reformed orders in particular, including the Carthusians, took these lay brothers into their communities who undertook the day-to-day tasks of the house. This ensured the choir monks, who by the late 12th century were more commonly priests, were not distracted from their continuing devotions and the specialised manual work they performed within their cells.

From the 14th century, laymen who wished to serve the community but not take monastic vows and serve under a contract of fidelity were known as donates or oblates. Outsiders who wanted to take a form of monastic vow and live within the community were called *redditi*. In England, the use of the term donates (or oblates) were occasionally confused with *redditi*.

The Carthusians were never a large, nor, in comparison to others, a popular or wealthy monastic order, but nevertheless maintained an exclusivity based on their reputation for severe discipline and asceticism.

1.2 Spread of the Carthusian Order

Bruno had not intended to found an order, nor that the Grande Chartreuse would become the mother house of a family of similar monasteries. He reluctantly left his new monastery in 1090 to become a counsellor to Pope Urban II, who had been his pupil at Rheims. He never returned to the monastery, but by 1091 he had persuaded the Pope to let him return to an eremitic life. He settled with new Italian followers in Calabria where he established a second monastery, St Mary de la Torre, modelled on the Grande Chartreuse. Bruno died in 1101 without having formalised his two monasteries within a rule or set of customs.

It was not until the election of Guigues (or Guigo) de Saint-Romain (d.1136) as the fifth prior of the Grande Chartreuse in 1110 that there was any move to organise Christ's Poor Men into a monastic order. Guigues was an exceptional organiser and knew and was respected by abbots Peter the Venerable of Cluny and Bernard of Clairvaux, the leading influences in the 12th-century monastic church. Under him the community of the Grande Chartreuse grew so rapidly that six new houses were established across France between 1115 and 1117, either by direct foundation or conversion.

Some formalisation of the community and its followers was clearly essential, and at the request of the new houses Guigues compiled, in about 1128, the *Consuetudines Cartusiae* (Carthusian Customs). These were a definitive collection of the customs observed at the Grande Chartreuse, which codified both religious and social practice for his own house as well as the others. These Customs, which effectively made the Grande Chartreuse the central authority of all Carthusian congregations, were ratified formally by Pope Innocent II in 1133, though his predecessors Calixtus II and Honorius II had also approved them and had referred to the new congregations as the 'Sacred Eremitic Carthusian Order'. The name was derived from Chartreuse.

Guigues' Customs owed a great deal to the advice of Peter of Cluny and Bernard of Clairvaux, and the Carthusians were to become as centralised as the Cluniac and Cistercian Orders, themselves also movements of reform. From 1140, at the request of the houses themselves, the Carthusians relied on an annual General Chapter of all priors held at the Grande Chartreuse to ensure that the Customs were being correctly interpreted or to extend them by statutes as the order grew. Between General Chapters, the prior of the Grande Chartreuse had executive authority, a system that combined Cistercian democracy with Cluniac centralisation. It is from this date that the Carthusians consider themselves to have been an order, with all houses, including the Grande Chartreuse, pledged to the General Chapter in perpetuity.

1.3 Carthusian Life

Solitude

The purpose of Carthusian life is total withdrawal from the world and its distractions to serve God by personal devotion and privation. The Monks live as hermits, without the communal life of the Benedictine and Augustinian traditions, setting themselves apart from the world to the extent that they discourage lay visitors to their monasteries. Though they dispense alms, they intentionally do little else to help those poorer than themselves, in obedience to the reminder given in Guigues' Customs: 'for it was not for the temporal cure of other folks' bodies, but for the welfare of our own souls, that we took refuge in the retirement of this desert'.

From the start, their eremetic style of life was apparent in the planning of their monasteries. Guibert de Nogent, a retired Abbot of the Benedictine house Nogent-sous-Coucy, visiting the Grande Chartreuse between 1101 and 1109, described the monastic buildings thus: 'there are 13 monks having indeed a cloister, sufficiently fit for coenobitic [communal monastic] custom, but not dwelling together like others cloisterwise, for they all have cells of their own round the cloister in which they work, sleep, and eat … Water … for drinking, as for other uses, they had by a conduit from the spring which goes into the cells of all, and through certain holes flows into each of their little houses' (Thompson 1930, 12–13).

Cells

The cells contain all the necessary requirements for monastic life and they, rather than the church, are the centre of Carthusian religious life. Life is strictly controlled by the Customs. No monk under the age of 20 is to be admitted to the order, and each member of the community has to undergo a probationary year before profession. On admission, each monk is assigned a cell and put under the supervision of a senior monk who might visit him to give instruction. Once professed, he accepts that he might do nothing without the prior's license, that he can own no property and that he must observe silence at all times.

The Customs give a basic list of his needs, which are all provided for by the monastery. This list remained unmodified throughout the Middle Ages, and specified for his bed straw, a felt cloth, a cushion, a covering of sheepskin and a coverlet of coarse cloth; for his wardrobe and personal use two hair shirts, two tunics, two pilches (outer garment of animal skin with the fur used as a lining), two cowls (hooded cloaks), three pairs of breeches, two loin cloths, shoes for night and day use, four pairs of socks, a hood, a girdle, a comb, a razor and whetstone; for the repair of his garments two needles, scissors and thread; for domestic use two plates, two cooking pots, a third pot, with a lid to it, for bread, a fourth pot, somewhat bigger, for washing up, two spoons, a bread knife, a flagon, a cup, a ewer, a salt cellar, a pan, a towel, tinder for his fire, wood and an axe; for writing he was to have a desk, pens, chalk, two pumices (for erasing marks on parchment), two inkhorns, a penknife, two parchment scrapers (for smoothing and cleaning sheets of parchment before use), a dry point (a lead pencil for ruling lines on parchment; a number of examples of which appear in the west range of cells, see Chapter 4), prickers (point used for marking parchment), a weight, a ruler and a stylus (writing point). He was also to have the necessary tools of his chosen trade (Thompson 1930, 33–4), for every monk was to have his own special skills to serve the house.

Diet

Diet remained strictly vegetarian, even for the sick and those who had been bled, an extreme austerity that was to bring the Carthusians into conflict with reforming Popes. From 13 September (the significance of the date is unclear, but it may have marked the end of harvest) to Easter only one meal was taken each day. Otherwise the monks ate twice daily. In the 12th century the monks were encouraged to fast during the summer on Monday, Wednesday and Friday, their diets restricted to white

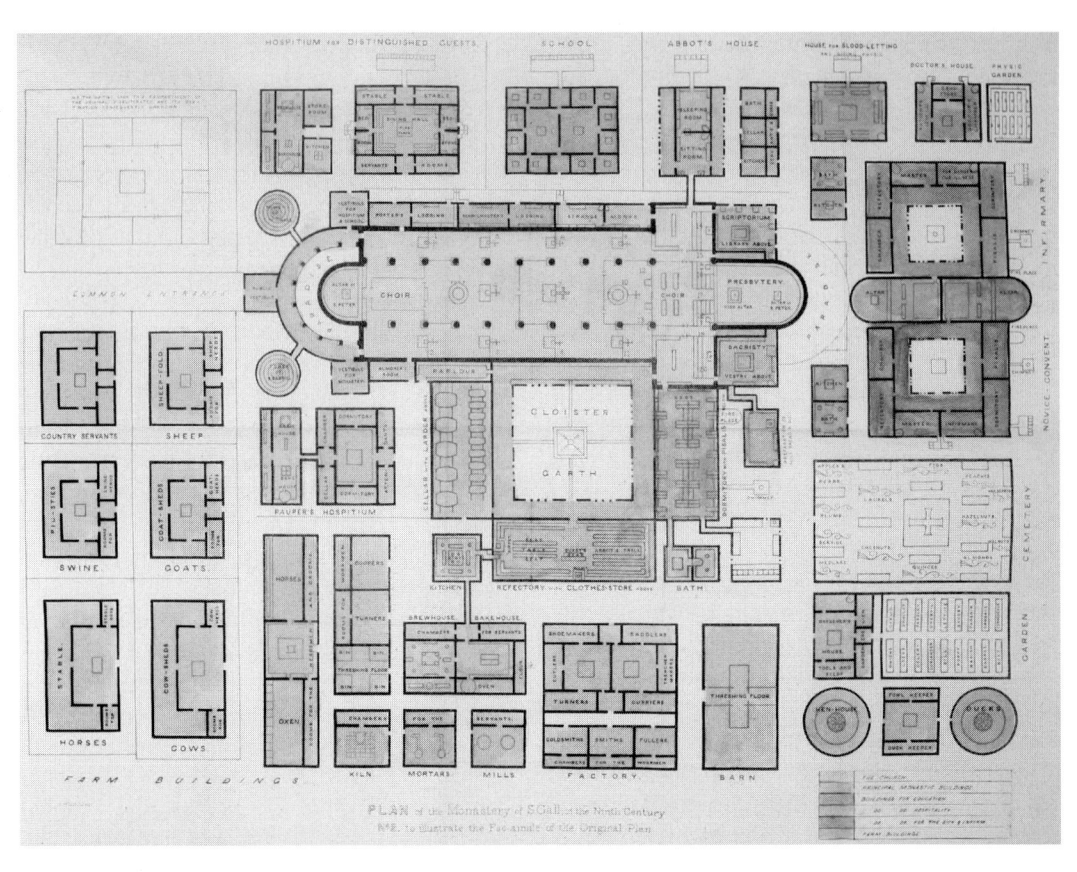

Figure 1.1 The early 9th-century plan of St Gall Abbey.

(good quality) bread, though by the mid-13th century this practice had been reduced to one day a week. Vegetables the monks cooked for themselves in their own cells, but for some meals eggs, cheese and fish were cooked in and supplied by the kitchen. The monks were able to supplement the monastery diet with herbs, additional vegetables and fruit, which they grew in their own cell gardens.

1.4 Layout of Carthusian Monasteries

Earliest Houses

The groups that came together using the Rule of St Benedict began to develop a distinctive layout for their buildings based essentially on the late Roman villa estate. This led, by the early 9th century, to a regular layout of monastic buildings around a cloister and enclosed courts, which is best exemplified by the early 9th-century plan that is held in the library of St Gall Abbey (see Figure 1.1), in what is now Switzerland, and which presents a schematic layout for a substantial Benedictine monastery (Horn and Born 1979, *passim*). As the teachings of St Benedict centred on communal living, with the monks eating, sleeping and worshipping together, monasteries following St Benedict's precepts required communal dormitories, refectories and cloisters.

The Carthusians, however, did not subscribe closely to the Benedictine rule but took their interpretation of monastic life from St Anthony of Egypt and his followers (see Chapter 1.1). They were almost alone among the monastic groups of western Europe in returning to the early ideals of the eastern church, practising the life of hermits and living in communities only for protection (Aston 1993; 2001, *passim*; Coppack and Aston 2002, 11–24). Such an emphasis is bound to be reflected in the physical plan of their monasteries.

Nevertheless, certain features, being necessary for the ordering of monastic life and its interfacing with the outside world, are common to the principal regular orders and the Carthusians: a cloister at the centre of the monastery, a church, a chapter house, a refectory and the cellular structure of enclosed inner and outer courts. As well as these purposeful similarities, a degree of commonality was imposed on the buildings of a Carthusian charterhouse and those of other religious houses simply because they were built by the same stonemasons. Carthusian ground plans, however, show that there are fundamental differences of design and in the weighting of individual structures that reflect the eremitic life of the community.

The charterhouse is in effect two monasteries: one for the choir monks, the other for the lay brothers – the 'upper' and 'lower' houses as they were first defined at the Grande Chartreuse. Initially, these two houses were distinct, the intention being to remove any distractions from the upper house where the monks were trying to achieve total solitude.

The upper house centred on the great cloister, which was bounded on three sides by the monks' individual cells and gardens. The fourth side comprised the communal buildings of the upper house: the refectory (for meals taken together on Sundays and on a small number of festivals), the chapter house (for the necessary corporate business of the monastery) and usually the cells of those monks who alone had business to conduct with laymen – the prior, the sacrist and the procurator (the financial manager of the house). Sometimes the kitchens, too, encroached onto this fourth side of the great cloister. Beyond these communal buildings lay the church, a small building, detached from the cloister, for the limited services attended in common.

Up to the 14th century the model of the Grande Chartreuse was followed, with a lower house forming a separate institution on a separate site. The lower house was also known as the *correrie*, after the location of the lower house of the Grand Chartreuse, which lay down the mountain from the upper house. The lower house might have its own church and included the lesser cloister (which accommodated the lay brothers), the guest houses and the farming and industrial buildings needed in an agricultural economy.

Changes in Planning

Later charterhouses, as in all those in England with the exception of only two, do not have lower houses, and so adopt the inner court common to other orders. This semi-public area lies, as at Mount Grace, beyond the church adjacent to the great cloister. It served many of the same functions as the lower house, including the lesser cloister, the guest house and some of the service buildings that would have been located in the lower house. The agricultural and industrial buildings were situated outside the walls of the central monastic complex, in the outer court.

This arrangement, as exemplified at Mount Grace, brought the overall plan more into line with those of other orders, but in essence it remains as established during Bruno's lifetime, with only slight modification, to the present day.

Originally charterhouses were intended only to house 12 monks and the prior, but increasing numbers led to the building of 'double houses', for 24 monks. The Grande Chartreuse became such a double house in 1324 and in 1595 even received a third '*ambitus*' (Braunfels 1972, 111), meaning an extension to the house.

The lay brothers and donates represented the domestic staff of the house, designed to minister to the needs of the choir monks and act as a buffer between them and the outside world in the day-to-day running of the house. They lived originally in communal buildings, but by the 15th century might live in individual cells in the same manner as the choir monks, although their cells were smaller, apparently with gardens but without an upper storey to accommodate a workroom: their workroom was the monastery. Their role was to manage and carry out the day-to-day affairs of the priory, dealing with tradesmen, with tenants on the lands owned by the house, with guests and with all other secular affairs, thereby shielding the monks from the outside world and allowing them to keep cell and solitude.

Influence of the Grande Chartreuse

The Grande Chartreuse as founded by St Bruno in 1084 was destroyed by an avalanche. Prior Guigues de Saint-Romain took the decision to rebuild it on a different site, a few hundred metres away, and its new church was consecrated in 1132. In the formative years of most orders, new houses would normally look to their mother house for inspiration and guidance for the layout of their buildings. Braunfels (1972, 113) suggests that it was Guigues who, through his rebuilding of the Grande Chartreuse, set the prototype that subsequent charterhouses were to emulate.

The Grande Chartreuse has never received detailed architectural or archaeological study, and indeed the extensive additions and alterations since the early 12th century would make such a task difficult. It is known, however, that new houses used its layout as a blueprint, adapting it as necessary to their specific topography and setting, and such was its timeless suitability that even 19th-century charterhouses, such as that at Parkminster, West Sussex, emulated it.

Braunfels also suggests (1972, 114–115) that the basic conservatism of the Carthusian order and the order's deliberate architectural plainness, which minimises any response to changing architectural fashions, encouraged the longevity and stability of the Carthusian plan. Conservatism in plan, however, was not peculiar to the Carthusians, and it is not without relevance that the planning of the second monastery at the Grande Chartreuse was established at just the time that the Cistercians were also defining the ideal layout of their monasteries, a development that culminated in the rebuilding of Clairvaux under Bernard des Fontaines from 1135. The plan adopted for Clairvaux survived without major change to the close of the 18th century.

1.5 The Carthusians in England (see Figure 1.2)

The order was brought to England by Henry II, who, as part of his penance for the death of Archbishop Thomas Becket, brought Carthusian monks to England from the Grande Chartreuse and settled them in a new house at Witham, Somerset, in 1178–9. Medieval Carthusian settlement in England was limited to nine houses, a single failed settlement and three projected settlements that did not materialise. They became known in England, via the Norman French, as charterhouses. All but two of the nine were founded towards the end of the medieval period, when the monastic church was otherwise in decline.

Compared with the 64 successful Cistercian houses, this might seem insignificant. The austere life of the Carthusians did not initially appeal to the English landed military class, which had flocked to support first the Augustinian canons who could serve appropriated churches, and then the Cistercians, an order happy to exploit vast areas of marginal land and one organised on military lines with which they felt in sympathy.

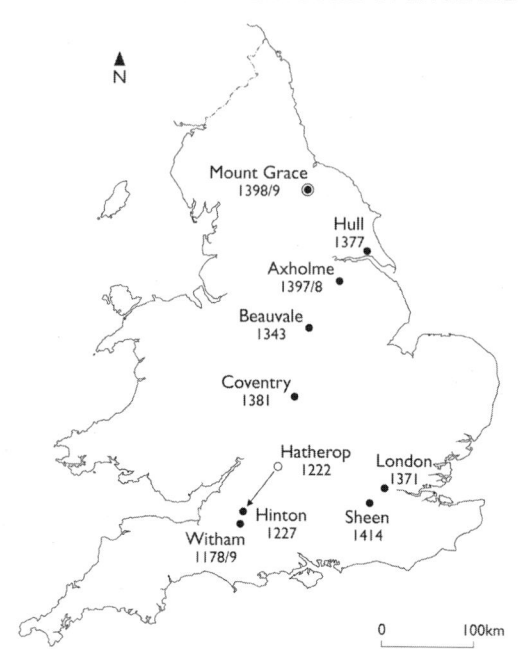

Figure 1.2 The English charterhouses with the dates of their foundation.

In contrast, the Carthusians aimed for self-sufficiency and peace. Their late arrival, a generation after the most intense period of monastic foundation in England, probably did not help, for most landed families supported at least one monastery already. Until the middle years of the 13th century, the Augustinians and Cistercians offered a better deal for patrons, who wished to be associated with a successful, as well as a reformist, movement.

It was the arrival in the early 1220s of the mendicant friars that marked the demise of the older orders. The friars brought about a change in the perception of a regular life by ministering to a broader band of society, depriving of recruits the Benedictines, Cluniacs, Cistercians and canons regular, but increasing the popularity of the Carthusians, whose uncompromising austerity set them apart from the other orders, but had much in common with the Franciscans and Dominicans. The revival of the Carthusian order in England directly followed the widespread founding of friaries in the 13th century. There had only been two successful Carthusian foundations before 1300, both supported by the Angevin royal house, but the first half of the 14th century saw an awakening of interest in the order: licences were

Table 1.1 Charterhouses of England

House	Foundation	Founder
Witham	1178/9	Henry II, King of England
Hatherop	1222	William Longespée, Earl of Salisbury (house transferred and refounded at Hinton)
Hinton	1227	Ela, Countess of Salisbury
Exeter	1331 (licence)	Licence granted to Richard Stapleton (house not built)
Beauvale	1343	Sir Nicholas de Cantilupe
Horne	c.1345 (licence)	Licence granted to Mary of St Pol, Countess of Pembroke (house not built)
London	1371	Sir Walter Maney
Hull	1377	Michael de la Pole, Earl of Suffolk
Coventry	1381	William, Lord Zouche, and Richard II, King of England
Monkskirby	1389 (licence)	Licence granted to Thomas Mowbray, Earl of Nottingham (house not built)
Axholme	1397/8	Thomas Mowbray, Earl of Nottingham
Mount Grace	1398	Thomas de Holand, Duke of Surrey
Sheen	1414	Henry V, King of England

sought and granted for three new charterhouses, although only one of these was built. After the Black Death, however, which in England raged from 1349 to 1350, a flurry of foundations came, the result of the panic and the increased piety that the pandemic had caused.

From the foundation of Beauvale in 1343 to the foundation of the royal house of Sheen in 1415, the founders of charterhouses in England were all courtiers or members of the royal family, an indicator of the level of society that now supported the order. Perhaps the Carthusians offered an exclusivity that the friaries denied the rich and powerful; certainly, they were not perceived as achieving the level of the austerity reached by the Carthusians, whose prayers, in consequence, were considered especially powerful.

The cellular structure of Carthusian monasteries permitted the endowment of individual cells, so enabling churchmen and the merchant class to be associated with the development of individual monasteries, and the founder to offset some of the cost without diminishing the benefit to his soul. Before 1343, all the English houses, as befitted the Carthusian desire to be apart from the world, were established on rural sites. After this date, only Axholme and Mount Grace were established on traditional sites, and Sheen was established alongside the royal palace of Richmond, hardly a 'desert' site in any sense of the word, but a royal monastery placed where it was for the benefit of Henry V.

The size and wealth of the English charterhouses is known for certain only in the mid-16th century from the *Valor Ecclesiasticus* of 1534/5, the valuation of Church property ordered by Henry VIII, and from the pension lists of dispossessed monks, lay brothers and donates, drawn up during the subsequent Suppression.

Charterhouses were not normally particularly richly endowed, partly because their Statutes insisted upon a subsistence economy (Thompson 1930, 91–2), partly because most were established after the Statute of Mortmain of 1279, which severely limited gifts of land, and partly because the Carthusians were in direct competition with the friars for alms.

Over 800 monasteries were valued in the *Valor Ecclesiasticus*. The richest was the Benedictine abbey of Glastonbury, which had an income of well over £1,000 a year and a community of 51. But most houses had less than £200, and some small nunneries survived on less than £8 a year. Of the charterhouses, only those of London (£642 a year), supported substantially by the wealthy city merchants, and of Sheen (£800 a year), funded by Henry V for the benefit of his own soul, could compare with the wealthier houses of other orders, such as the Benedictine monasteries of Chertsey and Malmesbury. The charterhouses of Beauvale, Coventry and Hull had net yearly incomes below £200 in 1535. Mount Grace, with a net income of £323, compares with a house like

Table 1.2 Carthusian communities derived from pension lists at the suppression, 1539–40

House	Net annual income	Monks	Novices	Lay brothers	Donates
Witham	£215 15s. 0d.	13	0	0	0
Hinton	£248 15s. 2d.	17	0	6	0
Beauvale	£196 6s. 0d.	9*	0	2	0
London	£643 0s. 4d.	12*	0	6	0
Hull	£174 18s. 4d.	12	1	1	0
Coventry	£131 6s. 4d.	13	0	3	(6 yeomen)
Axholme	£237 15s. 2d.	9*	0	0	0
Mount Grace	£323 2s. 10½d.	17	3	6	1
Sheen	£777 12s. 0½d.	18**	Numbers not recorded		

* indicates numbers had been reduced by executions in 1535, in which year Beauvale had had 19 monks, Axholme 13 monks and London 30 monks and 18 lay brothers
** number derived from a difference source

Great Malvern, though where that Benedictine house supported only a prior and 11 monks with such an income, Mount Grace supported a community of 27.

A brief summary of the history, and architectural development, where known, of each house is given below as background to the study of Mount Grace. This is based largely on a wider study of Carthusian houses in the British Isles undertaken by Mick Aston, Paul Everson and Glyn Coppack (for which see Coppack and Aston 2002, *passim*).

Witham, Somerset: 1178/9–1539
History
The Priory of the Blessed Virgin, St John the Baptist and All Saints, Witham, was founded by Henry II as part of his penance for the murder, by his followers, of Thomas Becket, his one-time friend, with whom he had quarrelled. The prior of the Grande Chartreuse sent his monk Narbert and two lay brothers, Gerard and a centenarian, Ainard, to England to establish this new charterhouse within the vill of Witham in the Royal Forest of Selwood (Thompson 1930, 49–53). The earliest documentary reference to the new house comes from the Pipe Rolls (26 Henry II, 106) where, in the accounts for the year 1179–80 for Baron Robert de Beauchamp, Sheriff of Somerset, there is an item of £10 to the 'brothers of the Order of Chartuse dwelling in the vill of Witham which William Fitz John had'.

The French Narbert, unable to cope (he disliked the people and the food and the king showed little support for the house), returned to France, and another monk, Hamon, was dispatched, but died of exposure shortly after his arrival (conditions must have been extremely harsh and the monks were probably still camping at the site, the first temporary buildings having yet to be constructed). Then, at Henry II's specific request, the Prior of Grande Chartreuse sent a renowned young monk, Hugh of Avalon (later St Hugh of Lincoln) in 1179. It was Hugh who began the construction of the first temporary buildings of the charterhouse in 1179/80 and formalised the community.

Henry II issued his charter of foundation on 6 January 1182. Permanent building work was to follow, but it was not until 1186, the last year of Hugh's priorate, that payments were received for the building of a church at Witham (Armitage Robinson 1918, 5–8), presumably marking the change from timber to stone. The kitchen, which burned down in 1199, was still of timber (Douie and Farmer 1985, I, 219).

The initial endowment of Witham comprised almost half the royal manor of Selwood, an area now identified as forming the whole parish of Witham Friary (McGarvie 1978, 5). To this were added substantial landholdings in Mendip, centred on granges at what is now Charterhouse-on-Mendip, at Hydon, and at Billerica.

Initially, it seems, the community lived off the produce of their own lands, supplemented by the proceeds of small-scale lead mining. In 1283 Edward I licensed them to profit from the lead resources within their lands, though there is no evidence to indicate whether or not these were commercially exploited. Only after the Black Death in the mid-14th century did they begin to accept, probably out of financial need, bequests of more distant properties and to benefit from their rents. By the 15th century they were even granting burial rights in their cemetery, in return for bequests, for laity living in the neighbourhood of Witham. The house was suppressed on 15 March 1539, its gross annual income valued at £227 1s. 8d.

Site

Being an early house – the earliest in England – Witham followed the early model of a split site, with an upper and lower house. The great cloister and choir monks' buildings were to the south of what is now Witham Hall Farm, at National Grid Reference (NGR) ST75804170, and the *correrie* was some 700 m further west, centred on the surviving 12th-century church of Witham Friary. The site of the great cloister was first identified in 1918 (Burrow and Burrow 1990, 144) and confirmed by excavation (Palmer 1923). Further excavations were carried out between 1965 and 1969 (Barlow and Reed 1966; 1967; and Burrow and Burrow 1990) and a tentative plan produced.

Interpretation of the results was confused by the failure to identify a major post-Suppression house of 1717, the south wing of which was misidentified as the monastic church.

The earthworks (see Figure 1.3) lie principally within a rectangular field (which occupies the site of the main garden of the post-Suppression house) on gentle north-facing slopes at 95 m OD (ordnance datum) on a spur between two valleys: that of the river Frome, flowing south-west to north-east, and that of an unnamed tributary flowing south–north. Both valleys were once used for water management in the form of ponds or lakes. The earthworks chiefly represent post-Suppression activity, but their orientation and basic structure suggest a strong continuity with the monastic layout, certainly into the 18th, and probably into the early 19th, century.

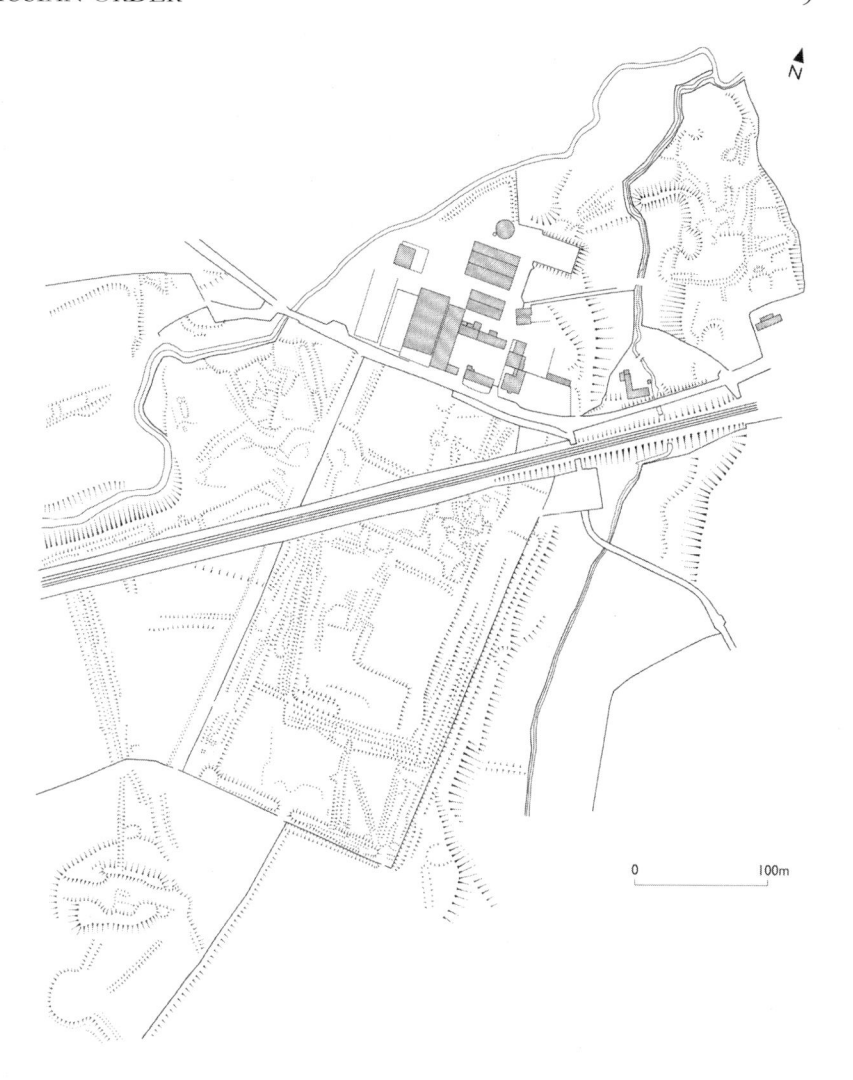

Monastery

The area of the monastic precinct corresponds in part to the rectangular field in which the bulk of the earthworks lie, though as some of the earthworks extend beyond it the full precinct must have been larger. The great cloister survives as a rectangular earthwork within the rectangular field. It forms a levelled area some 58 m by 73 m, cut into the gentle natural slope on the southern and western sides of the field. Geophysical survey confirmed that the cloister was rectangular and that it was defined by spreads of rubble marking the cloister alleys, by its walls, and by probable paving, some 5 m wide (Gaffney 1994, 2).

The east cloister range is marked by a massive west-facing terrace scarp, 1.2 m high, though this was certainly adapted as a garden terrace after the Suppression. The line of the east cloister alley, on the inner side of the

Figure 1.3 The charterhouse of Witham (after RCHM(E)).

terrace scarp, was revealed by excavation and is now visible as a low bank.

The west cloister alley wall is visible as a low bank. Beyond this bank, the west cloister wall and cells were identified by geophysical survey, as were others on the south side of the great cloister. The cells are within garden plots 18 m long, though their plans were not intelligible. One cell on the north-west side of the cloister was excavated and its plan partly recovered.

On the north side of the cloister was a range 38 m long and 13 m wide, with at least one room partitioned off at its west end.

The church can be identified as incorporated into the north wing of the house as altered after 1717, which is some 42 m north of the north wall of the cloister, suggesting that it was separated from the great cloister by a second cloister.

In the Frome valley to the west of the site are two linked substantial ponds, or lakes, which although post-monastic and ornamental in their present form probably perpetuate the sites of monastic fishponds. Burrow and Burrow (1990, 147) observed that 'the River Frome runs in a channel on the south side of the valley and has clearly been diverted to allow the fishponds to be created', and survey confirms this observation. In the valley to the east a pair of dams survives. Both appear to be substantially monastic in origin. When in use they would have flooded a 380 m length of the valley. Burrow and Burrow (1990, 147) equate the lowest of the two dams with the name 'Hach Stoch' in a document dealing with the initial grant of the site in 1179/80 and with a fishpond recorded in a charter of 1232. The upper dam lies 160 m to the south of the lower dam, and has been largely obscured, though it survives as an embankment 1.9 m high on which the present road runs. Its southern side has been confused by the construction of the railway embankment. This dam would have formed a reservoir some 200 m long.

Post-Suppression Development
HOUSE
In 1544 the charterhouse buildings and land were granted to Sir Ralph Hopton, who appears to have created the house on the site that subsequently passed to his great-nephew, Sir Robert Hopton. McGarvie (1989, 161–5) claims that both Robert and his son Ralph were resident there. The house was besieged three times during the Civil War campaigns in the south-west and was 'strengthened' (fortified) in 1644 (ibid.). While geophysical survey identified no evidence for this house or of Civil War activity, it did identify a potentially mid-17th-century layout of garden beds surviving in the grounds of the early 18th-century house that succeeded it.

The Witham site passed by marriage to John Wyndham in the late 17th century and remained in that family until it was sold to Sir William Beckford of Fonthill before 1763. In 1717 Sir William Wyndham commissioned William Talman to 'improve' his residence at Witham, work that was completed by James Gibbs. Drawings of the principal floor and an elevation of the house, made in about 1710 by the Scottish architect Colen Campbell (Campbell 1771, 344), show the planned addition of a southern wing (which excavation revealed was indeed built) and a western enclosing portico, or screen, to the existing house.

The earthworks of this house are still visible in the north-eastern part of the site, immediately to the south of the railway, the plan of the building being substantially confirmed by geophysics.

GARDENS
The surveyed formal garden relates closely to the house as altered from 1717. However, it is clear from the design that it is a mid-17th-century creation. The earthworks align well on plan with the building. The house was approached from the west. At the centre of the west front were Talman's new portico and steps, looking out onto a rectangular walled court, measuring 58 m by 40 m. This was later cut through obliquely by the railway. The main garden lay to the south of the house and corresponds with the area of the cloister garth within the rectangular field.

There was no access to the main garden from the principal suite of rooms in the south wing of the house, but only via a flight of steps on the east side that led to a long north–south walk that ran the length of the east side of the house and continued southwards along the east side of the former great cloister. Below the north–south walk, to the east, is a terrace where slight scarps indicate former garden features. Geophysical survey of this terrace confirmed the presence of foundations of a rectangular structure of unknown date, which had first been noted as parchmarks in 1921 (Palmer 1923, 91).

The great cloister was retained as a garden. The greater part of it, closest to the house, was retained as a privy, or walled, garden and the tiled cloister walks appear to have been maintained, as excavation produced a coin of 1672 associated with one of them (Burrow and Burrow 1990, 163) and a survey of 1761 (S'set CRO DD/WYp box 1 p. 15 pt 3) records 'the lead on the ridge and on the Cornish over the Terras Walk' and 'on the Terras Walk', suggesting either that the retained east cloister alley or its extension to the north was kept roofed after the Middle Ages. Geophysical survey confirmed that the privy garden contained a symmetrical arrangement of garden beds.

A ditch at the south end of the privy garden defines the north boundary of separate garden, called the 'south garden' by the Royal Commission on Historical Monuments for England. This area would originally have comprised the southern cells of the great cloister. It was defined by a massive terrace with an external ditch on the south and west sides, though the ditch on the west side has been filled. On the east, the field boundary itself marks a drop in level of 1.3 m to the continuation of the main terrace along the eastern side of both house and garden. This terrace overlooked the ponds in the valley below.

At the south-west corner of the south garden, on a corner of the main terrace, is a sub-rectangular mound 0.6 m high, which was the site of a summerhouse or pavilion at the highest point of the garden.

The stables and service ranges lay to the north of the house and now lie below the railway. To their west was the 'great garden', which extended the length of the forecourt on its south side. Its northern extent is obscured by the modern road and the buildings of Witham Hall Farm.

NEW HOUSE

Sir William Beckford began a new house at Witham in 1762, some 250 m to the south of Wyndham's house, to a design by Robert Adam. Its plan and elevation are recorded by Colen Campbell (1771, pls 38–42), and its site was located by survey.

The house had a central block of two storeys above a basement with a full-height portico connected by open colonnades to flanking pavilions. The central block, symmetrical wings and eastern pavilion can clearly be identified (Wilson North 1996). Between 1770 and 1788 Beckford demolished this new house and turned his energies instead to building Fonthill Abbey in Wiltshire.

Hatherop, Gloucestershire: 1222–7

Hatherop was founded from Witham by William Longespée, Earl of Salisbury and bastard son of Henry II, who, in 1222, gave the Carthusians his manor of Hatherop in Gloucestershire along with other lands and revenues, vestments from his private chapel, and 1,000 ewes, 300 rams, 48 oxen and 20 bulls. The site was settled for only five years and it is likely that only temporary buildings were constructed. The monks found the site unsuitable and persuaded Longespée's widow, Ela, Countess of Salisbury, to exchange it for her manors of Hinton and Norton in Somerset.

Hinton, Somerset: 1227–1539

History

Ela, Countess of Salisbury, re-established the Hatherop community at Hinton in 1227 and issued a new foundation charter on 16 May 1232 (BL Cotton MS Vitellius A.VIII). On the same day she also founded a house of Augustinian nuns at Lacock in Wiltshire, to which she would ultimately retire. At *Locus Dei*, God's Place, or the Priory of Sts Mary, John the Baptist and All Saints, Hinton, the monks built their charterhouse not in a wilderness, but in the middle of a deer park. Even here they were unhappy, complaining that their arable lands were hilly and the rents from their watermills slender.

The architectural detail of the surviving buildings indicates that building in stone was carried out more or less continuously from about 1230 to 1250, and that the new house was sufficiently complete for Hatherop to be finally abandoned in 1232.

Countess Ela gave the community the churches of Hinton and Norton to strengthen its endowment and, in 1254, Henry III licensed fairs at both places, enabling the monks to make an income from tolls and stall rents. In 1259, the monks obtained from the king right

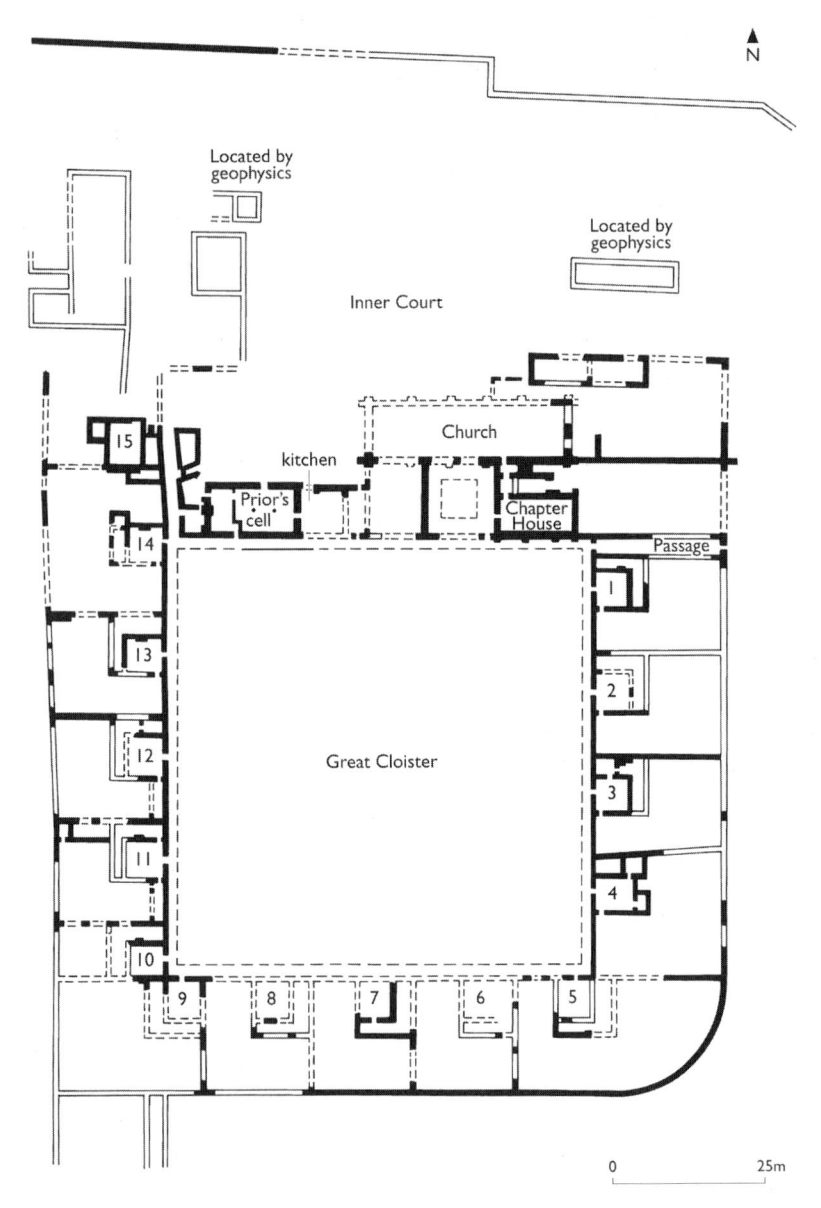

Figure 1.4 The charterhouse of Hinton (after Fletcher, with additions).

of a larger terrace above a north–south spur overlooking the river Frome. The plan of the charterhouse was partially recovered by Major Philip Fletcher and his son Robin between 1950 and 1959 as a result of numerous small, scattered excavations and a study of the surviving structures. Further detail has been provided by geophysical survey in the 1990s (see Figure 1.4).

The upper house, consisting of the great cloister and inner court, lay to the south of the manor house known today as Hinton Abbey (NGR ST778592), which was built in 16th century (and later modified) within the boundary of the medieval precinct wall, in what was the area of the inner court. The monastic church lay about 45 m to its south. There is no evidence that the manor house was a conversion of any of the monastic buildings, although the precinct wall formed the north wall of the house and much medieval masonry from the suppressed monastery was reused in its building. It remains a private residence.

About 1.5 km east of the great cloister was the lower house, or *correrie*, at NGR ST78845910, on the west side of the river Frome, still marked by earthworks and low walling.

The layout of the great cloister, particularly on the east and west sides, remains remarkably clear, with both cells and garden walls marked by low banks that have formed over the remaining walls and foundations below. The great cloister was 69 m² and surrounded by narrow alleys, 1.37 m wide on the east, south and west sides, and an alley 1.68 m wide on the north side.

Excavation revealed a total of 15 cells around the great cloister, of which two, Cell 10 and Cell 15 (as numbered by the Fletchers) on the west side, appear to be additions to an earlier layout. The north range of the great cloister contains two buildings which survive to their original height (though the roofs date from the 19th century): to the west a two-storey structure of which the ground floor comprised the prior's cell and the upper floor the refectory; and to the east the chapter house of three bays with three corresponding rooms above.

Forming part of the north range of the great cloister, and flanked by the prior's cell and kitchen to the west, and the chapter house to the east, was the lesser cloister, 11.74 m². It separated the church, which lay to its north, from the north alley of the great cloister, to its south.

of free warren on their lands at Hinton and Norton (Page 1911, 118–23). They traded in wool and perhaps also in cloth.

In the *taxatio*, the detailed valuation of English and Welsh Church property for the assessment of taxation, carried out for Pope Nicholas IV in 1291, the temporalities (secular possessions) of the prior of Hinton were valued at £41 5s. a year; at its suppression on 31 March 1539 they were valued at £248 19s. 2d. annually (Thompson 1930, 147–56).

Site

Like Witham, Hinton was built on a split site, with an upper and a lower house. The upper house lies within a trapezoidal field on relatively flat ground at 130 m OD and about 1 km north of the village of Hinton. The field forms part

Figure 1.5 The earthworks of Hinton charterhouse (after RCHM(E)).

The church was internally 29.26 m long and 7.93 m wide and divided into five vaulted bays. In the only surviving standing section of its walls – a section of the south wall – a tall lancet window in the second bay from the east indicates the form of the fenestration: paired lancets in each bay.

The Fletchers concentrated on the area of the great cloister and church (Fletcher 1951 and 1958–9; Hogg 1975); it is clear, however, from a few surviving earthworks and remains of substantial ranges of buildings further north (not visible, but known from geophysical survey), that they formed part of a much larger site (see Figure 1.5). This area to the north formed the inner court of the priory.

In the eastern half of the inner court, east of the modern drive to the manor house, a prominent bank marks the boundary between the inner court and the enclosed area of church and the great and lesser cloisters. Geophysical survey indicates that this bank marks a wall. On the south side of this bank is a building, apparently the sacrist's cell excavated by Fletcher but not included on his published plan.

Surrounding the entire site, from the great cloister to the inner court to the north, was a precinct wall. Unplanned excavations by Fletcher revealed the wall beneath to be approximately 0.75 m wide and that it lay 16.8 m to 18.4 m beyond the back walls of the cell gardens. Its remains are marked by a bank that runs east of the 16th-century manor house and the great cloister and south of the cloister's south range of cells, and by a scarp to the west of the western cells. It defined a precinct measuring some 185 m from north to south by 145 m from east to west. Within this boundary, and largely following the back walls of the cell gardens on the west, south and east, is an inner boundary which appears to post-date the Suppression, as it cuts across the garden of Cell 9 and probably accounts for the curved corner recorded by Fletcher of the garden of Cell 5. There are traces of activity between the precinct wall and the back wall of the cell gardens, with scarps marking slight terraces, probably evidence for cultivation.

Outside the precinct wall to the east, is a well-defined hollow way. For a short stretch immediately outside the precinct wall behind Cells 1 to 4, it forms a narrow terrace, before reverting to a hollow way. This must have been the road to the charterhouse and its position suggests the gatehouse was on the east side of the inner court. At the south-east corner of the precinct it reverts to a hollow way; its eastern bank is marked by a series of quarry pits of post-medieval date and one quarry pit in its west bank cuts into the precinct wall.

To the east of this roadway, and also served by it, is an enclosure some 30 m by 50 m with an entrance from the roadway 10 m wide on the west side. Within the enclosure are a number of irregular shaped platforms with evidence of buildings, almost certainly the outer court of the charterhouse, via which the roadway led on to the lower house or *correrie* further east.

To the west of the precinct on rising ground are three sub-rectangular ponds, modified but probably monastic in origin. The supply comes in from the south-west and enters the western pond at the centre of its west side. The west pond feeds the central pond at its south-east corner, the midpoint of the west side of the central pond, where there would have been a sluice. The central pond feeds into the large eastern pond at its south-east corner. This east pond contains two centrally placed small circular islands. It also has a channel entering at its north-west corner which appears to be a post-medieval addition associated with the surface drainage of the field to the west of the charterhouse buildings.

Post-Suppression modification of the earthworks to the north-west of the cloister is limited to the area around the 16th-century house and its farmstead. To the south of the manor house is a broad linear hollow some 10 m wide with a bank 8 m wide and 0.3 m high on its east side. Tree mounds were created to the west of the precinct boundary and within the fields to the west (they appear as circular features on the left of Figure 1.5). The great cloister was retained as a farmyard, with some cells adapted to serve as animal houses, their cloister doors blocked and back walls removed. Parts of the north range of the cloister were retained, but the church and buildings of the inner court were demolished. By the late 18th century the cloister garth had become an orchard and by 1849 the 'new garden' of the manor house.

Beauvale, Nottinghamshire: 1343–1539

History

The site of *Pulchra Vallis*, the Beautiful Valley, the Priory of St Mary and All Saints, Beauvale was given to the prior of Hinton by Sir Nicholas Cantilupe, Lord of Ilkeston and Greasley 'for founding a monastery of the Carthusian Order in my park at Gryselye in the county of Nottingham' (Thompson 1930, 158). It was founded on 9 December 1343 for 12 monks, but their numbers increased to 19 by the early 16th century. The initial endowment comprised 10 liberates (a local land measurement, of unknown extent) of land in Greasley and Selston and the advowsons of the churches in these vills. Cantilupe also provided the monks with building stone from his demesne for their charterhouse and its church (Thompson 1930, 159). This endowment was extended by Cantilupe, who was still endeavouring to fulfil his promised gift, in 1347 and 1360 with additional lands in Selston, Watnall, Kimberley and Newthorpe.

Sir William de Aldburgh granted further lands at about a mile to the north-east of the site at Willey Hay in Sherwood in 1362, and his sisters endowed a chantry at Beauvale on his death in 1394/5 with monies from their Yorkshire manors of Kirkby Overblow and Kereby.

Although the monastery was supported largely by agriculture, at least a part of its income was derived from coal mines. The net value of the priory given in the *Valor* at the Suppression was given at £196 6s. (Thompson 1930, 164), which was about average. The prior at that time, Robert Lawrence, was executed at Tyburn in 1535, leaving his reduced house of seven monks, who, with their new prior, finally surrendered on 18 July 1539 (Knowles and Hadcock 1971, 133–4). There had been an attempt to suppress the house in 1536, but continuance had been purchased by a substantial fine of £166 13s. 4d. (L&P HyVIII, xiii (3), 457).

Overall Site

The site chosen for the charterhouse (NGR SK492491) lay upon an artificially levelled field, with a wooded hillside rising to the north (Hill and Gill 1908, 71) at the head of an unnamed stream valley at a height of between 114 m and 130 m OD. The site is now occupied, in part, by Abbey Farm, whose farmhouse and several farm buildings occupy the sites of monastic buildings.

In May 1908 the site was partially excavated and the surviving buildings surveyed by the Thoroton Society of Nottinghamshire. The site remains well defined by earthworks, and the 1908 excavation (the only one conducted here until 2015) revealed the general layout of the great cloister ranges. Geophysical survey in 1995–6 extended the known plan (see Figure 1.6).

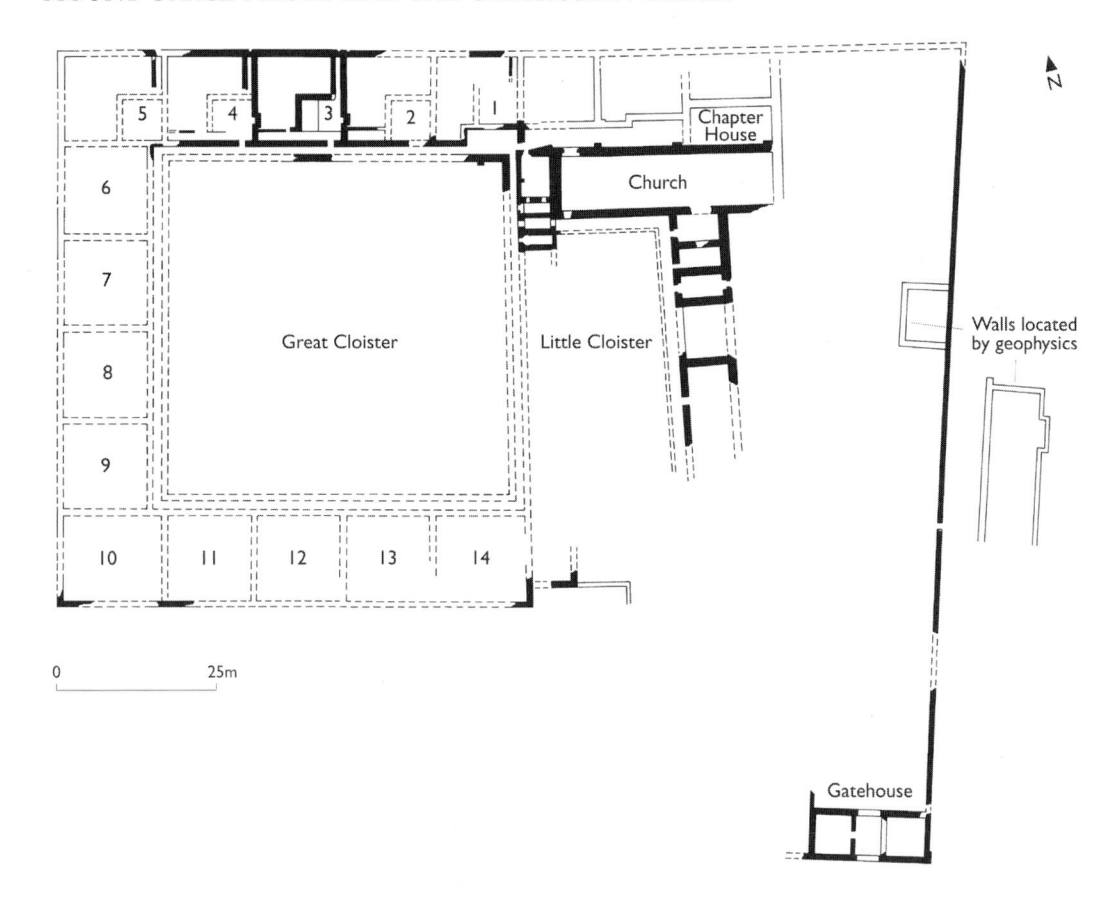

Figure 1.6 The charterhouse of Beauvale (after Hill and Gill 1908).

Great Cloister

The great cloister, which was placed at the centre of a much larger terrace, measured 58 m north–south by 56 m east–west, and was enclosed on the north, west and south sides by garden plots 13 m deep. In spite of post-Suppression development and the disturbance of the 1908 excavation, the earthworks of the great cloister remain remarkably clear, and this earthwork evidence, and the partial excavation of the north range in 1908, identified 14 cells around the great cloister.

The cloister garth survives as an orchard on the east of Abbey Farm farmhouse, and geophysical survey identified the site of a water tower at its centre. The northern range of cells and their gardens (Cells 1 to 5) are well preserved, as are those at the northern end of the west range. This west side falls from north to south, and its southern cells are more deeply buried. The southern range of cells has been obscured, but the masonry of the south-east corner of the garden of Cell 10, excavated in 1908, remains visible and the southern wall of the gardens of this range is still marked by a low scarp running the length of the range.

East Range and Church

The east side of the great cloister was closed by a range comprising the communal offices of the monastery and the prior's cell and, at the north end, a yard 4.53 m wide (the same width as the east range), which separated the west wall of the church from the east cloister alley.

Although the church and central part of the east cloister range were retained to form the basis of a post-Suppression house, it appears never to have been completed, and the site generally has no earthwork evidence for an associated garden. All that survives of the mid-16th-century house is the uppermost storey added to the earlier prior's house, which lay adjacent to the church on the south side of the yard that separated the church from the cloister.

The ground floor of the prior's house comprised three spaces: a storeroom to the north, the entry to the great cloister from the little cloister at its centre and the priory prison to the south. This southern bay also contained a spiral stair from the cloister alley to the prior's accommodation at first-floor level. After the Suppression, a second storey was added to this building.

South of the prior's cell was an open space, and south of that, occupying the site of the monks' refectory and kitchen, is a farmhouse first built in the last decade of the 16th century and extended in the 17th and 18th centuries reusing stone recovered from medieval buildings on site.

Both side walls of the church survive to almost full height and its full plan is known from excavation. It was a plain rectangular structure 30.48 m long and 8 m wide. On its north side towards its east end was the chapter house, abutting the north wall of the presbytery. Further north from the church and to its east a series of small terraces mark building platforms suggestive of buildings, doubtless of the inner and outer courts.

Little Cloister and Inner Court
To the south of the church, abutting the communal offices of the east range, was the little cloister, which was partially excavated in 1908. Its east side was closed by a north–south range of buildings that comprised a series of chapels and what was interpreted as a common dormitory for the lay brothers. The west wall of this range is still visible between the garden wall of the Abbey Farm farmhouse and the farm track that runs outside it. At the northern end of this range, a deep hole against the south wall of the church is the remains of a trench dug in 1908 to expose the chapel on the south side of the presbytery.

To the north and east of the church a series of small terraces mark building platforms, and a series of east–west walls located by geophysics indicate that the roadway led in from the north-east corner of the garden of Cell 5 and possibly along the west side of the western range of cells. There are additional structures to the north of this roadway in the north-east corner of the precinct (Gaffney 1994, figs 2–5). This area between the precinct wall and the access road is identified as the outer court.

The inner court lay to the south and east of the little cloister, and was separated by it from the great cloister. It was entered through a gatehouse that survives within a 19th-century farm building in the south-east corner of the precinct. Geophysical survey located traces of buildings within the inner court, particularly against the precinct wall. Against the east side of the east range slight earthworks indicate another building. A narrow doorway in the precinct wall to the east of this building is explained by the presence of a substantial building outside the wall that is not apparent on the surface but located by additional geophysical survey (Gaffney 1994, fig. 2).

Precinct
As at Hinton, the enclosure of the great cloister is contained within a larger walled precinct, defined on the north and west by a substantial bank 35 m distant from the back wall of the cell gardens, and on the east side by an extant length of precinct wall some 2 m high, which terminates at the gatehouse lying in the south-eastern corner of the precinct. The southern side is obscured by post-Suppression development. Between the precinct wall and the cells of the north and west ranges, there is evidence for the existence of a series of rectangular enclosures, served by a track than runs around the outside of the garden walls.

To the north of Cell 1, geophysical survey indicated an area of high resistance within a marked rectangular platform that appears to be a substantial building. Otherwise, these closes are devoid of traces of structures and, as at Hinton, may be additional gardens or orchards.

Wider Site
As at Hinton, the area known from excavation is only a part of a much larger site defined by earthworks (see Figure 1.7). The present access track to the site, which approaches from the south-east, is post-medieval, carried on a massive earthen bank. It has removed or obscured the original access, if there ever was one, on this side.

Three earlier roads are apparent in the landscape, two on the west side of the site and one on the east. To the south-west, a possible roadway can be observed crossing the breached dam of a pond, possibly a millpond, in the valley bottom and following the crest of a hollow towards the central buildings of the charterhouse. A second causeway can be observed leading west to east towards the south-west corner of the enclosed precinct and into an area which is disturbed by post-Suppression development. Either or both of these trackways could be the medieval access to the site.

MOUNT GRACE PRIORY AND THE CARTHUSIAN ORDER

The route of the third road, that to the east, is marked by a low bank that follows the site of a track which approaches from the south-east, turns west between two fields of ridge and furrow, and enters through a breach in the precinct wall to run along the back of the north cloister range, Cells 1 to 5. From here it appears to continue south along the back of the west cloister range, within the precinct, and possibly marks a separate access to the outer court (see below).

Geophysical survey also located sections of an east–west wall that ran east from the north-east corner of the precinct wall, at the back of the garden of Cell 5, flanking the roadway that approached from the east and then possibly turned south along the back of the western range of cells. There are additional structures to the north of this roadway in the north-east corner of the precinct. This area between the precinct wall and the access road is identified as the outer court.

The ponds on the south side of the great cloister relate to the farm that developed on the site.

Outside the precinct, the principal feature is a large, rectangular pond, held against the north side of the valley by a massive earthen dam 22 m wide and up to 2.5 m high that returns along its eastern side and carries the road leading from the outer court. Its western end has been disturbed by the farm access and a barn. It was presumably a fishpond associated with the monastery.

London: 1371–1537
History

The House of the Assumption of the Holy Virgin Mary (changed by the founder to the House of the Mother of God), London charterhouse, was founded in 1371 by Sir Walter Maney on land he had originally bought and given to the city as an overflow plague cemetery. Here he later built a chapel and supplied a group of priests to say masses for the dead. Finally, he was persuaded by the Bishop of London to found the charterhouse. Maney was an old soldier and courtier, typical of the class that professed, as stated on his foundation charter, a 'special devotion' to the Carthusian order. It was founded for a prior and 24 monks, and by 1535, if not from its foundation, was the largest and second wealthiest of the English charterhouses, with 30 monks and 18 lay brothers.

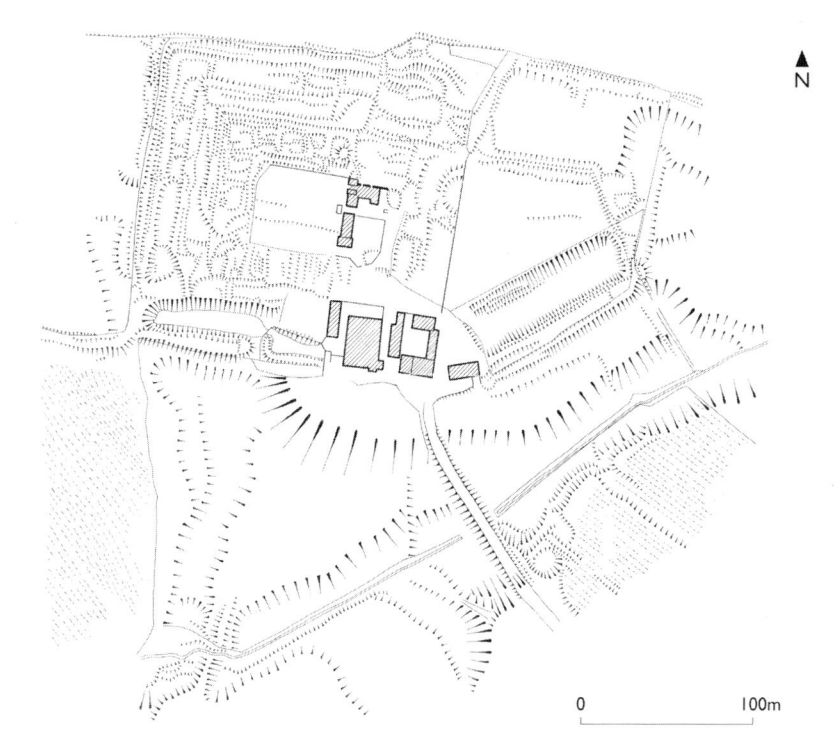

London and its monks suffered more than any other charterhouse at the Suppression: in 1535 its prior, John Houghton, and three of its monks were imprisoned, tortured and executed. Although, in 1537, the new prior and the majority of monks took the Oath of Supremacy, four choirmonks and six lay brothers still refused; they were imprisoned, nine of them starved to death and the one survivor was eventually executed. The house failed to surrender voluntarily, and in 1537 12 monks and six lay brothers were forcibly ejected (Knowles and Hadcock 1971, 135).

The charterhouse was converted to a mansion from 1545 by Lord North and after his death further altered by the new owner, the Duke of Norfolk. It still stands on the north-western post-Roman boundary of the city.

Site

In the early 20th century Sir William St John Hope and others studied, but did not excavate, the buildings of the converted charterhouse and concluded that substantial parts of the monastic church, lesser cloister and lay brothers' buildings survived within

Figure 1.7 The earthworks of Beauvale charterhouse (after RCHM(E)).

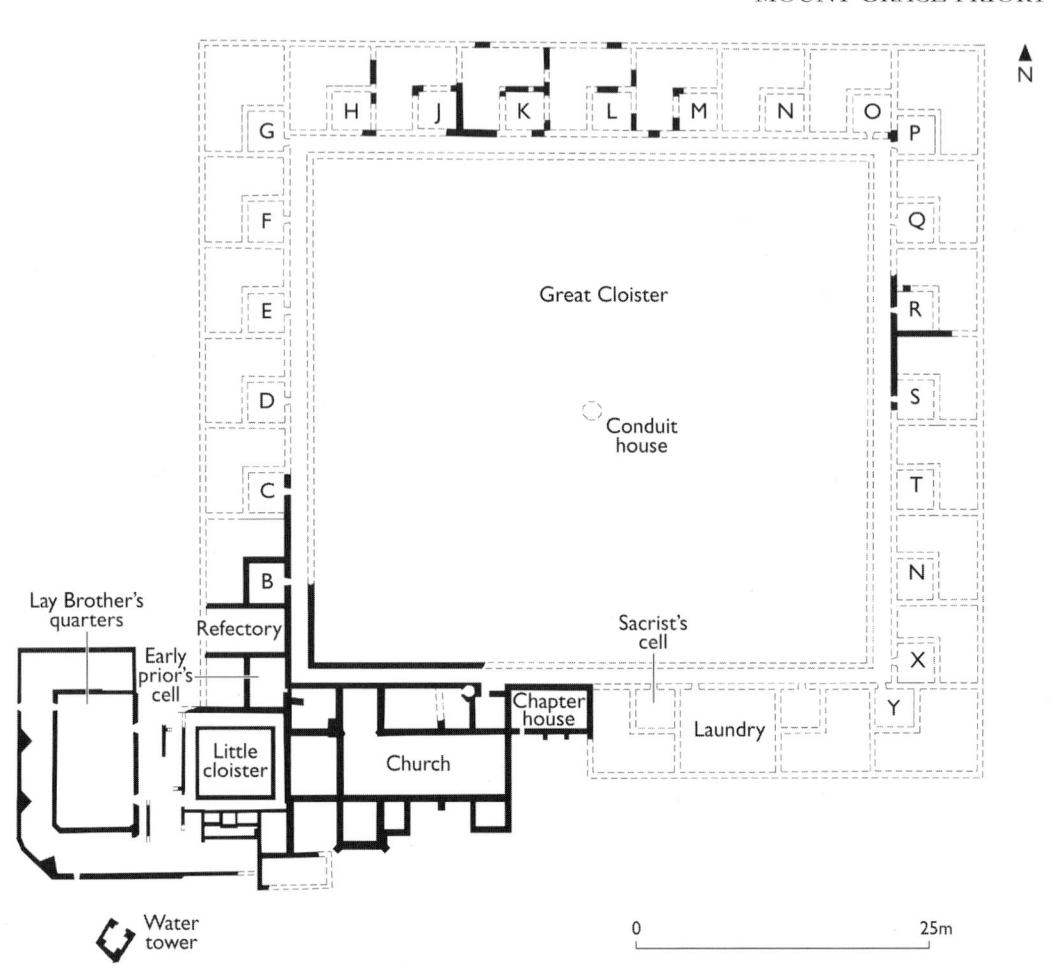

Figure 1.8 The charterhouse of London (after Grimes 1968, and Barber and Thomas 2002).

the later house (Hope 1925, *passim*). The site was seriously damaged by fire-bombing in 1941. In this damaged state, before its post-war reconstruction and the extension to St Bartholomew's Hospital Medical College on the site of the cloister's east range took place, it was partially excavated by W. F. Grimes in 1948–9 and 1959. Grimes produced a plan based on the evidence of his excavation and interpolated from the 1430s plan of the priory's waterworks (Hope 1903, pl. XXI), which was demonstrated to be remarkably accurate. Further excavation and recording by MoLA between 1988 and 2000 further refined the plan (see Figure 1.8).

Monastery
The plan shows the layout of 24 cells around the great cloister, the position of the church and chapter house, the location of the service ranges to the west of the lesser cloister and the location of the water tower at the centre of the great cloister. The great cloister was calculated to be 103.8 m from east to west and 93 m from north to south, each cell 5.4 m² internally, and the garden plots 13.7 m deep.

Grimes's excavation of the church recorded a complex building history. It may have been built during the site's existence as a plague cemetery and retained, or was newly built from 1371 with the charterhouse. It measured 12.85 m by 4.95 m, it was extended to the west by 4.50 m in the 15th century, and extended to north and south by chapels – at least five are documented – up to the early 16th century. At the centre of the presbytery, a brick-built vault containing a lead coffin was excavated by Grimes and found to contain Walter Maney's remains.

During post-war reconstruction, under the architects Seely and Paget, Cell A (numbered as such on a waterworks plan of 1431) and the refectory were discovered inside the late 16th-century buildings, which had been damaged in the Blitz. The side walls of the refectory are still standing, and part of the south alley of the cloister. Grimes further recorded elements of cells R and S in a rapid and incomplete excavation during the course of an extension of St Bartholomew's Hospital, which covers the eastern and northern ranges of the great cloisters.

More significant, but similarly under the imperfect conditions of another hospital extension, was the partial recording in 1990 of Cells H, J, K, L and M on the north side of the great cloister, which allowed the observance and recording of recognisable floor plans and the remains of the piped water supply that entered the precinct through the garden of Cell L (Barber and Thomas 2002, 20–5). Excavation in Preacher's Court against the western precinct wall has identified buildings of the inner court (Barber and Thomas 2002, 26–7 and fig. 28, 45–7 and fig. 40). It is unlikely that there was an outer court, as the community bought their food at the market, not having much space for storage.

Hull, East Yorkshire: 1379–1539
History
At Hull, Sir William de la Pole acquired a royal licence to found a hospital of chaplains for housing and ministering to poor persons and to endow it with both money and land (Horrox 1983, 40). A hospital was duly founded on a 7-acre site outside and to the north of the town, but, not happy with his foundation, William obtained another royal licence to refound the site as a house of Franciscan nuns. William de la Pole died before this new plan could be put into effect, and his son, Michael, decided instead to found a charterhouse. Its charter is dated 18 February 1379, and grants it the original hospital and chapel, which would have continued to be served by its own priests and master. The hospital was to house 13 men and 13 women under the authority of a master, each inmate was to receive £2 a year, and the master £10 (ibid., 41). The House of St Michael (Michael de la Pole's patron saint), Hull charterhouse, was intended to provide for 12 monks and the prior, but an additional cell was added before 1412.

In 1536 the house held the prior, 11 monks, a novice and a lay brother, although by its suppression in 1539 the number of monks had fallen to seven. Pension lists surviving give the names and ages of each (Page 1913, 191). Hull was always a small house, with a maximum of 13 monks and a prior and a net income of little more than £174 in 1535, it was the second poorest house of the order in England.

John Leland, the King's Antiquary, observed the site after its suppression: 'certein of the De La Poles wher buried yn this Carthusian monastery; and at the late suppressing of it were found dyverse trowehes of leade with bones in a volte under the high altare ther. Most part of this monastery was buildid with brike, as the residew of the buildinges of Hull for the most part be' (Toulmin Smith 1964, 1, 50).

Site
Nothing remains visible of the Hull charterhouse. It was buried below urban housing on the north side of the medieval town, in the vicinity of Manson, Sykes, Princess and Bourne Streets, in what was an extra-mural suburb north of the medieval town's defences. Trial excavation before redevelopment at NGR TA099293 (the location suggested by a prospect of Hull by Wenceslaus Hollar indicating land and buildings known to have occupied the site of the charterhouse) failed to locate any trace of the monastery.

Coventry, Warwickshire: 1381–1539
History
The impetus to found a charterhouse at Coventry is attributed to William, Lord Zouch, who, although he died in 1382 before work got fully underway, requested that his heirs put aside 100 marks a year for that purpose. In 1381 Zouch persuaded three monks from London, three from Beauvale and four newly professed (presumably local) to come to Coventry where they were accommodated in the hermitage of St Anne for the first seven years, while their new house was built. A 14-acre site was allocated at Shortley, in what are now Coventry's south-eastern suburbs at NGR SP34477823, and the charterhouse was to be endowed with the disputed manor of Shortley, a grant which was not finally secured until 1417 (Page 1908, 83).

In 1385 the new house, known as the Priory of St Anne, received royal patronage from Richard II, who personally laid the foundation stone of the church and announced that he would be the 'founder' of it. He and his successors continued to patronise the house, frequently temporarily transferring alien priory estates to Coventry to support its community. Royal patronage brought further support in cash, both from prominent and wealthy Coventry citizens

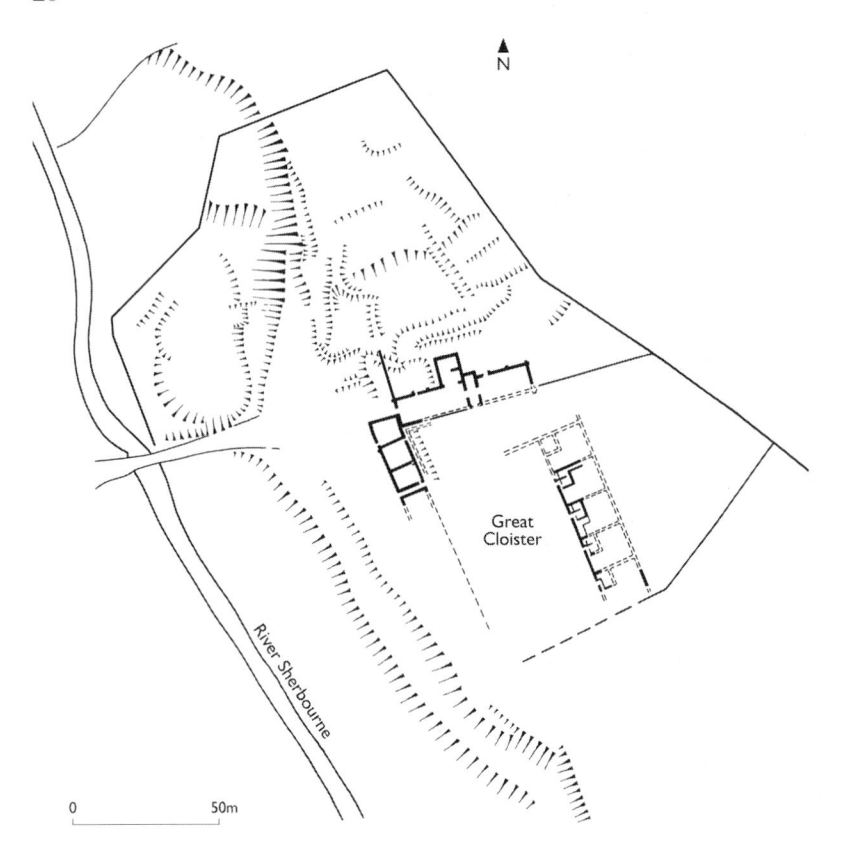

Figure 1.9 The charterhouse of Coventry (after Soden 1995 and RCHM(E), with additions).

and from courtiers in particular, who funded various works, from the four phases of building that completed the church to the building of individual cells.

It was not until 1387 that the statutory number of 12 monks and a prior was reached. The charterhouse is the only one known to have maintained a school: in 1399 the monks of Coventry undertook to educate (probably by employing a school master) 12 poor young clerks from the age of seven to 17 (Knowles and Hadcock 1971, 134). By the time of the *Valor* in 1535 the house contained the prior, 12 monks, 3 lay brothers, 6 yeomen servants and 12 children (ibid.). When the monastery was suppressed on 16 January 1539, having purchased a continuance in 1536 for £20, there was only the prior and nine others left to receive pensions.

Site

The site of the charterhouse on the east side of the river Sherborne, 0.5 km to the southeast of the medieval city, is still partly enclosed by its precinct wall which stands in places to full height (see Figure 1.9). Apart from the precinct wall, all that remains standing are the western two-thirds of the south wall of the church and the refectory and prior's cell, which were converted into a house after the Suppression.

The church and the east side of the great cloister were excavated by the Coventry and District Archaeological Society between 1968 and 1987 under the direction of Brian Hobley, Margaret Rylatt and Iain Soden (Soden 1995).

Their excavations revealed a church of five phases to the north of a rectangular cloister. Adjacent to the church on the west side of the cloister is the post-Suppression house, formed from the converted refectory and prior's cell, and aligned north–south. The refectory can be dated to no later than the early to mid-15th century by a wall-painting of the Crucifixion, which includes an inscription referring to the then prior William Soland (d.1437). The painting would have adorned the south wall of the refectory: the post-medieval addition of a floor means it now appears in the upper storey of the house.

At the north-west corner of the house was a wing that was demolished in the 19th century and is thought to have been the kitchen, of both the monastery and the later house, on account of a substantial chimney shown in a 19th-century drawing. Excavation of Cells 2 to 5 (so numbered in medieval documents) on the east side of the cloister (by Margaret Rylatt) revealed that they comprised houses 6.3 m wide and 5.7 m deep set at the corner of garden plots 10.4 m wide and 14.3 m deep. Cell 1 would have been 15 m south of the church, leaving space for the chapter house and a lesser cloister. The south and west sides of the great cloister have not been excavated, though the northernmost cell of the west range was identified in 1853 when a post-medieval building was demolished and replaced, and another cell of the west range was located in an evaluation trench dug by Soden. To the north-west of the church Soden's excavations revealed a medieval building. The excavators considered the area to the north of the nave to be the site of the lesser cloister, though it was more likely to have been part of the inner court.

The remains of the charterhouse are today approached from the west by a modern drive off the London Road and a bridge over the canalised river Sherbourne. The site occupies a raised terrace on the east side of the stream. North of the bridge over the Sherbourne was a cottage, now demolished, reputedly on the site of the porter's lodge at the precinct gate. Here the precinct wall survives only as its lowest courses for 7 m before it assumes its full height and encloses the northern end of the precinct. There are two medieval doorways in the precinct wall, one at the re-entrant angle of the wall on the north-west side of the site, now blocked, the second just above the terrace scarp on the north side. To the west of this door, a length of corbelling in the outer face of the wall is the remains of a latrine that discharged into a mill-leat that skirted the precinct wall here.

The wall remains substantially intact on the east side of the site and gently reduces in height as it disappears into the grounds of the Bluecoat School, which occupies the southern part of the precinct and has removed all trace of the monastic layout in this part of the site. Similarly, the playing fields of the school have removed any trace of the precinct wall on the west side of the great cloister.

The only remaining monastic earthworks lie in the northern part of the precinct to the north of the church and extending down the west side to the bridge over the stream. They are dominated by the redefined valley scarp of the Sherbourne, which is up to 3 m in height. Below this scarp and the terrace on which the charterhouse stands, and between it and the river, are traces of a pond 32 m wide and 60 m long. This has been partly filled with dumped material, but has traces of a mid-20th-century excavation trench running across it. A second trench is still evident against the precinct wall to the west of the pond.

Above the river terrace, the enclosed area is reasonably level. The earthworks indicate a series of buildings and yards to the north of the church, confirming the evidence of excavation that there was a building to the north-west of the church, its extent defined by a platform. W. G. Fretton, a local antiquarian, who did not excavate but published papers about the charterhouse, recorded ruins to the west of this building (1874, 42); there is slight earthwork evidence to support this. A series of scarps vertical to the eastern precinct wall indicate activity there, either a series of courts or possible garden plots.

Axholme, Lincolnshire: 1397/8–1538

History

The House of the Visitation of St Mary, Axholme charterhouse, was founded for a prior, 12 monks and an unspecified number of lay brothers by Thomas Mowbray, Earl of Nottingham and Earl Marshal of England (and later Duke of Norfolk) in 1397/8. The site chosen at Low Melwood was already partly occupied by a chapel to the Virgin, long known as the 'Priory in the Wood' (Hills 1961). Mowbray granted the site and its chapel, together with other properties in the possession of the chapel, to the new house 'in frank almoigne' (with perpetual rights of free tenure), as well as 100 acres in the manor of Epworth, a rent of 20 marks, and such rights of common, of pasture, of turbary and of fishery as other tenants held within the Isle of Axholme. Mowbray added to this the advowsons of Epworth and Belton, and the Benedictine priory of Monks Kirby in Warwickshire, where he had earlier failed to establish a charterhouse (Page 1906, 158).

Axholme's fortunes declined with the banishment of Mowbray in 1398, his death a year later and the execution of his son in 1405, but by 1449 had so well recovered that there were problems accommodating the numbers of monks within its cells. By the time of the *Valor* in 1535, however, numbers had fallen to the foundation figure. The prior at the time, St Augustine Webster, refused to take the Oath of Supremacy and was executed at Tyburn that year. In 1538 the new prior, Michael Mekeness, and eight monks surrendered and were pensioned (Knowles and Hadcock 1971, 134).

Site

The earthwork remains of Axholme Priory (NGR SE 8062501922) lie on the eastern side of the Epworth to Owston Ferry road, one mile south of Epworth, on the eastern edge of the Isle of Axholme (see Figure 1.10). Understanding of the site is complicated by two post-Suppression houses that occupied the north side of a cloister in succession, and the gardens of these houses, which were defined by a wet moat on the west (now backfilled), south and east sides. Only part of the second of these houses now remains standing.

The earliest of the mansions was built by John Candyssh (Cavendish) and was described by Abraham de la Pryme in 1698 from his recollection of the building from his youth:

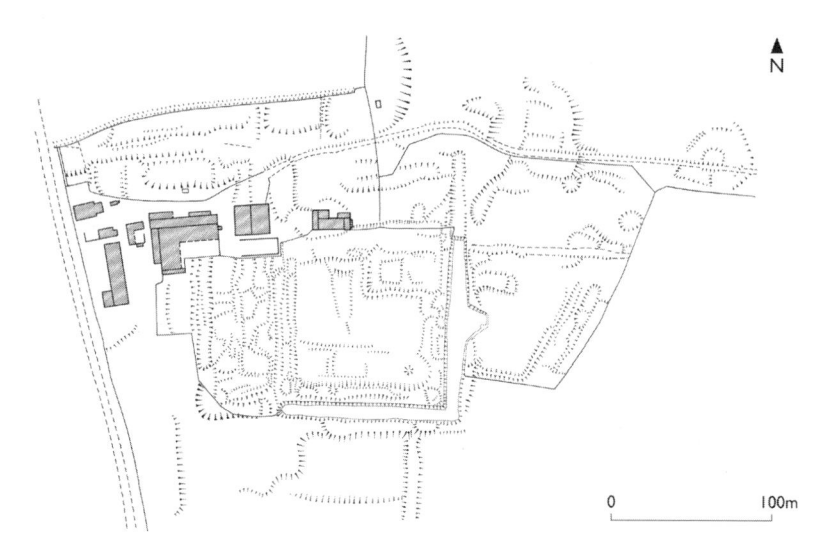

Figure 1.10 The charterhouse of Axholme (after RCHM(E)).

a great and most stately building of many stories high, all of huge squared stone, all wholly built so upon vaults and arches that I have gone under the same a great way. All was huge stone staircases, huge pillars, long entries, with the doors of both sides opening into opposite rooms. I remember the dining room also, which was at the end of one of those entries, had huge long tables in it, great church windows, with a great deal of painted glass. The outside of the house was all beautified with semi-arches jutting off the walls upon channeled pillars, and the top was all covered in lead. The doors were huge and strong, and ascended unto by a great many steps, and places made through the opposite turrets to defend the same, and the whole was encompassed with a huge ditch or moat … there was also the finest gardens, orchards and flowers there that I ever saw; but now there is, I believe, none of these things to be seen, for about 10 years ago, all or most part being ruinous was pulled down and a lesser house built out of the same. (Jackson 1870, 174)

A small part of this second post-Suppression mansion remains within a surviving farmhouse and one of its outbuildings.

The site of the first post-Suppression house appears to have occupied the whole of the north range of the great cloister and may have incorporated the priory church. A medieval pier surviving in the basement of the second house may still be *in situ*. To the south, the area of the cloister garth has been modified by the creation of a formal garden, features associated with which extend well beyond the moated area.

In spite of these later alterations, earthworks and geophysical survey identify at least 12 cells on the east, south and west sides of the cloister and the presence of a narrow cloister alley on the south and east sides. The cloister measures 72 m west to east and at least 52 m from south to north, with its south range within the moated garden area, its east range partly within the moated area and partly cut away lengthways by the moat itself, and its west range immediately outside the backfilled western branch of the moat.

This west range of the cloister survives as clear earthworks. It was excavated in 1968 by Peter Wenham, though his excavation trenches have not been located (Knowles 1977, 15), his work revealing five parallel walls. The first, Wall A, was the outer wall of a cell garden some 15 m inside the moat. The next, Wall B, was the back wall of the cell with an external evesdrip, and lay 12 m to the east. Wall C was an internal cill wall within the cell, and Wall D, furthest to the east, was the wall of the cell facing the cloister garth, demonstrating that the cell measured externally 11 m east to west.

Wall E, the cloister alley wall, lay 2.5 m to the east of the cell. Mortar floors with tile impressions were identified both in the cell and cloister alley, and all the structures were of brick with stone dressings.

The cells and gardens on the western side of the cloister are enclosed within a ditch some 20 m to the west of the back walls of the gardens. This area between ditch and garden wall is divided into a series of small enclosures by scarps at right angles to the ditch, as is the equivalent area at both Witham and Hinton. The enclosure ditch turns along the south side of the great cloister, but was otherwise destroyed or re-cut by the water-filled ditch that defines the south and east sides of the post-Suppression garden. It is likely, however, that it followed the same line as the existing ditch and was the boundary of the precinct. The earthworks between the ditch and the south and east ranges of the great cloister were all modified in the post-Suppression period.

To the east of the east range of the great cloister are a series of enclosures and building platforms. These do not follow the alignment of the post-medieval garden and are therefore probably all medieval and likely to be the remains of the monastic outer court. The area has been damaged by leveling, though it remains as pasture.

The earthworks continue along the northern side of the site as far as the modern road, and, though doubtless modified by post-Suppression development, they are, unlike the

MOUNT GRACE PRIORY AND THE CARTHUSIAN ORDER

area to the west, aligned on the great cloister and so almost certainly mark the location of the inner court, retained as the service ranges of the post-Suppression house. To the south of the great cloister and post-medieval garden, and under plough, are further traces of the post-Suppression garden layout.

Mount Grace, North Yorkshire: 1398–1539

History

The House of Mountgrace of Ingleby, or the House of the Assumption of the Blessed Virgin Mary and St Nicholas, the charterhouse of Mount Grace, was founded in 1398 by Thomas de Holand, Duke of Surrey and nephew of Richard II, on his manor of Bordelbi, which he held of the king, beside the medieval road from York to Durham, in the parish of East Harlsey. The chosen site was a perched terrace (natural terraces modified during the building of the manor of *Bordelbi*) on the western escarpment of the North York Moors, 7 km to the east of the existing town of Northallerton. The size of the intended community is unknown, but was probably for a prior and 12 monks.

The initial endowment, purchased for £1,000 from the Crown by de Holand, comprised the alien priories of Ware, Hinckley, Wareham and Carisbrooke, then in royal hands. But within two years the priory was without support: following Richard II's deposition in 1399 de Holand was deprived of his duchy by the new king, Henry IV, and in March 1400 was beheaded, and Henry IV reclaimed the valuable property of Ware, worth £251 a year. In 1415 the charterhouse was effectively refounded by Thomas Beaufort, Earl of Dorset and later Duke of Exeter, and uncle of the next king, Henry V. Beaufort increased the size of the community by five 'monk-chaplains' (his term perhaps indicating that he intended these monks to pray for him like the chaplains in a chantry), and persuaded the king to return the estates of Ware to Mount Grace, and find four further priories with which to endow the charterhouse. Mount Grace was suppressed in 1539, when the prior, 16 monks, three novices, six lay brothers and one oblate received pensions.

Site

The ruins of Mount Grace lie on the western edge of a sandstone escarpment at NGR SE 449985 on two prominent terraces. The site was substantially excavated by Sir William St John Hope between 1896 and 1900 (Hope 1905; see Preface). On the upper terrace (see Figure 1.11), substantial ruins remain of the great cloister, lesser cloister and inner court, while on the lower terrace to the west are the largely earthwork remains of the outer court. Although a 17th-century house was created within the ruins, the site remains largely in the form it assumed in the 16th century.

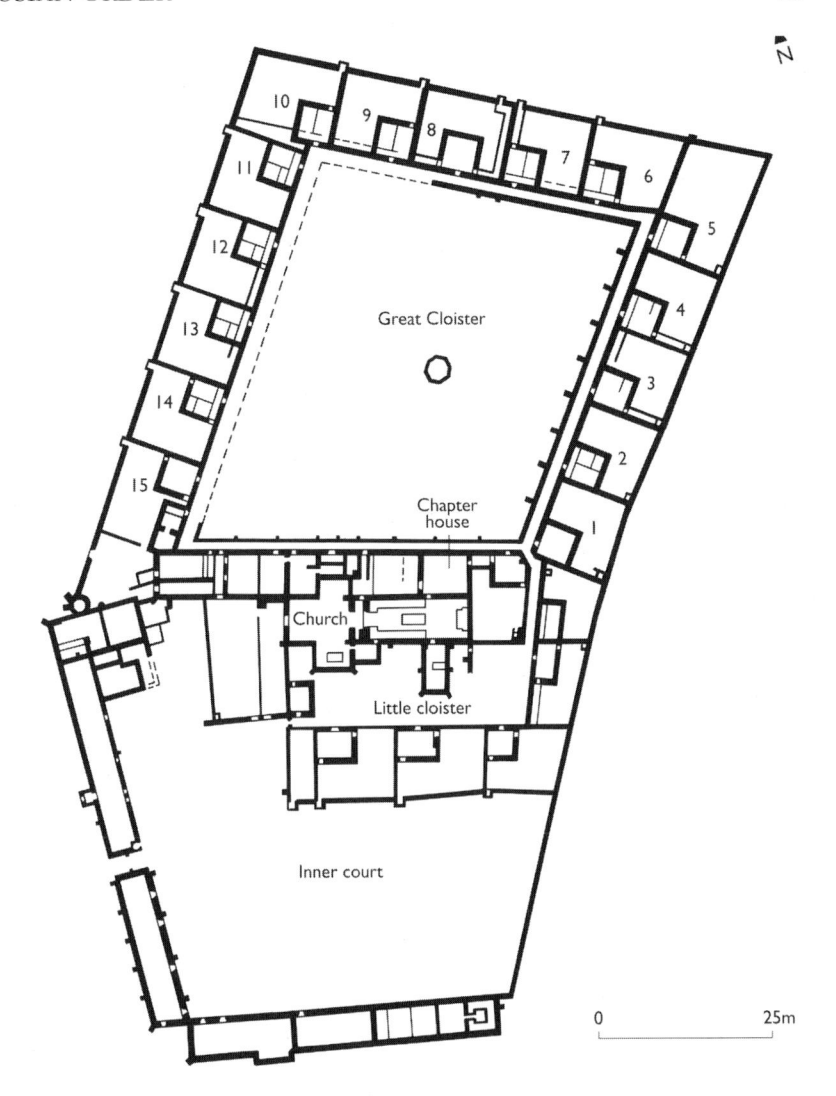

The north end of the upper terrace is occupied by a substantial trapezoidal great cloister; its central garth measures approximately 70 m along its north and south sides, 83 m on its west side and 70 m on its east side. The asymmetrical layout of the enclosures was the result of the piecemeal development of the site, which to begin with simply followed the largely natural shape of the terrace. Around the east, north and south sides of this cloister

Figure 1.11 The charterhouse of Mount Grace (after RCHM(E), with additions).

are 15 cells, each occupying a garden plot of about 15.25 m2. All these cells are visible above ground level and nine retain at least a part of their upper storeys. The south range of the great cloister comprised, from west to east, the prior's house, the refectory, two small cells without gardens, a small court, the chapter house and the sacrist's cell. Separated from the cloister by the small court and the chapter house was the church, of which survives the nave virtually to full height, with its central bell-tower complete but for its floors, and the greater part of the presbytery. To the east and south of the church is a second, or lesser, cloister that contains six cells, all reduced to low walling. The southern part of the upper terrace comprised the inner court containing service buildings, gatehouse, guest house and kitchen, all of which survive in part to full height.

Only one building, apparently a mill, remains visible on the lower terrace, though other buildings are documented. The principal feature of this area is a group of fishponds, two still containing water, and a dry moat, which probably belonged to the manor of Bordelbi granted to the house at its foundation.

Sheen, Surrey: 1414–1539, 1555–8

History

The House of Jesus of Bethlehem of Sheen was founded by Henry V in 1414 adjacent to the royal palace of Sheen (later Richmond) and endowed with the estates of the alien priories of Greenwich and Lewisham. In the following year he added the alien priories of Ware (seized from Mount Grace), Hayling, Noyon and Neufmarché in Normandy, and all the lands of the abbey of Lire except Hinckley. The prior of Sheen was to remit £100 per year to Mount Grace of the income of the farm of Ware so long as he held it.

Building of the charterhouse began between 1415 and 1418 and was still in progress in 1422. In 1457, further building work was underway and William the carpenter, a lay brother of Mount Grace, was loaned to Sheen until new cells were completed (Thompson 1930, 240).

This house was originally intended for 40 monks, but only 30 cells were built. At its suppression in 1539 the prior and 18 monks received pensions. In 1540 Henry VIII granted the site to Edward Seymour, Earl of Hertford and later Duke of Somerset, who partially converted the priory to a house. In 1555 the Catholic Mary I refounded Sheen, appointing a new prior and bringing back to England Carthusians who had gone abroad at the Suppression to Nieuwpoort in Belgium, where they had lived in a charterhouse renamed Sheen Anglorum. At least one of them had been a lay brother at Mount Grace. This rebirth was short-lived, however; with the accession of Elizabeth I in 1558 the house was again dissolved and the site subsumed into Richmond Palace, the buildings incorporated into the royal stables.

Site

The site of Sheen Priory lies at NGR TQ1705675646 below the fairway of the 14th hole of the Royal Mid-Surrey Golf Course, just south-west of the King's Observatory on the south bank of the Thames. Sheen Palace (renamed Richmond Palace in 1501) lay about 1 km further downriver.

William of Worcester visited Sheen in the 1460s or 1470s, and described the charterhouse thus: 'the cloister of the monks of the Charterhouse at King's Sheen, which has about 30 houses of the religious on the east, south, west, and north sides, is 200 paces long, and so in all 800 paces; and it is … wide. The height of the walls of the said cloister all round is 3 yards or 9 feet. The nave of the church, apart from the choir is about 60 paces' (Harvey 1969, 270).

Large parts of the monastic complex were still extant in 1649 when a Parliamentary survey was undertaken of the King's property there (TNA E. 317/53; Rowntree 1981, 457–66). The priory cells themselves can be reconstructed from this survey: 'one other brick tenem[t] formerly an Anchorits cell cont' two rooms below & two roomes aboue stairs, a long shed [or pentice], & a little garden' (Rowntree 1981, 466 quoting TNA E. 317/53, f. 2). Several buildings on the survey appear to retain their medieval names – the prior's cell, the monks' hall (the refectory), the church, the churchyard (the cloister garth) – or are referred to by their former use, as in the several anchorite's cells. Other buildings listed, particularly the great barn, granaries and stables within the Little Frayles, were almost certainly part of the original monastic complex.

Even the medieval water supply survived, for the survey of 1649 states: 'Memor[oran]d[um] the tenemen[ents] before ment[i]o[n]ed are very well accommodated w[i]t[h] water

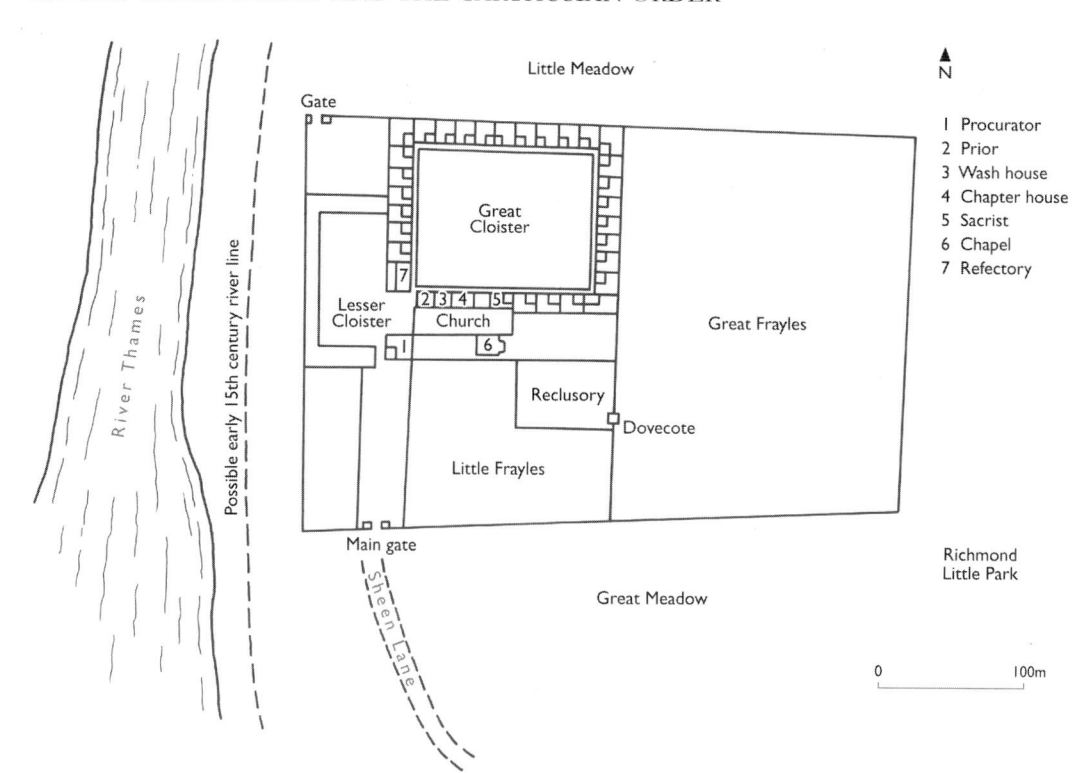

Figure 1.12 The charterhouse of Sheen (after Cloake 1990, with additions).

wh[ich] is brought and conueyed vnto them through severall small pipes of lead branched from one greate pipe of lead extending it selfe from the stop-cock or conduit head on Richmond greene vnto a greate cesterne of stone placed w[i]t[h]in the s[ai]d walls of Sheen' (TNA E. 317/53, f. 5).

There are no visible standing remains of the charterhouse, though a reconstruction of its plan has been attempted, based primarily on the 1649 survey (Cloake 1990). Slight earthworks and some parch marks can be seen, which indicate the location of individual buildings, and limited excavations in 2011–13 revealed well-preserved footings and lower walls.

The site comprised a walled precinct of a little over 32 acres, with, lying outside its walls, according to the 1649 survey (the names given on which may well be those used during the life of the monastery), the Lower Meadow to the north, Richmond Little Park to the east, the Thames to the west and the Great Meadow to the south. Within the precinct walls was the Great Frayles, a meadow of 10 acres comprising the eastern part of the precinct and separated from the rest of the enclosure by a brick wall. The south-western part of the precinct formed the inner court, or Little Frayles, and the north-western part the house itself (see Figure 1.12).

Chapter 2: History and Topography of Mount Grace Priory

The history of Mount Grace – its foundation, endowment and suppression – was originally researched in some detail by William Brown in the late 19th century (Brown 1882; 1905) and extended by Margaret Thompson (1930) in the 20th century. The following analysis borrows heavily from their work, though new material has been incorporated and mistakes corrected.

2.1 History of the Charterhouse

Foundation
The charterhouse of Mount Grace was founded on the manor of *Bordelbi*, near the early medieval town of Northallerton, by Thomas de Holand (*c*.1374–1400), 6th Earl of Kent and 1st Duke of Surrey, in 1398 (Knowles and Hadcock 1971, 133 and 135), following a licence granted for that purpose by his uncle Richard II on 18 February 1398 (Cal. Pat. R. 1396–9, 348).

Thomas de Holand claimed title, through his paternal grandmother, to large land holdings in Yorkshire that had once been part of the estates of the Wakes and Stutvilles. These holdings centred in the East Riding on the de Holand manor of Cottingham, some 50 miles from *Bordelbi*. The manor of *Bordelbi*, within the greater manor of East Harlsey, was not part of the de Holand fee as it was not held in chief, directly from the king, and did not require a licence in mortmain. De Holand must have made an arrangement with the Lascelles family, who were tenants in chief, in order that he could transfer it to his new charterhouse.

In 1301 lands in the manor of East Harlsey, including *Bordelbi*, had been settled by Edmund de Lascelles on Robert de Furneaux and his wife Maud Lascelles, having been held by the Lascelles family since the 12th century (Ft of Fines Yorks, 29 Edw I, no.193; De Banco R. 335, m.233). Maud's second husband was Geoffrey de Hotham, who is recorded as holding *Bordelbi* in 1316 (Skaithe 1866, 322). Maud paid subsidy for the manor in 1327 (TNA Lay Subsidy R., bundle 211, no. 6). She was succeeded by her son Richard de Furneaux, whose son Robert was in possession of *Bordelbi* in 1348 (ibid., no. 23). From Robert de Furneaux the manor descended to the Bentley family (BL Lansdowne MS 411) and in 1366 was conveyed by John de Bentley to, jointly, Richard de Ravenser, Marmaduke Constable and Robert de Elkyngton (ibid.).

William Brown concluded that the purpose of this conveyance was to alienate the manor to allow it be transferred to a religious establishment, as de Ravenser, Provost of Beverley, was a frequent intermediary in such land transfers under the Statutes of Mortmain. But whatever de Bentley's purpose, such a transfer never happened, for by 1370 a Thomas de Ingleby and Katherine, his wife, had made an agreement with one Ralph de Riplingham (no record survives of how he came to be in possession of the manor after 1366, nor does his name appear again) and his wife, Alice, in which they gained the manor of *Bordelbi* (De Banco R. 452, m.158d; Cal. Pat. R. 1369–74, 588).

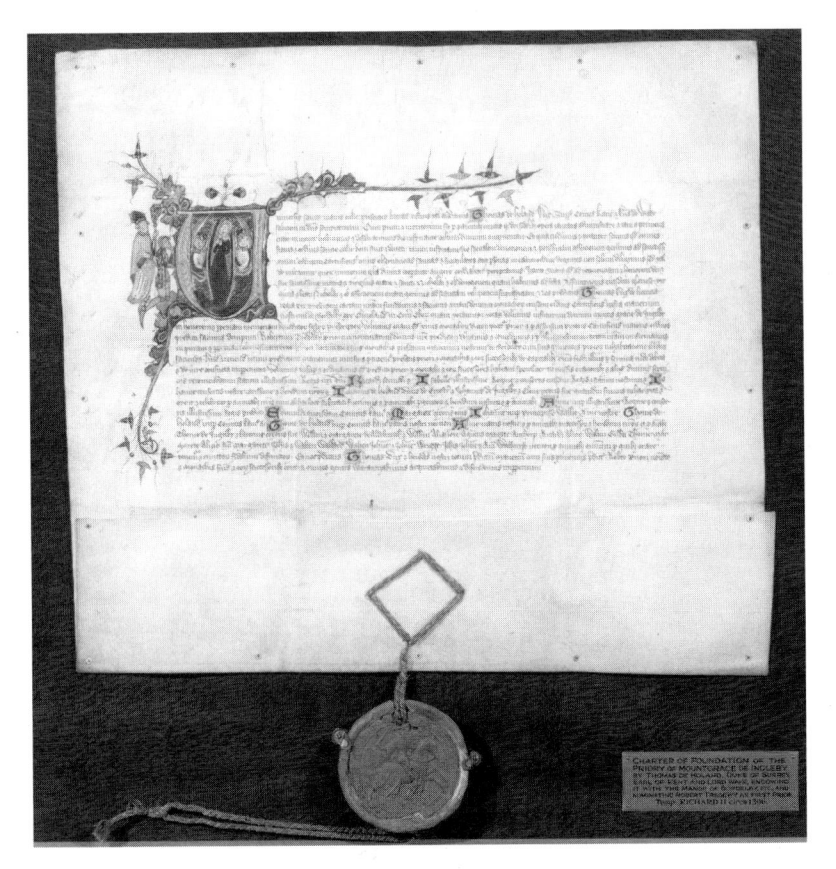

Figure 2.1 The foundation charter of Mount Grace Priory. This is the copy owned by the de Ingleby family and is now in the West Yorkshire Archives (Cat. no. Wyl230/25). The copies belonging to de Holand and the charterhouse are lost.

The de Ingleby family already owned other lands within the greater manor of East Harlsey, so *Bordlebi* was an expansion of their property. The family had first appeared in the area in 1362 when Thomas was granted lands in *Herleseye* (East Harlsey) (TNA Pat. R. 36 Edw III, pt i, m.17).

By 1397/8, and the time of the foundation of Mount Grace Priory, *Bordelbi* was evidently held by John de Ingleby, who was that year granted leave to hear mass in a chapel or oratory on his manor (Brown 1905, 259). Sometime between then and 18 February 1398, de Ingleby must have sold or transferred *Bordelbi* to de Holand. The patent roll makes it clear that de Holand did not hold the manor in chief (Calendar Patent Rolls 1396–9, 280).

The surviving foundation charter of Mount Grace (see Figure 2.1) details the initial endowment of de Holand's charterhouse. Though the charter is undated, it must post-date the licence in mortmain of 18 February 1398, without which licence de Holand would have been fined had he attempted to found a charterhouse, but is likely to have been drawn up shortly afterwards. The year 1398 was the first full year that Thomas held his father's estates, which provided him with the necessary income to endow his new charterhouse. It is also not surprising to see a new tenant-in-chief of substantial land holdings making provision for his soul and those of his forebears upon inheritance.

De Holand claimed that he had long wished to found a monastery, and his 'special devotion' (as he states in his charter) to the Carthusians was typical of his high social rank. His new house was to be dedicated to the Assumption of the Virgin and to St Nicholas, and was to be known as the house of Mount Grace of Ingleby. De Holand named Robert Trethewy (also Tredwye or Tredewy) as first prior with the consent of the prior of the Grande Chartreuse. The site of the priory was to be de Holand's manor of *Bordelbi*, and from internal evidence of the charter, John de Ingleby concurred. Indeed, amongst the list of those the priory was to pray for we find 'King Richard II, Queen Isabella, the founder, his wife, and heirs, the heirs of his uncle John de Holand, Duke of Exeter, and John de Ingleby and Eleanor his wife'. It would appear that part of the price de Holand paid to acquire the manor of Bodelbi from de Ingleby to found his charterhouse was to associate the Ingleby family with the foundation.

Further support for the new charterhouse was offered by the king himself (see Figure 2.2). On 20 April 1398, before the actual foundation of the new house, de Holand made a payment of £1,000 to Richard II, for which sum the king granted to Robert Trethewy, prior-nominate of Mount Grace, the alien priory of Ware in Hertfordshire, with all its possessions (Thompson 1930, 230). The king followed this endowment on 20 March 1399 with a charter of liberties and franchises, including freedom from taxation and a right to mine lead, in common with the charterhouses of London, Coventry and Axholme (TNA Charter R. 21–3 Richard II, no. 2).

Only a month later, on 22 May 1399, the king made a further grant at the request of de Holand. England was at this time at war with France and Richard II confiscated from the Normandy house of St Mary de Lire the three alien priories Hinckley, Wareham and Carisbrooke (TNA Pat. R. 22 Richard II, pt iii, m.11) and granted them to Mount Grace for the duration of the war. Such grants of alien

HISTORY AND TOPOGRAPHY OF MOUNT GRACE PRIORY

priories during wartime were not an ideal basis on which to endow a monastery, for following peace they were liable to be restored to their original owners. They did, however, provide an income at the critical period when the new monastery was developing its site.

Death of the Founder and Uncertainty

Having a founder who was one of the most powerful nobles in England, both on account of his great wealth and his close relationship with Richard II, and gaining as it did its various consequent endowments, the future of Mount Grace seemed assured. But such certainty was not to last. With the deposition of Richard II in 1399, de Holand was deprived of his duchy and most of his influence, and following his involvement in an abortive coup against the new king, Henry IV, which ended in a skirmish at Cirencester on 13 March 1400, he was executed on the battlefield together with the Earl of Salisbury and Ralph Lumley (Given-Wilson 1997, 237).

With de Holand's death and disgrace, the priory's right to its very site was in question, and the monks very insecure without the protection of a patron. They petitioned Henry IV, probably within weeks of de Holand's death, to confirm its title (TNA Anc. Pet. file 128, 6368). That it was confirmed is clear from the inquisition post mortem of de Holand finally taken in 1403/4, which, despite de Holand's acknowledged treason, gave the advowson of Mount Grace to his brother Edmund de Holand (IPM 5 Henry IV, no. 38). On the death of Edmund de Holand in 1408 the advowson passed to his widow, Lucy de Visconti (IPM 2 Henry VI, no. 35).

Despite Henry IV's confirmation of Mount Grace's title, he took the priory of Ware, which was valued at £251 a year – the date of this event is not known, but it is presumably the context of an appeal to the king and Parliament in 1412, in which the monks again requested confirmation of their right to the site of Mount Grace (TNA Anc. Pet. file 128, no. 6368). Henry IV made good at least part of the loss with an annual grant to Mount Grace of £100 from the exchequer and a tun (volume held in a barrel of that name) of Gascony wine, to be collected at Hull every Martinmas (11 November), until an equal endowment could be found (TNA Pat. R. 2 Henry IV, pt iv, m.121).

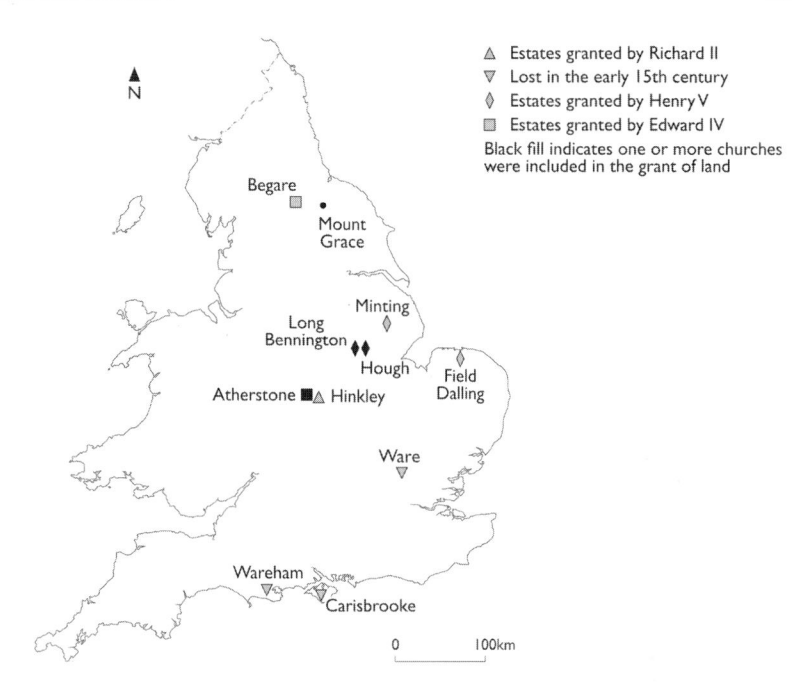

Figure 2.2 The national estates of Mount Grace.

At about the same time Mount Grace faced a difficulty in preserving their holding of the alien priories Hinckley, Wareham and Carisbrooke. The priory had apparently entered into an agreement with one William Hebard, monk, representing the Abbey of St Mary de Lire, who had agreed to pay rent to Mount Grace for the three alien priories. He reneged on the agreement and was initially supported by the Crown, but in the end Mount Grace retained the three alien priories, though for the time being on uncertain grounds.

In 1413 Henry V confirmed his father's award of £100, but stipulated that it should come from the farm of the Ware estates, which were obviously still in royal hands (TNA Pat. R. 1 Henry V, pt v, m.30). Mount Grace in return petitioned the Crown for the return of the estate (TNA Anc. Pet. file 186, no. 9299), but this was not to be.

Refoundation by Thomas Beaufort in 1415

The loss of de Holand patronage, although damaging, was mitigated by the interest of Thomas Beaufort, Earl of Dorset and later Duke of Exeter, uncle of Henry V. In 1415 Henry V took Ware and gave it to his own foundation of Sheen, which in return became responsible for paying the king's annual grant of £100 to Mount Grace. At about the same time he deprived Mount Grace of the priories of Wareham and Carisbrooke, transferring them, too, to Sheen.

Mount Grace's last alien possession, Hinckley Priory, was also threatened. For Mount Grace this final loss would have been disastrous. It was saved by the intervention of Exeter. At the very time that Henry V was removing Mount Grace's remaining endowment, Exeter succeeded in persuaded the king to confirm Mount Grace's possession of the Hinckley estates in what looks very much like an attempted refoundation (TNA Pat. R. 3 Henry V, pt ii, m.29). Exeter wished for his own charterhouse, and to augment the community by five 'monk-chaplains' (choir monks), and clearly saw himself as the new patron.

In 1417 the General Chapter granted Exeter the right to be buried in the priory church, a right usually reserved for a founder (Thompson 1930, 231). He is buried a little off-centre in the church, beside the first founder, de Holand. Exeter's further interest is apparent in 1421 when he persuaded Henry V to make good the loss of the Ware estates with the grant of the alien priories of Minting, Hough and Long Bennington in Lincolnshire, and Field Dalling in Norfolk (see Figure 2.2), and by reinstating Henry IV's annual grant of £100 (TNA Pat. R. 9 Henry V, pt ii, m.19). The new grant was far from ideal, for Hough (which, together with Long Bennington and Field Dalling, had originally been granted to Coventry Priory in 1399; TNA Pat. R. 21 Richard II, pt iii, m.9) and Minting were held by Henry IV's widow, the dowager queen, Joan of Navarre; Mount Grace would only receive the reversion on her death (TNA IPM 15 Henry VI, no. 48).

Edmund de Holand's widow Lucy Visconti died on 22 May 1424 (IPM 2 Henry VI, no. 35) and the advowson of Mount Grace passed to her heir, her cousin Gian Galeazzo Visconti, Duke of Milan (who, in fact, was already dead) and founder in 1396 of the Certosa of Pavia.

The next recorded holder of the advowson (though how he came to be so is unknown) was Sir William Ingleby, who died on 2 August 1438 (IPM 7 Henry VI, no. 9).

In 1437 Joan of Navarre died and Mount Grace took possession of its new estates at Hough and Minting. Yet despite this the monastery's situation remained insecure. The de Holand family appears to have shown little interest in the charterhouse since the death of its founder, Thomas de Holand, and with the death of its second founder, Thomas Beaufort, in 1426, and its return in 1438 to the Ingleby family, who lacked power and influence, the already struggling house must have felt in jeopardy.

The following year, in 1439, the monks petitioned both the king and Parliament for a confirmation of their title, claiming that building work had ceased with the death of the founder ('founder' at this date presumably referred to Thomas Beaufort) and that they dared not complete the house (TNA Rot. Parliament V, 22). An examination of the extant fabric (see Chapter 6) shows this to be an overstatement, but later events were to confirm their tenuous position.

On 19 November 1440 the king confirmed their title to the site (Brown 1905, 260). The value of this confirmation was limited, for with the loss of Thomas Beaufort's support, and its continued financial difficulties, the community remained insecure.

Mount Grace must have approached the General Chapter about the poor state of its finances for John Widrington, the prior of Sheen, agreed (the date is not recorded) that his house was well endowed and should not profit from Mount Grace's loss of Ware (Lambeth MS 413, f. 53). Widrington renewed Henry IV's annuity of £100 from the farm of Ware and in return Mount Grace relinquished any claim on the estates it had lost to Sheen (BL Cotton MS Otho B.xiv, f. 98).

Although Mount Grace was now entitled to enjoy the revenues from Hough and Minting, these alien priories continued to cause problems for the monastery. In 1483 Mount Grace petitioned Richard, Duke of Gloucester, Lord Protector of England (and soon to be Richard III), claiming that one John Burdett had been instituted to the Priory of Hough by the Abbot of Cherbourg in spite of Mount Grace's title to the site (Thompson 1930, 234). The outcome must have been successful, for the house still enjoyed the income of Hough's estates in 1535 (Caley and Hunter 1826, 84).

The Consolidation of Major Land Holdings

Although the first half of the 15th century was an unsure time for Mount Grace, the latter half of the century saw a period of consolidation and growth. In 1448, Henry VI licensed Prior Robert Leek to acquire in mortmain lands to the annual value of £40 (TNA Pat. R. 27 Henry VI, pt ii, m.9), an indication that the house was in a position to buy land for itself or was attracting patronage. It was at this period that further endowments began to accrue.

In 1423 Sir James Strangways bought land in East Harlsey and built Harlsey Castle. His son, also James, inherited, and in 1456 he and his wife Elizabeth were licensed to alienate the advowson of the church of Beighton in Derbyshire to Mount Grace for a fine of £10 (TNA Pat. R. 34 Henry VI, pt i, m.20), the first recorded endowment by a local family that was to remain a supporter of its neighbouring charterhouse until the Suppression.

In 1462 Edward IV granted the manor of Atherstone in Warwickshire to Mount Grace 'for the relief of the poor estate of the house and the expense of people gathering there weekly' (Cal. Pat. R. 1461–7, 120). In 1471 he further granted the priory the former estates in Richmond, Yorkshire, of the French Cistercian abbey of Begard (ibid., 1467–71, 304); these estates, as those of all other alien priories, had by 1414 either been made denizen or suppressed, and the lands remained with the Crown. The purpose of this second grant was to found a chantry within the monastery 'for the good estate of the king and for his soul after death, and for the souls of the king's father, the late Duke of York, and the king's brothers and sisters' (Cook 1947, 36). After this date there are no further major grants of land recorded.

Building Work and Land Purchase in the 1520s

Henry Clifford (1454–1523), 10th Baron Clifford, was a valuable patron to Mount Grace in the second and third decades of the 16th century, to judge from surviving letters of Richard Methley, a choir monk, and of Priors John Norton and John Wilson (see Chapter 2.3; Skeat 1957, pp. 4–6). Clifford's contact with the priory began as early as 1515, when Richard Methley returned a draft deed or bill to him for his approval (BL Add. MS 48965 f.10), after which he does not reappear in the house's recorded history until John Norton wrote to him on 27 August 1521, acknowledging Clifford's support for 'qwatt warkmen I haue in eu(r)y corner and now I muste go by more ledde for I thik to haue iij sellis thekyt wt lede a fore wynter, also I must pay for ccxxx wanscotts of this money xli' (ibid. f.v). Clearly, a substantial building campaign was underway largely funded by Clifford.

Norton's successor, John Wilson, wrote again to Clifford on St Lucy's Day (13 December) 1522 saying 'I thynk ther be as money stones hewen as will fynnych the houses, and I thynk best (th)at the walle that shall goo a boute the gardyn be made wt archelers stone for elles I cannot deuise as it may be made sure, wherin I wold glady know your lordships plesor. For pamente we may gytt masons now better to hew by grete than in sommer. Also I haue paid to masons gitters of stone and to ridders of the qwarrell xijli wich I shall make your lordship p(er)sie(n)t too when your s(er)uand comyth too hus'. He went on to say 'wee haue a propre lodgyng at our place wich a marchand of London did buld a(nd) he is now dep(ar)ted from hus a(nd) made knight at the roddes' (*idem*, f.6).

The 'knight at the roddes' can be identified firmly as Sir John Rawson, a Yorkshireman born at Fryston, though he was brought up in London where his father became an alderman and warden of the Mercers' Company. He joined the Hospitallers in 1497 and was appointed prior of the Hospital of Kilmainham in Ireland from 1511, a role that entitled him to sit in the Irish House of Lords and on the Privy Council of Ireland. He became Lord Treasurer of Ireland in 1517 (Cokayne 2000, 3, 334). He was also a pluralist who was preceptor of the preceptory of Ribston in Yorkshire from before 1529 (Page 1974, 262). He was at the defence of Rhodes in 1521/22, the year before this letter was written, and his connection with Mount Grace was through Dan Thomas Golwynne (see Chapter 2.3) who transferred there from London in 1519. Among Golwynne's possessions was a new mantel and a printed book, the gifts of Sir John Rawson. The 'propre lodgyng' that Prior John Wilson mentions in his letter must have been *le Inne* (see Chapter 2.2), but is not further identified.

On 4 January 1523 Wilson again wrote to Clifford, who had apparently asked that his chaplain be accepted as a member of the community. The prior was unwilling to take the man, explaining that our religion is strait wher for it is vere necessarye that he wich thinkith hymsellffe called of God therto shuld exersice hym a yere or two in the straitnes theroff as in ffasting, weering, waking, and in solitarie liffing wich is hard for wor[l]dlie men. Morouer my lord wee haue but too celles voide and for thone wee haue promysed to receyve shortlie affter th'fest of th'epiphanie a worshipfull man S[ir] Willm Malev[er]er and he is brether childer a[nd] also he is both Comissarie and officialle to the bushop of Rochester a[nd] may spend better than xlli beneffesse. His habbett is made redye for hym. And th'oder celle is not p[er]fetlie finished. Ther was a monke in it a yere a[nd] more and because I thought it nedefull to be mended putt hym in another celle. Albeit I had promised it to Mr Willm Stapilton who I here say is departed from this wretched liffe whos soule Ihs p[ar]done and affter hym wee grauntted the supp[ri]or of Burton Abbaye, and then the p[ar]son of sanct Saueyour in York, and then a yong prest wich was shaven w[t] huss v yere sence … and yesterday I receyuyd a l[ett]re from a graduett of Cambrige wich saithe he has a graunte in my predecessours tyme with diuersse other that makith grete instance. (*idem*, f. 7)

That there was a waiting list in January 1523 and that at least one cell was in need of repair indicates that the priory was both full and that building work was ongoing. Notwithstanding this thriving state, and Wilson's refusal to admit Clifford's chaplain, Wilson urged Clifford to continue his support of the community, for there was no wine to be had in that country and without his alms they would be unable to say Mass after Easter!

On 15 March 1523 building work still continued, for Wilson reported to Clifford:

> I haue paid since I was with your lordship to the masons a(nd) workmen vjli. I have ijM archlers hewyn a(nd) so we tare of nothing bot of lime wheroff I make all the haste that is possible for me for I can gitt noo cariage for the stone for no money be cawse the waye is fulle a(nd) up a grete hille a(nd) poore mens catell is so waike thei dar nott ventour albeit I make the best shifft w[t] our owne that I can a(nd) trustith to haue it bye the next weike afftir this. (*idem*, f. 8)

Reference to the priory's own cattle suggests that Mount Grace maintained an oxhouse either within the outer court or the home grange.

The same series of letters show that Wilson was keen to augment the priory estates, preferably at Clifford's expense. In his letter of 13 December 1522 (*idem*, f. 6), Wilson refers to the purchase of land in Teesdale already in hand, through payment by instalments begun by his predecessor, but for which payment of £21 was due and which he requested to borrow from Clifford. He also mentions the possible acquisition of land at Hutton Cranswick in Holderness: Wilson sought to borrow £70 from Clifford to lend to an improvident landowner in this village, on the security of the landowner's deeds, being fairly certain that the landowner must default. Clearly, he expected that Clifford would pay. As the land in Holderness was not held by the priory in 1539, Wilson's gamble may not have proved successful.

Wilson proposed a further purchase of land worth £25 a year to Clifford's son and heir, another Henry, on 27 November 1523. The prior was required to make a down payment of 100 marks, with the balance due on Lady Day following, when the land would be acquired (*idem*, f. 9). Its location is not specified. It is interesting to note, however, the extent to which the priory was seeking land at so late a date.

Once the house had acquired land, it was not always successful in keeping it. Land granted by Sir Robert Norton during his brother John's priorate was lost back to the Nortons of Bilborough because the deeds were imperfect (*idem*, f. 8) and the Nortons reenclosed the land.

2.2 The Estates, Demesnes and Site of Mount Grace Priory

Mount Grace, in common with the majority of medieval religious houses in England, depended for its continued existence on the temporal and spiritual income derived from substantial rural estates. The grants of major holdings (see Chapter 2.1) did not comprise the only lands from which the house derived an income. No cartulary survives, but it is possible to reconstruct the estates held in the early 16th century from two sources, the *Valor Ecclesiasticus* of 1534/5 (Caley and Hunter 1826, 84–5), and the Ministers' Accounts (the record of income from suppressed monasteries in the hands of the Court of Augmentations) of 1539–40 (TNA Min. Acc. 31 & 32 Henry VIII, no. 180).

Apart from the individual holdings identified by the *Valor* and the Ministers' Accounts, Mount Grace farmed land in

HISTORY AND TOPOGRAPHY OF MOUNT GRACE PRIORY

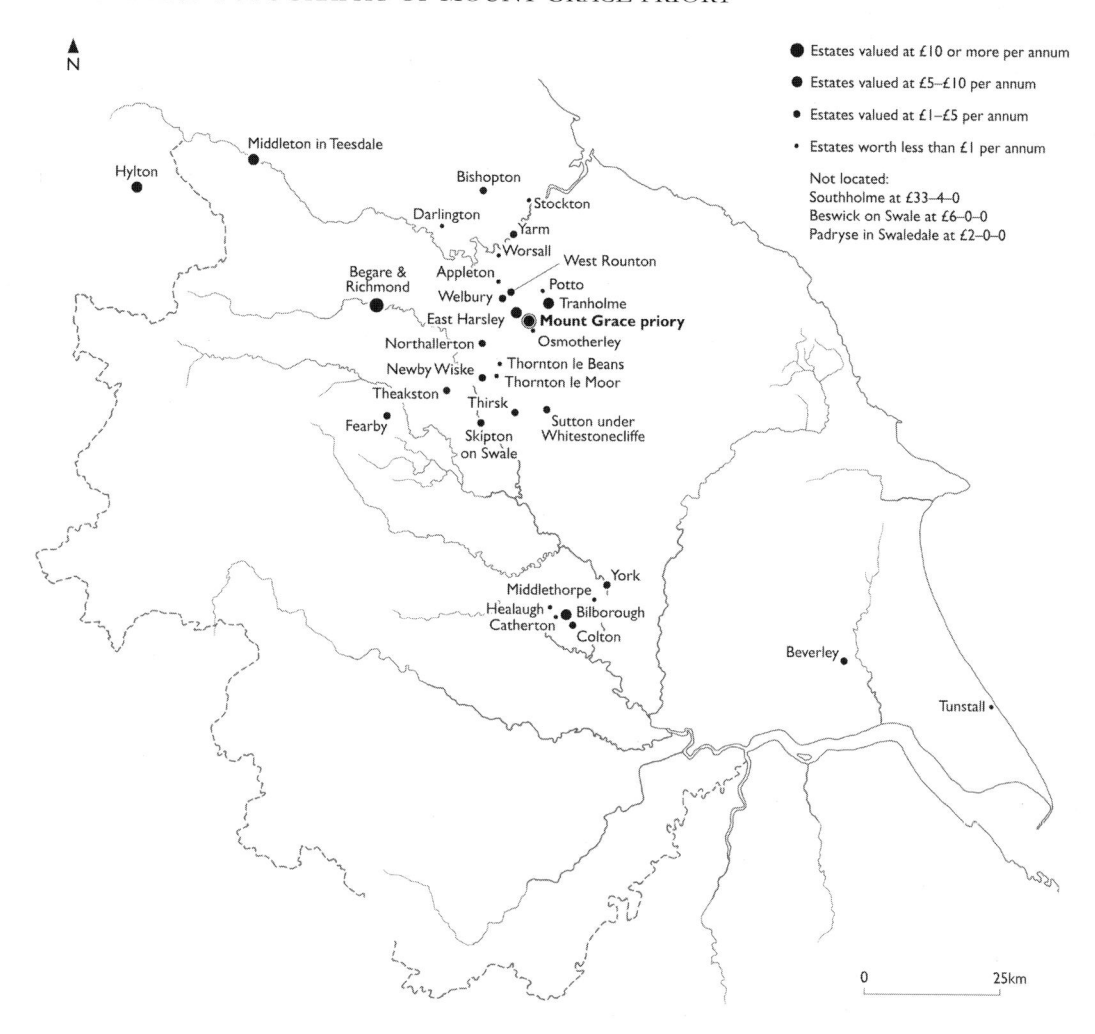

Figure 2.3 The northern, local estates of Mount Grace, from the Valor Ecclesiasticus *and Ministers' Accounts.*

demesne. These lands were attached to the immediate lands of the priory, and so are concealed within the first entry of the *Valor*: 'the site of the monastery'. A large part of these demesne lands comprised the original manor of *Bordelbi*. The priory itself occupied the south-east corner of the manor, which had been the site of *Bordelbi* village.

The land that comprised the manor is not defined by the foundation charter, but can be reconstructed from a lease of 1508, by which Prior Henry Eccleston secured Mount Grace's interest in the chapelry of *Bordelbi*. The chapel, located somewhere within *Bordelbi*, its advowson and the income it derived from the local population of *Bordelbi*, had been granted by Sir William Ingleby to Gisborough Priory before 1438 (Brown 1891, 289–92). The boundary of the chapelry was that of the vill of *Bordelbi* itself.

A further account remains of the priory demesnes in the grant of the site to Sir James Strangways in 1540 (TNA Pat. R. 32 Henry VIII, pt iv, m.45).

The Priory Estates

The priory estates that lay outside of the demesne lands can be split into two classes: the national estates, those well away from the priory and providing a clear cash income from rents (see Figure 2.2), and an extensive but less valuable group of properties which for the most part lay within 15 miles of the priory (see Figure 2.3). The total estates are listed in Table 2.1.

Temporalities totalled £277 19*s*. 3½*d*. and spiritualities £104 6*s*. 8*d*., providing a gross revenue of £382 5*s*. 11½*d*. Expenditure on rents and salaries totalled £59 3*s*. 1*d*. The value of the alien priory estates which had caused the priory so many problems in the earlier half of the 15th century is obvious. Six of the seven manors held by the priory were royal grants of seized monastic land.

Table 2.1 Mount Grace, Total estates from the Valor Ecclesiasticus and Ministers' Accounts, 1534/5 and 1540

| **Temporalities** | |
Valor Ecclesiasticus *(1534/5)*	Ministers' Accounts *(1540)*
Site of the monastery	
Manor of Beggare	The Mills
Demesnes and gardens in Rychmund	
Beverley	Beverley & Little Mautholme
City of York	In Ywbery (Jewbury)
Bilburgh	
Kennyngthwayte in Healaugh	Kennyngthwate Mede
Catterton	
Midlethorpfeld by Drynghowsez	Middilthorp & Sandwith
Estharlessay	
Westroughton	Westroughton
Thirske	Thirske & Bagby
Appleton	
Wrysell	East Worsall
Welbury	
Pottough	
Tranholme	
Sutton under Whystonclyff	
Thorneton in Mora	
Thorneton in le Beyns	
Northallarton	
Yarme	
Thekeston by Burneston	
Colton	
Manor of Southolme	
Beswyk super Waldam	
Boynton super Waldam & Skypton on Swale	
Sutton & Fearby by Masseham	
Newby on Wyske	Newby on Wyske
In Swaldale	Padryse in Swaldale
	Osmonderly
	Tunstall in Holdernesse
Stokton	
Bysshopton	
Derlyngton	Derneton
Midleton in Teasdale	
Hyltondale	
Wodham Ferers	
Manor of Hough with Gelston & Brandon	

(Continued)

Table 2.1 (Continued)

Temporalities	
Valor Ecclesiasticus (1534/5)	*Ministers' Accounts (1540)*
Manor of Myntyng with Gawdeby	
Foston in le deanry of London	
Barnebygate in Newark	
Manor of Hynckely	
Manor of Adderstone	
Manor of Feldallyng	
Spiritualities	
Valor Ecclesiasticus	*Ministers' Accounts*
Dyghton [rectory]	
Bennyngton [rectory]	
Hogg [rectory with tythes there & in Gelston & Brandon]	
Hogg [lands and glebe]	
Hynkley [rectory] with tythes there and in Wykyn, Dadlyngton, Stoke, & the mill of Dadlyngton	

How Southolme was acquired is not known, but it is the only manor not granted by the Crown.

The Priory Demesnes
The Manor of Bordelbi
The boundaries of the manor of *Bordelbi*, granted to the charterhouse for its foundation, are specifically described and can still be traced, for the most part, on a surviving 18th-century map of the Mount Grace estate (see Figure 2.4). They were defined by a bank and double ditch, which survived in part until the late 19th century (Smithson 1898, 7). Taken from the 1508 lease granted to Prior Henry Eccleston (see above), the boundaries were as follows:

Starting at the Staddlebridge across the river Wiske (formerly *Foulbrook*), the boundary ran north by the watercourse to the pasture called *lez pyttes* in the field of East Harlsey, and from there counterclockwise along the course of the *Foulbrook* to the bridge between Ingleby and East Harlsey called *Foulbrook* bridge, and from there along the *Foulbrook* to Warmdale, which was (and remains) the boundary of Ingleby, East Rounton, and East Harlsey; and then to the west along a ditch which marked the boundary between East Rounton and Low Siddle to the field of *Standfra* (now Stamfrey Farm) in the parish of West Rounton. From *Standfra* it followed the boundary of the field to the road which formed the boundary between Irby and East Harlsey, and from there the boundary between Irby Moor and East Harlsey as far as Irby Carr, and then the boundary ditch between Welbury and East Harlsey to the ditch of *Salcok*; and along the ditch between *Salcok* and *East Salcok* to Harlsey Moor.

From Harlsey Moor it ran eastwards along the boundary between *Salcok* and Harlsey by Fingay Hill. From there it ran between Fingay Ings and Holme Ings, following the line of the stream that ran southwards between East Harlsey and Harlsey to *Seggyngcroke*, and continued, following the same stream, to the road which led to Emcros, which formed the boundary between Harlsey and Morton Grange, and followed the road to the ditch of Ellerbeck, which it followed eastwards to Bruntcliffe dyke. From here it ran along the dyke to Bruntcliffe gate (a road), which lay on the south part of the field of Mount Grace, formerly called *Bordelbi* field, and then towards the east along the ditch between that field and the Clack Beck to Rowberry. Here it turned to the north along *le Stane Walle* on the brow of the escarpment, which was the boundary of the wood formerly called

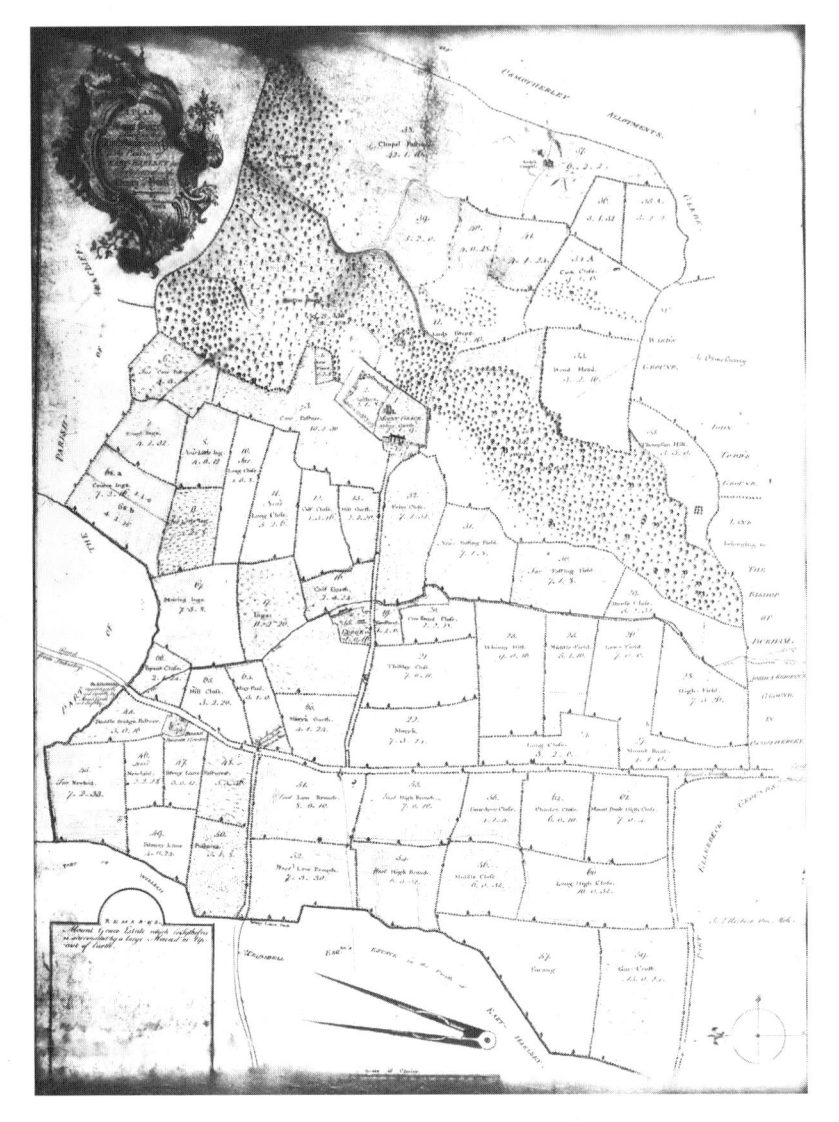

Figure 2.4 Plan of the estate of Mount Grace, 1768 (North Yorks County Record Office).

The common pasture of *Bordelbi* was parcel of Morton Grange.

In 1405, Rievaulx relaxed its claim to the common pasture in favour of Mount Grace, for an annual rent of 6s. 8d. (ibid., 219–20). Continued cooperation between the two monasteries in providing a local estate for Mount Grace can be seen in an agreement between Prior Thomas Lockington of Mount Grace and Abbot William Spencer of Rievaulx, dated Michaelmas 1436, concerning the lands of Morton Grange and their use by Mount Grace (ibid., 351).

Finally, in 1506 a lease was drawn up in which Morton Grange was to be let to Mount Grace at a rent of £13 6s. 8d. for a term of 79 years from the feast of the Invention of the Holy Cross in 1509, (ibid., 357); as such the grange effectively became a part of the demesnes of the priory, though it remained a parcel of the Rievaulx estate as far as the *Valor Ecclesiasticus* was concerned.

The extent and form of the lands of Morton Grange can be reconstructed from the detail provided in the grant of it to Sir James Strangways in 1540 (TNA Pat. R. 32 Henry VIII, pt iv, m.45). The grange comprised five closes of pasture: the *Stubbefelde*, the *Stackeclose*, the *Oxeclose*, the *Neweclose* and the *Leyfelde*; a large meadow called the *Grange-yng*; a sheepfold called the *Shepecote*; a large field called the *Cotefelde*; and that land called *Wykerlese* in the field of East Harlsey. There was also a messuage and three and a half bovates of arable land and one acre of land at *Forby lond* in the township of East Harlsey, a second messuage with four bovates of arable land and two acres of meadow in the *Grange-yng*, a third messuage with two bovates of arable land in East Harlsey, and a fourth messuage there with four bovates of arable land. In addition to this were two cottages with tofts and crofts in the village of East Harlsey.

All of this formed part of the demesnes of Mount Grace from 1509. In 1534/5, however, Mount Grace being 'determined and concluded to meddle with little husbandry' assigned this lease of the grange to Robert Wilson, already farmer of Morton Grange and servant of the Prior John Wilson (Atkinson 1889, 357), for a rent (amount unknown).

The demesne lands of Mount Grace can be reconstructed (see Table 2.2) from

Bordelbi wood (and later Mount Wood) and Osmotherley to Arncliffe park. Here it turned to the west by *le Parkedyke* back to the river Wiske (*Foulbrook*), and along the river to the Staddlebridge.

Wider Demesnes

When Mount Grace was established on the manor of *Bordelbi*, within the greater manor of East Harsley, much of East Harsley was already in monastic hands, limiting the monks' scope for developing their demesnes. One of the larger estates in East Harlsey, Morton Grange, within the manor of *Bordelbi*, had been granted to Rievaulx Abbey in about 1158 by Robert de Lascelles (Atkinson 1889, 53), and remained with Rievaulx when the rest of *Bordelbi* was settled on Mount Grace at its foundation.

Table 2.2 The demesnes of Mount Grace Priory Taken mostly from the 1540 grant to Sir James Strangways

Field	Use	Area (acres)
Calff Closes*	pasture	4
Brode Yng	meadow	30
Carter Closes*	pasture	3
Chapell Close	meadow	10
Chapell Close (alias Corne Close)	arable	4
Brottes	arable	16
Borncliffe	pasture	area not given
Gere [Gart] Crofte	pasture	20
Cowe Closes*	arable	23
Proctor Close	arable	6
Horse Closes*	pasture and meadow	10
Pryor Closes*	pasture	4
Butt Close	pasture	1½
Cater Close	pasture	3 roods (¾ acre)

* signifies two closes described together

post-Suppression sources, particularly the grant of the priory site to Sir James Strangways in 1540 (TNA Pat. R. 32 Henry VIII, pt iv, m.45). As these farmed lands all lay within the vill of *Bordelbi*, they presumably comprised a part of the initial grant of land made at the foundation of the house.

The 1540 grant identifies some 132 acres and 1 rood of land, plus the unknown acreage of the Borncliffe pasture, as forming the demesne lands of the priory, as well as buildings that are described as being outside the house, and its inner and outer court, but which were considered part of the house.

These outer buildings fall into two specific groups: *le graunge* (the home grange, or farm), with its barns, oxhouse, stables and dovecots, which lay 'near to' the priory; and *le Inne*, a tenement that lay between the home grange and the priory, its exact position is unknown, but it was probably on the north side of the precinct near the access road. The home grange, directly under the management of the priory, formed part of and managed the demesne lands. It probably also looked after the old *Bordelbi* field to the south of the priory and Mount Wood on the hillside above. *Le Inne* was tenanted, and fell outside of the demesne lands.

As indicated in Table 2.2, the demesne land constituted about 45 acres of meadow, more than 33 acres and 1 rood of pasture, and 49 acres of arable land. The location of most of the parcels of land are not known, although Butt Close lay next to the water corn mill, which can still be identified (see Chapter 6) on the lower terrace to the west of the priory buildings. In total, the demesne lands made up a relatively modest area to serve the needs of the house. In addition to these demesne lands was Mount Wood (the late medieval name), on the hillside above the priory to the east, which comprised roughly 100 acres of woodland.

The home grange can be identified today with a farm about 1 km to the west of the priory: Mount Lodge Farm. Its farmhouse, consisting of a hall between two cross-wings, is substantially 15th century in date. The rest of the farmstead now consists entirely of 18th- and 19th-century buildings that contain, not surprisingly, a large amount of reused medieval masonry. The farm extends almost up to the fishponds on the lower terrace of the priory site.

Le Inne is described as a tenement, or hostel, in the tenure of Richard Chapman. It lay adjacent to the two areas of demesne pastureland known together as Carter Closes, and within three closes of arable and pasture land, totalling 7 acres, which, like *le Inne* itself, were not counted with the demesne lands.

2.3 Priory Community and the Local People

Local Bequests

The high esteem in which the Carthusians were held for their piety and harsh life is evident from the number of bequests made in many northern wills from the middle years of the 15th century. Not all of the grants are substantial or conditional on burial at Mount Grace, and many were coupled with further bequests to the friars.

The earliest known bequest in 1401 was that of Dame Isabella Fauconbergh who left the prior her best furred mantle (Raine 1836, 282). In 1402 Sir John Dependen gave 10 marks '*pro reparatione j sellae*' (for the completion of one cell) not yet finished, in addition to a substantial bequest of £6 13s. 4d. and '*j tabulam cum crucificione pictam*' (one panel painted with the Crucifixion) for the prior (ibid., 294). In 1432, William de Authorp, rector of Kirk Deighton and a kinsman of John de Ingleby, desired to be buried in the church at Mount Grace, and in return left to the prior and monastery a silver cup, 12 silver spoons and a book called *Pupilla occuli* (Raine 1865, 351). John Paleman, alias Coke, left '*j towel de werk*' (one embroidered towel [probably for use during Mass]) to the house in 1435 (Smithson 1898, 19). In 1436, Thomas Lokwood of East Harlsey Grange, a tenant of Rievaulx Abbey, willed 20s. and requested that his body be buried in the church at Mount Grace (Raine 1865, 458d), and in July 1438, Eleanor de Roos was buried there, having left to the monastery in her will a silver vessel with a cover, and a noble apiece to the other eight English charterhouses (Raine 1855, 65).

It may have been Eleanor de Roos's burial that prompted the General Chapter to reiterate their proscription on women entering the church (while alive), even on the occasion of the burial of a prominent benefactor (Hogg 2008, 27 and 49). Presumably there had been complaints of female mourners on previous occasions.

Some bequests, however, were non-specific, singling out no particular monastery, but rather leaving small sums to many. For instance, Richard Russell, a merchant of York, bequeathed 5 marks amongst gifts to other houses on 1 December 1435 (ibid., 56). Similarly, Maud Clifford, the second wife of Richard of Conisbrough, Earl of Cambridge, left 5 marks to the 'religious men of Mount Grace', but requested to be buried at Roche Abbey, which she was, in 1446 (ibid., 120).

In 1458, William Banks, late of York, left the prior and monastery 20s. unless they reclaimed from him a book called '*Florarium Bartholomei*', which must have strayed from their library (ibid., 218). In 1474/5 Robert Est, a chantry priest of York, bequeathed 6s. 8d. to both the charterhouses of Hull and Mount Grace and returned letters of confraternity to both houses (Raine 1865, 159–60). Joan Ingleby, widow of Sir William Ingleby, died in October 1478, and although she made no pecuniary bequest to the priory, she willed her body for burial there, which implies she or her husband had supported the community while alive (ibid., 243).

Christopher Conyers, chaplain and rector of Rudby, in 1483 willed his body for burial at Mount Grace and left 20s. to the priory as well as many other bequests to other religious houses (ibid., 289). Other bequests of the late 15th century came from William Lambert, vicar of Gainford and Master of Staindrop hospital, who bequeathed 40s. to the priory (ibid., 255), and Agnes Withen, who left 26s. 8d. amongst other bequests to monastic houses (ibid., 266n), while Robert Kirton of Crathorne simply willed 'my body to be beryd at Mountegrace' (Raine 1884, 226d), indicating financial arrangements must have been made in his lifetime.

An idea of the services provided by Mount Grace for the laity can be gained from the will of Dame Joan Boynton of Yarm, who died in 1486. It reads, 'also I put in keeping of the prior and convent of Mount Grace 100 marks of money in my life to the finding of a priest 7½ years after my decease to say Mass in Yarm Friary yearly, 8 marks to be paid by the prior and convent of Mount Grace quarterly, the priest to be chosen by my executors and the prior of Mount Grace' (Raine 1868, 14).

Not only did Mount Grace hold money for laymen, on occasion it must have loaned money, for when Elizabeth de Ros, Lady Clifford (mother of Maud Clifford mentioned above), died in 1424, her inventory records a debt of £38 owed to the prior of Mount Grace (Raine 1865, 86).

From the 1480s the purpose of bequests becomes more specific. In 1488, John Carr of York left, amongst other bequests, 40s. to Mount Grace for 3 trentals (a trental is a set of 30 requiem Masses) of Requiem with note (*i.e.* sung) and 7d. to each of the monks (Raine 1868, 28), and in 1489 Robert Pynkey, former vicar of Kirkby Fletham and chantry priest of Hornby, left 6s. 8d. to the prior and a further 6s. 8d. to the monastery 'for to sing for my soule Placebo & Dirge with one obit mass' (ibid., 41). The prior of Mount Grace received 12d., each monk 8d. and each novice 4d. (as did the monks of the priories of Axholme and Beauvale) to perform a similar service for Edmund Talbot in August 1496 (Clay 1908, 66–7).

Thomas Darell of Sessay willed his body to Mount Grace in April 1500, and for the privilege of burial there gave *'priori et conv' Montis-Gratia terr' et ten' mea infra Est-Harlsey. Volo quod ij presbyteri celebrant pro an' mea per vij annos et uterque habebit viij marcas'* (to the prior and convent of Mount Grace, my land and tenement in East Harlsey. I will that two priests celebrate [Mass] for my soul for seven years and each will have 8 marks) (Raine 1868, 172). In May of the same year, Edmund Thwaites of Lund left, with bequests to other houses, 10 marks to the convent (ibid., 177), and later Dame Jane Strangways, who willed her body to the Dominican friars in York, left 10 marks to the community of Mount Grace to pray for her soul and that of her husband, who had been buried there in 1488, with one oblation (customary offering made on a particular occasion in church, especially during Mass) and a second a year afterwards (ibid., 188). Additionally, she left sums of 10s. to Dan Richard Methley and Dan Thurstan of the Mountgrace (ibid., 189).

Not all bequests were financial, however. In the will of Elizabeth Swinburne, proved on 19 October 1502, she left *'domni et conv' de Mountgrace unum par precularium, l earum de auro et c de la corrall cum omnibus le gaudyes de auro ac etiam j manile aureum dictis preculis pendens'* (to the lord and convent of Mount Grace one pair of beads [a rosary], 50 of them [the beads] of gold and 100 of coral, with all the gaudies [the larger beads between the decades of 'aves' in a rosary] of gold, and also one gold ewer from which the said beads hang) (ibid., 208) on the condition that both her mother and daughter, two further Elizabeths, 'be sisters of the same house for ever' (meaning, probably, that they received letters of confraternity).

Lady Jane Hastings bequeathed £6 13s. 4d. to Mount Grace in March 1504/5 so that a monk of the house should pray 'for ever more' for her soul and those of her first husband, Richard Pygott, her second husband, Lord Willoughby and Welles, and pray for her children and friends, while providing £3 6s. 8d. for the charterhouse of London and 40s. for Sheen without such an obligation (Clay 1908, 74).

In 1507/8, Robert Lascelles of Brakenburgh left 'to be delivered to Dan Richard Medley [Methley] 6s. 8d. and he to dispose of it to the prior and his brethren for the health of my soul' (Raine 1868, 270). The will of Martin Collins, treasurer of York Cathedral, contains only the second specific reference to building at Mount Grace: a codicil, proved on 18 August 1508, specifies *'Priori et conv' domus Cartusiensis de Monte Gratiae ad opera sive aedificationes suos x marcas'* (to the prior and convent of the Carthusian house of Mount Grace towards their works or buildings, 10 marks) (ibid., 279). A year later, Alison Clark bequeathed 10s. 'to the beilding of a glasse window' (York D. and C. Wills, ii, ff. 82r–83v).

In September 1532, two further Strangways burials were willed to Mount Grace. On 2 September, Sir Thomas Strangways of Harlsey Castle desired

> to be beriede at Mountgrace where as the Prior of the same house thynkes best. Also I gif to my corseprisaunce ['corpse price', or burial fee] my best horse. Also I give to the Mountgrace, if it please God that I be beriede there, on other horse. Also I gif to the saide house of Mountgrace, and the brether of the same, for to pray for my saull, lxs [60s.] … also I will that the Prior of the Mountgrace have, to pray for my saull and Cristen saulles that God wold have praid for xxs [20s.].

He also provided £4 for three years to support the priest 'that synges at our Lady chapell of Mountegrace' (Raine 1884, 155–6). Six days later, James Strangways of Westlathes in Whorlton parish willed 'to bee tumulate in the monasterie of the Mountgrace, and therfore I yeve theme xxs [20s.] in money' (ibid., 484n). The last recorded bequest came on 28 September 1538, when Richard Belasyse of Henknowle in County Durham left 20s. for the priory to pray for him (Clay 1908, 159). The prayers of the Carthusians of Mount Grace were seen as powerful right up to the eve of the Suppression.

Priors of Mount Grace

No formal list of the priors of Mount Grace has survived, though it is possible to reconstruct a reasonably complete list from secondary sources (see Table 2.3). In most cases, dates are only approximate.

Nicholas Love, or Luff, was a Benedictine monk in the Crowland Abbey cell of Freiston in Lincolnshire, according to the colophon on folio 121v in a copy of about 1400 of *'Meditationes vitae Christi'* (formerly Ripon Cathedral MS 6, now BL Add MS 62450), a work believed until the 19th century to have been written by St Bonaventura. At the foot

Table 2.3 Priors of Mount Grace

Prior	First mention as prior	Last mention as prior
Robert Trethewy (or Tredwye, Tredewy)	1398	
Edmund	1399	
Nicholas Love (or Luff, Louf, Lufe)*	1412	1424
Thomas Lockington (or Lokington, Lokynton)	1428	1447
Robert Leek (or Leke)	1448	1474
Thomas Atkinson (or Atkynson)	1475	1500
Henry Eccleston (or Egleston)	1501	1509
John Norton*	1509	1521
John Wilson	1521	
William Fletcher*	1532/3	
John Wilson*	1537/8	1539

* further information *given* below

of folio 3r of this same copy is written '*liber montis gracie*'. David Falls suggests that Love must have brought the book to Mount Grace when he became a monk of the house (Falls 2010, 313–15). It is possible Love used this copy of the *Meditations* as the basis for his later translation of the work into English, 'Mirrour of the Blessed Lyfe of Jesu Christ', which he wrote 'to the confusion of all fals Lollardes and heretikes' (note on Bodley MS 634 in Catalogue of Western MSS in the Bodleian Library, no. 27689), while at Mount Grace.

In 1410 his translation was endorsed by Thomas Arundel, Archbishop of Canterbury, whose friendship to Mount Grace had recently gained him a grant of confraternity from the priory (Thompson 1930, 339). Love was rector (effectively subprior) of the house for some years up to 1411, when he became prior, a post he held until 1421. He died in 1423 or early 1424, his death recorded in the obituary list compiled at the General Chapter of 1424 (Hogg 2008, 32).

John Norton of Bilborough entered Mount Grace in 1482/3 (Knowles 1971, 239). He became procurator and then prior of the house. When still only a monk of the house he received a bequest from Margaret Norton, presumably a relation (Raine 1868, 92n). He was a writer of some distinction and three of his works, '*De Musica Monachorum*', '*Thesaurus Cordium Vere Amancicum*' and '*Devotia Lamentacio*', survive (Lincoln Cathedral MS A 6.8). Knowles (1971, 239) claims that Norton was the sixth prior of the house, but his position on the list cannot be substantiated. It is only clear that he preceded John Wilson, who in 1521 acknowledged him to be his predecessor (BL Add. MS 48964, f. 8).

John Wilson appears to have served as prior twice. He was prior in 1521, when he named John Norton as his predecessor, and he appears again as prior on the pension list of November 1539, according to which he was granted a pension of £60 and the house and chapel of the Mount in Osmotherley. For some period between 1521 and 1539, however, William Fletcher was prior, as recorded on a lease of 1532/3 (Conventual Leases, Yorks, 524). With brother Leonard Hall and two lay brothers of the house – John Saunderson and Robert Shipley – Wilson was a member of the refounded charterhouse of Sheen from 1555. He died there on 10 September 1557 (Dickens 1959, 37, n96).

Others at Mount Grace

Some details, from various sources, are known of other members of the priory, as follows.

Dan Bryce was a monk of Mount Grace. While he was there, and sometime before 1426, he and the then prior of Mount Grace were sent up to Perth to look at the site for a new charterhouse in Perth to determine if it was suitable, suggesting Bryce was an experienced monk. The second prior of the new house at Perth was one Dan Bryce Montgomery – perhaps the same Dan Bryce of Mount Grace (Thompson 1930, 247).

John Wells, a monk of the London charterhouse, was sent to Hull in 1427. Such an action implies he was in some way troublesome, monks usually being sent away on disciplinary grounds and held at brother houses. But Wells was apparently sent as a guest rather than as a prisoner. It would appear he was not wanted back in London, but was passed from house to house. In 1439 he was at Mount Grace, and it was left to the discretion of the Visitors (provincial representatives of the Grande Chartreuse) whether he should return to London or to some other house. It would appear that he was finally sent to Hinton where he died in 1445 (Lambeth MS 413, ff. 57 and 163; Bodleian MS Rawlinson D.318, ff. 117 and 127).

John Fayrfax was a canon of the nearby Augustinian house, Gisborough Priory. He received papal approval in 1454 to transfer to Mount Grace or elsewhere (Cal. Papal Letters 1447–55, 672). It is not known if this transfer actually took place.

William, a lay brother of Mount Grace, was a carpenter, and was loaned to Sheen Priory by order of the General Chapter in 1454 to oversee building work then underway (Bodleian MS Rawlinson D.318, f. 140v).

Richard Methley (or Furth) was born in 1451/2 and entered Mount Grace in 1485. Knowles (1971, 224–6) suggested that he died shortly after 1491, but also quotes Kirchberger who suggests he died as vicar or subprior of the house in 1527/8, which is a date the Carthusian *cartae* (official records of the General Chapter) confirm. Methley was certainly alive in 1507/8, when he was mentioned in the will of Robert Lascelles of Brakenburgh (Raine 1868, 270), and in 1515, when he wrote to Henry Clifford (BL Add. MS 48965, f. 10).

Methley was an important mystical writer; an extant copy of the 'Book of Margery Kempe' from the Mount Grace library (Knowles 1971, 288n) contains marginalia that show that he read that copy extensively. He wrote a short autobiographical text, *'Refectorium salutis'*, which covers the period 6 October to 15 December 1487, in which he refers to two earlier works of his own (which do not survive): 'On the Name of Mary and the Sacrament of the Altar', and *'Trivium excellensie'*. He also wrote the tract *'Schola amoris languidi'* and translated into Latin 'The Cloud of Unknowing'. Additionally, he transcribed 'The Mirror of Simple Souls', his latest dated work, completed on 8 December 1491 (Pembroke Coll. MSS 198–9).

In his mystical *'Refectorium salutis'*, one of the most vivid of late medieval English Carthusian documents, Methley describes himself praying before a stone image of Our Lady above the altar in his oratory, feeling the wind that entered through the new but unfinished window 'he caused to be made to let in more light and air'. Methley also wrote for the world outside the cloister and his letter 'to Hew Heremyte' was clearly a reply to a request for spiritual guidance (Hogg 1977, 101).

Thurstan Watson, a Cistercian monk of Kirkstall Abbey, absconded without permission in 1485 and joined the community at Mount Grace, causing Abbot John Darnton of Fountains, the mother house of Kirkstall, to seek advice from the General Chapter of the order (Talbot 1967, 95–6). The outcome is unknown.

Thomas Golwynne was a monk transferred in January 1519/20 from the London charterhouse to Mount Grace (Thompson 1930, 327–8). He took with him the contents of his cell in London, for which the prior there, William Tynbegh, required an account.

The Contents of the Cell of Thomas Golwynne, 1520
Imprimis iij habyts as they come by cowrse
Itm ij newe stamyn shyrts and j olde
Item 2 new stammin shirts and 1 old
Itm ij newe stamyn colys and j olde
Itm ij newe hodys and j olde
Itm a newe coote lynyde and an olde mantell
Itm a wyde sloppe furryd to put ouer all my gere of the gyfte of my lady Conuay
Itm a newe cappe and an olde
Itm a newe pylche [outer garment of animal skin] of the gyft of Mr Saxby
Itm an olde pylche. And iij payer of hosen
Itm iij payer of newe sokks ij payer of olde
Itm iij olde sylces and a lumbare [body-cloth]
Itm a newe payer of korked shone lynyd [lined cork-soled shoes] and i payer of bobled solyd shone
Itm a payer of blanketts and ij goode pylows and ij lytell pylows and a kosshyn to knele on
Itm a newe mantell by the gyfte of syr John Rawson Knyght of the Roods
Itm a lytell brasyn morter wt a pestyll gevyn by the gyfte of a frende of myn
Itm ij pewtyr dysshes ij sawcers an a podynger [porringer] a lytell sqware dysshe for butter
Itm a new chafyng dysshe of laten gevyn to us and ij new tyne btylls gevyn by a kinsman of owres
Itm a brasyn chafer that ys to hete in water
Itm a brasse panne of a galon gevyn to us lyke wyse
Itm a lytell brasyn skelett wt a stele [handle]
Itm a payer of new felt boots and ij payer of lynyd sleppers for matyns
Itm a fayer laten sconse
These boks drawen to gether by lyne be in velome
(Itm a fayer wrytten yornall made by the cost of masters Saxby hauynge a claspe of syluer and an
(ymage of seynt Jerom gravyn ther yn. The seconde lef of aduent begynnyth ierusalem alleluia

(this boke standyth in makynge iijli
(Itm a fayer wrytten primer wt a kalendar and many other Rewls of owre religion ther yn
(Itm a fayer written sawter wt a fayer ymage of seynt Jerom theryn in the begynnynge the ijnd lef
(of the sawter begynnyth te erudimini
(Itm a large fayer boke wrytten wt the lessons of dirige and the psalmys of burying and letany
(and the Response theryn noted
(Itm a boke wrytten conteynynge certeyn masses wt the canon of the Masse and a kalendar in the
(begynnynge of the boke wt a fayer ymag of Jhesu standyng befor
(Itm a lytell penance boke wryttyn
(Itm a wrytten boke of prayers of diverse saynts wt ymags lymned and dirige wrytten ther yn
Itm a wryyten boke of papyr wt storeys of ars moriendi ther yn
Itm a printyd potews [pocket-sized breviary] by the gyft of mr Rawson
Itm a yornall a printyd primer gevyn by mr Parker
Itm a lytell legent aurey [Golden Legend] in print
Itm a shepds kalender in printe
Itm ysops fabylls in printe
Itm directium aurum in printe
Itm a complete frame for to wefe [weaving] wt corsys wt xix polysses of brasse and xix plumetts of lede
wt ij swordys [shuttles] of yryn to worke wt the frame
Itm a dowbyll styll to make wt aqua vite that ys to say a lymbeke wt a serpentyn [a condenser in the form of a coiled metallic tube] closyd both in oon [combined]

William Barker, monk of Mount Grace, was an apostate and was to be imprisoned at London charterhouse in 1529, but Prior William Tynbygh of London was not prepared to accept him unless Mount Grace took brother Alnett Hales (who had some nervous or mental disorder) in exchange on a non-charging basis. Hales survived a year at Mount Grace but obviously caused the house some distress, for he was then packed off to Axholme Priory without consent of the Visitors. Axholme found him equally troublesome and offered to exchange him for Barker. Hales was finally found a home at Witham Priory where he remained until the Suppression (Thompson 1930, 289–93).

Table 2.4 Pension list of Mount Grace, 1539

Choir monks, novices, lay brothers and oblates as given in the Pension List of 1539	
Robert Fletcher, priest	William Priest, priest
Henry Ayraye, priest	John Thorpe, priest
Geoffrey Hodgeson, priest	Leonard Hall, priest*
John Crise, priest	John Foster, novice
Robert Fuyster, priest	John Welles, novice
Augustine Fell, priest	Roger Tompson, novice
Robert Mersshall, priest	James Nelley, lay brother
William Bee, priest*	Richard Walker, lay brother
Robert Stell, priest	Peter Tutbagge, lay brother
Thomas Hargrave, priest	Robert Shipley, lay brother*
Richard Chyppyng, priest	John Saunderson, lay brother*
Thomas Dykenson, priest	Thomas Gellye, lay brother
Richard Mersshall, priest	John Tonge, oblate

* further information given below

Sir Richard Davy was a monk of Mount Grace, but left the cloister and served as curate of the church at Stanmore, near London. While there he was denounced, in 1538, to Thomas Cromwell, for not upholding the 'new doctrine' (probably referring to the collected pieces of reform legislation passed under Cromwell, going back to the Act of Supremacy of 1534) and for failing to suppress religious images (Letters and Papers Henry VIII 13 pt. 2, 142).

The 1539, the pension list (Letters and Papers Henry VIII 14 pt. 1, 258–9) named 26 individuals (see Table 2.4) under Prior Wilson.

A total of 16 choir monks, 3 novices, 6 lay brothers and 1 oblate, in addition to the prior, apparently made a full complement.

William Bee died at Newcastle in 1551. His will indicates that he was still in contact with his brother monks and that he bequeathed his books to Leonard Hall and his spectacles to John Wilson (Thompson 1930, 491–2).

Leonard Hall joined the refounded charterhouse of Sheen in 1555 and was expelled with the remains of that community to Bruges in July 1559. In 1551 he had inherited from William Bee, among other bequests, all but one of his books, perhaps the remains of the Mount Grace library (*ibid.*, 503).

John Saunderson, lay brother, joined the refounded charterhouse of Sheen in 1555 and was expelled with the remains of that community to Bruges in July 1559 (*ibid.*, 504).

Robert Shipley, lay brother, joined the refounded charterhouse of Sheen in 1555 and was expelled with the remains of that community to Bruges in July 1559 (*idem*, 504).

2.4 Suppression and Later History of Mount Grace

Suppression of the Priory

The suppression of Mount Grace in December 1539 followed five years of great uncertainty for the Carthusians, played out for the most part in London (Knowles 1971, 222–40; Thompson 1930, 379–95). This began in 1534 with the first Act of Succession. By this statute, all the king's subjects were to swear an oath before commissioners that they recognised the invalidity of Henry VIII's first marriage to Katherine of Aragon and declared the issue of his second wife, Anne Boleyn, legitimate. Given their respected reputation, Henry was particularly concerned to seek the Carthusians' approval, and especially that of John Houghton – the London and Visitor of the English houses. The Act came into force on 1 May 1534 and commissioners presented themselves at the London charterhouse on 4 May. Houghton and his procurator, Humphrey Middlemore, were asked to assemble the community and persuade them to take the oath. It was their view that the matter was not their concern, but moreover they were not persuaded that the king's first marriage was invalid. Both were dispatched to the Tower forthwith. Their imprisonment was reasonably gentle, and subtle pressure was applied, including the advice of Edward Lee, Archbishop of York. Houghton and Middlemore relented and agreed to allow the community to take the oath. They were released and, after some prevarication, the rest of their house affirmed the oath on 6 June.

The Act of Succession was followed in November 1534 by an Act of Supremacy, providing the king to be 'the only supreme head in earth of the church in England', and in February 1535 by the Treason Act, which included treason by word and specifically such speech as might 'maliciously' deprive the king of any of his 'dignities or titles'. The Act of Supremacy did not require an oath, but this did not stop commissioners being appointed to administer one. Prior Houghton, with Robert Lawrence, prior of Beauvale, and Augustine Webster, prior of Axholme, decided to forestall the commissioners by appealing directly to Thomas Cromwell, now the king's vicar general in matters spiritual, to ask to be exempted from the oath. This was refused, and the three were committed to the Tower after examination by Cromwell. On their refusal to swear a direct oath, they were sent for trial in Westminster Hall, from 28 to 29 April, on a charge of 'falsely, maliciously, and traitorously saying that the king our sovereign lord is not supreme head in earth of the church of England'. Their conviction resulted more from Cromwell's threats than the opinion of the jurors, and they were executed as traitors at Tyburn on 4 May 1535.

The martyrdom of the three Carthusian priors did not end the matter. On the day of the executions, Cromwell dispatched Dr Thomas Bedyll to the London charterhouse in an attempt to persuade the monks to swear to the Act of Supremacy. But on interviewing the three senior monks – Humphrey Middlemore, William Exemew and Sebastian Newdigate – Bedyll discovered that the community was unlikely to accept the royal supremacy, and dispatched the three monks to the Marshalsea prison for trial three weeks later. On 19 June they, too, were butchered.

The esteem in which the Carthusians were held was such that Cromwell could not act further against them. Instead, he intruded two of his servants into the house and imposed a life of great brutality on the remnants of the community. Immense pressure to conform was placed on individual members; four who were particularly opposed were packed off to Beauvale and to Hull. Eventually the community was split, and the ten remaining members who would not accept the supremacy were dispatched to Newgate in May 1537 where they were left to starve to death. Such was the example given to the other houses of the order.

At Mount Grace, second only in reputation to London, commissioners, including Sir Thomas Strangways, visited in the summer of 1534. Prior John Wilson swore to the Act of Succession, although two of his monks, Thomas Leyton and Geoffrey Hodgeson, refused to do so apparently without any penalty (Cal. Letters & Pps Henry VIII, 7, 358). The Act of Supremacy, however, Wilson was initially disposed to refuse. He consulted on the matter with Archbishop Lee of York and Bishop Tunstall of Durham, both conservative churchmen who had accepted the king's supremacy over the Church with different degrees of hesitation. On 9 July 1535 he had a personal interview with the archbishop, who reported to Cromwell that he was now compliant with the royal will (Cal. Letters & Pps Henry VIII, 11, 37). Wilson had some difficulty with his community, however, for Richard Marshall, priest, and James Newey, lay brother, fled to Scotland to avoid the supremacy oath. They were brought back and lodged in the priory prison where they were confined with Thomas Leyton and Geoffrey Hodgeson (who were still in the priory prison, having refused the first oath) until all four were compliant (Cal. Letters & Pps Henry VIII, 8, 409). Drs Richard Layton and Thomas Legh visited Mount Grace late in 1535 and found the community compliant (Cal. Letters & Pps Henry VIII, 10, 108).

With a net income of £323 2s. 10½d. in 1535, Mount Grace escaped suppression with the minor monasteries. Indeed, no Carthusian house was suppressed in 1536, though Hull, Coventry, Beauvale and Axholme all had incomes below £200 (which was the cut-off income, together with a community of fewer than 12, though the latter was not always applied) in the *Valor Ecclesiasticus*. Because suppression would have required the rehousing of the displaced monks in larger houses of the order, or persuading them to leave monastic life, closing the smaller houses was simply not practicable. There was no spare space available.

The Act of Supremacy of 1534 and the suppression of some 318 monasteries as a result of the first Act of Suppression of April 1536 were significant causes of popular revolt, first the Lincolnshire Rising of October 1536 and then the more general northern rising, the Pilgrimage of Grace, 1536–7. This latter did not involve Mount Grace, although John Wilson was invited to aid the rebels. He wisely kept his community on the sidelines, though the effect was to hasten the suppression of the greater monasteries. The Suppression commissioners Dr Thomas Legh, Dr Richard Layton, Sir George Lawson and William Blytheman arrived at Mount Grace late in 1539 to take its surrender.

Thomas Legh took the surrender of the charterhouse on 18 December 1539 and was generous with both the prior and the community. John Wilson, who had earlier complied with the royal will, was rewarded with a pension of £60 and the gift of the hermitage and chapel called the Mount in Osmotherley. Eight senior monks were paid a pension of £7, eight choir monks received £6 13s. 4d., three novices £3 6s. 8d., four lay brothers £2 and two other lay brothers four marks (£2 13s. 4d.). The single oblate received a pension of 26s 8d. In total, the pensions amounted to £195.

Mount Grace After the Suppression
The site of the former priory of Mount Grace, which included the cloister garth, church and cemetery, as well as various parcels of land that had been held by the monastery there, at East Harlsey, and elsewhere in Yorkshire, were leased to John Cheyne of Drayton in Buckinghamshire for a period of 21 years on 16 February 1540 (Ministers' Acts 4, 630). Cheyne must have returned the lease to the Crown, however, for in 1541 the reversion of the property was granted to Sir James Strangways of Harlsey Castle to be held in chief for a payment of £722 13s. 4d. (TNA Pat. R. 32 Henry VIII, pt iv, m.45).

Strangways also acquired the former Rievaulx grange of Morton at East Harlsey that had been leased to Mount Grace (ibid.). As he already had a substantial estate at West Harlsey, it would appear that he was not intending to convert the ruins of Mount Grace into a mansion, but that he was consolidating his estates as land became available. The demesnes of the priory comprised some 135 acres of meadow, pasture and arable land and some 100 acres of woodland.

Strangways died without a direct heir on 26 April 1541 (IPM 34 Henry VIII, pt ii, no. 31), and his estates were divided between his aunt Joan, wife of Sir William Mauleverer and his cousin Robert Roos of Ingmanthorpe.

By Act of Parliament in 1544, Mount Grace, with other properties, was granted to Robert Roos, who promptly sold the manor of Mount Grace to Ralph Rokeby (Brown 1882, 479–80).

It then passed to his son William Rokeby and became part of the settlement of his daughter Grace on her marriage to Conyers Darcy (1598/9–1689; later Baron Darcy and 1st Earl of Holderness) of Hornby Castle in 1616. The conversion of the guesthouse range to a modest house probably dates to the early years of their marriage.

In 1653, Darcy's son, another Conyers, sold the capital messuage (gentleman's house) of Mount Grace with the site of 'the late dissolved monastery' for £1,900 to one Captain Thomas Lascelles, who had fought in the Parliamentary army in the Civil War (ibid., 480). Thomas Lascelles came from a cadet branch of the Lascelles of Stank and Northallerton, the family that had held the manor of *Bordelbi* before 1301. His purpose in buying the site was to acquire a small country estate. He added a tower porch to the house; the porch bears the initials TL and the date 1654 above the lintel of its door. His purchase of the estate and its development appears to have strained his resources: in 1654 he was obliged to mortgage lands at Mount Grace for £200 and in 1660 he settled the estate on trustees to raise £2,000 for his seven children. The survival of so many ruined buildings on the site probably results from his inability to finance the completion of his house, its gardens and its service ranges.

In 1670, the estate passed to Lascelles's son, another Thomas, of Crossgate, Durham who settled the site on his wife, should she survive him, in lieu of dower. The last Lascelles to live at Mount Grace was his son, a third Thomas, who died there and was buried at East Harlsey in March 1701. From that date the house was tenanted, which is why it remained virtually unaltered until 1900. The Lascelles family continued to hold the manor of Mount Grace until 1744, when the Reverend Robert Lascelles sold the priory with 500 acres to Timothy Mauleverer of nearby Arncliffe Hall. It descended through the Mauleverer family to William Brown, a historian with a particular interest in Yorkshire monasteries (see Preface). In 1900 Brown sold the estate to Sir Isaac Lowthian Bell (Brown 1882, 480–1).

Chapter 3: The Site of Mount Grace Priory and its Archaeological History

3.1 Site of the Priory

Overview of the Site

Mount Grace Priory lies at the foot of the escarpment of the North York Moors National Park in the civil parish of Ingleby Arncliffe at National Grid Reference SE 453982. The site and its ruins are owned by the National Trust, and in the guardianship of the State through the Department for Digital, Culture, Media and Sport (DCMS), and managed on its behalf by the English Heritage Trust.

Two natural terraces at the base of the Cleveland Hills, at the north-west edge of the North York Moors, and at the eastern limit of the manor of *Bordelbi* (see Chapter 2.2), provided the site for the charterhouse in 1398. It was a site chosen with great care, not only large enough to accommodate the extensive buildings of a Carthusian monastery, but one which made the maximum use of existing water sources and natural drainage, while providing shelter on the north and east sides. The Jurassic deltaic sandstone of the Cleveland escarpment provided an easy source of good building stone (Senior 1989, 230), and an extant quarry 1.5 km to the north-east of the priory has been identified as the source of stone used for the priory buildings (John Senior, pers. comm.). It lies just within the bounds of *Bordelbi* and was thus on priory land.

The church, great cloister and inner court were laid out on the upper terrace at a height of approximately 100 m OD, while the outer court and home grange occupied the lower terrace at roughly 85 m OD (see Figure 3.1).

The site is marked by standing ruins, excavated low walling and substantial earthworks, which extend well to the west of the site. The priory was approached from the west by a raised causeway, which remains the modern access route, although now truncated at its west end by the A19 trunk road, which runs north–south about 650 m from the priory gatehouse, and which replaces a medieval and later road. About halfway between the A19 and the priory, just to the north of the causeway, is the 19th-century and later Mount Lodge Farm; its house is of 15th-century date with a central hall and cross-wings to north and south. The farm is almost certainly the site of the home grange referred to when the site was granted to Sir James Strangways in 1540.

Between the upper terrace and the farmstead of Mount Lodge Farm are extensive earthworks, surveyed by RCHM(E) in 1992 as part of a wider study of Carthusian monasteries. The analysis of the earthworks at Mount Grace that follows is based in part on that survey, but includes additional data provided by Glyn Coppack from his own field observations. The interpretation is therefore not exclusively that of RCHM(E), although the survey drawing itself is.

Upper Terrace: Great Cloister

On the upper terrace, the priory buildings are arranged about two trapezoidal enclosures; the great cloister and the inner court. The asymmetry of these enclosures is remarkable because it does not result from the difficulty of building on a constrained site. There was more than enough room on the terrace to have laid out rectangular enclosures, but this did not happen. Instead, the ground plan is notable for

48   MOUNT GRACE PRIORY

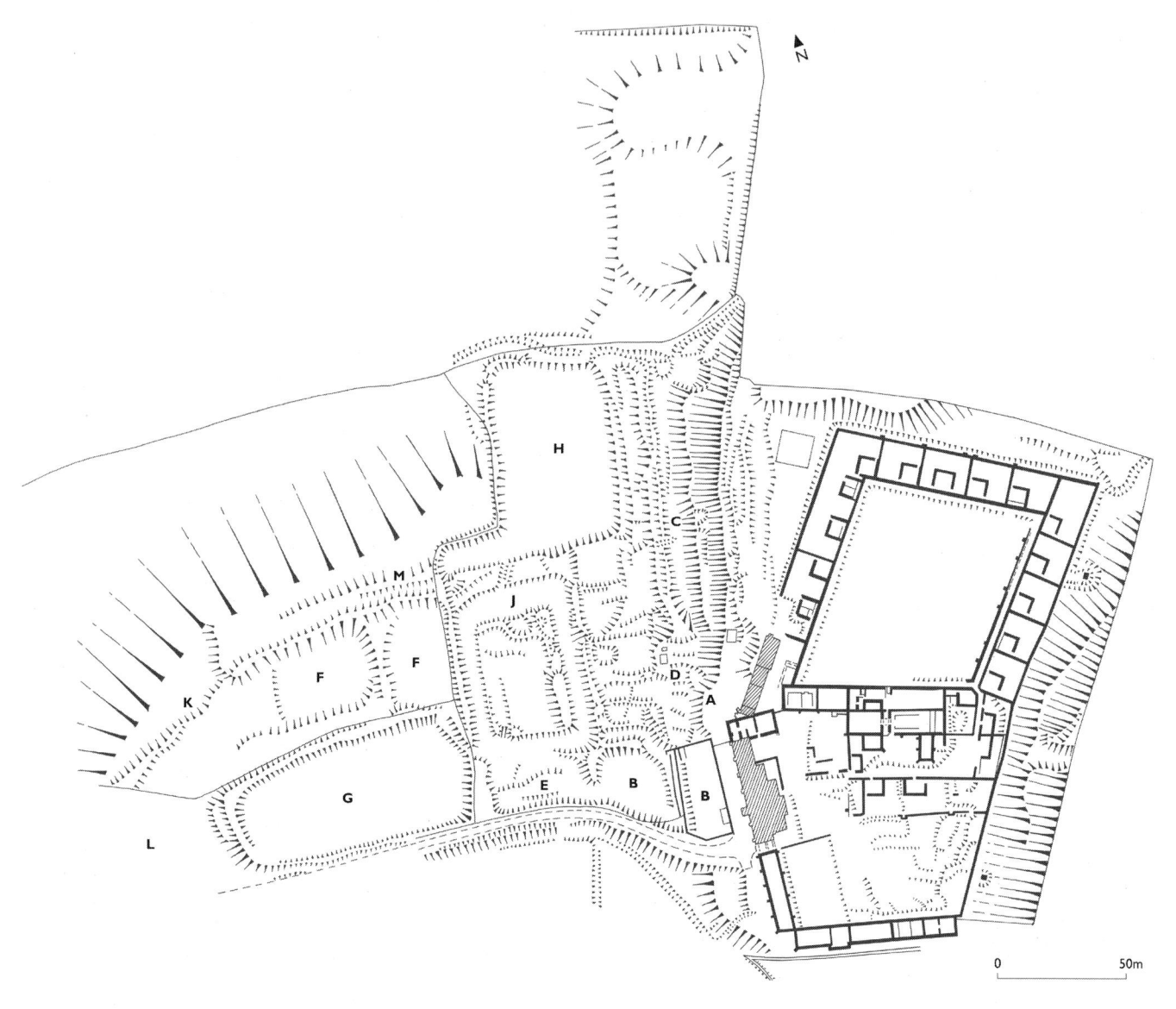

Figure 3.1 The precinct of Mount Grace Priory.

its lack of symmetry, with the east precinct wall following the base of the escarpment in a great curve. The irregular planning is particularly noticeable around the great cloister, which could have been more regularly aligned if the western precinct wall had followed the western edge of the terrace. There is some suggestion that this is what was originally planned, though it never actually happened.

The sequence of building (see Chapters 4, 5 and 6) offers a partial explanation for this asymmetric layout. The church, at the centre of the complex, the south range of the great cloister and the gatehouse were laid out and built at about the time of foundation. The south wall of the great cloister is in fact square to the western edge of the terrace and placed to allow east and west ranges at right angles to it to be added later. To this were added seven timber cells in ditched enclosures with the incomplete and unused enclosure of an eighth. It is reasonable to assume that the first five were laid out along the eastern edge of the terrace to gain the maximum shelter of the escarpment, and that they were conceived as a temporary measure, along with two further cells that began the north range. These cells, too, were aligned on the rising ground that defined the limit of the terrace, and so the temporary cells of the north range were not set at right angles to the temporary cells of the east range. Permanent buildings need not have followed their layout, though when the priory prison was constructed as part of the south cloister range, it was set out parallel to the temporary cells in the east range.

But in addition to this piecemeal, asymmetric growth, there must clearly have been considerations that developed while the first stone buildings were being raised that militated against a rectangular permanent cloister. Excavation and structural analysis gives a clue as to what those considerations were. The latrines of the temporary cells of the east cloister range were provided with sewers set within the great cloister terrace when it was modified to lay out the buildings at the foundation period. Their existence more or less dictated where the latrines of the permanent cells had to be, and the provision of a major water-flushed sewer along the line of the eventual east cloister alley would have discouraged building in stone across its line. What started as a logistical problem was compounded by the fact that the earliest cells were not replaced by a single campaign of building, but, as the architecture of the new cells shows, by a piecemeal development of individual units. Only the west range was free of earlier cells and was clearly built in a single campaign in the 1420s or 1430s, and it is significant that it was laid out more or less square to the north range. Its slight misalignment was caused by its having to line up with the existing prison building at its southern end.

Upper Terrace: Inner Court

The inner court to the south of the church is equally irregular, the result of trying to follow the east and west edges of the terrace. The line of the west precinct wall was dictated by the placing of the early gatehouse, though the remainder of the inner court was not built in stone for some 20 or 30 years. The southern boundary of the inner court (the south wall of the precinct) was built across slightly rising land and laid out more or less parallel to the church, which provided the northern limit of the inner court.

The surface of the inner court has been only partially modified by excavation and clearance, and retains at its centre and in its south-east quadrant well-preserved earthworks. The south-west quadrant is occupied by a tennis court of the early 20th century, partly terraced into the rising ground to the east, and by an orchard, which has done little to modify the topography of the court.

Against the inner side of east precinct wall are a series of sub-rectangular platforms (and in places visible traces of stone walls) that define a substantial range of buildings that is further identified by the sockets of first-floor joists in the inner face of the precinct wall. A linear scarp cutting across the inner court from the gatehouse towards the south range probably defines a roadway which may be medieval, though the eastern part of the range remained roofed into the 18th century (NYRO DN43) and the road may relate to the post-Suppression use of the site.

Medieval Road

Between the west precinct wall and the modified western edge of the upper terrace to the west of the great cloister are a series of low, parallel scarps. They continue the line of an existing and apparently medieval road that ran from outside the gatehouse along the western edge of the terrace. A public footpath from Arncliffe still follows the line of this road, which may pre-date the foundation of the priory and have served the village of *Bordelbi*, part at least of which has been located on the upper terrace (see Chapter 5). Minor terracing to its west marks the site of Ministry of Works hutting, which was relocated in 1988.

Lower Terrace (see Figure 3.1)

The majority of the earthworks lie to the west of the priory ruins on the lower terrace, an area that was heavily wooded until 1985, when diseased elms were felled. A number of oak trees remain that pre-date the modification of parts of this terrace to form the garden of the Bell house of 1900–1.

Scarp and Leat

The natural fall of the land, about 14 m from the upper to the lower terrace, is represented by a scarp (A), which lies roughly north–south. Towards the base of this fall, a narrow ledge is present for part of its length.

To the west of Cells 10 and 11 the ledge is obscured by dumped excavation spoil, the last vestiges of the 1960s spoil heap that was otherwise removed in 1988 to re-establish the profile of the scarp. The southern end of the scarp has been truncated by the terrace garden (B), created in 1900–1, though it re-emerges to the south of the road to the priory and returns towards the south-west angle of the precinct.

Further north along the scarp its base has been modified to create a perched leat (C), apparently to serve a substantial building (D), identified as a mill (see Chapter 6). The leat is between 1 m and 2 m in depth, below the top of the bank on its west side, but is partially filled with excavation spoil at its northern end. This outer, western bank, created by upcast from the leat, also served to retain water against the slope, keeping this water to serve the mill out of the fishpond to the west. The southern end of the leat, adjacent to the mill, has been partially filled from both sides by the creation in the 1950s of a terrace for a garage. The water course that fed the leat lies below the terrace garden (B), or has been destroyed by the sunken garden and pond (E) at the western end of the terrace garden (B), though its course is marked by a medieval culvert beneath the road to the priory where the northerly course of the Clack Beck now breaks.

Mill

The mill (D) is ruinous. Its south gable stands about 3 m high and the building can be traced northwards from it for some 20 m, but the building of an Anderson shelter in 1940 obscured the northern end of the building, and the north gable is not visible above ground. Between the mill and the terrace edge (A) are a series of minor scarps at right angles to the building; these are of uncertain significance, but almost certainly associated with the mill. West of the mill and its leat are a series of banked enclosures (I), aligned east–west and taking their alignment from the mill itself. They terminate against a north–south bank and define a series of yards that must have been an integral part of the outer court. There are slight traces of further buildings in these yards.

Ponds

The greater part of the lower terrace comprises a series of fishponds (F, G and H) that appear to represent at least two phases of development. The earliest of these, the two ponds F, are now dry; the creation of the manorial moat (J) before the foundation of the priory would have cut off their water supply, and they are likely to have gone out of use before the beginning of the 15th century. Ponds G and H are both water-filled.

The ponds (F) are represented by two shallow hollows on the brow of the lower terrace slope. They are defined to the north by a shallow, spread bank (K) up to 10 m wide that is now some 0.2 m above the external level, but is up to 0.5 m above the internal level of the ponds. The bank can be traced westwards beyond the ponds following the line of the landfall, in places broken by the paths created by farm traffic, and finally truncated by the steading of the 19th-century farm buildings at Mount Lodge Farm (L). North of this bank and running parallel to it is a relatively level area, which changes form to a shallow hollow (M) at its eastern end.

An estate map of 1768 (NYRO DN43; see Chapter 2, Figure 2.4) shows no ponds, but only fields in this area, defined by hedges. Adjacent to the access road, on its north side, between Mount Lodge Farm and the lower terrace of the priory, a rhomboid field is shown called Mill Garth. Its south boundary corresponds to the south bank of pond G on Figure 3.1, its east boundary to the bank spanning the east sides of pond G and the eastern pond F, and its north boundary corresponds to the north bank spanning both ponds F. In other words, at the end of the 18th century, the area that comprises both ponds F and G formed a field called Mill Garth. North of Mill Garth (north of the north bank of ponds F), was a field called Calf Close, the dog-leg eastern hedge line of which corresponds to the west bank of pond H.

As Calf Close is listed in this locality in the 1540 grant of the site to Sir James Strangways, these boundaries, as well as the two fields themselves, may well be monastic ones. Although Mill Garth is a post-medieval name, it appears to be simply a renaming of what was the medieval field Carter Closes, suggesting both ponds F were out of use by 1540. That they pre-date rather than post-date the 1768 plan is indicated by the remaining earthworks, which appear to be the earliest on the lower terrace. They may date from the first years of the monastic settlement, or even be part of the pre-monastic manor of *Bordelbi*.

The western of the two ponds F is sub-rectangular, about 40 m by 30 m, and is now less than 0.5 m deep. Its southern side forms a scarp that may represent its original edge or may have been created by upcast when pond G was dug in the late 19th century, creating the current water-filled pond to its south, and by later ploughing. Its east side forms a low bank about 0.4 m high, which separates it from the eastern pond. The east bank of this eastern pond was partly modified by the scarp created during the digging of the manorial moat (J) and the forming of its outer edge, and has been overlaid by spoil from the secondary clearing of the moat.

There is no clear relationship between these empty ponds (F) and the water-filled pond G.

This pond (G) was created by terracing into the gentle hill slope to the east and building a massive earth dam, up to 12 m wide, to the west. In its present form, the dam is faced with masonry and has two sluices. Both ponds F and pond G lie in the 18th-century Mill Garth (NYRO DN43). Pond G is fed by the streams that skirt the south side of the priory ruins. It is named the Mill Pond on an Ordnance Survey map of 1892 and was associated with a corn mill at Mount Lodge Farm. There is no evidence that this pond was associated with the priory, and is almost certainly a late 19th-century creation.

To the north-east of ponds F is another water-filled pond (H). Pond H is rectangular in shape, 72 m by 46 m, with a narrow, handle-like projection at its south-west corner. It is defined by a clear scarp to the east and the isthmus to the south. The other sides are formed by an earthen bank that becomes progressively more substantial towards the north-west corner where it is about 6.5 m wide. The bank has been breached in this corner to drain the pond. There are slight suggestions within the surviving earthworks that pond H was originally larger. Above the scarp marking its eastern side is a less clearly defined scarp running almost parallel to the lower one. The southern end of this scarp is disturbed, but it might be seen returning towards the northern branch of the moat, on its south side. If the isthmus between the pond and the moat represents a reduction of the pond, it would explain the presence of silts below it. Pond H was certainly dry in the 18th century (NYRO DN43), although now water-filled. It is presumed to be of monastic origin.

Moat and Island

The moated island between the early ponds (F) and the banked enclosures (I) associated with the monastic mill (D) has an uncertain relationship with the surrounding earthworks. The moat is rectangular in plan, 66 m by 35 m, and is partially cut away on its south side by the sunken, western area of the Bell-period garden and its pond. The west and north ditches of the moat have been recut and retain water, while the east and south ditches are partly filled, though they remain waterlogged and hold water at times of heavy rainfall.

On the island, two principal phases of activity can be identified. The earlier is represented by a series of smoothed scarps. At the northern end of the island is a shallow, dog-legged hollow around a sub-circular hollow on the inner edge of the northern arm of the moat. At the south-eastern corner of the island is a low, rounded mound, 23 m by 9 m, standing about 0.5 m above the centre of the island. Similar mounding occurs in the south-west corner, cut by a later access route.

Overlying this mounding in the southern half of the island are a number of parallel ridges at intervals of about 3.5 m, indicative of cultivation. A few remaining cherry trees suggest its use as an orchard, presumably within the context of a post-Suppression garden. The island is entered today across its eastern ditch where there is a break in the inner scarp towards the north-east corner. This does not appear to be an original entrance. Rewatering of the moat in 1995 and the dumping of spoil from the clearance of its ditches on the island has modified the earthworks.

The moat is separated from a the large pond (H) to the north by an isthmus of land 11 m wide, which may have been created when the pond was dug, but more likely when it was altered, as an auger survey shows that the primary silting of the pond appears to run below the isthmus (observed by Coppack). A drain, fairly recent in date, has been cut through this isthmus to drain the northern branch of the moat into the area of the pond.

3.2 Previous Archaeological Excavation at Mount Grace Priory

Nineteenth-century Excavation

Hope's First Season: 1896

The Yorkshire Archaeological Society (founded in 1863 as the Huddersfield Archaeological and Topographical Association, renamed in 1870, and again, as the Yorkshire Archaeological and Historical Society, in 2015) visited Mount Grace Priory on Wednesday 30 August 1882 at the invitation of the then owner, William Brown of Arncliffe Hall, for which visit a plan was prepared by one William Riley (see Figure 3.2a). There had clearly been no prior excavation, as the plan records only standing masonry and wall lines that could be surmised from scars left after demolition or from earthworks (Anon. 1882, facing 6).

In the same year, William Brown published a short paper on the history of Mount Grace

Figure 3.2 a) Plan of Mount Grace by William Riley, 1882. b) Plan of Mount Grace by William St John Hope, 1896.

that demonstrated the potential of the site for detailed study (Brown 1882). The combination of Brown's documentary research and the generally undisturbed nature of the site seen during its visit persuaded the Society to consider a programme of excavation.

Excavation began in the spring of 1896 and was conducted by William St John Hope, the Assistant Secretary of the Society of Antiquaries and the leading monastic archaeologist of the day. The Yorkshire Archaeological Society visited again on 16 September 1896 to inspect the site 'which is being excavated for the society by W H St J Hope' (Anon. 1896, 6). By the time of their visit Hope had produced a new plan (see Figure 3.2b).

Although based on Riley's original survey, the new plan was unmistakably in Hope's hand. When compared with Riley's plan of 1882, it shows that Hope had examined the presbytery and south-eastern chapel of the church, and the area to the north of the presbytery which contained the chapter house and a small courtyard. Additionally, he had dug out the sacrist's cell to the east and defined its garden. Hope had also cleared the area to the west of the church, exposing part of the south wall of what he was later to conclude was the prior's cell. He had also freed 'three of the houses on the north of the great cloister ... from the accumulated rubbish' (ibid., 8), and the new plan indicated that these included Cells 7 and 8. Additionally, Hope's plan shows the internal partitioning of Cells 3, 4 and 5 in the east range of the great cloister, suggesting that they, too, had been cleared to floor level during this season.

Hope's Subsequent Seasons: 1897, 1898 and 1900

A second season of excavation was conducted in 1897, concentrating on the south range of the great cloister (Hope 1905, 271). The buildings revealed were identified from east to west as the prior's cell, the refectory and the kitchen, buildings subsequently re-examined in 1988–92 when the scale of Hope's excavation was revealed (see Chapter 5). Further work was concentrated here in 1898, though Hope did not detail what was undertaken that season. No work was undertaken in 1899 (ibid.), presumably because the site was in the process of being sold by William Brown to Sir Lowthian Bell and permission to excavate had not been obtained.

Hope's excavation was resumed in 1900, however, for a final season, 'principally in the great cloister and the cells that surround it' and 'the whole of the eastern range of cells and their gardens were completely cleared of rubbish, and a number of interesting features brought to light, including many large pieces of the arcades of the destroyed cloister' (ibid.). The eastern cloister alley itself was examined in May 1900, before attention turned to the eastern cells (ibid., 303), when the site of the conduit house at the centre of the cloister was also examined (*idem*, 304).

Henry Stanley (1827–1903), Baron Stanley of Alderley, brother-in-law of General Pitt Rivers, the first Inspector of Ancient Monuments, subsequently excavated in the western part of the north alley and in the south alley (*idem*, 304). This concluded the archaeological examination of the site until the ruins were placed in the guardianship of the Ministry of Works in 1955.

Hope's Findings
The excavations of 1896–1900 appear to have been substantial, and that is certainly the impression that its early publication (Hope 1905, *passim*) seeks to create. For the period Hope was very good, but as was usual at the time he relied on sampling, not total stripping until his final season and he could be spectacularly wrong. Quite a bit has already been written about his excavations and enough of his work has been seen in recent excavations to be able to understand his method of working and to evaluate its successes and failures.

Hope was primarily excavating to recover building plans and to explore features within buildings that interested him. Mount Grace was one of the last excavations he undertook alone – subsequent work he undertook in partnership with Sir Harold Brakspear (1870–1934), whom he had first met when working on Fountains Abbey in the late 1880s – so it can be assumed that his methods at Mount Grace represented the extent to which he had personally developed his archaeological skills.

Hope's method of working was to use local estate labourers, who were given precise instructions but often left unsupervised whilst he continued his research elsewhere in the locality.

THE CHURCH
Hope's starting point was the standing ruin of the church (see Figures 3.2a and 3.2b), where he followed known wall lines without clearing the interior. He did not find the bases of the choir stalls or the tomb base between them, for they are not shown on his plan. He did, however, dig out the ruined south wall and surmised that because its plinth changed an extra bay had been added to the east end of the church. Hope no doubt followed his earlier practice at Fountains Abbey and so, to confirm the position of the primary east wall, dug a narrow trench across his assumed line of this wall.

Some areas he did properly examine. The high altar was dug out, presumably because it was encountered in the trenching of the east wall of the church, and the south and south-eastern burial chapels were completely cleared down to floor level. A trench was dug from the north-west corner of the church to reveal the south wall of the range of buildings that butted against it there, and an area to the south of this wall was also partly stripped, revealing a 17th-century pathway leading to the west door. This stripping was incomplete. It missed the porch outside the west door, but removed most of the evidence for its south wall. Hope was digging there because he had seen the sockets for the porch's wall plates to either side of the door, but he failed to see (or perhaps understand) what these revealed and did not record the porch on his plan.

NORTH AND EAST CLOISTER RANGES
Hope's 1896 examination of the monks' cells was restricted to the east and north ranges, with his principal work on the north range. His work on the cells has only since been re-examined in Cell 8. Cells 3 and 4 in the east range were cleared out to floor level. These were the most complete of the cells and he was clearly digging there to reveal their ground plans before he looked elsewhere. The gardens were not examined at this time, but he came back to them in 1900. From the plan he produced after the 1896 season it is apparent that he also dug

out the interior of Cell 5, at the corner of the north and east ranges.

In the north range he reduced the whole of the area of Cell 8, including its garden, to a uniform level that planed off demolition deposits to just below the top of the surviving pentice walls – just sufficient to recover their plan without removing the lower part of a deposit of fallen roof-slates. His plan of Cell 7 indicates the same process there. Unfortunately, Ministry of Works clearance of Cells 1 to 7 in the 1950s is likely to have removed any evidence of Hope's excavation in those areas. His work was reasonably non-destructive of significant archaeological deposits, and only small trenches, often only 2 ft by 1 ft, were dug to examine particular features. The Ministry clearance was much more damaging at a time when there was no excuse for it.

South Cloister Range

The later phases of Hope's work at Mount Grace were marked by the excavation of larger areas. In 1897 he examined the south-west cloister range, initially by trenching along suspected wall lines, and then by stripping the whole area of the building to what he considered to be the latest floor level. His trenching was based on his reading of the standing masonry, the trenches were barely wider than the walls they followed, but normally were dug down to the bottom of faced masonry removing any association with floors and demolition deposits. His examination of the eastern half of the range was remarkably successful, and re-excavation in 1988 (see Chapter 5) added very little to his conclusions.

Hope's examination of the western half of the range, however, revealed a major fault in his methodology. What he revealed were post-medieval garden features, aligned on the surviving walls of the structure, which incorporated medieval masonry. Hope's failing was his sheer brilliance. He created a late medieval reduction of the building that was feasible, but failed to appreciate that it stood on top of the demolition deposits associated with the ruination of the whole range. It was not the first time Hope had created a non-existent building from recognisable archaeological features; he was responsible for inventing a whole but robbed refectory at Furness Abbey by following the outside edge of the footpaces of the real building, a construct that was accepted until the early 1970s (Hope 1900, 269–71; Roy Gilyard-Beer, pers. comm.).

The demolition deposits within the south range were probed by small trenches, and many of Hope's conclusions about the western part of the range remain valid in spite of the economy of this excavation. The real bonus of his work here is that substantial demolition deposits survived for re-excavation.

Kitchen Range

The 1897 and 1898 seasons examined the kitchen range to the west of the south-west cloister range. As always, Hope worked outwards from the standing fabric, trenching along walls that were buried, and then finally stripping specific areas. Here he stripped an immense area to the latest floors and yard surfaces. Such extensive stripping was a new departure, for his previous work had been economical of earth moving. It is significant that he was working in a similar way in 1898 in partnership with Harold Brakspear at Waverley Abbey, where the infirmary was under excavation (Brakspear 1905, 2 and pl. 11). The stripping of large areas seems to have been influenced by Brakspear, and from 1898 it became the norm at Mount Grace.

The kitchen area was complicated and multi-phase, something which Hope failed to appreciate even in a large area excavation. His problems were partly caused by his flawed interpretation of the standing building: Hope's extensive knowledge of documentary sources, which required a brewhouse to exist somewhere in the vicinity, had him interpret the large kitchen chimney as a kiln associated with a brewhouse. Following this misinterpretation, the eastern part of the range became the bakehouse, a building normally associated with a brewhouse, and so the kitchen was forced into an unlikely series of timber-framed structures adjacent to the west end of the south-west cloister range (see Chapter 5, Figure 5.40).

The whole area was examined down to the latest floor level and planned in some detail. Within Hope's bakehouse was a substantial central hearth, which he failed to recognise. Only the kerb survived his excavation. With clear evidence of burning its function should have been obvious, but convinced as he was that this building was the bakehouse his judgement was coloured. But, having ruled out its function as a hearth he must have been perplexed by its purpose, for he had a large hole dug through it well into natural clay, without, however, recording the series of earlier floors that this sondage revealed.

To the south of this range he remarkably failed to see two rooms, of which the roof scar remained on the wall of the adjacent guest house, and missed a latrine shaft, half of which remained in the standing building. The cause was simple: he had not penetrated the demolition deposits and had let his reading of features in the surviving masonry cloud his judgement. He did locate a walled courtyard, the pavement of which survived, and several 17th-century features that he took to be medieval.

Here, as in other areas, Hope was careful to leave the greater part of the site's archaeology undisturbed. Unfortunately, those who followed him were less careful. The rebuilding of the guest-house range in 1900–1 was done before the excavation was backfilled, masonry was robbed for the new work and drains were cut through unexamined deposits. None of the features revealed by this work were reported to Hope.

Water Supply System
Hope's final, double, season in 1900 (he was at Mount Grace both over Easter and in May) was perhaps his most interesting and remarkable. He was applying the results of his work on the London charterhouse, which was largely document based, to Mount Grace. He had recently studied the London water-supply maps and wanted to see if Mount Grace had a similar water tower at the centre of the great cloister and, if so, to trace the supply pipes to individual cells. By excavating a rather irregular hole at the point at which the cloister's diagonals met, he did indeed find the water tower he was seeking, although it had been thoroughly demolished, leaving only fallen architectural detail. So much is apparent from his published report (Hope 1905, 304).

What is not apparent from the published account is what he did next. He actually found the rubble footings of the water tower, which were taken up, and below them found three rings of piles. No doubt in search of the inlet and outlet pipes, a deep hole was dug within the inner ring of piles. Because the pipes were not found and Hope was in a thick layer of wet peat, work was abandoned. Remarkably, his report mentions neither the *in situ* foundations nor the piles, yet it was clear from re-excavation that he saw both. Presumably they simply did not interest him.

At this point in the excavation Hope was working with Ambrose Poynter, architect of the rebuilt guest-house range, and Poynter was commissioned to draw some of the architectural detail Hope had recovered. Unaccountably, the material from the water tower was not included. However, as the east cloister alley was excavated, many fragments of the arcade were recognised and drawn by Poynter for publication.

Conclusion
Hope left the site in a reasonably intelligible state, with demolition material stripped from many areas. This process clearly continued after he left the site, and it is now impossible to identify areas for which he was not responsible. His rapid publication of the work, with a detailed plan and many perceptive conclusions, brought the charterhouse to national prominence. The fact that he had managed to do this with the minimum of excavation is a mark of his exceptional knowledge and ability. Subsequent work has largely supported his conclusions.

Twentieth-century Excavation
The 1950s and 1960s
The taking of the ruins of Mount Grace Priory into State care should have been the point at which its archaeology was reassessed. A small-scale excavation was conducted by Andrew Downing Saunders (1931–2009) in August 1957 (see Figure 3.3) to examine the latrine pentice of Cell 2, where clearance of the garden area by the Ministry of Works direct labour team had revealed a more complex development than Hope had assumed. Generally, however, the Ministry of Works approach was to remove post-Suppression deposits without archaeological supervision, a process that was to continue until 1968 under the general guidance of the late Roy Gilyard-Beer, then Principal Inspector of Ancient Monuments.

In this way, Cells 1 to 7 and their gardens were stripped to their present levels and the two northern well houses were dug out and reconstructed under the direction

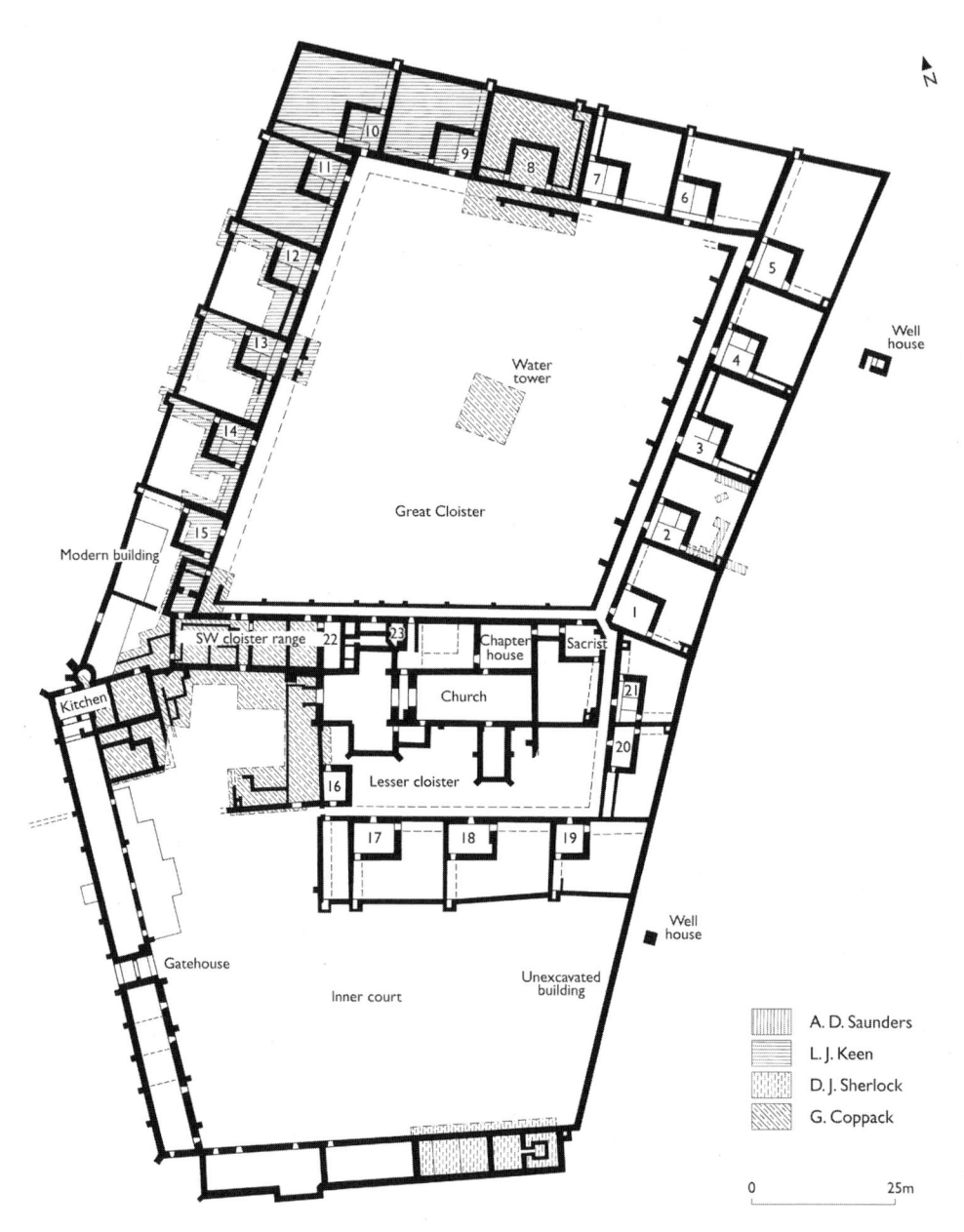

Figure 3.3 Location plan of excavations at Mount Grace since 1957.

of the then chargehand Albert Swainson (G. Hutchinson, pers. comm.) and supervision of Martin Biddle (pers. comm.). Finds from these cells collected during this work date mostly from within 20 years of the Suppression, suggesting that neither Hope's earlier work, nor the work of the direct labour team, destroyed anything beyond the 16th-century deposits. (Those few finds that were earlier had probably been displaced by earlier cultivation). Anecdotal evidence, however, suggests that the works team dug out, reconstructed and piped many of the medieval drains, seriously damaging any surviving archaeological deposits (G. Hutchinson, pers. comm.).

The somewhat cavalier approach to monastic sites in State care is suggested by the attitude of Dr Michael Thompson, an experienced Inspector and Principal Inspector of Ancient Monuments, thus: 'the amount of worthwhile information to be derived at a monastery from the mountains of debris accumulated since 1540 is probably fairly limited' (Thompson 1981, 52), and it was generally assumed that its removal by the direct works team under the intermittent supervision of an Inspector was sufficient. What mattered was the recovery of the ground plan to enable the presentation and display of a national monument.

In 1960 'removal of recent overburden from the latest medieval floor level of the church ... revealed the ashlar bases of the choir-stalls ... and the foundations for a large table-tomb' (Wilson and Hurst 1961, 314). The church was also land-drained, an action that revealed below the table-tomb at the centre of the monk's choir a body, which had remained undiscovered since Hope's excavation (T. Rudd, pers. comm.). The construction of toilets in 1957 within an existing building (now part of the holiday cottage) north of the guest house required the provision of a sewer across the site of the priory kitchens. Because the building had been excavated by Hope, re-excavation before this work took place was not considered, and the trench was dug from one manhole to another regardless of surviving medieval masonry. No record was made of the damage done and masonry that was removed was not reinstated. Even by the standards of the Ministry of Works at the time this is difficult to justify.

The 1970s
When, in about 1968, it was decided to conserve the largely buried western side of the cloister, John Weaver, Inspector of Ancient Monuments, commissioned Laurence Keen to excavate Cells 9 to 15 in advance of the work (see Figure 3.3). That work was carried out between 1969 and 1974 and included two trenches to examine the west cloister alley and a trench in the garden of Cell 8. The modern excavation of Mount Grace had begun. As Keen was constrained by the need to display (for the benefit of the visiting public) the features uncovered, excavation was restricted to the latest phase visible. Further excavation, again in advance of consolidation, was undertaken by David Sherlock, under the general direction of Keen, in the south range of the inner court in 1969, with a similar depth constraint. With the conclusion of this work, excavation was discontinued, while the consolidation of standing masonry was completed.

The State was well behind common archaeological practice in the 1960s and 1970s, and it is very much to the credit of John Weaver that the opportunity was taken to excavate Cells 9 to 15 before their conservation and display. The work was part of a wider campaign of research excavation begun on guardianship monuments in the late 1960s as a reaction to previous practice.

The importance of Laurence Keen's work was that he was able to identify individual collections of artefacts from individual cells that related to individual monks, and that he was able to recover two complete, and several partial, garden layouts, giving the first clear indication of Carthusian life in medieval England.

In 1974 Keen began the excavation of the garden of Cell 8, which was abandoned at an early stage. His appointment as County Archaeologist for Dorset effectively ended the first period of sustained research.

The 1980s Onwards
In 1983 the timber cover of a stone-lined tank in the garden of Cell 9 collapsed. It had not been examined by Keen because of depth constraints, but its collapse led to limited excavation by Rich Williams, again commissioned by John Weaver.

In 1984 Dr Glyn Coppack was persuaded by Dr Christopher Young to turn his attention from Fountains Abbey to Mount Grace Priory to restart the excavation of Cell 8. The newly established English Heritage had a proactive approach to monument presentation, and Cell 8 was to be reconstructed to enable the display of a 'typical' Carthusian cell (see Figure 3.3). In advance of its reconstruction, therefore, the excavation of Cell 8 and its garden was undertaken by Coppack in 1985. Its excavation was total, Coppack assuming that little or no archaeological material would survive the replanting of the garden or reflooring of the cell.

For the first time it was possible to examine the construction of the terrace on which the great cloister stood, and to locate evidence for the foundation period of the charterhouse. The commissioning of a monastic specialist allowed a forward research agenda to be established and research questions to be posed that preceded decisions on conservation and display. From this time onwards excavation at Mount Grace was addressing wider issues than those relevant to a single site (see Gilchrist and Mytum 1987, *passim*), returning to Hope's original research and allowing it to be updated.

No work was undertaken in 1986 or 1987, but the conduit house at the centre of the cloister was re-excavated in 1988, Hope's 'prior's cell' and the yards to its south in 1988–9, his 'refectory' in 1990 and his 'bakehouse' and 'kitchen' in 1991–2. Additionally, a detailed study was made of the surviving fabric by

Coppack in 1987–8, including the roofed guest-house range which was recorded by Steve Coll, and of the loose architectural detail by Dr Jackie Hall in 1989–90.

The excavation and associated analytical study of the ruins and architectural collections of 1987–92 was primarily research based, and sought to fill in fundamental gaps in understanding of the site. In particular, the pre-monastic use of the site and its modification at the foundation of the charterhouse was addressed with a remarkable degree of success. For the first time a clear picture was established of the chronological development of the site, area by area, throughout its active history, and individual buildings were dated. Additionally, from 1987, the principal communal buildings of the house were excavated, providing a contrast with the private areas of the cells and the connection between the eremitic lives of individuals and the coenobitic nature of the whole monastery.

Re-excavation of large areas previously examined by Hope permitted a re-evaluation of his research. In particular, the re-excavation of the water tower site and the location of pipe runs allowed the first proper study of water use in a Carthusian monastery, enabling comparison with the well-studied systems used by other orders. All of Coppack's excavations were by open area and (with limited exceptions) to the surface of natural clay.

While the site still contains considerable archaeological deposits, the decision was taken in 1989 to leave them intact for future research.

In 1985, Coppack persuaded Keen to delay the publication of his work until completion of excavation in 1992. The decision then to publish together and incorporate work by Andrew Saunders and David Sherlock further delayed his publication. Those decisions were undoubtedly correct, permitting the first full study of a medieval Carthusian monastery in Europe.

Chapter 4: The Archaeology of the Great Cloister

The 15 cells of the great cloister are now displayed at about their 16th-century ground levels, though only Cell 2 and Cells 8–15 have had any formal excavation since the completion of Hope's work in 1900. The remainder were cleared by the Ministry of Works and its successors primarily under the supervision of Roy Gilyard-Beer. Through the thoughtful and painstaking persistence of the then chargehand, Albert Swainson, finds from these cells (Cells 1 and 3–7) were originally carefully boxed cell by cell, enabling them to be studied in broadly contemporary groups and to be assessed against the more securely stratified material collected since 1968. Unfortunately, no such care was taken with the loose architectural detail recovered during clearance and that is described more generally in Chapters 6 and 7.

It is possible to ascribe the individual cells to a particular building phase either by the mortars used in their construction or by a study of the architectural development of the cloister ranges. Individual phases are more fully considered in Chapter 6, though, generally speaking, the cells, with the exception of the Sacrist's Cell (Period One) and Cell 8 (Period Three), belong to Period Two (the 1420s and 1430s). Date ranges for each period are given at the beginning of Chapter 6.

Excavation in the great cloister and elsewhere (see Chapter 5) comprised three separate campaigns and, while every effort has been made to standardise the presentation of the results, these must be seen against the development of British archaeology over three decades. In particular, the objectives of excavation changed from the requirement to reveal (for the purposes of display) the latest phase of building, to a requirement to understand the development over the whole course of its occupation. This has resulted in the description of the archaeology from top down by Saunders and Keen but from the bottom up by Coppack.

Where appropriate, the cultural and architectural collections from individual cells are presented after the discussion of the structural and archaeological evidence.

4.1 Note on Finds Numbering and Context Numbers

Because Keen and Coppack operated different methods of finds cataloguing, different methods of reference for small finds and stone are used here. All Keen's finds, both small finds and architectural fragments, have a unique find number (*e.g.* MG89); Coppack's small finds have individual find numbers (*e.g.* Fe116, Cu161), while architectural fragments from his excavation are referenced only to context (*e.g.* [37]). Note context numbers are used on the plans and in the text, although in some instances (indicated by italics in the text) they cannot be shown on the plans because they lie below contemporary features (*e.g.* floors or paths), or the context itself has since been removed. The numbers are still used in the text, however, as they relate the text to the extensive curated site archive.

Finds recovered from soil samples by the Ancient Monuments Laboratory, of the Department of the Environment (under whose management the site then was) and English Heritage, have been given their AML reference number where no find number was given on site.

All the finds from individual cells or structures are presented in a series of Finds Groups. In Cells 1–7 these comprise material recovered in clearance; from Cell 8 onwards they are composed of material from related contexts that were demonstrably contemporary.

A fuller discussion of the finds collections and their significance is given in Chapters 7 and 8.

4.2 The Monks' Cells

Sacrist's Cell (see Figure 4.1)

North (Cloister) Wall
The cloister wall of the cell is the Period One wall that retains the terrace of the great cloister (see Chapter 5), and as the cell is bonded into this wall it clearly belongs to the first phase of construction. Only two courses of masonry survive on the outer face of the cloister wall, and the door dressings have been robbed down to cloister alley floor level. The alley has, however, been raised by some 0.3 m and the lowest jamb sections and the bottom course of the internal splay remain, blocked with masonry that raised the door cill to the height of the cloister alley.

The cell floor is 0.40 m below the level of the cloister alley, and four courses of masonry remain on the internal face of the cloister wall, together with the lowest four courses of the jamb of a door to the garden pentice at its west end. The door was hung on the cloister wall where the sockets of two pintles remain.

West, South and East Walls
The west wall survives only one course high, as does the south wall, but the east wall remains substantially intact. In the centre of the east wall at ground-floor level is a fireplace with a monolithic lintel supported on corbels. The northern corbel has been dressed back and five pin-holes sunk into the jamb below the corbel suggest a crane (mechanism by which a cooking pot was suspended above the fire). There is no trace of the hearth or kerb, but it is possible that they are still buried, as the turf level within the cell is slightly above medieval floor level.

The southern end of the east wall is cut back on a slight chamfer to improve access to the latrine pentice door that occupied the south-east corner of the cell. No trace of the door itself survives.

Within the cell there is only slight evidence for partitioning. A lobby 1.05 m wide and 3.45 m long defined by fragments of its cill wall 0.2 m wide occupied the north-east corner of the cell. There was no trace of a stair within it, though this would be its logical location. The north-east angle of the cell was demolished in Period Three when access was created from the great cloister to the lesser cloister and as part of the same operation reconstructed on a splay that removed part of the lobby.

Nine courses above present ground level, 2.51 m high, is an offset 0.1 m wide that marks the level of the upper floor. Above the offset the east wall survives for a further 13 courses, and incorporates the greater part of the chimney flue.

Latrine Pentice
No trace remains of the latrine pentice, its location being confirmed only by the presence of a shallow latrine pit 0.50 m long and 0.35 m wide set in the south-east angle of the garden, with a drain running away to the west. The pit was not in the angle of the garden walls, but 0.45 m from the south wall and 0.70 m from the east wall. The garden walls were lined with a single remaining course of ashlar 0.2 m wide

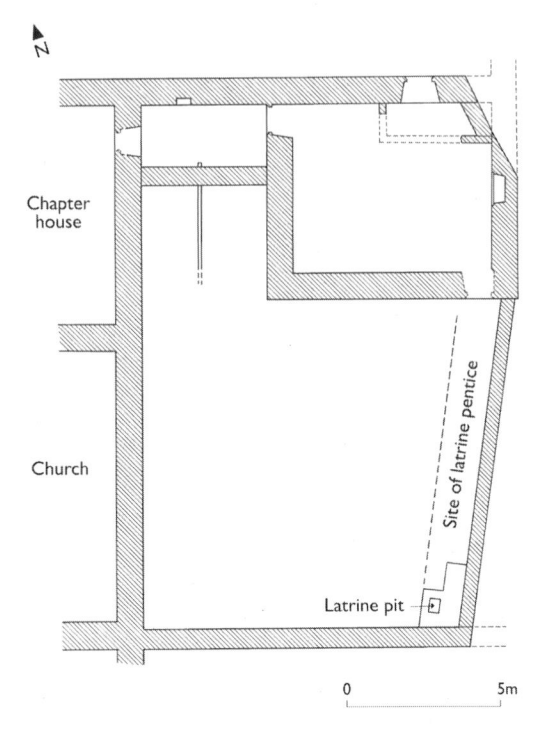

Figure 4.1 The sacrist's cell.

THE ARCHAEOLOGY OF THE GREAT CLOISTER

that may be the last remains of the latrine structure. Immediately to the north of the latrine pit is an area of paving.

Garden Pentice

The short garden pentice lay to the west of the cell, its floor 0.50 m below that of the cell, suggesting steps, though none remain. Its west wall was the east wall of the chapter house, for which the sacrist was responsible and the splays of a narrow door into that room remain. In the cloister wall, and nearer the chapter house than the cell, is a tap niche with the ghost of the lead pipe that fed the tap. Below it is a stone-lined gulley to catch the waste, which was channelled into the garden by a drain that passed below the pentice wall.

The pentice wall of this cell was of different construction to those of all the other cell pentices, being of double-skin construction and at least two courses high. It may well have been entirely of masonry and not of timber on low cill walls, as in all the other cells. It was not bonded to either the cell wall or the east wall of the chapter house, but as it butts the Period Two chapter house wall it cannot be a primary feature.

Garden

The garden is quite featureless, with only the lowest courses of its enclosing walls remaining.

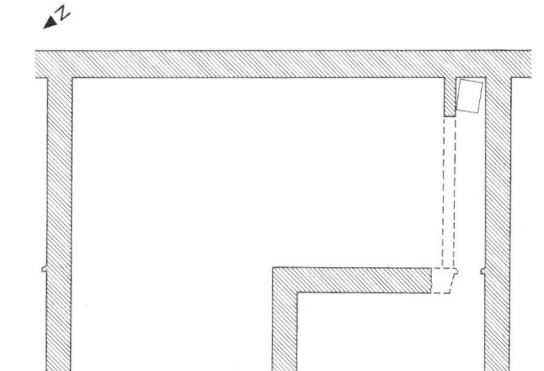

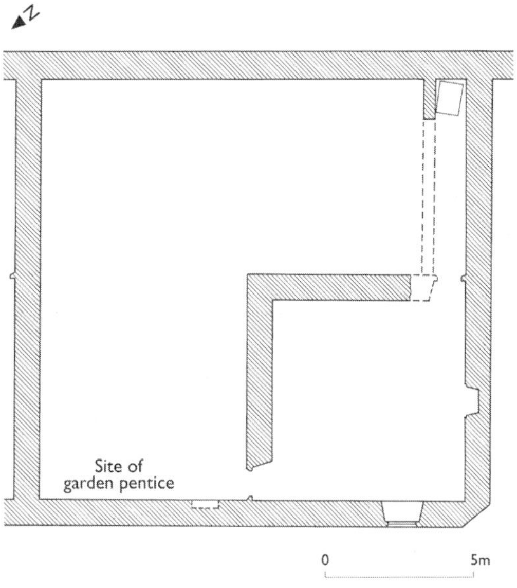

Cell 1 (see Figure 4.2)

West (Cloister) Wall

The cloister wall of Cell 1 stands to a height of ten courses, with the hatch to the south of the door (see Figure 4.3). Two blocked square putlog holes remain in the base of the sixth course above footings. The door to the cloister was hung on two pintles in the southern jamb, and there are a series of bolt and lock holes in the northern jamb. The inner part of the hatch was closed on the line of the door reveal by a wooden flap for which the hinge and latch fixings remain set in a rebate 20 mm deep. Within the doorway an area of stone paving remains.

No chasings exist for a turning stair in the south-west angle. Any stair must have been freestanding.

South Wall

The south wall of the cell survives to a height of two courses with a fragmentary fireplace at

Figure 4.2 Cell 1.

Figure 4.3 Cell 1: cloister door, bearing the arms of Archbishop Scrope on the label stops (G. Coppack).

its centre, of which only the damaged lower jambs survive.

East and North Walls

The east wall survives for most of its length to a height of two courses, but is robbed down to the top of the footings at its south end, where the door to the latrine pentice should be. Similarly, the north wall was demolished to two courses; only the lower part of the eastern jamb of the garden pentice door survived, though the western jamb survived to full height with

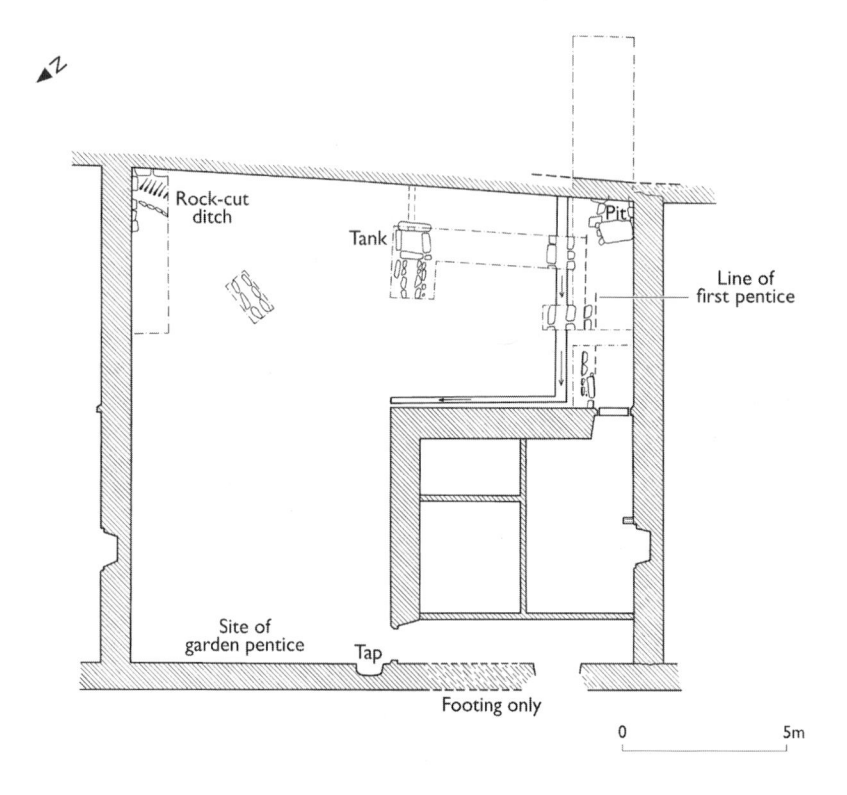

Figure 4.4 Cell 2.

sockets in the inner face of the west (cloister) wall for its door head and lintel. The door was hung on the cloister wall side.

Internally, there were no indications of the arrangements of the cell: no evidence of stairs and, similarly, no evidence in the form of cill walls or sockets for the fixing of internal partitions. Externally an ashlar-faced drain ran around the east and north walls of the cell and returned along and then below the garden pentice, running away into the south cloister alley.

Latrine Pentice

The latrine pentice was only traceable at its eastern end where the lowest course of its cill wall survived, enclosing a latrine pit within the precinct wall 0.80 m². The pit was not aligned with the pentice and presumably pre-dated its masonry construction. A timber seat over the privy was evidenced by two sockets 0.1 m wide and 50 mm high cut into the inner face of the precinct wall. At floor level in front of the pit a rough socket cut into the garden wall marked a timber step approximately 0.255 m wide and 0.13 m high. Clearance by the Ministry of Works revealed a foul drain running from this latrine towards the north-east corner of the cell and from there parallel with the north wall to a sewer below the east cloister alley.

Garden Pentice

No trace remains of the garden pentice, which contained a now-robbed tap niche in the cloister wall immediately outside the cell door. The cloister wall of the pentice is largely a recreation by Bell built in the first years of the 20th century.

Cell 2 (see Figure 4.4)

West (Cloister) Wall

The cloister wall to the south of the door of Cell 2 survives to only a single course of ashlar and, to the north of the door, only the footings remain. The superstructure of the wall is a rebuilding by Bell of before 1905 (Hope 1905, 297). Only the internal splays of the cell door remain.

Inside the cell, a cross-passage is defined by a cill wall set on the line of the inner reveal of the garden pentice door in the north wall. Slight traces remain of paving in the passage. The cill wall marks a change in level, for the floor of the remainder of the cell was 0.28 m above that of the passage, with three rooms defined by cill walls 0.18 m wide. The interior of the cell has not been excavated below the top of the cill walls.

South Wall

The south wall survives to a height of two courses with a damaged fireplace at the centre of the wall that retains a small fragment of its stone kerbing. There is no evidence for a stair in the south wall of this cell.

East Wall

The east wall survives through most of its length for a single course above footings, though there are two courses at its north end. It retains the lowest jamb stones and chamfered cill of the door to the latrine pentice at its south end. The door itself was hung on the southern jamb where the hole for its lowest pintle survives.

North Wall

The north wall is two courses high with the lower jambs of the door to the garden pentice at its west end. The door itself was hung from the cloister wall.

Latrine Pentice (Excavation by Andrew Saunders)

In August 1957 a small excavation was undertaken by the Ancient Monuments

THE ARCHAEOLOGY OF THE GREAT CLOISTER

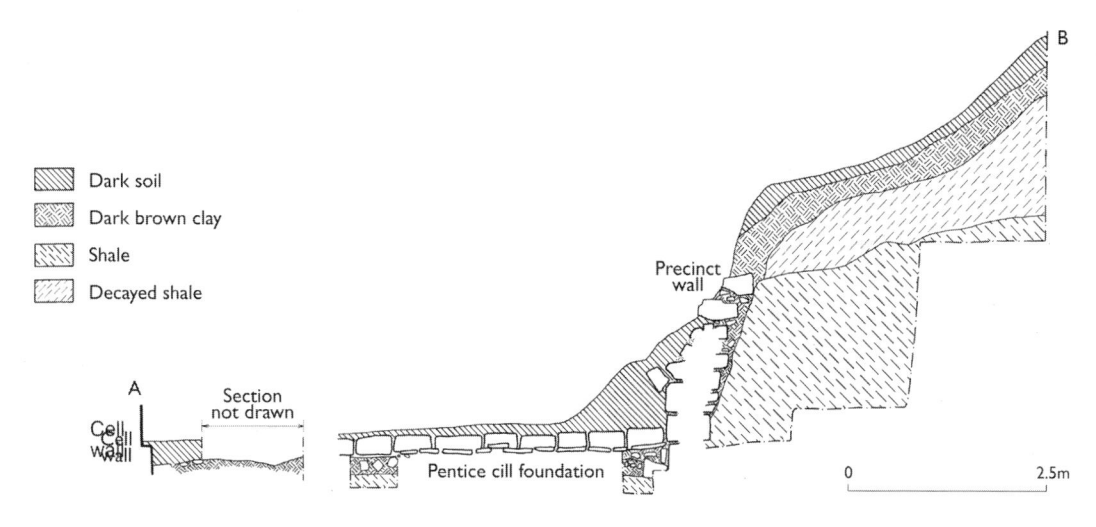

Figure 4.5 Cell 2: section through the precinct wall and latrine pentice.

Inspectorate of the Ministry of Works to establish the character of the east precinct wall of the great cloister before the work of consolidating the remains was begun. The purpose of this was to discover whether the wall had been freestanding and later engulfed by the slipping of the hillside behind, or had been built as a retaining wall.

At the same time it was hoped to learn something of the latrine arrangements in the eastern cells, of which Sir William St John Hope in his architectural description of the ruins wrote:

> It is somewhat uncertain how the latrines of the first four cells were arranged. Owing to the rise of the hill, the eastern wall of their gardens is practically a retaining wall to the hill itself, which has evidently been cut back to make room; there were consequently no external latrines as in other cells. The collapse of a good deal of the wall through the slipping of the ground behind has destroyed whatever evidence there may have been but it seems reasonable to suppose that the garderobes were framed of wood under the further end of the pentise. (Hope 1905, 298)

A trench 1.83 m wide was dug along the southern side of the garden of Cell 2 (see Figures 4.5 and 4.6) and into the hillside 3.2 m beyond the line of the eastern precinct wall. Below the humus and leaf mould on the tree-covered hillside was a dark brown soil that covered the remains of the outer face of the wall. Beneath the soil was natural orange-grey decomposed shale, which overlay, in varying thickness, grey shale of the Upper Lias.

Beside the wall the hillside had been cut back on an irregular line giving a slope of about 70 degrees. The base of the wall was built on a ledge of rock and, above the bottom two courses, rubble and mortar were packed against the sloping side of the cutting. The first course of ashlar of the outer wall face survived at the level of the change between rock and the decomposed shale, 1.61 m above the base of the wall and 2 m above the bottom of the internal wall face. Between the rubble core of the wall and the natural rock was dark brown soil, much darker than the layer above and mixed with black soil. The inner face of the wall survived for three courses and a fourth course was visible, though displaced. The internal height of this stretch of wall was 2.16 m above the footings. Where the wall became freestanding its width would have been 1 m.

The eastern wall of Cell 2 was 6 m to the west of this section of the precinct wall and occupied the south-western corner of a roughly square plot. The remaining L-shaped space served the cell's monk as a garden. The trench along the south wall of the plot produced evidence for the pentice walk that led from the doorway in the south-east corner of the cell. It was clear that this area had been excavated previously and the disturbed dark brown soil and decayed vegetation was sometimes more than 0.3 m deep. In this upper layer pieces of stone and many fragments of floor tiles, some of them glazed, were found, but it was impossible to assess their original position.

A single line of stones lay 1.70 m from the south wall of the plot, stretching from the cell to the precinct wall. Running parallel to this line of stones, on its south side, was a strip of thin, flat stone slabs (mostly reused roofing slates), about 0.3 m wide (see Figures 4.4 and 4.6). The stone slabs were the seating for a cill beam of timber on which stood a wooden wall or the supports for the pentice. The walk

Figure 4.6 Cell 2: east end of the latrine pentice as excavated, showing the latrine pit and evidence for the later pentice wall, scale imperial (A. Saunders).

itself was 1.49 m wide. The slabs were firmly bedded on a layer of small stones and black soil, 75–100 mm thick, and below these were more stones in a puddled grey clay about 0.15 m thick, with a thin spread of sooty black soil underneath.

These foundations were found to be later than a similarly constructed pentice walk only 0.92 m wide, and 0.2 m below the later line. The outer line of dressed stone, remaining at the west end, was about 1.22 m from the south wall of the plot; the slabs were from 0.28 m to 0.43 m wide.

The later raising of the level of the pentice walk was noticeable in the doorway of the cell. The earlier cill coincided with the lower level of slabs and the pentice wall of this period came close to the door jamb. With the raising of the floor level another cill, bricked up on small stones, was inserted into the doorway, masking the stops of the chamfered door jambs. The earlier cill and traces of the stone floor in the cell were on the same level as the earlier pentice. The earlier pentice foundations had been set on the natural shale and above this and below the stone slabs was a layer of grey clay of varying thickness.

Opposite the cell door at the eastern end of the pentice walk was a latrine covered by fallen rubble and stone slates, inside the garden, not outside the precinct wall such as those on the north side of the cloister. A large stone slab, roughly 1 m long by 0.66 m wide, served as a step. The footings for the garden wall and the precinct wall provided two sides of the latrine and a third was based on three large stones set at a slightly higher level than the step. The fourth side, with its wide step, may have been left open.

Sufficient evidence remained to indicate the existence of a wooden seat. The mortises for two horizontal beams at seat level were found. That in the garden wall was more of a notch hacked into the stone, 77 mm deep, 0.56 m from the south-east corner of the garden and 0.56 m above the step. The stone containing the mortise in the precinct wall was found displaced and was put back in its correct position. The mortise measured 0.153 m by 0.1 m and was 0.1 m deep; it was 0.71 m from the corner of the garden and was also 0.56 m above the step. The socket for the upright was less easily traced; it is likely to have been in the angle between the step and the footings on the north side.

Another stone with a mortise measuring 0.178 m by 0.153 m and 77 mm deep was found in the fallen rubble from the precinct wall and indicates another horizontal beam at a higher level, perhaps the wall plate of the pentice itself.

The latrine itself was a cesspool cut into the shale with a total depth of 1.42 m from the top of the step. The plan of the pit was irregular: about 1.37 m by 1 m, becoming squarer in plan about 0.6 m down, measuring 0.71 m by 0.79 m. There was no sign of a drain in excavation, although a channel was subsequently located, during land drainage work, running to the north-west around the cell and discharging into a major sewer below the east cloister alley. The pit itself was filled with grey-brown clay and rubble.

Garden (Excavation by Andrew Saunders)
A trench was dug in the north-east corner of the garden of Cell 2 to check whether the latrine in the adjacent Cell 3 was drained into a sewer or simply discharged into a cess pit. The results showed that its cess pit was provided with a small overflow drain cut only 0.15 m deep into the natural rock and led through a 0.3 m wide gap in the footings of the party wall

of Cells 2 and 3 directly below the first course of ashlar. This overflow drain was stone-lined on the west side and was 0.25 m wide. It had been opened in recent times, its cover slabs, if any, removed, and a land drain laid in its course with another land drain leading into it from the south-east.

Another trench dug 3 m away within the garden showed that the drain ran in a south-westerly direction across the garden. This stretch of drain had been undisturbed and 0.38 m below the present ground level were found the flat cover slabs over the stone lining. The drain was in a rock-cut gulley and was 0.2 m wide and 0.18 m deep. Subsequent conservation work by the direct labour team following Saunders's excavation traced this drain to its junction with the foul drain from the Cell 2 latrine.

On Sir William St John Hope's plan a small square tank is shown in the garden of Cell 2 and the top of this was visible below the leaf mould. This was examined and found to be built roughly 0.6 m², with four large pieces of reused building stone, two having a chamfered edge. The tank was 0.71 m deep and its bottom stone flagged so that it readily held water. In its north side was a hole 75–100 mm in diameter forming an inlet for water from the hillside. There was no outlet from the tank and water seeped out through the joints.

Running west of the tank was a stone-lined drain. It had two outer lines of pitched stones and was covered by very large slabs. Although the ends of the drain were flush against the tank, there was no connection between them. The tank appeared to be of post-medieval construction, probably cutting across the line of an earlier drain.

A drain with ashlar sides and a split stone base ran the length of the latrine pentice and returned along the east wall of the cell, where, at the north-east corner, it discharged into the foul drain from the latrine. It is now stopped off at the north-east corner of the cell. A widening of the drain at the west end of the latrine pentice suggests the location of a downpipe from the pentice roof, though it is far from certain that this is an original feature.

Garden Pentice
No trace remains of the garden pentice itself. A robbed tap niche remains in the base of the cloister wall immediately outside the cell door, with a runnel in the surviving paving below it. At the north end of the gallery, however, a number of features remain in a better-preserved section of the cloister wall (see Figure 4.7). A horizontal slot 0.80 m above the pentice floor marks a possible shelf 0.356 m wide and 0.56 m from the end wall of the gallery. Above it is an arched niche containing a smaller arched recess, probably for a candle. To the south are two pin-holes 2.16 m from the north end of the gallery. Perhaps there was a cupboard here.

Finds Group 1 (see Figure 4.8)
CERAMICS
In comparison with the pottery recovered from other cells, the Cell 2 pottery seemed comparatively humble, with few imported drinking vessels or Cistercian or other late medieval tablewares (Table 4.1). Jugs and jars comprised the bulk of the forms. There were also three urinals, all in the same fabric. This modest assemblage included nine sherds of pre-priory pottery: six jugs and three cooking pots. Cooking pots were on the decline by the 15th and early 16th centuries and were generally absent from those parts of the group contemporary with the use of the cells. The presence of pre-priory pottery in this area suggests that the settlement of *Bordelbi* may have extended to the foot of the escarpment.

Figure 4.7 Cell 2: sockets cut into the cloister wall at the north end of the garden pentice (G. Coppack).

Table 4.1 Cell 2, Finds Group 1: Ceramics

Fabric	Sherds	Total vessels	Cooking pot	Jar	Jug	Mug or cup	Pancheon	Tripod pipkin	Urinal
Brandsby type	4	1	0	0	1	0	0	0	0
Cistercian	2	2	0	0	0	0	2	0	0
Developed Humber	1	1	0	0	1	0	0	0	0
Gritty	9	6	3	0	3	0	0	0	0
Hambleton	16	1	0	0	1	0	0	0	0
Humber	6	2	0	0	1	0	0	1	0
Langerwehe	1	1	0	0	0	0	1	0	0
Late Gritty	7	3	0	0	0	2	0	1	0
Post-medieval Orange	24	13	0	7	4	0	2	0	0
Post-medieval Sandy	6	3	0	2	0	0	1	0	0
Raeren	1	1	0	0	0	0	1	0	0
Reversed Cistercian	1	1	0	0	0	0	1	0	0
Ryedale	45	10	0	0	7	0	0	0	3
Scarborough	4	2	0	0	2	0	0	0	0
Siegburg	4	1	0	0	0	0	1	0	0

1. Brandsby type cooking-pot rim. Pale yellowish surfaces and pale yellow core. Fairly hard and rough surfaced. Pre-priory.
2. Brandsby type cooking-pot rim. Cream coloured surfaces and whitish-yellow core. Pre-priory.
3. Brandsby type jug handle. Pale yellowish-buff outer surface and whitish-grey core. Greenish-yellow developed splashed glaze with orange highlights. Pre-priory.
4. Humber ware jug base. Dark red to bright orange outer surface, orange core and pale pinkish-orange inner surface. Two drips of clay slurry from a suspension glaze. 15th to early 16th century.
5. Ryedale ware urinal rim. White to blue-grey core and blue-grey inner surface. Olive-green glaze. Traces of a white deposit on inner surface. 15th to early 16th century.
6. Siegburg stoneware mug. Grey core with a silver-grey glaze to outer surface becoming tinged with brown towards the rim. Internally the glaze varies between a silver-grey and a bronze-brown. 15th to early 16th century.
7. Post-medieval Orange ware small jug. Purplish outer surface, blue-grey core with orange margins and purple-brown inner surface. Bright olive-green glaze. A thick, white deposit on inner surface suggests it was used as a urinal. 15th to early 16th century.

Small Finds

In addition to pottery, the cells were provided with wooden vessels, of which only those in the waterlogged conditions of the eastern cells survived. The single vessel from Cell 2 was recovered in a Ministry of Works' clearance and its find spot within the cell or garden was not recorded.

8. Bowl. Ash. Turned but now distorted. There are six pieces. Base: 73 mm by 55 mm; depth: 9 mm. Base bears a branded M (or B), H: 20 mm; W: 15 mm. The sides vary from 4–6 mm thick and below the everted rim there is a groove W: 1 mm and depth: 0.5 mm. AML 605004.

Cell 3 (see Figure 4.9)
West (Cloister) Wall

The cloister wall survives on the outside to a maximum height of 14 courses, with a further course remaining on the inner face at its south end. Above the cell door and to the north, the cloister wall is a rebuilding by Bell (see

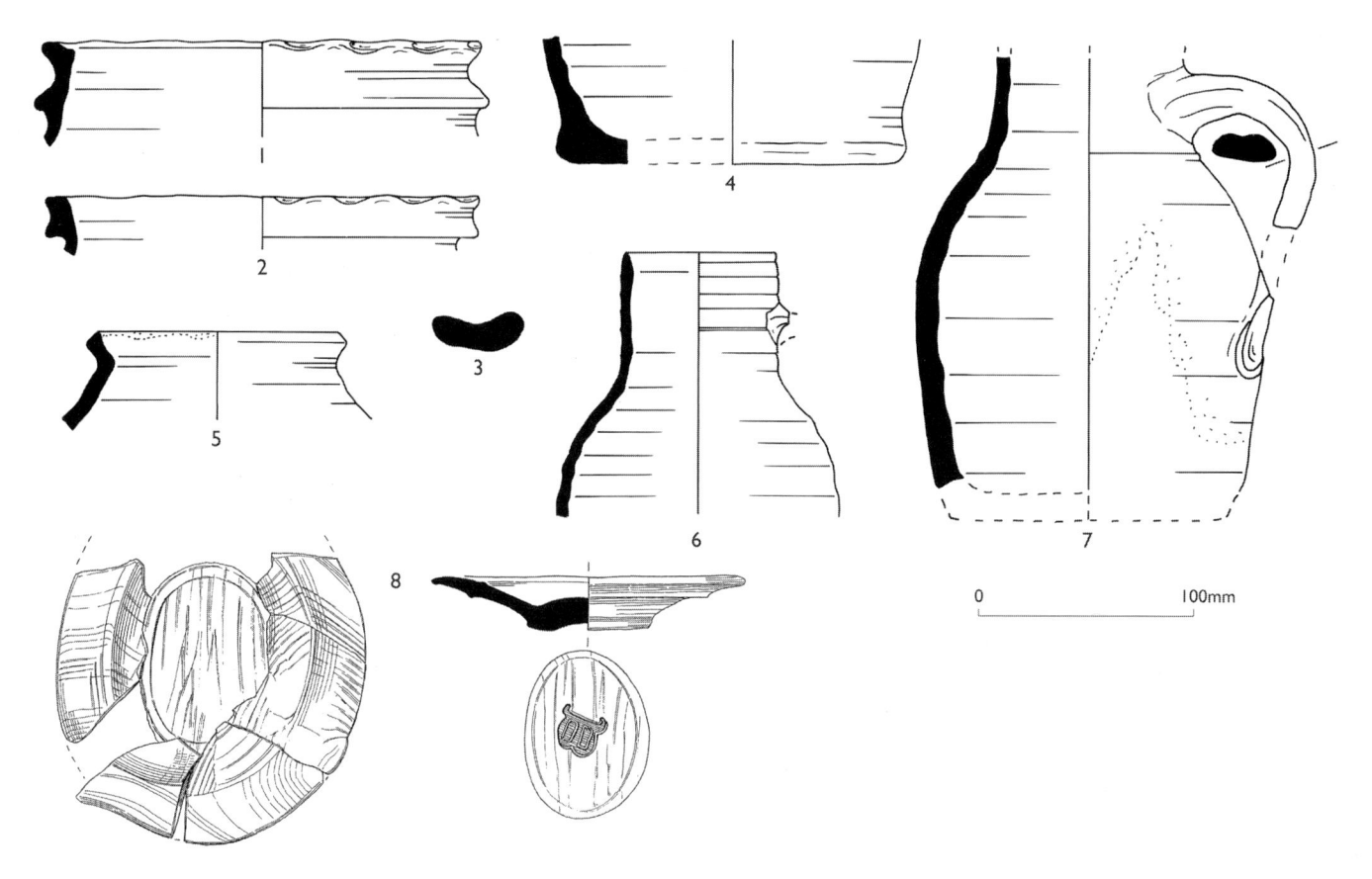

Figure 4.10). The door and hatch to its south are undisturbed and a single corbel to support the upper plate of the cloister roof remains below the string course that marks the cloister roof flashing.

South Wall
The south wall of the cell survives to a maximum of nine courses at its west end and three to the east. In the south-west corner of the cell, slots in the masonry indicate the treads and risers of a turning stair built within the end of the cross-passage. The lowest step is 0.60 m above the cell floor in the west (cloister) wall, suggesting further steps must have existed below it for which no evidence remains. A fireplace was provided at the centre of the south wall, with a hearth of slates set on edge and retained by a stone kerb.

The partial plan of the cell interior is provided by cill walls 0.18 m wide dividing the cell into three rooms (there is no trace of the partition for the cross-passage). The larger living room occupied the southern half of the cell and was 2.97 m from north to south.

East Wall
A small room, presumably the bedroom and oratory, occupied the north-east corner of the cell and was 1.65 m wide. The surviving masonry of the east and north walls provide the evidence for the lighting of these rooms and for modification of the partitioning (see Figure 4.11).

The east wall survives to eight courses at its north end and three at the south, where the lower courses of the latrine pentice door survive. The door itself was hung on the south jamb. Some paving survives in the door reveal.

To the north of the doorway is the lower part of a two-light window with evidence for shutters. The northern edge of its internal splay coincides with the south face of the east–west partition. Further north along the east wall, and lighting the bedroom, is a single-light window, now represented only by its cill.

Two sockets in the inner face of the east wall are associated with the partition between the living room and bedroom. The first, just above the cill wall and offset slightly to the south, is 0.1 m wide and 0.15 m high. The second, offset a further 50 mm to the south and 0.3 m above floor level, is 0.115 m high and 77 mm wide. A partition set in either would ruin the splay of the two-light window and it is therefore likely that they pre-date the stone

Figure 4.8 Cell 2: Finds Group 1 (pottery 1:4; wood 1:4).

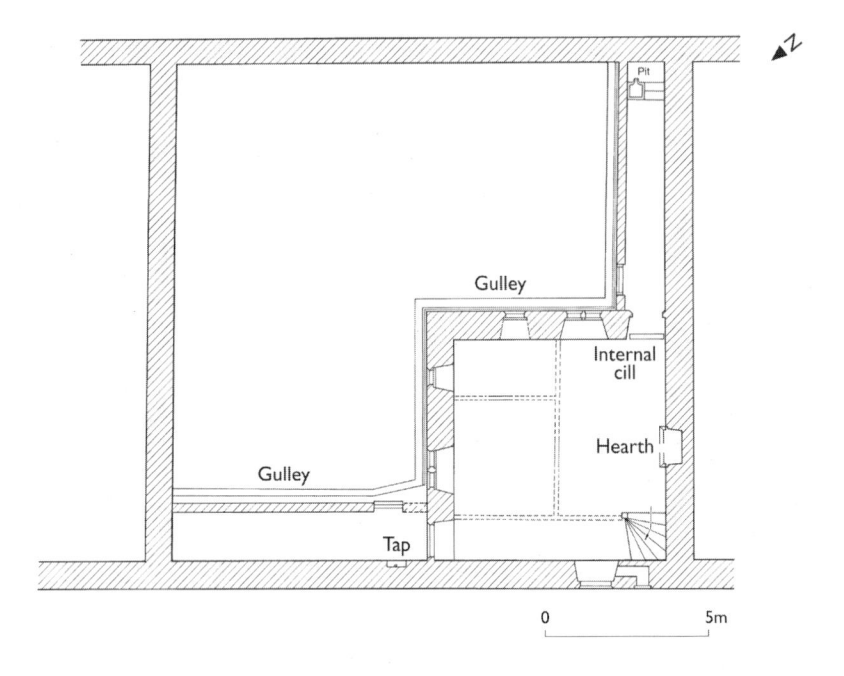

Figure 4.9 Cell 3.

Figure 4.10 Cell 3: the cloister door and hatch (G. Coppack).

cill wall, which must be contemporary with a refenestration of the cell.

North Wall
This re-windowing is evidenced in the north wall, which survives to a maximum height of 17 courses. A single-light window with evidence of bar holes and secondary glazing serves the bedroom and seems to be a later insertion. To its west, a four-light window remains largely complete (see Chapter 6); it was glazed above the transom and shuttered below before the lower lights were later fitted with glazing in wooden frames. This window is clearly a later insertion as its lintel is socketed for floor joists 0.46 m above the offset that marks the primary first floor of the cell. The larger room lit by this window was presumably the study. At the west end of the north wall, the door to the garden pentice remains complete, the pintles being set in the west jamb, and two square bolt fixings remaining in the east jamb.

The original first-floor level is established from an offset 0.1 m wide that remains in the north wall and at the south end of the west wall, ten courses above floor level. A single primary window of one light, shuttered and barred but not glazed, remains in the north wall just above floor level.

Latrine Pentice
The cill wall of the latrine pentice survives to the height of a single course of ashlar from the east wall of the cell to the precinct wall, where it survives to full height. At the west end, the chamfered cill of a door into the garden remains, its west jamb is 0.51 m from the cell and the doorposts were 0.15 m deep. Along the outside of the pentice was an ashlar-faced drain with a slate base that returned around the cell and discharged into the drain of the garden pentice. Where the drain runs around the cell its inner face is made of battered ashlars.

The latrine itself was the best preserved of the eastern cells (see Figure 4.12) and remained substantially complete but for its timberwork. It was contained within the eastern end of the latrine pentice and set over a masonry-lined pit, the base of which was 0.46 m below the level of the pentice floor. A hole in the precinct wall provided a flow of spring water to flush the pit, which was drained by a stone-lined drain that ran away to the south-west to join the foul drain from the latrine of Cell 2 close to the north-east corner of that cell.

Two stone steps up to the level of the latrine remain *in situ* providing an access 0.64 m wide on the south side of a carefully cut stone sink, 0.5 m^2, which discharged into the latrine pit. The top of the sink was set 0.33 m above the pentice floor. A socket 0.15 m high and 0.18 m wide in both the garden and pentice wall evidenced a third, timber, step that ran the

THE ARCHAEOLOGY OF THE GREAT CLOISTER

Figure 4.11 Cell 3: the interior showing the evidence for two phases of flooring in the north wall (G. Coppack).

width of the pentice, above the outlet of the sink, and through the thickness of the pentice wall. Set against the back of the step was a timber board 0.1 m thick, which formed the front of the latrine itself. The board did not extend the full depth of the timber step, to which it must have been nailed, but its slot in the garden wall showed that it extended 0.35 m above the top surface of the step. Level with the top of this board was the top of a substantial beam (0.15 m²) against the precinct wall that had supported the latrine seat, of which no other trace survived. The superstructure of the latrine was timber-framed and comprised a continuation of the pentice itself, though its cill beam was set 0.3 m above the cill beam of the remainder of the pentice. This raised section of cill extended 1.10 m from the precinct wall.

Garden Pentice

The garden pentice is defined by the single remaining course of its inner wall, which retains the chamfered threshold of a door 0.90 m long and set 0.71 m to the north of the cell. Opposite this doorway is a robbed tap niche, which retains the ghost of a lead pipe, 50 mm in diameter, rising through the cloister wall. The cloister wall is as largely rebuilt by Bell.

A socket in the north wall of the cell 1.66 m above floor level marked the timber wall plate of the inner gallery wall and would have accommodated a beam 0.165 m high and 0.178 m wide. Above this, traces of white mortar flashing indicated the approximate pitch of the pentice roof to be 45 degrees. An ashlar-lined drain ran along the east side of the pentice, meeting with the cell eavesdrip drain on the north side of the door into the garden, where both drains discharged into a deeper drain that ran below the garden pentice floor.

Finds Group 2 (see Figure 4.13)
Ceramics

This group (Table 4.2) illustrates a curious characteristic that is apparent in several other cells: the apparent duplication of certain vessel forms. For example, amongst the unillustrated material were Cistercian ware sherds that paralleled numbers 13, 15 and 17. The household goods of each cell would have been designed for the use of a single monk. Why should he require two or more of any particular tableware? In the case of these Cistercian ware vessels, the unillustrated duplicates are represented by far smaller numbers of sherds.

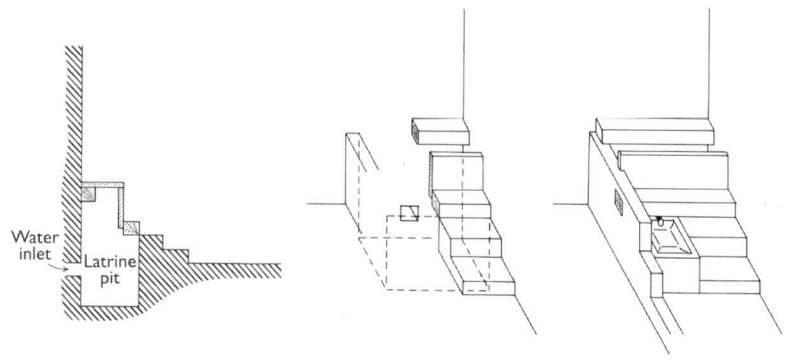

Figure 4.12 Cell 3: axonometric reconstruction of the latrine.

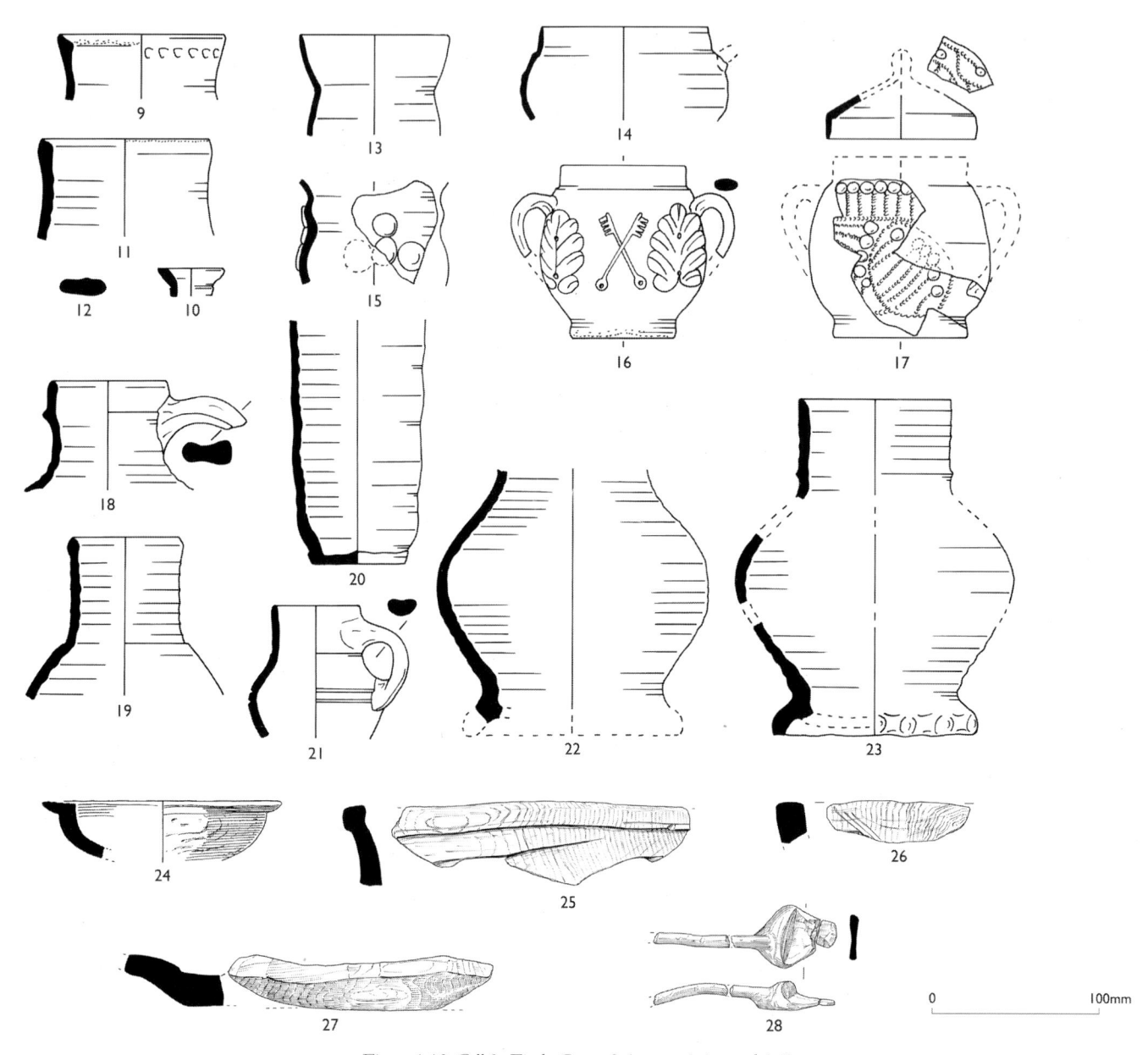

Figure 4.13 Cell 3: Finds Group 2 (pottery 1:4; wood 1:4).

Is it possible that what we are looking at is like-for-like replacements where a part of a broken vessel was left outside the cell and replaced by a lay brother from a central stock?

Amongst the unillustrated imported pottery was a single sherd from a Beauvais ware jug in a fine, white fabric with a bright yellow glaze on the outer surface turning orangish where the glaze thickens. There was also a sherd from a Pisa albarello in a soft, fine, orange fabric, with a thick cream-white glaze on the outer surface and very thin 'flashed on' orange-brown glaze to the inner surface. It was thin-walled and finely potted.

9. Scarborough ware II jug. Soft to hard white sandy fabric, yellowish-white core and cream inner surface. Deep copper-green glaze to top of rim. Crude roulette just below rim untypical of Scarborough ware, as is rim form itself. Probably pre-priory.
10. Humber ware drug jar. Orange fabric, purple-red surface patches, the rest of the outer and inner surface covered with a greenish-yellow glaze.
11. Ryedale ware jug. Hard, fine fabric with a white to dark blue-grey core and a dark blue-grey inner surface.

THE ARCHAEOLOGY OF THE GREAT CLOISTER

Table 4.2 Cell 3, Finds Group 2: Ceramics

Fabric	Sherds	Vessels							
		Total vessels	Albarello	Cistern	Drug jar	Jar	Jug	Mug or cup	Pancheon
Beauvais	1	1	0	0	0	0	1	0	0
Cistercian	20	6	0	0	0	0	0	6	0
Cistercian copy	4	2	0	0	0	0	0	2	0
Developed Humber	1	1	0	0	0	1	0	0	0
Hambleton	7	2	0	1	0	0	1	0	0
Humber	1	1	0	0	0	1	0	0	0
Langerwehe	8	3	0	0	0	0	0	3	0
Pisa maiolica	1	1	1	0	0	0	0	0	0
Post-medieval Sandy	1	1	0	0	0	1	0	0	0
Raeren	5	4	0	0	0	0	0	4	0
Ryedale	27	13	0	0	0	0	12	0	1
Siegburg	13	3	0	0	0	0	0	3	0

Olive-green glaze. The rim of a similar vessel is unillustrated.

12. Developed Humber ware jar handle. Fine, but very hard, blue-grey core. Dark and even olive-green glaze all over.
13. Cistercian ware cup. Purple-black glazed surfaces and dark purple-red core. Unillustrated was another rim of almost identical form.
14. Cistercian ware cup. Purple-black glazed surfaces and dark red core.
15. Cistercian copy cup. Bright orange-brown glaze on both surfaces and vermilion core. White pipeclay decoration appearing lemon-yellow under glaze. Appears as a rather crude design in comparison to the proper Cistercian wares.
16. Cistercian ware decorated posset pot. Purplish-black glaze on both surfaces and grey-black core. Applied pipeclay decoration appearing a very pale greenish-olive under glaze. Two-handled. Design takes the form of two pairs of St Peter's keys flanked on both sides by oak leaves.
17. Cistercian ware decorated posset pot and lid. Glossy purple-black glaze on both surfaces, dark red core. White clay decoration appearing a lemon-yellow under glaze.
18. Langerwehe stoneware drinking mug. Slightly glossy, but consistently coloured chocolate-brown outer surface, grey-blue core and matt, pale purple inner surface with pale orange highlighting.
19. Siegburg stoneware mug. Very pale purplish-buff surfaces and pale bluish-grey core.
20. Siegburg stoneware mug. Cream-buff fabric with whitish-buff core. Flashed-on, very thin, almost translucent greenish tinged clear glaze, which becomes greener wherever the glaze thickens.
21. Small Raeren stoneware mug. Matt, red-brown ash glaze, blue-grey core and dull buff inner surface with pale orange highlights.
22. Raeren stoneware mug. Pale grey core with a very pale grey-buff inner surface. Glossy, silver-grey glaze on the outer surface.
23. Raeren stoneware drinking mug. Blue-grey core with a matt, chocolate-brown outer surface and a glassy silver-grey glaze on inner surface turning greenish where the glaze thickens.

SMALL FINDS

Cell 3 also produced fragments of at least four wooden bowls and a ladle, recovered by clearance work and not located within the cell.

24. Bowl. Ash. In about ten pieces. The flat rim is 20 mm wide and the sides 8 mm thick. AML 605001.

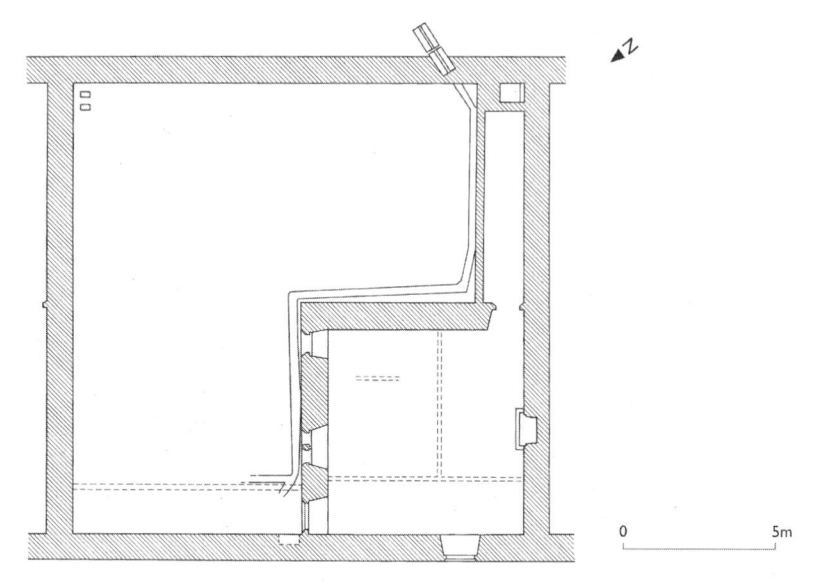

Figure 4.14 Cell 4.

Figure 4.15 Cell 4: the cloister door and hatch (G. Coppack).

25. Bowl rim. Ash. Turned. The rim has a square profile and the side is 12 mm thick. AML 605002.
26. Bowl rim. Ash. Turned. Plain rim with side with maximum depth of 18 mm. No groove or moulding. AML 605002.
27. Bowl base. Ash. Maximum interior diameter 123 mm. Base 16 mm thick. Slightly everted side suggesting shallow bowl. AML 605003.

28. Spoon or ladle. Ash. The spoon or ladle bowl is incomplete. There is about 20 mm of the handle remaining, which is circular in section and 4 mm in diameter.

Cell 4 (see Figure 4.14)

West (Cloister) Wall and South Wall

The cloister wall, including the door and hatch, was reset or reconstructed by Bell (see Figure 4.15). The south wall, however, survives to a height of eight courses at its west end and five at its east end. Deeply cut sockets in the south-west corner of the cell provide evidence for a stair matching that of Cell 3. The stair was built within the cross-passage of the cell, the location of which was fixed by two sockets, the first 0.178 m above the floor, 89 mm wide and 0.1 m high; the second 0.178 m directly above the first, also 89 mm wide, but 0.127 m high. The cross-passage was 1.0 m wide.

At the centre of the south wall is a fireplace that retains the corbels that supported its now-missing monolithic head (see Figure 4.16).

East and North Walls

The east wall survives to a height of only two courses with the lower jambs of the garden pentice door that indicate that the door was hung on the southern jamb. This jamb also retains the evidence of an internal locking bar.

The north wall of the cell was tolerably complete in 1900 but had fallen by 1905 (Hope 1905, 298 and pl. VII). It still survives to four courses above the first-floor offset at its west end and retains the complete door to the garden pentice (see Figure 4.17). The door was hung on the cloister wall and closed with a locking bar that fitted into a square socket in the east jamb (in the cell's north wall) and dropped into a long slot on the west jamb (in the cloister wall).

To the east of this door is the lower third of a two-light window lighting the study in the same manner as Cell 3, and to the east of that the cill of a single-light window lighting the bedroom. It is no longer possible to tell if these windows were inserted as they were in Cell 3. The upper floor of the cell had a single-light window in its gable wall that appears from Hope's published photograph as primary.

The internal arrangements of the cell can be reconstructed from the fragmentary evidence of cill walls still visible as parch-marks in the turf. The partition on the north side of the living room is further established by a socket in

THE ARCHAEOLOGY OF THE GREAT CLOISTER

the east wall at floor level, 0.127 m² and 2.77 m from the south wall.

Latrine Pentice

The latrine pentice was defined by its ashlar cill wall of largely one remaining course, though it remained to its full height of three courses where it abutted the precinct wall. Above the cill wall where it met the east wall of the cell was a 0.153 m² socket for the cill beam of the pentice gallery.

The latrine pit was 0.81 m wide and 0.61 m deep and set in the south-eastern angle of the pentice. West of the latrine pit was a stone step 0.24 m wide and 0.19 m high. Above the rear edge of the step, the garden wall was rebated to take a vertical wooden board 30 mm thick that formed the front of the privy. The rebate did not extend down to the step, but stopped 0.31 m above it. The seat of the privy was a board 0.12 m thick, rebated into the garden wall 0.63 m above the step. The space between the privy and the pentice wall, to the north of the latrine pit, was filled with a solid block of masonry that extended from floor level to the top of the pentice wall, some 0.53 m. The privy was drained from its north-west angle by a foul drain which ran away to the north-west around the cell and discharged into the sewer in the east cloister alley. This arrangement appears to have replaced a drain that ran to the south-west across the gardens of Cells 3 and 2 to meet the foul drain of the Cell 2 latrine; suggesting that the latrine was rebuilt when the cell was constructed in stone.

An unusual ashlar-lined drain ran along the outside of the pentice wall, being effectively one drain above another, separated by the slate floor of the upper drain. The lower drain was designed to take excess water from the spring house on the hillside above the garden and its eventual outfall is unknown, though it is still running. The upper drain returns along the east and north walls of the cell, discharging into the foul drain of the latrine in front of the garden pentice.

Garden Pentice

The cloister wall of the garden pentice is intact to the lowest course of its coping and has a set-back for the upper plate that carried the roof 3.0 m above the floor. Exceptionally, two corbels were provided in the outside face of this wall to carry the wall plate of the cloister roof in addition to rafter sockets at centres of 0.61 m. A robbed tap

Figure 4.16 Cell 4: corbelled fireplace in the south wall (G. Coppack).

Figure 4.17 Cell 4: the garden pentice door and the robbed location of the tap niche (G. Coppack).

niche exists just outside the cell door. No trace remains in the ground of the inner wall of the pentice, but the socket for its wall plate remains at its north end; the socket measuring 0.23 m wide and 0.204 m high for a timber with its soffit 1.54 m above the floor of the gallery. It indicated that the pentice was 1.40 m wide internally.

74 MOUNT GRACE PRIORY

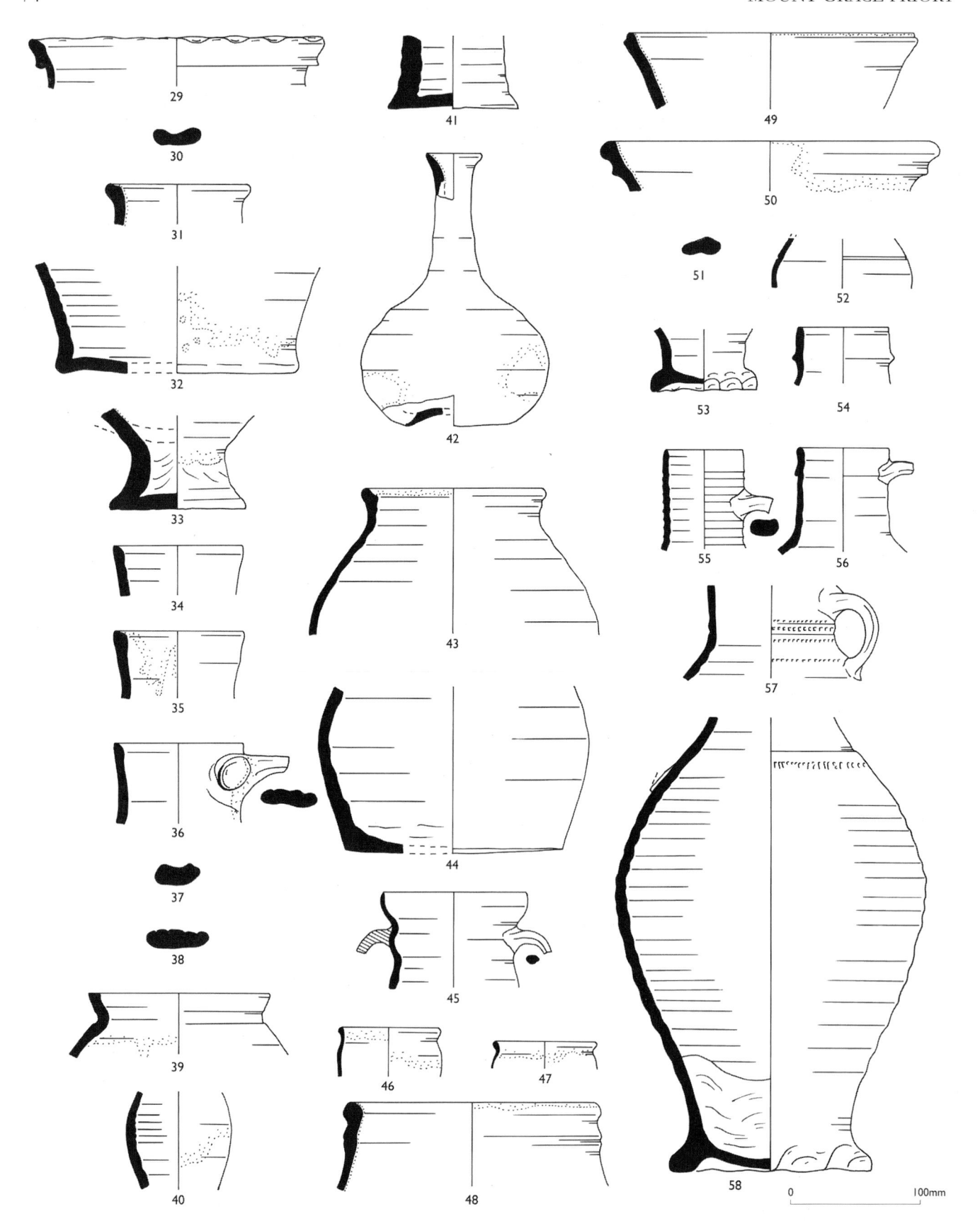

Figure 4.18 Cell 4: Finds Group 3 (pottery 1:4).

THE ARCHAEOLOGY OF THE GREAT CLOISTER

Table 4.3 Cell 4, Finds Group 3: Cell and Garden

Fabric	Sherds	Vessels							
		Total vessels	Bowl	Cistern	Jar	Jug	Mug or cup	Pancheon	Other
Brandsby type	3	3	0	0	0	3	0	0	0
Cistercian	9	4	0	0	0	0	4	0	0
Developed Humber	5	1	0	0	0	0	0	1	0
Gritty	1	1	0	0	0	1	0	0	0
Hambleton	7	3	3	0	0	0	0	0	0
Humber	1	1	0	0	0	1	0	0	0
Langerwehe	12	2	0	0	1	0	1	0	0
Post-medieval Orange	14	4	0	0	0	1	0	2	1 (chafer)
Post-medieval Sandy	8	5	0	0	1	0	0	4	0
Raeren	6	2	0	0	0	0	2	0	0
Regional Stray	2	2	0	0	0	1	0	0	1 (bottle)
Ryedale	90	53	0	3	0	47	0	0	3 (unknown)
Siegburg	29	11	0	0	0	0	11	0	0
Staffordshire	4	3	0	0	0	0	1	0	2 (drug jar)
Tudor Green	1	1	0	0	0	0	0	0	1 (bottle)

Table 4.4 Cell 4, Finds Group 3: Latrine

Fabric	Sherds	Vessels						
		Total vessels	Chafer	Cooking pot	Jar	Jug	Mug or cup	Urinal
Beauvais	1	1	0	0	0	1	0	0
Brandsby type	1	1	0	0	0	1	0	0
Hambleton	4	3	0	0	0	3	0	0
Humber	2	2	1	0	0	1	0	0
Gritty	3	3	0	2	0	1	0	0
Langerwehe	11	5	0	0	0	0	5	0
Late Gritty	4	2	0	0	0	0	0	2
Post-medieval Sandy	18	3	0	0	3	0	0	0
Reversed Cistercian	1	1	0	0	0	0	1	0
Raeren	1	1	0	0	0	0	1	0
Ryedale	37	18	0	0	0	17	0	1
Sieburg	20	8	0	0	0	0	8	0

Garden

The garden is featureless apart from two ashlar blocks in its north-east corner that appear to be the supports for a seat. A drain revealed during clearance ran along the inside face of the precinct wall, taking excess water from the spring house to flush the latrine of the adjacent Cell 5.

Finds Group 3
CERAMICS (SEE FIGURE 4.18)
During examination of the pottery from this cell and its garden it was noted that various sherds (all unmarked) in 'Cell 4' or 'Cell 4 Garderobe' boxes (Tables 4.3 and 4.4) were from the same vessels and that there had therefore been some pre-depositional or (more likely) post-depositional mixing. The pottery included pre-priory material and a comparatively full range of late medieval local and imported material. The late medieval local wares were heavily dominated by Ryedale ware, most of which represented fragments of jugs. This quantity of pottery, apparently from site clearance work, was higher than for all other excavated cells except

Cell 8. Quite why Cell 4 should have contained the remnants of so many jugs is unclear. Cell 4 also contained a more conventional range of late medieval local and imported tablewares. Among the finds not illustrated is a sherd of a Tudor Green ware lobed cup.

29. Gritty ware cooking-pot rim. Pale grey surfaces with orange highlighting (particularly on inner surface) with a pale greyish-blue core.
30. Gritty ware jug handle. Buff to off-white outer surface and off-white core. Lower handle attachment has no back fillet and is just smoothed on. Pocked traces of pale yellow glaze. Conventionally, this is an early form, probably pre-priory.
31. Brandsby type ware jug rim. Soft to hard, orange, sandy fabric. Orange glazed outer surface, and dark brownish-green glaze on inner surface.
32. Regional Stray ware jug base. Pinkish-orange outer surface skin, pale orange core and inner surface. Glaze margin mottled with green mottles on a greenish-orange background. Soft to hard, smooth textured fabric with sparse light grit (including grains of rounded orange sand). Glaze and surface resembles Orange ware. The whole character of this vessel suggests that it should be included amongst the pre-priory element of the Cell 4 group.
33. Humber ware chafing dish base. Purpled-red to pale orange outer surface and blue-grey core and inner surface. Flecked olive-green glaze with orange-brown to purple margins. Has an applied dish base to an otherwise single-piece construction. One sherd of this vessel was recovered from the Cell 4 latrine.
34. Ryedale ware jug rim. Dark blue-grey core and pale grey inner surface, dark olive-green glaze.
35. Ryedale ware jug rim. Olive-green glaze on outer surface, blue-grey to orange-red core with dull-red inner surface.
36. Ryedale ware jug rim. Fine, slightly micaceous fabric with pale orange outer surface, blue-grey core and dull orange-brown inner surface. Fairly consistent olive-green glaze with orange-brown margins.
37. Ryedale ware jug handle. Consistent olive-green glaze, dark blue-grey core and dull reddish surface.
38. Ryedale ware jug handle. Grey-black core with whitish margins. Yellowish-green glaze.
39. Ryedale ware urinal rim. Pale greyish-blue core and orange inner surface. Corroded olive-green glaze on outer surface and on inner surface as far down as neck.
40. Ryedale ware small jug or bottle. Pale orange outer surface, blue-grey core and pale grey inner surface with faint orange highlighting in places. Pale apple-green glaze.
41. Ryedale ware baluster jug (tall jug, with a height about three times its diameter) base. Dull buff outer surface, dark blue-grey core and inner surface. Traces of a pale greenish glaze scar on the base.
42. Regional Stray ware bottle, almost complete save for small chips to rim and a hole in the base. Hard, finely sand-tempered fabric with slightly roughened surfaces. Pale orange to buff surfaces with a pale greyish core. Bright olive-green glaze becoming yellower on the lower body. Fully glazed outer surface with the exception of two small areas and the upper part of the base. A small glaze scar on lower body. At the rim, the glaze is taken inside and all the way down the neck, stopping at the inner shoulder. Fired upright; the unglazed spots may be where the potter held the vessel when applying the glaze, or where two of three supports (the glaze scar representing the third) supported the vessel in the kiln during firing. Very close in form to contemporary glass bottles. The vessel appears to have been made in one piece, with no evidence of an applied neck.
43. Late Gritty ware urinal. Soft to hard, lightly and finely gritty fabric of rough texture. Corroded olive-green glaze, flecked with orange-brown on outer surface. White to blue-grey core, and blue-grey inner surface. Thin white deposit on inner surface. From the Cell 4 latrine.
44. Late Gritty ware urinal in a thick, very hard, gritty fabric. Pale red outer surface,

pale bluish core and orange inner surface. Fairly consistent olive-green glaze over outer surface to basal angle. From the Cell 4 latrine.
45. Cistercian ware two-handled cup. Usual metallic purple-black glaze on both surfaces and deep reddish-purple core.
46, 47. Staffordshire ware drug jars in a very thin, fine white fabric. Off-white surfaces and very watery yellowish-green glaze; that of number 47 in particular is lightly pocked.
48. Post-medieval Orange ware large jar rim. Dull reddish-purple outer surface, blue-grey core and olive-green glaze on inner surface.
49. Post-medieval Sandy ware bowl rim. Pale red to red outer surface, orange core and olive-green glaze on inner surface.
50. Post-medieval Sandy ware bowl rim. Very pale orange outer surface, buff core and glazed inner surface with copper-green mottles on an orange-yellow background.
51. Post-medieval Orange ware jar handle. Fine orange fabric with greenish tinged orange glaze.
52. Beauvais ware jug. Body sherd of a small vessel in a fine white fabric which, under a magnifying glass, appears very lightly sanded. Orange-yellow glaze on outer surface.
53. Siegburg stoneware drinking mug. Reddish-brown matt glazed to grey-buff outer surface and whitish-grey core.
54. Siegburg stoneware drinking mug. Pale grey core and dirty buff inner surface. Silver-grey glaze to outer surface. From the Cell 4 latrine.
55. Siegburg stoneware drinking mug. Matt chocolate-brown to glossy silver-grey ash glazed outer surface, blue-grey core and flashed-on glaze on inner surface, purplish at top and a sliver-grey from the neck down. Unusually tall-necked vessel.
56. Raeren stoneware mug. Glassy glaze on both surfaces, silver-grey on outer surface and brown on inner surface.
57. Decorated Siegburg stoneware mug. Pale, slightly bluish-grey core. Bright glassy silver-grey glaze on outer surface and buff-brown glaze to inner surface. Decorated with roulette around neck. From the Cell 4 latrine.
58. Langerwehe stoneware (underfired) jar. Largely matt red-brown to purple-brown ash glaze, becoming lustrous in places, particularly on the frills of the base, orange core and pale orange inner surface. Hard, smooth-textured, but not true stoneware. From the Cell 4 latrine.

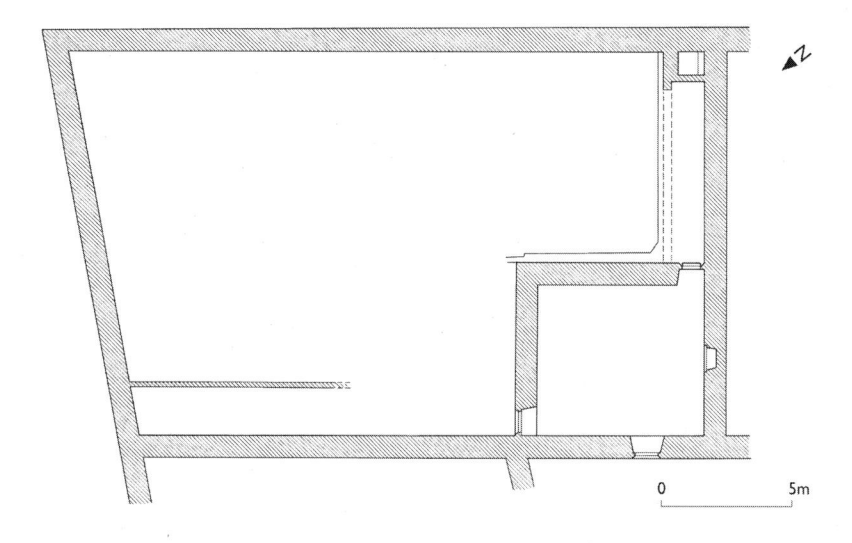

Figure 4.19 Cell 5.

SMALL FINDS (NOT ILLUSTRATED)
Clearance of Cell 4 recovered two pieces of oak board, both radially cleft. The larger piece is 720 mm by 98 mm (originally, now shrunk with drying out) by 10 mm, with one squared edge and the other rounded. A single bored hole, 12 mm deep, survives at one end. The other piece of board is 260 mm by 157 mm by 25 mm. Axe-trimmed at one end with sawing marks at the other; it appears to be an offcut from a larger piece.

Cell 5 (see Figure 4.19)

West (Cloister) Wall
The cloister wall, including the cloister door and its hatch to the south, was reconstructed by Bell using reclaimed medieval material that was scattered over the site. The hatch was fitted with a top-hinged shutter on its inner side, and the door was hung on the south jamb to open against the shutter. A series of bolt and latch fixings remain in the north jamb indicating a door 25 mm thick (see Figure 4.20).

South Wall
The south wall of the cell is largely intact, with an offset of 0.1 m above the tenth course that marks the height of the first floor. Above this, a maximum of ten courses survive well into the

Figure 4.20 Cell 5: cloister door and hatch (G. Coppack).

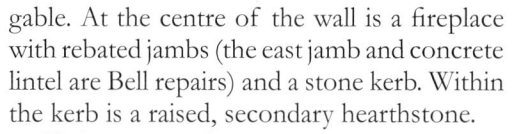

Figure 4.21 Cell 5: garden pentice door (G. Coppack).

gable. At the centre of the wall is a fireplace with rebated jambs (the east jamb and concrete lintel are Bell repairs) and a stone kerb. Within the kerb is a raised, secondary hearthstone.

Slight traces of a turning stair remain in the south-west angle of the cell and within the cross-passage, but evidence for it is largely obscured by Bell's rebuilding of the cloister wall. In the south wall, the undisturbed chases for the first three treads and two risers remain, the top of the first tread being 0.61 m above floor level. A slot 76 mm wide and 0.66 m high above floor level, 1.72 m from the south-west corner of the cell, may be associated with the stair as it lies well inside the line of the partition of the cross-passage and living room.

East Wall

The east wall survives to a height of two courses, with the door to the latrine pentice partially surviving at its south end. The door was hung on the south jamb, of which the lowest four courses survive, and was closed with a locking bar, the slot for which remains. An area of fine paving survives within the door splay, passing below the threshold. A second cill was set over the first one, an indication that the latrine pentice floor was raised in the same manner as Cell 2.

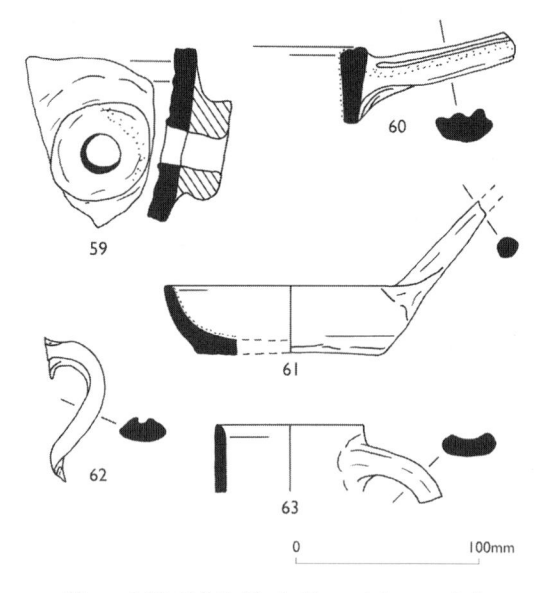

Figure 4.22 Cell 5: Finds Group 4 (pottery 1:4).

North Wall

The north wall is three courses high at its east end, but survives to retain the complete garden pentice door at its west end (see Figure 4.21) and the lower western jamb of a two-light window, from which it can be seen that the window had shutters but no glazing in its lower lights. The pentice door was hung on the west jamb, with a single square bolt hole in the east jamb.

THE ARCHAEOLOGY OF THE GREAT CLOISTER

Table 4.5 Cell 5, Finds Group 4: Ceramics

Fabric	Sherds	Total vessels	Cistern	Jar	Mug or cup	Skillet
Developed Humber	1	1	0	0	0	1
Post-medieval Sandy	1	1	0	1	0	0
Raeren	1	1	0	0	1	0
Ryedale	1	1	1	0	0	0
Scarborough	1	1	0	0	0	1

A locking bar 0.1 m wide and 0.125 m high was located in a socket in the east jamb; it pivoted in the socket to drop into a slot on the west side of the doorway. The door was 38 mm thick.

Latrine Pentice

The latrine pentice survives only at its east end, where the lowest course of the cill wall survives to enclose the latrine pit. The socket (0.18 m high by 0.153 m wide) for the cill beam of the timber gallery remains in the precinct wall, its position indicating that the internal width of the pentice was 1.30 m. The bottom of the cill beam was 0.40 m above the pentice floor. The cill wall formed the inner edge of the eavesdrip drain which had an ashlar outer face and slate bottom, falling towards the cell, where a localised widening suggested a downpipe. The drain then returned along the east wall of the cell.

Garden Pentice

The north end of the latrine pentice survived as a single course of ashlar blocks defining a passage 1.42 m wide.

Finds Group 4: Ceramics (see Figure 4.22)

Only five sherds were attributed to Cell 5 (Table 4.5) and are unlikely to be representative of the original group of the cell. All five pieces were larger than the average, suggesting that smaller, plainer sherds were either not retained or were subsequently discarded, and all five pieces were illustrated. The presence of two skillets amongst such a small sample is interesting, given that they are the only two examples of this form identified from the any of the cell groups.

59. Ryedale ware cistern. Greyish surfaces with bluish-grey core and dull olive-green glaze. Bung-hole rather crudely finished.
60. Scarborough II ware skillet. Orange fabric with orange-red surfaces and traces of a mottled copper-green glaze.
61. Developed Humber ware skillet. Purplish-grey surfaces and blue-grey core. Olive-green glaze on inner surface.
62. Post-medieval Sandy ware jar handle. Orange-yellow surface and yellow-buff core with traces of a bright apple-green glaze.
63. Raeren stoneware mug. Hard, pale grey core with brown ash glaze to outer surface.

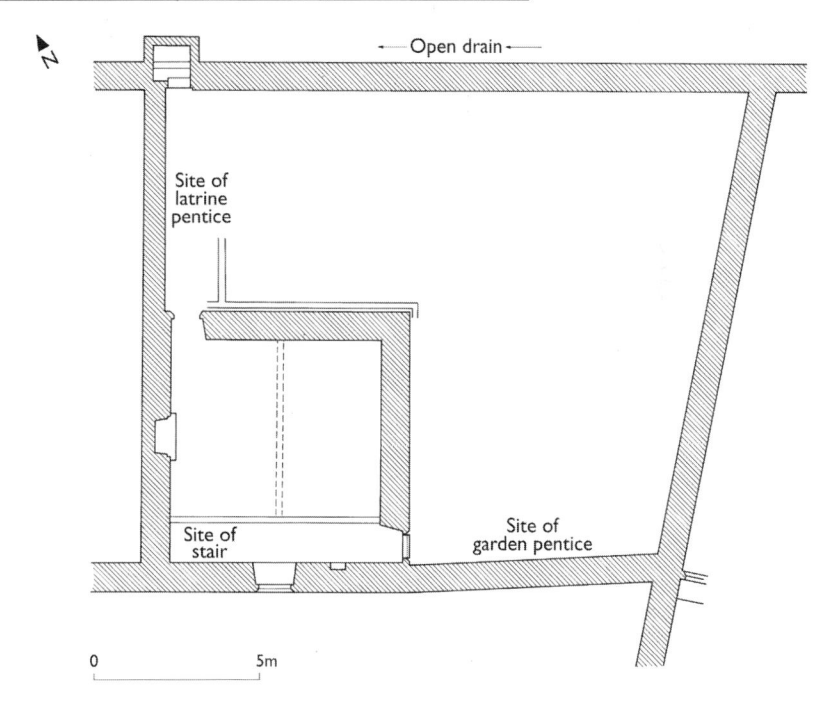

Figure 4.23 Cell 6.

Cell 6 (see Figure 4.23)

South (Cloister) Wall

The cloister wall, which was taken down and rebuilt by the Ministry of Works in the early 1960s, survives to a height of 19 courses, four courses above the string course that marks the level of the cloister alley roof. Below the string course are four equally spaced corbels to carry the wall plate of the cloister roof. The cloister door is centrally placed in the wall,

Figure 4.24 Cell 6: cloister door and hatch (G. Coppack).

with the hatch adjacent to the western jamb (see Figure 4.24).

A wooden shutter was hung on the cloister side of the hatch and a fixing for a bolt remains on its east side. The cloister door, which was only 25 mm thick, was hung on the west jamb, where the holes for the removal of its pintles remain. The fixings for no less than five square bolts remain in the eastern internal splay, providing evidence for the thickness of the door. Traces of limewash survive on the door reveals.

On the interior surface of the cloister wall there is no offset to mark the level of the first floor, which is evidenced instead by a centrally placed joist socket 0.305 m², 2.82 m above floor level. Just above the first-floor level and 0.79 m to the west of this cross-joist socket was a second socket 0.15 m wide and 0.23 m high.

The tap niche was placed between the cloister door and the door to the garden pentice, with the fixing of a hinged shutter above it. The base of the niche contained a badly damaged bowl of square plan with sloping sides (see Figure 6.51). A square channel cut into the wall below the niche would have contained a lead outlet pipe.

East Wall

The east wall survives only to the height of three courses, with the exception of the southern jamb of the garden pentice door, which remains to full height, with the stub of its square head and internal lintel. A single stone remains of the north jamb, together with the door cill set at the level of the passage floor. The inner edge of the passage is defined by a cill wall 0.23 m wide and aligned on the inner edge of the northern splay of this door, indicating that the passage was 1.16 m wide. The passage floor was 0.255 m below the level of the floor of the remainder of the cell.

North Wall

The north wall survived to a height of two courses and retained the lowest jamb stones of the latrine pentice door, though its cill was missing. As on the east wall, there remained traces of white internal plaster. A socket 0.18 m² at floor level, 3.20 m from the west wall of the cell, marked the partition that divided the living room on the west side of the cell from the study and bedroom on the east.

A slot 38 mm wide was cut into the inner face of the north wall, sloping slightly to the east and extending down to floor level, 2.79 m from the west wall.

An ashlar-lined eavesdrip drain ran along the north wall of the cell, its southern edge slightly battered, and falling to the east where it discharged into a deep drain at the north-east corner of the cell.

West Wall

The west wall remained to a height of three courses with the rebated jambs of the living room fireplace placed centrally. There was a flat hearthstone, but no kerb. The hearth had been relined and the fireplace back repaired with slate. A salt box 0.19 m high, 0.2 m wide and 0.15 m deep remained in the southern jamb, apparently a primary feature. The stair to the upper floor occupied the south-west corner of the cell, with rebates for its treads and risers cut into the west and cloister walls. It began on the line of the passage partition.

Latrine Pentice

The latrine pentice was only evidenced by the southern part of its ashlar drain that discharged into the drain on the north side of the cell. At its north end, the lowest two courses of the precinct wall retained the lowest jamb stones of the latrine door that hung on the west jamb. Three shallow steps set into in the thickness of the wall led to the latrine itself, which had been

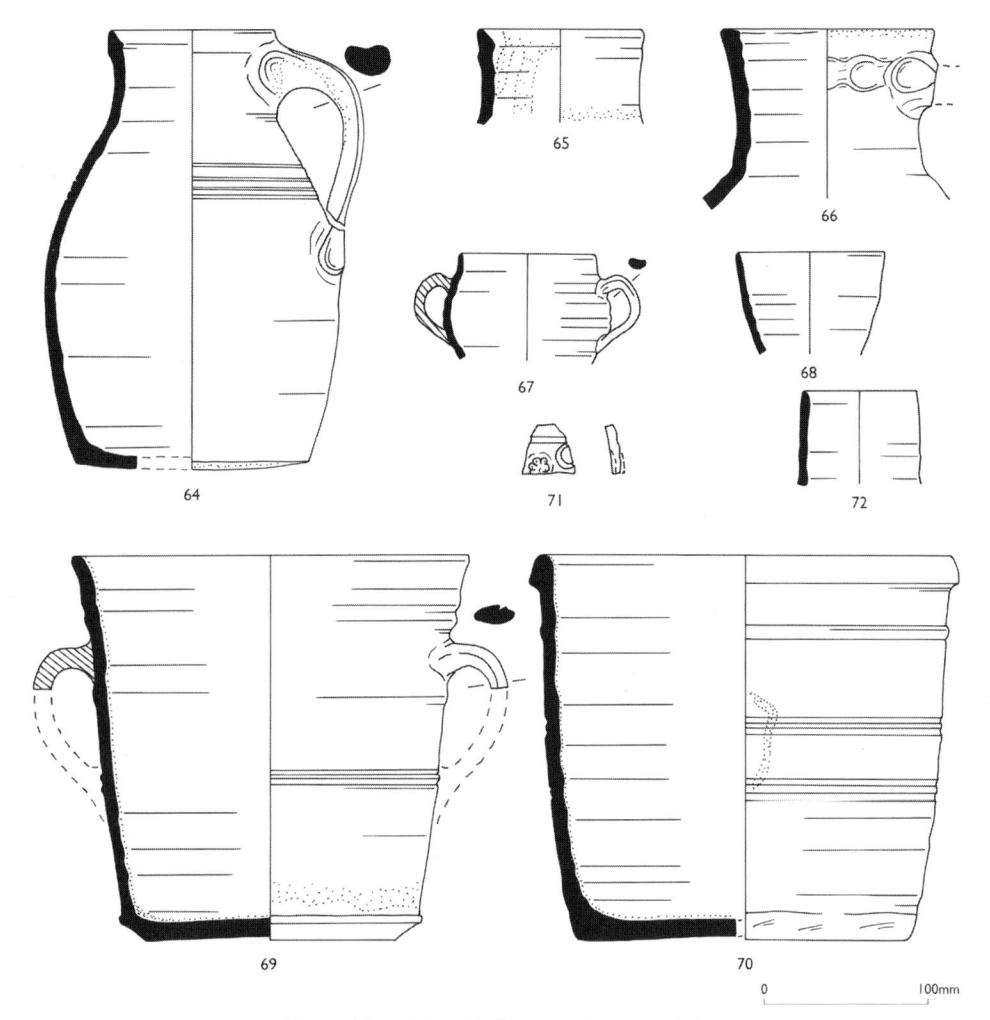

Figure 4.25 Cell 6: Finds Group 5 (pottery 1:4).

entirely destroyed. It was set above a stone-lined drain 1.14 m wide and 1.05 m deep that ran the full length of the northern precinct wall.

Garden Pentice
There were no visible remains of the garden pentice.

Finds Group 5: Ceramics (see Figure 4.25)
The Cell 6 group (Table 4.6) contained a comparatively high proportion of early post-medieval fabrics that must have derived from the final years of occupation of the priory. The pair of bucket-shaped jars (numbers 69 and 70) were unusual forms from the great cloister, though they may relate to some activity within the cell.

64. Ryedale ware jug in a soft, finely tempered, micaceous fabric. Pale yellow-buff outer surface, greyish-white core and black inner surface, slightly dusty to the touch. Fully and carefully glazed from the rim to the basal angle with a bright apple-green glaze thickening in places to a darker, more brownish green. Traces of light pock marks, especially on the upper surface. Upper handle attachment smoothed on with two lateral thumbings, the lower attachment with two thumbings. Lip and part of rim section missing. Rim glaze scar on base. Glaze flaking off outer surface.

65. Developed Humber ware. Soft heavily sand-tempered jug rim. Dull reddish-purple outer surface, pale buff core and orange inner surface. Yellowish olive-green glaze with spills down inner surface. Rough textured.

66. Hambleton ware jug rim. Smooth, grey surfaces and pale grey core. Soft to hard smoothish fracture. Brownish-olive glaze to outer surface to rim top. Traces of upper handle attachment with

Table 4.6 Cell 6, Finds Group 5: Ceramics

Fabric	Sherds	Total vessels	Chafer	Jar	Jug	Mug or cup	Other
Cistercian	4	1	0	0	0	1	0
Cistercian-copy	3	1	0	0	0	1	0
Developed Humber	3	3	0	0	3	0	0
Hambleton	18	2	0	1	1	0	0
Humber	1	1	0	0	1	0	0
Post-medieval Orange	21	4	0	1	3	0	0
Post-medieval Sandy	49	14	0	4	0	0	10
Raeren	1	1	0	0	0	1	0
Regional Stray	1	1	1	0	0	0	0
Ryedale	74	7	0	0	7	0	0
Scarborough	1	1	0	0	1	0	0
Siegburg	6	6	0	0	0	6	0
Staffordshire	1	1	0	0	0	1	0

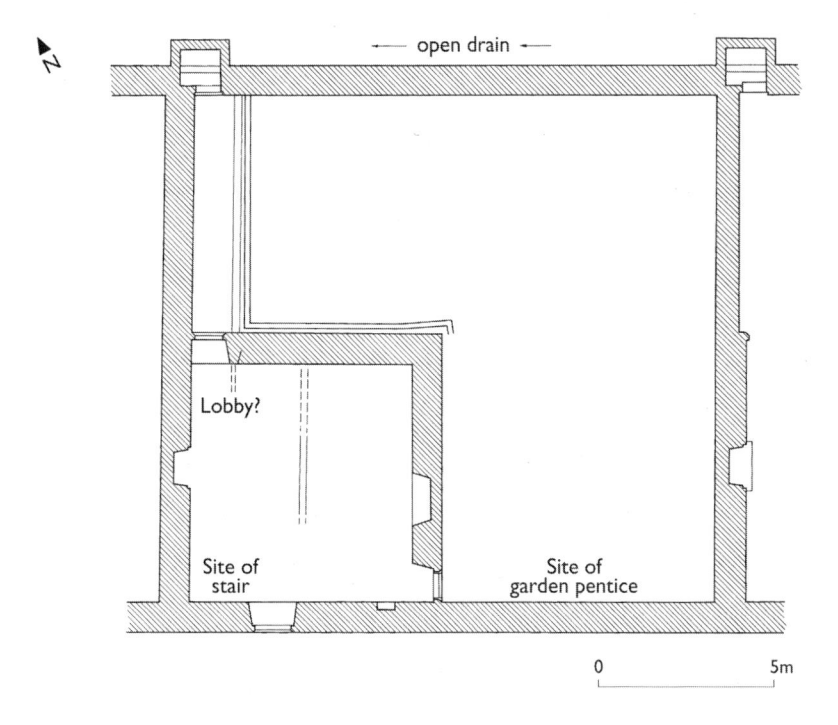

Figure 4.26 Cell 7.

two lateral thumbings. The size, crudity of the vessel and the unplugged handle would suggest that this was a cistern.

67. Cistercian ware cup. Purple-black to metallic purple glazed surfaces with a dark red core. Two-handled. Very hard fabric with a smooth fracture. Slightly pocked glaze on inner surface.

68. Cistercian ware flared rim cup. Bright glossy brown glaze on both surfaces with a hard, brick-red core.

69. Post-medieval Sandy ware two-handled jar. Pale orange surfaces and orange core. Soft to hard, finely tempered fabric. Full brownish-olive glaze on inner surface, pale olive-green glaze on outer surface with small, dark, metallic mottling (dense in places). Well of solid glaze in the basal angle indicates upright firing position. Scars confirm the position of two handles.

70. Post-medieval Sandy ware handled(?) jar. Dull red to grey outer surface and orange core. Fairly hard fabric with a spalling of the glaze from the inner surface. Fully glazed inner surface mostly a consistent olive-green glaze but becoming more orange-brown towards the rim. Area of olive-green glaze on outer surface, may be accidental or may be the area of a lower handle attachment. Fired inverted.

71. Midlands Yellow ware, relief-moulded cup. White core, with a crazed, watery yellow glaze on both surfaces. Relief-moulded design (the mould was held against the side of the vessel and then the inner wall of the vessel was pushed outward into the mould).

72. Siegburg stoneware mug. Bluish-grey core with flashed-on glaze, a silver-grey on the outer surface and a brownish-grey on inner surface.

THE ARCHAEOLOGY OF THE GREAT CLOISTER

Figure 4.27 Cell 7: latrine pentice door (G. Coppack).

Figure 4.28 Cell 7: sockets for the turning stair in the south-west angle (G. Coppack).

Cell 7 (see Figure 4.26)

South (Cloister) Wall

The cloister wall survived intact to the height of the cloister roof string course, below which four equally spaced corbel stubs can be identified. The cloister door was placed centrally with the hatch to the west of the door. The door, 25 mm thick, was hung on the west jamb, and four bolt fixings remained on the eastern splay.

Internally, the treatment of the wall was similar to the cloister wall of Cell 6. Above the cloister door and 2.59 m above the passage floor was the socket for a cross-joist 0.2 m wide and 0.25 m high, marking the level of the first floor. The tap niche was placed to the east of the cloister door. There was no evidence that it was ever fitted with a basin.

The stair occupied the south-west angle of the cell, and was identical in its fixings to that of Cell 6 (see Figure 4.28).

No trace remained of the passage partition, though from the location of the stair it was probably 1.12 m wide. Four inserted joist sockets in the inner face of the cloister wall at the east end of the passage suggest a loft 1.86 m above the passage floor extending 2.36 m from the east wall. A similar loft was inserted in Cell 8 in the same location.

East Wall

The east wall of the cell survived to a height of three courses and retained the lower jambs of the garden pentice door. The door itself was hung on the south jamb and was closed by a locking bar fixed in a square socket on the north splay and swung into a deep chase on the southern splay. To the north of the garden pentice door the splay of a two-light window in the southern room had been cut down to within one course of the cell floor.

North Wall

The north wall was reduced to a height of two courses, apart from its west end where the latrine pentice door with its square head remained intact below five courses of masonry (see Figure 4.27), and was featureless apart from a socket 0.18 m² at floor level that marked the north–south partition 3.16 m from the west wall of the cell. The lowest course of the western splay of a window remained 0.265 m to the east of the latrine pentice door. Between

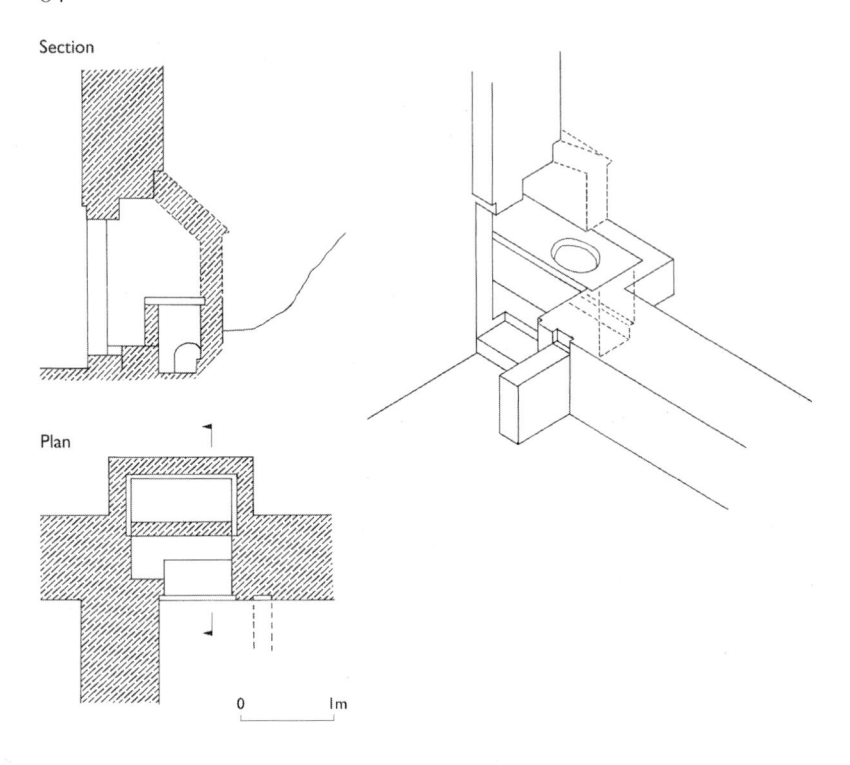

Figure 4.29 Cell 7: axonometric reconstruction of the latrine.

the window and door there was evidence for an internal porch or screen 70 mm east of the door reveal. At floor level there was the socket for a cill beam 90 mm wide and 0.15 m high. Level with its east face were two sockets, both 40 mm^2, and one 0.3 m and the other 0.74 m above floor level. The pentice door was hung on the west jamb and was closed by a locking bar. There were also four bolt fixings on the eastern splay, evidence of several alterations.

West Wall

The west wall survived 12 courses high at its south end, the top two courses being set back to mark the level of the upper floor, but was robbed down to two courses at its centre where the lowest rebated jambs of the living room fireplace remained. The wall was rebuilt to above first-floor level in 1990 and the fireplace restored.

Latrine Pentice

The latrine pentice was defined by its ashlar-lined drain that ran from the inner face of the precinct wall to the north wall of the cell where it turned to form the cell eavesdrip gulley. At the north-east corner of the cell it returned below ground along the outer face of the east wall. The lowest course of the cill wall remains along the length of the pentice. Sockets in the precinct wall show that the cill wall was originally 0.65 m high and carried a cill beam 0.18 m high and 0.2 m wide.

The top plate of the gallery fitted into a second socket 0.23 m^2 and 1.60 m above floor level. A matching socket remained in the north wall of the cell, but no socket for the cill beam exists, suggesting that a door into the garden existed at the south end of the pentice against the cell. The pentice was 1.01 m wide internally.

The latrine itself, set over a drain outside the precinct wall (see Figure 4.29), was well preserved. Two shallow steps in the thickness of the precinct wall led to the privy, the floor of which was 0.25 m above the pentice floor. The privy comprised a monolithic slab 0.43 m high and 0.15 m thick that supported a wooden seat 0.6 m wide and 0.18 m deep over the drain. The pitched stone roof of the latrine was missing.

Garden Pentice

No trace remained of the garden pentice.

Finds Group 6

CERAMICS (SEE FIGURE 4.30)

The group of Cell 7 was a most curious one, because the 254 sherds derive from only 11 vessels (Table 4.7). The sherds provide near complete profiles of the vessels, all of which are illustrated, and which suggest a large and representative group. The bigger jugs, numbers 77–9, each comprised a large number of sherds, but were missing their rims.

Other cells contained few examples of such large jugs. Their likely function within this cell is unclear. It is even possible that they were in the cell precisely because they had already been damaged. In this respect it is unfortunate that their location within the cell was not more precisely recorded. May such damaged vessels, for example, have fulfilled a function within the cell garden such as planters or water holders?

73. Humber ware jug. Pale orange outer surface turning to dull purple in patches. Orange core and inner surface. Dark olive-green patch of glaze with pale yellow margins. Glaze scar on base confirms it was fired inverted.

74. Humber ware jug. Pale orange outer surface turning a dull pinkish-red in places. Orange core and inner surface. Rather patchy orange-yellow glaze. One side of the pot is badly stained and discoloured.

75. Humber ware cruet body. Dull brick-red outer surface, pale orange core and

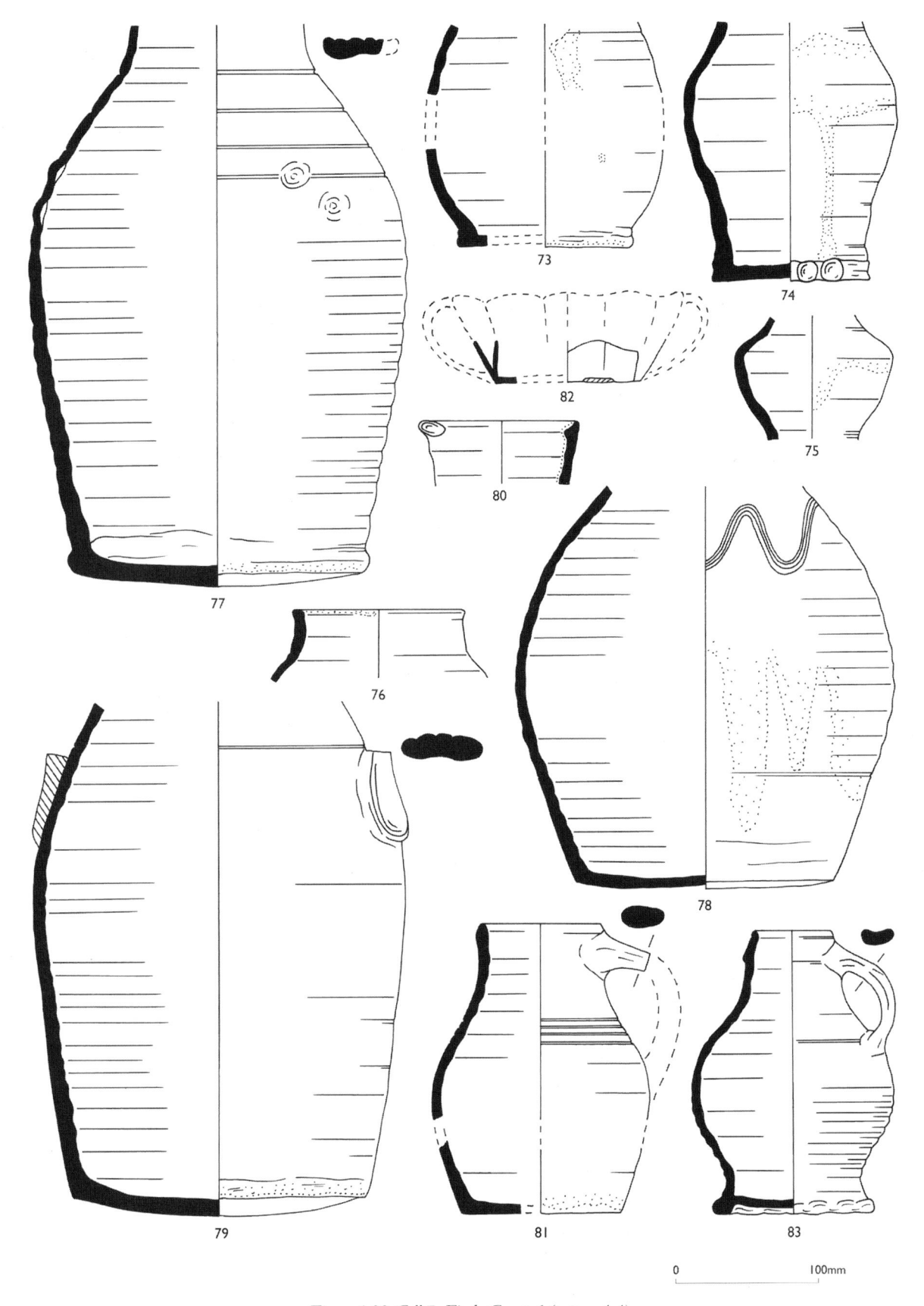

Figure 4.30 Cell 7: Finds Group 6 (pottery 1:4).

Table 4.7 Cell 7, Finds Group 6: Ceramics

Fabric	Sherds	Total vessels	Cruet	Jug	Mug or cup
Humber	11	4	1	3	0
Post-medieval Orange	12	2	0	2	0
Ryedale	214	3	0	3	0
Tudor Green	1	1	0	0	1
Siegburg	16	1	0	0	1

dull orange inner surface. Hard, sandy texture. Brownish-green glaze. Traces of sooting to outer surface.

76. Humber ware jug rim. Pale grey to blue-grey core and grey inner surface. Greenish-black glaze.

77. Ryedale ware jug. Fully glazed outer surface, basically olive-green, darker towards the top of the vessel, but more matt and lighter on the lower body. Grey-black core and slightly lighter inner surface. Sandy texture.

78. Ryedale ware jug. Hard, fine, smooth-textured fabric. Dull purple-red outer surface, pale bluish-grey core and inner surface. Brownish-purple glaze, thin and carelessly daubed on outer surface and going greenish in places. Fired inverted.

79. Ryedale ware jug or cistern. Pale silver-grey surfaces of very smooth texture. Yellowish-olive glaze, badly corroded in places and extending down as far as the basal angle.

80. Post-medieval Orange ware jug, with a small pinched lip. Bright vermilion core with a bright orange-brown glaze on both surfaces. Lip pinched out by means of two lateral thumbings.

81. Post-medieval Orange ware jug. Soft to hard, smooth to soapy textured micaceous fabric, seemingly without sand tempering. Pale orange surfaces, with the core just a shade darker. Bright but streaky copper-green glaze, inconsistently coloured, and turning a bright orange towards the margins. Some pockmarking of the glaze towards the lower margin. Upper handle attachment simply smoothed on.

82. Tudor Green ware lobed cup base. Badly burnt sherd. Off-white core and traces of greenish glaze on both surfaces. Trace of a lower handle attachment on basal angle.

83. Siegburg stoneware mug. Pale whitish-grey core, pale greyish-brown outer surfaces and a pale grey-buff inner surface.

SMALL FINDS (NOT ILLUSTRATED)

Cell 7 produced two pieces of oak. The first was a fragment of radially cleft board, 14 mm thick, with no surviving edges.

The second, from the latrine filling, was a piece of radially split board cut to form the left-hand side of a composite ogee arch, both arrises of which are chamfered. Two nail-holes, for fixing to an upright, remain. It measures at its maximum 198 mm by 132 mm by 16–17 mm. Probably derived from a piece of furniture.

Cell 8

Although Keen partially excavated the northeast corner of the garden of Cell 8 in 1974 (some 32.37 m^2), it was not until 1985 that the whole area of the cell, its garden and adjacent cloister alley (some 408.73 m2) was excavated by Coppack. The latter excavation was designed to recover sufficient information to enable the reconstruction of the cell and its garden for display, and involved the excavation to destruction of most archaeological deposits. Here, information recovered by Keen has been incorporated in the description of the 1985 excavation, so far as is possible given changes to the site since 1974. The earlier excavation was not backfilled and serious erosion of exposed features had occurred.

Period One (see Figure 4.31)

TERRACE

The earliest features encountered related to the construction of the terrace that was to carry the later buildings of the great cloister. Essentially, the terrace was cut back into the

THE ARCHAEOLOGY OF THE GREAT CLOISTER

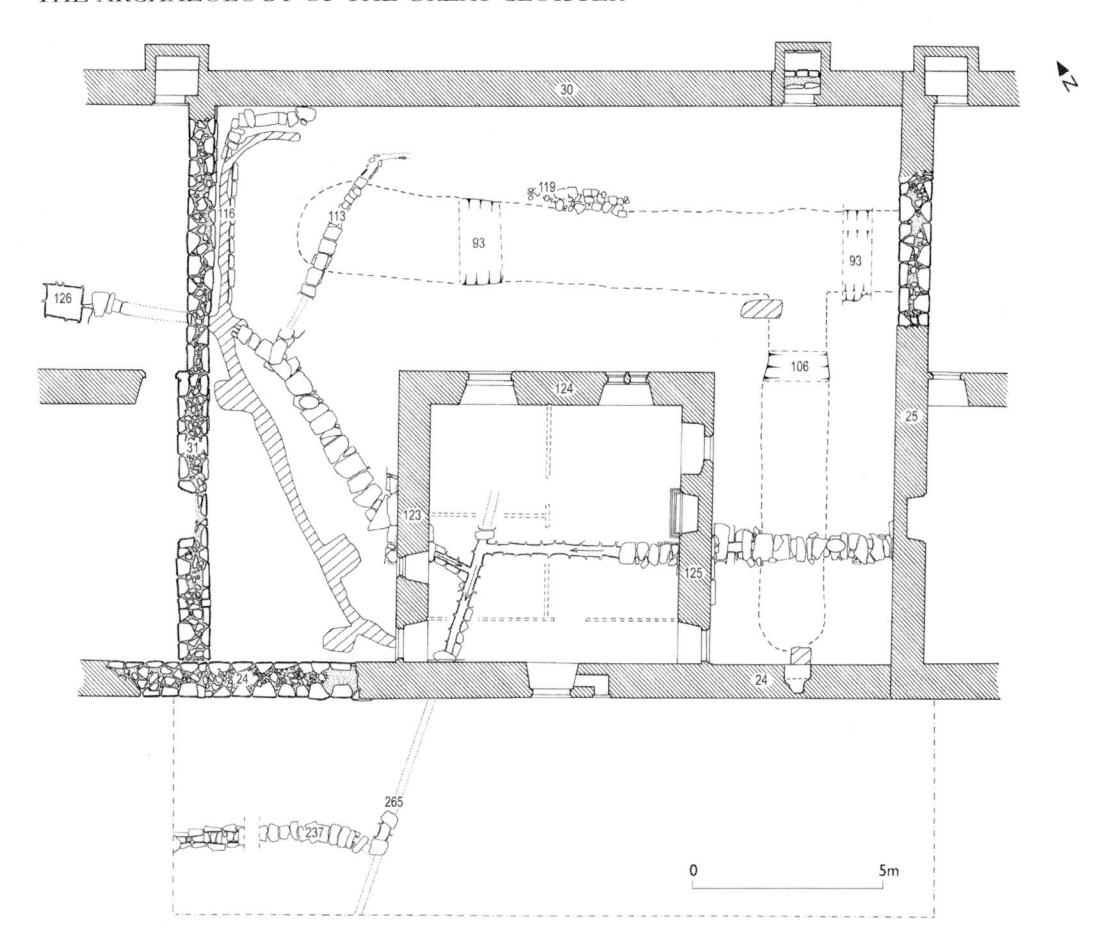

Figure 4.31 Cell 8: features in and on the great cloister terrace.

hillside to extend and level a pre-existing natural feature that apparently resulted from post-glacial landslip, and the interface between the negative and positive terracing ran through the area excavated.

The eastern half of the site was cut into the hill slope, exposing undisturbed natural pale brown clay with ferrous staining [*92*], while the western half was built up with mixed orange-brown and blue-grey clay [*117*]. A similar occurrence was observed less clearly in the area of the later north cloister alley where natural orange-grey clay [*255*] was overlaid in the western part of the excavated area by redeposited orange-grey clay [*243*].

DRAINS AND TANK

Built and sealed within the positive terracing were a series of stone-built drains that must have been primary to the construction of the terrace and occupation of the site. The first of these drains, [118], drained a stone-lined tank or cistern [126] in what was later to become the garden of Cell 9. This tank is still fed by an active spring of iron-rich water (not one of the springs that fed the well houses, for which see Chapter 6), which must have been tapped when the terrace was first constructed. Undiscovered by Keen, whose brief did not extend to deep excavation, it was examined by Rich Williams in 1983 at the request of John Weaver, following the collapse of its wooden cover.

The tank (see Figure 4.32) measured 0.92 m east to west, 0.80 m north to south and 0.68 m deep. It was lined with three courses of dressed stone, with a course of roof-slate packing between the first and second courses on its north side. Three blocks had masons' marks, two on the east elevation of types A1 and B5, one on the south elevation of type B5 (for analysis of masons' marks see Chapter 6), suggesting that the feature was constructed in this form when Cell 9 was built in Period Two.

The water outlet, 0.48 m above the natural clay base of the tank, was simply a gap of 40 mm between the two stones that comprised the upper course of the east side of the tank. Connecting with this outlet was the west end of drain [118], partly cut by the later drain

Figure 4.32 Cell 9: the spring chamber in the garden, showing the outlet in its east wall (R. Williams).

of the Cell 9 garden pentice that was built to discharge into it.

After the 1983 excavation, but before the 1985 work, the west end of drain [118] was effectively destroyed by the construction of a new land drain to carry away water from the tank. Where excavated, drain [118] comprised a single course of dressed stone set on or into the natural clay surface without a stone-lined bottom. At its west end, where it lay just below the surface of the terrace, it was simply capped for the first 2 m from the Cell 9 boundary wall with thin roof slates.

As the drain descended to the east it was more substantially capped with thick sandstone slabs. When one of these larger capstones was lifted in 1992 to insert a modern land drain, it was found to comprise an unused section of hood mould identical to that of the east cloister alley of Period Three (see Chapter 6), which suggests that these more substantial capstones of the drain at its east end were added above the original slate capping of the drain when Cell 8 was built in Period Three.

The drain filling of fine silt and gravel was heavily stained by the ferrous salts apparent in the spring water, which would have made it unsuitable for drinking. This source of water was clearly used to flush drains within the terrace. The construction of the drain was partially sealed by the unbroken levelling of the positive terrace, which extended below the western half of the later Cell 8.

A second drain [*127*] excavated within Cell 8 was also sealed within the terrace make-up and was apparently part of the same feature as drain [265], seen but not fully excavated to the south within the great cloister garth. It did not extend north of the later cell. Within the cell it had roughly dressed side stones a single course deep, a natural clay base and thick cover slabs (not illustrated). Drain [118] discharged through the west side of drain [*127*] and the two drains were clearly contemporary in their construction. The south end of drain [*127*] is known, however, for it discharges into an open drain on the far side of the great cloister between the north wall of the church and the east wall of Cell 22. It is still running and serves to drain most of the great cloister area.

A third drain, [237], within the cloister garth, and incorporated within the terrace levelling, was of slightly different construction, being set in a recognisable construction trench [*227*] and having a base of sandstone flags. It ran eastwards from outside the excavated area to feed into drain [265], though the junction had been damaged by the insertion of a later (though probably pre-Suppression) sump, [252] (see Figure 4.34).

The ferrous staining of the side stones and base of drain [237] would suggest that, like drain [118], it was fed by a spring in the terrace (this one, however, is now dry). Perhaps associated with the construction of this drain, for it lay just to the east of the junction of drain [237] and drain [265], and below the terrace levelling, was a shallow pit [*264*] packed with oyster shells (no doubt discarded after eating while construction was in progress). No other deposits of occupation debris were noted, but only limited areas of the cloister levelling were excavated.

PRIMARY TIMBER STRUCTURES

Once the terrace of the great cloister was levelled, the ranges of cells and the cloister alleys were laid out. Below the garden of Cell 8 and its cloister alley were found clear traces of a primary timber layout that can be fitted to existing documentation. Cut into the surface of the terrace were two ditches. The first, [93], clearly extends into the garden of Cell 7, from which party wall with Cell 8 it runs east–west, within the line of the later north boundary wall of Cell 8, to terminate in a butt end 1.10 m east of the party wall with Cell 9. The second, [106], runs south at right angles from ditch [93], 0.9 m west of the Cell 7 party wall and terminates 0.16 m north of the Period Two and later cloister wall of the north range. (Almost certainly, this stone cloister wall replaced a Period One timber screen enclosing the cloister area, though there is now no means of proving it.)

Neither ditch was excavated, although trial sections were cut to examine them. It is far from certain that they were bottomed. The two ditches define an area of roughly 115.2 m², though no closing ditch was ever dug on the west side and excavation to the west in the garden of Cell 9 did not suggest any continuation of the east–west ditch [93].

What the ditches excavated appear to represent is the last of a series of temporary enclosures (others presumably lie below the gardens of Cells 1–7) that would have contained Period One timber cells. The enclosure within the garden of the later Cell 8 does not appear to have been used, but it is known that there were nine monks present in 1412, including the prior and sacrist; the latter both had stone cells in Period One, leaving seven monks to be accommodated, and before an eighth cell was required building in stone on a larger scale had begun. There was no evidence of early occupation below Cell 8. There was, however, an area of split stone paving [119] on the northern edge of ditch [93].

Contemporary with the digging of the enclosure ditches and the suggested timber screen around the great cloister was the construction of a timber cloister alley (see Figure 4.34), represented simply by the stone packing for its cill beam [262], which was placed directly on the surface of the terrace levelling [242]. The stone packing survived only to a length of 1.46 m to the west of Cell 8, the remainder being cut away by the construction trench for a later stone arcade. Apparently, the primary timber arcade west of Cell 8 survived unaltered until the Suppression in 1539.

FINDS GROUP 7: CERAMICS (SEE FIGURE 4.33)
Found in the redeposited orange-grey clay [243] of the positive terrace in the later cell garden (Table 4.8).

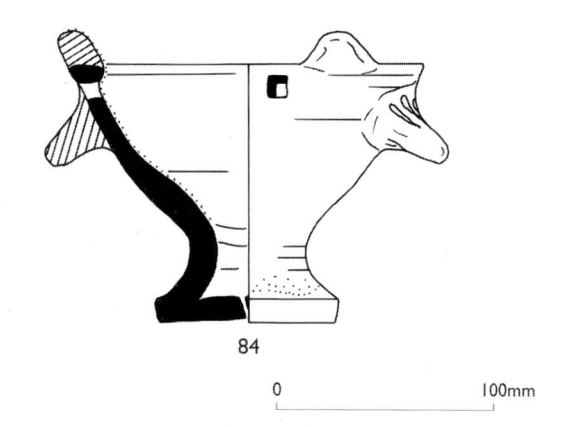

Figure 4.33 Cell 8: Finds Group 7 (pottery 1:4).

Table 4.8 Cell 8, Finds Group 7: Ceramics

Fabric	Sherds	Vessels	
		Total vessels	Chafing dish
Post-medieval Orange	5*	1	1

* includes residual material in the total

A single sherd from a chafing dish was found firmly stratified in the redeposited clay [243] of the positive terrace on the north side of the Cell 8 garden. This chafing dish was represented by a number of sherds from various locations, though this was its earliest finds context. However, ceramic chafing dishes are a predominantly 16th-century vessel form in North Yorkshire, and an early 15th-century date for this example would be surprising. It is difficult to see, all the same, how this sherd could be intrusive.

84.   Post-medieval Orange ware chafing dish.

Period Two (see Figure 4.31 and 4.34)
GARDEN WALLS
Both enclosure ditches were backfilled with rubble and brown clay, which had compacted, leaving slight hollows in the surface from which the Period Two enclosing garden walls [24], [25], [30] and [31] were constructed. Associated with the building of the garden walls was a deposit of builders' rubble [*93a*] which only survived in the top filling of ditches [93] and [106], comprising sandstone rubble, broken roofing slates and off-white mortar typical across the site of Period Two building. Elsewhere across the cell plot it had been scraped away when Cell 8 was built and its garden established.

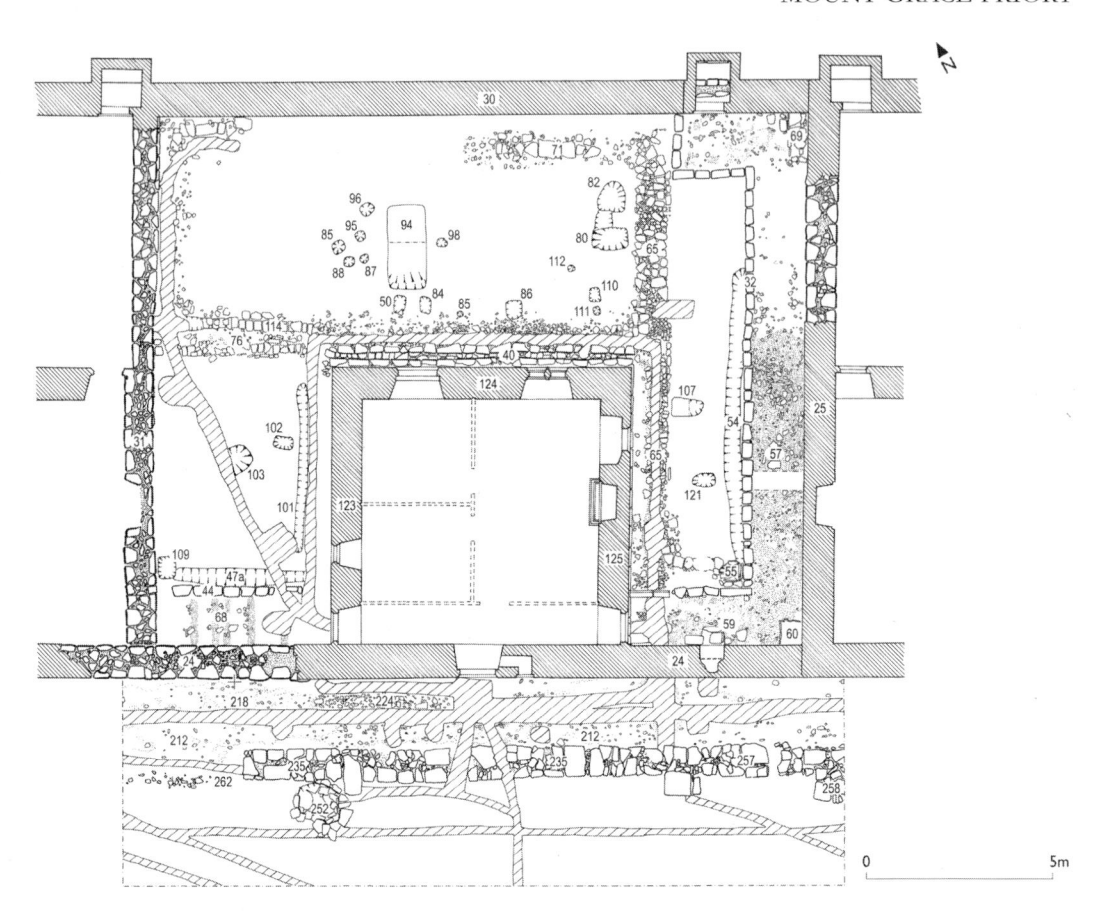

Figure 4.34 Cell 8: Period Two garden walls and Period Three cell and garden layout.

Drain

Cutting the backfilled ditch [106] and underlying the eastern garden wall [25] was a substantial drain [83]. It had previously been examined to the east by the Ministry of Works conservation team (T. Rudd, pers. comm.), and is known to extend as far east as Cell 5, but remained undisturbed within the garden of Cell 8. Its relationship with the builders' rubble in the upper filling of ditch [106] was unclear, but being sealed by the construction of wall [25] it must belong to Period Two.

Cut into the surface of the natural clay [*92*] of the negative terrace, the drain was substantially built of one or two courses of dressed masonry. Its unlined base was the natural clay and it was covered with substantial capstones (for a section of drain [83], see Figure 4.35a L–J). At its west end it intersected with the Period One drain [*127*]. Its fall very clearly was from east to west, confirming that, like drain [118], it fed the major drain [*127/265*] and served to drain the eastern part of the terrace, where stone cells were being constructed in Period Two.

North Range Passage

Although the Period Three insertion of Cell 8 into wall [24] and its latrine into wall [30] have slightly confused the issue, it is clear that when the enclosing walls [24], [25], [30] and [31] were built at this centre point of the north range there was no immediate intention of building a cell there. Instead, a passage was provided through the range adjacent to the east wall [25], and the eastern jambs of paired arches survive to springing height at the east ends of the north and south walls.

The chamfered south face of the western jamb of the northern door or, perhaps more correctly, gateway, can still be identified in the north wall [30] despite its being damaged by masonry of Period Three, showing that it was 3.60 m wide and 2.80 m high to its springing (see Figure 4.35b O–N).

The western jamb of the gateway in the south wall [24] did not survive rebuilding, but its surviving offset foundation course [*248*] did survive, showing it to be of like width (see Figure 4.35c A–B). The height of its springing was identical to the opening in the north wall of the range.

THE ARCHAEOLOGY OF THE GREAT CLOISTER

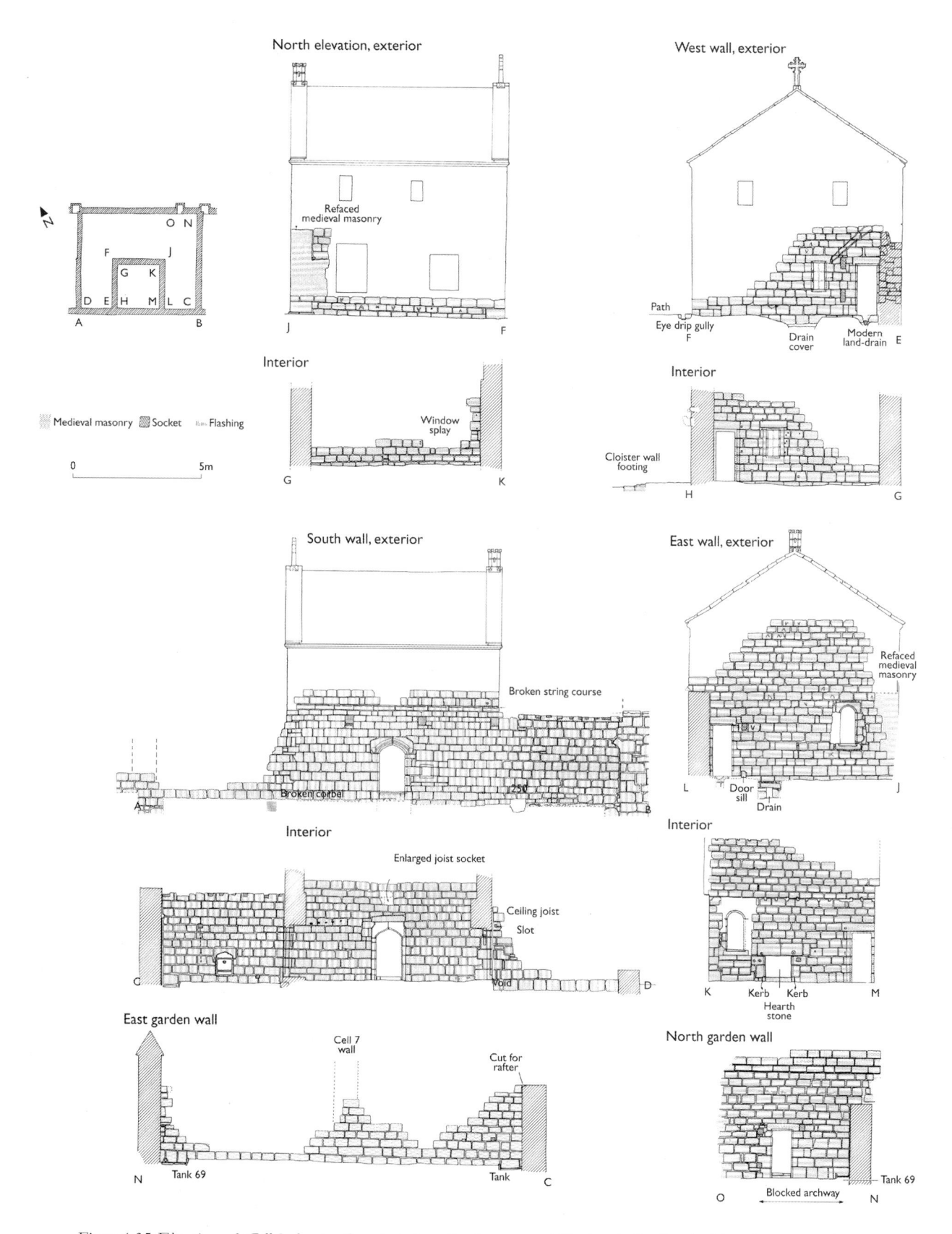

Figure 4.35 Elevations of Cell 8 showing the extent of medieval masonry within the rebuilt cell and evidence for its original form.

CLOISTER ARCADE

Contemporary with the Period Two enclosing walls was the building of a masonry cloister arcade to the south, enclosing an alley 1.92 m wide. Only the unmortared rubble footings [235] and the foundations of two shallow buttresses had survived post-Suppression robbing, but fragments found in destruction contexts (see Chapter 6) indicated that they had carried the Period Two cloister arcade, which can be reconstructed from its surviving elements. This arcade extended westwards only to within 2.6 m of the party wall with Cell 9, from which point the Period One timber arcade was left undisturbed. The footings [235] were packed into a narrow construction trench [263] cut into the surface of the clay terrace [259] and a layer of yellow-grey clay [242] was spread between the inner face of the arcade wall and the southern face of wall [24], sealing the construction of both. On top of this clay layer were deposits of rubble [224] in grey-brown soil, and of orange-brown clay and rubble [212] and [218], which comprised the subfloor of the Period Two cloister alley.

This area was badly disturbed by modern land drains, but within it was a deep and narrow trench [206], which had been cleared out in the late 19th century but which had probably contained a lead water main associated with Period Two. The trench appears to have been robbed out at the time of Hope's excavation or a little later, but because of modern disturbances it was impossible to be certain where it was cut from.

At the east end of the excavated alley wall was a gap, in both its footings and construction trench, 5.36 m wide, where the arcade wall had not existed. This was close to, but not directly opposite, the passage through the range. No metalled surface was traced within the range passage or the cloister alley, though the passage was wide enough to take wagons or sleds carrying building materials for the cloister ranges from the quarry that is still extant to the north-east of the priory. No heavy loads could have been carried through the range and over the backfilled ditches of Period One unless there was some form of surface, yet there seems to be no other purpose for the omitting of a cell at the centre of the range and the provision of a wide access into the heart of the priory. Perhaps a corded timber surface was provided, but no trace of this was encountered

Table 4.9 Cell 8, Finds Group 8: Ceramics

Fabric	Sherds	Vessels		
		Total vessels	Jug	Pancheon
Post-medieval Orange	2	2	2	0
Ryedale	2	2	1	1

in excavation. Reduction of the surface within the garden during Period Three construction may account for the lack of evidence, but no trace remained in the cloister alley either.

PIT

Associated with the construction of the cloister alley was a stone-lined pit [252], which was inserted in the angle between the footing of the arcade wall [235] and the footing of buttress [261]. This was dug down to expose the underlying drain [265] and also damaged its junction with drain [237]. It was filled with broken sandstone rubble, much of which was heavily burned and which functioned as a soakaway. A considerable quantity of water-washed silt had accumulated between the stones. Presumably the pit took water from the roof of the north cloister alley.

FINDS GROUP 8: CERAMICS

This group comprised material from the construction of drain [83], the subfloor levelling [212] of the Period Two cloister alley floor and the soakaway [252] associated with the Period Two cloister alley (Table 4.9). There was no pottery from the Cell 8 Period Two contexts that could be illustrated.

Period Three (see Figure 4.34)

CONSTRUCTION OF CELL 8 AND ITS GARDEN

In the third quarter of the 15th century, the central and eastern parts of the south wall [24] of the central section of the north cloister range were taken down to their footings, leaving only the east jamb of the wide opening, or throughway, in place. In the gap so formed was built Cell 8, not in the corner of the plot but placed centrally between the west and east walls [31] and [25], astride the junction of the negative and positive terraces.

Cell 8 was reconstructed by Sir Lowthian Bell before 1905 and its walls remain largely as he left them. The cell and its interior were examined in

1988 in the course of its restoration to a pre-Suppression appearance. The opportunity was taken during the repointing of the building to record the bedding mortars that differentiated Bell's work from the original build and to record the extent of the surviving medieval structure.

SURVIVING STRUCTURE (SEE FIGURE 4.35)

No construction deposits or traces of the internal cill walls and floors had survived Bell's reconstruction, but it was possible to examine the footings where they were cut into the clay surface of the terrace. Where the cell was footed onto the negative terrace, the footings of its east wall [125] and the eastern third of its north wall [124] comprised a single course of undressed blocks laid in a shallow foundation trench. The remainder of wall [124] and all of the west wall [123] were footed again on a single course of rubble laid in a foundation trench a full course (0.25 m) deeper. The trench had penetrated to the depth of the undisturbed natural clay below the positive terrace. Clearly, the builders were unhappy at building on the surface of made ground, however shallow. In spite of this precaution, the west wall had subsided 50 mm at the level of its first-floor offset. All of the masonry of the original structure was bedded in the pink mortar associated elsewhere with Period Three.

South Wall Remains (see Figure 4.35c): The south or cloister wall survived to two courses above the string course, which marked the pent roof of the cloister, apart from a small area above the cloister door at the centre of the wall where Bell had introduced a cross-joist in his reconstruction. In total the outer face of the south wall survived 15 courses to the west of the cloister door and 16 to the east.

The Period Two south wall of the range [24] appears to have been retained to form the lowest course of Cell 8's south wall, as it is continuous with the surviving Period Two south wall to the west of the cell. The junction between the Period Three masonry of the cell and this Period Two south wall to the west survives to the height of the string course just within the line of the west wall of the cell, where the coursing is broken.

To the east of the cell the south wall of the range, [24], is Period Three, contemporary with the building of the cell, up to the surviving east jamb of the Period Two north range passage gateway described above and the masonry courses through convincingly. The south wall of the cell survived to the same height internally, that is 13 courses to the west of the door and 14 to the east. This disparity between east and west is related to the bed heights of the cell door jambs: those on the east side were modified to course with the L-shaped hatch.

The doorway from the cloister was centrally placed in this wall and survives intact, the door being hung on the east jamb. Three corbels, now broken off, were set at centres of 2.80 m, the easternmost aligning with the east wall face of the cell, to carry the wall plate of the cloister alley roof. They were set 0.2 m below the string course that covered the lead flashing of the roof. To the east of the cell, sockets were cut into the topmost surviving course of the cloister wall at 0.46 m centres to accommodate the rafters of the alley roof.

East Wall Remains (see Figure 4.35a): The east wall of the cell [125] was the best preserved part of the building, surviving externally to a height of 20 courses (6.92 m) above its offset foundations and internally to a height of 18 courses (5.28 m). In the top three surviving courses of the outer face were five masons' marks of type C15 (see Chapter 6). Internally, there was a set-back of 0.1 m above the tenth course, which marked the height of the first-floor joists.

At its south end this wall contained a well-preserved square-headed doorway. The door hung on the southern jamb and was closed by both a sliding bolt and by a substantial locking bar, which swung when unlocked into a long rebate in the south jamb and was fixed into a hole in the north jamb.

At the north end of the wall was a single-light window of which the cill and north jamb survived. Although this did not course with the wall around it, and gave the impression of being inserted, the mortar used to set the masonry was the same as that of the walls. The window was subsequently altered in Period Four when it was given a semicircular head (see Figure 4.36) and its iron grille was replaced with a glazed panel set in a shallow secondary groove. Internally, its reveals were cut back square and the cill cut down to floor level, destroying the greater part of the original arrangement. The apparent reason for doing this was to fit panelling into the window splay, and a shallow slot 1.56 m above the internal

Figure 4.36 Cell 8: the round-headed window in the east wall in about 1890, before its repair by Bell (Canon J. C. Atkinson c. 1890).

floor level of the cell marked the top rail of the panelling. Above this slot, the window splays were not defaced.

At the centre of the east wall was a fireplace with a plain monolithic lintel. Two pin-holes in the lintel may relate to a low overmantle connected with the Period Four panelling of this room. A square hole in the right-hand jamb of the fireplace was perhaps a salt box, and two deep pin-holes in the left-hand jamb at the same level may indicate a crane. The hearthstone and its surrounding stone fender remain *in situ* at the level of the medieval floor.

North Wall Remains (see Figure 4.35): Of the north wall [124] little remains of the medieval structure. Externally, only two courses survive above the offset foundation, though the north-east angle of the building had been recased by Bell and contains more original fabric than might be thought on first examination. A small area of original facework can still be seen to the east of the four-light window that Bell inserted on the site of an original window.

Internally, the wall survives at its east end to a height of eight courses above footings, 2.40 m, but for more than half its length only the lowest three courses are original, and for the rest only two. The third course includes the lowest course of the internal splays of a four-light window and pin-holes to its east and west indicate the fixing of panelling around the window.

West Wall Remains (see Figure 4.35): The west wall [123] ranges from only two courses high at its north end to 11 courses (3.36 m) at its south end, both inside and out. Inside, an offset was provided above the tenth course to seat the first-floor joists. Settlement meant that this was 50 mm below the matching offset on the east wall. At the south end of the west wall is a door that matches that in the east wall, and at its north end a single-light square-headed window that retains evidence of its original iron grille and internal shutter rebate. Its grille was removed and it was glazed in Period Four, like the matching window in the east wall. In this instance, the window is coursed with the surrounding wall. The interior wall surface is largely plain, but a series of pin-holes around the window again indicate the fixing of panelling.

Cell Interior: No fixings remained in any of the internal wall surfaces for medieval partitions, though sockets had been cut by Bell's workmen to fix the modern pitch pine interior that was removed in 1988, after an attack of dry rot. Bell's workmen had already removed any evidence of the medieval floor and internal cill walls that excavation revealed in the other cells of the great cloister. However, the positioning of the surviving windows suggested that the cell had originally been divided on the ground floor into three rooms and a cross-passage.

The eastern room with its fireplace would have been the hall or living room, occupying some 40% of the ground floor of the building. Space would have been taken up by the cross-passage that ran between the two side doors. The remaining floor space was divided between a combined bedroom and oratory, with a single-light window, and a study with a large four-light window, although where that division fell is far from certain.

Roughly cut sockets in the inner face of the south wall indicate that a rather rudimentary loft was created at some time in the eastern part of the cross-passage, but there was no trace of the stair evidenced in almost all the other great cloister cells.

The placing of the cell at the centre of its garden and the effect this had on its planning is examined below in Chapter 6.

CONSTRUCTION OF THE LATRINE PENTICE
Pentice Walkway: Following the construction of the cell itself, all building materials were cleared from the garden area, which was scraped

down to a uniform level, removing evidence of Period Two features; only on the east side had some Period Two features subsided into the soft fillings of the Period One ditches, and been so preserved.

On this reduced surface a cill wall, [32], a single stone wide, was built of punched ashlar blocks. This wall survived to the height of a single course, except on the return along the south garden wall [24], where two stones from a second course survived. The lowest course was left undressed on its inner surface but the second course was dressed on all faces. This cill wall defined an L-shaped walkway, roughly 1.4 m wide, that led east from the east door of the cell and then north to an inserted latrine in the north wall of the range [30]. The cill wall had originally been two to three courses high and carried the cill beam of a timber gallery (see below).

The short southern branch of the walkway contained a door to the garden immediately next to the cell. The threshold of the door, 1.16 m wide, survived in place, its west end rebated to sit over the offset foundation of the cell wall. Its east end was flanked by a post, some 0.155 m^2, which was set in a brick-packed posthole, providing a jamb for the door against which the masonry of the cill wall was butted.

Within the long eastern branch of the walkway, and particularly in its southern half, was a dump of waste stone [79] that was sealed below a floor [57] of two layers of river-washed gravel, the upper layer fine and the lower coarse, set on a levelling layer of yellow-brown clay. The whole of the walkway had a gravel floor surface, but excavation and erosion at its north end meant only isolated patches of it survived there.

Tanks: In the angle of the south and east walls of the cell enclosure, and set in this floor, was a square tank [60], with a floor and sides both of split slate. Its base was set on a layer of ginger clay that was in turn set on a bedding of the same gravel used to surface the pentice walkway, though the whole tank structure was in place before the floor was laid. A second, rectangular tank [69], of identical construction, was provided in the north-east angle of the corridor (see Figure 4.35).

Both tanks contained only later demolition material and no evidence of their function was recovered. Both were only a maximum of 50 mm deep.

Pentice Roof: Good evidence remained for the form of the timber superstructure of this pentice walkway. Apart from the cill beam, sockets for the wall plate survived in walls [30], [24] and [125] showing that the wall plate measured 0.18 m^2 and was set 1.14 m above the cill beam. The mortar flashing of the pent roof remained on walls [30] and [125], and sockets for the rafter ends in the top surviving course of wall [24]. A single hole for a tie beam survived in wall [30] immediately above the level of the wall plate. In short, the exact disposition of the gallery, apart from its studs, was possible to recreate (see Figure 4.37).

The gallery was roofed with split stone slates, many of which were recovered from demolition spreads that buried the lowest course of the cill wall. There is no evidence to suggest that the walls of the gallery were enclosed or glazed.

The location of a stone-lined sump [55] in the angle of the east and south cill walls of the gallery, suggested that the pentice roof was provided with a gutter and a downpipe, which discharged at that point. The sump was packed with sandstone rubble and a stone-capped drain ran westwards from it to discharge between the capstones of the Period Two drain [83]. The drain from the sump [55] consisted simply of a channel cut into the filling of the Period One ditch ([106]; see Figure 4.31), with slates laid over it at the level of construction of the pentice. As the drain ran from the top of the sump, rather than the bottom, it was clearly intended to carry away any excess, rather than take all the water collected from the pentice roof.

Tap Niche: Set in the south wall of the gallery to the east of the cell door was a niche with a segmental head that contained the tap bringing piped water to Cell 8. Although both the tap and pipe had been robbed, the ghost of the pipe remained in the core of the wall. It emerged through the wall into the cloister alley where a rebate was provided in the lowest course of the wall to take the pipe. Unfortunately, Hope examined this area to trace the course of the pipe and his trench [260] removed any evidence for the pipe. It must have joined the ring main in trench [206]. Below the tap niche was a further intrusion [59], which probably also represents Hope's pipe-chasing. It coincided with a stone-lined pit and removed all of its filling. The pit had

Figure 4.37 Cell 8: the reconstructed latrine pentice (G. Coppack).

probably been a soakaway to take waste water from the tap. It was cut into the butt end of ditch [106], though its precise relationship with that feature had been destroyed.

Latrine: The latrine, partly rebuilt in the late 1960s, was inserted into the Period Two archway in the precinct wall. It was entered by a square-headed doorway, the jambs and head of which were rebated 50 mm to take a door that was hung on the western jamb. A single drilled hole on the east jamb evidenced a sliding bolt to close the door. A square-headed niche was provided in the west jamb for a candle or lamp. Two shallow steps, 0.1 m and 70 mm high, led to the latrine, which was set above a flushed drain outside the precinct wall in the same manner of those of Cells 6 and 7. The front of the privy comprised a monolithic slab, 0.39 m high and 0.16 m wide, above which were rebates for a timber seat 80 mm thick. All of the masonry above seat level was reset in the 1960s and, as it contains a series of seat and joist rebates, probably comes from other latrines.

CONSTRUCTION OF THE GARDEN PENTICE (SEE FIGURE 4.34)

To the west of Cell 8, and between it and the gable wall of Cell 9, was a second pentice, defined by a cill wall [44] that survived to the height of a single course. Like the latrine pentice, the wall was a single stone thick and the surviving course was not dressed on its inner face. It was set on the top of the redeposited clay [117] of the positive terrace. It had originally been three courses high (0.56 m), for both the substantial sockets of its cill beam survived, one in the west wall of the cell and the other in the gable wall of Cell 9. The socket size indicated that the cill beam had been 0.153 m^2. The wall plate socket (0.433 m high and 0.153 m wide) survived in the west wall of the cell, 1.04 m above the top of the cill beam, and a deep cut-out for the slate flashing of the roof above the wall plate socket indicated that the roof was pitched at 40 degrees.

The pentice was entered from the west door of the cell and had no access to the garden. Within the pentice, a series of shallow grooves [68] were cut into the surface of the positive terrace to take floor joists. This pentice had a suspended wooden floor similar to that provided in other cells of the great cloister and in their garden pentices, suggesting that it was of a higher quality than the latrine pentice. This was confirmed by the presence of a substantial quantity of window glass (607 pieces), including a number of whole quarries (diamond-shaped panes used in lattice widows), remaining from the 16th-century demolition of the gallery. The remarkable depth of the wall plate (just under 0.5 m) suggested that a series of window-heads had been cut into it and that this pentice, which served the monk as a private cloister alley, had been glazed in the manner of a late medieval cloister (see Figure 4.38).

THE ARCHAEOLOGY OF THE GREAT CLOISTER

An eavesdrip gulley [47a] was provided to the north of the garden pentice, cut into the surface of the clay of the positive terrace and leading to a soakaway [109] at its west end. This soakaway was packed with sandstone rubble.

CREATION OF THE GARDEN (SEE FIGURES 4.31 AND 4.34)

Once the cell and its pentices were built, the enclosed area of the garden was cleared of any construction debris and topsoil. The area was wet, with water seeping through the lowest courses of the north wall of the range. To deal with this problem, two stone-lined drains [113] and [116] were inserted, both discharging through the capstones of the Period One drain [118]. Drain [113] had sunk into the soft fill of the underlying Period One ditch [93] and cannot have remained effective for long. Drain [116] avoided the ditch and appears to have functioned up to the Suppression. It was badly damaged by a modern land drain.

Paths: The garden area was then divided into a series of raised beds by paths surfaced with split slates, which were laid on the surface of the clay terrace (see Figure 4.39). Access to the garden was via the door in the latrine pentice wall adjacent to the east wall of the cell. From there, a path, [65], ran northwards parallel to the east wall of the cell to within 0.40 m of the north wall of the range where it returned to the west as path [71]. A Bell-period land drain around Cell 8 had substantially damaged path [65] adjacent to the cell, but its northern extension was relatively undamaged, with a surviving kerb of slates set on edge, which had retained the raised soil of the garden beds.

Outside the latrine pentice door the split slates of the path were replaced by a setting of cobbles from where the monk would have stepped out onto the paved surface. An interesting aspect of this area was the evidence that the monk had cut his firewood there, for the threshold of the door was revealed on excavation to be scarred with the marks of an axe. A further path, [53], ran from path [65] along the cell's north wall, separated from it by an eavesdrip drain [40] of punched ashlar blocks with a split stone base. This gully was integral with the construction of the path. It discharged at the west end of the cell into a stone-lined drain [114], which ran to the west wall of the garden and itself discharged into drain [116], though the junction of these drains was severely damaged.

The capstones of drain [114] formed the northern edge of a western continuation [76] of path [53], which continued up to the west wall of the garden. An area of paving survived above drain [116] in the north-west corner of the garden, suggesting that this was a path that returned along the west wall to meet the now-destroyed western end of path [71].

The paths defined three rectangular beds and a fourth narrow strip along the north wall of the range that retained some evidence of their planting in Period Three.

Principal, or North, Garden Bed: The principal bed was that defined by paths [53], [65] and [71], and within it a number of holes cut into the surface of the clay terrace survived. These holes were either planting pits or holes for stakes that had supported plants.

The holes fell into two groups: a series of pits, associated with the edging of the plot [50], [80], [82], [84], [85], [86], [110], [111] and [112], which do not appear to have continued west of the cell itself; and a large rectangular planting pit [94] with six related features, [87], [88], [*89*], [95], [96] and [98], which occupied the central area of the plot. The fill of all these features was uniform: a dark brown clay-loam, to which compost had been added, consisting of decomposed leaf mould, wheat straw(?), heavily degraded root networks and quantities of oak and elm charcoal. No identifiable seeds, grains or fruit were recovered, as the level of mechanical destruction applied to the material during burial seems to have been too great.

Figure 4.38 Cell 8: the reconstructed garden pentice (G. Coppack).

Figure 4.39 Cell 8: the 15th-century garden as excavated (G. Coppack).

The large rectangular pit, [94], contained fragments of oak, elm and poplar, possibly the debris of construction or more probably from the cutting of firewood. It also contained a pair of tongs (see Figure 4.40).

East Garden Bed: The bed to the east of the cell, between path [65] and the latrine pentice contained similar features to those in the central bed. The main survival was a bedding trench [54] along the outside of wall [32]. The northern end of the trench was excavated by Keen in 1974, at which time it appears to have been at least partially edged with roof slates and was interpreted by him as an eavesdrip gully. It was examined in 1985, by which time it had been destroyed by erosion. No trace of the slates remained and it was found to have the same filling as the other bedding trenches. Two further planting pits [107] and [121] were found at the centre of this bed; others may have been lost to erosion further north.

West Garden Bed: A similar arrangement pertained in the bed to the west of the cell, where a narrow planting trench [101] was recorded to the west of and parallel to the cell wall [123]. A deep planting pit [103] occupied the centre of the plot, containing fragments of ash, perhaps from a stake. A second pit [102] containing fragments of elm, was found adjacent to trench [101]. All these features were sealed by a thin layer of developed topsoil [*62*], [*64*] and [*70*].

FINDS GROUP 9 (SEE FIGURE 4.40)
Ceramics
This groups consists of a collection of Period Three finds, excavated from the following garden features: eavesdrip drain [40], bedding trench [54], path [65], [*78*], pits [80], [*81*], [86], [*89*], [94] and [98], drain [113], the latrine pentice floor [57] and tank [60] (Table 4.10).

A small group of material was associated with the construction of the latrine pentice and the laying out of the garden. The albarello is a comparatively early example.

85. Siegburg stoneware mug. Silver-grey outer surface glaze, blue-grey core and pale purplish-grey inner surface.
86. Humber ware cistern. Grey to blue-grey core and blue-grey inner surface. Bright, flecked olive-green glaze turning more brownish at the upper glaze margin. A classic West Cowick (in East Yorkshire) product.
87. White Pisa slipware albarello. Soft, dull red, slightly micaceous fabric. Outer surface has a white slip and both outer and inner surfaces are glazed. The inner surface glaze is a pale ochre-brown, the glaze on the outer surface is a cream over the white outer-surface slip.

THE ARCHAEOLOGY OF THE GREAT CLOISTER

Table 4.10 Cell 8, Finds Group 9: Ceramics

Fabric	Sherds	Total vessels	Albarello	Cistern	Jug	Mug or cup
Hambleton	2	1	0	0	1	0
Humber	3	3	0	1	1	1
Langerwehe	1	1	0	0	0	1
Midlands Purple	1	1	0	0	1	0
Pisa Slip	2	1	1	0	0	0
Ryedale	110	4	0	1	3	0
Reversed Cistercian	2	1	0	0	0	1
Siegburg	5	3	0	0	0	3
Tudor Green	11	1	0	0	0	1

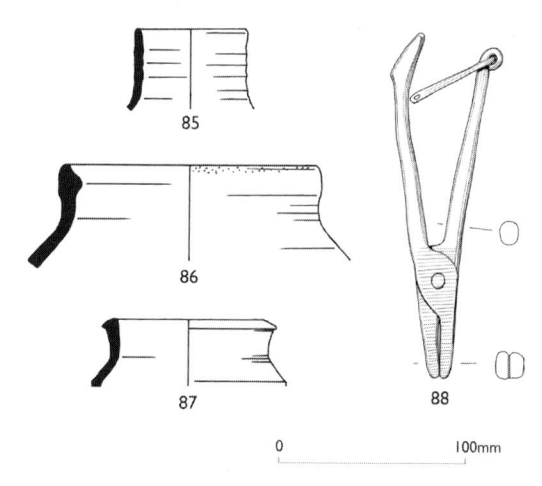

Figure 4.40 Cell 8: Finds Group 9 (pottery 1:4; iron 1:4).

Small Finds

In addition to the pottery find in the garden of Cell 8, a pair of tongs was found in the large planting pit of the principal garden bed.

88. Tongs. Fe. Total L: 182 mm. Jaws L: 31 mm; W: 13–14 mm. Arms oval in section, 12 mm at maximum diameter. A pair of tongs with one arm angled inwards, the other turned outwards with a locking clip (L: 50 mm) attached to its end. The clip would hold the tongs closed when secured over the bend in the other arm. Drawn from X-rays. Recovered from a soil sample from context [94]. It has no finds number. AML 854896.

Period Four (see Figure 4.41)
ALTERATIONS TO THE GARDEN PENTICE
The timber floor and supporting joists of the garden pentice were allowed to rot *in situ* and the collapsed timberwork was then deliberately buried beneath a reflooring of water-washed grey gravel [58] up to 50 mm thick that covered the whole floor area of the pentice. The incorporation of window glass in this gravel and beneath it would suggest that the glazing of the pentice was in poor repair.

The use of the pentice, originally designed as a private cloister alley, had changed by Period Four and on excavation it was found to have been used to store a considerable quantity of round, oakwood charcoal up to 30 mm in diameter, which still remained on the surface of the new floor at the western end of the gallery sealed by primary demolition material [40].

Following garden alterations (see 4.2.9.4.2), the Period Three eavesdrip gully [47a] outside the pentice was recut and lined with reused roof slates and continued to discharge into the Period Three soakaway [109].

ALTERATIONS TO THE GARDEN
The garden showed evidence of having been deserted for a time at the end of Period Three: the slate paths were all buried by soil, presumably washed from the raised beds, which suggests that the cell was temporarily unused.

At the start of Period Four, new paths were established, no longer of roof slate but of spreads of deliberately burned (to soften it) and crushed sandstone chips that were distinguished by their red colour. Mixed with the burned material were chips of pale cream mortar, presumably derived from demolition elsewhere on the site. The full length of the Period Three path [53] was resurfaced with this mixture of burned sandstone chips and mortar chips as path [41] and a new path [52] was laid

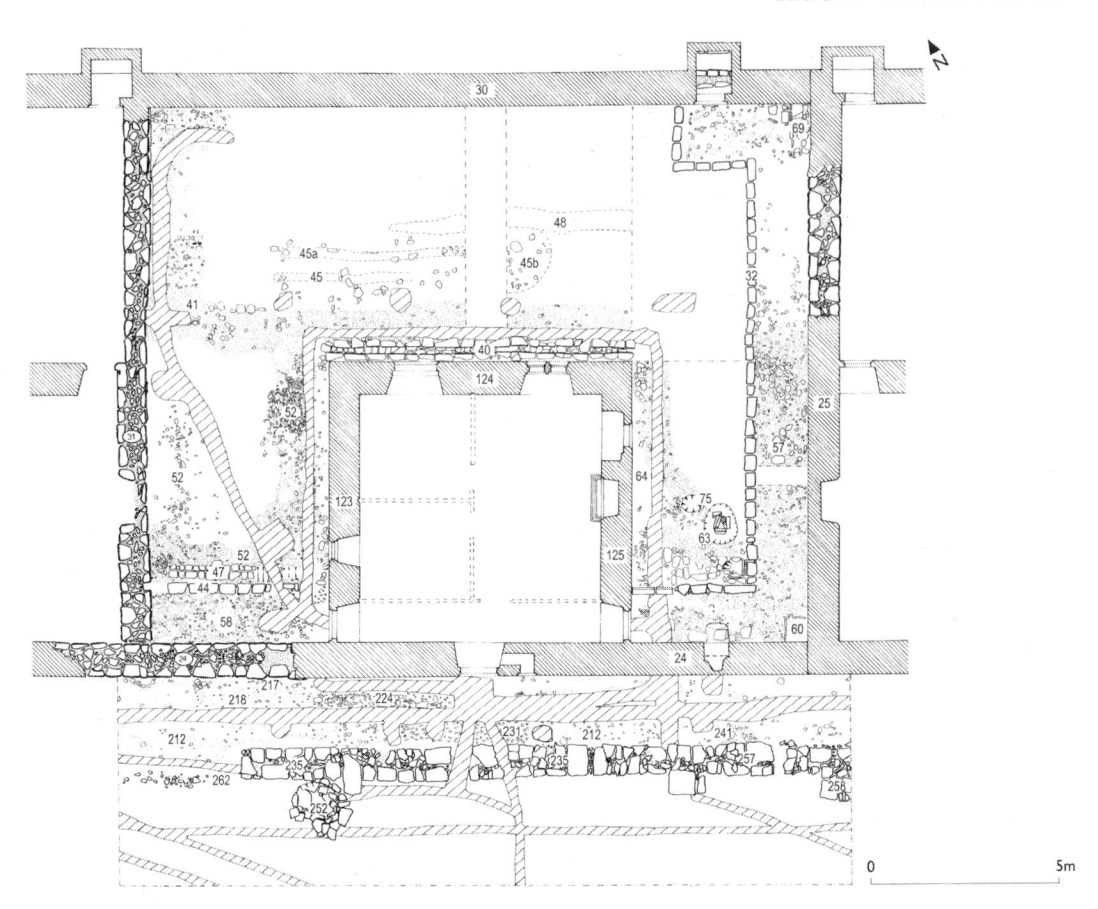

Figure 4.41 Cell 8: the early 16th-century garden and cloister alley.

using the same mixture onto a subsurface of mixed brown and grey clay [*67*], which covered the surface of the Period Three garden soil [*70*] around the bed to the west of the cell.

The Period Three eavesdrip gully, [*47a*], was recut, [*47*], into this surface, indicating that it post-dated the reorganisation of the garden.

To the east of the cell, a similar deposit of burned sandstone and mortar chips, [*64*], extended from the cill wall of the short southern section of the latrine pentice, where it sealed the capstones of the Period Three drain [*55*], to the north-east corner of the cell. The greater part of this new path had been removed by a modern land drain.

In 1985 the greater part of the Period Four garden was removed with the turf and topsoil, in which no features were detectable. The only evidence for gardening in Period Four was found where the bottoms of features that had penetrated into Period Three levels had survived. Such evidence remained in the bed to the north of the cell (see Figure 4.42), where a series of shallow features were found in the surface of the developed garden soil [*62*]. Three of these, [*45*], [*45a*] and [*48*], were parallel grooves containing fine rubble concentrated at and so defining their edges, which were otherwise indistinct. A fourth, shallow, sub-circular feature [*45b*], comprising a filling of topsoil and fine rubble similar to that found in the parallel grooves was also found. On this evidence the Period Four garden appears to have been cultivated in rows and to have been somewhat less sophisticated than its predecessor.

REMNANTS OF THE SUPPRESSION

To the east of the cell were a number of features that most properly belong to the end of Period Four, the demolition of the cell in 1539 at the suppression of the house. The first of these was a spread of pottery [*64*] on the surface of the Period Three path [*65*], immediately outside the latrine pentice door to the garden. Sherds of some 43 vessels that had evidently been discarded complete lay on the surface of the path and the adjacent garden soil (see Finds Group 11; Figures 4.44 and 4.45). It would appear that the pottery contents of the cell had been simply thrown out into the garden before the building was unroofed and stripped of its timberwork. In the corner of the plot, and cutting the pottery deposit (associated sherds were found in its fill)

THE ARCHAEOLOGY OF THE GREAT CLOISTER

Figure 4.42 Cell 8: the early 16th-century garden as excavated (G. Coppack).

was a substantial posthole [63] that retained the packing for a post 0.2 m². A second posthole [75] to its north-west appears to have accommodated an angled brace to the post in pit [63]. The two features suggest a small crane used in the process of demolition, perhaps for taking down the gable wall of Cell 7. All these features, as well as the cill wall of the latrine pentice, were sealed by a spill of fallen roof slates from the demolition of the pentice after the timbers in postholes [63] and [75] had been withdrawn. Amongst this fallen material was part of the chimney of Cell 7.

MODIFICATIONS TO THE NORTH CLOISTER ALLEY
Two minor repairs were noted within the floor makeup of the north cloister alley. Opposite the cloister door of Cell 8 a hollow in the subfloor had been made up with a spread of brown clay [231]. To the east, an ill-defined hole [241] against the alley wall [257] was packed with sandstone rubble in grey clay. The purpose of the hole, before it was filled, is unknown.

FINDS GROUP 10 (SEE FIGURE 4.43)
Ceramics
These finds were derived from the Period Four reflooring of the garden pentice [58] and the paths and gravel surfaces [41], [52], [64], [67], [70] and [77] of the Period Four garden (Table 4.11).

They are likely to be of early 16th-century date. The small bottle, 89, was an unusual local form and made more interesting by the small hole bored through the shoulder of the vessel. This may have been designed to enable the vessel to be suspended from a thong or similar device. The glazed Langerwehe costrel, 91, is a larger version of the same shaped vessel, although probably having a taller neck, while the fragments of 94 seem to represent a flat-sided or barrel costrel similar to the Martincamp forms. This sort of form, although comparatively uncommon in other contemporary groups in England, seems to be a common find amongst the Mount Grace cells.

89. Hambleton ware bottle. Orange-red outer surface, with pale orange to pale blue to pale orange core and pale orange inner surface. Olive-green glaze of good quality. The hole in the neck was bored through after firing.
90. Drug jar base. Soft white fabric with creamy surfaces and traces of yellow-green glaze splashes. Some burning and sooting to the base. More interestingly, perhaps, there was also burning and sooting to the inner surface bound by a tide mark implying the burning of a residue within the vessel.

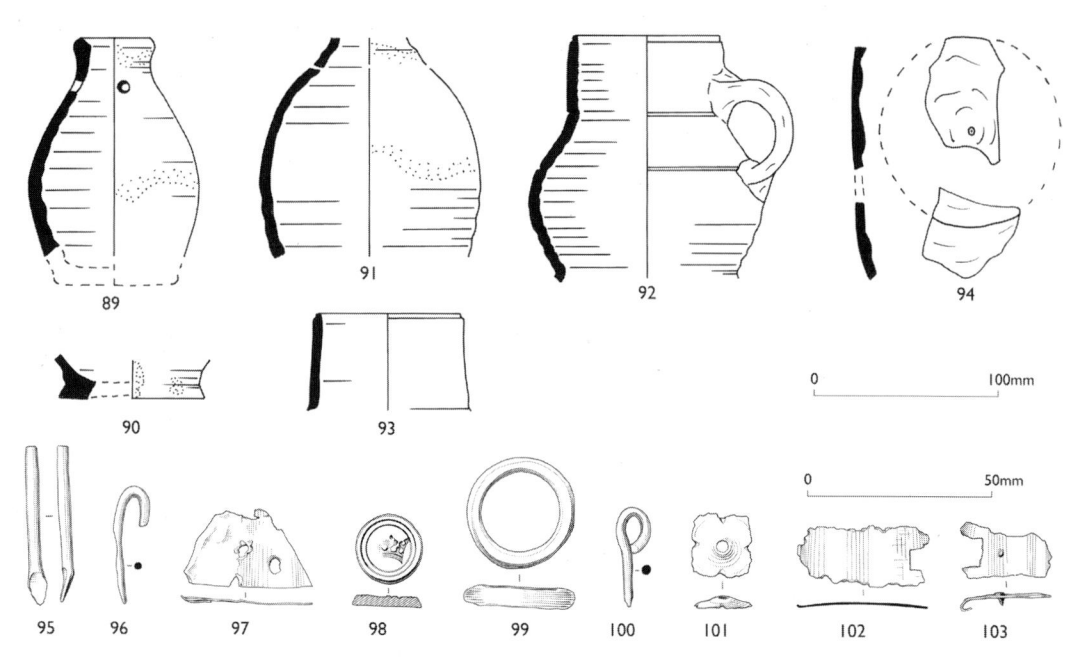

Figure 4.43 Cell 8: Finds Group 10 (pottery 1:4; copper alloy 1:2).

Table 4.11 Cell 8, Finds Group 10: Ceramics

Fabric	Sherds	Vessels						
		Total vessels	Bottle	Costrel	Drug jar	Flask	Jug	Mug or cup
Cistercian	4	3	0	0	0	0	0	3
Hambleton	7	1	1	0	0	0	0	0
Langerwehe	20	6	0	1	0	1	0	4
Raeren	6	1	0	0	0	0	0	1
Ryedale	10	1	0	0	0	0	1	0
Siegburg	3	1	0	0	0	0	0	1
Staffordshire	1	1	0	0	1	0	0	0

91. Langerwehe stoneware costrel. Pale grey outer surface, cream-white near core and inner surface. Upper body appears painted with a fairly consistent matt chocolate-brown glaze.
92. Langerwehe stoneware mug. Shiny dark brown outer surface glaze, blue-grey core and matt orange-brown inner surface.
93. Langerwehe stoneware mug. Grey glaze on both inner and outer surfaces and pale grey core.
94. Langerwehe stoneware flask. Pale greyish-white core with slightly greyer outer surface.

Small Finds

This group produced the first evidence for metalworking in the cell. Associated with the ceramic finds above was a substantial quantity of copper alloy book mounts and other fittings and a number of pieces of copper scrap were generally spread around the eastern side of the garden. This material should be seen in the same context as scrap material in Finds Groups 11 and 12, both of which date to the last occupation of the cell.

95. Small spatula. Cu. Handle L: 42 mm; diameter: 2.4 mm. The flattened end L: 8 mm; depth: 5 mm. Find no. Cu73.
96. Rod of circular section, bent over at one end. Cu. L: 48.5 mm; diameter: 2.25 m. Find no. Cu86.
97. Cut sheet. Cu. Maximum L: 35 mm; W: 20.5 mm; Th: 0.6 mm. There are two nail holes, 2 mm by 3 mm and 2 mm by 4 mm, and the sheet has been folded over at one end. Find no. Cu64.
98. Cast coin weight. Cu. Diameter: 18 mm; Th: 2.75 mm. Edges slightly bevelled. The weight has been unequally struck with a crown. Weight unrecorded. This object is now missing. Find no. Cu60.

THE ARCHAEOLOGY OF THE GREAT CLOISTER 103

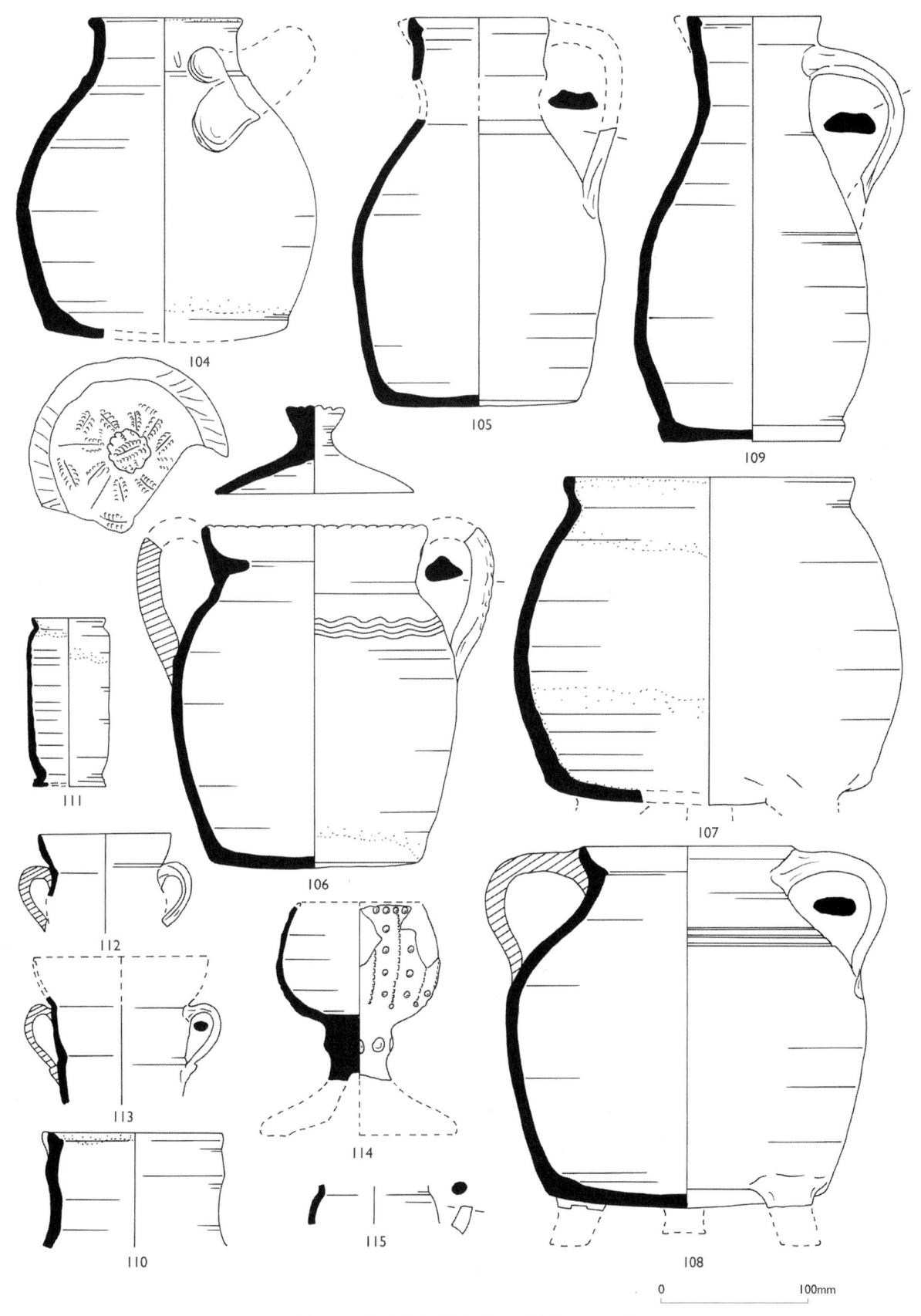

Figure 4.44 Cell 8: Finds Group 11 (pottery 1:4).

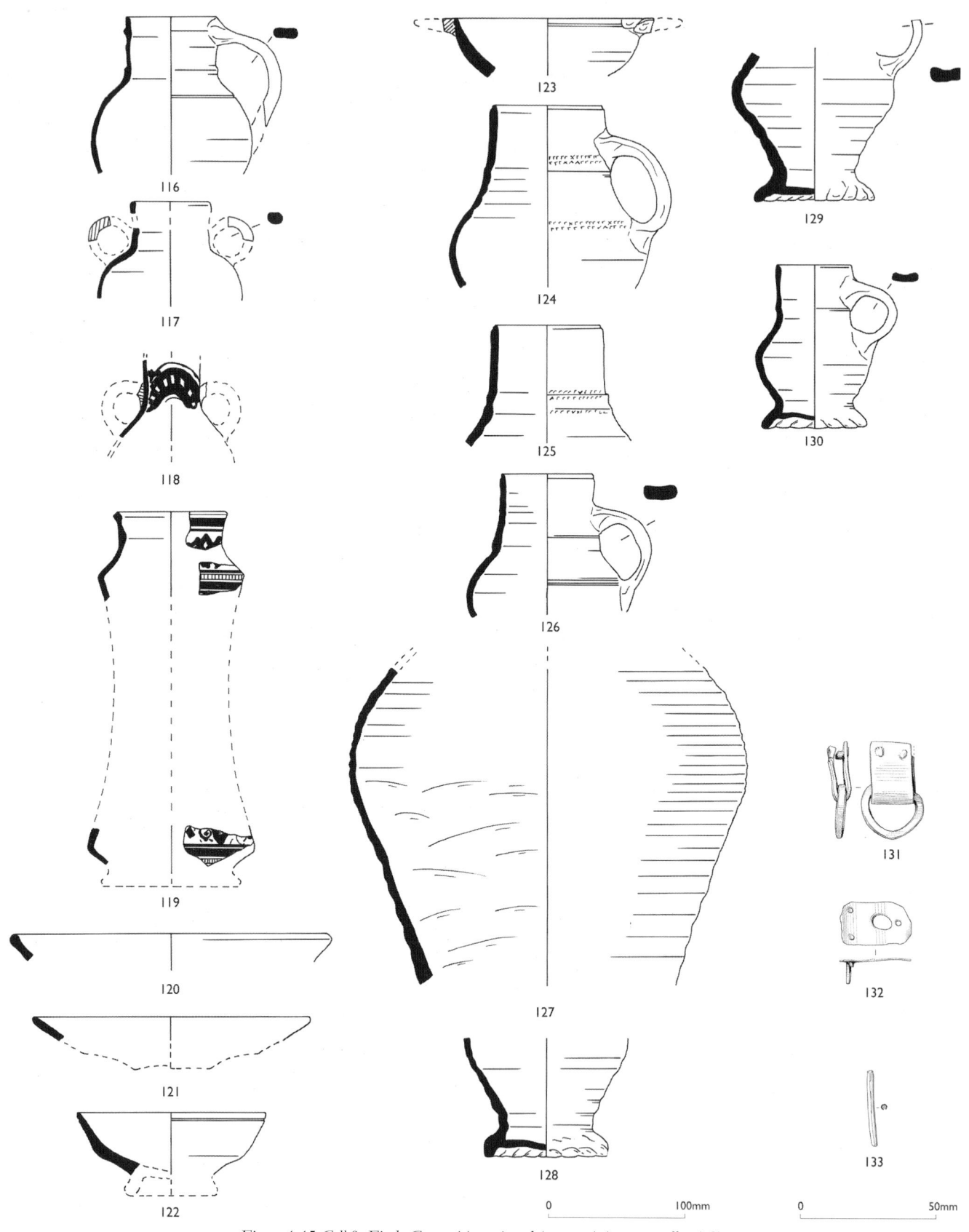

Figure 4.45 Cell 8: Finds Group 11 continued (pottery 1:4, copper alloy 1:2).

THE ARCHAEOLOGY OF THE GREAT CLOISTER

Table 4.12 Cell 8, Finds Group 11: Ceramics

Fabric	Sherds	Vessels							
		Total Vessels	Albarello	Jar	Jug	Mug or cup	Tripod pipkin	Urinal	Other
Beauvais	1	1	0	0	1	0	0	0	0
Cistercian	18	6	0	0	0	5	0	0	1 (chalice)
Columbia Plain	4	3	0	0	0	0	0	0	3 (dish)
Developed Humber	22	1	0	0	0	0	1	0	0
Hambleton	4	2	0	0	1	0	0	1	0
Humber	2	2	0	0	2	0	0	0	0
Langerwehe	46	8	0	0	0	8	0	0	0
Late Gritty	6	1	0	1	0	0	0	0	0
Midlands Yellow	3	1	0	0	0	1	0	0	0
Post-medieval Orange	20	1	0	0	1	0	0	0	0
Post-medieval Sandy	2	1	0	1	0	0	0	0	0
Raeren	11	3	0	0	0	3	0	0	0
Ryedale	53	7	0	0	6	0	1	0	0
Siegburg	12	1	0	0	0	1	0	0	0
South Netherlands maiolica	27	3	1	0	0	0	0	0	2 (vase)
Staffordshire	5	1	0	0	0	0	0	0	1 (drug jar)
Valencia Lustre	1	1	0	0	0	0	0	0	1 (dish)

99. Cast ring. Cu. Diameter (of ring): 29 mm; W (of band): 4 mm. Find no. Cu78.
100. Wire pin from a large buckle. Cu. L: 26 mm; diameter: 3 mm. Find no. Cu67.
101. Book mount. Cu. Slightly domed square sheet, 15 mm by 15 mm; Th: 1.5 mm. V-shape cut-out in each edge to form four roughly shaped leaves. Single central rivet hole diameter: 3 mm. Find no. Cu7.
102. Buckle plate. Cu. Front part only. L: 35 mm; W: 14 mm; Th: 0.8 mm. Find no. Cu49.
103. Buckle plate. Cu. Folded, but back part is missing. L: 24 mm; W 14 mm; Th: 0.8 mm. Two Fe rivets, of which one remains; diameter: 1 mm. Find no. Cu79.

FINDS GROUP 11

This group came from dump contexts [23], [55], [62] and [63] on the surface of Period Three path [65] and adjacent garden soil outside the latrine pentice door and assumed to have been deposited at the Suppression.

Ceramics (see Figures 4.44 and 4.45)

This material represents the most important pottery group recovered from the site. It has already been discussed in print (Roebuck, Coppack and Hurst 1987). However, since its early publication, there has been further analysis of both the site stratigraphy and the pottery itself. Several vessels that were omitted from the earlier report have been identified. It is the apparently intentional dumping of these largely complete vessels during the Suppression, and the possibility that they represent the set of pottery in use in Cell 8 during its last days of monastic occupation, that makes this such an important group. Further, the high number of imports – not so apparent in other cells, where only a small part of the household pottery has been recovered – and the origins of those imports, suggest an unexpectedly cosmopolitan status of at least one 16th-century Carthusian monk (Table 4.12).

The pottery came from dump deposits immediately outside the garden door of the pentice on the east side of Cell 8 and was confined to a spread of no more than 5m². This was an area already disturbed, archaeologically, by Hope's excavations and by the cutting of a drain through the deposit before 1905. Given these incursions, the relative completeness of the surviving vessels suggests that they may have been simply thrown against the cell wall to break them.

104. Hambleton ware urinal. Reddish-orange fabric with olive-green to brown glaze. Internal thick white deposit.
105. Ryedale ware jug. Pale orange outer surface, pale silver-grey core and silver-grey inner surface. Bright, pocked apple-green glaze.
106. Late Gritty ware handled jar and lid. Cream surfaces and pale grey core. Bright, pocked, green glaze, turning a yellow-green where the glaze thins. Crude stamped decoration on lid. A large rim sherd fitting to this vessel was recovered from the south-west cloister range, demonstrating how far a single sherd might travel in exceptional circumstances.
107. Developed Humber ware tripod pipkin. Orange-buff fabric, partly glazed internally.
108. Ryedale ware tripod pipkin. Dull orangish surfaces and pale grey core. Olive-green glaze. Feet, of uncertain length, applied as tubes.
109. Post-medieval Orange ware jug. Soft, micaceous orange fabric with bright brown-green to olive-green glaze.
110. Ryedale ware jug. Blue-grey core with a pale orange-buff inner surface. Very streaky brownish-green glaze taken to the top of the rim.
111. Staffordshire white ware drug jar. Soft off-white fabric with a thin but even pale yellowish-green glaze on rim and shoulder with some pocking to the more thinly glazed areas.
112. Cistercian ware cup.
113. Cistercian ware cup.
114. Cistercian ware chalice. Applied pipeclay decoration, appearing lemon-yellow under the glaze. A hitherto unrecorded form from the Wrenthorpe (near Wakefield in West Yorkshire) kilns.
115. Midlands Yellow ware cup. Soft white fabric with a thin, pale yellow glaze on both surfaces.
116. Beauvais earthenware jug. Fine white fabric with bright yellow glaze.
117. South Netherlands maiolica ware flower vase. White tin glaze on internal surface, external surface covered with cobalt-blue glaze.
118. South Netherlands maiolica ware flower vase.
119. South Netherlands maiolica ware albarello.
120. Valencia Lustre ware tin-glazed dish. The inner surface design is too faint to be recognisable.
121. Seville Columbia Plain earthenware dish with off-white tin glaze.
122. Seville Columbia Plain earthenware bowl.
123. Seville Columbia Plain earthenware dish. Heavily discoloured, but traces of tin-glaze and of one (or two?) applied handle lugs on the rim.
124. Langerwehe stoneware mug, silver-grey outer surface glaze, turning brown in places, pale grey core and chocolate-brown inner surface.
125. Langerwehe stoneware mug. Brown outer surface, grey core and pale purplish-grey inner surface.
126. Langerwehe stoneware mug.
127. Langerwehe stoneware(?) flagon. Silver-grey core with a silver-grey glaze on both surfaces that turns a very pale brown on parts of the outer surface. The lower inner surface is substantially knife-trimmed.
128. Raeren stoneware mug.
129. Raeren stoneware mug.
130. Raeren stoneware mug.

Small Finds (see Figures 4.45)

131. Loop and plate. Cu. D-shaped loop; W: 22 mm; Th: 2 mm. Loop join hidden within folded plate. Plate as folded L: 21 mm; W: 14 mm. Two Fe rivets on short edge. No pin, so suspension loop for satchel or bag. Find no. Cu19.
132. Belt plate(?). Cu. Rectangular and slightly rounded at one end. L: 24 mm; W: 15 mm. Three rivet holes, two at square end, one at rounded end, and a central larger oval hole 6 mm by 4 mm. Single Fe rivet surviving *in situ*, 8 mm long. Find no. Cu18.
133. Lace chape. Cu. Edge-to-edge seam, L: 27 mm; diameter: 2.3 mm. Leather(?) remains inside. Find no. Cu11.

Finds Group 12

The demolition levels of Cell 8, which in part sealed the dump of pottery described above, contained a considerable quantity of both pottery and metalwork derived from the final occupation of the cell. Most of the pottery could be related to that dumped outside the latrine pentice door and has been reunited with those vessels. Again, prominent in this collection are a number of book fittings that came mainly from the area of the latrine pentice.

Ceramics (see Figure 4.46)

This group was taken from contexts [7], [9], [13], [26], [37], [39], [42], [43], [209] and [225] (Table 4.13).

134. Ryedale ware jug. Blue-grey core and pale greyish-white inner surface. Pale apple-green glaze taken to the rim top.
135. Staffordshire white ware drug jar. Grey-buff outer surface, pale orange core with thick, off-white margins and a pale orange-buff inner surface. Band of pale yellowish-green glaze on the rim.

Small Finds (see Figure 4.46)

Material from demolition contexts primarily derives from the final occupation of the cell and indicates that the monk here was in possession of a considerable collection of scrap copper, many pieces deriving from book covers. The latrine pentice produced an enormous quantity of scraps of copper. They consisted of small pieces of sheet metal, short lengths of small diameter rods, tacks, pins, belt plates and strap ends; all clearly debris from salvaged material for book-binding, perhaps ready for melting down. Only identifiable pieces are illustrated.

136. Double-edged knife with whittle tang of square and tapering section. Fe. Overall L: 126 mm; maximum Th: 4 mm; W (of blade): 17 mm; Find no. MG1185.
137. Cramp. Fe. Overall W: 54 mm; overall depth: 17 mm. Square sectioned tails 3 mm by 3 mm. Th (of band): 11 mm. Find no. Fe78.
138. Ox-shoe. Fe. Complete; three rectangular nail holes in each arm. L: 100 mm; W: 22 mm; Th: 8 mm. Post-Suppression(?). Find no. Fe225.
139. Spatula. Cu. Overall L: 126 mm. Square-sectioned shaft 3 mm by 3 mm. Flattened end L: 34 mm; W: 16 mm. Find no. MG1014.
140. Ring. Cu. Overall diameter: 19.5 mm. Band diameter: 2–2.5 mm; Th: 1.5 mm. Find no. Cu94.8.
141. Ring, cast. Cu. Overall diameter: 23 mm. Band diameter: 3.5 mm. Find no. Cu59.
142. Book corner mount. Cu. Short side maximum L: 30 mm; long side maximum L: 57 mm. W: 14 mm. Edge folded over to depth: 7 mm. Two attachment holes diameter: 1.5 mm; each surrounded by two concentric punched circles, outer circle diameter: 6 mm. Find no. Cu56.
143. Book mount. Cu. Four roughly cut leaves with straight edges between V-cuts, decorated with medial incised lines. Overall 15 mm by 15 mm; Th: 1 mm. Central hole slightly elongated. Find no. MG944.
144. Book clasp. Cu. L: 34 mm; W: 10 mm; Th: 1 mm. One end with hook W: 4 mm, the other end splayed end and two ends cut. Main part is decorated with two depressed circles around central hole. Find no. Cu40.
145. Book clasp. Fe coated with Cu. Overall L: 40 mm long and W: 8 mm. Hook at one end W: 2 mm. Opposite end forked; W: 14 mm. Each fork with rivet hole and central V-cut at edge. Flush rivet top two-third along plate towards loop. Very little of the Cu coating survives. Find no. MG944.
146. Mount. Cu. L: 24 mm; W: 8 mm; Th: 0.5 mm. Pointed at one end with two rivet holes of diameter: 2 mm. Find no. Cu3.
147. Mount. Cu. L: 23 mm; W: 7 mm; Th: 0.5 mm. Pointed at one end with two rivet holes of diameter: 2 mm and 1 mm. Find no. MG1200.4.
148. Satchel loop and plate. Cu. Overall L: 58 mm. Oval loop L: 28 mm; W: 18 mm. Plate W: 22 mm, with a semicircular indent on each side. Three rivet holes of diameter: 2 mm through very thin plate. Width between plates is 3 mm. Circular bar diameter: 4 mm. Find no. MG947.1.
149. Strap end. Cu. L: 32 mm; W: 17 mm (maximum); Th: 2 mm. Front plate is slightly tapered, with serrated edge at top and awkwardly cut end. Back plate is much smaller. Two rivet holes near top and single central one near bottom. Find no. MG1162.
150. Belt plate. Cu. L: 36 mm; W: 23 mm; Th: 0.5 mm. Four small holes for rivets at each corner, diameter: 1.5 mm. One

108   MOUNT GRACE PRIORY

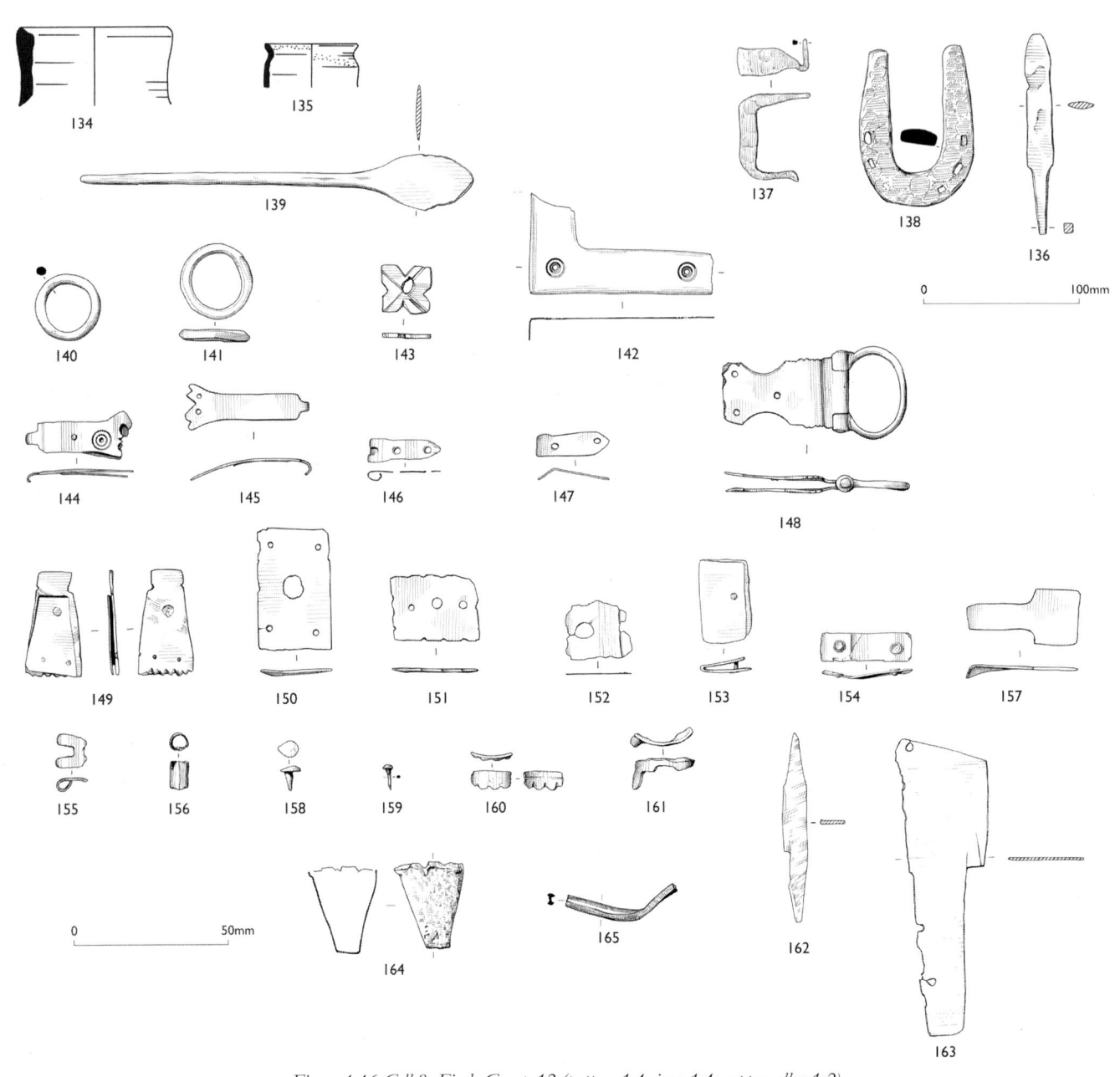

Figure 4.46 Cell 8: Finds Group 12 (pottery 1:4; iron 1:4; copper alloy 1:2).

Table 4.13 Cell 8, Finds Group 12: Ceramics

Fabric	Sherds	Vessels			
		Total vessels	Drug jar	Jug	Mug or cup
Cistercian	2	2	0	0	2
Cistercian copy	1	1	0	0	1
Ryedale	2	2	0	2	0
Staffordshire	1	1	1	0	0

larger central hole diameter: 7 mm. Find no. MG1200.1.

151. Belt plate. Cu. L: 27 mm; W: 20 mm; Th: 0.5 mm. Slightly scalloped edges. Two holes for rivets, diameter: 2 mm. Another, central, hole diameter: 3 mm. Find no. MG947.

152. Belt plate. Cu. Maximum L: 22 mm; W: 18 mm; Th: 1 mm. Central hole, diameter: 5 mm with a second, (?)rivet hole, diameter: 3 mm on one edge. Find no. Cu26.

153. Strap end. Cu. L: 25 mm; W: 15 mm; Th: 0.5 mm. Metal bent over with one Cu rivet. Find no. MG1200.10.
154. Mount. Cu. L: 29 mm; W: 9 mm; Th: 0.75 mm. Two rivet holes, diameter: 2 mm. Find no. Cu28.
155. Mount. Cu. Possibly the hinge end of a book clasp. L: 10 mm; W: 11 mm; Th: 0.75 mm. Find no. Cu29.
156. Tube. Cu. L: 8 mm; diameter: 6 mm; Th: 0.5 mm. Metal does not quite meet at seam. Could be cut from pen. Find no. MG1200.5.
157. Mount. Cu. Square-ended 13 mm by 17 mm, with narrower extension W: 8 mm; Th: 0.5 mm. Overall L: 37 mm. No rivets or attachments. Find no. MG1200.2.
158. Binding tack. Cu. L 8 mm. Slightly domed head, originally 4.5 mm in diameter. Find no. MG1011.
159. Binding tack. Cu. L: 8 mm. Slightly domed head, 4 mm in diameter. Find no. MG1200.83.
160. Top chape of a knife scabbard. Cu. Original diameter: 25–30 mm; L: 6 mm. The lower edge has been cut and filed to produce a carefully scalloped edge. Find no. Cu34.
161. Casting gate. Cu. W: 20 mm; H: 9 mm. Cut from a circular or segmental casting, with a single riser remaining. Find no. Cu35.
162. Scrap sheet. Cu. Overall L: 59 mm. Cut marks indicate the metal was being reused. Find no. Cu36.
163. Scrap sheet. Cu. Overall L: 93 mm. Originally part of plate with rivet holes. Cut marks indicate that metal was being reused. Find no. MG10112.
164. Paint/inkwell. Pb. Average diameter: 36 mm, tapering to 15 mm at base; H: 55 mm; Th: 3 mm. Formed of one piece of moulded lead. Top rim is very damaged. Bottom of inside and at least halfway up one side is covered with a thin layer of red pigment. Find no. MG1167.
165. Window came. Pb. L: 40 mm; W: 4.5 mm, with a glazing channel 2 mm wide. Find no. MG1152.

Post-Suppression Features of Cell 8
(see Figure 4.47)
Apart from the obvious post-Suppression and above-ground robbing of the cell there was no obvious disturbance of the site until the end of the 19th century, when a certain amount of clearance was carried out, presumably by Hope. The only exception to this was the building of a rubble wall [247] to retain a raised path around the cloister garth. This wall was uncovered in 1900 by Hope, who mistook it for a medieval wall and recorded it as such on his site plan (Hope 1905). No evidence of actual date was found for this wall, though it did seal 16th-century robbing of the medieval cloister arcade. In the light of work elsewhere on site it is most probably a 17th-century feature associated with a garden of that date in the retained area of the great cloister.

Within the garden of Cell 8 the demolition spreads of roof slate over the latrine pentice were found to have been truncated by levelling, which had revealed the surviving course of the pentice wall in places. This levelling appears to have been done by Hope because it pre-dated a trial hole, [59], cut by him to examine the area below the tap niche. Two further 'trenches', [260] and [233], in the cloister alley also appear to belong to Hope's campaign and indicate that he was searching, without success, for the course of the water pipe that supplied the cell. Following Hope's work in 1896, the next phase of disturbance is that associated with Sir Lowthian Bell's

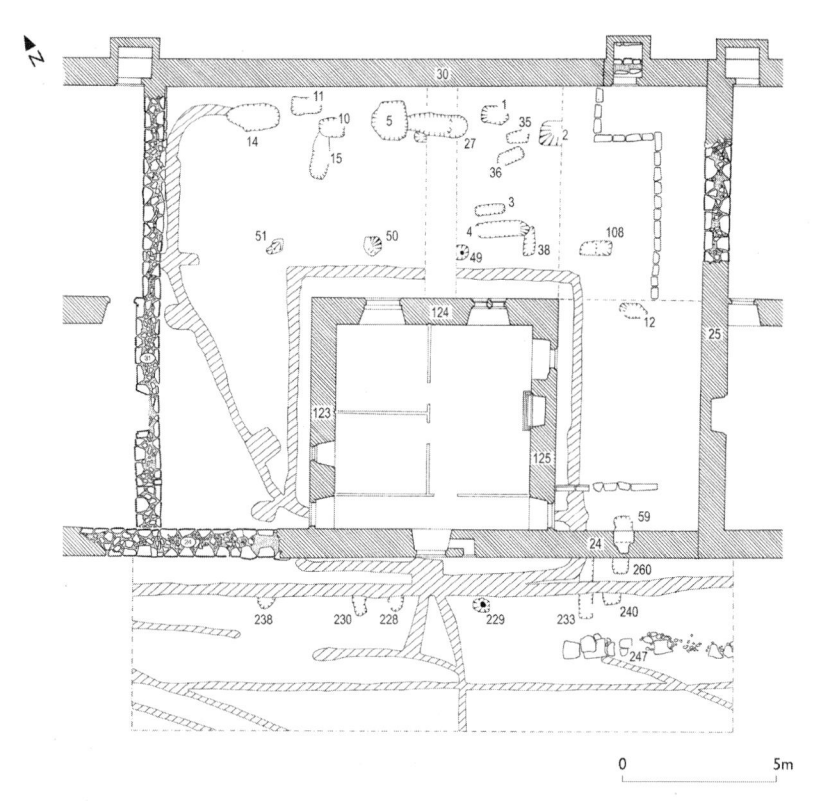

Figure 4.47 Cell 8: post-Suppression features.

reconstruction of the cell between 1900 and 1905. From Hope's published photograph of the north cloister range (Hope 1905, pl. I) it is clear that Bell demolished the standing remains of wall [31] on the west side of the garden and the section of cloister wall [24] to the west of the cell. This last section of wall [24] was taken down to provide access to the cell garden and its lowest courses were sealed by a surface, [202a] (not illustrated), of small sandstone chips, mortar and tile fragments.

Inside the garden to the west of the cell, this surface of sandstone chips, some 2.1 m wide, continued as a spread of cinders, [17]. The purpose of this track was to provide access for the masons engaged in rebuilding the cell. Two rows of postholes, to north and south, which had held the scaffolding during the rebuilding of the cell were found. The northern row comprised four postholes, [38], [49], [50] and [51], one of which, [49], retained the pipe of a post 0.1 m in diameter. The southern row also comprised four postholes, [238], [230], [228] and [229], and may have had a fifth setting, which did not survive, to the east. Posthole [229] retained the pipe of a post 0.2 m in diameter. The interior of the cell itself was then excavated to the top of the clay terrace, removing any evidence for its floors and partitions to create a void below a new timber floor.

The remaining features all dated between the reconstruction of the cell and about 1939, and comprised 14 rectangular or sub-rectangular rubbish pits, [1–5], [10], [11], [12], [14], [15], [27], [35], [36] and [108], associated with the catering for the Mount Grace Pageant, which was held over three days in September 1927.

ARCHITECTURAL DETAIL FROM THE DEMOLITION CONTEXTS (SEE FIGURE 4.48)

These finds were found in the latrine pentice of Cell 8 [37] and demolition contexts [206] and [209] in the cloister alley outside Cell 8.

1–3. Fragment of chimney cap (1) with a castellated moulding and two sections of shaft (2 and 3) from an octagonal chimney (each face: 190 mm). The flue is circular in plan and has been dressed with a punch. Externally, the chimney is finely bolster dressed. An assembly mark in the form of a plain St Andrew's cross remains on the lower bed of the upper

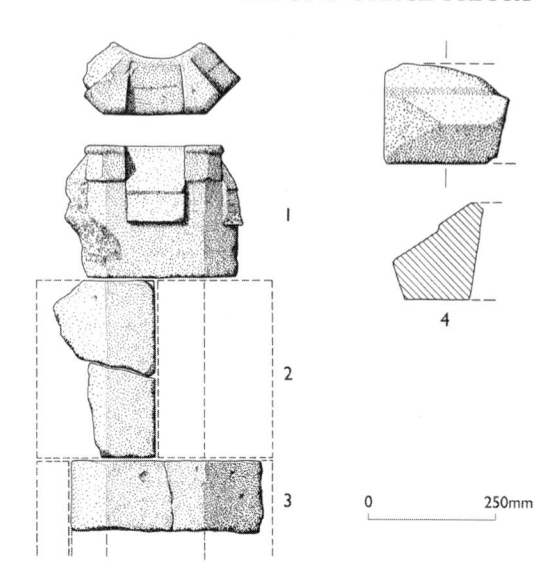

Figure 4.48 Cell 8: architectural detail from demolition deposits (1:10).

section (2) of shaft. From its location in the latrine pentice [37] of Cell 8 it had clearly fallen from Cell 7.

4. Weathering from the capping of a small buttress, perhaps from the north cloister alley. In all, four identical pieces were recovered, one from [206] and three from [209], both post-Suppression contexts in the cloister alley.

Cell 9 (see Figure 4.49)
Conditions before Excavation
Cell 9 was excavated in two seasons. The first, in September 1969, attempted to uncover the cell itself and to give some indication of the garden and garden pentices. The second, in July 1974, revealed the whole of the garden.

The cell had been partially cleared before the 1969 excavation took place, possibly by Hope in 1896. Both the doorway to the garden pentice and that to the latrine pentice were visible but their cills were not exposed. The doorway onto the cloister had been cleared to cill level and the recess to the fireplace was visible. The cell walls were standing about 0.50 m high above very waterlogged turf. Whilst the outline of the cell was apparent, the wall dividing the gardens of Cells 8 and 9 was not visible.

The waterlogged state of the ground prevented the total examination of the cell and the incomplete excavation was abandoned after several heavy falls of snow. The interpretation of the layers that were excavated was made particularly difficult because of this early

THE ARCHAEOLOGY OF THE GREAT CLOISTER

discontinuation due to the wet condition and also by the partial removal of deposits in the late 19th century. Because excavation was left incomplete, no plan was made of the interior of the cell and consequently none of the features described below are shown on Figure 4.49.

Cell Interior

Beneath the turf, a layer of dark yellow clay containing charcoal, modern glass, pottery and blocks of stone was revealed. East of the footings of the cell's central north–south internal partition the layer contained more sand, and to the west there were patches of light clay. Below this dark yellow clay layer was a layer of yellow-grey clay containing charcoal flecks, which extended over the whole of the cell except for the south-east corner. In that corner, patches of dark soil with flecks of white mortar were found beneath the upper clay layer, containing masonry blocks and modern material. The blocks and modern material overlay an area of pink mortar that extended over the internal east–west partition footings into the living room, where it was covered by the yellow-grey clay with charcoal flecks.

The same type of pink mortar was located in the vicinity of the cloister doorway, where again it was covered by patches of yellow-grey clay with charcoal flecks. The east–west partition footings were almost complete. Most of the stones had a flat face on the south, though in some cases the flat face was to the north. These footings were set into a yellow-grey clay, containing charcoal flecks, of exactly the same character and consistency as that which covered the pink mortar in the cloister doorway and the mortar extending into the living room. Since one of these clay deposits was earlier than the partition footings and the other later than the mortar that sealed the partition footings, it is impossible that these two deposits were the same. However, no junction line or intervening level was located. Adverse conditions prevented further excavation and subsequent elucidation of these layers.

The two areas of pink mortar suggest that the east–west passage to the north of the cloister doorway, as well as the rest of the cell, had mortar floors. Where the mortar extended over the partition footings in the south-east corner, it would appear that the floor had been laid before the timber partition had been constructed or reconstructed. Pink mortar suggests a repair of Period Three.

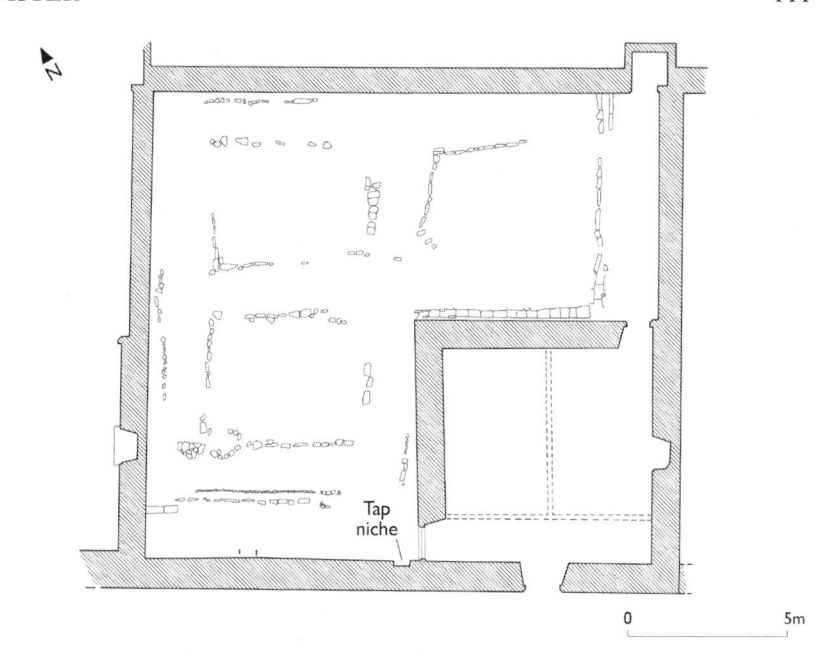

Figure 4.49 Cell 9.

South (Cloister) Wall

The cloister door was 1.90 m high above the floor with the lintel about 0.40 m above the top of the arch. The threshold of the door was about 0.12 m high; the door had its hinges on the east side. The hatch was on the east side of the doorway; it measured 0.37 m wide and 0.33 m high internally, and 0.37 m wide and 0.34 m high externally. The hatch had a rebate 80 mm wide and 70 mm deep at the cloister end of the turn.

Evidence for the staircase in the south-east corner of the cell existed only in the east wall (see below).

North and West Walls

The north and west walls of the cell had been demolished to within two courses of the approximate level of the floor, leaving the doorways to the garden and latrine pentices as the main surviving architectural detail. In the north wall, however, two square rebates were recorded, one more or less in line with the north–south partition. The bottom of the upper rebate, which measured 90 mm^2, was 0.35 m above floor level; the lower rebate was about 0.3 m below the top of the first and about 0.36 m to the east. This slot measured 0.1 m wide and 0.15 m high. These rebates were probably associated with partition construction and may indicate two structural phases.

Also in the north wall, 11 small circular holes were found. These were approximately 25 mm in diameter and 60 mm deep, the minimum distance between them was about 0.2 m and the greatest distance 0.3 m. They were arranged along the wall in two pendant curves with the lowest point about 0.5 m above floor level. It is possible that these served as peg holes to secure wainscoting.

East Wall
A number of structural features were associated with the east wall, which had been demolished to within three courses above floor level. A rebate extending 0.56 m above the ground, 35 mm deep and 90 mm wide had its north edge 1.63 m north of the inner face of the south wall, against which the east wall abutted. The rebate was not in line with the main east–west partition, but fell further north of it. Its purpose, without the excavation on the floor, was not possible to determine.

Evidence for the staircase in this wall consisted of the chasing for one tread, cut 30 mm into the wall, and indicating a tread 50 mm thick, 0.3 m deep; and one riser, similarly cut 30 mm into the wall and indicating a riser 50 mm thick, height unknown (the wall did not survive high enough). The fireplace in the east wall was at least 1.15 m wide, with a square rebate on the south.

Garden Pentice
Beneath the turf was a layer of brown-black clay containing flecks of mortar, sandstone fragments and blocks of worked stone. A spread of mortar within it was possibly the result of the repointing of the cloister wall shortly before excavations began in 1974. In the area of the doorway and on the level of the top of the door cill this layer sealed a patch of pink mortar. Elsewhere it lay over a yellow-grey clay, probably the same as that within the cell, at the same level as the mortar.

The layer of yellow-grey clay sealed the remains of a rough eavesdrip drain that lay north of the line of the pentice wall. The south edge of the drain was defined by a line of sloping slabs and its north edge by an irregular line of cobbles. The bottom of the drain was indicated by stone slabs and it was approximately 0.1 m deep. The yellow-grey clay also covered the two surviving stones as the west end of the pentice wall footing. The bottoms of these two large rectangular stones, 0.25 m high, were level with the top of the drain sides. Both these stones lay on a thin layer of white mortar.

The eavesdrip drain was constructed on a layer of yellow-grey clay containing sandstone fragments. Along most of the length of the garden pentice it was impossible to distinguish this layer from the clay above it. In the area of the garden doorway a difference was noticeable: the lower clay layer was paler and underlaid the door cill. The difference between the two layers was also apparent at the west end of the pentice. Here, the layer beneath the surviving stones of the pentice footings was slightly darker and underlaid the white mortar bedding for the footings.

The cloister wall of the garden pentice survived to a height of 12 courses on the inside and 15 courses plus coping on the outside, but neither the west wall of Cell 9 nor the east wall of Cell 10 survived sufficiently high to determine the structure of the pentice at a higher level.

The tap niche was situated immediately outside the garden door of the cell, with the bottom of the recess level with the pentice floor; no trace of a drain from this survived. A scar of a north–south wall 0.54 m wide was apparent on the inside of the cloister wall, 5.06 m from the west end of the pentice. The wall that was meant to fit here was never begun, just a toothing provided and then cut back to the wall face. Associated with this was a slot 0.25 m wide and 0.33 m high. It was situated 0.2 m to the east of the wall scar and 2 m above the floor. No indication of the wall or its function was found in the excavation of the pentice, but the scar probably marks an abandoned setting out of the original dividing wall between Cells 9 and 10.

Latrine Pentice
Along the line of the wall dividing Cells 8 and 9, immediately below the turf line, was a brown sandy soil containing small lenses of yellow sand and fragments of sandstone. To the west of the wall, in the area of the latrine pentice, the soil immediately below the turf contained more clay. This layer sealed a layer, 0.28 m thick, of orange-yellow clay containing sandstone fragments. In turn this layer overlay a layer of broken masonry, which was particularly concentrated in the area immediately south of the latrine. A number of stone fragments lay flat on the top of a layer of grey-brown clay and others protruded from it at random angles. Slightly further south along the pentice this underlying grey-brown clay appeared to

be more mixed, with patches of yellow clay, rubble, slag and some plain glazed floor tiles, suggesting this pentice had a tiled floor.

The eavesdrip drain of the pentice was cut into the layer of grey-brown clay. At its north end it had been filled with moist silver-grey clay and small stones. This drain was 0.25 m deep, had stone sides and was originally paved with flat stones. Five of the side stones had been burnt. Along most of its north–south length this drain had been reused by a ceramic field drain of the first half of the 20th century, which cut through the bottom. Approximately 1.25 m south of the north precinct wall this later drainpipe had cut through the side of the eavesdrip drain and been led west into the garden. No trace of pentice wall footings were found. The flat stone slabs lying immediately south of the latrine may have been remnants of a paved floor. Those lying at all angles, however, seem more likely to represent the collapse of the pentice roof.

The precinct wall along the north edge of the cell survives to its full height of 4 m, comprising 12 courses with two courses of coping. The square-headed doorway into the latrine is preserved in the wall. The sides and top of the doorway are rebated to the south for a wooden door. The beam hole for the wall plate of the latrine pentice survives to the west of the doorway and is about 0.19 m², and 1.55 m above the pentice floor. The mortar scar of the weathering runs from above this slot diagonally above the door to the top of the garden wall. The latrine doorway is 1.48 m high above the threshold. The cill was about 0.15 m higher than the paving. The doorway has an internal width of 0.75 m and there is a rebate for the seat about 0.50 m above the floor. The rebate is about 90 mm high and the clearance in the latrine was about 2 m.

The dividing wall between Cells 8 and 9 survived to only one course in height, except at the northern end where for the last 2 m it had retained two courses. It was rebuilt to full height in 1990.

Garden
The topsoil was a dark brown clay, approximately 0.1 m thick, containing small fragments of sandstone. This layer sealed an orange-yellow clay approximately 0.3 m thick, very similar to the layer below the topsoil in both the garden and latrine pentices. The clay was slightly greyer in colour in the south and west parts of the garden. A number of pieces of window tracery appeared in this layer; their size and form suggested that they came from the Period Two cloister arcade and were dumped here at the Suppression (see Chapter 6).

The orange-yellow clay layer covered a series of features outlined by stone settings (see Figure 4.50). These features themselves were set on a layer of grey clay, which was consistent over the whole area of the garden. Three of the features were approximately square; one lay to the north of the cell and west of the latrine pentice, a second in the north-west corner of the garden, and the third lay immediately to the north of the garden pentice. In the south-east corner of this last one was a small hollow about 1 m in diameter and 0.2 m deep, with a stone lining and a circular arrangement of stones.

The stones surrounding all these features were either regular shaped pieces of stone or cobbles. In addition there were three remnants of linear stone settings, one to the east of the garden wall, one to the west of the west wall of the cell and the third immediately inside the north precinct wall. Along the north wall of the cell was a drain, cut into the same grey clay layer in which the garden features were set. The drain had upright stone sides 0.17–0.18 m high and a paved bottom. It connected with the drain running along the edge of the latrine pentice and, like that drain, had been reused by the 20th-century field drain.

It seems probable that the features outlined by the stone settings were garden plots and the isolated linear settings the edges of garden paths. The small hollow and the circular feature associated with the southernmost square bed may have been settings for shrubs or bushes.

Figure 4.50 Cell 9: the garden as excavated, looking north (L. J. Keen).

Finds Group 13

CERAMICS (SEE FIGURE 4.51)

The pottery assemblages of Cells 9–15 differ from those of Cells 2–7 in several respects. Principal of these is that, although the pottery groups from Cells 9–15 are treated as single phase groups from the final phase (Period Four) of occupation, with some residual material, it derives from the careful excavation of parts of the cells and their gardens by Keen. All fragments were kept and it is therefore probably no coincidence that these cells are represented by a comparatively higher proportion of finer tablewares.

In comparison, only one sherd of maiolica was retained in the assemblages of Cells 2–7, such tin-glazed sherds perhaps having been dismissed and discarded as modern intrusions. So although the Cells 9–15 groups are not substantially bigger than those of Cells 2–7, they derive from a more restricted part of the cells and their gardens and, given their careful retrieval, their contents are more likely to be representative of the original cell contents.

To this extent, the Cell 9 group sets the pattern, with the remains of few, if any, larger jugs or other vessels (Table 4.14). Most sherds represent either tablewares or more modest sized jugs or jars. There are examples of urinals, pancheons and cisterns.

166. Hambleton ware jug. Cream core turning a blue-grey in thicker parts, with a pale yellowish-cream inner surface. Hard fabric with a smooth, but lumpy, surface covered with a bright, mottled yellow to copper-green glaze with some areas of surface pocking.
167. Ryedale ware jug. Dull orange-red core and grey-brown inner surface. Bright greenish-black glaze over outer surface and inner face of rim and neck. Glaze thins in places to a very dark olive-green. Handle smoothed on with no back fillet to the lower attachment.
168. Ryedale ware cistern. Grey-black core and pale grey inner surface. Outer surface covered with a partly corroded olive-green glaze. Applied and thumbed neck cordon, the thumbings decoratively stamped.
169. Ryedale ware jug. Pale grey core and pale cream-grey inner surface. Bright olive-green glaze badly corroded and fritted by the lip.
170. Regional Stray ware, lamp bowl(?). Very fine off-white fabric. Badly corroded green to yellow-green glaze on both surfaces. Outer surface glaze reminiscent of Saintonge ware.
171. Post-medieval Orange ware urinal. Very soft orange fabric reducing to a pale bluish-grey in the thicker parts of the core. Outer surface has a pale purplish skin with a grey (partly glazed) inner surface. Traces of a thin, watery olive glaze on inner surface. Much of the glaze and the vessel surfaces have worn away.
172–174. Staffordshire white ware drug jar rims. Whitish-buff fabric, pale yellowish green glazes.
175. Staffordshire white ware drug jar base. Fabric as above.
176. Cistercian ware copy posset pot lid. Grey core and dull purplish inner surface. Dark greenish-brown glaze over pipeclay decoration.
177. Reversed Cistercian ware cup. Off-white, near stoneware fabric with a pale, watery-greenish glaze. Outer surface decorated with applied 'petals' of iron rich clay appearing a dark greenish-brown under glaze.
178. Langerwehe stoneware mug. Matt, dull purplish outer surface with dull olive blotches. Very pale grey core. The inner surface has a very bright, lustrous, silver-grey glaze turning a semi-translucent olive wherever it thickens.
179. Langerwehe stoneware mug. Silver-grey to matt purplish outer surface, very pale grey core with a glossy silver-grey internal glaze.
180. South Netherlands maiolica ware flower vase. Soft creamy-yellow fabric, thin, white, heavily crazed glaze on the inner surface. Thicker (bluish) white glaze to outer surface over a cobalt-blue painted design.

SMALL FINDS (SEE FIGURE 4.51)

The small finds from Cell 9 were a mixed collection of devotional, personal and structural items that were reasonably typical of all the cells of the great cloister. Their sparse numbers indicate how thoroughly this cell was stripped, for all apart from the statue base 181 could be chance losses. Whatever the trade that the monk in this cell practised, it untypically

THE ARCHAEOLOGY OF THE GREAT CLOISTER

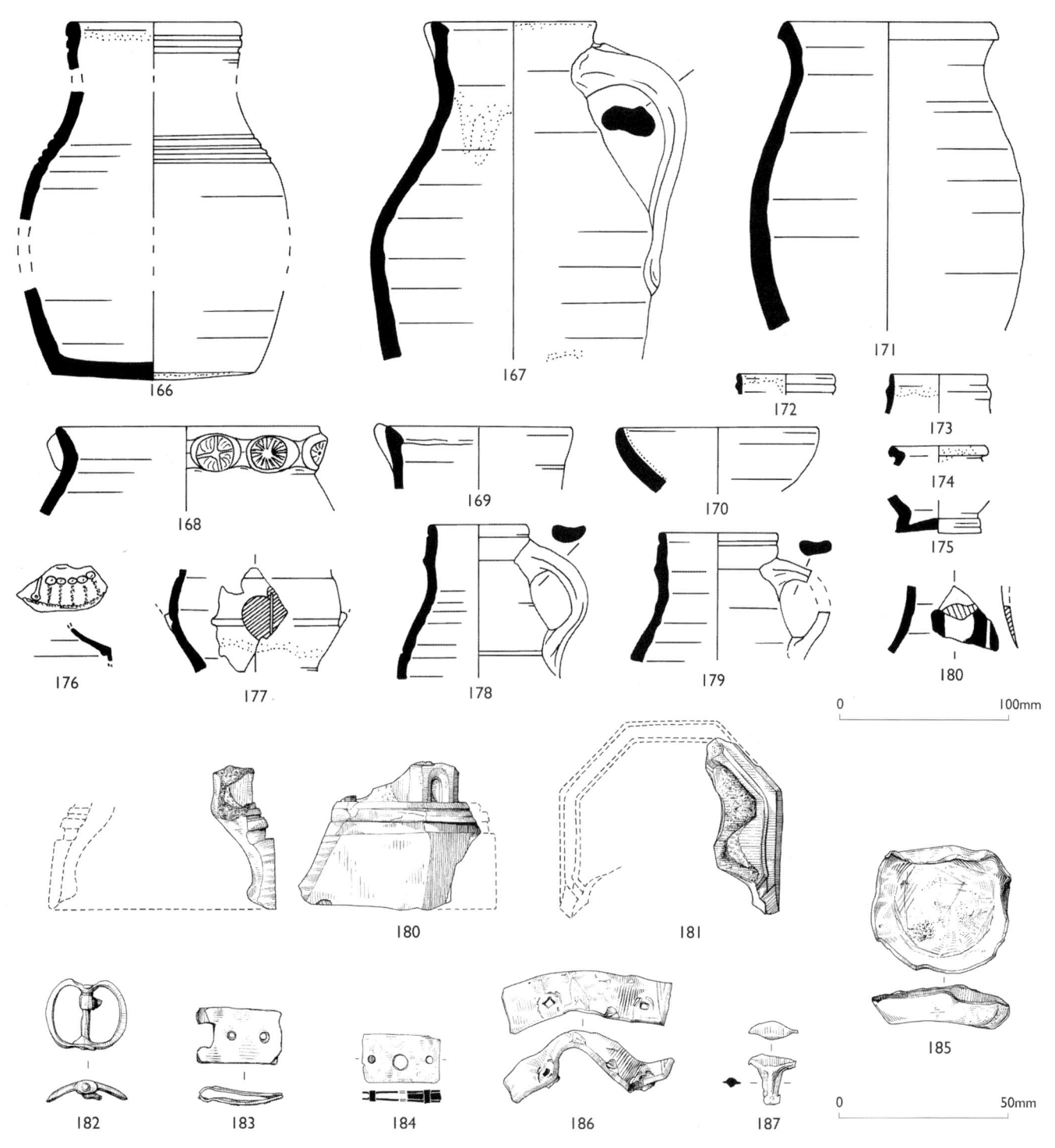

left no trace in the cultural collection. The statue is one of the few overtly spiritual objects recovered from any of the monks' cells.

181. Statue base, ceramic, white pipeclay. Octagonal, side: 54 mm and 70 mm with a plain, almost vertical base, H: 42 mm below a double-beak moulded plinth, H: 20 mm. Above the moulding, two faces, side: 32 mm and 48 mm. The narrower faces have deeply incised round-headed niches, H: 14 mm; W: 7 mm, with a bold external chamfer, W: 3.5 mm. The broader faces have the steeply sloping bases of much wider recesses, W: 30 mm; the most complete with a rounded back, the other piercing the wall. Neither has an external chamfer.

Figure 4.51 Cell 9: Finds Group 13 (pottery 1:4, pipe clay 1:2; copper alloy 1:2; lead 1:2).

Table 4.14 Cell 9, Finds Group 13: Ceramics

Fabric	Sherds	Vessels							
		Total vessels	Cistern	Jar	Jug	Mug or cup	Pancheon	Urinal	Other
Cistercian	7	7	0	0	0	5	0	0	2
Cistercian copy	2	2	0	0	0	1	0	0	1
Developed Humber	1	1	0	0	0	0	0	0	1
Hambleton	24	11	0	1	7	0	1	2	0
Humber	1	1	0	0	0	1	0	0	0
Langerwehe	4	4	0	0	0	4	0	0	0
Late Gritty	1	1	0	0	0	0	1	0	0
Post-medieval Orange	9	2	0	0	0	0	0	1	1
Raeren	1	1	0	0	0	1	0	0	0
Regional Stray	1	1	0	0	0	0	0	0	1
Reversed Cistercian	4	1	0	0	0	1	0	0	0
Ryedale	30	14	1	0	12	0	0	0	1
Siegburg	9	3	0	0	0	3	0	0	0
South Netherlands maiolica	2	1	0	0	0	0	0	0	1
Staffordshire	5	4	0	0	0	0	0	0	4
Tudor Green	3	1	0	0	0	0	0	0	1

The upper, round-headed niches may represent part of a castle, in which case the statue was probably of St Barbara, for whom the Carthusians had a particular devotion. Find no. MG11155.

182. Buckle, Cu. Double, independent, oval frames, with central Fe bar and pin. Overall W: 24 mm; H: 19 mm (maximum). Bar is L: 18 mm; diameter: 1.5 mm. Find no. MG33.
183. Buckle plate. Cu. Folded. L: 24 mm; W: 15 mm. Two rivet holes, diameter: 2.5 mm. Bar and pin missing. Find no. MG942.
184. Belt plates. Cu. L: 22 mm; W: 13 mm. Two identical plates with central hole, diameter: 3.5 mm, held together by two Cu rivets L: 4 mm; diameter: 1.5 mm. Small piece of leather survives between the plates. Find no. MG84.
185. Dish or pan. Pb. Maximum diameter: 44 mm; H: 15 mm; Th: 2 mm. Base is slightly convex. Bottom of inside has a number of scratched lines. May have been for holding a candle. Find no. MG1118.
186. Pipe clip. Pb. Approximate L: 120 mm; W: 26 mm; Th: 3 mm. Two rectangular holes. Find no. MG934.
187. Casting run. Pb. Top L: 27 mm; W: 9 mm. H: 14 mm. Find no. MG969.

Cell 10 (see Figure 4.52)

Conditions before Excavation
Very little of the cell itself was visible before the excavation, except a few stones of its north and west walls. The cloister door was partially blocked, but the blocking could only be seen from the cloister. A tree stump stood in the south-east corner of the cell plot, immediately to the south of the cell, in overburden up to 1 m deep.

Cell Interior
The first layer below the turf was a layer of fine black soil, containing rounded pebbles, fragments of worked stone, charcoal, tile, modern pottery, wood and mortar. The mortar content of this layer, which covered the interior of the cell, increased towards the south. Below it was a layer of loose stone and masonry in dark brown earth and mortar. The masonry consisted of dressed stone and fragments of chimney. This second layer was thinner at the centre of the cell and went right up to the cloister door blocking.

THE ARCHAEOLOGY OF THE GREAT CLOISTER

In the area of the doorway onto the garden pentice a small spread of dark grey earth underlay the rubble layer. Elsewhere, the rubble covered a layer of compact dark earth containing sandstone fragments. Large quantities of burnt wood of varying sizes, some round in section, others evidently fragments of cut timber, were found throughout this third layer. This layer sealed the stones of the north–south partition footing, which rested on a very similar layer of dark earth and charcoal, but without the overlying rubble of the higher layer.

Within this third layer a number of distinctive features [1]–[12], probably joist slots, filled with mortary soil, were cut into the underlying natural shale (see Figure 4.53). Features [1] and [2] ran north–south from the south-west corner of the cell and features [3]–[9] ran east–west from the east wall as far as the north–south partition footing. Three fragmentary but identical slots, [10]–[12], were recorded to the west of the north–south partition line.

Two stones of the east–west partition footing were revealed almost parallel to the south wall of the cell and about 1.20 m to the north of it. Between this setting and the cloister door was an area of paving into which a narrow gulley, 50 mm wide and 5 mm deep, had been cut. The remains of a second east–west partition footing, cut into natural rock, were revealed immediately to the north of features [1] and [2]. This footing did not align with the other east–west footing.

Cell Walls

Cell 10 was different from the others investigated. The most obvious difference was that it had a first-floor window overlooking the cloister. This had an interior splay of 1.20 m. The east edge was right up against the interior of the east wall and its most extant features were a groove for glass and square holes for glazing bars.

The ground plan of the cell was also different from that of the other cells. West of the north–south partition footing the house was divided into two parts: to the north a good-sized room and to the south a smaller area, from which a doorway led onto the garden pentice, suggesting it formed a wide passageway.

South (Cloister) Wall

The south wall survived to 15 courses, 4.5 m high, internally. Its east end constituted the cloister wall and its west extended beyond the line of the cloister into the cell grounds.

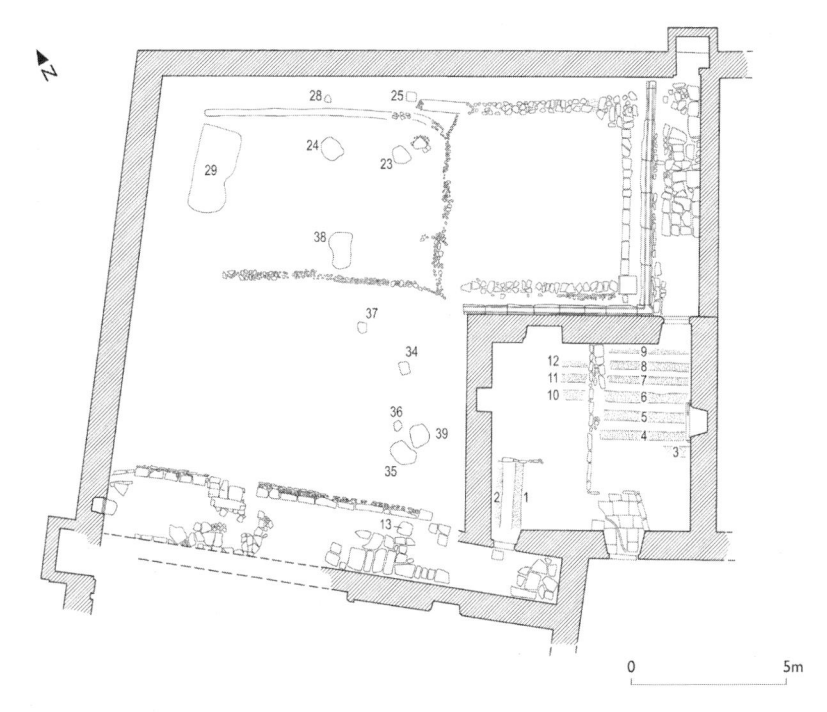

Figure 4.52 Cell 10.

Figure 4.53 Cell 10: as excavated, from the north-west (L. J. Barfoot).

Evidence of the staircase, which was situated in the south-east corner of the cell, was apparent in both the east and south walls. In the east wall were the chasings for a tread, cut 30 mm into the wall, indicating a tread 0.3 m deep and 60 mm thick; a riser cut 20 mm into the wall, indicating a riser 0.25 m high, 40 mm thick; and a second tread 0.3 m deep, 60 mm thick. In the south wall were the chasings for a tread beginning 1 m above ground level, 0.47 m deep and 70 mm thick; a riser 0.28 m high, 50 mm

Figure 4.54 Cell 10: the garden pentice as excavated, seen from the east, with the cill of the garden door and bridge over the eavesdrip gulley below the far scale pole (L. J. Barfoot).

thick; a second tread 0.38 m deep, 50 mm thick; a second riser 0.31 m high, 40 mm thick; and a third tread 0.38 m deep, 50 mm thick.

Further west along the south wall was the cloister door, 1.90 m high from the paving. The bottom of the internal lintel was about 0.22 m above the point of the arch. Within the door splay was the hatch through to the cloister, 0.34 m² internally and 0.36 m by 0.33 m externally, with a square rebate (80 mm wide and 70 mm deep) on the outside. The hatch was 0.77 m above the paving.

Approximately 0.6 m above the door lintel was a joist hole, 0.3 m². A second joist hole, 0.5 m high and between 0.35 m to 0.38 m wide, was apparent to the west of the first one. These presumably were for supports for the upper floor of the building.

Approximately 1 m west of the junction with the cloister wall was the doorway to the garden pentice.

East Wall

The east wall of the cell retained three courses and was 1 m high. East of the north–south partition footing was a large room with a fireplace, 0.97 m wide, with a floor made of stones. The sides and back of the fireplace were of bricks L: 0.24 m, W: 0.13 m, D: 40 mm, with their large faces to the front. Both the north and south front corners had square rebates. A fender 0.17 m high, with a chamfered edge, spanned the fireplace, projecting slightly from the line of the north–south wall. Beneath each of the short east–west arms of the fender was an underlying and projecting stone, suggesting an earlier fender and so possibly an earlier phase of fireplace.

Further south in the east wall, beginning 1.7 m from the south wall, was a rebate 0.46 m high, 60 mm wide and 20 mm deep. It was probably associated with an internal partition.

North and West Walls

The large, northern room to the west of the north–south partition had two window recesses cut into the north and west walls. These recesses were cut from ground level rather than from cill level and represent an alteration of existing windows. To the south of the western window recess was a 1 m long chasing, presumably for a bed against the partition wall.

The north wall of the cell survived to three courses, 0.75 m high, with the lowest courses of the doorway and its threshold onto the latrine pentice at its east end. The west wall only had two courses remaining.

Garden Pentice

In the south-east corner of the cell plot, at the east end of the garden pentice, a tree stump was removed to enable excavation. The digging disturbed the topsoil. The topsoil covered a layer of loose, pale brown, sandy clay flecked with rubble and mortar. This layer sealed the pentice paving and, alongside it, a second layer of pale brown sandy clay, containing fallen stone roof slates. This second sandy clay layer overlaid the line of the pentice drain running along the north side of the pentice and extended into the garden, but did not cover the area of the pentice and its surviving paving. Over the pentice paving in the south-west corner was a patch of charcoal and flecks of pink plaster. Much of the pentice paving had been robbed.

The outer, northern, edge of the pentice drain survived (see Figure 4.54), and consisted

THE ARCHAEOLOGY OF THE GREAT CLOISTER

of flat stone slabs sloping to the south, presumably forming one half of a shallow V-section drain, which sloped 0.14 m in 0.24 m. A number of small stone slabs were set vertically alongside the larger flat stones.

Towards the west end of the drain an elaborate sluice arrangement was found. Here the drain was 0.24 m wide and had vertical sides 0.18 m high and a flat bottom. It was capped by three stones adjacent to the threshold stone for the door from the pentice to the garden. Cut into the two easternmost stones of the drain were two vertical grooves 30 mm wide and 25 mm deep. These grooves must have carried a simple sluice. At the east of the pentice, in the east wall, was the water tap niche; all traces of its decorative masonry had been robbed. The V-section pentice drain continued to the west of the threshold stone, and passed under the precinct wall.

The threshold stone for the garden lay immediately to the south of the drain and was rebated to accommodate the upright posts of the pentice wall. The pentice wall footings at the west end were indicated by a rebate in the precinct wall, 0.25 m² and 0.25 m deep. At the east end the pentice wall footings survived up against the south-west corner of the house. Feature 13, a posthole, probably indicates the position of an upright timber, on the line of the surviving threshold stone. The threshold was socketed for two doorposts 0.15 m².

Set into the west precinct wall, at the west end of the pentice, was a recess about 0.6 m wide with three grooves: two vertical ones on the north and south sides of the opening, each about 0.45 m high, 40 mm wide and 30 mm deep, and the third horizontal one at the bottom of the recess connecting the two verticals. It appeared that the masonry at the top of this recess had been subsequently rebuilt.

Latrine Pentice

The turf was removed to reveal a topsoil of brown clay and stones. This sealed a layer of demolition rubble consisting of large pieces of dressed stone and smaller pieces of sandstone. Beneath this rubble was a thin spread of pinkish mortar, overlying a layer of brown earth and rubble, which in turn covered the large stone slabs of the pentice paving. The pentice paving did not cover the entire pentice (see Figures 4.55 and 4.56); it was missing from much of the southern half.

Here it was apparent that the paving rested on natural clay and had been patched in a number of places. On the outer edge of the paving, set face downwards, was a small limestone panel, which had served as a devotional object. It was carved with the figure of the wounded Christ and, below the figure, an indulgence in English (see Figure 4.60).

The pentice wall footing was indicated by a series of stones between the paving and the drain. The pentice drain was made of seven long, shaped stones forming a neatly cut gulley about 0.1 m deep. The channels in the stones were about 0.12 m wide at the bottom and about 0.21 m wide at the top. The direction of flow of this drain was from south to north (towards the precinct wall) without any apparent outlet at the northern end. At the southern end of the pentice the drain turned west and continued along the north wall of the cell. The corner stone, against the north wall of the cell, was

Figure 4.55 Cell 10: the latrine pentice and living room as excavated (L. J. Barfoot).

Figure 4.56 The latrine pentice looking north and showing the wall plate socket and the mortar flashing of the pentice roof above the door to the latrine (L. J. Barfoot).

bulged to the east, possibly to accommodate a downpipe. The direction of flow from the corner was to the west along the north wall of the cell. There were indications to the north of the drain of an earlier drain in structure similar to that alongside the garden pentice.

The latrine doorway survived in the precinct wall. It was 1.75 m high from the paving and 0.73 m wide with external rebates, 50 mm wide and 50 mm deep for a wooden door. A single step, 0.22 m high, led up to the latrine. The rebate for the seat was about 0.53 m above the step and about 0.13 m deep, and bore indications of the mortises for two north–south supports for the seat, 0.38 m apart and 70 mm wide. Maximum headroom in the latrine was about 1.82 m. To the west of the door, and level with the top of it, was the hole, 0.2 m wide and 0.24 m high, for the wall plate of the pentice wall. The mortar scar of the weathering ran from above this hole to the top of the dividing wall between Cells 9 and 10. This wall survived to two courses, 0.45 m high, along most of its length.

Garden

Across the garden the topsoil merged into a layer of brown-orange sand with clay streaks. Beneath this layer was a layer of grey-brown clay containing fallen roof slates. This layer was not consistent: at the west end of the garden the clay was more orange and contained no roof slates but some small gravel.

This clay layer covered a series of stone settings that can be interpreted as garden features (see Figure 4.57). One line of stones ran east–west along the north wall of the cell, turned at right angles and continued north along the pentice drain and then turned again at right angles and continued west along the precinct wall. The line of stones was well constructed, particularly along the latrine pentice, where a large squared stone marked the corner. These settings indicate a bed raised above the general level of the garden. A second line, of smaller stones, ran along the western half of the precinct wall, then turned at right angles and ran south to the north-west corner of the cell, and then again turned west and stopped some distance short of the west precinct wall. These stone settings were placed on natural.

Cut into natural, and sealed by the overlying clay layer, were a number of other features, of which several may be the settings for shrubs or bushes. One was a posthole [25], which was packed at its base with a broken stone mortar. All sealed contexts were sampled for seeds and pollen, but subsequent analysis by Professor Dimbleby identified only yew from the drain of the garden pentice, which could have blown in from outside the cell.

The precinct wall around the garden of Cell 10 survived to 12 or 13 courses, 4.75 m high, and had a number of scaffold holes in it.

Finds Group 14

CERAMICS (SEE FIGURE 4.58)

Cells 10 to 14 all produced pre-priory sherds. Vessel 188 from Cell 10 is an example of this date (Table 4.15). Clearly, all such pieces are residual from earlier settlement contexts. However, whether these sherds indicate that this earlier settlement covered this particular area of the site is uncertain. Any levelling of this or other parts of the site would have necessitated earth movement, and residual sherds such as

THE ARCHAEOLOGY OF THE GREAT CLOISTER

this could have been transported considerable distances from their original place of deposition.

Like that of Cell 9, this assemblage produced a range of ceramic tablewares. These included a bottle (193) and a barrel costrel (191), both in local fabrics not naturally suited to the production of such fine forms. German Langerwehe stoneware costrels were recognised from Cell 8 and from the prior's cell and vessels such as 191 may represent attempts by local potters to copy such imports. In the same way, 195 represents a local copy of a chafing dish. True chafing dishes were made of metal, usually bronze. Most ceramic copies were mere skeuomorphs. Even the ornate and finely potted Saintonge chafing dishes rarely show evidence of having held hot embers in their bowl. Local English copies were usually quite crude, with only token attempts at vent holes apparently included more for appearance than function. Certainly, none of the chafing dish fragments from Mount Grace seem to have been used with embers and were therefore presumably entirely decorative.

188. Gritty ware cooking pot. Orange outer surface, vermilion core and pale orange inner surface. Coil-built and partly wheel-finished. Probably pre-priory.
189. Ryedale ware urinal. Dull orange surfaces and pale blue-grey core. Plain olive-green glaze.
190. Ryedale ware urinal. Corroded olive-green glaze to outer surface, blue-grey core and pale orange inner surface. Rather a messily finished base. Traces of a handle scar.
191. Ryedale ware barrel costrel. Olive-green glaze on outer surface, blue-grey core and whitish-orange outer surface. Finger marks on inner surface.
192. Hambleton ware urinal. Orange fabric, reducing in thickenings to brick-red/blue-grey, with a dull red inner surface. Orange-brown glaze. Overfired to the point where vessel began to distort and the glaze turn a purple-black.
193. Hambleton ware bottle or flask. Outer surface covered with a rather corroded yellow-olive glaze taken neatly to the rim top, pale blue-grey core with pale grey margins and a pale orange inner surface.
194. Post-medieval Sandy ware two-handled jar. Grey-buff outer surface, buff core and a dark olive-green glaze on the inner surface.
195. Post-medieval Orange ware chafing dish. Soft whitish fabric with very pale pinkish-orange margins. Glaze of a quite consistent copper-green colour on the inner surface, turning to yellow-green on the lower parts of the outer surface with copper-green streaking. It appears from sherds present that the vessel had two opposing looped handles and, between them, two opposing lugs, while the rim had four smaller raised lugs.
196. Regional Stray ware jar rim. Hard orange to vermilion sand-tempered fabric. Orange-brown glaze on both surfaces.
197. Cistercian ware cup base. Red outer surface and dark red core. Purplish-black glaze which, on the inner surface, has thickened in the base confirming an upright firing position. Some glazed-mixed sand fritting adhering to the base. Parallel cut marks on base.

Figure 4.57 Cell 10: the northern part of the garden as excavated, seen from the west (L. J. Barfoot).

198. Cistercian ware tankard base. Dull red outer surface and orange-red core. Deep, bright, reddish-brown glaze. Traces of at least one handle.
199. Staffordshire white ware drug jar base. Off-white fabric with traces of a lemon-yellow glaze.
200. Staffordshire white ware drug jar base. Fairly hard, fine, white fabric of smoothish texture. Cream-coloured surfaces and off-white core. Dribble of clear, yellowish glaze on the basal angle.
201. Langerwehe stoneware mug. White flecked chocolate-brown glaze on the outer surface, grey core and dark brownish-black inner surface.
202. Raeren stoneware mug. Brownish glaze, lustrous on the outer surface on mid- to upper body, but more matt on lower outer surface. Paler matt brown glaze on inner surface. Pale grey fabric.

SMALL FINDS (SEE FIGURES 4.58, 4.59, 4.60 AND 4.61)

Cell 10 produced a remarkably rich collection of small finds. Some of these – two Cu pens (207 and 208), two Pb writing leads (219 and 220) and a piece of graphite – indicated the monk's trade: a copyist. All are rare finds, even in a monastic context. Fittings from book straps and from the book cover boards show that books were regularly handled in this cell. Two tape weights (221 and 223) could equally relate to manuscript transcription. Personal items like the bone ear-pick (213) and tweezers (205) are probably chance losses.

Two objects are exceptional. The first, the leg of a tumbrel (coin balance) (211); the second a piece of Caen stone with an image of the Crucified Christ and an indulgence text in English (227). The first indicates commerce, something Carthusian monks had no business to indulge in; the second potential involvement in the trade in indulgences.

203. Disk. Cu. Diameter: 23 mm, Th: 0.5 mm. Probably a corroded 19th–20th-century coin. Find no. MG28.
204. Wire. Cu. Twisted. Diameter: 2 mm. Five incised grooves at one end. Find no. MG99.
205. Tweezers. Cu. Single strip of metal, Th: 1–2 mm, folded to form tweezers L: 80 mm. Upper end formed into a loop, diameter: 16 mm. W (of loop): 6 mm. W (at neck): 9 mm, tapering to point W: 2 mm. Find no. MG20.
206. Buckle or belt plate. Cu. L: 11 mm; W: 8 mm. One Fe rivet. Find no. MG13.
207. Pen. Cu. L: 96 mm; diameter: 7 mm. Sheet alloy soldered edge-to-edge seam. Facetted nib end. Find no. MG23.
208. Pen. Cu. L: 118 mm; diameter: 3–5 mm. Cu sheet with edge-to-edge seam. The seam formed the central split of the pen end, which lacks its point. Find no. MG29.
209. Offcut. Cu. L: 20.5 mm. W: 5 mm, tapering to tip 2 mm. Th: 1 mm. Find no. MG14.
210. Ring. Cu. Diameter: 13 mm; Th: 0.7 mm thick; H: 1.5 mm. Broken. Find no. MG15.
211. Coin balance. Cu. Vertical arm only. L: 73 mm; W: 5–6 mm; Th: 1.8 mm. Slight taper at one end. Opposite, broader end rectangular in section. Main part has chamfered edges, the back is flat. Find no. MG19.
212. Book strap attachment. Cu. Roughly triangular, with vertex angle rounded. Maximum dimensions L: 17 mm; W: 16 mm. Th: 0.7 mm. Central rivet hole, diameter: 2 mm, above a slot, L: 11 mm; W: 2.5 mm, for cord or narrow leather strap. Find no. MG707.
213. Ear- and toothpick, bone. Overall L: 88 mm. Shallow scoop at one end, L: 31 mm, and pick at opposite end, L: 25 mm. Central section, L: 32 mm; W: 5–7 mm. Narrow ribs in sets of three, two, two and three, carved widthways around central body, but subsequently pared off on one side. Asymmetrically placed hole in central body, diameter: 2.5 mm. Find no. MG32.
214. Stud. Cu. Rounded head forming six sections above pin shaft. Head 10 mm from apex to line of outer edge, underside recessed to house top of shaft, L: 25 mm; diameter: 6 mm tapering to 2 mm. Find no. MG719.
215. Book mount. Cu. Slightly domed. W: 22 mm (maximum). Originally six lobes with two incised lines between each and central hole, diameter: 4 mm. Fe rivets on each alternate lobe. Find no. MG719.

THE ARCHAEOLOGY OF THE GREAT CLOISTER

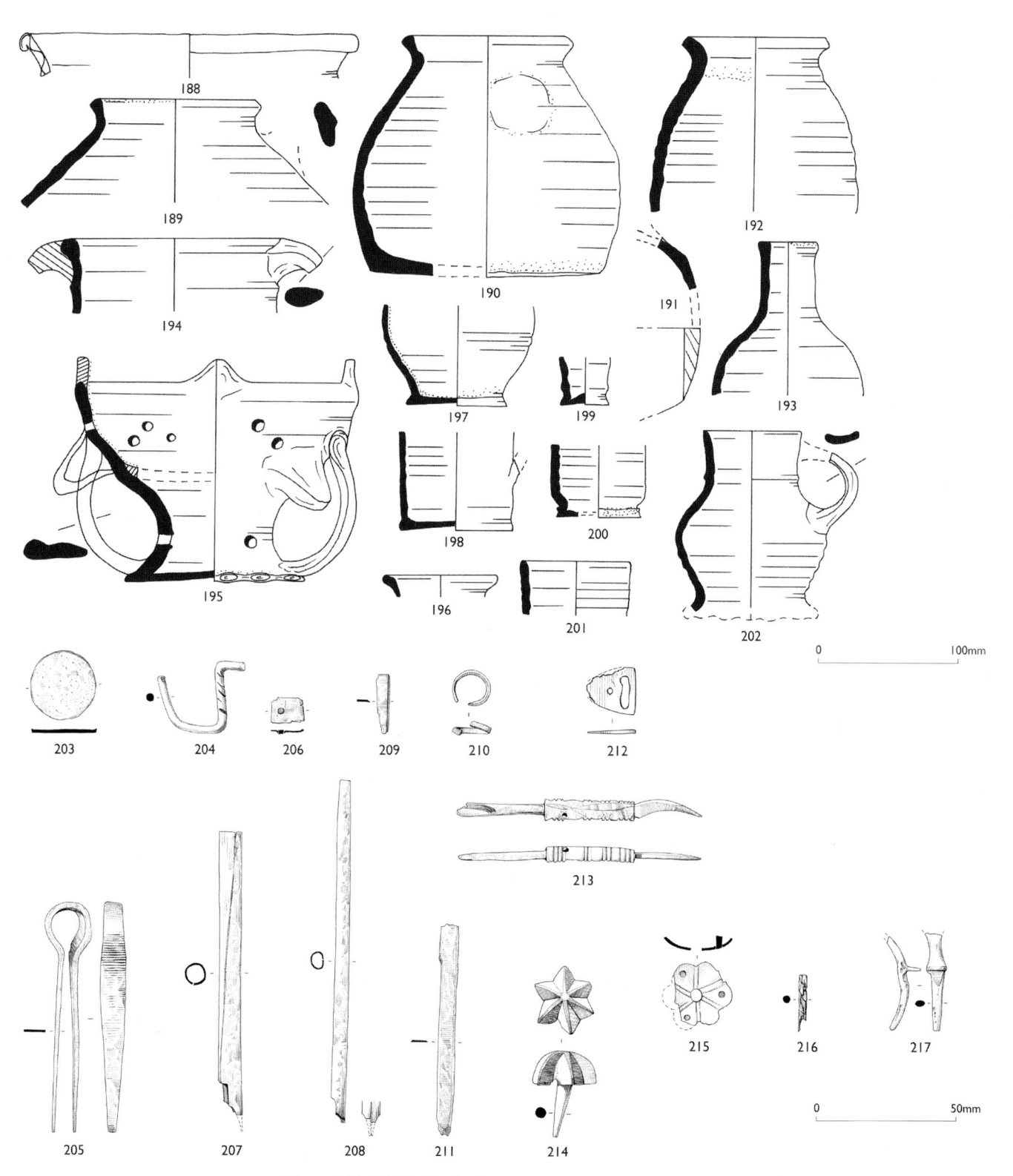

Figure 4.58 Cell 10: Finds Group 14 (pottery 1:4, copper alloy 1:2).

Table 4.15 Cell 10, Finds Group 14: Ceramics

Fabric	Sherds	Vessels							
		Total vessels	Bottle	Jar	Jug	Mug or cup	Tripod pipkin	Urinal	Other
Brandsby type	2	2	0	0	1	0	1	0	0
Cistercian	18	11	0	0	0	11	0	0	0
Cistercian copy	16	7	0	0	0	7	0	0	0
Developed Humber	9	1	0	1	0	0	0	0	
Gritty	1	1	0	0	1	0	0	0	0
Hambleton	8	4	0	0	2	0	0	1	1
Humber	1	1	0	0	1	0	0	0	0
Langerwehe	9	3	0	0	0	3	0	0	0
Late Gritty	1	1	0	1	0	0	0	0	0
Post-medieval Orange	39	7	0	3	2	1	0	0	1
Post-medieval Sandy	4	2	0	2	0	0	0	0	0
Raeren	8	2	0	0	0	2	0	0	0
Regional Stray	1	1	0	0	1		0	0	0
Ryedale	68	19	1	0	15	1	0	2	1
Siegburg	3	3	0	0	0	3	0	0	0
Staffordshire	2	2	0	0	0	0	0	0	2
South Netherlands maiolica	1	1	1	0	0	0	0	0	0

216. Lace chape. Cu. Edge to edge seam, L: 18 mm; diameter: 2 mm. Find no. MG98.

217. Glass fragment. Overall L: 40 mm; W: 6 mm narrowing to 4 mm. Lug projecting 6 mm from body. Might come from glass drinking vessel. Find no. MG712.

218. Pipe clip. Pb. L: 115 mm; W: 50–60 mm; Th: 2 mm. One end slightly folded over. Two rectangular nail holes 35 mm from one end. Rust stain on lead indicates nail heads of diameter: 20 mm. Find no. MG349.

219. Writing lead. Pb. L: 137 mm (maximum). Roughly six-sided in section, with top end roughly 14 mm by 6 mm. Find no. MG24.

220. Writing lead. Pb. L: 150 mm. Double-ended, with points roughly circular in section. Middle section, 6 mm² in section, with chamfered corners. One end was originally forked, with prongs, L: 54 mm, one of which has broken off. Find no. MG27.

221. Crudely decorated plate. Pb. L: 62 mm; W: 17 mm (maximum); Th: 2 mm. Two holes, 3.5 mm and 3 mm in diameter. Wider end roughly cut with stylised animal(?) heads on either side. Semicircular cut at narrower end. Possibly weight for bookmark. Find no. MG717.

222. Rod. Pb. L: 31 mm; diameter: 2.5 mm. Possibly a small writing lead. Find no. MG18.

223. Writing lead or weight. Pb. L: 63 mm; W: 12 mm, tapering to point; Th: 2 mm. Hole towards top 3 mm in diameter. Find no. MG18.

224. Offcut. Pb. Roughly triangular. Longest edge: 35 mm; Th: 2 mm. Two incised lines on top surface. Find no. MG22.

225. Came. Pb. L: 62 mm; W: 6 mm. Depth of plain-bottomed grooves 2 mm. Slight, thin moulding lines on each side. Find no. MG68.

226. Mould fragment, stone. L: 20.5 mm; W: 17.5 mm; Th: 8 mm. Two drilled holes, 3 mm in diameter, in the smoothed upper surface for locating pegs in the missing half of the two-piece mould. Find no. MG375.

227. Indulgence panel (Figure 4.60), Caen limestone, buried face down in the paving of the latrine pentice. Roughly 120 mm by 73 mm, with recessed panel 93 mm by 43 mm and 9 mm deep. Panel flush with

THE ARCHAEOLOGY OF THE GREAT CLOISTER

Figure 4.60 Cell 10: the indulgence panel (L. J. Barfoot).

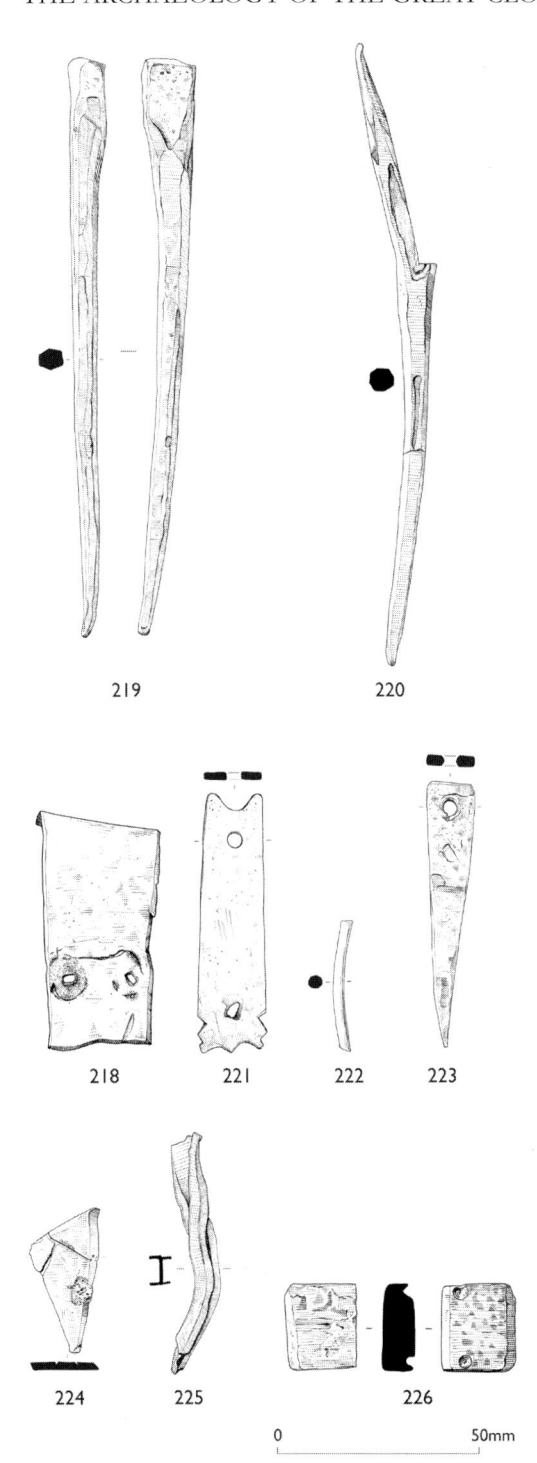

Figure 4.59 Cell 10: Finds Group 14 continued (lead 1:2; stone 1:2).

edge of the stone at the bottom and left, at top with border roughly 27 mm wide, and at right with border roughly 30 mm wide. Edges of recess slope slightly outwards. Two flush edges have either been cut off, remarkably neatly except that the bottom edge slopes slightly outwards while the left-hand edge is slightly undercut, or the border never existed on these sides. The border sides are rougher and at the top is a curved indentation, apparently carefully made though now partly broken. The borders have some irregularly incised cross-lines. No colour remains on the stone. On the indented panel is incised a crude representation of Christ, half-length, full-face, unclothed, beardless, with a cruciform nimbus, hair down to the shoulders, head bowed to His right, bleeding wound in His right side, and arms crossed at the waist. Above is inscribed the regular *titulus* of the Crucifixion, INRI (*Iesus Nazarenus Rex Iudeorum;* John 19.19). Below is a longer inscription:

The p'don for v p'
n'r & v aue ys xx
[vj M yeres] & xxvj daes

That is, the pardon for five Paternosters and five Aves is 26,000 years and 26 days.

The form of this piece is curious as it lacks a frame to the left and bottom. It is, therefore, unlikely to have been part of an

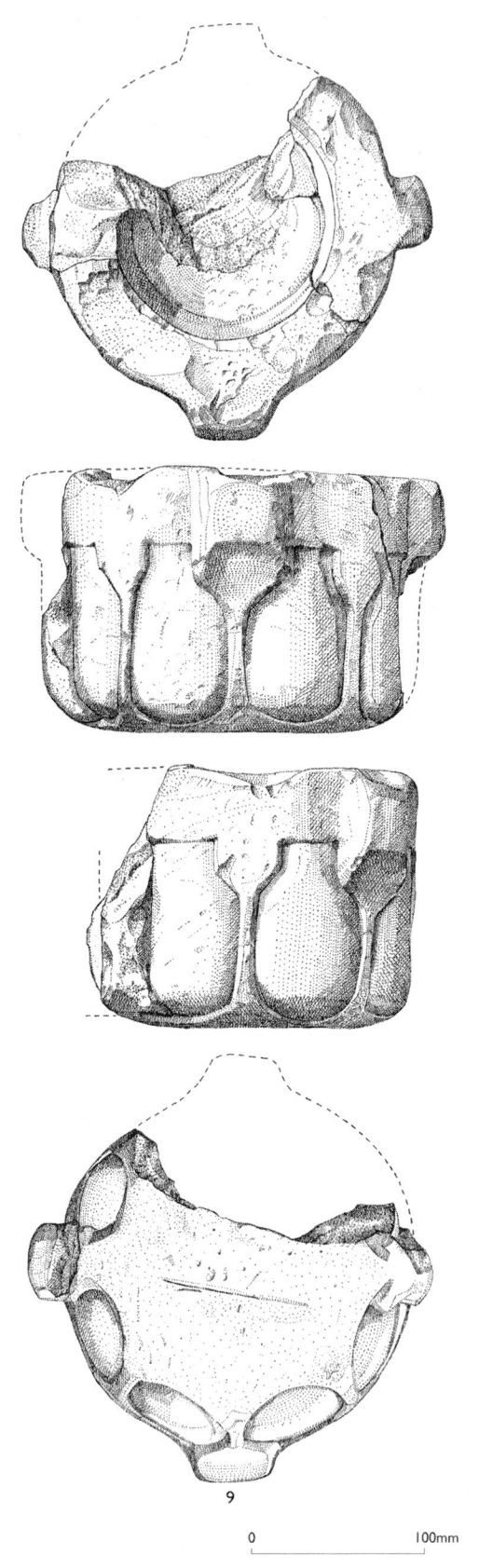

Figure 4.61 Cell 10: stone mortar (1:4).

iconographical set. The possibility remains that it might have been the positive for a mould which was capable of producing, not anything as sophisticated as a printing die, but, possibly, a clay cast for printing a rough representation on paper. That it should have been discarded, though perhaps, carefully hidden (in effect a respectful 'burial'), suggests that the experiment was not successful. The lack of colour precludes the idea of a devotional object and the lack of burning on the stone shows that it was not subjected to casting in metal.

The following small finds are not illustrated. Partial inscription. Pb. Cast. L: 36 mm; W: 24 mm. Reads '…arenu…' in retrograde. From same mould as 251 and 298. Find no. MG17.

Piece of shaped graphite. Find no. MG25.

Rod. Fe and Au. L: 31 mm; diameter: 2.5 mm. Top has thin layer of highly polished gold. Find no. MG26.

ARCHITECTURAL DETAIL FROM THE DEMOLITION CONTEXTS (SEE FIGURE 4.62)

5. Two fragments of the base of an octagonal chimney, with facets 190 mm wide, rising from a gable apex stone. In place of the usual pyramidal chamfer stops the angles are decorated with vertical 'spurs'. In the bottom half of the base the chimney flue is of square plan, but in the top half, where the shaft moulding projects, it is circular. Associated with this base were seven fragments of shaft (not illustrated). Find nos MG90 and MG91.

6. Fragment of castellated chimney cap. Similar to that found in Cell 8, but this piece had pierced openings, probably single lancets, in alternate sides. It has the same shaft dimensions as 5 above and no doubt came from the same chimney, probably that of Cell 10. Find nos MG2 and MG10.

7. Pivot stone for an upright timber of roughly 110 mm diameter. The timber would have functioned as the hinge of a harr-hung (held in place at the bottom by a pivot in the ground or on a cill, and at the top by a dowel fitted into the lintel of the doorframe, therefore not requiring hinges) gate or external door. Find no. MG124.

THE ARCHAEOLOGY OF THE GREAT CLOISTER

connects the three remaining lugs. These are proud of the rim by 16 mm. Between each lug are two slightly recessed panels with horizontal tops formed by the rim band and rounded bottoms extending around the rounded edge of the base to meet the flat bottom. Between each panel is a vertical shaft expanding to a straight-sided top, which becomes part of the collar band. This decoration complements the lower edges of the lugs, which are treated in a similar fashion. The interior bowl is 124 mm in diameter and 108 mm deep. Find no. MG1270.

Cell 11 (see Figure 4.63 and 4.64)

Conditions before Excavation

There was a central depression in the area of the cell, where a tree had been removed, and a mound of overburden between 1 m and 1.40 m deep against the cloister wall in the north-east corner.

Cell Interior

The topsoil in the cell was deepest in the centre of the northern room (the living room), where the tree had been removed. It covered a layer of mortar and rubble, which extended over most of the interior and included a springer from the Period Two cloister arcade. In the south-west room a small spread of loose cobbling lay at the bottom of this rubble layer and a spread of dark brown soil containing charcoal lumps lay beneath the rubble and cobbles. This soil layer covered all but the most northerly part of the cell and sealed three courses of blocking (probably of the 17th century) in the cloister doorway.

In the northern room a layer of clean, loose, pale brown sandy soil, containing small flecks of mortar and charcoal, sealed the paving in the north-east corner. In the passage area, to the east, underneath the staircase, this paving consisted of flat stones irregularly laid. In the living room, against the north wall, it continued up to the fireplace, where it consisted of very regular flagstones about 0.1 m thick. This paving must originally have continued all along the north wall, but to the west of the fireplace only one of the stones remained. The former presence of the paving in this area was indicated by a line along the bottom of the plaster rendering of this wall and a difference in the stratification about 0.92 m to the south of the wall.

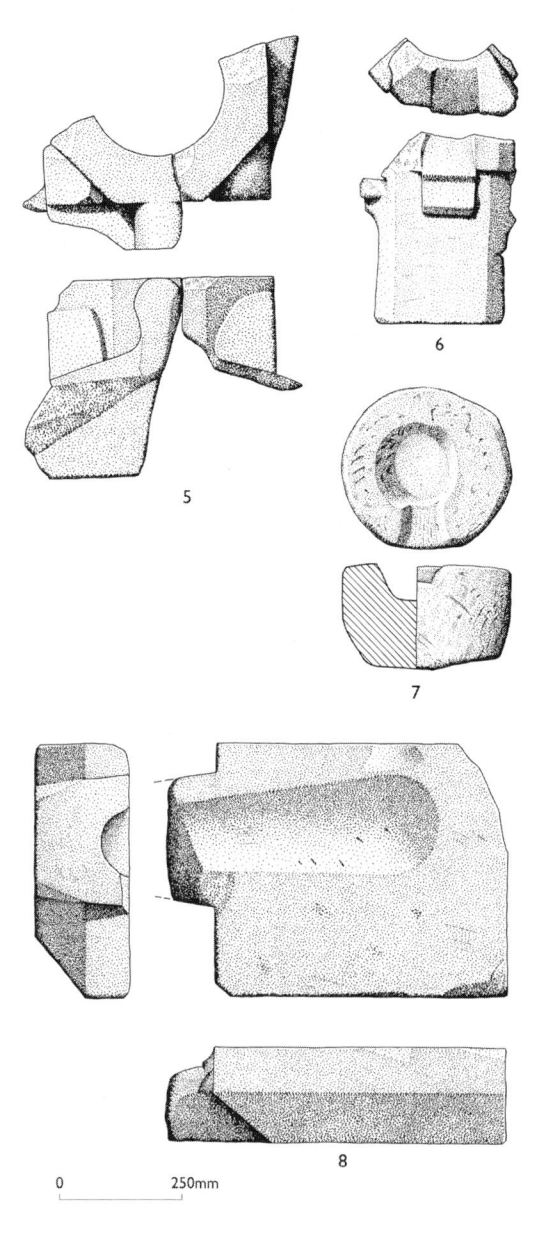

Figure 4.62 Cell 10: architectural detail from demolition deposits (1:10).

8. Waterspout for gutter. This would have been fixed on the corner of a building, as evidenced by the chamfered cornice moulding on two sides. The monks' cells have dripping eaves, so it is likely that this came from the parapeted roof of either the church or the prior's cell.

9. Mortar, limestone from the packing of posthole 25, 208 mm in diameter, 148 mm high. Broken, with one of the four lugs missing. This lug presumably had a lip for pouring. On the outside below the rim is a slightly raised band that

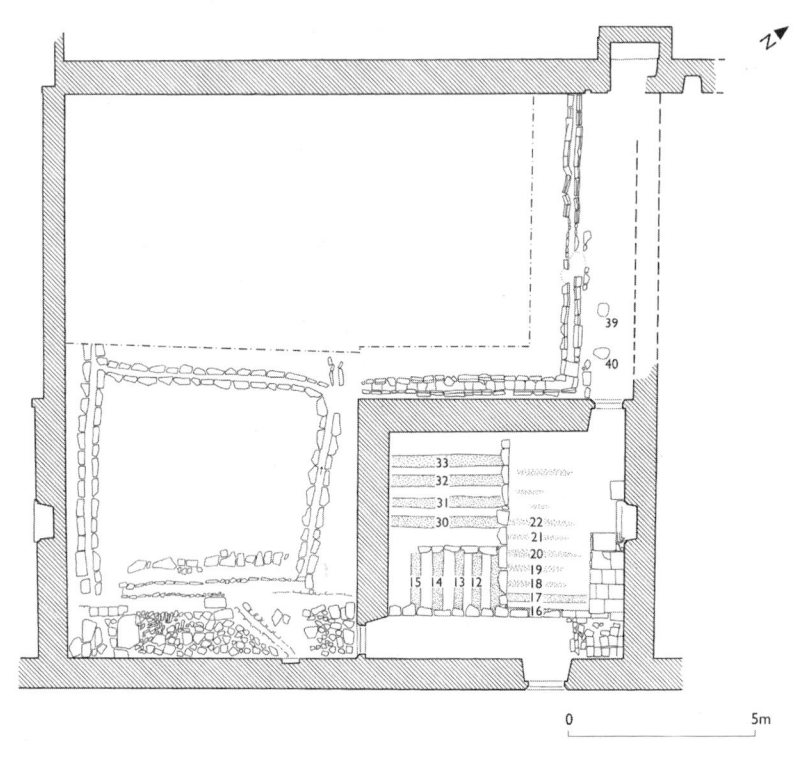

Figure 4.63 Cell 11.

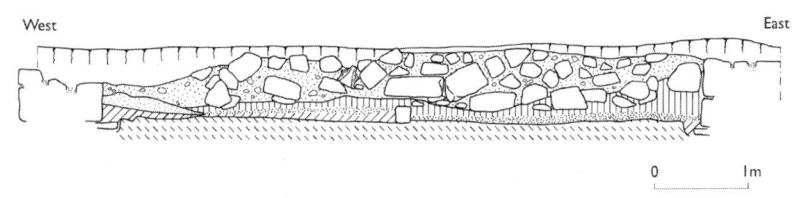

Figure 4.64 Cell 11: west–east section.

Removal of the layer of dark brown soil containing charcoal revealed the footings for the internal partitions of the cell (see Figure 4.65). Between the partitions and underlying the layer of dark brown soil was a spread of charcoal about 40 mm thick. This charcoal filled the slots where floor joists had been removed. The charcoal itself was of small fragments of rough timber which were unlikely to have come from the cell. In the living room the charcoal-filled joist holes, [16] to [22], ran north–south. In the south-west room, the joist holes [30] to [33] also ran north–south. In the small room in the south-east, however, the joist holes [11] to [15] ran east–west. In the two southern rooms the joist holes were cut into natural. In the living room they were cut through a thin spread of discoloured yellow clay above the natural.

To the north of the joist holes in the living room a layer of loose grey sand extended over the area where the paving had been robbed. This overlay a mixed sandy soil, which may have been the original bedding for the paving. The discoloured yellow clay was very distinct from the charcoal spread to the south and suggests that the charcoal lumps had been introduced before the paving was robbed.

East (Cloister) Wall
The full height of the cell survived on the cloister side, where the wall is 19 courses, 4.7 m, high. In the north-east corner of the cell was evidence for the staircase. The north wall (see Figure 4.66 and below) had chasings for three treads and two risers: the lowest began 0.12 m above the paving, and was for a tread 0.45 m deep, 60 mm thick; the first riser was 0.36 m high, 70 mm thick; the second tread was 0.48 m deep but its width was indeterminable; the second riser was 0.3 m high, 70 mm thick; and the third tread was 0.37 m deep, 80 mm thick. Evidence for the staircase continued in the east wall, where three more treads and two more risers were apparent: the first tread 0.35 m deep, 90 mm thick; the first riser 0.38 m high, 50 mm thick; the second tread 0.43 m deep, 60 mm thick; the second riser 0.36 m high, 80 mm thick; and the final tread 0.44 m deep, 0.1 m thick.

Further south along the east wall was the cloister doorway, about 2 m high, with the lintel another 0.17 m higher than the top of the arch. The rebate for the door suggested that the door was about 80 mm thick with its hinges on the north. The hatch, immediately to the north of the door, measured 0.36 m by 0.34 m internally, 0.35 m wide and 0.36 m high externally, and had a rebate measuring 80 mm wide and 60 mm deep. To the south of the cloister door and 0.1 m higher than the lintel is a hole for a floor joist, 0.28 m^2; it is in line with the internal east–west partition. There is another smaller hole, 0.23 m2, above the doorway.

North Wall
The north wall had up to three courses surviving. The internal plastering survived over most of this wall; it was about 10 mm thick, consisting of two layers: the first of pink plaster and the second of white. Traces of this rendering were also noticed along the west wall.

There was no rebate for the passage partition in the north wall, but the line of the partition was clear where the well-laid paving of the living room ended.

THE ARCHAEOLOGY OF THE GREAT CLOISTER

Figure 4.65 Cell 11: as excavated, seen from the north-west (L. J. Barfoot).

Towards the centre of the north wall was the fireplace, with a stone hearth and sides, and a brick and stone back. The bricks were roughly 60 mm thick. The fireplace was 1.05 m wide and 0.40 m deep. It had a chamfered stone fender and square rebates on the east and west corners.

Evidence for the staircase at the east end of the wall is described above.

South and West Walls

The south and west walls of the cell survived two courses high, roughly 0.5 m. At the east end of the south wall was the doorway onto the garden pentice. Part of the doorway survived on the cloister wall side, where the holes for the hinges were to be seen.

In the west wall at the latrine pentice doorway the threshold and bottom courses of the wall, including the door jambs, remained.

Garden Pentice

The tap niche of Cell 11 and the north wall of Cell 12 were revealed when the topsoil was removed. Beneath the topsoil was, at the north end of the pentice, a layer of rubble and mortar, and further to the south a layer of medium-sized rubble in dark clay.

This medium rubble and clay layer sealed a layer of rubble and mortar, which covered the entire length of the pentice and extended slightly into the tap niche. Finally, the rough cobbling of the pentice lay beneath this layer (see Figure 4.67). The cobbling was crossed by a small drain, 0.13 m wide and 50 mm deep,

Figure 4.66 Cell 11: evidence for the turning stair in the north-east corner of the cell (L. J. Barfoot).

Figure 4.67 Cell 11: garden pentice as excavated, looking south (L. J. Barfoot).

running from the tap niche. A single capstone survived *in situ* (not illustrated).

At the south end of the pentice were five plain, coloured tiles, each 0.24 m². These lay against the internal edge of the pentice wall, which is indicated by a narrow strip, about 0.25 m to 0.3 m wide, between the cobbling and the eavesdrip drain. This drain was constructed of irregularly placed stones and occasional bricks with an irregular bottom, and was blocked by a flat stone at its southern end. The side of the eavesdrip drain blocked an east–west drain running along the south wall of the cell.

The tap niche was 1.40 m from the south wall of the cell and had retained its decorative arched head; it was 0.75 m high and 0.48 m wide. The cloister wall survived 12 courses, 3.30 m, high.

Latrine Pentice
Turf and topsoil, 0.25 m deep, were removed to reveal a pale brown clay containing scattered patches of gravel, which covered the whole of the latrine pentice. This pale clay layer sealed a layer of rubble in dark brown clay, which, particularly on the southern side of the pentice, contained a large number of roof slates. The pale brown clay also filled the robbing trench of the party wall between Cells 10 and 11.

A drain ran along the south edge of the pentice, before turning at right angles and running south along the west wall of the cell. Along the pentice edge the drain contained a large number of slates and was also sealed by the layer of pale brown clay.

A layer of grey clay overlay the natural shale against the north side of the drain. This grey clay had been cut through by the robbing of the party wall. To the south of the drain a similar layer of grey clay sealed an area of cobbling (not illustrated), which ran the whole length of the pentice and may have been a garden path. The exact relationship between the cobbling and the drain was not investigated.

The flat-bottomed pentice drain was composed of fragments of shaped stones, including some window tracery. It was 0.15–0.16 m deep at the west end and 0.2 m deep at the east end. One capstone survived at the east end of the drain and may have acted as a step from a door into the garden. The drain had also been cut through by the later burial of an animal. Few indications of the pentice wall footings survived.

Two small pits, [39] and [40], were cut into the grey clay layer in the pentice and had a large patch of mortar lying between them.

The latrine doorway survived in the precinct wall and was 1.80 m high above the paving and 0.75 m wide, with a rebate 30 mm by 30 mm on the east side for a wooden door. The clearance inside the latrine would have been 2.10 m. A socket for the wall plate for the pentice wall was 1.55 m above ground level, and measured 0.22 m wide and 0.26 m high.

Garden
A layer of pale brown clay with scattered patches of gravel lay below the turf. This layer sealed heavy rubble in dark brown clay, which in its turn overlay a series of drains. These drains consisted of two east–west channels linked by a north–south channel, which was in line with the drain running along the west side of the cell.

The drains had flat capstones (not illustrated), which probably served as paths dividing the garden into three square beds. Beneath the capstones the drain, which was built of well-laid stones, was about 0.2 m high and 0.2 m wide.

The drain that ran along the west side of the cell and south side of the latrine pentice did not have capstones. It was also 0.2 m high, with vertical sides, but its flat bottom was 0.24 m wide. The relationship between this drain and the garden drains is uncertain, as the junction point of the two systems at the south-west corner of the cell was destroyed.

A line of irregularly laid stones running north–south on the west edge of the pentice eavesdrip drain may be interpreted as a garden path. Sandwiched between the north side of the northern east–west drain and the cell's south wall, was a mass of stones level with the capping of the drain, which may suggest rough paving. Two shallow depressions, filled mainly with thin stones, underlay the northern east–west drain, they were probably associated with the construction of the cell.

The precinct wall of this cell survived 12 courses, 3.70 m high.

Finds Group 15
CERAMICS (SEE FIGURE 4.68)
This was one of the larger cell assemblages, containing vessels in most of the local and imported fabrics represented at Mount Grace (Table 4.16). Jars, jugs, urinals and tablewares were all present. However, one particular characteristic was observable in this group. This was the cell of the 'polishing monk'. A number of the imported stoneware vessels either had their rims polished to a smoother finish or damaged vessels had their broken edges rubbed smooth. One damaged drinking mug (237), having lost its rim, neck and handle, had its upper edge and handle scar polished flat and smooth. This activity was not just restricted to the stonewares; cistern 229 had the rim above its handle smoothed flat. Only one other vessel from Mount Grace received such treatment and that was a stoneware drinking mug from the kitchen (see Chapter 5, Finds Group 40.

Had more such polished vessels been discovered elsewhere, it might have suggested that they were being repaired as a service to the priory, but a single vessel from the kitchen may instead represent part of the food chain to and from this particular cell. Other vessels from this assemblage had not been touched; perhaps there was a particular reason why this monk needed vessels with particularly smooth rims, for instance, dental problems.

228. Hambleton ware drinking mug or cruet. Dull pinkish-orange outer surface, blue-grey core and dull pinkish inner surface. Pale olive-green glaze.
229. Regional Stray white ware jar or cistern. Very fine off-white core with very pale orange surfaces. Inner surface covered with a copper-green glaze with some darker streaks, the colour mottling where the glaze thins. The top of the rim above the handle has been deliberately ground down, leaving a very smooth, polished finish.
230. Late Gritty ware chafing dish. Pale orange-white outer surface, pale orange core and pale reddish-orange inner surface. Orange glaze with blackish flecks. Small for a chafing dish, with cuts into rim rather than applied lugs. Rather curious evidence for large vents in the bowl itself.
231. Late Humber ware/post-medieval Sandy ware handled jar. Dull red surface, orange, to blue-grey, to whitish-grey core and streaked olive-green glaze on internal surface.
232. Post-medieval Orange ware two-handled cistern(?). Pale orange to orange sandy fabric with a brownish-green glaze on both surfaces.
233. Post-medieval Orange ware urinal. Orange fabric, traces of an orange-brown glaze on both surfaces. All the sherds were worn and abraded.
234. Cistercian ware copy cup. Purple-red core with dark, shiny blackish-brown glaze on both surfaces.
235. Staffordshire white ware drug jar rim. Usual very fine soft white fabric, which feels powdery to the touch. Lemon-yellow glaze to the rim top.
236. Tudor Green ware cup. Chalk-white fabric with a bright copper-green glaze, slightly watery with darker green mottles.
237. Siegburg stoneware mug. Silver-grey outer surface glaze that thickens in places to a dark olive-green flecking, pale grey core and a dull pale grey inner surface with pale orange highlights. This vessel is missing its upper body, but the top of the shoulder has been cleanly and carefully polished smooth and flat, while the scar of the lower handle attachment has also been polished out.
238. Siegburg stoneware mug. Pale whitish-grey surfaces and slightly paler core.
239. Langerwehe stoneware mug. Silver-grey to matt purplish-brown outer surface, pale grey core and purple-brown inner surface. Rim top and scar of upper

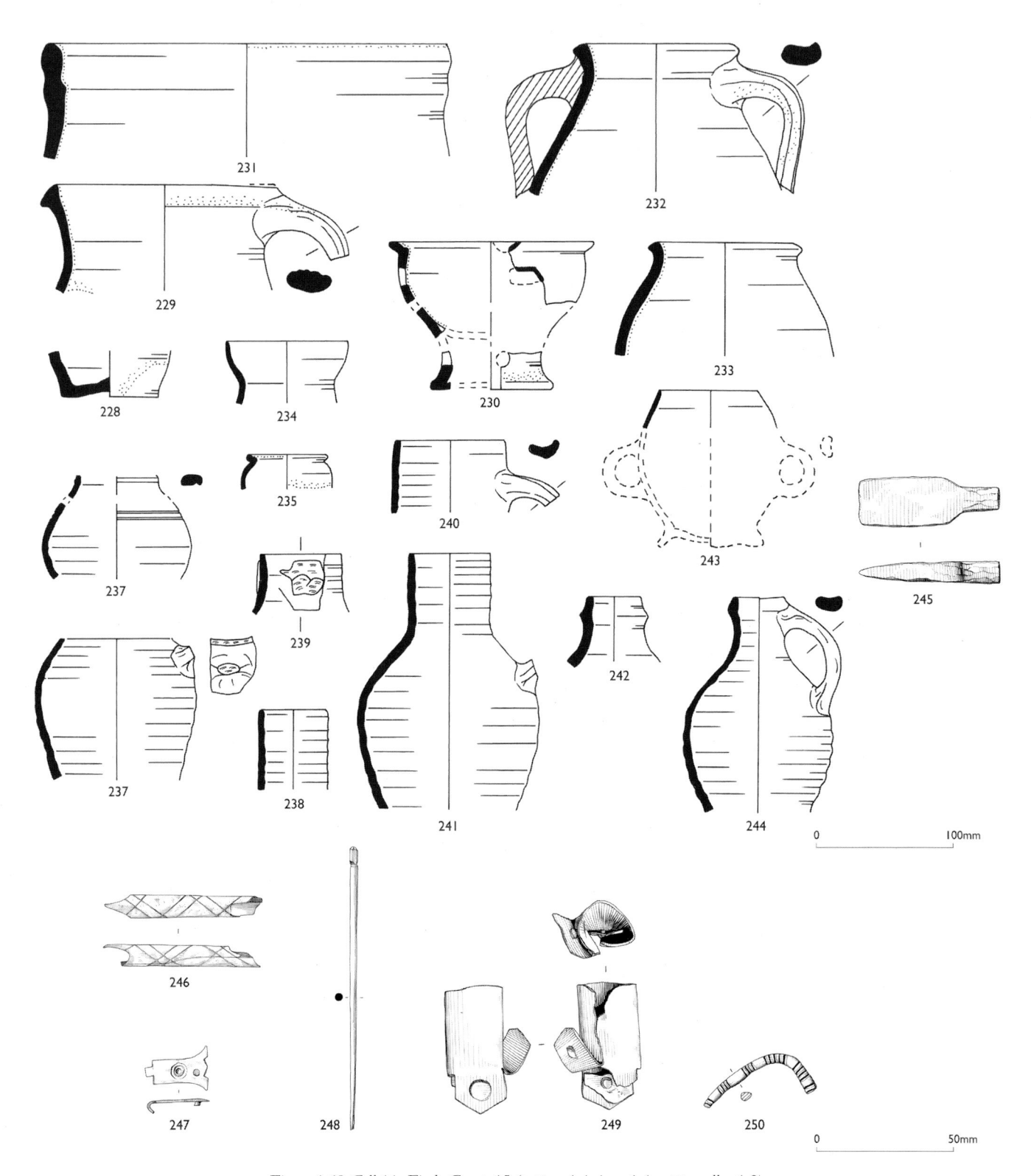

Figure 4.68 Cell 11: Finds Group 15 (pottery 1:4; iron 1:4; copper alloy 1:2).

THE ARCHAEOLOGY OF THE GREAT CLOISTER

Table 4.16 Cell 11, Finds Group 15: Ceramics

Fabric	Sherds	Vessels							
		Total vessels	Bottle	Cistern	Jar	Jug	Mug or cup	Urinal	Other
Brandsby type	2	2	0	0	0	2	0	0	0
Cistercian	18	13	0	0	0	0	12	0	1
Cistercian copy	5	5	0	0	0	0	5	0	0
Developed Humber	9	2	0	0	1	1	0	0	0
Hambleton	7	4	1	0	0	2	0	1	1
Humber	1	1	0	0	0	1	0	0	0
Langerwehe	60	17	1	0	0	0	16	0	0
Late Gritty	10	3	0	0	1	1	0	0	1
Low Countries Red	3	1	0	0	0	1	0	0	0
Post-medieval Orange	18	7	0	0	5	1	0	1	0
Post-medieval Sandy	6	4	0	1	2	1	0	0	0
Raeren	5	1	1	0	0	0	0	0	0
Regional Stray	1	1	0	0	1	0	0	0	0
Ryedale	69	27	0	0	0	26	1	0	0
Siegburg	72	15	0	0	0	0	15	0	0
Staffordshire	3	2	0	0	0	0	0	0	2
Tudor Green	17	2	0	0	0	1	1	0	0

handle attachment have been carefully and smoothly polished.

240. Langerwehe stoneware mug. Purple to orange outer surface with greenish blotches, pale silver-grey core and a slightly metallic purple inner surface. Rim top has been polished down to a smooth finish.
241. Langerwehe stoneware (underfired) mug. Pale chocolate-brown outer surface glaze, pale orange earthenware core and pale pinkish-orange inner surface. Top of the rim has been polished flat and smooth.
242. Langerwehe stoneware (underfired) bottle or flask rim. Matt purple outer surface, pale grey to orange earthenware core and an inner surface varying from purple towards the rim to dull, dark orange below. The proportion of surviving rim indicates that there could only have ever been one handle to this vessel.
243. Langerwehe stoneware cup. Glossy chocolate-brown glaze on both surfaces over a pale bluish-grey core.
244. Raeren stoneware (Aachen type) bottle. Silver-grey glazed outer surface turning to dull brownish colour around the neck. Pale silver-grey stoneware core and unglazed dull orange to grey inner surface.

SMALL FINDS (SEE FIGURES 4.68 AND 4.69)
The small finds from Cell 11 relate closely to those from Cell 10, with another Cu pen (246) and a Cu book clasp (247), suggesting that this cell, too, was occupied by a copyist. More remarkable is the mould (256) for casting gothic type, which is unique in Britain and suggests an attempt to print by casting moveable type (see Chapter 7). The cast Pb strip (251), with the retrograde script *jeſus nazarenus*, is one of three such castings from the western cells; the others are a fragment from Cell 10 (see Finds Group 14, unillustrated) and an unfinished casting from Cell 14 (see Finds Group 18, object 289).

245. Punch. Fe. L: 102 mm; W: 34 mm at broadest point. Short step and shouldered blade; blade tapering from Th: 14.5 mm to 2 mm at its rounded edge. Short step of circular section, diameter: 14.5 mm. Find no. MG417.
246. Pen. Cu sheet. L: 59 mm; diameter: 6 mm. Lightly incised double-lattice decoration. Nib at one end and evident

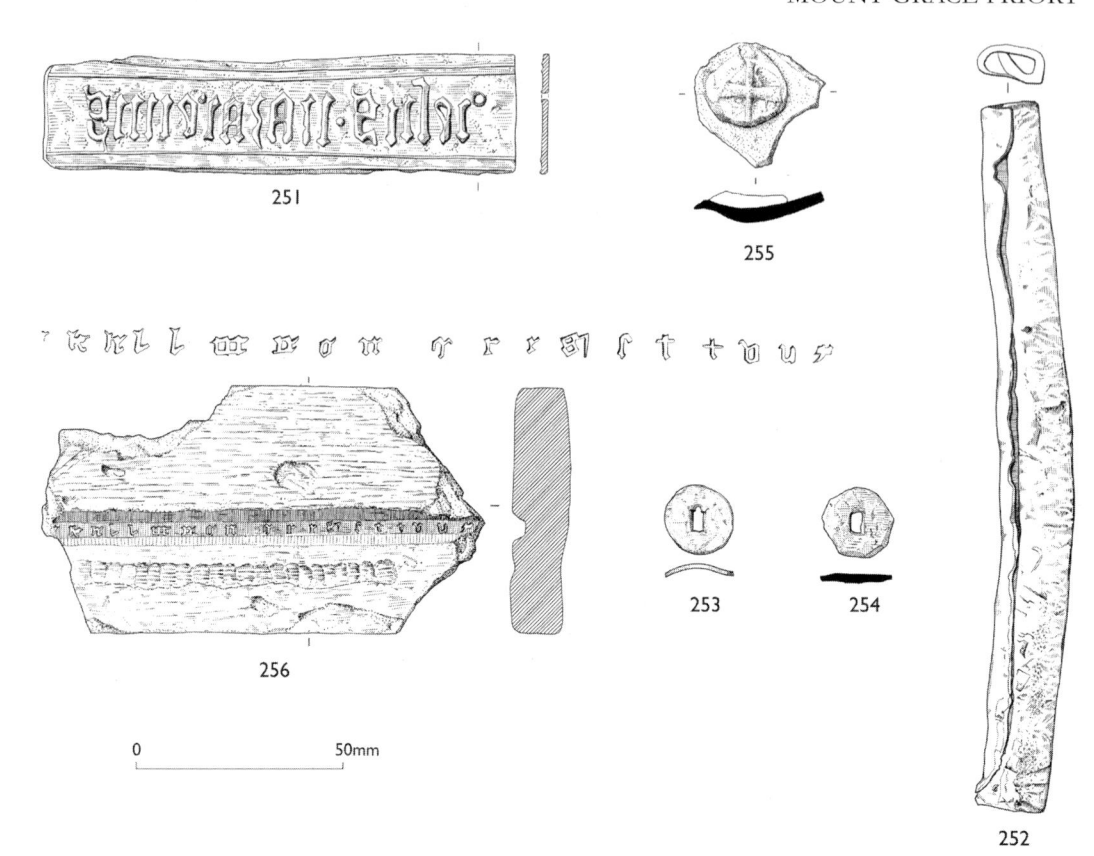

Figure 4.69 Cell 11: Finds Group 15 continued (lead 1:2; glass 1:2; stone 1:2).

reworking at opposite end to form point, perhaps for another nib. Find no. MG713.

247. Book clasp. Cu. L: 22 mm; W: 8 mm; Th: 1 mm. One end with hook, W: 3 mm, the other end splayed with two V-cuts in edge. Main part is decorated with two depressed circles around a central hole. One Cu rivet at splayed end. Back plate missing. Find no. MG716.
248. Needle. Cu. L: 100 mm; diameter: 2.5 mm, with a filed notch 5–6 mm from the top. Find no. MG16.
249. Candle holder. Cu. Sheet metal (Th: 0.5 mm) formed to make circular holder, with single Fe rivet (diameter: 0.9 mm) at base, which has angled sides. Overall H: 43 mm; diameter: 20 mm. Find no. MG513.
250. Buckle fragment. Cu. W: 3.5 mm; Th: 2.5 mm. Decorated with groups of four or five filed grooves between flat areas. File marks present on outer edge. 17th century (?). Find no. MG535.
251. Plaque, cast Pb. L: 111 mm; W: 24–27 mm; Th: 1 mm. Carries in relief the retrograde name *jefus nazarenus*. Pierced

hole (diameter: 2 mm) just to the right of the 'J'. Find no. MG1017.

252. Squashed tube. Pb. Could be damaged water pipe, but the seam is overlapping. L: 330 mm; diameter: 30–35 mm, Th (of sheet): 4 mm. Find no. MG389.
253. Washer. Pb. Diameter: 33 mm; Th: 2 mm. Central rectangular hole 9 mm by 5 mm, with narrower apsidal extension, L: 2 mm. Find no. MG420.
254. Washer. Pb. Maximum diameter: 32 mm; Th: 2 mm. Not exactly circular, several straight facets. Central rectangular hole 11 mm by 6 mm with slightly rounded ends. Find no. MG538.
255. Bottle(?), glass. A fragment of pale green vessel glass. Irregularly shaped fragment. Th: 2.5–3.5 mm. Oval pad (W: 20 mm; H: 18.5 mm; Th: 2–3 mm) of identical glass applied when molten and stamped with a square cross. One beam of the cross is narrow (W: 2 mm) and straight, the other is wider (W: 3–4 mm) and slightly flared at its ends. Find no. MG721.
256. An irregularly shaped piece of fossiliferous sandstone, smooth on the front face and at the top and bottom,

THE ARCHAEOLOGY OF THE GREAT CLOISTER

rough at the back and broken at each end. Maximum dimensions L: 198 mm; W: 104 mm; Th: 28 mm. Two grooves run the length of the face, the upper groove shallow, incomplete at one end and either unfinished or with detail roughly chiselled out. The lower groove is in the form of a rectangular trough, approximately 5–6 mm deep, 6–7 mm wide at the bottom and 11 mm at the top; its top arris is sharp, its lower edge is less so. Along the bottom of the lower groove are incised gothic small letters thus: k k l l m n o p q r r s ſ ſ t t v u x.

There is a fragment of a letter before the first k; both ks are divided, rather like the letter combination 'lc'; there is insufficient space for the tails of the p and q; and x is broken. A groove of this nature and size could only be used to cast in metal a strip of letters to be cut up and rearranged as required. These letters would be in raised reverse form, a primitive form of type. Find no. MG711.

Architectural Detail from the Demolition Contexts (see Figure 4.70)

10. Fragment of an octagonal chimney cap (each face: 175 mm), with traces of a conical hood on its upper surface above a roll and hollow moulding. Below the moulding are the beginnings of two pierced round-headed openings on alternating faces of the shaft. Their spacing close to the angles of the chimney suggests paired vents. As with the other chimney sections this fragment is bolster-dressed externally and punch-dressed internally.

11. Castellated section of octagonal chimney shaft (each face: 170 mm), bolster-dressed externally and punch-dressed internally. Instead of a moulded and castellated cap, merlons and embrasures have been crudely worked on the upper part of the shaft. A single cut-out indicates that alternate faces of the chimney were pierced with single round-headed vents. A second section of this chimney (not illustrated) was recovered, while a third, with the castellation broken off, was found in the Cell 11 garden pentice. This location explains the presence of two chimneys in Cell 11, since this one most probably fell from the north wall of Cell 12. Find no. MG174.

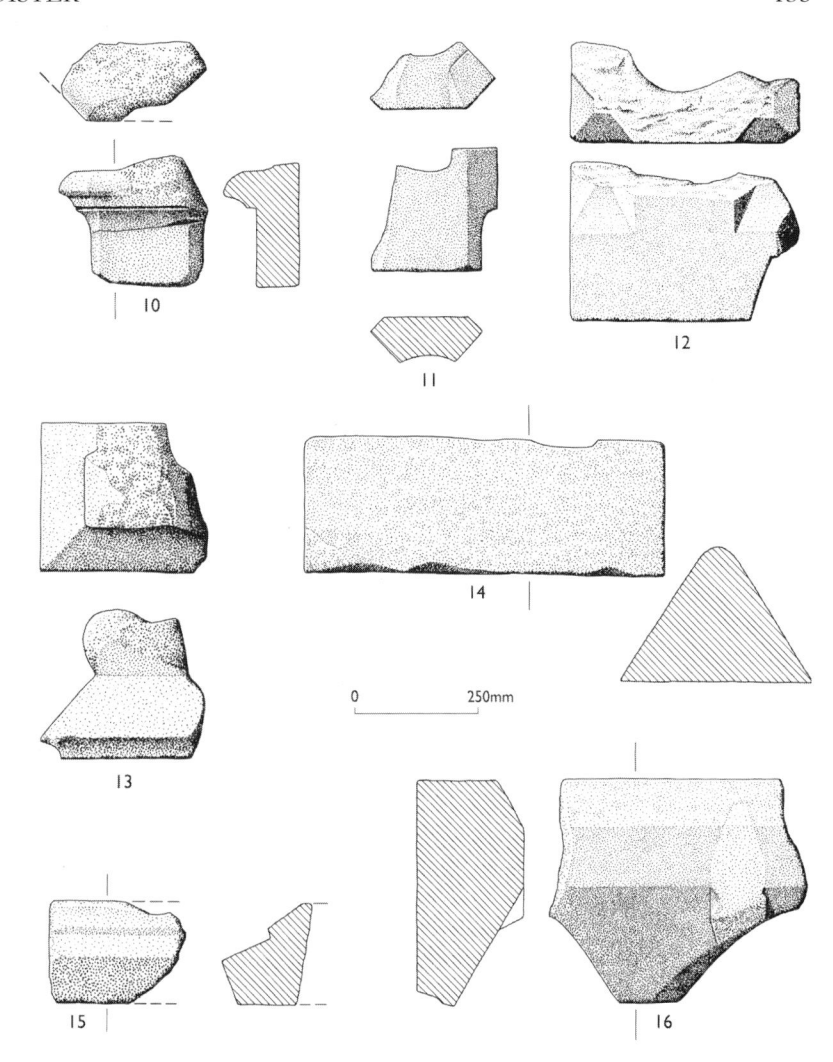

12. Fragment of square chimney base with the beginning of an octagonal shaft and pyramidal chamfer stops on the corners. Find no. MG144.

13. Corner section of a parapet with a hollow drip moulding at its base and a prominent upper roll above a splay. Although found in Cell 11, it may have originated in the prior's cell, which is known to have had a parapet (see Chapter 5). Find no. MG124.

14. Section of wall coping. Upper part of a compound coping from one of the garden walls of the cell. Find no. MG108.

15. One of three identical fragments of a buttress cap matching examples from the cloister alley outside Cell 8 and presumed to come from the Period Two cloister alley. Find no. MG103.

Figure 4.70 Cell 11: architectural detail from demolition contexts (1:10).

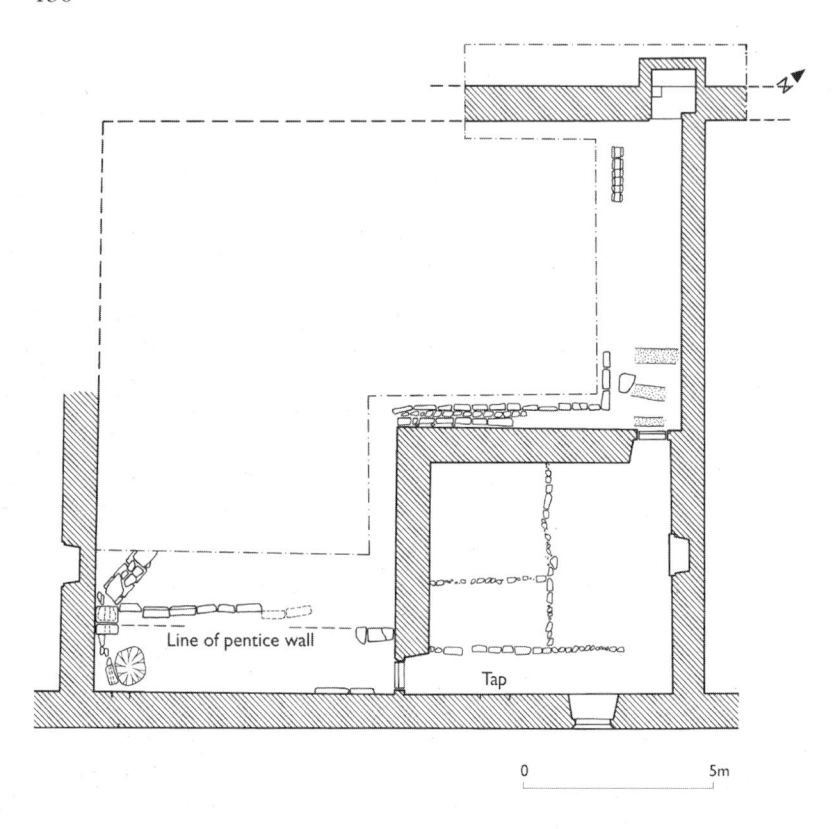

Figure 4.71 Cell 12.

the thin rubble layer beneath the topsoil. This clay layer did not seem to fill any joist slots as in the other cells, but sealed, in the south-west room, four stone alignments which were possibly pads for wooden joists. The stone footings for the cell's partition walls survived beneath the clay and charcoal layer. The partition footings and the stone alignments both seem to have been laid on natural clay.

East (Cloister) Wall
The cloister wall retained its full height, 22 courses.

In the north-east corner of the cell was evidence for the stairway. At the east end of the north wall (see below) survived the chasing for one tread and one riser. The chasings indicated a tread 0.2 m deep and 50 mm wide and a riser (which was in line with the passage partition) 50 mm thick. In the cloister wall the chasings of three treads and two risers remained (see Figure 4.72): the lowest tread would have been 0.4 m deep and 50 mm thick; the first riser 0.25 m high and 50 mm thick; the second tread 0.41 m deep and 40 mm thick; the second riser 0.24 m high and 40 mm thick; and the third tread 0.41 m deep and 40 mm thick.

The cloister doorway was 1.96 m high and had its hinges on the north side. The rebate for the door itself was 90 mm wide. The hatch measured 0.35 m wide and 0.34 m high internally and externally. Externally it had a rebate for the cover, 80 mm wide and 60 mm deep. Internally a hole for a joist, 0.18 m², had been cut one course above the top of the door lintel.

Further south along the east wall was the tap niche, 0.77 m wide and 1 m high, with no decorative features remaining.

Against the cloister wall the east side of the doorway in the south wall of the cell leading into the garden pentice survived. Associated with this door, in the cloister wall, was a rebate for a drawbar, 80 mm wide and 0.55 m high, which had a maximum depth of 80 mm tapering to nothing at the top. The holes for the hinges were also apparent in the cloister wall.

North Wall
The north wall survived only one course, 0.3 m, high. The fireplace had a brick hearth and back, apparently a relining. The maximum thickness of the bricks was 70 mm and their length was about 0.25 m. Nothing remained of the sides of the fireplace. In front of the fireplace

16. Section of cill from the Period Two cloister arcade (see Chapter 6 for full description). Find no. MG123.

A dump of architectural material was recovered from this cell, for in addition to the four sections of the cloister arcade from Cell 8 (Figure 4.48, no. 4), four more sections of associated cill, eight sections of mullion, two sections of jamb, seven sections of head and four sections of plinth were recovered from the same area. These are described in Chapter 6, as are three fragments of chimney base from the Period Two prior's cell found in the same dump.

Cell 12 (see Figure 4.71)
Cell Interior
The depth of overburden was only about 0.4 m. Removal of turf immediately exposed a thin layer of rubble covering the cell itself, which included scattered bricks from the fireplace. Immediately inside the cloister doorway this layer sealed the remains of a pink mortar floor about 0.3 m thick, and of an area 1 m by 0.3 m. This mortar overlay a more extensive area of bedding just inside the cloister door, made up of small cobbles and more pink mortar.

Elsewhere a layer of brown clay, with a considerable amount of charcoal in it, underlay was a square arrangement (not illustrated on Figure 4.71, but visible on Figures 4.72 and 4.73) of stone blocks about 0.3 m from the front of the fireplace. It appears to be the base of a hearthstone extending into the room, on which the fender would have stood.

South and West Walls
The south and west walls of the cell only had one course surviving, approximately 0.3 m high.

Garden Pentice
The stratification in the pentice was very similar to that within the cell; 0.25 m to 0.3 m of topsoil above a thin rubble layer, which overlay brown clay containing charcoal. This clay layer sealed the pentice wall footings, which consisted of a line of haphazardly set flat stones continuing a line established by a large squared stone cut through by the drain at the south of the pentice. A line of stones, presumably marking the west edge of the eavesdrip drain, was found, but the base of the drain and the other side were not found during excavation. No definite flooring to the pentice was found.

At the south end of the pentice a small shaped stone formed the start of a drain running across the pentice floor from a second tap niche, 0.48 m wide. This drain joined another larger drain outside the pentice, where a stone with a shallow depression marked the possible position of a downpipe from the pentice roof. It would seem that this outlet cut across the suggested line of the eavesdrip drain, showing that perhaps the eavesdrip drain went out of use once the guttering was constructed.

The cloister wall was rendered with plaster up to the height of the pentice roof. The wall was 12 courses high, 3.25 m.

Latrine Pentice
Beneath the topsoil a layer of rubble extended over the whole of the pentice and the drain along its edge. It also covered the footings of the party wall of Cell 12 and Cell 11; none of the wall courses survived. The approximate level of the pentice floor was indicated by a layer of small uneven stones (see Figure 4.73), into which three north–south slots had been cut. These were filled with a layer of brown clay and charcoal.

The layer of small stones extended south beneath the eavesdrip drain, which had been constructed on it. Three flat stones of the base of the drain survived at its east end and, at its west end, a short length of the drain with thin side slabs survives in place.

The only indication of the line of the pentice wall was a small posthole between the south end of one of the charcoal filled slots and the eavesdrip drain.

The latrine at the west end survived one to two courses high above the footings. The door was rebated on the east side, but had been blocked up (possibly in the 17th century) with two courses of large dressed stones. The rebate measured 40 mm wide and 50 mm deep, and the total width of the doorway was 0.76 m.

Excavation of a trench along the line of the precinct wall revealed the large stone-lined and capped drain (see Figure 4.74) just outside the line of the precinct wall, which ran beneath the latrine and connected all the latrines along the west

Figure 4.72 Cell 12: as excavated, looking east, showing the survival of the cloister wall with evidence for the stair, internal tap niche, cross-joist and fixings at first-floor level (L. J. Barfoot).

Figure 4.73 Cell 12: latrine and latrine pentice as excavated, looking east (L. J. Barfoot).

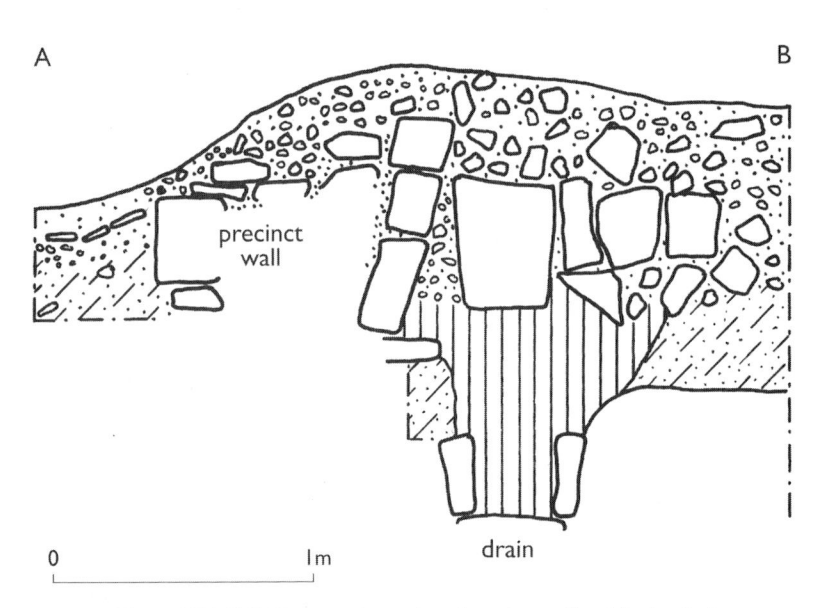

Figure 4.74 Cell 12: east–west section of precinct wall and latrine drain.

precinct wall. The capstones of the drain were at least 0.4 m below the bottom of the foundation stones for the precinct wall. It is therefore evident that the drain was entirely covered.

Garden

The surface level of the garden was reduced considerably at the beginning of the 20th century. Excavation suggested that this surface was lower than in the Middle Ages. A line of large stone blocks marked the north–south drain along the west side of the cell. The character of this drain was so completely different from that of the latrine pentice, to which it would have connected, that it may be wondered if the stones do no more than represent a recent idea of where the drain should be.

Finds Group 16

CERAMICS (SEE FIGURE 4.75)

Cell 12 produced a modest group, containing several pre-priory vessels, including cooking-pot rim 257 (Table 4.17).

The most striking vessel from this cell was the Developed Humber ware cucurbit, 260. This was a specialist vessel form used for distilling and commonly found on monastic sites in the 15th and 16th centuries, where it was used either for distilling spirits or chemical or medicinal products. This example is a comparatively late vessel, probably of the early 16th century, and may therefore have been associated with the work activities of one of the last occupants of this cell.

257. Gritty ware cooking pot. Burnt orange surfaces and pale grey core. Traces of burning and sooting to the outer surface. Coil-built and partly wheel-finished with lightly pinched 'pie crusting' to the outer edge of the rim.

258. Brandsby type baluster base. Orange outer surface, blue-grey core with whitish margins, and off-white inner surface. Badly worn with traces of a wire-pulled base.

259. Hambleton ware jar. Orange outer surface, blue-grey core and dull brownish-purple inner surface. Olive-green glaze. A hole was pierced through the centre of the base of this vessel after firing (probably drilled through from the outer surface). Although glaze had started to corrode slightly in places there is no indication that this

THE ARCHAEOLOGY OF THE GREAT CLOISTER

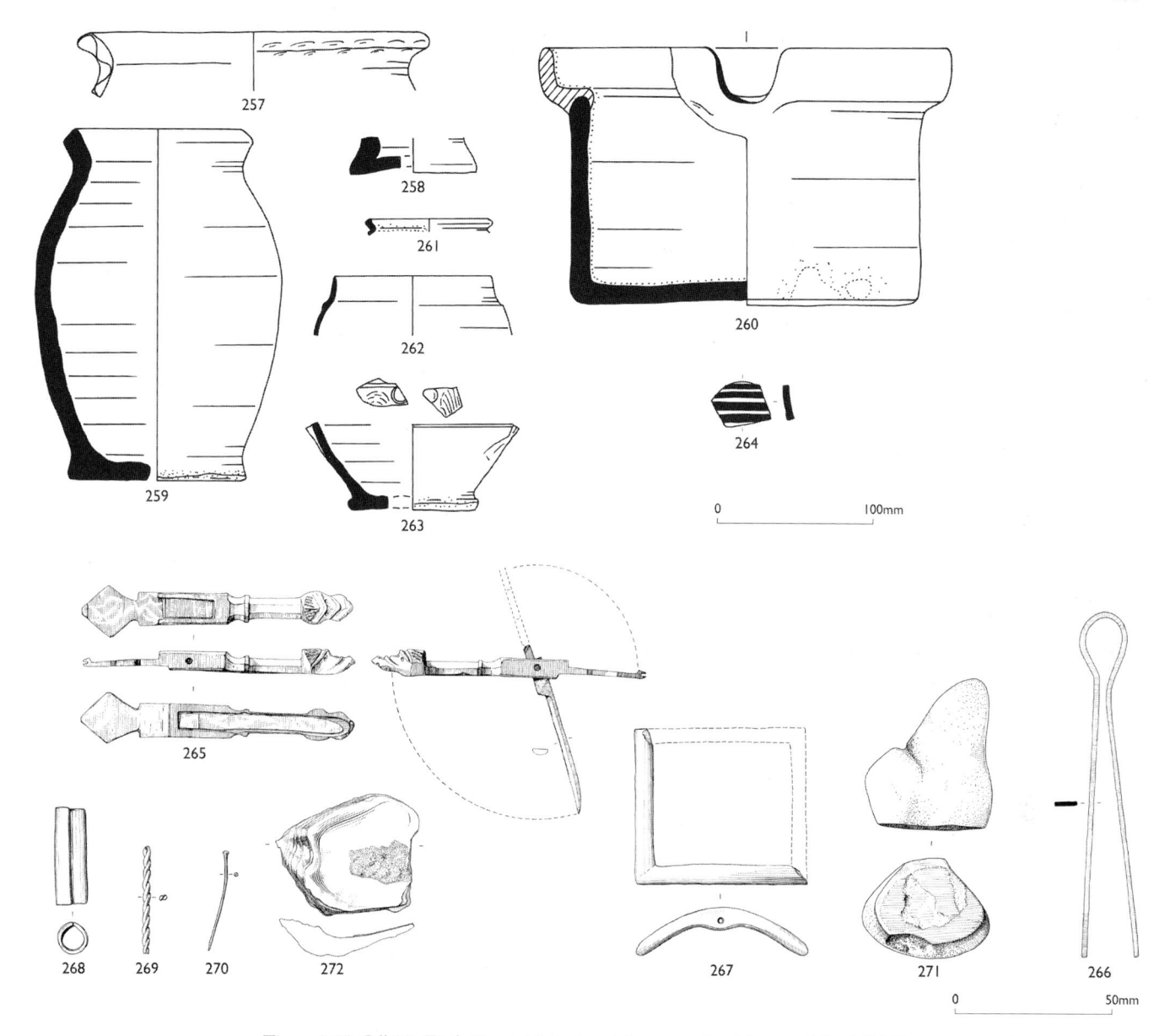

Figure 4.75 Cell 12: Finds Group 16 (pottery 1:4; copper alloy 1:2; stone 1:2; shell 1:2).

vessel had been kept outdoors for any length of time.

260. Humber ware cucurbit. Dull-orange outer surface, blue-grey core with pale orange margins. Almost complete surface cover with brownish-green glaze with thin orange-brown margins. Remains of a single cut-out on the rim.
261. Staffordshire white ware drug jar rim. Smooth, soft whitish-buff fabric, with a greenish-yellow glaze band to the rim top.
262. Cistercian ware posset pot. Blackish glazed surfaces and dark red core.
263. Cistercian ware posset pot. Off-white outer surface and core. Thick, watery, greenish-yellow glaze on both surfaces, heavily crazed where the glaze is thickest. Decorated with deeply impressed circles and traces of more lightly impressed 'ear of wheat' motifs, but overall design and decoration unknown.
264. Mediterranean, striped, black-painted jar. Hard, white, lightly sand-tempered fabric. Thick painted grey horizontal bands, apparently unglazed.

SMALL FINDS (SEE FIGURE 4.75)

265. Coin balance. Cu. The balance beam is L: 85 mm; W (at pivot point): 9 mm. The counterbalance, the heavier end,

Table 4.17 Cell 12, Finds Group 16: Ceramics

Fabric	Sherds	Total vessels	Bottle	Cooking pot	Jar	Jug	Mug or cup	Other
Brandsby type	2	2	0	1	0	1	0	0
Cistercian	6	5	0	0	0	0	5	0
Developed Humber	13	1	0	0	0	0	0	1
Gritty	2	1	0	1	0	0	0	0
Hambleton	7	2	1	0	1	0	0	0
Humber	3	2	0	0	0	2	0	0
Langerwehe	1	1	0	0	0	0	1	0
Post-medieval Orange	4	1	0	0	0	0	0	1
Post-medieval Sandy	2	2	0	0	1	1	0	0
Raeren	2	1	0	0	0	0	1	0
Reversed Cistercian	4	1	0	0	0	0	1	0
Ryedale	24	16	0	0	0	16	0	0
Siegburg	6	4	0	0	0	0	4	0
Staffordshire	2	2	0	0	0	0	0	2
Valencia	1	1	0	0	0	0	0	1

of the balancing arm is W: 6 mm with chamfered top edges and a stylised animal head, with eyes and snout, at the end. The opposite end, on which a coin would be placed, is trapezoidal, with a small stop at the end. A rectangular slot, L: 18 mm; W: 5.5 mm, receives the vertical arm, which is attached to the balance arm in the slot by two pins (diameter: 1.5 mm). When folded shut, the vertical arm is housed in a semicircular groove in the underside of the counterbalance.

The vertical arm is L: 48 mm from the pivot point to the opposite end; W: 5.5 mm (at pivot point), tapering to W: 3 mm (at opposite end). The pivot end is square in section and is housed in the slot. Below the pivot point the arm is round in section on its upper side, where it is housed when shut in the balance arm, and flat below. Find no. MG714.

266. Tweezers. Cu. L: 104 mm; W: 8 mm; Th: 1 mm. Single rod rectangular in section, bent to form a loop with a neck and two arms. Find no. MG715.

267. Buckle frame. Cu. Two adjacent sides only of rectangular frame; H: 48 mm; W: 56 mm; Th: 3 mm. Horizontal hole for central bar through the longer side, 1.5 mm in diameter. Possibly tinned. 18th century. Find no. MG561.

268. Tube. Cu. L: 29 mm; diameter: 9 mm; Th (of sheet): 1 mm. Edge-to-edge seam. Find no. MG676.

269. Twisted wire. Cu. Two single strands. As twisted together L: 33 mm; W: 2 mm; diameter (of each wire): 0.8 mm. Find no. MG651.

270. Pin. Cu. L: 31 mm; diameter (of pin shaft): 0.5 mm; diameter (of solid, flat-topped head): 1.5 mm. Find no. MG1209.

271. Grinding stone. Maximum H: 42 mm. Oval base, with maximum dimensions 26 mm by 35 mm, worn smooth by the use of the stone for grinding pigment. Find no. MG710.

272. Palette, oyster shell. Maximum dimensions L: 42 mm; W: 36 mm; Th: 6 mm. Shell contains visible traces of reddish pigment, which analysis showed to contain lead and mercury, indicating it had been vermillion pigment, which is comprised of red lead (lead tetroxide) or white lead (lead carbonate) and cinnabar (mercuric sulphide). Find no. MG721.

THE ARCHAEOLOGY OF THE GREAT CLOISTER

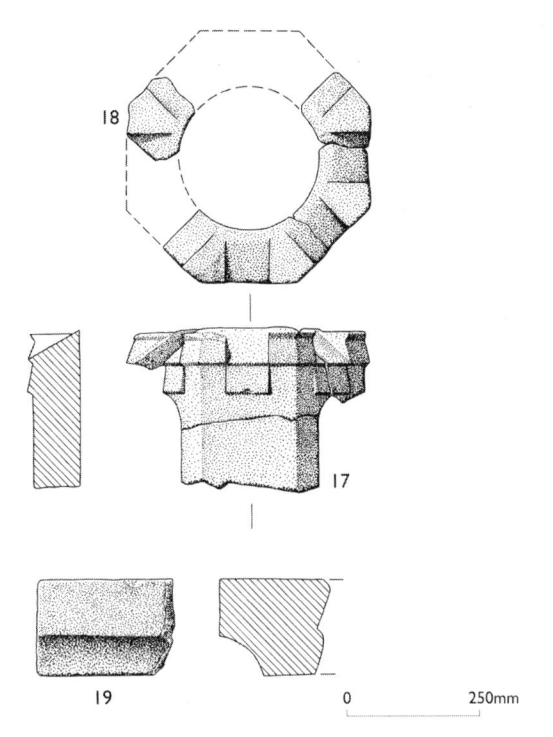

Figure 4.76 Cell 12: architectural detail from demolition contexts (1:10).

ARCHITECTURAL DETAIL FROM THE DEMOLITION CONTEXTS (SEE FIGURE 4.76)

17, 18 Chimney cap with castellated moulding from an octagonal chimney, with each face 185 mm. Design similar to stone 6 (Cell 10, Finds Group 14), but this is a more complete example. Like 6, this chimney has centrally placed lancet-headed openings in alternate faces immediately below the castellation. From its find-spot in the garden pentice of Cell 12 it is almost certainly derived from the north wall of Cell 13 (for the chimney of Cell 12, see fragments found in Cell 11). Sixteen plain sections of chimney shaft (not illustrated) were also found in the pentice, along with three further sections (not illustrated), which retain the edges of pierced vents and must have come from the top of the shaft. As with the other fragments, the finish of this particular chimney, which had apparently fallen complete, was of a very high quality, being dressed on the outer face with a bolster. Find nos MG184, MG194, MG195 and MG196.

19. Section of string course or cornice from the top of the cell wall. Normally these stones are chamfered on their lower angle, but in this case the lower half of the stone has a hollow moulding. Find no. MG175.

In addition, five sections of parapet coping were found, believed to have originated in the Period Two prior's cell. They are discussed in Chapter 4.

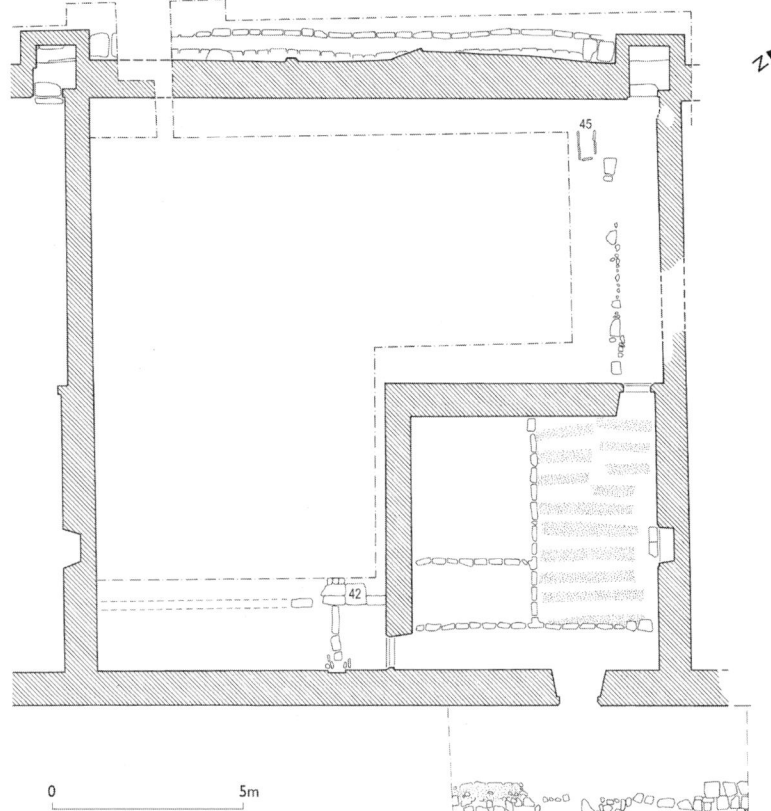

Figure 4.77 Cell 13 and adjacent cloister alley.

Cell 13 (see Figure 4.77)

Cell Interior

Beneath the turf, a layer of demolition rubble consisting of masonry, mortar and roof slates in a dark brown clay was revealed. The combined depth of the turf and rubble was about 0.7 m. Cut into the top of the rubble layer, but underneath the turf, a slight cobbled pathway ran diagonally from the cloister doorway across the north part of the cell (not illustrated). A number of modern (probably post-1957) water pipes in trenches were also encountered, cut into the rubble and the south wall of the cell.

Beneath the rubble layer was a concentrated charcoal spread, which in the area of the living

Figure 4.78 Cell 13: evidence for the floor joists in the living room, seen from the east (L. J. Barfoot).

room sealed and filled a number of north–south joist slots (see Figure 4.78). The charcoal layer also sealed the footings for the internal partitions, which divided the house into three rooms and a passage along the cloister wall. These partition footings were carefully constructed of shaped stones with special T-shaped stones (a technique apparent only in Cell 13) at the junctions of the east–west and north–south partitions. No joist slots were noticed in the two southernmost rooms, and here the layer of burnt wood and charcoal lay immediately over the natural clay.

East (Cloister) Wall
The east wall survived 20 courses high. In the north-east corner was evidence for the staircase. At the east end of the north wall (see below) were chasings for a tread 0.27 m deep and one for a riser 50 mm high. Evidence continued in the cloister wall, with three treads and two risers: the lowest tread was 0.36 m deep and 60 mm thick; the first riser 0.37 m high and 50 mm thick; the second tread 0.35 m deep and 60 mm thick; the second riser 0.26 m high and 60 mm thick; and the third tread 0.32 m deep and 50 mm thick.

Further south along the east wall was the cloister doorway. It was 2 m high with a Bell-period concrete lintel. The rebate for the door itself was 80 mm deep. Set into the wall to the north of the cloister door was the hatch, measuring 0.35 m wide and 0.33 m high internally, and 0.37 m wide and 0.35 m high externally, with a rebate 70 mm wide and 60 mm deep.

Just to the south of the door was a small pointed recess, 0.15 m wide, 0.34 m high and 80 mm deep; apparently a candle niche. Further south along the east wall was a slot, 0.2 m high, 0.25 m wide and 2.60 m above the ground. It was in line with the east–west partition, and was probably the socket for the cross-joist.

North Wall
The north wall of the house survived only a single course, 0.2 m high. Towards its centre was the fireplace, with a back of bricks 50 mm thick by 0.23 m long, and tiles. The surviving top course had three pieces of imported green glazed tile 35 mm thick set into it. The bottom and sides were of stone, and the overall fireplace width was 1 m. The front corners were rebated, and it had two stones, which together were 0.80 m long, and each 0.28 m wide and 80 mm thick, in front of it.

South and West Walls
Like the north wall, the south and west walls survived only one course: the south being 0.244 m high, the west 0.28 m high. In the south wall the door to the garden pentice retained its threshold stone, and the extant cloister wall, against which the doorway was set, showed that its hinges were on the east side. Also remaining in the east wall was a slot for its drawbar, similar to that in Cell 12.

In the west wall the door to the latrine pentice also retained its threshold stone, as well as the lowest courses of the door jambs.

Latrine Pentice
Turf was removed to reveal a layer of demolition rubble 0.5 m deep, consisting of brown sandy soil containing masonry and mortar. The concentrations of masonry and mortar were heaviest immediately to the west of the west wall of the cell, and immediately to the east of the precinct wall. The layer of brown soil and rubble overlay a very thin layer of brown clay, containing smaller fragments of rubble, particularly sandstone and mortar. This thin layer was confined to the area of the pentice path.

Immediately to the north of the pentice path was the robbing trench of the party wall of Cells 12 and 13. The wall appeared to have been robbed after the deposition of the thin layer of brown clay and small rubble. The filling of this robbing trench consisted of a mixture of loose, pale brown soil, rubble mortar and sandstone, which covered the foundation course of the party wall. The foundations were slightly wider than the wall above ground would have been. The thin layer of brown clay and rubble sealed a layer of grey clay covering the whole length of the pentice to a depth of 0.11 m, and burnt red in a small area in the middle of the pentice. This layer probably represented the surface of the path at the latest period of its use (Period Four).

Immediately beneath the grey clay layer was a layer of cobbling along the pentice path and above the masonry footings for the latrine pentice wall (see Figure 4.79), where they extended beyond the above-ground line of the wall face. This cobbling, only one stone thick over its whole area, was rather patchy at its west end. It was possibly an earlier floor to the pentice. The cobbling sealed a layer of yellow mortar, 90 mm deep, which extended under the line of the pentice footings. This must have been the bedding for the earlier pentice floor and wall footings. It was laid directly on the natural brown clay.

Both the drain and the footings for the pentice wall barely survived. The only vestige of the drain is one small piece of flat-laid pennant sandstone near the cell and a box-like structure [45] near the precinct wall. This structure had sides constructed of roofing slates set on edge, and measured 0.57 m by 0.93 m. The bottom was composed of rough cobbling. The whole feature had been cut through a thin layer of dark brown clay, containing crushed sandstone and some charcoal flecks, and into the natural brown clay. The filling of this structure was a similar dark brown clay containing small rubble and charcoal, a maximum of 0.22 m deep. The same thin dark brown clay layer overlay the garden. In the area immediately to the south of [45] a thin layer of charcoal, probably associated with the demolition, overlay the dark brown clay.

The latrine survives one course above ground level, with a step up through the doorway (see Figures 4.79 and 4.80). The doorway had a rebate 50 mm on the east side for the wooden door. The whole latrine block was filled with demolition rubble, sealing a layer of brown clay with fine grit lying in the drain bottom. This layer also contained a certain amount of demolition rubble. The inside of the latrine pit was lined with faced stones down to the bottom of the drain.

There was no evidence for a drain along the west wall of the cell.

Figure 4.79 Cell 13: latrine and latrine pentice as excavated, looking east (L. J. Keen).

Garden Pentice

Turf and topsoil were removed from above a layer of brown sandy soil containing masonry rubble and mortar. The rubble overlay a pale brown clay, which contained small fragments of sandstone, mortar, and charcoal, and was limited to the area of the pentice, extending no further west than the line of the wall footings. To the west of the line of the pentice footings

Figure 4.80 Cell 13: latrine, latrine drain and precinct wall as excavated (L. J. Keen).

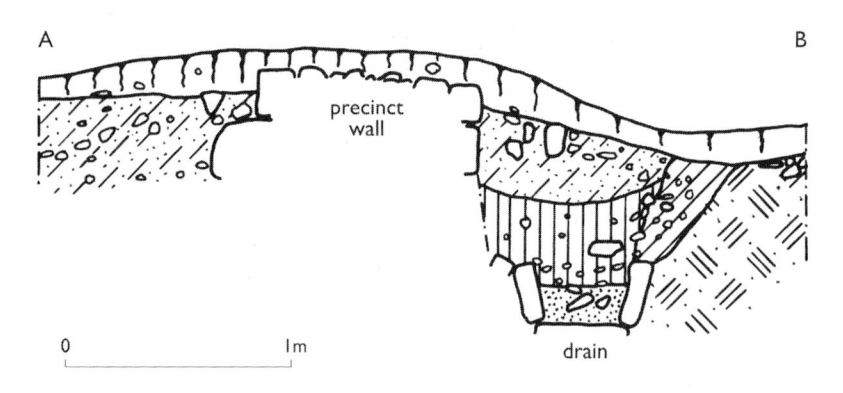

Figure 4.81 Cell 13: east–west section of the precinct wall and latrine drain.

very slight depression where the footings had been robbed.

On the east side of the garden pentice the cloister wall survived 11 courses, 3.30 m high. The tap niche was set into the cloister wall and had its base 0.70 m above the bottom of the drain. It measured 0.70 m wide and 1 m high and had a small round hole in the bottom from which a lead pipe had been withdrawn.

Precinct Wall

Turf covered the whole length of the precinct wall, which defined the west edge of the garden. Beneath the turf the top surviving course of the wall became apparent. On either side of the wall below the turf was a layer of rubble and pale brown clay. The rubble included post-medieval field drainpipes and pantiles. On the outside of the wall a layer of dark brown clay containing charcoal flecks and mortar underlay the rubble. A red-brown clay filling the drain lay underneath the dark brown clay. This lower clay layer also contained fallen masonry.

The precinct wall survived as a single course overlying footings (see Figures 4.80 and 4.81). The footings were offset approximately 0.2 m to 0.3 m from the above-ground face of the wall, and were one course high. The east face of the wall along this exposed length survived intact; the west face, however, had mostly collapsed. In parts its one remaining course leant steeply outwards, obscuring the footings, and in other parts it had fallen completely, partially covering the drain running along the outside of the precinct wall.

The drain itself did not follow a straight line, but curved slightly to the east at both its junction with the latrine of Cell 13 and that of Cell 14. The drain was constructed of faced stones forming its sides, with a flat stone bottom, and would have been capped along its length. The capstones had been robbed, however, except for the parts immediately adjacent to the latrines. In these areas, the tops of the capstones were approximately 0.2 m below the footings and the drain had been cut into the natural clay. The alignment of the drain, with its irregularities corresponding with the latrines of the individual cells, suggests that it was either laid out at the same time as the precinct wall, or with the plan of the west range in mind.

was a red-brown clay containing crushed sandstone and charcoal flecks.

Three stones on the line of the pentice wall footing remained at the north end, set on the natural red clay. One of these was a capstone for a drain running from the tap niche, and possibly served as a threshold stone. Along the line of the pentice wall footings a posthole [42], 0.75 m south of the cell wall, was cut through the pale brown clay. This was almost certainly part of the pentice wall construction. The line of the pentice wall was apparent as a

Cloister Alley

An area of the cloister alley was examined outside Cell 13 to examine its form and state of preservation. Turf and topsoil sealed an area of sandstone cobbling (not illustrated) along the line of the cloister alley. The cobbling had been cut recently by a trench containing a polythene water pipe running from the door of the cell across the cloister alley and into the garth. Its termination at the centre of the garth was recorded in 1988.

When the cobbles were lifted at the north end of the excavated area no trace was found of a medieval water pipe to the tap niche at the south end of the Cell 12 garden pentice, suggesting that the subfloor of the cloister alley had been disturbed. The eastern edge of the cobbling (which should perhaps be associated with the reuse of the cloister alley as a garden path in the 17th century) was marked by the foundations of the cloister arcade.

The cobbling, about 1.44 m wide, was separated from the west cloister wall outside Cell 13 by a gap of about 0.80 m, except in the area of the door to the cell, where the cobbling was continued to the cill.

The cobbling was set in a layer of dark brown soil that extended over the whole width of the cloister alley. The removal of this layer revealed a layer of dirty yellow clay, again extending over the whole width of the alley. The footings of the west cloister wall were also revealed at this level and the dirty yellow clay extended right up to them. The top of the footings were approximately 0.24 m below the top of the cloister door cill and 0.2 m below the top of the cobbling. These footings had been cut into the natural brown clay containing gravel, which underlay the dirty yellow clay. To the east of the cloister arcade footings, topsoil was about 0.17 m deep and seemed to cover a layer of topsoil that had been mixed up with the underlying natural dark brown clay: possibly the result of cultivation of the cloister garth during World War II.

The footings of the cloister arcade extended along the whole length of this trench, though they were rather less substantial immediately to the east of the cell door. Immediately to north and south of this short stretch of insubstantial footings were thickenings in the foundation course for a pair of buttresses. The coincidence of the placement of these buttresses with the slight nature of the footings between them strongly suggests a doorway into the garth at this point.

South of this probable doorway to the garth the arcade footings were roughly mortared; to the north they were not, and the foundations were clearly revealed, two stones wide, approximately 0.70 m.

Finds Group 17

CERAMICS (SEE FIGURE 4.82)

This assemblage contained the remains of only one early post-medieval vessel. In other respects it was typical of the cells of the great cloister, in that it contained a range of local and imported tablewares (Table 4.18).

273. Ryedale ware jug. Dull cream outer surface, white to blue-grey core and grey-black inner surface. Outer surface covered with an apple-green glaze. Upper handle attachment smoothed on.
274. Ryedale ware urinal. Orange surfaces and grey-white to blue-grey to orange core. All over yellowish-green glaze. Traces of salts deposit on inner surface.
275. Hambleton ware jug. Pale grey fabric with a full, but poor quality, greenish-brown glaze to the outer surface. Upper handle attachment simple and smoothed on. Base thick and lumpy with some internal paring away of the thicker parts.
276. Hambleton ware chafing dish. Dull orange-cream surfaces, off-white core turning a blue-grey in the thickenings. Yellow-green glaze with darker copper-green streaks; some pocking of the internal glaze surface.
277. Hambleton ware bottle. Orange outer surface and pale orange core and inner surface. Brownish-green glaze with some dark, slightly metallic, mottling.
278. Humber ware two-handled jar. Dull, deep-purple outer surface skin, otherwise a pale orange fabric. Glazed inner surface varies from olive-green at the rim and base to orange towards the central inner surface. Large, thick, orange-brown outer surface glaze drip. Probably fired upright.
279, 280. Cistercian ware cups. Both have metallic, purple-black glazed surfaces over dull, purplish cores.

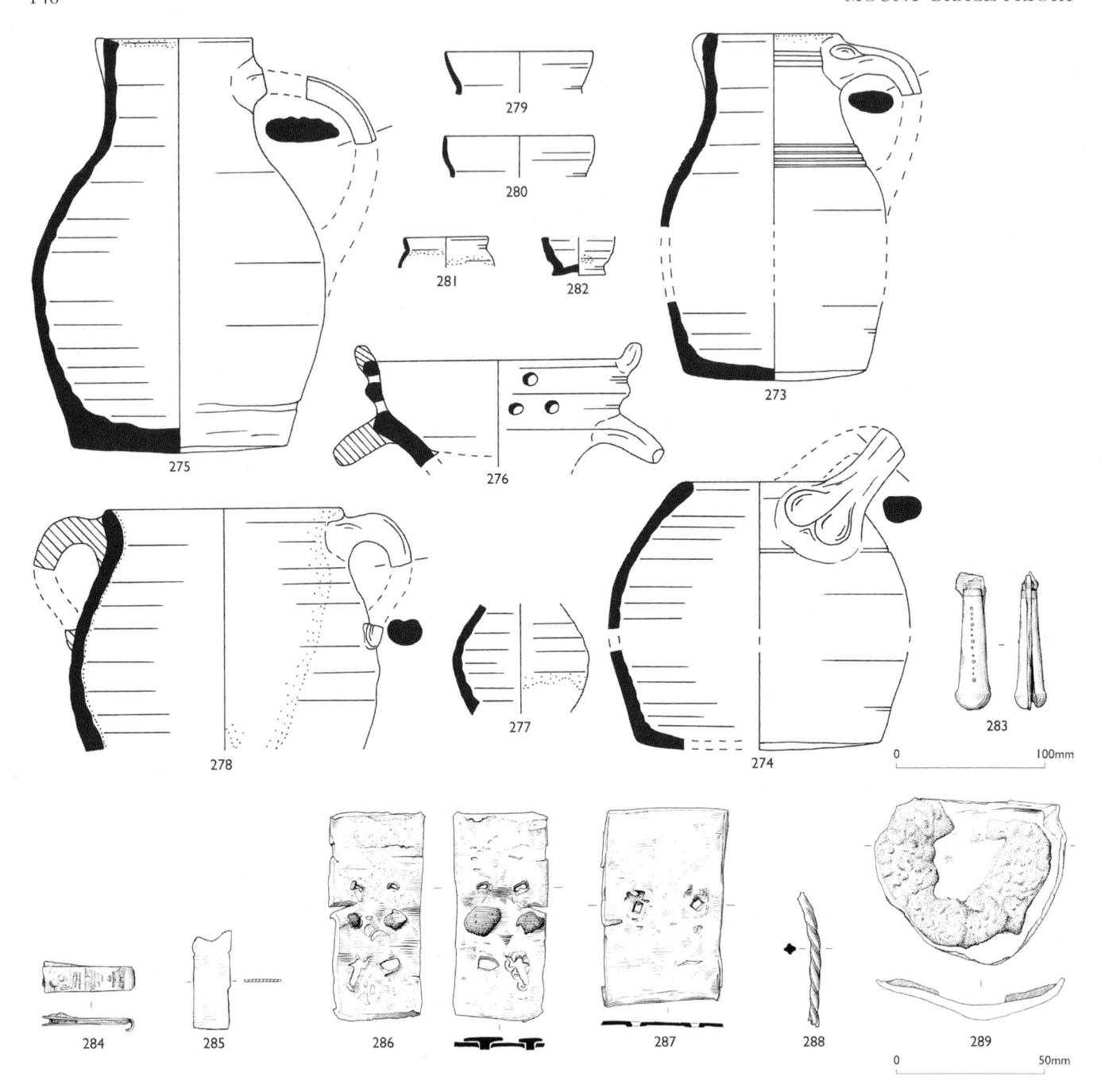

Figure 4.82 Cell 13: Finds Group 17 (pottery 1:4; iron 1:4; copper alloy 1:2; lead 1:2; shell 1:2).

281, 282. Staffordshire white ware drug jars. Soft white fabric with greenish-yellow glazed areas.

SMALL FINDS (SEE FIGURE 4.82)

283. Knife. Fe. Scale tang and fragment of blade. L: 90 mm; W: 19.5 mm (maximum); Th (of blade): 3 mm. Both bone scale plates remain, fixed by a row down the length of the handle of five Cu rivets, L: 12–16 mm; diameter: 1.5 mm. Between each pair of fixing rivets are two Cu pins of 1 mm diameter, eight in total. These penetrate the scale plates, but are purely decorative. Fragments of Fe plate 2.5 mm thick on either side of the blade appear to be the remains of a hammer-welded bolster. Find no. MG732.

284. Book clasp. Cu. L: 30 mm; W: 7–9 mm; Th (of each plate): 1 mm; Th (of clasp overall): 2–3 mm. Hook at one end – to fit over rod of fixed clasp. Separate plates

THE ARCHAEOLOGY OF THE GREAT CLOISTER

Table 4.18 Cell 13, Finds Group 17: Ceramics

Fabric	Sherds	Vessels						
		Total vessels	Bottle	Jar	Jug	Mug or cup	Pancheon	Urinal	Other
Brandsby type	2	2	0	0	2	0	0	0	0
Cistercian	11	8	0	0	0	8	0	0	0
Cistercian copy	23	5	0	0	0	5	0	0	0
Hambleton	36	5	0	0	3	0	0	1	1
Langerwehe	3	2	0	0	2	0	0	0	0
Post-medieval Sandy	1	1	0	0	0	0	1	0	0
Raeren	1	1	0	0	0	1	0	0	0
Ryedale	56	23	0	0	22	0	0	1	0
Siegburg	6	6	0	0	0	6	0	0	0
Staffordshire	2	2	0	0	0	0	0	0	2

have thin spacer to allow for leather strap, part of which survives. Three Fe rivets, two flush with the plates, the other slightly domed. Top plate decorated with three triangles formed of very lightly hammered lines 0.7 mm long. Find no. MG723.

285. Offcut. Cu. Maximum L: 32 mm; W: 12 mm; Th: 0.8 mm. Irregular cuts along one edge. Find no. MG676.

286. Pipe clip. Pb. L: 135 mm; W: 58–63 mm; Th: 2 mm. Two centrally placed holes with the remains of Fe nails; rust stain indicated nail head of 16 mm diameter. To either side of the pair of nail holes are two pairs of other irregular holes. Find no. MG664.

287. Pipe clip. Pb. L: 126 mm; W: 78 mm; Th: 2 mm. One end folded over. Two centrally placed roughly square holes. Impression marks in the lead indicate nail heads of 15–17 mm square. Find no. MG771.

288. Writing lead(?). Pb. L: 83 mm. Twisted, square-sectioned rod, 6 mm by 6 mm. Find no. MG664.

289. Palette, oyster shell. Maximum dimensions 62 mm by 50 mm by 4 mm. Contains green pigment, varying from yellowish to blueish-green. On analysis, the bluish-green area comprised lead, copper and tin in varying amounts, and the yellowish-green area comprised white lead and copper, the latter giving the green or yellow-green colour. Find no. MG737.

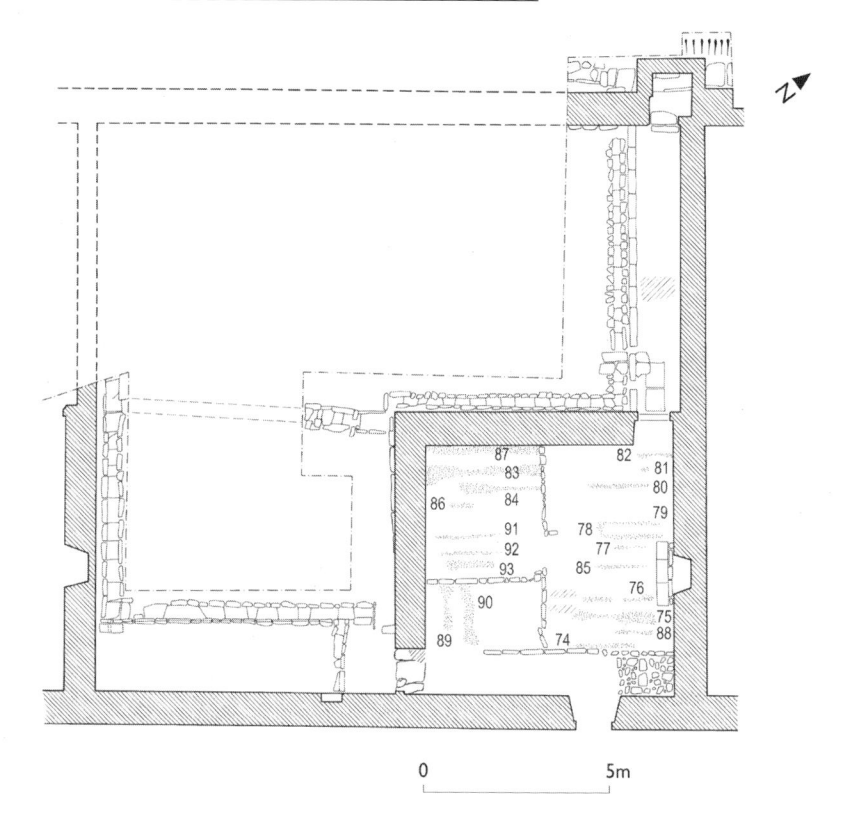

Figure 4.83 Cell 14.

Cell 14 (see Figure 4.83)

Cell Interior

Turf and topsoil were removed revealing a layer of earth and small rubble that extended over the whole of the interior of the cell. It was deepest in the northern part of the cell, where it had the appearance of relatively recent backfilling and levelling of the area. Over the southern half of the cell the earth and small rubble layer covered a layer of brown,

Figure 4.84 Cell 14 and its garden pentice as excavated, looking north (L. J. Keen).

sandy soil containing rubble and mortar, approximately 0.3 m deep. This sandy layer was absent from most of the northern part, with the exception of the north-west corner.

The footings for the internal partitions became apparent on the removal of the demolition layer (the layer of earth and small rubble that extended over the southern half of the cell interior; see Figure 4.84). They consisted of long, roughly square-edged stone blocks about 0.14 m high and divided the interior of the building into three rooms and a passage, as in the other cells. There was a break in the east–west line of footings, which may have marked the position of a door from the large north room to the south-west room. The footings dividing the south-west and south-east rooms overlapped the foundations of the south wall of the cell.

Also underlying the demolition layer was a dark brown soil containing heavy concentrations of charcoal. This lay immediately beneath the top level of earth and small rubble in the area where the demolition rubble layer was absent, and covered the whole of the cell except for the north end of the passageway where there was a small area of paving which was possibly a base for the staircase. This layer was also shown to fill a number of joist slots, [74] to [82], [85] and [88], of which faint traces remained. These joist slots were in the north room, aligned north–south, and cut into an underlying layer of yellow and brown sand and mortar.

In the south-west room were further north–south joist slots, [83], [86], [87] and [91] to [93], but these were cut into the natural brown clay, as were the two east–west joist slots, [89] and [90], in the south-east room.

Cut into the layer of dark brown soil and charcoal was an oval pit (not illustrated) about 1 m by 0.65 m containing the skeleton of an animal. The pit was filled with dark brown soil, but with no charcoal and was situated in the north-east corner of the south-west room.

Against the north wall, between the staircase footings and the fireplace, was a layer of small rubble, red clay and crushed mortar which extended south as far as the edges of the hearth, and was sealed by the dark brown soil with charcoal. This layer was probably a bedding material for paving similar to that immediately in front of the fireplace; the western range of cells seem to have had paving extending from the hearth as far as the foot of the stair, usually the first thing to be robbed at the Suppression. It would have been level with the boarded floor.

The cell floor level was indicated by the top of three stone flags in front of the fireplace and the bottom edge of the plaster rendering, with which these flags were level, on the inside of the north wall. Traces of this plaster were also apparent on the west and south walls.

The top of the partition footings also corresponded closely to the bottom of the plaster rendering.

Two patches of solid mortar lay between the joist slots [75] and [76] in the north room. The purpose of these is uncertain.

(Cloister) Wall

The east (cloister) wall of the cell had a ledge 11 courses above ground level, possibly to carry a joist for the upper floor. Above this ledge were a further eight courses.

Chasings for the staircase in the north-east corner of the cell existed in both the north and east walls. Those in the north wall (see below) indicated that the lowest tread of the stair was 0.27 m deep and 60 mm thick; the first riser 0.29 m high, 60 mm thick; the second tread 0.36 m deep, 90 mm thick; the second riser 0.28 m high, 70 mm thick; the third tread 0.53 m deep, 60 mm thick; and the third riser 0.26 m high.

Continuing in the east wall the chasings indicated the next a tread was 0.49 m deep and 70 mm thick, the first riser 0.32 m high, 90 mm thick, the second tread 0.41 m deep, 70 mm thick; the second riser 0.31 m high and 40 mm thick; and the final tread 0.4 m deep and 50 mm thick.

The cloister door was 2 m high to the top of the arch with a concrete lintel. The rebate for the door itself was 90 mm. The hatch measured 0.36 m wide and 0.36 m high internally, with a groove on the inside, 30 mm wide and 10 mm deep, presumably for an internal hatch cover. Also in the cloister wall, which survived to full height, was a joist hole for an upper floor in line with the east–west partition, measuring 0.28 m², and 2.65 m above floor level.

North Wall

The north wall of the cell had two surviving courses, 0.55 m high. The fireplace in the north wall was 0.93 m wide and 0.35 m deep. It had rebates 50 mm by 50 mm on either side at the front and a chamfered stone fender. It was relined with bricks 0.15 m deep. The bricks appear to be later relining as the stonework behind them was very burnt.

Further east along the north wall, in line with the north–south passage partition, was a rebate 0.17 m by 0.15 m.

South and West Walls

The south wall of the house retained one course, 0.35 m high, the west wall also had only one course, 0.32 m high.

Latrine Pentice

Turf and topsoil covered a layer of rubble in a dark brown soil extending over the entire area. This rubble and soil layer had its maximum thickness immediately to the west of the west wall of the cell, where it was 0.35 m deep, and immediately to the east of the precinct wall. It also sealed the garden wall, which had been robbed down to the top of the footings. The removal of the rubble and soil layer revealed the pentice wall footings and the eavesdrip drain (see Figure 4.85).

Within the area of the pentice, the soil and rubble layer sealed a layer of loose, fine, pale brown sand, mortar and rubble. This in turn sealed the natural dark brown clay, which had a trampled surface containing charcoal flecks and small fragments of sandstone.

The surviving pentice paving, which was laid on the natural dark brown clay, consisted of two large stone slabs immediately outside the doorway from the house to the pentice passage. Along the remaining length of the passage the heavily compacted dark brown clay possibly represented the actual floor level.

The pentice wall footings consisted of a regular line of large square blocks about 0.23 m by 0.2 m, extant along the whole length of the pentice. About 1.5 m west of the doorway from the cell was a slightly higher block, which was presumably the cill of the doorway to the garden. At this point the pentice paving continued across the eavesdrip drain, which elsewhere was open.

The eavesdrip drain was approximately 80 mm deep and 0.2 m wide, with regularly constructed sides and a paved bottom. At the east end of the pentice it turned through 90 degrees and continued south along the west wall of the cell until it reached the south-west corner, at which point it again turned 90 degrees, opening onto a larger box-like feature, possibly a tank (see Figure 4.86), against the south wall of the south-west corner of the house. This possible tank had upright stone sides and a paved base.

It appeared that the outlet from this tank could be blocked in order to retain water. The

Figure 4.85 Cell 14: latrine pentice and latrine as excavated, looking west (L. J. Keen).

Figure 4.86 Cell 14: tank and sluice at the south-east corner of the cell (L. J. Keen).

outlet was on the south side of the tank and led into a drain that ran south across the garden to meet an east–west drain along the south garden wall. Immediately to the south of the outlet from the tank the drain was covered over with stone slabs.

South of the pentice wall footings the layer of rubble sealed two layers of broken roof slates. The uppermost layer of roof slates were in dark brown soil, while the lower layer of slates were in a paler-brown soil which contained some mortar and charcoal. These two slate layers lay immediately on top of each other. The slates, deriving from the destruction of the pentice roof, lay on the natural dark brown clay, which must have represented the surface of the monastic garden.

The precinct wall survived one course, 0.3 m high, and contained the rebates (40 mm deep and 50 mm wide) for the latrine door and a door hinge hole on the north jamb.

Within the latrine, beneath the top layer of rubble, was a layer of red-brown clay containing a number of blocks of masonry, which sealed a pale brown compact clay, presumably a silting of the drain, lying immediately on top of the stone bottom of the drain. To the south of the latrine the red-brown clay layer sealed a loose, gritty mid-brown soil containing flecks of mortar, under which lay more of the pale brown clay silting.

Garden Pentice

Turf and topsoil, approximately 70 mm deep, were removed to reveal a layer of brown earth containing small fragments of masonry rubble. This covered both the pentice and the small area of garden excavated, and was approximately 40 mm deep. The brown earth and rubble sealed a layer of pale brown clay containing small rubble chippings and fragments of mortar. This layer represented

Table 4.19 Cell 14, Finds Group 18: Ceramics

Fabric	Sherds	Total vessels	Bottle	Cooking pot	Jar	Jug	Mug or cup	Other
Brandsby type	1	1	0	0	0	1	0	0
Cistercian	2	2	0	0	0	0	2	0
Cistercian copy	7	2	0	0	0	0	2	0
Gritty	1	1	0	1	0	0	0	0
Hambleton	3	3	0	0	0	3	0	0
Humber	3	2	0	0	0	2	0	0
Langerwehe	5	3	0	0	0	0	3	0
Late Gritty	1	1	0	0	0	1	0	0
Post-medieval Orange	1	1	0	0	0	0	0	1
Post-medieval Sandy	2	2	0	0	1	1	0	0
Raeren	14	2	0	0	0	0	2	0
Regional Stray	1	1	0	0	0	1	0	0
Ryedale	21	17	1	0	0	16	0	0
Staffordshire	1	1	0	0	0	0	0	1
Tudor Green	2	1	0	0	0	0	1	0

the trampled floor of the pentice and was the disturbed top of the natural clay.

The tap niche in the cloister wall was approximately 1.40 m south of the door to the garden pentice. It was 0.5 m wide and 0.9 m high. It had a decorative head with two beam slots, one on each side of the head of the recess on the face of the cloister wall. That to the south was 0.23 m wide and 0.36 m high, while the one to the north was 0.18 m wide and 0.31 m high. These may have carried a small canopy over the tap niche, though no trace of upright supports for this was found. Leading from the tap niche was a small drain, 0.1 m deep and 0.16 m wide, crossing the pentice to join the eavesdrip drain. The south side of the tap drain had been robbed.

The pentice wall survived only as two stones, approximately 0.25 m high, one at either end of the pentice, and both lying immediately inside the line of the eavesdrip drain.

Beneath the layer of brown earth and rubble, on the garden (west) side of the line of the pentice wall, was a layer of broken roof slates in dark brown soil, approximately 60 mm deep. This sealed, within the drain, a layer of loose red-brown clay, which extended along the whole length of the drain. To the west of the drain this red-brown clay layer lay upon the natural dark brown clay.

The eavesdrip drain started about 0.6 m to the south of the south wall of the cell and had regular sides of upright stones and a paved base. The sides were approximately 0.2 m high. At the south end of the pentice the drain turned through 90 degrees to run west along the party wall with Cell 15. It then connected with the north–south drain crossing the garden, but a north–south upright stone blocking suggested that water could be held up at this junction. The drain continued to the west beyond the edge of the excavation.

The cloister wall south of the cell is 12 courses, 3.30 m high, and has the eastern jamb of the pentice door extant in it. The west jamb has been robbed, but two hinge holes and a slot for a drawbar survived in the cloister wall.

Finds Group 18

CERAMICS (NOT ILLUSTRATED)

Despite a comparatively sizeable assemblage, most of the material from Cell 14 was very fragmentary and nothing merited illustration. The range of pottery spanned pre-priory fabrics to early post-medieval, with jugs, mugs and cups making up the bulk (Table 4.19).

SMALL FINDS (SEE FIGURE 4.87)

290. Pin. Fe. Elongated triangle-shaped pin. L: 122 mm; W: 19.5 mm, tapering to 3.5 mm; Th: 6–15.5 mm. Circular hole, 6 mm in diameter, at the wider end. Find no. MG1026.

152 MOUNT GRACE PRIORY

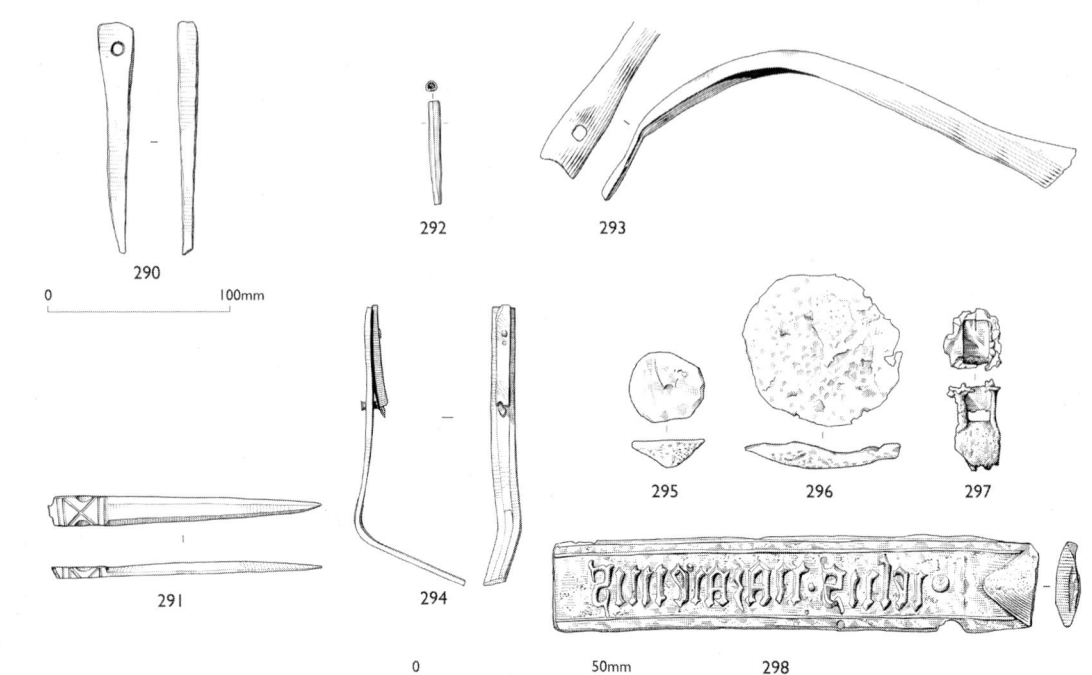

Figure 4.87 Cell 14: Finds Group 18 (iron 1:4; copper alloy 1:2; lead 1:2).

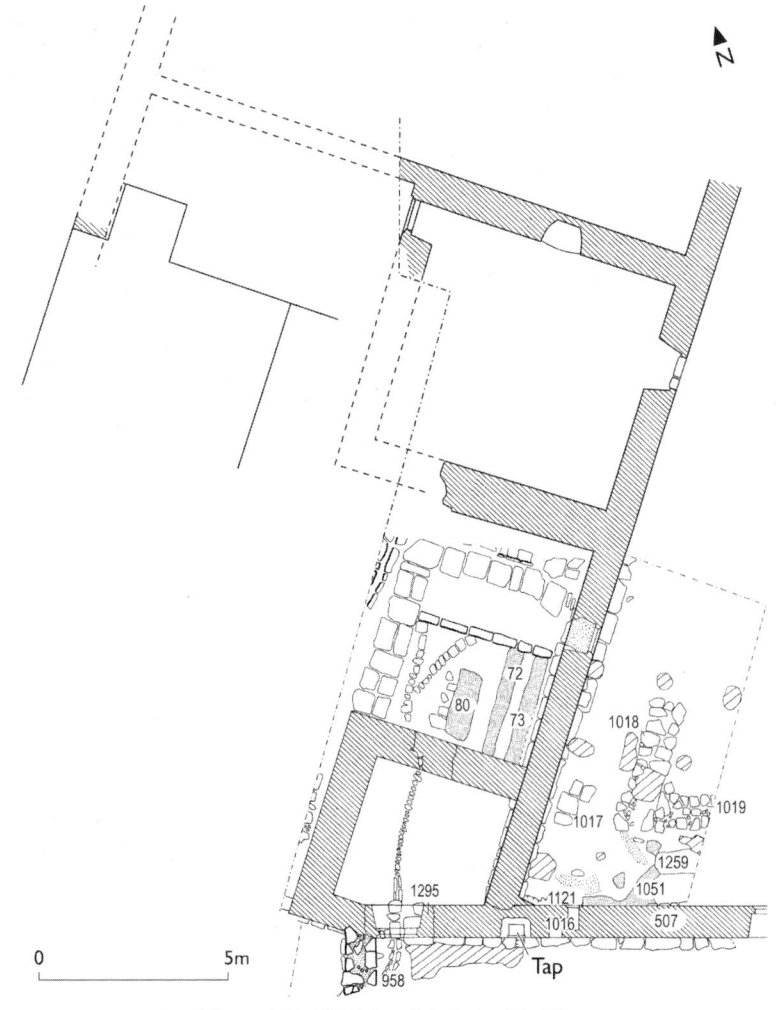

Figure 4.88 Cell 15 and the 'prison' building.

291. Coin balance. Cu. Vertical arm only. L: 75 mm; W: 8 mm tapering to point. Wider end has remains of pivot joint, W: 2.5 mm, and is decorated with incised lines and notches on the outside edges. Rest of top surface has chamfered edges. Back is flat. Find no. MG946.

292. Lace chape. Cu. L: 27 mm; diameter: 2 mm. Overlapping seam. Remains of leather inside. Find no. MG1257.

293. Binding strip. Cu. L: 147 mm; W: 8 mm (maximum); Th: 0.3 mm. Strip is folded together lengthways for 6–7 mm. Flat end has a hole 3 mm in diameter. Find no. MG1016.

294. Mount. Cu. Overall L: 90 mm; W: 6 mm; Th: 1 mm. Attached to the main strip is another strip, slightly smaller (W: 4 mm; Th: 2 mm), and attached to the larger strip by two Cu rivets. A soldering mark shows that the smaller strip originally extended along the full length of this piece. Find no. MG1030.

295. Pan weight. Pb. Flat base and roughly domed. Maximum diameter: 40 mm; H: 14 mm. Find no. MG785.

296. Cake. Pb. Diameter: 80 mm; H: 8 mm. Slightly concave. From casting. Find no. MG778.

297. Masonry plug. Pb. L: 45 mm; W: 22 mm. Recess to hold ferramentum, L: 23 mm; W: 15 mm; H: 22 mm. Find no. MG778.

298. Plaque. Pb. L: 128 mm; W: 24 mm wide; Th: 1 mm. Casting end 6 mm thick, extending into strip for 14 mm. Raised retrograde inscription *iefus.nazarenus* between two paired lines running the length of the strip. Casting bullet at one end. From same mould as 251 and another piece from Cell 10. Find no. MG1017.

Cell 15 (see Figures 4.88 and 4.90)

Cell Interior

Total excavation of this cell was prohibited by the access drive to the then works compound.

After removal of turf and topsoil, which were 70 mm thick, a very thin layer of light metalling was found to cover the western half of the cell. It appeared to have been a continuation of a post-Suppression trackway encountered in the excavation of the kitchens to the south (see Chapter 5).

Post-Suppression building debris, probably of the 17th-century and later, including rubble, pantiles and large numbers of nails, lay on this gravel metalling. To the east of this area, removal of topsoil revealed a thin layer of earth containing demolition rubble overlying the natural red clay, which covered the whole of the interior. The cell had been excavated by Hope and its plan determined (Hope 1905, 300).

East (Cloister) Wall

The east wall survived to a height of 22 courses (see Figures 4.90 and 4.91). The lower 17 courses, 5 m high above floor level, pre-dated the building of the cell and were built in Period One. The wall had shallow foundations, 0.16 m high, projecting 60–100 mm from the wall face, except immediately to the north of the cloister door, where they projected 0.33 m.

Evidence for the staircase that existed in the north-east corner of the cell survived only for the upper stairs, in the cloister wall. At the north end of this wall were chasings for two risers and two treads. Just south of these was the surviving hatch (0.36 m wide and 0.35 m high) and the cloister door, 2.15 m high with its hinges on the north reveal. Both door and hatch were inserted into the earlier wall, as was the lower part of the single-light window that survives at first-floor level.

This window is square-headed and may have been part of the original work (Hope 1905, 301). In Period Three the first floor of Cell 15 was altered. A second first-floor window, a large, low opening with a wide splay on the inside, was inserted into the east (cloister) wall just above first-floor level, and to its south a first-floor door, of which the jamb survives. This door provided access over a short bridge to the first floor of a new building that extended the Period One prison building to the north (see Figures 4.88 and 4.90). The low window has two beam sockets at its base, one on either side. Beneath these are two further beam sockets, the most northerly of which is vertically above another at floor level immediately to the south of the cloister door. Their function is unclear.

South Wall

The south wall survived as foundations only, and these had been robbed from its west end, leaving only about two-thirds of the foundations at the east end remaining. The south doorway to the garden pentice survived only as the east jamb in the cloister wall, which also contained the slot for a drawbar, all inserted into the earlier wall.

West Wall

Of the west wall of the cell only the doorway to the latrine pentice and about 0.90 m of wall to the south of this doorway could be excavated. The doorway has chamfered jambs and a cill 0.18 m high resting directly on foundations. Inside the doorway the recess was paved with three large stones.

North Wall

Of the north wall only one course remained, approximately 0.3 m high, resting on foundations that were contiguous with those under the west wall. The foundations were about 0.25 m deep and were cut through the natural clay. The fireplace in the north wall was constructed of burnt red sandstone blocks. The sides of the fireplace survive to a height of no more than 0.12 m. The front of the fireplace was destroyed. There were no surviving chasings for the staircase in the north wall. The only indication of a partition for the passage was a small rebate, 0.14 m wide and 0.2 m high, about 1.10 m west of the cloister wall: beneath this are four other features.

Table 4.20 Cell 15, Finds Group 19: Ceramics

Fabric	Sherds	Vessels			
		Total vessels	Jug	Mug or cup	Other
Hambleton	6	2	2	0	0
Post-medieval Orange	1	1	0	0	1
Siegburg	1	1	0	1	0

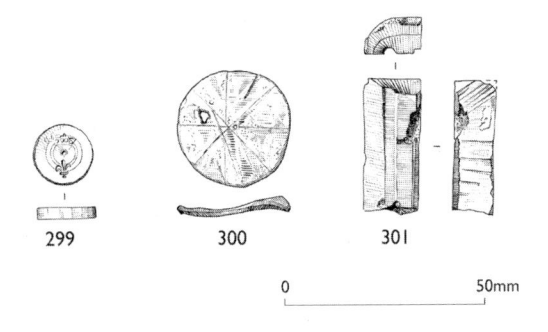

Figure 4.89 Cell 15: Finds Group 19 (copper alloy 1:2; lead 1:2; stone 1:2).

Latrine Pentice

Because of the access drive to the then works compound, no part of the latrine pentice could be uncovered. Of the section of party wall between Cells 14 and 15 backing the latrine pentice, no more than 0.5 m of it survived at its east end.

Garden Pentice and Garden

The tap niche is immediately outside the garden door of the cell and a rebate for a water pipe is apparent beneath the recess. There is no indication of the garden pentice along the cloister wall.

In Period Three part of the garden of Cell 15 was taken over to expand an earlier building in the south-west angle of the great cloister (see Chapter 6) contemporary with the first-floor alterations in Cell 15 (see Figure 4.90). The east garden wall of Cell 15 was heightened by three courses to stand one course higher than the east (cloister) wall of the cell, and this heightened wall was bonded with the inserted first-floor door of Cell 15. Against this raised wall, a new first-floor chamber accessible from the great cloister and the first-floor chamber of Cell 15 was built.

Finds Group 19

CERAMICS (NOT ILLUSTRATED)

Only a handful of sherds could be ascribed to Cell 15 with any confidence and none of these warranted illustration or further comment (Table 4.20).

SMALL FINDS (SEE FIGURE 4.89)

299. Weight. Cu. Diameter 14 mm, 2 mm thick and weight 3.4122g. Dr N. Mayhew, Heberden Coin Room, Ashmolean Museum, Oxford, reports that this is uniface (having one side blank) with fleur-de-lis and crown. The absence of any coin design raises uncertainty about whether this is a coin weight, though the weight would be about right for half a noble of 1412–64, and the crown and fleur-de-lis suggest an official role. Find no. MG960.

300. Disk. Pb. Diameter 23 mm, 1.5 mm thick. The centre of the disk is marked by the point of the compass that was used to mark it out, and a horizontal line has been cut through this mark. A vertical line dividing the disk roughly into quarters is cut 2 mm to the left of the centre mark. Diagonal lines dividing the disk into approximate eighths cross halfway between the centre mark and the junction of the vertical and horizontal lines. Find no. MG996.

301. Mould fragment, stone. Maximum dimensions 32.5 mm by 14 mm by 10 mm. In the smoothed upper surface there are two grooves, one 3 mm wide and 1.5 mm deep with a rounded bottom, the other at least 2 mm wide and 3 mm deep with a slightly sloping side and uneven base. The mould has broken along this deeper groove. Find no. MG997.

The Prison Block (see Figures 4.88, 4.90 and 4.91)

Condition before Excavation

Lying in the south-east corner of the garden plot of Cell 15 was a substantial structure which had been partially excavated by Hope and identified by him as a pair of cellars, with ground- and first-floor rooms above them, of at least two phases of construction.

Only the east (cloister) wall of this structure survived to full height (see Figures 4.90 and

THE ARCHAEOLOGY OF THE GREAT CLOISTER

4.91). A lower stretch, of about 6.5 m high, of the south wall remained above ground, buttressing the south-western corner of the south cloister range.

The southern half of the building, of irregular plan, bonded with the north wall of the Period One south-west cloister range (see Chapter 5 for a description and Chapter 6 for analysis of this range) and was of one build with it. Originally of three storeys of a single room, the southern half measured internally about 3.7 m from north to south on its longest, its west, side and 3.8 m from east to west.

In the east (cloister) wall of this room was a splayed recess, formed by blocking an earlier doorway. It was 1.05 m high and 1.07 m wide, with a slot for a wooden shelf at mid-height.

In the south wall at both ground- and first-floor levels were inserted doors communicating with the south-west cloister range.

Of the northern half of the building, only its east (cloister) wall survived to full height, with a narrow inserted door at its north end at ground-floor level and an inserted three-light window at first-floor level.

The Prison Block

Available Archaeology

In the southern room excavation revealed that the original floor had been dug out to a depth of about 0.80 m below the top of the footings, effectively destroying any construction or occupation deposits earlier than the date of that operation. The digging out of the floor was associated with the insertion of a door, [1295], in the north wall of the south-west cloister range in Period Three, and with the piercing of a door at the centre of the north wall of the block which was contemporary with the addition of a second room to the north. Thus, only the archaeology of the extended building of Period Three and later was available for excavation.

Northern Half

The northern room was a later addition to the earlier block and measured 4 m² internally with a partitioned passage 1.20 m wide to the north (see Figure 4.91). This passage was entered through an inserted doorway (which had originally served as the cloister door of the earlier prison block). The doorway was 1.95 m high and 0.64 m wide.

Only the footings of the northern half of the block survived, two blocks thick on the

Figure 4.90 Interior elevations of the 'prison' and adjacent buildings.

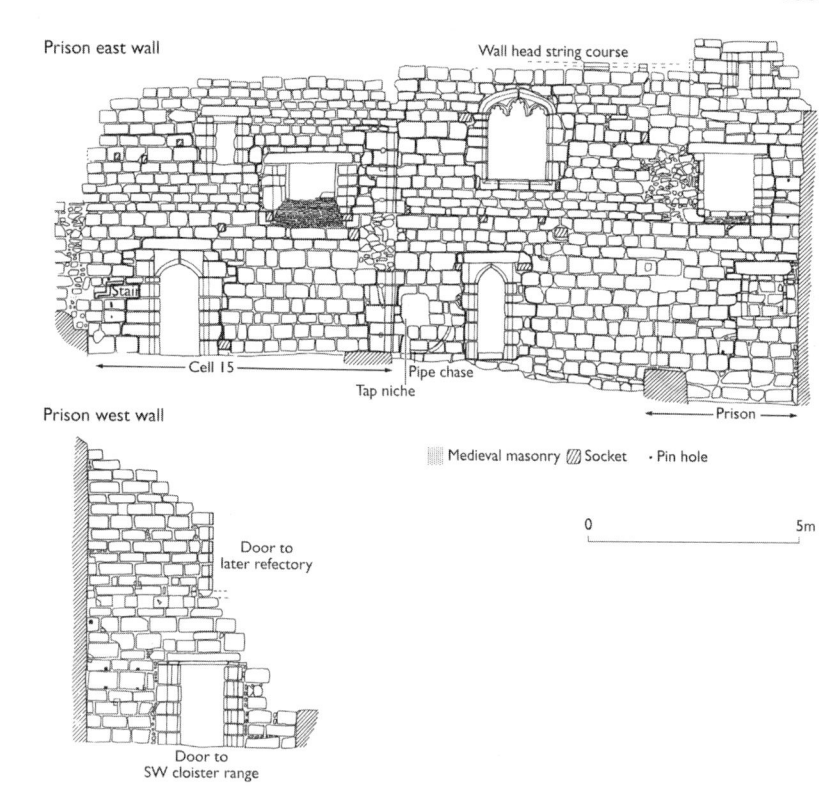

Figure 4.91 Prison block as excavated, looking south (L. J. Keen).

west side, but only a single block thick on the north. The passage partition at the northern end comprised a cill wall of a single course, some 0.21 m high, that had carried a timber partition.

To the north of this partition the clay floor, which was not excavated, was at the higher level of the west cloister alley, while south of it the floor level approximated to the passage on the north side of the south-west cloister range (see Chapter 5), though it sloped upwards slightly to the north.

The passage must have contained a stair to the chambers created at first-floor level. Other than this passage the building was excavated down to the surface of the natural red clay of the terrace, onto which the extension of Period Three was footed.

Cut into this material was a stone-lined and capped conduit, which emerged from beneath the cill of the passage partition wall and ran along the west side of the northern room, through the forced entry in the north wall of the original building, across that room and beneath the threshold of the inserted door into the south-west cloister range where it was further traced. This conduit had originally contained a lead water pipe and probably still does at its northern end, where its capstones remain in place. The source of the conduit is unknown, but there are two branches at its northern end, one leading from the general direction of the tap niche in Cell 15.

To the east of the conduit in the northern room were two linear features, [72] and [73], which look suspiciously like chases for floor joists, running parallel to the cloister wall and terminating at the line of the passage partition to the north, and the cross-wall to the south. They were filled with red clay and rubble, and it would appear that a timber floor in the northern room was abandoned in favour of a spread of clean red clay that sealed the conduit and the other features. This clay spread through the forced opening into the southern room, occupying its northern half.

Cutting the clean clay in the centre of the northern room was a rectangular pit, [47], measuring 0.57 m from east to west and 2.33 m from north to south, and 0.28 m deep with almost vertical sides. It was filled with compact red clay. On the surface of the red clay layer in this room was a patchy layer of compact mortar, which comprised the finished floor surface, butting up against the walls but spreading through the opening into the southern room. In the western part of the room the mortar floor overlay a small tip of clay, sandstone fragments and charcoal, possibly a levelling deposit.

Southern Half

In the southern room, to the east of the conduit and almost centrally placed, was a rectangular feature, [47], measuring 0.46 m north to south and 0.54 m from west to east, with vertical slides and a slightly sloping bottom. It had a maximum depth of 0.17 m and was filled with mixed grey and red clay, sandstone and brick rubble. A second feature, [48], in the extreme south-west corner of the room, was also cut into the surface of the natural clay. It measured 0.48 m north to south and 0.59 m from east to west, with vertical sides and a flat bottom. It was 0.29 m deep and was filled with grey-brown clay containing fragments of plaster, charcoal and sandstone rubble.

The Water Tower in the Great Cloister (see Figure 4.92 and 4.93)

Condition before Excavation

Hope excavated the central part of the great cloister in 1900 searching for a water tower or conduit similar to that shown on the early 15th-century plan of the London charterhouse (see Figure 4.93). His excavation remained until 1988 as a partly filled circular pit. Of what he found he gave the following description: 'a number of broken fragments of a small octagonal building, buttressed at the angles, with traceried openings in the sides. Some rough stones below may have served as foundations or footings. No pieces of piping or traces of drains were met with, and the worked stones lay as though thrown down' (Hope 1905, 304).

Re-excavation in 1988 was designed to enable the recovery of the structure that Hope revealed, to allow the waterlogged hole to be filled in, and to examine the construction of the great cloister terrace in an area already known to have been seriously disturbed and unlikely to contain burials or garden features. In all respects the excavation was successful.

The Structure of the Terrace (see Figures 4.92 and 4.94)

Deep excavation below the base of the 19th-century pit struck undisturbed natural clay some 3 m below the current surface of the great cloister. Above this was a deposit of peat, [455], sealed by a thin layer of grey clay, [444], that marked the depth of the Victorian

THE ARCHAEOLOGY OF THE GREAT CLOISTER

excavation. Above the clay was a further deposit of peat, [443]. In all, these water-laid deposits were 2.75 m deep (for a fuller discussion, see Chapter 7) and appeared to represent the progressive filling of a boggy hollow formed by a massive landslip towards the end of the last glaciation.

The extent of the peat deposit, and hence the extent of the hollow in the hillside, is not known, though it did not extend below the north range of the cloister, nor was it seen below the south-west cloister range. The likelihood is therefore that the great cloister terrace represents a modification of an existing natural terrace on the hillside at the foundation of the priory. Within the area examined this modification took the form of levelling deposits of redeposited natural blue to grey clay [446], and pale grey clay, [438] and [439], that sealed the peat deposit, which had continued to develop up to the foundation of the house.

Within the levelling material [438] was a complete plain floor tile and two fragmentary quarries of pale green window glass.

Above the primary levelling material [438] was a deposit of garden soil comprising a red to brown subsoil, [432], [434] and [435], which contained many small fragments of sandstone, perhaps masons' waste, and a cultivated topsoil [*423*], [*424*], [*426*], [*428*] and [*450*].

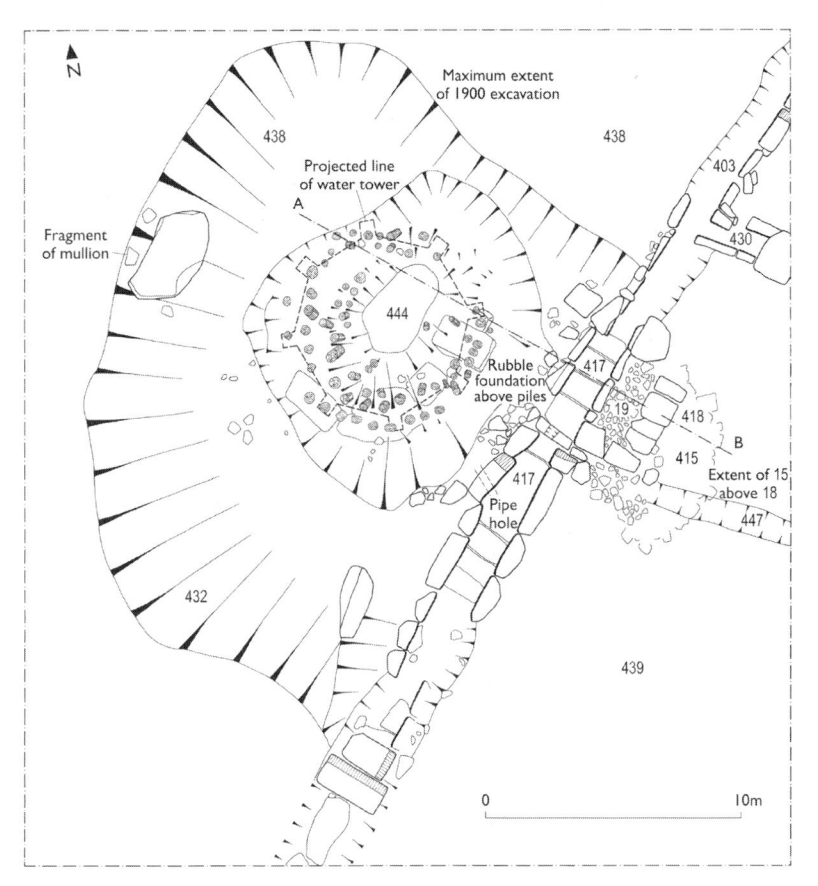

Figure 4.92 Water tower as excavated.

Figure 4.93 Water tower as excavated, seen from the north (G. Coppack).

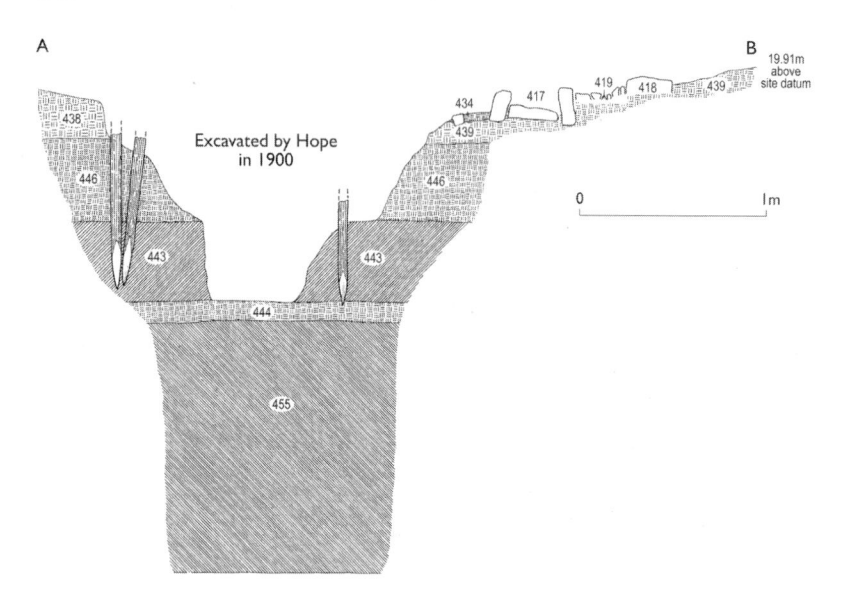

Figure 4.94 Water tower: section A–B.

In the area of excavation no garden features were traced in the garden soil or the top of the subsoil [438], but this may have resulted from extensive disturbance by Hope's excavation and more recent land drains. Within the upper levels of the garden soil was a considerable quantity of window glass, for the most part fragmentary: 27 quarries of blue glass, 2 quarries of red glass and 78 quarries of pale green glass, all apparently derived from the windows of the water tower at or before the Suppression.

The Construction of the Water Tower

A large, irregular hole at the exact centre of the cloister garth, [427] and [429], marked the extent of deep excavation in 1900, roughly 3.6 m in diameter, though excavation to the level of the medieval subsoil occurred over a greater area (see Figure 4.92). At the bottom of the excavation pit were a broken shovel and a Jardinson's mineral water bottle, but no trace remained *in situ* of the structure described by Hope. However, six undressed blocks of stone (shown in outline on Figure 4.92) survived above the heads of the piles on the south and south-east sides of the tower, where they had been reset after excavation, and several large undressed stones and three sections of chamfered plinth course had been thrown into the pit, the upper part of which was then left to fill up naturally. Sealing the stones that had been thrown into the pit was an organic deposit [413] that preserved a wooden bowl and a wedge, both of apparent medieval date, seemingly disturbed by Hope's labourers. The sections of plinth course and four fragments of window mullion found in the filling of Hope's pit, [400] and [401] (layers above [438], but since removed), all appear to be derived from the Period Two cloister arcade, but as the water tower itself had identical mullions they could as easily have come from there.

The pit had been dug by Hope to investigate three concentric rings of pine piles driven into the surface of the great cloister terrace to support a lost masonry structure some 2.5 m in diameter. Remarkably, they are not mentioned in Hope's report, though they were clearly revealed by his excavation. The piles, with axe-dressed points and retaining their bark, were not suitable for dendrochronological dating (no regional soft-wood curve is available). They appear to have been driven from the surface of the clay terrace levelling [438] and [439], though the 1900 excavation had removed virtually all overlying deposits and the upper ends of the piles had rotted away where they had been exposed. The undressed blocks thrown into the excavation pit are almost certainly the foundation-work recorded by Hope that must have been placed on the head of the piles, and which were displaced by his labourers.

Contemporary with the construction of the water tower foundations was the provision of a stone-lined drain [417], cut into the subsoil layer [434] and the underlying cloister levelling [439]. Its excavation by Hope and subsequent reuse as a land drain had effectively removed any sealing layers. Drain [417] was in fact two separate drains, [417/403], running from the south side of the step up into the water tower on its east side: [403] ran to the north-east, [417] to the south-west. The division between the two channels was marked by a single stone over which the supply pipe from the north well house approached the water tower along a cut [447] in the surface of the terrace levelling [439].

As is often the case at Mount Grace, the lead pipe and its protective stone channelling had been removed in the early years of the 20th century to be replaced by a modern land drain. Two sections of the pipe itself and two interlocking sections of the channel that it ran in had been redeposited in soil that sealed a modern land drain inserted into the northern part, [403], of drain [417/403]. This intrusion was dated by a second Jardinson's bottle and a George V farthing of 1920.

THE ARCHAEOLOGY OF THE GREAT CLOISTER

The northern section of drain [417/403] had been seriously damaged by the insertion of the modern land drain and only four of its bottom slabs survived at the south end, making it impossible to be certain of its direction of fall. Indeed, the bottom stones may never have existed, for it is difficult to see how they could have been removed without the total demolition of the feature. None of its capstones remained in place, and parts of both sides had also been removed when the modern land drain was inserted. A branch channel [430], at right angles to drain [417/403] on it east side, remained in better condition, though on the removal of its capstones it was found to contain another land drain. Like [417/403], it had side stones of ashlar, but its base had simply been the clay of the terrace levelling [439].

In comparison, the southern section, [417], of drain [417/403] was more substantial, with a paved bottom falling to the south-west. At its south end four capstones, one a reused section of hood-mould from the Period Three cloister arcade, appear to have been reset after clearing the drain in the early 20th century. The second stone from the north on the west side had a hole cut through it to take a lead pipe some 80 mm in diameter, perhaps the overflow from the water tower. Hope's excavation had removed all traces of the pipe run to the west of the drain and any trace of distribution pipes from the tower.

The water tower was clearly approached from the south-east where a solid foundation of cobbles [419] with a substantial kerb, [418], was inserted into the surface of the clay cloister levelling [434] and [439] laid up against the east face of drain [417]. Further rubble to the west of drain [417], largely removed by Hope's excavation, indicated that this feature extended in the direction of the water tower. Whether it was simply a path or the base for a water tank is uncertain. A path is perhaps most likely, for cultivation of the cloister garth led to the development of topsoil [*428*] which sealed the original structure, and a hard-standing of rubble sandstone [415] (shown in outline on Figure 4.92), which included a fragment of mullion from the Period Two cloister arcade, was laid in the garden soil to replace the lowest step, perhaps during Period Three when the eastern cloister alley was being rebuilt.

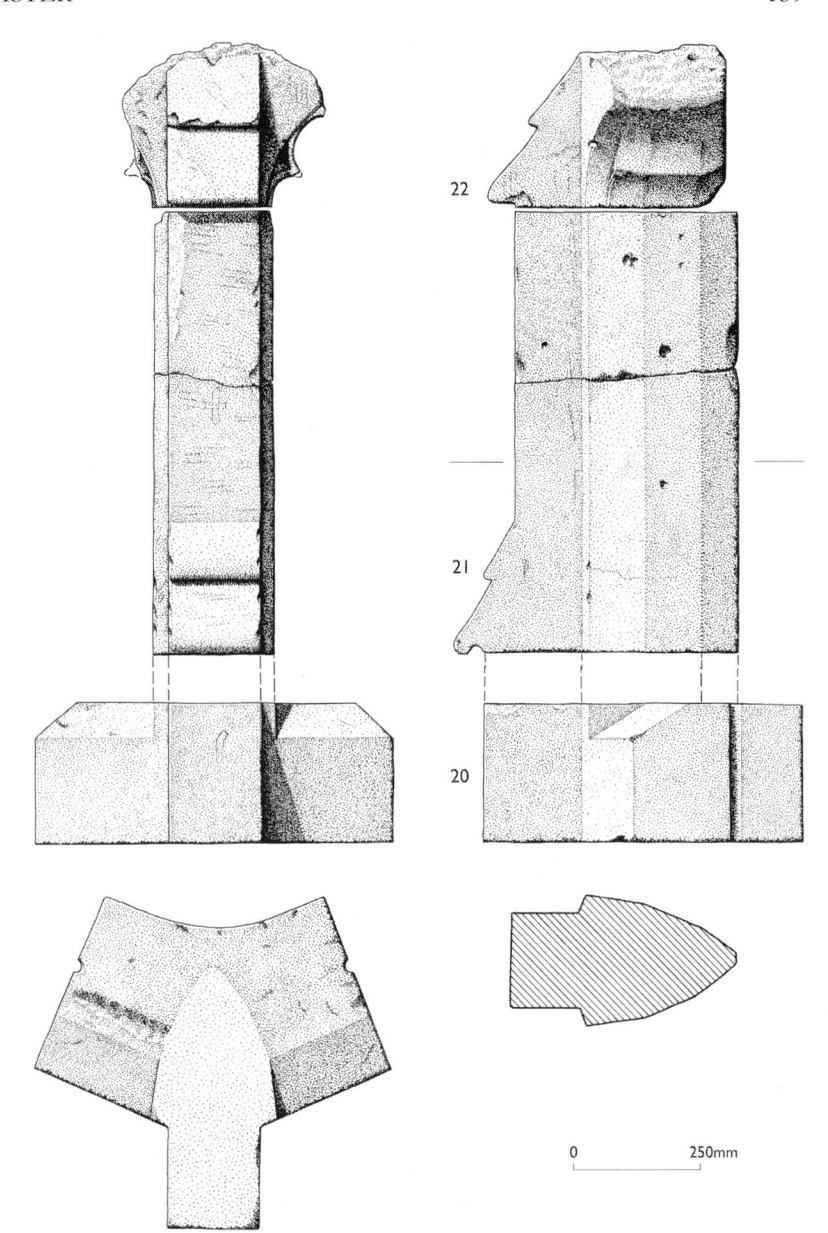

The Structure of the Water Tower

Although nothing remained *in situ* of the water tower on re-excavation, examination of the extensive collection of loose mouldings stored on site located three sections of a similar octagonal structure to that described by Hope (see Figure 4.95), a section of base course (20), a section of angle buttress (21), and a section incorporating the buttress cap and the springing of two window heads (22). Sufficient remains to reconstruct the precise form of the lower stage of the structure (see Figure 4.96).

In plan, the lower stage of the water tower was indeed octagonal, with sides of 0.86 m, each corner supported by a delicate buttress that reduced by twin set-backs to die into the

Figure 4.95 Water tower: architectural fragments from the ground storey (1:10).

160   MOUNT GRACE PRIORY

Figure 4.96 Water tower: reconstruction of the ground storey (S. Hayfield).

faces of the octagon at the level of the apex of the windows. The distance between the buttresses on each face was 0.682 m.

The height of the tower can be calculated from the detailing of the angle buttress. It is reasonable to assume that both stages above and below the set-back were equal, indicating that a section of buttress and jamb 0.32 m long is missing between the cill and the surviving section. If that was restored, the full height of the buttress would be 1.73 m. The structure must have had a plinth course, which has not been recovered, probably matching that of the Period Two cloister alley (see Chapter 6), giving a total height to the top of the buttress of 1.91 m.

The geometry of the window heads could be reconstructed from a full-size template taken from the better-preserved springer where fractionally less than half the trefoil head survived. From the template it proved possible to identify the centres of both the foils and the enclosing arch, and the original form of the head could be reconstructed. Each face of the octagon had a pair of lights 1.42 m high and 0.292 m wide to the outside of its chamfers, separated by a mullion 0.105 m wide with a nosing of 25 mm. The profile of the surviving jambs, and hence the central mullion, indicate that they were cut using the same template as the Period Two cloister arcade.

Cuts in the surviving stones show that the lights had originally been open but subsequently sockets had been cut for saddle bars and a rough and intermittent glazing groove provided. The considerable quantity of window glass, both plain and coloured, found in the garden soil that had survived Hope's depredations, was presumably derived from these windows.

In the south-east face opposite step [418] the paired lights would have been replaced by a door. Two mason's marks, one partly defaced and one (in the form of a black-letter 't', type B34) intact, remain on the structure and help to provide a date for the building of the water tower. The intact mark occurs in only one other location on the site: the arch over the lavatorium in the south cloister alley, an inserted feature in Period One masonry.

The detailing of the lower stage of the water tower has the same elegance as the Period Two cloister arcade, and, as the two structures share a common jamb and mullion template, it suggests that they are by the same workshop and thus likely to be contemporary, belonging to the building campaign of the 1420s. The fact that the mason's marks on the water tower do not occur on the cloister arcade would suggest it was the work of a specialist. The finish is of the highest quality, though the surviving fragments have become badly damaged and weathered. Clear evidence of bolster dressing remains on all surfaces but there are no traces of paint.

There is no reason to suppose that the upper stage of the water tower, which contained the tank itself, differed substantially from that shown in the contemporary London charterhouse drawing (a timber-framed structure that has left no trace in the archaeological record). Stone slates found in demolition contexts could be derived from its roof or from the cloister alleys and further afield, for they are ubiquitous at Mount Grace.

THE ARCHAEOLOGY OF THE GREAT CLOISTER

Table 4.21 Cell 2, Finds Group 20: Ceramics

Fabric	Sherds	Vessels	
		Total vessels	Jug
Ryedale	2	1	1

Other Architectural Detail Associated with the Water Tower (see Figure 4.97)

23, 24. Two interlocking sections of water-pipe casing with a semicircular cut-out in the upper surface in which a pipe with a maximum external diameter of 65 mm could be set. From the robbing of pipe trench [447].

25. Section of string course, with chamfered upper splay, large undercutting hollow and small lower roll. From Hope's excavation trench.

Pipes from the Water Tower (see Figure 4.97)

302. Water pipe. Pb. L: 130 mm; diameter: 60 mm; Th (of piping): 5 mm. Butted soldered seam, Th: 2–3 mm. Find no. Pb171.

303. Water pipe. Pb. Squashed at one end. Circular section with soldered butt seam. L: 150 mm; diameter: 30 mm; Th (of piping): 2–3 mm. Find no. Pb158.

304. Water pipe. Pb. Bent to near-right angle, L: 125 mm and 170 mm. Circular section with butted soldered seam, diameter: 18–30 mm. Th (of piping): 3 mm. Find no. Pb159.

Finds Group 20
From the primary levelling of the cloister [438] at the foundation of the priory.

CERAMICS (SEE FIGURE 4.98)

305. Ryedale ware jug. Very hard, grey to dull red core and grey inner surface. Dark blackish-green glaze on outer surface and on rim to shoulder of inner surface. Overfired (Table 4.21).

Finds Group 21
From late medieval garden soil [423], [424], [428] and [450] around the water tower (Table 4.22).

CERAMICS (SEE FIGURE 4.98)

306. Raeren stoneware mug. Faintly lustrous brown glaze on outer surface, pale

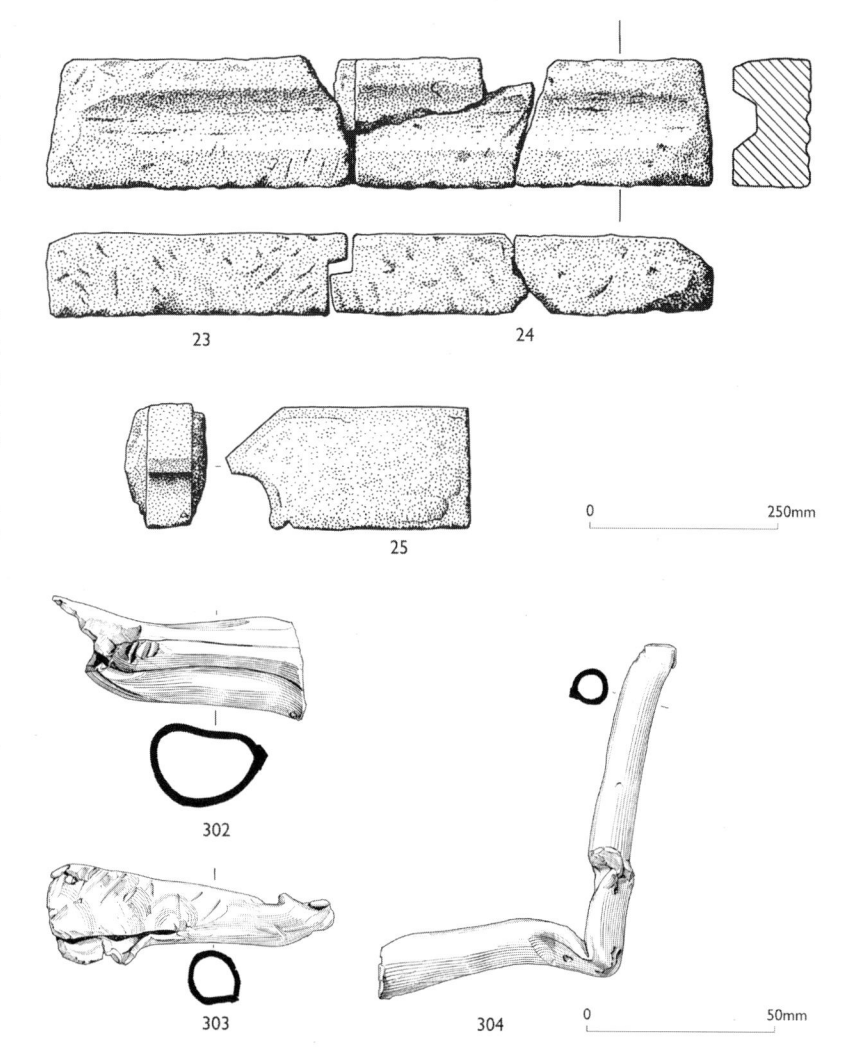

Figure 4.97 Water tower: architectural detail (1:10) and lead pipes (1:2).

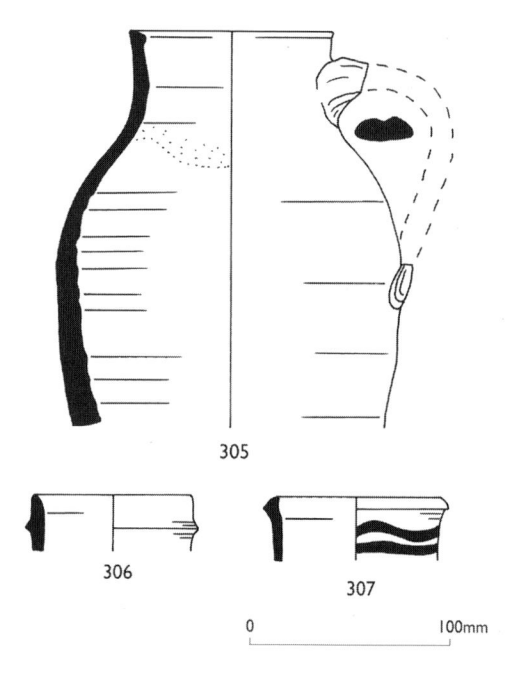

Figure 4.98 Water tower: Finds Groups 20 and 21 (pottery 1:4).

Table 4.22 Water Tower, Finds Group 21: Ceramics

Fabric	Sherds	Vessels				
		Total vessels	Albarello	Jug	Mug or cup	Pancheon
Cistercian	6	4	0	0	4	0
Gritty	1	1	0	1	0	0
Humber	1	1	0	1	0	0
Malaga	1	1	1	0	0	0
Post-medieval Orange	2	2	0	0	0	2
Raeren	1	1	0	0	1	0
Ryedale	6	2	0	2	0	0

silver-grey core and yellowish-buff inner surface.

307. Malaga, Late Andulusian lustreware albarello. Pale orange, slightly sandy fabric with paler buff margins. Both surfaces of this sherd were covered in a partly decayed and heavily crazed dirty lilac to white glaze with traces of blue to pale blue painted underglaze bands on the outer surface.

Cell 22

The north (cloister) wall of this cell was the south wall of the great cloister, which remained to full height. A narrow door with a two-centred head was inserted into this wall, with the door itself hung on the western jamb. A hatch was driven through the wall 2.4 m to the east, close to the cloister laver.

The cell was entered at the level of the cloister alley and was effectively a first-floor structure set over a cellar with masonry walls that now survive to a maximum height of four courses. The cellar communicated with the prior's cell to the west but not with Cell 22 itself. With the exception of its cloister wall, west wall (the east wall of the prior's cell) and its south wall (the north wall of the church), Cell 22 was a narrow timber-framed structure, the pitch of its roof demonstrated by a small gablet set on the top of the cloister wall (see Figure 6.30). A hole in the cloister wall to the west of the gablet drained the valley gutter between this cell and the gable wall of the prior's cell.

Internally (see Figure 6.31), an entry passage ran the full length of the cell, 0.92 m wide. To its east were two rooms of roughly equal size. The northern room was the living room, with a fireplace with rebated jambs and a monolithic lintel set in the cloister wall. The chimney associated with this fireplace was set

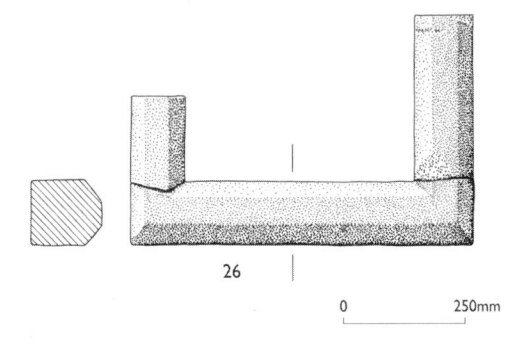

Figure 4.99 Cell 23: architectural detail (1:10).

on the apex of the gablet. To the east of this room was a latrine, the pit of which, flushed by a drain, remains at ground level.

The southern room, lit only by a small window inserted into the north wall of the church, and perhaps by windows in its missing eastern wall, may have been a study. To its east, and carried on a timber bridge, was a small bed chamber and oratory. The oratory itself was fashioned within the west wall of the north burial chapel of the church (see Figure 6.32). To the south of this was a narrow light well. The cell had no garden.

Cell 23

Contrived within a narrow and inconvenient space to the north of the church, Cell 23 (see Figure 6.31) was the least conventional of the monks' cells at Mount Grace. It was entered from the south cloister alley by an inserted door with a hatch on its west side. All the rooms of this cell were at first-floor level.

The north (cloister) wall remained intact and the south wall of the eastern part of the cell was the north wall of the presbytery. Otherwise, like Cell 22, this cell was of timber construction. The living room, some 1.23 m wide, was entered directly from the south cloister alley through the door in the centre of its north wall, without an intervening entry passage. To the east of this door was a narrow wall fireplace with rebated jambs and a monolithic lintel, a scaled-down version of the usual monk's cell fireplace.

On the west side of the living room was a latrine, the unexcavated pit of which survived at ground level. Exceptionally, a tap niche fed from the cloister laver supply was placed in the cloister wall within the latrine. To the east of the living room were two rooms, their floors at different levels, jettied out over the church entry. Because this cell occupied the site of an earlier two-storey building attached to the north side of the church, there was a confusion of joist sockets that made the interpretation of the southern room difficult in the extreme. There was some evidence that it had been altered at least once. A loft was provided over the southern room. Unless the monk in Cell 22 had access to the garden between the cell and the chapter house, this cell had no garden.

Architectural detail from Cell 23 (see Figure 4.99)

26. Kerb from the hearth of the living room of Cell 23 cut from a single stone. The fireplace of Cell 23 was smaller than any other cell fireplace and the kerb is only 0.70 m wide, though of standard section.

Chapter 5: The Archaeology of the Inner Court

5.1 The South-west Cloister Range

Lying between the west end of the church and the south-west corner of the great cloister are the remains of a substantial building first excavated by Hope in 1896–1900 and identified by him as the refectory (to the west) and the prior's cell (to the east) (Hope 1905, 281–3). Internally, the building measures 26 m from west to east and 7.9 m from north to south. Before re-excavation for consolidation and display in 1988–90 the western half of the north wall stood to its full height and the rest of its length to above first-floor level; the east wall stood to a maximum height of 19 courses at its north end, but to only two courses where it bonded with the north-west corner of the church. The west wall of the range was only partially visible, within unfilled excavation trenches, and only the easternmost 5.8 m of the south wall was visible, standing to the height of a chamfered offset.

Fragmentary masonry structures were visible in the turf within the area of Hope's 'refectory', and traces of cross-walls were apparent in his 'prior's cell'. An examination of the standing masonry (see Figure 5.1) indicated that the building had a complicated structural history, which included substantial alterations and rebuildings, and excavation was to demonstrate that the remainder of the buried structure was equally complex. As first built, the range was at least partially contemporary with the construction of the Period One nave of the priory church, with which its south-eastern corner bonded.

Pre-monastic Features (see Figure 5.2)

A number of features pre-dated the construction of the south-west cloister range but were demonstrably medieval. All [1173], [925], [950], [1287], [1149] and [791] were cut into natural but disturbed red clay, which occurred at the level of the great cloister in the north-west corner of the later range and fell away to the south and the east by at least 1 m, exposing an underlying clean yellow clay. Some early features had been truncated or obscured by later construction work and terracing, making it impossible to recover a total plan of them. The pottery from them indicates, however, that they date from the 12th and early 13th centuries and should be associated with the vill of *Bordelbi*.

The earliest of these features was a series of ditches, probably representing a sequence of drainage operations that can no longer be separated stratigraphically. The westernmost ditch, [1172], was seen only in a section below the later western alley of the great cloister. It was not traced within the later south range and it must have turned either west or east, where it could have joined a second ditch, [1148], which was seen inside the north wall of the later range and to the south of it, but was not fully excavated.

A third ditch, [837], ran south-west into ditch [1148], its course being defined by a depression in those later floors that were not removed. Where examined, it had almost vertical sides and a U-shaped profile. As with ditch [1172], the lower filling of this ditch was a fine silt, showing that it had been used to carry away water from the area later containing the great cloister, which excavation has shown was a boggy area until the foundation of the house.

A fourth ditch, [822], ran to the east of ditches [837] and [1148], and was perhaps dug to replace them. Certainly, it appeared to cut the fill of [1148] at the southern limit of

Figure 5.1 The south-west cloister range seen from the south-west before excavation (G. Coppack).

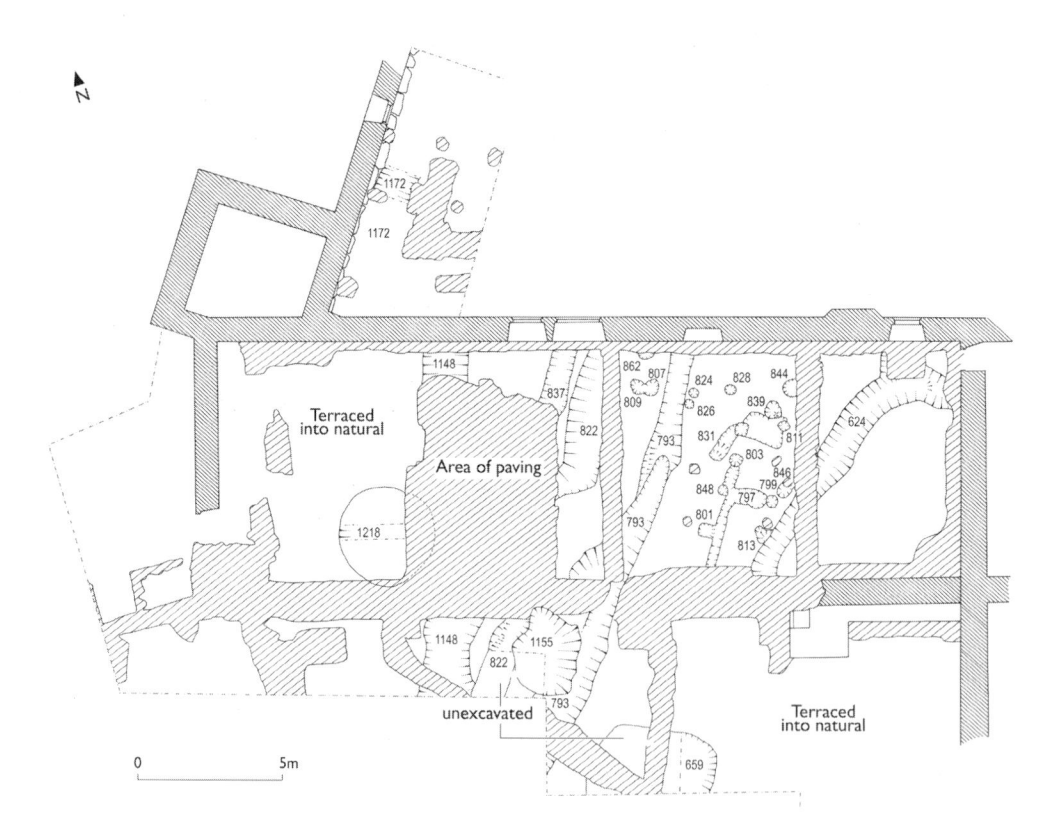

Figure 5.2 Pre-monastic features below the south-west cloister range.

excavation, suggesting that these two ditches were not contemporary. At its north end ditch [822] had been packed with rubble and brown loam, while at its southern end the filling consisted almost exclusively of brown loam. There was no evidence that it had carried water, although it may have been open for only a short time. It was apparently replaced by a fifth ditch, [793], which ran roughly parallel to it and was 1.6 m to the east of it. Its rather gritty lower filling again suggested that it had been used to drain the later cloister area.

To the east of ditch [793] were one or more small timber buildings (Building A), defined by postholes and slots [795], [797], [799], [801], [803], [807], [809], [811], [813],

THE ARCHAEOLOGY OF THE INNER COURT

Figure 5.3 Pre-monastic features below the eastern half of the south-west cloister range as excavated, seen from the north (G. Coppack).

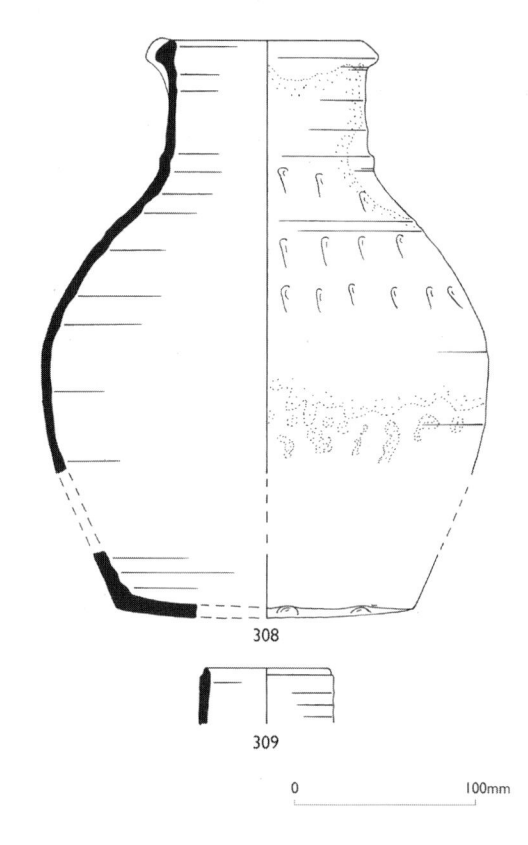

Figure 5.4 Finds Group 22 from the south-west cloister range (pottery 1:4).

[824], [826], [828], [831], [*834*], [839], [844], [846], [848] and [862] (see Figure 5.3). Three of these postholes lay to the west of ditch [793]. None of these features retained any evidence for the placing of posts, all of which had been withdrawn.

A thin spread of stained grey clay containing large quantities of charcoal, [657] and [*782*], was deposited over the eastern half of the area excavated, sealing the back-filled ditches [793], [822] and [837] and all of the postholes and slots to the east of ditch [793]. The building or buildings represented by these features must therefore have been demolished, although heavy spreads of butchered animal bone and pottery indicate that occupation continued in the area. These deposits, in their turn, were cut by a new ditch, [624], 1 m wide and 0.8 m deep, that ran away to the south-west more or less parallel to ditch [793]. This ditch was not open for long, as no silt had built up at its base before it was packed with yellow clay and sandstone rubble [*636*].

Three large pits that can be dated by their contents to the period of pre-monastic settlement had been dug in the area examined. Only one, [1155], was related to the series of ditches, certainly cutting through the filling of ditch [822] and less clearly cutting the fill of ditch [793], although it was not fully excavated. A second pit, [659], was dug to the east of ditch [793] in the surface of the natural red clay, but apart from being cut in an early surface it could not be related to any other feature. The third pit, [1218], lay below the western half of the south-west range, where it was traced as an area of dramatic subsidence sealed by the construction of the range itself. Although only a trial section into the west side of this pit was possible, it showed that the pit was at least 1.5 m deep and had near-vertical sides. A fire had clearly been lit in its base, the edge of which could be traced as a line of burned clay, but the pit's use, like that of the others, could not be ascertained.

Finds Group 22 (see Figure 5.4)
From the filling of ditch [837].

This small group from the filling of ditch [837] belongs to the pre-priory occupation of the site. Jug 308 would fit comfortably in a 13th-century date. However, such a date would be early for the Langerwehe stoneware mug rim sherd (309), which is more likely to be 14th-century in origin but still probably pre-dating the foundation of the priory (Table 5.1).

Table 5.1 South-west cloister range, Finds Group 22: Ceramics

Fabric	Sherds	Total vessels	Cooking pot	Jug	Mug or cup
Gritty	3	2	1	1	0
Langerwehe	2	1	0	0	1

308. Gritty ware jug. Orange-yellow to red outer surface, light vermilion core and inner surface. Bright greenish-yellow suspension glaze becoming greener as the glaze thickens and orange-yellow (and pocked) where the glaze thins. Token attempt at applied pellet decoration. Basal angle thumbed from underneath, as seen in other examples in this fabric.
309. Langerwehe stoneware drinking mug. Slightly shiny, red-brown outer surface glaze, pale greyish core and pale orange-grey inner surface.

Finds Group 23 (see Figure 5.5)
This material derives from the filling of pit [659] and ditches [687], [793], [849] and [1153].

With the exception of three probably intrusive sherds from pit [659], this pre-priory group comprises almost entirely Gritty ware vessels, most of which probably belong to the 13th century (Table 5.2). Cooking-pot rim 316 may be later, and jug rim 320, with its splashed glaze, is almost certainly 12th century. Many of the cooking-pot rims, such as 313–16, and bowl rim 317 are of very similar form to the sandy coarse wares produced at Staxton and Potter Brompton in the Vale of Pickering (Brewster and Hayfield 1992) and, although the fabrics differ, are part of the same North Yorkshire tradition.

Jug 322 was a substantial vessel. Its double-pinched basal angle seems characteristic of this particular fabric, while the applied thumbed strips hark back to late Saxon Thetford ware decorative styles. It was curious that the handle of such a large vessel had no plugged attachments or other attempts to provide additional strengthening.

310. Stamford ware cooking-pot base. Heavily burnt and sooted greyish outer surface, cream-white core and inner surface.
311. Gritty ware cooking-pot rim. Pale yellow-orange outer surface, orange-white core and inner surface. Traces of burning and sooting.
312. Gritty ware jug rim. Pale orange surfaces and orange core.
313. Gritty ware cooking-pot rim of a form very reminiscent of Staxton ware. Pale grey outer surface, off-white core and grey to off-white inner surface. Traces of burning and sooting to underside of rim.
314. Gritty ware cooking-pot rim. Dull orange-buff outer surface, pale orange core and pale orange-yellow inner surface. Burnt and sooted.
315. Gritty ware cooking-pot rim. Off-white surfaces and core.
316. Gritty ware cooking-pot rim. Orange outer surface, orange-red core and pinkish-orange inner surface. Burnt and sooted.
317. Gritty ware bowl rim. Pale pinkish-orange surfaces and grey-black core. Traces of an olive-green splashed glaze. Burnt and sooted.
318. Gritty ware pipkin. Pale orange fabric.
319. Gritty ware small cooking-pot rim. Pale yellowish outer surface (where not burnt to grey), creamy-yellow core and inner surface. Heavily burnt and sooted. Non-fitting profile.
320. Gritty ware jug rim. Pale orange-yellow surfaces and pale orange core. Yellow-olive splashed glaze.
321. Gritty ware jug rim. Pale grey-brown outer surface, orange core and light, pinkish-orange inner surface. Dull olive-green glaze.
322. Gritty ware jug, 83 sherds; pale orange-yellow outer surface, off-white core with thick pinkish margins. The inner surface is similar to the outer surface, but turning a pale purplish-pink in places. Bright yellowish-orange suspension glaze. Salts deposit attached to the lower body of the inner surface

THE ARCHAEOLOGY OF THE INNER COURT

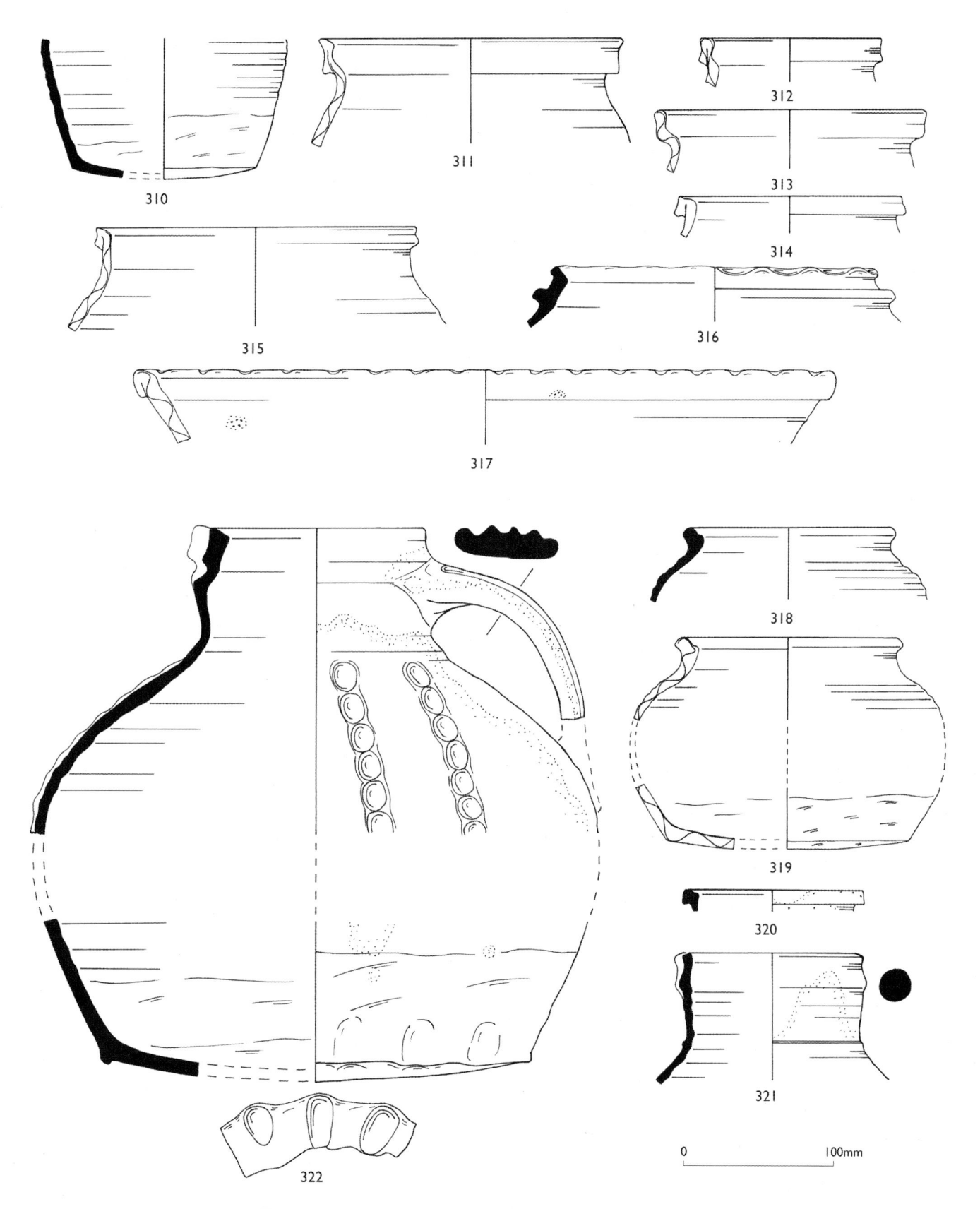

Figure 5.5 Finds Group 23 from the south-west cloister range (pottery 1:4).

Table 5.2 South-west cloister range, Finds Group 23: Ceramics

Fabric	Sherds	Vessels					
		Bowl	Cooking pot	Jug	Mug or cup	Pancheon	Pipkin
Gritty	173	2	59	22	0	1	1
Ryedale	2	0	0	2	0	0	0
Siegburg	1	0	0	0	1	0	0
Stamford type	1	0	1	0	0	0	0

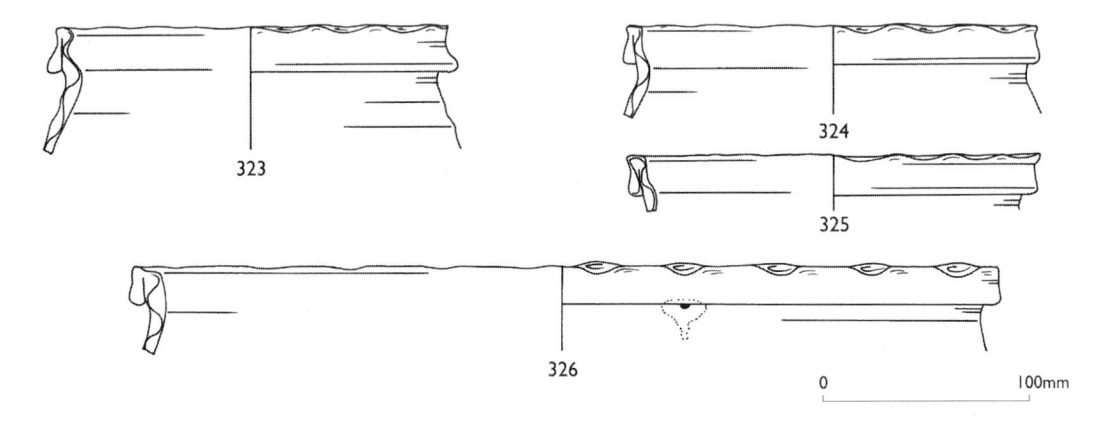

Figure 5.6 Finds Group 24 from the south-west cloister range (pottery 1:4).

and burning and sooting on the base and basal angle. Traces of applied thumbed vertical strips. Apparently typically for this fabric, the thumbings to the basal angle are made from the base rather than the lower body. Upper handle attachment smoothed on with no trace of any lateral thumbings. A well-used vessel; in addition to the burning and sooting there were traces of spalling on the lower body.

Finds Group 24 (see Figure 5.6)
From postholes and timber slots [663], [794], [796], [798], [812], [833] and [845] of Building A.

This group derived from the postholes and slots associated with Building A, one or more structures of apparent 13th-century date. Again, the Gritty ware fabric dominates the group and it is likely that the Ryedale ware, the Humber ware and the Siegburg stoneware material is intrusive and related to the withdrawal of posts rather than construction (Table 5.3). The form and thumbing of the illustrated cooking-pot rims suggest earlier dates for this material than for the bulk of Finds Group 23, which is supported to some extent by the splash of splashed glaze caught under the rim of 326. The form of this vessel suggests that it is unlikely to be a bowl. It could be an exceptionally large cooking pot, but its diameter and shape suggest a 'peat pot' (a cooking pot with a broad, flat base designed for use in a peat fire); if so, it is the only one to be recognised from this assemblage. A late 12th- or early 13th-century date could be suggested for this group.

323. Gritty ware cooking-pot rim. Pale orange surfaces and vermilion core. Burnt and sooted on the edge of the rim flange.
324. Gritty ware cooking-pot rim. Pale whitish-orange outer surface, off-white core and inner surface. Burnt and sooted.
325. Gritty ware cooking-pot rim. Yellow-cream outer surface, very pale yellow core and off-white inner surface.
326. Gritty ware 'peat pot'. Pale orange outer surface, off-white core and cream inner surface. Splash of olive-yellow splashed glaze under the face of the rim. Burnt and sooted.

Finds Group 25 (see Figure 5.7)
From the upper filling of ditch [793] and intersecting pit [1155].

This group, from the upper filling of ditch [793], and from pit [1155], which was cut into it, is probably of very similar date to Finds Group 24 and represents occupation derived

THE ARCHAEOLOGY OF THE INNER COURT

Table 5.3 South-west cloister range, Finds Group 24: Ceramics

Fabric	Sherds	Vessels		
		Cooking pot	Jug	Mug or cup
Brandsby type	1	0	1	
Gritty	67	32	4	0
Humber	2	0	1	0
Ryedale	2	0	2	0
Siegburg	1	0	0	1

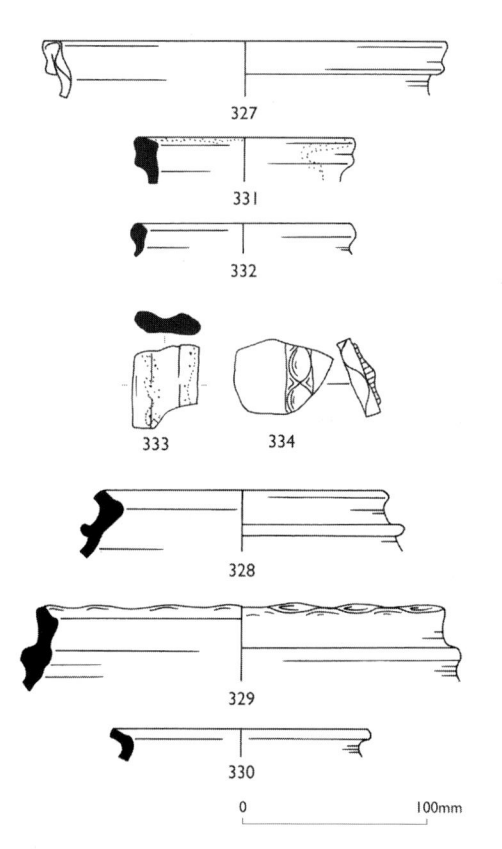

Figure 5.7 Finds Group 25 from the south-west cloister range (pottery 1:4).

from Building A. The splashed glazing of 333 indicates 12th-century material, while other rim forms suggest that the group extends into the 13th century (Table 5.4).

327. Gritty ware cooking-pot rim. Dull purplish-orange surfaces, becoming a more dirty purple colour towards the rim (particularly on the inner face), with a dull orange-buff core. Hard, rough textured.
328. Gritty ware cooking-pot rim. Pale lilac-white outer surface, yellow-buff core and cream inner surface.
329. Gritty ware cooking-pot rim. Vermilion outer surface skin, orange core with yellowish margins and orange-yellow inner surface.
330. Gritty ware cooking-pot rim. Pale yellow surfaces and grey-black core.
331. Gritty ware jug rim. Pale yellow-orange outer surface, off-white core and pale yellow inner surface. Clear, consistently coloured greenish-yellow suspension glaze becoming more orange at the margins.
332. Gritty ware pipkin rim. Grey-buff outer surface, orange-red core and pale orange inner surface.
333. Gritty ware jug. Yellow to pale orange outer surface, blue-grey core and inner surface. Olive-green splashed glaze with orange-yellow margins; a lightly pocked glaze, probably 12th-century.
334. Gritty ware curfew sherd with applied vertical thumbed strips. Pale orange outer surface, pale blue-grey core and brownish-buff inner surface.

Finds Group 26 (see Figure 5.8)
From the filling of ditch [624].

The Brandsby type fabric and rim forms 337–9 suggest the presence of material of late 12th- or probably 13th-century date (Table 5.5). However, 335 and 336 are of quite a different character and possibly residual; both are essentially handmade and decorated with a very crude roulette. They appear markedly earlier than any other medieval material from the site and may be of 11th- or early 12th-century date.

Amongst the unillustrated vessels were nine sherds from an early Gritty ware jug with a sparse and heavily pocked greenish splashed glaze with purplish margins and a very coarse fabric mix. The Ryedale ware jug sherd is almost certainly intrusive.

335. Gritty ware cooking-pot rim. Dull pinkish outer surface, grey-black core

Table 5.4 South-west cloister range, Finds Group 25: Ceramics

Fabric	Sherds	Bowl	Cooking pot	Curfew*	Jug	Pipkin
Brandsby type	1	0	1	0	0	0
Gritty	174	1	70	1	21	1

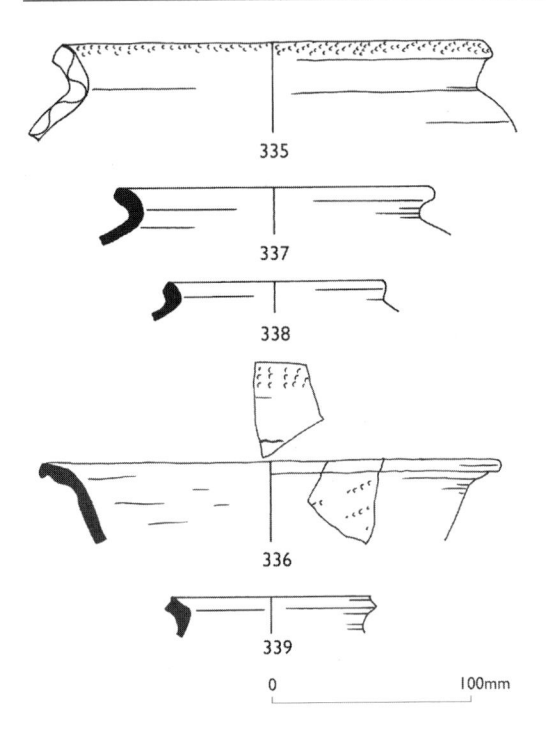

Figure 5.8 Finds Group 26 from the south-west cloister range (pottery 1:4).

and light orange inner surface. Only partly wheel-finished.

336. Gritty ware bowl. A very hard, slightly micaceous fabric with some haematite grits. No sign of coils, but appears to be fully hand-finished. Orange surfaces and pale orange to pale blue to pale orange core. Rough decorative stabbings in rows of four.

337. Gritty ware cooking pot, over-fired with some distortion, blue-grey outer surface and core, and pale blue-grey inner surface.

338. Gritty ware pipkin rim. Dull brick-red outer surface, vermilion core and inner surface. Slight traces of glaze on top of the rim.

339. Gritty ware small cooking-pot. Dull purplish-brown outer surface, pale orange core and inner surface. Burnt and sooted, probably accounting for the outer surface colour.

Period One (see Figures 5.9, 5.10 and 5.11)

Once ditch [624] was backfilled, the area to its east was also levelled up with similar yellow clay and rubble [622], which was cut by foundation trenches for the southern half of the range's east wall [512] and the easternmost 6 m of its south wall [872]. This corner of the building was then built as a buttress to the north-west angle of the adjoining church in advance of the construction of the main structure. A raking joint still visible in the east wall [512] of the range shows the extent of this buttressing, but the south wall survives only to plinth height. Its scar on the west wall of the church shows that it was, however, carried up to equal height.

The construction of the south-east corner of the range was marked by a spread of white mortar [525] that filled the construction trenches to a depth of 300 mm and gradually tailed out to the north-west, sealing the backfilled ditch [623]. Associated with this mortar was a group of 11 postholes [650], [648], [654], [652], [662], [644], [646], [680], [669], [663] and [629] and a series of 14 stakeholes [790a–n]. The stakeholes appear to have been associated with the construction of the south wall [872] and were all filled with the white mortar, but several of the postholes appeared to be contemporary with or later than the mortar.

Table 5.5 South-west cloister range, Finds Group 26: Ceramics

Fabric	Sherds	Bowl	Cooking pot	Jug	Pancheon	Pipkin
Brandsby type	14	0	2	2	0	0
Gritty	79	1	37	10	1	1
Ryedale	1	0	0	1	0	0

THE ARCHAEOLOGY OF THE INNER COURT

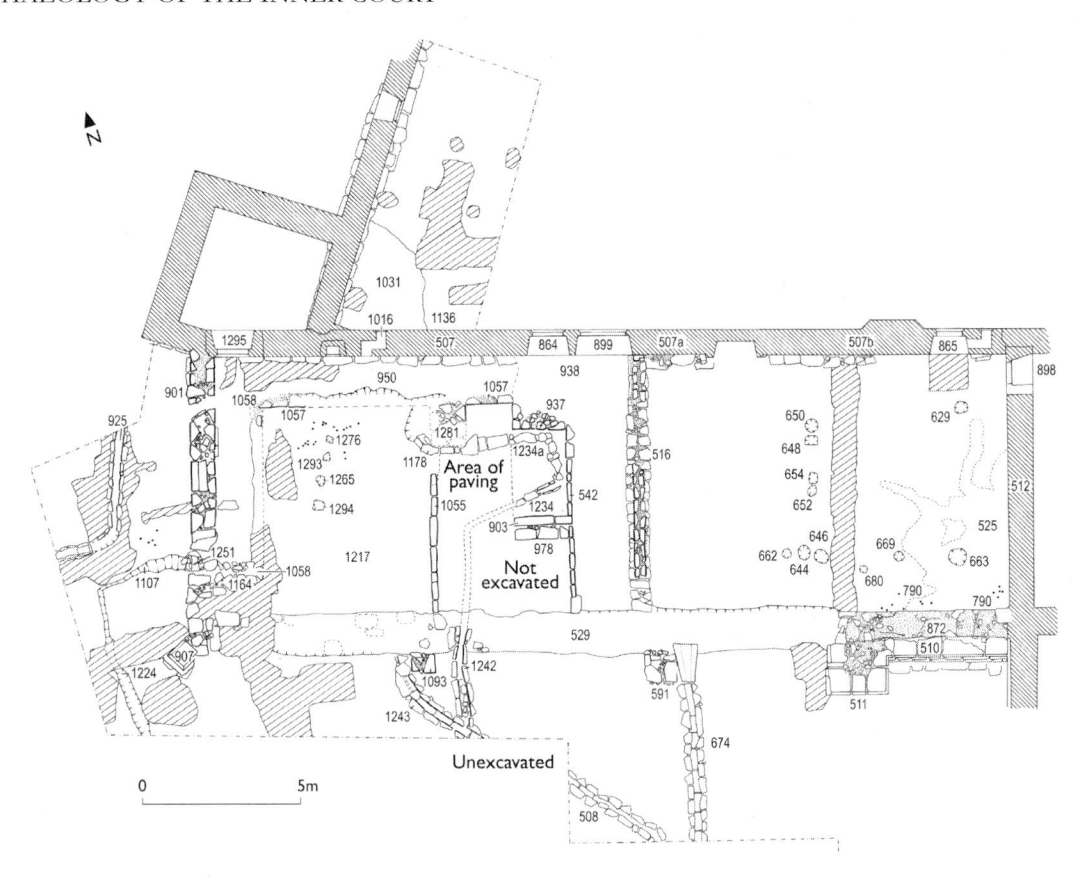

Figure 5.9 The south-west cloister range and 'prison', construction and sub-floor features.

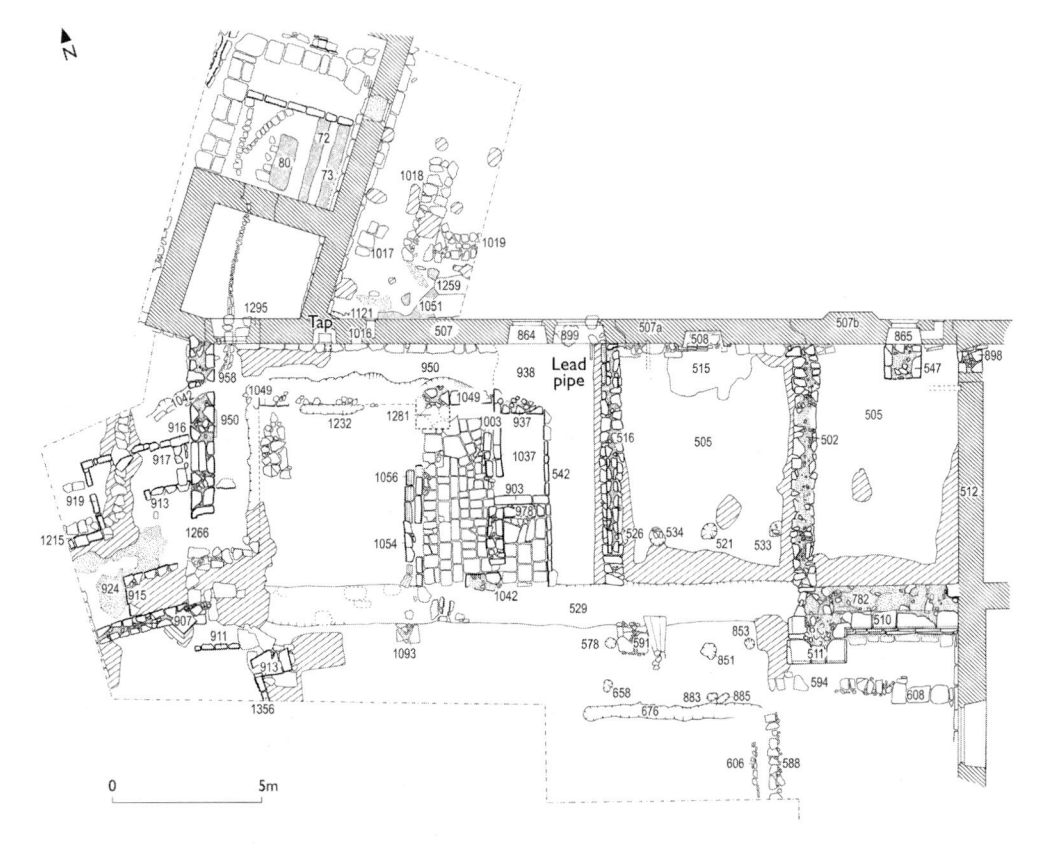

Figure 5.10 The south-west cloister range and 'prison', later features of Periods Two to Four.

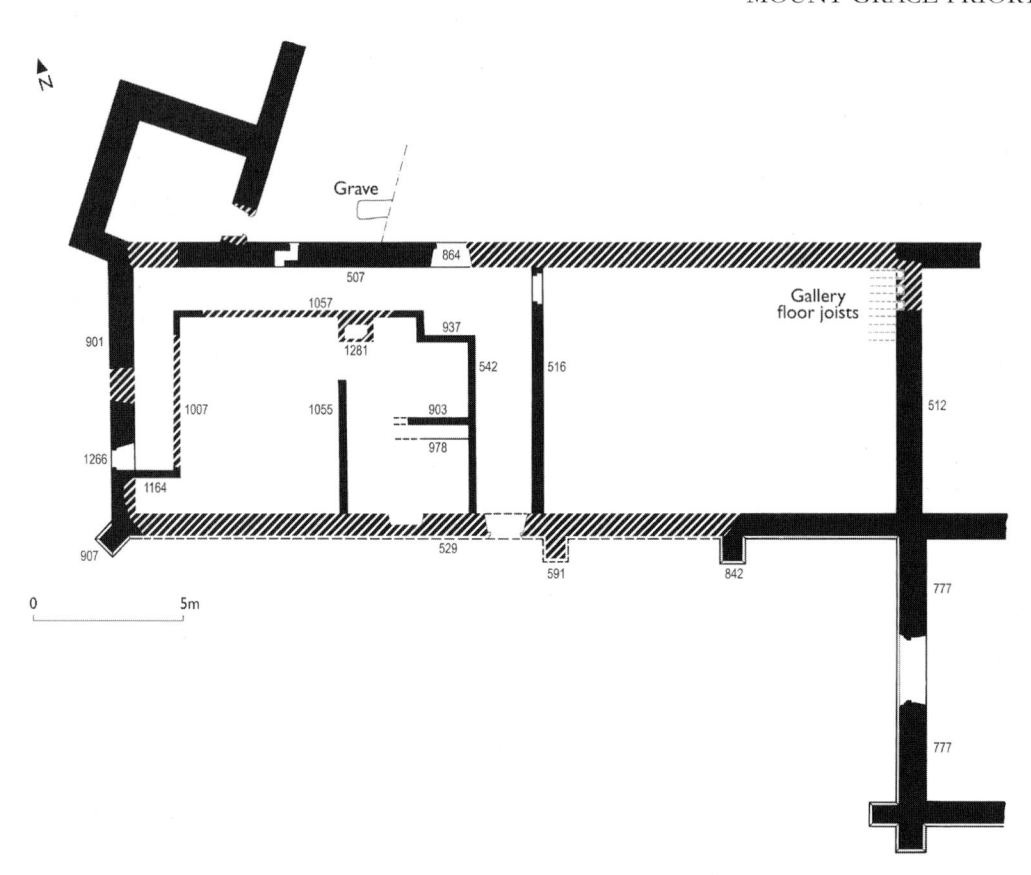

Figure 5.11 Plan of the south-west cloister range and 'prison' as built in Period One.

The postholes form the west and south sides of a light structure (Building B) that was apparently open to the north and was at least partially closed on the east side by wall [512]. None of the posts could have been for scaffolding, as they were sealed by the construction deposits associated with the lowest walling of the remainder of the south-west cloister range; they should probably be seen as some form of temporary shelter for the masons building the Period One church. Whatever their purpose, the posts, with the exception of that in posthole [629], were removed and their postholes sealed by spreads of stone chippings [628] and yellow clay [686]. Above these deposits, a mixed layer of red-orange clay and grey clay containing charcoal and rubble [600] and [602] was laid to level up the eastern part of the site before construction of the south-west cloister range began in earnest.

The site remained irregular, falling away quite steeply to the south, and the building was laid out on the slope. Foundation trenches 0.2 m deep and 1.2 m wide were dug for the north and south walls of the range and were filled with a single course of unmortared and undressed sandstone slabs. The west wall of the range was similarly footed, but the construction trench was dug in three stepped lengths down the slope. On the east side, where part of the east wall [512] had already been built, an irregular construction trench was cut from the new level to overlap with the earlier construction trench and this was filled with one or two courses of rubble.

On these insubstantial footings the north wall [507], west wall [901], south wall [529] and [872] and east wall [512] were built. All the walls were bonded with white mortar and were faced with punch-dressed ashlar. Some pink mortar in the west wall appears to relate to an area of later rebuilding. Dressings, where they survived, were bolster-dressed and of fine quality. The south wall was later entirely removed by post-Suppression stone robbing, apart from its eastern bay, but its construction trench survived to be compared with the others. Two buttresses [842] and [591] were provided at the east end of the south wall, at centres of 5.4 m. The easternmost buttress survived to the top of its plinth course and was 0.55 m wide, meaning that the wall space between the buttresses was 4.7 m. A further diagonal buttress, [907], was provided at the south-west angle of the building, where its plinth course had survived robbing. Above the plinth course the buttresses were 0.61 m deep. Two original doorways survived, one in the north wall [864] and one in the west wall [1266]. East of door [864] the north wall had been rebuilt above its footings at a later date. The range was divided into two parts by an original cross-wall, [516], that survived to a maximum height of two courses of dressed stone bonded with yellow-brown gritty mortar, above a foundation of unbonded and undressed rubble [589]. This footing followed the natural slope of the ground to the south and had been carried down into the fill of underlying ditches. Neither the wall nor its footings was bonded with the outer walls of the building, a practice noted elsewhere in the structure, which indicates that the fitting out of the interior was not carried out until the shell of the building was completed.

An original doorway with rebated ashlar jambs survived at the north end of cross-wall [516]. It was 0.58 m wide, with rebates 60 mm deep. To the east of this wall the range was levelled up to the top of the footings of the north wall with a deposit of reddish-brown clay [545] and [575] above a levelling layer of silty orange-red clay [600], which sealed all construction features. It was only after layer [545] had been laid that the post in the pre-building posthole [629] was finally withdrawn. Two postholes [556] and [558] were cut into the surface of layer [545], apparently for scaffolding. One, [556], was sealed by a patch of metalling, [536]. Above these deposits a thin, patchy deposit of brown loam, [505], comprised the primary floor of the eastern half of the building.

The eastern half of the range, with its two regular bays, was lit by traceried windows in its south wall; fragments of the tracery were recovered during the excavation of later demolition deposits. Limewash on the inner surface of the window tracery suggests that the room was whitelimed internally, but no trace of any paint survives on the remaining walls, all of which are now eroded. Substantial rebuilding in Period Three removed any internal features and large areas of the north wall, making the interpretation of this room difficult. However, its two regular bays with tall traceried windows in the south wall suggest that it was open to the roof, and therefore was probably the original refectory. At its east end, five regularly spaced joist sockets 11 courses or 3.0 m above floor level in the gable wall of the room, each of which was 0.25 m by 0.23 m, were clearly primary and may have held the joists of a loft or gallery. No trace was found of any support for the front edge of such a feature, but if it was supported by posts set on padstones their removal in Period Three would have left no obvious trace, as very little of the primary floor surface survived.

A narrow passage occupied the central area of the building, bounded to the east by wall [516] and to the west by a thin cill wall, [542], made up of a single thickness of accurately cut punched ashlar blocks set in white mortar. This wall did not extend to the north wall of the range [507], but returned to the west 2.32 m to its south. Like wall [516], it was footed on undressed rubble and simply butted against the south wall of the range. At its north end it survived to a height of three courses. Between the two walls, the passage was floored with reddish-brown clay [539] that ran level with the cill of the door at the north end of wall [516] to a point 3.20 m to the south of the inner face of the north wall of the range. From here, the passage surface sloped down to the south, falling 0.8 m in a distance of 5 m. The ashlar facing of walls [516] and [542] followed the slope of the passage floor. Post-Suppression robbing of the south wall had removed any trace of a door at the south end of the passage, and 16th-century gardening to the south of the range had destroyed any evidence of a path or door cill outside the building. That the floor slopes down to the level of the terrace to the south of the building can only indicate a through-passage. The passage floor sealed dumps of sandstone rubble and mortar [592] and [596] that were themselves later than the initial construction of the outer walls of the range.

To the west of the passage, the interior of the range was complicated by having its floors terraced into the natural clay surface onto which the building was constructed. Along the north wall of the range was a raised corridor retained by an ashlar wall [1057], in all 1.52 m wide. This retaining wall was later almost entirely removed by robbing, and only three facing stones remained at its western extremity and three at its east end. The stones and the rubble that backed them were set in yellow mortar. They retained a passageway that ran around the north and west sides of the range, for a return survived at the west end [1058] and the line of a north–south wall was marked by a post-Suppression robber trench [1007]. At the south end of the robber trench a single facing stone remained in place. This wall returned to the west as a line of rubble footings [1164] that aligned with the southern internal splay of door [1266]. The southern jamb of this doorway had been displaced by Hope's excavation (it is shown in place on his plan and has been reset in that location), but the remaining mortar bedding of its cill indicated that the opening was 0.91 m wide.

No floor remained in place within this corridor except at its east end, where the level floor of the central passage [*539*] continued along the north wall of the range for some 0.8 m. At this point, the corridor was widened to form a small lobby, 2.32 m wide, inside door [864]. Here, the retaining wall survived to its full height of three courses (0.89 m). Further west, post-medieval gardening and Hope's excavation had removed up to 0.3 m of the corridor floor, robbing and underlying natural clay, but the level of the floor appears to have been half a course above the top of the foundations of wall [507]. In the western corridor it sloped gently down to a step across the corridor, 0.56 m below the level floor of the north corridor, dropped 0.14 m and ran level at the height of the cill in door [1266]. Projecting from the south side of retaining wall [1057] was a rectangular block of masonry represented by a single return stone on its east side and the impressions of four other stones in the bottom of its robber trench [1281]. The function of this projection is unclear.

The area contained by these three corridors was floored at a lower level and divided into three rooms by a north–south cill wall, [1055], and an east–west cill wall, [903], both of a single-block thickness of finely cut ashlar, dressed on both faces. Wall [903] survived to its full original height of three courses, 0.76 m, and bonded with wall [542], while wall [1055] had been robbed down to a maximum of two courses, but had originally been of like height. It was not bonded with the robbed south wall of the range but simply butted up against its inner face. The central part of this wall had subsided into the backfilled pit [1218].

A gap of 0.88 m between the north end of this wall and the projecting block of masonry [1281] on the south face of terrace wall [1057] indicated the position of a door between the north-eastern room and the large west room. Wall [903] had been cut back at its west end, but subsidence in the later floor indicated a door of similar dimensions at its west end between the north-east and south-east rooms. The need to retain the latest structural features for display restricted excavation, and it was not possible to examine the majority of the primary levels of the eastern two rooms.

Approximately 40% of the north-eastern room was excavated to its primary floor or below. Below the floor was a stone-built drain [1234], the capstones of which were lifted to reveal a channel running south-west from wall [542]. It was cut into the surface of the natural red clay below the building and was sealed by a deposit of sandy brown soil [*1225*] that contained a considerable quantity of fish bones. This in turn was sealed by a patchy mortar floor. Drain [1234] disappeared below later masonry features, which were not removed, and appeared to run into a similar north–south drain, [1242], which was built in the backfilled pre-building ditch [1148] and was integral with the footings of the south wall of the building. This drain ran south out of the excavated area. One of its wall stones, where it passed through the footings of the south wall, was a reused architectural fragment not apparently derived from any building at Mount Grace.

No primary floor was excavated in the south-east room, as it was completely sealed by a later flagged floor that was not lifted. Centrally placed against the inner face of the south wall was a block of masonry comprising undressed blocks of sandstone set in white mortar [*1142*], apparently the base of a hearth. Sections of a hearth kerb matching those of other cells were found in the adjacent robber trench of the south wall, supporting this supposition.

Against the south face of cill wall [903] was a stone bench, [978], of which only the top surface was revealed. The seat was 0.45 m wide and 90 mm thick, and its lower edge was neatly chamfered. It was set on at least one course of punched ashlar blocks placed 40 mm back from its front edge. Like the wall it was built against, this bench had originally extended further west, but its west end was removed at a later date when the seat itself was incorporated in a floor. The seat appears to have originally extended to the full width of the wall.

The primary floor of the larger western room was fully excavated. Above the natural red clay was a levelling of red-brown to pink clay, [1217], containing small sandstone pebbles and patches of mortar, which sealed the construction trench of the south wall of the range and was laid up to terrace wall [1057] and cill wall [1055]. This subfloor was 0.25 m higher than the floors of the two eastern rooms, and was surfaced with a thin skimming of cream-coloured mortar, [1145]. The mortar surface sealed eight stakeholes [1267–75] and four small postholes [1265], [1276], [1293] and [1294]. A further 14 stakeholes were not sealed by the floor but were exposed by later robbing and should be associated with the others; they presumably represent some temporary structure erected during the fitting out of the range. Where the mortar surface and subfloor later subsided into the backfilling of the construction period pit [1218], an occupation deposit of ash and charcoal had built up on the surface of the floor during Period One. This material contained a large quantity of fish bones.

To the west of the range a spread of yellow-brown sandy loam, [1222], was laid above the natural red clay [882] on the completion of building work, sealing the construction trench of the west wall. Unfortunately, this area was substantially modified in Period Two and no further features of Period One were noted in that area.

The western half of the range comprised a two-storey structure, for the north wall survived virtually to full height, with evidence of joist sockets and a square-headed single-light first-floor window (see Figure 5.1). No trace of a stair to the upper floor was found in excavation, but one must have existed within the western half of the range.

Features in the surviving north wall of the range, in particular an inserted tap niche and a serving hatch, combined with the plan recovered by excavation, would suggest that this half of the building contained the original prior's cell. Like all other cells, it had an entry passage, three ground-floor rooms and an upper floor. The precise function of the individual spaces can no longer be identified.

In the south-west angle of the great cloister, to the north of the range, the natural red clay [1219] of the cloister terrace and the backfilled early medieval ditch [1172] were sealed by spreads of pink-brown clay [1031] and [1136]. These deposits were the subfloor levelling of the Period One cloister alleys, of which the arcade walls were presumably built of timber, if the pattern of events seen outside Cell 8 (see Chapter 4) was repeated here. Layer [1031] in the south alley sealed the construction trench [1262] of the north wall [507] of the range, and was in turn sealed by the surviving mortar floor of the alley, [1051], demonstrating conclusively that the early cloister was constructed after the south-west cloister range had been built. No trace of the timber cill beam of the alley wall had survived later reconstruction.

Cut into the floor of the primary south cloister alley and partially outside the area excavated was a single grave, [1259], placed centrally in the alley and aligned with the head to the west. The grave had vertical sides and a flat bottom, and was cut to a depth of 0.56 m from the alley floor. It contained a male burial (which was not lifted for examination) with slight evidence for a wooden coffin. It is one of a group of burials in the south alley; a second below the *lavatorium* was disturbed by emergency drainage works in the early 1970s (T. Rudd and L. J. Keen, pers. comm.), and excavation has revealed a comparable group at the London charterhouse (Knowles and Grimes 1954, plan). This burial was marked not with a stone ledger but simply by a repair in clay and mortar to the floor. As the grave-fill consolidated the floor was levelled up with a patch of yellow clay and charcoal [1138]. This anonymous grave contained no grave goods apart from two iron fragments that might be associated with the coffin, and it remains uncertain whether it is that of a prior or a benefactor. Its location outside the door of the prior's cell might suggest that the former is possible. If that is indeed the case, it is likely to be one of the first priors.

Finds Group 27 (see Figure 5.12)
Contexts [539], [543], [545], [575], [596], [597], [600], [613], [617], [622], [625], [663], [665], [678], [683], [686], [689], [693], [817], [855], [863], [867], [1144], [1145], [1147] and [1195], all associated with the construction of the south-west cloister range.

CERAMICS
This group derives from the initial construction of the south-west cloister range in the first years after the foundation of the priory in 1398. Certainly, there are a variety of vessel fabrics present that would be appropriate for

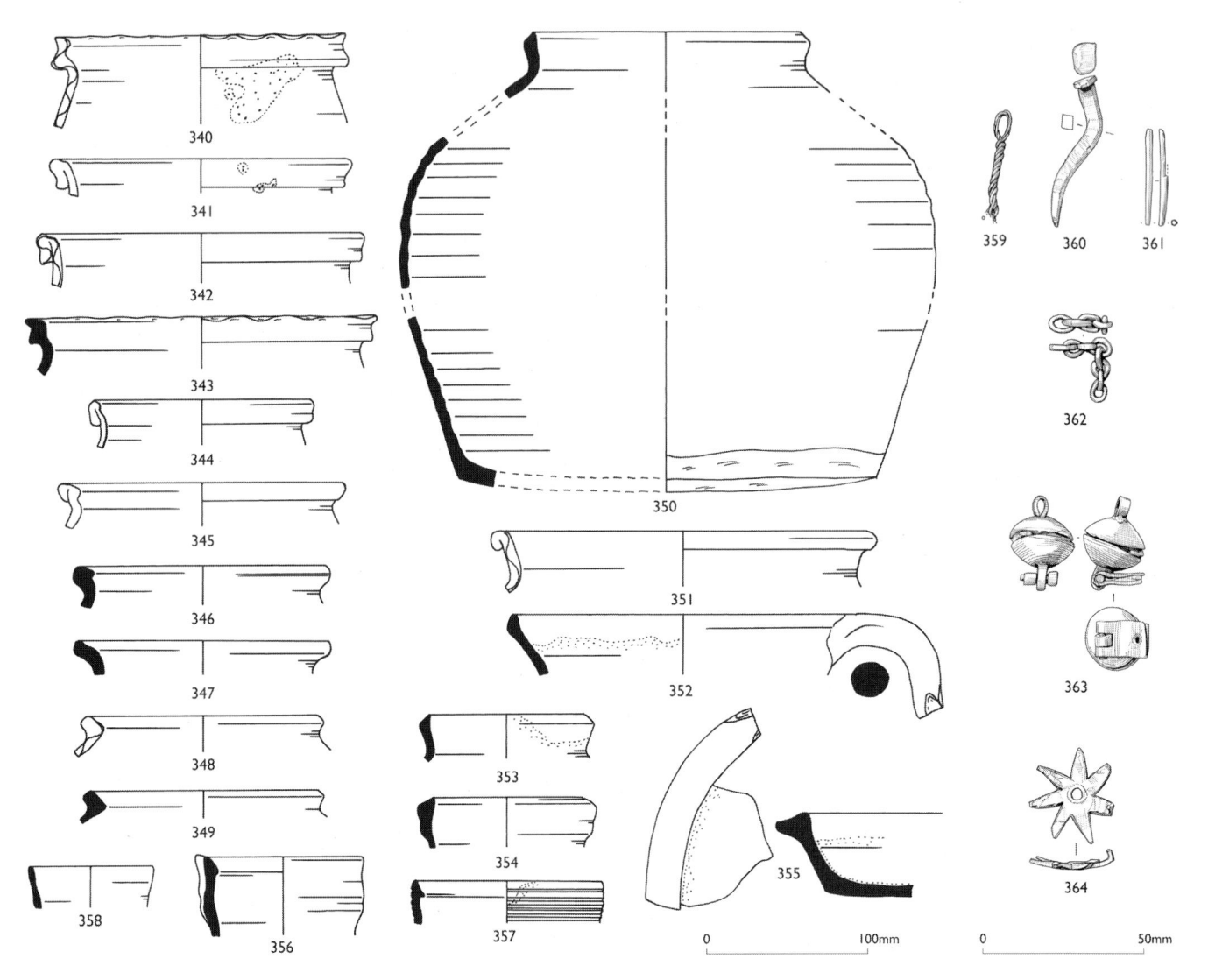

Figure 5.12 Finds Group 27 from the south-west cloister range (pottery 1:4; copper alloy 1:2; lead 1:2).

this date, including 356–7. However, the bulk of the group comprises vessels in the Gritty ware fabric, all of which are likely to be residual, derived from the disturbance of underlying occupation deposits that occurred when the range was being laid out and constructed in Period One. This material ranges from 12th-century cooking pots with splashed glazes, such as 340–1, to 14th-century vessels in the Brandsby type fabric, such as 348–55 (Table 5.6).

340. Gritty ware cooking-pot rim. Dull orange-buff outer surface, pale greyish-blue/orange core, and a creamy-buff inner surface. Classic, bright, light olive-green splashed glaze with orange-yellow margins to the splashes.

341. Gritty ware cooking-pot rim. Pale brown outer surface, grey core and brownish-grey inner surface. Splashes of a yellow-brown splashed glaze on the outer surface.

342. Gritty ware cooking-pot rim. Orange-buff outer surface, grey-black core and inner surface.

343. Gritty ware cooking-pot rim. Cream outer surface, pale orange-pink core and inner surface.

344. Gritty ware cooking-pot rim. Dull orange outer surface, blue-grey core and orange-brown inner surface. Very hard, rough-textured fabric.

345. Gritty ware cooking-pot rim. Light orange surfaces and grey-black core. Very gritty fabric.

346. Gritty ware cooking-pot rim. Orange surfaces and blue-grey core. Hard-fired, well-finished vessel.

347. Gritty ware cooking-pot rim. Orange surfaces and blue-grey core. Very gritty fabric.

THE ARCHAEOLOGY OF THE INNER COURT

Table 5.6 South-west cloister range, Finds Group 27: Ceramics

Fabric	Sherds	Total vessels	Bowl	Cistern	Cooking pot	Jug	Mug or cup	Pancheon	Tripod pipkin	Other
Brandsby type	18	10	0	0	4	4	0	0	2	0
Cistercian	6	4	0	4	0	0	0	0	0	0
Developed Humber	1	1	0	0	0	1	0	0	0	0
Gritty	284	167	1	0	119	39	0	2	1	1
Hambleton	4	2	0	0	0	2	0	0	0	0
Humber	1	1	0	0	0	1	0	0	0	0
Langerwehe	1	1	0	0	0	0	1	0	0	0
Low Countries Red	1	1	0	0	0	0	0	0	1	0
Post-medieval Sandy	4	3	0	1	0	0	0	0	0	2
Raeren	2	1	0	0	0	0	1	0	0	0
Ryedale	7	5	0	0	0	5	0	0	0	0
South Netherlands Maiolica	1	1	0	0	0	0	0	0	0	1
Stamford type	6	1	0	0	1	0	0	0	0	0

348. Brandsby type fabric cooking-pot rim with a slightly micaceous content. Dull orange surfaces and orange core. Burnt and sooted.
349. Brandsby type fabric small cooking-pot rim. Dull purplish outer surface, yellow-buff core and whitish-buff inner surface.
350. Brandsby type fabric cooking-pot (non-fitting profile). Orange outer surface becoming a cream colour from the shoulder upwards, orange-red core with orange margins and orange-red inner surface with spalling away from grits to reveal the orange margins of the inner core. Small cloth mark impressed on the basal angle.
351. Brandsby type fabric cooking-pot rim. Very pale orange surfaces and pinkish-orange core. Burnt and sooted.
352. Brandsby type fabric tripod pipkin rim. Light orange surfaces and pale orange core. Mottled green glaze, turning more yellowish where the glaze thins on the inner surface.
353. Brandsby type fabric pipkin rim. Orange surfaces and bright orange core. Olive-green glaze with orange-yellow margins.
334. Brandsby type fabric jug rim. Smoothed, orange outer surface, white/orange core and pale orange-yellow inner surface.
355. Brandsby type fabric basting dish. Orange surfaces and orange-buff core. Partially mottled yellow-green glaze on inner surface. Knife-trimming to base and lower body.
356. Ryedale ware jug rim. Pale orange outer surface, grey-white/blue-grey core and blue-grey inner surface. Olive-green glaze, very consistently coloured.
357. Ryedale ware jug rim. Pale orange outer surface, grey-black core and greyish-buff inner surface. Deep but clear olive-green glaze. The rim is ribbed, presumably as a decorative feature.
358. South Netherlands Maiolica bottle or flask. Very fine, hard, off-white core. Off-white tin glaze, thick on the outer surface, thinner on the inner surface, greyish hue to white glaze.

SMALL FINDS

The small finds from construction deposits, which were few in number, can be paralleled in monastic occupation deposits and are unlikely to be residual from earlier deposits. They indicate that religious must have been present on site during construction and that the colonisation of the site preceded rather

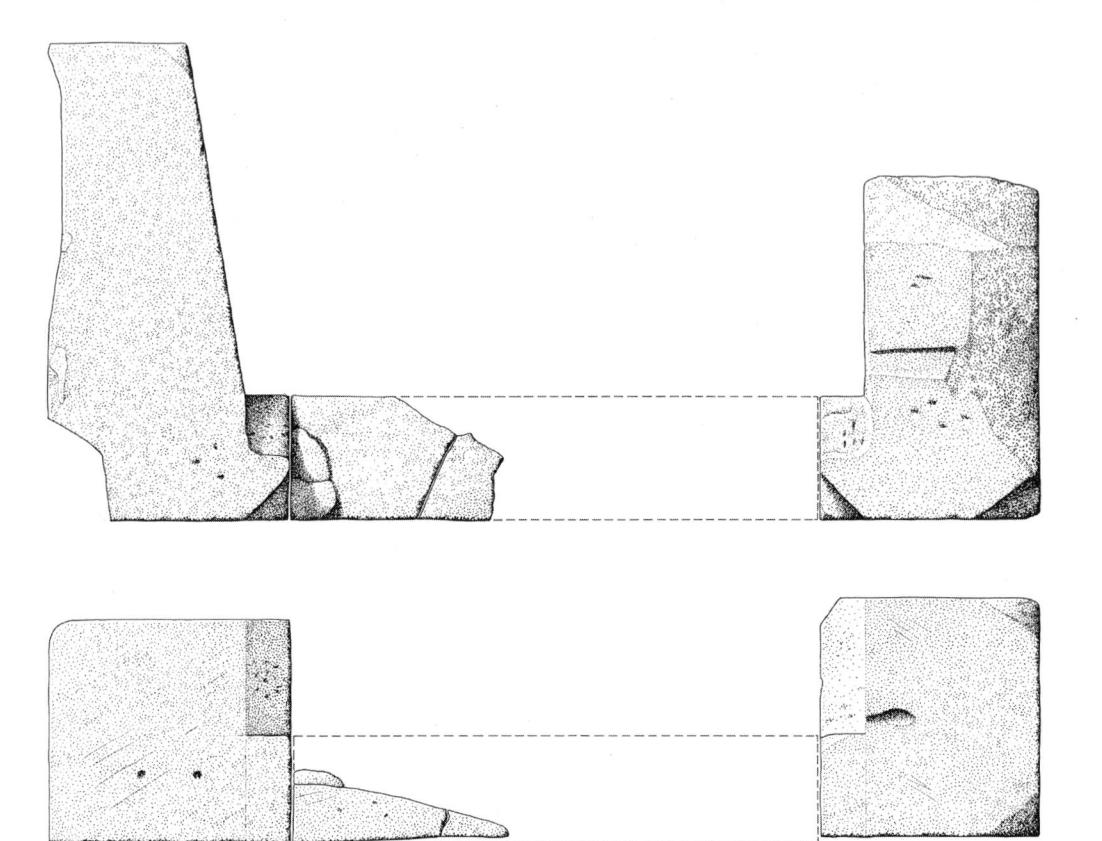

Figure 5.13 Jambs and cill (partly in situ*) in the west wall of the Period One south-west cloister range (1: 10).*

than followed the completion of the earliest stone buildings.

359. Twisted wire loop. Cu. L: 33 mm. Irregularly twisted double strand of wire D: 0.5 mm, with loop L: 0.9 mm at one end. Find no. Cu109.

360. Nail, (?) roofing. Cu. Flat rectangular head, 8 mm × 6 mm. Square section. Find no. Cu110.

361. Lace chape. Cu sheet. Edge to edge seam, slight taper. L: 30 mm; D: 1–2 mm. Find no. Cu120.

362. Strand. Cu. Four figure-of-eight interlocking links of round section. Overall L: 33 mm; L of links 13–15 mm; D: 1 mm. Find no. Cu126.

363. Rumbler bell. Cu. In two pieces. D: 18 mm. Top suspension loop, W: 4 mm, let into top and ends bent back. Base has similar arrangement, but with plate L: 15 mm; W: 10 mm, attached, held in place by central pin. End has single rivet hole. Find no. Cu119.

364. Star. Pb. Seven-rayed star cut from sheet. Th: 1.5 mm. Central hole D: 3 mm. Find no. Pb338.

ARCHITECTURAL DETAIL ASSOCIATED WITH PERIOD ONE (SEE FIGURES 5.13, 5.14 AND 5.15)

27, 28. Lowest jamb stones and fragmentary door cill from the primary door in the west wall [901]. The northern jamb remained *in situ*, as did the cill, but the southern jamb had been displaced by Hope's excavation. Externally, the door opening was chamfered and the chamfers were stopped off square 0.19 m from the base of the jambs, at the approximate height of the cill. Internally, the jambs were rebated to take a door hung from the southern jamb, where a wedge-shaped recess in the upper bed of the stone was cut to receive the lower hinge pintle. Subsequently, but before the Suppression, the door rebate was

THE ARCHAEOLOGY OF THE INNER COURT

roughly cut out to a depth of 90 mm to accommodate a wooden door frame. The internal reveal of the northern jamb was slightly splayed, but that of the southern jamb was square, so designed to continue the line of wall [1164] with which the tail of the jamb stone bonded. Both the jamb stones and the cill were finely bolster-dressed and retained tracing lines.

29. Section of chamfered plinth course from the south-west angle buttress of the range, reset *ex situ* in Period Four [911]. Its chamfer matches the surviving Period One plinth course at the east end of wall [529] and its buttress, both concealed by a localised Period Three widening. It indicates that the outer wall-face of the superstructure was offset 0.10 m from the face of the plinth course. This stone retains slight evidence of bolster dressing.

30–34. Five fragments from four stones comprising a hearth bounded by a raised kerb. Found together, they appear to derive from the same fireplace, presumed to be that of the Period One prior's cell, but on each stone the kerb has been cut to a different template. They were found in the robber trench [529] adjacent to the blocking of the fireplace [1042].

35. Chimney cap with castellated moulding in two sections (one not illustrated) from an octagonal chimney with sides of 0.225 m. This had apparently fallen from the south wall of the prior's cell [938] and was probably related to the hearth sections above. It is quite different from the chimney caps of the monks' cells, with a much larger shaft and a projecting moulding above a deep hollow with a neck-moulding at the bottom. It is, in fact, much more like the chimney caps of the lay brothers' cells and it is possible that, despite its association with a Period One fireplace, it is actually a Period Three replacement.

36–39. Three fragments of window tracery and one mullion associated with the south-west range. They are cut to almost the same template as the Period One church windows, but are slightly deeper. 36 and 37 are sections of jamb

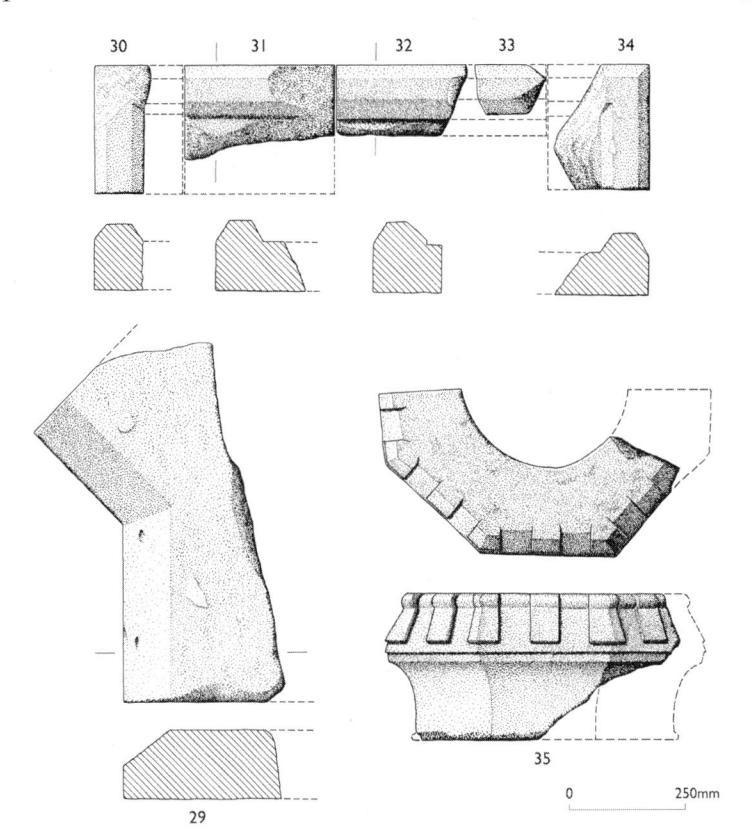

Figure 5.14 Architectural detail from the Period One south-west cloister range (1:10).

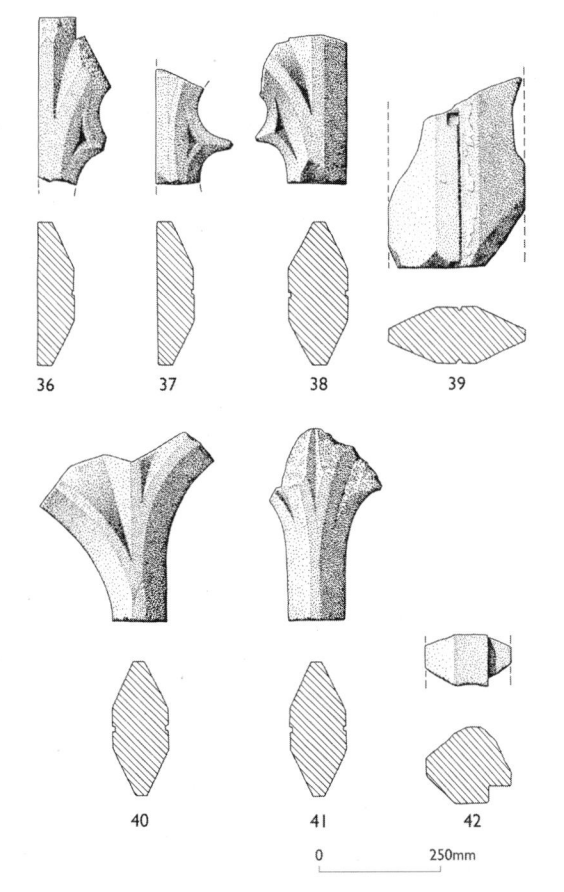

Figure 5.15 Window fragments from the Period One south-west cloister range (1:10).

with the springing of a cusped trefoil or cinquefoil head of a subsidiary light and 38 is a section of mullion with the springing of a similar light on one side only. 39 is a plain fragment of mullion retaining a single saddle-bar hole. Insufficient tracery was recovered to reconstruct the pattern of the window tracery. All fragments are neatly bolster-dressed and 36 and 37 retain whitelime on their inner faces up to the glazing grooves. 36–7 were found in demolition to the south of the refectory, [551], 39 was found in the robbing of its south wall, [529], and 38 was found among the unlocated collection and may have been recovered by Hope. Their provenance suggests they must have originated in traceried windows lighting the south wall of the Period One refectory.

40, 41. Two tracery fragments with the same template as the Period One nave windows. 40 is a mullion with uncusped tracery springing from both sides at different heights and 41 is a section of mullion with the springing of paired heads. They were found among the unlocated collection, but because they do not fit into the known Period One traceried windows from the church an origin within the refectory is possible.

42. Fragment of jamb with an external chamfer and internal rebate for a shutter or glazing frame. It was found in the demolition of the Period One prior's cell [938] and probably came from a square-headed single-light window.

Period Two (see Figures 5.10 and 5.16)
The building of the kitchen cross-wing at the north end of the guest-house range in Period Two seems to have been the stimulus for the prior to move his cell from the western half of the range into the original refectory. This entailed the removal of a section of the cloister wall [507] for a length of 6.8 m to the level of its foundation course and its rebuilding as wall [507a] with the inclusion of a wall fireplace, [508], 1.5 m wide at its centre (see Figure 5.17) and a now-blocked tap niche at its west end. The fireplace, of which only the east jamb and a fragment of the lintel survives, was more elaborate than those of the monks' cells, having hollow moulded jambs, a massive lintel and flanking conical lamp brackets. The area of the primary refectory was then divided into two separate rooms by the insertion of a cross-wall, [502], set just to the east of the buttress in the south wall that marked the bay divisions of the original building. All that remained of wall [502] was two courses of rubble foundation work set in white mortar, but the upper surface retained the bedding mortar for the first course of the superstructure, showing that the wall itself was only a single course of ashlar 0.4 m thick. Any doorway between the two rooms created could no longer be traced. Wall [502] was footed deeply to avoid settlement into the underlying pre-monastic ditch [624], but no trace of a foundation trench could be distinguished because the footings had been laid tight against the trench edge and the upper levels had been badly disturbed by Hope's excavation. In the east room, a thin deposit of yellow clay [*552*] and [*568*] was laid in hollows in the primary floor [*563*] and [*569*] to level the area up before a floor surface of pale yellow-brown clay [505] some 60 mm thick was laid. Significantly, the new floor surface ran over the footings of wall [502] and butted against the first course of its superstructure. Contemporary with this floor was the insertion of a door, [898], into the east wall to provide access to the area to the north of the church, which was being developed at this time (see Chapters 4 and 6). A socket cut into the face of wall [512] indicated a timber screen or lobby covering this door, which had left no trace in the floor.

In the western room an identical clay floor, [505a], was laid onto an irregular levelling of yellow clay, [*544*], though its relationship with wall [502] had been destroyed by Hope. It did, however, butt against the original west wall of the refectory, [516], showing that this wall, with the door at its north end, was retained unaltered. A disturbance, [515], in the floor in front of fireplace [508] suggested that a small area in front of the fire was flagged and that the flags were robbed out at the Suppression. Cut from the level of floor [505a] in the western room were four postholes [526], [534], [521] and [533] that defined a corridor along the south side of the room, suggesting a connecting door between the two rooms at the south end of wall [502]. The original door in the west wall, [516], was screened by a small lobby, the cuts for the top and bottom plates

THE ARCHAEOLOGY OF THE INNER COURT

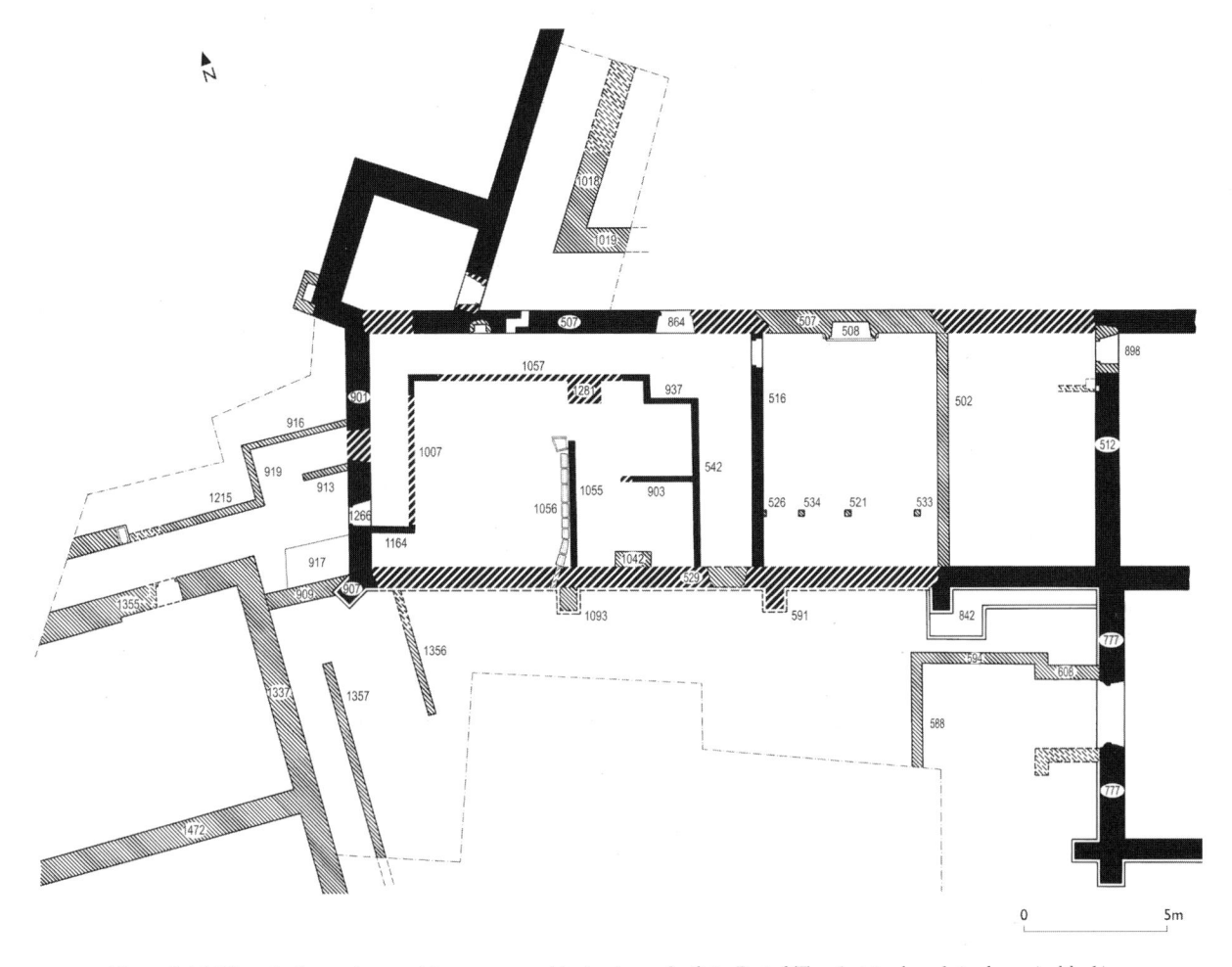

Figure 5.16 Plan of the south-west cloister range and 'prison' as rebuilt in Period Two (original work is shown in black).

of which survived to the west of the fireplace in wall [507a]. The new floor had not survived in the area of this lobby and its southern extent cannot be ascertained. A lead water pipe was introduced from the south cloister alley through the lowest course of wall [507] to the west of wall [516]. Post-Suppression robbing had removed all but a short stub of the pipe, but its course could be traced by a cut in the cill of the primary door at the north end of wall [516] leading in the direction of the blocked tap niche in wall [507a], ensuring that the new prior's cell retained a piped water supply.

It would appear that a floor was inserted within the old refectory supported on wall [502], which rose to a maximum height of 3 m, the height of the primary joist sockets in the east wall, [512], which were not reused. Instead, a corbel (the lone survivor of a series), was inserted into wall [512] to carry a cross-joist 0.43 m square. The north end of the joist was housed in a cut-out in the north wall that was subsequently

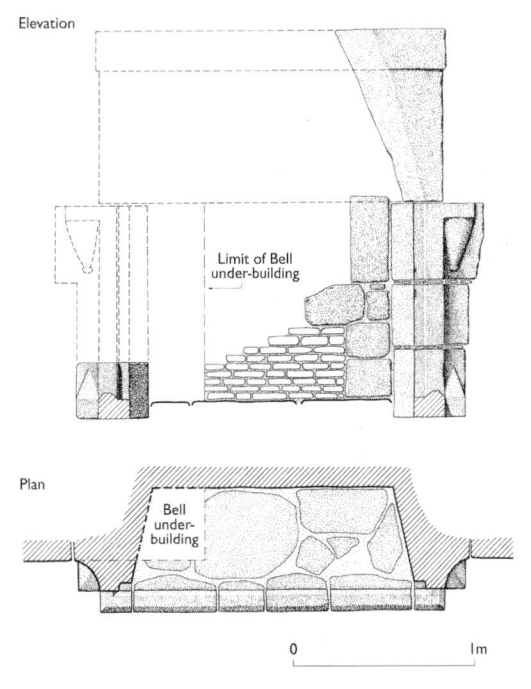

Figure 5.17 The Period Two fireplace in the prior's cell.

blocked, perhaps during Bell's repairs. The floor may have crossed the openings of the windows in the south wall, unless they were set high up. The windows were not apparently altered in the life of the building, making this a distinct possibility. This upper storey appears to have extended no further west than wall [516], and no trace remains of a stair by which it could be reached. The most likely location, following the example of the monks' cells being built in Period Two, would be at the west end of the screened passage in the western room.

The plan of this new prior's cell lacks the formality of his original accommodation, providing larger rooms at ground-floor level at the expense of abandoning the general layout of the other cells. The western room, with its fireplace, was obviously the living room, while the unheated eastern room would provide either a study or a bedroom and oratory, with access to a latrine in the yard to the north of the church. As the eastern room was not partitioned, one of these functions may have been relegated to the upper floor.

The removal of the prior from the western half of the range left his old apartments free for adaptation to new uses. In particular, a new refectory was required. Remarkably, the ground-floor structures were little altered, although the finds – in particular, great concentrations of fish bone – indicate that the rooms were given over to food preparation.

Externally, a buttress, [1093], was added to the south face of wall [529] just to the west of the cill wall [1055] that divided the original prior's apartments. In scale and positioning it matched the primary buttresses on the eastern half of the range, although its footings were bonded with the white Period Two mortar. Its purpose must have been structural rather than to balance the appearance of the range, though any movement must have been in the upper part of the wall. Pink mortar on the upper surface of the footings implied that the buttress was taken down and rebuilt from that level in Period Three, suggesting that sufficient movement occurred to cause the new buttress to fail and require reconstruction. Within the building the principal developments of Period Two occurred within the large western room. First, a lead water pipe was brought through the north wall [507] of the range from the south-west angle of the great cloister. Disturbance by Hope had destroyed its course across the northern corridor, but its line remained as the edge of a Period Three robber trench in the western edge of the western room's floor and as a stone-lined conduit, [1251], from which the pipe had been withdrawn where it returned to the west to exit through the primary door [1266] in wall [901]. The door cill had been reset in Period Two mortar. From there the pipe ran westwards for 3 m before returning south to run parallel with the east wall of the kitchen range in a cut [1107/1224]. It was rerouted in Period Three and this pipe was entirely withdrawn. In the course of Period Two a deposit of charcoal-rich ash [*988*] and [*1180*] built up on the primary floor of the western room, particularly against the dividing wall [1055] where the floor had subsided into the underlying pre-monastic pit [1218]. Next, a drain or gutter of carefully dressed ashlars [1056] was constructed against the east face of wall [1055] (see Figure 5.10) in a deep construction trench, [*1084*]. At its south end the gutter diverged from the line of the partition wall to pass through the wall to the west of the new buttress, [1093], and discharge into a new drain [1243] and [508] that ran away to the south-east (see Figure 5.9), truncating the Period One drain [1242] that still served the building and collecting its discharge. At the north end of the gutter was a stone-lined tank, [*1296*], set in the floor to the south of the doorway between the western and north-eastern rooms. This tank, the bottom of which was cut into the impervious natural clay, was 0.38 m deep. It contained a thick deposit of dark grey silt, but no cultural material to suggest its function. It was out of use by Period Three, when it was packed with rubble set in dirty yellow clay.

In the south-eastern room the primary wall fireplace was blocked, its filling including the greater part of the hearth kerb associated with it, and a rectangular masonry pier, [1141], was constructed against it. The purpose of this pier seems to have been to support the hearth of a fireplace at first-floor level that reused the original flue. The continued use of the flue would explain the survival of the chimney and its cap until the Suppression. A similar occupation deposit to that in the west room continued to build up throughout the phase; it was observed in the north face of the robber trench of wall [529], but was sealed below later stone floors that were not removed in excavation. A further similar occupation deposit, [*1225*], continued to build up in the north-east room, but was largely disturbed by later insertions.

The upper floor of the old prior's cell must have been adapted to serve as the new refectory. This appears to have caused access problems, for there is no evidence in the excavation record for a stair to reach it. However, the passage through the range between the original prior's cell and refectory was now redundant. Its door in the south wall of the range must have been blocked and a stair provided within the passage itself. There is some structural evidence to suggest that in Period Three a wide doorway, [899], was inserted in the north wall of the range opposite the passage, although it was obvious from the evidence of gardening to the south of the range that there was no doorway to match it there, and three sockets cut in the north wall of the upper storey to the west of the surviving Period One window suggest that the eastern part of the upper storey was partitioned off to form a lobby or screens passage (see Figure 5.1).

Period Two saw the development of the area to the west of the range associated with the construction of the kitchen complex in the cross-wing of the guest-house range. Hope's excavation of this area, a post-medieval cart track and the proximity of 18th-century and later buildings – not least a sewer inserted by the Ministry of Works in 1957 – caused severe damage to archaeological deposits there. The south-west cloister range and the new kitchen were linked by a timber pentice set on stone cill walls, built as a series of connected operations in the second quarter of the 15th century. First, and at the time that the lead water main was inserted into the south-west cloister range, a wall, [909], was built from the south-west angle buttress [907] of the range to the east wall of the cross-wing containing the kitchen. Its footings, [1226], which incorporated the water pipe, were set in a deep construction trench [1227] cut from the surface [1222] of the Period One yard on the west side of the range. Wall [909] sat on the southern edge of its foundations and the construction trench to its north was partially filled with a spread of sandstone metalling set in white mortar, [1221], which occurred only in the angle between walls [901] and [909]. This in turn was sealed by a spread of mid-brown sandy clay, [1185], that completely filled the construction trench of wall [909] and spread 2.5 m to the north of the wall, where it butted against a cill wall, [1215], that carried the pentice along the north side of the kitchen range. To the north, a stone-lined drain, [922], was inserted into the natural clay of the terrace to serve a latrine, observed by Hope (Hope 1905, 301) but outside the area of excavation, on the south-west angle of the prison block. This drain, which was partially excavated by Hope, comprised a base of natural red clay, roughly dressed side stones and a capping of flagstones. It turned to the west to run along the outer face of pentice cill wall 1215. Its construction was integral with the construction of the cill walls [916] and [919] (and most probably [1215]) that formed the base of the pentice along the west wall of the south-west cloister range (see Figures 5.10 and 5.16). The pentice walls were largely built of reused blocks, apparently embrasure cills from an embattled parapet, all marked with masons' marks of type B1. No floor or subfloors survived in the north end of this pentice because of Hope's disturbance, but a small area of the original floor was preserved at the south end against wall [909], where the subfloor material, [*1185*], was sealed by a further levelling of pink and yellow mortar [*954*] and a surface of yellow clay [*924*]. Access to the pentice from the south-west cloister range was limited to the primary doorway, [1266], in its west wall, yet the pentice extended to the north. The function of this extension was explained by a rectangular stone setting, [915], in the angle of walls [901] and [909]. Hope had removed the filling of this feature, which was set on the surface of the levelling layer, [*954*], exposing the undressed tails of the stones and showing that this was intended to be a solid structure that was primary to the pentice. It was associated with a masonry 'step', [913], placed 1.24 m to the south of the north wall of the pentice and sharing its alignment. These masonry features appear to be the base of a stair and landing leading both to the upper storey of a building that lay in the angle of wall [909] and the east wall of the kitchen range and to the new refectory.

The construction of a stone cloister arcade in Period Two was attested by excavation outside Cells 8 and 13. In the south-west angle of the great cloister (see Figures 5.10 and 5.16) this stone arcade was represented by the footings of its west [1018] and south [1019] walls. The construction trench for the south wall was difficult to distinguish, although it must have been cut from the level of the Period One mortar floor, [1051]. In the west alley it could not be identified at all, largely

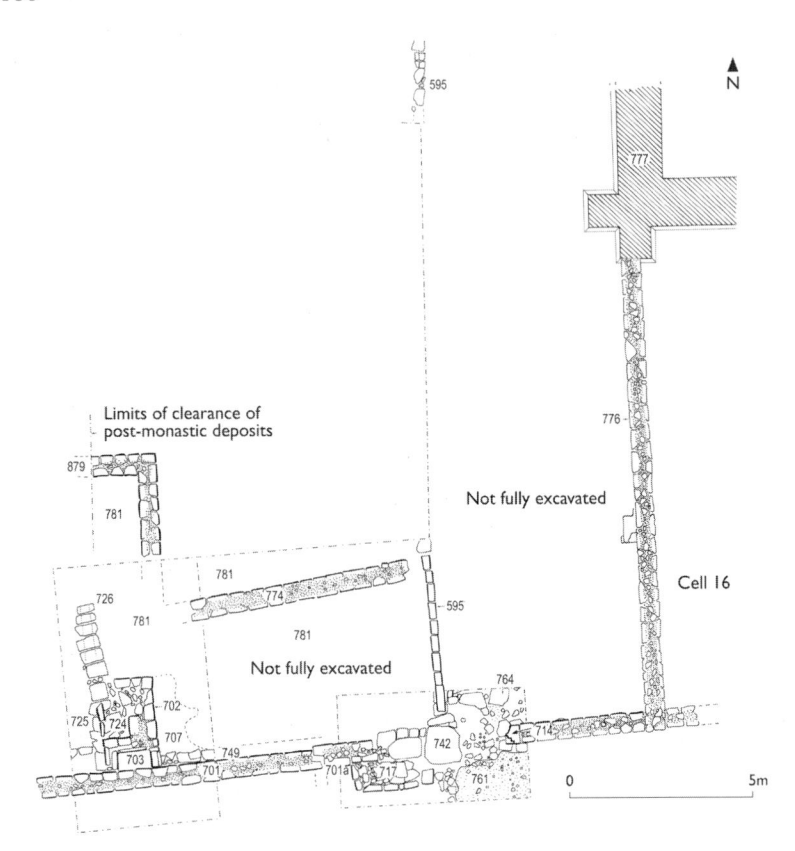

Figure 5.18 The yards to the south of the south-west cloister range as excavated.

because 17th-century gardening had removed most of the stratigraphy and, indeed, all but the southern 2.4 m of the wall footings themselves. Preservation was slightly better in the southern alley, where a fragmentary clay subfloor, [*1050*], survived, butting the north wall of the range but not extending to the cloister alley wall. It sealed the filling of grave [1259]. The floor surface had been destroyed, but a patch of four flagstones, [1017], in the west alley – though they had been lifted and reset, perhaps by Hope – may represent the Period Two alley floor.

An intermittent robber trench, [1121], along the north face of wall [507], was dug to remove a lead water pipe that ran to the south-west angle of the cloister and supplied a tap in the south face of the cloister wall. As the construction trench for the pipe survived for a short length, where the pipe had been withdrawn rather than dug out, and was sealed by the floor bedding [*1050*], but was cut into the surface of the Period One floor, the pipe was laid during the construction of the Period Two cloister. It was from this pipe, which must survive to the east of the excavated area, that a branch was taken through wall [509] to supply the new prior's cell.

The modification of the south-west cloister range in Period Two was associated with a number of features that were recorded in the open yard to the south and to the west of the church and which appear to belong to this period (see Figures 5.10, 5.16 and 5.18). The first was a shallow porch provided to cover the west door of the church. Only the foundation course of the north wall, [608], survived, which was made up of large undressed blocks of sandstone laid unmortared in a shallow trench cut into the natural clay of the terrace. The southern side of the porch had been robbed and all but the very bottom of its construction trench removed by Hope's recorded excavation in this area (Hope 1905, plan). The height of the porch can be ascertained from the sockets for its wall plates cut into the west wall of the church [777] adjacent to the springing of the door head, and its ridge line must have been below the cill of the west window. Contemporary with the building of the porch was the construction of a walled yard to the south of the south-west cloister range, bounded by a wall to the east, [776], that butted with the south-west angle buttress of the Period One church and a wall to the south, [701]; both were bonded with white mortar. Only two small areas associated with wall [701] were fully excavated before post-Suppression deposits were removed under archaeological supervision across the whole area of the yard, with the result that most medieval deposits remain unexcavated in this area. The yard was divided unequally into two parts (see Figure 5.18): a large garden to the west and a small paved enclosure leading to the church, the two being separated by a wall of punched ashlar a single block thick [595] set on a rubble foundation [588] and bonded with white mortar. The superstructure of this wall survived only at its southern end, and its footings did not extend as far north as the south wall of the south-west cloister range, but turned to the east as wall [594] to butt against the north wall of the new porch. This area was fully examined by excavation, showing that wall [594] convincingly cut construction deposits of Period One but was partially cut away itself in Period Three. The smaller enclosure was entered by a fine moulded archway, [714], in its south-west corner, closed by a door. The western jamb had been removed by robbing in the mid-16th century, but its massive footings,

THE ARCHAEOLOGY OF THE INNER COURT

Figure 5.19 Finds Group 28 from the south-west cloister range (pottery 1:4; iron 1:4; bone 1:2).

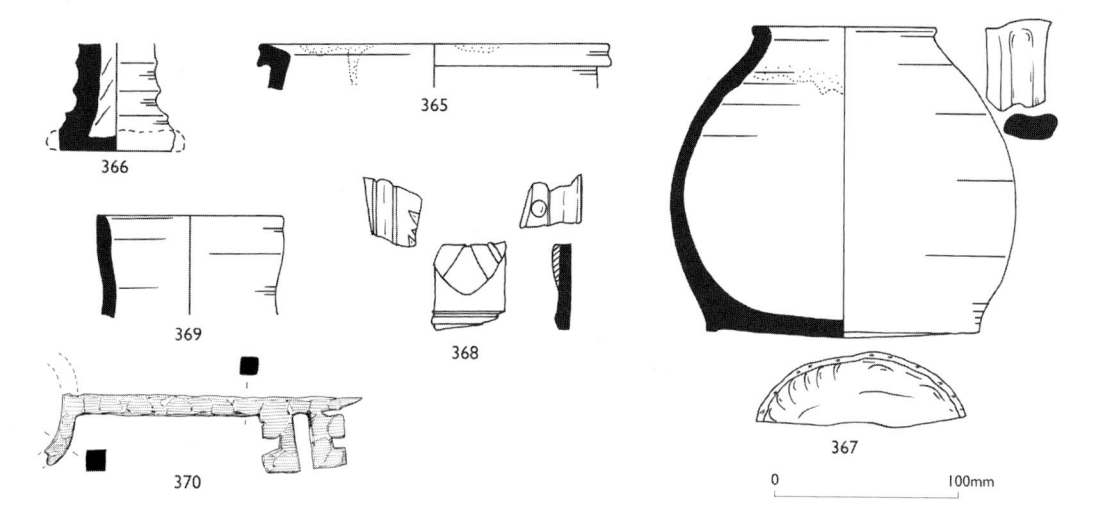

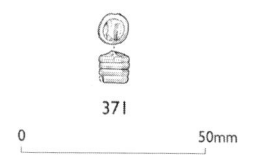

[742], survived and were demonstrably contemporary with the footings of wall [595]. Within this entrance, excavation revealed a flagged surface [761] and [764] somewhat disturbed by Hope and by its sinking into an underlying unexcavated feature, perhaps a pre-monastic ditch. Earlier than this surface was a spread of white mortar, [762], that extended to the west of wall [595] and a thick layer of charcoal and coal that extended some 5 m from the southern limit of excavation before it tailed out. It, too, extended to the west of wall [595] and both layers should be associated with activity in Period One.

Wall [701], which bounded the south side of the yards to the south of the south-west cloister range, continued westward to the limit of excavation, perhaps meeting the Period Two wall that separated the guest-house range from the remainder of the Inner Court (wall [1337] on Fig. 5.44). To its north, and west of wall [595], was a garden that was only partially examined. This area has been reduced to the base of 16th-century demolition deposits and the greater part of the garden soils remain undamaged for future research. The original laying out of the garden belongs to Period Two and it must be contemporary with the first occupation of the new prior's cell. In its north-east corner (see Figure 5.10) a raised bed was provided against the west face of wall [588], revetted by a line of roof slates set on edge [606]. This extended north from the limit of excavation to the line of a bedding trench, [676], cut into the natural clay and filled with light brown loam. This trench ran parallel to and 2.6 m from the south wall of the range. It reduced in depth to the west, where later gardening activity had removed the surface of the natural clay, and its western termination could not be recovered. Between it and the range were four postholes [578], [658], [851] and [853], two possible planting pits [883] and [885] and a single stakehole. All these features were sealed by a thick deposit of cultivated garden soil, [587], which contained pottery from manuring that demonstrated continuous cultivation up to the Suppression. In the south-east corner of the garden there was an area of metalling, [754], either a yard surface or a path, that butted both walls [701] and [595] and sealed their construction.

Finds Group 28 (see Figure 5.19)
From Period Two construction contexts [505], [520], [534], [732], [733], [754], [761], [765] and [1251].

CERAMICS
Finds Group 28 derives from Period Two construction deposits and contains a large amount of residual material from disturbed pre-monastic deposits as well as material contemporary with the 15th-century construction work. The ceramic stove-tile 368 is of a general class that has been recognised on other Yorkshire monastic sites, such as Fountains Abbey. Their function or range of functions is still uncertain, but their bright glazes and decorative designs would have made them striking features associated with high-status spaces (Table 5.7).

365. Gritty ware cooking-pot rim. Pink surfaces and off-white core. Orange-yellow suspension glaze on the rim top.

MOUNT GRACE PRIORY

Table 5.7 South-west cloister range, Finds Group 28: Ceramics

Fabric	Sherds	Vessels								
		Total vessels	Cistern	Cooking pot	Jar	Jug	Mug or cup	Pancheon	Tripod pipkin	Other
Developed Humber	11	2	0	0	0	0	0	0	0	2
Gritty	18	10	0	7	0	2	0	0	1	0
Post-medieval Sandy	7	5	0	0	3	1	0	1	0	0
Regional Stray	1	1	0	0	0	0	0	0	0	1
Ryedale	7	4	2	0	0	1	0	0	0	1
Siegburg	2	2	0	0	0	0	2	0	0	0

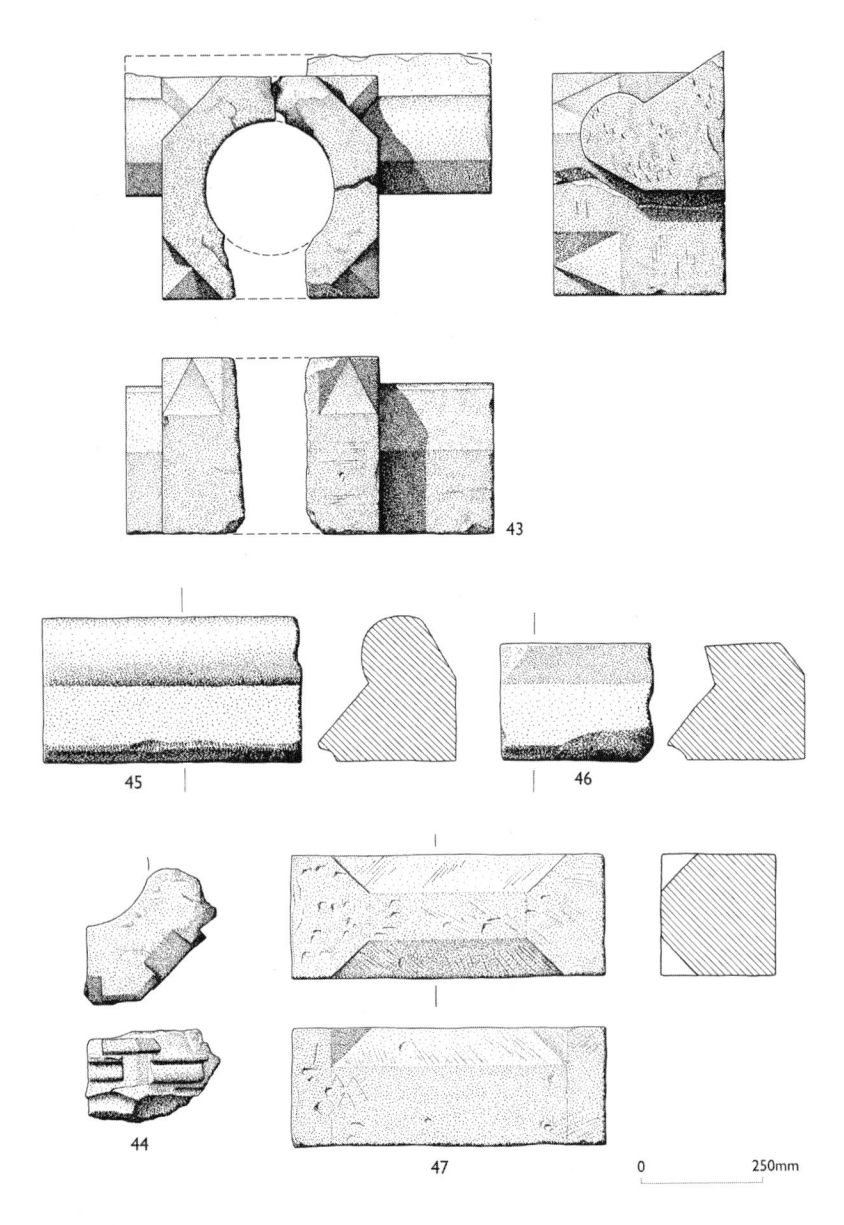

Figure 5.20 Architectural detail from the Period Two south-west cloister range (1:10).

366. Ryedale ware candlestick base, heavily worn. Pale orange outer surface, pale blue-grey core and inner surface. Olive-green 'developed splashed' glaze. At first sight this vessel looks as though it ought to be early, but the fabric of the base is too smooth (or smoothed?) to be the Gritty ware fabric, and the hard, fine Humber ware fabric often has pock-marked glazes.

367. Ryedale ware urinal (non-fitting profile). Dull purplish outer surface, very pale bluish-grey core and dull orangeish inner surface. Heavy white deposit on the inner surface, particularly thick on the base. Olive-green glaze. Knife-trimming to the underside of the basal angle and the central part of the underside.

368. Stove tile, off-white sandy fabric with a bright copper-green glaze. Produced from a mould?

369. Post-medieval Sandy ware jug. Dull orange-buff core and bright, deep olive-green glaze on both surfaces.

SMALL FINDS

370. Key. Fe. Broken bow, square section. L: 180 mm. Square section stem. Symmetrical clefts with short pin. Find no. Fe385.

371. Pin. Bone. Turned fragment H: 5 mm; D: 7.5 mm. Three shallow grooves. Find no. Bone132.

ARCHITECTURAL DETAIL ASSOCIATED WITH PERIOD TWO (SEE FIGURE 5.20)

43. (Found in the garden of Cell 11) Three fitting fragments from a chimney base

THE ARCHAEOLOGY OF THE INNER COURT

incorporating a section of wall parapet moulding (Find nos MG167, 168 and 169). The chimney base comprises an octagonal shaft of 0.19 m side and with pyramidal chamfer-stops rising from a square base. Internally, the flue is square in plan within the base, reducing to circular at the start of the octagonal shaft, identical to the monks' cell chimneys. The attached parapet moulding indicates that this chimney base comes from a side and not a gable wall, and it is this which identifies it as belonging to the prior's cell north wall, as this is the only location, apart from the surviving chimney in the east wall of the guest-house range, where a fireplace was set in a side rather than a gable wall. This chimney therefore additionally shows that the prior's cell was provided with a parapet and gutter, rather the dripping eaves of the monks' cells. Although the chimney belongs to Period Two, it is probable that the parapet coping dates to Period One.

44. Fragment of chimney cap with castellated moulding found in demolition material in front of the prior's cell fireplace and apparently fallen from its chimney [531]. Like 35 discussed above, this piece is more like the moulded chimney caps of the lay brothers' cells than the straight caps of the monks' cells.

45. Section of parapet coping matching that on chimney base 43 which comprises a heavy roll moulding above a 45-degree splay with a hollow drip mould on the lower, outer edge [938]. The rear of the roll is chamfered off above a vertical inner face, which itself formed the outer edge of a parapet gutter. A mason's mark of type B21 occurs on the inner face (for the definition of masons' marks, see Chapter 6). A number of identical parapet sections were recovered from elsewhere on site: three from Cell 10, five from Cell 11, three from the Cell 12 latrine (where they had been used to partly block the door) and one from the garden pentice. Two sections were recovered from Period Four construction in the south-west cloister range and demolition.

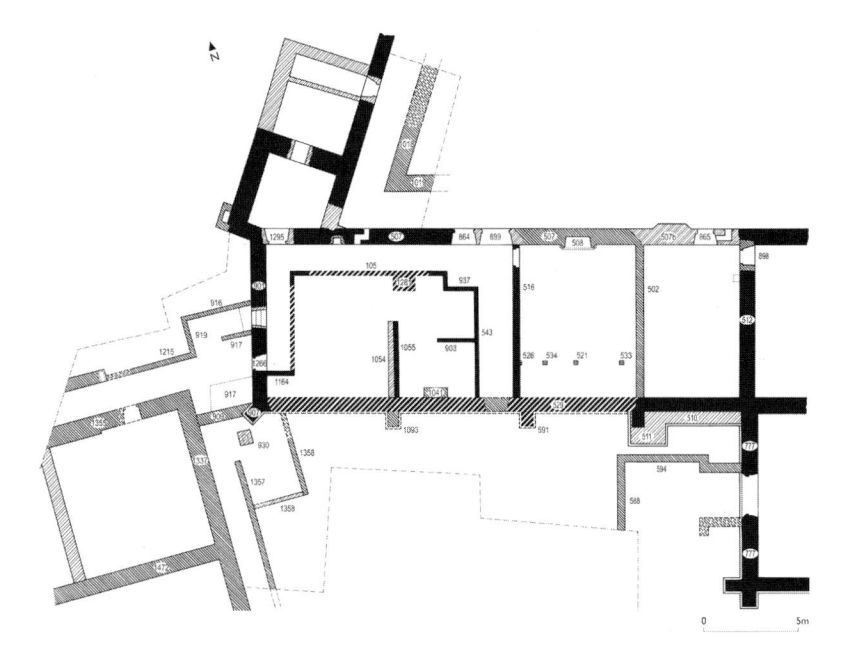

46. Section of parapet coping matching 45, but with the upper part of the roll-moulding dressed off, apparently for reuse in a post-Suppression context [938].

47. Section of chamfered cill that, from its small size (the opening is only 0.65 m wide), may have come from an embattled parapet. It is one of five similar sections reused in cill walls [916] and [919]. One block has a longer seating for its right-hand side (0.73 m), although the embrasure is of the standard width. All five blocks have traces of being drafted out with a 13 mm chisel, but were finished with a bolster. All carry mason's marks of type B1.

Figure 5.21 Plan of the south-west cloister range as rebuilt in Period Three.

Period Three (see Figures 5.10 and 5.21)

The south-west cloister range was further modified in the late 15th century, when substantial alterations were made to both the new prior's cell at the east end of the building (see Figure 5.22) and the service rooms below the new refectory at its west end (see Figure 5.23). The major building work of this period can be identified by the use of good-quality bolster-dressed ashlar that contrasts with the punch-dressed masonry used for all other phases.

The eastern bay of the building was substantially rebuilt from its foundations, an operation that left virtually no trace in the archaeological record. The cloister wall [507] was taken down between walls [502] and [512]

Figure 5.22 The Period Three prior's cell as excavated, seen from the west (G. Coppack).

and rebuilt as wall [507b], containing a new door and hatch at the raised level of the south cloister alley (see Figures 5.1 and 6.30). The lower part of the wall reused old masonry, with white lime plaster smeared into the wide joints, but this gave way to fine, unplastered ashlar at the level of the door cill. Passing through wall [507b] was a small conduit, 0.14 m², for a water pipe that turned east along the wall face and passed through the north jamb of the Period Two door, [898], to serve Cell 22, which was being built in Period Three directly to the east of the prior's cell. The purpose of the rebuilding of the eastern bay of the cloister wall was not simply to provide the prior with a new access to the cloister; incorporated within its north face was a canted respond that corbelled out to carry a monumental oriel window (of which two elements survive in the loose architectural collection) at first-floor level that looked out over the cloister garth. The oriel was screened off from the first-floor chamber in timber, and a stair of three risers was provided within the thickness of wall [507b] to give access to its higher floor level. It possibly provided the prior with an oratory. The south wall, [782], between the west wall of the church and the first buttress, [842], was widened by 0.51 m to a total thickness above plinth level of 1.37 m by the addition of a skin of masonry, [610] (see Figure 5.24). The chamfered plinth of this new work was 0.12 m higher than the corresponding plinth course of wall [529]. Additionally, the original buttress, [842], was cased in new masonry to measure 1.48 m wide by 1.36 m deep. The purpose of widening the south wall was to incorporate a mural stair to the upper floor, although the demolition of the wall to below contemporary floor level had removed any evidence of the stair itself. No archaeological deposits could be associated with the widening because wall [782], the surviving part of the original south wall, had been thoroughly cleared by Hope, but the construction trench [816] for the enlarged buttress [511] remained, cutting through and displacing the foundation course of wall [594], and demonstrating that it post-dated Period Two. All the new ashlar work was set in a hard white mortar.

At the centre of the range a wide new doorway, [899], was inserted into the north wall opposite the original through-passage that must now have contained the stair to the refectory from Period Two. Because it was set so close to the original prior's cell doorway, [864], the eastern jamb of that door was replaced with a new jamb cut on the back of the west jamb of the new door. This masonry, inserted into work of both Periods One and Two, is ascribed to Period Three simply by the finish of its dressings. No archaeological deposits were associated with it and it had been thoroughly repointed by the Ministry of Works.

The western part of the range saw equally intense activity at this time, but there it was better evidenced in the archaeological record. A sequence of interconnected events can be identified. First, the narrow cill wall [1055] that divided the old prior's apartments was widened by the addition of a skin of punched ashlar [1054] against its west face, set in a distinctive pink mortar which was usually associated with the use of punch-dressed masonry in Period Three. This widening was footed onto Period Two ashlar drain [1056], which must have gone out of use, as its channel was completely filled with mortar where wall [1054] had survived later robbing. The door at the north end of the wall was slightly widened at the same time. The pit served by drain [1056] was packed with rubble and clay, and was sealed by a pad of pink mortar associated with the construction of the wall widening. The widening of the wall may have been to strengthen it, as the original cill wall was still sinking into pre-monastic pit [1218]. If this was the case, it is perhaps surprising that no attempt was made to provide proper foundations for the new work.

A substantial flagged stone floor, [976], was laid in the two small eastern rooms (see Figure 5.23) to the east of cross-wall [1055].

THE ARCHAEOLOGY OF THE INNER COURT

Wall [903], which had divided the north-eastern and south-eastern rooms, and bench [978], to the south of that wall, were cut back before the new floor was laid, as it seals their levelled remains. The flags were laid approximately level with the remaining seat of the bench. This new floor, which survives intact and was not lifted in excavation, occupied the western half of the north-eastern room and all of the south-eastern room. In the eastern part of the north-east room, no flagstones were provided and the floor stopped with a straight edge. The unpaved area must have had an earth floor, but this had been removed in Period Four, when a new drain was inserted. The principal feature of the new floor was a carefully constructed surface drain or runnel, [1031], running parallel with wall [1055] and 0.72 m from it, that discharged between the flags at its south end into the Period One drain [1242]. Grooves in the surface of the floor directed water from east and west into the runnel. Between runnel [1031] and wall [1055] was a wooden bench, its legs 75 mm^2 and set into sockets cut into the stone floor. The bench, which was positioned immediately to the south of the door that communicated with the western room, measured 2 m long and 0.72 m wide. From its placing, it would appear that the runnel in the floor was designed to serve it, and that whatever function was served by the bench required it to be regularly swilled down with water. No occupation deposits associated with this phase survived, as the floor had been kept scrupulously clean, but Period Four occupation would suggest that the bench was used for the gutting and filleting of fish.

The western room was also refloored at this time with a series of thin trampled deposits of charcoal, burned clay and ash [988], which appeared to be the rake-out material from an oven. No such oven was found in the room, and it must have been derived from elsewhere on site, perhaps the adjacent kitchen. Scouring of the floor throughout the phase had removed most of this deposit.

The Period Two water pipe that ran from the tap niche along the west side of the western room and out through door [1266] was removed in this phase and rerouted. First a door, [1295], was inserted into the west end of the north wall [507] of the range, communicating with the old prison block to the north, which was remodelled in this phase, and a stone-lined conduit that had originally contained a lead pipe was brought through this door from the north. Once through the new door, the conduit, [958], turned towards wall [901] where a hole [1042] had been cut at an angle through the footing course to take the pipe. Outside the wall, conduit [958] had survived the subsequent robbing of the pipe. The course of the pipe from there, substantially removed by Hope's excavation, could be traced as cuts made through cill walls [916] and [919] to take the pipe and by its robber trench, which extended intermittently between wall [919] and the north door of the kitchen. At the same time as the insertion of the pipe through wall

Figure 5.23 The Period Three paving in the eastern room of the first prior's cell, with sockets for a fitted bench and drainage channel, seen from the north (T. Gledhill).

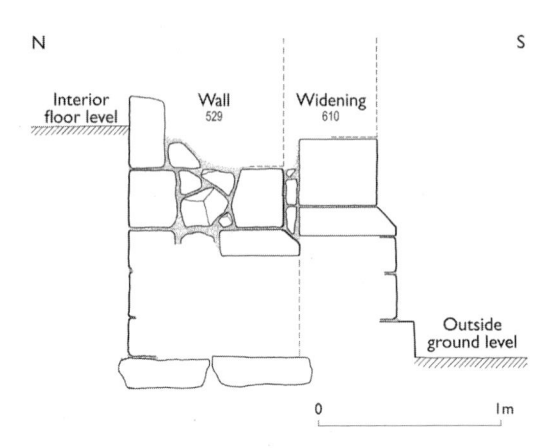

Figure 5.24 The widening of the south wall of the prior's cell in Period Three.

[901], which was marked by a repair in the ubiquitous pink mortar of Period Three, a flight of three steps set in identical mortar was inserted through the west wall of the range. The lowest step was simply the footing course of the wall, but the second and third steps were purpose-made in finely cut ashlar. These steps imply a new door inserted into the wall, of which no trace now remains apart from the ashlar lining of the north reveal, which was cut out to sit over the first and second steps. It was found loose, displaced by Hope, but discovered to fit perfectly on the north side of the steps, where it has been reset. The new door lay just to the south of the north cill wall [916] of the pentice against the west wall of the range and just to the north of the Period Two stair up to the refectory it contained. Strangely, it emerged 0.64 m above the floor of the pentice and a step down [917] was provided against the west face of the wall that overlay the surviving lower step of the Period Two stair.

At first-floor level a square-headed doorway was inserted into the west end of the north wall, its splay running at an angle through the corner of the range to provide access to the upper level of the old prison block (see Figure 5.1). The similarity of its dressings to door [1295] below would suggest that it also belongs to Period Three.

Apparently associated with Period Three was a curious structure [702] butted against the north face of the yard wall [701] that enclosed the area to the south of the south-west cloister range (see Figure 5.18). Hope had examined this structure thoroughly, although rather ineffectually, and interpreted the feature as a latrine, but his interpretation is far from certain. His removal of critical deposits has not aided reinterpretation. The prior's latrine of Period Two was taken over by that of Cell 22, inserted to the east of the south-west cloister range in Period Three, and a new latrine was needed. Only a limited area was examined in 1989 before consolidation, revealing that the structure had been set on a spread of brown clay and rubble [747] that was dumped against the north face of wall [701] to provide a solid foundation. Cut into the surface of this deposit was a stone-lined drain [749] that used the north face of the yard wall as its south edge. Above this was built the ashlar structure [702], which contained a rectangular shaft 0.92 m by 0.48 m with a square opening in its east side through which drain [749] passed. The floor of this drain comprised the base of the shaft. Drain [749] appears never to have been covered over, although it had been revealed and damaged by Hope, and ran along the face of wall [701] for 4.2 m before it turned through 90 degrees and passed through a square hole in a rebuilt section [701a] of the wall. If the shaft and drain comprise a latrine, it is the only one of two cases recorded at Mount Grace where the drain was not water-flushed and set below ground level.

Structure [702] is a complex construction, for the shaft occupies only the south end of a substantial block of masonry 1.56 m wide and 2.44 m long. Exceptionally, the masonry is bonded with a hard white mortar, although the structure can be stratigraphically related to Period Three across the site. It survives to a maximum height of three courses, the single stone of the upper course being a section of chamfered plinth. That it post-dates wall [701] is clear from the way it is butted up against that wall, with only a single stone, the capstone of the drain in the east face, being roughly bonded into the earlier construction. Integral with the structure and accessed from its north side is a wedge-shaped oven, [724], the base and walls of which are burned red. It had been entirely cleared out by Hope, but spreads of coal and charcoal [706] and [707] to its north and east belonging to Period Four were probably associated with the continued use of this feature. From the north-west corner of the masonry block and adjacent to the flue of the oven a wall of a single thickness of ashlar, [775], ran northwards on a foundation course of rubble slabs, [726], dividing the

THE ARCHAEOLOGY OF THE INNER COURT

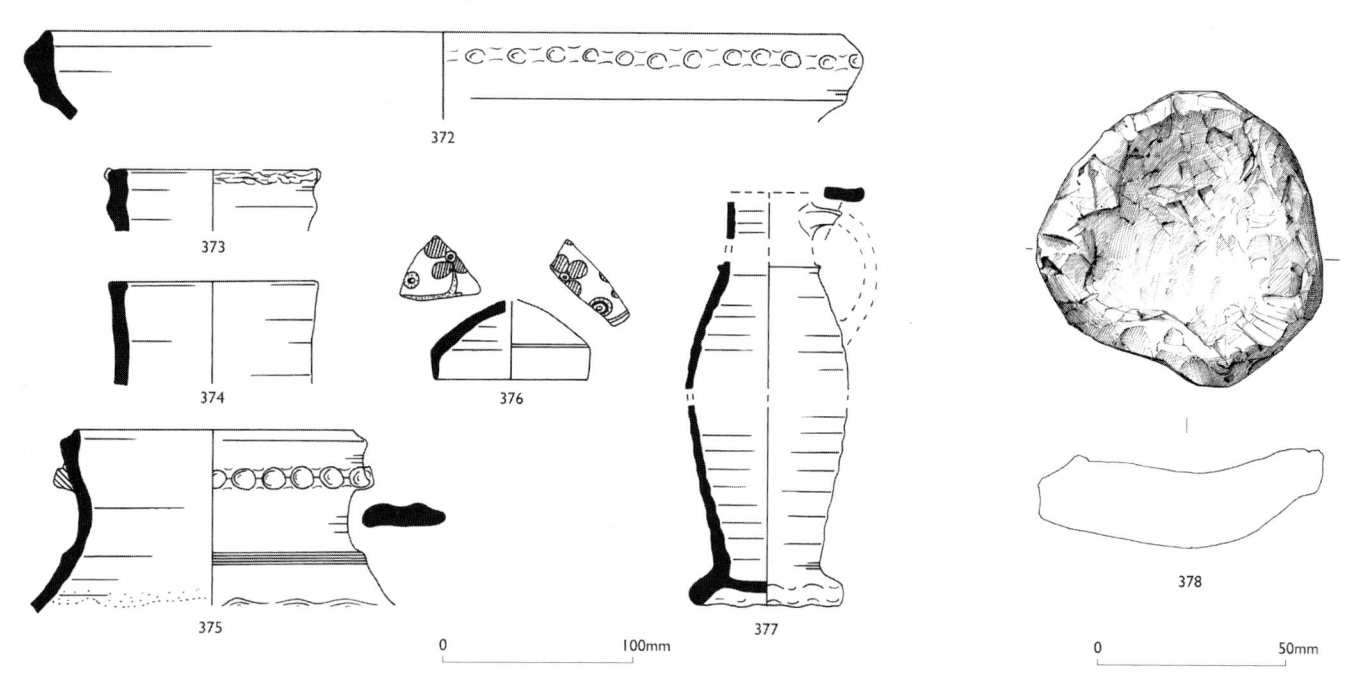

Figure 5.25 Finds Group 29 from the south-west cloister range (pottery 1:4; lead 1:2).

Table 5.8 South-west cloister range, Finds Group 29: Ceramics

Fabric	Sherds	Vessels						
		Total vessels	Bowl	Cistern	Cooking pot	Jug	Lid	Mug or cup
Gritty	13	11	1	0	5	5	0	0
Hambleton	3	2	0	1	0	1	0	0
Humber	2	2	0	0	0	2	0	0
Langerwehe	8	3	0	0	0	0	0	3
Midlands Yellow	1	1	0	0	0	0	1	0
Post-medieval Orange	2	1	0	0	0	1	0	0
Ryedale	12	8	0	1	0	7	0	0
Siegburg	2	2	0	0	0	0	0	2

Period Two yard into two unequal parts. To its west a deposit of kitchen waste built up, most probably derived from the guest-house kitchen, as it contained animal bones.

Finds Group 29 (see Figure 5.25)
From construction deposits [609], [747], [919], [1150] and [1181] of Period Three.

CERAMICS
Finds Group 29 comes from Period Three construction deposits in the south-west cloister range and the yards to the south of it, and was deposited in the third quarter of the 15th century (Table 5.8). The residual Gritty ware fabric element is reduced to about one-third in this group and, with the exception of one vessel, 376, the group seems uncontaminated with intrusive material. 376 is a lid to a cup or posset pot. Its style and decoration is closely related to Cistercian ware, which is generally thought to have been introduced towards the end of the 15th century. However, this sherd is in a white fabric with a yellowish glaze perhaps more reminiscent of early Staffordshire yellow wares.

The Siegburg stoneware mug, 377, is typical of the many German stoneware vessels from

Figure 5.26 Architectural detail from the Period Three south-west cloister range (1:10).

the site. However, the proportion of these vessels was lower in the occupation levels of the south-west cloister range than it was in the monks' cells, perhaps suggesting that other non-ceramic drinking vessels were used here.

372. Gritty ware bowl rim. Orange/yellow/pale brown outer surface, orange-red core and orange-pink inner surface.
373. Gritty ware jug rim. Orange vermilion surfaces and orange core. Orange-brown glaze. Thick crust of glaze/sand and other firing debris around the top of the rim.
374. Humber ware rim. Pale blue-grey core and dull orange inner surface. Yellow-olive glaze.
375. Ryedale ware cistern. Whitish-orange/pale bluish core and light orange inner surface. Copper-green glaze that thins on the inner surface to a watery greenish colour with pocking where the glaze thins further.
376. Staffordshire yellow lid. Rather discoloured sherds, but off-white outer surface and core, cream-white inner surface. Crazed yellow glaze, but with a greenish tinge probably caused by the applied iron-rich clay decoration, which appears as a dark brownish-green under glaze. The centres of the flowers are in a self-clay.
377. Siegburg stoneware drinking mug. Matt outer surface finish varying from a pale grey-buff to orange-brown. Whitish-grey core and inner surface.

SMALL FINDS

378. Cake. Pb. Solid with slightly dished top surface. D: 75 mm max.; Th: 20 mm max.; Wt: 715.45g. Finds no. Pb32.

ARCHITECTURAL DETAIL ASSOCIATED WITH PERIOD THREE (SEE FIGURE 5.26)

48, 49. Two sections of window-head from the oriel window of the prior's cell of Period Three, one section from an angle and one from the front elevation of the window. The oriel had four cinquefoil lights to its front elevation at 0.65 m centres, with two identical lights to each canted face. The individual sections of window-head were fixed together with iron cramps, the sockets for which remain in the upper surface. Externally, the window was framed by a roll and hollow drip-mould, which returns down the corner angles. The spandrels of the individual lights comprise blind sunk panels that replicate the compound chamfer and hollow mouldings of the jambs and mullions. Centrally placed glazing grooves indicate that the upper lights of the oriel were glazed. Although both pieces of the window are heavily weathered, traces of fine bolster dressing remain. They were found in the loose collection.

Period Four

Further modifications to the range were carried out in the early part of the 16th century, and documentary sources suggest that this work

THE ARCHAEOLOGY OF THE INNER COURT

Figure 5.27 The western half of the south-west cloister range showing its appearance in Period Four, seen from the south (G. Coppack).

might be identified with the priorates of John Norton or John Wilson.

Within the new prior's cell at the east end of the range a number of modifications could be identified. The timber stair that had led down from the Period Three door [865] to the cell was replaced by a block of masonry [547] cased with punched ashlar blocks set in a dense white mortar and with a rubble core. Associated with this was a new floor of grey-brown clay, [528], which survived only towards the centre of the eastern room. It had been disturbed by a post-medieval tree-planting pit and the 20th-century burial of a dog. In the western room a patch of similar grey-brown clay, [515], in front of the wall fireplace may be associated with Period Four and was possibly the bedding for an area of stone paving subsequently robbed. Post-Suppression robbing and Hope's clearance of the eastern half of the range had effectively removed all other features of this phase.

At the west end of the range (see Figures 5.9–5.10 and 5.27), where Hope had substantially failed to penetrate 16th-century demolition spreads and the survival of Period Four features was excellent, the principal modification was the widening of the passage that ran along the north side of the building. The Period One terrace wall, [1057], that supported the passage was taken down and replaced by a new wall, [1059] and [1049], 2.04 m to the south of the inner face of the north wall of the range. The shorter section of wall, [1049], was associated with the re-laying of part of the Period Three flagged floor in the north-east room (see below). The western section, [1059], was footed on a single course of reused roof slates, [1257], laid onto the underlying floor. Presumably the partition carried on wall [1057] was moved to the line of the new terrace wall, although no trace of its setting had survived post-Suppression robbing in the 16th century and Hope's excavation. A considerable number of floor tiles associated with this robbing would suggest that the floor of the widened passage had been tiled, but not a single tile remained *in situ*. The continuation of the passage along the west wall of the range was not altered in Period Four, although it may have been at that time that a wooden frame was inserted into the rebates of the Period One door [1266] in the west wall.

The floor of the western room had continued to subside into pre-monastic pit [1218], and the Period Three widening [1054] of wall [1055] had begun to lean seriously to the west. Nothing was apparently done to correct this, but the sinkage in the floor was made good with a dump of yellow clay [1179] below a thick packing of rubble in mid-brown loam [1039], which contained quantities of white-painted wall plaster, lumps of white mortar and burned red friable soil. Above this deposit, and sealing the Period Three floor deposits in the western room, a floor surface of stone roof slates was laid. None of the slates was pierced for hanging. In the north-west corner of the room a rectangular patch of this floor surface remained undisturbed, perhaps because it was below a timber stair into the room from the corridor to the north. Elsewhere the floor surface was badly broken up and it was initially difficult to tell if the slates were actually a part of the floor or had fallen from the roof during demolition. Apparently contemporary with this new floor surface was a narrow slot, [1232], parallel to the south face of the new terrace wall, [1059], with a number of stakeholes in its base. Whatever the slot had contained was removed during the stripping and demolition of the building.

A new drain, [1178], was provided in the north-east corner of the western room. It could not be examined because it ran below floor surfaces that could not be removed. However, it appears to be the same drain as drain [1234a], which was observed further east, running along the northern side of the north-eastern room and turning south to meet an existing drain [1234]. This earlier drain appears to have been a primary feature of the building, and its existence must have been known when the new drain was inserted. The course of drain [1234a] could be traced in the flagged floor of Period Three where it had been patched; this was particularly noticeable in the area of the doorway between the western and north-eastern rooms, where the patching had been done with large roofing slates. Further east, the regular nature of the stone floor had been disrupted by the insertion of the drain.

Following the construction of drain [1178]/[1234a] the earth floor in the eastern part of the north-eastern room was relaid as a deposit of friable dark brown sandy silt containing large quantities of fish bones and charcoal [*1186*], and purple sandy silt containing patches of organic matter [*1118*]. Following the re-laying of this floor a wall of reused punched ashlar blocks of unmortared construction, [1003], was built on the surface of the earlier flagstone floor, [976], and the earth floor, [*1118*]. Robbed at its northern end, it had originally butted against the terrace wall [937] and stopped 0.6 m to the north of cill wall [903], where a single socket, [1099], was cut into the flagstone floor, indicating a harr-hung door in the opening. Wall [1003] survived to a height of a single course. The floor surface within this room was soft and friable and showed no evidence of wear except in the area of the doorway, and it is suggested that it contained a lead-lined tank removed at the Suppression (L. J. Keen, pers. comm.). To the south of cill wall [903] a second room was created by building a short length of wall, [904], in line with wall [1003] from wall [903] to the projecting block of masonry [1041] against the south wall of the range. Wall [904] was placed directly on the clean surface of the flagged floor. Again, this section of wall, which survived to a maximum height of two courses, was not bonded with mortar and it was largely composed of reused punched ashlar blocks, though some roughly dressed rubble was used in the second course. Towards its south end a section of Period One or Two parapet had been reused in the bottom course as a through-stone. As there was no opening into this 'room', it is again suggested that wall [904] enclosed a lead-lined tank. Three further sockets ([*1084*], [*1058*] and [*1086*]; see Figure 5.23) cut into the Period Three flagged floor suggest that the bench against wall [1055] was partitioned off from the rest of the room at this time.

To the south of the building there was evidence for the continued use of the enclosed yard to the west of the church entry as a garden, presumably associated with the prior's cell. The features encountered within it are described in the discussion of Period Two (above), but the pottery from the manuring of the soil indicated that cultivation continued through this phase as well. Within the garden, a large pit, [*699*], was dug to expose the capstones of drain [1243], which was draining water from the flagged room in the western part of the range and which must have become blocked in Period Four. To the south of the garden (see Figure 5.18), a new wall, [774], was footed onto the surface of the garden soil [781], slightly out of parallel with wall [701], which closed the yard to the south, and approximately 4 m to its north. It survived to the height of a single course of punched ashlar (most blocks bearing a mason's mark of type C16) and had been bonded with white mortar. At its east end it butted against the wall [595] that separated the garden to the

THE ARCHAEOLOGY OF THE INNER COURT

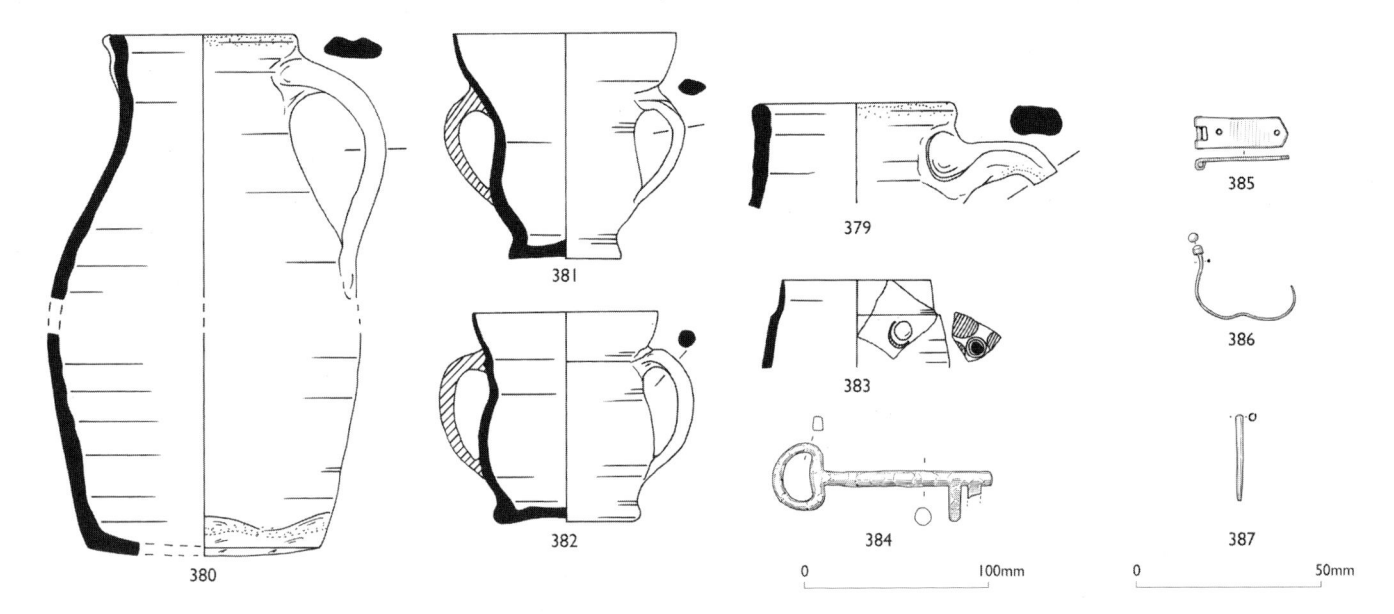

Figure 5.28 Finds Group 30 from the south-west cloister range (pottery 1:4; iron 1:4, copper alloy 1:2).

south of the range from the church entry, but at its west end it returned to the north and then to the west to meet the Period Three wall [726]. This deflection appears to have been caused by the continued existence of structure [702], which butted the original yard wall at that point. Occupation spreads [720] and [745], associated with that feature in Period Four, butted up to the south face of wall [774]. Also associated with Period Four was a block of masonry set in white mortar [717] that buttressed the south face of wall [701] to the west of the doorway into the church entry, where subsidence had caused it to lean outwards.

Finds Group 30 (see Figure 5.28)
From construction deposits of Period Four [528], [642], [699], [759], [781], [1039], [1047], [1118] and [1186].

CERAMICS
This material belongs to the early 16th-century construction of Period Four and, with the exception of the residual Gritty ware fabric, represents a homogeneous group. The post-medieval fabrics were in each case represented by only a single sherd, but it seems likely that they were becoming current well before the Suppression.

It is also interesting that a group such as this should have produced Cistercian ware, Reversed Cistercian ware and Cistercian ware copies in an apparently contemporary setting. There is evidence that a number of contemporary late medieval potteries, such as West Cowick, eventually attempted to produce a range of fine ware forms similar to the Cistercian ware potteries. However, it is now becoming clear that these local potteries were quick to respond to the new Cistercian ware forms. The differences here between the true Cistercian ware cup, 381, and its copy, 382, seem minimal (Table 5.9).

379. Humber ware jug rim. Pale orange-red outer surface, blue-grey core and dull brick-red inner surface. Flecked brownish-orange suspension glaze. The handle is of classic Humber ware type, perhaps more reminiscent of Holme-upon-Spalding-Moor types than Cowick.

380. Hard, fine Humber ware jug profile. Light, dull purple outer surface, greyish-white core with a matt grey-black inner surface. Typical Hard, fine Humber ware fabric, slightly micaceous, not too hard with a smooth texture. Rather crude, but well-covered olive-green glaze, pocked in places where the glaze thins, but becoming more lustrous where the glaze thickens. Fairly crudely produced vessel; the handle, for example, is very simply smoothed on.

381. Cistercian ware flared-rimmed, three-handled cup. Brick-red fabric. Bright, glossy, dark brown glaze on both surfaces (some iridescent vertical

Table 5.9 South-west cloister range, Finds Group 30: Ceramics

Fabric	Sherds	Total vessels	Bowl	Cooking pot	Jar	Jug	Lid	Mug or cup
Cistercian	2	2	0	0	0	0	0	2
Cistercian copy	1	1	0	0	0	0	0	1
Gritty	14	11	1	8	0	2	0	0
Humber	6	2	0	0	0	2	0	0
Post-medieval Orange	1	1	0	0	1	0	0	0
Post-medieval Sandy	1	1	0	0	0	1	0	0
Raeren	1	1	0	0	0	0	0	1
Reversed Cistercian	7	2	0	0	0	0	1	1
Ryedale	20	1	0	0	0	1	0	0
Siegburg	5	5	0	0	0	0	0	5

streaking down the outer surface of the glaze). The glaze adhesion of some sand on the basal angle confirms that this vessel was fired upright. Wire-pulled base.

382. Cistercian ware copy. Orange outer surface and vermilion core. Bright brownish-orange glaze (with small blackish spots within the glaze) on both surfaces with a sand-fritted glaze edge on the outer face of the base. This is a nicely turned vessel whose base has been cut (but not wire pulled), and whose handles are identical to those of the proper Cistercian wares.

383. Reversed Cistercian ware cup. Very hard (near stoneware) fabric. The outer surface glaze is a glassy-looking, watery, greenish-yellow applied fairly thinly. On the inner surface, however, the glaze becomes thicker, more yellowish and crazed. There is an applied decoration: the bulk is in an iron-rich clay (appearing a dark blackish-brown under glaze), but some elements are in self-clay.

SMALL FINDS

The small finds appear to be derived from the occupation of the prior's cell. It is interesting to note the occurrence of a key, as, although every cell cloister door had a lock, keys were found only in the south-west cloister range. The other small finds could have come from any of the monks' cells.

384. Key. Fe. L: 120 mm. D-shaped bow of squarish section. Round stem. Bit with central cleft L: 20 mm. Short pin. Find no. Fe954.

385. Book clasp. Cu. Fixed end. L: 25 mm; W: 6.5 mm. Receiving end D: 2.5 mm with Cu pin. Two aligned rivet holes along long axis. Th: 0.8 mm. Find no. Cu141.

386. Pin. Cu. Spiral wound head D: 2 mm. Shank bent D: 0.8 mm. Find no. Cu142.

387. Lace chape. Cu sheet. Edge to edge seam. L: 22 mm; D: 1 mm. Find no. Cu139.

Finds Group 31 (see Figure 5.29)
From garden soil deposits [574], [577], [587], [607], [638], [671], [766], [850], [854], [1088], [1090], [1114] and [1125].

CERAMICS

A very mixed group from the garden beds to the south of the refectory and prior's cell, which had been cultivated up to the Suppression and contained a large residual element, most clearly seen in the number of Gritty ware sherds. This is perhaps not too surprising given its recovery from a garden soil that had probably been the subject of repeated cultivation that may have disturbed pre-priory deposits. Cooking-pot rim 390 was hard fired and in a very coarse version of the Gritty ware fabric; it has all the appearances of a local late Saxon or Saxo-Norman product (Table 5.10).

388. Gritty ware bowl rim. Pale orange outer surface, orange-red core and orange inner surface. Burnt and sooted.

THE ARCHAEOLOGY OF THE INNER COURT

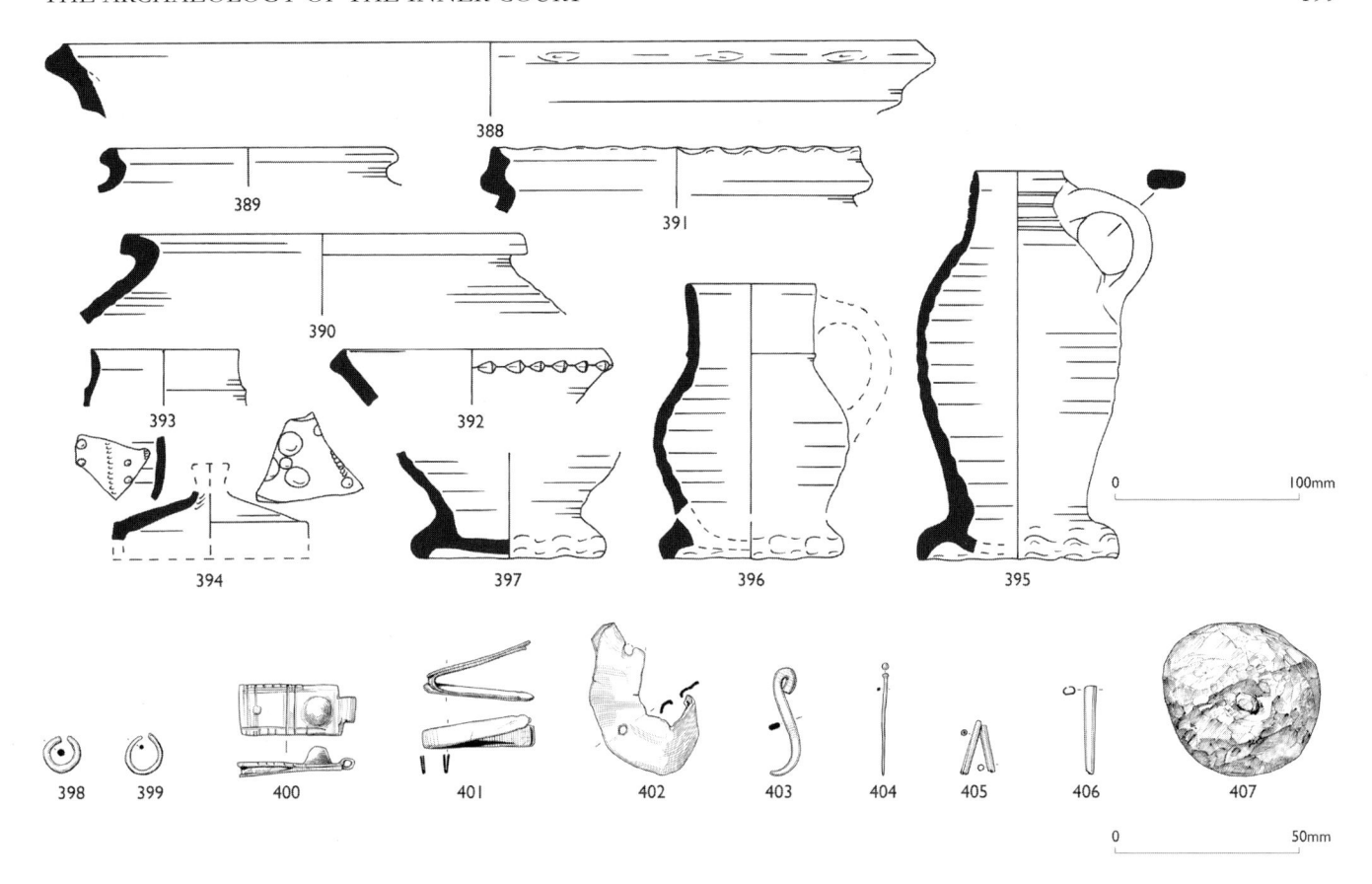

Figure 5.29 Finds Group 31 from the south-west cloister range (pottery 1:4; copper alloy 1:2, lead 1:2).

389. Gritty ware cooking-pot rim. Orange surfaces, where on the outer surface at least the orange is a dense highlighting to an otherwise grey background, and a blue-grey core. Very hard, with a rough to harsh texture. All the apparent characteristics of a late Saxon form.
390. Gritty ware cooking-pot rim. Yellow-cream outer surface, yellowish-white core and inner surface. Well-potted, competently thrown vessel.
391. Gritty ware cooking-pot rim. Light yellow surfaces and pale blue-grey core.
392. Post-medieval Sandy ware fabric lamp? rim. Off-white fabric with a bright (yellowish) green glaze on both surfaces. Notched rim edge decoration.
393. Cistercian ware cup. Purple fabric and purple-black glaze on both surfaces.
394. Cistercian ware copy lid. Brick-red fabric with a bright deep brown glaze on both surfaces of body (and only the outer surface of the lid). Applied pipeclay decoration.
395. Siegburg stoneware drinking mug. Buff-white outer surface, creamy-grey core and inner surface.
396. Raeren stoneware drinking mug. Lustrous orange-brown glaze on the outer surfaces which thins in places to a silver-grey. Grey core. The inner surface glaze is similar to that of the outer surface but thinning more readily to a beige–grey.
397. Raeren stoneware drinking mug. Brown glazed outer surface, flecking where the glaze thins, pale grey core and a thicker, glassy greenish-grey glaze on the inner surface.

Small Finds

Like the pottery above, the small finds from the garden soil are almost certainly derived from the prior's cell and represent chance losses.

398. Link. Cu. Round section. Overall D: 10 mm. Find no. Cu103.
399. Link. Cu. Round section. Overall D: 10 mm, of link 0.7 mm. Find no. Cu104.
400. Belt hasp plate or book-strap fitting. Cu. Folded sheet. L: 31 mm; W: 12.5 mm. End is narrower (6 mm). Top with substantial dome and single

Table 5.10 South-west cloister range, Finds Group 31: Ceramics

Fabric	Sherds	Vessels								
		Total vessels	Bowl	Cistern	Cooking pot	Jar	Jug	Mug or cup	Pancheon	Other
Brandsby type	6	5	0	0	3	0	2	0	0	0
Cistercian	17	10	0	0	0	0	0	10	0	0
Developed Humber	5	2	0	0	0	2	0	0	0	0
Gritty	213	57	1	0	37	0	16	0	2	1
Hambleton	25	5					3		1	1
Humber	6	5	0	0	0	1	4	0	0	0
Langerwehe	5	3	0	0	0	0	0	3	0	0
Post-medieval Sandy	14	6				2	2			2
Raeren	15	3	0	0	0	0	0	3	0	0
Ryedale	76	15	0	1	0	0	14	0	0	0
Siegburg	18	9	0	0	0	0	0	9	0	0

rivet. Surface decorated with roughly incised lines and edge nicks. Back plain and unused hole D: 2 mm. Leather strap survives inside. Find Cu115.

401. Binding. Cu. Folded sheet. L: 30 + 28 mm; W: 4.5 mm. Find no. Cu114.
402. Mount. Cu folded sheet. Originally square with diagonal corners. Three of the four fixing holes remain. Th: about 1 mm. ?cover for lock. Find no. Cu106.
403. Fish-hook. Cu moulded. Rectangular section. Plain hook and attachment end bent over. L: 30 mm; W: 2 mm. Find no. Cu143.
404. Pin. Cu. L: 27 mm; D: 0.6 mm. Spiral-wound head. Find no. Cu113.
405. Lace chape. Cu sheet. Broken. Edge to edge seam. L: (original) 27 mm; D: 1.5 mm. Find no. Cu116.
406. Lace chape. Cu sheet. Edge to edge seam. Slight taper. L: 24 mm; D: 1–2 mm. Find no. Cu180.
407. Weight. Pb. Of spherical form, D: 40–2 mm, roughly hammer-dressed to shape, with the remains of an attached hanging loop. Find no. Pb295.

Finds Group 32 (see Figure 5.30)
Latest occupation deposits 703, 720, 745, 1037, 1065, 1094, 1097, 1115, 1119, 1158, 1165, 1203 and 1284 from the western half of the south-west cloister range.

CERAMICS
Finds Group 32 came from the final occupation of the rooms below the late refectory and seems to contain no identifiable pre-priory material. There were no cooking-pots or bowls, instead the group consisted principally of jugs and smaller tablewares such as mugs and cups. Interestingly, these are all drinking vessels and there is no evidence of ceramic platters or dishes, suggesting that these must have been provided in other materials (Table 5.11).

Amongst the unillustrated material were two small rim fragments from a Tudor Green lobed cup. These were in a greyish-white fabric with bright copper-green glazed surfaces thinning to pale green.

408. Regional Stray bottle neck, soft orange fabric with a white slip over both surfaces. Bright, pale yellow glaze on outer surface and also, spread much more thinly, on the inner surface.
409. Cistercian ware cup in a reddish-brown fabric with a deep orange-brown glaze over both surfaces. The decorative sherd illustrated has white pipeclay decoration appearing yellow under glaze.
410. Cistercian ware small decorated lid. Brick-red fabric with purplish-black glaze and pipeclay decoration; classic Cistercian ware. No deliberate glazing of the inner surface.

THE ARCHAEOLOGY OF THE INNER COURT

Small Finds

Although the pottery from this deposit all appears to be contemporary with the final occupation of the south-west cloister range, pin 412 is almost certainly of 12th-century date and must be derived from the pre-monastic occupation known to exist below the building. The lead outlet pipe, 414, from a wooden tub, supports the use of this area for food preparation.

411. Key-hole cover. Cu with Fe pin. L: 30 mm; W: 10 mm. Simple design with two bands dividing central section from ends. Back of central portion is hollow. Fe fixing pin through top end. Find no. Cu135.
412. Pin. Cu. L: 65 mm. Tapering shank D: 2.5 mm at neck. Top is of two outward turning spirals formed from the metal being split and bent over. Ends are rectangular in section W: 2 mm. Find no. Cu134.
413. Lace chape. Cu sheet. Edge to edge seam. L: 28 mm; D: 2. Remains of ?leather inside. Find no. Cu137.
414. Water pipe. Pb. Slightly squashed. Flange at one end, other end bent inwards. Butted soldered seam. L: 72 mm max; W: 28 mm. Find no. Pb505.

Demolition

Demolition of the range appears to have begun immediately after the Suppression and was highly selective. As Hope removed virtually all the destruction deposits from the interior of the eastern half of the building, it is necessary to interpolate from what survived in the area of the original prior's cell. First, it would appear that, after the internal spaces were stripped of any furnishings, any glazing was removed from the windows, for very little window glass or cames survived, especially from the substantial windows of the first refectory. Next the slate roof and presumably the timber framing of the roof was dismantled, and again there was little evidence that the slates were discarded. Indeed, very few slates pierced for hanging pegs were recovered from the surviving demolition spreads, although many nails from the fixing of the slating battens had survived at floor level, where they had been discarded. Lead flashings and the valley gutters implied by the Period Two parapet copings and presumably the sections of water pipe that were recovered were then melted down, apparently in the prior's cell fireplace, where a circular lead ingot was found in the floor where it had been cast [514]. Next the internal partitions were removed, with some desultory robbing of the cill walls in the western part of the range [1007], [1029], [1046], [1120] and [1103]. Once anything of value had been recovered, the decision was taken to demolish the south wall of the range only, rather than to quarry the whole building. That was done in such a way as to ensure that the north and east walls and the north-western angle of the church were not destabilised. The west wall seems to have been left as a raking buttress to support the north wall, and the eastern end of the south wall was left to buttress the corner

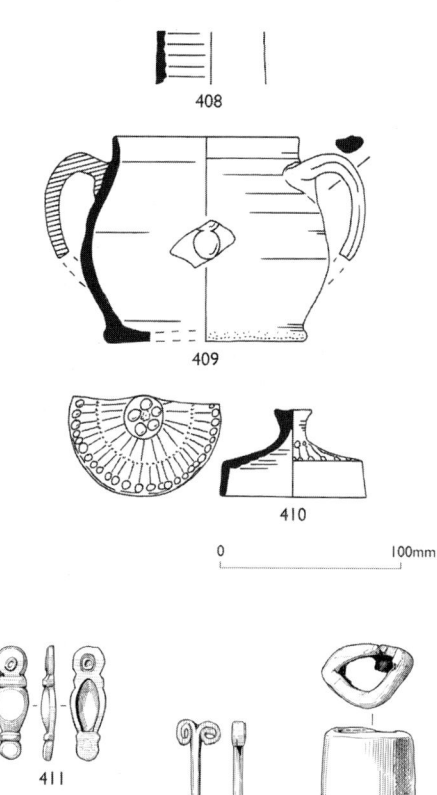

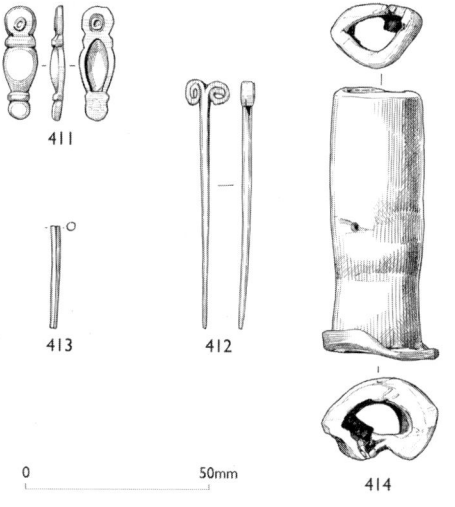

Figure 5.30 Finds Group 32 from the south-west cloister range (pottery 1:4; copper alloy 1:2, lead 1:2).

Table 5.11 Cloister range, Finds Group 32: Ceramics

Fabric	Sherds	Vessels						
		Total vessels	Bottle	Cistern	Jug	Lid	Mug or cup	Other
Beauvais	1	1	0	0	1	0	0	0
Cistercian	24	10	0	0	0	2	8	0
Cistercian copy	16	2	0	0	0		2	0
Hambleton	3	3	0	1	2	0	0	0
Humber	3	2	0	0	2	0	0	0
Langerwehe	2	2	0	0	0	0	2	0
Midlands Yellow	1	1	0	0	0	0	1	0
Post-medieval Orange	4	1	1	0	0	0	0	0
Raeren	6	3	0	0	0	0	3	0
Ryedale	13	9	0	1	7	0	0	1
Siegburg	1	1	0	0	0	0	1	0

of the church. Otherwise, the south wall was totally removed, right down to the bottom of its construction trench, where only a handful of stones and the imprints in the clay of many others remained [531], [591], [926] and [1005]. Pottery from the robbing included many sherds from vessels associated with the last occupation of the building and included no material later than the late 1530s, indicating that demolition was rapid. The south wall was taken down from the outside of the building, as evidenced by the build-up of rubble and mortar cleaned from the walling stones that built up against the south face of the wall [504], [551], [562], [921] and [928]. Spread across the floor of the western room of the range were fallen wall plaster [1038] and displaced floor tiles, apparently derived from the partition between the passage along the north wall and that room and the floor of the passage itself. Rubble from the wall core was then spread across the inside of the building [926], [927], [931], [934], [935], [938], [981] and [989], particularly at its west end, sealing the inner face of the robber trench and the Period One chimney cap, which had been thrown down from the wall inside the building. The intention of this exercise appears to have been to infill the terracing at that end of the building. Late occupation debris from the building or from its demolition [778], [779], [780] and [893] was spread across the yards to the south, sealing the remains of the southern yard walls, which had all been removed, and partially sealed in turn by spreads of demolition from the south wall. To the south of wall [774] further spreads of rubble and occupation debris [704], [707], [708], [715] and [894] were associated with the demolition of the south yard wall, [701], and the associated structure, [702].

The careful demolition of the south-west cloister range implies rather more than the intentional slighting of the site, because it was done in such a way as to retain two of the building's walls and avoid any unnecessary disturbance to the church. It is at odds with the usual policy of widespread damage normally associated with suppression wrecking. It is difficult to see any context for such an action apart from the reuse of selected parts of the site to form a post-Suppression house. However, there is no other indication that this was intended to be the case at Mount Grace before the early 17th century.

Finds Group 33

Demolition contexts [504], [531], [551], [562], [704], [707], [708], [715], [778], [779], [780], [894], [926], [931], [934], [935], [936], [938], [981], [989], [1005], [1029], [1046], [1089] and [1103].

CERAMICS (SEE FIGURE 5.31)

Like most demolition groups, this contains a large and varied selection of pottery largely dominated by the Post-medieval Sandy ware fabric which had clearly been in use in the priory in the years preceding its suppression. Indeed, the group contains sherds from almost all the late-medieval fabrics represented at Mount Grace. In addition to the usual stonewares,

THE ARCHAEOLOGY OF THE INNER COURT 203

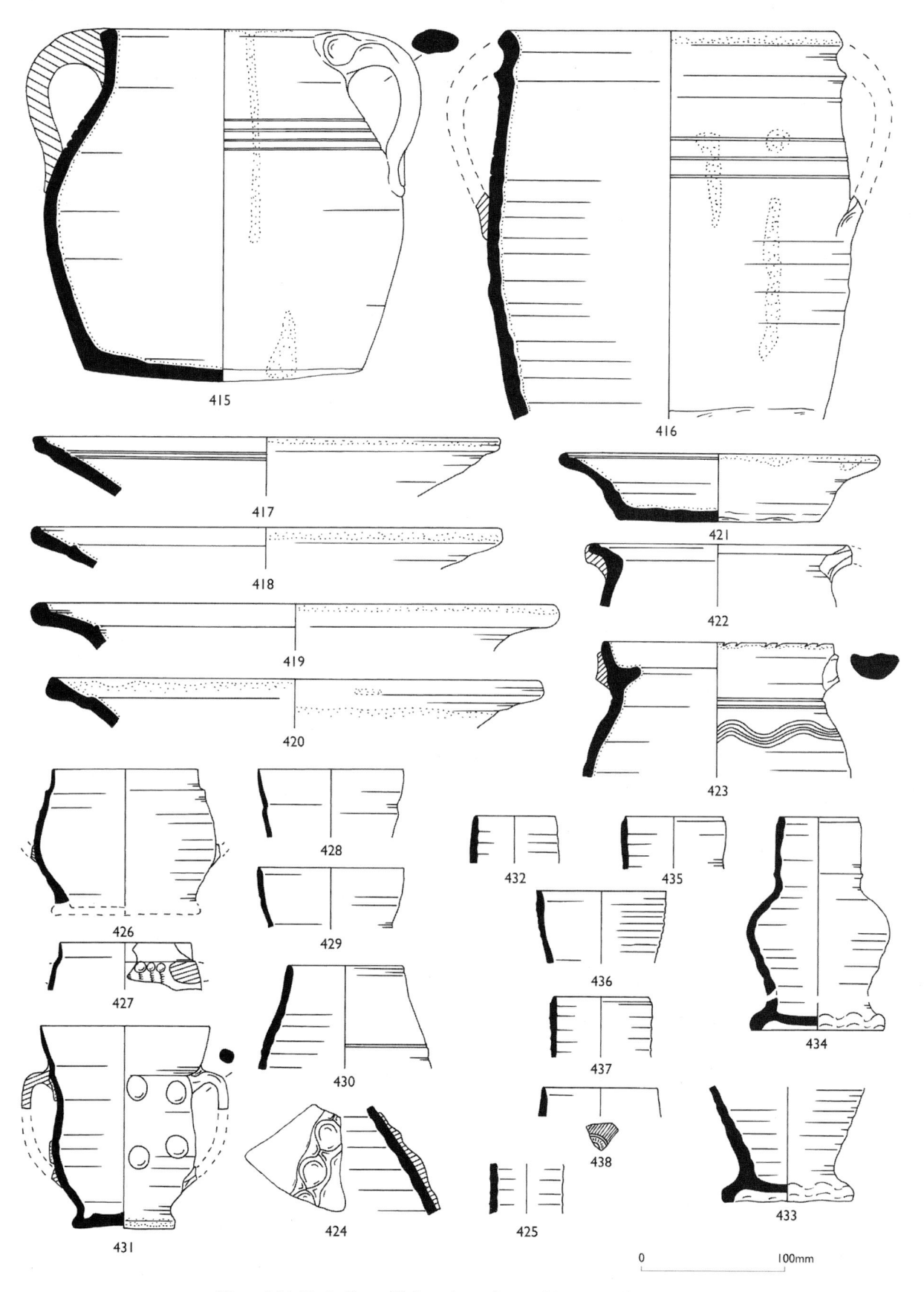

Figure 5.31 Finds Group 33 from the south-west cloister range (pottery 1:4).

Table 5.12 Cloister range, Finds Group 33: Ceramics

Fabric	Sherds	Total vessels	Cistern	Cooking pot	Jar	Jug	Mug or cup	Pancheon	Other
Cistercian	55	29	0	0	0	0	27	0	2
Cistercian copy	9	3	0	0	0	0	3	0	0
Developed Humber	2	2	0	0	0	2	0	0	0
Gritty	21	18	0	14	0	4	0	0	0
Hambleton	5	5	2	0	0	3	0	0	0
Humber	7	6	0	0	0	5	1	0	0
Langerwehe	14	10	0	0	0	0	8	1(?)	1
Midlands Yellow	1	1	0	0	0	0	1	0	0
Post-medieval Orange	2	2	0	0	0	1	1	0	0
Post-medieval Sandy	119	63	6	0	24	9	0	9	15
Raeren	8	5	0	0	0	0	5	0	0
Reversed Cistercian	1	1	0	0	0	0	1	0	0
Ryedale	40	29	0	3	0	25	0	0	1
Siegburg	19	13	0	0	0	0	12	0	1
Unidentified stoneware	1	1	0	0	0	0	1	0	1
Westerwald	1	1	0	0	0	0	1	0	1

there were sherds from a highly decorated Westerwald mug. Again, the preponderance of vessels was tablewares, this time including dishes and platters. These latter vessels were of some size and may have been serving dishes rather than individual plates, which were perhaps more likely to have been wooden (or bread) trenchers (Table 5.12).

415. Post-medieval Sandy ware two-handled jar. Yellowish-cream outer surface, yellowish-white/orange core and fully covered bright yellowish-green glaze on the inner surface. The glaze becomes a darker, more coppery green at the inner rim and on external glaze drips, presumably where the glaze thickens.
416. Post-medieval Sandy ware fabric large jar. Orange (dull red) outer surface, orange/blue-grey core and full olive-green glaze on the inner surface.
417. Post-medieval Sandy ware platter rim. Pale orange outer surface, cream-buff core and full olive-yellow suspension glaze to the inner surface. The rim and top 50–60 mm of the outer surface are heavily burnt and sooted.
418. Post-medieval Sandy ware platter rim. Orange-red outer surface and blue-grey core, with a full olive-green glaze on the inner surface.
419. Post-medieval Sandy ware platter rim. Purplish outer surface, pale orange core and full, deep, rich, brownish-green glaze to the inner surface. Some traces of sooting under the rim.
420. Post-medieval Sandy ware fabric pancheon/dish rim. Purplish-red outer surface and light blue-grey core, with a dark green glaze on the inner surface that becomes lighter in colour where the glaze thins towards the margin. There was also a band of glaze around the lower body of the outer surface. This glaze band has been seen on several such vessels from Mount Grace and seems characteristic of the type.
421. Post-medieval Sandy ware fabric small dish. Pale orange outer surface, orange core and full greenish-orange glaze on the inner surface.
422. Post-medieval Sandy ware fabric small, handled jar rim. Brownish-orange core

THE ARCHAEOLOGY OF THE INNER COURT

with bright apple-green glaze on both surfaces.

423. Late Gritty ware fabric handled jar?, yellow-cream outer surface, off-white core. Fine, smooth-textured fabric, fired hard. Mottled copper-green splashed glaze on inner surface. The glaze is smooth around the face and lip of the rim, but becomes markedly more pocked on the inside lower body. This sherd fits and is therefore the same vessel as a near complete pot from Cell 8 demolition (Finds Group 11, 106), a rare example of pottery that could be shown to have migrated in a historic context.

424. Ryedale ware cistern sherd with an applied thumbed strip. Off-white core and pale bluish-grey inner surface. Pocked, light olive-green glaze.

425. Stray, soft, lightly sanded vermilion fabric both under glaze and on its own on the inner surface. Bright copper-green glaze over this slip on the outer surface.

426. Cistercian ware cup. Dull purplish core. Lustrous purple-black glaze on both surfaces.

427. Cistercian ware posset pot. Purple fabric with bright, deep purple glaze on both surfaces. Applied pipeclay decoration. Scar of upper handle attachment springing from the top of the shoulder.

428. Cistercian ware cup. Dark red fabric with bright, deep orange-brown glaze on both surfaces.

429. Cistercian ware cup. Red fabric, glaze appears blackish, but is in fact a very deep brown.

430. Late Cistercian ware cup. Buff fabric with dark greenish-olive glaze on the outer surface and top part of inner surface, thinning about halfway down the illustrated sherd.

431. Cistercian ware copy handled cup. Pale brick red outer surface (base) and brick-red core. Rich and deep orange-brown glaze on both surfaces that becomes almost blackish-brown where the glaze thickens. Decorated with large applied spots in a white pipeclay that appear lemon yellow under glaze.

432. Langerwehe stoneware drinking mug rim with a handle scar. Purple-brown ash glaze on both surfaces, with a pale grey core. The unillustrated base of this vessel was 100 mm in diameter.

433. Langerwehe stoneware drinking mug. Lustrous chocolate-brown glaze on outer surface, thinning to a lighter mottle in places. Blue-grey core and dull purplish inner surface with faint orange highlights.

434. Siegburg stoneware drinking mug. Bright silver-grey ash glaze turning a light brown in places. Base has been ground flat after firing.

435. Siegburg stoneware drinking mug. Shiny greenish-grey-brown outer surface glaze, grey core and a light, matt, grey-brown inner surface.

436. Siegburg stoneware drinking mug. Pale silver-grey glaze on both surfaces. The glaze contains minute black specks, particularly apparent on the inner surface. Pale grey core. Slightly flared rim.

437. Raeren stoneware drinking mug. Shiny brown ash glaze on outer surface, grey core and silver-grey inner surface glaze. Pronounced turning (not throwing) marks.

438. Westerwald stoneware. Pale whitish-grey core. Embossed design with dark blue painted background within the design area.

SMALL FINDS (SEE FIGURE 5.32)

As with the pottery, the small find collection represents the residue of the contents of the south-west cloister range in the late 1530s, a combination of personal objects such as the book furniture (446 and 447), which could have come from any cell, and obvious fittings of the food preparation areas of the first prior's cell, the lead outlet pipe (452) and the lead strainer from a water tank (453) being standard 'kitchen' objects.

439. Key. Fe. L: 110 mm. Round-sectioned oval bow, Ht: 28 mm; W: 26 mm. Round stem, but with symmetrical clefts, slightly tapering pin L: 18 mm. Find no. Fe815.

440. Key. Fe. L: 46 mm. Short length of stem only, and bit with asymmetrical clefts. Find no. Fe809.

441. Clasp knife. Fe. L: 83 mm; W: 16 mm (maximum). Fe cover plate with Fe rivets. Find no. Fe338.

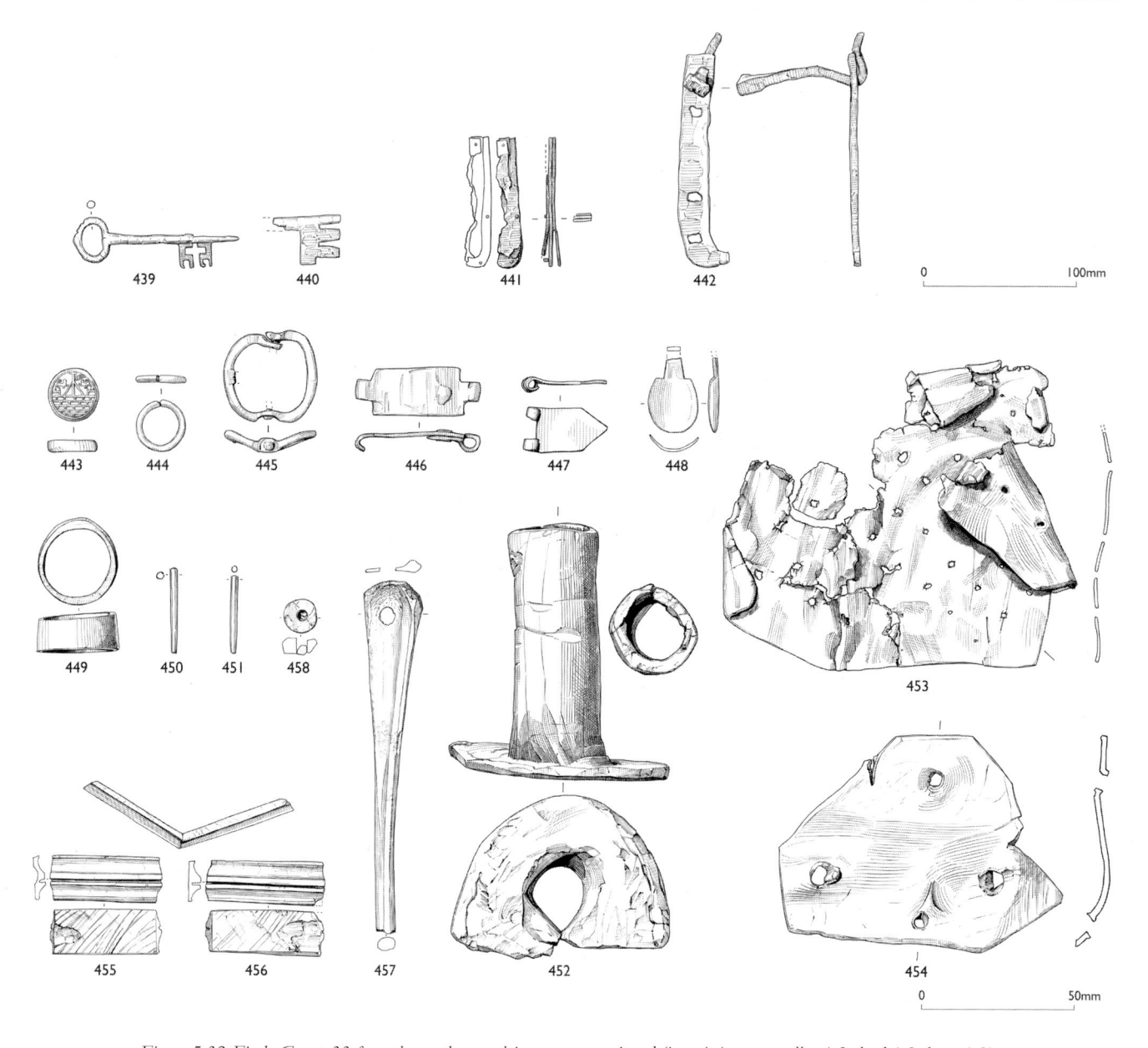

Figure 5.32 Finds Group 33 from the south-west cloister range continued (iron 1:4; copper alloy 1:2, lead 1:2; bone 1:2).

442. Mount with hanging attachment. Fe. Suspension arm L: 83 mm with hooked end Ht: 34 mm. Mount L: 136 mm; W: 20 mm, with three rectangular holes 8 mm × 4–6 mm. Find no. Fe802.
443. Coin weight. Cu. D: 16 mm; Th: 3 mm; Wt: 6.710g. Dr N. Mayhew, Heberden Coin Room, Ashmolean Museum, Oxford, reports that this is uniface, ship with a mast and flag between two lions. The design and weight suggest that this is a weight for an English noble (6s. 8d.) struck at about 7g in the period 1412 to 1464. Find no. MG959.
444. Ring. Cu wire. Overall D: 16 mm, of wire 1.3 mm. Find no. Cu88.
445. Buckle. Cu. Double D-shaped frames, central bar and pin missing. W: 30 mm; H: 29 mm. Bar W: 2 mm; Th: 1.8 mm. Bottom of frame is integral. The higher part of one side overlaps the other to enable the central bar to be inserted. Find no. Cu87.
446. Book clasp. Cu. L: 40 mm; W: 15 mm. End for attachment to fixed plate W: 6 mm, the sheet being turned over to

form the loop and fixed with a single fixed rivet. Clasp end W: 6 mm. Central plate area L: 30 mm. Find no. Cu95.

447. Hinge-plate for book clasp. Cu. L: 26 mm; W: 13 mm. Two closed loops at one end for attachment bar. Other end pointed (for insertion in wooden cover board). Find no. MG962.

448. Scoop. Cu. Shallow spoon-like end L: 17 mm; W: 16 mm. Stem is broken. Find no. Cu89.

449. Cut ring. Cu. Irregularly cut section of Cu piping. D: 37 mm; Ht: 9–13 mm; Th: 0.75–2.5 mm. Find no. Cu90.

450. Lace chape. Cu sheet. Edge to edge seam. L: 28 mm; D: 2 mm. ?Leather inside. Find no. Cu138.

451. Lace chape. Cu sheet. Edge to edge seam. Slight taper. L: 24 mm; D: 1.5 mm. ?Leather inside. Find no. Cu138a.

452. Water pipe. Pb. Butt soldered seam. Flange at one end 20–23 mm wide. L: 76 mm; D: 30 mm; Th: 4 mm. Find no. Pb391.

453. Perforated sheet. Pb. Large and irregular shape with parts of edges turned over, approx. 220 mm × 210 mm. Th: 2 mm. Covered with irregularly shaped holes, square to circular D: about 3–4 mm. Sieve for water-tank. Find no. Pb393.

454. Sheet. Pb. Irregular cut lead sheet with four holes 7 mm². Th: 2 mm. Find no. Pb394.

455 and 456. Inlay. Bone. Two fitting sections of bone inlay L: 19 mm; H: 14 mm; Th: 4 mm; from an octagonal box. Find nos Bone 3 and 4.

457. Needle. Bone. L: 110 mm, W: (head) 20 mm, (shaft) 6 mm; with a drilled eye D: 5 mm at the upper end. Made from a pig fibula. Find no. Bone5.

458. Offcut. Bone. D: 10 mm; L: 5 mm; with a central hole D: 3 mm. Find no. Bone6.

ARCHITECTURAL DETAIL ASSOCIATED WITH PERIOD FOUR (SEE FIGURE 5.33)

50. Fragment of small basin or piscina, with the halves of two drilled holes remaining in the base (504). Its roughly dressed quality is unusual in the context of both other piscinas and the very high quality of the architectural fragments at Mount Grace. It is possible that the rough dressing was meant to provide a key for a plaster finish.

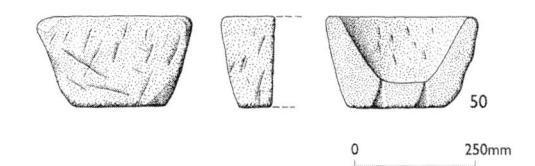

Figure 5.33 Stone object from the period four south-west cloister range (1:10).

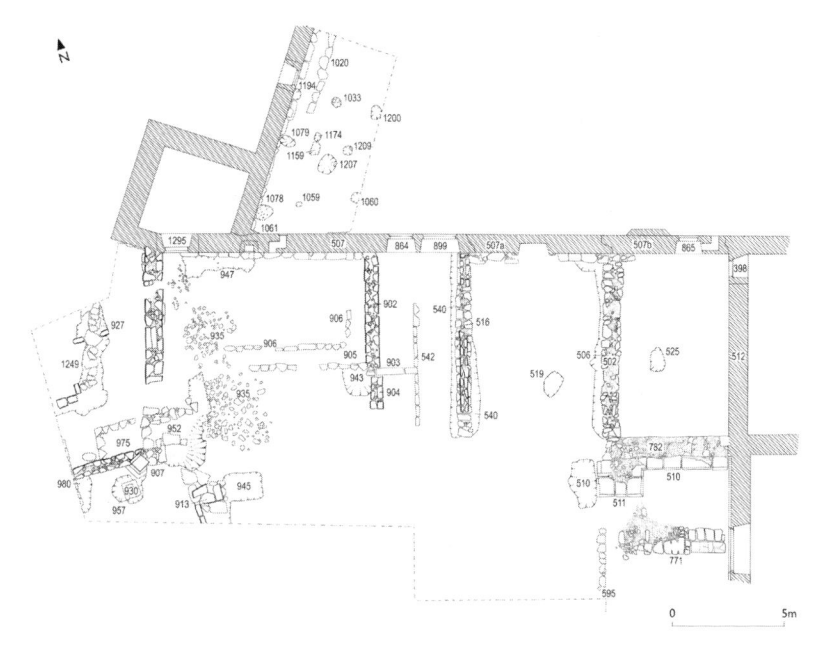

Figure 5.34 The south-west cloister range and 'prison', post-medieval features.

The 17th Century (see Figure 5.34)

Associated with the post-medieval occupation of the site were a number of garden features (see Figure 5.35) that were superimposed on the site of the south-west cloister range and its yards. All were badly damaged by Hope's excavation and had been identified by him as medieval, although in every case they were demonstrably later than the demolition of the building. The masonry used was, however, all derived from monastic buildings.

A wall, [902], was built immediately to the west of the Period One prior's cell door [864], directly onto the surface of the demolition material that sealed the western half of the building. Hope had removed any deposits associated with it in 1897 or 1898, and the wall had incorporated the remains of the Period One cill wall [903] and the Period Four unmortared wall [904], both of which appeared through the demolition deposits. Wall [902] appears to have revetted a raised garden that occupied the higher area of the western half of the demolished range. Edgings of reused medieval masonry, including a mullion from a four-light cell window, marked out cultivated beds, while edging [905] continued westwards the line of cill wall [903]. The inner edge of the beds, [906], lay some 0.6 m inside the line of wall [902] and edging [905] and was parallel to them. Hope had removed all deposits associated with these structures and presumed incorrectly that they marked the footpaces of a late layout of the refectory. The edge stones [905] and [906] did not survive over the full extent of the raised area, but appear to have terminated at a metalled pathway which emerged from the surviving doorway, [1295], in the north-west angle of the range. A similar flower bed was encountered in the west alley of the great cloister, [1020], which extended from south of the door to the prison cell northwards out of the area excavated, retaining a raised bed of grey loam and rubble. In neither did any evidence survive to date these features securely, and it is only presumed that they are of 17th-century date.

One feature that could be identified as 17th century was a wall, [595], running from the south-west corner of the enlarged Period Three buttress on the south wall of the range to wall [701], its foundation trench cutting through the demolition deposits associated with wall [588] between the church entry and the prior's cell garden. Hope had mistaken it for a medieval wall, as it more or less followed the line of the earlier wall [588], but 17th-century pottery was associated with its construction. A little earlier than the construction of this wall was the provision of a paved surface, [771], which ran from the west door of the church to the base of the wall and which incorporated an apparently 13th-century floriate grave slab and a section of cell window cill (see below). This appears to have been provided for bringing building stone out of the church for use in the 17th-century house.

Figure 5.35 The 17th-century garden overlying the western half of the south-west cloister range, seen from the south (G. Coppack).

Finds Group 34 (see Figure 5.36)
From deposits associated with the 17th-century house, [595].

CERAMICS

A comparatively small group of material from the garden associated with the 1654 house, which contains a high proportion of residual material. The illustrated vessels are probably 17th century and may therefore have been associated with the Lascelles' occupation of the site. Certainly, the tigerware posset pot would fit comfortably into a date in the later 17th century (Table 5.13).

Table 5.13 Cloister range, Finds Group 34: Ceramics

Fabric	Sherds	Total vessels	Cistern	Cooking pot	Dish	Jar	Jug	Mug or cup	Pancheon
Brandsby type	6	5	0	2	0	0	3	0	0
Cistercian	2	2	0	0	0	0	0	2	0
Developed Humber	1	1	0	0	0	0	1	0	0
Gritty	10	10	0	10	0	0	0	0	0
Post-medieval Sandy	19	9	0	0	2	3	3	0	1
Regional Stray	1	1	0	0	0	0	1	0	0
Ryedale	6	3	1	0	0	0	2	0	0
Siegburg	3	1	0	0	0	0	0	1	0
Tigerware (17th century)	1	1	0	0	0	1	0	0	0

459. Developed Humber ware jar. Light orange outer surface, blue-grey core with a finely pocked olive-green glaze on the inner surface. Not an applied pad, but a deeply thumbed decorative ring.
460. Post-medieval Sandy ware fabric lid rim. Smooth-textured, slightly micaceous fabric. Pale yellow-orange surfaces and a pinkish-orange/pale blue/pinkish-orange core. Odd tiny spots of yellow-orange glaze.
461. Post-medieval Sandy ware fabric pancheon rim. Grey outer surface with orange highlighting, orange-buff core and orange-green glaze on inner surface. Outer surface slightly sooted.
462. Post-medieval Sandy ware small, two-handled dish. Pale orange/dark red outer surface, orange core and full, pockmarked, orange glaze on the inner surface.
463. Staffordshire tigerware posset pot base. Light orange outer surface skin, cream core and full orange-yellow glaze on the inner surface. Externally, the glaze is a yellow base with chocolate-brown feathering typical of this class of pottery.

The Evidence of Hope's Excavation (see Figure 5.34)

Hope's excavation of the south-west cloister range was conducted in 1897, when the area of the building was stripped down to what he considered to be its latest floor levels (Hope 1905, 271). He returned to do further work in 1898, although its extent was never recorded. Re-excavation revealed his methodology.

Once the site had been cleared of topsoil and obvious demolition rubble, he examined the standing north and east walls for evidence of cross-walls and the location of the missing south wall. Cross-wall [502] was evidenced by its mortar scar on the south face of wall [507a] and [507b], which still remains, and he dug a trench [506] along its length, revealing its footings and recording the impression of the lowest course of ashlar. On the west side of the wall his trench was deepened to reveal the depth of the foundations. The southern end of trench [506] encountered the south wall [782] of the building, which was then cleared back to its junction with the north-west corner of the church, and a large hole was dug outside the wall extending to the south of the west door of the church, revealing the 17th-century path that incorporated a grave slab. This also revealed the Period Three widening [510] and extended buttress [511] of the south wall of the range. To the west, wall [516], which divided the original refectory from the Period One prior's cell, was similarly exposed in a narrow trench, [540], which was carried down to examine, but not bottom, the footings. No attempt was made to find the robbed south wall of the range, and Hope's examination of what he correctly identified as the (later) prior's cell was concluded with minimal excavation. Almost certainly, this work was carried out in 1897, when the western half of the range was similarly stripped.

The western half of the range proved difficult for Hope to understand. Stripping had revealed a mixture of medieval and post-medieval walls separated by a thick layer of obvious demolition rubble (see Figure 5.35). His excavation did not originally penetrate this rubble, and he satisfied himself with recording the medieval walls [542], [903] and [904] that could be seen through it. The west wall of the range was dug out in a series of rather confused pits that were subsequently left open to reveal the course of the wall. Only one, [952], was deep enough to penetrate pre-16th-century deposits, and revealed the internal junction of the west and south walls of the range and the external angle buttress [907].

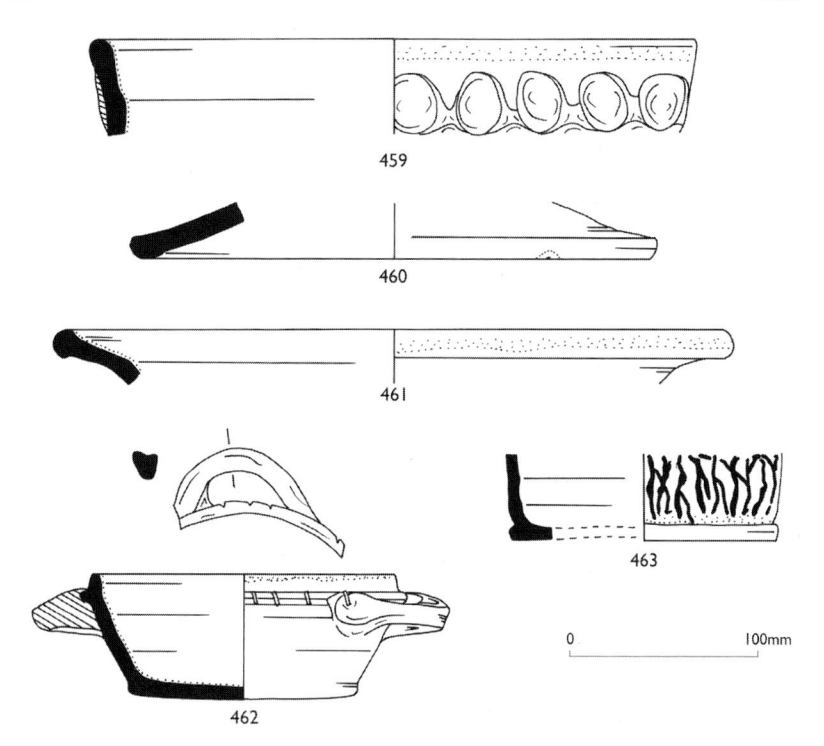

Figure 5.36 Finds Group 34 from the south-west cloister range (pottery 1:4).

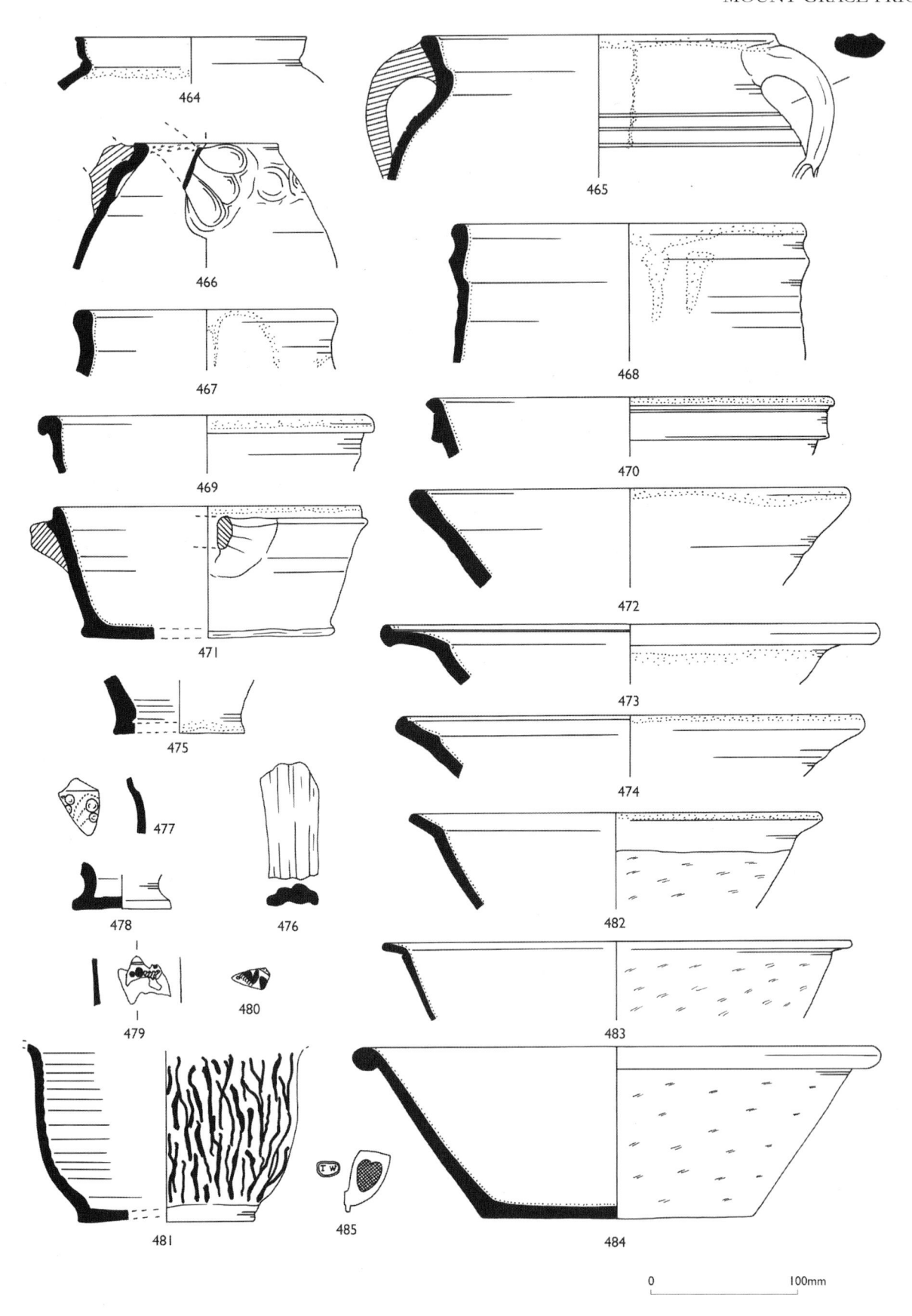

Figure 5.37 Finds Group 35 from the south-west cloister range (pottery 1:4).

THE ARCHAEOLOGY OF THE INNER COURT

Table 5.14 Cloister range, Finds Group 35: Ceramics

Fabric	Sherds	Total vessels	Bowl	Cistern	Cooking pot	Dish	Jar	Jug	Mug or cup	Pancheon	Urinal
Brandsby type	4	4	0	0	2	0	0	2	0	0	0
Cistercian	33	26	0	0	0	0	0	0	26	0	0
Cistercian copy	4	3	0	0	0	0	0	0	3	0	0
Delft	2	2	0	0	0	0	2	0	0	0	0
Developed Humber	1	1	0	0	0	0	0	0	0	0	1
Gritty	131	114	3	0	93	0	0	19	0	0	0
Hambleton	20	7	0	1	0	0	0	6	0	0	0
Humber	11	11	0	0	0	0	0	10	0	0	1
Langerwehe	5	4	0	0	0	0	0	0	4	0	0
Late Gritty	2	2	0	0	0	0	0	2	0	0	0
Midlands Yellow	6	1	0	0	0	0	0	0	1	0	0
Post-medieval Orange	20	7	0	0	0	0	5	1	0	1	0
Post-medieval Sandy	238	140	0	11	0	7	28	35	0	58	1
Raeren	5	4	0	0	0	0	0	0	4	0	0
Ryedale	87	32	0	0	0	1	0	30	1	0	1
Siegburg	9	8	0	0	0	0	0	0	8	0	0
Tigerware (17th century)	1	1	0	0	0	0	0	0	1	0	0
Tudor Green	1	1	0	0	0	0	0	0	1	0	0

Otherwise, Hope recorded the 17th-century garden wall, [902], and single lines of stones [905] and [906], and dug a sondage, [943], in the angle between the stone alignment [905] and the medieval wall [904], exposing a small area of the Period Three paving. Subsequent work in this area related to work he was doing in the kitchen: a small trench, [947], was dug along the north wall to look for a water pipe, and holes were dug to examine a drain, [927], and a complex series of stone structures against the south-west corner of the building, [975] and [957]. This was almost certainly the work done in 1898.

Finds Group 35
Material from Hope's excavation and backfill.

CERAMICS (SEE FIGURE 5.37)
A large, mixed group of pottery spanning the entire range of the assemblage, from a Roman sherd (this time a grey ware jar sherd), to a range of 19th-century domestic and garden ceramics. Pancheons 472–4, which were 19th century in origin, were in a cream-glazed red earthenware and suggested a domestic function. The tigerware vessel (481) and possibly some of the delft ware (479 and 480) can be associated with the Lascelles' occupation of the house (Table 5.14).

Otherwise, the illustrated material has been largely selected from the early post-medieval fabric, the largest single component of the group, to illustrate a further range of forms that can probably be associated with the final occupation of the refectory area of the priory.

464. Developed Humber ware cooking-pot rim. Blue-grey/orange core and brick/purple-red inner surface. Olive-green glaze on outer surface and on upper part of inner surface. The glaze colour darkens to an olive-brown where the glaze thickens.

465. Developed Humber ware handled jar. Orange/dull reddish-orange outer surface, orange/blue-grey core, and full, pocked, olive-green glaze with purplish margins on the inner surface. Upper handle attachment smoothed on.

466. Ryedale ware urinal. Crude brownish-orange glaze to outer surface, pale blue-grey core and grey-black inner surface. Crude, pinched shoulder decoration. The crudity of the vessel is tempered only by the post-firing smoothing of the inner rim of the vessel.
467. Post-medieval Sandy ware fabric jar. Dull purplish-grey outer surface and buff/grey core. Bright brownish-green glaze covering the inner surface and large parts of the outer surface.
468. Post-medieval Sandy ware fabric jar. Light orange outer surface, orange/pale blue-grey core and glazed inner surface. Light apple-green glaze on inner surface with some areas of pocking; the same glaze extends a little way down the outer surface and is heavily pocked.
469. Post-medieval Sandy ware fabric bowl. Dull purple-red outer surface skin, orange core, full orange-brown glaze on inner surface.
470. Post-medieval Sandy ware fabric. Soft orange outer surface, pale yellow/orange core, full, bright orange-green glaze to inner surface.
471. Post-medieval Sandy ware fabric handled bowl. Pale orange outer surface, buff/very pale blue-grey core, full, pocked, yellow-green glaze on inner surface. Traces of an attachment for one (presumably of two) lateral handle.
472. Post-medieval Sandy ware fabric pancheon rim. Soft orange outer surface, pale bluish-grey core and full, light, lightly pocked olive-green glaze on the inner surface.
473. Post-medieval Sandy ware fabric pancheon. Purplish-red fabric. Bright orange-green glaze on inner surface and on the outer surface of the lower body.
474. Post-medieval Sandy ware fabric pancheon rim. Orange outer surface, orange/pale greyish-blue core, full, bright olive-green glaze on inner surface.
475. Stray/late Gritty ware fabric. Orange/purplish outer surface, blue-grey core and pale orange-buff inner surface. Lower margins of an olive-green glaze, flashed on, although seeming to thicken towards the top of the sherd.
476. French?, fine, smooth-textured fabric, fired hard. Pale cream outer surface and off-white core. Consistently coloured greenish-yellow glaze, all very matt.
477. Cistercian ware posset pot. Purple-red fabric with bright blackish-brown glaze on both surfaces. Pipeclay decoration.
478. Cistercian ware pedestal base. Brick-red core, dark purple-brown glaze on both surfaces, fired upright with sand fritting on the base. Wire-pulled base.
479. Delft? flask neck or drug pot. Soft, friable cream-coloured fabric, crazed bluish-white tin glaze, now mostly spalled off. What little glaze remains shows a design encircled at the top by a pale blue horizontal line below which yellow and dark blue spots linked with a faint brown line and an apple-green leaf of fern-like shape.
480. Delft?. Soft, pale yellowish fabric with straw-coloured glaze on outer surface. Bluish tinged white glaze on inner surface with orange/green/pale blue underglaze design.
481. Staffordshire tigerware chamber pot/spittoon(?). Light orange outer surface skin, cream core and fully yellow-glazed inner surface. External glaze is the typical yellow to treacle-brown feathering.
482. 19th-century red earthenware bowl. Dark purple-red outer surface, brick-red core. Slipped inner surface with pale yellow-coloured glaze, decorated with a darker, brown dappling over the slip.
483. 19th-century red earthenware pancheon. Dull brick-red outer surface with slightly lighter coloured core. Tick pale yellow glaze on the inner surface with a deliberate and decorative? dark brown mottling on the upper face of the rim. The lower body of the outer surface has been cut to produce a thin wall to this part of the vessel.
484. 19th-century red earthenware pancheon. Soft brick-red outer surface, vermilion core. White slip on inner surface with a clear glaze to produce a bright, light lemon-yellow glaze.

THE ARCHAEOLOGY OF THE INNER COURT

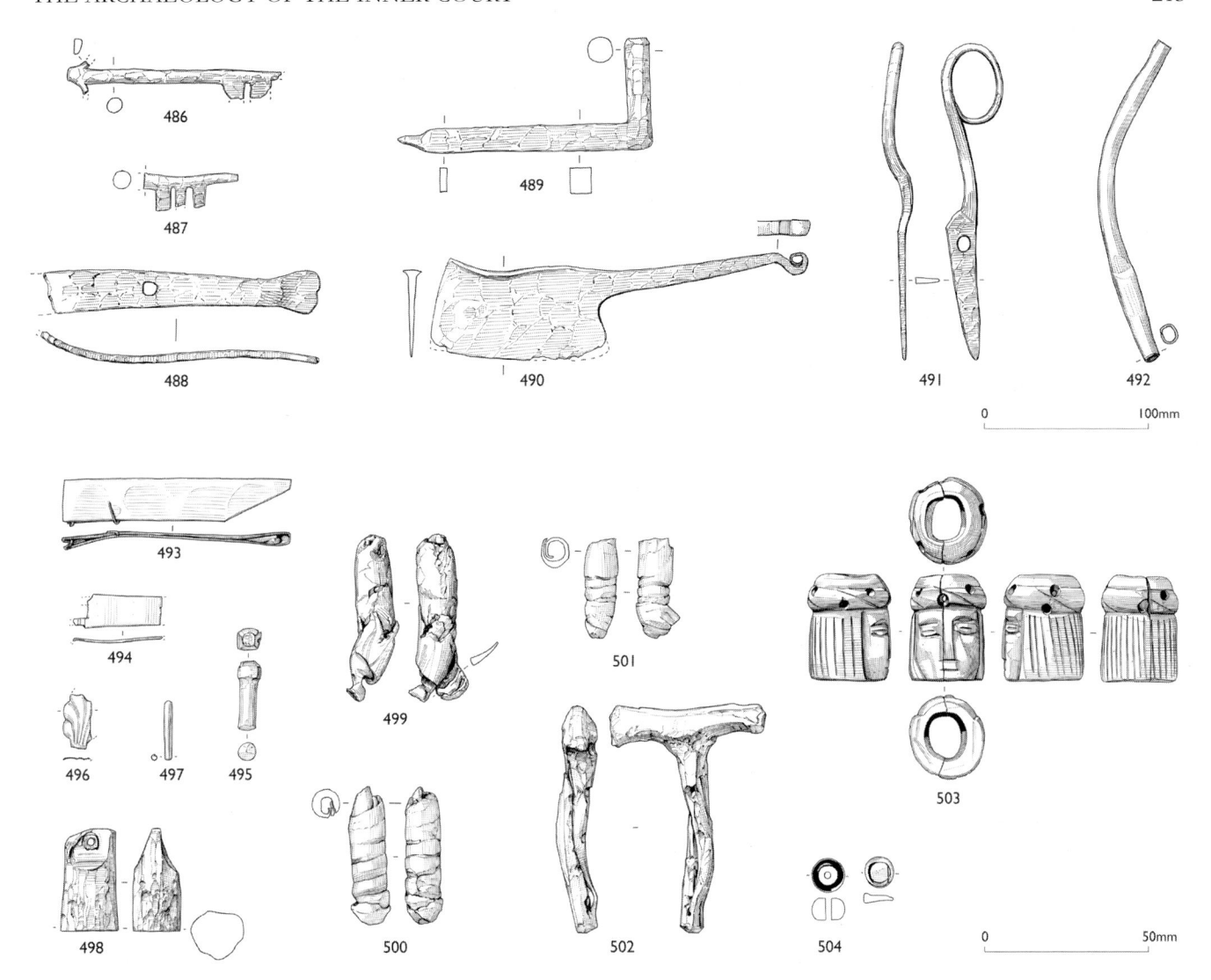

485. Clay pipe bowl. Moulded design of a heart (on one side only) with neat, regular diagonal hatching. On edge of pipe (facing stem) are the poorly impressed initials T W.

SMALL FINDS (SEE FIGURE 5.38)
Derived from demolition and late occupation deposits but disturbed by Hope's excavation, all of these objects come from either Prior John Wilson's cell or from the latest use of the first prior's cell. The most significant object is the walrus ivory head of Christ (503) from a rosary, which was derived from the late prior's cell, where it was found with a single jet rosary bead, 504. The keys 486 and 487, scissor blade 491 and cleaver 490 come from the rooms below the late refectory. Most of the remaining finds are associated with the building itself and must come from general demolition deposits.

486. Key. Fe. L: 130 mm. Broken kidney-shaped bow, roughly rectangular in section. Round stem. Broken bit with central cleft. Broken tip. Find no. Fe958.

487. Key. Fe. Part of bit and pin L: 58 mm. Bit W: 30 mm with two vertical clefts. Pin L: 20 mm. Remains of circular stem D: 10 mm. Find no. Fe933.

488. Strap-hinge. Fe. L: 166 mm; W: 24 mm (maximum), tapering to kidney-shaped end. Th: 4 mm. One square hole 8 mm × 8 mm. Find no. Fe766.

489. Pintle. Fe. Spike L: 156 mm. Square (12 mm) section tapering to 4 mm. Pivot H: 66 mm, round section D: 15 mm. Find no. Fe316.

Figure 5.38 Finds Group 35 from the south-west cloister range continued (iron 1:4; copper alloy 1:2, lead 1:2; bone 1:2; jet 1:2).

214   MOUNT GRACE PRIORY

497. Lace chape. Cu sheet. Overlapping seam. L: 17 mm; D: 1.5 mm. Find no. Cu111.
498. Plumb-bob. Pb. Roughly circular D: 16 mm (maximum); Ht: 29 mm. Shouldered top to W: 2 mm at apex. Circular hole. Find no. Pb183.
499. Packing. Pb. Circularly wound Pb strip with hollow centre. L: 50 mm (maximum); D: 11 mm. Could be plumb-bob, but there is no hole or attachment. Find no. Pb203.
500. Packing. Pb. Circularly wound Pb strip with ?hollow centre. L: 41 mm (maximum); D: 10 mm. Similar to 499. Find no. Pb204.
501. Packing. Pb. Circularly wound lead strip with hollow centre. L: 30 mm (maximum); D: 10 mm. Similar to 499 and 500. Find no. Pb205.
502. ?Packing from masonry clamp. Pb. T-shaped with roughly circular sections. Head L: 46 mm. Split stem L: 66 mm; D: 9 mm. Find no. Pb194.
503. Head of Christ. Walrus ivory. H: 31 mm; D: (max) 24 mm. Christ's face is fairly crudely carved, and his hair is schematically drawn by a series of vertical grooves. A raised band above forehead level has eight drill holes, D: 1.5 mm in two bands marked with bronze staining showing that a Crown of Thorns in copper alloy has become detached and lost. The soft centre of the tooth has been drilled out, D: 10–12 mm. The head was broken into two pieces. Find no. Bone1.
504. Bead. Jet. Highly polished. D: 10 mm; Th: 6 mm. Central hole D: 1.5 mm. Find no. St 1.

ARCHITECTURAL DETAIL ASSOCIATED WITH THE DEMOLITION (SEE FIGURE 5.39)

51. Fragment of tank with a small base and shallow sloping sides [901]. Externally it has a chamfer along one side and a narrow platform along the top of the same side. It is very similar in design and dimensions to stone 98, a piscina, and it is possible that it was originally intended to be a piscina, since there are signs of a drainage hole begun but not finished.
52. Incomplete section of parapet, with the same moulding as that on the

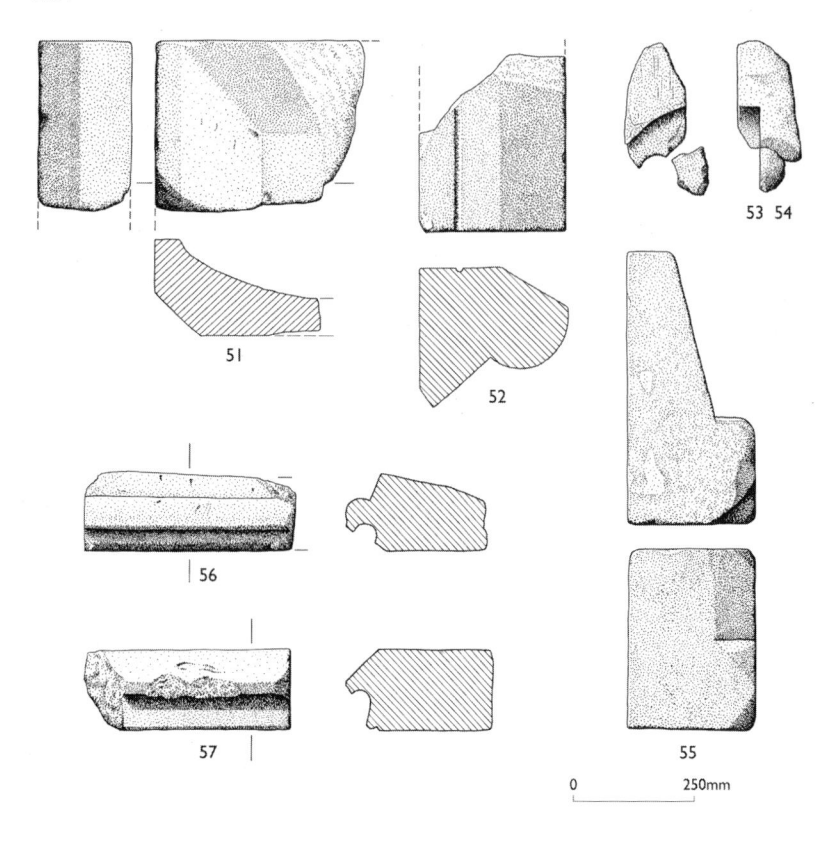

Figure 5.39 Architectural detail from demolition contexts in the south-west cloister range (1:10).

490. Cleaver. Fe. L: 240 mm. Blade H: 30 mm (maximum), with overhanging slightly convex top W: 10 mm. Handle, square sectioned and L: 30 mm, with looped end. Find no. Fe248.
491. Scissor blade. Fe. Blade L: 70 mm; W: 18 mm tapering to point; Th: 3 mm. Handle L: 120 mm; W: 7 mm, rectangular arm section, oval loop. Pivot hole 6 mm × 8 mm. Find no. Fe726.
492. Tube. Cu sheet. Edge to edge seam. L: 101 mm; D: 5 mm. Find no. Cu133.
493. Binding. Cu. Folded sheet, cut diagonally at one end, the straight end with 6 mm of sheet inturned. L: 68 mm (maximum); W: 12 mm. Find no. Cu128.
494. Clasp-mount. Cu. Unfixed part. L: 27 mm (maximum); W: 9 mm. Find no. Cu91.
495. Spoon terminal. Cu. L: 20 mm; D: 5 mm. Cut from terminal end of spoon. Terminal is roughly formed but with four sides W: 7 mm. Find no. Cu107.
496. Mount. Cu with gilt. H: 16 mm; W: 8 mm. Very thin, decorated with three leaves and part of a fourth. Incomplete and no fixing shank or rivet. Find no. Cu93.

THE ARCHAEOLOGY OF THE INNER COURT

prior's cell (see stones 43 and 45 above) [938]. In this instance, though, a glazing groove has been neatly cut into one side, showing reuse as a window jamb probably after the Suppression.

53 and 54. Fragments from the base of a shallow basin with a circular cut-out for a lead waste pipe [501].

55. Lower jamb stone with front chamfer and rear rebate and splay [901]. The chamfer is stopped 0.18 m above the base.

56, 57. Two sections of string course with different moulding designs. 56 has a demi-roll and fillet, a bottom chamfer and a hollow in between. Above the moulding is a splay that suggests that this was part of a ground-course or offset of some kind. 57 is a typical perpendicular and later moulding with an upper splay, hollow and ogee roll.

5.2 The Guest House and Kitchen Ranges

The northern end of the guest-house range and a cross-wing at its north end were examined by Hope in 1900 before the ruined parts of the range were incorporated in the Bell house of 1901 (Hope 1905, 275–7 and 280). He interpreted the northern half of the guest house as the guest hall and its kitchens, the former open to the roof and the latter below two chambers. The cross-wing was partially excavated and identified as the brewhouse to the west (with its substantial chimney and west gable wall surviving) and the bakehouse to the east, ruined to its footings. He also examined the area to the south of the cross-wing and east of the guest house, which he concluded from the lack of windows in the guest-house elevation must have been covered by buildings. Here he identified two enclosed yards and a stair to the rooms over the guest-house kitchen. Hope's excavation of the ruined elements of the building was superficial and in most areas failed to penetrate medieval deposits. As a result his conclusions were at least suspect and it is difficult to make sense of his plan (see Figure 5.40).

Since 1900, the whole of the area to the north of the 17th-century house that occupies the southern half of the guest-house range has been altered substantially by terracing and the construction of service buildings associated with the Bell house. The insertion of a sewer by the Ministry of Works in 1957, which runs diagonally across the cross-wing and the area between it and the guest house, has caused further substantial damage. This sewer was laid without archaeological supervision and the course chosen was unfortunate in that it removed a series of critical wall intersections that could easily have been avoided by reference to Hope's published plan. Before analysis of the surviving masonry in 1988–9 and re-excavation of the buried structures in 1991–2 the site was under turf and an access road, with short sections of wall visible on the surface. The area to the south of the cross-wing was strewn with detached architectural detail, some at least of which had been dumped there to form a rockery in the 1950s. The western part of the cross-wing was incorporated in a series of service buildings dating to 1901, which were demolished in 1988 to enable the display of the medieval structure.

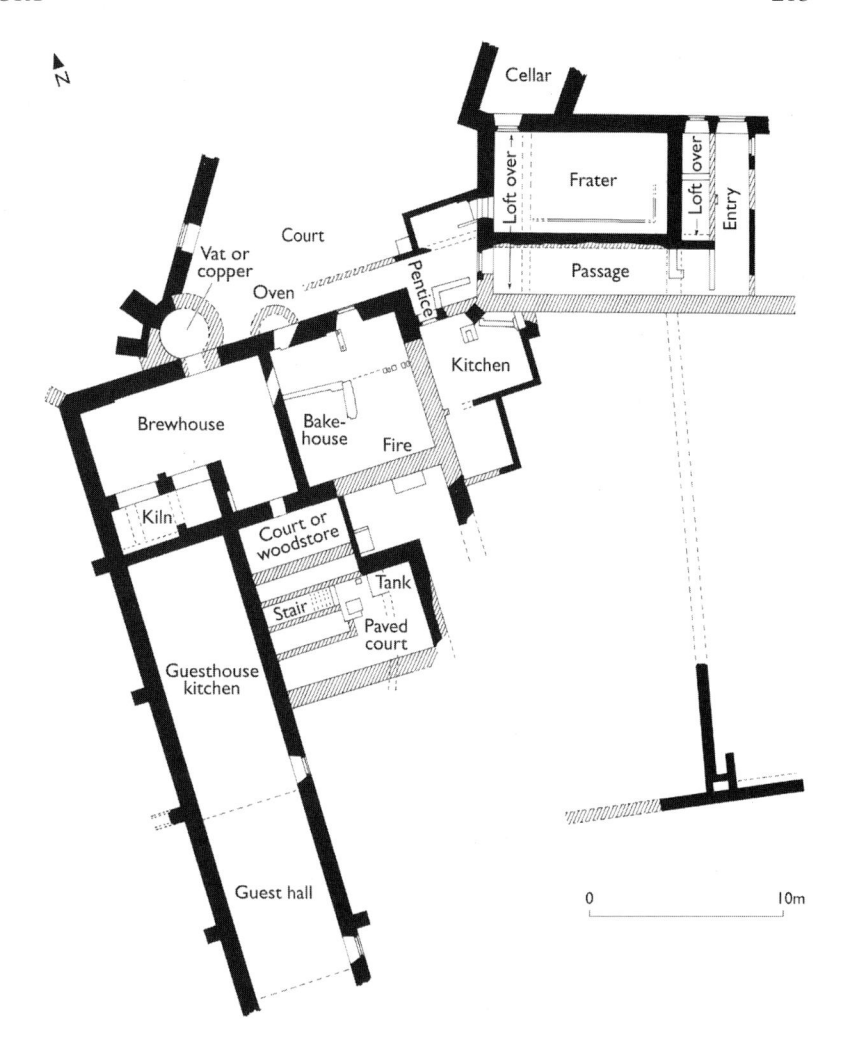

Figure 5.40 The kitchen area and 'refectory' as excavated and interpreted by Hope.

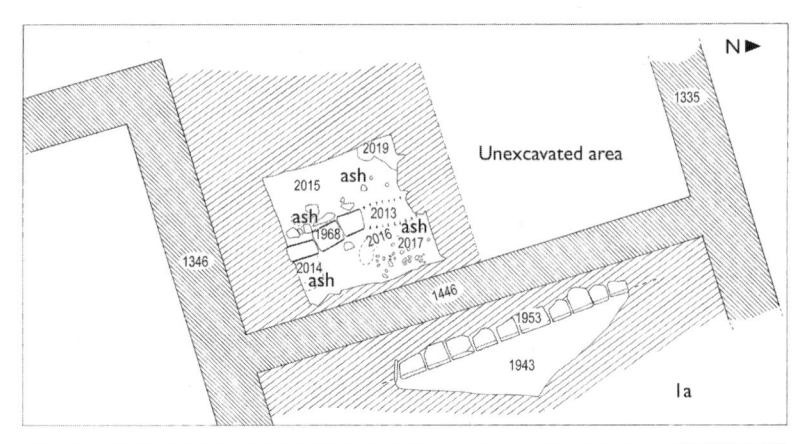

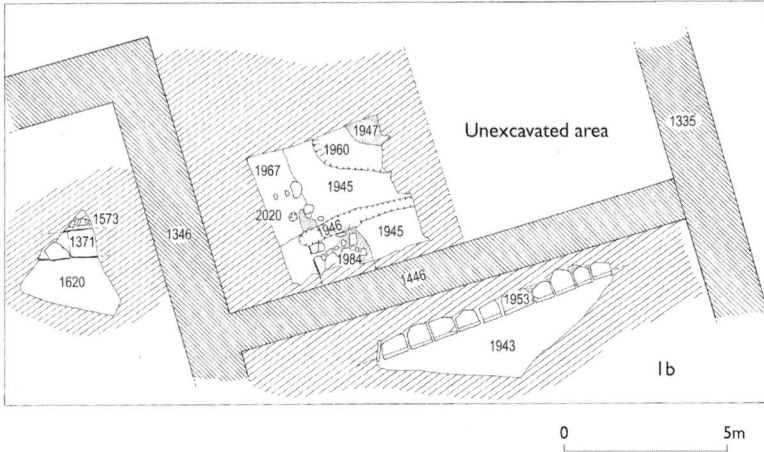

Figure 5.41 The Period One kitchen.

Excavation revealed the same four phases of development as were apparent on other parts of the site, as detailed below.

Period One (see Figure 5.41)

Although only sample areas were examined down to Period One levels, traces were revealed of an early 15th-century building of two phases below the western part of the 1420s cross-wing. The greater part of this building, apparently a freestanding kitchen, is likely to survive below the Bell-period paving in Room I of the cross-wing, but it could not be examined in 1992 because of time and cost constraints. It has been left protected for future research.

The Period One kitchen was represented only by the external plinth course [1953] of its east wall and by two distinct floors (see Figure 5.41A and B), indicating that it was a stone building refitted at least once in its short life. A deposit of red-brown silt, [1943], had built up to the east of the building, covering the ashlar plinth course, and this in turn was sealed by an occupation deposit of burned organic matter, coal and charcoal, [1954], which must have come from the kitchen. An identical silt build-up, [1620], was noted on a small island of surviving stratigraphy to the south of the later cross-wing, and this was cut by a fragment of wall, [1371], running approximately north–south. This wall pre-dates Period Two, as a fragment of it appeared to be incorporated in the south wall of the cross-wing. It was apparently an external wall, as the rubble levelling [1573] of a floor butted against its west face. Although later disturbance had removed any relationship with the Period One kitchen, it must represent an adjunct on the kitchen's south side, perhaps contemporary with its latest fitting out.

In its first phase the kitchen had a timber partition orientated north–south some 1.4 m to the west of wall [1953], which was set on an ashlar cill wall, [1968], of which three stones remained. Its line could be traced northwards as a shallow robber trench, [2013]. To its west was a floor of light brown clay, [2019], sealed by a thick deposit of ash and charcoal, [2015]. This material spread up to the line of the partition but did not cross it. Some large fragments of sandstone laid within this build-up are best seen as temporary floor surfacing. To the east of the partition wall the floor comprised a spread of light brown clay and rubble, [2017]. On the surface of this was a linear deposit of burned material, [2016], and a thin patch of ash, [2014], which butted against the partition cill wall. Its northern extent was truncated by later features.

The ash deposits, floors and partition wall were levelled off when the building was refitted and a new floor of orange clay, [1945], was laid across that part of the building examined. This sealed the partition cill wall, showing that the timber structure above had been removed. The new floor was then cut by the construction trench, [*2001*], of an east–west wall that must have extended to the inner face of wall [1953]. The foundation course, [1984], remained, although the superstructure of this new wall was removed in Period Two. Also cutting floor [1945] was a timber slot, [1946], for the 0.30 m-wide cill beam of a new partition wall that extended just to the south of wall [1984], where there was perhaps a door. This new partition lay just to the east of its predecessor. A single posthole, [2020], cut the floor in the western room, aligned on the south face of wall [1984] and the end of slot [1946]. It coincided with a patch of orange-grey clay and sandstone rubble that appeared to be a repair of the floor and whose northern edge appeared to mark

THE ARCHAEOLOGY OF THE INNER COURT

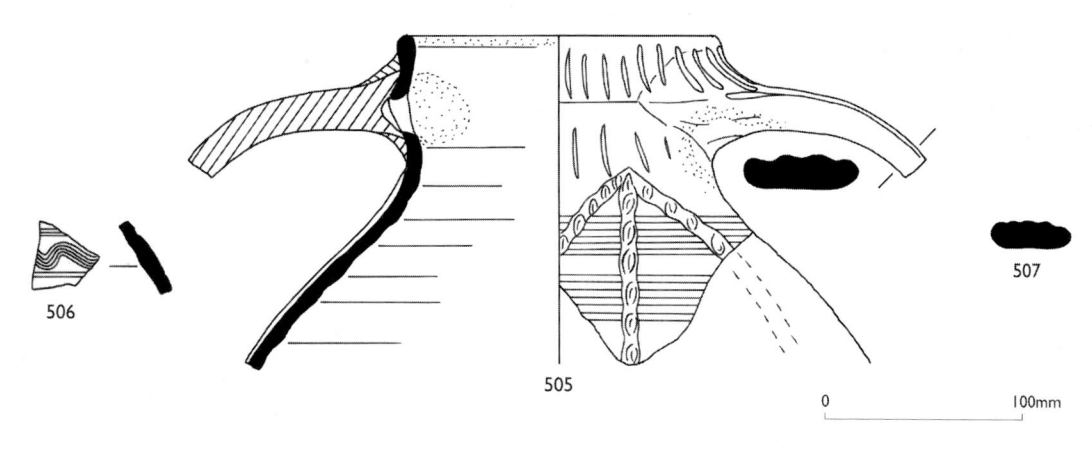

Figure 5.42 Finds Group 36 from the kitchen (pottery 1:4).

Table 5.15 Finds Group 36: Ceramics

Fabric	Sherds	Total vessels	Bottle	Cistern	Cooking pot	Jug	Pancheon
Brandsby type	3	3	0	0	1	2	0
Gritty	1	1	0	0	0	1	0
Regional Stray	2	1	0	1	0	0	0
Ryedale	48	12	2	1	0	8	1

a partition line. A shallow cut, [1960], in the north-western part of floor [1945] contained a hearth, [1947], with multiple patchings of white mortar. A substantial spread of ash, [1936], sealed both the hearth and the adjacent floor.

Kitchen, Finds Group 36 (see Figure 5.42)
Phase One kitchen construction and occupation from contexts [1821], [1844], [1894], [1936], [1937], [1943], [1945], [1954], [2009] and [2024].

CERAMICS

As elsewhere on the site, Brandsby type and Gritty ware fabrics form the principal pre-priory residual element in this and all subsequent groups from the kitchen area. Conversely, the Ryedale ware is contemporary with the early 15th-century Phase One occupation of the site. In terms of number of sherds and relative completeness of vessels, the Ryedale ware cistern, 505, is the dominant vessel in this Finds Group (Table 5.15).

505. Ryedale ware cistern. Orange (darkening to red by glaze margins), grey/blue-grey/grey core and purple-brown inner surface. Good-quality (consistent and even) brownish-green glaze. At least two, almost certainly three, broad, heavy handles. Upper handle attachments formed by fingers being inserted into neck and pushed into the handle, the resulting cavity being filled with a small plug of clay, smoothed down, and, in at least one case, the scar being rather carelessly daubed with a smear of glaze. Decorative vertical slashes to rim and neck applied after handle and applied body decoration added. Large, probably very heavy, and for its period quite an elaborate cistern.

506. Ryedale ware jug. Grey/blue-grey core and grey inner surface. Dark olive green glaze. Lightly incised horizontal bands and wavy comb decoration.

507. Regional Stray jug. Heavily sand-tempered fabric, ribbed oval handle, fairly hard and of rough surface texture. Pale yellowish-buff to grey-buff outer surface cream core, turning first bluish-white and then blue-grey towards centre of handle core. Lightly pocked, fairly watery, olive-green glaze. Possibly Upper Heaton.

ARCHITECTURAL DETAIL FROM THE PERIOD ONE KITCHEN (SEE FIGURE 5.43)

58, 59 Two sections of trefoil-topped coping. The smaller section, cut from the whole stone, was found in a 17th-century context at the south-west angle of the church; the larger part of the stone was found below the Period Two kitchen yard and is possibly associated with the Period One kitchen.

Period Two (see Figures 5.44 and 5.45)

The Kitchen Range
The cross-wing at the north end of the guest-house range was built in two stages around the Period One kitchen, which obviously remained in use for as long as possible. Initially, the eastern part of the cross-wing was laid out to the east of wall [1953] and slightly terraced into the rising surface of the natural red clay. The footings followed the rising ground for the most part and consisted of no more than two courses of substantial sandstone slabs, not trench-laid but constructed on the surface. The footings of the south wall, [1561], were actually laid onto the surface of a Period One cobbled yard [1958] and [2009] to the east of the original kitchen.

The north wall, [1355b], was trench-built, but only at its western end, where its construction trench was cut from the surface of a deposit of red-brown silt that was probably the same deposit as the Period One silt [1943] to the east of the original kitchen. It was backfilled with cream mortar [1904] and [1971] and was topped with a dump of mixed clay and silt, [1970]. A doorway, [2030], was provided towards the east

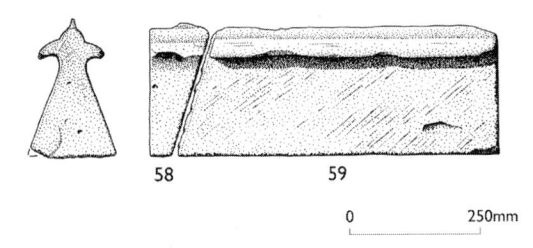

Figure 5.43 Architectural detail from the area of the Period One kitchen (1:10).

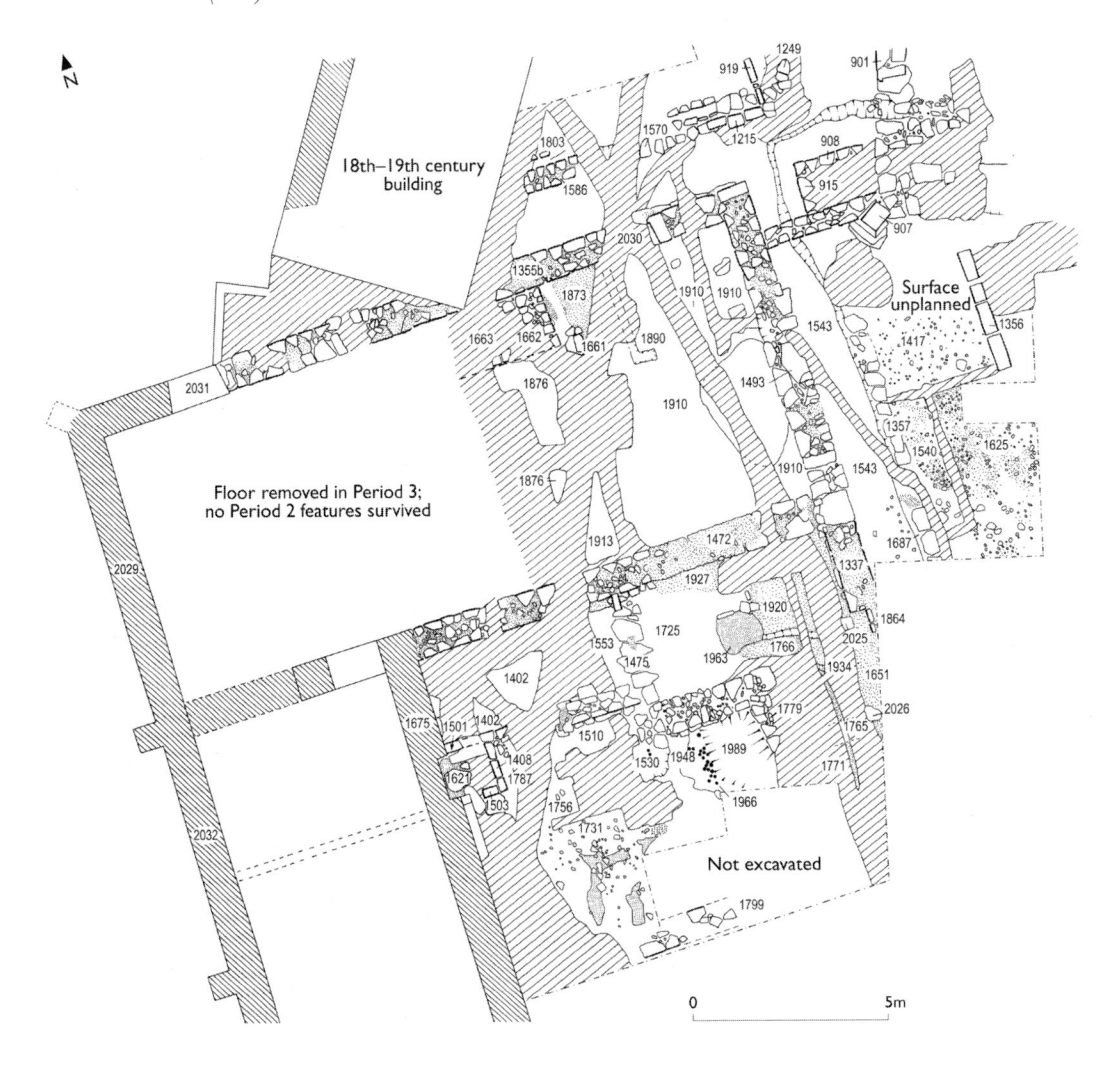

Figure 5.44 The Period Two kitchen as excavated.

Figure 5.45 The Period Two kitchen and its offices as excavated, seen from the east (T. Gledhill).

end of the wall, its eastern jamb remaining a single course high, although the sewer of 1957 had removed its western jamb and cill (both of which were recorded *in situ* by Hope). The north wall returned to the south as wall [1337]; this was footed onto two courses of substantial slabs [1493] and its external angle dressed with finely bolstered ashlar quoins. The footings [*1561*] of the south wall [1472] bonded with those of the east wall, and this wall was continued up to a point 1 m east of the original kitchen. The east wall, [1337], extended southwards beyond the new building (see Figure 5.44).

Once the shell of the eastern part of the cross-wing was completed, but before it was fitted out, the original kitchen was demolished. The destruction of wall [1953] was marked by a thick deposit of broken sandstone rubble, white mortar and roof slates, [1942], thrown down within the shell of the new building to the east and which built up against the outer face of the wall before its lowest courses were removed. The north wall was then extended to the west [1335a], the west gable wall [2029] was built and the remainder of the south wall [1346] was built from west to east in a single operation. These three walls all bond at their junctions, but there is a break in the coursing of the north and south walls where they meet the earlier work. There is also a slight misalignment in the south wall. A doorway, [2031], which was provided towards the west end of the north wall [1335a], was blocked in the 17th century. Although the dressings of this door have been robbed, it still retains its western splay and rere-arch, as well as a section of its cill that indicates the intended floor level of the building. The western wall is complete to the springing of its gable and has two square-headed lights at ground-floor level and a single light at first-floor level (see Figure 5.46 A–B and C–D). The south wall retains a tall archway, now blocked, which communicated with the north end of the guest-house range. A single surviving corbel in the south wall indicates both the presence and level of an upper floor.

The cross-wing was built before the remainder of the guest-house range, but as part of a continuing campaign. The west wall, [2029], courses with a short stub of the west wall of the guest house, [2032], the junction being marked by a buttress that differs in design from the other buttresses of the west facade of the guest house (see Figure 5.46 A–B). Similarly, the eastern wall of the guest house, [1675], bonds with the western part [1346] of the south wall of the cross-wing. The short wall stubs buttressed the cross-wing until the guest-house range was completed (see Figure 5.46 B–A). The east wall of the guest house was examined by excavation on its outer face only. Although serious damage had been

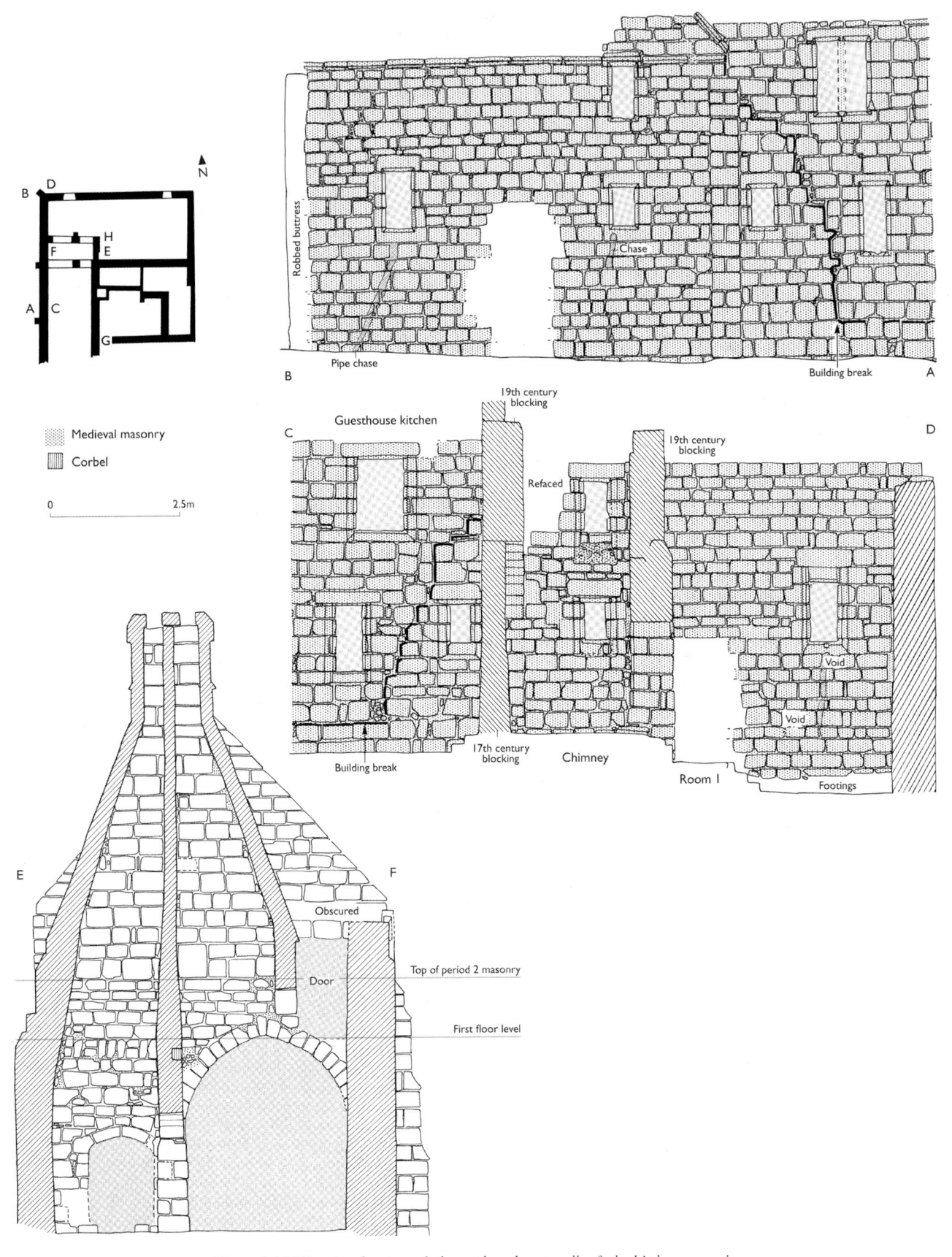

Figure 5.46 Elevation drawings of the north and west walls of the kitchen cross-wing.

done in 1900, when a pipe drain, [*1444*], and a lead water pipe, [*1348*], had been inserted parallel to the east wall to serve the Bell house, sufficient remained to identify the method of construction. A shallow construction trench, [1668], was cut into the surface of the natural dirty red clay, [*1643*], its bottom levelled up with a packing of orange-brown clay, [*1633*]. Two courses of large undressed sandstone blocks set in hard white mortar filled the construction trench and extended 2.2 m to the south of wall [1346]. The natural surface fell away to the south at this point, the construction trench and two courses of footings following this fall in ground level. The break in foundation level was concealed by the construction of an external latrine tower integral with wall [1675]. The west side of the latrine shaft, which survives, was recessed 0.3 m into the guest-house wall for the full height of the tower, with a contemporary square-headed doorway at first-floor level. The construction of the lower part of the latrine tower preceded the construction of the adjacent wall faces of the guest house, as it was built in a pit [*1667*] cut through the partly completed footings of wall [1675]. In the bottom of this pit were placed huge slabs of sandstone, [*1621*], which were both the floor and foundations of the tower. The floor was not continuous and gaps in the stones were made up with the same hard cream mortar used throughout the superstructure in this phase. The north wall [1501] and [1504], east wall [1408] and south wall [1502] and [1503] of the tower were a single stone thick, faced on both sides and placed directly on the stone floor. The latrine shaft was 1.2 m from east to west and 1.12 m from north to south, and appeared to be drained to the south, where the floor slabs extended beyond the tower. Any opening there had been destroyed in 1900 by the insertion of the modern pipe drain, [*1444*]. There was no sewer associated with the latrine, a rare occurrence at Mount Grace.

Only when the outer walls of the cross-wing were completed was the building fitted out. A mistake had been made in setting out the floor level at the west end of the building. Presumably the floor was intended to approximate to the level of the cill of door [2031]. The ground level rose to the east, however, and the footings of the east wall were higher than this cill. The interior of the building was levelled up with a packing of red-brown clay, [*1981*], which butted against the south wall and extended to cover the lowest footings [1493] of the east wall [1337], although it did not reach the north wall. This was in turn sealed by a clay floor surface, [1983], which sealed the construction of the north wall. Because of the rising ground surface, this floor visibly rose towards the east gable, where the upper course of footings was left exposed. It also sloped down slightly to the south, again because of the behaviour of the natural surface below. In Period Three the floor level was reduced in the western half of the building and no Period Two deposits survived.

On the surface of floor [1983], against the east gable wall, was a substantial hearth, [1980], and a spread of occupation debris, [*1941*], that occurred only in the southern half of the room, where the floor level was slightly lower (see Figure 5.45). This deposit contained a substantial quantity of articulated fish bones and mussel and cockle shells (for the analysis of fish bones and other foodstuffs from the kitchen, see Chapter 7).

A new floor of sticky red clay [1879], [1910], [1930] was laid over floor [1983] and the occupation debris on it. Fish bones and shell incorporated in this material was probably trodden in. Cut into the new floor was an east–west timber slot, [1890], for a screen inside doorway [2030]. Its return towards wall [1355] had been destroyed by the 1957 sewer trench, although its junction with the east–west slot survived. On this floor a substantial fire had burned against the centre of the east wall, although no proper hearth was provided and the floor surface was heavily burned. There was no evidence of a chimney, although indications to the north and in the south wall suggested that the cross-wing was two-storeyed at its east end and at least a timber chimney hood would have been required. The east wall was sufficiently substantial to have supported a corbelled masonry hood. From this fire a spread of ash, [*1911*], sealed floor [1910] and a deposit of fish bones, [1925], that lay on it. A further spread of refuse, [*1913*], with many fish bones and ash, in the south half of the building, sealed the spread of ash from the hearth. Sealing all these deposits was an ashy deposit [*1833*], [*1882*], [*1883*]. Vast quantities of fish bone, including a lot of articulated material, were noted in this occupation layer, which was up to 0.10 m thick. Layer [*1833*] was a laminate deposit with 'shiny' trampled surfaces that were impossible to separate but could be distinguished as the deposit was lifted.

A third floor, [*1832*], of orange-brown sandy silt was laid in the centre of the room, sealing [*1833*]. Similar patches [*1872*] and [*1876*] were probably part of the same surface, making up hollows in the general floor surface. On this surface a raised platform defined by walls [1662] and [1664] and bonded with yellow clay was probably contemporary with this surface. Built against the north wall, its western side was destroyed in Period Three. Although only the lowest course of masonry survived, it is likely that this platform could have been up to 1 m high, providing the base for one or more bread ovens. On Hope's plan (see Figure 5.40) an external oven is shown to the north of wall [1335b] at this point. If it existed, it now lies below the corner of the adjacent building of 1900–1 and was not re-excavated. From its recorded position it is most likely to be associated with this feature. A mortar surface, [*1873*], to the east was probably associated with this structure; it sealed a sandy levelling dump, [*1868*], in a hollow above the second Period Two floor.

The Southern Outshut
At the same time as the building of the kitchen range in Period Two, an outshut of two rooms was begun against its south wall [1346] and [1472]. It was to occupy a slightly lower terrace, for the ground surface fell away to the south and was followed by the footings of the guest-house range. The sequence of construction was complicated in the extreme, its interpretation not being aided by the destruction of most of the western room by early 20th-century drains and the 1957 sewer trench, and by the incomplete nature of the 1991–2 excavation. Although the constructional sequence was recorded in the sections provided by modern intrusions, it was not possible to examine it all in plan.

As originally planned, the south wall of the outshut, [1393], was constructed in a deep cut, [*2010*], which survived only in the eastern two-thirds of the building and which created a lower terrace. The lower level of the natural surface at the western end of the site adjacent to the guest-house range obviated the need for a deep cut there. Wall [1393] and its footings [*1534*] were set in a shallow cut, [*1830*], that penetrated a thin layer of occupation material, [*1541*], which had built up in Period One on the surface of the natural subsoil, [*1606*]. Wall [1393] and its footings [1534] were aligned on the north face of the latrine tower in the east wall of the guest house and extended as far east as a partition wall, [1475], a single course of ashlar 0.20 m thick set on substantial footings of four courses that had been built free-standing in the terracing cut [*2010*]. The footings of wall [1475] appeared to bond with those of wall [1472] and the one surviving freestone block was effectively bonded with the south face of the kitchen range wall, demonstrating contemporaneity. The east wall of the kitchen range, [1337], was continued to the south of the building to finish with a return, [2025], that aligned exactly with the inner face of wall [1393]. The extended wall [1337] lay outside the terracing cut, [*2010*], which skirted its west face, suggesting that it had been built before the cut was made, and construction material [*1951*] and [*1952*] associated with the building of wall [1472], which bonded with it, was actually truncated by the cut. The south wall of the eastern room, [1424], was not aligned with wall [1393] but was set further to the south, its awkward junction with walls [1393] and [1475] being covered by a substantial buttress, [1530], that sat on the surface of the Period One occupation deposit [*1541*]. Wall [1424] did not extend to the east as far as the east wall [1337], but returned to the south as wall [1779], with which it bonded, all within the terracing cut [*2010*], suggesting a major change of plan during construction. The east wall, [1337], was continued to the south by a narrower wall, [1864], that simply butted up against its southern return, and the return was partially dismantled, leaving a single block at its inner angle. This L-shaped room apparently extended as far south as a yard wall, [1799].

The western room (Room III) was then levelled up with a dump of dark orange-brown clay loam [*1538*] and [*1552*] 0.4 m deep that seal the construction of walls [1475] and [1393] and which contained at least two rejected ashlar blocks. In turn, this levelling layer was sealed by a small fragment of orange-brown clay floor, [1553], which butted the inner face of wall [1393], while two small islands of similar material, [1402], also sealed subfloor levelling material. There was no evidence of access doors in the west, north or south walls of this room, and it must have communicated with the room to the east, though only a single stone of the party wall survived above floor level and no door could be located.

In the eastern room (Room IV), terracing cut [*2010*] was filled with a series of dumps of constructional material [1725], [1963] and [*1964*], predominantly clay and rubble. Further debris, [2028], had built up from the construction of wall [1864], filling the upper part of the cut, and a stone block, [2026], was actually set in this material. With the dismantled remains of the original south-east corner of Room IV, [2025], this block provided a seating for a timber post set on the line of the inner face of wall [1337]. In the eastern and south-eastern parts of the room the primary floors survived in small areas, sealing the backfill of the terracing cut. To the north was a floor of yellow clay, [1920], bounded on its southern edge, 0.8 m from wall [1424], by a beam slot [1918]/[1924] that appears to have defined a narrow passage along that wall. To the south of this and at a lower level was a floor surface of yellow sandy silt, [1766], that extended as far as a second timber slot, [1765], that defined a second partition that must have run between walls [1779] and [1864]. To the south of this was a further floor of yellow plastic clay, [*1771*], that had been largely destroyed by the insertion of a septic tank in 1901. Cut into the surface of the central floor, [1766], was a shallow slot, [1934], 0.25 m wide and 30 mm deep, of unknown extent and function. Sealing the upper floor, [1920], was a thin layer of occupation debris [*1915*] and [*1955*], while a similar deposit [*1967*] and [*1969*] sealed floor [*1766*]. A door in the partition wall at some point was suggested by the fact that layer [*1967*] also occurred above floor [*1771*]. In the northern half of the room this occupation was in turn sealed by a thin layer of charcoal [*1919*] and [*1916*].

Within Period Two, the primary floors at the north end of Room IV subsided into the soft backfilling of the terracing cut [*2010*], and in the central part of the room a subfloor levelling of brown clay, [1933], was sealed by a further deposit of mid-brown silty clay [1927], apparently the make-up for a new floor which had been removed in Period Three. Against the east wall of the room the primary floor had been dug out and replaced by a new surface [1651] and [*1907*], which had survived – a thick deposit of orange to red-brown clay that had no levelling deposits beneath it because it was on the edge of the construction cut for the terrace. This floor was laid around the posts set on stylobates, [2025] and [2026], sealing their upper surfaces. A Bell-period septic tank, pipe trench and cable trench had removed almost all of the interior of the southern continuation of the room along wall [1864], an area that had also been badly disturbed by Hope above the primary floors, and no evidence of reflooring had survived there.

To the south and west of the outshut was a small yard, enclosed to the south by a wall, [1799], that had probably butted against the east wall of the guest house. Hope had recorded the existence of this wall in 1900 (see Figure 5.40). Unfortunately, its western part had been destroyed by a manhole and drain outfall associated with the Bell rebuilding of the guest house in 1900–1. What remained of wall [1799] was footed onto the surface of the redeposited natural clay, [*1606*], that represented the level from which the guest-house range was constructed and which had assumed its present form in Period One. A thin spread of metalling, [*1821*], between wall [1799] and the underlying clay was almost certainly associated with the first kitchen. Butting against the north face of wall [1799] and sealing its construction was a thick deposit of red clay, rubble and roof slates [1510], [*1592*], [1731] and [1787], either waste from the construction of the guest house, or more probably, from the demolition of Period One buildings. It skirted the great pit cut to accommodate the outshut buildings, [*2010*], and so must have been laid during their construction. The pit itself was then filled up with a deposit of ash, [*1990*], and a dump of red and green plastic clay, [1898], leaving a deep depression or tank, [1778], at the east end of the yard along wall [1779]. The filling of the pit effectively sealed the construction of walls [1779] and [1424]. The western edge of tank [1778] was flanked by a double row of stakeholes, [1966a–o], driven into the surface of layer [1989]. A spread of pebbles in yellow clay, [1948], to the south of the outshut was all that remained of the surface of this yard. There must have been a stair from the yard to the primary door at first-floor level in the east wall of the guest house, just to the south of the latrine tower. This was reconstructed in Period Three and no trace of it was recovered.

The Northern Pentice

Along the north side of the cross-wing and parallel to wall [1355b] was a pentice 1.48 m wide, extending westwards from the pentice that covered the west gable of the south-west cloister range. At its eastern end it comprised a cill wall of one course of ashlar, [1570], set on a foundation of roughly dressed sandstone occupying a construction trench, [1682], that was cut into the surface of the natural red-brown clay, [1574], seen across the site. Wall [1570] had apparently carried a timber gallery at its east end that extended as far west as door [2030] in wall [1355b]. Most of the cill wall had been robbed, leaving only its foundation course in place. To the west of door [2030] the natural ground surface fell steeply away to the west, and the structure of wall [1570] changed dramatically. The wall there was of coursed construction and was 0.56 m wide. Up to four courses of foundation work remained where the surface of the natural fell away. The wall was subsequently rebuilt above this point, but may well have been intended to be entirely of stone construction. The junction between the narrow cill wall and the wider foundation was unfortunately destroyed by the intersection of a Bell-period drain trench and the 1957 sewer.

That the construction of the pentice was contemporary with the building of wall [1355b] there can be no doubt. Between the two walls, and sealing construction debris [1763] from the lower levels of the cross-wing to the west of door [2030], was a working surface of small cobbles and metalling [1710] and [1728] that butted both walls. This surface showed evidence of heavy wear, but was sealed by a thick dump of red clay, [1709], that roughly levelled up the floor of the pentice within the area excavated. Spreads of ash, [1707], on the surface of this clay were sealed by a further clay layer, [1700]. On top of this, and extending the length of the pentice, was a further metalled surface, [1578], crushed into which were the remains of a pottery vessel (Finds Group 37, 515). The surface was again a temporary one that was sealed by the final yellow clay floor of the corridor, [1573], a surface that remained in use throughout the life of the building and which was at about the level of the cill of doorway [2030].

Outside the pentice wall was a drain, [1431], that was a continuation of the Period Two drain [922] that ran across the pentice on the west side of the south-west cloister range. Its eastern 1.08 m was lined with ashlar blocks and capped with slates, extending only to the line of the eastern gable of the cross-wing. Its base was the natural red-brown clay, [1574]. From that point its construction changed and it took the form of an open eavesdrip gulley, lined and floored with split stone slates. This drain occupied the same construction trench, [1682], as the pentice wall [1570] itself.

The Eastern Pentice

To the east of the cross-wing in Period Two and parallel with its eastern gable wall, [1337], a pentice wall, [1357], was constructed, shallowly footed onto natural red clay [1574]. Only the lowest courses of split stone slates remained, bedded on a skim of white mortar. Between the pentice wall and the east wall of the cross-wing, [1337], was a spread of yellow-brown sandy clay, [1543], which comprised the pentice floor. It sealed the wide construction trench, [1686], of wall [1337]. Along the inside face of the pentice wall was the narrow cut for a water pipe, [1215], which was lined with red clay in which the lead pipe had been bedded. This pipe was the continuation of the water main that ran out under the western door cill of the early prior's cell and which was removed and realigned in Period Three. The pipe trench had later been packed with rubble. To the east of the pentice was a cobbled surface [1540] and [1625] that again sealed the natural clay surface. The pentice stopped some 2.2 m to the south of wall [909], which closed the gap between the south-west cloister range and the kitchen range, and a second cill wall, [1356], 0.34 m wide and built of ashlar blocks faced on all six sides, was built parallel to [1357]; it ran south from the south wall of the south-west cloister range, survived to a maximum height of two courses and outlined a structure 4.25 m square. There was no trace of a cill wall on the south side. The area between these walls was levelled up with a mixed deposit of brown, red and yellow clay with spreads of sandstone rubble, [1417], topped with a surface of pebbles. To the east of this structure and to the south of the south-west cloister range lay the cultivated soils of the prior's cell garden, which were not excavated.

Kitchen, Finds Group 37 (see Figure 5.47)

From Period Two construction contexts [1417], [1434], [1552], [1573], [1578], [1663],

THE ARCHAEOLOGY OF THE INNER COURT

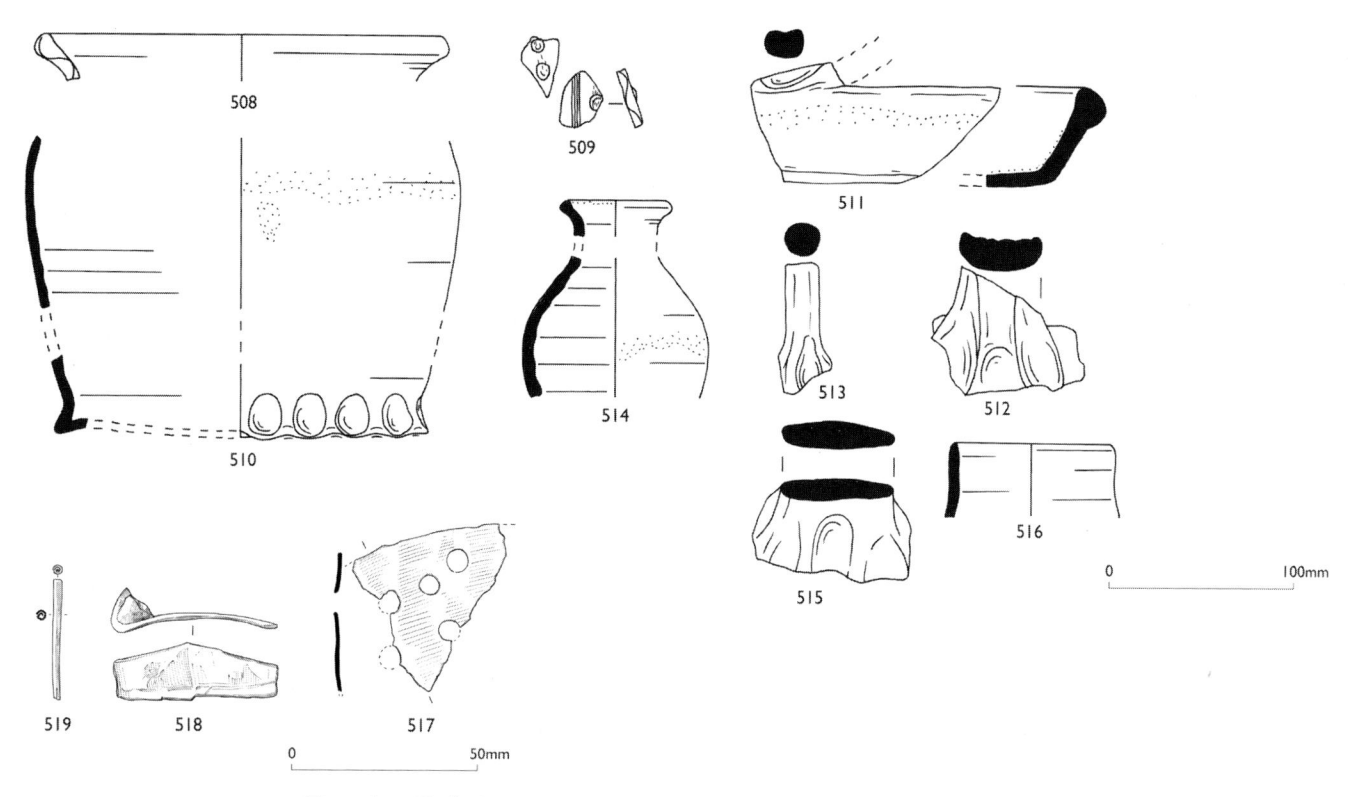

Figure 5.47 Finds Group 37 from the kitchen (pottery 1:4; copper alloy 1:2, lead 1:2).

Table 5.16 Finds Group 37: Ceramics

Fabric	Sherds	Total vessels	Bottle	Bowl	Cooking pot	Dish	Jug	Mug or cup	Pancheon	Pipkin
Brandsby type	15	10	0	1	4	0	4	0	0	0
Gritty	37	25	0	0	11	0	12	0	1	1
Humber	1	1	0	0	0	0	1	0	0	0
Post-medieval Sandy	2	2	0	0	0	1	0	0	1	0
Raeren	2	2	0	0	0	0	0	2	0	0
Ryedale	265	24	1	0	0	0	22	0	1	0
Siegburg	1	1	0	0	0	0	0	1	0	0
*										

[1664], [1677], [1692], [1700], [1709], [1717], [1727], [1731], [1810], [1835], [1854], [1879], [1933], [1942], [1948], [1949], [1970], [1971], [1981], [1999] and [2011].

CERAMICS

The Period Two construction work represented by Finds Group 37 had clearly disturbed pre-priory deposits and thus introduced a considerable residual element to the group, principally the Gritty ware and Brandsby type fabrics represented by illustrations 508–10 and probably 511. Among the contemporary pottery is the bottle 514, paralleled in the Period Two occupation deposits of Finds Group 38 below. Bottles are not a particularly common late-medieval form, but, given their association with both local and imported stoneware handled drinking mugs and their general similarity of body form, they are probably best considered as handleless drinking mugs. Mug rim 516 is a particularly early example of the Raeren stoneware products (Table 5.16).

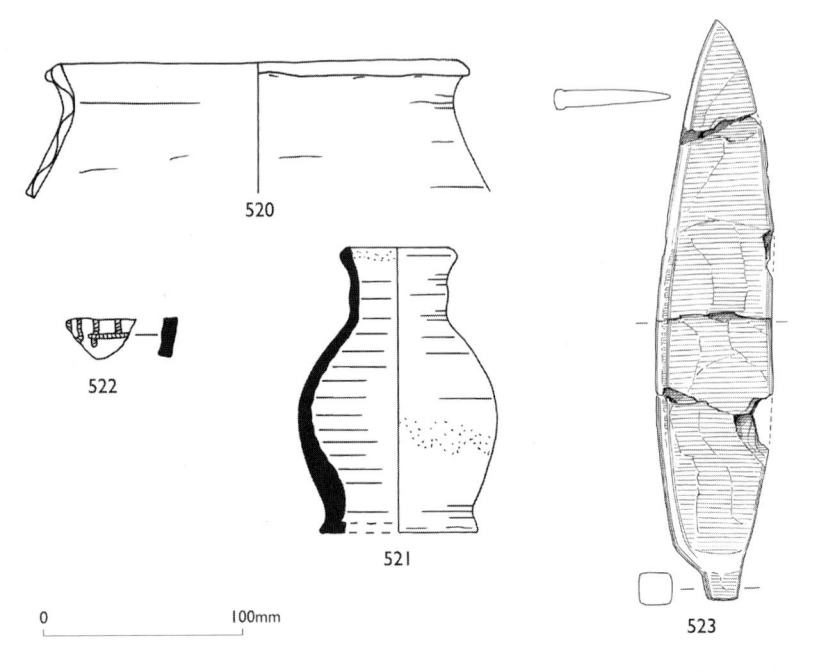

Figure 5.48 Finds Group 38 from the kitchen (pottery 1:4; iron 1:4).

508. Gritty ware cooking pot. Brownish-orange surfaces and orange core. Traces of burning to the outside edge of the rim only.
509. Gritty ware jug. Light orange-buff surfaces and, in places, a blue-grey core. Olive-green glaze. Lightly incised vertical lines and applied spots in an iron-rich clay.
510. Gritty ware/Brandsby type fabric jug. Pale orange surfaces, the inner surface having darker red streaks, and orange core. Orange glaze with green mottles, traces of pocking at margins but not on fully glazed sherds. Deeply thumbed base.
511. Gritty ware? handled basting dish. Light orange-brown surfaces and orange-vermilion core. Orange-brown glaze on inner surface. Traces of a substantial loop handle following the profile of the rim, with one handle attachment surviving, held on by a single deep thumbing. Heavily burnt and sooted on outer surface and on rim top. Not that far removed from the Ryedale ware fabric; slightly rough-textured but thick-walled and fairly hard.
512. Ryedale ware jug. Grey-black core and inner surface. Olive-green glaze, bright and clear, some minor pocking. Upper handle attachment (unillustrated) smoothed on, lower attachment also smoothed on with deep central thumbing pushing the lower body wall inwards, and then with two conventional lower thumbings.
513. Ryedale ware drinking mug. Orange outer surface over-fired to purple-black in patches, pale orange/blue-grey core and purple brown inner surface. No trace of glaze.
514. Ryedale ware bottle. Dull pale red outer surface, blue-grey core and pale orange inner surface. Light olive-green glaze with some pocking where glaze thins.
515. Ryedale ware jug. Grey-black core and inner surface with a thin white skin of core immediately under the glaze. A rough textured surface with an inclination to dust, particularly with the more abraded sherds. A consistent rather thin olive-green glaze with varying degrees of surface pocking. This was clearly a very large vessel, represented here by some 200 sherds, but all of small size with no trace of rim or basal angle.
516. Raeren stoneware drinking mug. Pale purplish-grey core. Matt brown outer surface, with paler inner surface.

SMALL FINDS

517. Skimmer/strainer. Cu, probably cast. Fragment with irregularly placed holes. D: 5.5 mm; Th: 1 mm. Find no. Cu186.
518. Sheet. Cu. Irregularly cut, one end folded over. L: 45 mm; Th: 1.5 mm. Find no. Cu198.
519. Lace chape. Cu sheet. Edge to edge seam. L: 33 mm; D: 2 mm. Find no. Cu194.

Kitchen, Finds Group 38 (see Figure 5.48)

Occupation of the Period Two kitchen, contexts [1777], [1833], [1904], [1910], [1913], [1915], [1930] and [1941].

CERAMICS

This comparatively small group is dominated by two vessels, a hand-finished sandy fabric cooking pot 520, which is residual from the 11th or 12th centuries, and a Ryedale ware bottle

THE ARCHAEOLOGY OF THE INNER COURT

Table 5.17 Finds Group 38: Ceramics

Fabric	Sherds	Vessels					
		Total vessels	Bottle	Cooking pot	Jar	Jug	Posset pot
Brandsby type	1	1	0	1	0	0	0
Cistercian copy	1	1	0	0	0	0	1
Early medieval Sandy	4	1	0	1	0	0	0
Gritty	16	12	0	9	0	3	0
Post-medieval Sandy	2	2	0	0	2	0	0
Ryedale	23	5	1	0	0	4	0

521. In many ways more interesting, however, is the Cistercian ware copy posset pot sherd 523, which, coming from a 15th-century group, is a particularly early example (Table 5.17).

520. Early medieval Sandy ware fabric cooking pot. Orange-brown to brown outer surface, orange core and dull orange inner surface. Coil-built and hand-finished. Outer surface probably burnt, while the inner rim face has a sooted 'tide-mark' between 10 and 15 mm below the top; below that mark the inner surface is unburnt – indications, perhaps, of some sort of lid constraining any burning?

521. Ryedale ware bottle. Light orange outer surface, blue-grey core and pale to whitish-orange inner surface. Light olive-green glaze to mid-body.

522. Cistercian ware copy cup or posset pot sherd. Bright brownish glaze over a thick vermilion core. Thin trails of white clay decoration appearing a bright yellow under glaze.

SMALL FINDS

523. Knife. Fe. Blade L: 270 mm; W: 60 mm; Th: 8 mm, edge and back curve to meet, back slightly overhanging blade. Whittle tang broken, square section W: 18 mm. Find no. Fe1582.

Period Three (see Figure 5.49)

The Kitchen Range

In Period Three the ground floor of the kitchen range was divided into two rooms (Rooms I and II) by the insertion of a cross-wall, [1446], the masonry of which was set in pink mortar. Associated with this was the excavation of the western 9.25 m of the building down to just above the level of the floors of the underlying Period One structure. The eastern extent of this excavation, [1789], survived, cut from the level of the last Period Two red clay floor, [1879]. Wall [1446] was constructed in this cut on two courses of undressed and unmortared footings, [1743]. At the centre of the wall was a square opening, [1748], which was part of the original construction.

ROOM I

To the west of wall [1446] a new floor of yellow-brown plastic clay, [1412], was laid, and the cill of doorway [2031] in the north wall was cut down to the level of the new floor, which appears to have been set at the level of the floor in the guest-house kitchen.

Figure 5.49 The Period Three kitchen as excavated.

In the western half of the room relevelling during the Bell reconstruction had destroyed most archaeological deposits and in places cut down below the foundation level of the Period Two range. Only a small area of floor was available for excavation in the south-east corner of the room. Here it was found to seal the construction of a stone-lined drain, [1479], that ran westwards from the square aperture at the centre of wall [1446]. This drain appears to have functioned as an open gutter, as there was no evidence that capstones were ever provided. The base of the drain comprised a series of six squared blocks, [*1901*], above which was a deposit of primary grey-brown sandy silt, [*1867*].

Constructed from the surface of floor [1412] or the underlying cut [1987] (the relationship had been destroyed by under-building of the foundations in concrete in 1900–1) was Hope's great 'brewhouse' chimney (see Chapter 6 for a full structural analysis). A second archway was inserted into the west wall of the room to enable its western hearth to be accessed from the guest-house kitchen to the south, and the original opening was blocked. Its masonry was bonded with pink mortar where it had not been substantially repointed in 1900–1. The height of the arched openings in the north wall of the chimney implies that the upper floor over Room I was removed. Additionally, no floor joist sockets were provided in the masonry of the chimney. As there was no direct communication with Room II, to the east, it would appear that Room I serviced the guest house rather than the great cloister, suggesting a formal segregation of diet. A second feature, inserted in the north wall of the building and originally recorded by Hope (Hope 1905, 280) as a circular vat, was identified as work of this period by its use of pink mortar. No occupation deposits had survived Hope's excavation and parts of the structure lay under a building of 1900–1 and were not available for re-excavation. Hope had identified the building as a circular buttressed structure (see Figure 5.40), but re-excavation in 1992 demonstrated that the structure was in fact three-sided externally and buttressed at the angles, but sub-circular within. It retained a rough masonry surface of sandstone rubble bonded with yellow sand, [1790]. This butted against the curving inner face of Hope's structure and neither it nor the inner wall face showed any sign of burning or heat-scorching. The surface was too rough to have functioned as a floor, and the use of the structure cannot be determined from the small area re-excavated. It was, however, substantial, and the buttresses were clearly an addition to the primary structure, as they were straight-jointed to the external angles and only bastard-bonded above plinth level. Whatever function this feature served, it appears to have been two-storeyed.

Room II

To the east of wall [1446] construction cut [*1987*] was filled with a mixture of red-brown clay and sandstone rubble to the level of the latest Period Two floor. Room II was then provided with a new clay floor, [1451], which sealed both all earlier deposits and the construction of the Period Three cross-wall. A centrally placed stone tank, [1816], was incorporated within this floor and was contemporary with it. Originally, the stone lining had projected above the surface of the floor but it had been roughly dressed back to floor level in Period Four. Beneath this new floor was the clay-lined cut for a lead water pipe, [1600], which entered the room in a cut below the cill of doorway [2030] and exited through a roughly cut hole, [1487], in the south wall, [1472]. This pipe continued the Period Three line that began in the cellars to the north of the south-west cloister range, passed through the west wall of that range and continued across the pentice between that range and the kitchen range, a realignment of the Period Two water supply to the kitchens and guest house. A shallow robber trench, [1591], truncated by the 1957 sewer trench, suggests a branch pipe to feed a tap on the east side of the dividing wall [1446] at the point where drain [1749] passed through the wall. Although the floor in this area had been destroyed by a French drain in 1900–1, there was no evidence to suggest that the drain had extended eastwards into Room II, although there may well have been a gulley against the wall to take waste from this tap.

The oven base, now in the angle of walls [1446] and [1355b], was extended by the widening of walls [1664] and [1674], both set in pink mortar. A skim of white mortar, [1615], to the east of this enlarged platform ran up to the outer face of the widening [1674] and sealed

THE ARCHAEOLOGY OF THE INNER COURT

the mortar surface [1873] that was associated with the earlier structure. This deposit was truncated by the 1957 sewer trench and could not be directly related to the Period Three floor in the remainder of Room II.

Some 34 stakeholes were recorded along the southern margin of clay floor [1451], together with a single post setting, [1636]. A small cut to its north might have been a second post setting, but is more likely to have been one or more damaged stakeholes. These settings made no obvious pattern. To the west, and separated from the stakeholes, was the base of an oven, [1465], cut into the surface of floor [1451]. It was largely destroyed by a sub-square pit, [1637], within this phase, but retained some of its fill, a large quantity of fish bones mixed with ash. It was also cut by a post setting, [1438]. Three stones placed in line were set into the surface of floor [1451], and their alignment, if continued to the north, would have coincided with the west side of tank [1816] (which shared their axis) and the now-missing western internal splay of door [2030] in the north wall. A large excavation trench attributed to Hope and the 1957 sewer trench had removed the remainder of what must have been the cill for a timber partition that extended to within 2 m of the south wall. Its alignment, out of square with the building, is curious.

A substantial paved hearth was provided against the centre of the east wall, cut into clay floor [1451] and perpetuating the location of the Period Two hearth in this room (see Figure 5.50). It was relined on at least two occasions. The earliest hearth consisted of stones set in mortar [1893] at its south end and stones and brick laid in mortar [1892] at its north end, possibly a repair. Three depressions in the stone that formed the south-west angle of the hearth seem to have been caused by the constant abrasion of a metal tripod vessel. Although the hearth was bisected by a 1900–1 service trench and a power cable of the same date, sufficient remained to show that it was L-shaped in plan. There was no evidence to suggest how a canopy or smoke-hood was supported. The hearth was resurfaced with buff mortar and rubble [*1893/1931*] (not shown on Figure 5.49) and a fireback, [*1732*], bedded onto mortared rubble, [*1931*], within Period Three – clear evidence that it was heavily used. A thick spread of ash and charcoal associated with this hearth covered most of floor [1451] in the eastern half of the room, extending as far west as the suggested partition. A new floor surface [*1734*] of red clay at the east end of Room II was associated with the latest relining of the hearth. Sealing the ashy spread [1508], it lapped the edges of the latest hearth and was cut by three postholes, [1752], [1753] and [1775], that formed a line along the east wall face.

Figure 5.50 The hearth of the Period Three kitchen, seen from the north. The hollows worn by a metal tripod cauldron can be seen at its south-west corner (T. Gledhill).

The Southern Outshut

No modifications of Room III were identified, but given the slight nature of surviving deposits this is hardly surprising.

In Room IV substantial alterations were made. First, a chimney stack, [1378], was built against the south face of wall [1472], the masonry of both its footings and superstructure being set in the pink mortar typical of Period Three work. This chimney did not serve the eastern room, and must be associated with an upper floor over Room II in the kitchen range, as the outshut was obviously only of a single storey. Its footings were set in a construction trench, [*1921*], which was cut from the level of the later Period Two floor and backfilled with pink mortar droppings. The upper fill of the construction trench was filled with stone rubble, [1714], that had been disturbed when the Period Two floor surface had been dug out to be replaced by a new floor of yellow clay, [1820] and [1857], that convincingly sealed the masonry of the chimney breast. This new floor extended up to the south wall, [1424], of the room, and was also recorded [1860] against the extended east wall, where it had been substantially removed by one of Hope's trenches in 1900. Two stakeholes, [1885a] and [1885b], in the surface of the floor appear to have marked out a partition, [1870], a single course high and set onto the floor surface 0.72 m north of wall [1424]. Seventeenth-century and modern disturbances had removed both ends of the cill wall, which mirrored the arrangements of the primary Period Two partition on this line. To its north, a further floor surface of brown clay, [1869], was laid, its surface lapping over the edge of cill wall [1870] and defining the northern edge of the cill beam it carried.

Within the yard to the south, a new stair was provided to the first-floor chambers above the guest-house kitchen. Two cill walls, [1384] and [1394], were built parallel to the south wall of the outshut, [1393]. The northern wall, [1394], which survived to a height of two courses, was faced on its south side only and occupied a construction trench, [1612], cut into the pre-existing yard surface from the southeast corner of the Period Two latrine tower to the south-west corner of buttress [1530]. Twentieth-century intrusions having destroyed the western 1.5 m of wall [1394] completely, the junction at its west end with the latrine tower existed only in the form of the wall's insertion scar. The space between this wall and wall [1393] was filled with rubble and white mortar, [1471], which also filled construction trench [1612]. Hope's excavation had truncated this layer, which probably extended originally to the full height of wall [1394]. Next, a dump of red clay, [1756], was laid against the south face of the wall, and this in turn was cut by the construction trench [1776] of wall [1384], which was constructed from the surface of the Period Two yard. It had originally butted against the east wall of the guest house, where the sockets of cill beam and wall plate, each 0.20 m², remained of the timber-framed wall it had carried. The western 2 m of the wall had been destroyed by 20th-century intrusions, and

Figure 5.51 Stair base [1395] seen from the west. The socket for the timber stair string is on the left (J. Hall).

only a single course of neatly dressed ashlar blocks remained at its eastern end of the three courses that the cill wall would originally have comprised. Like wall [1394], it was bonded with white mortar rather than the usual pink mix of Period Three and this also filled its construction trench. Between the two walls were the lowest two ashlar risers of a stair [1395 and 1396] backed by a mass of rubble, [1532] (see Figure 5.51). The second riser was of double depth, and at its north end was the socket for the string of a timber staircase. A second socketed stone, presumably from the south end of the second riser, was found loose. This stair rose to a landing outside the first-floor door in the guest-house range that was marked by a series of heavily weathered joist-sockets set just above the wall-plate level of wall [1384], suggesting a jettied upper storey. At the foot of the stair was a projecting porch represented by its west [1385], south [1836] and east [1618] cill walls. One of the blocks used in wall [1385] had a mason's mark of type C24. The area enclosed had originally been paved and slight remains of the stone flagging,

THE ARCHAEOLOGY OF THE INNER COURT

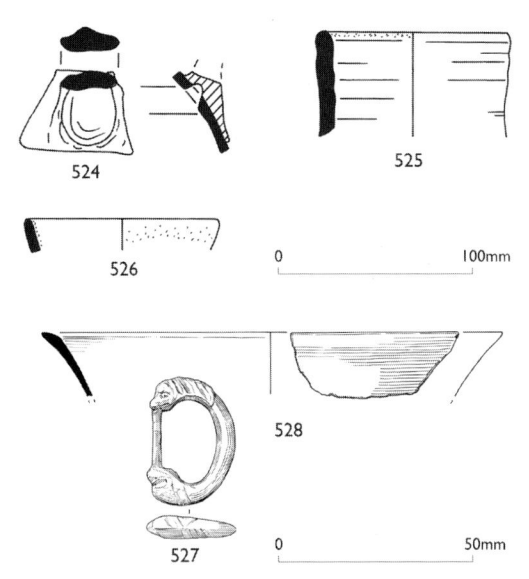

Figure 5.52 Finds Group 39 from the kitchen (pottery 1:4; copper alloy 1:2).

[1593], remained at the foot of the stair (see Figure 5.51). The remainder had been removed by Hope's workmen. They had also lifted some of the porch walling, which had been reset on a layer of topsoil.

To the south of the porch and cill wall [1384] the yard had been relevelled with a spread of clay, rubble and mortar [1413] and [1507] that was almost certainly the bedding for the paved surface that Hope recorded in this area (Hope 1905, 276), but which no longer survived. Slight traces of further yellow clay bedding, [1835], remained to the east of the porch on the edge of the tank, [1778], which remained open throughout this period.

The Eastern Pentice
The building in the angle between the south-west cloister range and the kitchen cross-wing was modified by the addition of an ashlar cill wall, [1358], on its south side. Wall [1358] was bedded on a skim of pink mortar set on the surface of the Period Two floor [1417]. This wall was 0.20 m wide and the Period Two east wall of the building was cut back by 40 mm on its inner face to reduce its thickness to 0.30 m. A return for wall [1358] was left on the southernmost block of wall [1356]. A doorway some 1.12 m wide was provided at the west end of wall [1358]. Within the room, a large stylobate block, [930], was set centrally in the floor at the north end of the room (see Figure 5.45) in a deep construction pit, [1027]. A slot in its upper surface 0.26 m wide and 50 mm deep evidenced a post of that scantling, perhaps the newel post for a stair to the upper floor of the cross-wing to the west. Unfortunately, Hope was fascinated by this post setting and his excavation destroyed any deposits associated with it in the northern half of the building. However, he had not penetrated significant levels in the southern half of the structure, where a floor, [1392], of mixed yellow and brown clay loam with spreads of burned stone and occupation debris apparently derived from the adjacent kitchen range survived, spreading out through the door in wall [1358]. Outside the building, a similar deposit, [1400] and [1497], and a spread of charcoal, [1533], built up throughout Period Three. These deposits contained Jetton 1.

Kitchen, Finds Group 39 (see Figure 5.52)
Period Three reconstruction and refitting of the kitchen and its offices from contexts [1412], [1451], [1541], [1756], [1820] and [1988].

CERAMICS
This is a small group that is contaminated by both a residual element, in the form of the usual fine Sandy ware and Gritty ware fabric, and an obviously intrusive 19th-century white earthenware sherd. The Ryedale ware cup rim is similar to, if slightly thicker than, the Type IV Cistercian ware cup rims and is a reminder that local potters were quick to try and emulate these new tableware forms (Table 5.18).

524. Brandsby type fabric jug. Brown outer surface, grey-black core and light orange inner surface. Rather corroded olive-green glaze that appears full except immediately under handle. Two lateral thumbings for upper handle attachment and one deep single thumbing for the lower. In each case the inner wall of the vessel has been pushed into the attachment and left untidied.
525. Ryedale ware jug. Blue-grey core and pale grey inner surface. Outer surface, to rim top, in a greenish-brown glaze.
526. Ryedale ware cup. Purplish (glaze margin) outer surface and light orange core. Bright olive-green glaze on upper, outer rim and on inner surface.

Table 5.18 Kitchen, Finds Group 39: Ceramics

Fabric	Sherds	Vessels				
		Total vessels	Cooking pot	Jar	Jug	Mug or cup
Brandsby type	2	2	0	0	2	0
Developed Humber	1	1	0	1	0	0
Gritty	1	1	1	0	0	0
Ryedale	7	7	1	1	4	1

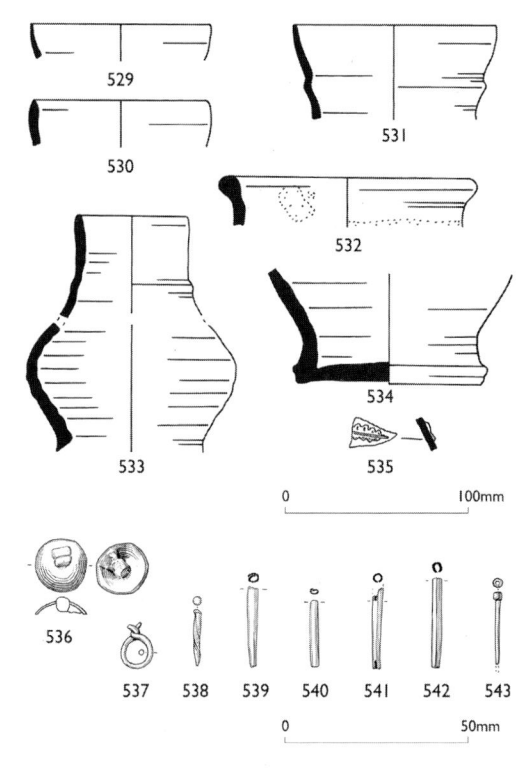

Figure 5.53 Finds Group 40 from the kitchen (pottery 1:4; copper alloy 1:2).

Ceramics

As the table below suggests, this is a badly mixed group containing both clearly residual and intrusive material, and it is difficult to isolate pottery that can, with any certainty, be regarded as contemporary with the Period Three occupation of this area. Most of the illustrated vessels could be contemporary, with the exception of the Cologne stoneware sherd with its applied leaf design, which must surely be intrusive. Certainly, the late 15th- or early 16th-century occurrence of Cistercian wares, and even Reversed Cistercian wares, is confirmed both from other areas of this site and from elsewhere in Yorkshire (Table 5.19).

The base of stoneware mug 534 has been polished, removing the rougher areas common on many of these vessels. Together with similar examples of such modification from vessels in Cell 11, this perhaps suggests the work of a single monk.

529. Cistercian ware. Bright blackish glaze over a dull reddish-purple fabric.
530. Cistercian ware. Metallic purple glaze over a dull reddish fabric.
531. Cistercian ware copy. Rich, glossy dark brown glaze over a dull reddish fabric.
532. Low Countries Redware tripod pipkin. Orange-red surfaces and orange core. Bright orange glaze, with a tendency to splash on margins. Traces of applied handle.
533. Raeren stoneware mug. Bright silver-grey outer surface turning a speckled brown in places, grey core and slightly lustrous chocolate-brown inner surface.
534. Raeren stoneware mug base. Chocolate-brown outer surface turning a silver grey in places, grey core and a bright silver-grey inner surface glaze. The base is complete and has been ground

Glazing crack through rim, through which the glaze has seeped.

Small Finds

527. Buckle. Cu. D-shaped frame H: 31 mm; W: 21 mm with integral bar. Frame is W: 4.5 mm (maximum) and each end has a stylised animal head with snout and grooves for eyes. The bar runs between the two chins and is L: 15 mm; D: 2 mm. Residual, 12th century. Find no. Cu196.
528. Rim of vessel. Cu cast. Probably from shallow bowl. D: 240 mm; Th: 2–4 mm. Find no. Cu197.

Kitchen, Finds Group 40 (see Figure 5.53)
Period Three occupation from the kitchen and its offices [1400], [1413], [1449], [1497], [1507], [1508], [1584] and [1867].

THE ARCHAEOLOGY OF THE INNER COURT

Table 5.19 Kitchen, Finds Group 40: Ceramics

| Fabric | Sherds | Vessels ||||||||
		Total vessels	Cooking pot	Jar	Jug	Mug or cup	Pancheon	Tripod pipkin	Other
Brandsby type	1	1	1	0	0	0	0	0	0
Cistercian	11	7	0	0	0	7	0	0	0
Cologne	1	1	0	0	0	1	0	0	0
Gritty	1	1	0	0	1	0	0	0	0
Hambleton	1	1	0	0	1	0	0	0	0
Humber	1	1	0	0	1	0	0	0	0
Langerwehe	1	1	0	0	0	1	0	0	0
Low Countries Red	1	1	0	0	0	0	0	1	0
Post-medieval Sandy	4	4	0	2	0	0	2	0	0
Raeren	8	5	0	0	0	5	0	0	0
Regional Stray	1	1	0	0	0	0	0	0	1
Reversed Cistercian	1	1	0	0	0	1	0	0	0
Ryedale	4	3	0	0	3	0	0	0	0

down (in fact, polished down) in similar fashion to several vessels from Cell 11.

535. Cologne stoneware mug. Chocolate-brown surfaces, slightly metallic, with pale grey stoneware core. Applied decoration, neatly fashioned.

SMALL FINDS

536. Rumbler bell. Cu. Top half of dome with remains of loop. D: 15 mm. Find no. Cu183.
537. Ring. Cu. Wire with single twist. Overall D: 8 mm, of wire 0.5 mm. Find no. Cu190.
538. Wire. Cu. L: 15 mm; W: 2 mm. Twisted and worked to a blunt point. Find no. Cu187.
539. Lace chape. Cu sheet. Edge to edge seam. Slight taper. L: 21 mm; D: 2–3 mm. Find no. Cu180.
540. Lace chape. Cu sheet. Edge to edge seam. L: 18 mm; D: 2 mm. Find no. Cu179.
541. Lace chape. Cu sheet. Edge to edge seam. Slight taper. L: 20 mm; D: 2 mm. Find no. Cu182.
542. Lace chape. Cu sheet. Edge to edge seam. L: 23 mm; D: 2 mm. Find no. Cu193.
543. Pin. Cu. Spiral-wound soldered head. Shank L: 18 mm; head D: 2 mm. Find no. Cu191.

Figure 5.54 The Period Four kitchen as excavated.

Period Four (see Figures 5.54 and 5.55)

Developments of Period Four were restricted to Room II, the north pentice and the east pentice. Elsewhere, Period Three represented the latest medieval development.

Figure 5.55 The Period Four kitchen and its offices as excavated, seen from the east (T. Gledhill).

The Kitchen Range

Room II

All of the Period Three fittings of the monks' kitchen were ruthlessly swept away and a new stone floor, [1429], was laid. This floor survived only in the northern half of the room and particularly in its north-east corner, and was made up largely of reused elements, many of which retained the pink mortar of Period Three or the off-white mortar of Period Two, laid in a grey-brown clay loam. In the southern half of the room the floor had been removed by Hope, whose excavation penetrated to the Period Three floor (see Figure 5.55). It is uncertain how far to the west the floor extended, because the north-west corner of Room II was modified during the phase. The surviving paving did, however, extend to the west of door [2030].

Placed centrally in this new floor was a substantial open hearth kerbed with massive chamfered blocks, [1410], which remained on the north and west sides. The south side was traceable only by its remaining foundations, all the kerb having been robbed. The eastern side of the kerb had been moved in the 17th century, though its original setting, [1626], was recovered by excavation and it is shown in its primary location in Figure 5.54. This feature was encountered by Hope, who excavated a deep square trench within it, removing most of the hearth itself. A small area of heavily burned paving, [1427], remained at the west end, suggesting that the hearth extended up to dividing wall [1446]. The hearth was not aligned on the building, its deflection to the south-east apparently being required to keep the access to door [2030] clear. To the north of the hearth and partly cut into the inner face of wall [1335b] was a small circular oven, [1615]. Only its floor of white mortar remained. At some point in its history the floor was relined with thin sandstone slabs, [1673]. This operation was contemporary with the construction of a localised widening, [1614], of wall [1355b], which reduced the oven in size. Along the widened wall, and incorporating this oven, was a low bench, [1428]. Part of the oven and the southern end of the bench were removed by the 1957 sewer trench, but the bench appears to have terminated against a low cill wall, [1659], socketed at either end for timber uprights. This feature, which stood on floor, [1429], was recorded by Hope and would have aligned with the western splay of door [2030]. The screen set on this cill wall would thus have

THE ARCHAEOLOGY OF THE INNER COURT

Table 5.20 Kitchen, Finds Group 41: Ceramics

Fabric	Sherds	Vessels					
		Total vessels	Cistern	Jug	Mug or cup	Pancheon	Vase
Langerwehe	1	1	0	0	1	0	0
Post-medieval Sandy	1	1	0	0	0	1	0
Raeren	1	1	0	0	1	0	0
Ryedale	5	4	1	3	0	0	0
Siegburg	3	1	0	0	1	0	0
South Netherlands Maiolica	1	1	0	0	0	0	1

kept draughts from the door away from the oven.

The Northern Pentice
The wider, western section of the pentice wall was dismantled to floor level and rebuilt. This rebuilding, [1586], incorporated the eavesdrip gulley outside the wall, which was packed with rubble and white mortar. The rebuilt wall was wider than the original structure, at 0.64 m, and incorporated the base of a stone tank, [1430]. Mortar on the inside of the tank demonstrated that it had been packed with rubble and had no function other than as a walling stone. Robbing had removed all but the lowest course of this new wall.

The Eastern Pentice
In the early 16th century a substantial fireplace, [913], was inserted in the north-east corner of the room, its hearth defined by a kerb, [911]. The fireback was in part the outer wall face of the south-west cloister range and, as the plinth course of the range's angle buttress was removed and reset in the hearth itself, the structure of that wall must have been altered. Post-Suppression robbing has unfortunately removed any further evidence of that modification and Hope had removed any occupation associated with the hearth.

To the south of the building, and alongside the Period Two pentice, a long, narrow structure was created that blocked the door in wall [1358]. Enclosed by walls [1379], [1380] and [1666], all 0.24 m thick, was a space 0.88 m wide that can only have contained a stair, as it had no floor. To the east garden soil, [1364], had built up throughout this period over a spread of broken roof slates, [1365], and mid-brown sandy loam, [1496].

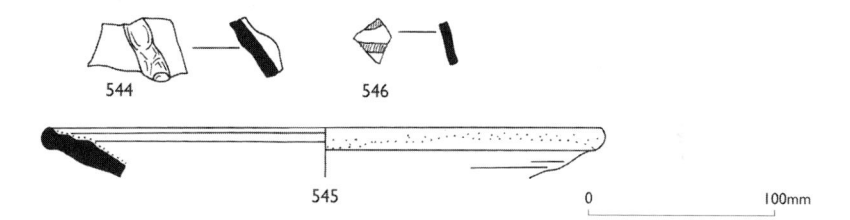

Kitchen, Finds Group 41 (see Figure 5.56)
Period Four construction in the kitchen area, contexts [1365], [1463], [1703], [1734], [1745], [1753] and [1826].

CERAMICS
This small group belongs to the Period Four construction work of the early 16th century (Table 5.20).

544. Ryedale ware jug/cistern. Blue-grey core and light brownish-orange inner surface. Brownish-olive glaze and thick crude applied thumbed strip.
545. Post-medieval Sandy ware fabric dish. Thin orange-purple outer surface skin and yellow-buff core. Brownish-olive glaze on inner surface.
546.. South Netherlands Maiolica vase/jar? Cream-coloured fabric. Outer surface white with dark blue painted bands under glaze. Inner surface white glaze with just a hint of purple.

Figure 5.56 Finds Group 41 from the kitchen (pottery 1:4).

Kitchen, Finds Group 42 (see Figure 5.57)
Period Four occupation of the kitchen area from contexts [1364], [1498] and [1575].

CERAMICS
This group reflects the final occupation deposits from the kitchen area from the decades of the 1520s to the 1540s. The dominating presence of the Post-medieval Sandy ware fabric surely

confirms its currency during the first half of the 16th century (Table 5.21).

547. Cistercian ware copy cup. Orange-brown glaze over a vermilion core. Applied pipeclay spots appearing lemon-yellow under glaze.
548. Post-medieval Sandy ware fabric cup. Pale grey fabric and bright olive-green glaze on both surfaces.
549. Post-medieval Sandy ware fabric jar. Pale orange surfaces and cream-buff core. Light olive glaze thinning extensively to a yellowish-orange, all heavily pocked.
550. Post-medieval Sandy ware fabric jar. Thin purple-brown outer surface, and pale orange core. Marginal (yellowish) traces of olive-green glaze. Traces of burning and sooting to outer surface.
551. Post-medieval Sandy ware fabric small flanged bowl. Light orange-yellow outer surface and core. Apple-green glaze on inner surface.

SMALL FINDS

552. Pan weight. Pb. D: 38 mm (maximum); Th: 4 mm. Unweighed Find no. Pb552.

The 17th Century and Later (see Figure 5.58)

As virtually no demolition deposits survived 17th-century disturbance or Hope's excavation of this area, it is impossible to say when the kitchen cross-wing was demolished to ground level or below. There are certain pointers, however, to suggest that the eastern part of the cross-wing and the southern outshut were demolished before 17th-century work began on the guest-house range, although the western half of the cross-wing was retained after that. The blocking of the door at the west end of the north wall would not have been necessary if the wall to its east had been demolished previously, and the kitchen chimney was retained intact together with the west wall of the wing, which still stands to above the springing of its gable. Wall [1446] was sealed only by the construction of a new yard wall in 1900–1 and was recorded by Hope (1905, plan) in a better-preserved state than it was found on re-excavation. The south wall of the cross-wing, [1346], was sealed only by topsoil and remained to a maximum height of two courses above foundation level,

Figure 5.57 Finds Group 42 from the kitchen (pottery 1:4; lead 1:2).

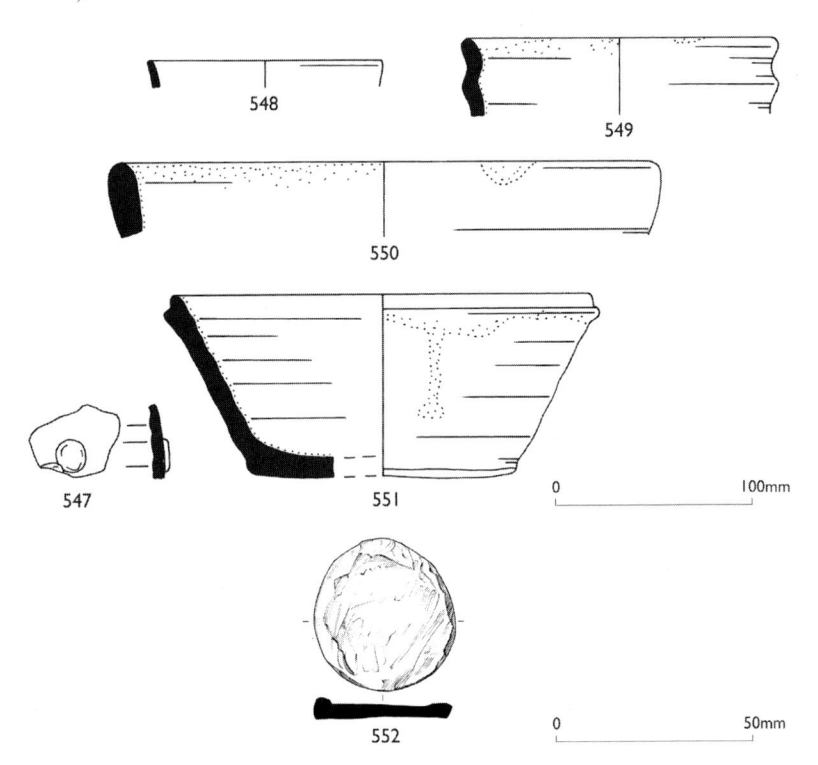

Table 5.21 Kitchen, Finds Group 42: Ceramics

Fabric	Sherds	Vessels					
		Total vessels	Jar	Jug	Mug or cup	Pancheon	Other
Cistercian	2	2	0	0	2	0	0
Cistercian copy	1	1	0	0	1	0	0
Developed Humber	1	1	1	0	0	0	0
Langerwehe	1	1	0	0	1	0	0
Post-medieval Sandy	22	18	5	0	1	7	5
Ryedale	2	2	0	2	0	0	0
Siegburg	2	2	0	0	2	0	0

THE ARCHAEOLOGY OF THE INNER COURT

although this wall was thoroughly robbed down to its footings to the east of wall [1446]. In comparison, demolition deposits [*1604*], [*1603*] and [*1642*] did survive around and within the latrine tower against the east wall of the guest-house range, suggesting that it was at least partially demolished at the Suppression, and its lower filling contained a large amount of coloured and enamelled glass that was presumably derived from the windows of other buildings, the most likely contender being the church.

Kitchen, Finds Group 43 (see Figure 5.59)
Post-Suppression robbing of the kitchen area from contexts 1382, 1391, 1432, 1433, 1443, 1455, 1456, 1483, 1494, 1496, 1513, 1519, 1555, 1632, 1650, 1691, 1780 and 1801.

CERAMICS
A widely mixed group of material typical of demolition deposits. The comparatively large sherds of residual gritty fabric, as seen in illustrations 553 and 554, for example, reflect the degree of robbing that would seem to have disturbed the underlying pre-priory deposits (Table 5.22).

553. Gritty ware/fine Sandy ware cooking pot. Light yellowish surfaces and pale blue core.
554. Gritty ware fabric bowl. Pale orange-pink surfaces and orange core. Burnt and sooted outer surface.
555. Gritty ware/Brandsby type fabric jug. Hard orange gritty fabric of rough texture. Yellowish-green glaze, some darker mottling and pock-marking. Traces of a white pipeclay slip under glaze and also used for applied strip.

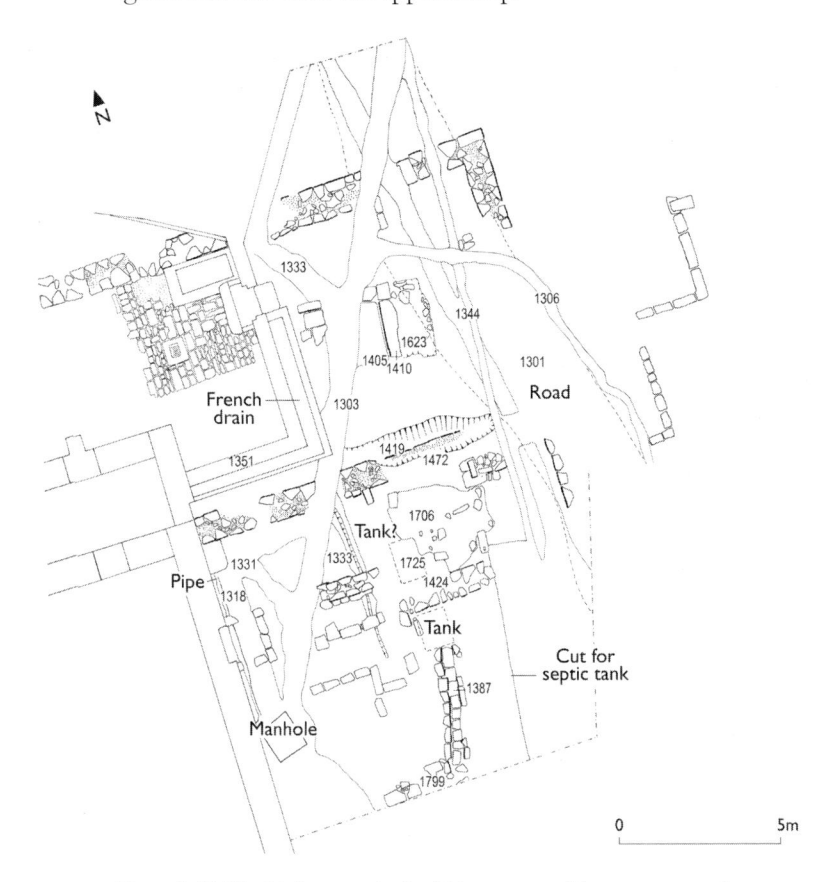

Figure 5.58 The kitchen area in the 17th century and later as excavated.

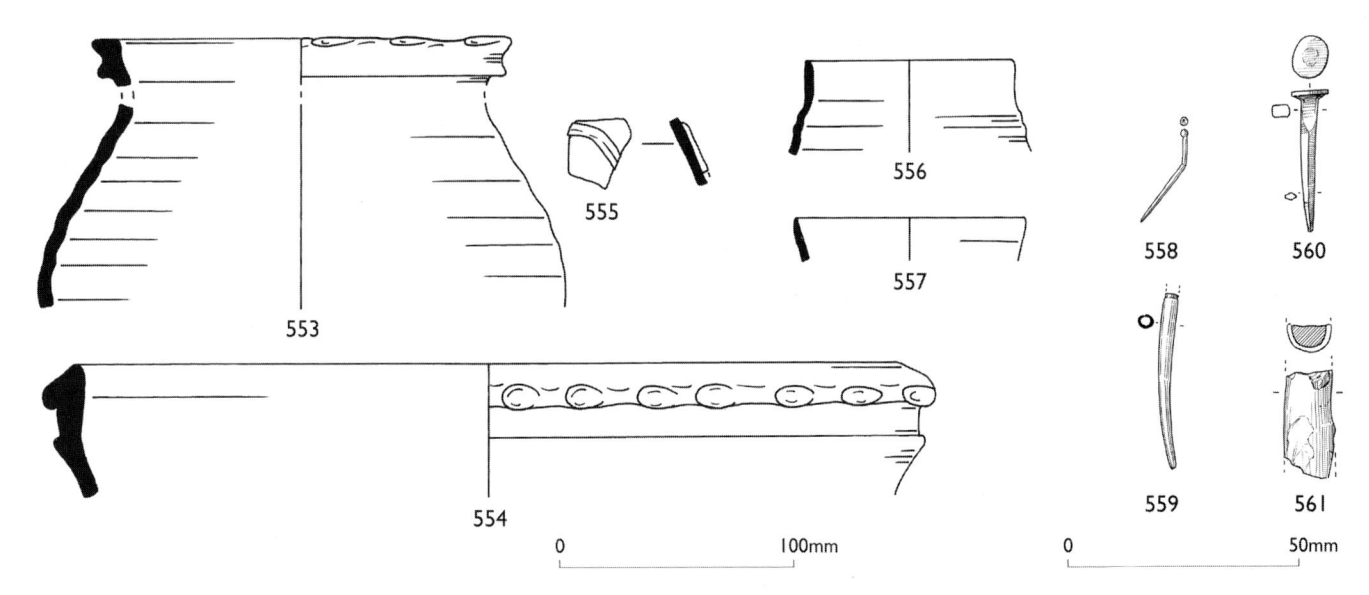

Figure 5.59 Finds Group 43 from the kitchen (pottery 1:4; copper alloy 1:2; lead 1:2).

Table 5.22 Kitchen, Finds Group 43: Ceramics

Fabric	Sherds	Vessels									
		Total vessels	Bowl	Cistern	Cooking pot	Jar	Jug	Lid	Mug or cup	Pancheon	Other
Brandsby type	6	6	1	0	2	0	3	0	0	0	0
Cistercian	9	5	0	0	0	0	0	1	4	0	0
Cistercian copy	1	1	0	0	0	0	0	0	1	0	0
Developed Humber	1	1	0	0	0	0	1	0	0	0	0
Gritty	2	2	0	0	2	0	0	0	0	0	0
Hambleton	1	1	0	1	0	0	0	0	0	0	0
Langerwehe	2	2	0	0	0	0	0	0	2	0	0
Post-medieval Sandy	10	7	0	1	0	2	0	0	0	3	1
Raeren	1	1	0	0	0	0	0	0	1	0	0
Ryedale	13	10	0	0	0	0	9	0	0	1	0
Siegburg	2	2	0	0	0	0	0	0	2	0	0

556. Cistercian ware copy cup. Brownish-purple glaze and orange fabric.
557. Cistercian ware copy cup. Bright dark orange-brown glaze over a reddish-purple fabric.

SMALL FINDS

558 Pin. Cu. Solid head. Shank L: 13 mm; head D: 1 mm. Find no. Cu160.
559. Lace chape. Cu sheet. Edge to edge seam. Slight taper. L: 36 mm; D: 1.5–3 mm. Fibre remains inside. Find no. Cu175.
560. Nail. Cu. L: 29 mm. Circular head with casting lines below D: 8 mm. Find no. Cu169.
561. Tube fragment. Cu. Semicircular piece. L: 22 mm; W: 12 mm (maximum). Find no. Cu168.

Seventeenth-century Works in the Area of the Kitchen and its Offices

Although the eastern part of the cross-wing, the southern outshut and the yard to its south had all been cleared before the guest-house range was remodelled in 1654, the builders of that date were certainly aware of the layout of the demolished building, suggesting that demolition was fairly recent or that the walls still remained above ground level. In particular, a large but shallow rectangular pit, [1599]/[1641], was excavated in the centre of Room IV in the southern outshut, respecting all its walls. This pit was used to mix mortar for the guest-house conversion, and its base retained the remains of the last mixes, [1706], a hard light brown mortar that was identical to the mortar used in Lascelles' building work, containing fragments of brick, which can also be matched in mid-17th-century work in the guest-house range. A square ghosting of 0.7 m side, [1725], remained in the mortar on the floor of the pit in the south-west angle of the room where Hope recorded a tank (see Figure 5.40), which was removed after his excavation. It had been placed there prior to the mortar mixing and perhaps related to the builders' water supply. On completion of the building work the pit was backfilled, first with a deposit of yellow/brown clay, broken bricks, cobbles and waste mortar, [1692], and then with a levelling of brown loam, [1611], and red-brown silt and sand [1585].

Apparently related to this work was the provision of a tank immediately to the south of that set in the ghosting [1725] and separated from it only by the lowest courses of wall [1424], the south wall of the outshut and a substantial drain, [1387], that ran away to the south across the yard and over the levelled remains of its south wall, [1799]. Both these features were recorded by Hope (see Figure 5.40), but only the drain remained. It had not been backfilled after excavation in

Table 5.23 Kitchen, Finds Group 44: Ceramics

Fabric	Sherds	Vessels						
		Total vessels	Cooking pot	Jar	Jug	Mug or cup	Pancheon	Other
Brandsby type	3	2	2	0	0	0	0	0
Cistercian	3	2	0	0	0	2	0	0
Developed Humber	1	1	0	0	0	0	0	1
Gritty	4	4	1	0	3	0	0	0
Late Gritty	1	1	0	0	1	0	0	0
Post-medieval Sandy	2	2	0	0	0	0	2	0
Ryedale	4	4	0	0	4	0	0	0

1900, and had suffered from gardening activity and the dumping of loose masonry before re-excavation in 1991. A degree of stratification survived sufficient to demonstrate that the construction of the drain and its associated tank sealed the backfilling of the robber trench [1535] of wall [1424], the south wall of the outshut, which had very clearly been removed before the 17th-century building work began. Drain [1387] ran over the levelled remains of wall [1799], although that precise relationship was not examined. The drain itself occupied a cut, [1479], in the medieval yard surface, which was too deep simply to contain the drain and was possibly an earlier gulley. This was packed with mixed red and green clay, [1480], into which a shallow construction trench, [1469], was cut. The stone-lined drain was then built into this feature using reset medieval masonry throughout. The east side of the drain incorporated a section of pipe channel identical to those recovered from the centre of the great cloister (see Chapter 4 and Figure 4.97, 23 and 24). Everything above the construction level of the drain had been removed, either during Hope's excavation or during the subsequent building campaign.

Within Room II, at the east end of the medieval kitchen cross-wing, 17th-century interference within the demolished building was curiously restricted to a reduction in the size of the central hearth. The eastern kerb [1410] of the hearth was carefully removed from its original bedding and moved 1 m to the west. The resulting hole was then filled with dark brown loam, [1623], incorporating a number of reused paving slabs and large blocks of rubble stone. The purpose of this alteration was not obvious.

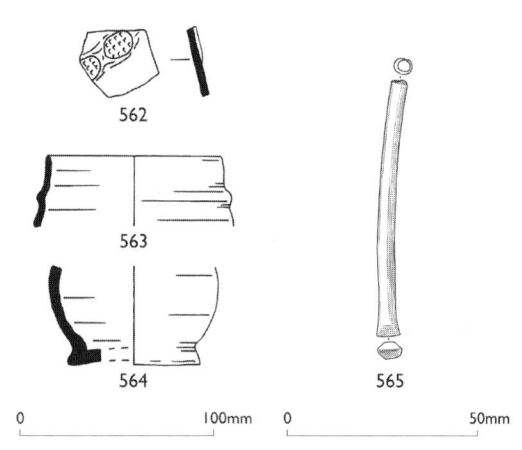

Figure 5.60 Finds Group 44 from the kitchen (pottery 1:4; copper alloy 1:2).

Kitchen, Finds Group 44 (see Figure 5.60)
Building activities of 1654 associated with the construction of the Lascelles' house, contexts [1442], [1480], [1535], [1563], [1585] and [1611].

CERAMICS
A group from contexts associated with the 17th-century Lascelles' building work, although pottery diagnostic to that period was hard to detect (Table 5.23).

562. Ryedale ware jug. Pale blue-grey core, corroded greenish glaze on both surfaces. May have been a cistern, as there are traces of applied horizontal strips with stamped design.
563. Cistercian ware cup. Metallic purple glaze and dull reddish-purple core.
564. Cistercian ware cup. Bright brownish-black glaze over a dull purplish fabric. Glaze down to basal angle.

Small Finds

565. Tube. Tinned Cu. Edge to edge seam. L: 65 mm; D: 4 mm. ?Modern. Find no. Cu187.

Hope's Excavation and the Rebuilding of 1900–1 (see Figure 5.58)

After the completion of mid-17th-century building work a road surface, [1301], was laid across the eastern part of the excavated area, covering the eastern pentice, the north-east corner of the cross-wing and a substantial part of the northern pentice. Made up substantially of demolition material, it remained in use well into the present century, being resurfaced on a number of occasions and its deep ruts packed with both rubble and broken bricks. Its surface included the reduced north-east corner of the cross-wing, which remained visible at the time of excavation. This service road appears to be associated with the construction of a small building against the eastern precinct wall, built apparently in the 18th century.

The next event to be recorded in the archaeological record was the excavation of the area by Hope in 1900. He appears to have begun by trenching along the south wall, [1472], of the cross-wing, from the 'brewhouse' chimney to the western margin of the track, and the base of a shallow excavation trench, [1419], remained to the north of the wall. As the north-east corner of the building was visible in the metalling of the track he had no need to locate the north or east walls by trenching, and his next operation was to strip the eastern room of the cross-wing to its latest floor level or below; in doing so he cut into the trackway that sealed the north-east corner of the room. To the east and north of the cross-wing he appears to have been content simply to remove topsoil and demolition deposits to reveal the east and north pentices, and his only deep excavation was around the post-base in the eastern pentice. Within the kitchen he was similarly fascinated by the kerbing for the Period Four hearth. A square trench, [1405], was sunk through this feature to a depth of at least 1.2 m. It was not fully re-excavated in 1992, but was cut well into natural red clay. Visible in its south section, but not recorded by Hope, was the sequence of floors and fish-bone deposits that indicated the archaeological importance of the building.

To the south of the cross-wing and east of the guest house, Hope stripped a large area down to the levels of the latest floors and yard surfaces, removing all but the last vestiges of any Period Four occupation, but redepositing some of it with his later backfill. His only deep excavation was within the porch at the foot of the stair to the first floor at the north end of the guest-house range.

The next event was the reconstruction and extension of the guest-house range by Ambrose Poynter in 1900–1 for Sir Lowthian Bell. It is clear that this work was carried out before the excavated building was backfilled and that there was a deliberate attempt to cause as little damage as possible to the medieval buildings. The west end of the cross-wing was retained to form a boiler house 3.3 m wide for the new house. The floor of this new room was dug out to a depth of 1.2 m, the medieval masonry being underbuilt in brick, resulting in the removal of all archaeological deposits from the west part of Room I. A door was then forced through the north wall at its west end to provide access to a coal store that contained the remains of Hope's 'oven', [1790]. The remainder of Room I was taken up by a walled yard that contained servants' lavatories and stores. The stone surface of the yard was not lifted, but was seen to lie directly over the Period Three floor of the room. On the south side of the room the kitchen chimney was underbuilt with a new concrete foundation. Wall [1446], which separated Room I from Room II, was reduced in height and a new wall, [1351], was built directly above it. This wall returned to the west against the kitchen chimney, some 1 m to the north of the south wall of the cross-wing. Outside this wall (which was demolished to two courses of its base before excavation to provide stone for the reconstruction of Cell 8) was a brick and cement-lined French drain that cut through the west end of wall [1446] and divorced it from all medieval stratification in Room II. A land drain, [1518], ran from the south-east corner of this drain to discharge in the hole that Hope had created by his excavation of the porch at the base of the stair to the upper floor of the guest-house range.

Contemporary with the construction of this walled yard was the insertion of a ceramic drainpipe that ran from a drain at the centre of the yard along the east side of the guest house to a manhole at the south end of the excavated area. This drain, which cut through the remains

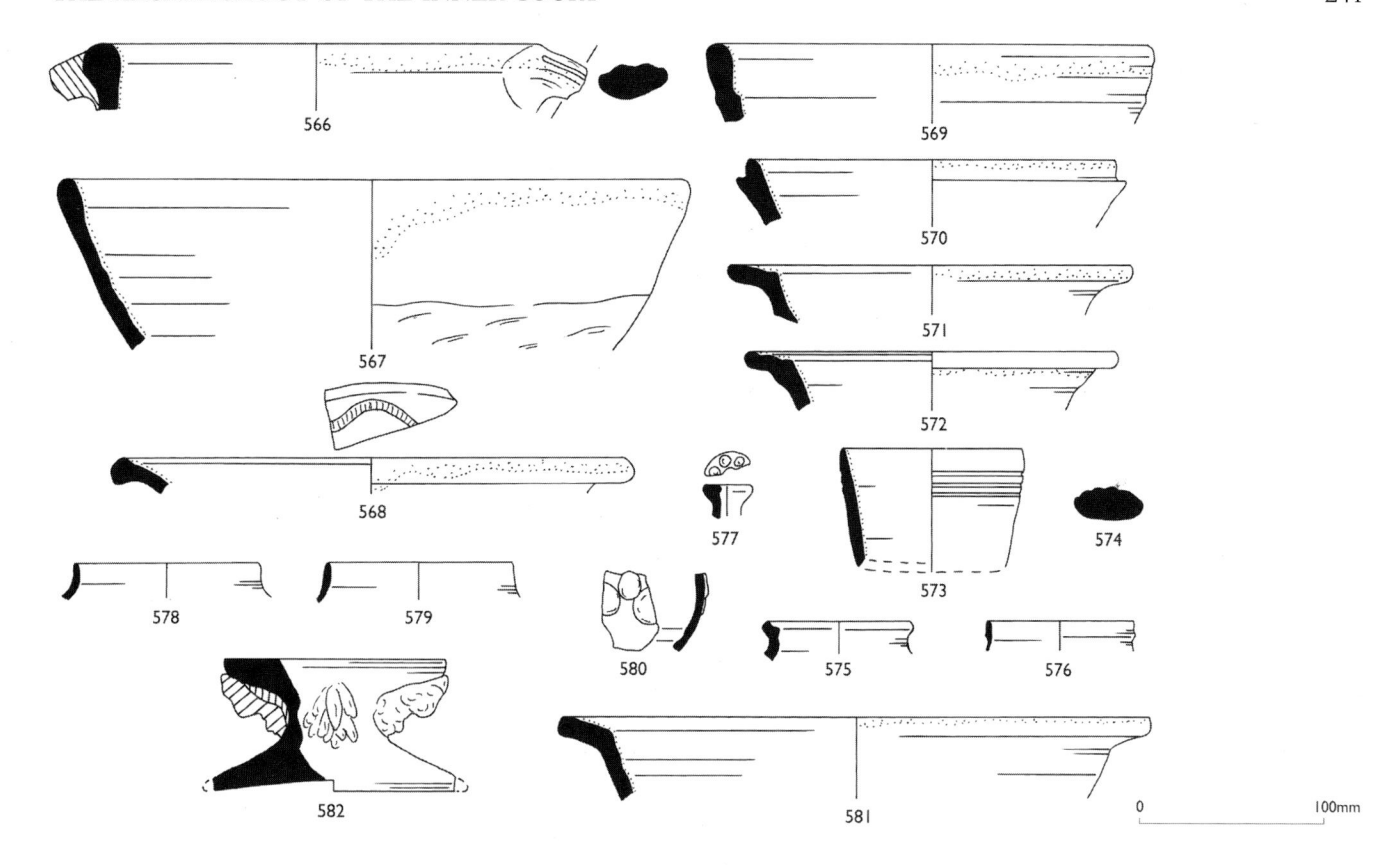

THE ARCHAEOLOGY OF THE INNER COURT

Figure 5.61 Finds Group 45 from the kitchen (pottery 1:4).

of the latrine tower, served a downpipe on the east wall of the guest house. Inserted in a parallel trench was a lead water pipe, protected by wooden boards on either side. Both passed below the south wall of the cross-wing.

Also contemporary with the Bell-period reconstruction was the provision of a large concrete septic tank at the south-east corner of the excavated area. This was not re-excavated, but a sewer was recorded passing through door [2030] in the north wall of the kitchen and out below the south wall of the room to this tank. Cutting its fill was a cable trench, [1344], that cut the walls of the cross-wing. The damage this trench had caused to the structure indicates that it was dug long after Hope's excavation had been backfilled. It was in its turn cut by service trenches dug by the Ministry of Works in 1957.

The latest features were well documented: the insertion of a sewer, [1303], by the Ministry of Works, which entered the cross-wing through doorway [2030], removing its west jamb, and exited through the south wall, [1346], with spurs to gulleys [1331] and [1333] along its length. It ended at the Bell-period manhole at the south-west corner of the excavated area and was capped with concrete throughout its length. It had caused a great deal of damage, and was not planned to avoid parts of the building that Hope had demonstrated survived well above floor level. Further minor damage was caused by the laying of alkathene water pipes, [1306], in the 1980s.

Kitchen, Finds Group 45

Unstratified material from the kitchen area from contexts [1300], [1302], [1304], [1309], [1312], [1317], [1320], [1324], [1334], [1339], [1342], [1353], [1361], [1362], [1363], [1366], [1370], [1372], [1373], [1375], [1390], [1398], [1399], [1401], [1405], [1406], [1409], [1415], [1418], [1435], [1438], [1439], [1462], [1515], [1516], [1558], [1567], [1730], [1764], [1772], [1788], [1840] and [1865].

CERAMICS (SEE FIGURE 5.61)

Pottery from unstratified and unphased contexts whose sherds reflect the full range of pottery from the site. Illustrated vessels have been chosen for their intrinsic interest and to more widely reflect the range of forms in the Post-medieval Sandy ware fabric that occurred from the site. The terracotta tazza stand, 582, is probably of 19th-century date and a form of garden ornament (Table 5.24).

Table 5.24 Kitchen, Finds Group 45: Ceramics

Fabric	Sherds	Total vessels	Cistern	Cooking pot	Jar	Jug	Mug or cup	Pancheon	Tripod pipkin	Other
Brandsby type	14	12	0	5	0	6	0	0	1	0
Cistercian	13	12	0	0	0	0	10	0	0	2
Cistercian copy	3	2	0	0	0	0	2	0	0	0
Gritty	15	13	0	8	0	3	0	0	0	2
Hambleton	1	1	0	0	0	1	0	0	0	0
Humber	2	2	0	0	0	2	0	0	0	0
Langerwehe	3	2	0	0	0	0	2	0	0	0
Late Cistercian	3	2	0	0	0	0	2	0	0	0
Late Gritty	2	2	0	0	0	2	0	0	0	0
Low Countries Red	1	1	0	0	0	0	0	0	1	0
Post-medieval Orange	3	3	0	0	2	0	0	1	0	0
Post-medieval Sandy	54	45	1	0	14	4	0	15	1	10
Raeren	2	2	0	0	0	0	2	0	0	0
Ryedale	57	30	2	0	0	27	0	0	0	1
Siegburg	2	1	0	0	0	0	1	0	0	0
Tudor Green	1	1	0	0	0	0	1	0	0	0

566. Post-medieval Sandy ware fabric large handled jar. Orange outer surface, turning purplish towards glaze margin. Orange core turning lighter at margins. Brownish olive-green glaze, becoming more orangish where the glaze thins.

567. Post-medieval Sandy ware fabric bowl. Purplish outer surface skin, orange/blue-grey core. Bright olive-green glaze on inner surface, extending over top of outer surface.

568. Post-medieval Sandy ware fabric slip-decorated dish. Dull orange/purplish outer surface, light orange core. Olive-green glaze with white pipeclay wavy band appearing a dull greenish-yellow under glaze. Heavily burnt and sooted on the outer surface under the rim, inner surface glaze heat crazed.

569. Post-medieval Sandy ware fabric jar. Pale orange outer surface and blue-grey core. Consistently coloured apple-green glaze with some light pocking in places. Traces of a rim handle.

570. Post-medieval Sandy ware fabric, flanged bowl. Grey-buff surfaces and orange-buff core. Yellowish-olive developed splashed glaze on inner surface, with a worn band about 8 mm wide around inner face of rim where glaze is missing, which might just represent the presence of a lid. Outer surface heavily burnt and sooted.

571. Post-medieval Sandy ware fabric bowl. Pale orange outer surface and pale orange/pale blue (under glazed areas) core. Clear, even apple-green glaze on inner surface.

572. Post-medieval Sandy ware fabric bowl. Reddish-purple outer surface skin, orange/blue-grey core. Olive-green glaze on inner surface.

573. Post-medieval Sandy ware fabric cup? Blue-grey core. Consistent, light, olive-green glaze fully covering both surfaces.

574. Hambleton ware jug. Badly corroded surfaces, but appears to have dull grey surfaces and grey-black core. Traces of heavily corroded greenish glaze. Ribbed oval handle with smoothed-down lower handle attachment with no apparent use of a back fillet.

575. Late-medieval Sandy ware bottle? Light orange-buff outer surface, grey-black core and inner surface. Rich olive-green glaze to rim top.

THE ARCHAEOLOGY OF THE INNER COURT

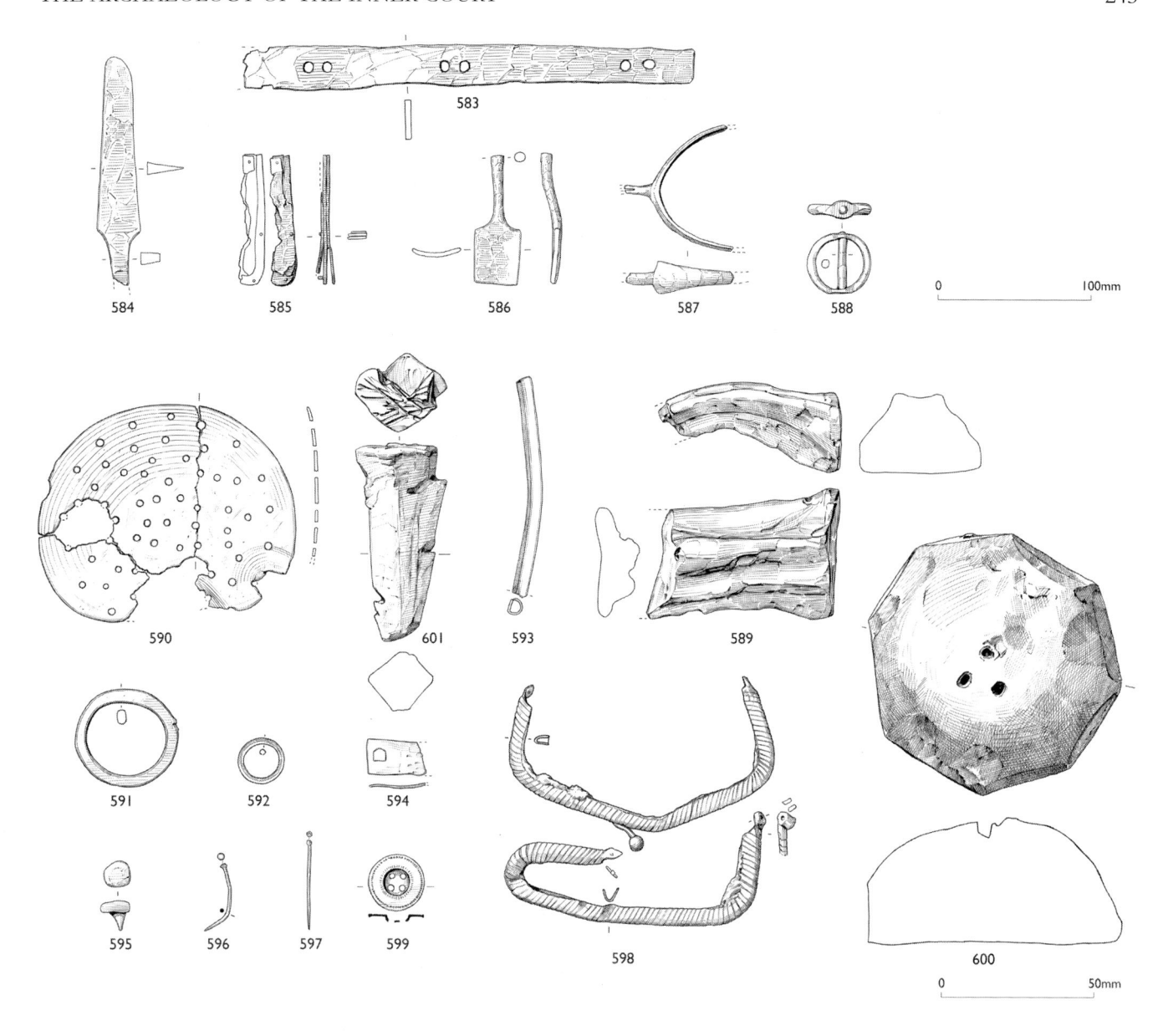

576. Tudor Green ware cup? Fine, white fabric covered on both surfaces with a light, mottled, copper-green glaze.
577. Cistercian ware lid knop. Bright glossy black glaze on outer surface, dull brick-red core and inner surface. Applied pipeclay spots on top of knop. There also may have been a hole at top of knop, about 5 mm in diameter.
579. Cistercian ware cup. Metallic purple glaze over a dull reddish a dull reddish fabric.
579. Cistercian ware cup. Metallic purple glaze over a dull reddish fabric.
580. Cistercian ware copy cup sherd. Bright reddish-brown glaze over a vermilion core. Applied spots in a white pipeclay appearing lemon-yellow under glaze.
581. 19th-century Blackware pancheon. Hard, smooth orange-red fabric with thick black glaze to inner surface.
582. 19th-century terracotta plant pot stand. Orange-red terracotta, with four sets of applied decoration, two opposing ears of wheat and two opposing lion's heads? Traces of an off-white/cream paint to the pedestal and applied designs.

SMALL FINDS (SEE FIGURE 5.62)

583. Strap-hinge. Fe. L: 290 mm; W: 28 mm; Th: 4 mm. Three pairs of holes D: about 5 mm. Find no. Fe1257.

Figure 5.62 Finds Group 45 from the kitchen continued (iron 1:4; copper alloy 1:2; lead 1:2).

584. Knife. Fe. L: 146 mm. Blade with tapered section L: 116 mm; W: 28 mm; Th: 8 mm. Whittle tang broken L: 36 mm. Find no. Fe1143.
585. Folding knife. Fe with bone handle. Broken thumb piece. Handle L: 82 mm; W: 20 mm with three iron rivets D: 3 mm. Find no. Fe1143.
586. Gouge. Fe. L: 84 mm. Hollow shank L: 44 mm; D: 6 mm. Slightly concave end L: 14 mm; W: 28 mm; Th: 5 mm. Find no. Fe1137.
587. Spur. Fe. Rowel and terminals missing. Tapering from 2 mm to 8 mm. Overall L: 90 mm. Span 82 mm. Neck L: 16 mm. ?Post-Suppression, 17th century. Find no. Fe1338.
588. Buckle. Fe. Single loop frame with central inserted circular bar. D: 23 mm. Frame D: 5 mm. Bar D: 5 mm. Find no. Fe1224.
589. Vessel foot. Cu cast. Two raised lines on outer face. Plain back. W: of base 40 mm. Ht: from base 60 mm. Find no. Cu161.
590. Skimmer/strainer. Cu. Probably cast. D: 168 mm (maximum); Th: 1.5 mm. In three pieces. Irregularly spaced holes D: 3 mm. Broken area is presumably where handle was attached. Find nos Cu166, Cu172 and Cu173.
591. Ring. Cu. D: 33 mm (maximum); W: 3 mm; Th: 2.5 mm. Find no. Cu162.
592. Tubular ring. Cu. Thin sheet with join on one side. D: 9 mm; Th: 1 mm. Possibly modern. Find no. Cu150.
593. Tube. Cu sheet. Edge to edge seam. L: 70 mm; D: 5 mm. Find no. Cu177.
594. Sheet. Cu. Piece of thin sheet with irregularly shaped hole. Find no. Cu176.
595. Stud. Cu. Head with Fe shank. Circular head D: 9 mm; H: 2.5 mm. Shank L: 9 mm. Find no. Cu154.
596. Pin. Cu. Integral head with fat top D: 1 mm. L: 23 mm (over bent length). Find no. Cu165.
597. Pin. Cu. Solid head. L: 28 mm; D: 0.8 mm (shank), 1 mm (head). Find no. Cu163.
598. Purse frame. Cu with ?silver. Two sides of purse frame with incised lines on outer faces: inner surfaces are flat, outer slightly rounded. One piece has one side of fastening clip which is lacking on other piece. Each has rounded ends with attachment holes. Corroded Fe of main structure survives in each part of frame. W: 90 mm (maximum); H: 35 mm; Th: 2.5 mm. 19th century. Find nos Cu151 and Cu152.
599. Button. Cu. Dished with four central perforations. Face has two concentric lines, the outer of dots, the inner of short lines. Possible black enamel remains. D: 17 mm. 19th century. Find no. Cu1361.
600. ?base for candlestick. Pb. Cast and roughly octagonal with vertical or sloping sides. Three attachment holes on top surface. W: 80 mm (maximum). Wt: 1377.48g. Find no. Pb1316.
601. Masonry plug. Pb. Roughly square in section. L: 62 mm (maximum). Void (for iron) on one side has right angle and is 33 mm long. Find no. Pb1331.

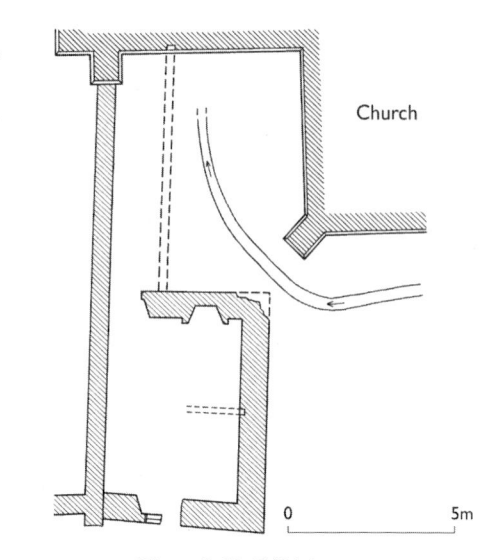

Figure 5.63 Cell 16.

5.3 The Cells of the Lesser Cloister

Six cells were arranged around the lesser cloister (for a discussion of their phasing and development see Chapter 6). All apparently were excavated by Hope, though he does not record the fact, but none has been examined since. It is certain that these cells were occupied by lay brothers in the 16th century.

Cell 16 (see Figure 5.63)

Inserted against the outer face of the east wall of the yard that fronted the church, Cell 16 occupied a limited space between the nave and

THE ARCHAEOLOGY OF THE INNER COURT

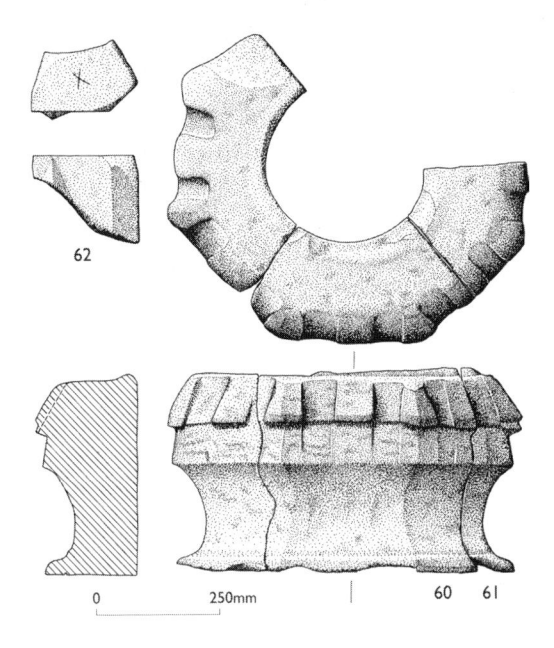

Figure 5.64 Architectural detail from cell 16 (scale 1:10).

south burial chapel. Its south wall, surviving to a maximum of two courses, retained the western jamb and splay of its cloister door. Part of the cill also remained. The east wall survived at its northern end to two courses, but only to a single course in its southern half. The north wall remained to a height of two courses and contained at its centre the lowest projecting jambs of a fireplace. At its west end was the lowest course of the eastern jamb of the garden pentice door. Within, the cell retained evidence for two partitions. A socket 0.165 m wide and 0.20 m high for a cill beam in the east wall just above floor level marked a partition across the cell 2.65 m from the north wall, defining the living room, from which a passage 1.5 m wide was partitioned on the west side, evidenced by a socket 0.18 m wide on the line of the splay of the garden pentice door. Thus the cell had only two ground-floor rooms and there was no evidence for a stair to an upper floor.

The only evidence for the garden pentice was a series of slots cut into the south wall of the church that indicated two phases of construction. The earliest, not shown on Figure 5.63, was a slight structure only 1 m wide, defined by a socket 0.15 m² cut into the lowest plinth course of the nave at ground level. This structure was replaced by a pentice 1.48 m wide, marked by the 0.23 m2 sockets of its cill beam and wall plate, 0.75 m and 2.2 m above ground level respectively. No trace of its cill wall or eavesdrip gulley remained.

Cell 16 was forced into a very small space, and its garden, uniquely, was placed opposite the cell across the lesser cloister alley. Its enclosing walls survived to only a single course. At its south-west angle, rather inconveniently placed for the occupant of the cell, was a latrine examined by Hope but no longer exposed. Although a sewer ran past the corner of the cell itself, it must have been deemed inappropriate to place a latrine so close to the church.

ARCHITECTURAL DETAIL FROM CELL 16 (SEE FIGURE 5.64)

60, 61. Cap from an octagonal chimney, fitting a chimney shaft of 0.25 m side. One full half of the cap and a fragment of the other half survive, one fitting fragment being recovered from Hope's stone dump. The cap has a crenellated moulding above a deep hollow collar with a small neck-moulding at the bottom. Both halves have a plain cross assembly mark on the lower bed. Two sections were recovered from the walled yard immediately to the west of Cell 16, from which they had clearly fallen.

62. Fragment from the base of an octagonal chimney matching the above cap, with the top of a tall pyramidal spur on one face. There is a plain cross assembly mark on the upper bed. Found with the above cap.

Cell 17

Cell 17 survived for the most part to a height of a single course of masonry, although the cloister wall remained two courses high. The cell was clearly added to the pre-existing lesser cloister wall, as a thickening 0.25 m wide was added to its south face within the cell. The cloister door itself did not survive and the cell had been dug out to below floor level by Hope. The lowest jambs of the garden pentice door, at the north end of the east wall, and the latrine pentice door, at the west end of the south wall, survived, but there was no trace of the fireplace that should have occupied the central part of the west wall. An entry passage 1.22 m wide was defined along the north side of the cell by

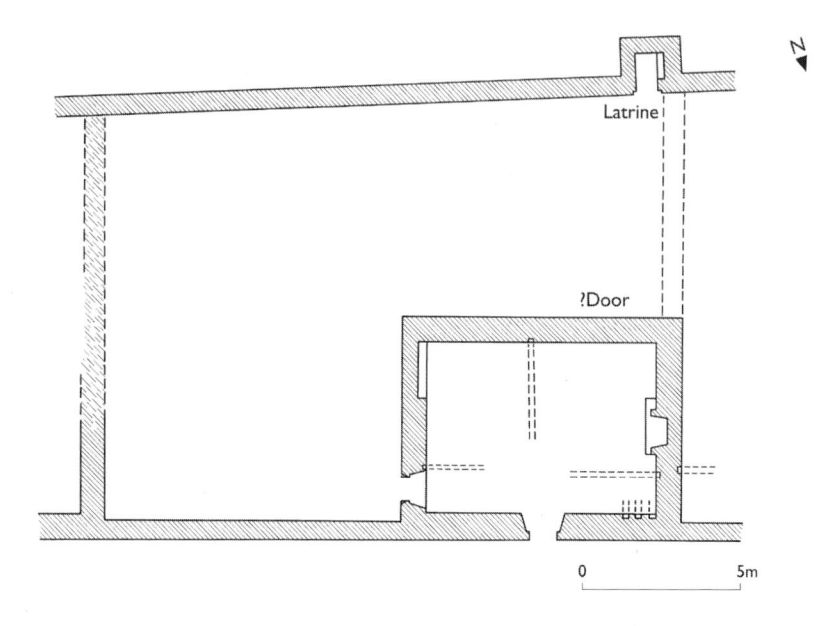

Figure 5.65 Cell 18.

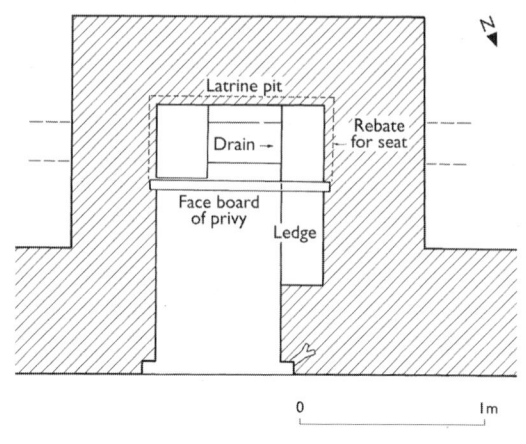

Figure 5.66 Cell 18 latrine.

the socket of its cill beam, 0.15 m wide, just outside the splay of the garden pentice door, and the ground floor was divided by a partition 4.02 m from the west wall set on a cill beam 0.20 m wide.

The garden pentice ran along the cloister wall and was evidenced by the socket of its cill beam, 0.255 m square and 0.45 m above ground level in the west wall of Cell 18 (see Figure 5.65). No trace remained of the cill wall. The pentice was 1.52 m wide internally.

The garden was featureless, only its west wall being visible above the turf. The south wall, which contained a latrine recorded by Hope (1905, plan), and the east wall remained buried.

Cell 18 (see Figure 5.65)
Like Cell 17, this cell was excavated by Hope to the depth of a full course below floor level. The cloister wall survived to a height of two courses and had a centrally placed door, the linings of which were integral with an internal widening identical to that seen in Cell 17. The door was hung on the western jamb, where the keying for the hinge pivot still remained. The west wall, also two courses high, retained the lowest jambs of a projecting fireplace, the hearth of which had been relined with roof slates set on edge. The south wall was robbed down to its foundation course at its west end, where the latrine pentice door had been, although it retained its second course from its mid-point and a third course at the east end. The east wall was three courses high and retained the lowest courses of the garden pentice door at its north end. At its south end a recess 1.75 m wide and 0.3 m deep had been cut into the top two courses of the inner face and lined with ashlar, presumably marking the position of a window, the cill of which had been cut down to floor level. An entry passage on the north side of the cell, 1.04 m wide at its west end and 1.33 m at its east end, was defined by sockets 0.18 m² at floor level in the west and east walls. To the west of the cloister door four joist sockets 0.20 m wide indicated a sprung floor some 0.15 m above the general floor level of the cell. The ground floor of the cell was divided into two rooms by a partition 4 m from the west wall, marked by a socket at floor level in the south wall 0.127 m wide and 0.165 m high. There was no evidence for a stair to an upper floor.

The garden to the south and east was featureless and apparently unexcavated. Its east wall remained buried, but the south wall, a single course high, was exposed. At its west end it contained the well-preserved lower courses of a latrine (see Figure 5.66). The jambs were rebated for a door 70 mm thick that was hung on the western jamb, where the seating for a hinge pivot remained. The privy, 0.4 m square, was centrally placed against the back wall and fronted by a vertical board 0.10 m thick fixed in a rebate. To either side of the privy was a solid block of masonry that supported the seat, a board 0.10 m thick rebated into the side and rear walls of the latrine. The privy was placed over a stone-lined drain with sloping sides that ran outside

Table 5.25 Kitchen, Finds Group 46: Ceramics

Fabric	Sherds	Vessels								
		Total vessels	Cistern	Cooking pot	Jar	Jug	Mug or cup	Pancheon	Urinal	Other
Brandsby type	5	5	0	0	0	5	0	0	0	0
Cistercian										
Cistercian copy	2	2	0	0	0	0	1	0	0	1
Deveeloped Humber	1	1	0	0	1	0	0	0	0	0
Gritty	1	1	0	0	0	1	0	0	0	0
Hambleton	7	4				3				1
Post-medieval Orange	17	4	0	0	3	0	0	0	0	1
Post-medieval Sandy	8	8	0	0	5	0	0	2	0	1
Ryedale	63	30	1	1	0	25	0	2	1	0
Siegburg	25	9	0	0	0	0	8	0	0	1

the line of the garden wall. Between the privy and the door a ledge one course high was provided against the west wall. The external walls survived to a maximum height of three courses.

Cell 19

Although trenched by Hope, this cell remained largely unexcavated and only its cloister wall and a short length of its south wall with the east jamb of the latrine pentice door remained exposed. The cloister wall, robbed below the level of the cloister door, was 0.6 m wide and had an internal widening of 0.25 m, identical to the cloister walls of Cells 17 and 18.

The south garden wall survived to a height of a single course with the remains of a latrine at its western end. Of similar form to that of Cell 18, its privy was placed on the western side with a solid block of masonry on its east. Two vertical slots 0.10 m wide evidenced two phases of seat, but only the lowest two courses of the structure survived, with no evidence for the fixing of the seat itself. The privy was served by a drain that ran outside the garden wall, the covering slabs of which were exposed to the west of the structure. The latrine was floored at the level of the latrine pentice and most of its stone paving remained *in situ*. A short length of the cill wall of the pentice, 0.4 m wide, was exposed. The width of the pentice was unknown, as the west garden wall remained buried. It must have butted against the south wall, as the inner face of that wall is unbroken between Cells 18 and 19.

The east wall of the garden was the precinct wall that retained the hillside to the east of the site and it survived to a height of 15 courses. It bore traces of two phases of garden pentice flanking the cloister wall. The earliest, evidenced by the rather damaged socket of its wall plate 2.15 m above ground level and the chase for the lead flashing of its roof, was 1.5 m wide. In its later form, marked by its cill beam and wall-plate sockets, both 0.255 m square and set 0.3 m and 1.7 m above ground level respectively, it was 1.9 m wide. A series of eight sockets in the east wall at the height of the wall plate suggested that the pentice returned along the full length of the precinct wall.

Cell 20

Cell 20 was heavily robbed and only partially preserved in plan, although it was apparently a mirror image of Cell 21. Exceptionally, these cells were semi-detached, sharing a party wall. The cell was entered from the cloister alley via a centrally placed door of which the lowest course of its northern jamb survived. Only the northern half of the cloister wall remained, to two courses high. The north wall was also preserved to a height of two courses. The east wall survived to a height of three courses only at its northern end and was otherwise reduced to its footings. The south wall remained only partially to the height of a single course, retaining the remains of a projecting fireplace, the eastern jamb of the garden pentice door and its cill. The fireplace was fronted by a surviving kerb – the only one to survive in the lesser cloister cells – and a small area of stone paving. An entry passage 1.03 m wide occupied the western side of the cell, evidenced by cill beam fixings 0.15 m wide and 0.20 m high in the north and south walls just above floor level. Three irregularly spaced joist sockets averaging 0.20 m wide in the cloister wall to the north of the door indicated a sprung floor slightly above the general floor level of the cell, a feature also seen in Cell 18. The ground floor was divided into two rooms by a partition 3.45 m from the south wall marked by a similarly sized cill beam socket. The remaining three courses at the north end of the east wall were the blocking of the latrine pentice door, the jambs of which had been removed.

The latrine pit remained at the north-east corner of the garden. It was 1.3 m long, 0.6 m wide and set within a pentice 1.48 m wide, evidenced by a cill beam socket 0.15 m wide and 0.255 m high some 0.30 m above garden level. No trace of the cill wall remained. To the south along the precinct wall was a raised planting bed faced with a single course of ashlar. This was set parallel with the back wall of the cell and not the precinct wall, and was therefore 1 m wide at its north end but only 0.55 m wide where it butted against the rubble footings of the south garden wall.

An ashlar-faced eavesdrip gulley ran along the east wall of the cell and returned along the south gable wall to meet the eavesdrip of the garden pentice that ranged along the west garden wall. This pentice was 1.13 m wide and retained up to two courses of its cill wall, which was 0.3 m wide.

A wedge-shaped tank lined with ashlar was set over a drain on the south side of the garden. Its function was uncertain.

Cell 20, Finds Group 46: Ceramics
(see Figure 5.67)
This was the only pottery collection to be recovered from the lay brothers' cells and it immediately invites comparison with the pottery from the monks' cells. The anticipation might be that it would not be of quite the same quality as that of the monks. Certainly, there does not seem to be either the quantity or the range of tablewares apparent from the great cloister cells. There were only two vessels of pseudo-Cistercian ware and, although there were a number of stoneware mugs, they were of a single basic type. There was no Westerwald, no maiolica, no Tudor Green or Midlands Yellow, no trace of the highly decorated Cistercian ware or Reversed Cistercian ware cups and posset pots. Indeed, at first sight this group does seem to represent a poorer standard of pottery.

However, the ceramic assemblages from the great cloister did vary from cell to cell to a certain extent, dependent on the extent and quality of archaeological work carried out. The pottery from Cell 20 was recovered during unsupervised clearance work and it would be unwise to presume on its representativeness (Table 5.25).

602. Brandsby-type fabric strap handle. Dull grey-brown outer surface and light orange-buff core. Dark olive-green glaze with purplish margins.

603. Ryedale ware urinal. Light orange outer surface, pale blue-grey core and inner surface. Outer surface neatly and almost fully covered with an olive-green glaze.

604. Hambleton ware urinal. Bluish-grey core and silver-grey inner surface. Almost totally covered in an olive-green glaze on the outer surface. Very crude and lumpy textured fabric fired quite hard.

605. Ryedale ware cooking pot. Yellow-green glazed outer surface and brownish-green glazed inner surface over a sandy orange-red core.

606. Ryedale ware jug. Hard, lightly sanded orange fabric with pale orange outer surface and orange-red inner surface. Orange-brown glaze.

607. Ryedale ware jug. Pale orange outer surface, blue-grey core and buff/blue-grey inner surface. Corroded traces of an olive-green glaze. Traces of an upper handle attachment with lateral thumbings.

608. Regional Stray ware bottle. Soft, sandy, orange core with orange-pink surfaces.

609. Unidentified. Very hard, vitrified grey core, becoming more of a pale orange-yellow in the thinner, central part of the base. Silver-grey glaze to outer surface and a yellowish-grey glaze on the inner surface. Rim form resembles that of a small cucurbit.

610. Post-medieval Sandy ware fabric large jar. Pale orange outer surface and orange-red core. Olive-green glaze.

THE ARCHAEOLOGY OF THE INNER COURT

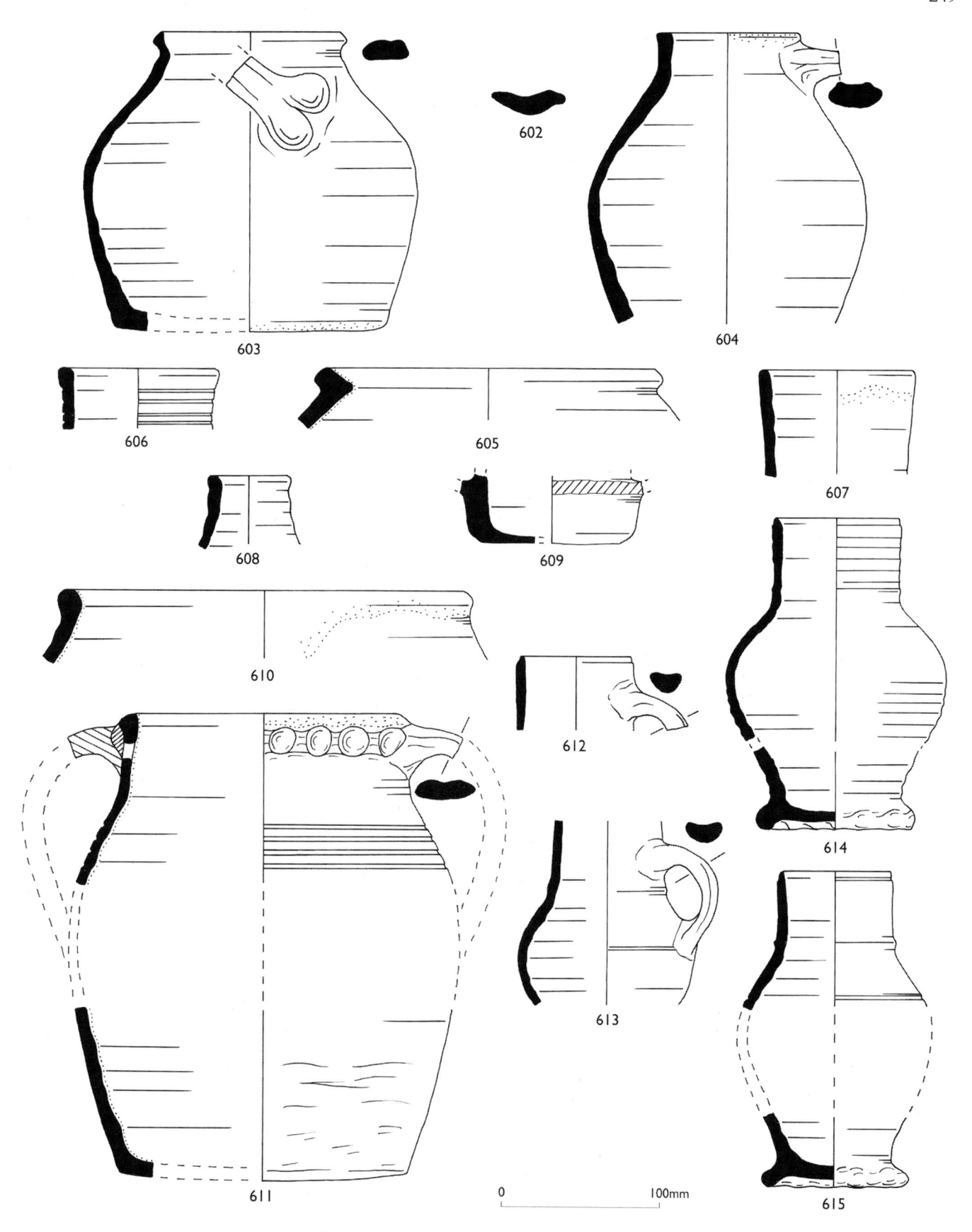

Figure 5.67 Finds Group 46 from Cell 20 (pottery 1:4).

611. Post-medieval Orange ware two-handled jar. Pale orange outer surface and soft, micaceous orange core fabric. Copper-green glaze on inner surface thinning to more of a yellow-green, but conversely thickens to a dark copper-green. Upper handle attachments plugged.
612. Siegburg stoneware mug. Pale grey core with silver-grey glaze on both surfaces.
613. Siegburg stoneware mug. Pale whitish-grey core and inner surface. Silver-grey outer surface glaze with brown patches.
614. Siegburg stoneware mug. Pale grey core. Inner surface grey with slight orange highlights. Silver-grey glaze on outer surface.
615. Siegburg stoneware mug. Pale grey core and slightly shiny orange-buff inner surface. Outer surface glaze varies from silver-grey to patches of a more matt brown colour.

Cell 21 (see Figure 5.68)

This cell was entered by a door at the centre of its west wall that survived to a height of two courses. The north wall remained to a maximum height of three courses at its east end. At its west end was the door to the latrine pentice, where the lowest two courses of the jambs and its cill survived. At the centre of the north wall were the lower jambs of a projecting fireplace with a relined hearth. The east wall was equally well preserved, being three courses high at its north end and two at the south, where it retained the lowest two courses of jamb stones and cill of the garden pentice door. This door had been partially blocked with masonry, apparently to convert it to a window. The south wall stood to a maximum height of three courses.

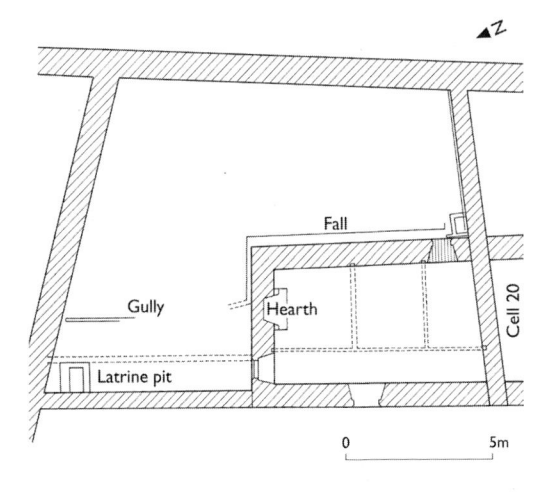

An entry passage 1.14 m wide was defined on the west side of the cell by sockets 0.20 m wide and 0.16 m high in the north and south walls just above floor level. The interior of the cell was divided by partitions, evidenced by sockets 0.16 m² in the east wall, into three roughly equal-sized rooms. A small area of stone paving, perhaps associated with the hearth, remained in the north-east corner of the northern room. There was no trace of a stair to an upper floor.

The latrine pentice, which was 1.02 m wide, flanked the cloister wall to the north of the cell and was defined by the socket of its cill beam, 0.18 m wide and 0.15 m high, set just above ground level in the south wall of Cell 1, which formed the northern boundary of the garden. An ashlar-faced latrine pit, flushed by a stone-lined drain, was set within the northern end of the pentice.

Outside the blocked garden pentice door was an ashlar-lined tank 1.03 m deep, which was partially overlaid by the garden wall between Cells 20 and 21 and was demonstrably earlier than the building of either cell. Its function was not certain. No trace remained of the garden pentice and an ashlar-faced eavesdrip gulley started against the upstanding lining of the tank and ran along the east wall of the cell across the presumed line of the pentice. It returned along the northern gable wall before turning away from the cell and running away below ground. A second drain, starting against the south wall of Cell 1, ran across the garden well to the east of the latrine pentice. Otherwise, the garden was featureless.

5.4 The South Range of the Inner Court

The central and eastern buildings of the south range of the inner court, identified by Hope (1905, 273–4) as a stable and a granary, were re-excavated by David Sherlock for Laurence Keen in 1969–70 and 1973 in advance of their conservation and display. The eastern building, Hope's 'granary', retained its roof as late as 1768, when it was shown on an estate plan (NYRO DN43). Excavation confirmed Hope's conclusions in the main but added considerable detail, including the identification of a kiln house at the east end of the granary. It also

Figure 5.68 Cell 21.

THE ARCHAEOLOGY OF THE INNER COURT

demonstrated that the stable at the centre of the range was constructed in Period Three and that the granary to its east was a later construction, apparently of Period Four (see Chapter 6 for a discussion of the phasing of this range).

Stables (see Figures 5.69 and 5.70)

The earliest masonry encountered was the south precinct wall, which formed the north wall of the building. This survived to a maximum height of two courses above an offset plinth. Hope identified an inserted door 1.1 m wide at the west end of the building. Two further doors were located, towards the centre and east of the building. The eastern door retained its cill – though its western jamb had been destroyed by a modern land drain – showing that its opening was also 1.1 m wide. The central door was more badly damaged and its width could not be ascertained. All three doorways were set in pink mortar, indicating that they were inserted into the earlier precinct wall in Period Three. The north, west and south walls of the building bonded at their junctions and were clearly contemporary, and it was noticed that the west wall was laid in pink mortar where it had not been repointed before excavation. The west and east walls were butted against the precinct wall. Within, the building was levelled up with a dump of orange and blue clay that sealed both the offset foundations of the precinct wall and the lowest courses of the west wall where it was examined. The underlying natural surface was not examined, but it must have risen to the east, as the east wall was footed 1.12 m above the contemporary west wall. As with other buildings at Mount Grace, the foundations of the stable followed the slope and were not cut into it.

Figure 5.69 The stables in the south range of the inner court as excavated.

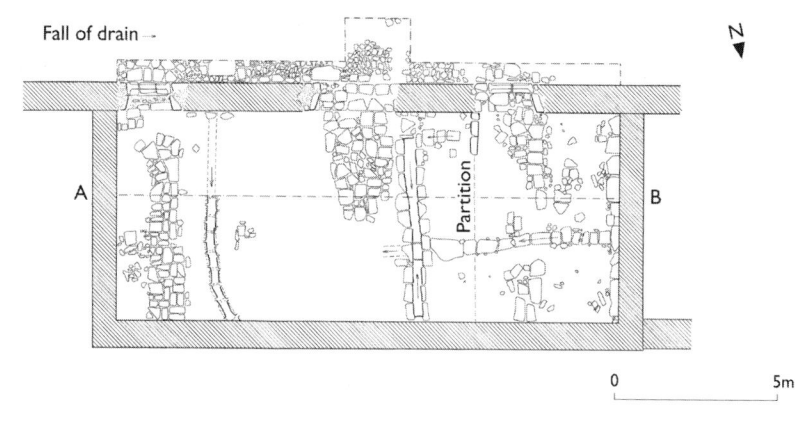

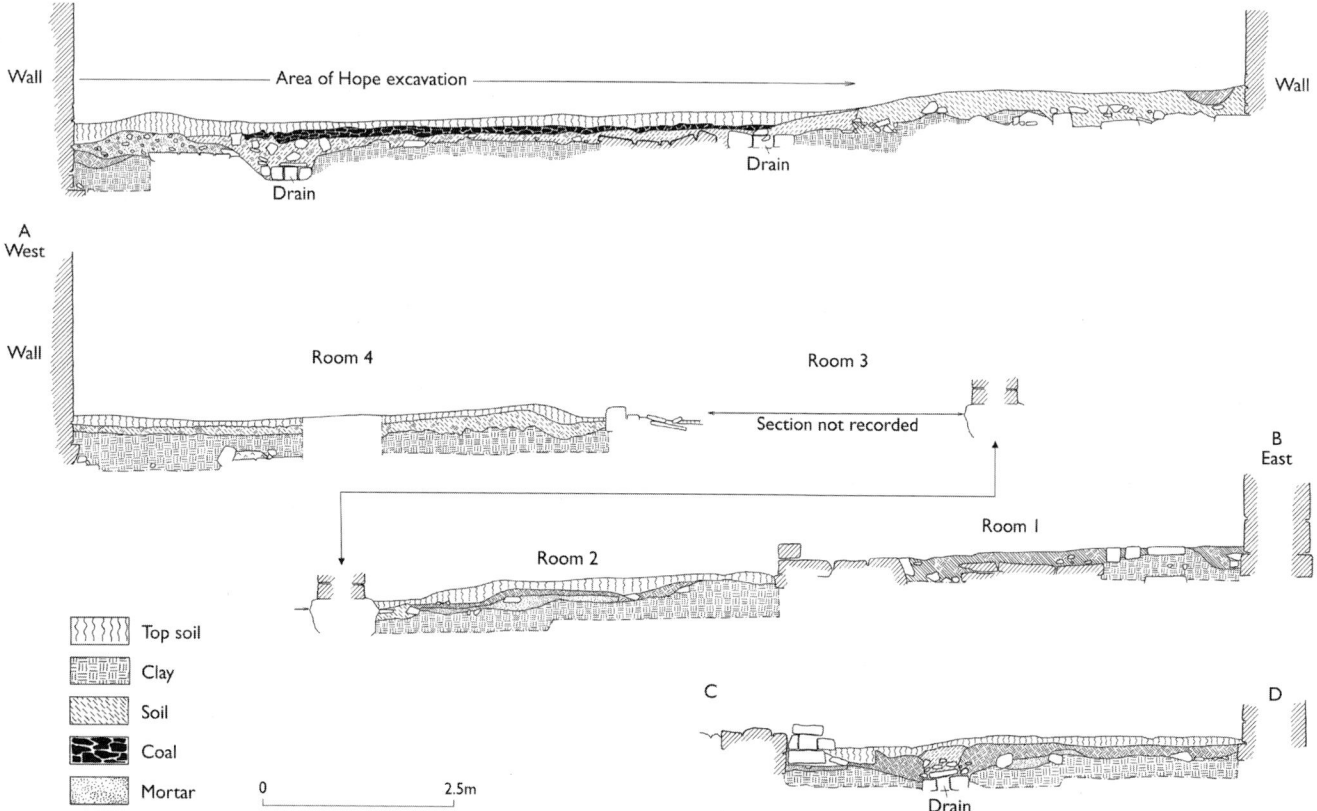

Figure 5.70 Sections of the stable, granary and kiln house in the south range of the inner court.

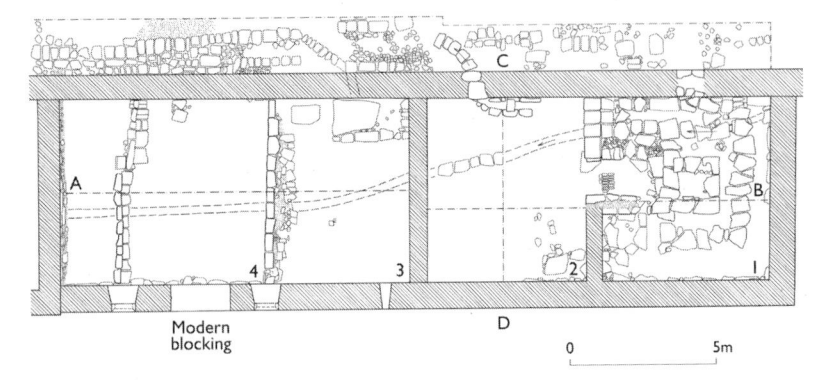

Figure 5.71 The granary and kiln house in the south range of the inner court as excavated.

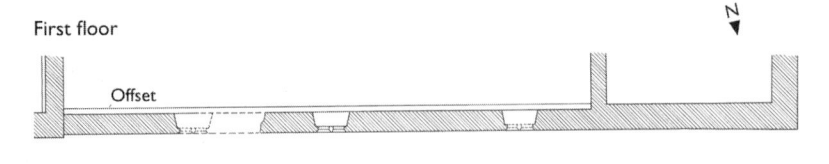

manger was associated with a timber partition 4.4 m to the west, evidenced by a socket and a vertical chase in the south wall 1 m short of the floor. The northern end of this partition was evidenced by three stones in line: the last remains of a cill wall. The third manger, identical to the first, implies a partition for which no evidence remains 4.4 m east of the west gable wall.

Most of the interior of the stable had been cleared down to floor level or below by Hope, but small areas of secondary flooring comprising yellow clay and mortar remained, associated with the western door and the paving inside it. This material sealed the inner face of the door cill and overlay the edge of the stone paving. Further patches indicated that it had originally covered the stone paving, but had been largely removed by the earlier excavation. There was no indication elsewhere in the building of this secondary floor, which may have been restricted to the west end, where the original floor was somewhat lower than the remainder of the building.

Outside the building to the north was revealed the surface of the inner court, principally of small water-rolled cobbles set in clay. Outside the three doors to the stable were more substantial areas of paving.

Within the building very little occupation material remained, although there were spreads of window glass on the floors that indicated that its windows were glazed. The windows must have been in the north wall, as the south wall survives to a sufficient height to show that it had no windows at ground- or first-floor levels. The room above is evidenced by an offset in the east gable wall that carried its floor joists. There was no evidence from excavation for its function or to suggest how it was entered. It was almost certainly a granary.

Granary and Kiln House (see Figures 5.70 and 5.71)

In Period Four a substantial building 24 m long and 6 m wide internally was butted against the eastern gable wall of the stables and the south face of the southern precinct wall. This was the building depicted on the 1768 estate map. Today, its south wall survives up to 1 m above the level of the first-floor window cills and both its gable walls are substantially intact, with vestigial evidence of its roof form, although the northern wall is reduced

Dug into the orange and blue clay levelling were two drains that ran from north to south. The western drain was set below floor level and was capped with thin roof slates. Its outfall was not examined. The eastern drain, which was not capped but set at floor level, fell from both the south and north walls to an east–west drain 1.8 m to the north of the south wall. The western part of this latter drain was not excavated but found in later conservation work. The east–west drain ran down the slope from the line of the eastern precinct wall and was seen in the excavation of the building to the east. It passed below the east gable wall of the stables. A short drain ran westwards into the northern end of the eastern north–south drain. Once the drains had been constructed the stable was floored with large sandstone flags, three areas of which survived. These areas of stone flooring were associated with the three doors in the north wall to the extent that they extended into the door splays. All three have definable edges, suggesting that they represent passages across the building and were not the last remains of a continuous floor. Elsewhere within the building the floor appears to have comprised the dumped orange and blue clay.

Associated with the areas of apparent clay flooring were three mangers, evidenced by slots cut in the masonry of the south wall. The best preserved was that against the east wall of the building, which was further supported by regularly spaced joists set 0.85 m to 0.9 m above floor level in the east wall itself. The second to its lowest courses or footing level. It was originally divided into two spaces at both ground- and first-floor levels by a cross-wall that bonds with the south wall 5.7 m from its eastern end. A second cross-wall, which occurs at ground-floor level only at the mid point of the building, is probably also medieval, although it butts against the south wall and was not bonded. Two further cross-walls towards the west end of the building would have cut across the ground-floor windows that survive there and it is presumed that they date to the post-medieval use of the building. Only one of these walls was visible when excavation began, and the excavation was carried out in the four 'rooms' (numbered 1–4 on Figure 5.71) that were apparent. Unfortunately, conservation work had already begun, and some critical relationships were damaged or destroyed. Most apparent is the lack of post-medieval floor surfaces.

The surface from which the building was constructed was a deposit of blue clay that was assumed to be natural. Dug into its surface was a drain that was traced from the north-east corner of the building to the east gable wall of the stables, where it passed below the lowest course of ashlar. This drain was further examined in the stables and was identified as a primary feature of the building. It must therefore belong to Period Three. Its function is uncertain, although it was identified at the time of excavation as the drain of a latrine outside the east gable wall of the Period Four building (Edgar Barker, pers. comm., who provided David Sherlock with a plan showing his observations made during conservation work). An examination of this plan suggests that the drain is more likely to be associated with the overflow of the central well house outside the east precinct wall (see Figure 6.53).

The primary floor of the western two-thirds of the building was of reddish-orange mortar that survived in Room 2, where it was observed to butt against the inner face of the north wall and seal the surface of the natural clay. Its relationship with the unbonded cross-wall had been destroyed by the rebuilding of that wall before excavation. Similarly, the drain had been dug out and cleared, though it did appear to be sealed in places by the floor. In Room 4, small patches of the floor remained above a layer of yellow-orange clay that formed the natural surface there. An area of stone paving in the north-east corner of Room 3 was associated with a drain inserted into the old precinct wall that ran away into the inner court. The eastern edge of this paving underlay the unbonded cross-wall and is thus likely to be primary.

The use of this building is determined from the partitioned room at its east end. Though severely damaged by post-medieval relevelling and by enthusiastic conservation before excavation, sufficient remained on the surface of the natural blue clay to identify the base of a grain-drying kiln. A heavily burned opening in the cross-wall provided the flue for a square grain dryer with a central pedestal that supported a raised floor. All that was recovered by excavation was the footing of thin slabs on which the kiln had been built, but the form was typical of a late medieval monastic grain dryer, of which the best-known example is the late 14th-century kiln excavated at Thornholme Priory (Coppack 1989, pl. 9). The unbonded cross-wall between Rooms 2 and 3 separated the working area of the grain dryer from a second room to the west that had two square-headed single light windows and a narrow loop. There must have been three doors from the inner court in the north wall, but only the easternmost was traced in excavation, where the masonry of the Period Two precinct wall was smoothed where it had acted as the door cill perhaps as late as the 18th or 19th century, when the floor level in the eastern room was reduced and the door cut down. A raised floor around the kiln and its primary date is demonstrated by the exposed footings of the east gable wall, which protrude some 0.5 m above post-medieval floor level. Set in the north side of the flue are the base and one side of what appears to be a hatch from one of the monks' or lay brothers' cells. It must be reused in this context as it would have been buried below the medieval floor level of Room 1. To the north of the building the cobbled surface of the inner court was exposed.

Kiln houses are invariably associated with granaries (see Brown 1887, *passim*), and the floor above the kiln and possibly the loft above that must have served that purpose. More problematic are the rooms in the western end of the building. The ground-floor room was probably a service room, given the simplicity of its surviving windows, but the first-floor room had three two-light windows in its south wall that suggest it was something more than a granary. These windows were barred and shuttered, although there is no evidence that they were glazed. Because the windows are not regularly disposed, it is possible that the upper floor was divided into two or more rooms by timber partitions. The roof was of principal rafter construction, with two purlins to each side, the chases for which survive in both gable walls.

The post-medieval refitting of the building barely survived its consolidation and what may be clearance by Hope. The cross-wall between Rooms 3 and 4 and that encountered in Room 4 both sit on the surface of the natural clay and were sealed only by demolition debris consisting primarily of fallen roof slates, presumably from the roof known to have existed in 1768. Because they would have cut across the windows it is almost certain they are not medieval. Additionally, the western wall was footed at its north end on a pair of mullions derived from the Period Two cloister arcade. A door was cut in the south wall midway between these walls, later blocked in Bell's restoration, and must be associated with them. No dressings survive. The opening into the kiln flue was blocked with masonry obviously derived from the demolition of monastic buildings, and this must have been done before the kiln was dismantled. In Room 2, the floor level was raised and an area of flagging was recorded at this higher level in the south-east corner of the room. At a similar level, a drain was built along the inner face of the north wall; it was roughly cut through the wall and discharged into the inner court. The cobbled surface of the inner court was replaced by regular paving, some of it obviously reused monastic masonry. It would appear that the building survived the Suppression and was converted to serve the 17th-century house, possibly as a stable.

Chapter 6: The Buildings and Infrastructure of Mount Grace Priory and their Development

Braunfels has suggested (1972, 112–24) that the study of Carthusian architecture, which was plain in the extreme, has little to offer the serious monastic scholar, and indeed William St John Hope was unable to phase the buildings at Mount Grace with his normal consummate skill (Hope 1905, *passim*). However, the ruins of Mount Grace Priory, which represent approximately one quarter of the house in its latest phase of development, are the most complete and accessible of the nine English houses of the order. Recent study of the remains, which has been greatly simplified by their excavation and clearance, has shown that the development of the house is clearly discernible and that it can be related to the house's known historical background (see Figure 6.1).

A study of the masonry joints and an analysis of the surviving architectural detail reveal four distinct periods of medieval building. Period One, encompassing the first quarter of the 15th century, relates to the foundation period; Period Two, the second quarter of the 15th century, relates to the patronage of Thomas Beaufort, Duke of Exeter; Period Three, the later 15th century, to the relative stability achieved after the middle of the 15th century; and Period Four, *c.*1520–30, to the documented patronage of Henry, Lord Clifford in the 1520s. Two post-Suppression phases are also apparent: Period Five, from *c.*1616, represents the first rebuilding of the guest-house range as a house, and Period Six the extension of the post-Suppression house in 1900–1. All six phases are identified in the archaeological record (see Chapters 4 and 5), and a series of masons' marks can be identified to buildings of Periods One, Two and Three (see Table 6.1 and Figures 6.2, 6.3 and 6.4).

In work of Periods One and Two, despite the rough surface of the blocks, virtually every walling stone was marked with a mason's mark. The same marks were used both freehand for punch-dressed blocks and from a template on fine ashlar. In Period Three marking was much more haphazard, but the same habit of marking both punched blocks and fine ashlar was apparent. There was also wide-scale evidence of the reuse of masonry of all periods, the list above indicating only the earliest occurrence of a particular mark. The only marks to be found on Period Four work were on reused material of Periods One to Three, which confirms Prior Wilson's remark that he was employing masons 'by great': that is, by contract (BL Add. MS 48965, f. 6).

Although the development of the charterhouse was a slow and apparently painful process, excavation has demonstrated that the two great terraces now occupied by the claustral buildings and the inner court were constructed during the foundation period, and there is plain evidence for a temporary arrangement of timber buildings on at least the upper terrace (see Chapter 4). This suggests that the final development of the house did indeed accord with the intentions of the founding community and that the slow pace of building in stone reflects only financial difficulty. The lack of stone buildings in various parts of the precinct in the first two periods does not indicate that the necessary structures were not provided, only that they were constructed of timber in those periods, being replaced in stone subsequently.

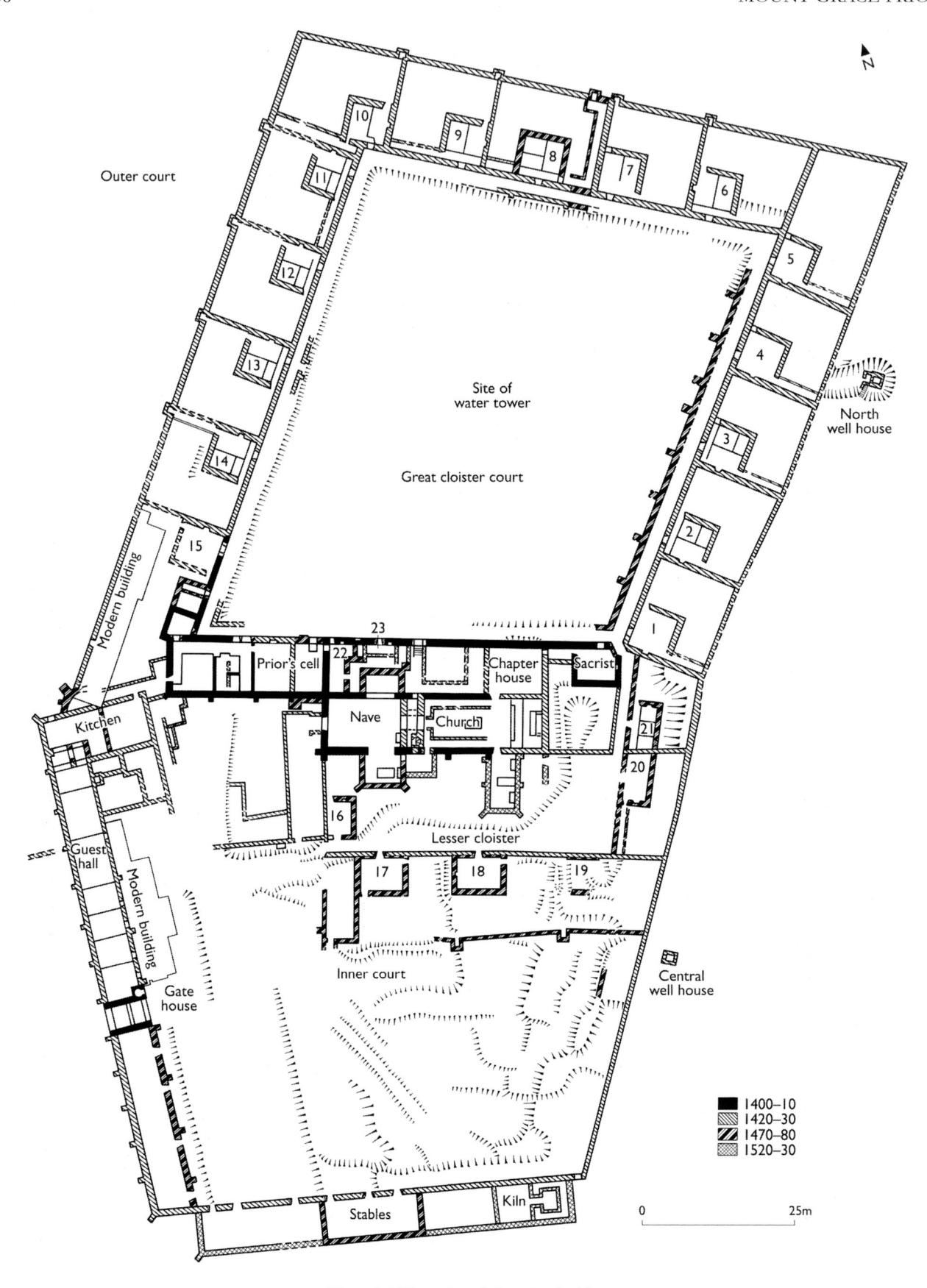

Figure 6.1 Phase plan of the priory buildings.

Table 6.1 Masons' marks on fabric of Periods One, Two and Three

Period	Mark	Location
1	A1	Church north and west walls; sacrist's cell; prison
1	A2	Church west wall
1	A3	Church north and west walls
1	A4	Church nave window
1	A5	Church north wall
1	A6	Sacrist's cell
1	A7	Sacrist's cell
1	A8	Sacrist's cell
1	A9	Sacrist's cell
1	A10	Church north wall; sacrist's cell
1	A11	Church west wall
1	A12	Church west wall, prior's cell
1	A13	Church nave window and north wall
1	A14	Church north wall
2	B1	Church tower; Cell 1; Cell 10; Cell 12; Cell 13
2	B2	Cloister arcade
2	B3	Cloister arcade
2	B4	Cloister arcade
2	B5	Cloister arcade
2	B6	Church east window; Cell 4; Cell 5; Cell 6; Cell 7; Cell 9; Cell 10; Cell 11
2	B7	Cell 5
2	B8	Church tower; Cell 9; Cell 12
2	B9	Cell 9
2	B10	Cell 4; Cell 5; Cell 7; Cell 9; Cell 10; Cell 11
2	B11	Church east window; cloister arcade; lesser cloister wall
2	B12	Church east wall
2	B13	Church east wall; Cell 10; sacrist's cell north-east angle rebuild
2	B14	Church presbytery
2	B15	Church presbytery
2	B16	Chapter house east wall
2	B17	Cloister arcade; Cell 10
2	B18	Church presbytery
2	B19	Sacrist's cell latrine pentice
2	B20	Guest house
2	B21	Church tower, south precinct wall
2	B22	Cell 10
2	B23	Cell 4
2	B24	Cell 5
2	B25	Cloister arcade, Cell 10, lavatorium
2	B26	Church east window, cloister arcade

(Continued)

Table 6.1 Masons' marks on fabric of Periods One, Two and Three (Continued)

Period	Mark	Location
2	B27	Guest house
2	B28	Guest house, Cell 11 window
2	B29	Guest house
2	B30	Cloister arcade, Cell 23 door
2	B31	Church east window
2	B32	Cloister arcade
2	B33	Water tower, lavatorium
2	B34	Water tower
2	B35	Cloister arcade or water tower
2	B36	Church tower
3	C1	Church south chapel, prior's cell door, Cell 22
3	C2	Church south chapel, Cell 12 drain, Cell 16, Cell 17
3	C3	Lesser cloister wall, Cell 21
3	C4	Cell 20, Cell 21
3	C5	Cell 20
3	C6	Church south chapel
3	C7	Church south chapel
3	C8	Church north chapel
3	C9	Church south chapel, Cell 21
3	C10	Church south chapel, Cell 20, Cell 21
3	C11	Church south chapel, Cell 22 oratory
3	C12	Cell 8
3	C13	Cloister arcade, Cell 16
3	C14	Church south chapel
3	C15	Cell 8
3	C16	Blocked prison door, Cell 21
3	C17	Church south chapel, Cell 22 oratory
3	C18	Cell 18
3	C19	Cell 18
3	C20	Cell 18
3	C21	Cell 17, Cell 21
3	C22	Cell 17
3	C23	Cell 21
3	C24	Cell 16, Cell 17
3	C25	Blocked prison door
3	C26	Cell 16, Cell 17; Cell 19
3	C27	Cell 21
3	C28	Cell 18
3	C29	Cell 12 drain, Cell 17
3	C30	Cell 18

(Continued)

THE BUILDINGS AND INFRASTRUCTURE

Table 6.1 (Continued)

Period	Mark	Location
3	C31	Cell 18
3	C32	Cell 18
3	C33	Cloister arcade
3	C34	Cloister arcade
3	C35	Cell 21
3	C36	Cell 8
3	C37	Cell 17
3	C38	Cell 17
3	C39	Cell 22
3	C40	Cell 22

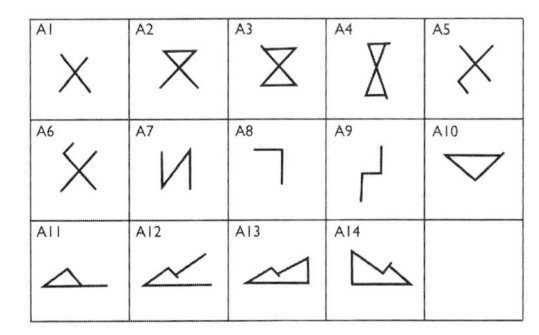

Figure 6.2 Masons' marks of Period One.

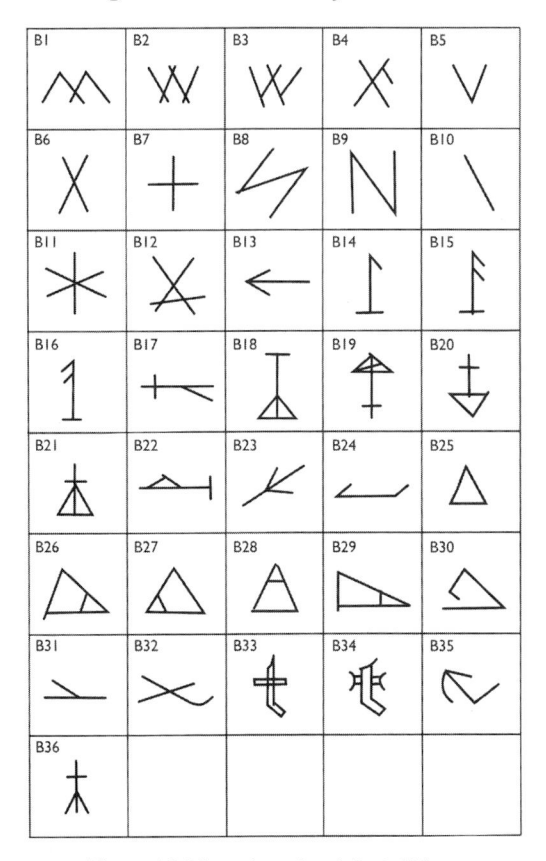

Figure 6.3 Masons' marks of Period Two.

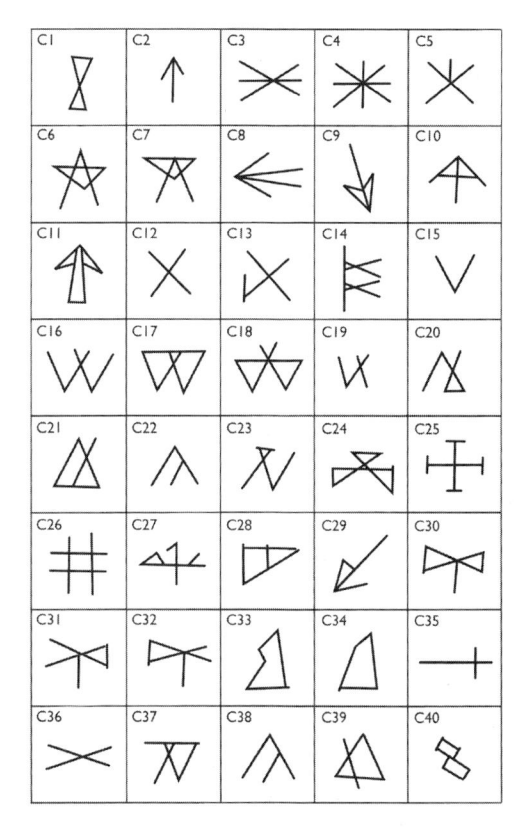

Figure 6.4 Masons' marks of Period Three.

The development of the house is outlined below:

Period One saw the development of the gatehouse and the initial building of the church and most of the south range of the great cloister. Apart from the prior's and sacrist's cells, all cells were of timber.

Period Two saw the construction of the cells of the great cloister except for Cell 8, the extension of the church, the enclosure of the inner court and the provision of the guest-house range.

Period Three saw the provision of Cell 8 and an additional cell in the south range of the great cloister, the building in stone of the lesser cloister cells, the further extension of the church and the provision of stone ranges to replace the timber buildings of the inner court.

Period Four saw the further extension of the church, the provision of an additional cell in the south range of the great cloister and the construction of further buildings in the inner court.

The following description follows the order of Hope's analysis (Hope 1905, *passim*), which it develops and corrects. Where architectural detail from the loose collection can be identified only to classes of building or broad areas of the site it is presented after the analysis of those structures.

6.1 The Development of the Priory Buildings 1398–1539

The Inner Court

The West Range of the Inner Court

THE GATEHOUSE

The priory was entered by a small gatehouse of two bays, which was originally freestanding but later set centrally in the west range of the inner court or service area. This building, of Period One, had a vaulted ground storey comprising an outer porch entered via a plain, chamfered four-centred archway, and an inner gate-hall. Between the two, a massive two-leaf door was mounted on the inner face of the responds of the dividing arch. The sockets for its lower pivots remain in the surface of the threshold. An upper storey was reached via a stair turret in the north-east angle, the blocked door of which remains. The upper storey was demolished in 1654, when the range to the north was remodelled, and its form is unknown. Unusually, no provision appears to have been made for a porter.

THE GUEST-HOUSE RANGE

The guest-house range, to the north of the gatehouse, now comprises the house probably built within it for the marriage of Grace Rokeby to Conyers, Lord Darcy in October 1616, extended and altered by Thomas Lascelles in 1654 and extended and repaired by Sir Lowthian Bell in 1900–1 (Coppack and Douglas 2014, 35–8). Despite its dramatic remodelling over the years, this structure remains principally a building of Period Two. Its southern end is butted up against the north wall of the pre-existing gatehouse with straight joints. The east wall survives virtually intact, with numerous primary window and door openings, while critical areas of the west wall, which retains its original buttresses, also survived the 17th-century refenestration (see Figure 6.5). The timber-framed partitions of the cells at Mount Grace were often not fixed to the masonry of the external walls, and it seems likely that the same technique was employed in the guest-house range, as no trace remains of any original cross-walls within the building: neither toothing for stone partitions nor sockets for framed divisions are present.

As originally built, the guest-house range provided accommodation for guests in the form of four individual suites at ground-floor level. Each had a plain, chamfered four-centred doorway and a single square-headed light facing onto the inner court. Accommodation of a better quality was provided on the floors above, and the chambers associated with the upper suite appear to have comprised a third floor at the south end of the building. The windows of the upper suite were all of two lights below a square head; one partial head survives in the west wall. Access to the first-floor suite was by means of a wooden stair from the inner court; the socket for the fixing of its handrail remains against the northern jamb of the surviving four-centred door. The means of access to the second floor is unclear.

To the north of the guest suites was a hall open to the roof, which presumably served the guests and was entered by a doorway in its north-east corner. In its east and west walls tall, transomed windows cut across the floor levels of the remainder of the building. To the north of the hall the guest-house range was of two storeys, with a servery and kitchen on the ground floor and chambers above. This part of the range, which lies outside the 17th-century house and underwent no modifications until it was reroofed and floored in 1900–1, retains all its medieval features. The floor level of the kitchen was approximately 0.5 m above that of the hall, following the rise in ground level to the great cloister terrace to the north, and the five surviving square-headed lights in the west wall, one of which has been enlarged since the

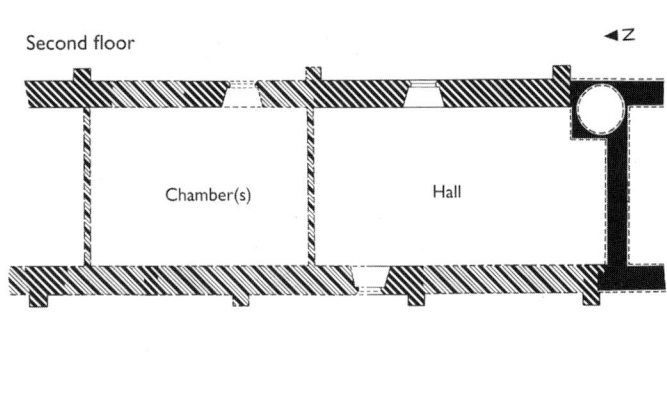

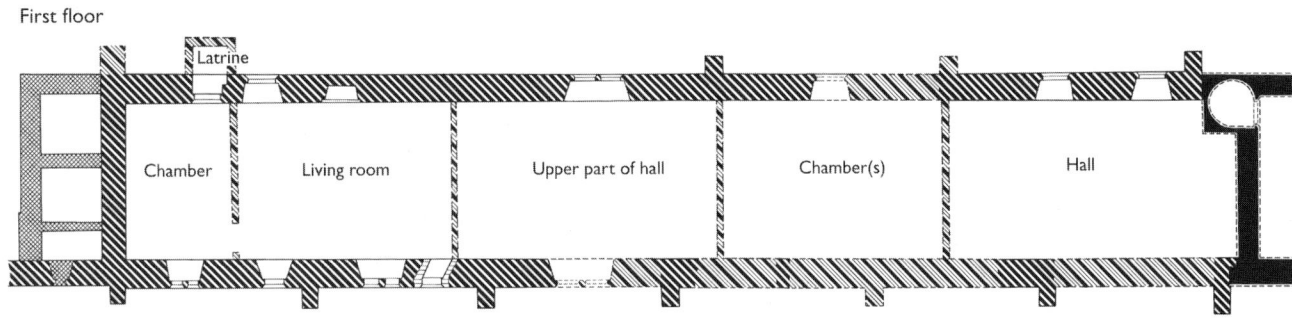

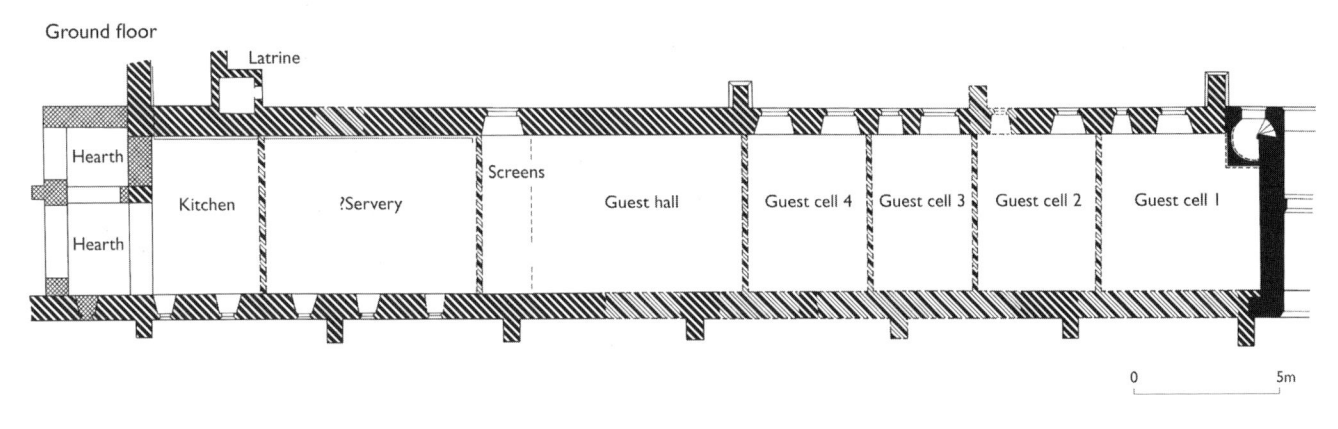

THE BUILDINGS AND INFRASTRUCTURE 261

Figure 6.5 The guest-house range, medieval phases only.

Suppression to form a door, also indicate this rise in level. Above the servery and kitchen were two rooms. That to the south, which was entered by an external stair rising from an enclosed yard on the east side of the range (see Chapter 5), retains an original transomed window in the west wall and a small, inserted fireplace of early type in the east wall, suggesting that it was a living room. Above, the base of an octagonal chimney stack remains. A second door was inserted in the west wall in Period Four to provide access from the outer court, although no trace remains of fixings for a stair. The northern room, apparently a bed chamber, retains a square-headed window in its west wall and a partially blocked square-headed door in its east wall that led to a latrine tower on the outside of the building, the shaft of which partly remains as a recess in the east wall of the range below the door (see Chapter 5). These two rooms presumably provided the accommodation of the procurator responsible for guests and the external affairs of the house.

The north end of the range, which comprised a substantial cross-wing also of Period Two, was re-excavated in 1991–2 (see Chapter 5). A study of the masonry coursing suggests that it had already been built to full height when only the lower courses of the guest-house range had been completed. Its eastern part has been demolished to ground level and is known only from Hope's account (Hope 1905, 280). The western part was identified by Hope as the brewhouse: a great embattled chimney in its south-west corner (see Figures 6.6 and 6.7) is shared with the guest-house kitchen to the south and still survives to full height, the scar of the demolished 'brewhouse' wall and the cut for the lead flashing of the roof of the cross-wing still visible on its east face. Recent analysis by Steve Coll (see Figure 6.8)

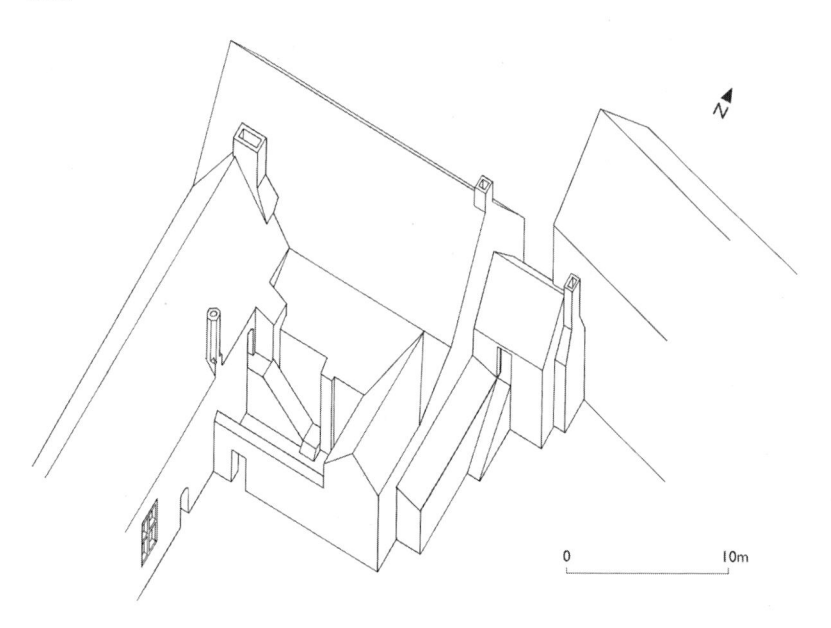

Figure 6.6 Axonometric reconstruction of the kitchen cross-wing and related buildings as it was developed in Period Four.

has demonstrated that the chimney is an insertion into Hope's 'brewhouse' and that it has a complex relationship with the kitchen to the south. It appears to belong to Period Three and replaces a Period Two kitchen chimney. Contemporary with its construction the large pointed arch in the western half of the north wall of the guest-house kitchen was blocked up and a smaller round-headed arch was inserted into the eastern half of the wall to replace it. This itself was blocked before the Suppression. The chimney was built from the first with two flues, each with a four-centred arch opening to the north separated by a two-stage buttress (see Figures 6.7 and 6.8).

As originally built, the cross-wing was of two storeys. The upper floor was carried on corbels, one of which remains in the south wall, incorporated into the wall dividing the flues; these presumably carried plates into which the floor joists were fixed. Before the chimney was built there was no gable at the north end of the guest-house range, its roof being common with that of the cross-wing, with valley gutters where the south side of the kitchen roof met each side of the guest-house range roof. The insertion of the chimney required the building of a new gable, against which the chimney itself was butted; the junction between the old wall-head and the new work is clearly demonstrated not only by a mortar change but also by a change in the character of the masonry. The insertion of the chimney also fouled the southern windows of the west wall of the cross-wing and they

Figure 6.7 The guest house and meat kitchen chimney in the 1890s before its repair, showing the scars of the kitchen roof (Canon J. C. Atkinson).

were consequently blocked. This blocking has since been removed, but the soot on the inner edges of the reveal shows that the inner face of the blocking was set back 50 mm. In spite of Hope's identification of this building as the priory brewhouse, the insertion of the chimney suggests that it functioned as a kitchen with two hearths, one of which was shared with the guest-house kitchen. Both hearths have heavy traces of burning on their surrounding masonry, but concrete underpinning has destroyed any evidence at ground level.

The north face of the chimney has a number of blocked sockets that show the form of the cross-wing roof (see Figures 6.7 and 6.9), which must pre-date the chimney because elements of it were incorporated within the new masonry. A rectangular socket 0.16 m wide and 0.42 m high carried the south end of a tie-beam that originally extended to the south wall line. Its centre line was 2.97 m east of the inner face of the west gable wall of the cross-wing. Allowing for the regular spacing of tie-beams, the next in the series would have been just to the east of the chimney, explaining a curious set-back in the masonry at that point. Above the socket for the tie-beam was a second

THE BUILDINGS AND INFRASTRUCTURE

fixing, this time to take the truncated end of a principal rafter, the raking section of which was 0.16 m wide and 0.36 m high. Set just above the principal rafter are the seatings for six more or less equally spaced common rafters 0.12 m wide and 0.10 m high. On the sides of the chimney were the sockets to take the first in a series of three equally spaced purlins. A deep cut in the east face of the chimney indicates the lead flashing of the roof, its pitch conforming exactly to that determined by the remains of the west gable of the cross-wing. An interesting detail was the provision of a boxed valley gutter between the roof of the cross-wing and the north face of the chimney, with a steep fall to the east. Four sockets for the joists that carried the floor of the gutter remain in the masonry of the chimney, each set above a rafter socket; the easternmost is virtually level with the point at which the roof covering would have met the chimney.

A large, buttressed polygonal structure, recorded as circular by Hope (Hope 1905, 280) and interpreted by him as a vat, was inserted into the north wall of the cross-wing in Period Three, just to the east of a primary door that led to the outer court. It was probably as tall as the cross-wing itself and perhaps carried a chimney. To the east, beyond a masonry cross-wall, was the 'bakehouse', re-excavated in 1991–2 and identified as a further kitchen (see Chapter 5). A door in the north wall led to a pentice giving access to the south-west cloister range and what Hope took to be the convent kitchen. Hope noted a fireplace in the south wall, although this was found not to exist on re-excavation (Hope 1905, 280). No trace remains in either room of a stair to the upper floor. A passage on the west side of the inserted chimney from the first-floor chamber in the guest-house range was probably the only access to the upper storey of the cross-wing.

On the south side of the cross-wing was a series of rooms within an outshut, rebuilt at least once and extending as far south as the latrine tower on the east side of the main building. They were excavated in 1991–2 and are described in Chapter 5 above.

THE SOUTH-WESTERN INNER COURT RANGE

To the south of the gatehouse the ruined remains of a three-storeyed range extend to the south-west corner of the site. The earliest masonry, that of the heavily buttressed west or

Figure 6.8 Axonometric cut-away drawing of the kitchen chimney (J. Dobie after S. Coll).

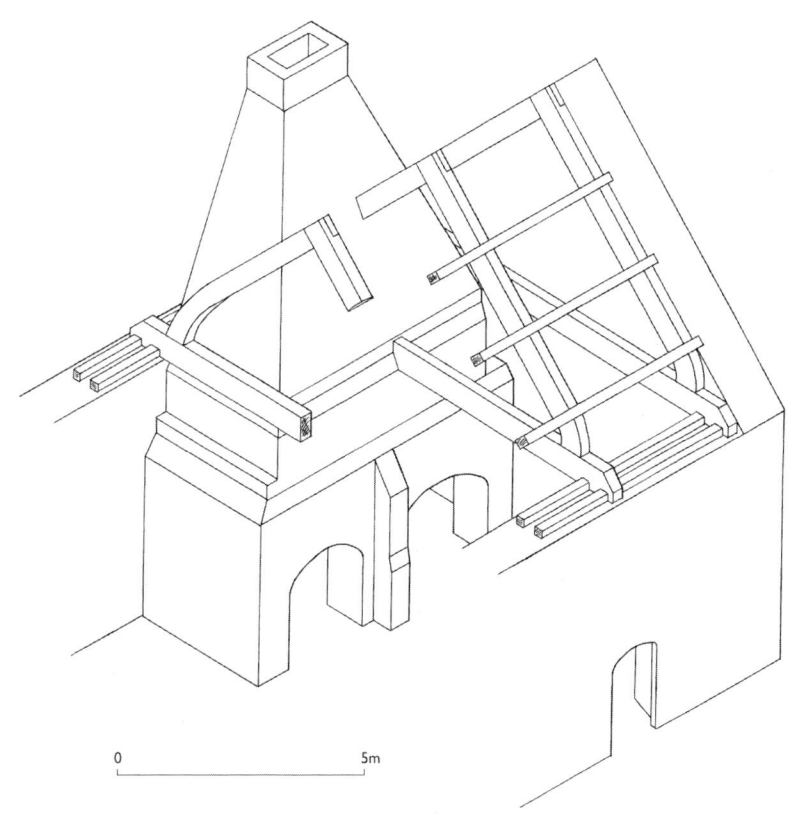

Figure 6.9 Axonometric reconstruction of the kitchen cross-wing showing the form of the roof.

outer wall, clearly belongs to Period Two and buts up to the earlier gatehouse. As originally built, it was the enclosing wall of the inner court and, as it has four windows and a door at first-floor level and a set-back to carry floors at both first- and second-floor level, there must have been a contemporary timber range built against its inner face. In Period Three this range was rebuilt in stone. At ground level four doors open into the inner court, suggesting that the range was divided into four units by timber-framed partitions, very much as the guest-house range must have been divided, for there is no trace of masonry partitions. Each room or division had one or more windows, although only the northernmost retains a part of its head, a cusped ogee closely comparable with the Period Three cloister arcade (see below), suggesting that this work also dates to the latter part of the 15th century. It has been suggested (L. J. Keen, pers. comm.) that these small rooms were additional guest chambers of a better quality than those on the ground floor of the Period Two guest-house range. In Period Four or later a door was inserted into the west wall of the range, which is a continuation of the enclosing wall of Period Two. On the first floor, entered via a door with a shouldered lintel in the centre of the west wall and reached from outside the inner court by a wooden stair, was an open space lit by four square-headed two-light windows primary to the west wall and a matching single light set in the south wall. Chases in the west wall mark the seatings of base-crucks that divided the room into eight equal bays and framed the roof above. Nothing remains of the east wall at first-floor level. Each surviving window retains evidence of shutters and iron grilles, suggesting that this room was not a granary but had a domestic use, perhaps as a common dormitory for poorer guests. Of the upper floor, which occupied the roof-space, all that survives is the lower part of the south gable wall, including a single-light window and the set-backs in the side walls that carried the floor. The side walls stood to a height of at least five courses. The use of this space and its means of access cannot now be identified.

The South Range of the Inner Court
Closing the south side of the inner court was the Period Two precinct wall, now reduced to its footing except at its eastern end, where it was partially rebuilt by Bell early in the 20th century. There may originally have been timber ranges against its inner face, but in Periods Three and Four three stone buildings were added against its outer face, access from the inner court being provided by doors inserted into the Period Two wall.

THE WESTERN BUILDING
The westernmost building was the latest, dating to Period Four, and was of two storeys. Three doors led from the inner court to partitioned rooms, and cuts in the masonry indicate the fixings of timber partitions. The upper floor is extensively ruined and, apart from two square-headed two-light windows in its western gable, little can be said of its arrangements.

THE STABLE BLOCK
The central building of the range is also the earliest surviving, of Period Three, and is again of two storeys. It was excavated in 1969–70 (see Chapter 5). Although the north wall has been demolished more or less to its footings and the south wall to below first-floor level, the west gable wall survives to full height and includes a set-back on which the first-floor joists were supported. At ground-floor level the building had a wide central doorway and narrower doors to east and west giving access from the court to what was apparently a stable, with floor drains and cuts in the masonry of the south wall indicating at least two and possibly three mangers. Above the stable was a granary, which must have been reached from the inner court by a timber stair.

THE EASTERN BUILDING
The eastern building, of Period Four, was excavated in 1970 and 1973 (see Chapter 5). Its surviving eastern gable wall suggests that it was of three storeys, and its ground floor was divided into two separate units by a centrally placed cross-wall. Although this wall does not bond with the side walls of the building, there is nothing to suggest that it is not primary. The western half of the ground floor was a granary that was lit from the south by at least three windows, all of which have been altered in the post-medieval period. A post-Suppression breach at the west end of the south wall has been closed with modern masonry. The eastern half comprises the priory kiln-house or grain-dryer. The ghost of the kiln itself can still be seen in the stone-paved floor of the

THE BUILDINGS AND INFRASTRUCTURE

Figure 6.10 The church at Mount Grace seen from the south-west (G. Coppack).

eastern room of the range – the floor of the kiln would have been perhaps a metre above the present floor level of the room – and the heavily burned stokehole from which it was heated remains in the low wall that crosses the room. The upper floors of the eastern building probably comprised granaries. Certainly, kiln-houses were normally associated with areas of grain storage (Coppack and Hayfield forthcoming; Coppack 1986, 128), and much of the south range of the inner court appears to have been reserved for the handling of cereals.

At the east end of the south range, and contemporary with the last building, was a single latrine presumably provided for the court servants. Its door, destroyed by Bell after observation by Hope, was inserted into the Period Two enclosure wall.

The East Range of the Inner Court

Against the Period Two precinct wall, which returns along the east side of the inner court and retains a terrace cut back into the hillside, are clear traces of a major building. The sockets for the principal joists of an upper floor can be traced over six bays, and the uneven ground surface indicates the unexcavated remains of a substantial stone building, perhaps one matching that on the west side of the court. The bakehouse and brewhouse, which should lie in the inner court, are unidentified, and this range is almost certainly their location.

To the south-east of this buried building is a stone-lined tank set into the yard surface of the court. It is fed by a spring further up the hill, and must have been one of the principal sources of water for industrial and agricultural use.

The Church

In common with other Carthusian churches, the church at Mount Grace was a small and relatively plain structure when compared with the churches of other orders. It clearly shows four periods of building (see Figure 6.10) and, despite its small scale, was a complex building, with clear traces remaining of its fittings and furnishings. There has been no modern excavation, and details of its archaeology have been adapted and extended from Hope's description.

Period One

The earliest phase of the church (see Figures 6.11 and 6.12) was a relatively plain rectangular structure 28.03 m long and 8.54 m wide internally, with stepped buttresses and a moulded plinth visible on its west and south sides only (see Figure 6.13). The plinth rises in the third and fourth bays from the west, following the natural rise in the ground and emphasising the choir and the sanctuary. The eastern half of the north wall, which survives to full height, is capped with

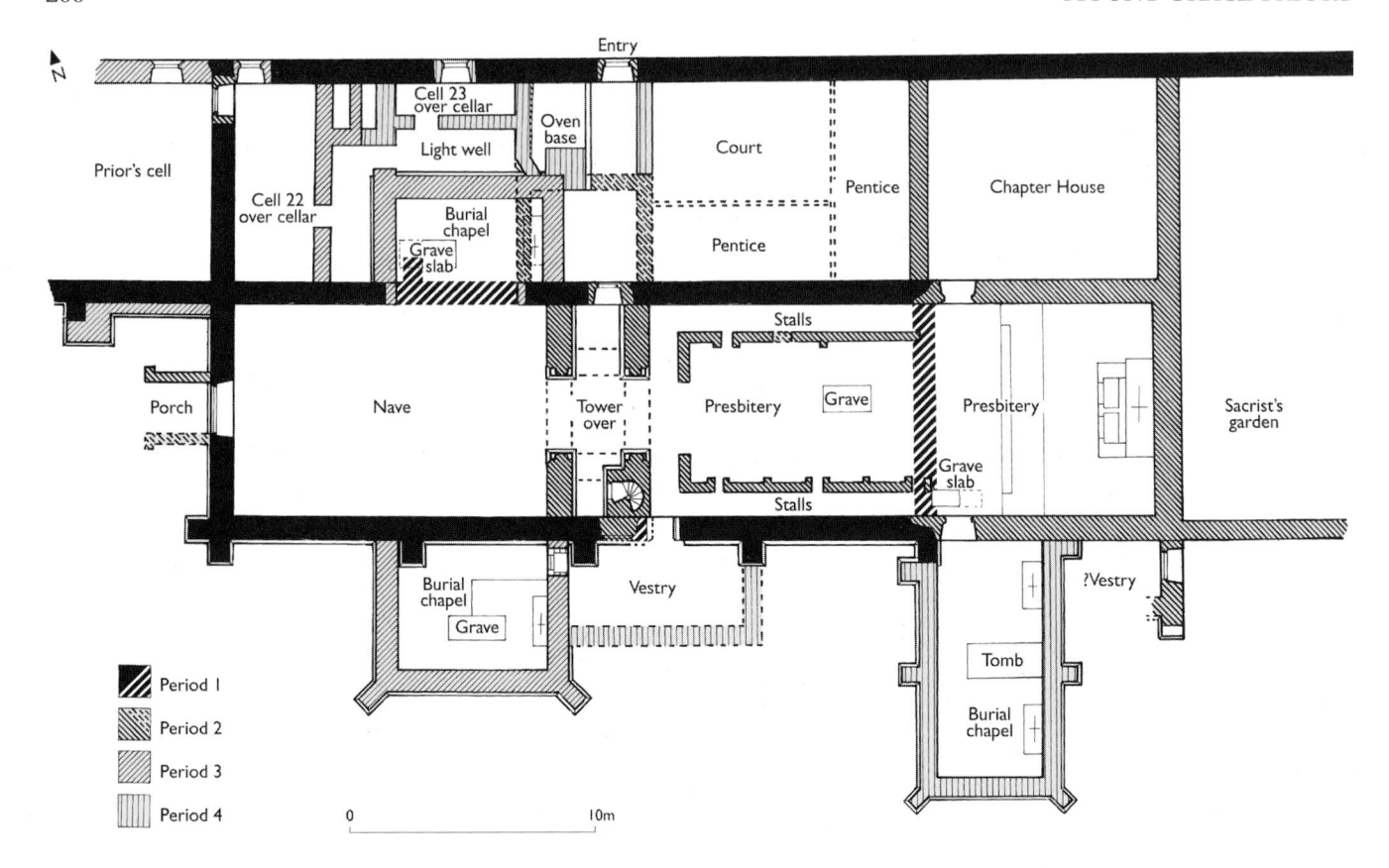

Figure 6.11 The church at Mount Grace, showing masonry of all four phases of development.

through stones that are dressed inside and out on their lower angle with a bold hollow chamfer. Built 7.8 m to the south of the wall that retained the great cloister, the church was a detached building and was entered from the inner court through an enclosed yard. The Period One door in the west wall, of two leaves, was closed with a substantial wooden bar, the slot for which survives. A small square-headed window to the north of the door, later blocked, also belongs to Period One. Any window of this period above the west door has been lost in the insertion of a later window. Two further primary doors were set into the north and south walls of the church just east of its centre line; that on the north side, the monks' entrance to the church, had an integral holy water stoup. In Period Two the door on the south side was blocked and the north door was moved a little way to the west. These doors led into a cross-passage, screened to east and west, which comprised the pulpitum, dividing the monks' choir to the east from the church of the lay brothers to the west. The screens carried a loft, the sockets for the bressummer of which can still be seen immediately to the west of the later-inserted tower, 2.65 m above the church-floor level. Above the bressummer is a shallow slot 80 mm wide into which the panelled front of the screen was fitted; this was at least 0.8 m high, but its upper part was destroyed by the insertion of a later rood beam.

Traces of two Period One windows of identical design survive. In the north wall, between the third and fourth bays from the west, is the lower part of a blocked window that lit the monks' choir, its cill set 2.4 m above the choir floor to avoid the stalls. Why it was placed at the bay division is unclear. In the western bay of the south wall of the nave the jamb and springing of the head of a large window are clearly part of the first building. Early excavation and clearance recovered tracery from two windows of this design, suggesting that at least one must have survived in the eastern bays of the south wall until the Suppression. It appears that there were no windows on the north side of the nave.

The first church was apparently completed by 1411, when Thomas de Holand was reburied there in accordance with his will (Cal. Pat. R. 1408–13, p. 416).

Period Two

In Period Two the church was substantially enlarged (see Figures 6.11 and 6.12), apparently as the burial place of Thomas Beaufort, whose tomb base remains within the choir. Beaufort

THE BUILDINGS AND INFRASTRUCTURE

effectively became the second founder in 1415 and was granted the right of sepulture at Mount Grace in 1417 (see Chapter 2). The timber screens of the pulpitum were rebuilt in stone and carried up to support a small tower, which was reached by a stair turret set against the south wall and between the two screen walls. The building of the new structure caused the original door in the south wall of the church to be blocked and the northern door to be moved slightly to the west, as noted above. Between the screen walls and above the north church door was a timber loft just over 2.1 m above floor level that was closed off from the passage through the pulpitum by a wooden screen. Both floor and screen, which may belong to a later phase, have left clear traces on the stonework. On the nave side of the new stone pulpitum, 3.45 m above the floor, are the fixings for a wooden rood beam and loft: four small sockets, two in the masonry of the west tower arch and two above, indicate the fixings of the Rood itself. Below this were two altars, one on each side of the arch that led below the tower; the base of the southern altar still remains. A tall single-light window was inserted high in the south wall of the church to light the space between the screen walls, which supported the tower. The tower, which survives intact but for its floors and roof, has three stages. The lower stage, reached from a turret stair within the pulpitum, comprised a chamber with openings into both nave and choir. That on the west was little more than a window, for its lower third was blocked with matching masonry, but that to the east was somewhat larger and might have led to a small loft overlooking the choir. The second stage, like the belfry above it, had a similar opening into the roof-space of the choir and small trefoil-headed lights in the north and south walls. The belfry has a cinquefoil window on each face below an embattled parapet with corner pinnacles and waterspouts. At the Suppression it contained at least two bells: one was removed to St Peter's, Osmotherley, where it survived until c.1890; the second, with the inscription *IN MULTIS ANNIS RESONAT CAMPANA IOHANNIS*, remained in the tower until it fell and was removed to Northallerton, where it was broken and recast in 1802 (Smithson 1898, 20).

Contemporary with the building of the tower and stone pulpitum was an eastwards extension of the choir. The east wall of the

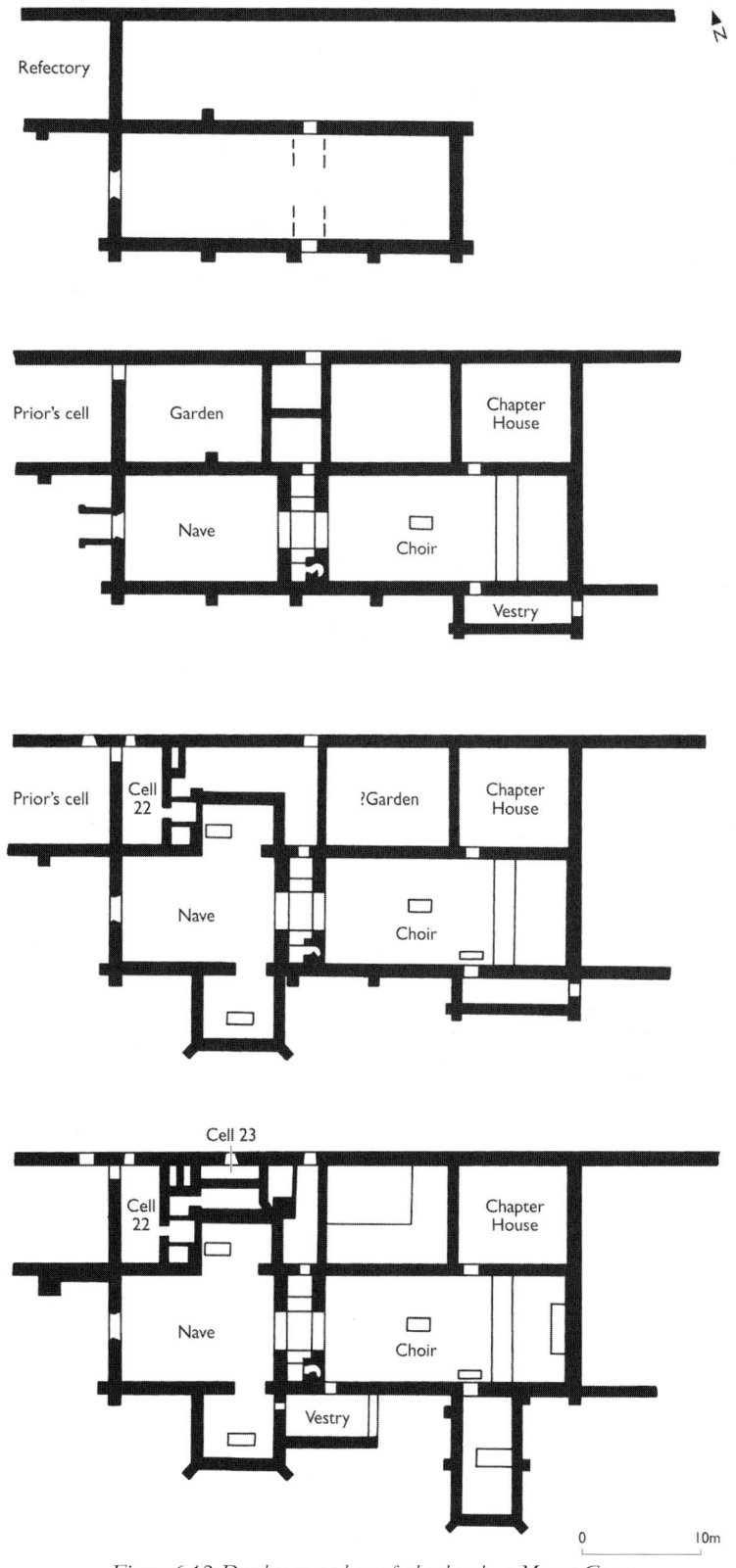

Figure 6.12 Development plans of the church at Mount Grace.

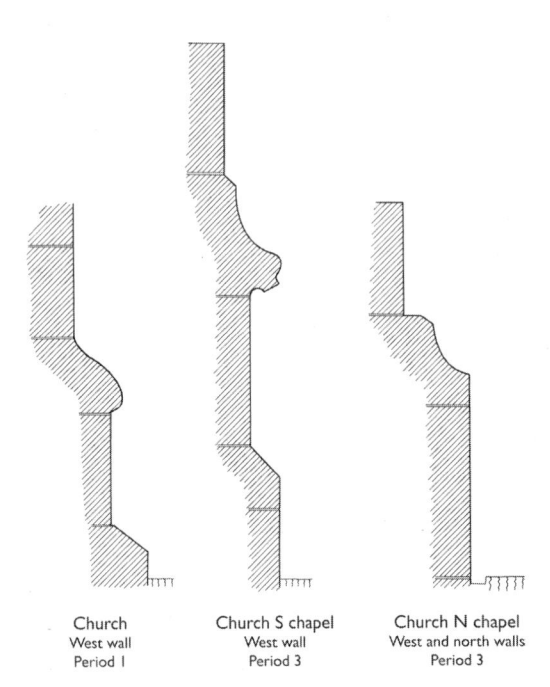

Figure 6.13 Plinth details of the Period One church and its Period Three burial chapels.

sanctuary was a tiled floor within which is the base of a large tomb, perhaps that of the second founder, Thomas Beaufort; when disturbed by drainage works, the body was found to be intact and so not that of the executed Thomas de Holand (*ex inf.* T. Rudd and G. Hutchinson). To the east of the choir doors in the north and south walls led to the chapter house and what may have been a vestry of this phase. Above the presbytery steps was a tiled platform on which is the lowest course of a stone altar – represented by its northern edge today – that is set against the east wall; a later altar was built up against its west face. The altar against the wall belongs to Period Two: when it was first excavated, the white paint on the inner face of the east wall was found not to continue behind it.

A two-storey structure with internal measurements of (according to Hope's plan) 4.45 m from west to east and 3.66 m from north to south was added to the north wall of the church, covering the relocated cross-passage door. It was demolished in Period Three and the only visible traces now are the sockets of its first-floor joists, roof creasing on the outer face of the north wall of the church and a short section of the footings of the structure's north wall. There must have been a second room of identical dimensions further to the north that Hope did not see, for the blocked sockets of its first-floor joists remain in the south face of the cloister wall. The upper floor of the southern room contained a chapel, evidenced by a piscina inserted into the church wall and reused within the 16th-century Cell 23.

The west door of the church was enclosed by a small porch in Period Two. Its stone walls reached to the level of the springing of the west door itself, their height being clearly marked by the sockets for both wall plates.

Period Three

Period Three, towards the end of the 15th century, saw the further development of the church (see Figures 6.11 and 6.12). First, a chapel was built against the south side of the nave with a large window of five lights in its south wall, another off-centre in its west wall and a tall moulded plinth (see Figure 6.13). The east wall was solid and against it is the base of an altar, high above which are the fixings of an elaborate reredos. Below the south window are the blocked remains of a piscina. At the centre of the chapel is the base of a built tomb. Access to the chapel

Period One church was removed and two further bays of a total length of 9.78 m were added. The new work, being concealed to the south by a vestry and to the north by the chapter house, lacked a moulded plinth. New paired windows of three lights were inserted in the north wall of the choir. Their cills were set very high in the wall because the monk's stalls, now canopied, were placed against the walls of the choir, precluding full-length windows. Though of one phase, the three surviving windows differ slightly in the detail of their cills and hood-mouldings. The east and south walls of the choir extension survive to little more than 1.5 m high and no windows survive in place. On the east face of the tower the weathering of the choir roof is visible, and below it the clear ghosting of the choir ceiling in the form of a pointed barrel (see Figure 6.14). This feature is not repeated on the west side of the tower, suggesting that the construction of the tower was contemporary with the remodelling of the choir.

The ritual arrangements of the choir are evidenced by the features that survive in its floor (see Figure 6.11). To north and south are the stone bases of the wooden choir stalls, the fixings for whose canopies can be seen to a height of 3 m on the surviving north wall of the choir. The north and south banks differ in detail, but there is no evidence to suggest that they were not contemporary. Between the stalls and extending as far east as the step up into the was provided by cutting down the Period One window that had occupied the second bay of the nave. Following the construction of the south chapel, a second chapel was built on the north side of the nave directly opposite, again with a moulded plinth, albeit different in its detail (see Figure 6.13). A wide, barely pointed arch closed by a wooden screen was inserted into the north wall of the nave to give access to this chapel, which had a large window in its north wall and a three-light window high up in its west wall (see Figure 6.32). Again, the east wall is solid and has traces of an altar against it, above which there are the fixings of an elaborate canopy. To the south of the altar is a small damaged bracket piscina. Both chapels were built to receive burials, graves being clearly visible in their floors. A large window was inserted in the west wall of the church at this time, presumably to compensate for the loss of lateral light caused by the removal of at least one window in the nave.

Period Four

The final phase of building in the church, dating to the first quarter of the 16th century, comprised the construction of a chapel to the south of the presbytery and a vestry in the angle between the Period Three chapel to the south of the nave and the choir (see Figures 6.11 and 6.12). The building of these two structures may well be connected, as the door that leads into the new chapel clearly belongs to Period Two, its east jamb coursing well with the masonry of the extended presbytery and its west jamb being inserted into the south wall of the original church. It is most likely that it originally led to a vestry that was destroyed when the chapel was built and thus required replacement. Undoubtedly, the pressure for further space for lay burial within the church was the reason for the building of the chapel. Against the east wall are the bases of two altars, and between them the base of a table tomb.

Architectural Detail from the Church

PERIOD ONE WINDOWS FROM THE NAVE (SEE FIGURE 6.15)

The western jamb, the cill, the lower part of an external hood-mould and the springing of the rear arch of the westernmost window on the south side of the nave survive *in situ*, and a straight section of hood-mould, 5 sections of tracery, 12 fragmentary mullions and 2 sections of window-head cut to the same template can be traced in the unprovenanced collection, from which a segmental-headed window with four major lights can be reconstructed and dated with certainty to Period One, *c.*1400 (stones 63–8, illustrated). The tracery comprised a mullion that sprang from the head of one of the major lights and four double springers with central diamond piercings that formed the heads of a second tier of two full and two half-lights and the bottom of an upper tier of six foiled lights. The full height of the window from the upper surface of the cill to the springing of the head was 4.40 m, and from the cill to the springing of the heads of the major lights 2.27 m. Unlike the elements illustrated, which were crisp and unweathered externally, two of the pierced springers were badly eroded and, as a four-light window would require only three, it is likely that they come from another window, the only possible location for which was the west end of the south wall of the monks' choir, where Period One masonry survived to the Suppression. The western splay of this window survives *in situ* immediately east of the tower.

The quality of the window, which retained its tracing lines and clear evidence of bolster tooling, was high. All the lights had well-cut glazing grooves, and the major lights had external saddle-bars at variable centres, though there were no bars in the upper lights. Masons' marks of types A4, and A14 were recorded

Figure 6.14 The monks' choir before 1900, showing the ghost of the wooden barrel vault evidenced by whiteliming of the walls that no longer survives (Canon J. C. Atkinson).

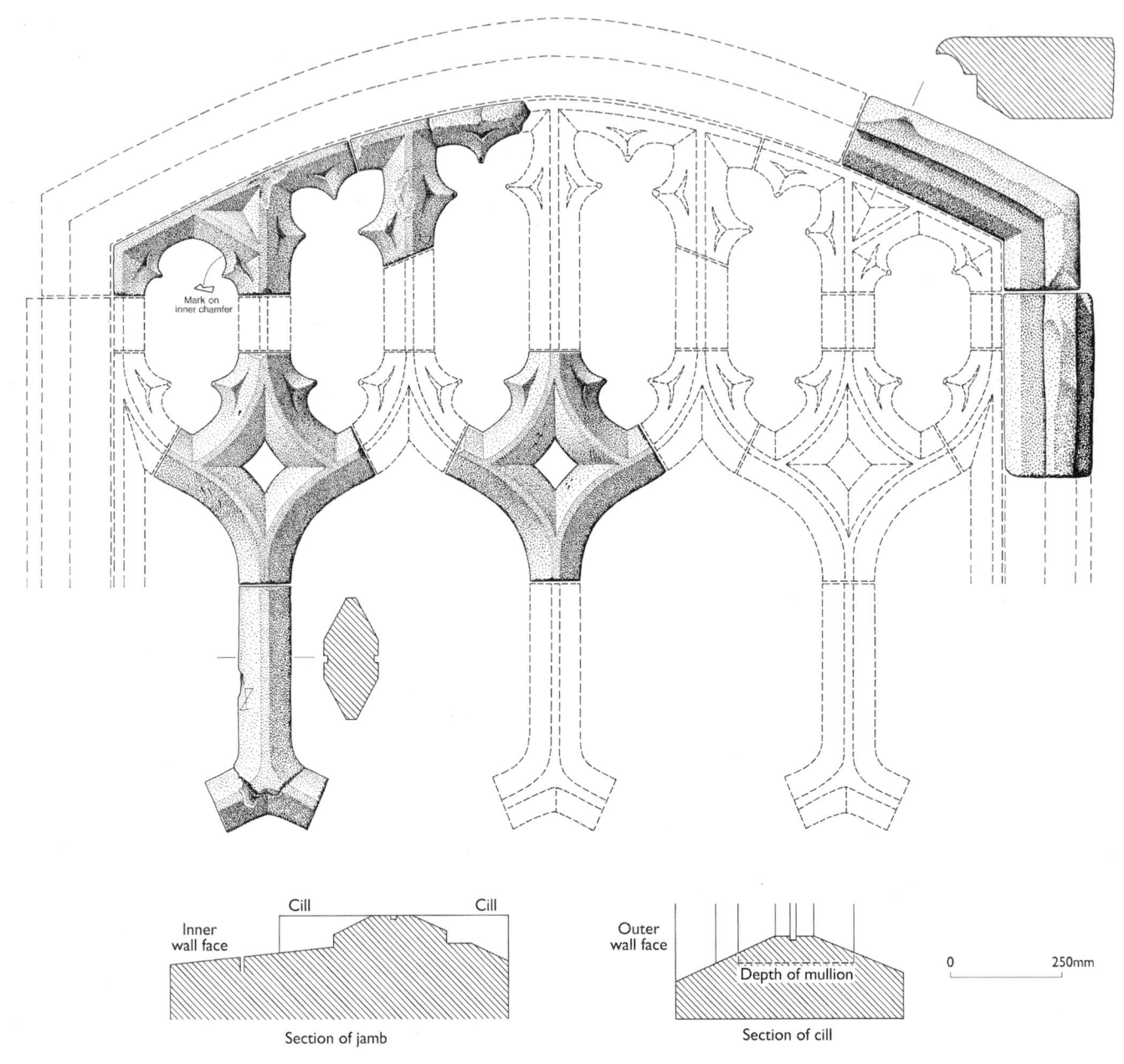

Figure 6.15 Period One window from the south wall of the nave (1:10) (G. Coppack, J. Hall and S. Hayfield).

on the surviving elements, and the sections of head retained a coating of limewash on the inner surface, which extended only to the glazing groove.

THE PERIOD TWO EAST WINDOW (SEE FIGURES 6.16 AND 6.17)

Twenty-one elements (69–89, all illustrated) were identified within the unprovenanced collection from a major window that was so large that the only wall it could have occupied was the east gable wall of the church built in Period Two, when the church was extended to the east. In all, five pieces of window head survive, comprising two almost complete sections, most of a third now in two pieces and two fragments. Additionally, there were five sections of embattled transom with the seatings of passing mullions that in two cases break the line of the transom; one complete and four fragmentary heads from major lights; one matching double springer; two mullions with a side springer; two mullions with multiple springings; and a single section of plain mullion. No jamb or cill sections were recovered, and the poor condition of many of the surviving fragments suggests that the window tracery had collapsed before the east wall was demolished and its materials reused. This would also account for the absence of any sections of hood-mould.

THE BUILDINGS AND INFRASTRUCTURE

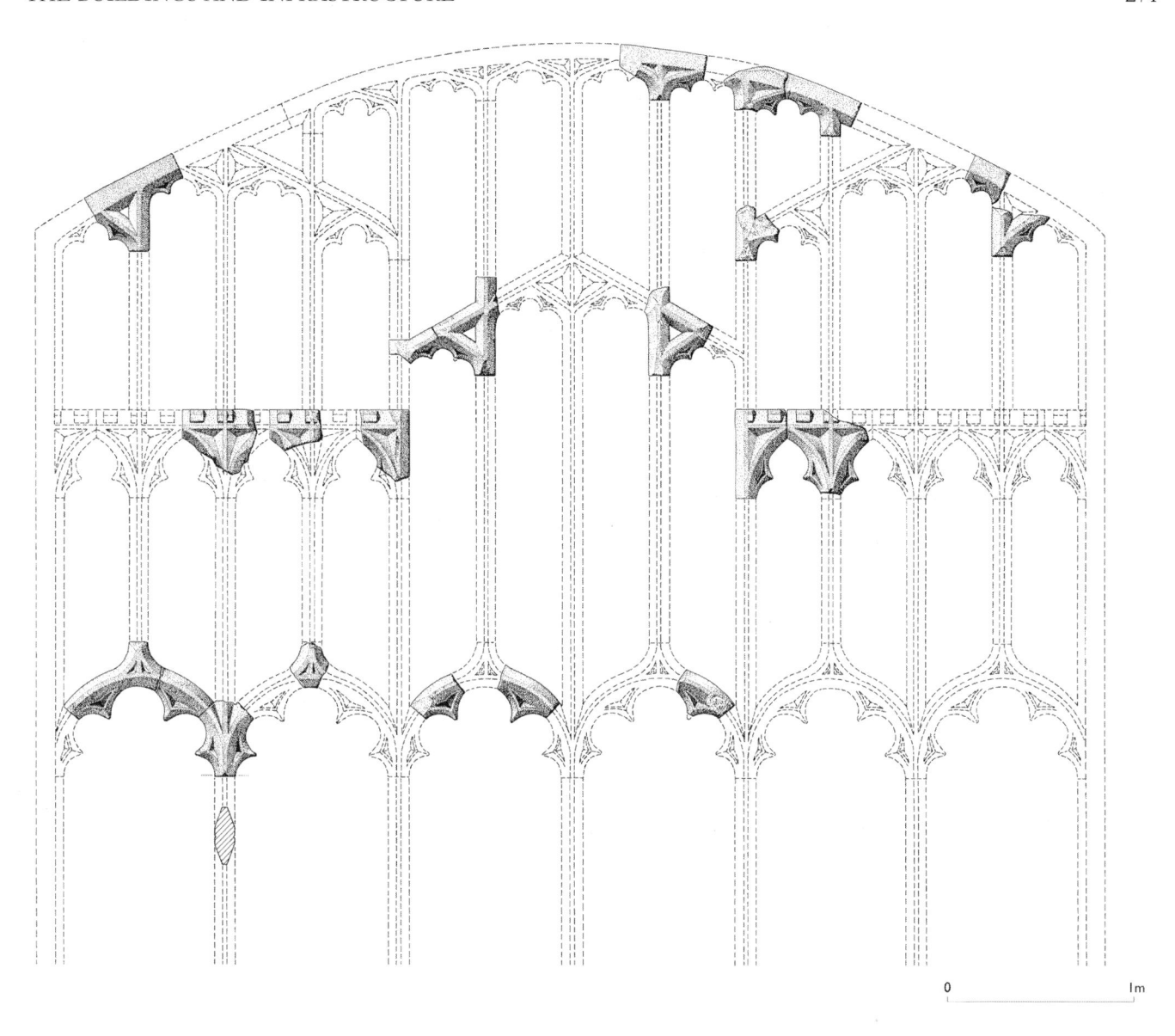

Paper reconstruction revealed a window of panel tracery with six major lights at centres of 0.92 m and groups of 12 lights above. It would fit easily into the east wall of the church with roughly 1.25 m of masonry to each side. If a standard proportion of 3:1 for each light is assumed, then the height of the window must be at least 7 m. Again, this easily fits into the east wall, as the ceiling of the choir, evidenced by paint on the east face of the tower (see Figure 6.14) is about 10 m above floor level. The cill of the window must have been at least 1.3 m from ground level, as this is the height of the extant walling; while, to allow for the height of the altar and its retable or reredos, the cill is hardly likely to have been less than 2 m above the floor of the altar platform.

Two possible reconstructions can be demonstrated from the surviving fragments. In the first (see Figure 6.16), the window consisted of three and, in places, four tiers of lights. The main lights in the lowest tier had semicircular cinquefoiled heads the upper surfaces of which formed the ogee cills of the next tier of lights. In the second tier the four lights (half the width of the lower lights) on each side of the window had pointed trefoiled heads below an embattled transom, the castellation occurring on both sides of the window. This transom was interrupted by the four central lights of this tier, which rose through it to form a secondary window with pointed trefoiled heads below a third tier of trefoil-headed lights. Similar secondary windows of four lights were

Figure 6.16 Possible reconstruction of the Period Two east window of the church (1:20) (J. Hall and S. Hayfield).

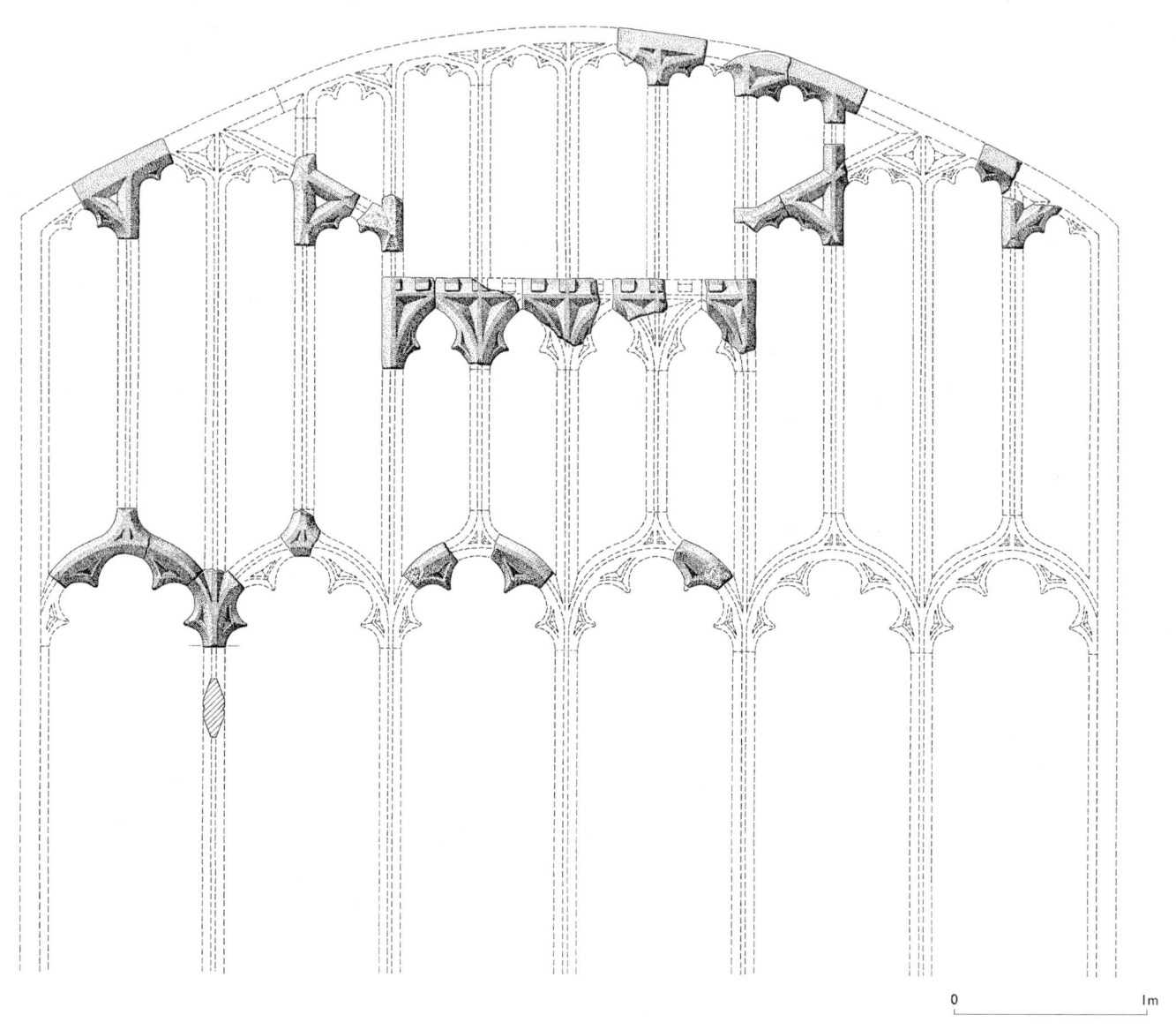

Figure 6.17 Alternate reconstruction of the Period Two east window of the church (1:20) (J. Hall and S. Hayfield).

provided above the embattled transom in the upper tier of the window, the remaining space between the secondary window heads and the segmental head of the window being filled with a fourth tier of lights, all bar two glazed triangles with round trefoiled heads. All the lights, with the exception of minor triangular piercings, had a centrally placed glazing groove. No fixings for saddle bars were recorded on the surviving pieces, but as these would have occurred only on straight lengths of mullion it is hardly surprising.

Given the fragmentary nature of the surviving tracery, an alternative reconstruction (see Figure 6.17) is proposed. Here, the same elements are combined to give a window of two and, centrally, three tiers of lights by placing the interrupted transom above the two central main lights of the main window, with subsidiary windows of four lights to left and right. This would give a more typical Perpendicular design, but it presupposes that the elements of the interrupted transom were more likely to survive than any of the other major elements of tracery, particularly the heads and springers of the main lights. The precise form of the window would have been dictated by the iconography of the glass it contained.

In the form of its tracery, and particularly its cusping, this window has the same restrained elegance as the contemporary Period Two cloister arcade (see Figure 6.24 'The Period Two Arcade'), and its elements were bolster dressed to an extremely high standard. Despite damage and erosion, tracing lines, presumably deeply cut, survived

THE BUILDINGS AND INFRASTRUCTURE

on 15 of the pieces. Limewash, evidenced elsewhere in the church, was detectable on only three pieces. Fifteen stones had assembly marks on bed surfaces (13 simple crosses and two in the form of an asterisk), and four masons' marks, of types B6, B11, B26 and B31, were recorded.

Window Tracery from the South Burial Chapel

The south burial chapel had two windows of plain panel tracery in which each light extended the full height of the window and terminated in pointed cinquefoil heads. The south window of five lights (see Figure 6.10) survives without its mullions, but with head, jambs and cill intact. Of the west window, only the southern jamb remains. Its placing, well to the north of centre in the west wall of the chapel, leaves room for only three lights. Two fragments of tracery from its head, which match the surviving detail of the south window, were recovered (see Figure 6.18, stones 90 and 91), as were 30 sections of matching hollow-chamfered mullion (not illustrated), which could be from either window – apart from those in the east burial chapel, these are the only windows extant on the site to utilise hollow chamfers. Both fragments of tracery consist of a mullion with a side springer, and are consistent with having been broken from a section of window-head. From stone 90 it was possible to ascertain that the lights were placed at centres of 0.69 m, a spacing identical to that of the lights in the surviving south window, while the surviving jambs and mullion fragments indicate that saddle bars were provided at centres of 0.29 m. Where beds survive, assembly marks in the form of a plain cross were found. No masons' marks or paint were recorded, though all the fragments were severely eroded.

Window from the North Burial Chapel

Three sections of mullion matching the jamb moulding of the north window of the north burial chapel were recovered from Hope's stone dump. One of these (see Figure 6.18, 92) has a mason's mark of type C2 on its inner chamfer, while two have plain cross assembly marks on their lower beds.

Windows from the Eastern Burial Chapel

Three sections of window survive that can be assigned to the fenestration of this Period Four addition to the church. This identification, which

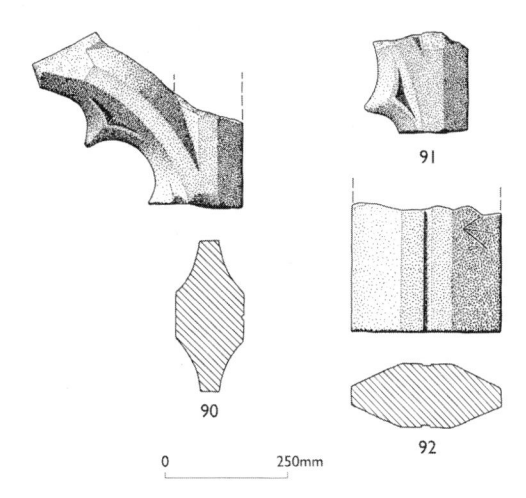

Figure 6.18 Window tracery from the south and north burial chapels (1:10).

was originally based on the size and style of the windows, was confirmed by the width of the chapel walls, 0.66 m, which was identical to two elements that can be identified as through stones. At least two windows are represented. The first (see Figure 6.19, 93) was a window of panel tracery with trefoil-headed lights of approximately 0.45 m centres, the head being integral, with internal and external splays. A second element of head cut to the same template (see Figure 6.19, 94) did not have the integral internal splay, but this might have been worked on a separate stone. Both pieces were badly abraded and, although they retained glazing grooves, no evidence of surface tooling or masons' marks remained. The bay-spacing of the east and west walls of the eastern burial chapel would allow for windows of five or six lights.

The third stone is an altogether more interesting piece (see Figure 6.19, 95), being derived from a circular window that had an internal radius of approximately 0.83 m and 12 round foils relieving its soffit. This stone has identical inner and outer splays to those of the panel tracery window described above, and the two windows very clearly belong to the same structure. The most likely placing for the circular window was in the south gable of the burial chapel. This stone was too badly damaged to identify its surface finish or any tracing lines or mason's mark, although the glazing groove remained at the top of the one surviving foil.

Piscinas from the East Burial Chapel (see Figure 6.20)

In the Period Four eastern burial chapel Hope recorded the discovery 'close by the south end

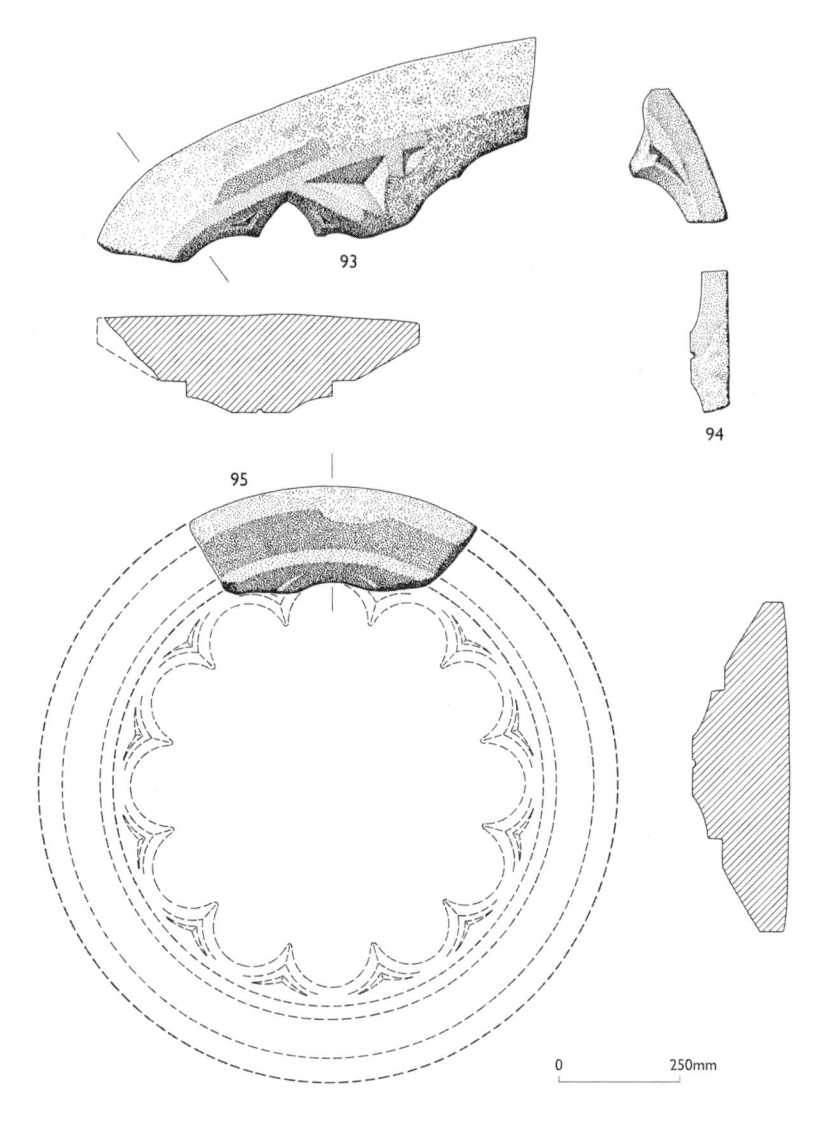

Figure 6.19 Windows from the east burial chapel (1:10).

way. In elevation, both below the basin and the set-back bracket are deeply chamfered, and the stone has every appearance of a bracket piscina, although the bottom part is broken away. Hope must have found the two stones together and drawn the wrong conclusion. The situation is confused by the occurrence in the loose stone collection of a large piscina (stone 98) that *would* fit on the existing pillar and should probably be associated with it. This piscina has a shallow and slightly irregular square basin with a raised hemisphere at its base. Where the arrises of the sinking meet the hemisphere there are four drilled drain-holes that emerge within a square sinking in the bottom surface of the stone, provided to receive the belled end of a lead pipe. The lower front edge of the piscina block is boldly chamfered, a treatment not accorded to the sides. If it was supported on the surviving pillar it must have been set into a wall recess some 0.11 m deep.

OTHER ARCHITECTURAL DETAIL DERIVED FROM THE CHURCH (SEE FIGURES 6.21 AND 6.22)

99–101. Three sections from a stone screen, comprising a section of chamfered plinth, a second section of plinth with the base of a buttress 0.19 m wide and 0.155 m deep above the chamfer and a section of blind traceried panelling with one of a series of trefoil-headed gablets between unchamfered standards. Although the section of panelling, 101, is badly damaged, the two sections of plinth retain their fine bolster finish and stone 99 has a mason's mark of type B17.

102. Step section rebated to a depth of 25 mm on the riser for tiling.

103. Step section 0.245 m high, lightly chamfered on the front arris and rebated to a depth of 25 mm on the upper surface to take tiles. The stone is finely bolster dressed and has a mason's mark of type B18 on the upper surface of the front lip. The upper face of the stone is incised with graffiti, for the most part medieval, principally a series of Rs.

104. Grave cover with a floriate cross and calvary base found immediately outside the west door of the church in a 17th-century context. The design of this

of the northernmost altar … [of] a curious shaft, 22½ins high, of a pillar piscina, with a deep oblong drain on top, and beside it a projection to carry the cruets' (Hope 1905, 286). Both the pillar and the piscina were subsequently removed from site, but can be identified in the loose stone collection. The pillar (stone 96), which is cut out at the back for a lead pipe, has prominent hollow chamfers on its front angles, with long arrow-stops to top and bottom that are further emphasised by triangular sinkings. Along its bottom edge is a band of white mortar some 30 mm thick, where the floor had butted against the pillar.

The piscina itself (stone 97), with its bracket for the cruets, has a square, rather than a rectangular, sinking in its upper surface, with a square drain-hole placed at the back of the basin. Its dimensions are such that it is difficult to associate it with the pillar in any

THE BUILDINGS AND INFRASTRUCTURE

incised slab is a very simple 'bracelet' type typical of the late 12th or 13th centuries (Gittos and Gittos 1989; Ryder 1985) that had certainly gone out of use long before the foundation of Mount Grace Priory. An early date is reinforced by the tapered plan of the slab, as it is much more usual to find rectangular slabs in the 15th century. How it arrived at Mount Grace is a matter for speculation.

105–7. Three fragments of gargoyle. 106 survives only as a lock of hair, while 105 and 107 each have an eye and a single lock of hair. The absence of hair behind this shows that the Mount Grace masons wasted no energy on what was not going to be seen from the ground. Although the most likely location for these fragments is the church, it should not be forgotten that the prior's cell also had a parapet and would have been provided with waterspouts of some kind.

The Great Cloister (see Figure 6.1)

To the north of the church, on a great terrace levelled into the hillside, is the great cloister, around which were built the principal communal buildings of the priory and the cells and gardens for 17 members of the convent, the sacrist and the prior. Excavation has demonstrated that the terrace was laid out during the initial phase of building (Period One) and that it incorporated a series of substantial drains and watercourses, indicating the intention to build from the first on the scale that is apparent today. However, the first phase of building appears to have been largely of timber, with cells set in gardens defined by ditches, and the construction of the east, north and west ranges in stone did not begin until Period Two. In contrast, much of the south range was built in stone from the first.

The great cloister garth itself comprised an enclosed garden surrounded by alleys covered by pent roofs that were carried by a variety of methods. In the south and east alleys, the first to be surrounded by stone cells, a continuous wall plate was carried on prominent corbels set in both the cell walls and the cloister walls between the cells. The detailing is particularly interesting in the latter, where a course of ashlar separated the corbels from a continuous string course (see Figure 6.23A). Above the string course were a second course of ashlar and two courses of coping. This detail is best seen in the cloister wall between Cells 4 and 5. A different approach was adopted for the north and west ranges, in which a wall plate was provided only against the front wall of each cell. No corbels were provided in the garden walls and the upper ends of the rafters were simply lodged in sockets cut in the masonry (see Figure 6.23B). Directly above the sockets was a continuous string course capped by a single course of ashlar and two courses of coping. The best-preserved example of this technique can be seen in the cloister wall between Cells 13 and 14. These alleys, the centre of communal life in the houses of other orders, were essentially corridors linking individual cells with the church, chapter house, refectory and kitchen. Their relative lack of importance at Mount Grace is reflected in their piecemeal development. Originally built of timber, the north alley remained in large part in that form until the Suppression, although its eastern half, along with the west

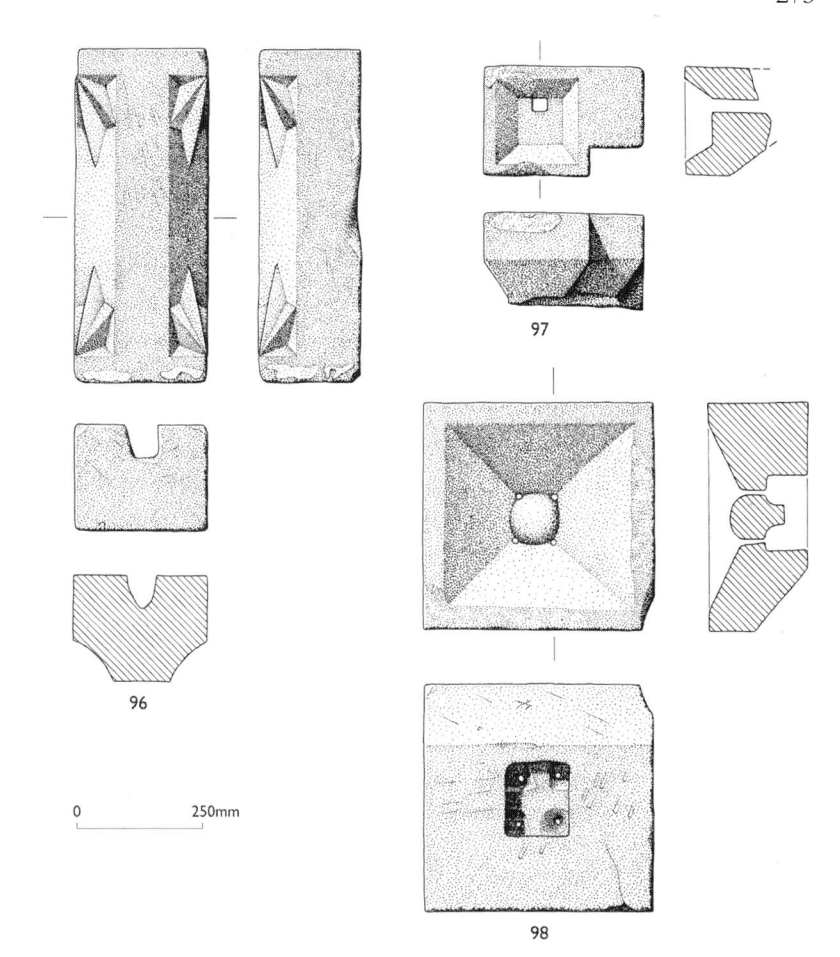

Figure 6.20 Piscinas from the east burial chapel (1:10).

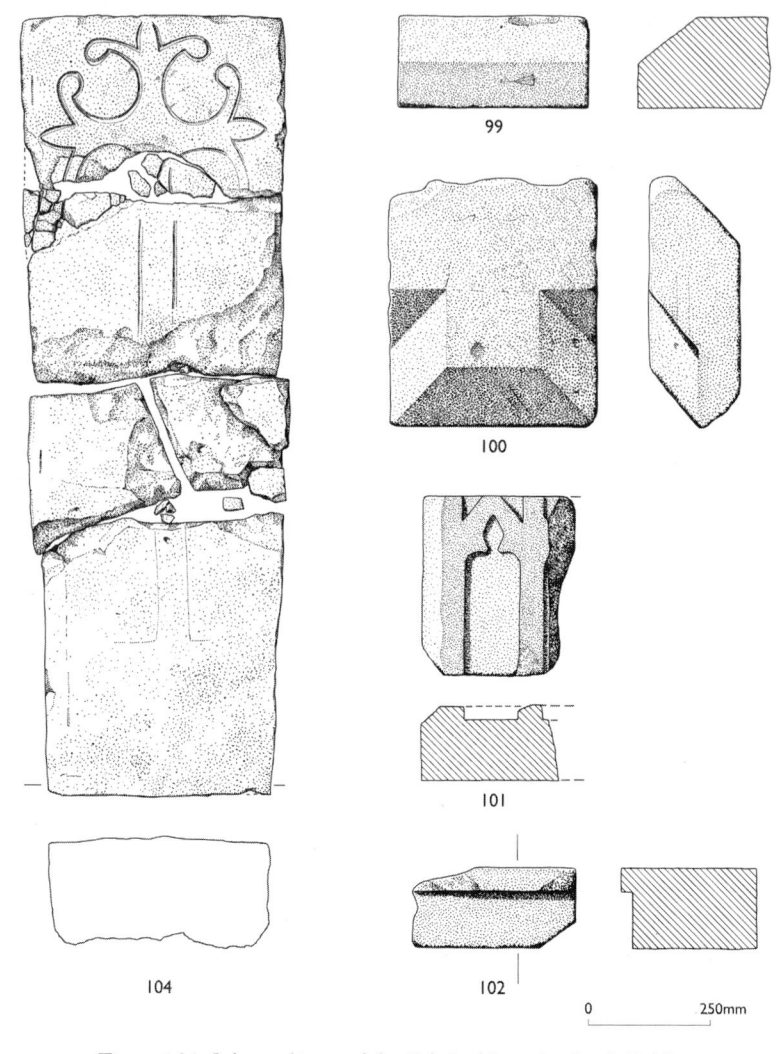

Figure 6.21 Other architectural detail derived from the church (1:10).

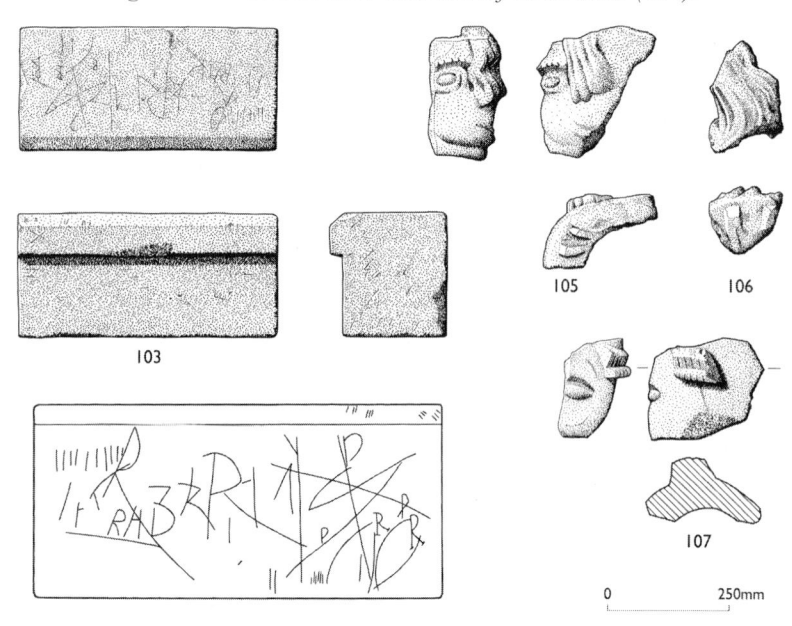

Figure 6.22 Other architectural detail derived from the church (1:10).

alley and the south alley, was rebuilt in stone in Period Two. Excavation in the north alley has shown that this rebuilding was carried out in short sections that differed in form. It was not until Period Three that a unified rebuilding began in the east alley, with the provision of three windows of three lights with ogee heads grouped between deep projecting buttresses. These windows were glazed and the work was of high quality. Although this rebuilding was carried around into the north and south alleys, it was never completed. Excavation by Hope in 1900 recovered considerable fragments of this alley, enabling its reconstruction in some detail (Hope 1905, fig. 10).

Contemporary with the building of the Period Two stone cloister arcade was the construction of an octagonal conduit house in the centre of the garth (see Chapter 4), its site marked until 1988 by a deep depression. From here, water was carried to each cell by a series of lead pipes, and each monk had his own tap set in a recess either inside or just outside his cell. Also of Period Two was a small lavatorium in the south wall of the great cloister (see Figure 6.52). Chases in the sides of the opening mark the position of a tank placed above the basin and fed by a lead pipe, the chase for which survives on the west side of the laver.

The Great Cloister Arcades

THE PERIOD TWO ARCADE (SEE FIGURES 6.24 AND 6.25)

No trace of the Period Two cloister arcade can now be seen above ground level, although it was partially examined in the north alley outside Cell 8 in 1985, in the west alley outside Cell 13 and the prison in 1971 and 1989 (see Chapter 4) and by Hope in both the north and south alleys in 1900 (Hope 1905, 304). No obvious evidence of the superstructure was recovered in 1985 and Hope did not describe or illustrate anything that he might have uncovered. Analysis of the loose stone collection in 1988–9, however, identified 53 elements (13 illustrated, stones 108–20) from an elegant arcade found either by Hope or in subsequent clearance of the site by the Ministry of Works that was capable of paper reconstruction. Some elements were also recovered by excavation since 1969. In all, 8 sections of jamb (4 found by Keen in Cells 10 and 11), 4 engaged springers, 14 detached

THE BUILDINGS AND INFRASTRUCTURE

springers, 11 largely fragmentary keystones, 7 sections of cill (4 found by Keen in Cell 11, 1 found in the cloister alley outside Cell 8 [210]) and 9 fragments of mullion (5 found by Keen in Cell 11, the longest being 0.57 m in length but broken; and 1 0.34 m in length that came from the cloister alley outside Cell 8 [210]) were identified. Four further mullion fragments were recovered from the backfill of Hope's water-tower excavation [400], [401] and [415], but these could as easily have been derived from the tower as from the cloister alley. One unlocated section of cill had been recut for the fitting of glazing in a wooden frame, which, remarkably, was inserted from the outer face by rebating the cill and dressing back the outer chamfer of the jamb (see Figure 6.25, 121).

In form, the arcade consisted of three or more lights with cusped ogee heads below a continuous plain chamfered string course that was integral in some cases with the substantial keystones, but in most cases worked on a separate stone. Between the groups of lights were buttresses that were little more than shallow pilasters at the height of the springers and upper jambs. As plain ashlar blocks had not been retained during conservation work, it was not possible to reconstruct the form of these buttresses, but their projection at foundation level, where excavated outside Cell 8 (see Chapter 4), was 0.36 m. Internally, the bay divisions were marked by shallow pilasters of the same width as the buttresses that simply died into the internal chamfer of the cill, a fragmentary section of which was found in excavation outside Cell 8 [210]. A further section of cill (see Figure 6.25, 122) was found among the loose stonework retaining the seating of a mullion, which was not set centrally, as would be expected, but with its internal nosing set towards the inner edge of the cill. The external chamfer of the cill was

Figure 6.23 Details of the cloister roof fixings on the south and north walls of the great cloister.

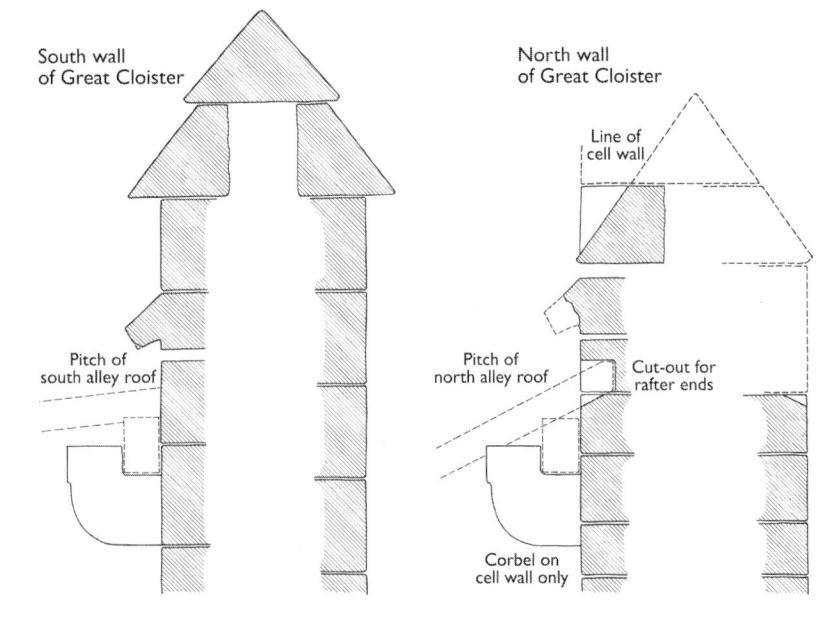

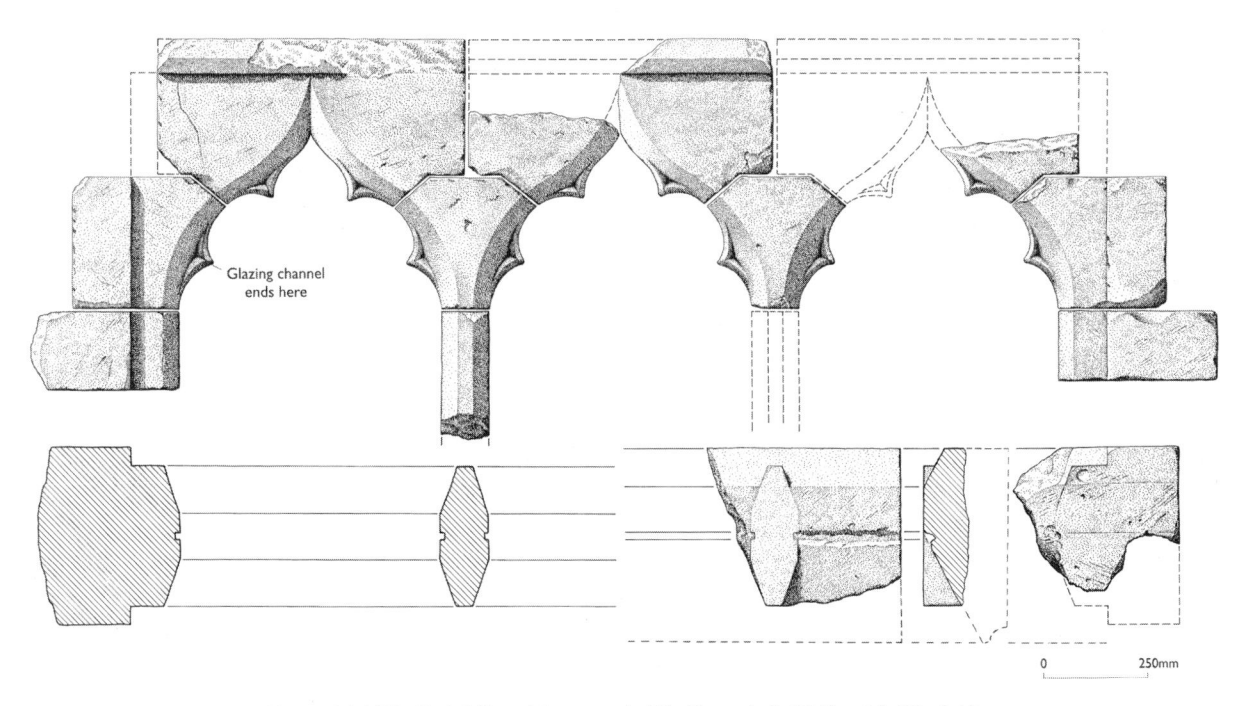

Figure 6.24 The Period Two cloister arcade (G. Coppack, J. Hall and S. Hayfield).

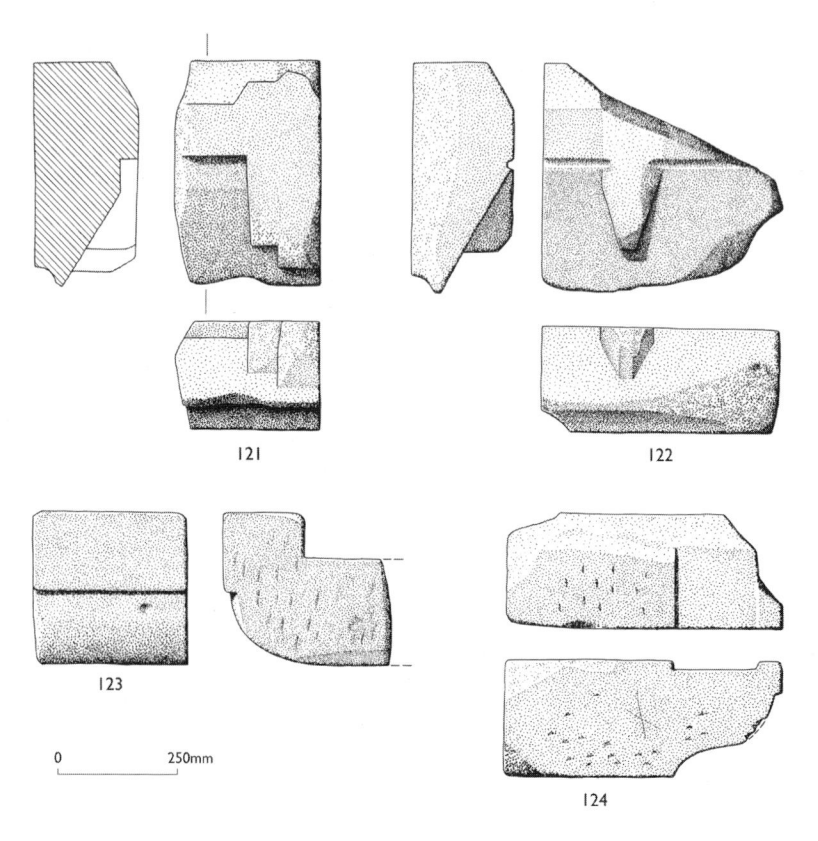

Figure 6.25 Architectural detail from the Period Two cloister (1:10).

The wall plate of the Period Two cloister roof was carried on corbels (see Figures 6.23 and 6.25, 123) that are still extant in the contemporary masonry of the south, east, west and north cloister walls. These are cut to a simple quarter-round profile and have a prominent square block on the front that is emphasised by the chamfering of the arrises of the rounded lower face. The upper surface is cut out to a depth of 90 mm to accommodate the wall plate. The corbels of this type in the south alley are clearly contemporary with masonry of Period One and must be reused from the earlier timber cloister alley, but they also occur elsewhere in masonry of Period Two. A single unlocated example survives with very similar dimensions but an ogee rather than a quarter-round profile (see Figure 6.25, 124). Its size and proportions, particularly of the rebate for the wall plate, strongly suggest, however, that it also originated in the cloister roof.

THE PERIOD THREE ARCADE (SEE FIGURE 6.26) The rebuilt eastern arcade was excavated by Hope in 1900 and his account describes it in some detail (Hope 1905, 302–4 and fig. 10). Some 33 elements (10 illustrated, stones 125–34) can still be identified, comprising some 11 engaged springers, 8 double springers, 5 sections of hood-mould, 4 jamb sections, 4 superordinate mullion sections (3 with a bed height of 0.370 m and one with a bed height of 0.320 m) and 1 fragment of mullion. The sections of hood-mould from the recent excavations comprise two sections that fit above the jambs, one recovered from the modern recapping of drain [417] in the water-tower excavation and one from the capping of drain [118] that ran below Cell 8 (see Chapter 3), which continued the central nosing of the superordinate mullion between two engaged springers. Two plain sections of hood-mould recorded by Hope can no longer be traced, but, as good walling blocks, were probably reused by Bell.

Although the Period Three arcade lacks the elegance of its predecessor it is similar in form, with three windows of three lights grouped between deeply projecting buttresses and divided by substantial superordinate mullions. The windows were recessed and the deeply chamfered hood-mould that continued the outer order of the superordinate mullions carried the masonry of the wall-head some

carried back to the back edge of the glazing line, and the cill projected inwards behind the mullion to the depth of the internal pilaster. All lights bar one (one mullion section with no glazing groove found in Cell 10, not illustrated) were glazed, but the irregular nature of the glazing groove, which did not extend above the soffit of the lowest cusps in the heads, and the conspicuous absence of saddle-bar holes in the surviving jambs and mullions suggest that the glazing was secondary. Drilled holes in the heads on the glazing line indicate that thin iron bars had been sprung in to fix the glazing where no groove existed. Most instructive was the treatment of the cill, however, which had been mutilated to take the bottom of the glazing panel, a rough channel being literally hacked into the upper slope of the external chamfer.

The quality of the arcade was exceptionally high, all the sections being dressed to a fine surface with a bolster. In many cases tracing lines were still apparent and masons' marks of types B2, B3, B4, B11, B17, B25, B30 and B31 were recorded. No traces of paint survived, even on the unweathered inner face, although it might have been expected in the tracing lines, deeper bolster marks and the undercutting of cusps, and it seems unlikely that the arcade was ever limewashed.

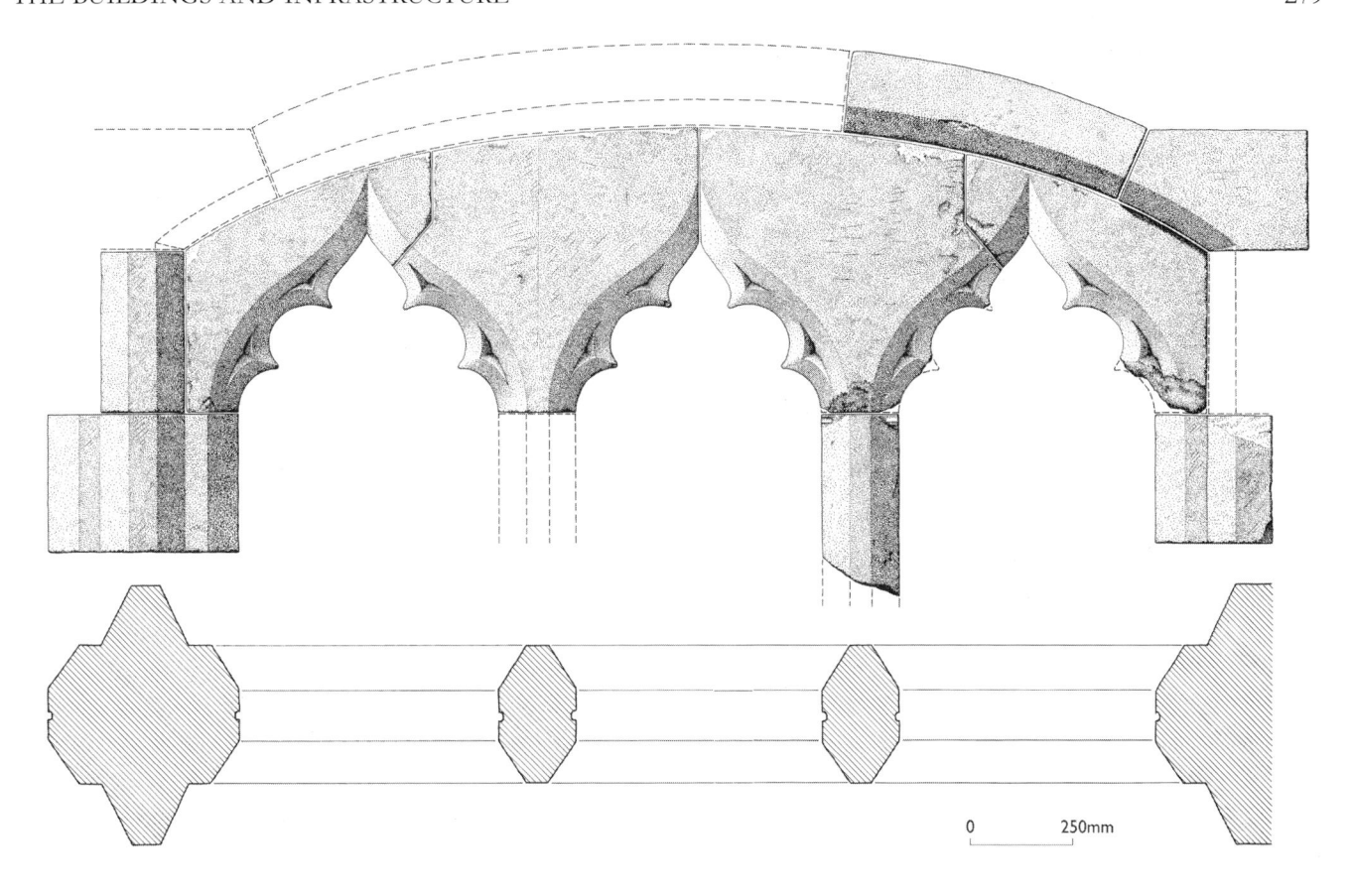

0.153 m beyond the inner and outer faces of the plate tracery of the windows. The jambs of the outermost lights engaged with the buttresses that defined the bays of the arcade, the lowest courses of which remain *in situ*. The treatment of the window tracery, although monumental in its scale, is clumsy in the extreme, comprising two side and two central springers. The size of the central springers was such that it was necessary for them to be edge-bedded, resulting in a tendency for them to split vertically with the grain of the stone. The sequence of building can be observed in the way in which the sections interlock. Two identical but mirrored springers were placed on their mullions and simply butted together at the apex of the central light, with no evidence of pinning or cramping. Next, the smaller side springers were fitted to the jambs or superordinate mullions and interlocked with the central springers. Finally, the head was tied together by its hood-mould or, more correctly, its chamfered outer order.

The lights, like those of the Period Two arcade, were all of a common height, although they were set rather uncomfortably within their segmental hood-mould. Also like those of the earlier arcade, they had cusped ogee cinquefoil heads and were of identical width. The layouts of the heads of the two arcades share a common geometry, suggesting a deliberate attempt to copy that detail of the Period Two arcade that survived, although the larger scale of the new work led to a coarsening of detail. The surviving elements show that the Period Three arcade was finely finished, with fine bolster tooling and laying-out lines surviving on the less weathered inner face and a carefully cut glazing channel, clearly a primary feature, set just forward of the centre line. Such a feature does not, however, occur on every light: at least one superordinate mullion, two double springers and four engaged springers have no glazing grooves. Additionally, the glazing groove is not present on the soffits of the cusps or in the central foil. It seems likely, but cannot be proved, that the Period Two west, north and south alleys were glazed at the time that the eastern alley was rebuilt. No traces of whitelime remained on any stone, even where weathering was only slight, which would suggest that, like the Period Two work, the eastern cloister alley was not painted. Masons' marks of types C13, C33 and C34 were recorded on the surviving elements.

Figure 6.26 The Period Three cloister arcade (G. Coppack, J. Hall and S. Hayfield).

Figure 6.27 Door to the Period One prior's cell in the south-west cloister range (G. Coppack).

The South Cloister Range

The range to the south of the great cloister consists of the communal rooms of the convent; the entry into the cloister itself from the inner court; cells for the prior and sacrist; an entry from the cloister to the church and chapter house; a garden; and two cells of unusual form. All these structures are built up against the wall that retains the cloister terrace. Much of this wall dates to Period One, although it was partially rebuilt in Periods Two and Three, especially between the entry from the inner court into the cloister and the entry into the church from the cloister.

THE SOUTH-WEST CLOISTER RANGE

At the west end of the range, its wall towards the cloister surviving to full height to the west, was a rectangular building identified by Hope as being divided between the refectory to the west and the prior's cell to the east. Re-excavation in 1988–90 (see Chapter 5) has shown Hope's interpretation to be flawed. As originally built in Period One, the prior's cell occupied the western half of the building, which was entered from the cloister by a four-centred door, the label stops of which bear the badly eroded arms of Redman quartering Aldeburgh (see Figure 6.27). Above the door is a primary square-headed window that lit the first floor, above the cloister roof. On the ground floor the prior's cell (see Figure 6.28) comprised three rooms that lay 0.75 m below the level of the great cloister and were divided by thin cill walls that originally carried timber partitions. A corridor at the same level as the great cloister that ran around the north and west sides of the cell led to a garden door in the west wall. A hatch or turn was provided from Period One in the centre of the north wall and an adjacent small recess for a water tap shows that piped water was provided here in Period Two, just as it was in the monks' cells. The passage widened adjacent to the cloister door, forming a small lobby. A sloping passage to the east of the prior's cell provided access from the inner court to the south alley of the great cloister and was so placed to be controlled by the prior. Apart from the settings of three cross-joists, no details of the upper storey of the prior's cell survive.

To the east of the cloister entry passage described above the range was divided by a primary cross-wall, beyond which was the original refectory of two bays. This was open to the roof and lit by traceried windows in its south wall, which no longer exists. It was entered from the lobby of the prior's cell and the base of a door remains at the north end of the dividing wall. Sockets for joists in the east wall suggest a gallery or ceilure at the upper end of the room.

In Periods Two and Three the range was substantially remodelled (see Figure 6.29). In Period Two a fireplace with fine candle brackets was inserted into the cloister wall in the western half of the refectory and the old refectory was divided into two rooms by a cross-wall. As the scar of this wall extends only to first-floor level, a floor was also inserted at the same time. It would appear that the prior had taken over the original refectory as his cell. In Period Three the cloister wall of the old refectory was partly rebuilt to incorporate both a new door from the south cloister alley, complete with a turn or hatch, and an oriel window that served the first floor, the base of which survives (see Figure 6.30). The eastern bay of the south wall was also substantially rebuilt and widened to the south, perhaps to incorporate a mural stair to the upper floor; the arrangements can no longer be recovered totally. The western room was clearly the hall or living room. The eastern room, with its door and hatch, was undivided, and may have been his bedroom:

THE BUILDINGS AND INFRASTRUCTURE

it was provided with a forced door in its east wall that gave the prior private access to the church and to a latrine. The oriel window above was screened off from the remainder of the upper floor to form an oratory. It is not possible to identify the layout of the remainder of the upper floor.

To the west of the new prior's cell, the cloister entry was remodelled. The door in the south wall of the range was blocked and a wide door inserted into the previously blank cloister wall, providing access to a wooden stair from the cloister alley to the upper floor of the original prior's cell, which must have been converted to use as the refectory.

The ground floor of the former prior's cell was converted to service use, heavy flagstone floors complete with substantial drains being inserted into its eastern rooms. Its partition walls were modified to suit this new use and appear to have been carried up in stone to support the upper floor. Timber corridors linked this building with the cross-wing of the guest-house range. At first-floor level the only work of Period Three that can be identified is the insertion of a square-headed door leading from the north-west angle of the range to the first floor of the old prison building.

Cell 22

Also of Period Three and adjacent to the new prior's cell, Cell 22 (see Figure 6.31) was built at the same time as the chapel on the north side of the church; its oratory was placed within the thickness of the west wall of the chapel, with a window looking down at the altar there (see Figure 6.32). In addition, a window was inserted into the north wall of the nave to borrow a little light for what must have been a very dark cell. Accommodation, all at the level of the cloister, was set over the cellars, which connected with the prior's cell, and, with the exception of the north, south and west walls, was timber-framed. A door, turn and fireplace were inserted into the Phase Two cloister wall and, exceptionally, a gable was added to that wall, the fireplace chimney emerging at its apex. This cell was a long, narrow building with a living room at the northern end and a study at the south end, against the church. A small cross-wing between the cell and the north chapel of the church carried on a 'bridge' comprised of the bedroom and oratory. A latrine was provided in the angle between the cell and the cloister wall, superseding what had been the prior's latrine in Period Two. There was initially space for a small garden to the east.

Cell 23

East of Cell 22 lay Cell 23, inserted in Period Four into a very difficult site (see Figure 6.31).

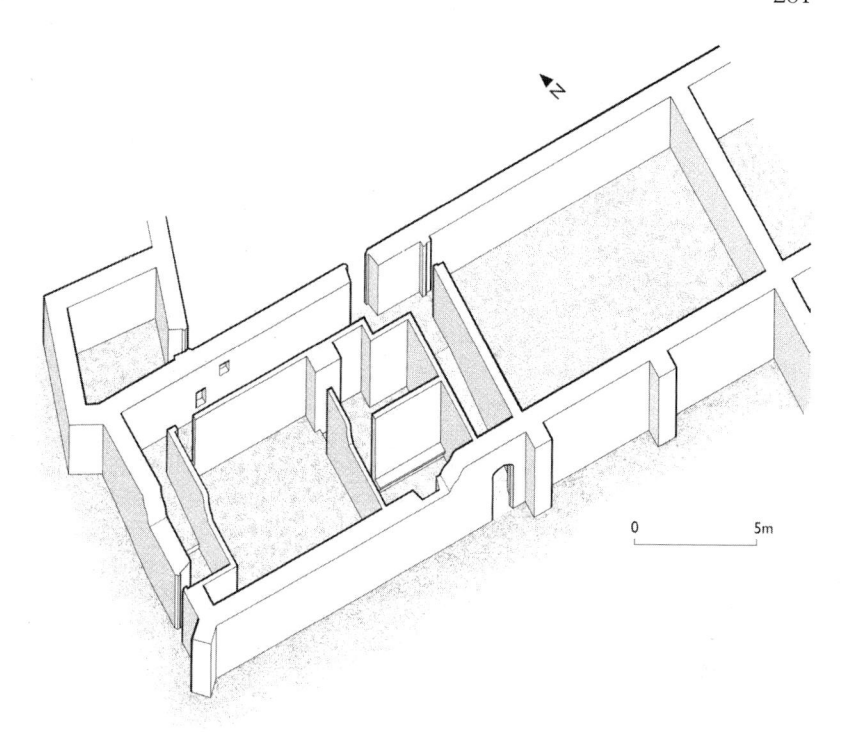

Figure 6.28 The south-west cloister range as originally built in Period One (G. Coppack and S. Hayfield).

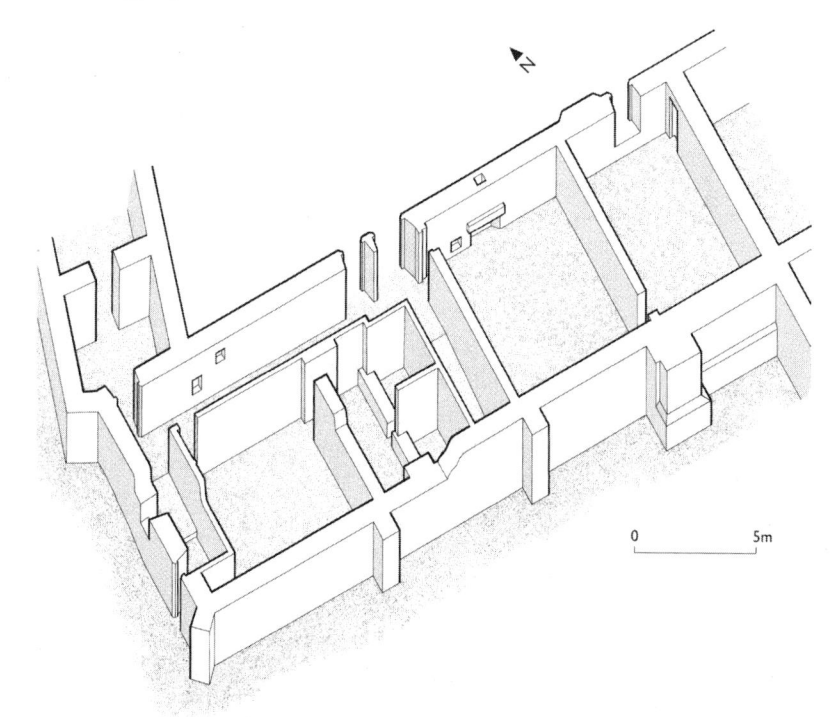

Figure 6.29 The south-west cloister range as modified in Periods Two to Four (G. Coppack and S. Hayfield).

Figure 6.30 The south wall of the great cloister with (from left to right) the church entry, the door to Cell 23, the lavatorium, the door to Cell 22, the door to the later prior's cell and the base of his oriel window (G. Coppack).

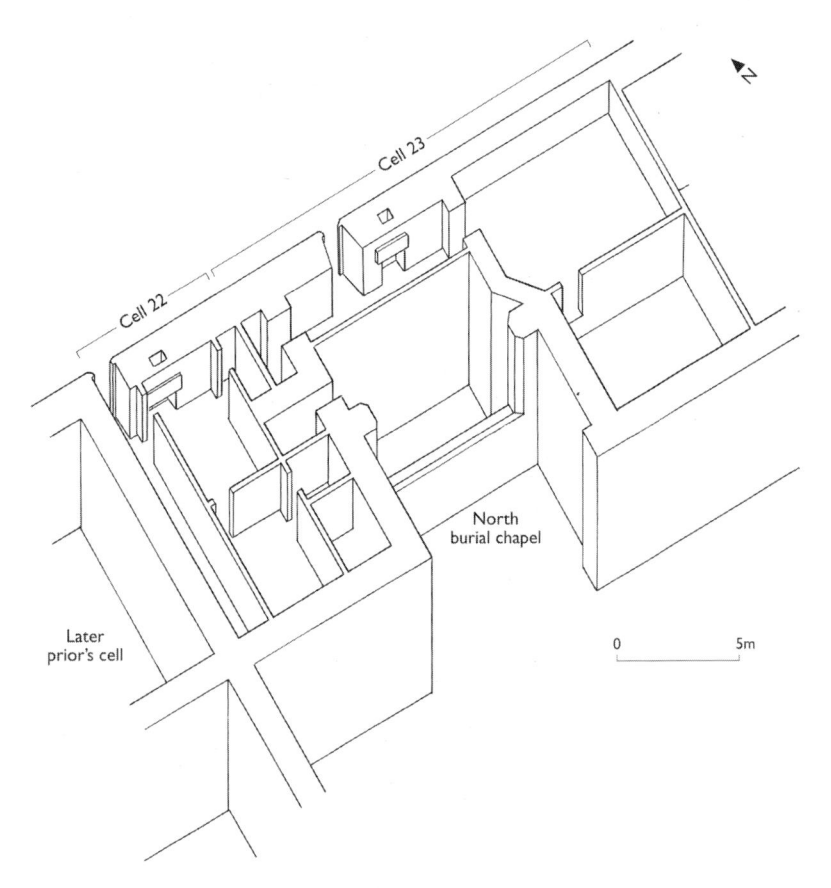

Figure 6.31 Axonometric reconstruction of Cells 22 and 23.

This is possibly the cell referred to by Prior John Wilson as being built or rebuilt in *c.*1523 (BL Add. MS 48965, f. 7). It occupies the area between the north chapel of the church and the cloister wall and, like its neighbour, was of a single storey, either at the level of the cloister or a little above it. The cell was entered by a door inserted into the earlier cloister wall, which led into a long, narrow living room (see Figure 6.33). A fireplace was inserted to the east of the door. To the west of the living room was a latrine that occupied half the latrine block initially built for Cell 22. The line of the inserted partition can still be seen and the tap-niche in the surviving cloister wall probably belonged originally to Cell 22. Below the living room of Cell 23 was a cellar. The remainder of the cell was at a higher level, its floor being partially set over the entry to the church from the cloister. So tight was the space available that the cloister wall was cut back to provide extra room, the rough core of the wall being plastered over, and the fact that this cutback extends beyond the east wall of the church entry below indicates that this part of the cell at least was timber-framed and its floor jettied out over the garden to the east. The pitch of the roof can be seen on the north wall of the church, as can indications of at least one phase of flooring. However, the evidence for the floor against the cloister wall shows it to be at a different level, indicating more than one room. The southern room, with a loft over, was apparently the bedroom and oratory, as a damaged piscina is present in the north wall of

THE BUILDINGS AND INFRASTRUCTURE

the church, reused from the Period Two first-floor chapel there, which had been removed in the late 15th century. The western part of the northern room was carried upon a basement that appears to have functioned as a sacristy, for an oven was built into an external buttress at the corner of the adjacent chapel for the baking of sacramental wafers. This room was entered from the church entry.

The Period Three church entry was simply a corridor leading from the south alley of the cloister to the north door of the church. In the north wall of the church, adjacent to the door, is a small recess for a holy water stoup. A similar feature was provided next to the blocked Period One door. To the east of the church entry was a small garden in which was a pentice against the north wall of the church leading to the chapter house. This returned against the west wall of the chapter house and there are clear marks on the cloister wall to show that this part of the covered passage had a double-pitch roof.

THE CHAPTER HOUSE

Further to the east came the chapter house, which was constructed in Period Two. It has lost all of its internal features, but retains a door into the presbytery of the church in its south wall, while steps lead up to a door in the east wall which gave access through a pentice to the sacrist's cell.

ARCHITECTURAL DETAIL FROM THE CHAPTER HOUSE (SEE FIGURE 6.34)

135–7. Three fragments of tracery, all with the same mullion profile, and one mullion (not illustrated). Although these fragments come from the unprovenanced collection, the profile matches none of the church windows nor the stones associated with the south-west cloister range. The only remaining potential location for traceried windows at Mount Grace is the chapter house. The fragments comprise one detached springer (136) and two engaged springers of different geometry, either from different windows or from different tiers of the same window.

THE SACRIST'S CELL

To the east of the chapter house, and of a single build with the Period One retaining wall of the great cloister terrace, was a two-storey cell reserved for the sacrist and set in a large walled garden. All but the east gable wall of the cell has been reduced to low walling, but it is clear that this cell was of very similar design to the remaining cells around the great cloister. In its east wall is a fine fireplace, its monolithic lintel supported on corbels, and a set-back in the masonry marks the height of the upper floor, some 2.67 m above ground level. The north-east angle of the building was taken down late in Period Two, when an entry was forced in the south-east angle of the

Figure 6.32 The oratory of Cell 22 in the west wall of the Period Three north burial chapel of the church (G. Coppack).

Figure 6.33 The interior of Cell 23 (at first-floor level and above) (G. Coppack).

great cloister to provide access from the lesser cloister, and the corner was rebuilt askew. The sacrist's cell was linked to the chapter house by means of a short gallery or pentice against the south wall of the cloister. A door must have existed in the east wall of the chapter house at this point, as the fragmentary remains of a stone stair leading down from the sacrist's cloister pentice are present in the chapter house at the point at which the sacrist would have entered. Within the pentice is an inserted tap recess of Period Two. The south door of the sacrist's cell gave access into his garden, from where a pentice led to a latrine in the garden's south-east angle. Although the latrine has been altered – seemingly in Period Two, when the lesser cloister was first constructed – it is probably an original feature.

The Great Cloister Ranges

Around the east, north and west sides of the great cloister were 15 two-storey cells, each set in its own garden. With the exception of Cell 8, they all belong to Period Two. Although there are minor differences between individual cells, all were built to a common pattern, providing standard accommodation for the monks in the form of a miniature monastery (see Figure 6.35). The cell itself was normally set in one corner of the garden, and was entered from the cloister by a four-centred door. Next to the door was a small 'L'-shaped hatch or turn, where food could be left for the monk without disturbing his solitude. Most of these retain evidence of hinged flaps to close off their outer ends. Within, the cell was divided by timber partitions into a cross-passage, hall, study and combined bedroom/oratory. The partitions, set on stone cill walls that survive for the most part, were occasionally fixed into the stonework of the cell walls and have left clear traces. Excavation has demonstrated (see Chapter 4) that the ground floor was, in most cases, of timber, its joists set into the surface of the clay terrace. On entering the cell, the cross-passage led to a door into a short pentice that ran along the inside of the cloister wall and which was essentially a private cloister for meditation and reading. A second door led into the living room or hall, a room lit by a four-light window. The hall was provided with a wall fireplace and in several instances, particularly Cell 8, was panelled in timber. From the hall, doors gave onto the study, lit by a four-light window, and the chamber and oratory, lit by one or two single lights. An external door from the hall opened onto to a pentice leading to a latrine set in or against the back wall of the garden. Opposite this door a stair was provided to give access to the upper floor. With the exception of Cell 8, this occupied the closed end of the cross-passage and rose by three turns, its treads and risers being cut into the stonework of the outer walls. The upper space was a workroom, apparently unpartitioned and lit by two or more single-

THE BUILDINGS AND INFRASTRUCTURE

light windows normally placed in the gable wall that did not carry the chimney flue. The first prior's cell and Cells 10 and 15 were exceptional in having one single-light window looking out over the cloister. In every case the upper floor was carried on a centrally placed binder and set-backs in the side walls. Internally, the cells were whitelimed, in some cases onto plaster.

The sequence of building can be ascertained from both the structural sequence of masonry joints and surviving architectural detail. The first cells to be built in Period Two were Cells 1–4, which were built as a group (although Cell 1 is the only one to contain masonry with the Period One masons' marks A5 and A7 and the Period Two mason's mark B15, suggesting that it was the first to be built). Although heavily ruined and in part reconstructed by Bell, these cells are distinguished by the detailing of their cloister doors with large and distinctive label-stop shields (see Figure 4.3). Those that remain on Cell 1 bear the arms of Archbishop Scrope, who died in 1405 (Hope 1905, 297) and was perhaps the giver of the original endowment. The surviving shields on the door of Cell 3 are plain, and those of Cell 4 have Gascoigne's arms. The garden doors of these cells, only two of which now survive *in situ* in Cells 3 and 4, had four-centred heads (see Figures 4.10 and 4.15). No original windows survive in this group, but the monolithic lintels of the wall fireplaces are supported by corbelled jambs (see Figure 4.16), a feature first noted in the sacrist's cell of Period One. Next to be built, in an orderly sequence, was Cell 5. Its cloister door head shows a change of detail, with small label-stop shields, again with the arms of Gascoigne, and the introduction of a keystone not present in the earlier door heads (see Figure 4.20). The garden door that survives in this cell has a flat head with radiused corners (see Figure 4.21), again showing an architectural development, and the corbelled fireplace of Cells 1–4 has been replaced by one with plain rebated jambs. Next built were Cells 6 and 7 and 9–15, in two distinct groups. The garden doors of these cells have square heads with mitred angles. The cloister wall from Cell 7 to the south-west angle of the cloister was erected before Cells 9 and 10 were built, although Cells 11–15 bond with it and must therefore be contemporary with its construction, and there are indications of a change in plan in the western half of the north

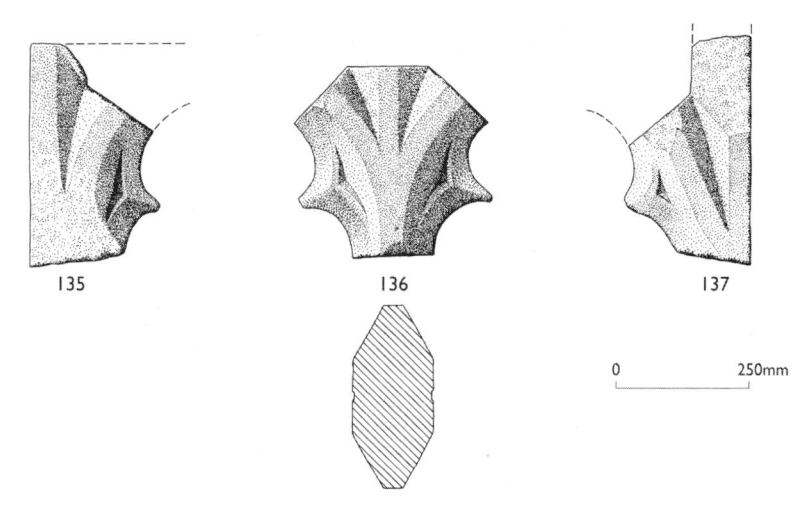

Figure 6.34 Architectural detail from the chapter house (1:10).

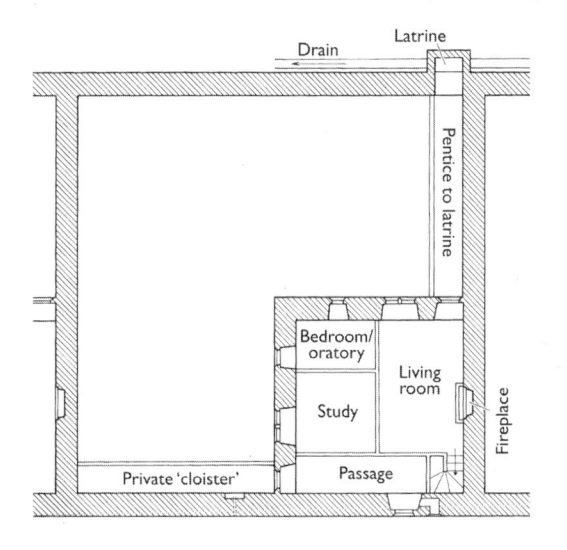

Figure 6.35 A 'typical' cell in the great cloister at Mount Grace.

range of the cloister. Initially, a passage 3.60 m wide was left through the range, immediately to the west of Cell 7, apparently to bring building stone into the cloister area in Period Two, and to its west provision was made at first to build Cell 9 further to the east. The scar left by the initial toothing for the original Cell 9's west garden wall can still be seen on the inside of the cloister wall, 5.06 m to the west of the present Cell 9. Excavation has demonstrated, however, that the wall itself was never built. According to the masonry joints, Cell 10 was built soon after the completion of Cells 11–15 and Cell 9 was constructed after that. Finally, the passage through the north cloister range that had caused this confusion was abandoned and in Period Three a final cell, Cell 8, was constructed on its site. Although all the cells of the great cloister had a reasonably short life, they were altered on a number of occasions,

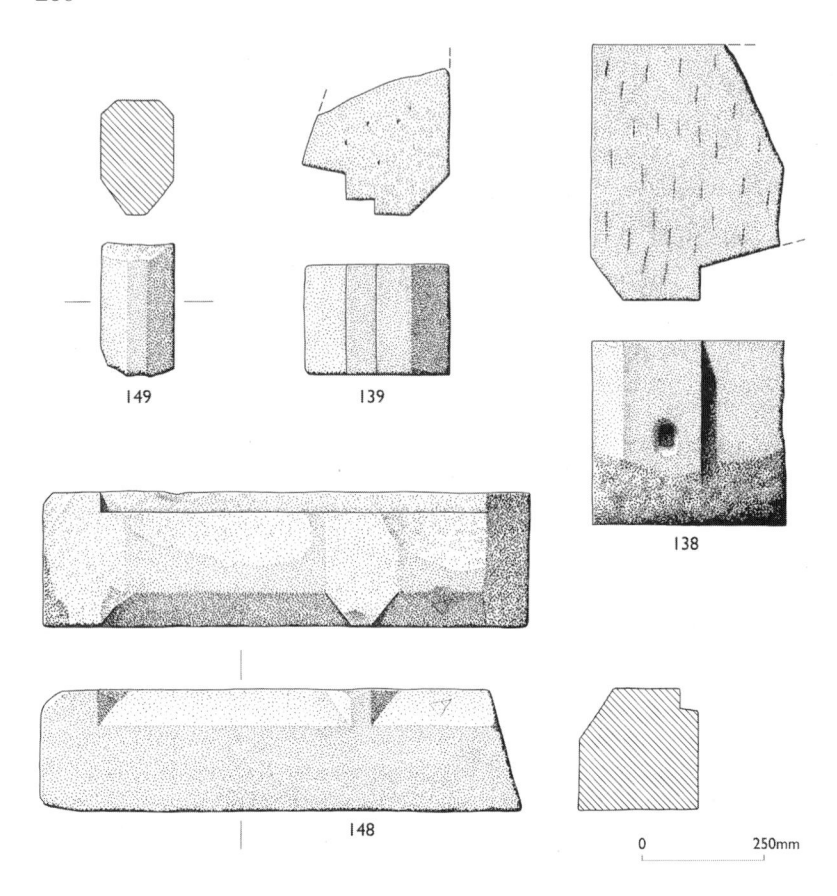

Figure 6.36 Windows from the cells of the great cloister (1:10).

Windows (see Figures 6.36 and 6.37)

Each cell was lit by two types of window, as evidenced by the surviving medieval fabric of Cells 3 and 8: a small square-headed single-light window and a large square-headed four-light window.

Single-light Windows

Five sections of jamb can be identified as coming from single-light windows, which conform to two types:

138. Simple jamb section from a window with a plain external chamfer and an internal rebate for a shutter. A centrally placed rectangular socket is provided for the fixing of an iron grille. Of the four examples recovered, in two cases the grille had been superseded by a glazing groove, indicating that windows that had originally been unglazed were provided with glass at some point before the Suppression. This sequence of events can be identified in the single-light windows of Cell 8.

139. Single jamb section of a window with a plain external chamfer and an inner face rebated to take a wooden window frame 30 mm thick. A second rebate was provided on the internal splay for a wooden shutter.

Four-light Windows

140–3. Transom, two mullion fragments and one jamb section (recovered from Cell 11 (MG121) in 1970) of a four-light window with a shallow external chamfer and internal rebates for shutters (see Figure 6.37 left). The transom, which bears a mason's mark (type B28) not identified elsewhere at Mount Grace, has an apparently primary glazing groove on its upper surface only, suggesting that the lower lights were not glazed. At least two windows are represented, as the mullions are socketed for an iron grille but the transom is not.

148. Cill and mullion fragment from a four-light window of similar form to that above, but with deeper external chamfers. The inner face of the cill, which bears a mason's mark of type B26, is rebated for shutters, but this rebate continues past the stooling for

leaving evidence both on the structure and in the archaeological record. The most significant of these changes was refenestration, best evidenced in Cell 3 (see Figure 4.11). The excavation of Cell 8 recovered fragments of a four-light window similar to that in Cell 3, the examination of which demonstrated that the surviving cill and splays were primary, suggesting that the provision of new windows was a feature of Period Three. Matching jamb and mullion sections from all parts of the great cloister show that this was a general refitting, not restricted simply to the oldest cells.

ARCHITECTURAL DETAIL FROM THE CELLS OF THE GREAT CLOISTER

Although all the cells of the great cloister were built to a common design there was obviously a great deal of variation in their architectural detailing, as might be expected given the extended time-span over which they were constructed. A considerable quantity of loose architectural detail, principally from the east range, was recovered by Hope or by Ministry of Works clearance prior to 1968. Very little of this material can now be identified to a precise location.

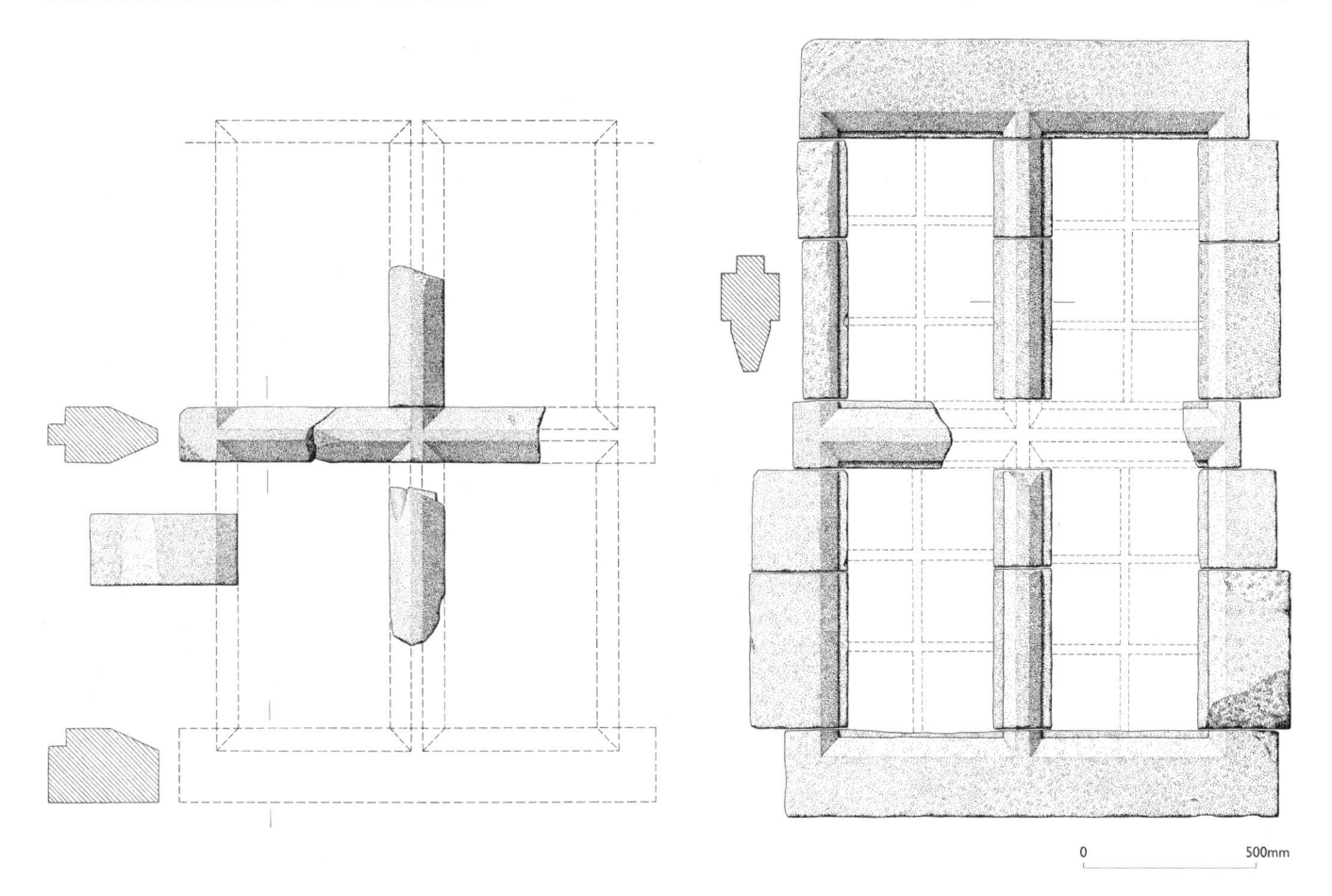

THE BUILDINGS AND INFRASTRUCTURE

the mullion. The mullion itself has no shutter rebates, but its back face aligns with the inner edge of the rebate on the cill and its arrises have been lightly chamfered. There is no evidence to suggest that the lower lights of this window were glazed; however, they were barred, the single, mortar-filled socket for a grille surviving in the left-hand light. The shutters must have closed against the back of the mullion.

Cell 3: Nine sections of mullion, two fragments of transom and one fragment of cill matching the extant four-light window in the north wall of Cell 3 were recovered and are shown as a composite reconstruction of the Cell 3 window (see Figure 6.37 right). Externally, the window is chamfered, with a shallow rebate worked on the chamfer, and an internal rebate is provided for shutters in the same manner as on window 140 above. The one remaining loose section of cill retains a socket for an iron grille and has no glazing groove, and the two fragments of transom have glazing grooves in their upper surfaces only. In common with the other four-light windows, the lower lights of this window type were originally unglazed. Several sections of mullion and the surviving jambs of the Cell 3 windows have secondary holes drilled into the inner edge of the shutter rebate to enable the fixing of wooden window frames within the openings of the lower lights, and the surviving jambs of the Cell 3 windows show that the openings were enlarged slightly to take the frames. As the Cell 3 window is an insertion into earlier fabric, its more elaborate form may post-date the plainer forms described above. Identical windows can be identified in Cells 4 and 5, although consolidation there has destroyed any evidence of insertion.

149. Two fragments of mullion cut from the same template as the Cell 3 window, but with the arrises of the internal shutter rebate chamfered.

Chimneys (see Figures 6.38, 6.39 and 6.40)

Each cell had an octagonal chimney rising from the apex of one of its gables. Nine fragmentary gable apex stones with chimney bases were recovered from the clearance of Cells 1–6

Figure 6.37 Windows from the cells of the great cloister (1:20).

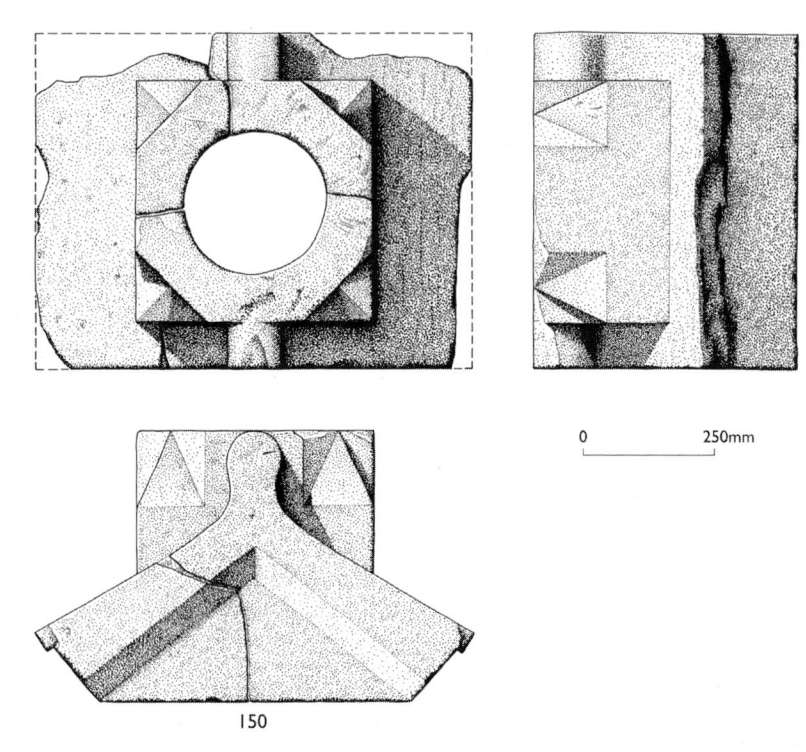

Figure 6.38 Chimney base from the great cloister cells (1:10).

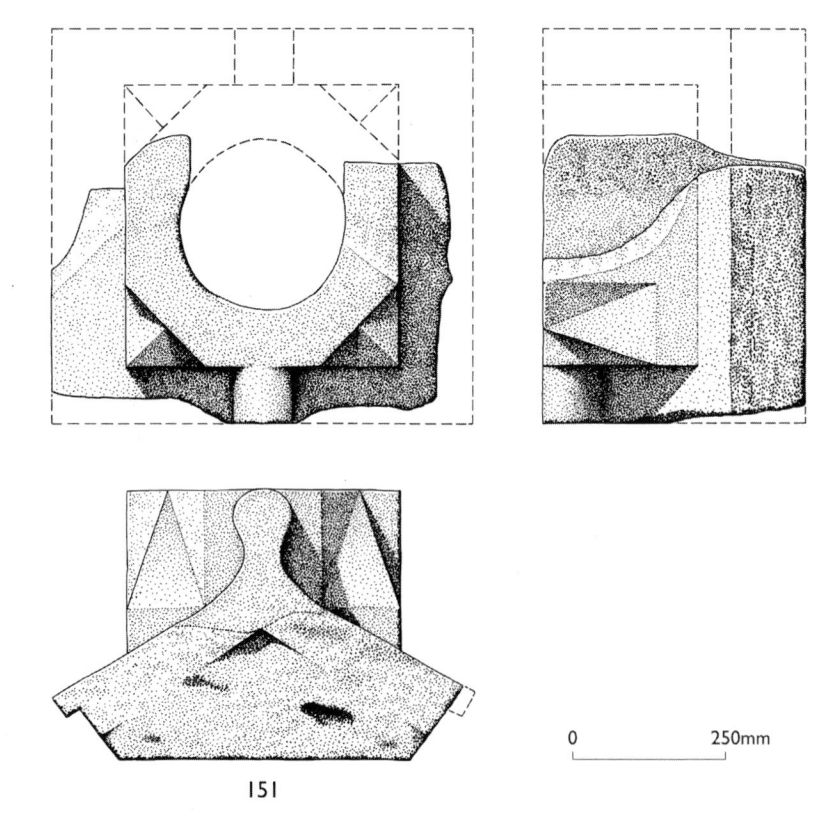

Figure 6.39 Chimney base from the great cloister cells (1:10).

and from Hope's excavation. These conform to two types; a third type was found in Cell 11 (see Chapter 4).

150. Square chimney base reducing to octagonal plan with short pyramidal chamfer-stops. Within the apex stone the chimney flue is square, reducing to round in the chimney base, and is very roughly punch dressed. The exterior surface is finely finished with a bolster.
151. As 150, but with taller pyramidal chamfer-stops on the square chimney base.

The clearance collection contained six identifiable octagonal chimney caps and ten sections of octagonal chimney shaft. Almost all had evidence of smoke-vents, indicating that plain fragments had not been collected. Four variant chimneys were identified:

152–4. Chimney with an embattled cap of equally spaced merlons and embrasures recovered by Hope (1905, fig. 8). The detailing of the cap is clumsier than that of the other chimneys, the merlons being incompletely moulded. Below the crenellations on alternating faces are lancet-headed smoke-vents. The chimney shaft has sides measuring 0.180 m, and enough survives to indicate that it was three or more courses high.
155. Similar chimney cap to 152, but with finely cut merlons and embrasures, and with round-headed smoke-vents.
156. Fragmentary chimney cap with narrow merlons, broad embrasures and lancet-headed smoke-vents. The detailing of the crenellation is simple and slab-like, akin to that of 152.
157. Fragmentary chimney cap with the stub of a conical cover above a moulded rim. This example was recovered by Hope (1905, fig. 9) and illustrated with the remains of the conical cover, which can no longer be traced. Below the moulded rim the remains of round-headed smoke-vents can be seen on alternating faces of the octagonal shaft.

Gable Crosses and Bases (see Figures 6.41, 6.42 and 6.43)

With a single exception (see stone 165), the other cell gable was decorated with a cross set in a socketed apex stone. In all, 19 cross

THE BUILDINGS AND INFRASTRUCTURE

fragments (representing no fewer than nine crosses) and six bases were recovered. Two basic forms of gable cross were represented: a plain Maltese cross and a more elaborate cross fleury, of which Hope (1905, fig. 7) published a composite example.

158. Head and upper shaft of a plain Maltese cross comprising two fitting fragments. The head itself is boldly chamfered, but the shaft retains its arrises. Although the layout of the cross-head is slightly irregular, it was finished with a bolster to a high standard. The shaft of the cross was found in the robbing of the precinct wall in Cell 13 (MG 832).

159. Four fitting fragments of a cross fleury. The base has the remains of a square tenon of 0.14 m side that fitted into the socket of the apex stone. The shaft of the cross is lightly chamfered, a treatment that extends to the head and arms, and the chamfer terminates in tall arrow-stops that rise from the base. Shaft, arms and head have bold cusps with blind eyes. No terminals remain.

    Five variants of apex stones with cross bases survive. All are finely bolster dressed, but are somewhat eroded by their exposure to the weather.

160. A plain square-socketed base rising from a standard apex stone. Cross 159 would fit the mortise in the upper surface of the base.

161. A large socketed base with a chamfered upper edge rising from a standard apex stone. The sides of the base are decorated with the same hood-mould design seen on the outer face of the apex stone. The mortise is cut for a tenon of 0.180 m side.

162. A large socketed base similar to 161 but rising from a non-standard apex stone with a tall ridge-rib.

163. A socketed base similar to 161 but with a mortise cut to take a tenon of 0.140 m side. Cross 159 would fit this base.

164. A fragment of cross base decorated with a false hood-mould in the manner of bases 161, 162 and 163. In this case, the ridge-rib is not a simple roll-moulding but has a worn trefoil profile.

    Not every cell had both a gable cross and a gable chimney, as one apex stone survives without a cross-base.

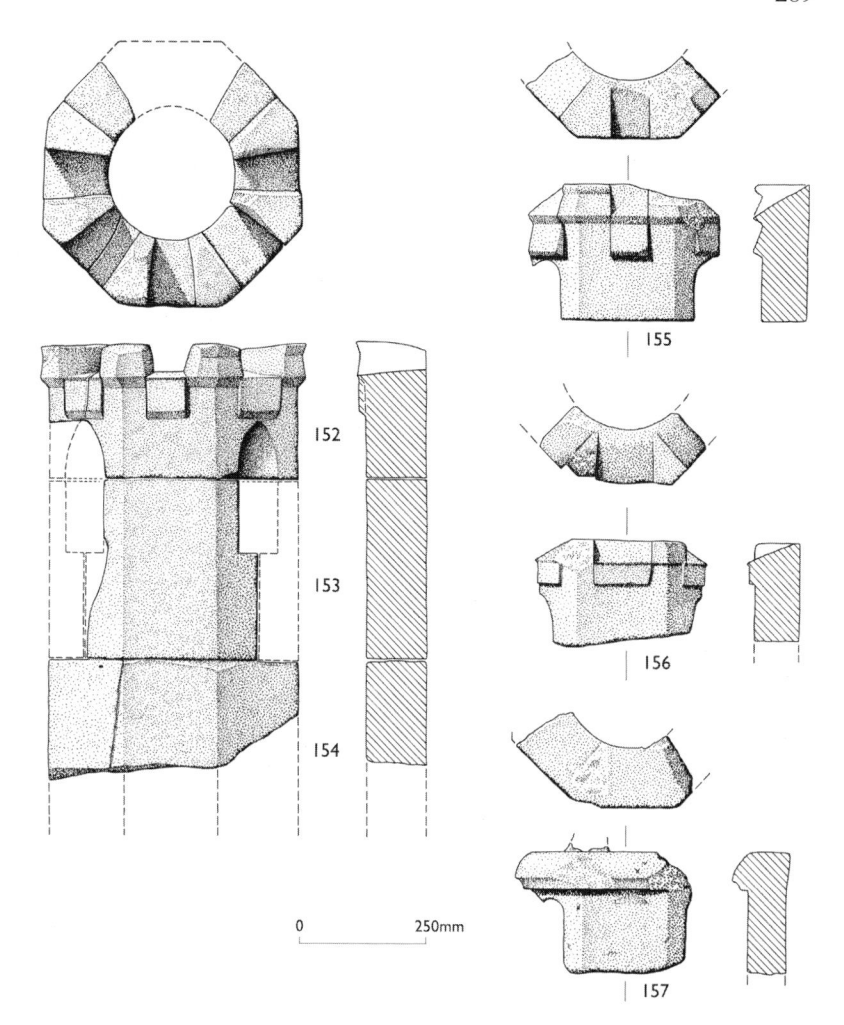

Figure 6.40 Chimney shafts and caps from the great cloister cells (1:10).

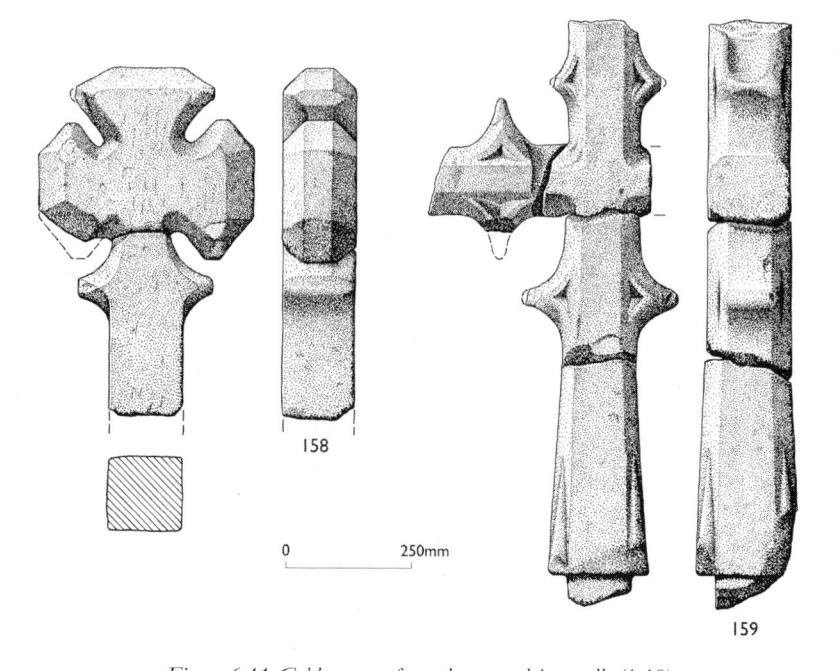

Figure 6.41 Gable crosses from the great cloister cells (1:10).

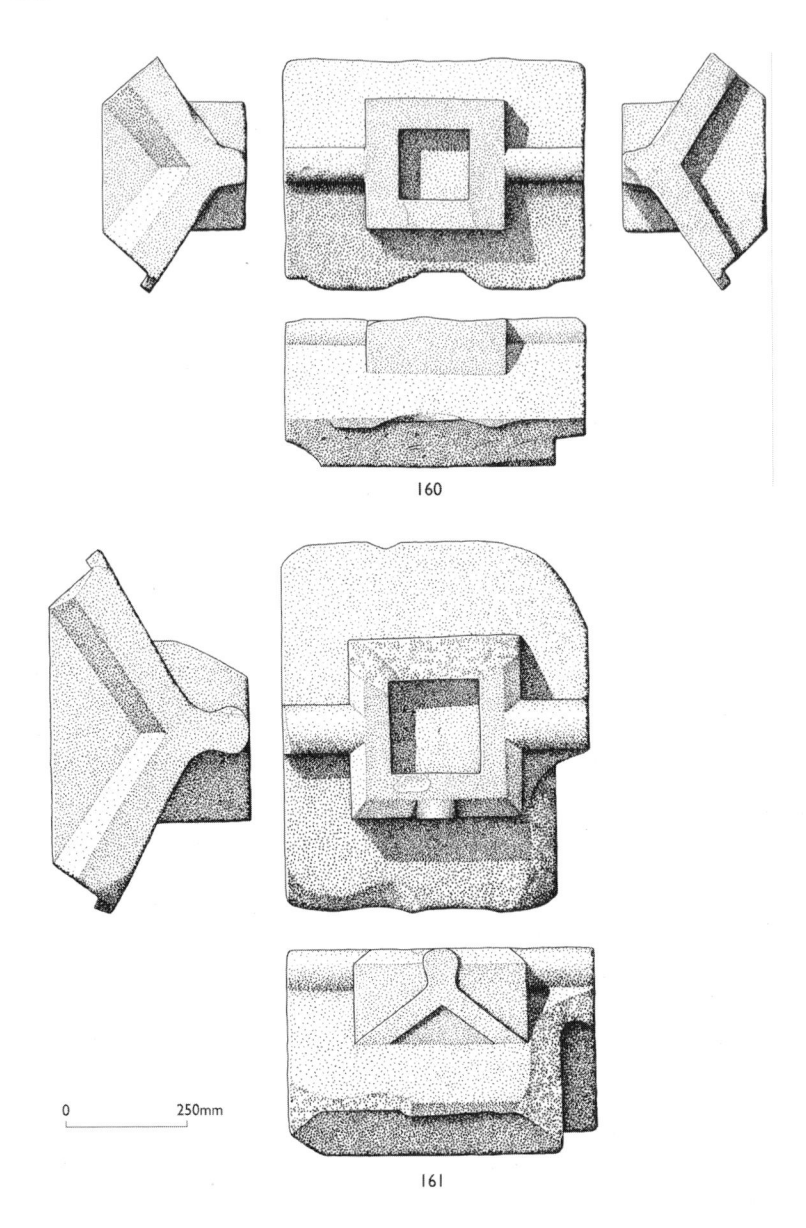

Figure 6.42 Gable cross bases from the great cloister cells (1:10).

165. Standard apex stone from a cell gable, with a square rebate on the inner face to cover the roof flashing and a chamfer below the external hood-mould with a continuous ridge-rib of trefoil section.

Buildings at the South-west Corner of the Great Cloister

Integral with the Period One masonry of the north wall of the south-west cloister range was a three-storey structure dating to the early years of the 15th century with a single small room on each floor. It was entered from the south-west corner of the cloister alley by a narrow door that was later blocked. Although its north and west walls have been demolished to foundation level, the east wall against the cloister remains to full height, retaining the stub of the north wall and the south wall remains to second-storey height. Subsequent alterations make the building difficult to understand (see Figures 4.89 and 6.45), but sufficient remains to reconstruct its original form.

The ground-floor room was featureless apart from the provision of a door in its north-east corner, where the socket for a monolithic lintel remains in the east wall. This door appears to have led to a latrine, perhaps of timber as it has left no trace against the cloister wall, which remains Period One masonry as far north as the Period Two Cell 15. That it was an internal door is shown by the lack of a proper jamb, the masonry simply being cut back to provide a shallow check against which the door would close below the lintel. The joist sockets for the first floor survive, showing it to have been 3.2 m above the later ground-floor level. No evidence of a stair between the ground and first floors exists in the surviving structure. An inserted window of Period Two or Three in the first-floor east wall does not appear to replace a primary opening, and the unbroken scar of the north wall shows that there was no door above that on the ground floor. The second floor was evidenced by joist sockets in the south wall, some 2.3 m above the first floor. The jamb of a door survived in the north-east corner of the room, and a cut-out in the east wall was provided for the door to open into. Again, it must have given access to the putative latrine. A square-headed single-light window in the east wall, looking over the cloister, was the only primary fenestration in the building.

This building might be interpreted as the priory prison, given its rather forbidding appearance and its location within the great cloister. Whatever its primary use, it was substantially remodelled in Period Three, when it was converted into a much larger building directly connected with both the south-west cloister range and Cell 15 (see Figure 4.90).

The Period Three remodelling doubled the structure in size by the addition of a two-storey block to the north. The low ceiling of the Period One ground floor was eased by the digging out of the floor of the original structure to expose its foundations. At this reduced level, doors were inserted into both

THE BUILDINGS AND INFRASTRUCTURE

the north and south walls of the primary structure. The casing of the Period One door from the cloister was removed and reinserted further north in the Period One cloister wall to serve the new extension, and its original position was carefully blocked. The internal blocking contained a small cupboard. A new door was inserted in the south wall so that this room could be accessed directly from the corridor along the north side of the south-west cloister range. Pin-holes in the east and south walls that post-date both the blocking of the cloister door and the insertion of the south door indicate that the room was panelled at this time or later. Only the footings of the north and west walls of the extension remain, and the north wall may have been timber-framed, as two sockets remain in the east wall where the north wall met the earlier masonry. The east, cloister wall survives to full height and retains sections of the wall-head string course that match those of the Period Two cells; five courses of new masonry were added to its Period One masonry to bring it up to this height, the shallow bed-heights matching exactly those of Cell 15 to the north and demonstrating the contemporaneity of the work. The repositioned cloister door led to a narrow timber-screened lobby at the north end of the extended building, which appears to have contained a staircase to the upper floor. The masonry cill wall of the partition and the fixing of its top plate remain. The remainder of the extension at ground-floor level was entered from the ground floor of the Period One building by a new door that was cut through the centre of the north wall. Presumably, the original door in the north-east corner of the room, evidenced in the masonry, must have been blocked at this time. At first-floor level was a single chamber, its floor set three courses higher than the first floor of the Period One block and at the height of the first floor in Cell 15. It must have been entered from the upper floor of that cell by way of a bridge over the narrow passage that separated the two buildings, as the jamb of an inserted door remains in the stub of the south wall of the cell, its cill at exactly the height of the upper floor. This first-floor chamber, which was obviously a room of some importance, was lit by a three-light window with a four-centred head that was inserted into the Phase Two heightening of the east wall. The window is not centrally placed within the room, but offset to the north, presumably to make space for a stair to the second floor of the prison block at the south end of the room. Also of Period Three was an inserted door leading from the second floor of the primary building to the upper floor of the south-west cloister range. No use can be suggested for this remodelled structure, which lay within the garden of Cell 15 and was at least partially accessible from the cell. Hope suggested (1905, 301) that the ground floor simply provided cellarage accessible only from his 'refectory', but that the upper

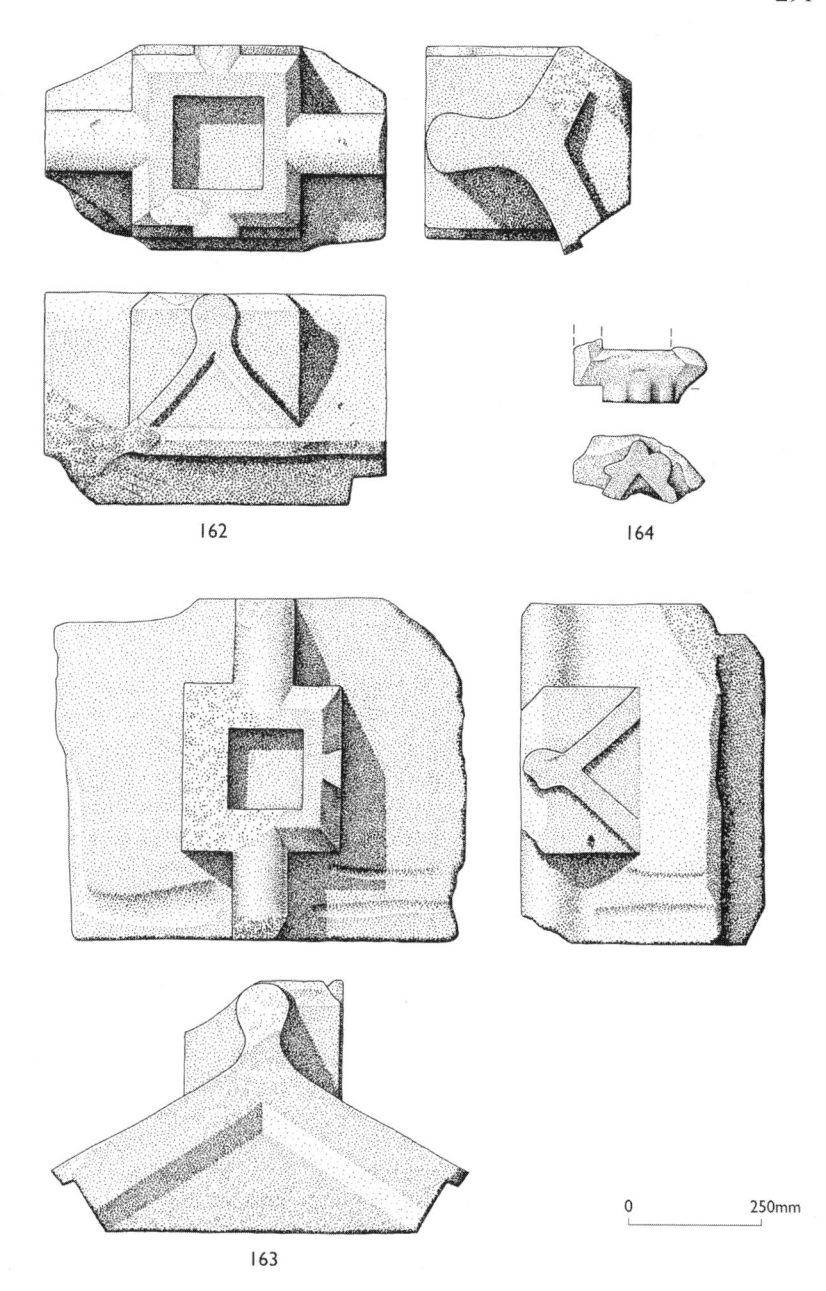

Figure 6.43 Gable cross bases from the great cloister cells (1:10).

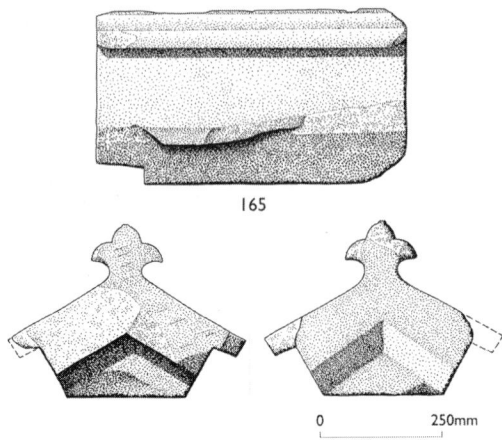

Figure 6.44 Gable coping from the great cloister cells (1:10).

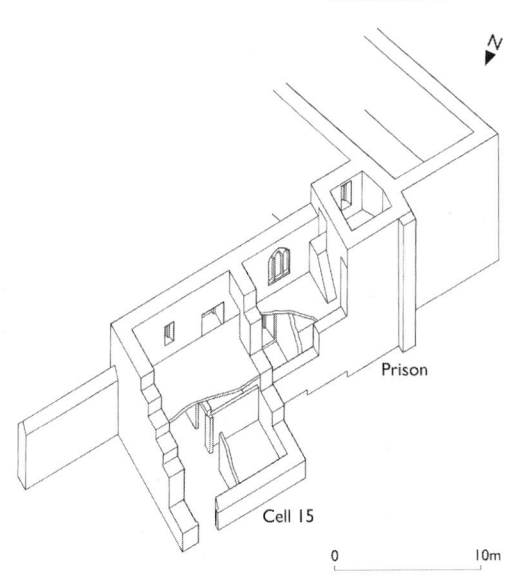

Figure 6.45 Axonometric reconstruction of the 'prison' and associated rooms.

file 186, no. 9299), leaving sufficient space for more cells about the great cloister. The pension list of 1539 (Letters & Pps, Henry VIII, xiv, f. 258) provides the required explanation for the lesser cloister. The house is known to have had a full complement in its closing years and in 1539 pensions were granted to the prior, procurator, 15 monks, three novices, six lay brothers and an oblate. The cells of the great cloister and the accommodation in the guest-house range would have accommodated all the choir monks, leaving the six cells of the lesser cloister to the *conversi*.

Access to the lesser cloister, which lay to the east and south of the church, was provided by a forced doorway in the south-east corner of the great cloister, which entailed the rebuilding of the north-east angle of the Period One sacrist's cell and the modification of the Period Two masonry of Cell 1. Accordingly, the building of the lesser cloister, at least in stone, might also be ascribed to Period Three, although it could equally have been begun in Period Two. Against this is the evidence of prolific banker marks, many of which cannot be identified elsewhere in Period Two work. The surviving low walling suggests that building was a slow process. Masonry joints indicate that the earliest work was the back wall of the cloister alley, itself built in sections. Nothing remains of the cloister arcade, which may have remained in timber, but its width was dictated by the width of the passage cut from the sacrist's garden. It enclosed a garth or garden the length of the church and was closed at its west end by a door that gave access from the inner court. The doors of Cells 17–21, where they survive, bond well with the cloister wall and appear to be primary. However, some of the cells themselves are clearly additions to a pre-existing wall and perhaps represent a gradual replacement of timber buildings.

The first cells to be built in stone, Cells 20 and 21, may well be of one build with the cloister wall. Certainly, they share common banker marks. Although considerably smaller than the cells of the great cloister, these cells have the same general disposition, with evidence of timber partitioning dividing each one into three rooms and a cross-passage on the ground floor; however, there is no evidence of a staircase to an upper floor. From the cross-passage a door led to a latrine and, in the east wall, another gave access to a garden pentice.

rooms comprised domestic accommodation served by a latrine pit, no longer visible, at the south-west angle of the building. Accessible from the west cloister alley and from the upper floor of the original prior's cell, this room might have been the library.

The Lesser Cloister (see Figure 6.1)

Thomas Beaufort's grant of 1415 (TNA Pat. R, 3 Henry V, pt ii m 29) specified an increase in the number of the community by five monk-chaplains, and it has long been assumed that additional accommodation was provided for them in addition to the cells of the great cloister. It is very tempting to believe that the cells of the lesser cloister, first built in stone in Period Three, filled this need, especially as five cells were originally provided there. Such an explanation does not, however, accord with the surviving documentation. In 1412 there were only *dix en ordre en la dit priorie* (TNA Anc. Pet.,

THE BUILDINGS AND INFRASTRUCTURE

The door in the east wall of Cell 21 was later blocked. The fireplaces placed at the centre of the gable walls differed substantially from those of the great cloister cells in that they projected into the room.

Next to be built, against the south side of the lesser cloister, were Cells 19–17. In each case, the cells' north wall was placed against an earlier cloister wall, creating a wider wall at these points. Cell 19, left undisturbed for future excavation, was partially examined by Hope, who described it as 5 m² (1905, 305), while 17 and 18 were almost as large as those of the great cloister. All bear traces of internal partitioning, including a cross-passage, with side doors to a private cloister and a latrine pentice. All the lesser cloister cells, with the exception of Cell 19, were rectangular in plan – unlike the square monks' cells – and, though well-built, were obviously of a second quality. Their garden walls, with the exceptions of Cells 20 and 21, were built very much as an afterthought, the back wall running haphazardly from east to west and not bonding with the side garden walls, which themselves were straight-jointed to the cells. Cells 19–17, like the monks' cells, were each provided with a latrine in the back wall of the garden.

After the completion of the lesser cloister in Period Three, a further cell, Cell 16, was added at the west end of the cloister alley between the alley and the south wall of the church. Its white mortar is typical of Period Four work, and this may be one of the cells built by Prior Wilson in 1523–4. Space was clearly at a premium, for its private cloister ran along the north–south wall, closing off the lesser cloister from the inner court, sockets for the pentice's wall cill and top plates being clearly visible in the masonry of the church itself. Remarkably, the garden of Cell 16 was placed to the south of the lesser cloister alley, just west of Cell 17, and the occupant would have had to leave the confines of his cell to use the latrine. It is unclear why the cell was not built in its garden.

Architectural Detail from the Lesser Cloister (see Figure 6.46)
Generally, it is not possible to separate architectural detail arising from the lay brothers' cells from that from the cells of the monks. A large octagonal moulded chimney cap design has already been identified for Cell 16. In addition, another distinctive design, embattled

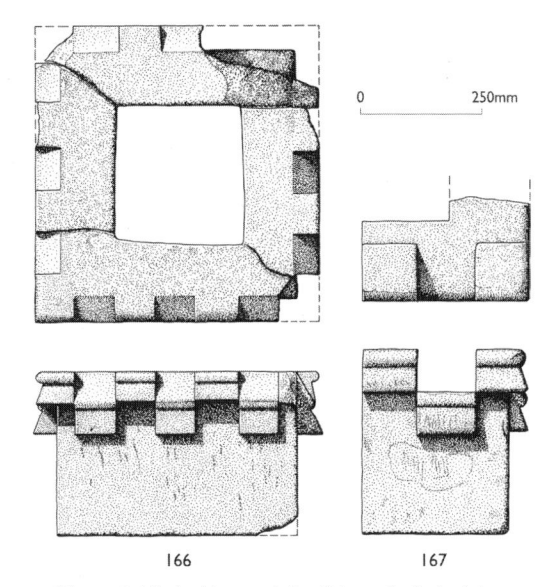

Figure 6.46 Architectural detail from the little cloister.

with a square shaft, can be identified, and it can be tentatively suggested that these originated in the lay brothers' cloister.

166. A square chimney cap with a crenellated moulding cut from a single stone, with equally spaced and carefully moulded merlons and embrasures. The square shaft has sides of 0.490 m. The outer face is very carefully cut and bolster finished, but the square flue is very roughly dressed with a punch.

167. A fragment from the cap of a square chimney made up of at least two sections with boldly moulded crenellations. In this instance, the embrasures are cut through the stone, rather than an illusion of embrasures being provided by the moulding.

6.2 Water Supply and Drainage

Mount Grace Priory required a regular and abundant supply of water for washing, brewing and food preparation, for flushing its drains, for filling its fishponds and for powering its mill. The chosen site, at the foot of the Cleveland escarpment, might have provided the monks with the wilderness and solitude that they sought, but it did not provide a sufficiently powerful stream to serve their needs. In the absence of an adequate water supply one had to be brought to the site, and existing watercourses in the locality were successfully

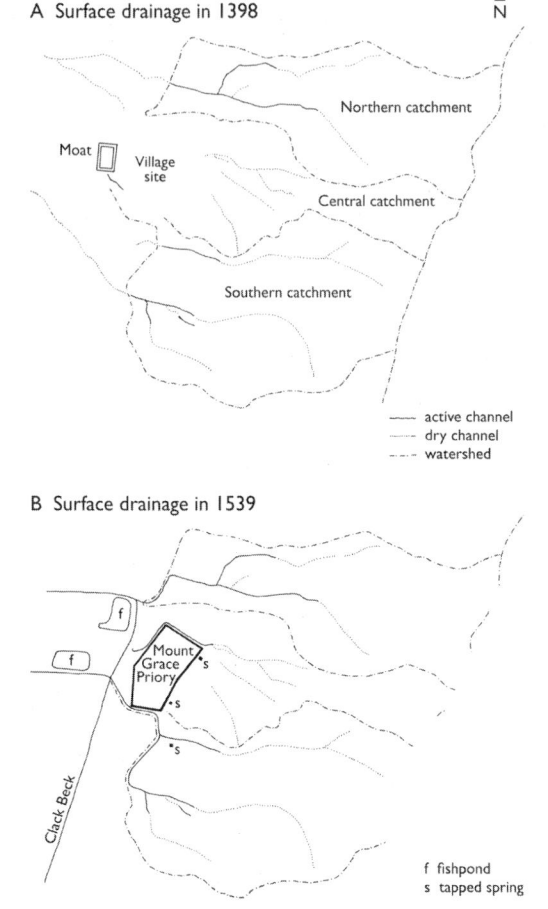

Figure 6.47 The surface drainage of the priory site (a) before the priory was built and (b) as it was modified to serve the needs of the house.

modified and exploited. Essentially, three separate supplies were needed: a reliable source of clean potable water; a supply to flush the foul drains; and a powerful and dependable source to service the mill and fishponds. The means by which these needs were met has been ascertained by a combination of ground survey, excavation and carefully monitored site clearance, demonstrating that the site was provided with a sophisticated hydraulic system from the very beginning.

The construction in the foundation period of the two great terraces on which the priory stands substantially modified the natural drainage pattern of the area. Detailed ground survey by J. Rose and J. R. Elliot between October 1985 and February 1986 and excavation in 1988 has established the nature of the pre-monastic landscape and analysed its modification. Before 1398, the escarpment above the site of Bordelby comprised three catchment areas supporting a network of streams draining to the west, which remain traceable as active watercourses or dry channels both above and below the site of the priory (see Figure 6.47A). The northern catchment provided a substantial flow of water, but the central catchment area was less reliable, most of the surface water disappearing into the underlying strata before it reached the priory site and feeding a number of springs at the foot of the escarpment. It can be no accident, however, that the priory was placed on the spring-line fed by this catchment. The southern catchment area supported the greatest run-off, with a powerful stream capable of industrial exploitation. It would seem, however, that the three catchments alone were insufficient to serve the house's needs, and a further supply had to be engineered.

The construction of the priory buildings had a dramatic effect on the natural surface drainage in the central catchment (see Figure 6.47B). The levelling of the terraces on which the priory was to be built destroyed any run-off channels, but also revealed at least three springs, one on the northern terrace in what was to become the garden of Cell 9, another in the area of Cell 5 and a third on the southern terrace within the inner court. That in the garden of Cell 9 was canalised (see Chapter 4), its channel being clearly incorporated in the construction of the terrace itself. The northern run-off channel in the central catchment was diverted, apparently in Period Two, to flush the latrines on the north and west sides of the great cloister, while the spring in the garden of Cell 9 and others as yet untraced fed a supply that flushed the latrines of the cells on the east side of the cloister garth. As these drains were incorporated in the construction levels of the terrace, their provision was allowed for in Period One. The main function of the central catchment was to provide a source of piped water for the convent, two of the three well houses being fed by ground water in this area. The stream supported by the northern catchment was diverted in its lower part into the central catchment to feed the fishponds below the priory, with a bypass channel running off to the west in a new cut.

The most dramatic hydraulic engineering can be observed in the southern catchment,

THE BUILDINGS AND INFRASTRUCTURE

Figure 6.48 The southern well house (St John's Well) as it was in 1900 (Canon J. C. Atkinson).

where a strong watercourse was diverted from Osmotherley to the south in a straight cut following the natural contour. This stream, the Clack Beck (*le Clak* of the 1508 agreement with the prior of Gisborough), appears to have been diverted to serve the priory mill, and its course cuts across the natural drainage channels of the southern catchment, implying that its diversion post-dates the diversion of those watercourses. The movement of those streams is connected with the construction of the lower or southern terrace, on which the buildings of the inner court stand. The intention appears to have been to combine the water flow of the southern catchment with the Clack Beck to provide a substantial head of water; at the junction of the two systems a stone conduit below the access road to the priory gatehouse fed water into the deep mill leat that still flanks the ruins of the mill itself. The southern part of this leet is obscured by a modern garden, but its northern end survives as a deep earthwork channel skirting the fishpond and discharging into the diverted course of the stream in the northern catchment. When the mill was not running, the waters of the Clack Beck and the southern catchment were diverted into the present stream bed, a channel running parallel to the priory access road.

The southern catchment also supported a spring, St John's Well (see Figure 6.48), a dedication that almost certainly pre-dates the foundation of the house and might have had some bearing on the choice of the site. It was enclosed within a stone well house in Period Two, and survived in use until 1900 as the supply for the 17th-century house. Sir Lowthian Bell used the southern catchment to provide water for his house, replacing the well house with a large cast-iron tank that still serves farms on the estate.

Piped Water Supply

One of the prerequisites of a monastic house was a clean supply of potable water, collected centrally in a conduit house and distributed by lead or ceramic pipes to the various offices of the convent (Coppack 1990, ch. 4). The Carthusians differed from other orders in supplying water to a tap in each cell, and an elaborate supply system can thus be presumed. It is fortunate that two near-identical plans of the London charterhouse, which enjoyed close associations with Mount Grace, survive and have been extensively studied (Hope 1903; Coppack 1996b). At the house of the Salutation in London water was brought from a distance to feed a stone and timber conduit house at the centre of the great cloister, and from this a feed was taken to each cloister range and distributed to every cell as well as to the refectory laver and the domestic offices. Hope studied Mount Grace in the light of the London plan, excavating at the centre of the great cloister to locate the conduit house and trenching to locate pipe-runs. He found an octagonal conduit with angle buttresses and traceried windows in its lower storey at the centre of the cloister garth, but his trenching failed to find any lead pipes *in situ*. He mistakenly assumed that the source of water was St John's Well, as two more spring-houses remained buried by landslip until the 1960s. The discovery in the early 1960s of both the northern, principal well house (see Figure 6.49) and a stone channel still containing sections of lead pipe running below the garden of Cell 4 and the east cloister alley in the direction of the conduit house suggested that it was this spring that was tapped to supply the conduit house (Edgar Barker, pers. comm.). The outlet of the spring itself was only 1.89 m above the level of the cloister garth, however, hardly ensuring an adequate gravity feed to a tank in the upper part of a centrally placed conduit,

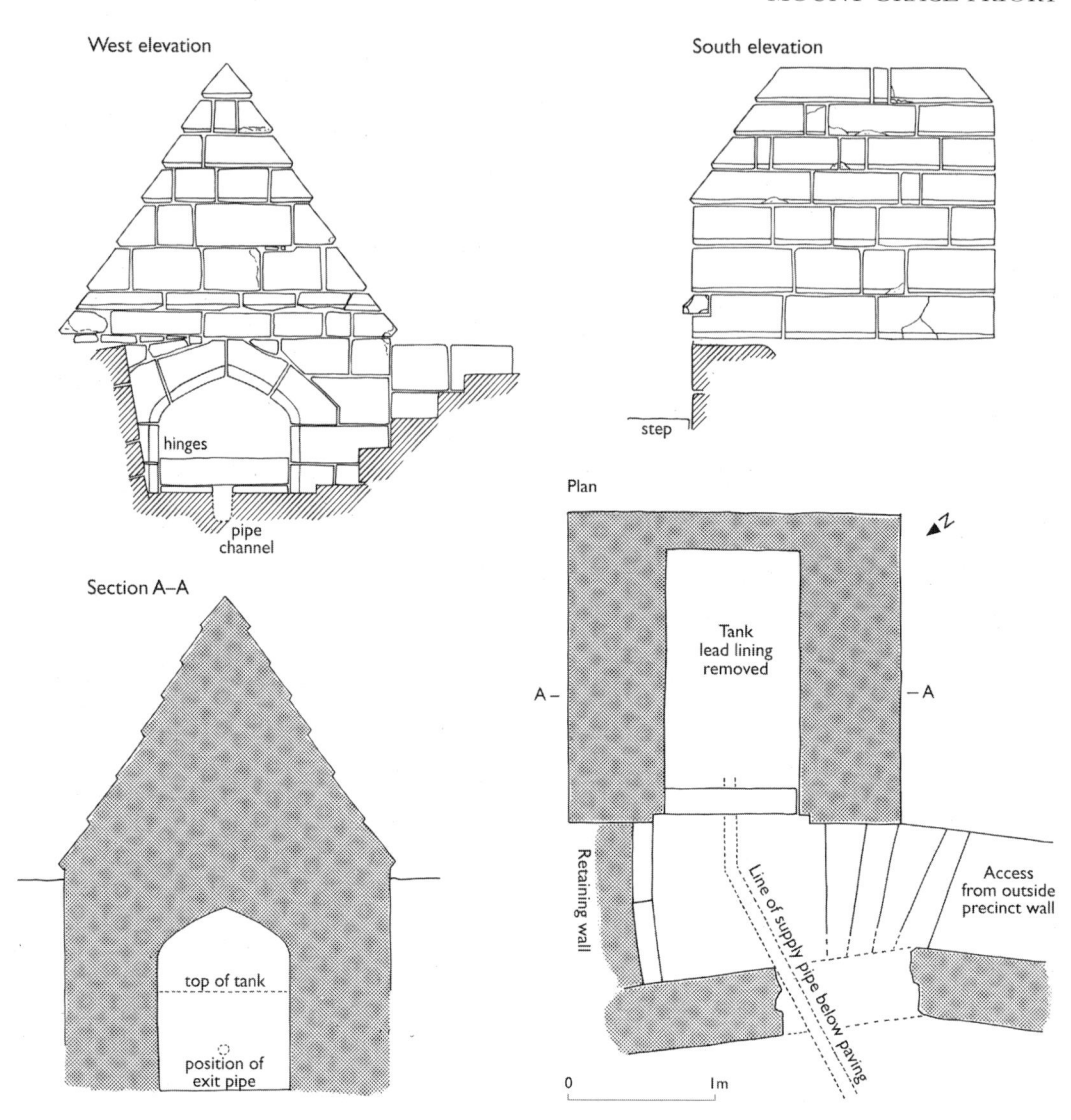

Figure 6.49 The northern well house.

and water must therefore have been pumped in some way.

The well houses, all of Period Two, are contemporary with the construction of the majority of cells within the great cloister. As they stand, only St John's Well is a truly medieval construction: a cylindrical water tank surmounted by a pyramid roof and entered by a round-headed door. The rebate for a wooden door that opened outwards is a feature it shares with the other two well houses. The central well house, unknown to Hope, was found in a collapsed state when the precinct wall on the east side of the inner court was dug out and consolidated, and it was rebuilt with additional stone (G. Hutchinson, pers. comm.). The rebuild probably replicates the original form, a square structure with a steeply gabled roof (see Figure 6.50) set over a circular well. It was fed by a stone channel that ran down the hillside and pierced the back wall. The collapsed state of the structure seems to have been the result of the robbing of a lead tank, and subsequent reconstruction has obscured any outlet for a pipe. The northern well house was a more substantial affair (see Figure 6.49) that was also rebuilt from fallen masonry in the early 1960s (M. Biddle and G. Hutchinson, pers. comm.). Again, it lay adjacent to the precinct wall, but differed from the other two well houses in that it had a small enclosed yard to the west of it approached by steps from the cobbled path that ran from the central well house and along the outside of the precinct wall. Below the flagstones that lead to the well house door is an accurately cut channel of pear-shaped section that was designed to protect a lead pipe with an external diameter of 75 mm and which ran

THE BUILDINGS AND INFRASTRUCTURE

through the east precinct wall. Since excavation, its precise form when it passes through the wall has been modified and the pipe channel that ran from it towards the garden of Cell 4 changed beyond all recognition: the capstone of the channel where it passed through the wall was recovered in excavation, but not reset in its original location on the instructions of Roy Gilyard-Beer (E. Barker, pers. comm.). The reasons for this decision remain unclear, but the resulting interpretation of the supply from this well house has been unnecessarily obscured. How the pipe emerged through the precinct wall remains uncertain, but it must have turned down the wall-face to be led below ground in a stone channel that ran towards the conduit house. A complicated series of drains (see Figure 4.14, Chapter 4) adjacent to the Cell 4 latrine suggest a stop-cock on the supply pipe just inside the precinct wall, and when water was not required to fill the tank in the conduit house it was led away in a channel below the pentice gutter which helped to flush the foul sewers, a course still taken by water from this spring.

The method by which water was distributed from the conduit house appears to be broadly similar to the London model, although the robbing of pipes at the Suppression and later has removed most of the detail. A pipe trench running along the north alley of the great cloister outside Cell 8 was found to have been robbed as recently as the late 19th century and, where a pipe had been taken off this main to feed the Cell 8 tap, one of Hope's trenches dug to answer the same question had removed any evidence of the pipe's line. A pipe still exists in the south cloister alley in an identical location, with a branch taken through the door to the west of the later prior's cell. The size of the pipes feeding individual taps can be gauged from their impression in surviving medieval mortar in the wall core and from the surviving pipe that supplied the prior's cell: the average external diameter was 50 mm. A section of pipe some 2 m in length found *in situ* in the garden of Cell 21 had an external diameter of 28 mm. This was apparently a section of main, complete with a termination; the plate or flange at the end of the pipe suggest that it fed a tank or pressure box, the detail described on the London plan as a 'suspirel'. The fragmentary remains of the water supply system at Mount Grace suggest that it was at least as sophisticated as that of its London sister house.

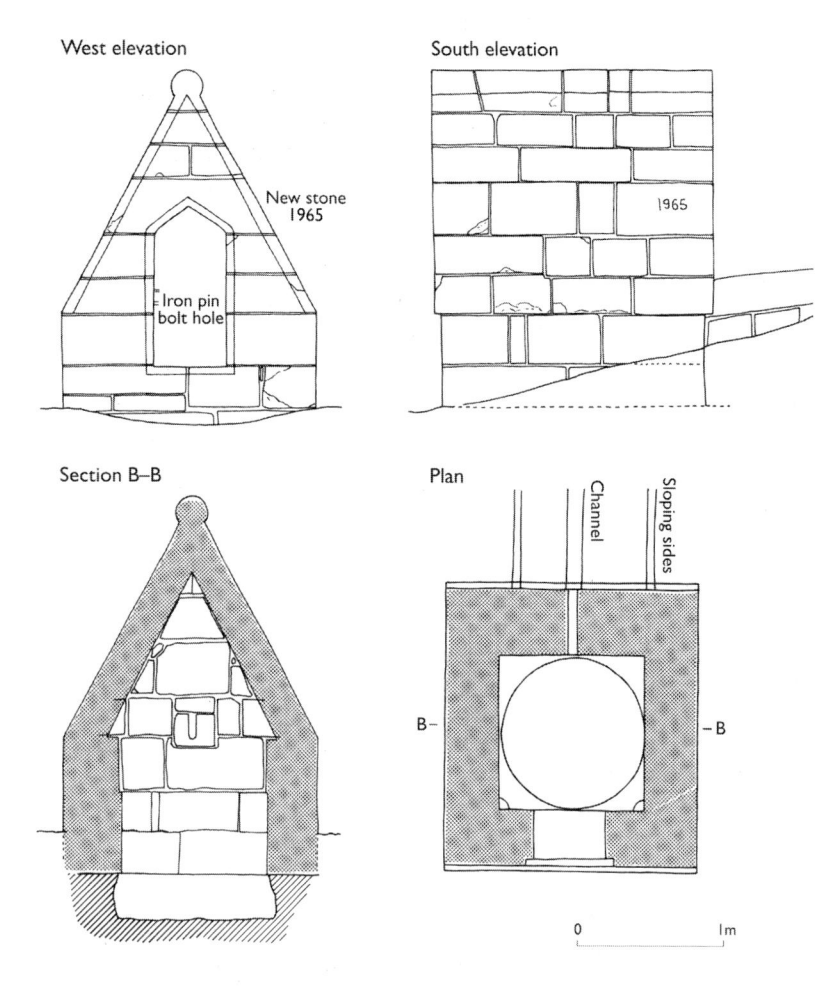

Each of the cells of the great cloister had its own tap set in a niche, normally within the garden pentice but occasionally within the entry-passage of the cell itself (see Figures 6.51 and 6.53). A further tap is evidenced by its cut in the east face of the sacrist's cell, serving the lesser cloister alley, and a similar cut in the south-west corner of the great cloister suggests a tap there as well. A square-headed niche rebated for a door in the north wall of the original prior's cell also appears to have had a tap. A supply that served the kitchen and guest hall was taken off the main that ran around the great cloister, and excavation (see Chapter 5) indicated that it had been altered when the kitchen itself was remodelled in Period Three. It is probable that the system was modified elsewhere as the needs of the house developed, and that excavation might ultimately show that the piped supply has a number of identifiable phases. It is significant that there

Figure 6.50 The central well house.

Figure 6.51 The tap niche in Cell 6 (G. Coppack).

was no evidence for a piped supply in Period One, presumably because its development was possible only as the community grew and stone buildings were provided. No evidence has survived or been excavated to demonstrate that the cells of the lesser cloister had an individual water supply apart from the section of water main from the garden of Cell 21; nor have any taps been recovered by excavation. This section of main may well have related to a supply elsewhere.

Contemporary with the installation of the piped water supply was the provision of a small lavatorium in the south alley of the great cloister. A supply pipe, evidenced by the cut for it in the masonry to the west of the laver, filled a lead tank 0.370 m high and 0.210 m deep above and behind a shallow stone basin (see Figure 6.52). The basin was filled from one or more taps set in the front of the tank, which was supported by a wooden board 25 mm wide set in shallow grooves in the sides of the laver recess. A central drain from the basin, also apparently of lead, as it was robbed, took waste water and returned it to the system, a practice as old as Prior Wybert's supply of the 1160s at Canterbury cathedral priory. It is interesting to note that the chase for this waste pipe had been miscut initially by the masons to one side of its correct location, and the miscut was subsequently carefully blocked. The contemporaneity of the laver and the water tower at the centre of the great cloister was demonstrated by common masons' marks.

Foul Drainage (see Figure 6.53)

Each cell of the great and lesser cloister was provided with a latrine that was water-flushed. Three water sources were used for this: springs within the terraces, surface water and the steam of the northern catchment.

The first latrines to be built were those of Cells 1–5 and the sacrist's cell. These consisted of deep stone-lined pits with an outlet drain that ran to a sewer that still runs down the centre of the east cloister alley and below the sacrist's cell, emerging into the garth of the lesser cloister and skirting the south side of the church. In its present form the southern end of this sewer must be a realignment, as it is deflected around the eastern burial chapel of Period Four. The latrine pits and their drains, however, are a primary feature of the terrace construction and must therefore belong to Period One. The sewer is fed by a spring, probably in the garden of Cell 6, which has not been investigated. A second sewer, also of primary construction, runs south-west from below Cell 8 across the Great Cloister and emerges to the east of the south-west cloister range. At its north end it is fed by a spring in the garden of Cell 9 and a drain that carries surface water from the garden of Cell 5. In Period Two waste water from the conduit tower was diverted into this drain. This second sewer disappears below the Period One church, where it must join the first sewer, and both outfall to the west. The course of the outfall has not been traced, although it is still running: dyed water emerges on the lower terrace to the west of the guest-house range.

The earliest latrines, of which Cell 3 provides the best example (see Figure 4.12), were flushed by springs tapped through the precinct wall. As stone cells were provided in Period Two, the eavesdrip gutters of the cells and their pentices were not used to flush the latrine itself but diverted into the sewer to help keep it scoured. The concept was remarkably sophisticated and shows a particular regard for hygiene even at the foundation stage of the house, when the community was living

THE BUILDINGS AND INFRASTRUCTURE

in timber cells. The system was obviously not foolproof, and there is some evidence that additional sewer runs were provided to redirect the foul drainage when the original runs were found to be less than effective (see Figure 6.53 and Chapter 4). However, the topography of the eastern range, terraced back into the hillside, prevented the adoption of a more satisfactory system. The slightly later north and west ranges, however, were freestanding, and it was possible to provide a single drain to serve the latrines of Cells 6–15 that ran immediately outside the precinct wall. The stream of the northern catchment was diverted to flush this drain, which was open along the north side of the priory but buried along the west side of the site, as its fall increased. After it had passed through the latrine of Cell 15 it turned to the south-west to discharge into the mill race on the lower western terrace. Just as the cells of the north and west side of the great cloister were built individually, the drain appears to have been built from latrine to latrine, with slight variations in its line and fall. Stone-lined throughout its length, it has slightly inclined sides and its fall is marked by a series of steps rather than a sloping base, a design perhaps intended to speed the flow and discourage silting. The new latrines, to the west and north sides of the cloister, were all built over the external drain to a common pattern, which is best seen today in the latrine of Cell 7 (see Figure 4.29). Cell 8 is a reconstruction dating to the 1960s, part of a scheme, never completed, to reconstruct the whole garden. The effectiveness of this new system was such that it was not found necessary to alter it or any of the latrines between Period Two and the Suppression. The Period Three latrines of the lesser cloister, with the exception of Cells 20 and 21, adopted a similar system, the covered drain running along the north side of the inner court, where it could easily be recovered without disturbing the occupants of the cells. Cells 20 and 21, because of their location, adopted the earlier system of drains within the terrace, which must link with the sewer that ran below the east cloister alley and the sacrist's cell.

No trace has been found of a latrine associated with the prior's cell in its original location, or of a drain that could serve it. There must have been a latrine from Period One, perhaps associated with the sewer that was

Figure 6.52 The lavatorium in the great cloister (G. Coppack).

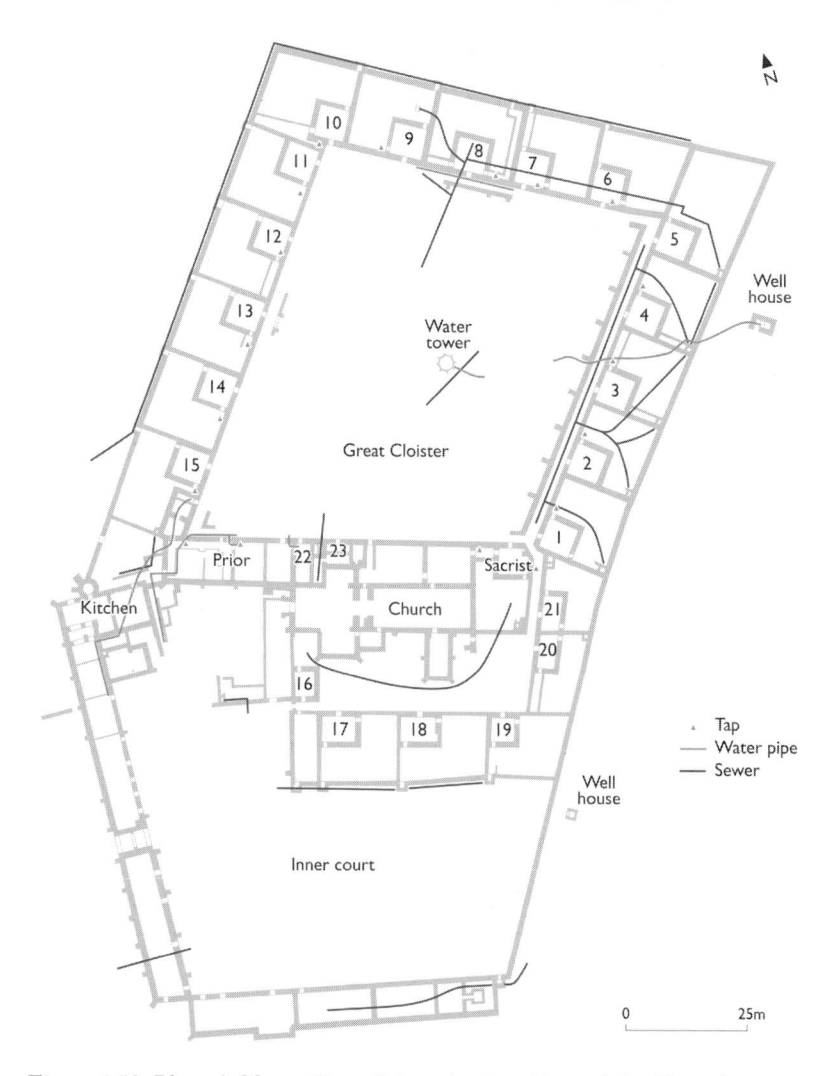

Figure 6.53 Plan of Mount Grace Priory showing all recorded evidence for water management.

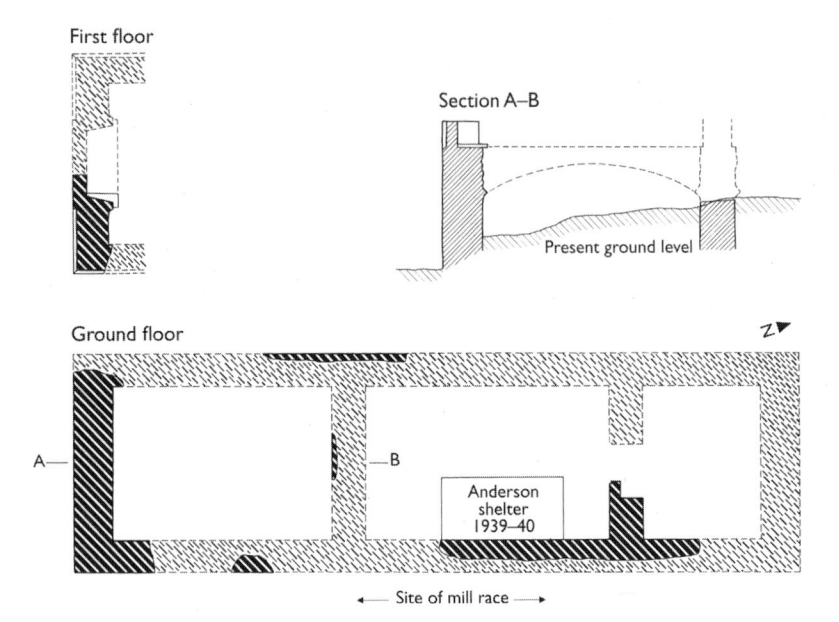

Figure 6.54 Plan and section of the water mill in the outer court.

fed by the two foul drains that meet below the nave of the church and which must discharge towards the west. Remarkably, no trace of it was seen in excavation to the west, although it must be remembered that a substantial area to the west of the church has been cleared only down to Suppression-period levels. What is clear is that it did not extend as far west as the yard on the east side of the guest-house range, where substantial modern intrusions into the natural clay of the terrace revealed no trace of a sewer. If the presumed line of the drain is projected to the west it would run close to the latrine tower on the east side of the guest house, which was, significantly, a pit latrine, the only one identified at Mount Grace. The foul drainage was obviously a very sophisticated system of which only a small part has been observed to date.

The Carthusian plan, with its provision of individual privies for each monk and lay brother, is partly responsible for the complexity of the foul drainage at Mount Grace. Some provision must also have been made for the inner court and particularly for the guest accommodation, but this has not been traced.

Surface Drainage (see Figure 6.53)

Mount Grace is a remarkably wet site because of its location at the foot of an escarpment that seems to catch every passing cloud and, because the subsoil is impervious, elaborate drainage was absolutely essential. Great attention was paid from the earliest period to the collection of surface water. Surface water, which includes run-off from roofs, was obviously an important source of additional water, and it is significant that very little of it was wasted. In the eastern range of the great cloister its primary function was to flush the foul drains and supplement the supply from tapped springs, and this appears to have also been the case in the north range. It was also collected for use in the cell gardens, and the tanks that would have stored it survive in the gardens of Cells 2 and 3. The provision of gutters on most pentices, evidenced in some instances by the widening of drains to take the discharge from a downpipe, could also allow the collection of water in butts for garden use. The latrine pentice in Cell 8 had only a single soakaway to take water from its extensive roof, and it is quite possible that a second downpipe filled a barrel in the north-east angle. Because this would have been above ground level, no trace has survived in the archaeological record. It is a testament to the medieval water engineers that their drains, cleaned and repaired after excavation, are still used to keep the site dry.

The Water Mill and its Water Supply

Lying on the west side of the canalised Clack Beck are the unexcavated ruins of a two-storey masonry building approximately 23.5 m long and 6.80 m wide (see Figure 6.54). Part of its south gable wall stands to a height of 0.80 m above first-floor level; otherwise, it has been reduced to ground level or below. It was not examined or described by Hope. Its lower storey was filled to an unknown depth with demolition material, which was disturbed only by the insertion of an Anderson shelter in 1939–40. Only short lengths of the side and cross-walls were visible through the turf, though sufficient could be traced to reconstruct the ground-floor plan of the building with some certainty. The exact location of the north wall, marked by a prominent earthwork, is not precisely determined, for no facing stones were visible on the surface. The Anderson shelter was removed and the hole backfilled in 1995.

The ground floor comprised three rooms in line, of which the southernmost was the best preserved. Although the gable wall was deeply buried in rubble, a maximum of three and a half courses of masonry, some 1.15 m in height, were visible below the finely dressed springing of a segmental vault. The apparent sturdiness of the internal cross-walls suggested

THE BUILDINGS AND INFRASTRUCTURE

that each of the three rooms was similarly vaulted, providing the building with a very substantial sub-structure. No door could be traced between the southern and central rooms, though only a small part of the dividing wall was visible, but the east jamb of a door between the central and northern rooms remained exposed at the centre of the building; if exactly central, the door would have been 1.15 m wide. It was hung on the south side of the cross-wall in a 50 mm rebate similar in detail to those of the latrine doors of Cells 6–15. No openings were observed in either side wall, although a substantial length of the inner face of the east wall remained visible. As the mill race lay on this side of the building, no doors are likely to have existed there. The west wall, which appeared to be substantially robbed at its north end, provided no evidence at all.

All that remained of the upper floor was the eastern half of the south gable wall and a short length of the inner face of the east wall, a singularly informative fragment. Internally, the wall-face was set back 0.120 m from the line of the ground floor wall-face and was ashlar-faced only above the spandrel of the vault. Externally, the first-floor level was marked by a chamfered offset, again of 0.120 m. At the centre of the gable wall was a fireplace, of which the east jamb, fireback and a section of hearth stone remained. Externally this was marked by a widening of the wall and the omission of the chamfered offset course. The east jamb of the fireplace coursed with the masonry of the inner wall-face, its external edge radiused in the same manner as the Period Two fireplace in the prior's cell, although it lacked the spurred base seen there (see Figure 5.17). Reconstructed, the fireplace was 2.38 m wide. It must be presumed that the ground-floor cross-walls were continued up into the upper storey, dividing the first floor into three rooms of unequal size. The southern room, with its fireplace, was probably the office of the miller.

There can be little doubt that this building, aligned on the mill race and directly adjacent to it, was the mill. Constructed throughout in good-quality ashlar, the few details it retained suggested that it was a construction of Period Two. As all of the visible masonry was laid to common bed heights, there is every indication that it was a single-period structure. Only excavation will confirm its use and date.

6.3 The Development of the Guest-house Range 1540–1901

The medieval guest-house range survives today as the shell of an important post-Suppression house. It was surveyed by Ambrose Poynter and Pieter Rodeck in 1899 (for the context of this survey, see Morrison 2003, 126) and large parts of it were further recorded by Steve Coll in 1988 during its repair for public display. This analysis draws heavily on both those surveys. Coll's survey is held in the English Heritage Archaeology Store in Helmsley with the excavation archive.

The Period Five Rebuilding of the Guest-house Range by Conyers, Lord Darcy in c.1616

It is unclear whether the guest-house range remained roofed at the Suppression, although surviving reset roof trusses in the southern half of the building, derived from base crucks, could be of 15th-century date. No date could be determined by dendrochronological dating. There is no evidence for immediate post-Suppression conversion to a house and the survival of the greater part of the medieval fenestration and doors in the east wall argue against conversion. The original purchaser, John Cheney, was simply a dealer in monastic estates, and Sir James Strangways, who acquired the reversion of the property, already had a major house at East Harlsey Castle and was unlikely to have required a second house in the immediate locality. Against this needs to be set the partial and controlled demolition of the south-west cloister range, which does appear to be the start of a planned redevelopment of the site.

The most likely context for the new house was the marriage of Conyers, Lord Darcy, to Grace Rokeby in 1616, the Mount Grace estate being part of her marriage settlement (Coppack and Douglas 2014, 35). The principal alteration made was the turning of the building around: in its medieval form it faced into the inner court and its west wall was essentially a continuation of the precinct wall that enclosed the central buildings of the priory. The 17th-century house was designed to face away from the priory ruins, with its principal fenestration inserted into the west wall, looking out over the lower terrace (see Figure 6.55). Its plan was unremarkable (see Figure 6.56), with

Figure 6.55 The Lascelles house as it appeared in the late 1890s before its repair and extension by Sir Lowthian Bell.

three rooms on the ground floor (kitchen, hall and parlour), bed chambers on the first floor and garrets above. The northern half of the original building, including the kitchen chimney of Period Three, was left as an unroofed yard. As part of this rebuilding, the upper storey of the gatehouse to the south was demolished and the south gable of the range rebuilt. Cross-walls were also inserted, built entirely out of reused monastic masonry, and original openings in the east wall were largely blocked up. Much of this blocking was, confusingly, removed after 1900.

On the west facade the medieval buttresses were retained to define the bay divisions, but most of the masonry between them was taken down to allow the insertion of large, square-headed and transomed windows of three lights. The four lowest courses below the ground-floor windows remain undisturbed. Because the early 17th-century bay spacing differed from that of the original building, there is a certain lack of symmetry. The placement of the windows was structured by the contemporary cross-walls, the parlour to the south having paired windows, the hall having a window to each side of its central door and the kitchen having paired windows separated by a buttress, while the windows of the first floor mirrored those below. A slight change in detail is apparent in the three first-floor windows at the north end of the house, where the hood-moulds of the windows are carried back through the thickness of the wall to form the head of the window splay – all the other windows had timber safe-lintels that were replaced in 1901, when the southernmost first-floor window was also renewed. This change in detail may indicate that these were the last windows to be inserted in the west wall of the old guest house. Originally, three dormer windows lit the garrets, but the southern one had been removed before *c.*1890 (see Figure 6.55) and the northern one was reconstructed using original material in 1900/1. Only the central dormer remains as built, although it too was adapted in 1654.

The south wall of the building at ground-floor level is the north wall of the Period One gatehouse, which survives to the springing level of the gate-passage vault; at first-floor level and up into the gable the south wall is all of early 17th-century date and almost exclusively built of reused medieval masonry. Within the house a stair turret at the north-east corner of the gate was removed and medieval ashlars were used to reface the wall from the straight joint where the east wall of the guest house had

THE BUILDINGS AND INFRASTRUCTURE

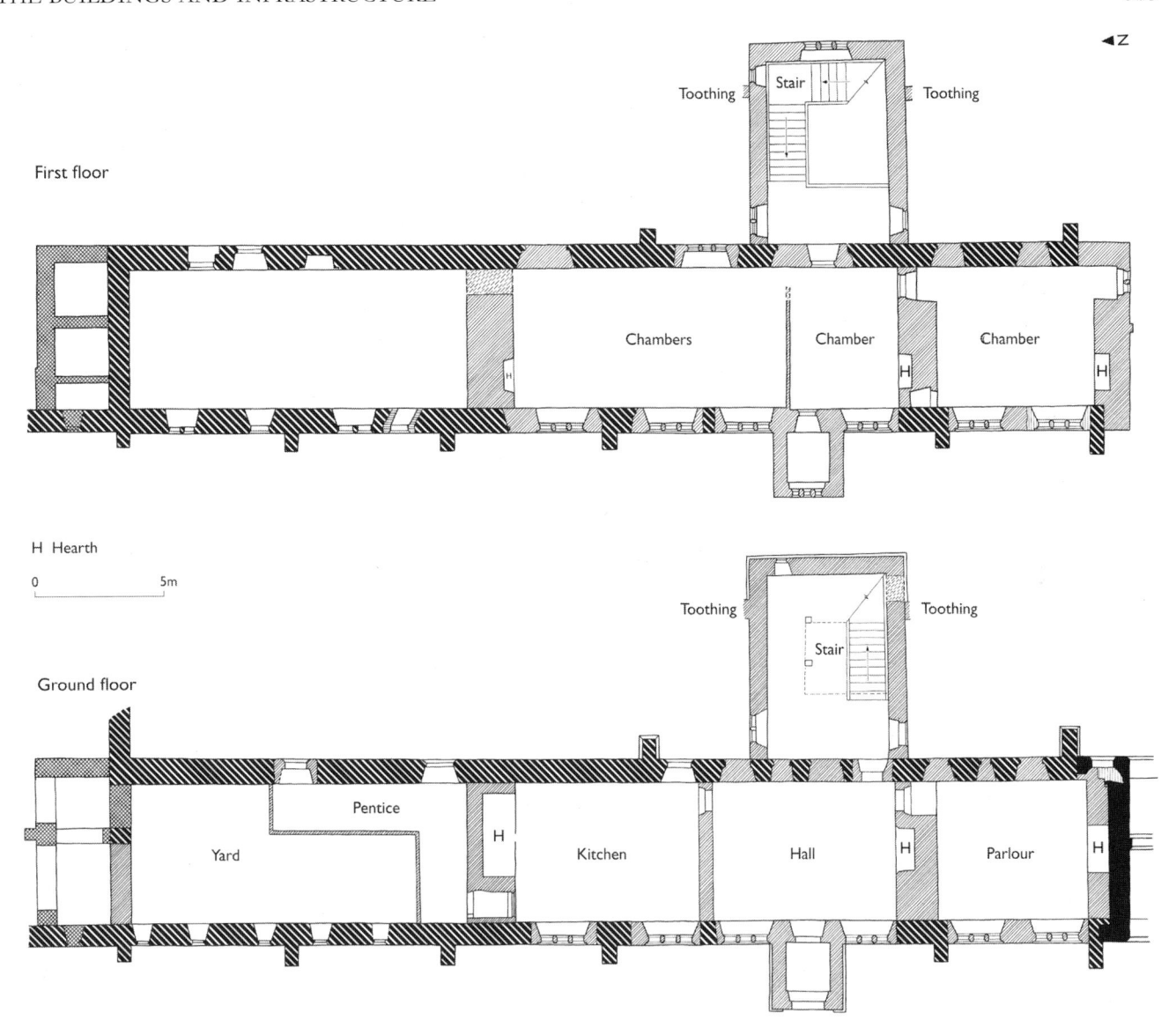

butted against the turret. The south wall was widened internally to take a fireplace at ground-floor level, which remains. There are two early 17th-century fireplaces at first-floor level.

The east wall of the old guest house remained substantially unchanged apart from the blocking of almost all its original openings. Again, the medieval buttresses were allowed to remain. A single first-floor window was inserted in the east wall to light a passage at first-floor level.

Internally, a great deal of the early 17th-century house can still be traced. The parlour is divided from the hall by a thick wall, again built of reused medieval ashlar, which contains a fireplace at its centre and a square-headed door at its east end. This wall is carried up to the full height of the house, with, at first-floor level, a door to the chamber above the parlour at its east end and a small fireplace serving the chamber over the southern half of the hall. A narrow wall, carried up only to first-floor level, separated the hall from the kitchen to the north. Again, the square-headed communicating door was at the east end of the wall. The kitchen was a substantial room, with a great joggled segmental-headed fireplace set in the thick north wall of the house, which is all of early 17th-century date. A 15th-century window in the east wall of the kitchen was cut down to form a door leading to a small yard on the east side of the house, and a passage with a door at each end was provided through the north wall to the west of the fireplace. This led to a pentice that ran along the outside of the north wall and returned along the east wall of

Figure 6.56 Ground- and first-floor plans of the house of 1652 built in the shell of the guest-house range.

the old guest-house kitchen. The 15th-century door of the old guest hall was retained to serve this pentice and a new door with a square head was inserted into the east wall at its north end. The pentice was a substantial affair with a sprung timber floor and a steeply pitched roof, both of which have left clear traces on the surviving masonry. In 1899/1900 Ambrose Poynter recorded two small partitioned rooms, possibly a pantry and buttery, on the south side of the kitchen; these may have been of early 17th-century date, as he illustrates them using the same convention as the masonry of that period.

The first floor must have been reached by a stair from the hall, but this has not survived further building in 1654 (see below). At first-floor level, with the exception of the southern chamber, which appears to have been the principal room on this floor, the house was divided by timber-framed partitions, one of which remains *in situ*. Ambrose Poynter recorded a timber partition running from just west of the door to the southern chamber to this surviving partition, which extended up to the east wall of the building and had a door at its east end into a corridor that ran up to the north wall of the building. That corridor was widened in 1900/1, destroying the original partition and cutting back the one remaining timber-framed partition wall. Reset in the new corridor wall at its south end is a 17th-century baluster grille that may have come from the original corridor wall. The remainder of the first-floor partitioning that survives dates to 1900/1, but Poynter also recorded a further partition wall that ran from the northern splay of the inserted window in the east wall to the southern mullion of the opposite window in the west wall. No trace of this partition was found when the building was examined by Steve Coll, although there is no reason to suppose that it was not 17th century in date. The northern chamber on the first floor has a substantial fireplace in its gable wall, offset to the west of the kitchen chimney flue.

The Extension of the House by Thomas Lascelles in 1654

In 1653 Conyers, Lord Darcy succeeded his father as 8th Lord Darcy of Knaith and sold Captain Thomas Lascelles his capital messuage of Mount Grace 'with other houses, buildings, barns, stables, dovecote, out-houses, gardens [and] tofts'. Lascelles set out to extend the house (Coppack and Douglas 2014, 35), building both the two-storey porch on the west side of the house that carries his initials and the date 1654 over the porch door and a substantial stair wing on the back of the house.

The porch is very clearly an addition, being straight-jointed to the house and sealing the inserted masonry of the south hall window. Its construction required the removal of the third buttress from the south. Curiously, the porch is built out of vertical, following the pronounced outward lean of the medieval wall apart from the five courses below the parapet, which were set vertically. The first floor of the porch was a closet entered from the bed chamber over the hall via a new door case inserted in the west wall. The oak door of 1654 survives. A second door was provided in the central dormer to give access to the flat roof of the tower porch. Although the present door is a replacement of 1900/1, it appears to be a faithful copy of the original.

The stair wing is also butted up to the original building. A new door inserted into the east wall of the house in the south-east corner of the hall led to a small lobby at the west end of the stair wing. In the north wall of the lobby a door led to the yard outside the house. The stair, slightly remodelled in 1900/1, survives, serving both the first floor and garrets above. Behind the balusters of the stair the masonry is painted with a red ochre wash, which appears to have been used throughout the building in this phase where walls were not panelled: traces remain on all the 17th-century fireplaces and on window and door splays and heads. The first floor was entered from the stair wing through a new wide square-headed door in the medieval east wall. Pin holes around this door indicate that it had an elaborate door case that had been removed by 1899.

Toothings for the east wall of flanking rooms at ground- and first-floor level to north and south of the stair wing were provided when the stair wing was built, but were not used, probably because of Lascelles' death in *c.*1658.

The Period Six Remodelling and Extension of the 17th-century House by Bell

Sir Lowthian Bell acquired the site in 1900 and, on the advice of Philip Webb, who had remodelled his first house, Washington Hall, in 1854 and built his later house, Rounton Grange, between 1872 and 1876, commissioned Ambrose Macdonald Poynter to remodel and extend the 17th-century house at Mount Grace. Poynter, a leading light of the Society for the Preservation of Ancient Buildings, was also to work with Hope on the architectural detail from the site and provided drawings for his report. His approach was to record and understand the earlier building, and he restored and extended the house with a remarkable degree of care (Morrison 2003, *passim*). The early 20th-century house survives largely as he left it, the scale of his intervention being identified internally by Steve Coll and externally from Poynter's survey drawings. The work was done after Hope had studied the building (Hope 1905, 274–80), and Ambrose Poynter's careful approach ensured that no surviving medieval features were lost, although some were modified. The house was extended into the northern half of the range to provide service rooms on the ground floor, a back stair and accommodation on the first and attic floors. Poynter also added the rooms to either side of the stair wing, using the toothing provided by Lascelles.

The extent of the work, while thoughtful, was substantial. Internally, the timber lintels of all the 17th-century windows were cut out and replaced with steel joists jacketed with tiles packed in a hard cement mortar, and the inner wall-face between the ground- and first-floor windows was taken down and reset when the lintels of the lower windows were renewed. The southernmost first-floor window, blocked in the 1890s (from the evidence of Poynter's survey), was renewed in its entirety, the inscription 19 ILB 01 on its head firmly dating the reconstruction. Within the 17th-century house the wall-head was taken down to the top of the first-floor windows and rebuilt. The binders and joists of the 17th-century first floor survived throughout the house, but the attic floor and roof were both renewed, together with the roof of the stair wing. In the northern half of the range, less work was necessary. The missing elements of the west window of the Procurator's chamber were accurately replaced, the door to his now-missing latrine was partly blocked to become a window and the door through the west side of the Period Three kitchen chimney to rooms over the western half of the kitchen cross-wing was carefully blocked. Cross-walls were built to divide the space up, simply butted up against the medieval side walls, and doors and windows had their joinery replaced in good Arts and Crafts style. This careful repair, which retained the maximum amount of information, is in stark contrast to the heavy-handed repair of the 17th-century house and indicates that a much higher value was placed by Poynter and his client Sir Lowthian Bell on the medieval structure than on the 17th-century modifications. The care taken extended to the great chimney stack at the north end of the house, which was effectively redundant space. Its footings were underpinned with concrete and its junction with the north-east corner of the guest-house range, where the scar of the demolished south kitchen wall remained, was carefully refaced with reclaimed medieval stone to the extent that it is now virtually impossible to see where it was. Fortunately, it was photographed in the 1890s. Waterproof leaded roofs were provided in the chimney flues, with a downpipe taking away the run-off.

The care shown in the treatment of medieval fabric continued into the western end of the kitchen cross-wing, where the west and part of the north wall survived and were reused in a new boiler house with virtually no modification. The western half of the kitchen was then enclosed by a new wall footed on the remains of the dividing wall between medieval rooms I and II of the kitchen cross-wing, and the small yard that resulted contained lavatories for the male and female servants. The care lavished on the surviving walls did not extend to the archaeology, however: the western half of room I was dug out to a depth of over a metre and the standing walls were underpinned with brick and new masonry to provide headroom for the central heating boiler. Wrapped around the north-west corner of the boiler room was a coal house that contained the remains of Hope's 'vat', which was permitted to remain below a heap of coke. The digging of service trenches and the installation of a septic tank in the area of the medieval kitchen and its offices made no attempt to avoid buried archaeological features, even though most of them had previously been revealed by Hope.

Chapter 7: The Cultural Collections

Although most of the finds have been presented in Chapters 3, 4 and 5, the wider significance of the cultural collections is presented here, together with the environmental evidence for both the setting of the priory and the food waste from the kitchen and other areas.

7.1 The Setting of the Site Evidenced by Insect Remains

by Mark Dinnin

Introduction

Mount Grace Priory stands on a levelled terrace of tamped-down clay, a feature made necessary by the boggy nature of the land in that location. The flat area that the priory covers is situated on the back slope of a late Devensian landslip, one of many at the foot of the steep scarp slope of the North Yorkshire Moors (see, for example, Blackham *et al.* 1981). The opportunity to examine sealed deposits immediately below the levelling of the great cloister terrace came in the summer of 1988, when Hope's excavation trench on the site of the water tower was reopened, revealing three concentric rings of pine piles that had been driven through the clay terrace levelling and the underlying peat fen and into a second layer of clay (see Chapter 4 and Figure 4.92) that was, at the time, thought to represent the bottom of the basin. Since saturated peat deposits are conducive to the preservation of fossil insect material, it was decided to deepen the excavation and take a series of samples for fossil insect analysis, work that was undertaken by Professor Paul Buckland and the writer. On deepening the excavation it was found that there was, in fact, a *c.*3 m succession of peats and clays, from which 27 samples were taken (see Figure 7.1). Samples weighing 5 kg were taken at 100 mm intervals or at a change in stratigraphy. The base of the profile consisted of a grey clay, as yet undated but possibly belonging to the Late Glacial or early Flandrian period. The middle of the section, composed of unconsolidated fibrous peat with sandy and clayey lenses, represented inwash material brought into the basin by the streams that dissect the scarp, the peat forming *in situ*. Coppack's excavation of Cell 8 and earlier work by the Ministry of Works' direct labour team had indicated that the terrace was drained at the foundation of the priory in or about 1398, suggesting that the ground was still relatively marshy at that time. Therefore, while the majority of the samples remain unstudied in the Department of Archaeology, University of Sheffield, the peat sample from immediately below the clay terrace levelling was examined with the aim of reconstructing the landscape setting of the Mount Grace site at the time of the foundation of the priory. Particular research questions were:

- How wet was the site before building took place?
- How open was the site at this time; in particular, was there any woodland in the vicinity?
- What land management systems were in place?

The Recovery of Fossil Insect Material

In order to recover fossil insect material from peat samples it is first necessary to concentrate them. This was accomplished using the

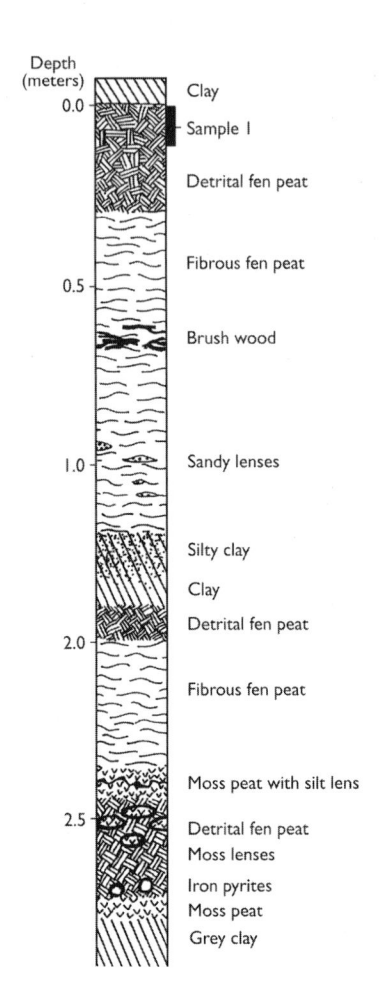

Figure 7.1 Schematic section of the peat column from the water-tower excavation.

now-standard technique developed by Coope and Osborne (1968). The samples were disaggregated in warm water over a 300 μm sieve and then concentrated by paraffin (kerosene) flotation. After washing with detergent to remove excess paraffin, the insect fraction was separated from the plant macrofossil float (in this case quite small). Sorting was carried out in alcohol under a low-powered microscope and the disarticulated insect remains were identified using the standard entomological keys and an extensive reference collection. The insects recovered are listed in Table 7.1; taxonomy follows Kloet and Hinks (1977).

Environmental Interpretation

The number of species recovered has enabled a detailed environmental reconstruction to be carried out. The vast majority of taxa are associated with wet, boggy ground and vegetation characteristic of it. *Esolus parallelepipidus,* the smallest and most common member of the Elminthidae (riffle beetles), inhabits gravel- or stony-bedded streams and rivers. The two individuals recovered probably lived in one of the streams that drained the scarp slope, where the water flow was fast enough to prevent the deposition of silt. The presence of some standing water is indicated by at least six species of beetle. *Coelostoma orbiculare* and *Chaetarthria seminulum* are found at the edges of stagnant, eutrophic, well-vegetated ponds and in shallow water among plant debris; the former species is also found in shallow water among vegetation and is considered to be a typical fenland species. Similarly, *Anacaena globulus* inhabits the grassy edge of running or stagnant water, where it can be seen in submerged vegetation (Balfour-Browne 1958), although it has been recorded from grass and litter in woodland as well as from cut hay (Donisthorpe 1939). Members of the genus *Laccobius* live in slowly running or stagnant water, *L. bipuntatus* being found mainly on clayey or silty water margins, frequently only sparsely covered with vegetation. A second member of the genus recovered could not be confidently identified to species, but seemed to match *L. minutes* most closely. Often found in association with the preceding species, this beetle has very similar ecological preferences. Additional evidence for the occurrence of areas of muddy, sparsely vegetated water margins is provided by the presence of two Dryopids in the sample. These beetles are notoriously difficult to identify and the species names assigned to those recovered must remain tentative. *Dryops* spp. are found on land, on open muddy banks, and in water, either still or running, in which they breathe by trapping air on their hairy bodies. Likewise, the small rovebeetles of the genus *Carpelimus* are difficult to identify, but nearly all are associated with areas free from vegetation, such as pond and river banks. Species of the genera *Hydroporus, Helophorus* and *Hydraena* are to be found in various aquatic habitats, mostly involving stagnant pools. There is no indication of extensive open water being present, as would have been suggested by the occurrence of the larger dytiscids. A variety of other hygrophilous species was recovered from the sample: of the carabids (ground beetles), *Patrobus septentrionis* is frequently seen among litter on muddy shores of stagnant pools in the north of Britain. The more eurytopic *Bembidian bruxellense* is another inhabitant of moist, lightly vegetated river or pond banks. Similarly, *Dyschirius globosus* shows a preference for humid soils with rather sparse cover.

Rich water-side vegetation is indicated directly by the phytophagous component of the fauna and indirectly by the predatory Carabid fauna. The iridescent reed beetles *Plateumaris affinis* and *P. discolor/sericea* live on and develop in *Carex* spp. The larvae of the small weevil *Thryogenes festucae* live in the stems of various Cyperaceae, *Carex, Scirpus* and possibly *Phragmites* (Hoffman 1958), all of which grow in swampy localities. Likewise, the weevil *Limnobaris pilistriata* lives in and on swamp grasses such as sedge (*Carex* and *Cladium*) and rushes (*Scirpus*), over-wintering in the stems (Hoffman 1954; Lohse 1983b). *Notaris acridulus* is found in the roots of aquatic grasses such as reed sweet-grass (*Glyceria aquatica* (L.)), as well as amphibious biswort (*Polygonum amphibium* (L.)) (Hoffman 1958) and bur-reed (*Sparganium ramosum* (Huds.)) (Lohse 1983a), all of which are marsh plants. A beetle belonging to the genus *Phtobius*, whose members generally feed on *Polygonum* sp., was also recovered, but could not be identified to species level. The Pselaphid *Reichenbachia juncorum* is not, as its name would suggest, a common inhabitant of rushes but of moss and grass tussocks (Pearce 1957). This kind of habitat is also favoured by the carnivorous ground beetles *Bembidion guttula, Agonum thoreyi, Pterostichus nigrita* and *P. vernalis* (Lindroth 1985), which feed on springtails and other small arthropods. Apart from the previously mentioned *Carpelimus*, a number of other Staphylinid beetles recovered are common to water-side situations, including *Olophrum piceum, Lesteva heeri, Anthophagus caraboides* and *Lathrobium* spp. In Britain, *A. caraboides* is restricted to hills and upland areas of the north and west and is found, often in numbers, on shrubs and plants beside water (Harde 1984). *Acidota cruentata* lives in moist localities in moss and under leaf litter. The remains of a click beetle belonging to the genus *Selatosomus* could not be positively identified to species level; the candidates were *S. nigricornis*, which is often numerous in water-side locations, and *S. impressus*, which is found in mountainous areas in decaying birch and conifers. In the light of this habitat data it seems that *S. nigricornis* is a more likely candidate for a deposit in this situation.

The reed swamp was apparently flanked by carr-type vegetation growing on drier soils. An indication of its composition is given by the shiny Chrysomelid *Plagiodera versicolora*, the larvae of which attack willows (and sometimes poplars), stripping the leaves down to the ribs (Donisthorpe 1939; Mohr 1966). *Bembidion clarkii, Pterostichus strenuous* and *Agonum assimile* are all litter-layer species of damp, deciduous forests on clayey, mull-rich soil, occurring particularly in the drier parts of *Alnus* and *Salix* swamps or on the shaded edges of eutrophic ponds (*i.e.* among sedges and grasses). *A. assimile* hibernates in fallen trees and behind the bark on stumps (Lindroth 1985), where the rove beetle *Hapalaraea pygmaea* lives (Lohse 1964). Likewise, *Pterostichus diligens*, although generally distributed in wet habitats, is especially typical of shaded boggy sites such as alder carr; it occurs in euthropic fens, but is most frequent in oligotrophic bogs (Lindroth 1985). *Pterostichus minor*, only tentatively identified, is often very abundant on the shores of eutrophic lakes and in *Sphagnum* bogs and alder swamps (Lindroth 1985). Despite the absence of any species that actually feeds on alder, the presence of some shade-giving trees can be assumed, be they willow, alder or other fenland species.

There is much evidence for a rich, damp, open ground flora containing plants often associated with waste ground and wet meadows. The leaf beetle *Prasocurius phellandrii* feeds on aquatic Umbelliferae, which would have flourished in the boggy environment. Marsh marigold (*Caltha palustris* (L.)) and some species of buttercup, host plants of *Hydrothassa marginella* (Mohr 1966), grow in marshy areas and in wet woods; the partial shade provided by fen carr would have encouraged luxuriant growth in marsh marigold. Two members of the genus *Phyllotreta* were present in the sample. Many of these, including *P. exclamationis*, feed on members of the Cruciferae family in damp situations. Other open-/rough-ground plants indicated include *Lotus uliginosus* (Schkuhr.) and/or *L. corniculatus* (L.), large birds' foot trefoil and birds' foot trefoil, which grow in grassy places and are the food plants of the weevil *Lotus uliginosus* (Lohse and Tischler 1983). *S. macularius* is found on vetches (*Vicia*) and clovers (*Trifolium*) and *S. lineatus* on *Lotus* sp., *Trifolium* sp. and *medico* sp., again waste-ground plants. *Leiosoma deflexum*, a feeder on *Ranunculus* spp. (buttercups, creeping buttercups and wood anenome) further supports the evidence for open ground. Chrysomelids can be found on a variety of different herbs, and members of the genera *Aphthona* and *Longitarsus* present in the sample could not be identified to species. Longitarsus spp. live on the the Boraginacae, Scrophulariaceae and Labiatae families, many of which are flowering herbs occurring in open areas or at the sides of walks or ponds in relatively unshaded areas. Adults of *Aphthona* spp. feed on *Euphorbia* (spurges), which are found in arable, wood and hedge situations, and less often on *Linum* (flaxes), plants of grassland and moorland.

The presence of a large amount of rotting vegetable refuse within these habitats is indicated by the hydrophilids *Cercyon atomarius*, *Cercyon* spp. and the tiny *Megasternum obscurum*, all ubiquitous insects of decaying vegetable matter. The rove beetles of the genera *Megarthrus*, *Anotylus*, *Xylodromus*, *Gyrohypnus*, *Xantholinus*, *Quedius*, *Gabrius*, *Tachyporus* and *Tachinus*, and the species *Micropeplus porcatus*, *Omalium rivulare*, *O. caesum*, *Rugilus orbiculare* and *Encephalus complicans*, are all fairly eurytopic creatures, being found in all kinds of vegetable refuse, including that in damp places, which would have been a feature of all the habitats previously described. *Xylodromus concinnus* and *X. depressus* are normally associated with rotting hay residues (Harde 1984; Lohse 1964), which would have accumulated in damp, lush meadows, although the latter has also been recorded from decaying trees, stumps and birds' nests (Palm 1959). Members of the Latridiidae, which include *Stephostethus*, *Enicmus* and *Corticaria*, are colloquially referred to as mould beetles and are found wherever fungi grow; as a result, they are common in all manner of habitats. They are often numerous under bark and particularly in mildewy hay and grass cuttings. In summer they can often be seen in numbers on flowering plants, along with adult *Nitidula* spp. Latridiids often occur with the genus Cryptophagus, although the latter appears to prefer slightly drier material.

There is a continuum between the elements of rotting compost fauna and that of herbivore dung. *Anotylus* spp. are equally common in both these substrates, as are *Cercyon* spp., *Cryptopleurum* spp. and *Megasternum obscurum*. The members of the genus *Platystethus* are almost impossible to identify to species level as fossils, but most live in dung, particularly on muddy river banks (Tottenham 1954), where several hundred may be found in a single pat. The best indicators of animal dung are the dung beetles of the genus *Aphodius*. *A. ater* is not restricted to dung, also living in compost; however, it does show a preference for open habitats. The larvae and adults of *A. contaminatus* develop only in dung; it is a common species especially numerous in horse dung. *A. rufipes* and *A. depressus* live in all kinds of dung and are common and widespread (Jessop 1986).

Comparison with West Cowick moat

The Mount Grace fauna can be compared to another medieval Yorkshire insect assemblage of similar date from the moat at West Cowick (Hayfield and Greig 1989), although the open water of the Cowick moat resulted in a pond-type element within the fauna that was absent at Mount Grace. There is a large overlap between the riparian and compost faunas of the two sites, but the Cowick faunas differ in two significant ways. Direct evidence of human habitation in the vicinity of the moat is provided by the grain pests *Oryzaephilus surinamensis* (L.) and the usually synanthropic *Myceteae hirta* (Marsh.), *Tipnus unicolor* (Pill. and Mitt.) and *Ptinus fur* (L.), suggesting the close proximity of grain stores. Secondly, the occurrence of species such as *Rhynchaenus quercus* (L.), *Polydrusus pterygomalis* (Boh.), *Ermotes ater* (L.), *Rhyncolus lignarius* (Marsh.), *Hylesinus crenatus* (F.), *Leperisinus varius* (F.) and *Ancrantus vittatus* (F.) indicate the proximity of deciduous and coniferous trees of differing ages and in various states of decay. It was these elements of the fauna that were notably absent from the Mount Grace sample. Given this, the evidence for a cleared landscape at Mount Grace becomes all the more conclusive.

Summary

The insects indicate a swampy local environment fed by calcareous springs emerging at the foot of the scarp. There is evidence of small areas of slowly running water and shallow eutrophic standing water with fairly extensive areas of exposed mud. The water was bordered by reed and rush beds supporting their own distinct beetle fauna. Marsh grasses and sedges grew on the adjacent boggy ground, with flushes

THE CULTURAL COLLECTIONS

of herbs associated with wet areas. Although only one species-specific phytophage was recovered, the presence of carr-type shrubs and trees is suggested, with *Salix* and perhaps *Alnus* and *Betula* growing on the drier ground away from the water. The large compost fauna suggests a rich litter accumulation, as is usual in reed swamps.

Meadow or at least rough open ground is apparently present, with grass and grassland weeds indicated. Although there is evidence for large herbivores, it is not possible to determine whether they were deer, cattle, horses, sheep or another domestic animal.

There is no evidence, however, of the mature woodland that covers the scarp today, although the extensive and valuable Mount Wood was certainly in existence by 1538. It is difficult to determine whether this absence is a true reflection of the landscape or just a result of taphonomic processes. If woodland had been as close to the site as it is today, it would be surprising if none of the woodland stenotypes had become incorporated into the deposit. However, many of the woodland beetles are poor dispersers and may not have strayed far enough from their habitats to be included in the catchment area of the swamp. Other than this fact, there is very little information available on the dispersal of woodland beetles and an obvious need for research in this area.

There is no indication of the presence of the village of *Bordelbi,* excavated elements of which lay within 40 m of the area sampled, and it fair to assume that this part of the village had been long abandoned by the close of the 14th century. The site of the priory was a boggy and uneven terrace drained only by the natural streams that crossed it, but it had the undoubted advantage of being a large area of relatively flat land that was not under cultivation and was large enough to accommodate the great cloister and inner court of a Carthusian monastery and, by the end of the 14th century, such sites were actually hard to find. Levelling and drainage were major undertakings, but were secondary to the location of a large enough plot of marginal land and the cost of raising stone buildings. It was certainly not the first monastery to be built under such circumstances: the construction of Byland Abbey from the 1150s required the draining of a mere, and Winchester cathedral priory was raised on a marsh in the 1070s.

7.2 Pottery

by Colin Hayfield

Introduction

Mount Grace, which was occupied for just 141 years from its foundation in 1398 to its suppression in 1539, provides a valuable opportunity to study the transitional developments in English late medieval and early post-medieval pottery production, an important and poorly understood period of ceramic change beginning in the second half of the 15th century. In addition, as a Carthusian charterhouse, in which the religious undertook a solitary life, the site was likely to provide discrete groups of pottery that related directly to individual members of the community.

This relatively short period of occupation can be divided into four well-defined and -dated building and occupation periods and a final phase associated with the post-Suppression demolition of the priory buildings. The four medieval construction phases (defined in Chapter 6 above) are:

Period One: *c.*1398–*c.*1412
Period Two: 1420s and 1430s
Period Three: 1460s and 1470s
Period Four: 1520s

Coppack's excavation of Cell 8, the water tower, the south-west cloister range and the kitchen area has provided a series of well-stratified finds groups related to the construction and occupation that occurred within those four main periods, while Keen's excavation of Cells 9–15 produced predominantly occupation material dating only to Period Four. Pottery from Ministry of Works clearance work before 1968 is presumed to come from the later periods of occupation of Cells 1–7, but is unstratified.

Although the pottery resulting from clearance in the great cloister was not recovered archaeologically, the monks' cells and their gardens were separated by walls some 3 m high, circumstances that would mitigate against discarded pottery spreading far from its original point of deposition. And, although the quantities of pottery from each cell were far from even, the chance was nevertheless provided here to observe the character of the pottery from 14 of the 15 cells, indicating the preferences or needs of individual members

Table 7.1 Coleoptera recovered from Sample 1

Taxa	H	T	LE	RE	MNI
CARABIDAE					
Dyschirius globosus (Herb.)	0	0	1	0	1
Patrobus ?assimilis (Chaud.)	0	0	1	0	1
P. septentrionis (Dej.)	0	0	4	4	4
Trechus obtusus (Erich.)	0	1	1	1	1
Bembidion ?bruxellense (Wes.)	1	0	1	1	1
B. clarkii (Dawson)	0	1	0	0	1
B. quinquestriatum (Gyll.)	1	1	1	1	1
B. guttula (F.)	1	1	2	1	2
Bembidion sp.	0	0	1	1	1
Pterostichus diligens (Sturm)	5	6	4	5	6
P. ?minor (Gyll.)	0	0	0	3	3
P. nigrita (Payk.)	0	1	0	0	1
P. strenuus (Pz.)	1	2	2	3	3
P. ?vernalis (Pz.)	0	0	0	1	1
Pterostichus sp.	0	0	1	1	1
Calathus sp.	0	0	1	0	1
Agonum assimile (Payk.)	0	1	1	1	1
A. thoyeri (Dej.)	2	0	4	2	4
CARABIDAE spp.	2	0	0	0	2
DYTISCIDAE					
Hydroporus sp.	0	1	0	0	1
HYDROPHILIDAE					
Helophorus ?brevipalpis (Bed.)	4	3	1	1	4
H. ?porculus (Bed.)	0	0	1	0	1
Helophorus sp.	0	1	2	2	2
Colostoma orbiculare (F.)	4	10	15	10	15
Cercyon atoarius (F.)	3	4	4	2	4
Cercyon spp.	11	12	10	0	12
Megasternum obscurum (Marsh.)	5	10	8	7	10
Cryptopleurum crenatum (Kug.)	3	4	5	3	5
Cryptopleurum sp.	0	0	0	1	1
Anacaena globus (Payk.)	0	1	0	0	1
Laccobius bipunctatus (F.)	1	2	1	0	1
L. minutes (L.)	0	2	1	1	2
Chaeterthria seminulum (Herb.)	12	15	20	4	20
HYDRAENA					
Hydraena sp.	10	1	0	0	1
PTILIIDAE					
Ptenidum sp.	0	0	1	1	1

(Continued)

THE CULTURAL COLLECTIONS

Table 7.1 (Continued)

Taxa	H	T	LE	RE	MNI
STAPHYLINIDAE					
Micropeplus porcatus (Payk.)	3	2	1	1	3
Megarthrus denticollis (Beck)	8	7	14	13	14
M. ?depressus (Payk.)	6	3	1	2	6
Megarthrus sp.	0	0	0	1	1
Olphrum piceum (Gyll.)	2	11	5	3	11
O. ?fuscum (Grav.)/*piceum* (Gyll.)	0	1	0	0	1
Acidota cruentata (F.)	1	0	1	0	1
Lesteva heeri (Fauv.)	0	0	1	1	1
Anthophagus caraboides (L.)	0	0	0	1	1
Acrolacha sulcala (Steph.)	0	3	8	6	8
Omalium caesum (Grav.)	1	1	1	1	1
O. rivulare (Payk.)	3	4	4	6	6
Omalium sp.	0	0	2	1	2
Xylodromus ?concinus (Marsh.)	0	0	0	1	1
X. depressus (Grav.)	0	0	1	1	1
Caepelimus spp.	13	12	20	18	20
Aploderus caelayus (Grav.)	0	1	0	0	1
Platystethus ?nodifrons (Mann.)/*nitens* (Sahl.)	1	2	2	0	2
Anotylus nitidulus (Grav.)	0	1	0	0	1
A. rugosus (F.)	19	28	23	27	28
A. sculpturatus (Grav.)	0	0	3	2	3
A. tetracarinatus (Block.)	2	3	0	0	3
Stenus spp.	34	39	35	46	46
Lathrobium spp.	5	3	5	4	5
Rugilus ?erichsoni (Fauv.)	3	4	2	3	4
Othius spp.	3	4	9	7	9
Xantholinus ?linearis (Oliv.)/*longiventris* (Heer)	0	1	0	0	1
Xantholinus spp.	4	3	7	5	7
Philonthus ?cephalotes (Grav.)	0	0	1	3	3
P. marginatus (Strom)	0	1	0	0	1
P. splendens (F.)	0	1	0	0	1
Philonthus spp.	5	4	8	9	9
Gabrius spp.	7	16	43	38	43
Staphylinus olens (Mull.)	1	1	1	0	1
Staphylinus sp.	0	1	1	0	1
Quedius curtipennis (Bern.)	1	2	4	4	4
Q. ?umbrinus (Erich.)	3	4	1	3	4
Quedius spp.	8	2	14	11	14
Mycetoporus ?lepidus (Grav.)	0	0	0	1	1

(Continued)

Table 7.1 Coleoptera recovered from Sample 1 (Continued)

Taxa	H	T	LE	RE	MNI
Tachyporus sp.	0	0	0	1	1
Tachinus marginellus (F.)	0	0	2	3	3
T. signatus (Grav.)	1	1	0	3	3
Bolitochara sp.	1	0	0	0	1
Encephalus complicans (Steph.)	0	0	0	1	1
Aleocharinae sp. *et gen. indet.*	24	25	60	45	60
PSELAPHIDAE					
Reichenbachia juncorum (Lch.)	2	2	3	1	3
SCARABAEIDAE					
Aphodius ater (Deg.)	3	1	1	1	1
A. contaminatus (Herb.)	1	2	6	8	8
A. depressus (Kug.)	0	2	1	2	2
A. rufipes (L.)	0	1	1	1	1
Aphodius spp.	0	0	1	3	3
SCIRTIDAE gen. et sp. indet.	4	7	14	11	14
DRYOPIDAE					
Dryops ?ernrsti (des Gz.)	3	4	2	1	4
D. ?nitidulus (Heer)	0	0	0	1	1
ELMINTHIDAE					
Esolus parallelepipedus (Mull.)	1	2	1	1	2
ELATERIDAE					
Athous vittatus (F.)	0	1	1	1	1
Selatosomus ?impressus (F.)/*nigricornis* (Pz.)	1	1	1	1	1
NITIDULIDAE					
Brachyptrerolus sp.	1	1	0	0	1
Meligethes sp.	2	3	4	1	4
RHIZOPHAGIDAE					
Monotoma sp.	0	0	1	0	1
CRYPTOPHAGIDAE					
Cryptophagus sp.	2	1	1	1	2
Atomaria sp.	1	0	0	1	1
LATRIDIIDAE					
Stephostethus ?lardarius (Deg.)	0	2	2	2	2
Enicmus sp.	0	3	1	1	3
Corticaria sp.	0	0	1	2	2
Cortinicara ?gibbosa (Herb.)	0	0	1	0	1
CHRYSOMELIDAE					
Plateumaris affinis (Kunze)	3	3	6	8	8
P. discolor (Pz.)/*sericea* (L.)	0	0	2	1	2
Phaedon ?concinnus (Steph.)	0	0	1	0	1

(Continued)

THE CULTURAL COLLECTIONS

Table 7.1 (Continued)

Taxa	H	T	LE	RE	MNI
Hydrothassa marginella (L.)	1	1	1	1	1
Prasocuris phellandrii (L.)	7	5	3	2	7
Plagiodera versicolora (Laic.)	0	1	1	0	1
Phyllotreta excalamationis (Thun.)	0	1	2	1	2
P. nigripes (F.)/*nodicornis* (Marsh.)	2	7	4	3	7
Aphthona spp.	4	3	5	4	5
Longitarsus spp.	2	4	6	7	7
Altica ?ericeti (All.)/*brevicollis* (Foud.)	1	0	1	0	1
Chaetocnema confusa (Boh.)	1	0	0	2	2
Chaetocnema sp.	3	1	2	2	2
APIONIDAE					
Apion spp.	12	11	13	15	15
CURCULIONIDAE					
Phyllobius sp.	0	1	1	0	1
Sitona cambricus (Steph.)	2	0	2	5	5
S. lineatus (L.)	5	2	2	4	5
S. macularius (Marsh.)	0	0	1	0	1
Liosoma deflexum (Pz.)	0	1	1	0	1
Notaris acridulus (L.)	2	1	1	1	1
Thryogenes festucae (Herb.)	0	0	1	1	1
Ceutorhynchus spp.	0	3	2	2	1
Phytobius sp.	1	2	0	0	2
Limnobaris pilistriata (Steph.)	3	2	2	1	3

Key: H = head; T = thorax; LE = left elytron; RE = right elytron; MNI = minimum number of individuals

of the community with a degree of precision not possible elsewhere. Only in Cells 8 and 10, however, was the excavation total.

The pottery assemblage includes fabrics and forms that apparently belong to much earlier periods. This was first noticed in the cell groups, although no archaeological features were recorded at the time that could be associated with the pre-monastic use of the site. It was only in 1990 that indisputable pre-priory occupation was discovered below the south-west cloister range. This was identified as part of the medieval settlement of *Bordelbi*, which was cleared to make way for the charterhouse. These early deposits (Finds Groups 22 to 26) confirmed the suspicion that the pottery assemblage had a far wider date range than that which might be assumed from the foundation date of the priory, as residual elements from them were identified in many of the stratified groups associated with monastic occupation. Such unexpected complications do not detract from the overall significance of the Mount Grace pottery, however, particularly as the site occupies an area of North Yorkshire with a general dearth of well-stratified ceramics (McCarthy and Brooks 1988).

The Extent of the Collection and its Provenance

Clearance and excavation since 1954 have recovered 6,053 sherds of pottery representing a minimum of 2,490 vessels. This material may be divided into four groups: pottery recovered by Ministry of Works clearance and stored by cell; stratified medieval pottery from excavations by Keen and Coppack; stratified 17th-century pottery from excavations by Coppack; and unstratified pottery of all periods recovered predominantly from topsoil, Hope's excavation trenches and modern disturbances. Although the first group is not strictly stratified and there is some evidence (from fitting sherds and contradictory labels) that subsequent reboxing has caused some contamination, the groups are sufficiently secure to present them as the contents of eight cells (Cells 2–7 and Cell 20). The erratic retention of body sherds from some cells (Cell 5 has only five feature sherds, all capable of illustration: see Chapter 4) suggests selective retention in some instances. Pottery from Andrew Saunders' excavation of Cell 2 has not been identified and it may now be mixed with the clearance material from that cell. This material, in spite of its less than perfect method of recovery, is particularly useful in that it can be related to and contrasted with groups from those cells that were examined archaeologically.

The pottery from Keen's excavation of Cells 9–15 and from the south range of the inner court is all from stratified contexts or can be related to stratified contexts by identifiable vessels or fitting sherds. It all comes, however, from the latest archaeological deposits, and the identification of residual material from earlier, unexcavated, deposits is not particularly easy. Keen's excavation did not identify Pre-monastic occupation features in the natural surfaces. In contrast, all of Coppack's excavations (with the exception of the yards to the south of kitchen) reached the natural red clay surface of the terrace and the full ceramic sequence was recovered. By identifying individual vessels in specific fabrics, it is possible in some cases to restore residual material to the group from which it had originally come (in the pottery incidence tables in Chapters 4 and 5 the inclusion of residual material from later groups is marked by an asterisk). Coppack's excavation was the only one to identify mid-17th-century deposits associated with the construction of the 1654 house and, although these groups were small, they were securely stratified and closely dated. The pottery from them, however, contained a very high residual element.

The unstratified material came from three sources: turf and topsoil; service trenches dug by the Ministry of Works (predominantly in the area of the kitchen); and Hope's excavation of 1896–1900 and the construction and service trenches of the Bell house of 1901. The problem of relating unstratified material to stratified groups was particularly difficult in the kitchen, where Hope had removed almost all the Period Four deposits but included most of the material in his backfilling. The likelihood is that the greater part of this material does relate to the final use of the kitchen, but there can be no certainty that spoil was directly returned to the area from which it came. Indeed, there is good archaeological evidence to suggest that his excavation in this area was not backfilled until work on the Bell house was largely completed, and that material from elsewhere was incorporated in the levelling of the site. The unstratified material from the kitchen was studied, however, because it presents a series of vessel forms that are peculiar to that area.

In seeking to make comparisons between the pottery profiles from different cells, the varying assemblage size, the differing techniques of recovery and the extent of excavation within each cell are all significant constraints. Additionally, only Cells 8 and 10, the south-west cloister range and the kitchen area were fully excavated to natural, and all of these areas except Cell 10 had been previously examined by Hope. Nevertheless, comparison appears to be worthwhile. The pottery from the cells and the south-west cloister range divides consistently into three groups: utilitarian vessels; pottery that was indicative of an individual monk's special requirements; and 'display' wares. It is noticeable that this last group does not feature in the only lay brother's cell, Cell 20, from which pottery was collected in clearance. In comparison, the pottery from the kitchen area was almost exclusively utilitarian, as might be expected.

Methodology
The study of the pottery progressed from the stratified material from Coppack's excavations through Keen's material (originally examined by Jean le Patourel) and finished with the finds from the Ministry of Works clearance. From Coppack's excavation, the site matrix was used to define a series of both construction and occupation deposits that formed the basis of a discrete series of Finds Groups, a method first established at Thornholme Priory, Lincolnshire, in 1976 (Coppack and Hayfield forthcoming) and used subsequently at Sawley Abbey (Coppack et al. 2002). Each Finds Group contains a number of related contexts that were examined together (they also include metalwork, glass and worked bone). A pottery type series was then established, the pottery was separated by fabric type and each fabric type was sorted into discrete vessels.

THE CULTURAL COLLECTIONS

The number of sherds in each fabric type was then recorded, as were the number of vessels and vessel types in each fabric. Because each excavation area was examined *in toto* it was possible to identify some, but not necessarily all, of the residual material and relate it back to its earliest occurrence. Individual vessels were then selected for drawing. Unillustrated material largely consisted of body and base sherds or duplicate vessels.

The statistical analysis is based on vessel numbers rather than sherd numbers, and a distinction is drawn between the pre-priory and the priory pottery. In this respect it is fortunate that two of the major fabrics were demonstrably pre-monastic in their currency and thus form an easily identifiable residual element in subsequent deposits. As might be expected, one or two pottery fabrics bridge the two strands of occupation, but as the vessel numbers are relatively tiny the overall distinction between the pottery in use by the priory and that of the preceding settlement of *Bordelbi* remains convincing.

Pottery Fabrics

The pottery fabrics come from three broad sources: relatively local coarse ware products with a high incidence of Yorkshire fabrics, including factory-produced wares such as Humberwares; finer-quality tablewares such as Cistercian and Tudor Green wares; and imported wares, some of them exotic but the majority from the Rhineland.

Coarse Wares
GRITTY WARE
An oxidised, predominantly coarse ware fabric tempered with rounded and sub-rounded quartz grits up to 1 mm in size that vary from a semi-translucent pinkish colour to colourless. The overall fabric colour ranges from pale orange and buff to darker shades of orange in the core, which is occasionally reduced to pale grey or blue-grey. Cooking pots predominate, although some bowls, dishes and glazed jugs are also present. The earliest deposits produced sherds from splash-glazed jugs.

Most cooking pots had folded, squared rims, often with shallow thumbings along the outer edge to give a 'pie-crust' effect; vessels from Finds Group 24, 323–6 illustrate the type. There were some variants; Finds Group 31, 388 was of Saxo-Norman form, while a cooking pot and a bowl with rouletted decoration on their rim edges (Finds Group 26, 335 and 336) are probably of 11th-century date. Jug forms varied: the splash-glazed rims, such as Finds Group 23, 320, had a small square shape, but later jug profiles, such as Finds Group 22, 308 or Finds Group 23, 322, show a variety of shape, decoration and rim form. Other identified forms include pipkins (Finds Group 23, 319) and basting dishes (Finds Group 37, 511).

At Mount Grace, the earliest forms in this fabric are late 11th or early 12th century, and the fabric continued well into the 13th century, becoming progressively finer. It occurred residually in the first monastic construction deposits and remained an easily identifiable residual element in all subsequent groups. Numerically, with 733 vessels, it was the most common fabric to be found at Mount Grace, but only 261 vessels were stratified. Of the residual remainder, 398 came from the south-west cloister range.

BRANDSBY TYPE WARE
A light-coloured oxidised sand-tempered fabric type found widely across much of the Vale of York and the Tees Valley. Vessels are tempered with fine semi-translucent quartz particles generally less than 0.5 mm across (though larger grits are occasionally used sporadically) and soft, powdery, burnt orange/red grog, producing a hard fabric with roughly textured surfaces. The surfaces range in colour from light orange to orange/pink and orange/red, the core either a slightly darker shade or reduced to blue/grey. The earliest vessels have splashed glazes, but most have suspension glazes, olive green predominating.

While the Gritty ware vessels were predominately cooking pots, the vessels in the Brandsby type wares were more evenly divided between cooking pots and jugs. The variety of shapes and rim forms reflects the fact that this fabric probably derived from a number of production sources. One cooking-pot rim form from Cell 2 (Finds Group 1, 1 and 2) seems quite diagnostic.

Although Brandsby type ware is present among the earliest pre-priory deposits at Mount Grace, the 90 vessels that were recovered are substantially overshadowed in number by the Gritty wares, and seem, here at least, to be a predominantly 13th- and

14th-century product. Although one production source has been identified at Brandsby, the wide distribution of this fabric type and the variations within it suggest, as noted, that other kiln sites await discovery. At York, Brooks found this type of fabric in groups from the 13th century (in very small numbers) to the end of the 14th century (Brooks 1987). At Mount Grace, it belongs to the pre-monastic occupation of the site and occurs residually in Period One and subsequent deposits.

Humberwares

A group of hard, sand-tempered fabrics produced in south and east Yorkshire that provides the bulk of late medieval pottery in the county (Hayfield 1992). The principal kiln source for the Mount Grace examples appears to be West Cowick, near Snaith. The fabric is a hard/very hard, rough-textured, sandy fabric, usually oxidised pale orange to brick red. The core and inner surface, particularly in the case of jugs, are often reduced to blue/grey or grey, while most vessels are glazed with an olive-green suspension glaze with a light orange/brown surface flecking.

Most of the 58 Humberware products from Mount Grace were jugs. From Cell 7 Finds Group 6, 73 and 74 illustrate two typical jug shapes, while Finds Group 29, 374 and Finds Group 30, 379 show two classic Humberware jug rim forms (Hayfield 1985; Hayfield and Grieg 1990). Cistern rims, such as Finds Group 6, 76 and Finds Group 9, 86, and a chafing dish (Finds Group 5, 33) demonstrate other forms.

Humberware was never a numerically important fabric at Mount Grace, but is found stratified in pre-priory deposits (Finds Group 24) and across all four periods of the monastic occupation.

Late Gritty Ware

A hard, usually well-potted fabric heavily tempered with larger quartz grits, producing a rough/harsh textured surface, particularly on the inside of the vessel. Typically, vessels in this fabric have orange outer surfaces, pale blue/grey cores and grey/buff inner surfaces. Some vessels are fired almost to the point of vitrification. Glazes, from orange/brown to brownish green, are usually even-coloured. These late medieval gritty fabrics may have a number of sources, but share a similar tradition to the Firsby/Rawmarsh fabrics, which began life in the high medieval period as an oxidised gritty fabric at Firsby (Buckland and Hayfield 1989) and became harder and reduced by the 15th century (Hayfield 1985). The Late Gritty ware may have developed from the local Gritty ware or Brandsby type ware traditions rather than farther afield.

The bulk of examples found at Mount Grace were glazed jugs. Few were illustratable, but the lidded jar form from Cell 8 (Finds Group 11, 106 a and b) was quite an impressive form. A second jar rim of this type was Finds Group 33, 423. A rather basic chafing dish form from Cell 11 was also in this fabric (Finds Group 15, 230). The only firmly stratified examples came from Finds Group 11, the Suppression-period dump deposit in Cell 8, suggesting a general late medieval currency at Mount Grace.

Hambleton Ware

A fairly soft, thick-walled, sand-tempered fabric principally characterised by its smooth but uneven surface. It is tempered with tiny rounded grains of quartz, orange/red grog and specks of white ?limestone, and occasional lumps in the fabric are caused by large (up to 5 mm) and irregular grit and grog. The few harder fired examples show that the fabric has a tendency to laminate. Outer surfaces are usually oxidised to orange, although the inner surface tends to be darker: either partly reduced to dull purple/brown or fully reduced to grey. Glazes are consistent in colour and between olive green and brownish green (often with more orange margins). A distinct variety of this fabric has white to cream surfaces with internal and core reduction to grey or blue-grey, and fairly bright copper green glazes. Hambleton Wares also have a tendency to erode.

Jugs, jars, urinals, cisterns, bottles and even a chafing dish (Finds Group 17, 276) were made in this fabric type. The most common vessel forms are jugs and urinals. Jug forms vary, as shown by Finds Group 13, 166 and Finds Group 17, 275. The jars seem to be more consistent in form (Finds Group 14, 192; Finds Group 16, 259), while the only near-complete urinal profile (Finds Group 11, 104) is typical of late medieval forms. Two types of bottle form were recovered: one with a tall neck (Finds Group 14, 193) and the other shorter and stubbier (Finds Group 10, 89).

This fabric first appears at Mount Grace around 1400, in construction deposits of

Period One in the south-west cloister range (Finds Group 27), and remains current through to the Suppression.

Ryedale Ware

A hard sand-tempered fabric with traces of mica and surfaces that tend to dust when dry. It varies in colour from pale orange to pale grey. Occasional vessels are fully reduced internally to grey/black and below the glaze there is often a whitish margin. Vessels tend to be glazed from rim to base. Bright, shiny olive green and apple green glazes are the most common, and a pockmarked surface is frequently found on the glaze, although some vessels have smooth and consistently coloured suspension glazes. Ryedale ware is a broad fabric tradition that extended from east Yorkshire through the Vale of York and into the Tees valley, presumably being produced from a number of kiln sites within its distribution area. With 483 identifiable vessels (21.86% of priory pottery), it forms the dominant coarse ware fabric type in all phases of the priory occupation.

Given the nature of this fabric tradition it is hardly surprising that a wide variety of forms is indicated by the illustrated sherds. Medium-sized jugs predominate, as demonstrated by Finds Group 17, 273; Finds Group 5, 64; Finds Group 11, 105; Finds Group 13, 167; and Finds Group 30, 380. Cell 7 produced a small number of very large jugs in this fabric (Finds Group 6, 77, 78 and 79), but sadly all without a surviving rim. The elaborate nature of Finds Group 36, 505, the neck and rim of a very large two-handled jug with applied strips of finger-impressed clay, from a Period One occupation deposit, represents one of the earliest examples of this fabric from Mount Grace. Urinals seem to have two basic rim types, a simple (and perhaps kinder) rim (Finds Group 17, 274; Finds Group 28, 367), and a more everted form (Finds Group 14, 189 or 190). A tripod pipkin (Finds Group 11, 108), bottles (Finds Group 37, 514; Finds Group 38, 521), a candlestick base (Finds Group 28, 366) and even a barrel costrel (Finds Group 14, 191) make up the vessel range identified in this fabric type from Mount Grace.

Pre-monastic Finds Groups 23, 24 and 26 all contain a very small number of vessels in this fabric type, which, if they are not intrusive, might suggest that this fabric tradition may have originated in the late 14th century. However, this is essentially a late medieval fabric tradition that extended across much of north and parts of east Yorkshire.

Developed Humberware

Seemingly derived from the Humberware tradition, this fabric is usually harder and thinner walled, and has a more consistent olive green glaze. Its forms, too, are more akin to early post-medieval types.

With only 26 vessels, this was never a common fabric type at Mount Grace, and the range of illustrated forms suggests the use of the more specialised vessels. There were several examples of tripod pipkins (Finds Group 11, 107; Finds Group 17, 278; Finds Group 35, 464 and 465). Finds Group 34, 459 suggests a far larger form, perhaps a deep jar or 'bucket'. The skillet (Finds Group 4, 61) was one of only two such forms from the priory, both from Cell 5. However, the most specialised form from a technical viewpoint was the cucurbit from Cell 12 (Finds Group 16, 260).

Within the kitchen range this fabric first appears in Period Three (Finds Group 39). In the south-west cloister range single vessels are represented in Periods One (Finds Group 27) and Two (Finds Group 28), but here there seems a possibility of intrusion. In Cell 8 it occurs only in Suppression-period deposits (Finds Group 11). Elsewhere it seems to begin in the late 15th century and is thought to be a post-medieval successor to the late medieval Humberware tradition.

Post-medieval Orange Ware

A fine, soft to hard, micaceous fabric with outer surface colours that range from bright orange to dull purple/red (or even occasionally an off-white colour), with slightly darker colours on the inner surface. Glazes vary from olive green on the earliest vessels to a bright, glossy copper green on later examples. Vessels are thick-walled and occur in both 'medieval' and 'post-medieval' forms.

The majority of forms in this fabric from Mount Grace are jugs: Finds Group 1, 7, Finds Group 6, 81 and Finds Group 11, 109 illustrate the range. Jar forms include Finds Group 3, 48, Finds Group 13, 171 and Finds Group 15, 232 and 233, the handles on 232 suggesting a cistern form. Two chafing dishes are illustrated: Finds Group 14, 195 and, from the Period One terrace levelling in Cell 8, Finds Group 7, 84. The attribution of this vessel to

Period One was a little ambiguous, as its sherds came from various contexts in Cell 8; that apparently earliest, a single sherd from Period One, could be intrusive, as disturbances in the redeposited natural clay of the great cloister terrace were notoriously difficult to spot unless soil conditions were ideal. The next recorded occurrence is from the Period Three Finds Group 29, from the south-west cloister range. Kiln assemblages at West Cowick included a small number of vessels in this fabric, usually small tablewares that seemed to be copying contemporary Cistercian ware forms, and these early examples from Mount Grace, again single vessels, might well belong to this early phase of production. Overall, however, this is essentially a post-medieval fabric that is most in evidence in the 16th century, at the closing stages of the Mount Grace sequence.

POST-MEDIEVAL SANDY WARE

Similar to the post-medieval Orange ware and probably produced in Ryedale, this is a fine, fairly soft fabric with fine sand tempering and orange/buff to yellow buff surfaces which reduce to whitish grey. Glazes are predominantly light green or apple green. Internally glazed vessels such as open jars, bowls and dishes predominate.

Given the numerical dominance of this fabric during the final periods of occupation and desertion at Mount Grace (especially Finds Groups 33 and 35), it is surprising that so few jug forms were recognised; Finds Group 28, 369 is one of the few illustrated rim forms. Instead, the vessel range in this fabric type consisted largely of dishes, bowls and jars. The bowls ranged from fairly small examples, such as Finds Group 42, 551 – some with handles, such as Finds Group 34, 462 – to larger, shallow dishes/bowls such as Finds Group 41, 454. Most jars were large, two-handled forms of two types: a more conventional Yorkshire form, such as Finds Group 33, 416, and almost straight-sided, bucket-like forms, such as the pair from Cell 6 (Finds Group 5, 69 and 70). Generally, Finds Groups 33, 34, 35 and 45 show a broad range of vessel forms in this fabric type.

Small numbers of vessels in this fabric, possibly intrusive, come from Period One deposits in both the south-west cloister range and the kitchen range and from Period Two in Cell 8 (Finds Group 8). Vessel numbers rise substantially towards Period Four and the Suppression period, however; it is, again, a predominately post-medieval fabric type.

Fine Wares
CISTERCIAN WARE

A hard, finely sand-tempered ware with a red–purple body often fired to the point of vitrification and glazed on both surfaces with a lustrous purple/black glaze. A variant is less hard fired, with a red/brown body colour and a reddish-brown or even an orange glaze. The forms used are identical, however, suggesting that the latter vessels are simply under-fired. Both variants occasionally have under-glaze decoration in white pipe clay in a manner identical to products of the Potovens kilns (Moorhouse and Roberts 1992). This fabric was used mainly for cups, although a single chalice was recorded in Cell 8.

Cell 3 produced two highly decorated type 2 cups and a single cover (Finds Group 2, 15, 16 and 17); Cell 8 produced a decorated chalice (Finds Group 11, 114) alongside five plain type 2 and type 4 cups; and the later prior's cell produced two highly decorated type 2 cup lids (Finds Group 32, 410). Because the same forms were available without decoration, and were recorded in virtually every cell, the occurrence of decoration has to be an indication of individual taste, something rarely recorded on monastic sites.

The earliest example of this fabric from Mount Grace is technically from the Period One Finds Group 27, suggesting a date in the early 15th century – substantially earlier than anywhere else in the country. However, Finds Group 27 produced several other surprisingly early examples of fabrics, suggesting an element of intrusion or disturbance within this Finds Group. It is difficult, however, to see how this could have happened. Elsewhere within the priory Cistercian ware does not appear before Period Four, although there are indications (see below) that it might have been current from the latter part of the 15th century (Period Three), in closer agreement with its suggested date range elsewhere in Yorkshire.

CISTERCIAN WARE COPIES

Copies of Cistercian ware forms occur in a number of fabrics, but the most common one at Mount Grace is a fine, soft to hard, sand-tempered fabric with lighter orange-brown or reddish-brown glazes. Vessel walls are often slightly thicker than those of true Cistercian wares.

The most complete profile of a Type 4 cup was Finds Group 33, 431, although other examples, such as Finds Group 43, 556 and 557, demonstrate other known Cistercian ware forms.

The earliest Cistercian ware 'copy' at Mount Grace came from Finds Group 38, from the kitchen range, and date to the first half of the fifteenth century. Such evidence is slight, but, as it occurs a period earlier than the true Cistercian wares, it does raise the delicate question of who was copying whom. It has always been assumed that these items were local copies of the new Cistercian ware forms, but it is possible that they were in fact prototypes of the new forms.

REVERSED CISTERCIAN WARE

Similar in form and decoration to Cistercian ware, these vessels have a buff to grey body and are glazed on both surfaces with a lustrous watery green glaze that is darker where the glaze has thickened before firing. Under-glaze decoration was done with iron-rich slip, which fires red/brown below the glaze.

The earliest examples of this fabric occur in the Period Three Finds Group 9 from Cell 8 and the Period Three Finds Group 40 from the kitchen range. It is also present in Period Four and Suppression-period groups.

TUDOR GREEN WARE

A fine white fabric, often fairly soft and friable, with a fairly patchy light-green copper-rich glaze. It was used predominantly for tablewares, particularly lobed cups, which are also copied in Midlands Yellow wares (below).

Only one lobed cup is illustrated (Finds Group 6, 82), but there are also two examples of small jugs (Finds Group 15, 236; Finds Group 45, 576). This fabric is thought to be a 16th-century type, and no stratified examples came from either the south-west cloister range or the kitchen area. However, 11 fragments from one cup were recovered from Period Three deposits in Cell 8 (Finds Group 9).

MIDLANDS YELLOW WARE

A soft, powdery white to cream fabric with a clear, watery but bright lemon yellow glaze that becomes orange/yellow where the glaze has thickened. The glaze has frequently crazed in firing. This fabric was used predominantly for cups, but candlesticks are also recorded.

A single stratified example came from the Period Three Finds Group 29, from the south-west cloister range excavations. The latest occupation deposit in the south-west cloister range (Finds Group 32) contained three sherds from the same cup.

STAFFORDSHIRE WHITE WARES

A fine white fabric with virtually no tempering used almost exclusively, at Mount Grace at least, for small drug pots. A thin yellow or greenish-yellow glaze is apparent only on the rim and shoulder of these vessels.

The only stratified examples in this fabric came from the Period Four Finds Groups 10 and 11 in Cell 8; Finds Group 11, 111 illustrates the only reconstructable profile. All 20 items found came from small drug pots and were entirely confined to the cells of the great cloister. No examples in this fabric were recovered from the kitchen range or the south-west cloister range.

Imported Wares

Mount Grace produced 290 examples of imported pottery representing 17.56% of the priory pottery. These were heavily dominated by the three main German stoneware products of Siegburg, Langerwehe and Raeren. The nature of these wares is generally well known and the whole range has been adequately defined elsewhere, especially by Hurst *et al.* (1986). Two fragments of Siegburg mugs and one of Langerwehe were found in pre-priory deposits, but the remainder were post-foundation (1398). South Netherlands Majolica, Pisa Majolica, Valencia Lustreware and Colombia Plain make up the less common late medieval imports, almost all of which came from the monks' cells. Any one of these examples would have been an appropriate find on a late medieval manorial site, and the numbers here, although small in relation to the size of the priory pottery assemblage, nevertheless indicate the high status of Mount Grace.

Finds Group 11 from Cell 8 illustrates the broadest range of imported forms, with a wide range of other examples coming from the other cells of the great cloister. Indeed, imports made up 22.07% of the combined assemblages from the monastic cells, the highest proportion across the entire site. Within Cell 8, 33 of the 84 vessels recovered were imported, representing 39.29% of the total.

Table 7.2 Numbers of stratified pre-priory vessels by fabric and by form (Finds Groups 22–6)

Fabric	No.	%	Form	No.	%
Stamford type	1	0.36	Cooking pot	201	71.53
Gritty wares	261	92.88	Bowl	4	1.43
Brandsby types	10	3.56	Jug	67	23.84
Humberwares	1	0.36	Pipkin	3	1.07
Ryedale wares	5	1.78	Pancheon	2	0.71

Discussion

Pre-monastic Pottery

The pottery from pre-monastic contexts is presented by fabric and form in Table 7.2. Gritty ware was the predominant fabric in all the deposits that pre-dated the construction of the south-west cloister range. The earliest material, quite possibly of late 11th- or early 12th-century date, came from ditch [624] (Finds Group 26), where two of the Gritty ware vessels were roulette decorated and all the profiles in this fabric were typologically early. Brandsby type fabric was also present in this group, not simply from the upper filling but mixed with the Gritty ware, suggesting that the two fabrics might be contemporary in this context. Splashed glazes on both fabrics suggest that some of the material is no later than the early 12th century, and the occurrence of Stamford ware in the filling of pit [659] indicates, similarly, that at least some of the material in the pit dates from the 12th century, rather than later. For the end of pre-monastic settlement the evidence has to come from pottery incorporated in the construction deposits of the south-west cloister range, dating to around 1400. Here, the bulk of the pottery comprises Gritty ware that is clearly residual and compares closely with stratified material dated to the 12th century. Indeed, six sherds of the Stamford ware cooking pot found in pit [659] came from earth derived from the foundation trenches of the range. The Brandsby type fabric, however, is present in both early and late forms, with the latest material being not much earlier than the end of the 13th century, suggesting that this part of the medieval settlement of *Bordelbi* was deserted by that date.

The mix of vessel types, with many cooking pots, pipkins and bowls and a relatively small number of jugs, is highly suggestive of domestic occupation. Although the quality of the pottery is good, it is no better than the general run of wares generally available in North Yorkshire for this period, and it would appear that all of this pottery is associated with the occupation of a part of *Bordelbi* that is known to have covered the site later developed by the charterhouse, its spread probably indicating the extent of earlier settlement. Vessels in the Gritty and Brandsby fabrics were recorded from Cells 2, 4, 6, 10, 11, 12, 13 and 14, from the water tower at the centre of the great cloister, and from Cell 20, on the lower terrace of the inner court. The single vessel from Cell 6 comprised no fewer than 56 sherds, and although this was recovered in clearance it must represent a genuine findspot of some significance. Predominantly, however, the spread indicates a concentration across the southern half of the great cloister terrace and it is presumably significant that not a single sherd was recovered from the deep excavation of Cell 8, its garden or the cloister alley. The six vessels from Cell 20 indicate that the settlement seen on the lower terrace below the south-west cloister range continues across this area.

Pottery from Monastic Deposits

The pottery from monastic deposits can be divided into two groups: vessels associated with construction, which normally involved the use of outside contractors, and vessels related to the everyday life of the community. As construction involved the digging of foundation trenches and the levelling of the site, it inevitably disturbed the remains of the pre-monastic settlement.

The pottery finds from the earliest construction deposits of Period One associated with the first monastic Period One stone buildings in the south-west cloister range were predominantly residual and largely of 13th-century date. Only a small number of the Ryedale ware sherds found were contemporary with the building. Significantly, in view of the high status of the settlement, there was also a single rim sherd from a South Netherlands Majolica flask. Excavation did not extend below the Period One kitchen.

The enclosed nature of the cells and their gardens suggests that the pottery found in them was almost certainly used there. The exception to this is the pottery from construction deposits, but only in Cell 8 and the prior's cells were construction deposits found and excavated. The pottery found entered the deposits via two routes: rubbish produced in the cell and used to fertilise the garden; and occupation debris associated with the latest use of the cell before the suppression of the house. Pottery, of course, comprised only one component of the monk's household equipment and was the cheapest element of it, simply not worth recording in any surviving account. Metal vessels played a more important role, as is suggested by their documentation: Thomas Golwynne (see Chapter 2), for example, brought with him to Mount Grace from London in 1519/20 a brass pestle and mortar, two pewter dishes, two pewter saucers, a porringer, a butter dish, a new latten chafing dish, two tin bottles, a brass chafer heated with water, a brass pan and a little brass skillet with a steel handle. He also had a double still – that is, an alembic and serpentine combined in one vessel for distilling spirits. In contrast, the fact that pottery was used for storage, cooking, tablewares and the ubiquitous urinals is known only from the archaeological record.

Given the eremitic life of the Carthusian monk, who left his cell only to pray and occasionally to eat in common, it is safe to assume that the ceramic contents of the cells represent what the monk was supplied with from a central distribution point in the house or what he brought with him on entering his cell or religion, and that they accurately reflect his daily needs or the trade he followed. The most important collection of pottery is Finds Group 11, which comes from the latest occupation of Cell 8. Somebody appears to have collected the complete contents of the cell, taken them outside and smashed them against the east wall of the building; not so much vandalism, perhaps, as a conscious attempt at disposing of unwanted material that was not worth selling. A similar occurrence is recorded outside the kitchen at Denny Abbey in Cambridgeshire (Coppack 1980, 235–6 and figs 38–43) in a Suppression context. A total of 227 sherds representing 43 vessels – the highest sherd-to-vessel ratio recorded on the site – was recovered from the surface of the garden path and the soil. With the exception of the fragile tin-glazed wares and two single sherds of Humberware, all the vessels were substantially complete, and missing sherds from them can be accounted for in three ways: Hope's excavation had skimmed the surface of the deposit; a modern land drain was cut through it; and the soil from this area was not sieved on excavation. The Humberware sherds are probably residual, derived from the garden soil. The 43 vessels in Finds Group 11 consisted of a urinal, 8 jugs, 2 tripod pitchers, a handled lidded jar, 2 jars, a drug jar, a chalice, at least 6 cups, a small Beauvais jug, 2 South Netherlands Majolica flower vases and an albarello, 3 bowls and a dish from Spain and 12 drinking pots and a flagon from the Rhineland. The 21 imports in this group represent a remarkably high number even for a high-status site. In particular, the inclusion of Spanish vessels, and especially the three vessels in Columbia Plain, is remarkable. It is unclear whether these reflect the taste of an individual monk or were brought with him, or whether Mount Grace acquired a batch of these rare imports, but to find three such vessels in the same deposit is without parallel in England (Roebuck *et al.* 1987).

That individual vessels related closely to individual members of the community is shown by a number of vessels from Cell 11 (Finds Group 15). Here – and, with one exception, only here – the rims and occasionally the handles of damaged vessels had been carefully ground down. In one instance a Siegburg drinking pot had lost its rim, handle and neck, yet the broken base of the neck had been ground flat, along with the handle stub, so that the vessel could be used as a beaker. In other circumstances this might be seen as an indication of poverty or of a need to make-do-and-mend, but this cell produced the same general quantity and quality of pottery as the others and the practice must reflect the character of an individual monk. The one ground vessel not found in Cell 11 came from the kitchen, a communal building in an otherwise segregated community, and was probably brought there as part of the distribution of food and drink. In general, however, the consistency of the pottery groups from the monks' cells suggests that there was a standard issue of pottery for cooking and table use, and that broken vessels were replenished from a central store. Although it is not possible to prove this theory, perhaps it was the case that a monk would place part of a broken vessel in the cell hatch to indicate that he required a new vessel, thus explaining why no complete vessels have been recovered from the garden soil, despite the fact that this is the only place where they could otherwise have been discarded. The lack of excavation in the cloister garden, apart from the area around the water tower, is unfortunate, for this was also being manured with domestic rubbish, as the occurrence of a single sherd from a Malaga albarello demonstrated. The source of this material cannot be determined.

Apart from Cells 8 and 11, which provide the full range of pottery used by members of the community, important collections also come from Cells 3, 4, 6, 7, 9, 10, 12 and 13 and from the garden of the later prior's cell. Imports are generally restricted to Siegburg, Raeren and Langerwehe stonewares, along with Beauvais jugs and a small number of vessels in South Netherlands Majolica. It is interesting to note than no tin-glazed wares were recovered from Cells 1–7, possibly because the archaeologically unskilled labour force considered them to be modern and discarded them.

Tables 7.3 and 7.4 summarise the fabrics and forms of the priory pottery by area. In essence, the pottery divides into two types: coarse ware forms and finer tablewares, the latter made up of local wares and imported vessels. Across the whole site tablewares comprise 33.85% of the pottery assemblage, with 16.29% being local and 17.56% being imports. Although there has been no study of vessel forms in the region around Mount Grace, a study of the stratified groups around Humberside in the late medieval period (Hayfield 1988) shows that jugs comprised 73.7% of vessel forms, with cups and mugs at 5%. At Mount Grace jugs comprised only 37.54% of the priory pottery and cups and mugs 30.09%. The percentage of almost every vessel form from Mount Grace differs from the Humberside regional norms, and this must surely reflect the special nature of the monastic community.

The pottery from the cells of the great cloister only emphasised these differences, for here tablewares reached 39.16%, with imports at 22.07% and local products at 17.09%. Although there are substantial variations in the size of the assemblage from each cell, it is possible to make certain observations about their ceramic profile. For example, almost every cell produced the remains of at least one urinal; many had a chafing dish; while all of the more carefully recovered cell assemblages had at least one drug pot. Almost all had a selection of mugs and cups in both local Cistercian wares and Siegburg or Langerwehe stonewares. Most of the larger assemblages produced at least one vessel of majolica or lustreware; Cell 8 had several. Among the coarse wares, almost all cells produced jugs and jars, while some had pancheons and cisterns.

Armed with these generalisations relating to the cell assemblages, it is possible to identify those cells where the pottery varied. In Cell 11 several vessels had rough or broken edges carefully polished. Cell 5 produced (among its very small assemblage) the only two skillet forms from the whole site. Cell 6 had two large 'bucket'-shaped jars; Cell 7 three unusually large jugs; and Cell 12 a cucurbit. These minor differences hint at the individual taste or foibles of monks, perhaps even at individual skills or trades, a trait that is also apparent in the small find collections.

Altogether, Mount Grace has produced an exceptional assemblage of late medieval pottery, much of it well stratified, with many vessels sufficiently complete to allow relatively full profiles to be drawn. It makes a substantial contribution to our understanding of ceramic development in this part of northern England and is directly comparable with later medieval groups from other Yorkshire monastic sites, such as Fountains Abbey (Coppack 1986, 72–80 and figs 15–17) and Kirkstall (Moorhouse and Wrathmell 1987, 59–116), although it differs substantially in its make-up. Only at Mount Grace can the needs and preferences of individuals be identified.

7.3 Coins and Jettons

by Kevin Leahy

Excavation recovered only two coins and a single jetton.

Coin 1

Long cross silver penny, inscription largely obliterated. Initial mark obliterated. York mint.

Edward III, post-treaty coinage, 1369–77.

The coin is clipped and damaged but not worn, and may be residual from Period One construction. It was found in the Period Four

THE CULTURAL COLLECTIONS

Table 7.3 The number of vessels in each fabric by area

Fabric	South-west cloister	Kitchen	Cells	Total
Humberwares	29	4	24	57
Late Gritty wares	2	3	12	17
Hambleton wares	24	3	50	77
Ryedale wares	107	101	270	478
Developed Humberware	8	4	14	26
Post-medieval Orange ware	12	3	50	65
Total	182	118	420	720

Table 7.4 The number of identifiable pottery vessels from monastic contexts

Fabric	South-west cloister	Kitchen	Cells	Total	%
Cooking pot	4	0	1	5	0.3
Jug	201	99	325	625	37.54
Tripod pipkin	1	3	4	8	0.48
Pancheon	72	35	18	125	7.51
Cistern	30	8	10	48	2.88
Jar	84	33	60	177	10.63
Urinal	5	0	17	22	1.32
Lids	4	3	0	7	0.42
Bucket	0	0	2	2	0.12
Skillet	0	0	2	2	0.12
Cucurbit	0	0	1	1	0.06
Cup/mug	178	61	262	501	30.09
Chalice	0	0	1	1	0.06
Posset pot	0	1	3	4	0.24
Bottle	1	4	14	19	1.14
Flask/costrel	0	0	2	2	0.12
Drug pot	0	0	20	20	1.2
Chafing dish	0	0	11	11	0.66
Lamp/candlestick	0	0	1	1	0.06
Vase	1	1	2	4	0.24
Dish	25	6	7	38	2.28
Albarello	0	0	4	4	0.24
Other	10	13	15	38	2.28
Totals	616	267	782	1665	

garden soil [62] in Cell 8, and is associated with Finds Group 10.

Coin 2
Long cross silver penny, small flan, inscription almost totally absent. Annulet by neck on Obv., quatrefoil in centre of Rev.

Edward IV, Irish, light issue, probably Waterford, 1473–8.

From topsoil [700] in the yard to the west of the church.

Jetton 1
Copper alloy jetton.

Obv. Heater shaped shield of France modern with three pellets above and one to each side, inscription: +AVE MARIA:GRACIA [PL]ENA.

Rev. Long cross of three strands *fleurdelisee* with a quatrefoil in the centre. In each angle a fleur de lys. Inscription: mute.

French, 15th century.

From Period Three occupation material [1497] in the eastern pentice of the kitchen.

7.4 *The Ceramic Floor Tiles*

by Laurence Keen

Introduction

Jenny Stopford's catalogue of northern medieval floor tiles summarises the floor tiles that remain *in situ* and which she found loose on site, but she did not examine any of the floor tiles from Keen's or Coppack's excavations (Stopford 2005, 316–18). This report summarises the results of the examination of the floor-tile material from those excavations, every fragment of which was retained (although some very small pieces were discarded during the post-excavation work), of the loose material collected over the years and displayed on site, and of a decorated tile *in situ* in the church. The tiles have been grouped by size, fabric – based on examination with a ×10 magnifying glass – and general character (see Figure 7.2). Petrological analysis of several tiles from some of the groups has been carried out by Dr David Williams (English Heritage Ceramic & Lithic Petrology Project, Department of Archaeology, Southampton University), and his results are mentioned in the text. The full text of his report is included in this section as Appendix A. The glazes were analysed by Sarah Paynter of the English Heritage Centre for Archaeology and her report appears as Appendix B. The distribution of tiles, where the group is more certainly identified, is shown on Figure 7.3.

The provenance of individual tiles is identified for Keen's excavation by finds number, expressed in round brackets, and for Coppack's excavation by context number, expressed in square brackets.

The Tile Groups

Group 1

The fabric is a well-mixed earthenware. The thin sectioning of two examples showed that the clay matrix is tightly packed, with well-sorted angular to sub-angular, mainly monocrystalline quartz grains less than 0.33 mm in size and fairly frequent flecks and strands of mica, most of which were muscovite, although a little biotite was also present. The tiles have nearly straight sides and sandy backs. There are two main colours: yellow or a dark green to brown. To produce the yellow the surfaces were coated with a white slip that appears yellow under a lead glaze: brush marks are frequently present where the slip has not been generously applied. Small nail holes are sometimes present near the corners. The fabric is well oxidised and the slip often has a flaky appearance, suggesting that the tiles were fired twice: once before slip and glaze were applied and again afterwards. The dark green to brown tiles are similarly well oxidised and nail holes, either four or five (see Figure 7.2, 16 (MG 373), 17 (MG 1141)), are often visible. The colour was achieved by the addition of some copper or iron to a lead glaze. The tiles vary from 105 mm^2 to 110 mm^2, with thicknesses ranging from 20 to 26 mm.

PROVENANCE

Cell 8 latrine pentice (MG 1141); Cell 10 (MG 41, 43–5, 47–8, 53–5, 232); Cell 10, garden (MG 266); Cell 10, latrine pentice (MG 373); Cell 10, garden pentice (MG 424); Cell 12, garden pentice (MG 558); Cell 13 (MG 665); topsoil over earlier prior's cell [900]; demolition of earlier prior's cell [926 and 938].

Group 2

Like Group 1, the fabric is well mixed, but has a tendency to be slightly more sandy. The thin sectioning of four samples showed that the fabric is similar to Group 1, but that the size-range of quartz grains is slightly larger. In all other respects the manufacturing characteristics are similar, but larger circular or rectangular nail holes, up to 5 mm, are visible on the dark glazed tiles. The tiles of this group, however, are distinguished by a larger size and greater thickness. Because of the former there are far fewer complete surviving examples. Complete tiles range from 240 mm^2 to 255 mm^2, with thicknesses ranging from 30 to 42 mm. A few slipped tiles have the remains of a diagonal incision that is rarely more than 1.5 mm deep.

PROVENANCE

Cell 9 (MG 804); Cell 9 garden (MG 1119); Cell 10 (MG 46, 56, 232); Cell 10 garden (MG 333, 350); Cell 10 latrine pentice (MG 383); Cell 11 garden pentice (MG 384, 385, 395, 1259); Cell 13, three dark tiles *in situ*, garden

THE CULTURAL COLLECTIONS

Figure 7.2 Floor tiles from Mount Grace and Sawley (1:3).

pentice; Cell 14 (MG 847); Cell 14 garden (MG 1020); Cell 15 (MG 1003); topsoil over earlier prior's cell [900]; earlier prior's cell [1047]; demolition of earlier prior's cell [926, 927, 931, 934, 938, 981, 1005, 1039]; garden soil, Period Four, prior's cell occupation [577]; demolition of later prior's cell [713]; topsoil over kitchen [1362]; demolition of Period Four kitchen [1363].

Group 3
A few tiles are characteristically the same as Groups 1 and 2. No complete examples survive, but with sizes of more than 120 mm^2 or 170 mm^2 they cannot belong to Group 1, and because the thicknesses vary from 26 to 32 mm the tiles do not appear to belong to Group 2. As a result, a group that falls between Group 1 and 2 in terms of size is suggested.

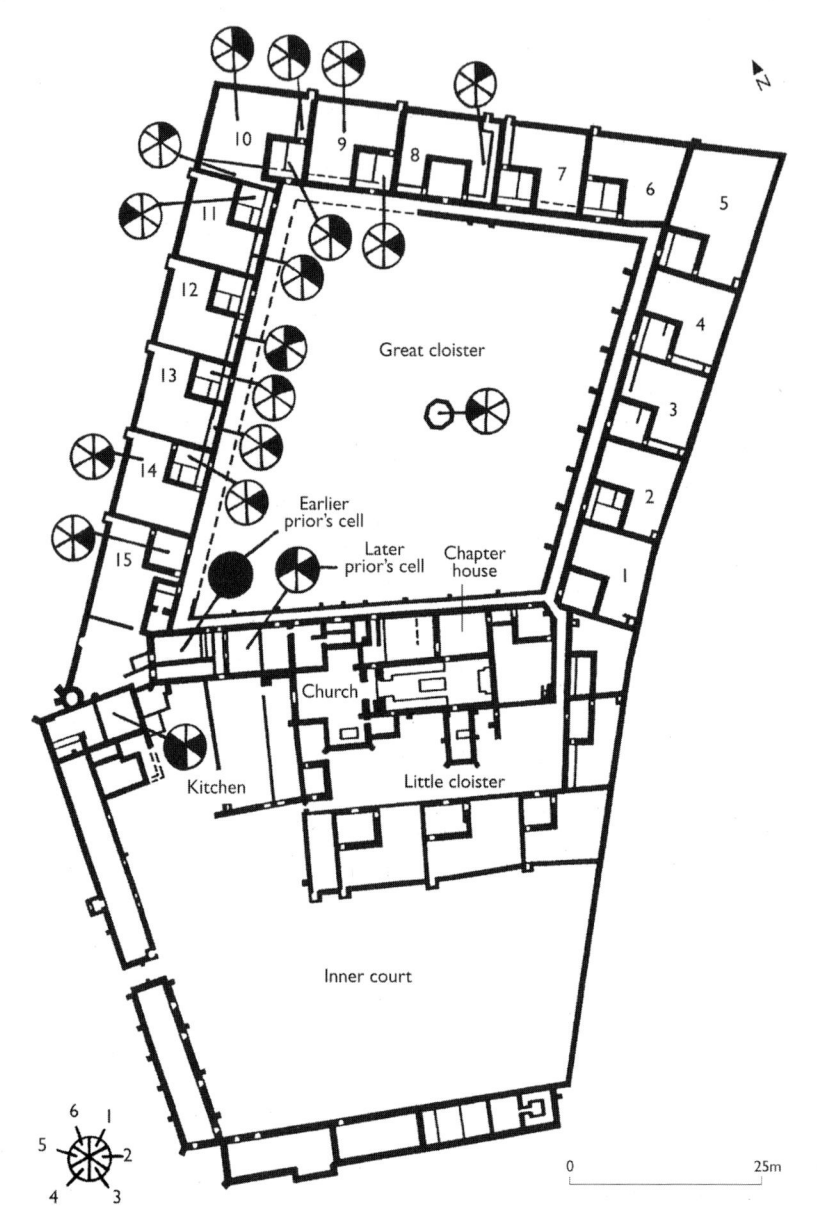

Figure 7.3 Location of floor tiles at Mount Grace.

Group 5

This group consists of both decorated and plain tiles in a well-mixed, fully oxidised red earthenware fabric. Thin sectioning of one of the decorated tiles (MG 487) showed frequent, mostly well-sorted, angular to sub-angular monocrystalline quartz grains generally below 0.20 mm in size, with a few slightly larger grains. Also present are some flecks of mica, a few pieces of siltstone and chert, some clay pellets, the odd small grain of felspar and some opaque iron oxide. Local production is a possibility. The decorated tiles have a thin layer of white slip over a line-impressed design about 1 mm deep (see Figure 7.2, 2 and 3). The tiles are about 110 mm^2, with nearly straight or slightly chamfered sides, and are 30 to 38 mm thick, with plain rough backs. Design 2 appears on a triangular tile from Cell 12, garden pentice (MG 558), that was broken from a whole tile; the diagonal length has an inclined knife cut from 8 to 32 mm deep. A complete example is in the unprovenanced loose collection from the site. Examples of slipped Design 3 come from Cell 11 (MG 487), the demolition of the later prior's cell [713] and the demolition of the earlier prior's cell [935], the last two on triangular half-tiles. One example from [935] is on a slightly larger tile, 120 mm^2, with a copper green glaze over the white slip. A plain tile 114 mm^2 and 32 mm thick found during the water tower excavation (see Chapter 4) in the Period One levelling of the cloister [438] has three nail holes, each near a corner, and an irregularly applied dark green glaze that incompletely covers the surface and has flowed over the sides. The demolition of the kitchen [1365] contained a plain dark green glazed tile 115 mm^2 with a diagonal cut. It is 38 mm thick and has nail holes near the corners.

Group 6

The fabric of this group is generally highly reduced, except near the sides and back, contains numerous inclusions and is laminated with thin lenses of clay. The thin sectioning of two examples from context [938] showed strong lamination in the clay matrix, suggesting that the clay received minimal wedging before shaping and firing took place. The clay matrix is fairly fine-textured, consisting for the most part of a fine, silty, slightly micaceous clay. Also present were a modest scatter of poorly sorted monocrystalline quartz grains, often concentrated in streaks, the odd piece of chert

Provenance

Demolition of earlier prior's cell [713, 927, 938]. Other examples may be present, but large pieces are necessary to allow the positive identification of tiles from this group.

Group 4

Other plain tiles were found in contexts [931] (the demolition of the earlier prior's cell), [1362] (topsoil over kitchen) and [1363] (the demolition of the Period Four kitchen). The few examples present have a dull red well-oxidised earthenware fabric. The plain, unslipped and unglazed surfaces are very smooth and the straight sides have distinctive wire or cut marks. The backs are plain. The tiles are 220 mm^2 and from 45 to 50 mm thick.

and some opaque iron oxide. Local production is likely. The sides are roughly moulded, not cut, and the back is extremely uneven and appears to have been pressed with fingers. One tile from the demolition of the earlier prior's cell [938] is 112 mm^2 and 33 mm thick, and has a slight chamfer. A brownish glaze covers part of Design 3, which is so indistinct that it cannot be drawn. The general characteristics of badly made tiles are found on plain tiles and identify a distinct group. From the demolition of the earlier prior's cell: context [938] has another example of Group 6 160+mm^2 and 32 mm thick, with a yellow/green surface, five other fragments, a complete warped example 120 mm^2 with a kiln stacking mark on the top surface and a fragment 32 mm thick with fused glaze, probably a kiln waster; context [926] has a piece 135+mm^2 and 34 mm thick, with white slip running over the sides, and two pieces 28 mm thick and about 130 mm^2 with dark brown glaze; context [1037] contains a fragment 35 mm thick with white slip, which does not cover the whole surface, and a brownish glaze; another piece from context [963] is overfired and 36 mm thick. There are also other fragments from the topsoil over the later prior's cell [550] – two pieces with a nail hole – and [700]; from the Period Four prior's cell occupation [577]; and from the demolition of the earlier prior's cell [710]. Other pieces from contexts [574], the demolition of the later prior's cell, and [894], the demolition of the earlier prior's cell, could belong to this group.

Group 7
Only one tile, from the demolition of the earlier prior's cell [704], is assigned to this group (see Figure 7.2, 1). It is 33 mm thick, with a mottled dark brown glaze, some on the straight sides, and has a sandy back. The fabric is well mixed and fired. This is the only example of a mosaic tile from the site. A 13th-century date, in this Yorkshire context, would probably be correct, so this tile must surely come from another monastic context. Rievaulx Abbey had an interest in *Bordelbi* from the 12th century.

Group 8
Nine decorated tiles apparently belong to this group, all of which have the same shallow stamped design and thinly inlaid white slip. The well-mixed fabric is oxidised and the tiles have almost straight sides. No petrological analysis has been carried out. With one exception they came from the collection of loose tiles on site, and their provenance is extremely doubtful. They are certainly from the site, however, and an original location in the church is probable. The single example of Design 4 has a reversed design (the design is dark, the background white) and the remains of a patchy glaze, with some flecks of copper; no complete measurements can be obtained, but the overall size was some 109 mm^2. Design 8 is represented by a single example *in situ* in the church. Design 9 occurs on two fragments that are 30 mm thick and have a steep chamfer, poor inlay and no surviving glaze. There is one example of Design 10, which has straight sides, shallow inlay and a badly worn brown glaze. Design 12 is represented by two fragments and one whole example with applied slip and a yellow or dark brown glaze. Nail holes are present near the corners. Design 13 occurs on two pieces 35 mm thick with straight sides, very shallow inlay and a brown glaze. Design 14 is found on three complete tiles and one half-tile with straight sides and a thickness of 30 to 35 mm. The inlay is poor and does not completely fill the stamped impression. A tile with Design 15 comes from the demolition of the earlier prior's cell [926]. It has a slight chamfer and is 32 mm thick. The surface is worn, but a mottled green glaze is present on the sides. The inlaid decoration is very shallow and worn. The drawing here is based on a tile in the Yorkshire Museum (HB 188).

Discussion
The character of Groups 1–3, with evidence for biscuit firing and nail holes, suggests that these tiles are imports from the Low Countries. The two main sizes, 105 mm^2 to 110 mm^2 and 240 mm^2 to 250 mm^2, and the consistent yellow or dark green/brown colour support this conclusion. Large numbers of these tiles are found in England and Scotland, but no tiles have ever been thin sectioned to establish how many production centres might be involved and whether the different sizes of tile come from the same source. The thin sectioning carried out on three tiles from Group 1 and on five tiles from Group 2 shows a generally similar fabric and suggests a common production source.

Such tiles are common and widespread along the south and east coasts and in Scotland (Norton 1994, 150–3). They were imported in their thousands and are referred to frequently in customs books and port books (records of customs duties paid on overseas trade) and in account rolls. But *in situ* imported tiles can rarely be linked to specific documentary references. The exceptions are tiles in Winchester College, bought from Flanders and dated to 1396–7 (Norton 1976, 23–42), and in the crypt of York Minster (*largis tegulis Flaundrensibus*), bought in 1415 (Raine 1859; Keen 1971, 148). At Exeter the earliest reference is of 1437–8, when large Flemish tiles were bought for the cathedral (Keen and Allan 1984, 240). The port books of Southampton are particularly illuminating because the destinations of the tiles – sites in the Southampton hinterland – are recorded. In 1443 tiles were destined for Romsey, Salisbury, Winchester and St Cross (Coleman 1960–1, 16, 30, 41, 307). London must have received hundreds of thousands of tiles, particularly for royal works: in 1368, 8,000 'tiles of Flanders' at 6s. 8d. a thousand were supplied by Henry Yeveley for work at Westminster Palace (Salzman 1952, 145). Dr Williams was asked to compare the Group 1 and 2 specimens with imported tiles found in London, and found that the Mount Grace specimens matched the London examples very well.

For Yorkshire, the Hull customs accounts of the late 15th century list tile imports (Childs 1986), and in 1471/2 a shipmaster of Edam brought in 700 paving tiles (Knight and Keen 1977, 74; Keen 1971, 148). There is a tendency to call these tiles 'Flemish', but, given that both Flanders and Holland are documented as sources, a 'Low Countries' appellation is preferable even to 'Netherlandish' (Eames 1983) until the Continental source(s) can be identified.

In York, imported tiles have been published from the excavation of the Gilbertine priory at Fishergate, with sizes of 265 mm and between 105 mm^2 and 117 mm^2 (Stopford 1996, 298–300). An unpublished floor of tiles about 125 mm^2 is *in situ* in the Consistory Court, York Minster, and dates to the late 14th century (Norton 1994, 170 n. 61; Stopford 1996, 299). Tiles from Gisborough Priory are either about 100 mm or 250 mm^2 (Knight and Keen 1977, 74). At Horsham St Faith, Norfolk, the imported tiles are 107 mm^2 and were associated with architecture of *c.*1400 (Keen 1976, 215).

Given the documentation referred to above establishing that tiles were imported from the Low Countries from the late 14th century and throughout the 15th century, the material from Mount Grace would sit happily in a general 15th-century context. The archaeological evidence suggests that the floors of the cells were of timber, so the use of tiles was probably limited to areas in front of fireplaces, or in the garden or latrine pentices. This is, in fact, demonstrated by the archaeological contexts (see Figure 7.3). A greater concentration of imported tiles occurs in the archaeological contexts associated with the earlier prior's cell and this, with the presence of tiles from other groups, suggests not only a greater use of tiles from Groups 1–3 but a significant general use of ceramic floor tiles. Whether this is simply because the floors in the prior's cell were not of timber, or because tiles were considered to be a more luxurious commodity, or even a status symbol, cannot be determined.

The Group 4 plain tiles are present in only a few examples: with no glaze or slip they might be post-Suppression.

Tiles from Group 5 are both decorated and plain. Design 2 is paralleled at Fountains Abbey, whence tiles are found in the Yorkshire Museum (HB 124–9), and from excavations carried out at Fountains in 1979–80 (Gilyard-Beer and Coppack 1986, figs 12, 18). The infirmary at Fountains still has a floor with tiles of this design, some with nail holes, and they have also been found in the refectory and the floor of the south crossing aisle at Fountains; the latter, if in a primary context, are 1490s in date (G. Coppack, pers. comm.). Further examples are recorded from Rievaulx (BM *Catalogue,* 6130–6) and Kirkham (Stopford 1995, fig. 7.1). Design 3 is also found at Fountains (G. Coppack, pers. comm.). The interesting point about this group is that there is evidence for nail holes in both decorated and plain examples. While nail holes are a Low Countries feature, there is an increasing body of evidence to show that nail holes appear on locally made products, as must be the case here, where a local, Yorkshire, kiln must surely be involved. The greater number of tiles in this group was found in the earlier or later prior's cell, suggesting a more lavish interior decoration than in the brothers' cells, as was also the case with tiles of Group 6.

The Group 6 tiles are linked to those of Group 5 by the use of the same line-impressed design. However, the tiles are so badly made that they might not come from the same workshop or, if they did, they might have been made by a novice labourer. The use of nail holes should be noted. A local, Yorkshire, source is probable. In general character this group appears to be linked with other tiles from the county. Designs 5 and 6 do not appear at Mount Grace, although Design 4, of Group 8, appears to be an earlier version of Designs 5 and 6. Design 6 is found at Fountains Abbey (Gilyard-Beer and Coppack 1986, figs 12, 13), but lacks the central cross found there: an example is in the British Museum (BM *Catalogue*, 1754). Exceptionally, the design occurs twice on one tile in the Yorkshire Museum (HB 130[a]), which has a large scoop on the back reminiscent of the published Fountains Abbey example, and four times on two tiles measuring 260 mm^2 and 255 mm^2 and with a large scoop on the back, one of which came from Parliament Street, York (Yorkshire Museum, HB 1 and HB 5). The same design, but without the central cross, is found on tiles from Meaux Abbey (Beaulah 1929, fig. 36). The fabric and glaze of the tiles in the Yorkshire Museum appear to be similar to those of a tile found on North Cliff, Scarborough in 1855 (Yorkshire Museum, 2000.4262), with Design 5, and a very similar stamp is found on tiles from Meaux Abbey (BM *Catalogue*, 2105, 2997–3001, 12372–5). The example from Scarborough is accompanied by plain and glazed roof tiles and fused wasters (2000.4261, 4263, 4264). A year earlier, in 1854, the discovery was made by E. D. Nesfield of a kiln site on Castle Road, North Cliff, Scarborough, and glazed and unglazed tiles were found in 1855 (Rutter 1961, 51). Rutter presumed that these tiles were roof tiles, 'which are frequently associated with medieval glazed wares in the town'. Unfortunately, the manuscript catalogue of Charles Rooke, which Rutter cites as evidence, cannot be located and there are no similar tiles in the Scarborough Museum's collection. If the tile with Design 5 did come from the kiln site it was probably made there. This, in turn, would suggest that the Fountains, Meaux and York material may derive from Scarborough, which is well known as a centre of pottery production (Farmer and Farmer 1982). However, the thin sectioning of samples from Group 6 suggests that the fabric is quite different in terms of clays and temper from Scarborough Ware (see Appendix A), so, unless the fabric used for tiles at Scarborough was distinctively different from that used for pottery, another local production centre might be responsible.

The single tile in Group 7 is a curiosity, as no other mosaic tiles have been found. Given a possible 13th-century date, it is most likely to be a stray or even the result of monastic pilfering.

The decorated tiles in Group 8 appear to belong together, as they all have the same general appearance. Unfortunately, none has a secure provenance in the priory, although the church is a likely candidate. As has been noted above, Design 4, which is paralleled by a tile from Bolton Priory, Yorkshire (BM *Catalogue*, 7663), is linked typologically to designs that appear to belong to Group 6, but the fabric of Group 8 is clearly different and the tiles are more expertly made. Design 8 is found at Rievaulx (BM *Catalogue*, 6099–100) and Kirkham (Stopford 1995, fig. 7.6); Design 9 at Rievaulx (BM *Catalogue*, 6101–4) and, with dots in the two-line circular frame, at Sawley (Yorkshire Museum, HB 186); and Designs 10 and 11 at Sawley (Yorkshire Museum, HB 163, 170). The episcopal or abbatial staff with the letter W may represent William Gower, abbot of Fountains 1369–84 (Gilyard-Beer 1970, 21). Design 12 is found only at Mount Grace; John Goodall FSA has kindly identified the arms as *three swords points downward* (2.1) and attributes them to Kirkstall Abbey or William St Paul of Todwick, whose family members were benefactors of Roche Abbey. Design 13 is found at Fountains and Sawley Abbey (Yorkshire Museum, HB 159, 162), while 14 is found at Sawley (Yorkshire Museum, HB 163) and Kirkham (Stopford 1995, fig. 7.4). Design 15 is found on an unprovenanced example in the Yorkshire Museum (HB 188) and goes with two tiles of a 16-tile pattern from Sawley Abbey (HB 166) or tiles from Tanner's Moat, York (HB 231). HB 188 was found in 1888, along with a number of floor-tile wasters, suggesting the possibility of a kiln site.

Within this group a large proportion of the designs, as noted, are found at Sawley Abbey and, remarkably, one tile (Design 7) from Sawley in the Yorkshire Museum (HB 165) bears the sgraffito inscription *iohos Sallay abbas christus iehus*. The Abbot John referred to is probably the John mentioned in 1376 (Preston Record Office K/9/29 – *ex inf.* G. Coppack) and 1377 (Dugdale 1825, 516). This tile is almost certainly a waster, but it is clear that the abbot was somehow linked directly with tile production.

The example of Design 15 from Tanner's Moat, York, may be from a kiln there, but many of the other tiles found are directly linked by their designs to Fountains Abbey. Design 11, if correctly attributed to Abbot William Gower of Fountains (Stopford 2005, 227 and figs 22.2, 23.24), implies a Fountains–Sawley link in this group, so perhaps a joint production centre is not entirely out of the question.

Whatever the source of this group, the designs were somehow carried to Cheshire. Part of Design 15 is found in Chester (BM *Catalogue,* 1719), which has also produced Design 9 without inlay and a version of Design 15 (Rutter 1990, figs 177 44/304, 180 37/312).

Conclusion

For floor-tile studies generally the Mount Grace material has the distinction of being confined to a relatively short period starting in *c.*1400–10. There is nothing here that should pre-date the start of the first construction phase, with perhaps the majority of the imported material belonging to this or subsequent phases of building. As yet, local floor-tile production in Yorkshire is not understood. It is not surprising that York appears to be a likely source, and Scarborough could be another candidate, although a kiln site on the Fountains or Sawley Abbey estate is a distinct possibility. Significantly, while nail holes are not a definitive indication of imported tiles, their occurrence on obviously locally made material does suggest the possibility that tile-makers from the Low Countries had become part of the growing community of alien artisans, unless indigenous craftsmen had deliberately copied foreign techniques. Despite its relatively small size, this collection adds considerably to national studies.

Appendix A: A Note on the Petrology of Medieval Tiles from Mount Grace Priory, North Yorkshire

by D. F. Williams

I) INTRODUCTION

A small programme of thin sectioning and study under the petrological microscope was undertaken on the clay fabrics of 13 samples of glazed and plain tiles recovered from Mount Grace Priory. The main object of the examination was to see how any possible groupings of the tiles on the basis of their fabrics related to the groupings based on design, visual appearance of fabrics and typology. A secondary aim was to suggest possible sources for the tiles on the basis of their characteristic fabrics. Mount Grace Priory is situated in an area dominated by a range of Jurassic formations and close to glacial boulder clays and alluvium (Geological Survey, 1 inch Map of England, sheet no. 42).

II) PETROLOGY

Group 1

Sample tiles (1) MG 558 and (2) MG 262. Thin sectioning showed that both tiles have a very similar fabric, containing the same range and texture of non-plastic inclusions. The clay matrix in each case is tightly packed, with well-sorted angular to sub-angular mainly monocrystalline quartz grains less than 0.33 mm in size, together with fairly frequent flecks and strands of mica, most of which are muscovite, although a little biotite is present as well. Also present are some small pieces of chert, small discrete grains of felspar (mainly plagioclase), occasional small grains of ferro-magnesian minerals and a little opaque iron oxide.

Sample tile (3) from context [939]. This tile has a somewhat similar range and texture of non-plastic inclusions as tiles (1) and (2) but, in addition, contains moderately frequent small well-rounded cryptocrystalline pieces of limestone. A fresh fracture visible under hand lens showed a positive reaction to the application of a small drop of dilute hydrochloric acid. Tiles (1) and (2) did not.

Group 2

Sample tiles (4) MG 333, (5) from context [938], (6) from context [1119] and (7) from context [1259]. These four tiles appear to be in a generally similar fabric to numbers (1) and (2) above, but a slightly larger size-range of quartz grains is present.

Sample tile (8), from context [1259]. The range of non-plastic inclusions present in the fabric of this tile is similar to those in numbers (4) to (7), except that this tile is slightly finer textured than the latter examples.

Group 5

Sample tile (9), MG 487. Thin sectioning showed frequent, mostly well-sorted, angular to subangular monocrystalline quartz grains generally smaller than 0.20 mm, with a few slightly larger grains. Also present are some flecks of mica, a few pieces of siltstone and chert, some clay pellets, the odd small grain of felspar (generally plagioclase) and some opaque iron oxide.

Sample tiles (10) MG 558 and (11) MG 438. In thin section both of these tiles show a similar range of non-plastic inclusions to that noted for (9), although the quartz grains tend to be more closely packed and the clay matrix is slightly more micaceous in these two examples. A large fragment of cryptocrystalline limestone was present in (10).

Group 6
Sample tiles (12) and (13) from context [938]. Both tiles are clearly in an identical fabric, which in the hand-specimen has a distinctive variegated dark grey core with light red surfaces. Thin sectioning showed strong lamination in the clay matrix, suggesting that the clay received minimal wedging before shaping and firing took place. The clay matrix is fairly fine-textured, consisting for the most part of a fine, silty, slightly micaceous clay. There are also a modest scatter of poorly sorted monocrystalline quartz grains, often concentrated in streaks, the odd piece of chert and some opaque iron oxide. This fabric is quite different in terms of its range of inclusions from the predominantly sandy fabrics of (9)–(11) above and also from the clays and temper used for Scarborough Ware (Williams and Tomber 1982).

III) COMMENTS
Through the good offices of Dr Ian Betts of the Museum of London Archaeological Service, the majority of the tiles described above were compared in the hand-specimen with imported medieval and post-medieval tiles from the Low Countries held in the reference collection of the Museum of London. The three tiles from Group 1 matched very well with early Low Countries tiles from the collection. It was interesting to see that the petrological evidence suggests that there is a non-calcareous fabric among the Museum of London collection as well as the calcareous one previously noted by Dr Betts in the hand-specimen. The petrological descriptions of the two fabrics from Group 1 noted above should further help to characterise these imported tiles. The four tiles from Group 2 ((4)–(7)) appeared similar to slightly later imported tiles from the collection, which tend to be somewhat thicker than the earlier tiles. The distinctive variegated fabric of the two tiles from Group 6 was noted among some of the imported tiles from the collection, but a close examination of the latter under a compound microscope showed that they contain large distinctive inclusions of light-coloured mudstone/clay pellets that are lacking in the Mount Grace tiles. In view of this, if the Mount Grace tiles were made locally, the source of their material could have been one of the silty estuarine clays that occur in the area.

Appendix B: A Note on the Glazing of Medieval Tiles from Mount Grace Priory, North Yorkshire

by Sarah Paynter

The tiles were analysed using X-ray fluorescence spectrometry (XRF), which is a rapid and non-destructive analytical technique. Three combinations of glaze/slip decoration had been used on the tiles: an amber-coloured glaze applied directly over the clay, a dark green/black glaze applied directly over the clay and a white slip applied over the clay followed by a transparent amber glaze. All of the glazes were lead fluxed, containing in excess of 70 wt% lead oxide. The white slip used was silica rich and probably consists largely of fine quartz mixed with a small amount of clay. The results of the petrological examination may enable this to be investigated further. The dark glazes were coloured by high concentrations of intentionally added copper and iron oxides. Traces of zinc oxide and nickel oxide, compounds likely to have entered the glazes with the colourants, were also detected in several of the dark glazes (the latter in tiles 6a/b and 7). The amber glazes were coloured by small amounts of iron oxide. The analytical results are given in Table 7.5.

On analysis, the clay of tile MG 558 was found to have a composition typical of an earthenware clay: about 50 wt% silica, 11 wt% iron oxide, 12 wt% aluminium oxide, 8 wt% Calcium oxide, 3.5 wt% magnesium oxide and 3 wt% potassium oxide.

7.5 Fish Remains from the Kitchen and South-west Cloister Range

by Brian Irving and Andrew Jones

Introduction and Background
The excavation of the kitchen and the western part of the south-west cloister range between 1989 and 1992 recovered substantial stratified deposits rich in fish remains that could be related to identified structures and to three of the four basic phases of the site's development.

Table 7.5 Composition of the tile glazes and slips, as determined by XRF analysis (all values as wt %, normalized)

No.	Sample	Description	Area	Al_2O_3	SiO_2	K_2O	CaO	TiO_2	MnO	Fe_2O_3	NiO	CuO	XnO	PbO
1	MG 558	Amber glaze over slip, decorated	Glaze	3.9	18.6	0.4	1.5	0.5	0.1	1.9	0.0	0.1	0.0	73.0
2	MG 487	Amber glaze over slip	Glaze	14.9	54.0	1.6	1.1	1.6	0.0	4.4	0.0	0.1	0.4	21.8
			Slip	19.6	72.6	1.9	0.5	2.6	0.0	2.5	0.0	0.0	0.0	0.1
3	MG 266	Amber glaze over slip	Glaze	4.8	21.9	0.5	0.9	0.9	0.1	1.1	0.0	0.1	0.0	69.7
			Slip	14.9	72.5	1.1	0.3	3.0	0.0	4.5	0.0	0.1	0.0	3.7
4	MG 558	Amber glaze over slip	Glaze	3.5	17.2	0.5	4.0	1.0	0.0	1.7	0.0	0.1	0.0	72.0
5	[438]	Dark glaze	Glaze	4.7	22.1	0.5	4.5	0.5	0.1	6.7	0.0	3.0	1.5	56.5
6a/b	MG 1259	Dark glaze	Glaze	6.7	30.3	5.2	2.3	0.6	0.1	3.6	0.2	2.3	0.1	48.7
7	[938]	Dark glaze	Glaze	1.6	12.9	0.4	2.4	0.5	0.1	2.0	0.2	5.9	0.1	73.0
8	[938]	Amber glaze nearly whole	Glaze	4.7	15.3	0.5	1.3	0.4	0.0	2.8	0.0	0.1	0.0	74.9
9	[938]	Amber glaze	Glaze	3.9	13.2	0.5	1.3	0.4	0.0	2.4	0.0	0.1	0.0	78.2
10a	[938](1)	Dark glaze	Glaze	3.6	24.7	0.5	1.0	0.4	0.0	2.9	0.0	3.4	0.6	62.9
10b	MG 1119	Dark Glaze	Glaze	3.5	23.0	0.5	0.9	0.5	0.1	3.9	0.0	2.2	0.6	64.7
10c	[333]	Amber glaze	Glaze	3.7	17.9	0.3	1.0	1.1	0.0	1.6	0.0	0.1	0.0	74.4

This discussion is an edited version of two reports issued by the Environmental Archaeology Unit of the University of York (Bailey *et al*. 1994 and Irving and Jones 1994).

Both documentary sources and the evidence of fishponds and fisheries associated with rural monasteries bear witness to the importance of fish in the monastic diet and economy. The Carthusian Order was, and remains, strictly vegetarian in its diet and, although other orders ate meat in the later Middle Ages in spite of St Benedict's rule forbidding the consumption of quadrupeds, fish remains are commonly found on most monastic sites. The importance of fish, often eaten on festival days if not more frequently, is not matched by their frequency in the published archaeological record (Jones 1989, *passim*). The recovery of large numbers of fish remains at Mount Grace from the kitchen and elsewhere (Bailey *et al*. 1994) provides, perhaps for the first time in Britain, the opportunity to examine a large body of evidence from a major rural monastery, and the first opportunity to examine a major group of fish remains from any Carthusian site.

A notable aspect of the research on the fish remains from Mount Grace was the involvement of the general public in the sorting of samples in the interactive Archaeological Activity Area of the Archaeological Resource Centre (ARC) at York.

This report deals with the full analysis of fish bones from eight bulk samples selected from the 33 collected during excavation, chosen because of their size and the primary nature of the deposits. It has identified a wide range of fish species. The level of analysis, and thus the amount of material examined, was dictated by the timescale, the overall project research design and the funding available. Full analysis of the material is planned at a later date.

Methods

Complete deposits were lifted from the clay surface of the kitchen floors in metre squares based on the site grid, with only obvious pottery sherds and metal small finds being removed in the process. The limits of individual deposits were planned. From the earliest Period Two kitchen floor came bulk sample [1941] and from the surface of the first reflooring of this phase came bulk samples [1909], [1913] and [1925]. The largest deposit collected, [1833], was taken from the surface of the third floor of the Period Two kitchen. Sample [1508] was taken from the Period Three kitchen floor. No Period Four deposits were recovered from the kitchen because they had been removed by

Hope's excavation, but a contemporary dump of fish-processing waste, [1037], was recovered from the floor of a small 'room' at the centre of the south-west cloister range. Thus substantial quantities of fish waste were recovered from a series of discrete but related deposits that covered the period c.1420–1539.

The processing of material was carried out in two phases. In the first the dried sediment residues after bulk-sieving to 1 mm were first sorted at the ARC, York, under the supervision of Dr Andrew Jones, and the bulk of the sorting was done by parties of schoolchildren and members of the general public, who were provided with illuminated magnifiers and tweezers. The sorting was supervised by experienced ARC demonstrators and all finds were checked before being bagged. The experience of the sorting activity for the members of the public was enhanced with photographs and plans of the excavation, together with a short piece of text describing the nature of the work. Meanwhile, in the second phase 100 g sub-samples of each sample were sorted by trained archaeological demonstrators away from the public sorting area to determine whether any kinds of fish remains were being systematically overlooked by visitors and whether the sorting done by visitors was recovering fish remains not present in the 100 g sub-samples.

The fish remains assemblage is large in comparison with those from other sites of this type and, as the research design required an overview rather than a full analysis of the collection, the following protocol was developed with a view to maximising the information recovered.

The bones from the dried residues were sorted into four main categories at the ARC: head and tail bones; vertebrae; ribs and fin spines; and others (scales, teeth, otoliths and scutes). The first three categories were weighed separately; the data for each sample analysed are given in Table 7.6. Weights for identifiable head bones from those samples selected for full analysis were also recorded to determine the ratio of identifiable to unidentifiable material from each context. Recording of the cranial elements was based on the best-preserved and most diagnostic fragments, which are the maxilla, the premaxilla, the articular, the dentary, the quadrate, the ceratohyal, the urohyal (for flatfish), the opercular, the cleithrum, the post-temporal and teeth. These 11 elements permitted the identification of a range of species and are all bio-symmetrical paired elements, except the urohyal, so also provided data for the estimation of the minimum number of individuals. In addition, they are sufficiently robust in British teleosts to allow comparison across families. As a consequence of this strategy more time could be taken in identifying fish remains to the lowest taxonometric level. Other cranial elements examined were recorded where they could be identified to species or family, and vertebrae were generally recorded to family; however, a small number were determined to species. Systematic nomenclature follows Wheeler (1969) and skeleton element nomenclature follows Wheeler and Jones (1989).

Measurements were taken only on articulars and quadrates, which were present for most species, as follows:

Articular

1. Greatest dorso-ventral length of articular surface
2. Greatest latero-medial width of articular surface

Quadrate

1. Greatest dorso-ventral length of articular surface
2. Greatest latero-medial width of articular surface

Evidence of butchery was sought for all recorded elements. Generally, fish bones are cut with knives, except in the case of large fish, which are chopped into segments; chopped vertebrae are usually very obvious in archaeological material, as they show both a clean cut and some compression of the vertebral body. Aberrant and pathological bones were recorded, the most obvious pathology being hyperostosis in haddock cleithera and mackerel vertebrae. Post-mortem attrition of the fish bone was scored for individual bones using a five-point system:

1. Complete, 100% of bone present
2. Slight damage, 80–95% of bone present
3. Moderate damage, 40–79% of bone present
4. High damage, 20–39% of bone present
5. Identifiable simply as fish bone, 1–19% of bone present

Table 7.6 Quantities of fish bone recovered from kitchen deposit

Context		Total wt (g)	Cranial wt (g)	% Cranial	Vertebrae wt (g)	% Vertebrae
[1941]	1	113.5	48.6	42.82	42.7	37.62
	2	223.2	99.2	44.44	68.3	30.60
	3	56.2	28.4	50.53	15.6	22.76
[1909]		75.7	32.4	42.8	24.3	32.10
[1913]	1	64.6	31.6	48.92	22.2	34.37
	2	219.2	104.3	47.58	69.7	31.80
	3	84.3	38.8	46.03	26.8	31.79
[1925]	1	66.1	26.7	40.39	22.0	33.28
	2	166.1	78.7	47.38	49.3	29.68
[1833]	1	31.2	16.4	52.56	6.0	19.23
	2	58.7	27.6	47.02	17.8	30.32
	3	44.1	23.3	52.83	13.1	29.71
	5	10.4	5.4	51.92	2.3	22.12
	6	260.7	93.0	35.67	105.2	40.35
	7	70.6	25.3	35.84	22.4	31.73
	8	53.2	19.2	36.09	18.3	34.40
	10	18.9	5.8	30.69	5.7	30.16

The taphonomic variables that may have caused bone breakage and loss are considered within each sample description. The main influences on bone survival/attrition within the Mount Grace assemblages are as follows:

1. Excavation and storage damage
2. Chemical damage
3. Old breaks and erosion
4. Human and carnivore damage in antiquity

Identification of category of attrition:

1. Fresh breaks
2. Bone surface etching
3. Rounded break points
4. Gnaw marks and deformities

Other evidence that directly relates to the taphonomic histories is provided by descriptions of fish bones *in situ* from both the excavation record and personal observation. These consist of statements about, for example, articulating vertebrae and head bones found in approximately the correct anatomical relationships, which give primary information on taphonomy.

The fish bone assemblage is considered in two stages: the first covers the quantification of the bulk material and the second covers the fully recorded samples.

Quantification

The material from bulk samples, once sorted, was weighed as skeleton element groups, as described above. The results are given in Table 7.6.

The results show some variation in both skeletal part representation and weight of fish bone per volume/weight unit of deposit. There is wide variation in the number of fish bones per sample, the lowest concentration coming from the Period Four deposit in the south-west cloister range. The largest bone assemblage, from context [1833] in the kitchen, shows, as might be expected, a wide variation in fish bone concentration across the floor of the building, the result of a discard pattern reflecting the location of furniture and the hearth. The percentages of cranial elements, vertebrae and ribs/fin spines, when plotted, show a similar pattern across all samples.

Analysis

Nine bulk samples were recorded using the above criteria. They were chosen to represent context type, room function and each recorded development phase. The samples chosen from

Table 7.7 Numbers of fish bones from the samples studied in detail

Context	Building	Date	Period	No. fish bones
[1941]	Kitchen	c. 1420	2(a)	603
[1909]	Kitchen	c. 1440	2(b)	190
[1913]	Kitchen	c. 1440	2(b)	377
[1833]	Kitchen	c. 1460	2(c)	2095
[1508]	Kitchen	c. 1480	3	116
[1037]	South-west cloister range	c. 1520	4	113
Total fish bones				3494

the kitchen were [1941] 2, [1909] 1, [1913] 2, [1833] 6 and 16, and [1508] 1 and 2. From the south-west cloister range, both [1137] 1 and 2 were recorded for comparison with the kitchen material. The material is described here by chronological phase.

Kitchen Deposits
A total of 3,381 fish bones was fully recorded from the kitchen floor deposits and a further 113 came from the south-west cloister range.

The deposits were described initially by the excavators as 'food waste'. In the light of the evidence presented here in the form of *in situ* descriptions of articulating vertebrae and skeletal representation from the laboratory analysis (see below), this description can be revised to 'kitchen processing waste', a term more accurately reflecting the handling and butchering of the fish that was carried out in the locations concerned.

Period Two (a), context [1941]
Fourteen identified species and three families are represented in this single context, which is dominated by marine species. Haddock and flatfishes make up the bulk of the material. Bones of ling, mackerel and grey gurnard are recorded from this phase only. There is a general paucity of freshwater material, with the exception of the Cyprinidae (carp family). Also worthy of note is the absence of both herring and eel, two species that are well represented in later phases.

Period Two (b), contexts [1909] and [1913], and Period Two (c), context [1833]
This material, although dominated by herring, haddock, other gadids and flatfishes, contains a very broad diversity of species. There is an increase in the range and frequency of freshwater species. Salmon is represented throughout the three contexts, as is eel, suggesting a local fishery, perhaps on the river Wiske, that concentrated on migratory species. The family Cyprinidae is represented by six identified species, which may have been cultured in the extensive fishponds on the lower western terrace of the site.

Period Three, context [1508]
A single context from the Phase Three kitchen produced only 116 identifiable bones. The commonest species was eel. Marine species predominated, the cod family (Gadidae) and herring being well represented. Only a very small amount of freshwater material was present. An unusual species is the cuckoo wrasse, which is not an important food fish but is, nevertheless, edible. The pollack also occurs exclusively within this phase.

Period Four, context [1037]
The fish remains from the floor of the original prior's cell in the south-west cloister range came from a context representing occupation within what was probably a servery or preparation area associated with the refectory at first-floor level or with the later prior's cell to the east. The fish remains were more fragmentary, with far fewer cranial bones, suggesting that the mode of disposal differed from that of the earlier samples. There was a complete absence of primary freshwater fishes. Migratory fishes, though, were represented by both salmon and eel. Marine fish included thornback ray, herring, flatfishes and gadids. Initial assessment of this deposit (Bailey *et al.* 1994) revealed one species not recorded in the selected samples: scute fragments of sturgeon (*Acipenser sturio* L.) were noted.

The *in situ* kitchen floor assemblages showed the articulation of vertebrae and head bones, indicating that the fish had been thrown down onto the floor surface and demonstrating what by today's standards would have been a filthy and unhygienic environment. This material was generally in attrition states 2–3, which is an unusually good state of preservation for medieval fish remains.

The kitchen material covers the greater part of the occupational history of the site, from the 1420s to 1539, and is clearly characteristic of the site as a whole (Bailey *et al.* 1994), showing trends in both species diversity and species utilised. This information is summarised in Table 7.8.

Discussion

The occupation period represented by the contexts examined spans a little over a century, and within this short timespan the structural phasing of the site permits extremely accurate dating and presents a unique opportunity for the study of change in the food economy of Mount Grace between 1420 and 1539.

A striking feature is the changing frequency of cyprinid bone fragments and species numbers. Two obvious factors may have influenced such variation: sample size (which may cause the bias in species represented, for the bigger the sample the more likely it is to contain a true cross section of the species utilised) or a real change in the dietary preference of the monks. This latter factor may also explain the provision of fishponds within the monastery. The cyprinid material peaks in Period Two (c), in the 1460s, is barely present in Period Three and was not represented at all in Period Four. Unfortunately, the sample size was small in both Periods Three and Four, and a lack of representation does not necessarily mean that cyprinids ceased to be available or eaten.

There are other general trends through the phases. The most common species were eel, haddock, whiting and herring, giving the economy of the site a maritime flavour. The utilisation of marine fishes at this site on such a scale may seem puzzling, given the geographical location of Mount Grace – some 20 miles from the nearest fishing port – and the presence of fishponds. However, the work of economic historians such as Littler (1979) and Harvey (1993) has confirmed the importance of marine fishes in the monastic diet. The medieval towns along the east coast of England all had fishing fleets taking herring, cod and other species from the North Sea and beyond in the 14th and 15th centuries, and the Cistercian abbey of Fountains, 40 miles from the nearest port, regularly bought fish at Yarm, Scarborough and Grimsby, as well as having important river fisheries on the rivers Swale, Wiske, Ouse and Derwent, and at Malham Tarn and Derwentwater (Coppack 1993, 85). The assemblages at Mount Grace contain many of the same species of fish that were found at Valle Crucis (Barker 1976), Taunton (Wheeler 1984), Westminster (Jones 1976), the Austin friary at Leicester (Thawley 1981), Battle (Locker 1986) and Om in Denmark (Rosenlund 1984). Close comparison of the Mount Grace material with the fish remains from these sites is not possible, however, because of the significant differences in the nature of the deposits recovered, the local topography and the methods of recovery.

The assemblage of fish bones most similar to that from Mount Grace comes from the abbey of St Salvator, at Ename in Flanders (Ervynck and Van Neer 1992), located on the river Schelt. Freshwater taxa dominate this assemblage but many of the marine taxa present at Mount Grace also occurred. At both sites the methods used to recover fish remains from kitchen floor deposits produced large representative samples of bones, scales and other remains that provide an accurate picture of the fishes present at each site. Ervynck and van Neer (1992) assumed, because the bones were so well preserved, that the accumulation of fish remains at Ename occurred under a boarded floor. No such evidence for a sprung floor was recovered at Mount Grace, and the polished and laminate appearance of deposits such as [1833] suggest that they were constantly walked on; thus it seems likely that the rapidly accumulating layers of ash and charcoal provided excellent conditions for the preservation of fragile bones.

The freshwater taxa from the Mount Grace assemblage have also been found at other monastic sites, such as Owston, where the evidence came from the fishponds (Shackley *et al.* 1998), and Om in Denmark (Rosenlund 1984). Quite clearly, medieval monasteries

Table 7.8 Identified fish species from the kitchen area by context and phase

Context	1941	1913	1909	1833	1508	1037	
Period	2a	2b	2b	2c	3	4	Total
Raja clavata L. Thornback ray	3	59	2	12	2	4	82
CYPRINIDAE (carp family)	57	32	23	138	4	0	254
Tinca tinca (L) tench	0	0	0	1	0	0	1
Abramis brama (L) common bream	0	0	0	1	0	0	1
Blicca bjoerkna (L) silver bream	0	0	0	1	0	0	1
Leuciscus leuciscus (L) dace	0	1	0	1	0	0	2
Leuciscus cephalus (L) chub	1	1	0	0	0	0	2
Rutilus rutilus (L) roach	0	0	0	2	0	0	2
Salmo salar (L) atlantic salmon	0	2	10	10	0	3	25
Salmo trutta (L) sea/brown trout	3	0	0	1	0	0	4
Perca fluviatilis (L)perch	0	1	2	0	0	0	3
Anguila anguila (L) eel	0	28	15	72	51	11	177
Esox lucius (L) pike	0	0	4	0	1	0	5
Conger conger (L) conger eel	2	0	0	0	2	0	4
lupea harengus (L) herring	0	2	0	1318	11	39	1370
GADIDAE (cod family)	169	59	62	69	11	26	396
Gadus morhua (L) cod	1	6	0	23	3	0	33
Melanogrammus aeglefinus (L) haddock	140	104	20	155	12	2	433
Merlangius merlangus (L) whiting	26	4	4	59	9	0	102
Pollachius pollachius (L) pollack	0	0	0	0	1	0	1
Molva molva (L) ling	17	0	0	0	0	0	17
Merluccius merluccius (L) hake	0	0	1	0	0	0	1
LABRIDAE (wrasse family)	0	0	0	0	1	0	1
Labrus mixtus (L) cuckoo wrasse	0	0	0	0	1	0	1
Scomber scombrus (L) mackerel	3	0	0	0	0	0	3
TRIGLIDAE (gurnard family)	0	0	0	2	3	0	5
Eutrigla gurnardus (L) grey gurnard	1	0	0	0	0	0	1
Scophthalmus maximus (L) turbot	3	7	0	6	1	1	18
PLEURONECTIDAE (flatfish family)	33	13	4	72	1	8	131
Platichthys flesus (L) flounder	2	2	0	11	1	1	17
Pleuronectes platessa (L) plaice	3	15	0	11	1	1	31
Solea solea (L) sole	1	0	0	1	0	0	2
Indeterminate	138	41	43	129	0	17	368
Total	603	337	190	2095	116	113	3494

exploited a wide range of species and might trade fish over considerable distances.

Fresh or Preserved Fish?
The presence of the articulated skeletons of marine fish suggests that whole animals were being brought onto the site. A small number of bones of large gadids, mainly cod, showed clear evidence of butchery, all consistent with the kinds of processing common in a kitchen. One dentary bore two large chop marks, suggesting that the fish had been roughly chopped prior to being cooked perhaps in a soup or stew. Some gadid vertebrae had been split anterio-posteriorly in a manner reminiscent of cutlets being divided in half. No clear evidence for stockfish was observed.

The size of the haddock and whiting, reconstructed by the comparison of quadrate measurements with specimens of known length, is around 0.5–0.6 m. Cod and ling measured up to 1.2 m.

Season at Death
Migratory species, such as salmon and eel, occurred throughout the later deposits. The salmon was represented by well-preserved vertebrae, permitting the identification of season at death. The annual growth bands ('annuli') on fish vertebrae provide information on both growth and time of death, and the standard technique used in modern fisheries analysis was readily adapted to the archaeological material. By 'reading' the growth bands it has been established that the salmon died during the autumn, probably during October or November. Salmon would probably spawn in the local river Wiske, a tributary of the Swale, during the auttumn. Small rivers such as the Wiske are typical spawning places and, while spawning, salmon become an easy target for fishermen.

Conclusion
The most obvious feature of the Mount Grace fish remains assemblage is the dominance of marine species over freshwater forms. The evidence from the kitchen and south-west cloister range makes it clear that, despite the maintenance of extensive fishponds at the site, the monks were heavily dependent on imported sea fish, notably herring, cod, haddock and whiting. Other species, although represented by only small numbers of bones, demonstrate that the monks had access to a wide variety of species, including highly prized fishes such as turbot and sturgeon.

Other Food Debris from the Kitchen and South-west Cloister Range
The samples lifted from the kitchen floors and from the small 'room' in the south-west cloister range were bulk sieved to 1 mm with a wash-over sieved to 500 µm, primarily to recover the fish remains (above), larger plant remains and shells. The results indicate that survival at Mount Grace was poor, the deposits being devoid of organic matter other than bone and charcoal. Some slight evidence for diet was, however, apparent (Bailey *et al.* 1994).

Other Food Stuffs
Although shellfish were well represented in virtually every sample taken, showing that they made up a significant element in the monks' diet, cockles were recorded only in Period Two (a) deposits, suggesting that they were not consumed after the first quarter of the 15th century. Mussels predominated in the collection, with oysters coming a close second, as might be expected. Significantly, shellfish were not recovered from the putative servery in the south-west cloister range, but were restricted to the kitchen itself, suggesting the preparation of dishes in which the meat was actually removed from the shells during the cooking process. Because food was prepared centrally and because the Carthusian Order had strict dietary rules, the material from the kitchen should shed light on the major elements of the convent's daily diet (Table 7.9).

Perhaps unsurprisingly, eggshell, indicative of the use of eggs in cooking, was recorded in the majority of contexts throughout Periods Two and Three, apart from those from the south-west cloister range. Samples with abundant eggshell – as opposed to moderate amounts – were [1914] 3, [1833] 11, [1913] 3 and [1908] 1.

Evidence for seeds and legumes was sparse, although this should be attributed primarily to soil conditions. Sample [1833] 20 contained several eroded and very fragile charred (?) cereal grains, [1913] 1 a fragment of elderberry (*Sambucus nigra*), [1508] 1 a trace of toad rush (*Juncus bufonius*), and [1307] 1 a single charred pea (*Pisum*) seed and three fragments of (?)bed straw (*Galium* sp.).

THE CULTURAL COLLECTIONS

Mixed into all deposits were substantial quantities of coal and clinker and a lesser amount of wood charcoal, all derived from the kitchen hearth, demonstrating that coal was the principal fuel used.

Mammal bone was significant by its absence in the kitchen and south-west cloister range deposits. A single bird bone was recorded in sample [1833] 13 and a single tibia from a juvenile rodent, probably *Mus* or *Apodemus* sp. in sample [1833] 06. However, occupation deposits from this area did produce some evidence of meat preparation and eating. Particularly significant were six fragments identified as Phocidae (seal): a metapodial from context [1835] (Period Two), a phalanx from context [1449] (Period Three), a metacarpal from context [577] in the Period Three prior's cell, two canines from contexts [1513] and [1519] (Period Four), and a fibula (tentatively identified as seal) from context [1826] (Period Four). It would appear that marine mammals were considered to be fish for dietary purposes.

The remainder of the animal bone was made up of 118 fragments from Period Two deposits, 72 fragments from Period Three deposits and 511 fragments from Period Four deposits (which included material from the initial post-Suppression stripping of the site). None came from the kitchen deposits, and all material from Period One deposits (175 fragments principally from construction deposits) is presumed to be either residual from the pre-monastic village occupation of the site or food debris left by the masons. Meat was not permitted as part of the convent diet, even for the sick, but was allowed for guests. The collection was unexceptional, comprising:

- cattle 28.9%, 97 fragments
- sheep/goat 31.8%, 107 fragments
- pig 15.2%, 51 fragments
- horse 12.2%, 41 fragments
- deer 1.2%, 4 fragments
- bird 10.7%, 36 fragments

Additional species represented included small canid (probably fox, cf. *Vulpes vulpes* L.) domestic cat and dog, hare (*Lepus,* cf. *europaeus* Pallas) and hedgehog (Erinaceus europaeus L.), the majority from Periods Three and Four. Bones of small mammals were also present in very small numbers, and included the femur of a black rat (*Rattus rattus L.*) from the Period Three context [1899]. In short, there was slight evidence for the everyday feral occupation of the site.

7.6 Small Finds

by Laurence Keen

The small finds are presented within individual Finds Groups in Chapters 4 and 5 above without any discussion of their significance. Here they are discussed by class and use.

Pre-priory Residual Objects

The presence of residual 12th- and 13th-century pottery in Carthusian contexts might suggest that some of the other finds were also residual. Remarkably, this is restricted to a very small number of objects.

The copper-alloy spiral-headed pin (Finds Group 32, 412) has out-turned spirals. It may belong to the class of Type D pins from Southampton, published by Hinton, in which case it would be Saxon in date, but the Southampton pins have inturned spirals (Hinton 1996, 29–30). Hinton notes a pin with out-turned spirals from St Augustine's, Canterbury (Sherlock and Woods 1988, figs 70, 86, citing parallels from Lyveden, Northants and Rievaulx). The Rievaulx pin was found in 1925 between the refectory and the dormitory (Dunning 1965, 62 and fig. 10), and with the lack of any other pre-Conquest material from the site is likely to be medieval in date. A similar pin in known from the Free Grammar School, the Whitefriars, Coventry (Woodfield 1981, figs 5, 40). A further parallel is a pin from South Street, Dorchester, Dorset, thought to be a Continental Late Bronze Age type (Farrar 1966, 111). The dating bias lies with the Rievaulx pin, so the Mount Grace item may well belong to the Carthusian occupation of the site.

The copper-alloy buckle (Finds Group 39, 527) with stylised animal heads has a close parallel with a buckle from Norwich which is dated to the late 11th/early 12th century because of its archaeological context (Margeson 1993, 25, no. 127 and figs 13, 127).

The bone needle from demolition of the south-west cloister range (Finds Group 33, 457) made from a pig fibula has parallels with a similar 11th-/12th-century date range from Norwich (ibid., 13), and with undated examples from Old Sarum, now in the Salisbury and South Wiltshire Museum (MacGregor 2001, 24, nos 14–17).

Table 7.9 Other foodstuffs

Context	Sample	Period	Egg	Mussel	Cockle	Oyster	Seed	Legume
[1941]	1	2a	X	X	X	X	O	O
	2	2a	O	O	X	O	O	O
	3	2a	X	X	X	X	O	O
[1909]	1	2b	O	X	O	O	O	O
[1913]	1	2b	O	X	O	O	X	O
	2	2b	O	O	O	X	O	O
	3	2b	X	X	O	X	O	O
[1925]	2	2b	O	O	O	X	O	O
[1833]	3	2c	O	X	O	X	O	O
	5	2c	O	X	O	O	O	O
	6	2c	O	X	O	O	O	O
	8	2c	X	X	O	O	O	O
	10	2c	O	X	O	X	O	O
	11	2c	X	X	O	X	O	O
	12	2c	O	X	O	X	O	O
	13	2c	O	X	O	O	O	O
	14	2c	X	X	O	O	O	O
	15	2c	X	X	O	O	O	O
	16	2c	X	X	O	X	O	O
	18	2c	X	X	O	X	O	O
	19	2c	O	X	O	O	O	O
	20	2c	X	X	O	X	X	O
	22	2c	X	X	O	O	O	O
[1508]	1	3	X	X	O	X	O	O
	1	3	X	X	O	X	O	O
	3	3	X	X	O	X	O	O
[1037]	1	4	O	O	O	X	X	O
	2	4	O	O	O	O	O	X

Key: X = present; O = absent

Personal Accoutrements, Distilling, Weaving, Books and Book Production

Fortunately, there are two important documents that give an idea of what a Carthusian brother might have had in his cell. The first, in the statutes of 1259, but taken directly from Guigues de Saint-Romain's Customs of the early 12th century, lists the bedding and clothing and then domestic items, objects for writing and eating utensils (Hope 1905, 294–5). The inmate of a cell 'has two needles, thread, scissors, a comb, a razor for the head, a hone or stone, and a strop for sharpening'. For writing, there was to be 'a desk, pens, chalk, two pumices, two inkhorns, a penknife, two razors or scrapers for scraping parchment, a pointer, an awl, a weight, a rule, a ruler for ruling, tables, a writing style'. It was then noted that if a brother was engaged in another craft, 'which very rarely happens among us, for almost all whom we receive, if it can be done, we teach to write, he has suitable tools for his craft'. The utensils for meals and other necessary items included 'two pots, two plates, a third for bread, and a lid for it. And there is a fourth, somewhat bigger, for washing up. Two spoons, a knife for bread, a flagon, a cup, an ewer, a salt, a pan, a towel, tinder for his fire, fuel, a strike-a-light, wood, a chopper. But for works, an axe'.

As Hope has observed (1905, 295), it is interesting to compare this list with the inventory of items brought by Dan Thomas Golwynne from the London charterhouse to Mount Grace, when he moved to Yorkshire in January 1519/20 (see Chapter 2). In addition to bedding and clothes, it itemises (ibid., 296) a little brass mortar with a pestle, two pewter dishes, two saucers, a porringer and a little square dish for butter, a new chafing dish of latten, a brass chafer, a brass pan of a gallon capacity, a little brass skillet with handle and a 'fayer laten sconse'. He lists also seven books in vellum, one with a silver clasp, 'a wrytten boke of papyr with divers storeys of ars moriendi ther yn', a printed breviary, a journal and a printed primer and other printed books, including Aesop's Fables. All of these books must have been intended for the Mount Grace library because Carthusian monks were not permitted to own their own books. The list concludes with a complete weaving frame with courses, 19 pulleys of brass and 19 plumettes of lead, and two iron swords 'to worke with in the frame', and then a double still to make aqua vita 'that ys to say a lymbeke with a serperntyn closyd both yn oon'.

Thomas Golwynne's books need to be considered with the evidence for the books known to have been in the monastery. Brown (1905, 259, 264–5) noted that several of these books can be identified: a copy of *Speculum Spiritualium* in the Minster Library, York; a copy in Latin of Bonaventura's *Meditations on the Life of Christ* in Ripon Minster Library (now BL Add. MS 62450; Watson 1987, 49); a copy of Mount Grace's prior Nicholas Love's English translation of Bonaventura's text in Ripley Castle, the home of the Ingleby family, where it was presumably taken at the Suppression along with the foundation charter and the main gate's lock and key; and another, autograph copy of Love's translation in the British Library (Add. MS 30031). To these may now be added the *Mirror of Christ* in Cambridge (UL Add. 6578), Trinity College, Dublin, 318, British Library, Harley MS 237 and 2373, a copy of the works of St Anselm in Ridley Hall, Cambridge (RHL, E2) and a copy of the works of Margery Kempe (BL Add. MS 61823) (Ker 1964, 132; Watson 1987, 49). Of the three printed books from Mount Grace, two are in the Bodleian Library, Oxford. One is a bible printed in Rouen in 1512 (MS Antiq. d. F 1512/1) (Coppack 1988, 13, exh. 55), the other Thomas Seld's *Fortalicium fidei* printed in Nuremberg in 1494 (Ker 1964, 132).

Nicholas Love's translation of Bonaventura's meditative *Life of Christ* as *The Mirroir of the blessed lyf of Jesu Christ* is indicative of the Carthusians' contribution to the transmission of the spiritual teaching of the 14th century. As Dom David Knowles has observed, the list of surviving manuscripts of the English mystics is a demonstration of this contribution. The London charterhouse had two copies of *The Cloud of Unknowing*, two of Walter Hilton's works and *The Mirror of Simple Souls*. At Sheen there were two works of Richard Rolle and two Hiltons, Beauvale had a Rolle and Mount Grace *The Cloud, The Mirror* and *The Book of Margery Kempe* (Knowles 1961, 198n, 222–3). It is perhaps not surprising to consider that Rolle's origins in Yorkshire, at Thornton-le-dale, near Pickering, and his life as a hermit (Allen 1931, xiv–xvi; Wolters 1972, 11–14), would not have gone unnoticed by the brothers at Mount Grace.

Mount Grace had a special place in Carthusian spirituality and is considered by Knowles above all other charterhouses 'to have absorbed most fully both the old English teaching and the spirit of the Flemish mystics and the *devotio moderna,* with its direct, loving, almost pietistic approach to Jesus, the crucified lover of the soul' (Knowles 1961, 223). In addition to Nicolas Love's presence at Mount Grace and his seminal translation of Bonaventura, Mount Grace, in the late 15th century, housed another brother, whose work as a translator is well documented. Richard Furth, or Methley, was born in 1451/2 and became a Carthusian at 25. He spent much of his free time writing in his cell. A short autobiographical text *Refectorium salutis,* covers, almost day by day, the weeks 6 October to 15 December 1487, and refers to texts 'On the name of Mary and the Sacrament of the Altar', and on the Compassion of the Blessed Virgin. There are also the text *Scola amoris languidi,* a Latin translation of *The Cloud of Unknowing* and a copy in his writing of *The Mirror of Simple Souls.* The manuscripts are in Trinity

College and Pembroke College, Cambridge, and are cited by Knowles, on which this paragraph relies (Knowles 1961, 223–6). The texts contain 'a number of autobiographical passages in which he describes experiences which, if not in the full sense mystical, are at least on the fringe and threshold of the contemplative life' (ibid., 225). Knowles observes that 'We see him praying before the stone statue of Our Lady above the altar in his oratory, feeling the wind that entered through the new unfinished window he caused to be made to let in more light and air, thanking God each morning, as he put on his habit, for the gift of his Carthusian vocation, and bearing witness to the esteem in which the order was held by all' (ibid., 226).

The surviving works of Nicholas Love and Richard Methley illustrate vividly the literary activity of two of the brothers and the spiritual and devotional aspirations that were their cause. Together with Thomas Golwynne's list of items and books brought from the London charterhouse they provide an exceptional picture of the way the contemplative life at Mount Grace was run. There are hardly any other monasteries where such striking insights are available. Except, perhaps, at the Cistercian abbey of Forde, Dorset, where the literary output of Baldwin and John of Forde in the 12th century gives that house a special distinction (Holdsworth 1979; 1989).

Dress

A large number of lace chapes must indicate that the monks wore shoes or boots with laces. Indeed, Thomas Golwynne brought two pairs of shoes with him from London. They derive from many contexts: Finds Group 11, 133; Finds Group 14, 216; Finds Group 18, 292; Finds Group 27, 361; Finds Group 30, 387; Finds Group 31, 405–6; Finds Group 32, 413; Finds Group 33, 450–1; Finds Group 36, 497; Finds Group 37, 519; Finds Group 40, 539–42; Finds Group 43, 559. These are of the standard form and are generally have edge-to-edge seams. They occur on many sites and the literature is extensive: the major sources are Margeson 1993, 22–4; Egan and Pritchard 1991, 281–90; Biddle 1990, 581–9.

Other personal items of dress include, for example, a number of belt plates: Finds Group 11, 132; Finds Group 12, 150–1; Finds Group 13, 184, and buckles: Finds Group 12, 148; Finds Group 13, 182, and strap ends: Finds Group 12, 149. All these are of standard 16th-century form. The belt plates, for example, have very close parallels at Norwich (Margeson 1993, fig. 22 nos 263–6) and Coventry (Woodfield 1981, fig. 5, no. 46). But those that occur in Cell 8 are in contexts which suggest that they were waste, or ready to be recycled into bookbindings.

Palettes, Paint-pot and Inkwell

Mount Grace's exceptionality is advanced still further by the archaeological discovery of objects and material that result from its literary activity, giving outstanding witness of manuscript and book production.

Two oyster shells containing pigments were found, one from Cell 12 (Finds Group 16, 272), the other from Cell 13 (Finds Group 17, 289). That from Cell 12 was a vermilion shade of red, and that from the garden pentice of Cell 13 a green, varying from yellow to blue. Analysis by Dr Justine Bayley showed that the red pigment gave a strong X-ray fluorescence for lead and a weaker one for mercury, the colour being due to cinnabar (mercuric sulphide) and the lead to red lead (lead tetroxide) or white lead (basic lead carbonate). The bluish area of the green pigment showed a strong presence of lead, with copper and tin giving weaker signals. The lead in the green pigment was almost certainly due to white lead, the green being partly due to copper compounds.

It is interesting to note that cinnabar, red and white lead, along with gold and silver leaves, were listed in the treasurer's accounts, among the items purchased for work at Ely (Chapman 1907, II, 73, 83, 136). These purchases, however, were for wall-paintings and the new bell tower. Oyster shells were common and useful containers for pigments, and it is not surprising, therefore, that many have been found in contexts dating from Roman to modern times. Over 20 oyster shells containing pigment have been found on medieval and Tudor sites in Britain (Howard and Park n.d.). With few exceptions it is not certain for what type of decoration the pigments were used. At St Aldates, Oxford, an oyster shell containing pigment was found with pens and other tools associated with book production (Donovan 1991, 13). And an oyster shell found in Boynton parish church, Wiltshire, in 1956–62, was painted on both sides and contained gold, as well as red and blue pigment. It was associated with the tomb of Lady Margaret Nevill, who died in 1338, so the shell is thought to date to *c.*1330 or earlier. The colours are the same shades as the paint on the tomb-chest (Alexander and Binski 1987, 391). There are also two oyster shells with red paint from Hugh Braun's 1939 excavations at Sempringham, Lincolnshire, now in the Grantham Museum, associated with the northern or canons' cloister (Lincs HER, Pointon and Sempringham Parish File/the Clinton Mansion).

The Mount Grace oyster shells are certainly associated with the illumination of books and are, therefore, of importance, because of these associations and the known part the charterhouse played in writing and translation. There is one book, shown on internal evidence to have been produced at Mount Grace (BL Add. MS 37049), which has coloured drawings using red, a pale brown, green and a very pale blue (Coppack 1991, 35, 37).

The lead container from Cell 8 (Finds Group 12, 164) has on its inside what is clearly red paint, and was used, therefore, as a paint pot. Its tapering form and uneven base shows that it can never have been used freestanding. It must have been housed in a desk, and could have been used equally well as an inkwell.

Grinding-stone

The flat-faced stone (Finds Group 16, 271) from Cell 12 was clearly intended for grinding. With the pigment palette from the same cell, it is most likely to have been used for the preparation of pigment. It is interesting to note that the 1259 statutes refer to 'two pumices' for writing, so this is likely to have been one of these.

Illumination

The palettes, however, are only one indication of the book decoration. Two tweezers (Finds Group 14, 205 and Finds Group 16, 266) were no doubt used for handling gold leaf. This is perhaps illustrated further by two tubes (Finds Group 35, 492 and Finds Group 45, 593), which may well have been used to moisten the size on which gold leaf was to be placed, and render it sticky (Johnston 1946, 120 and fig. 102). Once gold leaf had been correctly positioned, a burnisher, of which there is unfortunately no example, or a metal or ivory point, would have been used to work around the letter or shape to be illuminated (ibid., 122). In this regard, the bone ear- and tooth-pick, which would otherwise seem to be a somewhat strange item for a monk to have, emerges as a possible object for using in laying gold leaf: the sharp point would have been ideal. The writing pens considered below, could also have been used to lay size on the forms to be gilded (ibid., 115).

Writing Leads

'First, if you would paint miniatures you must first draw with a leaden style figures, foliage, letters, or whatever you please, on parchment, that is to say, in books: then with a pen you must make the delicate permanent outline of what you have designed' (from Chapter 157 of *The Book of Art of Cennino Cennini*, early 15th century, quoted Johnstone 1949, 131).

There are two writing leads and another possible one, from Cell 10 (Finds Group 77, 219, 220 and 223). They conform generally with those published from Winchester (Biddle 1990, 735–8, 743–6).

Pens

Three tubular sheet copper alloy pens, with split and faceted nib ends were found: two from Cell 10 (Finds Group 14, 207, MG 23, 208, MG 29), and one from Cell 11 (Finds Group 15, 246, MG 713). They are of a rare type and this group is the largest identified to date. Comparable examples are known from Fountains Abbey (Coppack 1988, 16, exh. 80) and from London (Museum of London, A2405, *ex inf.* G. Egan). The provenance of this London find is not known. Another London example, but with a scoop at one end, was found near the north end of Southwark Bridge (Alexander and Binski 1987, 384, no. 424). A rolled Cu sheet object from Norwich looks a very likely candidate (Margeson 1993, fig. 12, no. 123). The pens are of special importance in highlighting the activities of the brothers in Cells 10 and 11 in manuscript production. These pens are presumably representative of the 'writing style' referred to in the 1259 statutes. Although they were clearly capable of being used for writing, their use in gilding, as discussed above, should be remembered.

Book Mounts and Clasps

The many book mounts and clasps from the site are the result of losses and, significantly, from finds in Cell 8, of actual bookbinding.

Archaeological reports rarely consider these items in their original contexts on books. A worthy exception is the discussion of clasps from London (Egan 1998, 277–80), Norwich (Margeson 1993, 74–7) and Winchester (Biddle 1990, 755–8). They are rarely found in any great numbers on monastic sites: those from Saint Frideswide's, Oxford, are noteworthy (Goodall 1990). A recent publication adds considerably to their study (Szirmai 2001, 251–62 for fastenings, 263–71 for furnishings). It would appear that, in general terms, English books did not have clasps that were very different from those bound on the Continent, as can be seen, for instance, on several early 16th-century books of Erasmus in the Erasmus house, Alternach, Brussels. From these it is clear that copper-alloy attachments, sometimes of simple, flat and undecorated form, could often be mounted on leather strips to ensure that book covers were securely held together. So the length of any particular metal clasp cannot be assumed to indicate the thickness of the book to which it was attached. Unfortunately, studies of medieval bookbindings generally concentrate on the leather, often stamped, covers. But publications on bindings are nonetheless extremely useful for showing the design and position of clasps, and of decorative bosses (for instance, Brassington 1891; Gibson 1903; Goldschmidt 1928; Hobson 1929; Oldman 1943 and Needham 1979). For the need for the study of binding structures, too, Sheppard has demonstrated the potential of a thorough study, which is in its infancy (Sheppard 1998). While the leather covering the wooden cover boards is sometimes stamped with decoration, Goldschmidt has noted that 'any effort at artistic ornamentation of the outside, if attempted at all, is confined to the fitting of engraved and embossed metal centre- and corner pieces and clasps' (Goldshmidt 1928, 3). The fore-edge of books was subject to most wear and tear and two clasps were generally used to hold the boards together and, when the book was on a shelf with other books, to act as a handle. But surviving volumes illustrate that clasps were not always used, leather straps or simple ties, held in place by rivets or small riveted strips, being an alternative. As far as the cover-board decoration is concerned, bosses are not always present: decoration with groups of domed or flush rivets, or simple mounts, were suitable adornment.

The finds from Mount Grace include clasps: Finds Group 12, 144, 145 MG 944; 146, 147 MG 1200.4; Finds Group 15, 247 MG 716; Finds Group 17, 284 MG 723; Finds Group 33, 446; bosses or mounts: Finds Group 12, 143 MG 944; Finds Group 14, 215 MG 710; decorative tacks: Finds Group 12, 158 MG 1011, 159 MG 1200.83; and a corner binding strip: Finds Group 12, 142.

Other Bookbinding Objects

There are three objects that are probably associated with bookbinding: from Cell 11 a small punch (Finds Group 15, 245), which would be suitable for decorating leather, and a needle (Finds Group 15, 248), which is robust enough for sewing gatherings together. The third item is a small gouge (Finds Group 45, 586), which is probably a wood-working tool. If so, it may have been used for cutting the grooves in wooden cover boards for the spine heading bands.

Wooden Vessels and Spoon/Scoop

The parts of the wooden vessels (Finds Group 1, 8; Finds Group 2, 24, 25, 26, 27) and the spoon/scoop (Finds Group 2, 28) are all identified by Jacqui Watson as of ash. No vessel is complete and all the fragments are distorted. Only one (Finds Group 1, 8) has a privy mark – a branded M or B. If it is a B, then it probably belonged to Cell B (see the London charterhouse waterworks plan for the lettering system). They are parts of bowls or platters and may be compared with the collection of ten vessels from the Austin Friars, Leicester (Clay 1981, 139 and figs 52: 76–82, 53: 83–5), the 18 from the Priory and Hospital of St Mary Spital, London (Egan 1997, 203–5, figs 47 and 73), some of which have scratched privy marks on the base, and the collection from Southampton (Platt and Coleman-Smith 1975, 228–31), many with scratched marks on the bases. The most thorough surveys of lathe-turned vessels are those for material from London (Egan 1998, 198–210) and of the collection found at Winchester (Biddle 1990, 959–65). A useful comparison with the Mount Grace material are the lathe-turned bowls from Beverley, most of which are of alder (Morris and Evans 1991, 189–90, 193 and fig. 92; Foreman 1992, 174–5 and fig. 121). The techniques of manufacture are usefully described by Morris (1984, ch. 8, cited in Morris and Evans 1991, 189). It should be noted that neither the 1259 statutes nor Thomas Golwynne's list refer to any wooden vessels, though it is likely that they formed a significant part of the original cell contents. Furthermore, it seems highly probable that wooden bowls and platters were most likely to have been made at Mount Grace. They would have been quick and easy to make, and cheaper than pottery.

Cell Effects and Fittings

A few rings may well have been for curtains or drapes (Margeson 1993, 82): Finds Group 10, 99; Finds Group 12, 140–1. The copper alloy candle holder (Finds Group 15, 249) is the only lighting item, except for the lead base (Finds Group 45, 600), which may have been for a candle stick. The shallow lead pan (Finds Group 69, 185) may have been a primitive candle stick.

Weighing and Weights

The almost complete coin balance (Finds Group 16, 265), and the two broken off vertical arms from similar objects (Finds Group 14, 211; Finds Group 18, 291) give a surprising insight into the monks' monetary affairs, which is even more startling with the evidence of pan and coin weights.

A coin balance designed for use with sterlings of the 13th and 14th century, weighing about 14 grains when new, has been published by Mayhew (1975), who has reviewed Continental examples. MacGregor has reconsidered this object and published other balances in the Ashmolean Museum (1985). He concludes that the general features of the balances are that 'the balance-arm proper pivots about a fulcrum, having to one side an elongated tail and to the other a flattened platform or tray to support the coin, the positioning of which is regulated by a raised lip or stop: this horizontal arm is supported by a vertically oriented stirrup or pivot-arm, the two being arranged so that they fold flat'. This is just how the Mount Grace balance would have operated. MacGregor notes, too, that the balance of 14.9 grains achieved by Mayhew's example equates with silver pennies issued between 1279 and 1344, while another, balancing at 11.5 gm, corresponds to reduced issues current between 1351 and 1412. The Mount Grace item balances at 6.82 gm or 105.23 grains, which would have been just under the weight of a noble of 1412–64.

Dolley and Ketteringham (1976) note that, despite punitive measures against improper use of tumbrels (cited in MacGregor 1985, 443), the increasing numbers being recognised suggest that their use was more widespread than has seemed likely. Other provenanced English examples of this copper-alloy type are from Pembroke College Oxford (ibid., 442), Foel Farm Park, Anglesey (Department of Culture, Media and Sport 2002, 79 and fig. 57) and Salisbury (Algar and Egan 2001, 120 no. 6 and fig. 42). Chris Marshall has published a catalogue of all the balances known to him (1987/8). One from London, made of pewter deserves mention (Egan 1998, 328–9).

The excavations produced three coin weights and three pan weights. The coin weights are Finds Group 10, 98; Finds Group 19, 299 and Finds Group 33, 443. These represent the weights for coins then current: 299 a half-noble of 1412–64, 443 an English noble (6s. 8d.) of the same period. The three pan weights are Finds Group 18, 295 MG 785; Finds Group 31, 407 and Finds Group 42, 552.

The surprising thing about this collection is that it would be exceptional for one coin balance to be found. With the extra two pieces the site becomes unique. But this evidence for handling money is not something that one would expect in a Carthusian house. Added to this, the presence of three coin weights and three pan weights, raise the site to one of exceptionality, without parallel in Britain.

Devotion and Essays in Printing

The carved bone human head (503) and the jet bead (504) are most likely to have come from a rosary. Dr Geoff Egan has offered a comparable example: a head of similar size, from Spain, is a rosary bead, or top of a rosary, and shows the head of Christ with a crown of thorns, but with a skull on the opposite side to that of Christ. The Spanish object is dated to the last quarter of the 16th century (de Osma 1916, 29, no. 35).

The broken base of a ceramic statue from Cell 9 (Finds Group 13, 181) has little to determine what the statue might have been. If it were a saint, as seems likely, the one round-headed niche might suggest that it is part of a statue of St Barbara.

Three cells (10, 11 and 14) each produced an example of a lead plaque with the inscription *Iehus nazarenus* in reverse (Finds Group 15, 251; Finds Group 18, 298 7 and not illustrated MG 17 from Cell 10). To say the least these are very curious objects indeed, without parallel. As the inscription, which must be regarded as devotional, is in reverse, the only possible answer to what use they were put is that they must have been intended to produce a positive image. The most likely material would have been cloth or paper, though it would have been possible to produce a positive in clay that would then have been fired. These three items can be considered with the demi-figure of Christ and the indulgence inscription from Cell 10 (fig. 78, Finds Group 14, 227). This object is not in itself a devotional item, but it could have been used for producing a clay mould, which would then have been used to print images on paper. The result would not have been entirely successful. But it would have suited the passing pilgrim, wayfarer trade, as would the paper, cloth or ceramic products from the lead plaques. What is surprising is that the monks in Cells 10, 11 and 14 were all turning out souvenirs for the passers-by.

The grooved stone with letters from Cell 11 (Finds Group 15, 256 MG 711) raises several important questions. With nearly half of the alphabet missing it is difficult to conclude much about the letter-forms being used. What seems clear is that the letter-forms are based on contemporary handwriting and compare well with the typefaces in printed books with which the monks would have been familiar. Comparisons are easy enough to find: the printed books of Caxton (see, for example, the samples of black-letter gothic Bastardas: Dowding 1961, fig. 7).

With the assistance of William Sessions of the Ebor Press, York, and Jim Spriggs of the York Archaeological Trust, experiments were arranged by Keen to establish if the mould could have been used for the casting of metal type. The experiments showed that this was, indeed, the case, that there was sufficient space between the letters for the alphabet to have been cut up and, furthermore, that after smoothing and a little attention, metal letters would have had a suitably flat-top profile for them to have produced satisfactory impressions on paper after inking.

But to what purpose might the type have been put? It seems unlikely that the monks would have even contemplated full-scale book printing. One is surely looking at a much smaller and less exacting enterprise. As it is clear that the charterhouse was giving out letters of confraternity (two examples are cited in Clark-Maxwell 1929, 208 – one for 1515, the other for 1520), and such letters were being printed for other monasteries and gilds (Clark-Maxwell 1924–5, 47 for letters of fraternity issued for the Boston gild in 1519 and 1521). The possibility emerges, therefore, that the monks might have attempted to print their letters of confraternity. The proof, however, must await the discovery of a printed Mount Grace example.

Kitchen Equipment

The 1539 list of kitchen equipment at the Cistercian Dieulacres Abbey (Chapter 8), must be close to the minimum requirements of the Mount Grace kitchen, if the meat utensils were excluded. Some of the items listed have, indeed, been found at Mount Grace. There is part of the rim of a latten vessel (Finds Group 39, 528) and the broken-off leg of a cauldron or skillet (Finds Group 45, 589), both of standard types. From the same kitchen area are an almost complete strainer/skimmer and part of a second (Finds Group 37, 517; Finds Group 45, 590). They are of the standard type (Biddle 1990, no. 3404; Margeson 1993, 118; Christie and Coad 1980, fig. 53 no. 52).

For a kitchen that processed nothing but fish, it is surprising that only one fishhook was found (Finds Group 31, 403). More substantial reminders of fish preparation are the iron cleaver (Finds Group 35, 490) (see Biddle 1990, no. 2543), and the fish-knife (Finds Group 38, 523) (see Cowgill *et al*. 1987, nos 112 and 113).

Building Fittings

For a site where the buildings seem to have been so carefully emptied of their salvageable material, it is surprising that the list of fittings is reasonably large. For ironwork (excluding the large collection of keys from the kitchen area) there is the strap-hinge and pintle (Finds Group 35, 488 and 489) and another strap-hinge (Finds Group 45, 583) (for pintles, see, for example, Biddle 1990, nos 557–651). There is also a substantial numbers of pipe-clips, from Cells 8, 10, 11 and 12, probably associated with lead downpipes on the pentices

(Finds Group 14, 218; Finds Group 17, 286–7). Lead water piping is well represented, considering its worth: Water Tower, 302–4, Finds Group 32, 414, Finds Group 33, 452. Excavation has shown that large parts of the water system remain in the ground unrobbed. The associated filter or sieving leads are rare survivals: Finds Group 33, 453–4.

Metalworking

The pair of tongs (Finds Group 9, 88) appears to be the only find associated with metalworking. There are no other tools from a smith's kit at Mount Grace. So this item may well have been used in the manufacture of bookbindings (see (g) and (h) above). It can be paralleled at Tattershall Thorpe, Lincolnshire, by a similar object of Saxon date without a locking clip. This does not appear to have serrated jaws, like modern pliers, which is unlikely because serrations would cause damage to objects such as a sheet of beaten copper alloy or a length of wire being held during working (Hinton 2000, 24 and fig. 15.5, 104). Leahy republishes the Tattershall Thorpe tongs alongside another pair from Flixborough, Lincolnshire – these have a locking clip – and cites other Saxon examples from Sibertswold, Kent, Shakenoak, Oxfordshire, and Ramsbury, Wiltshire (Leahy 2003, 117 and fig. 58). The Flixborough tongs were thought to be used for small items of metalworking during filing or forging (Coatsworth and Pinder 2002, 50–3). They are also illustrated by the excavator (Loveluck 2001, fig. 5.13.D). It is clear that such things were current throughout the medieval period and later. Theophilus describes large and small pincers and medium pincers used in the filing of objects, with a clip with perforations into which a thin handle is inserted to lock the pincers in position and so hold securely small objects being filed (Dodwell 1961, 68–9). Brian Read has kindly brought to the writer's attention a large pair of tongs with a locking clip, shown being used to hold a horseshoe in a 1568 woodcut of a smithy published in Nuremburg (Sachs 1973, no page no.)

Summary

The significance of the finds from Mount Grace is that they can be related to individual monks, living in their own cells. It is possible, therefore, to relate these finds to particular craft activity. With the exception of the monk in Cell 9, all of the others in Cells 8 to 14 were engaged either in writing, illuminating, making trinkets for wayfarers or, as for the monk in Cell 8, bookbinding. The monk in Cell 8 was probably engaged in manuscript production, too, if the paint pot (164) is evidence, just as the monk in Cell 11 seems to have been doing some bookbinding. These activities are not a surprise for a monastery. What is a revelation is the large quantity of the material, its relationship with the individual monks and, indeed, with the buildings. It must be a unique occurrence to discover that the reduction of the walls beneath the windows on the ground floor of Cell 10 was due, no doubt, to that monk's wish to have his writing and illuminating, for the finds show that this is what he was doing, carried out with more daylight.

The evidence for producing devotional items for pilgrims and travellers appears at first sight to be inexplicable. But when it is shown that the guest accommodation at Mount Grace was exceptional in the scale and form that it took, probably due to its location on the major north–south road, this activity is put into perspective. But if the evidence has been read correctly, at least three monks were engaged in this souvenir production. Whether or not the souvenir and devotional trinket sales produced the coinage that was clearly being weighed and tested, the scale of this coin handling, either as individuals or as the result of commerce, is clear from the finds.

It is these several different strands of evidence that make the Mount Grace material so interesting on the national and international stage.

7.7 *Architectural Detail*

by Jackie Hall and Glyn Coppack

Excavation and clearance at Mount Grace since 1896 has produced one of the most comprehensive collections of architectural detail from any monastic house in England, and one of particular importance for its limited time span. With the exception of a handful of recorded stones from Beauvale (Hill and Gill 1908, pl. 4), the rather disappointing collection from Coventry (Soden 1995, 122–6 and figs 32–4) and a small pile of worked stone still lying on the site at Axholme, it is the only significant collection of architectural detail from any Carthusian house in Britain. Most significantly, the items can in most cases be identified to individual buildings within the charterhouse.

The Methodology of Study

The Mount Grace architectural collection was initially studied by Jackie Hall in 1989–90 and a fully integrated catalogue was prepared for deposition in the English Heritage archaeology store at Helmsley, together with the greater part of the collection. Architectural fragments came from four separate sources on site: a substantial dump of material resulting from both Hope's excavation and Ministry of Works clearance; a collection of material that had been selected for display in the site custodian's office (and which probably came from the dumped material); a collection of stones recovered in excavation by Keen between 1968 and 1972; and a smaller collection recovered between 1985 and 1991 by Coppack. Keen's material had been stored in the open and many stones had lost their labels by 1989 (a persistent problem with stone collections), but it was possible to re-identify almost every piece.

Every stone was examined, identified by type and recorded on a standard English Heritage stone record form. Approximately 80% of the collection was photographed and 75% drawn at a scale of 1:5. Individual moulding templates were also recorded at actual size to determine any degree of variation. Repeat examples of window mullion from the unprovenanced collection were reburied within the eastern room of the south-west cloister range after recording; all other material was removed to a secure store or displayed on site. Window elements were separated into groups defined by template profile, which enabled the definition of three specific phases of construction. The jamb profiles of individual surviving windows were then used to assign individual window elements to a specific period of construction. Individual windows could in part be identified, and paper reconstruction was initially undertaken by Jackie Hall. As no major window survives with its tracery at Mount Grace this provided a major addition to the architectural evidence from the site and enabled the context of architectural development to be identified (see Chapter 6).

Some identifications had been made by Hope, but during the analysis of the architectural collection it became apparent that the elements he recorded, with drawings made by Ambrose Poynter in 1905, were somewhat generic, rather than based on individual pieces that could still be identified. Hope had concentrated on gable crosses and chimneys from the cells of the east and north ranges of the great cloister (1905, figs 7–9) and appears to have missed the degree of variation that is apparent within the unprovenanced collection. His reconstruction of the east cloister alley (1905, fig. 10), again drawn by Ambrose Poynter, is, however, drawn accurately from individual stones, four of which can still be identified. Because of the inadequacy of the original record it was decided to repeat the exercise and produce accurate reconstructions from identifiable elements, specifically an earlier cloister alley, together with elements from the water tower that Hope had removed from his excavation at the centre of the great cloister. This process was greatly aided by the recovery of additional elements by Keen from destruction deposits on the west side of the great cloister, which had not been available to Hope. The reconstruction of these elements was undertaken by Glyn Coppack and Jackie Hall, using additional material that had been recovered by Keen from the east range of the great cloister.

Material derived from the excavation of individual buildings has been presented with the discussion of the finds groups in Chapters 4 and 5 above, and the accurate recording of find-spots enabled the identification of stones that had fallen from adjacent buildings. The presence of stones that had clearly come from another source, such as elements of the great cloister arcade of Period Two or the chimney base from the later prior's cell, indicated the process of demolition and sorting of reusable material, which had not been realised at the time of excavation, but was capable of reconstruction. The whole exercise identified the importance and potential of loose material that has lost its archaeological context in providing the fine detail that allows an understanding of the development of individual buildings.

Unlocated Architectural Fragments (see Figures 7.4–7.8)

As far as possible, architectural fragments from the unprovenanced collection were related either to individual buildings, such as the church, or to types of building, such as the

THE CULTURAL COLLECTIONS

great cloister cells. This material is presented in Chapter 6. Excavated material from both the great cloister and the inner court, along with the elements of Hope's water tower, are discussed in the excavation contexts in Chapters 4 and 5. A small part of the unprovenanced collection is not possible to locate on site but is, nevertheless, still important for the understanding of the site. That is presented here.

168. Sandstone paving slab (see Figure 7.4) measuring 0.684 m by 0.485 m and 0.110 m thick, with tracing lines for the laying out of an 'early' Perpendicular window or more probably screenwork that is closely related to the window tracery from the nave of the Period One church (see Figure 6.15). In particular, it shows two panels of tracery separated by a plain band 50 mm wide; each panel has a lower tier of lights with ogee heads, an intermediate tier of four lights with trefoil heads below a transom and an upper tier of four lights again with trefoiled heads. The upper tier on the right side of the composition is confused by a series of alterations indicating different forms of tracery; the left side is worn down and no evidence of alteration is apparent there. If the laying out is at actual size, this is likely to be a design for an altar frontal or retable. The slab has been cut for use as a paving stone. Although originally identified by Roy Gilyard-Beer, its find-spot is not recorded. Its upper surface, however, has a thick deposit of calcite sealing the design, which suggests a connection with the piped water supply.

169. Corbel with a small undecorated shield cut on the face. It is cut down from a larger corbel taken from the wall of the great cloister, identical to those shown in Figure 6.23. It is too small to have been reused in the cloister.

170. Part of the lintel of a square-headed door with rounded corners below a square and plain hood-mould. The spandrels have blind triangular sinkings. This detail is not recorded anywhere in the standing ruins.

171. Part of the two-centred head of a tap niche, similar to the Period Three

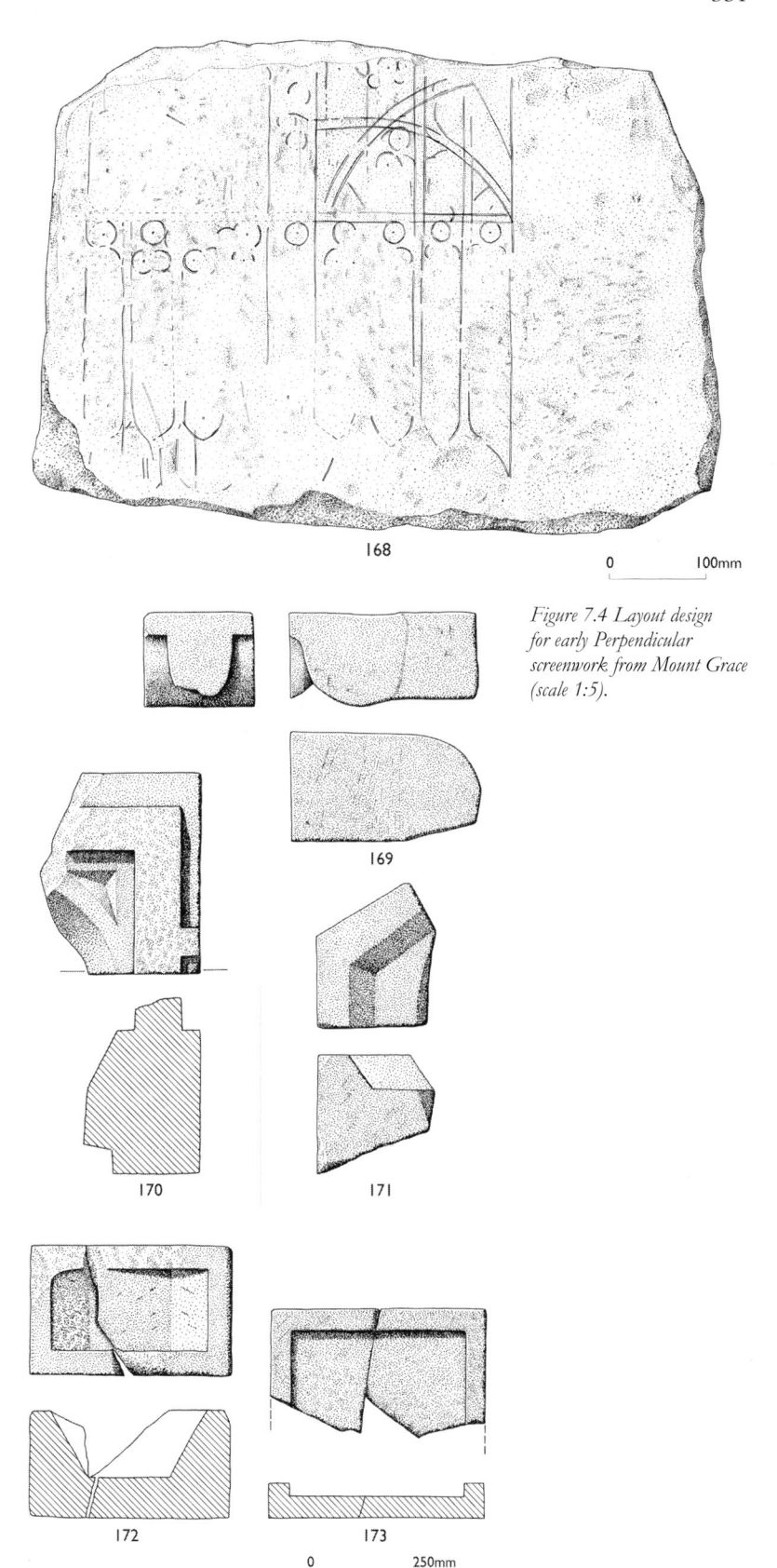

Figure 7.4 Layout design for early Perpendicular screenwork from Mount Grace (scale 1:5).

Figure 7.5 Unlocated architectural detail (1:10).

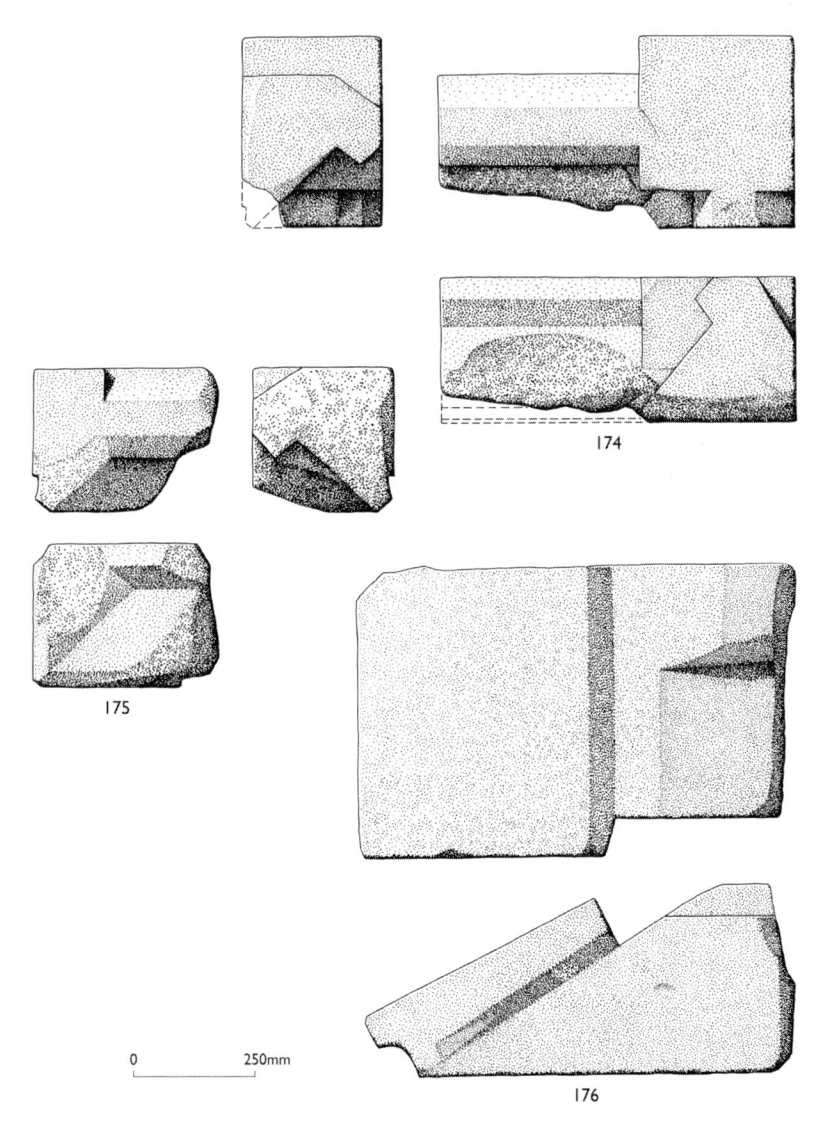

Figure 7.6 Unlocated architectural detail (1:10).

example from Cell 8, but from an unrecorded location.

172. Small stone water tank, probably from a tap niche.
173. Shallow stone 'tray' with upstands of 25 mm, probably from the floor below a tap niche.
174 and 175. Two sections from a parapet coping similar to that of Period One or Two on the south-west cloister range (see Figure 5.20, 45), and of a similar scale, but with an angular rather than a rounded profile. Stone 174 marks an outward return; stone 175 is cut for the profile of the parapet to rise vertically. Perhaps associated with one or both of the Period Three burial chapels.
176. Kneeler from the springing of a cell gable; the chamfer on the bottom of its coping has a long arrow stop. This stone was published by Hope (1905, fig. 6) and provenanced to an unidentified great cloister cell.
177. Wall coping cut for the north-east corner of the precinct wall in the garden of Cell 5, and matching the profile of the upper course of the compound coping of the north precinct wall.
178. Section of wall coping matching stone 177, from either the east or the north precinct wall.
179. Section of coping finished with a roll moulding from an unknown location.
180. Section of wall coping cut to two different pitches, apparently from a parapet wall.
181. Section of the lowest course of a compound wall coping with a prominent semicircular drip cut into the bottom bed that indicates the overhang.
182. Section of the lowest course of a compound wall coping with a hollow chamfered nosing.
183. Section of the lowest course of a compound wall coping with a plain chamfered nosing.

7.8 Window Glass

by Glyn Coppack

Most of the window glass from excavation at Mount Grace comprised fragmentary quarries of pale green glass typically diamond-shaped and 1.5–2.0 mm thick. The majority was recovered from the garden pentice of Cell 8 (see Chapter 4), but it appears to have been used generally in the monks' cells and the cloister alleys.

Four groups of decorated window glass were recovered: three in excavation and one in clearance by the Ministry of Works, all from demolition contexts. The quantity was small and, as all fragments were derived from borders or tabernacle work, the indication is that the glass had been sorted and some sold. All had been broken out of the cames and very little lead came was recovered anywhere on site. The process of breaking up glass windows is well recorded at Rievaulx Abbey in 1538–9, where 'the glasse was to be sortyd into iij partes: one, the fairest to be sortyd; the second sort to be sold; the iij sort to be

THE CULTURAL COLLECTIONS

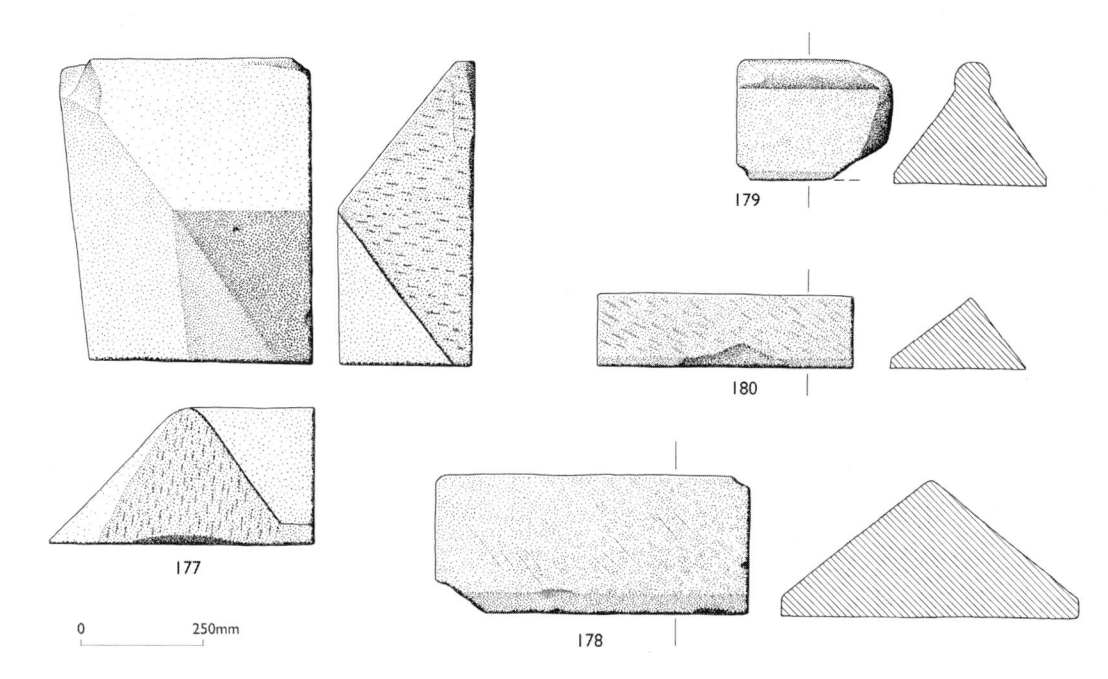

Figure 7.7 Unlocated architectural detail (1:10).

taken out of the lede and the lede molten' (Coppack 1986, 108). It would appear that the same process was followed at Mount Grace, and what remained was glass of the third sort, discarded close to where the lead was scrapped and not necessarily indicating material from a particular window.

The majority of the glass found in clearance work is clear pale green metal, and of two distinct qualities: one has remained almost as deposited, but the other is heavily devitrified and now totally opaque. Some 90% of the glass was 2.5–3.0 mm thick, the remainder being much thinner, at 1.5–2.0 mm thick. None of this latter material had devitified: it was all clear, and had bands of yellow or gold flashed onto its inner surface. The thicker glass had grozed edges, but the thin metal appears to have been cut.

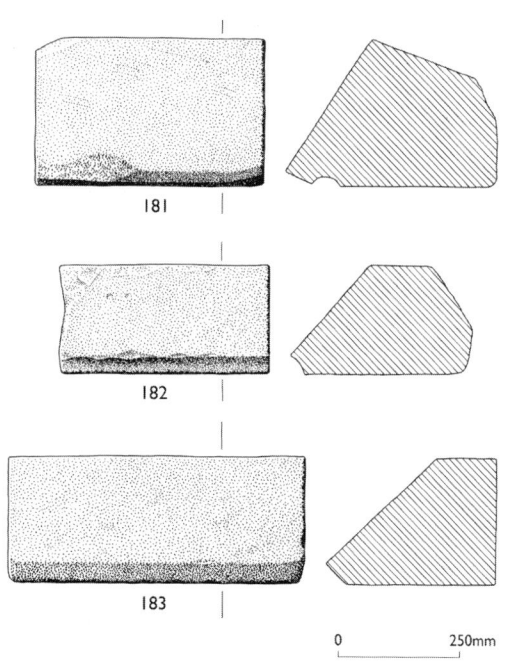

Figure 7.8 Unlocated architectural detail (1:10).

Group 1 (see Figure 7.9)
From the great cloister ranges.

1. Fragment of a tabernacle and border design. Cell 14 demolition.
2. Fragment of border. Cell 14 demolition.
3. Fragment of border with scale decoration. Cell 14 demolition.
4. Fragment of border, matching 2. Prison, demolition.
5. Lower part of a diamond-shaped quarry with painted borders and the lower part of a leaf stem. Prison, demolition.
6. Fragment of a diamond-shaped quarry with the lower part of a leaf stem. Prison demolition.

Group 2 (see Figure 7.9)
From the demolition of the south-west cloister range, contexts [504], [531], [938] and [1039].

7. Fragment of border [938].
8. Fragment of border [531].
9. Fragment of a quarry with leaf

354

MOUNT GRACE PRIORY

Figure 7.9 Window glass from Mount Grace, Groups 1–4 (1:2).

THE CULTURAL COLLECTIONS

10. Fragment of a quarry with leaf decoration [504].
11. Fragment of a border with leaf decoration [504].
12. Fragment of a quarry with leaf decoration [531].
13. Fragment of a border with an inscription in black letter reading ?{I}HS [1039].

Group 3 (see Figure 7.9)
From the latrine pit on the east side of the guest-house range, contexts [1443], [1455] and [1456].

14. Fragment of a border with leaf decoration [1443].
15. Fragment of a border with leaf decoration [1456].
16. Fragment of a border with a tall-stemmed double flower [1443].
17. Fragment of a quarry with a composite flower head. The centres of the flower heads are flashed yellow. Thin glass [1456].
18. Fragment of a quarry with the edge of a tabernacle [1455].
19. Section of border with arcading; the central and right-hand niches are flashed yellow. Thin glass [1443].
20. Fragment of a quarry with border detail, with the first letter, M, of an inscription [1443].
21. Fragment of a quarry with border detail, with part of an unintelligible inscription [1443].
22. Fragment of a quarry with border detail, with the letter, M, part of an inscription [1443].

Group 4 (see Figures 7.9 and 7.10)
Found in clearance below the west window of the priory church, but not necessarily derived from there. More than 500 quarries or part quarries were recovered; most were badly devitrified and had lost any evidence of decoration. Fewer than 30 pieces remained recognisable and all identifiable material has been drawn.

23. Whole quarry from a border.
24. Whole quarry from a border.
25. Fragment of border.

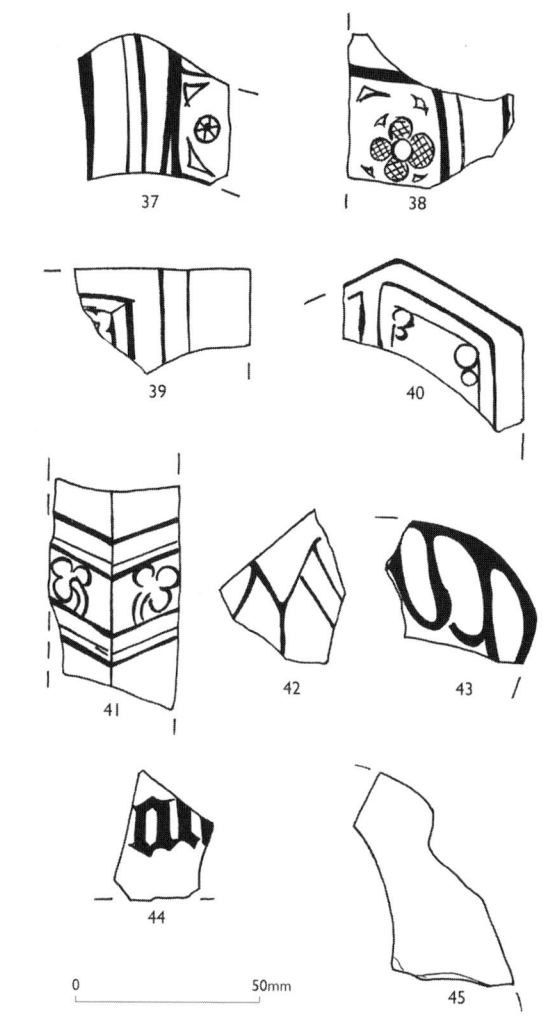

Figure 7.10 Window glass from Mount Grace, Group 4 continued (1:2).

26. Fragment of border.
27. Fragment of border and tabernacle, the latter with part of a cross-hatched window.
28. Fragment from a tabernacle with parts of two cross-hatched windows.
29. Fragment from a tabernacle with the upper part of a cross-hatched window.
30. Part of a border quarry with diaper decoration, where alternate squares have quatrefoil leaf decoration.
31. Part of a border quarry with a quatrefoil and two circles in a broad band of enamel.
32. Fragment of border.
33. Fragment of a border with leaf decoration.
34. Fragment of a border with leaf decoration.

35. Fragment of a border with leaf decoration.
36. Fragment of a border with leaf decoration.
37. Fragment of tabernacle work.
38. Fragment of tabernacle work.
39. Fragment of tabernacle work.
40. Fragment of tabernacle work.
41. Part of a tabernacle with stemmed trefoil decoration.
42. Fragment of ?tabernacle.
43. ? part of a figure panel.
44. Part of a panel with a fragmentary black letter inscription.
45. Fragment of deep blue glass with no over-paint. ?Drapery or background for a figure.

In no instance is it safe to assume that the painted glass recovered comes either from the location in which it was found or indeed from individual windows. The discard pattern implies the organised and careful recovery of saleable glass and the recovery of lead cames. Most, if not all, of the glass probably came originally from the church, and it is closely comparable with glass recovered from the church at Coventry (Soden 1995, 119–20 and fig. 30), of like 15th-century date. There is nothing particularly Carthusian about it, and closely comparable glass has been recovered in a Cistercian context at both Fountains and Rievaulx (now held in the English Heritage archaeology store at Helmsley). Particular windows may well have been the gifts of individuals, although only one such gift is recorded at Mount Grace: in 1509 Alison Clark bequeathed 10s. 'to the beilding of a glasse window' (York D & C Wills, ii, ff. 82r–83v).

Chapter 8: The Significance of the Mount Grace Project

8.1 Mount Grace Priory and its Significance

The extensive nature of the archaeological and architectural research made possible at Mount Grace by the Department of the Environment and by English Heritage, coupled with the good survival of historic fabric and earthworks, places the house among the most thoroughly researched monastic sites in Europe. It is no accident that it was one of the sites chosen by Sir William St John Hope in his attempt to define the medieval monastic plan, for it was the best preserved of the English charterhouses, perhaps the Carthusian equivalent of the Cistercian Fountains Abbey or Benedictine Canterbury cathedral priory. The second house of its order in England, according to Dom David Knowles' assessment, it was similar in scale and endowment to the preponderance of European charterhouses established before the end of the 15th century. Architecturally, it is comparable with the houses of its own order and with those of other orders, both nationally and across Europe.

The Village of Bordelbi

The village of *Bordelbi*, which occupied the site of Mount Grace Priory before the house's foundation, was held jointly at Domesday by the king, Roger de Poitou and Robert de Bruis, each with a holding of two carrucates to the geld (Williams and Martin 2002, 792, 854 and 855). The king also held Morton and East Harlsey (ibid., 792), and his lands were tenanted by Madalgrim. Roger of Poitou's man in *Bordelbi* was Svartkollr (ibid., 854). By the second quarter of the 12th century the vills of *Bordelbi* and Morton were in the possession of Robert de Lascelles, who granted the common pasture and the land that became Morton Grange to Rievaulx Abbey around 1150 (see Chapter 2). The vill of *Bordelbi* was held until 1398 by Thomas de Ingleby, who was resident in 1397/8, when he was licensed to hear mass in the chapel of his manor there (Brown 1905, 259). The extent of the manor (which enclosed Morton Grange) can be reconstructed from Gisborough Priory's 1509 lease of the chapelry of *Bordelbi* to Mount Grace (see Chapter 3).

Until the excavations reported here the precise location of the village of *Bordelbi* was unknown and the date of its desertion uncertain. Excavation below the south-west cloister range and adjacent cloister alley, however, located positive evidence for pre-monastic settlement on the terraces that were occupied by the great cloister and inner court. Although the evidence is fragmentary, it was possible to define ditches and earth-fast timber buildings dating from the early 12th century to the end of the 13th century, and a comparison of the pottery from these early features with pottery groups from the cells of the great cloister demonstrated the extent of the settlement (see Figure 8.1). Crucial to the understanding of the settlement is the existence of a large pond at the centre of the great cloister terrace, probably fed by the southernmost stream of the central catchment (see Figure 6.47). Settlement was possible only on the margins of the upper terrace, as is clearly demonstrated by 12th- and 13th-century pottery found within the enclosures of Cells 2, 4 and 6 on the east side of the cloister and Cells 10–14 on the west side. It is significant that Cell

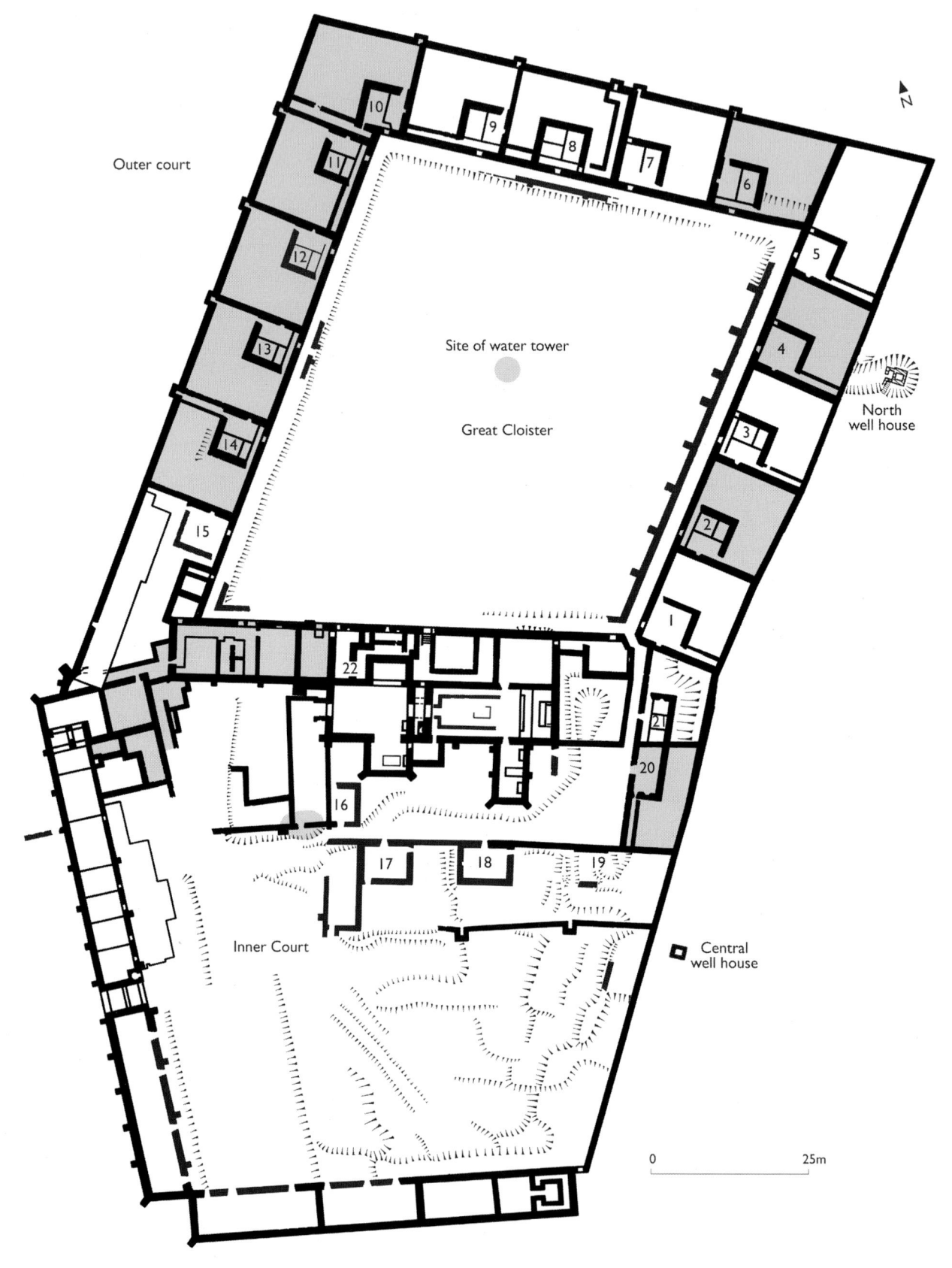

Figure 8.1 The extent of the village of Bordelby that preceded the priory. The shaded areas represent those parts of the site that have produced pottery from the 12th to late 13th century.

8, which was totally excavated to the surface of the terrace, produced no early pottery at all. That this area had no evidence of occupation before the foundation of the charterhouse is clear from the environmental evidence, which suggests unmanaged reed-swamp and meadow or rough open ground, with indications of the presence of herbivores (see Chapter 7). That pre-monastic settlement existed on the slightly lower terrace of the inner court was demonstrated by early pottery from Cell 20 and underneath the kitchen and its offices. Only a lack of modern excavation and the failure to collect finds from Ministry of Works clearance in the inner court limits our knowledge of the likely extent of settlement there.

Earthwork survey on the lower terrace (see Chapter 3) identified a moat and a series of fishponds (see Figure 3.1). The moat has been modified and shows evidence of use as a gardening area in the post-medieval period. There is a reasonable chance that the fishponds, F on Figure 3.1, which appear to have gone out of use before the suppression of the charterhouse, are pre-monastic, and relate to the Ingleby manor at *Bordelbi*. The moat itself contains evidence of buildings that pre-date the gardening activity, and in construction appears to pre-date the monastic mill and the closes associated with it. It may, indeed, have been the site of the Ingleby manor house, which was then retained within the outer court of the new charterhouse. It is also a possible location for *le* inne, an early 16th-century building known only from the lease of the site to Sir James Strangways in 1540 (TNA Pat. R. 32 Henry VIII, pt iv, m.45). Only excavation would confirm this, but the likelihood is that the village of *Bordelbi* occupied both major terraces on which the priory stood and was bounded to the south by Bordelby Field and, on the hillside to the east, by Bordelby Wood, both located by the 1509 lease (see Chapter 3).

The Planning and Development of the Monastery

The development of Carthusian monasteries is less well understood than that of other orders for two reasons: the apparent simplicity of Carthusian architecture and a distinct lack of archaeological research, both in England and further afield. Although substantial plans have been recovered by excavation at Witham, Hinton, Beauvale, London and Coventry, no attempt has yet been made to analyse the planning of these sites or, with the exception of Coventry, to identify the sequence of building or recover extensive cultural collections.

Sir William St John Hope had great difficulty in phasing the standing ruins at Mount Grace and so was unable to describe the development of the house with any degree of conviction (Hope 1905, *passim*). He had used excavation alone to recover the ground plan and his study of the standing fabric was limited by the surviving identifiable architectural detail. He discerned only three periods of building – *c.*1400, 1420, and 1450 and later – and failed to consider the likelihood of timber buildings in any phase. By the standard of his time, however, his analysis was good and it has remained the classic interpretation of a Carthusian charterhouse in England, informing all subsequent research, including that published here.

The key to understanding the development and planning of Mount Grace is the levelling of the three great terraces on which the charterhouse was built and the placement of its earliest stone buildings. Excavation in the great cloister and particularly around Cell 8 has demonstrated that the terraces are largely natural features, resulting from a massive post-glacial landslip. It was this unplanned form that dictated the slightly irregular plan of the house. The great cloister terrace (the only one examined archaeologically) was levelled and extended upon the foundation of the monastery, however, indicating that the extent of the great cloister had already been planned (see Figure 8.2). Critical to the understanding of how the first stone buildings were laid out is the east wall of the south-west cloister range where it abuts the north-west corner of the church. The church was built first, on the lower of the two upper terraces, and might possibly have been complete in time for the foundation in 1398. Although there is evidence of earlier medieval settlement in this area in the form of the documented village of *Bordelbi*, this part of the settlement had been deserted by the end of the 13th century if the pottery evidence is to be believed, and the church was built on a greenfield site on the natural surface of the terrace. Only after the church was raised to a substantial height was the south-west cloister range built, and with it the south wall of the great cloister, which was to retain the

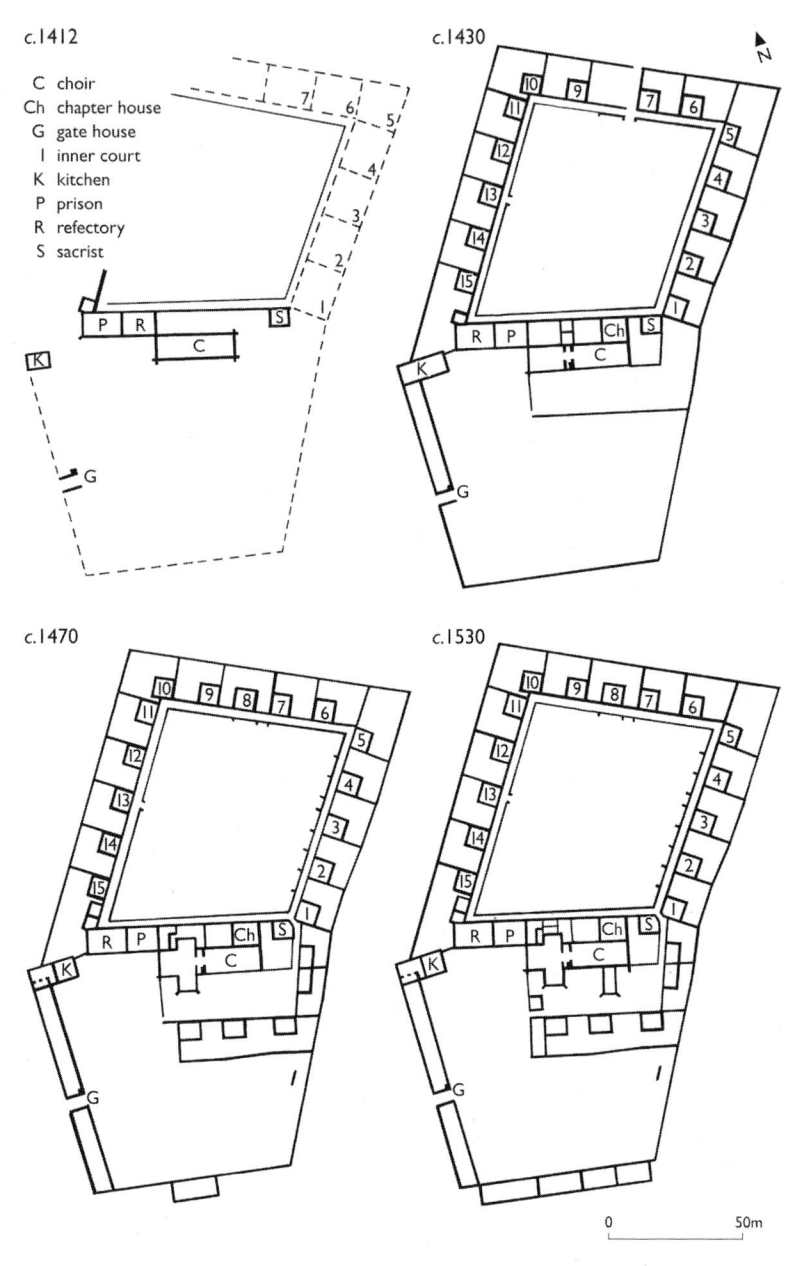

Figure 8.2 The development of Mount Grace Priory: c.1412; c.1430; c.1470; c.1530.

upper terrace, relevelled after the church was built. This sequence of events is convincingly supported by the raising of the door cill of the sacrist's cell from the level of the unmodified terrace to the level of the great cloister terrace at some point after the raising of the south cloister wall. The first offices to be provided in the south range of the great cloister were the most important buildings after the church: a detached kitchen, the convent prison, the prior's cell, the refectory and the sacrist's cell, but not the chapter house, unless this began its life as a timber building.

The relevelling of the natural surface of the great cloister after the building of the south range included the provision of substantial drains that tapped a series of springs within the terrace, both draining the site and providing sewers that would later serve the earliest stone cells. The precise location of these drains in relation to the stone buildings of the monastery suggests that the final layout had already been planned and that the progress of building was dependent on only two factors: the availability of patronage and the growth of the community. The uncertainty of the years following the death of Thomas de Holand explains the delay in building permanent cells, but it is hardly surprising that temporary accommodation was provided from the first. Other orders had done precisely the same thing, replacing timber buildings as the house achieved economic stability. This is well known from Cistercian sites in the 12th century, the process being clearly documented at Meaux (Fergusson 1983, 133) and Fountains (Walbran 1862, 47) and identified in excavation at Fountains (Gilyard-Beer and Coppack 1986, 151–4) and Sawley (Coppack *et al.* 2002, 30–45 and 101–5). It has also been seen in a 12th-century Augustinian context at Norton (Greene 1989, 73–9) and in a 13th-century context at the Augustinian friary at Leicester (Mellor and Pearce 1981, 9–10 and 14) and the Dominican friary in Beverley (Forman 1996, 20–31 and 234–9). In some cases, timber or other vernacular materials such as clay or cob were used for permanent cloister buildings, as at the Augustinian canonesses' house of Brewood in Shropshire (Gilyard-Beer 1987, 34), the Benedictine nunnery of Wilberfoss in East Yorkshire (Brown 1887, 204–6) and the Cistercian nunnery at Torksey in Lincolnshire (Maurice Barley, pers. comm.). Timber was used for the first buildings at the Grande Chartreuse and at Witham (below), and it should hardly come as a surprise that it was used for temporary provision at Mount Grace even in the first years of the 15th century. Indeed, it is likely – although as yet unexamined by excavation – that the inner court at Mount Grace, which occupied the lower terrace to the south of the church, was also laid out in timber and provided with some sort of enclosure; otherwise, there seems little point in the provision of a two-storey stone gatehouse at the centre of its west side at this early date.

The permanent form of the charterhouse became apparent only in the 1420s, the result of an apparent refoundation by Thomas Beaufort, whose stated intention was to increase the size of the community by a further five monks (see Figure 8.2). The first manifestation of this was the extension and remodelling of the church (discussed below) and the building of a permanent chapter house. Fourteen permanent cells were also built, not in a single campaign but as required. The central cell of the north range was obviously planned but not at first built, its site providing instead a convenient entrance to the great cloister for the builders. It was only now that a permanent enclosure, a wall some 4 m high, was provided for the great cloister and inner court. This was also the time that the water supply was engineered and work began on the permanent cloister alleys. In the inner court the only masonry building to be built in Period Two was the substantial guest-house range and its kitchen cross-wing, to the north of the earlier gatehouse. Other buildings there were initially of timber, particularly the range to the south of the gatehouse and at least three lay brothers' cells. Other buildings are suspected but have yet to be sought by excavation. At this point the community could have housed 17 monks, with the procurator accommodated at the north end of the guest-house range.

It was not until the third quarter of the 15th century that the monastery achieved the conversion of its remaining temporary buildings to stone, with the building of Cell 8 and five permanent lay brothers' cells to the east and south of the church in the inner court (see Figure 8.2). This was the result of additional patronage – on this occasion, generous grants from Edward IV – and the continued expansion of the community. At this time the great cloister was fully developed and the building of an additional cell to the north of the church (Cell 22) is the first obvious sign that the original plan had been inadequate. Another indication can be seen in the inner court, where the south range was moved from inside to outside the precinct wall, giving more working space to that semi-public area, probably to replace the additional space taken up by the lay brothers' permanent accommodation. By the 1480s the monastery could have housed 19 monks and five lay brothers. The story of the early 16th century is one of well-documented expansion and the continued provision of permanent buildings, as the charterhouse matured in what was obviously a period of reasonable prosperity (see Figure 8.2). These indications that the monastery was continuing to grow, even as support for other orders was rapidly falling away, demonstrated the continued popularity of the Carthusians.

To what extent Mount Grace is typical of Carthusian monasteries remains uncertain, however, because no other medieval charterhouse in England has been studied so intensely. Comparison with other sites, where the evidence exists, shows a remarkable similarity of planning, regardless of date, something hardly surprising in an order that has remained true to its earliest principles. It is only in the detail that differences can be seen – the result of developing ideas, innovative architecture, patronal interference or local custom. Common factors abound: the small-scale planning of churches and their separation from the cloister by a small court; the provision of common offices in the cloister range closest to the church; the planning and layout of the great cloister; and the engineering of a sophisticated clean water supply and foul drainage. How Mount Grace compares with other houses is examined in detail below.

The Development of the Church

Of the ten medieval Carthusian churches built in England, five retain standing fabric: Hinton, Beauvale, London, Coventry and Mount Grace. Excavation has recovered extensive ground plans of these buildings and enabled at least rudimentary development plans to be drawn up. In addition, a partial ground plan has been created of the church at Witham, which was incorporated within the north wing of a house built on the site by William Talman and James Gibbs in 1717 and demolished in 1762 (Campbell 1771, pl. 91). Taken as a group, they show a consistency in the planning of the initial church of each house that was not affected by date or wealth. There was, however, a difference in the way that churches of houses established after the middle of the 14th century developed: that is, between those houses where a *correrie* and church were provided for the lay brothers on a separate site and those where the lay brothers were housed within the same enclosure. Among the later churches there was also a remarkable consistency. Initially, each house had a simple church of either four or five bays, comprising a nave used by the lay brothers, a choir used by the monks – these separated at London and Mount Grace by an identifiable cross-passage defined by timber screens – and a small presbytery to the east of the monks' choir.

All Carthusian churches were small and, at least in England, unaisled. Regardless of date, or the absence or presence of lay brothers, they were all remarkably consistent in scale and planning, as is apparent from Table 8.1. The church at Witham (see Figure 8.3) was described by J. Strachey in an undated account probably of the 1720s or 1730s (*ex inf.* R. Wilson North):

> The house is mostly new built & forms a quadrangle but the Old Dark Vaulted Carthusian Chapell is on the N side & now [a] Convenient Cellar, but the Pillars and Niches for Images and Holy Water plainly discover what it hath been but Instead of it there is a more light and Beautiful Chapell built which forms the south Side of the Quadrangle.

The chapel, which can be identified on Colen Campbell's plan of the piano nobile, even though it shows only the upper parts, had walls some 1.2 m thick, which can be traced on its north, east and south sides. Its west end was truncated by the facade of the 1717 house. Its width is virtually the same as the later church at Hinton and, assuming that there was a family resemblance between these two churches, the three eastern bays of a vaulted five-bay church had survived in recognisable form within the house as late as the 1760s, the two westernmost bays having been demolished upon the house's construction. The Witham church lay some 49 m north of the north cloister alley identified by the excavation of Barlow and Reid in the 1960s (Wilson-North 1996). The 'church' identified in that excavation (Burrow and Burrow 1990) was in fact the south wing of the 1717 house, and its 'south transept' the 18th-century chapel.

The church at Hinton (see Figure 8.4) was an unaisled rectangle of five vaulted bays; a part of its south wall survives to the springing of its paired lancet windows. It dates to the mid-13th century and appears not to have been modified. It was separated from the north alley of the great cloister by a small court and the chapter house, which was separated from the church by a sacristy, in the English rather than the Continental style (Gilyard-Beer 1958, 43).

The greater part of the north and south walls of the church at Beauvale survive and its partial excavation in 1908 recovered the plan of its demolished eastern end (see Figure 8.5). The excavators' plan does not accord with their text, but there are indications that the plan was produced after the text was completed and it may show features uncovered too late to be included in the text. At a distance of 19.80 m from the inner face of the surviving west wall the excavators recorded the inner face of what can only be the east wall of the original church. This first phase was separated from the east alley of the cloister by a small court and was entered by opposed doors at the west end of the north and south walls. The lesser or little

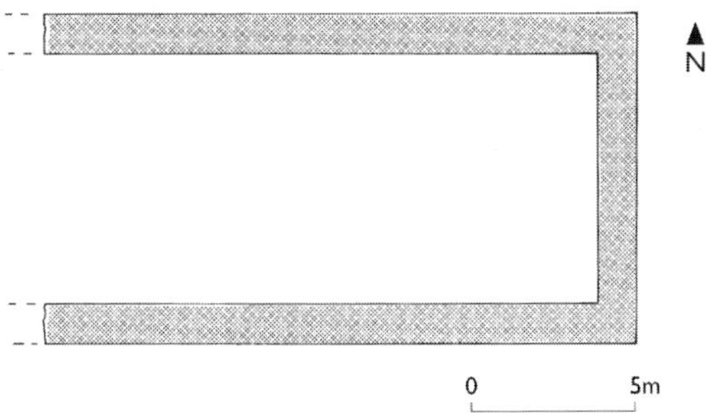

Figure 8.3 The church at Witham (from Campbell 1771).

Table 8.1 Dimensions of first-phase Carthusian churches

Charterhouse	Date	Length (m)	Width (m)	Bays
Witham	c.1186	>17.30	7.65	>3
Hinton	c.1227	28.03	7.93	5
Beauvale	1344	19.80	8.4045	?4
Coventry	c.1385	26.50	6.00	5
Coventry	c.1385	26.50	6.00	5
Mount Grace	1398	28.04	7.32	4

cloister lay on the south side of the church and extended along its full length.

The three churches built before the middle of the 14th century are simple and conform to the early requirements of the order, although they could be, like Hinton, architecturally distinguished. There, triple wall-shafts rose from the string course below the window cills to support a ribbed vault. The church, however, in common with the other buildings of the charterhouse, was built of coursed rubble with ashlar dressings. Beauvale is also built of coursed rubble, but with surviving architectural detail of some quality in fine sandstone. It was never vaulted, however, and lacks any vertical or horizontal articulation. The only surviving windows are late 14th-century insertions. Central to the plan form is a distinct lack of chapel space, with room only for the high altar and two altars below the pulpitum.

The Carthusian churches in England that can best be compared directly with the church at Mount Grace are those of the London and Coventry charterhouses, both of which have been excavated. At London, excavated by W. F. Grimes (Knowles and Grimes 1954), the church (see Figure 8.6) was either that first laid out by Henry Yeveley for Sir Walter Manney in 1371, when the first permanent buildings of the house were begun (Hope 1925, 14; Harvey 1946, 31), or the pre-existing chapel of the plague cemetery, built between 1350 and 1361, reused (Barber and Thomas 2002, 14). Shown in elevation in its original form on the charterhouse waterworks plan of 1431–2 (Hope 1903, pl. XXI; Coppack 1996b, fig. 1d), it was a simple, rectangular single-cell building of four bays, measuring 27.43 m by 9.14 m internally, with an octagonal belfry topped by a tall spire above the second bay from the east. It was separated from the south wall of the great cloister by a narrow court. At its north-east corner was a low tower, also shown on the waterworks plan, that still survives and which linked the church to the cloister and chapter house.

The church at Coventry (Soden 1995, 35–58), excavated between 1968–74 and 1984–7, was a long, narrow structure with at least five phases of construction (see Figure 8.7). Part of its south wall survives in a heavily modified state. Its earliest phase, dated to *c.*1385, when Richard II laid the first stone, was a single-cell structure approximately 15 m long and 6 m wide internally that was divided into three slightly unequal bays by buttresses. The west wall of this first phase was not traced and the excavators concluded that it was a temporary timber construction, removed when the remainder of the nave, planned from the first, was built in *c.*1411–17 (Soden 1995, 38). The west wall of the completed nave was of light construction, suggesting that it too was a temporary closing, and it was built out of square with the remainder of the structure. The completion of the nave brought the internal length of the church up to 26.5 m.

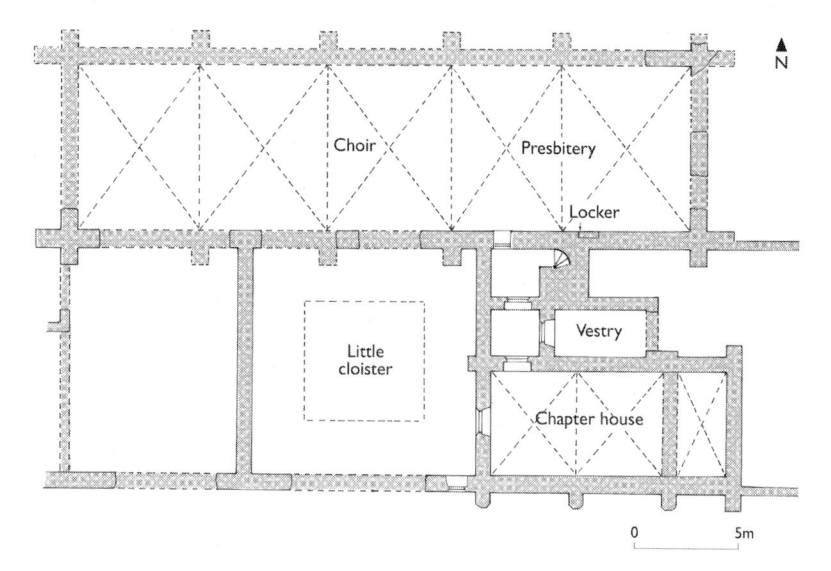

Figure 8.4 The church, chapter house and lesser cloister at Hinton (after Fletcher 1958–9).

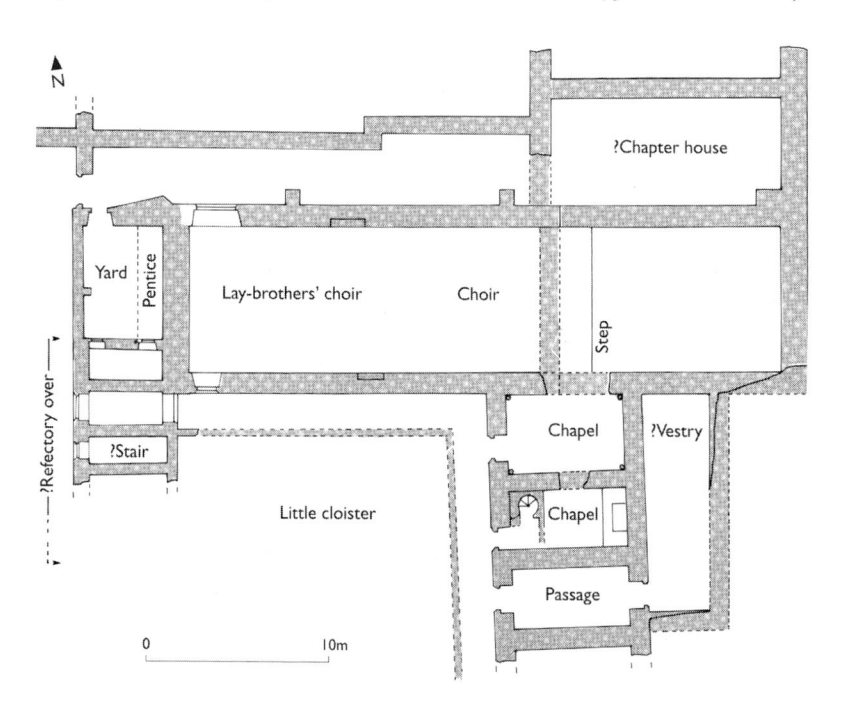

Figure 8.5 The church, chapter house and lesser cloister at Beauvale (after Hill and Gill 1908).

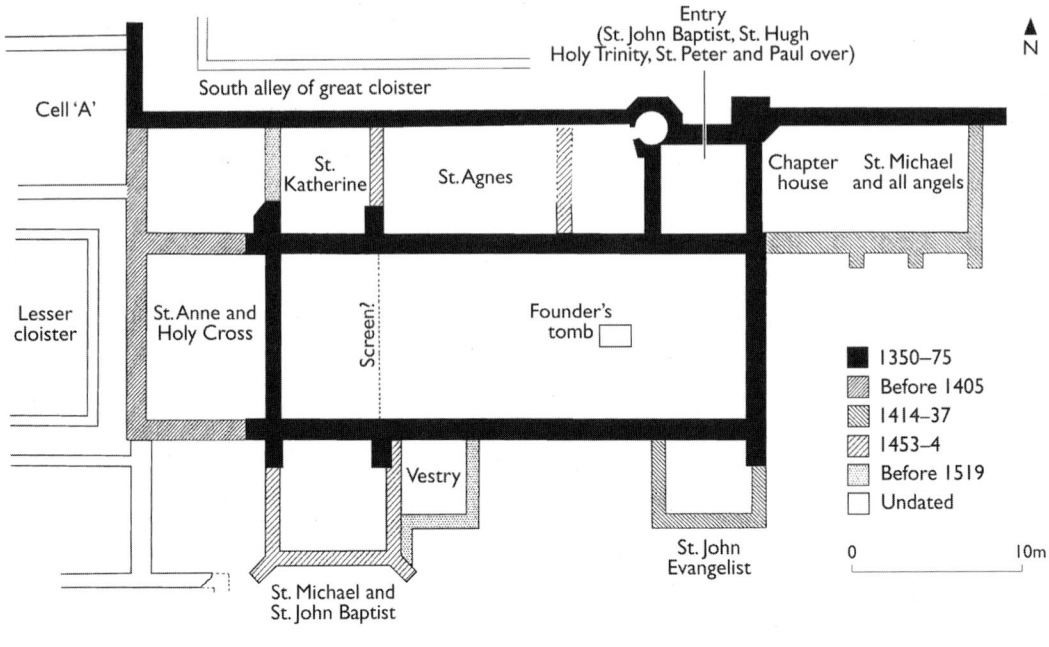

Figure 8.6 The church, chapter house and lesser cloister at London (after Knowles and Grimes 1954).

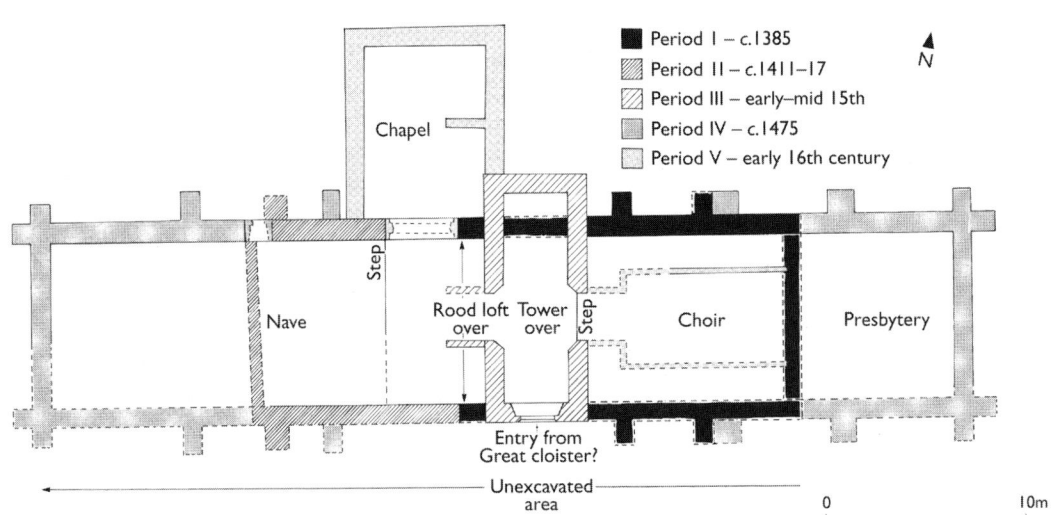

Figure 8.7 The church at Coventry (after Soden 1995).

At Mount Grace (see Figures 6.10 and 6.11) the four-bay church was divided into two unequal parts by a cross-passage at the west end of the second bay from the east. No internal features of this church survive and, apart from Hope's location of its east wall, there has been no excavation. The form of the cross-passage, destroyed by the insertion of a later tower, is unknown, but the feature was a common one in European Carthusian churches; examples are recorded at Cologne, Nuremberg, Gdansk, Basle, Ittingen, Jülich and Buxheim (Braunfels 1972, 116). The western part of the church is presumed to have been used by the lay brothers, although the low cills of the windows in its south wall preclude the provision of anything other than wall benches. To the east of the cross-passage, the cill of a blocked primary window in the north wall some 1.9 m above present ground level at the west end of the eastern bay suggests that the monks' stalls placed against the walls were not originally canopied. The church was linked to the great cloister by a two-storey structure perhaps similar to the tower at London. The first floor obviously contained a chapel, as at London, as a piscina remains in the north wall of the church at that level.

All the first-phase churches, regardless of date, follow the same basic pattern: an unaisled single-cell building with average internal dimensions of 29.11 m by 7.65 m. Only the 12th- and 13th-century churches of Witham and Hinton were vaulted, although this was the norm with European churches of the order. The vaulting of such simple spaces in stone was not a problem technically, and its omission is perhaps an indication of simplicity, a characteristic that English Carthusian churches share with those of the Cistercian order in the United Kingdom. Both the Cistercians and Carthusians framed statutes to ensure that their buildings should be plain and humble (Gilyard-Beer 1958, 15) and, like the 12th-century churches of the Cistercians in England, Mount Grace appears to have had a boarded ceiling that mimicked a barrel vault. If so, it is a very English approach, unlike that taken in the European churches of the order, such as Pavia, Champmol and Nuremberg. The size of the churches is proportionate to their use, the lack of side altar space being explained by the fact that each monk could say private masses in his own oratory. In planning and scale, these first-phase churches are closest to those of the great majority of nunneries or the earliest friaries, such as Hulne, or the 14th-century reduced church of the Gilbertines in York (Kemp and Graves 1996, 165–9 and fig. 68).

The extension of Carthusian churches to suit changing needs can be seen only at London, Beauvale, Mount Grace and Coventry. In no case was this caused directly by a growth in the size of the community, which in any case was restricted by the availability of cells. There are only two other reasons why monastic churches needed to grow: the provision of additional altar space for the saying of private masses, which was not a concern in a Carthusian house because each monk had his own oratory; and the growing pressure of lay burials and the provision of obits, which resulted directly from the perceived value of the community's prayers. At London the sequence is known from contemporary documents and from the structural sequence recovered by excavation; at Coventry simply from the evidence of excavation; and at Mount Grace from the archaeology of the surviving structure.

At London (see Figure 8.6) the extension of the original church began before 1405, when the nave was extended to the west by some 8.8 m to increase the size of the lay brothers' church (Knowles and Grimes 1954, 51–63). The monks' choir and presbytery, focused on the founder's tomb (Luxford 2011a, 262–5), remained structurally unaltered throughout the life of the church. The next addition, built between 1414 and 1437, was a small chapel dedicated to St John the Evangelist at the south-east corner of the presbytery. The space between the north wall of the church and the south wall of the great cloister had originally contained the parlour and a garden, but this had been relocated by 1453, when a large chapel dedicated to St Agnes was built on the north side of the church. The excavator concluded that the space between this chapel and the tower to the east remained in use as a slightly smaller sacristy. At the same time, a transeptal chapel containing altars dedicated to St Michael and St John the Baptist and similar in form to the south burial chapel at Mount Grace was built on the south side of the nave, and, to the east of this, a smaller chapel dedicated to St Jerome and St Bernard of Clairvaux was built some time later. A smaller transeptal chapel was added on the north side of the nave, probably dedicated to St Katherine or St Margaret, before 1519, completing the development of the church. The early 16th-century history of the house, which prefaces the cartulary (TNA Land Revenue, Misc. Book 61) makes it clear that either the altars or the chapels in which they were set were the gifts of patrons. The chapel of St Jerome and St Bernard was built at the expense of Sir John Popham, who was buried there in 1453, while the altar of St John Evangelist was funded by Robert Botler in 1437 and that of St Agnes by William Freeman in 1475 (Thompson 1930, 181). If the Carthusians were accepting the bodies of lay people for burial, they also had to accept the buildings that came with them.

The church at Beauvale (see Figure 8.5) was extended to the east by 13.41 m in the late 14th century, apparently to provide an extended presbytery that contained a centrally placed stone-built tomb just east of the new presbytery step. Contemporary with this extension was a long range orientated north–south that butted against the south wall of the original church but bonded with the extension, and which contained at its north end two chapels, a passage from the lesser cloister and possibly a vestry. The northernmost chapel was entered from the presbytery and was vaulted, suggesting that it was of more than one storey. Unsurprisingly, its tiled floor had been extensively disturbed by burials. The second chapel, which had retained its altar upon excavation, was originally entered from

Figure 8.8 The charterhouse of Nieuwlicht in the Netherlands, c.1725.

the lesser cloister. A spiral stair added later, when a door was forced through from the northern chapel, suggests that this chapel, too, was of two or more storeys, not unlike the structures provided on the north sides of the churches at London and Mount Grace at about the same time.

The church at Coventry (see Figure 8.7) was a complicated structure that grew spasmodically from the third quarter of the 15th century. The first addition was a tower at the centre of the original church. Its sub-structure extended to the north of the original church, perhaps to contain a stair, but was otherwise virtually identical to the contemporary provision of the tower and screen walls at Mount Grace. The next alteration, in about 1475, was a major event: the extension of the presbytery to the east by 9.0 m and the nave to the west by 9.5 m. The whole church was then rebuttressed, indicating that the old bay divisions had been suppressed and that the building was probably refenestrated. The extension of the presbytery contained a single central highstatus burial. The extension to the nave, however, contained at least 16 burials, which, when added to the 21 found within the early 15th-century nave, show the pressure for lay burial within the church. That pressure continued into the early 16th century, when a large chapel was built on the north side of the nave. Remarkably, however, it was never used for burial; perhaps it was never completed. The south side of the church was not available for excavation, although the inner face of the nave wall was seen to be unbroken opposite this transeptal chapel, suggesting that it was not matched on the south side. It is not known whether other chapels or the chapter house existed on the south side of the presbytery.

The development of the Mount Grace church (see Figures 6.10 and 6.11) is fully described in Chapter 6. The eastward extension and remodelling of the presbytery at Mount Grace can only have resulted from the desire of Thomas Beaufort to provide himself with a suitable burial place, and the insertion of a bell-tower is probably also associated with this. Indeed, the provision of no fewer than three separate burial chapels between c.1470 and 1520 indicates the pressure that was placed on the community by their local patrons. Such developments would be understandable in an urban context, but are less so in the rural context of Mount Grace. However, they show a remarkable degree of similarity with those taking place at other developed Carthusian churches, as described above, suggesting that there was a degree of agreement within the English province (and perhaps further afield) on how churches might be extended and modified.

Perhaps the clearest evidence for the development of a Continental charterhouse church comes from the charterhouse of Nieuwlicht (see Figure 8.8), outside the city of Utrecht, in the Netherlands.

Closely contemporary with the church at Mount Grace, and a good comparison owing to its date and similarly difficult start in life, its first phase was begun on 6 July 1396, over four years after the foundation of the house, and was sufficiently complete by 1407 to be dedicated, which took place on 15 January (Gumbert 1974, 29). Parts of the nave, choir and presbytery have been excavated (Hartog 2013, 39–44). As was the norm with Continental Carthusian churches in the early 15th century, the church was unaisled, and was of seven equal bays terminating in an apse (Fig. 8.8A). The western three bays were the nave, or lay brothers' church, which was divided from the monks' choir by a substantial pulpitum screen with two chapels to the west of it. The choir occupied the next two bays, and the presbytery a further two bays and the apse. The easternmost five bays of the church barring the apse survived until c.1725 (see Figure 8.7B). This simple church was intended

THE SIGNIFICANCE OF THE MOUNT GRACE PROJECT

for the burial of its founder, Lord Sweder van Apcoude, who was initially buried before the altar on the chord of the apse; after his death Arnoldus van Dorp, a major patron, was buried in the choir, and to the east of him, below the bell-turret, was buried Otto Koudaver van Geervliet, the Heer van Apcoude's steward and another major benefactor. In 1447 the Lady Joletta, the founder's daughter, was buried in front of the northern return stall in the choir, 'where the Gospel is read in the convent masses', and her father's bones were exhumed and buried with her. Her son, Lord Jacobus van Gaasbeek, was buried in the same grave in 1459. The final burial, between those of Arnoldus van Dorp and Otto Koudaver, 'below the lamp', was Johannes Wilhelmus, son of Arnoldus van Dorp. Only one burial is recorded in the nave: that of Ghijsbertus Pau, who was buried before the altar of the martyrs in front of the pulpitum in 1521 (HUA HSA18151, f. 104).

An inserted door in the south wall of the second bay of the nave from the west led into the New Chapel, which was consecrated on 24 November 1438. This was intended as a burial chapel, and three altars were sponsored by lay donors: Bertold van Assendelf, Knight of the Diocese of Utrecht; Nicolaas Jacobzoen of Amsterdam and his wife Fye; and Alijt Hasselt, mother of the house's clericus-redditus, Johannes van Cleves. The building appears to have been commissioned by the house rather than by the donors, for when Bertold van Assendelf failed to pay his full share of the costs the house had to find the money where it could. The individual altars – from north to south, of the Holy Cross, the blessed Virgin and St John the Evangelist – were intended as the focus of family burials (Hasselt 1886, 182–3). The first and only burial before the altar of the Blessed Virgin was that of Alijt Hasselt, before the sedile in the perpent wall; the Jacobzoen family burials were clustered around the altar of the Holy Cross. There were two burials before the southern altar of St John the Evangelist, neither of them Bertold van Assendelf (HUA A18151, f. 105). The majority of lay burials were concentrated in the west alley of the great cloister and the east, south and west alleys of the little cloister.

The Nieuwlicht Calendar (HSA 18154, de kalender origineel, sub. ii id. Oct) records the dedication of a new building on 13 October 1446, simply 'above the pulpitum' (super doxale), with stacked chapels dedicated to St Barbara and St Katherine, and St Michael and All Angels. This is likely to have been on the north side of the presbytery, west of the apse. Balancing this, on the south side of the church, was an earlier two-storey sacristy for which Sir William van den Rijn, provost of Eembrugge, 'gave us all the windows … both upper and lower' (Geer 1857, 138).

Central to all of the later group in England, as it was at Nieuwlicht, was a 'founder's' tomb, placed either in the choir, as at Mount Grace, or at the focus of the presbytery, as at London, Beauvale and Coventry. None of these churches was to develop an aisle, and only Coventry and Mount Grace were to have axial towers. Added chapels were either transeptal or were entered by a door in the fashion of a Saxon *porticus*. At London and Mount Grace planning appears to have been rather *ad hoc*,

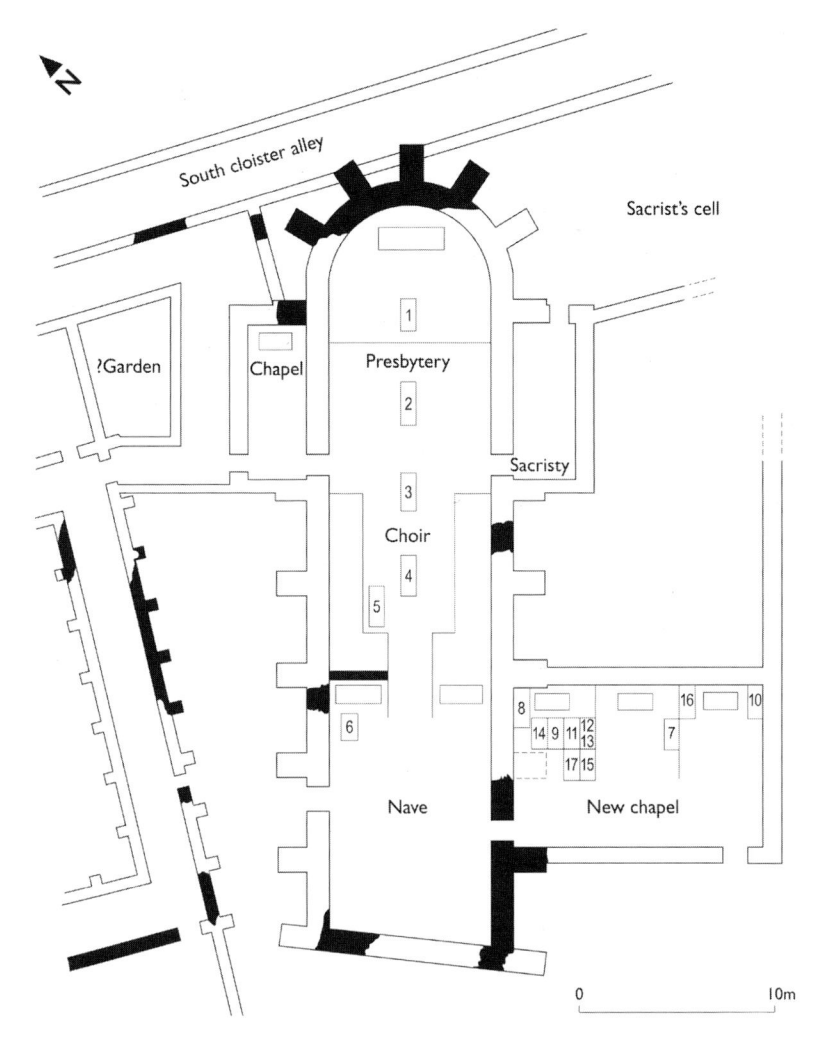

Figure 8.8 A Plan of Nieuwlicht church showing burials (after Hundertmark and den Hartog).

Figure 8.9 Reconstruction of the church at Mount Grace based on the surviving fabric and detached architectural detail (G. Coppack and S. Hayfield).

expansion being limited by the proximity of other buildings and the distance the church was originally placed from the great cloister. The original intention to separate the church and cloister was abandoned as the pressure to increase chapel space grew, making necessary a degree of ingenuity that the original builders had not required. Why it should have been the later charterhouse churches that required lateral expansion is not at all clear, unless it was because they had no *correrie* churches in which to concentrate lay burial. If this was the case, Beauvale may have been the last charterhouse in England to have had a *correrie*, and thus the latest foundation not to have been forced to expand its church substantially because of lay pressure.

Within the limits of Carthusian planning, and the accretions to this demanded by patronal needs, what is known of the superstructure of the Mount Grace church is strictly contemporary. Surprisingly, given the Carthusians' tenacious tendency to cling to their original ideals, there is little sign of any archaism, harking back to an earlier, ideal time. The modernity of Carthusian building is demonstrated by the employment of Henry Yeveley at the London house (although this was related to patronage) and at Mount Grace by features such as the tower, the tracery design and the related cloister arcades.

Of the Period One church at Mount Grace, the principal known architectural feature is the fenestration of its south wall, the western window of which has been reconstructed on paper (see Figures 6.15 and 8.9). In many ways this is an unusual window, with early, late and idiosyncratic traits of perpendicular tracery. On the one hand, its setting beneath a very flat arch, with the subsequent dropping of the tracery below springing level, is suggestive of advanced perpendicular. On the other hand, the reticulated and sub-reticulated middle and upper tiers with ogee heads are more reminiscent of an earlier style. Additionally, the division between the middle and upper tier of lights is unusual, as is the form of the upper lights. The horizontal division between the two tiers is formed half by the lights below (reticulation) and half by diamond-shaped eyelets interrupting the main mullions. In this respect it partly resembles what Harvey described as a 'latticed transom', where diamond-shaped eyelets are placed between all lights (Harvey 1978, 71–2 and 165): not common at any time, and never so in the north of England. The upper lights are also unusual, with cusped trefoils at the bottom and cusped quatrefoils above (except for the side lights, which have trefoil heads).

Inspiration for the semi-latticed transom might have come from the latticed transoms visible in the clerestorey of the western part of the choir of York Minster, although no other features are shared with these windows (albeit the York Minster choir aisle windows below are reticulated). The quatrefoil-headed lights above are harder to place, as such features are usually found only beneath a transom. In the region, the closest tracery to the Mount Grace south nave windows appears to be that of the east windows of Catterick and Burneston churches (see Figures 8.10 and 8.11). Both have ogee lower lights with sub-reticulated lights above and both have quatrefoil-headed lights, although set at an intermediate level under transoms; Catterick, additionally, has dropped tracery. Neither has latticed transoms and neither has the lower part of any light cusped. Nonetheless, as Catterick was built in 1412–15 (Pevsner 1966, 119) and both Burneston and Catterick also have close stylistic links with the Period Two work at Mount Grace, it is possible to posit the work of a single mason, Richard de Cracall (ibid.). The Period One

THE SIGNIFICANCE OF THE MOUNT GRACE PROJECT

Figure 8.10 The east window of Catterick church (G. Coppack).

Figure 8.11 The east window of Burneston church (G. Coppack).

work at Mount Grace might then represent the tentative steps of a young mason–architect, eclectic and unsure, though aware of important works elsewhere, perhaps as far as the cloisters of Gloucester cathedral priory, while the parish churches and later work at Mount Grace show the development of a more mature style.

Richard de Cracall's work at Catterick comprised the chancel and both aisles of the church, structures that share a second feature with Mount Grace: the parapet gutters. Although these do not survive on the church at Mount Grace, they are implied by the survival of fragments of water spouts and by the surviving sections of parapet coping from the contemporary Period One and Two south-west cloister range (see Figure 5.20, 43 and 45). These are of near-identical form to the copings still in place at Catterick and support the suggested connection.

In Period Two, it is the tower that is of the greatest significance (see Figures 6.10 and 6.14). Although small in scale and with no overly decorative embellishments, everything about this tower is nicely done: the tiny diagonal buttresses with statue niches, the bold string courses and parapet, the pinnacles and gargoyles on the corners (now mostly broken off), the graceful single-light openings of the belfry and the framing of the small ogee lights below with a label that has a vertical link with the string course above. It is, altogether, a pleasing composition. The comparison of towers is not easy (see Harvey 1978, 228–30), and the Mount Grace example is both small and centrally placed, in contrast with most of the perpendicular towers in the region. The tower of the Richmond Franciscans (see Figure 8.12), however, provides a very interesting comparison. Typically for English mendicant architecture (Martin 1937, *passim*) and like that of Mount Grace – though it is taller – the tower is centrally placed and modestly sized. It, too, has tiny buttresses (here paired), bold string courses and a small opening framed by a label below the belfry stage. In its multiple pinnacles, open-work parapet and traceried belfry openings, the Richmond tower is more ornate that that of Mount Grace, yet the two towers have a remarkably similar feel to them. At Richmond, the stair from the belfry stage to the parapet is handled in exactly the same way as that in the upper stages of the Mount Grace tower, both pointing up, and being largely the result of, the close but largely unexplored links between the design of friary churches and Carthusian churches generally.

Figure 8.12 The tower of the Greyfriars' church at Richmond from the west (G. Coppack).

The stylistic similarities between the Richmond and Mount Grace towers are too close, though, for this to be sufficient explanation. The two sets of tower arches in particular are very similar, with plain shafts, polygonal moulded capitals and two-centred moulded arches above. It is hard to believe that one tower did not inspire the other. The influence of the friars' houses of York and other lost local friaries should also not be forgotten, although it cannot be assessed.

Also belonging to Period Two is the east window (see Figures 6.16 and 6.17), which has the most complex tracery of the known windows at Mount Grace. Before discussing details, it should first be remembered that the design is not completely known and that it is possible to reconstruct a number of differently designed windows from the surviving fragments. Nonetheless, certain features are irreducible: the broad round-headed cinquefoil lights at the bottom, of which the uppers cills are treated as an ogee; the threefold division of the main design without any intersecting arches; the interrupted embattled transoms; and the arch of the window head, either four-centred or basket.

Looking at perhaps the most important local centre first, Westminster-influenced York (see Harvey 1978, 172), a remarkable lack of clear parallels emerges. There is a near-absence of ogee features and embattled transoms, although a threefold division of the main design and broken transoms are common, most notably in the eastern transepts and choir clerestorey of the Minster. Unsurprisingly, the later windows of the clerestorey, already noted for their latticed transoms (probably contemporary with Period One at Mount Grace: see Pevsner and Neave 1995, 136), are more similar to the Mount Grace east window than are the earlier ones, with their overtones of flamboyance. The parish churches of York, especially St Michael-le-Belfry (a 16th-century building with a reset east window), St Saviour's and All Saint's, Pavement, closely follow the later windows of the Minster. However, an intriguing parallel with Mount Grace might be found in St Mary Castlegate, with its ogee main lights (above and below) and embattled transoms, although much of this may belong to the restoration of 1867–70 (Wilson and Mee 1998, 117). Comparisons in the East Riding and Malton are no better than those in York. Indeed, the Mount Grace window has far fewer parallels with the one perpendicular window surviving in Old Malton Priory, with its intersecting arches and dagger quatrefoils between the main lights and the transom, or with the great east window of Beverley Minster (dated to shortly after 1416: see Pevsner and Neave 1995, 285), whose main features are intersecting arches defined by enlarged mullions and light upon light of panel tracery.

A tour of the perpendicular churches in the immediately surrounding area, by contrast, reveals some pertinent comparisons. Burneston church, on the eastern edge of the Dales, is perhaps the closest of all, especially to the second reconstruction (see Figure 8.11). It has a fine series of perpendicular windows culminating in the east window, which, like Mount Grace, has a basic threefold division, ogee lower lights (though here the lights as well as the cill are ogee) and interrupted embattled transoms. In fact, it would be possible to construct a very similar window indeed with the surviving elements from Mount Grace, with short transoms at three different levels. The most notable differences from the Mount Grace window are the square-headed quatrefoils below the transoms and the two-light window head. Unfortunately, there is no good dating evidence for the Burneston windows. However, the bulk of Catterick church is closely dated to 1412–15, as discussed above, and its east window is similar enough in its details and design to that of Burneston, with ogee cinquefoil lights, embattled interrupted transoms (here stepped) and square-headed quatrefoils, to identify it as being by the same master, Richard de Cracall. Unlike at both Mount Grace and Burneston, there is no overall threefold division of the space, but the window head is much flatter than that at Burneston and, as at Mount Grace, the tracery is dropped below the springing level.

In a milieu in which designs and techniques were rapidly exchanged, it cannot be confirmed absolutely that Mount Grace was also the work of Richard de Cracall, but he still remains a strong contender. Nevertheless, it is fairly clear that the architecture of the first two periods of the Mount Grace church is firmly within regional norms and may have played a significant part in developing the late perpendicular architecture (or at least the tracery designs) of the area. Interestingly, this analysis of the architecture demonstrates a disregard for the patron. Both of Mount Grace's early patrons were close to the Crown, yet there is no obvious Westminster influence in either Period One or Period Two. While this is perhaps less surprising in the case of Thomas de Holand, whose association with the house was very short, it is more remarkable in the context of Thomas Beaufort, who was converting the church as his burial place. Perhaps the scope of the building was decided by the patron, but the design was left to the community. The appointment of a local master, possibly twice, emphasises the appropriateness of a competent parish church style in a Carthusian context. It is perhaps not without significance in this context that Richard de Cracall built the chancel at Burneston for St Mary's Abbey at York and was thus known in monastic circles.

The possible influence of Mount Grace and its architect may be seen in other churches of the region. Guisborough church, although probably rather later (late 15th century), has very similar tracery in its western windows. Its aisles almost form a facade with the small west tower, giving it an appearance very like that of a central tower, especially with its super arch over both window and door, aping a tower arch. This parish church was owned by the Augustinian Gisborough Priory, which had very close links with Mount Grace. The Inglebys were patrons of Gisborough (see Chapter 2), and at least one Gisborough canon was licensed to join the Carthusians (Cal. Papal Letters 1447–55, 672). The similarity of some aspects of the parish church, which lay immediately outside the priory precinct, to features of the Mount Grace church further suggests a close relationship between the neighbouring houses. The east window at Thirsk (*c*.1460: see Pevsner 1966, 365) has interrupted stepped transoms (not embattled), a shallow arch and dropped tracery, although no threefold division. The side chancel and clerestorey windows are perhaps more similar, along with those of Coxwold church (with panel tracery in the middle and beneath sub-arches to either side), but with only three main lights these are not complex enough for a really useful comparison. The Northallerton south transept gable window (*c*.1440–55: see Pevsner 1966, 270) shares some features with the east window of Thirsk and with Mount Grace, although the tracery is below a steep two-centred arch. There are plenty of broken transoms with minute battlements, and on either side of a broad central section of panel tracery two of the super-lights are enclosed within sub-arches.

The next significant change to the church at Mount Grace was the addition of the north and south burial chapels. Although there were at least three recorded burials in the 1430s (see Chapter 2), these could easily have been accommodated in the nave, as happened at Coventry (see above). Requests for burials seemed to pick up again from the 1470s, and at the same time there were many specific requests for obits, trentals and prayers, which continued right up to the Suppression. It may be these, as much as the burials, of which only a few are known, that prompted the new chapels, with their consecrated altar space for the saying of masses and prayers for the priory's benefactors. The south burial chapel is in many ways similar to the Thirsk chancel (c.1460), with a large four-centred window and stepped diagonal buttresses. The windows, though, unlike the nave window they replaced, have no tracery to speak of, the south window having five uninterrupted cinquefoil lights and the west window probably three. Although the lack of tracery could be indicative of both economy and Carthusian aesthetics, the move towards plain windows was widespread. The window in the west wall is set asymmetrically towards the nave, possibly to compensate for the loss of the nave window or to accommodate the interior fittings. The east wall had no window at all, although it provided scope for a substantial reredos or painting. The north chapel, of which even less remains, was similarly plain.

The east burial chapel, built in Period Four, must have had the same impetus behind it as the earlier chapels, with ever increasing obligations on the monks to pray for the dead. Architecturally, even less is known about this annex, as only the foundations survive. There is evidence for at least two windows (see Chapter 6 and Figure 6.19), one with trefoil-headed lights but no evidence either way for tracery, and the other a roundel. It has been reconstructed here as a circle with twelve cusps, although in fact the fragment could represent a number of designs. Although rarely remarked upon, the round window is a feature that seems to persist throughout the later Middle Ages. It is in the east gable at Catterick (see Figure 8.10), for example, but also at Arundel in Sussex (late 14th century: Harvey 1978, pl. 60), Burwell in Cambridgeshire (1454–64: ibid., pl. 157), King's Lynn in Norfolk (early 16th century: Pevsner and Wilson 1962, pl. 34) and doubtless elsewhere.

In summary, it is clear that the architectural designs seen at Mount Grace's church belong firmly in the mainstream of the time and link closely with regional developments, particularly those of the immediate vicinity, and less so to those of York and the East Riding. The regional links appear to have continued throughout the church's 120-year building history and to have been more important than patronal influence.

The church at Mount Grace is the only Carthusian one in England to retain evidence of its fixtures and fittings, which are mainly evidenced by the cuts in the masonry that held their fixings (for a fuller discussion of these fittings, see Coppack and Hall 2008). According to the Carthusian statutes (Thompson 1930, 23), churches were to be undecorated, without paintings and carpets, with a single crucifix in a prominent place as well as one over each altar. At Mount Grace, however, the evidence of fixings for altar dressings and screens suggests a closer similarity with the churches of other orders, or indeed with parish churches and chapels. Fortunately, Dr Richard Layton, in company with Drs Thomas Legh and Francis Cave, Harry Polstead and Thomas Thacker, recorded in detail the fittings of the church at London in 1539, when they were still in place, and this information (Hope 1925, 184–6) is directly relevant to the disposition of furnishings at Mount Grace:

The Quere
The hyghe alter of the storye of the passyon of bowne, wrought wyth smalle Imagys Curyouslie, at ether ende of the sayd alter an Image the on of saint John Baptyste and the other of saint Peter and above the sayd alter iij tabernacles, the nether fronte of the alter of alabaster wyth the Trinitie and other Imagys, at the South Syde of the same at thende of the alter a Cupparde painted wyth the pycture of Cryste. On the northe syde of the alter an ambry wyth a letter. In the same quere a lampe and a bason to bere waxe both of latten, the Stalles of the sayd quere on ether syde wyth a lectern, undefacyd.

Saint Johns Chappell
In the Southe syde of the Churche a chappell of saint John thavaungelyste wyth an alter and a table of the Resurrecyon of alabaster with ij Imagys of saint John Evaungellyst and the other of saint Augustyne at eyther ende of the said alter. Item the sayd chappel is scealyd wyth oke waynscotte and other borde Rounde abougte thre quarters hygh.

The bodye of the Churche
The Rodelofte wyth an Image of Cryste Crusyfyed a mownteyne with ij alters on eyther syde of the quere dore. On the southe syde an alter with a table of the assumption of Our Lady gylte there remaynynge.

The chapell of saint Jerome
An alter table wythe a Crucyfyx of Marye and John. ij Imagys at ether ende of the sayd alter, the one of Irone the other of saint Barnard, the sayd Chappell being partelye scelyd wyth wayn skotte. Item ij seates and a lyttell Coffer.

[no heading]
Item. An alter of St Mychell wythe a ffayre table of the Crucyfyx marye and John and at eyther ende of thalter an Image the on of Seint Mychell thother of saint John.

> Mr Redys Chappell
> An alter wythe a table of the Trinite the iij Doctors of the Churche the same chappell beinge selyd wyth waynskot and ij Covers all remaynynge undefaced.
> Item nyghe unto the sayd Chappell a pewe wyth ij seates of waynscott.
> The North syde of the Quere
> An alter wythe a table of saynt anne gylte wyth certeyn other Imagys gylt and payntyd. Item a table wyth an auter of saint anne and owr ladye with certeyn other Imagys above the sayd alter at ether ende an Image wyth a tabernacle and betwyxte every on of the sayd alters above wrytten there ys a partysyon of waynskotte.
> The weste end of the Church
> On the north syde an alter in the myddes of mary and John, fayer paynted. Item on the southe syde an alter wyth a table of the passyon of Cryste fayr painted.
> Item in the myddes of the sayd ende a particion of tymber wyth pykes of Iron above.

Also in the nave were 'vij Seatys and settells' for the lay brothers, whose church this was (Hope 1925, 189).

It is clear from the above that the Carthusians of London dressed their altars in much the same way as anyone else. The list indicates that some of the dedications had changed since the 15th century; while the dedications of the Mount Grace altars remain unknown, the evidence that they were similarly fitted is perfectly clear.

The statutes permitted only a single chalice and reed of silver; otherwise, gold and silver were to be avoided (Thompson 1930, 23). Again at London, and hinted at in Mount Grace wills, there had been some movement away from the ideal by the early 16th century. Layton removed from the London charterhouse 12 chalices, a censer, a pix, an incense boat, 22 cruets, 3 crucifixes, 2 reliquaries (of St Sithe and St Barbara), 2 paxes and 8 spoons: in all, some 4,047 ounces of plate (Thompson 1930, 184). To this can be added rich altar cloths, vestments, Turkey carpets and cushions, all out of keeping with the rule. Yet, although London was a wealthy house, its collection of church plate was not considerable when compared to those of Benedictine houses or even the richer Cistercian monasteries. The likelihood is that a considerable proportion comprised gifts or bequests to the house that it would have been impolitic to refuse.

The windows of the Mount Grace church contained, rather than plain metal quarries, pictorial glass that was equal in quality to that of other monastic churches in Yorkshire. Some or even all of the windows could have been gifts or provided by the founders, and would thus reflect their taste, rather than that of the community. Only one bequest is recorded, however: the gift of a window by Alison Clark in 1509, the location of which in the monastery is not recorded. At Coventry Dame Margery Byry of Newark, founder of the fourth cell in the great cloister there, provided £10 'towards the window at the head of the choir, that is the east window', after 1385 (Dugdale 1825, 16–17). This suggests she was one of several donors. At Nieuwlicht, the register of great donors records the gifts of many of the first-phase windows of the church there, together with their prices and occasionally their location. The first recorded was a gift of 129 florins of Gelhre by Evaert Foec (d.1418), Dean of the Church of St Saviour in Utrecht, for a glass window in the church. Willem Buser, high canon, gave a further five French *scutae* towards a window funded by Sir Hermann de Lochorst, High Dean (Dean before 1400, d.1438), which contained the donor panels of both these men and was located in the second bay of the north wall of the nave, over the lay brothers' door to the church. Heer Willem van der Rijn, who had glazed the sacristy, gave money for several windows. The Dean and Chapter of St Saviour collectively paid for the great west window of the church, while Bishop Frederick van Blankenstein gave about 39 florins towards another window. Then come three windows funded by laity. The first of these donors was the knight Heer Theodericus van Zuylen, who paid 52 florins for a window on the south side of the church; the second an unnamed gentleman of Montfoord, paying the same for a window on the north side; and the third Sophie Minneboden, who bought a window on the south side of the nave. It was moved into the New Chapel after its construction, where it survived with her donor panel intact. In every case it seems that the payment was for the glazing, not the construction of the windows, and that the money was raised during or immediately after the building of the church (Geer 1857, 134–9). Clearly, benefactors could either contribute to the fabric of the church or provide for its decoration. At Nieuwlicht at least three pictorial windows associated with groups of family burials were provided in the great and little cloisters (HUA A18151, ff. 106 and 111). It is perhaps significant that, with a few exceptions from Cells 14 and 15 (which could be derived from elsewhere) and the later prior's cell (where it was clearly derived from the adjacent church), excavation of the monks' cells at Mount Grace produced only plain window glass.

The Origins and Parallels for the Carthusian Cell

The earliest mention of a Carthusian cell comes from Guibert de Nogent's description of the Grande Chartreuse, written before 1109:

> there are 13 monks ... not dwelling together like others cloisterwise, for they have cells of their own round the cloister in which they work, sleep, and eat. On Sunday they receive their food from the dispenser, that is bread and vegetables, which, their only pottage, is cooked by each of them in their own quarters. Water, however, for drinking as for other uses, they have by means of a conduit from the fountain, which goes to the cells of all, and through certain holes passes into each of their little houses. (Thompson 1930, 12)

The form of the Carthusian cell, with its provision for sleeping, cooking, prayer, manual work and solitude, was thus established by the first years of the 12th century.

When the first Grande Chartreuse – save a single cell – was destroyed by an avalanche in January 1132, Peter the Venerable of Cluny recorded that it was built *again* of timber (ibid., 19), presumably indicating that the original cells there were of wooden construction. The *Magna Vita S Hugonis*, written by Adam of Eynsham in the early 13th century (Douie and Farmer 1985), describes the state of affairs Hugh of Avalon found at Witham when he arrived as prior in 1180: the brethren were living in cells built of logs enclosed by ditches and a pale, although it was admitted that these were temporary buildings, pre-dating the formal establishment of a cloister. The founding group at Witham came from the Grande Chartreuse and Portes, and it would be surprising if they had not brought the traditions of their mother houses with them. The provision of formal buildings began in 1180/1 and is evidenced by small grants (Thompson 1930, 53) that again suggest timber buildings, with the exception of the church, which was still in building in 1186–7, as confirmed by the *Magna Vita*. The documentary evidence for the first cells at Coventry (below) and the evidence from Cell 8 at Mount Grace (see Chapter 4) suggest that the tradition of initially building in timber continued into the early years of the 15th century. This was not only a Carthusian practice, however, for the Carmelites of Esslingen occupied timber houses up to the rebuilding of their friary on more conventional lines at the close of the 15th century (Elders 1996). And, with the exception of Mount Grace, no Carthusian house has in fact produced any archaeological evidence for initial timber cells, though admittedly the evidence has not been sought.

The plan of late medieval Carthusian cells in England is best known from the Period Two and Three cells at Mount Grace and also from Axholme (Wenham unpublished). The earliest cells excavated in England were at Hinton, dating from the middle years of the 13th century (Fletcher 1958/9). Between these two points are cells of the mid-13th century at Beauvale (Hill and Gill 1908, 72–7), of the final quarter of the 14th century at London (Grimes 1968, 177–8; Barber and Thomas 2002, 19–25 and 34–7), and of the last decade or so of the 14th century at Coventry (Soden 1995, 58–63). Generally, the cell comprises a two-storey house set in the corner of a walled garden and occupying about a quarter of the enclosed space. Attached to the house were two corridors, one a private cloister ranging along the garden side of the cloister wall, the other a pentice leading from the back door of the house to a latrine in the back wall of the garden. This plan is common to all the English houses where cell plans have been recovered. The planning of the house, however, can be seen to change through time (see Figure 8.13). Excavation at Witham (Burrow and Burrow 1990) revealed a single cell that appears to date to the second half of the 14th century, and we have no knowledge of the cells of the primary phase of the first charterhouse to be established in England in the last decades of the 12th century. Two basic cell plans can be identified in England, one apparently of the 13th century, best shown by Cell 11 at Hinton, though it is common to Cells 1–13 there; the other most completely developed in Cell 3 at Mount Grace, though it can be seen in the single undated cell excavated at Witham, in

THE SIGNIFICANCE OF THE MOUNT GRACE PROJECT

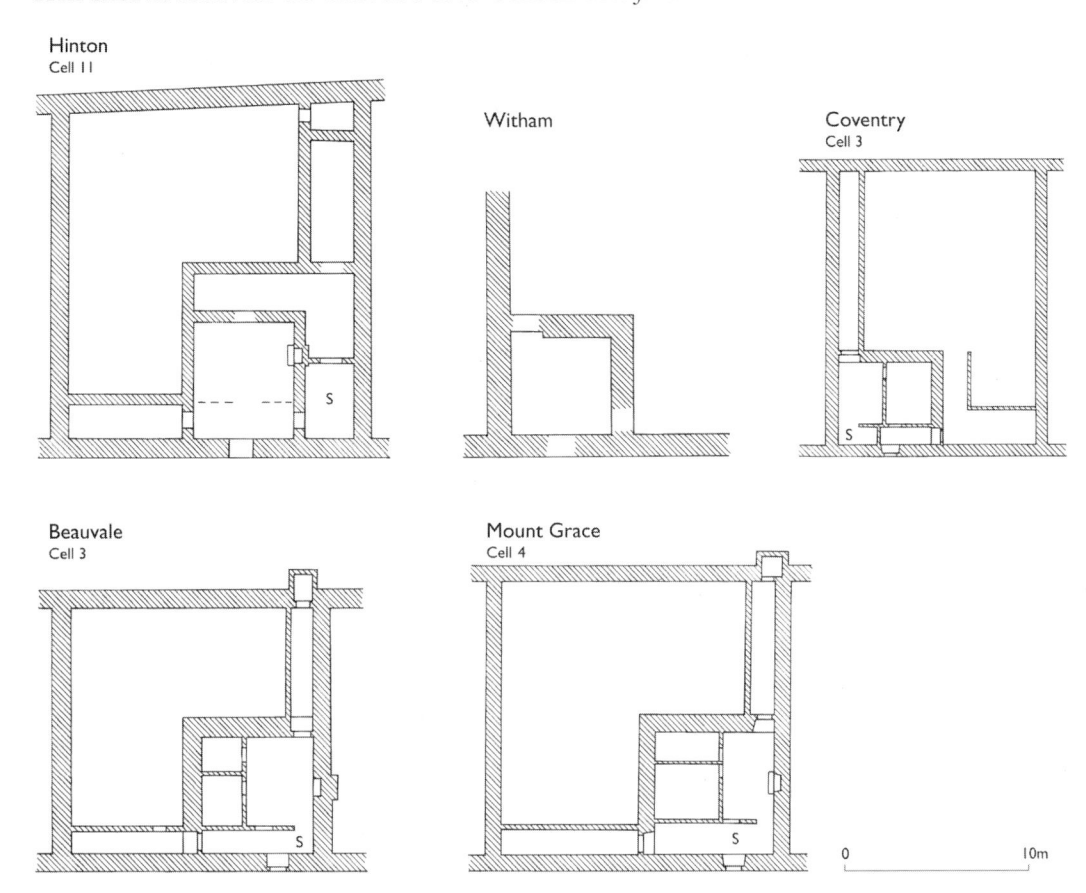

Figure 8.13 Comparative cell plans from English charterhouses. Hinton, Cell 11 (after Fletcher 1958–9); Witham (after Burrow and Burrow 1990); Beauvale, Cell 3 (after Hill and Gill 1908); Coventry, Cell 3 (after Soden 1995); and Mount Grace, Cell 4.

Cell 3 at Beauvale, and in Cells J–M, R and S at London.

Interpretation of the Hinton cells is complicated by the way they were excavated: trenches were dug along walls and no attempt was made to uncover floors. No complete cell plan was recovered and it was assumed that walls not recovered in some cells because robber trenches were not identified would have followed the general layout seen in cells where walls were located. Timber partitions were not sought or even, it would appear, anticipated. The excavator claimed that

> the cells are uniformly 31ft 6in wide and rather less in depth. They consist of one large room, 20ft square, the rest of the cell usually forming a peculiar 'dog-leg', which measured 8ft at the side and 6ft at the end. It seems probable that this was a pentice, but how it was divided up remains a mystery, as this part of the cell has usually been badly knocked about … the large room invariably has the hearth, where it still exists, in the same relative position on the side internal wall. (Fletcher 1958/9, 77–8)

However, an examination of the ground plan of Cell 11 (see Figure 8.13), the most complete cell plan recovered, indicates a very different interpretation. Critical to the understanding of the form of the building is the location of the chimney stack. In the later medieval Carthusian cell this would be expected to occupy a central position in one of the gable walls of the cell, but at Hinton it does not. It does, however, lie in every case on the centre line of the building, so that the chimney passed through the ridge-line of the cell on the line of an internal wall. Cell 11 measured 9.1 m by 7.7 m internally, of which the living room or hall occupied an area 6.6 m by 5.9 m. If the fireplace was centrally located in the north wall of the hall, then there would have been space for a lobby some 1.8 m wide between the hall and the door from the cloister and the hall would thus have been 4.8 m wide. In Cell 11 there was a door at each end of this lobby, that at the south end leading to an external gallery and that to the north leading into the narrow room between the gable wall of the cell and the wall containing the hall fireplace. This space was 2.25 m wide and in Cells 3, 4 and 12 it was curtailed by a north–south cross-wall aligned with the chimney stack, defining a room approximately 3 m long; in Cells 4 and

12 this cross-wall had a centrally placed door. Because this space can have had no windows at ground-floor level, it is most likely that it was the location of the stair to the upper floor, perhaps with a cupboard below. It most certainly was not a pentice, as Fletcher claimed. Another 'corridor', a narrow space along the garden side of the hall, appears never to have been seriously investigated. Where its outer wall was investigated it was found to be the same width as the other external walls of the cell. Its inner wall was thinner, suggesting it was carried up only to the first floor, while the internal wall that contained the chimney flue was carried up to the ridge. This 'corridor' was only 1.4 m wide. In Cell 7 there was a centrally placed door from the hall.

At Witham, the single cell excavated in the west range of the cloister was somewhat smaller (see Figure 8.13) and differs from the Hinton cells in its plan form. It seems to have been placed in the south-east corner of the garden plot, although this was not checked by excavation. Internally, it measured 5.49 m from north to south and 5.18 m from east to west. The wall footings were 1.22 m wide. The cloister wall had been robbed out and the location of the principal door was not recovered. Robbing suggested a door at the east end of the north wall, leading to the unexcavated garden pentice, and an off-set in the south end of the foundations of the west wall suggests a door to the latrine pentice. Paving outside this door was sealed by the construction of an ashlar tank with a sluice at its west end, implying that this door had been blocked (as in Cell 20 at Mount Grace). The interior of the cell was not examined and the fireplace was not located. The planning of the cell suggests that it was a late medieval structure and did not date from the 12th or 13th century.

At London, Grimes (1968, 178–80) was able to examine parts of Cells R and S in the east range of the great cloister, which were built before 1381 (see below). Both cells were approximately 6.4 m wide internally, had cloister doors placed slightly north of centre and were placed in the south-west corner of their garden plots. The gardens were approximately 14 m square. A garden pentice placed against the cloister wall to the north of each cell was entered, as at Mount Grace, from the lobby. Unfortunately, it was not possible to recover the depth of the cells or any detail of their internal layout. This lack was, to a certain extent, rectified by the excavation under difficult circumstances of Cells H to M in 1990 (Barber and Thomas 2002, 19–25). Sponsored between 1372 and 1376 (below), these cells were built to a common plan, probably in a single operation, as they were all built on foundations constructed in the same manner. They were approximately 6 m square internally, divided into two rooms and a passage (which in the case of Cell L was also divided by a cross-partition) and set in the south-east corner of a garden 14 m deep. Both the garden and latrine pentices were traced.

At Beauvale only one cell, Cell 3, was fully excavated (see Figure 8.13) and its plan was claimed to be almost identical to those recorded at Mount Grace by Hope. To what extent that results from the excavators having Hope's plan of Mount Grace in front of them as they worked is unclear (Hill and Gill 1908, 74). Cell 3 measured 6.1 m square internally, with walls 1.0 m thick, and lay in the south-east corner of a garden plot some 13.1 m square. The cloister door of the cell was not placed centrally, but towards the east gable wall, and led into a lobby 1.2 m wide. The east end of the lobby contained a wooden turning stair to the upper floor. Beyond the lobby the cell was divided internally, by timber partitions set on stone plinths, into two rooms. The tiled living room, which was a step above the lobby floor, occupied the east end of the cell, with a fireplace in the east wall, its stack projecting into the neighbouring garden plot on the centre line of the cell. A castellated octagonal chimney was recovered from the cell. To the west was a second room, a bedroom and oratory, and a study. Though the excavators looked for a partition dividing these two function areas, they failed to find one, and it almost certainly did not exist. Fragments of window detail suggested trefoiled lights below square heads, but the masonry of the walls did not survive to a height sufficient to locate the windows or demonstrate their size. Some window detail had fallen from the upper floor, suggesting a three-light window in the east gable wall. The roof was of low pitch and slated, as at Mount Grace, and fragments of a gable cross were recovered. A door from the lobby led into a gallery 1.2 m wide, built of timber and set on a stone plinth, which ran along the inside of the cloister wall. Within this gallery was a tap niche (better evidenced in Cell 2, where the lead water pipe survived). A second door in the north wall of the living room led to the latrine pentice. The latrine itself was thought to be of timber, as no trace was found of it in excavation. It is more likely, however, to have been of stone and corbelled out over an open drain.

At Coventry four cells on the east side of the great cloister – Cells 2 to 5, as described in contemporary documents – were excavated in 1980–2 (Soden 1995, 58–63). All shared a common plan, being some 4.25 m deep and 4.60 m wide and set in the north-west corner of a garden plot 10.8 m wide and 13.8 m deep. Each had a door placed centrally in their cloister wall. Internally, they were divided into a lobby and two rooms by timber partitions set on stone sleeper walls, their planning being very similar to that of the Beauvale cells. Cell 3 was the most complete example. Figure 8.13 shows a composite plan of Cells 2 and 3 (Soden's IV and III). Immediately inside the cloister door was a lobby 0.8 m wide that was divided into two parts by a timber partition. The northern part was paved and was probably the site of the stair to the upper floor with a cupboard below, while the southern part was tiled and led to the garden pentice door in the south wall of the cell. Opposite the cloister door was a door into the living room, which occupied the southern half of the cell. No trace was found of a fireplace, but there was a door in the south-west corner of the room leading into the garden. A door towards the east end of the partition led into the northern room, which the excavator considered to be the bedroom and oratory because it had no external door. Cell 2, however, had a door in its north-east corner leading to the latrine pentice. To the south of Cell 3 was a garden pentice some 1.9 m wide that returned along the south wall of the cell and appears to have continued towards the east precinct wall, where the latrine must have been situated. This east–west gallery was only 1.5 m wide. In Cell 2, the place of this pentice was taken up by a room the full depth of the cell.

The form and plan of the Mount Grace cells (see Figure 8.13) are fully discussed in Chapters 4 and 6. The 15 cells on the east, north and west sides of the great cloister demonstrate a remarkable consistency of planning. Variation is normally explained by date of building, and the order of building has been determined by analysis of the standing ruins. Every cell was entered through a corridor or lobby that led to the garden pentice at one end and contained the turning stair to the upper floor, usually with a cupboard below it. Off the lobby was a living room with a wall fireplace and a door to the latrine pentice. Entered from the living room were two further rooms, one usually larger than the other: the study, and the bedroom and oratory. Mount Grace is exceptional in that several cells retain evidence of fenestration, at least for the latest phase of occupation: the living room had a large four-light window, the study had a similar four-light window and a single-light window and the bedroom/oratory had a single-light window. The site also demonstrates a curious fact of Carthusian life that remains unexplained. While the cloister door was invariably locked with a key, which ensured the monk's solitude, the doors to the garden and latrine pentices were secured with locking bars. Access to the outside of the cell, which lay in a garden surrounded by walls at least 3.5 m high, was extremely unlikely in any event. All the same, the community believed that these doors had to be secured in this rather cumbersome way. Keys, a common find on monastic sites, are rare at Mount Grace, other than in the kitchen area, and are conspicuous by their absence. The indication is that doors against other members of the community were locked, but that the more drastic resort of barring other doors was perhaps an act undertaken against demons, which were very real in the medieval Carthusian mind.

Two cells, 22 and 23, on the south side of the great cloister, are atypical (see Figure 6.31). Both were forced into cramped spaces on the north side of the church between the prior's cell and the chapter house; both were at first-floor level above cellars to which they had no access; and both had no evidence of a workroom on an upper floor. Both, too, were largely timber-framed buildings. Cell 23, like Cell 8 built in Period Three, maintained a standard passage-and-three-room layout, with roughly half the floor area of a standard cell, but had no garden or pentices. It did, however, have a latrine entered directly from the living room. Having no stairs and no garden, it might have been designed for an older member of the community. Cell 23 was different. There was no entry passage; the cloister door led directly into a living room little more than 2 m wide and with a tiny fireplace. Two rooms to the east provided a large study and a bedroom and oratory, maintaining the tripartite division of rooms seen elsewhere in the great cloister as late as the 1520s. This cell might have had the use of the garden between it and the chapter house, but, again, there was no private cloister and the latrine was *en suite* with the living room. Although these cells are planned differently from the 16 standard cells about the great cloister, they still maintain, with some difficulty, the three-room division common to those cells.

Aside from the two cells just described, in every case, and regardless of date, the monks' cells were two-storey structures with living accommodation on the ground floor. The upper floor was used as a workroom. Unfortunately, no first-floor plan remains in England and the form and layout of the workroom remains unknown. The original or early form of the Carthusian cell in England, or indeed elsewhere in Europe, remains unknown, as none of the early cells at Witham have been excavated. Starting with the cells at Hinton, their plan appears to be reasonably consistent, but no individual cell was completely excavated and the plan was recovered by wall chasing, with no attention paid to flooring or evidence for timber partitioning. They must have remained suitable for use because they do not appear to have been altered or modified before the Suppression. However, the founding party of monks at Beauvale came from Hinton, and when they began building permanent cells in the third quarter of the 14th century did not choose the plan they knew well from Hinton, and neither did Prior John Luscote and the Hinton and Beauvale monks who settled at the London charterhouse in or before 1371. They adopted the cell plan at Beauvale with slight variations. The founding monks at Coventry came from London and Beauvale, and were using the same basic plan of two rooms and an entry passage; if there was a change here, it was that the cells were smaller and thinner-walled. At Mount Grace, where the earliest cells were built in the first decade of the 15th century, the division of the cell into an entry passage and three rooms was well established. Unfortunately, it is not known where the founding community came from, but London is a strong possibility. At least one cell in the north range at London had a living room, bedroom and oratory, and a separate study, the norm at Mount Grace until the Suppression. Only at Mount Grace do we have evidence for alterations being made to cells to suit the needs of individual monks, and this must have happened at all houses from time to time.

The charterhouse of Delft in Holland, excavated and observed by H. H. Vos during the construction of a hospital on the site, provides a comparable contemporary cell plan outside England in the late Middle Ages (Vos 1975, *passim*). There the common pattern (see Figure 8.14) was of a cell some 8 m wide and 6.5 m deep set in the corner of a garden plot some 17 m square and divided into two equal-sized rooms on the ground floor (Vos 1985, afb 15).

The living room was entered directly from the cloister, there was no lobby, and a single door in the back wall led directly to a latrine pentice that also accessed the garden. A door at the centre of the partition wall accessed a combined bedroom, study and oratory. There was no garden pentice in any of the 20 cells examined, nor any door leading into one. The excavator postulated a workroom on the upper floor, though no trace was found of a stair. The excavation of great cloister cells at Nieuwlicht in both the north and south ranges confirms both the detail recorded at Delft and the development of the Carthusian cell from the first decade of the 15th century to the closure of the house in 1579 (Hoogendijke 2012, 62–84; Hartog 2013, 35; Hartog 2016, 29–44). This general plan had a long currency, and is still recognisable in the 17th-century cells of the charterhouse of La Verne, in the southern Alps of Var, excavated by J.-L. Mordefroid and J. H. Escobar (1996, 184–90). Cell 4 at La Verne was a two-storey structure 9.34 m wide and 10.86 m deep set in the corner of a garden plot 14.15 m wide and 21.73 m deep (see Figure 8.15). The cell was entered from the cloister alley through a door at the centre of its west wall that led into a lobby. At the north end of the lobby was a turning stair to the upper floor, and at the south end a door that led into a workroom, at the south end of which was a latrine. The cell itself was partitioned at ground level into a heated living room, a small bedroom and oratory, and a larger study. In the east wall of the living room a door led into a gallery, the descendant of the Mount Grace garden pentice or private cloister alley.

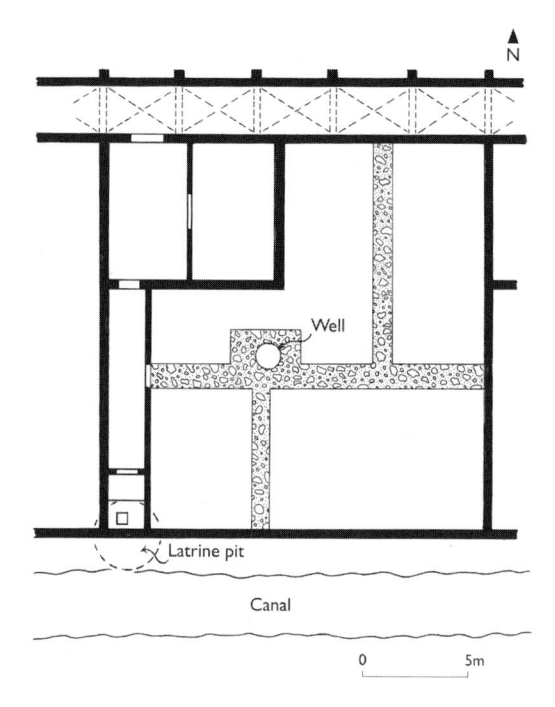

Figure 8.14 Reconstructed cell plan at the charterhouse of Delft in Holland (after Vos 1975).

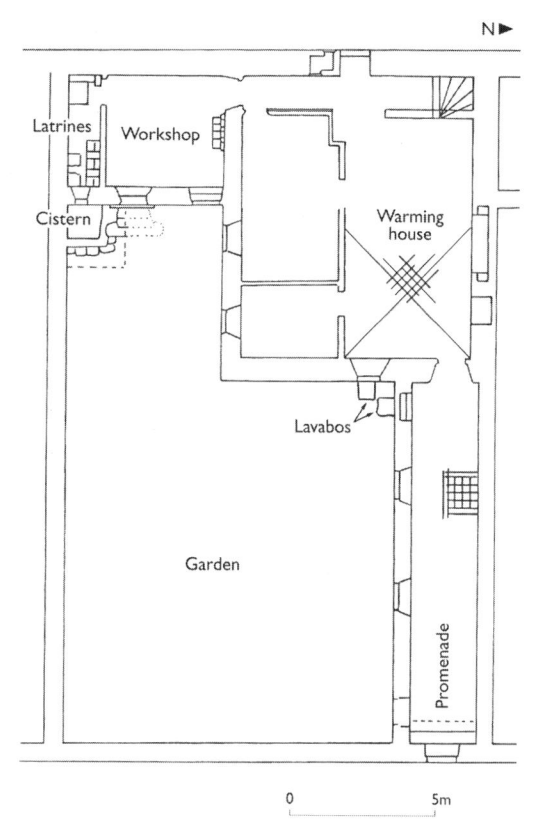

Figure 8.15 Cell 4 at the charterhouse of Notre-Dame-de-la-Verne, Var, France (J.-L. Mordefroid).

How and where the 'later' plan developed is far from clear, but the form and scale of accommodation it provided is not unique to the Carthusian order in England; similar provision can be seen in lodgings ranges from the early 14th century. The earliest known example is the south range of the college of the Vicars Choral at Lincoln (Wood 1951), where six single and undivided rooms, each with an attached latrine, were provided on two floors in about 1310. In 1370 Henry Yeveley was commissioned to build a college of chantry priests at Cobham in Kent, adopting for the first time individual cells on two floors for the priests. In the following year he secured the contract for the first buildings of the London charterhouse and was responsible for the first cells to be built there (Harvey 1946, 30–1). The accommodation provided by the contemporary Carthusian cells should be compared with similar contemporary provision made for retainers and priests in great households, for vicars choral or chantry priests, for colleges and for hospitals.

Henry Yeveley's college at Cobham, begun in 1370, provided six individual cells, each with a fireplace and entered separately from a cloister, but with a common latrine, and the similarity of the design of the earliest cells at London, also designed by Yeveley, is obvious (Harvey 1946, 31). At Dartington Hall, Devon, built by Thomas de Holand's brother John in c.1385–90, the lodging range of 16 chambers on two floors survives little modified (Emery 2007a, 232–5). Each chamber was approximately 6.6 m square, lit by a single window and provided with a wall fireplace and a latrine: basic accommodation for a senior member of the household who would have eaten in hall but who required sleeping and office space. Similar, if slightly less generous, provision was made in the lower court at Haddon Hall in Derbyshire (Pantin 1959, 253), where two qualities of lodging were supplied. Of the better quality was the chaplain's accommodation, which was divided into a living room and a chamber. Here the living room was heated and, again, supplied with a latrine. This form of accommodation had a long life, beginning in the middle years of the 14th century and continuing with little modification into the early years of the 17th century. At the hospital of St Cross in Winchester, in Cardinal Beaufort's range of c.1445, accommodation consisting of a heated room and two chambers, one of which had a latrine, was provided on two floors. The parallel was close enough for Walter Godfrey to observe that St Cross was one of the earliest hospitals to be organised 'upon the Carthusian plan of separate dwellings or cells' (Clapham and Godfrey 1913, 220–1). At Ashby de la Zouch Castle, Lord Hastings built a new collegiate chapel and a lodging for his priests in the late 1480s (Jones 1984, 8). In all, there are four sets of lodgings, two at ground-floor level and two above, each comprising a heated living room with access to a latrine, and a chamber.

From a monastic context, one of the closest analogies to the Carthusian cell of the 'late' type remains in the south range of Worcester College, Oxford. Built by the Benedictines of Gloucester in the 15th century to be occupied by individual houses of the order, the accommodation comprised individual chambers and studies on two floors. The chamber was a combined living room and bedroom with a wall fireplace and one- and two-light windows; the study had a single-light window. There was, however, no internal latrine (Pantin 1959, 246–7). A number of similar arrangements can still be detected within the claustral nucleus or infirmary of several monasteries, where communal living had begun to break down in the later Middle Ages. At Cleeve Abbey (Gilyard-Beer 1990, 30–1) the ground floor of the south range, rebuilt in the late 15th century by Abbot David Juyner, contains a living room with a wall fireplace and a bed chamber with a latrine, presumably occupied by a senior member of the convent. While Gilyard-Beer considered this to be a corrodian's lodging, he was not aware of a similar and somewhat earlier development at Byland Abbey (Harrison 1990, 15–18), where a series of two-room apartments was constructed on the ground floor of the east range and the site of the infirmary in the late 14th or early 15th century to provide accommodation for individual monks. Similar arrangements can be seen in the infirmary at Fountains Abbey (Coppack and Gilyard-Beer 1993, 49–50; Coppack 2002, 200–2). Here, individual lodgings, many of them two-storeyed, were created in the aisles of the infirmary hall and provided with fireplaces and latrines. Other examples exist, as within the infirmaries at Tintern and Kirkstall, but a general lack of archaeological research into later medieval monastic life means that the evidence for the partitioning up of old communal ranges has yet to be sought. Generally speaking, however, there is sufficient evidence to suggest that even the communal orders were providing individual accommodation for their monks from the late 14th century and that they were moving closer to the concept of the Carthusian cell.

At Mount Grace, the plan form of the prior's cell was different from that of the monks' cells (see Figure 8.16B and C), probably because the prior needed additional space for his administrative duties. Few examples of comparable president's lodgings of medieval date exist, and only two other Carthusian prior's cells can be identified in England. The prior's cell at Hinton (see Figure 8.16A) remains today at the west end of the north cloister range, a building of 1280–90 first identified by Fletcher (1958/9, 78), with the refectory above.

It was of four bays and comprised two rooms: a heated living room to the west vaulted in three bays and entered through a baffle porch from the cloister alley, and, to the east, a larger room vaulted in three double bays. This latter room may have been partitioned in timber. A hatch to the east of the cloister door served the eastern room, although this was later blocked and replaced by a hatch inside the baffle entry. The living room was lit by small square-headed windows to either side of the fireplace and had a narrow door in its north-west corner that probably led to a latrine (a major drain was located just to the north of the cell). A wide archway at the north end of the east wall of the living room led into the larger space, which had a wide door at the centre of its north wall flanked by windows that are now blocked. A narrow square-headed door in its south-east corner led into what was probably a garden pentice, but this was blocked when the kitchen was placed there.

At London, the prior's cell was originally the Cell A recorded on the London waterworks plan, which was recorded by Sealey and Paget during the clearance of bomb debris (Knowles and Grimes 1954, 45–6; Barber and Thomas 2002, 20). One of the cells built by Henry Yeveley, it was rectangular in plan, measuring 7.96 m by 6.12 m, and occupied the full width of its plot against the cloister. In the late 1530s, however, the prior's cell was referred to as 'new built', suggesting that it had moved to a new location, which is unknown.

At Coventry, the prior's cell of the early 15th century survives together with the contemporary refectory to the south-west of the church (see Figure 8.15D and E). The original range, in which the prior's cell and refectory were situated, was dated by Soden to before 1417 (Soden 2005, 90), but is more likely to date to the 1430s (Luxford 2011b, 252). It was 8.10 m wide and, after the demolition of its southern end in the 19th century, is now 24.5 m long internally, with walls, on average, 0.75 m thick. At ground-floor level at the south end a cross-passage has a primary door at its east end and an archway at its west that led to a contemporary building, no longer surviving, to the west of the range. Immediately to the north, a traceried window is a relatively modern insertion in what is otherwise undisturbed medieval walling as far north as the south wall of the church. The west wall is largely refaced at ground-floor level, but at first-floor level is substantially as built, with a partially blocked medieval window towards its southern end. A cross-wing at the south end that survived until the 19th century is evidenced by the obviously internal arch of two orders at the west end of the cross-passage, while a second cross-wing at the north end, south of the church but west of the refectory, is known from map evidence and is normally interpreted as the convent kitchen.

The prior's cell, entered from the cross-passage through a square-headed door, occupied the southern half of the building and was arranged on two floors. At ground level was a room 5.80 m by 8.00 m, with a spiral stair to the upper floor in its north-eastern corner. The stair turret intrudes into the room and, apart from the door in the south wall, is the only visible medieval feature. The fireplace and window in the west wall are obvious insertions of the late 19th or early 20th century, and the east wall was originally somewhat narrower than it currently is. The west wall at ground-floor level has been largely destroyed by the insertion of three large late 18th-century sash windows and the north, east and south walls are concealed by panelling of the same date. This space was originally more than one room and would have been divided by timber partitions. Typically, there would have been a passage that would have run along the east wall, connecting the door from the passage to the stair turret, and two rooms: a study lit by a fairly large square-headed window in the west wall, and a bedroom and oratory lit by a smaller one. Almost certainly, the traceried light in the east wall replaces a simpler medieval window that lit the passage. The upper floor consisted of a single room 8 m square that extended over the cross-passage and contained a substantial 14th-century fireplace with a corbelled and moulded lintel in its east wall and, originally, the top of the stair turret in its north-east angle. This room was the prior's hall, where he might entertain or conduct business. It was originally a tall room, open to the roof, and its true proportions are hidden by a late 16th-century inserted ceiling. One medieval window remains opposite the fireplace, and this appears to have been the only source of light. Its lower part has been destroyed by the insertion of a later window, but its elaborately moulded splays are still visible on the top floor of the present building. It was a mullioned and transomed window with a square head, the form of which is still patently clear on the outside face of the west wall. On the upper floor, two tie-beams that relate to the medieval

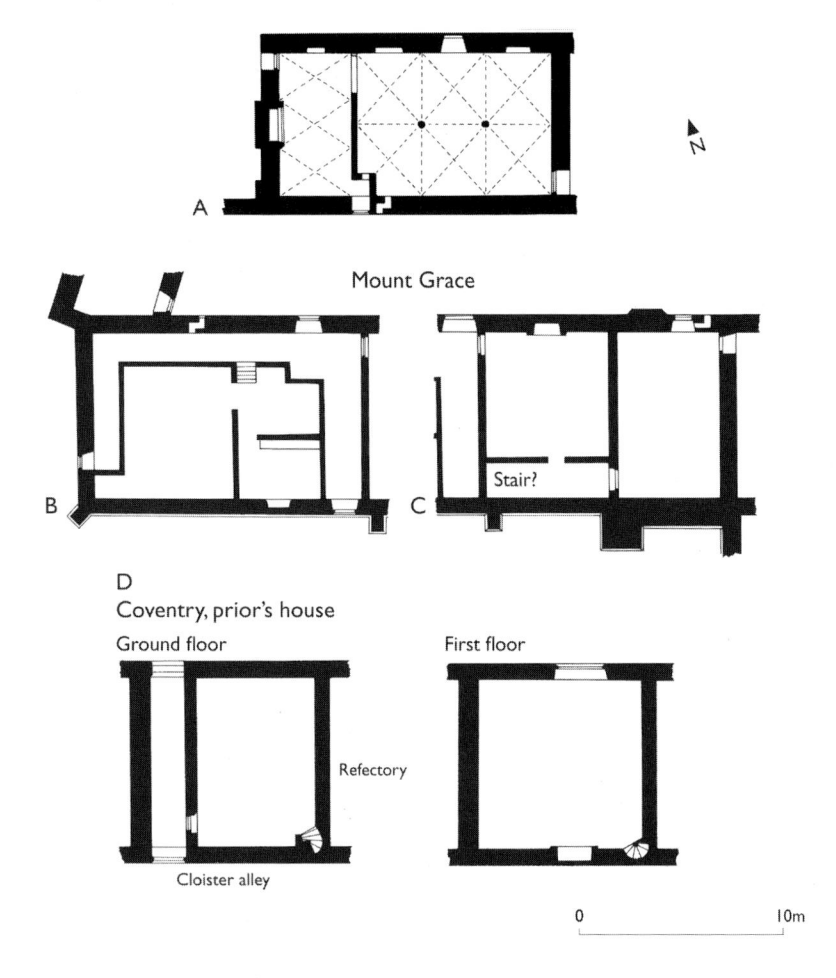

Figure 8.16 Comparative plans of prior's cells. A: Hinton; B: Mount Grace, the early cell; C: Mount Grace, the later cell; D: Coventry.

roof remain within this room; these are carved with a foliate design that suggests replacement in the late 15th or early 16th century, but could conceivably be as early as the first quarter of the 15th century. The room was clearly one of some sophistication. The tie-beam, which is south of the chimey-piece and the window in the west wall, stands on wall posts set on corbels. This tie formed the basis of a roof truss that was set slightly off-centre to avoid the chimney stack, another indication that the first-floor fireplace is primary to the structure.

At Mount Grace, two prior's cells are known from excavation (see Figure 8.16B and C). The first, from Period One, was probably built before 1405. The second belongs to Period Two, possibly dating to the 1430s. The plan of the first prior's cell has a number of similarities with the slightly later prior's cell at Coventry, with an entry passage and three rooms, one heated, at ground-floor level, and a single room above. As at Coventry, the entrance to the great cloister is adjacent to the entrance to the prior's cell, indicating that the prior directly controlled access into the inner enclosure of the house. As at London and Coventry, the refectory was also immediately adjacent, continuing the association between the prior and communal eating that is implicit in the placing of the prior's cell below the refectory at Witham. The prior's cell at Mount Grace was approximately half as large again as the cells of the choir monks, an indication that the prior was little more than first among equals within the community, but needed extra space because of his duties on behalf of the community. The fact that his living quarters were almost identical to those of the other monks indicates that, unlike the presidents of other orders, the Carthusian prior was provided only with a standard cell for his spiritual use, the one concession to his role in wider society as representative of the house being the exchange of his workroom for a small hall. The second prior's cell, built within the shell of the refectory from the 1420s, was precisely the same size as the original cell. There were some changes, however. The entry to the cloister was closed, although the same relationship was maintained with the new refectory. In Period Three, however, the entrance to the cell was moved to the east side of the building, where a new door that communicated directly with the south cloister alley was inserted, and the original entrance from the lobby of the first prior's cell became a secondary door. It was at this time, too, that the first-floor hall was remodelled, with the addition of an oriel window looking out over the cloister and possibly a second overlooking the court in front of the church. The prior's hall was thus moving closer to the halls of laymen and away from the simplicity normally associated with the order, and was thus becoming more similar to those of other abbots and priors.

Common to both the cells of the community and that of the prior was the provision of an enclosed garden that provided scope for manual work as well as a spiritual context for the religious life. The symbolism of the *hortus conclusus* as a metaphor for chastity, taken from the Song of Songs, had, by the 12th century, been translated to the cult of the Virgin and adopted by the reforming orders. In the 1150s Abbot Aelred of Rievaulx had established a garden in his abbey's cloister with fruit trees and flowers, which he described lovingly in his *de spiritualia amicitia* (Fergusson and Harrison 1999, 65): it was a garden intended to promote spirituality, rather than the sort of functional medicinal garden shown in the infirmary cloister of Canterbury cathedral priory on Prior Wybert's waterworks plan of *c*.1160 (Trinity Coll. MS R.17.1, ff. 284v/285r; Fergusson 2011, fig. 3). Central to Cistercian thinking on gardens were Bernard of Clairvaux's sermons on the Song of Songs (Meyvaert 1986, 51; Newman 1996, 89–94), which were widely read outside the Cistercian order. The garden was not simply a Marian metaphor; it was an aid to contemplation that was an essential part of the *lectio divina* which made up a third part of monastic life, and it provided an opportunity for *opus manuum*, which comprised another third within the confines of the cloister. For the Carthusians, who looked back to the origins of eremitic life in the Egyptian desert, gardens also provided a tangible link with the past and with monastic purity. There was, however, an inconsistency, for the creation of an earthly paradise was somewhat at odds with attempts to re-establish a desert life.

The point at which the Carthusians adopted individual gardens is not recorded. The first monastery at the Grande Chartreuse did not apparently have gardens attached to its cells, although each member of the community was given a piece of ground, carefully selected to ensure that no one benefited over his peers. In Prior Guigues de Saint-Romain's Customs of 1121–8 the only reference to a garden is in the lower house, where it was to be tended by a solitary converse (Thompson 1930, 44). The adoption of individual gardens, however, is critical to the development of the overall Carthusian plan, as it conditions the scale of the great cloister, and it might be assumed that the provision of gardens was already well established when Hugh of Avalon began the construction of Witham in the 1180s, where he specifically created a cloister with cells. Certainly, by the time that Hinton was laid out in the early 13th century the garden and its relationship with the cell was fully established to a pattern that survives to the present day. There is a remarkable consistency in the size of Carthusian gardens in England (see Figure 8.13), suggesting that the plan was maintained from its first establishment with very little change, in spite of the development of the cell itself.

It is highly regrettable that Mount Grace is the only site at which any serious attempt has been made to study individual gardens. Indeed, Keen's excavation of the gardens of Cells 9 and 10 was among the earliest garden excavation in England and identified the potential for the study of Carthusian gardens generally. Remarkably, it was not followed up until 1985, with the excavation to destruction of the garden of Cell 8. The later excavation demonstrated that the garden layout in individual cells might change over time, as monks came and went, and that the Carthusian garden had no specific layout, something that is not particularly remarkable in such a context. The gardens in fact show a remarkable degree of individualism, each one reflecting the interests or needs of the member of the community who tended it. Excavations in Cell 9 revealed the latest garden layout, while those in Cell 10 demonstrated probable elements of two distinct gardens. Both these cells produced evidence for well-defined beds and, in the case of Cell 10, a series of planting pits dug into the natural clay and filled with soil, features that are notoriously difficult to see at Mount Grace unless the clay is wet. Both garden layouts appear to follow a common pattern seen in the late 15th and early 16th centuries, characterised by square raised beds or knots separated by grass paths. The early garden of Cell 8 was similarly formal, but differed in having carefully paved paths and raised rectangular beds revetted with roofing slate. Here, though, the principal bed shared the proportions of the garden beds depicted on the early 9th-century schematic Benedictine plan at St Gall in Switzerland (Stifts-bibliotek St Gallen, Cod. Sang. 1092; Horn and Born 1979, *passim*). Like the western part of the garden of Cell 10, the early garden of Cell 8 had deep planting pits that were filled with fertilised soil. All of the gardens were carefully drained and considerable effort had been expended in developing them. They were designed as 'gardens of delight', not simply for the production of food or herbs, and thus fulfilled the ideal for contemplation first recorded by St Aelred at Rievaulx. The later garden of Cell 8, however, was very different: the raised beds were suppressed and it appears to have been used for the cultivation of vegetables, as it was dug in rows. The neat paths of the earlier garden were replaced with spreads of crushed stone, and the garden was transformed to a place of manual work and food production. As the latest gardens of Cells 8 and 9 were demonstrably contemporary, both being sealed only by spreads of demolition material, both forms of garden were obviously to be found together, indicating the outcomes of personal preference rather than requirements of the house.

Some other detail survives in those cells that have not had their gardens excavated. Cells 2 and 20 have water tanks within the garden, presumably for watering plants without recourse to the piped water supply. A further tank was excavated in the garden of Cell 14, where water from the eavesdrip drain of the cell could be retained by operating a sluice. In the Dutch houses of Nieuwlicht and Delft every garden had its own well, comprising a small barrel with its ends knocked out sunk into the natural sandy clay, which provided water for the garden (see Figure 8.14). Cell 4 retained the stone supports of a seat against the north wall of the garden and Cell 20 had a raised bed against the precinct wall. In Cell 10 there was a raised bed around the knot in the angle of the latrine pentice drain and the eavesdrip drain of the cell, and the garden of the prior's cell had raised borders on its north and east sides. With the exception of the water tanks, which may have been supplemented with the use of butts fed by downpipes from the pentice roofs (suggested in Cell 8), all of these features imply something more than a vegetable garden. While this would not be surprising in the cells of the choir monks, Cell 20 lay in the lesser cloister, suggesting that at least one lay brother had a 'garden of delight'.

The Form and Construction of the Monks' Cells

At Mount Grace nine of the 16 cells around the great cloister that can be described as 'standard', along with those of the prior, have been at least partially excavated, and all 17 cells have had their standing masonry closely examined. While no two are exactly alike, there are a number of common factors that indicate how the cells were built, fitted out, modified to suit individual tastes and decorated. In this they are no different from those cells excavated at Witham, Hinton, Beauvale, London or Coventry, although the only cells they match closely in plan are those of Beauvale and London, which share the same overall design. In terms of building details, the cells of individual houses appear to have followed local building models.

All the cells at Mount Grace were divided by timber partitions into an entry passage, living room, bedroom/oratory and study. While there is evidence that a number of cells had their partitions modified over time, there is no evidence for a radical change of plan or for the overall plan changing between *c*.1400 and 1538. All the cells of the great cloister were of two storeys, with parts of the upper storey surviving in Cells 3, 4 and 6–15. The earliest cells, those of the prior, sacrist and Cells 1–2, have no evidence in their structure for a stair to the upper floor, although this was almost certainly within the closed end of the entry passage in Cells 1–4 and accessed from the living room. Because Cell 8 had doors at both ends of its entry passage, there had to be a freestanding stair in the living room. Otherwise, all cells had turning stairs fixed into their walls.

Entry passages tended to be paved with stone slabs (Cells 2–4, 10, 11 and 14); the paving extended below the stair and, in the case of Cells 10, 11 and perhaps 14, also along the fireplace wall of the living room to the latrine pentice door. Only Cell 10 and the early prior's cell produced a substantial number of plain glazed floor tiles from inside the cell. None were *in situ*, but in Cell 10 they could have been derived from the paving inside the latrine pentice door and in the early prior's cell from the passage along the north wall. At Coventry, where Cells 2–5 have been excavated (Soden 1995, 58–63), all the entry passages were tiled, although the area below the stair to the upper floor might be paved with stone. At Mount Grace the ground-floor rooms of Cells 10, 11, 13, 14 and probably 8 and 15 had timber floors on substantial joists set into the natural ground surface or cut through construction deposits; Cells 9 and 12 had mortar floors, as did the early prior's cell. Cell 3 at Beauvale had a tiled floor in its living room (Hill and Gill 1908, 76), while Cell 2 at Coventry had both tiled and wooden floors, although the other cells had clay floors (Soden 1995, 61 and fig. 21). In three instances at Mount Grace where timber joists were traced in excavation (Cells 10, 11 and 13) the floor cavity was filled with roundwood charcoal that in some instances sealed the partition footings. Keen was of the opinion that this had been introduced when the floor was removed, perhaps being the remains of brushwood insulation in the roof. Coppack, however, also found roundwood charcoal between the joists of the garden pentice of Cell 8, which was stratified below a 16th-century floor. His initial interpretation (see Chapter 3) was that this charcoal had fallen through a rotted floor. The possibility remains that brushwood was used as insulation below the timber floors. A similar deposit was recorded in Cell 4 at Coventry in a room that may have had a timber floor (Soden 1995, 60). The lack of evidence from the sacrist's cell and Cells 1–7 is regrettable, because this means that the manner in which the earliest cells were floored is unknown.

The treatment of the pentice floors was more varied. In the sacrist's cell and Cells 1 and 3–7 no flooring was recorded. In Cell 2, although no floor was traced in the latrine pentice, Saunders noted a quantity of floor tile that had been displaced by earlier excavation. In Cell 8 the latrine pentice was surfaced with gravel and the garden pentice was originally floored in wood, which was replaced in Period Four by gravel. The latrine pentice of Cell 9 produced loose floor tiles, but both pentices of Cell 10 and the latrine pentice of Cell 14 were paved with sandstone flags. Cell 10 also produced loose floor tiles that may have come from the pentice floors. The garden pentice of Cell 11 and the first latrine pentice of Cell 13 were cobbled, while the latrine pentice of Cell 12 appears to have had a suspended wooden floor. The later latrine pentice of Cell 13 had a clay floor, as did the garden pentice of Cell 14. Cell 15 was not examined outside the walls of the cell itself. The flooring of the galleries appears to have been as varied as the structure of the galleries themselves, and no common pattern emerges.

No evidence has been recovered by excavation for the fixtures and furnishing of the cells, although both Cells 8 and 9 retain evidence for panelling. At London, most if not all of the cells were panelled with wainscot, some of which was taken away by the brothers at the Suppression. According to William Dale, who was charged with accounting for the site in the days following its closure, 'certeyne brethren take away ther selles as they stooyd' and '[one] of the sayd brederne toke away ... sertayn boordys of waynscote whyche dyffacyd the Cellys very sore' (Hope 1925, 167). In Cell 8 the panelling was not a primary feature but post-dated the insertion of a round-headed window in the east wall of the cell, probably in the early 16th century; previously, the walls had simply been white-limed. The internal splay of this window was cut down to floor level, a feature noted again in Cell 7, where a window in the east wall had been cut down, and Cell 10, where both the windows of the study had been cut down to floor level. Cells 6, 11 and 14 retained evidence of internal plaster finishes. Elsewhere, no evidence survived the processes of weathering and repointing.

The Order and Sponsoring of Cells

It is clear from the evidence of form and structure that the great cloister at Mount Grace was not developed in a single operation, but in stages that can be related to developing patronage. Taking the evidence of door heads, the only primary evidence that remains, the order of building was the prior's and sacrist's cells, followed by Cells 1–2, 3–4, 5, 6–7, 9, 10–15 and, finally, Cell 8 (see Chapter 6). Apart from the Period One prior's and sacrist's cells, all but Cell 8 were built in Period Two, between about 1420 and 1450. Cells 1–7 replaced temporary timber cells that were indicated by the documented extent of the community in 1412 (see Chapter 2). The rebuilding of these cells in stone appears to follow on from the patronage of Thomas Beaufort in 1417, for he 'built and endowed five cells in the same [place]' (Bodleian MS Rawlinson D.138, f. 108v). Endowment and building need not have been contemporary events, however, in spite of this statement. Cell 1 bears the arms of Archbishop Richard Scrope of York, who died in 1405, at least a decade before the cell was built. Cell 4, although the evidence is no longer clear, had label-stop shields with the arms of Gascoigne (Hope 1905, 297) and Cell 5 has smaller shields with the same charge (ibid., 298), making the likely founder Sir William Gascoigne, chief justice of the King's Bench and a friend of Scrope, who died in 1419. This probably dates the endowment of these two cells, but, again, it is not contemporary with their construction. The arms of Redman quartering Aldburgh found on the label-stops of the door to the first prior's cell in the south-west cloister range are those of Sir Richard Redman, MP for Yorkshire between 1405 and 1421 and Speaker of the Commons in 1415, and there can be little doubt that he was at least associated with the building of that cell in Period One. It is known that his wife's family was associated with the foundation of the house, being included in the list of supporters of the founder in his charter of 1398 (see Chapter 2).

The sponsoring of individual cells was not peculiar to Mount Grace, and one of the appeals of the Carthusians was that the sponsoring of individual cells allowed a large number of people, including the merchant classes, to take an active part in the endowment of their chosen house. At the London charterhouse the names of the founders are recorded for all of the cells, with, in most cases, an indication of the date and cost (Hope 1925, 155–7). Here, the cells were identified by a letter, the normal method used by the Carthusians, which was originally recorded on the waterworks plan of 1431–2 (see Figure 1.8). At Hinton, the letter was actually incised in the door jamb. The construction of the great cloister at London was begun by founder Sir Walter Manney in 1371/2 to the design of Henry Yeveley (TNA Pat. R. 50 Edward III, pt ii, m.13), and his initial investment in Cell A (the prior's cell) was completed by Sir William Walworth, who also sponsored Cells B, D, G, H and J in 1372, and

Adam Fraunceys, who built Cells C, E, F, L and M in 1374. In both cases the endowment was 1,000 marks (£666), or 200 marks (£132.66) per cell. In 1376, Mary de St Pol endowed the house with a gift of £2,000, which included the building of Cell K, and in 1378 Felicia Aubrey and Margaret Tilney built Cells N and O, each at the cost of 260 marks (£173.33). This completed the west and north sides of the great cloister and provided lodging for the prior and 13 monks. The cells of the east and south sides of the cloister were provided in a more piecemeal way, suggesting a slowing in the growth of the community. However, the order of building can still be determined reasonably accurately. First, Cells R and S were built by Bishop Thomas Hatfield of Durham before 1381 at a cost of 600 marks (£400); Cell T followed, built by William Ufford, Earl of Suffolk, in 1382 with an endowment of 460 marks (£306.66). Next came Cell Q, sponsored by Bishop John Bokyngham of Lincoln, followed by Cell P, financed by Sir Robert Knolles in about 1389. At this point there was a pause in building. When construction recommenced, Cell V was sponsored by Richard Clyderhowe before 1419 and Cell X by his kinsman John Clyderhowe, who had funded the construction of the lesser cloister in 1436, after that date. The corner cell, Cell Y, was built at the cost of William Symmes (who had funded the conduit with Anne Tatershale in 1431) before his death in 1439, beginning the south range. Cell Z was built at the cost of Dame Joan Brenchley before her death in 1453, the building of the cell not being included in her will of that year (Hope 1925, 72). The sacrist's cell to the east of the chapter house was built by Robert Chamberlayn, when the endowment promised by Robert Manfeld in 1419 had failed to materialise. Its date is not known, but Chamberlayn was a contemporary of William Symmes.

At Coventry, the same process can be seen (Rowntree 1981, 82). This house had uncertain beginnings in 1375, when three monks from London occupied the hermitage of St Anne without any endowment and only the promise of a site (Dugdale 1830, 6, 16). They were joined by three brothers from Beauvale and by four recruits gathered locally. They were not to occupy their permanent site until 1382 and work began on a permanent church in 1385, Richard II laying the foundation stone and claiming to be the founder. Before 1385 seven cells had been built or at least endowed, the scale of the endowment, when compared with the costs of the London house, suggesting that these were temporary cells. Cells 1–3 were sponsored by Richard Luff and John Botener, who also contributed to the cost of the church. Their contribution, which can only have partially covered the cost, was 40 marks (£26.66). Cell 4 was endowed by Dame Margaret Byry of Newark at a cost of £20 and Cell 5 was built with £20 from Dame Margaret Tilney, who later financed Cell O at London and who also provided £10 towards the window 'at the east end of the choir' at Coventry. Cell 6 was sponsored by Bishop John Bokyngham of Lincoln, again for £20, and Cell 7 by Thomas Beauchamp, Earl of Warwick, at the same cost. Cells 8–11 followed after work had begun on the church: Cell 8 was endowed by Adam Botener of Coventry; Cell 9 from the estate of Sir Nigel Loryng procured by Bishop Robert Braybroke of London; Cell 10 from the goods of William Tilney, husband of Dame Margery and sometime deputy butler of Boston, through John Holmeton, his executor, who had himself contributed £180 to the building of the church; and Cell 11 from the estate of Sir John Morten, canon of Lichfield. In each case the endowment was £20 (Dugdale 1830, 16–17).

Sponsorship could take another form. At Hull, John Colthorpe, who had been mayor in 1398, and his wife Alice endowed a cell in the early 15th century with an annual rental of 20s. from a manor in Essex (Page 1913, 191), enough to ensure the sustenance of the monk without providing the structure of the cell itself.

A similar process of cell endowing and building at the Nieuwlicht charterhouse is recorded in a mid-15th-century List of Great Donors (HUA HSA18153, de Grote Schenkers; Geer 1857, 129–46). Building began in 1392 with the lesser cloister, which was to form a temporary monastery while money was raised for the building of the greater part of the house, and there must have been temporary cells, as there were four monks in 1194 and six two years later. Before 1404 Mechtildis van Nes funded the building of two cells, at about the same time Agaat Russchen built a third and, between 1400 and 1407, the founder's brother

Willem van Abcoude built the seven cells of the east range of the great cloister. This accords well with the 11–12 monks who are thought from documentary sources to have comprised the community by 1406. Financial problems then resulted in the dispersal of some of the monks to other houses in 1412, but Willem van Merode built two additional cells around 1416. Further cells may also have been built from money accruing to the community from a whole host of major and minor donors, but before 1440 Alijt Hessel and Elizabeth Emerici had both built cells for their sons. The growth of the community was slow, and Johan Dirckssoen is recorded as building a wooden cell, presumably a temporary structure that would be replaced as money accumulated (Gumbert 1974, 54–5). This may indicate that the community was finding it easier to attract recruits than to raise the money to build permanent cells. The latest record of a new cell being funded comes from the will of Sophia 't Scrooden in c.1500 (HUA HS 1006–3, Oude of Eerste cartularium, ff. 113v–114r).

The Great Cloister

It is difficult to find comparison for the ultra-plain details of the two phases of the great cloister at Mount Grace, particularly as no other Carthusian cloister has been recovered in England. The Period Two cloister arcade consisted of groups of probably three cinquefoil ogee lights, all of the same height beneath a straight hood-mould. The lights were probably not originally glazed, and it should be remembered that the narrow cloister alleys were only passages to the church and other communal buildings in a Carthusian house, not the living room of the community. The Period Three cloister arcade appears to be a less finely worked copy of the earlier arcade, though here the lights were glazed from the first and sat below a segmental arch. By contrast, the majority of perpendicular cloisters extant elsewhere (for example, at Gloucester, Wells, Norwich and New College, Oxford; see Harvey 1978, pls 29, 88, 158 and 129) continued the earlier fashion of having ornate tracery in their arcade lights resembling those found in aisle or clerestorey windows. In addition, the majority of such grand cloisters are covered in an equally impressive way with stone vaulting, something that was apparently never considered at Mount Grace, although it does occur in Continental houses of the order. Some institutions had plainer designs; Magdalen College, Oxford, had cloisters almost as plain (and contemporary with the Period Three work at Mount Grace), with three lights and open spandrels beneath a four-centred arch. More similar, though, is the cloister of St Giles' Hospital of Norwich, built in 1448–57 by Robert Buchan (Harvey 1978, pl. 159; Rawcliffe 1999, 63–4 and pl. 5). Aside from the blind worked spandrels, it could almost have come from Mount Grace in Period Two, being unglazed with three cinquefoil lights per bay set beneath a label externally and a four-centred arch internally. Grand indeed for a hospital, albeit one with rapidly changing function, a cloister such as this would seem restrained in most monastic and cathedral contexts. Yet in a Carthusian great cloister fine architecture would have served no function: the monks' business was with God, not with display, and there would be no one else to appreciate it. Indeed, once in their cells the majority of monks could not even see into the cloister.

The Lay Brothers' Cells

Mount Grace has produced the only evidence for lay brothers' cells in Britain. From the 12th century it was usual for the lay brothers to occupy a separate 'lower house' or *correrie* detached from the 'upper house' of the monks to ensure the monks' seclusion, and this is the pattern of development known at both Witham and Hinton, where *correries* have been identified. In the 12th century the Carthusians had been dependent on substantial numbers of lay brothers; indeed, in the 1160s the Grande Chartreuse itself had some 16 lay brothers to a maximum of 14 choir monks, figures established in Prior Guigues de Saint-Romain's Customs (Farmer 1989, 9; Cowdrey 1989, 43). As communities grew, the *conversi* were supplemented by hired servants. Although the reasons for it are unclear, there was a move to combine both groups within the same house by about the middle of the 14th century; Beauvale is presumed to have been the last English house where the two communities were so divided. By this date lay brothers had already ceased to be a significant element in houses of other orders, including the Cistercians, and monastic agriculture was firmly in the hands of lay servants or tenants. Quite possibly, the small numbers of lay brothers and their lost functions outside the monastery enabled the two houses to be combined, greatly increasing efficiency. Any disturbance this might have caused the monks was more than compensated for by the fact that the lay brothers' presence within the monastery enabled the monks to keep to their cells. Both London and Mount Grace had six lay brothers; Coventry had three; Beauvale had two; and Hull only one in the 1530s.

By analogy with Continental houses it has been presumed that the lay brothers were housed communally and not in individual cells, although there is no positive evidence in England to support this. At London, the lay brothers were apparently housed in the early 16th-century west range of a court to the west of the lesser cloister, although this has yet to be tested by excavation. The identification of the six cells of the lesser cloister at Mount Grace is a simple matter of arithmetic. The great cloister had cells for the prior, sacrist and 17 monks. There was also accommodation for the procurator (who was a monk) at the north end of the guest-house range. At the Suppression Mount Grace had 20 monks, each with an identifiable cell. There were, in addition, six lay brothers and an oblate, and at least a further six cells have been traced.

None of the lay brothers' cells at Mount Grace have been excavated since their partial clearance by Hope, though the plans of five have been recovered and their masonry examined. Five date to Period Three – the later 15th century – and they post-date all the cells of the great cloister apart from Cell 8. They are, however, all added to a pre-existing lesser cloister wall and it is likely that they replaced timber cells dating to Period Two. They are slightly smaller than the monks' cells but share a common ground plan, with an entry passage and two or three rooms defined by timber partitions. Lay brothers had no need of an oratory, for they were not priests, or a study, for they were not scholars. The basic cell plan was altered to suit their needs. Each cell was set in a garden, with the exception of the Period Four Cell 16, which was the last to be built on a cramped site between the lesser cloister and the church, and each had its own latrine. Cell 16 had its garden and privy on the opposite side of the lesser cloister, which can hardly have been convenient. All six cells differ in two ways from those of the great cloister:

none has any evidence for a stair to an upper floor, and all have fireplaces that project into the living room. The cells appear to have been of a single storey, for the lay brothers had no need of a workroom. Their duties lay in the great cloister, the kitchens, bakehouse and brewhouse, the granaries, the guest house and the outer court.

If lay brothers could be accommodated in cells that were close in their layout to those of the monks by the later 15th century it is quite possible that at Beauvale and Coventry empty cells in the great cloister evidenced by the numbers of religious in 1535/6 could have been occupied by the few lay brothers in these houses, obviating the need to provide them with distinct accommodation. Only further excavation will resolve this issue.

The Kitchen and its Offices

Monastic kitchens are well represented in the claustral plans of virtually all the orders in England, and their layout has been established by clearance and early excavation. Modern excavation, however, has provided detailed evidence from very few sites, notable exceptions being Benedictine Shrewsbury (Baker and Cooper 1988; Baker 2002, 71–86) and Coventry cathedral priory (Hobley 1971, 97), Augustinian Norton (Brown and Howard-Davis 2008, 61–3 and 87–9) and St Gregory's, Canterbury (Hicks and Tatton-Brown 1991), Cistercian Kirkstall (Moorhouse and Wrathmell 1987) and Sawley (Coppack *et al.* 2002, 65–9 and 77–9), the Lincoln Franciscan friary (Jarvis 1995, 9) and the Guildford Dominican friary, as well as subsidiary kitchens associated with the misericord at Benedictine Westminster (Black 1976) and the infirmary at Cluniac Bermondsey (Dyson *et al.* 2011, 42, 44 and 61, and fig. 23). No other Carthusian kitchens have been identified in England, with the exception of Hinton (Fletcher 1958–9, 78), although the kitchens at the London charterhouse are well known from documentary sources (Hope 1925) and can partially be traced in the west range of the surviving Washhouse Court (Barber and Thomas 2002, 38; *ex inf.* Stephen Porter). Small quantities of food waste associated with the kitchen at London have been recovered (Barber and Thomas 2002, 61–5).

In the later Middle Ages, middle range and larger monasteries would typically have had between two and five kitchens: the cloister kitchen directly associated with the refectory, a meat kitchen associated with the misericord, a kitchen within the infirmary, a kitchen attached to the president's lodging and a kitchen associated with guest facilities. Each was intended for a discrete diet although, in smaller houses, some kitchens might be shared between two or more groups of users. The Carthusians rejected the eating of meat, even for the sick, and provided no infirmary because the old and infirm were tended in their cells. Their monasteries should thus have a single kitchen analogous to the cloister kitchen of other orders, where it was usually a vegetarian kitchen and the refectory a vegetarian hall. A separate diet might be provided for guests and it comes as no surprise that the London charterhouse had two kitchens, a fish kitchen associated with the refectory and great cloister, and a flesh kitchen (called 'Egypt' on the waterworks plan in a reference to the starving children of Israel passing through the desert of Sin and thinking of the flesh-pots of Egypt, where they had bread to the full (Exodus XVI, 1–3)) and meat hall in the inner court to serve the guest house. The kitchen at Hinton, a room some 7 m² with a large tile-lined hearth against its north wall, lay to the east of the refectory in the north range of the great cloister (see Figure 1.4). Although only partially excavated and undated, it would appear to resemble a standard late medieval monastic kitchen. Perhaps the closest comparison of plan form for the kitchen and its offices should be sought in the late medieval kitchens of the reformed orders, as at Kirkstall and Sawley, or of the friars.

Mount Grace has seen one of the most substantial excavations of any monastic kitchen (see Figure 8.17) in England or Europe, providing clear indications of the development of the cloister and guest kitchens from about 1420 to the Suppression (see Figure 8.17B–D), but the form of the buildings that comprised the kitchen and its offices are difficult to interpret without the documentary evidence provided by the charterhouse of London. London has provided good parallels for other buildings at Mount Grace, and there is a strong likelihood that there was a 'family' relationship here, too. At London, the kitchen was a group of closely related rooms that retained their contents in 1539: the fish kitchen with 'iiij Cisternes of leade all in on, a lyttell ffurnasse of brasse, a shyppynge borde, [and] ij hanginge shelves'; the larder with 'xiiij shelves'; and the buttery

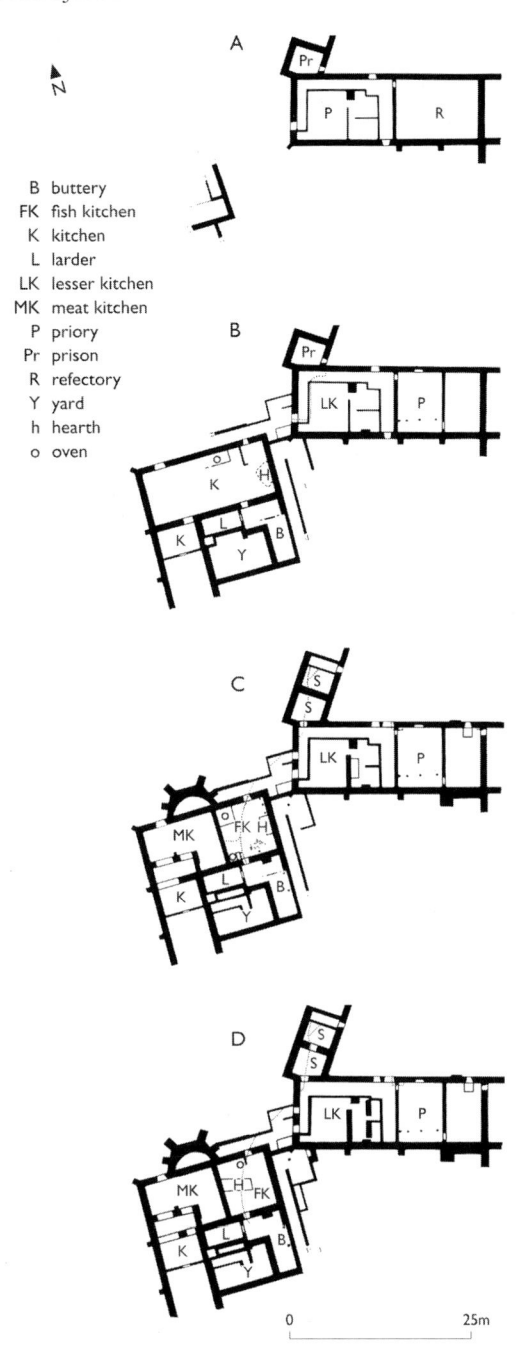

B buttery
FK fish kitchen
K kitchen
L larder
LK lesser kitchen
MK meat kitchen
P priory
Pr prison
R refectory
Y yard
h hearth
o oven

Figure 8.17 The development of the kitchen and its offices at Mount Grace from c.1420 to c.1530.

with 'xij tubes, grete and small cubbordys, with certeyn old bordys and a long table' (Hope 1925, 188). At Mount Grace, as originally built in Period Two, the cross-wing at the north end of the guest-house range was the 'fish kitchen' and the rooms of the southern outshut were the larder (Room III) and buttery (Room IV). Only the eastern half of the kitchen survived (see Figure 8.17B), with the hearth against the east wall and a platform for a battery of ovens (or 'furnaces and cisterns') along the north wall.

The deep deposit of food-processing waste on the floor, which comprised almost exclusively fish, indicated a table along the south wall at the kitchen's west end.

Kitchen equipment is well documented in the sale particulars regularly recorded by the auditors of the Court of Augmentations after the Suppression, although lists do not survive for Mount Grace or London. At Cistercian Dieulacres Abbey the contents of the kitchen in October 1539 comprised 'v grete braspottes & iiij smale panes, j Cauderoune, iij spyttes, j skyelett, ij Cupbordes, j fyerforke, j fleshoke, j fryenpanne, ij cressettes, ij gryderoune, xxxviij platters, dysshes, and saucers, j brazen morter w^t a pestell, ij Choppyngknyues, j dressing knyffe, j Almery, j grater, ij dressing bordes, ij Chafyngdyshys, & Skimmer of brass' (Hibbert 1910, 239). If the meat items – the spits, gridirons and flesh-hook – are ignored, this list must be close to the minimum requirements of the Mount Grace kitchen. Dieulacres housed a community of 14, less than half the size of the Mount Grace community.

The development of the fish kitchen was directly related to the provision of a kitchen at the north end of the guest-house range and to the migration of the prior's cell and the refectory in the south-west cloister range in the course of Periods Two and Three. Initially, the guest kitchen must have been within the northern end of the guest-house range, communicating directly with the fish kitchen, and this remained the case until the 1470s. The fish kitchen was provided with direct access along the northern pentice and up a stair against the south-west cloister range to the Period Two refectory on the upper floor of the range, as well as access through the ground-floor door and along the corridor of the old prior's cell to the great cloister to service individual cells. In Period Three a new door was cut in the west wall of the south-west cloister range to avoid this dog-leg. From the very beginning a piped water supply was provided for the kitchen, almost certainly with a tap in the buttery, as was the case at London (Hope 1903, 310).

The need to separate the fish kitchen from the meat kitchen became apparent only in Period Three (see Figure 8.17C), and resulted in the building of both a wall that divided the kitchen into two unequal parts and a massive chimney against the gable wall of the guest-house range. The fact that the monks' kitchen occupied the smaller of these spaces suggests that the functions of preparation and cooking had been separated, the former being removed to the redundant space of the old prior's cell that lay below the new refectory. The fish kitchen was still floored over (though the flesh kitchen was not), and a first-floor fireplace was provided at the east end of its south wall. The use of the upper room remains unknown, although it can have been accessed only from the timber-framed building that lay in the angle between the kitchen and the south-west cloister range. Rooms above kitchens are not rare in Yorkshire houses in the early 16th century: at the small Benedictine nunnery of Thicket the room over the kitchen was the cheese house (Brown 1887, 202–3) and in the Cluniac nunnery at Arthington the chamber over the kitchen, of unspecified use, was fitted with a fireplace (ibid., 213). This rearrangement of the kitchen was accompanied by a rerouting of the piped water supply from the direction of the Cell 15 tap. The new pipe entered the fish kitchen through its door and the supply split in the middle of the room, one branch going to a tap against the new dividing wall (and possibly through the wall to a tap in the meat kitchen), the other into the buttery, where its course was lost. One of these pipes also served a tap in the screens passage of the guest hall, although its route could not be recovered because of post-Suppression disturbance. The detailed layout of this kitchen was recovered by excavation: the room was divided into two parts by a timber partition that separated the cooking area of the hearth from a space that contained a raised oven platform in the north-west corner and a small oven against the south wall. A stone-lined tank was placed in the floor against the partition, and the location of a bench against the west wall was marked by a large number of stakeholes that probably represent the position of raised duck-boards in front of it. The kitchen floor was still the preferred receptacle for food-processing waste. Three substantial postholes to the north of the hearth suggest a bench or 'board' in that location. In Period Four (see Figure 8.17D) all the earlier kitchen fittings were swept away and a central hearth was installed, implying the removal of the first floor above this room and the provision of a smoke-hood. Unfortunately, no evidence for the functioning of this kitchen had survived the earlier excavation.

Food preparation was evidenced in the old prior's cell from Period Two, but was best seen in Period Three, when a new stone floor with an integral drain was inserted into the two eastern rooms and a timber bench installed against the west wall. Unusually, the floor had been kept clean, but a large quantity of fish waste had found its way into the western room. The use of the western room remains uncertain; it could have been a store for fuel for the kitchen fire and ovens, and for dry goods needed in the kitchen. A similar use is ascribed to the rooms below the refectory at the charterhouse of Gaming in Lower Austria (Hogg 1975, 83). Additional storage was provided in the ground-floor rooms of the old prison block. Further evidence of food preparation is seen in the provision of two tanks for live fish in the eastern rooms of the old prior's cell, to the east of the Period Three bench. Almost identical provision was made at the Guildford blackfriars, where a Suppression-period survey records 'ij frameis of leade to water fische [and] dressing bordis' in the lesser kitchen (Poulton and Woods 1984, 37–8), and in the kitchen at Abingdon Abbey's grange of Dean Court in a late 14th-century context (Allen 1994, 289–301), while at the Wookey Palace of the Bishops of Bath and Wells '2 stone trowes for to kepe and water fyshe' stood outside the kitchen in 1552 (Hasler and Luker 1993, 115).

Perhaps the closest analogy for the Mount Grace kitchen in the archaeological record is the Guildford blackfriars (Poulton and Woods 1984), where the great kitchen occupied the ground floor of the north range of the cloister below the refectory and the lesser kitchen a ground-floor room in the east range adjacent to it. At Guildford there was no obvious larder or buttery, although heavy post-Suppression disturbance meant that partitions were not found in excavation and only one of a pair of wall fireplaces without obvious hoods, known from a 16th-century survey, was recovered. Evidence was recovered for a piped water supply and drainage. The kitchen at the Lincoln greyfriars, a building detached from the refectory, was identified from its tile-on-edge hearth, which survived virtually intact, including slight evidence for a timber firehood (J. Wilford, pers. comm.). At Kirkstall, the cloister kitchen remained a fish kitchen to the Suppression. Excavation has demonstrated that it had two attached offices: a larder on the south side and a buttery attached to its south-west corner, an arrangement similar to the disposition of offices at both London and Mount Grace. The cloister kitchen at Sawley was refitted in the second half of the 14th century, when the great central stack typical of Cistercian kitchens of the 12th and 13th centuries was removed and a tiled hearth set in the centre of the room below a timber smoke-hood carried on stone cill walls and earth-fast posts. The location of furniture was evidenced by postholes both outside and inside the smoke-hood. Water appears to have been piped into the kitchen in its north-east corner via a pipe in the adjacent refectory, while waste was carried off by a substantial drain that left the kitchen through a door inserted at the east end of its south wall. This door led into a rectangular building along the west side of the refectory that was almost certainly a buttery or larder. Unfortunately, 19th-century excavation had removed any occupation material in this room and its function remains unclear. Compared with the kitchens at Kirkstall and Sawley, the Mount Grace kitchen appears to be unexceptional, conforming to near-contemporary types in Cistercian houses and having much in common with the friars' kitchens at both Guildford and Lincoln. A late medieval monastic kitchen type seems to be appearing, common to both monks and friars.

Where the Mount Grace kitchen complex is remarkable, and unique in Britain, is the direct association with food-processing waste. The sheer quantities of fish processed and the squalor in which it was cooked are remarkable in a monastic context, where cleanliness was normally axiomatic. Usually waste was disposed of off-site or into the monastic drainage system. Where it was dumped outside the building it tended to be mixed with waste from other areas, and in such cases it is of little use for determining the diet of individual members of the convent. At Thornholme Priory, for example, vast quantities of obvious kitchen waste were spread in both the inner and outer courts to help raise levels on a wet site (Coppack and Hayfield forthcoming). Thornholme had at least two kitchens, and it is by no means clear where this material came from. Only two other kitchens have produced a comparable collection of food waste, those at Kirkstall (Ryder 1961a and 1961b) and Westminster (Black 1976). In both cases the food waste was associated with the meat kitchen of the misericord, although in the latter case large quantities of fish waste were also produced. This form of midden deposit related to the misericord was also recorded at Fountains Abbey as early as 1851, where vast quantities of animal and bird bone were found mixed with 'bushels of oyster, mussel, and cockle shells' (Walbran 1876, 136–7). At Mount Grace, however, there had been no attempt to remove the waste from the kitchen and the midden deposits seen outside the buildings at Kirkstall and Fountains simply did not exist.

The late medieval Carthusian diet can be reconstructed to a certain extent from the London charterhouse's procurator's accounts of 1492–1500. The accounts list not the produce of the house's estates but foodstuffs purchased for the house. In the first year £104 17s. 8½d. was spent on sea and freshwater fish; £8 1s. 11d. on milk, cheese, butter and eggs; 18s. 8d. on salt, honey and oil; 2s. on pease; 11s. 6d. on oatmeal; and £5 1s. 0d. on spices, figs, raisins, apples and pears. Additionally, £5 5s. 0d. was spent on flesh for guests and servants (Thompson 1930, 193). Quite clearly, fish was the major item, and in this there is a close parallel with Mount Grace. That sea fish were preferred is apparent from the lease of a fishpond by the charterhouse of Hinton in 1525 because the monks 'never eet Flesshe but contynuaally vse Fysshe for ther sustentacion and lyuyng', and in case they should not be able to obtain fish from the sea (Gribbin 2001, 201). The Mount Grace kitchen of Periods Two and Three also produced slight evidence for peas, cereals and eggs (Bailey et al. 1994, 9–11) in quantities that would suggest that they were not used commonly in the kitchen. The Carthusian pittance of five eggs or their equivalent, provided on Mondays and Wednesdays (Gribbin 2001, 204), was more likely to have been distributed to the monks in their cells, and their remains were not recovered from the gardens because contexts were not sieved on site.

The reliance of the community on the convent kitchen was not complete, for each member of the community had his own hearth in his cell and the produce of his garden to supplement his diet. Mount Grace has produced little in the way of artefactual evidence to support the transport of food from a central kitchen to individual cells. For instance, the numerous handled pipkins that identified doles of food at Thornholme Priory in the 13th and 14th centuries are lacking and, more to the point, cooking pots within the cell assemblages are, with the exception of the cooking vessels from Cell 8, almost entirely residual from pre-priory levels. Metal vessels, as evidenced in the list of equipment transferred from London to Mount Grace in 1508 (see Chapter 2), are most likely. The kitchen produced parts of at least one latten cooking pot, and the lack of cooking vessels among the mobilier céramique would be explained by the use of metal vessels that simply did not get broken. Wooden vessels are evidenced in Cells 2 and 3, where waterlogged deposits ensured their survival, and it may be that wooden containers were used to deliver food. Large vessels would not fit into the cell hatches, indicating that food must have been supplied in individual meal portions or messes.

Bread and ale, the two basic comestibles, were supplied directly from the bakehouse and brewhouse, although again the mechanics of the operation are not discernible in the archaeological record. As the average daily allowance in English monasteries in the early 16th century was 2 lb of bread and seven to eight pints of ale of varying strengths (Bond 2004, 43–4), the supply of the brethren was a sizeable undertaking. The drinking pots and cups that can be identified in every cell provide evidence for consumption, but the large jugs used to carry and store the ale are lacking. The quantities that must have been consumed by the community and guests explain the extent of the granaries in the inner court.

The Refectory

The Carthusian refectory differs in several respects from the refectories of other orders, partly because it was used only on festivals, on Sundays and on the day of burial of one of the brothers. Only five survive: at Hinton, at Coventry, at London and the two at Mount Grace.

Early refectories tended to be placed on the first floor, a habit adopted by the Carthusians from the Benedictines in the late 11th and 12th centuries, but also copying the late 11th- and 12th-century aristocratic halls of their early patrons. The biblical model was, of course, the upper room of the Last Supper (Fergusson

1986, 173–9). Other reforming orders, such as the Cluniacs and the Cistercians, placed their refectories on the ground floor, a perverse form of humility that allowed them to develop large buildings open to the roof. It was not until the 15th century that the Carthusians in England were to move their refectory to the ground floor.

The Hinton refectory (see Figure 8.18A), a room 14 m long and 7 m wide on the floor above the prior's cell, survives with the exception of its upper walls and roof, and was converted to a granary in the 17th or 18th century (Hogg 1975, 83). Its original door survives at its north-east corner and the partly blocked remains of two of its three original windows look out over the great cloister. The central window has been destroyed by the insertion of a door for the granary. There are two lancet lights in the west gable wall to either side of the prior's cell chimney. Otherwise, the room is featureless.

At Coventry (see Figure 8.18B), the refectory is still at first-floor level, between the prior's cell and the west end of the church, and it survives almost complete, a building of two bays lit on its east side by two large windows, now blocked. These are large enough to have had elaborate tracery below their four-centred heads. The refectory stands above two service rooms, one of which must have contained a stair up to it, and in the outer face of the east wall just above ground level is the blocked niche of a small laver. The south wall of the refectory retains a wall painting, the lower half of a depiction of the Crucifixion that originally extended up into the gable, showing that the refectory was open to the roof in the standard English manner. The roof above has three finely carved tie-beams. The wall painting of the Crucifixion was not a Carthusian peculiarity; the Cistercians used the same imagery at Cleeve in the late 15th century, and it was seen as a suitable reminder of the monks' daily purpose. At Coventry it was also used to demonstrate patronage: the Roman centurion Longinus' supporter has a pennant on his lance with the arms of Langley, patrons of the house, and to the left of the cross was a figure of St Anne, the house's patron saint. The wall painting of the Crucifixion is of exceptional quality, with exquisite figures rendered with soft, delicate draperies and carefully observed naturalistic details, which has avoided all but a light clean

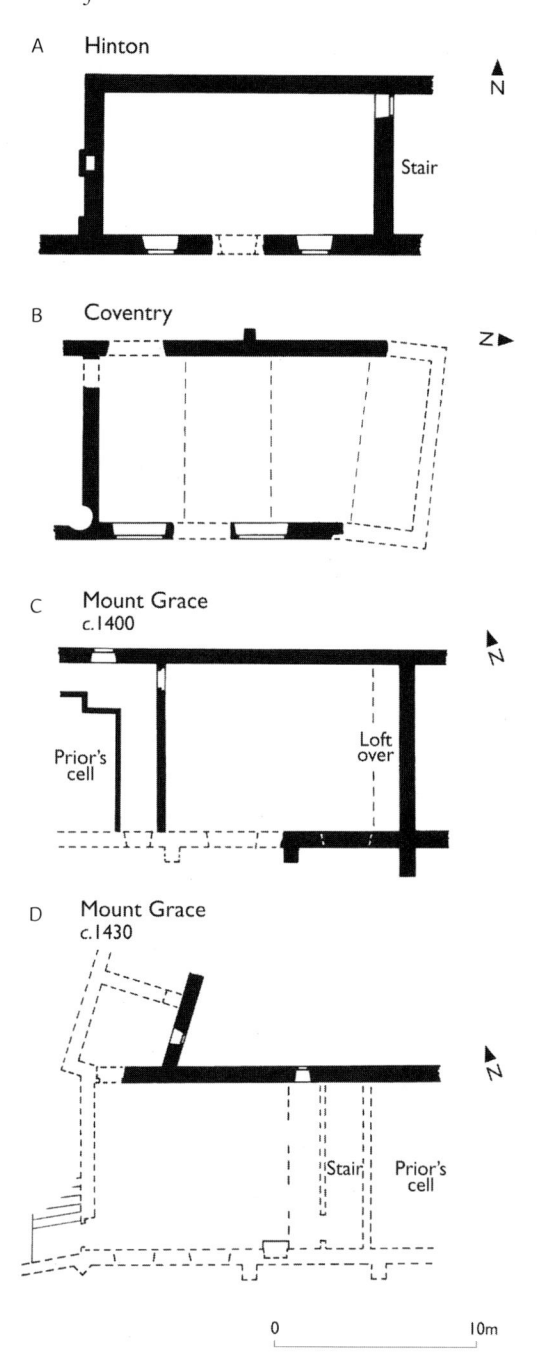

Figure 8.18 Comparative plans of refectories. A: Hinton; B: Coventry; C: Mount Grace c.1400; D: Mount Grace c.1430.

since it was first uncovered. Few wall paintings of this quality survive from the period *c.*1350–1450, and this is the only monumental work to survive from an English charterhouse (Naydenova-Slade 2011, 271–2). In a most unCarthusian manner, the painting also carries an inscription recording the completion of the monastery by Prior William Soland: *Fuit domus hec completa – Laus sit Christo assueta – Sic faventi homini[bus] … rior Solonde ram sudar[i]t – Thomas Lambard procuravit – Postponens fallacias Post quem lic …*, which translates as 'This house has been finished. The accustomed praise be to Christ thus helpful to men. ... Prior Soland had hard labour indeed. Thomas Lambard attended to it, forgiving small faults. After this ...'. Iain Soden dated the inscription to before 1417, and had interpreted 'house' to mean the refectory, but more recently Julian Luxford has suggested that 'house' refers to the whole of the charterhouse buildings, and pointed out that William Soland was still alive and prior in 1437, a more likely date for the wall painting (Luxford 2011a, 251–2).

Both the Hinton and Coventry refectories have lost all their fittings in their conversion to reuse, and they give no indication of how they were used. They do, however, lack one feature that is common to the refectories of other orders: there is no pulpit from which readings were made during meals. Carthusian meals were taken in silence.

At London, the refectory was retained within the house built in 1571 by Thomas Howard, and its north and south walls survive substantially intact. The eastern, cloister wall can be safely presumed, and only the west wall is untraced. Apparently at first-floor level, the refectory was 7.5 m wide and probably 14 m long and was built in the early 15th century (Hope 1925, 41), possibly replacing an earlier building on the same site (*ex inf.* Stephen Porter). No internal features can be identified, although its location next to the prior's cell is typical of Carthusian planning.

At Mount Grace the original refectory (see Figure 8.18C) was at ground-floor level in the same range as the prior's cell, and was 10.5 m long and 8 m wide, with two large traceried windows high up in its south wall. It was not entered directly from the cloister alley, but through a small and undistinguished door in a corridor that crossed the range. Open to the roof, it was a substantial space, with white-limed walls and plain glass in its windows. Its floor was of earth, and in the floor and sub-floor levelling that survived across the building there was no evidence whatsoever for the features regularly found in other monastic refectories. In the refectories of other orders benches were placed against the side walls with tables in front of them, their legs set into raised platforms or foot-paces, while the prior's table was placed on a raised dais at one end of the room, from where he could see every member of the community. The only distinction given to the upper end of the refectory at Mount Grace was a loft or ceilure 3 m above floor level. Nor are there the normal cupboards for the storage of napkins, towels and spoons next to the door. The Carthusians simply placed their tables and benches on the floor, and did not have the expensively tiled or paved floors of other orders. The impression created by the building at Mount Grace was of both quality, for it was a fine building, and simplicity, for it was devoid of any decoration. In comparison, the individual monks' cells were elaborate. Their refectory thus gives every indication that they regarded eating communally as a penance. In the 1430s the community gave up their refectory to the prior, who moved his cell there, and took over his first floor-hall as their new refectory virtually unaltered.

This later refectory (see Figure 8.18D) had a screens passage at its eastern end that was lit by a small square-headed window in its north wall, and probably had two larger windows in the missing south wall. A door was forced though the south end of the west wall, where a broad stair and landing provided access from the convent kitchen. A hearth that remained at ground-floor level indicated the placement of a fireplace in its south wall, hard up against the screens passage. A further door at the west end of the north wall led into the upper floor of the old prison building, which must have changed use by the 1470s, when the door was inserted.

While other orders treated their refectories as the third most important building of the cloister after the church and chapter house, the Carthusians treated it as little more than a hall, like that of a college or even a manorial hall. Its anonymity within the cloister was intentional and its provision basic.

Guest Accommodation

The Carthusian order was not noted for the welcome that it extended to guests because of the interference they could cause to religious life, but remained aware of its charitable obligations. Normally, guests were housed in the *correrie* and used its church, but, with the combination of the upper and lower houses at Mount Grace, guest accommodation had to be provided within the inner and outer courts of the monastery, as was customary among other regular orders. What makes Mount Grace exceptional in the context of Carthusian monasteries across Europe is the scale and survival of the guest accommodation and the form that it took.

The principal guest house was built in the 1420s between the gate to the inner court and the kitchen. Four small guest chambers were provided on the ground floor, while a suite of rooms on two floors above housed more important guests. The central part of the range comprised the guest hall, which was some 5 m wide, 9 m long and open to the roof, and the northern part of the building consisted of the kitchen and the accommodation of the procurator, who was responsible for the guests. This is a reasonably modest provision compared with that at houses of similar wealth in Yorkshire. The guest hall at Kirkstall, one of two known there, provided more substantial accommodation from the early 13th century and grew throughout its life (Wrathmell 2018, 23–48), while the guest hall at Fountains was an aisled hall of seven bays of *c.*1230 associated with two earlier guest houses (Coppack and Gilyard-Beer 1993, 59–61). At Mount Grace the building survives almost complete and is significant because it is contemporary with the bulk of the choir monks' cells, a part of the monastery refounded by Thomas Beaufort, and indicates the scale of guest provision thought necessary for a house of this size and income. Its location is also significant. Documentary sources (such as Brown 1887) normally place guest houses within the inner court of monastic houses, associating them with the stables, granaries, brewhouse and bakehouse, all ancillary to the cloister. The guest-house range at Mount Grace lies immediately inside the inner court gate in an area where access was controlled, but is separated from the church and south-west cloister range by walled courts. It is literally on the periphery of the inner court. All the same, it faces into the inner court and is accessed from there.

The Period Two guest house had proved inadequate by the third quarter of the 15th century and was augmented in Period Three by a second building to the south of the gatehouse within which were provided a further four ground-floor guest chambers entered from the inner court; above was at least one and possibly two floors of what appears to be dormitory accommodation, entered by a stair from the outer court. Larger monasteries in Yorkshire did have 'hostels' for the poorer sort of traveller, usually in the outer court, as at Fountains and Kirkstall, and this appears to be what was provided at Mount Grace. The first floor provided 145 m^2 of space, which would be doubled if the attic floor was also used. Effectively, the guest provision had been tripled within half a century of the construction of the original guest house. This was not the end of the story, however, for in the 1520s Prior John Wilson wrote to Henry, Lord Clifford, referring to a 'proper lodging' built by a London merchant and Knight of St John (BL Add. MS 48965, f. 6), and it is probably this building that is called 'le Inne' in the grant of the priory site to Sir James Strangways in 1540 (TNA Cal. Pat. R. 32Hy8 pt 4, m.45), lying between the home grange and the priory itself. It would appear that this was further accommodation for travellers built by the Hospitaller Sir John Rawson before he left for the siege of Rhodes in 1522.

Why a Carthusian charterhouse should need so much accommodation is not immediately clear, particularly as the entertainment of guests was not a high priority within the order. It is probably more to do with the location of the monastery, a day's ride north of York on the road to Durham, where it provided a convenient stopping place. One problem, however, remains. Neither within the guest-house range nor in its southern extension are there any latrines, and no evidence exists of direct access to latrines outside the enclosure of the inner court. A single privy in the south-east corner of the inner court would not have been sufficient, and the quality of the guest accommodation was too good for the guests to have been required to use the stable or dung heap. There must be a latrine building somewhere outside the inner court gate, but it has not been found.

The Cultural Collections

Monastic sites normally produce collections of finds that indicate the high cultural status that is implied by their buildings, even though poverty and simplicity of life were required by the rule followed by the house. In this, Mount Grace is no different from any other monastery that has seen extensive excavation, although the collections do differ in a number of ways from contemporary collections deriving from monastic houses of other orders. This is partly because individual items can be related to individual members of the community in a way that has not previously been seen in an archaeological context, but is possible here because of the planning of a Carthusian monastery, with its dominant layers of enclosure, and partly because the Carthusians espoused a life that differed materially from that of other monks.

Central to the understanding of the cultural collections at Mount Grace is an appreciation of Carthusian life, lived not communally but in the isolation of the cell. Essentially, the cell was a miniature monastery that provided the basis of the monk's life, and its contents were prescribed by the rule (see Chapter 1). Thus, if monastic life was being conducted according to the rule, there should be a similarity in the finds from individual cells. Any variation would result from the particular trade a monk practised and from the acquisition of objects that indicated personal tastes or preferences. To balance this, it must be understood that the cultural collection is not intact; whole classes of object are not present because they have not survived on this largely dry site or were not disposed of within the monastery. Essentially, what has been recovered represents chance breakages of pottery, small objects that had become detached from apparel or books, broken (and therefore useless) personal objects and pieces of scrap that had survived being recycled. The nature of the eremitic life seems to have ensured that lost or misplaced items were generally recovered by the monks. Central to our understanding of the contents of a cell is the list of objects brought by Thomas Golwynne from London in January 1519/20 (see Chapter 2). If the books, which must have been destined for the Mount Grace library – as monks were not permitted to own books and could have only two books from the library at a time – are excluded, the remaining objects must have been the contents of his cell.

As Colin Hayfield has demonstrated (see Chapter 7), there is a degree of consistency in the ceramic collections from those cells that were cleared or excavated that suggests uniformity. The standard pottery provision seems to consist of a urinal, several jugs, at least one jar, a surprising number of cups, a bottle, at least two drug jars and a chafing dish. The Suppression-period group from Cell 8 (Finds Group 11, see Figure 4.44) is of considerable importance because it appears to represent the whole ceramic assemblage of a particular cell at a known date (Roebuck *et al.* 1987). Otherwise, the pottery represents breakages within the cell over a century or more, chance disposal in the garden or incorporation in early demolition and construction deposits. Only three gardens were fully excavated and, as a result, the pottery collections from Cells 8, 9 and 10 are of particular significance. There is a high incidence of tablewares, a number of jugs and several urinals. Cooking vessels are noticeable by their absence, but Thomas Golwynne had a latten chafing dish, a small brass pan, a brass skillet with a steel handle and a little brazen pestle and mortar, all virtually unbreakable and of some resale value, so unlikely to be abandoned. Given the amount of ceramic tablewares, it is perhaps surprising to find that Thomas also had two dishes, two saucers, a porringer and a butter dish in pewter, along with two tin bottles. The evidence is that each monk was well provided for and, in terms of pottery, appeared to have spare vessels in case of breakage. The numbers of drinking pots and mugs is, as noted, high. Finds Group 11, taken to be the entire contemporary ceramic collection in Cell 8, had no fewer than 18. It may be that breakage rates were high, or that washing up was not a high priority. Imported wares were common, even more so than usual on monastic sites – an indication, supported by documentary evidence, that the Carthusians drew their recruits from the middle and upper levels of society.

In comparison with Mount Grace, the Carthusians of Coventry were seemingly less well provided for in terms of pottery (Soden 1995, 83–99; 2005, 97). The size of the groups recovered was much smaller, and only Cells 4 and 5 (or III and IV, as they are numbered by Soden) produced groups of any size. In no case was a garden area fully examined. Tablewares predominated, as at Mount Grace, and, although imported stonewares and South Netherlands Majolica were represented, the incidence of non-local pottery was much lower than at Mount Grace. This was taken to suggest that either the more valuable pottery had been removed by theft or by the monks themselves, or that Coventry, being an austere house, did not buy the more expensive and elaborate imports (Soden 1995, 91). It is more likely, however, that insufficient of the site has been examined to determine its ceramic profile. At London, which is not directly comparable because most of the stratified pottery came from service areas, the bulk of the pottery was of a mundane and domestic nature, although Dutch redwares, stoneware drinking vessels, Saintonge and a single sherd of Andalusian lustreware were recovered. This was a range of fabrics, as Lynne Blackmore noted, that was consistent with pottery from other London monastic sites, particularly the neighbouring monasteries of St John and St Mary of Clerkenwell (Barber and Thomas 2002, 68–9).

Locally, comparison is possible with late medieval groups from three Cistercian sites. At Fountains, late 15th-century deposits in the abbey's wool house produced pottery comparable in type and quality to the pottery from Mount Grace, including decorated Cistercian wares and German stonewares found in a semi-industrial context (Coppack 1986, 75–80). At Sawley Abbey, where the latrine, main drain and south cloister range were excavated, the stonewares were absent, but Cistercian ware, reversed Cistercian ware and Tudor Green tablewares were well represented in the latest occupation deposits (Coppack et al. 2002, 83–93 and 96). At Kirkstall Abbey late medieval deposits from the refectory and warming house provide the best comparison with the Cistercian wares found at Mount Grace, but lack the imports that were common at the latter, even though they are directly associated with the monastic community (Moorhouse and Wrathmell 1987, 75–6 and figs 45 and 55).

Central to the understanding of the pottery from the Mount Grace cells is the fact that they come from totally enclosed units and that any pottery broken within the cell is unlikely to have migrated except in the supply of food from the kitchen. Colin Hayfield has identified one instance of migration (see Chapter 7), where a stoneware mug with its broken neck ground down found in the kitchen could be directly compared with a number of vessels from Cell 11, where the same treatment of damaged vessels was apparent. Any variation from the norm, therefore, is likely to indicate personal preference or differing needs. It is perhaps significant that the only pottery group to be associated with a lay brother, from Cell 20, lacked the finer tablewares and the decorated Cistercian wares common in the choir monks' cells. It is to be regretted that the excavation of a lay brother's cell was not included in the post-1988 research programme.

It is the non-standard objects in the cell collections that are of particular significance. Within the monks' cells a number of finds related directly to the 'trades' of individual members of the community. Pre-eminent were items relating to the production and copying of books, both for the house and for the wider world, a practice that began in the early years of the order and continued in England up to the Suppression (Gillespie 1998, 172–5). At Mount Grace there is evidence to suppose that the copying of books was carried out in an organised way, with an element of the production line being apparent. Cells 10 and 11 produced copper alloy pen nibs and Cell 10 lead dry points; Cells 12 and 13 had oyster shells containing coloured pigment; and Cell 12 also produced a stone 'rubber' for grinding pigment or polishing parchment. Thus there was, in these four cells, evidence for both copying and illumination. The last occupant of Cell 8 appears to have been a bookbinder, for many book cover fittings and clasps were scattered around the garden, some unfinished, others probably scrap from covers that had been renewed. The bookbinder monk had a close contemporary at the Nieuwlicht charterhouse, for the burial list of the monks there recorded Dan Henricus van Bolzward, who was 'most obliging in the binding of our books and other needs of our brothers' (Hasselt 1886, 356). The type mould from Cell 10 suggests that the community was experimenting in a small way with basic printing in the early 16th century. Although Mount Grace possessed printed books in its library, there is no evidence that it ever produced its own printed works, although the community could well have been producing certificates of confraternity known to be associated with Coventry and other houses (David Bell, pers. comm.). While it is unexceptional that monks should be copyists, and all were bound to be able to write in both Latin and English, no other British monastic site has produced such clear evidence that it was individual members of the community who were responsible for book production, and one could be forgiven for imagining that here at least two monks were copying books, which were then taken to the cells of two others, who added the colour, and then to Cell 8, where the parchment or paper leaves were bound in permanent covers. Nor is it beyond the bounds of possibility that books were being produced for use outside the monastery. We know that Richard Methley wrote for Hew Hermyte (Hogg 1977, 101), and members of the community were corresponding with people outside the charterhouse. An unknown member of the community wrote

> in this last yere I sent to a devoute preeste of my knowlegge a copy of the Reuelacion ... Which ye [a monk of the London charterhouse] sende me. And the same preste sent dyuers copies to certeyn of hys Frendes, of whom ther was a good husbond man harde of the grete vartu and grace of the forsaid prayers he vsed it dayly as deuoutly as he coulde. (Wormald 1936, 181)

Effectively, Carthusian teaching, which made great use of the vernacular, as opposed to Latin, could be spread outside the monastery without monks leaving the enclosure of the great cloister. Other finds from the great cloister also indicate that the community was closer to society than one might expect.

Two classes of object relate closely to commerce: coin balances from Cells 10, 12 and 14 and coin weights from Cell 8, the cloister alley outside Cell 15 and the early prior's cell. Only one coin was found in the great cloister (Cell 8) and that is likely to derive from the levelling of the great cloister terrace, but the presence of balances and weights indicate that money must have been present. Individual members of the community were receiving money from outside the monastery: so much is clear from wills (see Chapter 2). At London, such bequests were vested in the prior and used for the purchase of books, repairs to the fabric and other 'approved' uses, even though this was specifically forbidden by the statutes (Gillespie 1989, 171). There was no lessening of this rule, although it appears to have been more honoured in the breach up to the Suppression, and members of the Mount Grace community appear to have been handling coin as individuals. Four further objects may have some bearing on this conundrum: cast lead strips with the retrograde legend *iehus nazerenus*, three from Cells 10, 11 and 14 and one from unlocated clearance. These strips appear to have no purpose within the cell: they are not mounts from furniture, as they have no evidence of fixing, and they are not obviously devotional objects within the cell, like the pardon plaque from Cell 10. It has been suggested (Keen, Chapter 7) that they are moulds for making 'pilgrim' objects, a result of Mount Grace's location on the pilgrimage route between York and Durham. Certainly, the charterhouse has more guest accommodation than is usual for a Carthusian monastery, and it is difficult to see why the regular guest house, the additional dormitory accommodation in the inner court and the unlocated 'inne' in the outer court were required unless it was to house pilgrims. Perhaps the expense of housing guests was offset by selling them mementoes of their visit made by one or more members of the community.

Other trades are evidenced by both documentary sources and the cultural collections. Thomas Golwynne brought a loom and a still to Mount Grace (see Chapter 2). Weaving and tailoring were necessities of the house, provided in other orders by servants, and London had previously supplied a weaving frame to the charterhouse of Coventry (Blackmore 2000, 327). The production of *aqua vitae* was considered medicinal (Gribbin 2001, 207 quoting BL MS Sloane 1584, ff. 6v, 41v–45 and 88), and pottery cucurbits from Cells 12 and 20 (a lay brother's cell) imply distillation there. This was a common enough practice on monastic sites of any order (for example, Moorhouse 1972, 111–15), evidencing the production of alcoholic spirits or medicines or alchemical research. The collection of urine, implied by the ubiquitous spread of urinals, also indicates medicinal preparation (Ogden 1938, 10). In the finds collection tools or fragments of tools are rare: a pair of pliers from Cell 8, pairs of tweezers from Cells 10 and 12, an iron punch from Cell 11 and an iron gouge from the kitchen. Only the area of the kitchen and its offices produced items related to the preparation of food, with chopping and paring knives, brass skimmers and latten cooking vessels (Finds Groups 35, 37, 38, 39 and 45). This, though, was an area restricted to the lay brothers, and the finds collection is strictly utilitarian. This is also the only area of the site to produce keys, normally among the most common of iron objects from monastic sites and indicative of accountability for supplies within the various common offices of the house. While every cell where the door case survives had a lock on its cloister door, not a single key was recovered from the excavation of Cells 8 to 15, although the kitchen and early prior's cell produced no fewer than six.

The Piped Water Supply
The Carthusians' particular use of piped water was well known and at least partially understood before the excavation of Mount Grace (Hope 1903; Knowles and Grimes 1954). It differs from the water systems developed by the Benedictines and Cistercians in the second half of the 12th century, best illustrated by the contemporary surviving waterworks plan of Canterbury cathedral priory from the early 1160s (Trinity Coll. MS R.17.1, ff. 284v/285r; Grewe 1991), in one significant way. Both Benedictines and Cistercians brought their piped supplies into the infirmary and from there to a series of lavers before taking water, including recycled waste, to the kitchen, bakehouse and brewhouse, implying that the use of expensively conduited and cleaned water was intended for ritual washing in the first instance. The Carthusians, however, appear to have been much more pragmatic in their use of water. The London charterhouse waterworks plan of the 1430s (Hope 1903; Coppack 1996b) indicated that water was initially treated in the same way – collected from a distant source, filtered and cleaned – but that it was then taken to a central conduit house and distributed on an equal basis to individual cells, the great cloister laver, the kitchen and even buildings outside the precinct. While the technology was the same, the significance of piped water was clearly different. The spiritual use of water in monastic life is an area that has not been examined in any detail. Unlike the generality of monastic communities in Britain, the Carthusians alone drank water on fast days and in Lent. This alone might explain why the supply was direct to the cell and why there is no evidence within the great cloister for the recirculation of waste that is common on other sites.

A water supply was important, as the engineering to provide it at Mount Grace indicates, but it is surprising that it was not supplied from the beginning of the settlement. It may well be that springs tapped in the course of levelling the great cloister were used by the founding community, although no evidence for this has been seen in the admittedly limited excavation of that area; and the spring seen in the garden of Cell 9 was iron-rich and thus unusable. At Sheen, Henry V had granted permission at the foundation of the monastery for the spring of 'Hillesdenwell' to be tapped to supply the house, and this was supplemented in 1466 by a grant from Edward IV for the convent to make an underground conduit from the spring of 'Welway *alias* Pickwelleswell' (Gribbin 2001, 199). Similar provision can be assumed at other houses, but is not recorded. That a piped supply was not a prerequisite of the order is clear from the charterhouse of Delft, in the Netherlands. Excavation there revealed that each cell had a brick-lined well in its garden (Vos 1975, 22–4 and afb. 15) and no indication of pipes was found, though the site was almost completely stripped.

Until the early 1990s London stood alone as a model of Carthusian hydraulic engineering, and the Mount Grace system had not been seriously studied, even though parts of it had been recorded as early as the 1960s. Atypically, Mount Grace was not supplied from a distant source, being placed instead on the spring line at the base of the escarpment of the North Yorkshire moors. In addition, unlike the single source identified at London, it had three sources of spring water that seem fortuitously related to three distinct use areas: the great cloister, the lesser cloister and the inner court. Although not common, a similar phenomenon can be observed in Yorkshire on three Cistercian sites. Fountains Abbey had two distinct sources, one to the south-east of the house that supplied the monks' infirmary and cloister *lavatorium*, and one to the south-west that supplied the lay brothers and the inner court (Walbran 1876, 136; Coppack 1986, 55 and fig. 4). At Sawley Abbey (Coppack *et al.* 2002, 32, 36–7 and 104), excavation has identified separate supplies from as early as the 1150s, serving the first temporary accommodation of the monks and lay brothers and retained in modified form until the suppression of the house. At Kirkstall Abbey, separate supplies have been identified for the choir monks and the lay brothers and inner court (Stuart Wrathmell, pers. comm.).

It may very well be that this is more common than has so far been recognised, and that the Carthusians of Mount Grace were simply copying the traditions of other orders on a site where it was easy to do so. Even so, the provision of three well houses just outside the eastern precinct wall in the 1420s is without parallel in England.

There is nothing exceptional in the technology of water engineering at Mount Grace; the methods used can be seen in houses of any order from the 1150s onwards. What is exceptional, and peculiar to the Carthusians, is the scale of the undertaking. Each cell required its own supply because of the nature of the community's eremitic life, and this required far more pipework and 'suspirels', or pressure valves, to make the system work. It is significant that the piped supply is contemporary with the first substantial phase of stone building in Period Two, and that no supply has been identified for the first period of occupation. Similarly, it appears that the London house did not have a piped supply before 1430, when John and Margery Feriby conveyed the source at Overmead in the manor of Barnersbury in Islington to the house (Hope 1903, 296), and it may have become a priority only as the size of the community increased. The origins of the piped supplies at Witham and Hinton remain unknown, although Fletcher believed that the supply at Hinton was carried in a stone conduit that was traced throughout the gardens of the great cloister (Fletcher 1958/9, 79–80), being described as 'a stone channel, 15 inches square, from 3 to 5 feet below the present ground surface, beautifully cut and mortared and roofed with very large flat stones'. Almost certainly, however, Fletcher's 'conduit' is part of the foul drainage system and has nothing to do with potable water. Contemporary photographs of the excavation indicate the presence of a series of cut stone channels to take lead pipes that were not identified at the time (Hogg 1975, pls 62 and 68). That Mount Grace and London were not atypical is demonstrated by Beauvale. Excavation revealed a lead pipe connecting Cell 2 to a ring main in the cloister alley (Hill and Gill 1908, 77). Geophysical survey of the site in 1995 by Geophysical Surveys of Bradford (Adam 1995a, figs 5 and 6) located not only a conduit house or water tower at the centre of the great cloister, but also the lines of lead pipes leading to and from it. The pipes are presumably protected by cut stone channels similar to those recorded at Hinton and Mount Grace, which is why they can be traced by resistivity. Geophysical survey at Hinton (Wilson-North 1995, figs 3–6) failed to find any trace of a central water tower or the 'conduits' identified by Fletcher. At Axholme charterhouse a substantial building, possibly a post-medieval structure, occupied a large part of the eastern half of the cloister and had obscured any evidence for a water tower there (Gater 1995, figs 3–7).

Water towers do not survive on any of the English charterhouse sites, and their form can be reconstructed only from the drawing of the London 'age' (from the Latin *augea*) and the loose architectural detail recovered by Hope at Mount Grace in 1900. The caption on the London drawing reads:

> M^d that thys age ys made viijth square and in that [erasure] which ys ~~from the~~ north warde dyrectlye from the suspyrell the mayne pype doth come & Rysythe up into the age in the middth of a fayre square Cestron of leade. Wh' yt Runnythe downe out of the [erasure] in the top of the age into a ~~pyp~~ another pype on the weaste side of the same Wills whyche doth s've the howse. Md that the doore Goyng into the age benethe doth stand dyrectlye southe warde and the doore into the age above Openythe east warde and the Goyng up thereunto ys by a ladder and abovev ys a Greate ~~Md that~~ Cestron square of leade and in the middth therof dothe Ryse the mayne pype and at the heyht. (Hope 1903, 308)

The drawing shows three faces of an octagonal structure, stone below and timber-framed above, with a tall pyramid roof surmounted by a cross. The roof covering appears to be lead and the timber-framed upper walls are divided by a mid-wall plate, above and below which are paired leaded windows. The ground storey has a bold plinth but no angle buttresses and apparently no openings, and the upper storey is jettied out on projecting dragon beams that are shown in detail at the angles of the tower. It appears to be an accurate representation. Although the captions have been altered and are mainly in a 16th-century hand, there is every indication that the tower is as originally drawn in the 1430s. This would make it a near contemporary of the Mount Grace water tower.

The age at Mount Grace was similarly octagonal and probably roughly the same size as the London water tower. It also appears to have had a timber-framed upper storey, for no evidence was found for it in excavation either by Hope or, later, by Coppack. The fragments recovered suggest that it was a considerably more sophisticated structure than that recorded at London, its first stage having angle buttresses, two-light windows and presumably a door into the ground floor. Its windows were glazed and its design was *en suite* with the Period Two cloister arcade. Nothing remains in Britain for comparison, but its model is clearly the detached laver house evidenced in Benedictine and Cluniac houses from the later 12th century to the later Middle Ages, and perhaps best seen in the late 14th-century example from Sherborne now used as a market cross or the excavated example at Durham cathedral priory (Hope and Fowler 1903). The structure has simply been scaled down to suit its use here.

The well houses are much easier to parallel, as they belong to a series of late medieval well houses known across England. There is nothing particularly Carthusian about them. The closest comparisons are with Haughmond Abbey in Shropshire and Llanthony Secunda Priory in Gloucester (Bond 1996, 461 and fig. 5), both Augustinian houses, and Monkton Farleigh in Wiltshire (Bond 1989, 87), a Cluniac house. Others are known at Augustinian Canons Ashby in Northamptonshire and Cistercian Valle Crucis in Clwyd. In every case they are small vaulted chambers covered with a steeply pitched roof enclosing a substantial tank filled by water canalised from a nearby spring, and do not contain the spring itself. They represent close sources and not a distant spring, such as those at Islington depicted and described on the London charterhouse plan, and as a result do not require the settling and filtration tanks associated with highly engineered supplies.

Latrines

The provision of water-flushed latrines at Mount Grace provided a degree of sophistication not seen in the monasteries of any other order in England. No information is available from any other British charterhouse, as they have not been found in excavation at London, Axholme, Coventry, Hinton or Witham, and excavation failed to locate any at Beauvale, although an open watercourse was identified along the outer face of the northern precinct wall in the likely location of the latrines of Cells 1 to 5 and its existence was confirmed by resistivity (Hill and Gill 1908, 77; Adam 1995a, fig. 2).

The excavators presumed wooden privies set over the drain. Mount Grace is exceptional in that only one pit latrine has been identified on the entire site and a preference for flushed privies was identified from the period of foundation. Gribbin (2001, 200) claims that this was an indication that the Carthusians, in common with other orders of monks, whose sanitary arrangements were considerably more sophisticated than those of the laity, associated human excrement with disease. The evidence from Mount Grace is that other orders were less concerned than the Yorkshire Carthusians.

The great 12th- and 13th-century latrine blocks that typified the Benedictines, the Cluniacs, the Cistercians and the major houses of canons were not necessarily in use in the later Middle Ages. Excavation of the latrines at Cistercian Dundrennan (Ewart 2001) and Cluniac Bermondsey (Dyson *et al.* 2011, 90–5 and fig. 65) and Paisley (Malden 2000, 177) indicate that the great water-flushed latrines of these houses had been converted to pit latrines by the 15th century. Lack of modern excavation hinders our understanding of late monastic communal latrines, but, in any case, communal life had broken down in many houses, with monks living in small apartments usually carved out of the infirmary hall or even the claustral ranges. These apartments can be identified by two features essential for life: a wall fireplace and a latrine. Perhaps the clearest example of this is the infirmary at Fountains Abbey (Coppack 1993, 71–3 and fig. 58). Here rooms were created within the east and west aisles of the hall on two levels, providing accommodation for a household of at least 12 monks; many of the rooms were heated, and some were provided with latrines, some of which served the ground floor, while others can only have serviced rooms at first-floor level. As the infirmary is carried on four tunnels over the river Skell, providing chutes into the river was not a problem, but this option was ignored in favour of the far less hygienic pit latrine. The same provision is still apparent in the infirmary at Kirkstall and the south range at Cleeve Abbey. The Carthusians at Delft chose to build brick-lined domed latrine pits below their privies that could be emptied into a boat using the canal that skirted the precinct wall (Vos 1975, afb. 12 and 13). Human waste was a useful material for manuring and even tanning, and its recovery might therefore outweigh the inconvenience of its collection in evil-smelling stone-lined pits. It would appear from these examples that Mount Grace was exceptional in its removal of human excrement from the vicinity of the living areas and only paralleled in its sophistication by Beauvale. Was this because the community had no need for its own fertiliser or no market for it? One possible explanation is that a flushed system obviated the periodic need to empty latrine pits, an obvious source of disturbance to life in the cell.

8.2 Future Research

All modern excavation undertaken at Mount Grace Priory has been conditioned by the requirements of site display, and this has concentrated on specific areas where buildings were not apparent on the surface or where 19th-century excavation had been limited or non-existent. All the same, some 25% of the site has been studied, and analysis of the standing ruins has extended our knowledge of the site to more than 75%. Mount Grace does not stand alone; the excavation of the church and five cells at Coventry and the limited excavation of Witham, Hinton and London provide a national context for the site that has been substantially extended by a reappraisal of the work carried out at the turn of the 20th century. There remain, however, substantial areas of ignorance that need to be addressed before our knowledge of the Carthusians can approach our knowledge of the other regular orders.

Carthusian monks remain, for the most part, anonymous, and no Carthusian cemetery has ever been excavated (apart from the discovery of five graves in the cloister of the London charterhouse and two graves in the south cloister alley at Mount Grace). At Nieuwlicht in the Netherlands, the scale and location of burials is known from the record of burials maintained by successive sacrists (see Figure 8.8A). There the graves of the choir monks and priors were located in the south-east corner of the great cloister opposite the sacrist's cell, extending as far as the west wall of the convent church. Between 1420 and 1580 120 religious were buried more than 1 m apart in four well-spaced rows (Hasselt 1886, 354–60). Five burials from the first and second rows have been excavated, including a monk clearly uncoffined, buried in his habit and clutching a rosary in his right hand (Hartog 2013, 33 and afb. 3.10–13). To the north of the choir monks, and separated by a gap, 21 lay brothers were buried in a single row. West of the monks' cemetery at Nieuwlicht was another burial plot, opposite the cell of the procurator and the kitchen, where servants and donates were buried in two or more ranks. Part of this plot has been excavated (Hoogendijk 2012, 85–104 and afb. 62–74). The graves here were far from orderly, with a lot of intercutting, suggesting that, unlike those of the religious, they were probably unmarked.

The evidence from Nieuwlicht does not aid in a clear understanding of a Carthusian cemetery. Burials are, however, a major resource for our knowledge about the community itself. Little is known about the age or health of the communities (Gribbin 2001, 204–7), although documentary evidence suggests that longevity was more common in a charterhouse than in contemporary Benedictine houses, where life expectancy was falling in the 15th and early 16th centuries (Hatcher 1986; Harvey 1993, 115–19, 135–41, 144–5). Carthusian burials are likely to remain undisturbed within the identifiable cloister gardens of all the English houses, uncontaminated by patronal burials and easily accessible for excavation.

The development of the Carthusian cell and its garden remains substantially unstudied, although it is central to the understanding of how the order developed. In contrast, the process of development is well understood in other reformed orders and among the friars. Although the Carthusian order proudly maintains that it is *nunquam reformata quia nunquam deformata*, it is clear that there is a development (above), but the process has not been examined by excavation. At Witham it is likely that the full progression from documented timber cells to the 'late' cell-type identified by excavation is present, while the cells at Hinton probably demonstrate development throughout the 13th century and there remains the possibility that the known cell plan at Beauvale represents a rebuilding to match the 'late' design first seen at London. There is also variation in the planning of cells within individual contemporary houses, which needs to be addressed. Similarly, the development of the lay brothers' accommodation from *correrie* through communal quarters (as suggested at London) to the individual cells at Mount Grace remains unexplored. There has been no modern excavation of any lay brothers' accommodation on any site, partly because the lay brothers have been seen as a less important manifestation of Carthusian life, although that indicates a failure to understand the organisation of Carthusian communities. The re-excavation of Cell 19 at Mount Grace remains a very high priority.

The development of water systems remains unclear. While London, Beauvale, Mount Grace and probably Sheen (Cloake 1990, 12) had a central water tower, it would appear that Witham, Hinton and possibly Axholme did not. A water supply was established in the early years of the Grande Chartreuse, and the technology was generally available from well before the foundation of Witham. At Hinton, supply and drainage appear to have been confused by the excavators, while at Witham neither system has been identified. Different houses appear to have widely differing methods of dealing with human excrement, yet monks moved between the houses of the order in England and must have been aware of the different provision they found in individual houses. The Carthusians were a highly centralised order, like the Cistercians, yet there does not appear to be a common approach to something as basic as water management. This could be a result either of differing levels of development or of the simple fact that it was not important within the order. Given the care evident in the engineering of supply and waste provision at Mount Grace, however, the latter seem unlikely.

The place of the Carthusians in the late medieval monastic church has yet to be established, partly because too much emphasis has been placed on the development of other orders in the 12th and 13th centuries. Historically, a great deal is known, but this has not been matched by archaeological research. It is clear that there was a renaissance in monastic life generally from the late 14th century and evidence exists that the communal orders were beginning to favour individual cells on the Carthusian or collegiate model. The Carthusians were attracting both Augustinian and Premonstratensian canons to their cloisters, but it is uncertain how far the Carthusian ideal had already spread outside their houses. Mount Grace has provided some insight into the means by which the Carthusians interfaced with society, but it remains to be seen if this was typical of the order (Coppack 2008). Mount Grace has also established that Carthusian monks enjoyed as good a lifestyle as other monks, and that the use of imported pottery was consistent with its use by other orders. Generally, there was a movement away from the strictness of the early 12th-century Customs, but this was common to other orders as well. The Carthusians remained at heart 'Christ's Poor Men', although the framework of their religious lives reflected their high social status. The obvious link with the friars and particularly the Franciscans remains to be made.

Although considerable energy has been expended on understanding how other orders created and managed their estates, this work has not been carried out for the Carthusians, in spite of the fact that they were managing estates at a time when the survival of documentary evidence is good. That they were doing it in a different way from the Benedictines, Augustinians and Cistercians is apparent from the dispersed nature of their holdings, reflecting their endowment with alien priory estates. Precisely how they were doing it, however, remains a mystery, yet half the houses of the order in England enjoyed a high level of income that is apparent in their buildings and material culture.

Mount Grace Priory has demonstrated the development of a late medieval charterhouse in a way that is exceptional. It points the way to a better understanding of the order in England and further afield and demonstrates the potential of other houses for research. The excavations of 1896–1900 and 1957–92 have demonstrated the potential for archaeological research on any Carthusian site and the architectural study of the ruins has shown the process of development with remarkable clarity. These processes need to be extended to other houses of the order, not simply in England but across Continental Europe. The Mount Grace project, an exemplary study of a major monastic order, is of international significance. It cannot stand alone.

Bibliography

1. Manuscript Sources

Bodleian MS 634
Bodleian MS Rawlinson D.318
British Library Additional MS 48964
British Library Additional MS 48965
British Library Cotton MS Otho Bxiv
British Library Cotton MS Vitellius Aviii
British Library MS Lansdowne 411
Het Utrechtse Archief HS 18151, Necrologium
Het Utrechtse Archief HSA 8154, de kalender originaal
Het Utrechtse Archiev HSA18153, de Grote Schenkers
Het Utrechtse Archief HS 1006–3, Oude of Eerste cartularium
Lambeth Palace MS 413
Lincoln Cathedral MS A6.8
North Yorks County Record Office DN43
Pembroke College MS 198–9
Preston Record Office K/9/29
Somerset County Record Office DD/WYp box 1
Stifts-bibliotek St Gallen Cod. Sang. 1092
TNA Ancient Petitions Files 128 and 186
TNA de Banco Rolls 335 and 452
TNA Charter Roll 21–3 Richard II
TNA Feet of Fines, Yorkshire, 29 Edward I
TNA Land Revenue Misc. Book 61
TNA Lay Subsidy Roll, bundle 211
TNA Patent Roll 36 Edward III, part ii
TNA Patent Roll 50 Edward III, part ii
TNA Patent Roll 1 Henry
TNA Patent Roll 2 Henry IV, part iv
TNA Patent Roll 3 Henry V, part ii
TNA Patent Roll 9 Henry V, part ii
TNA Patent Roll 27 Henry VI, part i
TNA Patent Roll 32 Henry VIII, part iv
TNA Patent Roll 34 Henry VI pt i, m. 20
TNA Patent Roll 21 Richard II, parts ii and iii
TNA Patent Roll 22 Richard II, part iii
TNA Pipe Roll 26 Henry II Pipe Rolls 27–33 Hy II
TNA Land Revenue Misc. Book 61
TNA Ministers Accounts 31 & 32 Henry VIII
TNA State Papers Domestic, Henry VIII, ix, lii, and xcii
Trinity College, Cambridge, MSR.17.1 Trinity Coll. MS R.17.1.
York Dean and Chapter Wills, ii

2. Calendared Sources

Calendar Patent Rolls 1369–74
Calendar Patent Rolls 1396–9
Calendar Patent Rolls 1408–13
Calendar Patent Rolls 1461–7
Calendar Patent Rolls 1467–71
Calendar Papal Letters 1447–55
Calendar State Papers xiii
Calendar Inquisitiones Post Mortem 5 Henry IV
Calendar Inquisitiones Post Mortem 2 Henry VI
Calendar Inquisitiones Post Mortem 7 Henry VI
Calendar Inquisitiones Post Mortem 15 Henry VI
Calendar Inquisitiones Post Mortem 34 Henry VIII
Letters and Papers Henry VIII 8
Letters and Papers Henry VIII 10
Letters and Papers Henry VIII 13, part 3
Letters and Papers Henry VIII 14, part 1
Rotuli Parliamentorum v

3. Printed Sources

Adam, C. R. 1995a 'Report on geophysical survey, Beauvale Priory, Nottinghamshire', *Geophysical Surveys of Bradford* 95/10.
Adam, C. R 1995b 'Report on geophysical survey, Beauvale Priory, Nottinghamshire II', *Geophysical Surveys of Bradford* 95/52.
Alexander, J. and Binski, P. 1987 *Age of Chivalry: Art in Plantagenet England 1200–1400* (London).
Alexander, J. J. G., Brown, T. J. and Gibbs, J. 1988 *Francis Wormald Collected Writings*, II, *Studies in English and Continental Art of the Later Middle Ages* (London).
Algar, D. and Egan, G. 2001 'Balances and weights', in P. Saunders (ed.), *Salisbury Museum Medieval Catalogue* 3, 119–31.
Allen, H. E. (ed.) 1931 *English Writings of Richard Rolle Hermit of Hampole* (Oxford).
Allen, T. G. 1994 'A medieval grange of Abingdon Abbey at Dean Court Farm, Cumnor, Oxon', *Oxoniensia* 54, 219–447.
Anon 1882. *Yorkshire Archaeological Society and Topographical Association Excursion Programme and arrangements at Mount Grace Priory and Northallerton, Wednesday August 30 1882* (Worksop).
Anon 1896. *Excursion to Mount Grace Priory, September 16 1896: Programme and Arrangements* (Wakefield).

Armitage Robinson, J. 1918 'The foundation charter of Witham Charterhouse', *Proceedings of the Somerset Archaeological & Natural History Society* 64/2, 1–28.

Armstrong, P., Tomlinson, D. and Evans, D. H. 1991 *Excavations at Lurk Lane Beverley 1979–82* (Sheffield Excavation Reports 1, Beverley).

Aston, M. 1993 'The development of the Carthusian order in Europe and Britain: a preliminary survey', in M. Carver (ed.), *In Search of Cult: Archaeological Investigations in Honour of Philip Rahtz* (Woodbridge), 139–51.

Aston, M. 2001 'The expansion of the monastic and religious orders of Europe from the eleventh century', in G. Keevil, M. Aston and T. Hall (eds), *Monastic Archaeology: Papers on the Study of Medieval Monasteries* (Oxford).

Atkinson, J. C. (ed.) 1889 *Cartularium Abbathie de Rievalle* (Surtees Society 83, London).

Bailey, S. *et al.* 1994 *Assessment of Biological Remains from Excavations at Mount Grace Priory, North Yorkshire* (Environmental Archaeology Unit, report 94/10, York).

Baker, N. (ed.) 2002 *Shrewsbury Abbey* (Shropshire Archaeological and Historical Society Monograph 2).

Baker, N. and Cooper, M. 1988 'Shrewsbury Abbey', *Current Archaeology* 102, 59–62.

Balfour-Brown, B. 1958 *British Water Beetles* 3 (Ray Society of London, London).

Barber, B. and Thomas, C. 2002 *The London Charterhouse* (MoLAS Monograph 10, London).

Barber, J. 1984 'Medieval wooden bowls', in Breeze 1984, 125–47.

Barker, G. 1976 'Diet and economy at Valle Crucis', in L. A. S. Butler, 'Valle Crucis Abbey: an excavation in 1970', *Archaeological Cambrensis* 125, 80–126.

Barlow, P. 1967–8 'Witham Priory', *Wells Natural History & Archaeological Society*, 122, 7–11.

Barlow, P. and Reed, R. D. 1966 'Wells Natural History and Archaeological Society', *Proceedings of the Somerset Archaeological & Natural History Society* 110, 7–8.

Barlow, P. and Reed, R. D. 1967 'Wells Natural History and Archaeological Society', *Proceedings of the Somerset Archaeological & Natural History Society* 111, 7–8.

Beaulah, G. K. 1929 'Appendix. Paving tiles from Meaux Abbey', *Transactions of the East Riding Antiquarian Society* 26, 116–36.

Biddle, M. 1990 *Artefacts from Medieval Winchester. Object and Economy in Medieval Winchester* (Winchester Studies 7/ii, Oxford).

Biddle, M. and Smith, D. 1990 'Mortars', in Biddle 1990, 890–908.

Black, G. 1976 'Excavations in the subvault of the misericord of Westminster Abbey', *Transactions of the London & Middlesex Archaeological Society* 27, 135–78.

Blackham, A., Davies, C. and Flenley, J. 1981 'Evidence for late Devensian landslipping and late Flandrian forest regeneration at Gormire Lake, North Yorkshire', in J. Neale and J. Flenley (eds), *The Quaternary in Britain* (Oxford), 184–93.

Blackmore, L. 2000 'The medieval and later accessioned finds from Charterhouse: specialist report', unpublished MoLAS report.

Blades, W. 1861 *The Life and Typography of William Caxton England's First Printer with evidence of his typographical connection with Colard Mansion the printer at Bruges* (Bibliography and Reference Ser. 74, New York).

Bond, J. 1989 'Water management in the rural monastery', in Gilchrist and Mytum 1989, 83–111.

Bond, J. 1996 'Les systèmes hydrauliques monastiques dans la Grande Bretagne médiévale', in Bonis and Wabont 1996, 457–73.

Bond, J. 2004 *Monastic Landscapes* (Stroud).

Bond, M. F. 1947 *The Inventories of St. George's Chapel, Windsor Castle 1384–1667* (Historical Monograph 7, Windsor).

Bonis, A. and Wabont, M. (eds) 1996 *L'hydraulique monastique* (Grâne).

Bowers, R. 2001 'The music and musical establishment of St George's Chapel in the 15th century', in Richmond and Scarff 2001, 171–214.

Brakspeare, H. 1905 *Waverley Abbey* (London).

Brassington, W. S. 1891 *Historic Bindings in the Bodleian Library, Oxford: with reproductions of twenty-four of the finest bindings* (London).

Braunfels, W. 1972 *Monasteries of Western Europe* (London).

Breeze, D. (ed.) 1984 *Studies in Scottish Antiquity Presented to Steward Cruden* (Edinburgh).

Brewster, T. C. M. and Hayfield, C. 1988 'Cowlam deserted village: a case study of post-medieval village desertion', *Post-Medieval Archaeology* 22, 21–109.

Brewster, T. C. M. and Hayfield, C. 1992 'The medieval pottery industries at Potter Brompton and Staxton, East Yorkshire', *Yorkshire Archaeological Journal* 64, 49–82.

Brewster, T. C. M. and Hayfield, C. 1994 'Excavations at Sherburn, East Yorkshire', *Yorkshire Archaeological Journal* 66, 107–48.

Brooks, C. M. 1987 *The Archaeology of York, The Pottery 16/3, Medieval and Later Pottery from Aldwark and Other Sites* (London).

Brown, F. and Howard-Davis, C. 2008 *Norton Priory: Monastery to Museum. Excavations 1970–87* (Lancaster).

Brown, W. 1882 'History of Mount Grace', *Yorkshire Archaeological Journal* 7, 473–94.

Brown, W. 1887 'Descriptions of the buildings of twelve small Yorkshire priories at the Reformation', *Yorkshire Archaeological Journal* 9, 197–215 and 321–33.

Brown, W. 1891 *Cartularium Prioratus de Gyseburne* II (Surtees Society 89, London).

Brown, W. 1905 'History of the priory', *Yorkshire Archaeological Journal* 18, 252–69.

Brunon, C. 2011 'Deux vaisseliers de peintre Étude sur les contenants des pigments', *Histoire et Images Médiévales* 49, 21–4.

Buckland, P. C. and Hayfield, C. 1989 'Late-medieval pottery wasters from Firsby, South Yorkshire', *Transactions of the Hunter Archaeological Society* 15, 8–24.

Buckland, P. C., Dolby, M. J., Hayfield, C. and Magilton, J. R. 1979 *The Medieval Pottery Industry at Hallgate, Doncaster* (Doncaster).

Buckland, P. C., Hayfield, C. and Magilton, J. R. 1989 *The Archaeology of Medieval Doncaster* (British Archaeological Reports, Brit. Ser. 202, Oxford).

Burrow, I. and Burrow, C. 1990 'Witham Priory: the first English Carthusian monastery', *Proceedings of the Somerset Archaeological & Natural History Society* 134, 141–82.

Caley, J. and Hunter, J. 1826 *Valor Ecclesiasticus Temp Henrici VIII Auctoritate Regia Institutus 5* (London).

Campbell, C. 1771 *Vitruvius Britannicus* (London).

Casselman, M. 1987 'Determination of age and growth', in A. H. Weatherley and H. S. Gill, *The Biology of Fish Growth* (London).

Cather, S. 2006 'Oyster shell palette', in Wallis 2006, 72–3. Chapman, F. R. 1907 *The Sacrist Rolls of Ely* (Cambridge).

Childs, W. R. (ed.) 1986 *The Customs Accounts of Hull 1453–1490* (Yorkshire Archaeological Society Record Ser. 144, Leeds).

Christie, P. M. and Coad, J. G. 1980 'Excavations at Denny Abbey', *Archaeological Journal* 137, 138–279.

Clapham, A. W. and Godfrey, W. H. 1913 *Some Famous Buildings and their Story Being the Results of Recent Research in London and Elsewhere* (London).

Clark-Maxwell, W. G. 1924–5 'Some letters of confraternity', *Archaeologia* 75, 19–60.

Clark-Maxwell, W. G. 1929 'Some further letters of fraternity', *Archaeologia* 79, 179–216.

Clarke, H. and Carter, A. 1977 *Excavations in King's Lynn 1963–1970* (Society for Medieval Archaeology Monograph 7, London).

Clarke, M. 2011 *Medieval Painters Materials and Techniques: The Montpellier 'Liber diversarum arcium'* (London).

Clarke-Maxwell, M. 2012 'A unique 12th-century illuminator's treatise: an original composition incorporated in the Brussels *Compendium artis picturae*', in Eyb-Green *et al.* 2012, 54–9.

Clay, J. W. (ed.) 1908 *North Country Wills 1383–1558* (Surtees Society 116, London).

Clay, P. 1981 'The small finds – non-structural', in J. E. Mellor and T. Pearce, *The Austin Friars, Leicester* (CBA Research Report 35, Leicester/London), 130–45.

Cloake, J. 1990 *Richmond's Great Monastery: The Charterhouse of Jesus of Bethlehem of Shene* (Richmond Local History Society Paper No. 6, Richmond).

Coatsworth, E. and Pinder, M. 2002 *The Art of the Anglo-Saxon Goldsmith: Fine Metalwork in Anglo-Saxon England: its Practice and Practitioners*, Anglo-Saxon Studies 2 (Woodbridge).

Cokayne, G. E. 2000 *The Complete Peerage*, 6 vols. Reprint (Gloucester).

Coleman, O. 1960–1 *The Brokage Book of Southampton 1443–1444* (Southampton Records Ser. 4 and 5, Southampton).

Cook, G. 1947 *Medieval Chantries and Chantry Chapels* (London).

Coope, G. R. and Osborne, P. 1968 'Report on the Coleopterous fauna of the Roman well at Barnsley Park, Gloucestershire', *Transactions of the Bristol and Gloucestershire Archaeological Society* 86, 84–7.

Coppack, G. 1980 'Medieval and post-medieval pottery', in P. M. Christie and J. G. Coad, 'Excavations at Denny Abbey', *Archaeological Journal* 137, 138–279.

Coppack, G. 1986 'Some descriptions of Rievaulx Abbey in 1538–9: the disposition of a major Cistercian precinct in the early sixteenth century', *Journal of the British Archaeological Association* 139, 100–33.

Coppack, G. 1988 *Abbeys: Yorkshire's Monastic Heritage: An Exhibition Drawn from the Modern Counties of Cleveland, Durham, Lancashire, Yorkshire and Humberside* (London).

Coppack, G. 1989 'Thornholme Priory: the Development of a Monastic Outer Court' in Gilchrist, R and Mytum, H. 1989.

Coppack, G. 1990 *Abbeys and Priories: The Archaeology of the English Monastery* (London).

Coppack, G. 1991 *Mount Grace Priory* (London).

Coppack, G. 1993 *The English Heritage Book of Fountains Abbey* (London).

Coppack, G. 1996a 'La chartreuse de Mount Grace, le système hydraulique du 15e siècle: l'adduction, la distribution, et l'évacuation des eaux', in Bonis and Wabont 1996, 157–67.

Coppack, G. 1996b 'The contribution of the Carthusians to monastic hydraulics: the evidence from England', in J. de Mascarenhas, M. H. Abecasis and V. F. Jorge (eds), *Hidráulica Monástica Medieval e Moderna* (Lisbon), 51–63.

Coppack, G. 2002 'The planning of Cistercian monasteries in the later Middle Ages: the evidence from Fountains, Rievaulx, Sawley and Rushen', in J. G. Clark (ed.), *The Religious Orders in Pre-Reformation England* (Woodbridge), 197–209.

Coppack, G. 2008 '"Make straight in the desert a highway for our God": Carthusians and community in late medieval England', in J. Burton and K. Stöber (eds), *Monasteries and Society in the British Isles* (Woodbridge), 168–79.

Coppack, G. and Aston, M. 2002 *Christ's Poor Men: The Carthusians in England* (Stroud).

Coppack, G. and Douglas, M. 2014 *Mount Grace Priory* (London).

Coppack, G. and Gilyard-Beer, R. 1993 *Fountains Abbey, North Yorkshire* (London).

Coppack, G. and Hall, J. 2008 'The church of Mount Grace Priory: its development and origins', in J. M. Luxford (ed.), *Studies in Carthusian Monasticism in the Late Middle Ages* (Medieval Church Studies 14, Turnhout), 299–322.

Coppack, G. and Hayfield, C. forthcoming *Thornholme Priory: The Archaeology of an Augustinian House* (Nottingham).

Coppack, G., Harrison, S. and Hayfield, C. 1995 'Kirkham Priory: the architecture and archaeology of an Augustinian house', *Journal of the British Archaeological Association* 148, 55–136.

Coppack, G., Hayfield, C. and Williams, R. 2002 'Sawley Abbey: the architecture and archaeology of a smaller Cistercian abbey', *Journal of the British Archaeological Association* 155, 22–114. Cowdrey, H. E. J. 1989 'Hugh of Avalon, Carthusian and bishop', in M. G. Sargent (ed.), *De Cella in Seculum* (Cambridge), 41–57.

Cowgill, J., de Neergaard, M. and Griffiths, N. 1987 *Medieval Finds from Excavations in London*, 1, *Knives and Scabbards* (London).

Curteis, A., Morris, C. A., Martin, C., Wright, D. and Bogden, N. Q. 2012 'The worked wood', in *Perth High Street Archaeological Excavations 1975–1977*, fasc. 2 (Tayside and Fife Archaeological Committee, Perth), 223–316.

de Osma y Scull, G. J. 1916 *Catálogo de Azabaches Compostelanos* (Madrid).

de Hamel, C. 2018 *Making Medieval Manuscripts* (Oxford).

Department of Culture, Media and Sport 2002 *Portable Antiquities Annual Report 2000–2001* (London).

Dickens, A. G. 1959 *Tudor Treatises* (Yorkshire Archaeological Society Record Ser. 125, Wakefield).

Dickens, A. G. 1963 'The writers of Tudor Yorkshire', *Transactions of the Royal Historical Society*, 5th ser. 13, 49–76.

Dodwell, C. R., trans. 1961 *Theophilus: De Diuersis Artibus* (Medieval Texts, London).

Dolley, M. and Ketteringham, L. 1976 'The thirteenth-century *trebuchet*-type coin balance', in L. Ketteringham, *Alsted: Excavations of a Thirteenth-Fourteenth Century Sub-Manor House with its Ironworks in Netherne Wood, Merstham, Surrey* (Surrey Archaeological Society Research vol. 2, Guildford), 62–3.

Donisthorpe, H. St J. K. 1939 *A Preliminary List of the Coleoptera of Windsor Forest* (London).

Donovan, C. 1991 *The de Brailes Hours: Shaping the Book of Hours in Thirteenth-century Oxford* (London).

Douie, D. L. and Farmer, D. H. 1985 *Magna Vita SHugonis*, 2 vols, 2nd edn (Oxford).

Dowding, G. 1961 *An Introduction to the History of Printing Types* 3 (London).

Doyle, A. I. 1953 'A survey of the origins and circulation of theological writings in English in the 14th, 15th, and early 16th centuries with special consideration of the part of the clergy therein', thesis submitted for PhD degree, University of Cambridge.

Dugdale, W. 1825 *Monasticon Anglicanum* 5, ed. J. Caley, H. Ellis and B. Bandinel (London).

Dugdale, W. 1830 *Monasticon Anglicanum* 6 pt 1, ed. J. Caley, H. Ellis and B. Bandinel (London).

Dunning, G. C. 1937 'A fourteenth-century well at the Bank of England', *Antiquaries Journal* 17, 414–18.

Dunning, G. C. 1965 'Heraldic and decorated metalwork and other finds from Rievaulx Abbey, Yorkshire', *Antiquaries Journal* 45, 53–63.

Dunning, G. C. 1977 'Mortars', in Clarke and Carter 1977, 320–47.

Dyson, T., Samuel, S., Steele, A. and Wright, S. M. 2011 *The Cluniac Priory and Abbey of St Saviour Bermondsey, Surrey: Excavations 1984–95* (MOLA Monograph 50, London).

Eames, E. S. 1980 *Catalogue of Medieval Lead-glazed Earthenware Tiles in the Department of Medieval and Later Antiquities, British Museum* (London).

Eames, E. S. 1983 'Floor tiles', in J. Wordsworth, 'Friarscroft and the Trinitarians in Dunbar', *Proceedings of the Society of Antiquaries of Scotland* 113, 478–89.

Egan, G. 1997 'Non-ceramic finds', in C. Thomas, C. B. Stone and C. Phillpotts, *Excavations at the Priory and Hospital of St Mary Spital, London* (Museum of London Monograph 1, London), 201–10.

Egan, G. 1998 *Medieval Finds from Excavations in London*, 6, *The Medieval Household Daily Living c.1150–c.1450* (London).

Egan, G. and Pritchard, F. 1991 *Medieval Finds from Excavations in London*, 3, *Dress Accessories c.1150–c.1450* (London).

Elders, J. 1996 'Farmers, friars, millers, tanners: the Oberrtorvorstadt in Esslingen am Necker, Germany', unpublished PhD thesis, University of Nottingham.

Emery, A. 2007a 'Dartington Hall: a mirror of nobility in late medieval Devon', *Archaeological Journal* 164, 227–48.

Emery, P. A. 2007b *Norwich Greyfriars: Pre-Conquest Town and Medieval Friary* (East Anglian Archaeology 120, Dereham).

Ervynck, A. and van Neer, W. 1992 'De voedselvoorieing in de Sint-Salvatorsabdij te Ename (staad Oudenaarde, prov. Oost Vlaanderen) I:

Beenderen onder een Keukenvloer (1450–1550AD)', *Archeologie in Vlaanderen* 2, 419–34.

Ewart, G. 2001 *Dundrennan Abbey: Archaeological Investigation Within the South Range of a Cistercian Abbey in Kirkcudbrightshire (Dumfries and Galloway, Scotland)* (Scottish Archaeological Internet Reports 1), https://doi.org/10.5284/1017938.

Eyb-Green, S., Townsend, J. H., Clarke, M., Nadolay, J. and Kroustallis, S. (eds) 2012, *The Artist's Process: Technology and interpretation* (London).

Falls, D. J. 2010 'Reading prior to translating: a possible Latin exemplar for Nicholas Love's Myrrour of the Blessed Lyf of Jesu Christ', *Notes and Queries* 57/3, 313–15.

Farmer, D. H. 1989 'Hugh of Lincoln, Carthusian saint', in M. G. Sargent (ed.), *De Cella in Seculum* (Cambridge), 41–57.

Farmer, P. G. and Farmer, N. C. 1982 'The dating of the Scarborough ware pottery industry', *Medieval Ceramics* 6, 66–86.

Farrar, R. A. H. (ed.) 1966 'Archaeological notes and news for 1966', *Proceedings of the Dorset Natural History and Archaeological Society* 88, 102–21.

Fergusson, P. J. 1983 'The first architecture of the Cistercians in England and the work of Abbot Adam of Meaux', *Journal of the British Archaeological Association* 136, 74–86.

Fergusson, P. J. 1984 *The Architecture of Solitude: Cistercian Abbeys in Twelfth Century England* (Princeton).

Fergusson, P. J. 1986 'The twelfth-century refectories at Rievaulx and Byland Abbeys', in C. Norton and D. Park (eds), *Cistercian Art and Architecture in the British Isles* (Cambridge), 160–80.

Fergusson, P. J. 2011 *Canterbury Cathedral Priory in the Age of Becket* (New Haven and London).

Fergusson, P. and Harrison, S. 1999 *Rievaulx Abbey: Community, Architecture, Memory* (New Haven and London).

Fletcher, P. C. 1951 'Recent excavations at Hinton Priory', *Somerset Archaeological & Natural History Society* 96, 160–65.

Fletcher, P. C. 1958–9 'Further excavations at Hinton Priory', *Somerset Archaeological & Natural History Society* 103, 76–80.

Foreman, M. 1991 'The bone and antler', in Armstrong *et al.* 1991, 183–96.

Foreman, M. 1992 'The wood', in D. H. Evans and D. G. Tomlinson, *Excavations at 33–35 Eastgate, Beverley 1983–96* (Sheffield Excavation Reports 5: Sheffield), 174–82.

Foreman, M. 1996 *Further Excavations at the Dominican Priory, Beverley, 1986–89* (Sheffield Excavation Reports 4: Sheffield).

Fretton, W. G. 1874 'Memorials of the Charter House, Coventry', *Transactions of the Birmingham and Warwickshire Archaeological Society* 5, 26–45.

Gaffney, V. 1994 'Report on geophysical survey: Witham Priory, Somerset', *Geophysical Surveys of Bradford* 94/73.

Gater, J. 1995 'Report on geophysical survey: Axholme Priory, Lincolnshire', *Geophysical Surveys of Bradford* 95/12.

Geer, B. J. L. de 1857 'Begifters en bezittingen van het Carthuizer-convent bij Utrecht', *Kroniek van het historisch genootschap gevestigd te Utrecht*, 3rd ser., 3, 129–46.

Gibson, S. 1903 *Early Oxford Bindings* (Oxford).

Gilchrist, R. and Mytum, H. 1989 (eds) *The Archaeology of Rural Monasteries* (British Archaeological Reports, Brit. Ser. 203, Oxford).

Gillespie, A. and Wakelin, D. (eds) 2011 *The Production of Books in England 1350–1500* (Cambridge Studies in Palaeography and Codiology 14, Cambridge).

Gillespie, V. 1998 'Cura Pastoralis in Deserto', in M. G. Sargent (ed.), *De Cella in Seculum* (Cambridge), 161–82.

Gilyard-Beer, R. 1958 *Abbeys* (London).

Gilyard-Beer, R. 1970 *Fountains Abbey, Yorkshire* (London).

Gilyard-Beer, R. 1987 'White Ladies Priory', in O. J. Weaver, *Boscobel House and White Ladies Priory* (London), 35–8.

Gilyard-Beer, R. 1990 *Cleeve Abbey, Somerset* (London).

Gilyard-Beer, R. and Coppack, G. 1986 'Excavations at Fountains Abbey, North Yorkshire, 1979–80; the early development of the monastery', *Archaeologia* 108, 149–88.

Gittos, B. and Gittos, H. 1989 'A survey of East Riding sepulchral monuments before 1500', in C. Wilson (ed.) *Medieval Art and Architecture in the East Riding* (British Archaeological Association Conference Transactions 9, Leeds), 91–108.

Given-Wilson, C. (ed.) 1997 *The Chronicle of Adam of Usk, 1377–1421* (Oxford).

Goldschmidt, E. Ph. 1928 *Gothic & Renaissance Bookbindings Exemplified and Illustrated from the Author's Collection*, 2 vols (London).

Goodall, A. R. 1990 'Non-ferrous metal objects', in C. Scull, 'Excavations in the Cloister of St. Frideswide's Priory, 1985', in J. Blair (ed.), *Saint Frideswide's Monastery at Oxford Archaeological and Architectural Studies, Oxoniensia* 53 (1988), 39–40.

Goodall, I. H. 2011 *Ironwork in Medieval Britain: An Archaeological Study* (Society for Medieval Archaeology Monograph 31, London).

Greene, J. P. 1989 *Norton Priory* (Cambridge).

Grewe, K. 1991 *Die Wasserversorgung im Mittelalter* 4 (Mainz am Rhein).

Gribbin, J. 2001 'Health and disease in the English charterhouses: a preliminary study', *Analecta Cartusiana* 157, 198–209.

Grimes, W. F. 1968 *The Excavation of Roman and Medieval London* (London).

Gumbert, J. P. 1974 *Die Utrechter Kartäuser und ihre Bücher im frühen fünfzehnten Jahrhundert* (Leiden).

Hamerow, H. and MacGregor, A. 2001 *Image and Power in the Archaeology of Early Medieval Britain: Essays in Honour of Rosemary Cramp* (Oxford).

Harde, K. W. 1984 *A Field Guide in Colour to Beetles* (London).

Harrison, S. 1990 *Byland Abbey, North Yorkshire* (London).

Hartog, C. M. W. Den 2013 *Nieuw Licht op de Marnixlaan: Een archeologisch Onderzoek naar het kartuizersklooster Nieuwlicht* (Basisrapportage Archeologie 66. Utrecht: Afdeeling Erfgoed gemeente Utrecht).

Hartog, C. M. W. Den 2016 *Herinrichting Klokkenveld: Archeologisch Onderzoek naar het kartuizersklooster Nieuwlicht op de Marnixlaan (MRL 5) te Utrecht* (Basisrapportage 86, Utrecht).

Harvey, B. 1993 *Living and Dying in England, 1100–1540: The Monastic Experience* (Oxford).

Harvey, J. H. 1946 *Henry Yeveley: The Life of an English Architect*, 2nd edn (London).

Harvey, J. H. (ed.) 1969 *William Worcestre: Itineraries* (Oxford).

Harvey, J. H. 1978 *The Perpendicular Style 1330–1485* (London).

Hasler, J. and Luker, B. 1993 'The site of the Bishops' Palace, Wookey', *Proceedings of the Somerset Archaeological & Natural History Society* 137, 111–22.

Hasselt, L. van (ed.) 1886 'Het Necrologium van het Karthuiser-klooster Nieuwlicht of Bloemendaal buiten Utrecht', *Bijdragen en Mededeelingen van het Historisch Genootscap Gevestigd te Utrecht* 9, 126–392.

Hatcher, J. 1986 'Mortality in the fifteenth century: some new evidence', *Economic History Review*, 2nd ser. 39, 19–38.

Hayfield, C. 1980 'Techniques of pottery manufacture in East Yorkshire and North Lincolnshire', *Medieval Ceramics* 4, 29–43.

Hayfield, C. 1984a 'Excavations on the site of the Mowbray manor house at the Vinegarth, Epworth, Lincolnshire, 1975–1976', *Lincolnshire History and Archaeology* 19, 5–28.

Hayfield, C. 1984b 'Wawne, East Riding of Yorkshire: a case study in settlement morphology', *Landscape History* 6, 41–67.

Hayfield, C. 1984c 'An early-medieval splashed-glazed pottery kiln at Market Place, Doncaster', *Yorkshire Archaeological Journal* 56, 41–3.

Hayfield, C. 1984d 'A late-medieval pottery group from Humberstone Abbey, Lincolnshire', *Lincolnshire History and Archaeology* 19, 107–10.

Hayfield, C. and Slater, T. R. 1985 *The Medieval Town of Hedon: Excavations 1975/1976* (Barton-on-Humber).

Hayfield, C. 1985 *Medieval Pottery from the Humberside Region* (British Archaeological Reports, Brit. Ser. 140/1 and 140/2, Oxford).

Hayfield, C. 1986 'Medieval pottery', in R. Gilyard-Beer and G. Coppack, 'Excavations at Fountains Abbey, North Yorkshire, 1979–80: the early development of the monastery', *Archaeologia* 108, 164–8.

Hayfield, C. 1988 'The popularity of medieval vessel forms in Humberside', *Medieval Ceramics* 12, 57–68.

Hayfield, C. 1992 'Humberware: the development of a late-medieval pottery tradition', in D. Gaimster and M. Redknap (eds), *Everyday and Exotic Pottery from Europe, c. 650–1900: Studies in Honour of John G. Hurst* (Oxford), 38–44.

Hayfield, C. and Grieg, J. 1989 'Excavation and salvage work on a moated site at Cowick, South Humberside, 1976: Part 1', *Yorkshire Archaeological Journal* 61, 41–70.

Hayfield, C. and Grieg, J. 1990 'Excavation and salvage work on a moated site at Cowick, South Humberside, 1976: part 2: the finds', *Yorkshire Archaeological Journal* 62, 111–24.

Heale, M. 2009 *Monasticism in Late Medieval England, c. 1300–1535* (Manchester).

Hibbert, F. A. 1910 *The Dissolution of the Monasteries: As Illustrated by the Suppression of the Religious Houses of Staffordshire* (London).

Hicks, M. and Tatton-Brown, T. 1991 'St Gregory's Priory, Canterbury', *Current Archaeology* 123, 100–6.

Hill, A. du Boulay and Gill, H. 1908 'Beauvale Charterhouse, Notts', *Transactions of the Thoroton Society* 12, 70–94.

Hills, P. J. 1961 *The Priory of the Wood* (Gainsborough).

Hinton, D. A. 1996 *The Gold, Silver and Other Non-Ferrous Alloy Objects from Hamwic* (Southampton Finds 2, Stroud).

Hinton, D. A. 2000 *A Smith in Lindsey: The Anglo-Saxon Grave at Tattershall Thorpe, Lincolnshire* (Society for Medieval Archaeology Monograph 16, London).

Hirst, S. M., Walsh, D. A. and Wright, S. M. 1983 *Bordesley Abbey II: Second Report on Excavations at Bordeley Abbey, Redditch, Hereford-Worcestershire* (British Archaeological Reports Brit. Ser. 111, Oxford).

Hobley, B. 1971 'Excavations at the cathedral and Benedictine Priory of St Mary, Coventry', *Transactions of the Birmingham and Warwickshire Archaeological Society* 84, 46–139.

Hobson, G. D. 1929 *English Binding Before 1500* (Cambridge).

Hoffman, A. 1954 *Coléoptères Curculionides, Faune de France* 59 (Paris).

Hoffman, A. 1958 *Coléoptères Curculionides, Faune de France* 62 (Paris).

Hogg, J. 1975 'The Architecture of Hinton Charterhouse', *Analecta Cartusiana* 25, lxxi–xcvi and 1–70.

Hogg, J. (ed.) 1977 'Richard Methley: to Hew Heremyte, a pystyl of solytary lyfe nowadayes', *Analecta Cartusiana* 31, 95–104.

Hogg, J. 2008 'Life in an English charterhouse', in J. M. Luxford, *Studies in Carthusian Monasticism in the Late Middle Ages* (Medieval Church Studies 14, Turnhout), 19–60.

Hoogendijk, T. 2012 *Karthuizerklooster Nieuwlicht: de archeologie van een Utrechts klooster* (Zandijke).

Holdsworth, C. J. 1979 *'Another Stage ... A Different World': Ideas and People around Exeter in the Twelfth Century* (Inaugural Lecture 27 October 1978, Exeter).

Holdsworth, C. J. 1989 'Baldwin of Forde, Cistercian and Archbishop of Canterbury', *Friends of Lambeth Palace Library: Annual Report 1989*, 13–31.

Holdsworth, J. 1978 'Selected pottery groups AD 650–1780', in *The Archaeology of York, The Pottery* 16/1 (London).

Hope, W. H. St J. 1900a 'Fountains Abbey', *Yorkshire Archaeological Journal* 15, 269–402.

Hope, W. H St J. 1900b 'The Abbey of St Mary in Furness, Lancashire', *Transactions of the Cumberland and Westmoreland Antiquarian and Archaeological Society* 16, 221–302.

Hope, W. H. St J. 1903 'The London charterhouse and its old water supply', *Archaeologia* 58/1, 293–312.

Hope, W. H. St J. 1905 'Architectural history of Mount Grace charterhouse', *Yorkshire Archaeological Journal* 18, 270–309.

Hope, W. H. St J. 1925 *The History of the London Charterhouse from its Foundation until the Suppression of the Monastery* (London).

Hope, W. H. St J. and Fowler, J. T. 1903 'Recent Discoveries in the Cloister of Durham Abbey', *Archaeologia* 53 pt. 2, 437–57.

Horn, W. and Born, E. 1979 *The Plan of St Gall*, 3 vols (Berkeley).

Horrox, R. 1983 *The De La Poles of Hull* (East Yorkshire Local History Ser. 38, Beverley).

Howard, H. 2007 'Medieval oyster shell palette' and 'Appendix 5: Medieval paint palettes', in Emery 2007b, 139–43, 240–1.

Howard, H. and Park, D. n.d. 'A medieval oyster shell palette from the Greyfriars, Norwich', unpublished typescript.

Hurst, J. G., Neal, D. S. and Van Beuningen, H. J. E. 1986 *Pottery Produced and Traded in North-west Europe 1350–1650* (Rotterdam Papers 6, Rotterdam).

Irving, B. and Jones, A. K. G. 1994 *Technical Report: Fish Remains from Mount Grace Priory, N Yorkshire* (Environmental Archaeology Unit Report 94/54, York).

Jackson, C. (ed.) 1870 *The Diary of Abraham de la Pryme* (Surtees Society 54, London).

Jarvis, M. 1995 'Lincoln central library', in M. J. Joes (ed.), *Lincoln Archaeology 1995–1994* (Lincoln).

Jenkins, J. G. 1978 *Traditional Country Craftsmen* (London).

Jennings, S. 1992 *Medieval Pottery in the Yorkshire Museum* (York).

Jessop, L. 1986 *Dung Beetles and Chafers. Coleoptera: Scarabaeoidea*, new edn (Handbooks for the identification of British insects 5/11, London).

Johnstone, E .1946 *Writing & Illuminating, & Lettering* (London).

Jones, A. K. G. 1976 'The fish bones', in G. Black, 'Excavations in the subvault of the misericord of Westminster Abbey', *Transactions of the London & Middlesex Archaeological Society* 27, 170–6.

Jones, A. K. G. 1989 'The survival of fish remains at monastic sites', in Gilchrist and Mytum 1989, 173–84.

Jones, T. L. 1984 *Ashby de la Zouch Castle, Leicestershire* (London).

Keen, L. 1971 'Medieval floor-tiles from Campsea Ash Priory', *Proceedings of the Suffolk Institute of Archaeology* 32/2, 140–51.

Keen, L. 1976 'Floor tiles', in D. Sherlock, 'Discoveries at Horsham St. Faith Priory, 1970–1973', *Norfolk Archaeology* 36/3, 214–17.

Keen, L. J. 1984 'The Medieval Floor tiles in J. P. Allen 'Medieval and Post-medieval Finds From Exeter, 1971–80', *Exeter Archaeological Reports* 3, 232–46.

Kemp, R. L. and Graves, C. P. 1996 'The church and Gilbertine priory of St Andrew, Fishergate', *Archaeology of York* 11/2 (York).

Ker, N. R. (ed.) 1964 *Medieval Libraries of Great Britain: A List of Surviving Books* (Royal Historical Society Guides and Handbooks 3, London).

Kloet, G. S. and Hinks, W. D. 1977 *A Checklist of British Insects*, 2nd edn (revised) (Royal Entomological Society of London Handbook 4 pt 2, London).

Knight, S. and Keen, L. 1977 'Medieval floor tiles from Guisborough Priory, Yorkshire', *Yorkshire Archaeological Journal* 49, 65–75.

Knowles, D. 1961a *The Religious Orders in England* II (Cambridge).

Knowles, D. 1961b *The Religious Orders in England* III (Cambridge).

Knowles, D. and Grimes, W. F. 1954 *Charterhouse: The Medieval Foundation in the Light of Recent Discoveries* (London).

Knowles, D. and Hadcock, R. N. 1971 *Medieval Religious Houses of England and Wales*, 2nd edn (London).

Knowles, D. and Smith, D. M. 2008 *The Heads of Religious Houses England and Wales, 1377–1540* III (Cambridge).

Knowles, G. C. 1977 entries in J. May (ed.), *East Midlands Archaeological Bulletin* 11, 15.

Kroustalis, S. 2011 'Quomodo decoretur pictura librorum de la iluminación medieval', *Anuario de Estudios Medievales* 41/2, 775–802.

Leahy, K. 2003 *Anglo-Saxon Crafts* (Stroud).

Le Patourel, H. E. J. 1968 'Documentary evidence and the medieval pottery industry', *Medieval Archaeology* 12, 101–26.

Lindroth, C. H. 1985 'The Carabidae Coleoptera of Fennoscandia and Denmark', *Fauna Entomologica Scandinavica* 15/1, 1–232.

Littler, A. S. 1979 'Fish in English economy and society down to the Reformation', unpublished PhD thesis, University College, Swansea.

Locker, A. 1986 'The fish', in J. Hare, *Battle Abbey – The Eastern Range and the Excavations of 1979–80* (HBMC Archaeological Report 2, London), 185–7.

Lohse, G. A. 1964 'Familie: Staphylinidae', in H. Freude, K. W. Harde and G. A. Lohse (eds), *Die Käfer mitteleuropas* 4 (Krefeld).

Lohse, G. A. 1969 'Familie: Elateridae', in H. Freude, K. W. Harde and G. A. Lohse (eds), *Die Käfer mitteleuropas* 6 (Krefeld), 103–86.

Lohse, G. A. 1983a 'Unterfamilie: Notarinae (Erirhinae)', in H. Freude, K. W. Harde and G. A. Lohse (eds), *Die Käfer mitteleuropas* 11 (Krefeld), 59–78.

Lohse, G. A. 1983b 'Unterfamilie: Barinae', in H. Freude, K. W. Harde and G. A. Lohse (eds), *Die Käfer mitteleuropas* 11 (Krefeld), 171–283.

Lohse, G. and Tischler, Th. 1983 'U. Familie Mecininae', in Freude *et al.* 1983b, 259–78.

Loveluck, C. 2001 'Flixborough and its importance', in H. Hameroe and A. MacGregor (eds), *Images of Power in the Archaeology of Early Medieval Britain: Essays in Honour of Rosemary Cramp* (Oxford), 79–130.

Luxford, J. M. 2008 *Studies in Carthusian Monasticism in the Late Middle Ages* (Medieval Church Studies 14, Turnhout).

Luxford, J. M. 2011a 'The charterhouse of St Anne, Coventry', in L. Monckton and R. K. Morris (eds), *Coventry: Medieval Art, Architecture and Archaeology in the City and its Vicinity* (British Archaeological Association Transactions 33), 240–66.

Luxford, J. 2011b 'The space of the tomb in Carthusian consciousness', in F. Andrews (ed.), *Ritual and Space in the Middle Ages* (Harlaxton Medieval Studies 21, Donington).

McCarthy, M. R. and Brooks, C. M. 1988 *Medieval Pottery in Britain AD900–1600* (Leicester).

McGarvie, M. 1978 *The Bounds of Selwood* (Frome History Research Group Occasional Papers 1, Frome).

McGarvie, M. 1989 *Witham Priory: Church and Parish* (Frome Hist Research Group Church Histories 1, Frome).

MacGregor, A. 1985 'Coin balances in the Ashmolean Museum', *Antiquaries Journal* 65, 439–43.

MacGregor, A. 2001 'Objects of bone, antler and ivory', in P. Saunders (ed.), *Salisbury Museum Medieval Catalogue* 3 (Salisbury), 14–25.

Malden, J. (ed.) 2000 *The Monastery and Abbey of Paisley* (Glasgow).

Margeson, S. 1993 *Norwich Households: The Medieval and Post-medieval Finds from Norwich Survey Excavations 1971–1978* (East Anglian Archaeology 58, Norwich).

Marshall, C. 1987/8 'The medieval tumbrel', *Treasure Hunting*, March 1987, n.p.; June 1987, 38–9; January 1988, 26–7.

Martin, A. R. 1937 *Franciscan Architecture in England* (Manchester).

Mayes, P. and Hayfield, C. 1980 'A late medieval pottery kiln at Holme-upon-Spalding-Moor', *East Riding Archaeology* 6, 97–113.

Mayhew, N. J. 1975 'A tumbrel at the Ashmolean Museum', *Antiquaries Journal* 55, 394–6.

Meech, S. B. and Allen, H. E. (eds) 1940 *The Book of Margery Kemps: The Text from the Unique MS. Owned by Colonel W. Butler-Bowden* I (Early English Text Society, Orig. Ser. 212, Oxford).

Mellor, J. E. and Pearce, T. 1981 *The Austin Friars, Leicester* (CBA Research Report 35, Leicester).

Mellor, M. 1994 *Medieval Ceramic Studies in England: A Review for English Heritage* (London).Meyvaert, P. 1986 'The medieval monastic garden', in E. MacDougall (ed.), *Medieval Gardens* (Washington, DC).

Mohr, K. H. 1966 'Familie: Chrysomelidae', in H. Freude, K. W. Harde and G. A. Lohse (eds), *Die Käfer mitteleuropas* 9 (Krefeld), 95–280.

Moorhouse, S. and Roberts, I. 1992 'Wrenthorpe potteries', *Yorkshire Archaeology* 2.

Moorhouse, S. and Wrathmell, S. 1987 'Kirkstall Abbey I: The 1950–64 excavations – a reassessment', *Yorkshire Archaeology* 1.

Mordefroid, J.-L. and Horrilo Escobar, J. 1996 'Archéologie et hydraulique cartusienne, Notre-Dame-de-la-Verne du XIIe au XVIIIe siècle (Var, France)', in Bonis and Wabont 1996, 169–91.

Morris, C. 1984 'Anglo-Saxon and medieval woodworking crafts – the manufacture and use of domestic and utilitarian wooden artifacts in the British Isles 400–1500AD', unpublished PhD thesis, University of Cambridge.

Morris, C. A. 2000 *Craft, Industry and Everyday Life: Wood and Woodworking in Anglo-Scandinavian and Medieval York*, in *The Archaeology of York*, 17/13 (York).

Morris, C. A. and Evans, D. H. 1991 'The wood', in Armstrong *et al.*, 189–209.

Morrison, A. 2003 'Mount Grace Priory: the rediscovered historic interiors of the Manor House', in J. Bryant, *Collections Review* 4 (London).Naydenova-Slade, M. 2011 'A "body full of wounds": The 15th-century mural at St Anne's Charterhouse, Coventry', in L. Monkton and R. K. Morris (eds), *Coventry: Medieval Art, Architecture and Archaeology in the City and its Vicinity* (British Archaeological Association Transactions 33), 271–2.

Needham, P. 1979 *Twelve Centuries of Bookbinding 400–1600* (New York and London).

Newman, M. 1996 *The Boundaries of Charity: Cistercian Culture and Ecclesiastical Reform* (Stanford).

Norton, E. C. 1976 'The medieval pavingtiles of Winchester College', *Proceedings of the Hampshire Field Club and Archaeological Society* 31, 23–42.

Norton, E. C. 1994 'Medieval floor tiles in Scotland', in J. Higgitt (ed.), *Medieval Art and Architecture in the Diocese of St Andrews* (British Archaeological Association Conference Transactions 14), 137–73.

Ogden, M. (ed.) 1938 *Liber de Diversis Medicinis* (Early English Text Society 207, London).

Oldman, J. B. 1943 *Shrewsbury School Library Bindings: Catalogue Raisonné* (Oxford).

Page, W. (ed.) 1906 *Victoria History of the County of Lincolnshire II* (London).

Page, W. (ed.) 1908 *Victoria History of the County of Warwickshire II* (London).

Page, W. (ed.) 1910 *Victoria History of the County of Nottinghamshire II* (London).

Page, W. (ed.) 1911 *Victoria History of the County of Somerset II* (London)

Page, W. (ed.) 1913 *Victoria History of the County of York III* (London).

Palm, T. 1951 'Die Holz- und Rinsdenkäfer der nordschwedishen Laubbaume', *Medd. Stat. Skogfors. Inst* 40, 2.

Palm, T. 1959 'Die Holz- und Rinden-Käfer der süd- und mittelschwedischen Laubbäume', *Opuscula Entomologica Supplementum* 16, 1–374.

Palmer, T. F. 1923 'The site of Witham Priory or charterhouse', *Somerset and Dorset Notes & Queries* 17, 90–2.

Pantin, W. 1959 'Chantry priests' houses and other medieval lodgings', *Medieval Archaeology* 3, 216–58.

Pearce, E. J. 1957 *Coleoptera (Pselaphidae)* (Handbooks for the identification of British insects IV (9), London).

Pevsner, N. 1966 *The Buildings of England: Yorkshire, the North Riding* (London).

Pevsner, N. and Neave, D. 1995 *The Buildings of England: Yorkshire, York and the East Riding* (London).

Pevsner, N. and Wilson, B. 1962 *The Buildings of England: Norfolk I: Norwich and North East* (London).

Platt, C. and Coleman-Smith, R. 1975 *Excavations in Medieval Southampton 1953–1969, Vol 2, The Finds* (Leicester).

Poulton, R. and Woods, H. 1984 *Excavations on the site of the Dominican Friary at Guildford in 1974 and 1978* (Research volumes of the Surrey Archaeological Society 9, Guildford).

Pouzet, J.-P. 2011 'Book production outside commercial contexts', in Gillespie and Wakelin 2011, 212–38.

Raine, J. (ed.) 1836 *Testamenta Eboracensia I* (Surtees Society 4, London).

Raine, J. (ed.) 1855 *Testamenta Eboracensia II* (Surtees Society 30, London).
Raine, J. (ed.) 1859 *The Fabric Rolls of York Minster* (Surtees Society 35, London).
Raine, J. (ed.) 1865 *Testamenta Eboracensia III* (Surtees Society 45, London).
Raine, J. (ed.) 1868 *Testamenta Eboracensia IV* (Surtees Society 53, London).
Raine, J. (ed.) 1884 *Testamenta Eboracensia V* (Surtees Society 79, London).
Rawcliffe, C. 1999 *Medicine for the Soul* (Stroud).
Richmond, C. and Scarff, E. (eds) 2001 *St George's Chapel, Windsor, in the Late Middle Ages* (Historical Monograph 17, Windsor).
Roberts, A. K. B. 1947 *St. George's Chapel, Windsor Castle 1348–1416: A Study in Early Collegiate Administration* (Historical Monograph 6, Windsor).
Robinson, J. A. and James, M. R. 1909 *The Manuscripts of Westminster Abbey* (Cambridge).
Roebuck, J., Coppack, G. and Hurst, J. G. 1987 'A closely dated group of late medieval pottery from Mount Grace Priory', *Medieval Ceramics* 11, 15–24.
Rosenlund, K. 1984 'The fish bone material from a Danish monastery and an 18th century mission station in Greenland – an investigation of materials with a known key', in N. Desse-Berset (ed.), '2nd Fish Osteology Meeting', *CNRS Centre de Recherches Archaéologiques, Notes & Monographies Techniques* 16, 145–53.
Rowntree, C. B. 1981 'Studies in Carthusian history in later medieval England; with special reference to the order's relations with secular society', unpublished DPhil thesis, University of York.
Rutter, J. G. 1961 *Medieval Pottery in the Scarborough Museum: 13th & 14th Centuries* (Scarborough and District Archaeological Society Research Report 3, Scarborough).
Rutter, J. A. 1990 'Floor tile catalogue', in S. W. Ward, *Excavations at Chester: The Lesser Medieval Religious Houses* (Grosvenor Museum Archaeological Excavation and Survey Reports 6, Chester).
Ryder, P. F. 1985 *The Medieval Cross Slab Grace Cover in County Durham* (Durham).
Ryder, M. L. 1961 'Report on Animal Remains' in Mitchell, C. M and Bellamy, C. V. (ed.) *Kirkstall Abbey Excavations 1955–1959*, Publications of the Thoresy Society 48, 41–50, 67–77, 98–100 and 130–132.
Sachs, H. 1973 *The Book of Trades. Ständebuch. [Woodcuts by] Jost Amman and [text by] Hans Sachs*. With a new introduction by Benjamin A. Rifkin (New York).
Salzman, L. F. 1952 *Building in England down to 1540: A Documentary History* (Oxford).
Sargent, M. G. 1976 'The transmission by the English Carthusians of some late medieval spiritual writings', *Journal of Ecclesiastical History* 27/3, 225–40.
Saunders, P. (ed.) 2001 *Salisbury Museum Medieval Catalogue* 3 (Salisbury).
Schenkluhn, W. 2000 *Architektur der Bettelorden* (Darmstadt).
Senior, J. R. 1989 'The selection of dimensional and ornamental stone types used in some northern monasteries', in Gilchrist and Mytum 1989, 223–50.
Shackley, M., Hayne, J. and Wainwright, N. 1998 'Environmental analysis of medieval fishpond deposits at Owston Abbey, Leicestershire', in M. Aston (ed.), *Medieval Fish, Fisheries, and Fishponds* (British Archaeological Reports Brit. Ser. 182, Oxford), 301–8.
Sheppard, J. M. 1998 'Some 12th-century bindings from the library of Bury St Edmunds Abbey: preliminary findings', in A. Gransden (ed.), *Bury St Edmunds: Medieval Art, Architecture, Archaeology and Economy* (British Archaeological Association Conference Transactions 20), 194–203.
Sherlock, D. and Woods, H. 1988 *St. Augustine's Abbey: Report on Excavations, 1960–78* (Kent Archaeological Society Monograph Ser. 4, Maidstone).
Skaithe, R. H. (ed.) 1866 *The Survey of the County of York taken by John de Kirby* (Surtees Society 49, London).
Skeat, T. C. 1957 'Letters from the reign of Henry VIII', *British Museum Quarterly* 21/1, 4–8.

Smith, D. M. 2006 'The phantom prior of Mount Grace', *Monastic Research Bulletin* 12, 37–9.
Smithson, C. W. 1898 *History and Guide to the Ruins of the Carthusian Monastery called Mount Grace*, 7th edn (Northallerton).
Soden, I. 1995 *Excavations at St Anne's Charterhouse, Coventry, 1968–87* (Coventry).
Soden, I. 2005 *Coventry: The Hidden History* (Stroud).
Standing, G. 2010 'A Saxo-Norman oyster colour-dish from St. Mary's Church, New Shoreham, Sussex', *Journal of the British Archaeological Association* 163, 16–23.
Stopford, J. 1995 'Floor tiles at Kirkham Priory', in Coppack *et al.*, 75–81.
Stopford, J. 1996 'The floor tiles', in R. L. Kem and C. P. Graves, 'The church and Gilbertine priory of St Andrew, Fishergate', in *Archaeology of York* 11/2 (York), 298–301.
Stopford, J. 2005 *Medieval Floor Tiles of Northern England, Pattern and Purpose: Production between the 13th and 16th Centuries* (Oxford).
Szirmai, J. A. 2001 *The Archaeology of Medieval Bookbinding* (Aldershot).
Talbot, C. H. 1967 *Letters from the English Abbots to the Chapter at Cîteaux, 1442–1531* (Camden Society 4th Ser., 4, London).
Thawley, C. R. 1981 'The mammal, bird, and fish bones', in J. E. Mellor and T. Pearce, *The Austin Friars, Leicester* (CBA Research Report 35, Leicester), 173–5.
Thompson, E. M. 1930 *The Carthusian Order in England* (London).
Thompson, M. W. 1981 *Ruins: Their Preservation and Display* (London).
Tottenham, C. E. 1954 *Coleoptera Staphylinidae section (a) Piestinae to Euaesthetinae* (Handbooks for the identification of British insects 4/9, London).
Toulmin Smith, L. (ed.) 1964 *The Itinerary of John Leland in or about the Years 1535–1543* I (London).
van Acker, L. 1972 *Petri Pictoris Carmina, nec non Petri de Sancto Andemero de coloribus faciendis Librum* (Corpus Christianum: Continuatio Medievalis 25, Turnhout).
Vos, H. H. 1975 'Archeologisch onderzoek naar het voormalig Kartuizer Klooster buiten Delft', in R. Rothfusz *et al.* (eds), *De Kartuizers en hun Delftse klooster: Een bundle studiën verschenen ter gelegenheid van het achtste lustrum van het Genootschap Delfia Batavorum* (Delft), 17–36.
Walbran, J. R. 1862 *Memorials of the Abbey of St Mary of Fountains, I* (Surtees Society 62, London).
Walbran, J. R. 1876 *Memorials of the Abbey of St Mary of Fountains, II* (Surtees Society 76, London).
Wallis, H. 2006 *Excavations on the site of Norwich Cathedral Refectory 2001–3* (East Anglian Archaeology 116, Dereham).
Watson, A. G. (ed.) 1987 *Medieval Libraries of Great Britain: A List of Surviving Books* (ed. N. R. Ker), Supplement to the 2nd edition (Royal Historical Society Guides and Handbooks 15, London).
Watts, L. 1983 'Books, book fittings and writing', in Hirst *et al.* 1983, 200–6.
Wheeler, A. 1984 'Fish bones', in P. Leach (ed.), *The Archaeology of Taunton* (Western Archaeological Trust Excavation Monograph 8, Bristol), 193–4.
Wheeler, A. and Jones, A. K. G. 1989 *Fishes* (Cambridge).
Wheeler, A. C. 1969 *The Fishes of the British Isles and North-west Europe* (London).
Williams, A. and Martin, G. H. (eds) 2002 *Domesday Book* (London).
Williams, D. F. and Tomber, R. 1982 'Petrological examination of Scarborough Ware and other medieval pottery', *Medieval Ceramics* 6, 111–19.
Wilson, B. and Mee, F. 1998 *The Medieval Parish Churches of York, The Pictorial Evidence* (York).
Wilson, D. M. and Hurst, D. G. 1961 'Medieval Britain in 1960', *Medieval Archaeology* 5, 309–39.
Wilson-North, R. 'Report on geophysical survey at Hinton Priory, Somerset', *Geophysical Surveys of Bradford Report* 94/12.
Wilson North, R. 1996 'Witham: from Carthusian monastery to country house', *Current Archaeology* 148, 151–6.
Wolters, C. (trans. and ed.) 1972 *Richard Rolle: The Fire of Love* (London).

Wood, M. 1951 'Number 3, Vicars' Court, Lincoln', *Lincolnshire Historian* 7, 281–6.

Woodfield, C. 1981 'Finds from the Free Grammar School at the Whitefriars, Coventry, *c*.1545–*c*.1557/58', *Post-Medieval Archaeology* 15, 81–159.

Woodfield, C. 2005 *The Church of Our Lady of Mount Carmel and Some Conventual Buildings at the Whitefriars, Coventry* (British Archaeological Reports Brit. Ser. 389, Oxford).

Wormald, F. 1936 '"The Revelation of the Hundred Pater Nosters": a fifteenth-century meditation', *Laudate* 14/55, 165–82.

Wormald, F. 1965 'Some popular miniatures and their rich relations', republished in Alexander *et al.* 1988, 139–46.

Wrathmell, S. (ed.) 2018 *Kirkstall Abbey II, The Guest House* Yorkshire Archaeology 12 (Leeds).

Zeeman, E. 1955 'Nicholas Love – a fifteenth-century translator', *Review of English Studies* n.s. 6/22, 113–27.

Index

Numbers in *italic* denote pages with figures, those in **bold** denote pages with tables.
Small finds are listed by material: bone, copper alloy, glass, iron, lead, pipeclay, silver, stone, and wood.

Acts of Succession and Supremacy (1534) 43, 44
Adam of Eynsham 374
Aldburgh, Sir William de 14
ale 392
altars 53, 267, 268
animal bones 341
    see also fish bones
animal burial 148
Anthony of Egypt, Saint 1, 4
arcades, cloister
    cell 8 *90*, 92
    cell 13 145
    great cloister 276–80, *277–9*, 387
    south-west cloister range 185–6
architectural fragments *see* stone, architectural
Arthington, W. Yorks. 390
Ashby de la Zouch Castle, Leics. 380
Atherstone, Warwicks. 29, 31
Authorp, William de 38
Axholme, Lincs. **xvii**, *6*, **7–8**, 21–3, *22*, 374, 400

bakehouse 54, 263, 265
Banks, William 38
Barker, William 42
Bayley, Justine 344
Beaufort, Thomas, 1st Duke of Exeter 23, 29, 30, 266–7, 268, 361
Beauvale, Notts. **xvii**, *6*, **7–8**, 14–17, *15*, *17*
    books 343
    cells 374–5, *375*, 376–7, 378, 384
    church *15*, 16, 362–3, *363*, 365–6, 368
    latrines 401
    lay brothers 387, 388
    water supply 400
Beckford, Sir William 11
beds, garden
    cell 8 97–8
    cell 9 113
    cell 10 120, *121*
    cell 20 248
    prior's *173*, 187
    south-west cloister range 208, *208*
Bedyll, Thomas 43
Bee, William 42, 43
Beighton, Derbys. 31
Belasyse, Richard 39
Bell, Sir Isaac Lowthian 109–10, 240, 295, 304–5
bells 267
benches 176, 191, *191*, 234, 390, 391
Benedict, Saint 1, 2, 4
bequests 37–9
Bernard of Clairvaux 2, 382
Beverley Minster, E. Yorks. 370
Biddle, Martin 56
Blackmore, Lynne 397
bone objects
    ear- and toothpick 122, *123*, 345
    head of Christ *213*, 214, 347
    inlays *206*, 207
    needle *206*, 207, 341
    offcut *206*, 207
    pin *187*, 188
'Book of Margery Kempe' 41
books
    in a cell 41–2
    library 38, 41, 43, 343
    production of 122, 133, 344–6, 397
        book clasps 107, *108*, *132*, 134, 146–7, *146*, *197*, 198, 206–7, *206*
    book corner mount/strip 107, *108*
    book mounts *102*, 105, 107, *108*, 122, *123*
    ear- and toothpick 122, *123*
    gouge *243*, 244
    grinding stone *139*, 140
    needle *132*, 134
    paint pot/inkwell *108*, 109
    palettes, shell *139*, 140, *146*, 147
    pens 122, *123*, *132*, 133–4
    punch *132*, 133
    tacks, binding *108*, 109
    tubes *213*, 214, *243*, 244
    tweezers 122, *123*, *139*, 140
    writing leads 124, *125*, *146*, 147
    written at Mount Grace 40, 41, 343–4
Bordelbi, N. Yorks. 27–8, 33, 35–6, *36*, 37, 165, 315, 357, *358*, 359
Boynton, Joan 38
Brakspear, Sir Harold 53, 54
Braunfels, W. 5, 6, 255
bread 3–4, 392
'brewhouse'/kitchen 261–3, *262–3*
Brown, William 27, 45, 51–2, 343
Bruno of Cologne, Saint 1, 2
Bryce, Dan 40
building fittings 348–9
    pintle *213*, 213
    pipe clips *115*, 116, 124, *125*, *146*, 147
    pipes 201, *201*, *206*, 207
    sieves/filters *206*, 207
    strap-hinges *213*, 213, *243*, 243
Burdett, John 30
burial chapels 366, 371–2
    piscinas 273–4, *275*
    windows 265, 273, *273–4*, 372
burials 38–9, 177, 367, 371, 402

Burneston, N. Yorks. 368, *369*, 370–1
Burrow, C. & I. 10
Byland Abbey, N. Yorks. 310, 380

Campbell, Colen 10, 11, 362
candle niches 65, 96, 142
Candyssh (Cavendish), John 21
Canterbury Cathedral, Kent 298, 382, 399
Cantilupe, Sir Nicholas 14
Carisbrooke, Isle of Wight 28, 29, *29*, 30
Carr, John 38
Carthusian Order 1–6, *4*
    in England 6–25, *6*, **7–8**
    spirituality 343
Catterick, N. Yorks. 368, 369, *369*, 371, 372
cell 1 61–2, *61*, 285, 385
cell 2 62–6, *62–5*, **66**, *67*, 383
cell 3 66–72, *68–70*, **71**, 287, *287*
cell 4 72–3, *72–4*, 75–7, **75**, 285, 383, 385
cell 5 77–9, *77–8*, **79**, 285, 385
cell 6 79–82, *79–81*, **82**
cell 7 82–5, *83–4*, 86, **86**, 385
cell 8 86–110
    architectural frags. 110, *110*
    cell interior 94
    cloister alley 89, *90*, 92, 99, *100*, 101
    cloister arcade *90*, 92
    drains and tank 87–8, *88*, 90, 95, 97
    Finds Group 7 89, **89**, *89*
    Finds Group 8 92, **92**
    Finds Group 9 98, 99, **99**, *99*
    Finds Group 10 101–2, **102**, *102*, 105
    Finds Group 11 *103–4*, 105–6, **105**, 323
    Finds Group 12 107–9, **108**, *108*
    garden *87*, *90*, 97–8, *98*, 99–100, *101*, 383
    garden pentice *90*, 96–7, *97*, 99
    garden walls *87*, 89, *90*
    latrine pentice 94–6, *96*
    north range passage 90
    pit *90*, 92
    post-suppression 109–10, *109*
    suppression 100–1
    terrace 86–7, *87*
    timber structures 88–9
    walls *91*, 92–4, *94*, 385
cell 9 *88*, 110–16, *111*, *113*, *115*, **116**, 285, 383
cell 10 110–27
    architectural frags. 126–7, *126–7*
    cell interior 116–17
    ceramics 120–2, *123*, **124**
    garden 120, *121*, 383
    garden pentice 118–19, *118*
    latrine pentice 119–20, *119–20*
    small finds 122, *123*, 124–6, *125*
    walls 117–18
    window 385
cell 11 127–36
    architectural frags. 135–6, *135*
    cell interior 127–8, *128*
    ceramics 131, *132*, 133, **133**
    garden 130–1
    garden pentice 129–30, *130*
    latrine pentice 130
    small finds *132*, 133–4, *134*
    walls 128–9, *129*
cell 12 136–41, *136–41*, **140**
cell 13 141–7, *141–4*, *146*, **147**
cell 14 147–53, *147–8*, *150*, **151**, *152*, 383
cell 15 *152*, 153–4, **154**, *154*
cell 16 244–5, *244–5*, 293, 388
cell 17 245–6, 293
cell 18 246–7, *246*, 293
cell 19 247, 293
cell 20 247–8, **247**, *249*, 250, 292, 383, 384
cell 21 250, *250*, 292
cell 22 162, 192, 281, *282–3*, 377
cell 23 162–3, *162*, 281–3, *282*, *284*, 377–8
cell, sacrist's 60–1, *60*, 283–4
cell, prior's 280–1, *280–2*, 299, 380–2, *381*
    first 177, 201, 382, 385
    second 182, 184, 189–90, *190*, 195, 382
    gardens *173*, 187, 196
    water pipes 183, 184, 186, 191
    windows 190, 194, *194*, 280, *282*
cells, discussion of 374–88, *375*, *379*, 402
    contents of 41–2, 323, 342–3, 398
    gardens 382–4
    other lodgings 379–80
    prior's cells 380–2, *381*
cells, fittings 347
    candle holder *132*, 134
    candlestick base? *243*, 244
    curtain/drape rings *102*, 105, 107, *108*
    dish or pan *115*, 116
ceramic floor tiles 326–33, *327–8*, **334**
    conclusion 332
    discussion 329–32
        imported tiles 329–30
        locally made tiles 330–1
    glazes 333
    petrology 332–3
    tile groups 326–9, *327–8*
ceramic forms
    albarello
        Malaga lustreware *161*, 162
        White Pisa slipware 98, *99*
    barrel costrel, Ryedale 121, *123*
    basting dishes
        Brandsby type *178*, 179
        Gritty? *225*, 226
    bottle neck, Regional Stray 200, *201*
    bottle or flask
        Hambleton 121, *123*
        Langerwehe *132*, 133
        South Netherlands maiolica *178*, 179
    bottles
        Hambleton 101, *102*, 145, *146*
        late-medieval Sandy 241, 242
        Raeren *132*, 133
        Regional Stray 74, 76, 248, *249*
        Ryedale *225*, 226, *226*, 227
    bowls
        Gritty 168, *169*, 172, *172*, *193*, 194, 198, *199*, 237, *237*
        19th cent. red earthenware *210*, 212
        post-med. Sandy 74, 77, *210*, 212, 236, *236*, 241, 242
        Seville Columbia Plain earthenware *104*, 106
    candlestick base, Ryedale *187*, 188
    chafing dishes
        Hambleton 145, *146*
        Humber *74*, 76
        Late Gritty 131, *132*
        post-med. Orange 89, *89*, 121, *123*
    chalice, Cistercian *103*, 106
    chamberpot/spittoon? Staffordshire tiger *210*, 212
    cisterns
        Humber 98, *99*
        post-med. Orange 131, *132*
        Ryedale *78*, 79, 114, *115*, *193*, 194, *203*, 205, 217, *217*
    cooking-pot bases, Stamford 168, *169*
    cooking-pot rims
        Brandsby type 66, *67*, *178*, 179
        Developed Humber *210*, 211
        Gritty *74*, 76, 168, *169–72*, 170–2, *178*, 178, 187, *187*, 199, *199*
    cooking pots
        Brandsby type *178*, 179
        early medieval Sandy *226*, 227
        Gritty 121, *123*, 138, *139*, 172, *172*, *225*, 226
        Gritty/fine sandy 237, *237*
        Ryedale 248, *249*
        Staxton? 168, *169*
    costrels, Langerwehe *102*, 102
    cruets, Humber 84, *85*, 86
    cup/posset pot, Cistercian copy *226*, 227
    cups
        Cistercian 70, *71*, *81*, *82*, *103*, 106, 121, *123*, 145, *146*, 199–200, *199*, *201*, *203*, 205, 239, *239*, 241, 243

INDEX

Cistercian copy *70*, 71, 131, *132*, 236, *236*, *237*, 238, *241*, 243
Langerwehe *132*, 133
Late Cistercian *203*, 205
Midland Yellow *81*, 82, *103*, 106
post-med. Sandy 236, *236*, *241*, 242
Reversed Cistercian 114, *115*, *197*, 198
Ryedale 231, *231*
Tudor Green 131, *132*, *241*, 243
cups, handled, Cistercian copy *203*, 205
cups, two-handled, Cistercian *74*, 77
cups, three-handled
Cistercian 197–8, *197*
Cistercian copy *197*, 198
cups, lobed, Tudor Green *85*, 86
curcurbits
Humber 139, *139*
unid. 248, *249*
curfew, Gritty 171, *171*
dishes
post-med. Sandy *203*, 204, 235, *235*, *241*, 242
Seville Columbia Plain earthenware *104*, 106
Valencia Lustre *104*, 106
dishes, two handled, post-med. Sandy 209, *209*
drug jars
Humber 70, *70*
Staffordshire *74*, 77, 101, *102*, *103*, 106, 107, *108*, 114, *115*, 122, *123*, 131, *132*, 139, *139*, 146, *146*
flagons, Langerwehe(?) *104*, 106
flask or drug pot, Delft? *210*, 212
flasks, Langerwehe *102*, *102*
handles, Brandsby type 248, *249*
jar and lid, Late Gritty *103*, 106
jar handles
Developed Humber *70*, 71
post-med. Orange *74*, 77
post-med. Sandy *78*, 79
jar or cistern, Regional Stray 131, *132*
jar rims
post-med. Orange *74*, 77
Regional Stray 121, *123*
jars
Developed Humber 209, *209*
Hambleton 138, *139*
Langerwehe *74*, 77
Mediterranean 139, *139*
post-med. Sandy *203*, 204, *210*, 212, 236, *236*, *241*, 242, 248, *249*
jars, handled
Developed Humber *210*, 211
Late Gritty *203*, 205

Late Humber/post-med. Sandy 131, *132*
post-med. Orange *81*, 82
post-med. Sandy *203*, 204–5, *241*, 242
jars, two-handled
Hambleton 145, *146*
post-med. Orange *81*, 82, *249*, 250
post-med. Sandy 121, *123*, *203*, 204
jug bases
Humber 66, *67*
Regional Stray *74*, 76
jug handles
Brandsby type 66, *67*
Gritty *74*, 76
Regional Stray 217, *217*
Ryedale *74*, 76
jug rims
Brandsby type *74*, 76, *178*, 179
Developed Humber 81, *81*
Gritty 168, *169*, 171, *171*, *193*, 194
Hambleton 81–2, *81*
Humber *85*, 86, 197, *197*
Ryedale *74*, 76, *178*, 179
jugs(?), Ryedale *74*, 76, *85*, 86, 235, *235*
jugs
Beauvais *74*, 77, *104*, 106
Brandsby 231, *231*
Gritty *167*, 168, *169*, 170, 171, *171*, *225*, 226
Gritty/Brandsby *225*, 226, 237, *237*
Hambleton 114, *115*, 145, *146*, *241*, 242
Humber 84, *85*, 197, *197*
post-med. Orange 66, *67*, *85*, 86, *103*, 106
post-med. Sandy *187*, 188
Ryedale 70–1, *70*, 81, *81*, *85*, 86, *103*, 106–7, *108*, 114, *115*, 145, *146*, 161, *161*, 217, *217*, *225*, 226, 231, *231*, 239, *239*, 248, *249*
Scarborough 70, *70*
jugs, baluster
Brandsby type 138, *139*
Ryedale *74*, 76
lamps
post-med. Sandy 199, *199*
Regional Stray 114, *115*
lids
Cistercian 200, *201*, *241*, 243
Cistercian copy 199, *199*
post-med. Sandy 209, *209*
Staffordshire *193*, 194
mug or cruet, Hambleton 131, *132*
mugs, Ryedale *225*, 226
mugs, stoneware

Cologne *232*, 233
Langerwehe *70*, 71, 102, *102*, *104*, 106, 114, *115*, 122, *123*, 131, *132*, 133, *167*, 168, *203*, 205
Raeren *70*, 71, *74*, 77, *78*, 79, *104*, 106, 122, *123*, 161–2, *161*, 199, *199*, *203*, 205, *225*, 226, *232*, *232*
Siegburg 66, *67*, *70*, 71, *74*, 77, *81*, 82, *85*, 86, 98, *99*, 131, *132*, *193*, 194, 199, *199*, *203*, 205, *249*, 250
Westerwald *203*, 205
pancheons
19th cent. Blackware *241*, 243
19th cent. red earthenware *210*, 212
post-med. Sandy *203*, 204, 209, *209*, *210*, 212
peat pot, Gritty 170, *170*
pedestal base, Cistercian *210*, 212
pipkins
Brandsby type *178*, 179
Gritty 168, *169*, 171, *171*, 172, *172*
plant pot stand, 19th cent. terracotta *241*, 243
platters, post-med. Sandy *203*, 204
posset pot lids, Cistercian copy 114, *115*
posset pots
Cistercian *70*, 71, 139, *139*, *203*, 205, *210*, 212
Staffordshire tiger 209, *209*
skillets
Developed Humber *78*, 79
Scarborough II *78*, 79
stove tiles *187*, 188
tankards, Cistercian 122, *123*
tripod pipkins
Brandsby type *178*, 179
Developed Humber *103*, 106
Low Countries redware *232*, *232*
Ryedale ware *103*, 106
urinals
Hambleton *103*, 106, 121, *123*, 248, *249*
Late Gritty *74*, 76–7
post-med. Orange 114, *115*, 131, *132*
Ryedale 66, *67*, *74*, 76, 121, *123*, 145, *146*, *187*, 188, *210*, 212, 248, *249*
vases, South Netherlands maiolica *104*, 106, 114, *115*, 235, *235*
unid. frags.
Cistercian *232*, *232*
Cistercian copy 232, *232*
Delft? *210*, 212
French? *210*, 212
Humber rim *193*, 194

post-med. Sandy *210*, 212
Stray *203*, 205
stray/late Gritty *210*, 212
ceramics
collection and provenance 315–16, 396
discussion 322–4, **322**, **325**
fabrics 317–21
Brandsby type 317–18
Cistercian 320
Cistercian copy 320–1
Developed Humber 319
Gritty 317
Hambleton 318–19
Humber 318
imported wares 321
Late Gritty 318
Midlands Yellow 321
post-med. Orange 319–20
post-med. Sandy 320
Reversed Cistercian 321
Ryedale 319
Staffordshire 321
Tudor Green 321
introduction 311, 315
methodology 316–17
chapter houses
Mount Grace *23*, 283, *285*, 360, *360*
other sites 5, 12, *12*, 15, 16, 18, *18*, *363–4*
charcoal 99, 117, 128, 141–2, 148, 384
charterhouses, English **xvii**, xvii–xviii, 6–25, **7–8**
Cheyne, John 44
chimneys
'brewhouse'/kitchen 228, 229, 261–3, *262–3*
cells 287–8, *288–9*
see also stone, architectural, chimneys
choir monks 2, 3–4, 5, **8**, **42**, 131
church 265–75, *265–7*, 364, 365, 366, 367–8, *368*
period one 265–6, *268*, 368
windows 269–70, *270*, 368
period two 266–8, *269*, 369, 370–1
windows 270–3, *271–2*, 370
period three 268–9, *268*
period four 269
architectural frags. 274–5, *276*
burial chapels 371–2
windows *265*, 273, *273–4*, 372
Hope's excavation *52*, 53
piscinas 273–4, *275*
churches, other charterhouses 5, 361–74, **362**
Beauvale *15*, 16, 362–3, *363*, 365–6, 368
Coventry 20, 363, *364*, 366
Hinton 13, 362, 363, *363*

London 18, *18*, 363, *364*, 365, 367–8, 372–3
Witham 10, 361, 362, *362*
Cistercians 6
Clark, Alison 356, 373
Cleeve Abbey, Somerset 380, 393, 401
Clifford, Elizabeth de Ros, Lady 38
Clifford, Henry, 10th Baron 31, 32
Clifford, Maud 38
cloister alleys
cell 8 89, *90*, 92, 99, *100*, 101
cell 13 *141*, 145
south-west cloister range 177
cloisters
Mount Grace 23, 24, *52*, 53–4
other sites 9–10, 11, 12, *12*, 15, 16, 18, *18*, 22
typical layout 3, 4, 5
see also great cloister; lesser cloister cells; south-west cloister range
clothing 3, 41
coal 14, 341
Cobham, Kent 379
coins 324–5
Coll, Steve 58, 261–2, 301, 304, 305
colleges 379, 380, 387
Collins, Martin 39
commerce, evidence for 347, 349, 398
conduits 156, 190, 191
see also water pipes; water supplies; water tower
context numbers 59
conversi (lay brothers) 2, 5, **8**, 41, **42**, 387–8
see also cells 16–20
Conyers, Christopher 38
Coppack, Glyn *56*, 57–8
copper alloy objects
belt hasp plate/book-strap fitting 199–200, *199*
belt plates *104*, 106, 107–8, *108*, 115, 116, 344
binding strip 152, *152*
bindings *199*, 200, *213*, 214
book clasp hinge-plate *206*, 207
book clasps 107, *108*, *132*, 134, 146–7, *146*, *197*, 198, 206–7, *206*, 346
book corner mount/strip 107, *108*, 346
book mounts *102*, 105, 107, *108*, 122, *123*, 346
book strap attachment 122, *123*
buckle frag. *132*, 134
buckle frame *139*, 140
buckle loops and plates *104*, 106, 107, *108*, 344
buckle or belt plate 122, *123*
buckle pin *102*, 105

buckle plates *102*, 105, *115*, 116, 344
buckles *115*, 116, 206, *206*
animal-headed 231, 232, 341
button *243*, 244
candle holder *132*, 134, 347
casting gate *108*, 109
clasp-mount *213*, 214
coin balances 122, *123*, 139–40, *139*, 152, *152*, 347
coin weights 102, *102*, 154, *154*, 206, *206*, 347
disk 122, *123*
fish-hook *199*, 200, 349
jetton 325–6
key-hole cover 201, *201*
lace chapes *104*, 106, *123*, 124, 152, *152*, *178*, 180, *197*, 198, *199*, 200, 201, *201*, *206*, 207, *213*, 214, *225*, 226, *232*, 233, *237*, 238, 344
links 199, *199*
mounts 107, *108*, 109, 152, *152*, *199*, 200, *213*, 214
nails *178*, 180, *237*, 238
needle *132*, 134, 346
offcut 122, *123*, *146*, 147
pens 122, *123*, *132*, 133–4, 345
pins *139*, 140, *197*, 198, *199*, 200, *232*, 233, *237*, 238, *243*, 244
spiral headed 201, *201*, 341
purse frame *243*, 244
rings 122, *123*, 206–7, *206*, *232*, 233, *243*, 244
curtain/drape *102*, 105, 107, *108*, 347
rod 102, *102*
rumbler bells *178*, 180, *232*, 233
scabbard chape *108*, 109
scoop *206*, 207
sheets 102, *102*, *108*, 109, *225*, 226, *243*, 244
skimmers/strainers *225*, 226, *243*, 244, 348
spatulas 102, *102*, 107, *108*
spoon terminal *213*, 214
strand *178*, 180
strap ends 107, *108*, 109, 344
stud 122, *123*, *243*, 244
tacks, binding *108*, 109, 346
tubes *108*, 109, *139*, 140, *237*, 238, *239*, 240
size moistening *213*, 214, *243*, 244, 345
tweezers 122, *123*, *139*, 140, 345
vessel foot *243*, 244, 348
vessel rim *231*, 232, 348, 392
wire, twisted *139*, 140, *178*, 180
wires 122, *123*, *232*, 233

INDEX

correries (lower houses) 5, 9, 12, 361, 368, 387
Coventry, Warwicks. **xvii**, *6*, **7–8**, 19–21, *20*
    cells 20, *375*, 377, 378, 384
    ceramics 396–7
    church 20, 363, *364*, 366, 373
    endowments 19, 386
    lay brothers 388
    prior's cell 381–2, *381*
    refectory 20, 393–4, *393*
Coxwold, N. Yorks. 371
Cracall, Richard de 368–9, 371
crane mechanisms 60, 94, 101
Cromwell, Thomas 43

Darcy, Conyers, 1st Earl of Holderness 45, 301
Darcy, Conyers, 2nd Earl of Holderness 304
Darell, Thomas 38–9
Dartington Hall, Devon 379
dating of the priory 255, *256*, 259–60
Davy, Sir Richard 42
Delft, Netherlands 378, *379*, 383, 399, 401
demesnes 35–7, **37**
    see also estates; landholdings
Denny Abbey, Cambs. 323
Dependen, Sir John 37
desert fathers 1, 4
devotional objects 347–8, *349*
    indulgence panel 119, 124–6, *125*
    lead plaques 134, *134*, *152*, 153
    rosary beads *213*, 214
    statue base 115–16, *115*
    type mould 134–5, *134*
diet 3–4, 334, 340–1, *342*, 389, 392
Dieulacres Abbey, Staffs. 390
distilling equipment 42, 138, 343, 398
ditches
    pre-monastery 165–6, *166*, 167
    temporary enclosure 88–9, *88*
donates 2, 5, **8**
doors
    cell 1 61–2, *61*
    cell 2 64
    cell 3 67, 68, *68*, 69
    cell 4 72, *72–3*
    cell 5 77, 78–9, *78*
    cell 6 79–80, *80*
    cell 7 83, *83*, 84
    cell 8 90, *91*, 93, 94, 95, 96, 97
    cell 9 110, 111, 113
    cell 10 118, 120
    cell 11 128, 129, *129*, 130
    cell 12 136
    cell 13 142
    cell 14 148, 149, 150, 151

    cell 15 153
    cell 18 246
    cell 22 162
    cell 23 163
    cell gardens *68*, *72*, 285
    cell, sacrist's 60
    church 266
    guest-house range 304
    kitchen 219
    prior's cell 280–1, *280*, *282*
    prison block 155
    south-west cloister range 175, 176, 182, 186, 190, 192, 196
    stables 251, 252
double houses 5
drains 298–300, *299*
    cell 1 62
    cell 2 64–5
    cell 3 68, 69
    cell 4 *72*, 73, 75
    cell 5 79
    cell 6 80, 81
    cell 7 84
    cell 8 87–8, *87*, 90, 95, 97
    cell 9 112, 113
    cell 10 118–19, *118*, 119–20
    cell 11 129–30, 131
    cell 12 137–8, *138*
    cell 13 143, 144, *144*
    cell 14 149, 150, 151
    cell 21 250
    granary and kiln house 253, 254
    kitchen area 224, 228, 238–9
    south-west cloister range 176, 184, 185, 190, 191, 196
    stables 252
    water tower *157*, 158, 159
dress items 344
    belt plates *104*, 106, 107–8, *108*, *115*, 116
    buckle plates *102*, 105, *115*, 116
    lace chapes *104*, 106, *123*, 124, 152, *152*, *178*, 180, *197*, 198, *199*, 200, 201, *201*, *206*, 207, *213*, 214, *225*, 226, *232*, 233, *237*, 238
    strap ends 107, *108*, 109

earthworks 47–51, *48*
East Harlsey, N. Yorks. 27, 36, 44
east range of the inner court 265
Eccleston, Henry 33
Edward IV, King 31, 399
Egan, Geoff 347
eggshell 340, **342**
Ela, Countess of Salisbury 11
Elizabeth I, Queen 24
Elliot, J. R. 294
Ename, Belgium 338

endowments 7, 385–7
    Mount Grace 23, 28, 29, 30, 31, 385
    other sites 8, 11, 14, 17, 19, 21, 24, 385–7
equipment 3, 41–2, 138, 323, 342–3, 348, 398
Ervynck, A. 338
Escobar, J. H. 378
Est, Robert 38
estates 33, *33*, **34–5**, 35, 44–5
    see also demesnes; landholdings
excavations, previous 51–8
experimental archaeology 348

Falls, David 40
Fauconbergh, Isabella 37
faunal remains *see* animal bones; fish bones; insect remains; shellfish
Fayrfax, John 41
Field Dalling, Norfolk *29*, 30
finds numbering 59
fireplaces
    cell 1 61
    cell 2 62
    cell 3 67, *68*
    cell 4 72, *73*
    cell 5 78
    cell 6 80
    cell 8 94
    cell 9 112
    cell 10 118
    cell 11 129
    cell 12 136
    cell 13 142
    cell 14 149
    cell 15 153
    cell 18 246
    cell 20 247–8, 293
    cell 21 293
    cell 22 162
    cell 23 163
    cell, sacrist's 60
    kitchen pentice 235
    mill 301
    south-west cloister range 182, *183*, 184
firewood 97, 98
fish bones 333–40, **336–7**, *339*
fish tanks 196, 391
fishponds
    Mount Grace 24, *48*, 50–1, 359
    other sites 10, 14, 17, 21, 392
Fletcher, Philip 12, 13, 380, 400
Fletcher, William 40
floor tiles 326–33, *327–8*, **334**
floors
    clay 182, 195, 221, 222, 223, 227, 228, 229, 230, 252

cobble 143, *143*, 145
earth 196
mortar 111, 136, 177, 185, 253, 384
silt 222, 223, 224
slate 196
stone
    cells 64, 118, 119, *119–20*, 127, 148, 149
    kitchen 216, 234
    prior's cell 191, *191*
    stables 252
tile 113, 195, 384
timber 384 *see also* joist slots
food-processing waste 391–2
foul drains 298–9, *299*
foundation of Mount Grace 27–30, *28–9*, 385
founders of charterhouses 7, **7**
founders' tombs 367
Fountains Abbey, N. Yorks.
    accommodation 380, 395
    building of 360
    ceramics 397
    diet 338, 392
    floor tiles 330, 331, 332
    latrines 401
    water supply 399
Fretton, W. G. 21
friaries 6

Gaming, Austria 391
gardens and garden pentices 24, 382–5 75 247
    cell 1 62
    cell 2 64–5, *65*, 383
    cell 3 69
    cell 4 73, *73*, 75, 383
    cell 5 79
    cell 8 *87*, *90*, 96–100, *97–8*, *101*, 383
    cell 9 112, 113, *113*, 383
    cell 10 118–20, *118*, *121*, 383
    cell 11 129–31, *130*
    cell 12 137, 138
    cell 13 143–4
    cell 14 150–1, 383
    cell 15 154
    cell 16 *244*, 245
    cell 17 246
    cell 18 246
    cell 20 248, 383, 384
    cell, sacrist's 61
    doors *68*, *72*, 285
    other sites 10, 15, *15*, 18, 20, 383
    prior's *173*, 187, 196
    sacrist's 61
Gascoigne, Sir William 285, 385
gatehouses *15*, 16, 260, 302
geology 47

Gibbs, James 10
Gilyard-Beer, Roy 55, 59, 297, 351, 380
Gisborough Priory, N. Yorks. 33, 371
glass
    bottle? 134, *134*
    vessel frag. *123*, 124
    see also window glass
Godfrey, Walter 380
Goldschmidt, E. Ph. 346
Golwynne, Thomas 31, 41–2, 323, 343, 396
graffiti 274, *276*
granary and kiln house 252–4, *252*, 264–5
Grande Chartreuse, France
    authority of 2
    buildings 3, 5, 360
    cells 374, 382
    influence of 5–6
    lay brothers 387
    monks, number of 387
    site of 1
grange 37, 47
great cloister 47–9, *48*, 59–163, 275–93, 387
    arcades 276–80, *277–9*, 387
    cells 284–6, *285*
    chapter house 283, *285*, 360, *360*
    roof fixings 275, *277*
    south-west range 280–1
    see also cell, prior's; cell, sacrist's; cells 1-15, 22, 23; prison block; water tower
Grimes, W. F. 18, 376
guest accommodation 260, *261*, 264, 394–5
guest-house range 215, 260–3, *261*, 301–5, *302–3*
Guibert de Nogent 3, 374
Guigues de Saint-Romain 2, 5, 342, 383
Guildford, Surrey 391
Guisborough, N. Yorks. 371

Haddon Hall, Derbys. 379
Hales, Alnett 42
hall, guest-house range 260
Hall, Jackie 350
Hall, Leonard 42–3
Hartenfaust, Bruno, Saint 1, 2
Harvey, J. H. 368
Hastings, Jane, Lady 39
hatches
    cell 1 61, *61*
    cell 3 67, *68*
    cell 4 72, *72*
    cell 5 77, *78*
    cell 6 80, *80*
    cell 9 111

cell 10 118
cell 11 128
cell 13 142
cell 14 149
Hatherop, Gloucs. **xvii**, *6*, **7**, 11
hearths
    cells 67, *68*, 80, 94, 129, 136–7, 246
    kitchen 217, 221, 229, *229*, 234, 239
    south-west cloister range 176, 181, *181*
Hebard, William 29
Henry II, King 6, 8
Henry III, King 11
Henry IV, King 23, 29
Henry V, King 24, 29, 30
Henry VI, King 31
Henry VIII, King 24, 43
Hinckley, Warwicks. 28, 29, *29*, 30
Hinton, D. A. 341
Hinton, Somerset **xvii**, *6*, **7–8**, 11–14, *12–13*
    cells 374, 375–6, *375*, 378, 385
    church 13, 362, **362**, 363, *363*, 364
    fishponds 14, 392
    gardens, cell 383
    kitchen 389
    prior's cell 380, *381*
    refectory 393, *393*
    water supply 400
history of Mount Grace 27–32, *28–9*
Hobley, Brian 20
Hodgeson, Geoffrey 44
Holand, Edmund de, 4th Earl of Kent 29
Holand, John de 379
Holand, Thomas de, 1st Duke of Surrey 23, 27, 28, 29, 30, 266
Hope, Sir William St John
    arcades 276, 278
    architectural frags. 350
    cell 8 109–10
    cell 19 293
    granary and stable 250
    guest-house range 261
    inventory 343
    kitchen 263
    latrines 63
    London, study of 17
    Mount Grace excavations 52–3, *52*, 255, 359
    piscina 273–4
    prison block 291
Hopton, Sir Ralph 10
Hopton, Sir Robert 10
Hough, Lincs. *29*, 30
Houghton, John 17, 43
Hugh de Chateau-Neuf, Saint 1

INDEX

Hugh of Avalon (St Hugh of Lincoln) 8, 374, 383
Hull, E. Yorks. *6*, **7–8**, 19, 386

income 7, **8**
Ingleby, Joan 38
Ingleby, John de 28
Ingleby, Thomas de 27, 357
Ingleby, Sir William 30, 33
inner courts 5
    Mount Grace 24, *24*, 49, 165–254
    other sites 12, 13, 16, 19, 20, 23, 25
inscriptions 348
    graffiti 274, *276*
    indulgence panel 124–6, *125*
    lead plaques 126, 134, *134*, *152*, 153
    type mould 134–5, *134*
insect remains 307–11, *308*, **312–15**
insulation, charcoal 384
iron objects
    buckle *243*, 244
    cleaver *213*, 214, 248
    cramp 107, *108*
    fish-knife *226*, 227, 348
    gouge *243*, 244, 346
    keys *187*, 188, *197*, 198, 205, *206*, 213, *213*, 377, 398–9
    knife, clasp 205, *206*
    knives 107, *108*, 146, *146*, *243*, 244
    knives, folding *243*, 244
    mount *206*, 206
    ox shoe 107, *108*
    pin 151, *152*
    pintle 213, *213*, 318
    punch *132*, 133, 346
    rod, gold finished 126
    scissor blade *213*, 214
    spur *243*, 244
    strap-hinges 213, *213*, *243*, *243*, 348
    tongs 99, *99*, 349
island *48*, 51
ivory objects, head of Christ *213*, 214, 347

jet objects, bead *213*, 214, 347
jetton 325–6
Joan of Navarre 30
joist slots
    cells 117, *117*, 128, *128*, 142, *142*, *147*, 148, 384
    prison block *152*, 156
joist sockets 60, 246, 248

Keen, Laurence *56*, 57, 86, 383, 384
kiln, grain drying 253, 264–5
Kirkstall Abbey, W. Yorks. 391, 392, 395, 397, 399, 401
Kirton, Robert 38

kitchen equipment 348
    cleaver *213*, 214
    fish-hook *199*, 200
    fish-knife *226*, 227
    skimmers/strainers *225*, 226, *243*, 244
    vessel foot *243*, 244
    vessel rim *231*, 232
kitchen excavations
    period one 216–17, *216*
        architectural frags. 217–18, *218*
        ceramics 217, **217**, *217*
    period two 218–23, *218–20*
        ceramics 225–7, **225**, *225–6*, **227**
        small finds 225–6, 226–7
    period three 227–31, *227*, *229–30*
        ceramics 231–3, *231–2*, **232–3**
        small finds *231–2*, 232–3
    period four 233–5, *233–4*
        ceramics 235–6, **235–6**, *235–6*
        pan weight 236, *236*
    17th cent. and later 236–7, *237*
        ceramics 237–8, *237*, **238**
        small finds *237*, 238
    17th cent. works 238–40
        ceramics 239, **239**, *239*
        tube *239*, 240
    fish bones **336–7**, 337–8, **339**
    Hope's excavation 54–5, *56*, 215, 240
    rebuilding, 20th cent. 240–1
    unstratified and unphased
        ceramics *241*, 242–3, **242**
        small finds 243–4, *243*
kitchens 388–92, *389*
Knowles, D. 40, 41, 343, 344

La Verne, France 378, *379*
label stops *61*, 285, 385
Lambert, William 38
landholdings 28–31, *29*
    see also demesnes; estates
Lascelles, Robert de (1150) 357
Lascelles, Robert (1507/8) 39
Lascelles, Robert (1744) 45
Lascelles, Thomas 45, 304
latrines and latrine pentices 298–9, *299*, 384–5, 401–2
    cell 1 62
    cell 2 62–4, *62–4*
    cell 3 68–9, *68*, *69*
    cell 4 73
    cell 5 79
    cell 6 80
    cell 7 84, *84*
    cell 8 94–6, *96*
    cell 9 112–13
    cell 10 119–20, *119–20*
    cell 11 130

    cell 12 137–8, *138*
    cell 13 142–3, *143–4*
    cell 14 149–50, *150*
    cell 16 245
    cell 18 246, *246*
    cell 19 247
    cell 20 248
    cell 21 250
    cell 22 192, 281
    cell 23 163, 282
    cell, sacrist's 60–1, *60*
    guest house tower 221, 237, 261
    south-west cloister range 192
lavatorium 276, 298, *299*
Lawrence, Robert 14, 43
lay brothers 2, 5, **8**, 41, **42**, 387–8
    see also cells 16–20
Le Inne 37, 359, 395
lead mining 9, 28
lead objects
    cakes 152, *152*, *193*, 194
    candlestick base? *243*, 244, 347
    casting run *115*, 116
    dish or pan *115*, 116, 347
    disk 154, *154*
    masonry plug 152, *152*, *243*, 244
    offcut 124, *125*
    packing 213, 214
    paint pot/inkwell *108*, 109, 345
    pipe clips *115*, 116, 124, *125*, 146, 147, 348–9
    pipes 158, 161, *161*, 201, *201*, *206*, 207, 297, 349
    plaques 126, 134, *134*, *152*, 153, 348
    plate (bookmark weight?) 124, *125*
    plumb-bob *213*, 214
    rod 124, *125*
    sieves/filters *206*, 207, 349
    star *178*, 180
    tube 134, *134*
    washers 134, *134*
    weights 152, *152*, *199*, 200, 236, *236*, 347
    window cames *108*, 109, 124, *125*
    writing leads 124, *125*, 146, 147, 345
Leahy, K. 349
leat, mill 49–50, 295
Leek, Robert 31
Legh, Thomas 44
Leland, John 19
lesser cloister cells 244–50, *244–6*, **247**, *249–50*, 292–3, *293*
letters of confraternity 348
Leyton, Thomas 44
library
    books 38, 41, 43, 343
    building 292
lighting 347

candle holder *132*, 134
candlestick base? *243*, 244
dish or pan *115*, 116
Lincoln, Lincs. 379, 391
locking bars 72, 78, 79, 83, 84, 93, 377
Lockington, Thomas 36
Lokwood, Thomas 38
London charterhouse **xvii**, *6*, 7, **7–8**, 17–19, *18*
    cells 374, 376, 378, 379
    ceramics 397
    church 363, *364*, 365, 367–8, 372–3
    diet 392
    endowments 39, 385–6
    kitchens 388, 389
    lay brothers 388
    panelling 385
    prior's cell 380
    refectory 394
    and suppression 43
    water supply 295, 399, 400
Long Bennington, Lincs. *29*, 30
Love, Nicholas 39–40, 343
lower houses 5, 9, 12, 361, 368, 387
lower terrace *48*, 49–51
Luxford, Julian 394

McGarvie, M. 10
MacGregor, A. 347
Magdalen College, Oxford 387
Magna Vita S Hugonis 374
Maney, Sir Walter 17, *18*
mangers 252
Marshall, Chris 347
Marshall, Richard 44
martyrs 43
Mary I, Queen 24
mason's marks 255, **257–9**, *259*
masses 38–9, 371–2
Mauleverer, Timothy 45
Mayhew, N. 154, 206, 347
Meditationes vitae Christi 39–40
Mekeness, Michael 21
metalworking tongs 99, *99*, 349
Methley, Richard 31, 39, 41, 343–4, 398
Middlemore, Humphrey 43
mill 50, 300–1, *300*
mill leat 49–50, 295
Ministry of Works 55–7
Minsters' Accounts **34–5**
Minting, Lincs. *29*, 30
moat *48*, 51, 359
monastery
    layout 4–6, *4*
    planning and development 359–61, *360*
monastic living 1–2, *3*
money, handling of 347, 349, 398
monks 2, 3–4, 5, **8**, **42**, 131

Mordefroid, J.-L. 378
mortar mix pit 238
Morton Grange, N. Yorks. 36, 44, 357
Mount Grace, N. Yorks. *6*, 7–8, **7–8**, 23–4, *23*
    estates, demesnes and site 32–7, *33*, **34–5**, *36*, **37**
    excavations, previous 51–8, *56*
    history 27–32, *28–9*
    people 37–43, **40**, **42**
    site 47–51, *48*
    suppression 43–4
Mount Lodge Farm, N. Yorks. 37, 47
Mowbray, Thomas, 1st Duke of Norfolk 21

Neer, W. van 338
Newey, James 44
Nieuwlicht, Netherlands xx, 366, *366–7*, 373–4, 378, 383, 386–7, 397, 402
Northallerton, N. Yorks. 267, 371
Norton, John 31, 40
Norton, Sir Robert 32

Old Malton Priory, N. Yorks. 370
oratories 365, 384
    cell 22 162, 281, *283*
    cell 23 282
    prior's 190, 281, 381
outer courts 5, 16, 17, *17*, 22, 23
ovens 192, 222, 228, 229, 234, 283

Paleman, John 38
panelling 92, 94, 111, 385
paths 97, *98*, 99–100, 131
paving *see* floor tiles; floors
pensioners 42, **42**, 44
petrology of floor tiles 332–3
phases 255, *256*, 259–60
piles, pine *157*, 158
Pilgrimage of Grace 44
pilgrims 348, 349, 398
pipeclay objects
    pipe bowl *210*, 213
    statue base 115–16, *115*, 347–8
pits *90*, 92, 167
plant remains 340, **342**
plaster 80, 128, 137, 148–9
Pole, Michael de la, 1st Earl of Suffolk 19
Pole, William de la, 1st Duke of Suffolk 19
polishing monk 131
ponds *see* fishponds
porches 53, 186, 230, 268, 304
postholes
    crane mechanism *100*, 101
    kitchen 216, *216*, 390

pentice wall *141*, 144
plant holes *117*, 120
scaffolding *109*, 110, 175
south-west cloister range 166–7, *166*, 172, *173*, 174
Poynter, Ambrose 55, 301, 304, 305, 350
precinct walls
    cell 13 144, *144*
    other sites 13, *15*, 16, 20, *20*, 21
priors 39–40, **40**
prison block *152*, 154–6, *155*, *174*, 290–1, *292*
Pryme, Abraham de la 21–2
Pynkey, Robert 38

Rawson, Sir John 31, 395
Read, Brian 349
recesses 119
    see also candle niches; tap niches; windows
Redman, Sir Richard 385
refectories 5, 392–4, *393*
    Mount Grace 175, 182, 184, 185, 280, *393*, 394
    other sites 12, 18, 20, 393, *393*, 394
Refectorium salutis (Methley) 41
research design xix–xx
Richard II, King 19, 27, 28
Richard III, King 30, 386
Richmond, N. Yorks. 31, 369–70, *370*
Richmond Palace, Surrey 24
Rievaulx Abbey, N. Yorks. 36, 341, 352, 382
Riley, William 51, *52*
roads 49, 240
Robert of Molesme, Saint 1
Rodeck, Pieter 301
Rokeby, Ralph 44
Rolle, Richard 343
Roos, Eleanor de 38
Roos, Robert 44
Rose, J. 294
rubbish pits *109*, 110
Rule of St Benedict 2, 4
Russell, Richard 38
Rutter, J. G. 331
Rylatt, Margaret 20

sacristy 283
salt boxes 80, 94
Saunders, Andrew Downing 55, *56*
Saunderson, John 43
Sawley Abbey, Lancs. *327*, 331, 391, 397, 399
Scarborough, N. Yorks. 331
school, Coventry 20
Scrope, Richard, Archbishop *61*, 285, 385

INDEX

Sessions, William 348
sewers 298–9, *299*
Seymour, Edward, 1st Duke of Somerset 24
Sheen, Surrey *6*, *7*, **7–8**, 24–5, *25*
    books 343
    endowments 29, 30
    expulsion of 42, 43
    water supply 399
shell palettes *139*, 140, *146*, 147, 344–5
shellfish 340, **342**
Sheppard, J. M. 346
Sherlock, David *56*, 57, 250
shields, label stop *61*, 285, 385
Shipley, Robert 43
silver coins 324–5
sink, cell 3 68
site overview 47–51
Soden, Iain 20, 381, 394
Song of Songs 382
south range of the inner court
    eastern building 252–4, *252*, 264–5
    granary and kiln house 252–4, *252*, 264–5
    stables 251–2, *251*, 264
    western building 264
south-west cloister range 165–215, 280–1, *281–2*
    pre-monastery 165–72
        ceramics 167–72, *167*, **168**, *169–72*, **170–2**
        ditches 165–6, *166*, 167
        pits 167
        timber buildings 166–7, *167*
    period one 172–82, *174*
        architectural frags. 180–2, *180–1*
        bench 176
        buttresses 174–5
        ceramics 177–9, *178*, **179**
        cloister alley 177
        corridors 175–6
        doors 175, 176
        drains 176
        floors 176
        foundation trenches 174
        hearth 176
        passage 175
        prior's cell 177
        prior's garden *173*
        refectory 175
        small finds *178*, 179–80
        south-east corner 172
        timber building 172, *173*, 174
        walls 174, 175, 176
        windows *166*, 175, 177
    period two 182–9, *183*
        arcade 185–6
        architectural frags. 188–9, *188*
        buttresses 184

ceramics 187–8, *187*, **188**
corridors 182
doors 182, 186
drains 184, 185
fireplaces 182, *183*, 184
floors 182
garden *173*
pentice to kitchen 185
porch 186
prior's cell 182, 184
prior's garden 187
refectory 182, 184, 185
small finds *187*, 188
stairs 185
tank 184
upper floor 183–4
walls 182
water pipes 183, 184, 186
yard 186, *186*
period three 189–94, *189*
    architectural frags. 194, *194*
    bench 191
    ceramics 193–4, **193**, *193*
    conduits 191
    doors 190, 192
    drains 190, 191
    floors 191, *191*
    latrine? 192
    oriel window 190
    oven 192
    prior's cell 189–90, *190*
    small find, lead cake *193*, 194
    stairs 190
    water pipes 191
period four 194–201, *195*
    ceramics 197–8, *197*, **198**, 200, **200**, *201*, **202**
    corridor/passage 195
    doors 196
    drains 196
    prior's cell 195
    prior's garden 196
    small finds *197*, 198, 201, *201*
    tank rooms 196
demolition 201–7
    bowl or piscina 207, *207*
    ceramics 202, *203*, 204–5, **204**
    prior's cell 201
    small finds 205–7, *206*
    south wall 201–2
17th century 207–9, **208**, *208–9*
Hope's excavation 209–15
    architectural frags. 214–15, *215*
    ceramics *210*, 211–13, **211**
    excavations 209, 211
    small finds 213–14, *213*
souvenir production 347, 349
Spencer, William 36
Spriggs, Jim 348

St Cross, Winchester, Hants. 379–80
St Gall Abbey, Switzerland 4, *4*, 383
St Giles' Hospital, Norwich 387
St John's Well 295, *295*, 296
St Salvator Abbey, Ename 338
stables 251–2, *251*, 264
stairs
    cell 1 61
    cell 3 67, *68*
    cell 4 72
    cell 5 78
    cell 6 80
    cell 7 83, *83*
    cell 9 112
    cell 10 117–18
    cell 11 128, *129*
    cell 12 136, *137*
    cell 13 142
    cell 14 149
    cell 15 153
    guest-house range 304
    kitchen area 223, 230, *230*, 231, 235
    south-west cloister range 185, 190, 195
Stanley, Henry 53
stone, architectural 349–50
    arcades, cloister 276–80, *277–9*
    basin 215, *215*
    basin or piscina 207, *207*
    buttress caps 110, *110*, 135, *135*
    chimney bases 188–9, *188*, 245, *245*, 288, *288*
    chimney caps 110, *110*, 126, *127*, 135, *135*, 141, *141*, 181, *181*, *188*, 189, 245, *245*, 288, *289*, 293, *293*
    chimneys 126, *127*, 135, *135*
    cills *135*, 136, *188*, 189
    coping, trefoil-topped 217–18, *218*
    corbel 351, *351*
    gable coping 290, *292*
    gable crosses and bases 288–90, *289–91*
    gargoyle 275, *276*
    grave cover 274–5, *276*
    head, tap niche 351–2, *351*
    hearth 181, *181*
    jamb and cill 180–1, *180*
    jambs *181*, 182, 215, *215*
    kerb *162*, 163
    kneeler, gable 352, *352*
    label stop shields *61*, 285, 385
    layout design for screenwork 351, *351*
    lintel 351, *351*
    mullions *181*, *181*, 182, 287, *287*
    parapet 135, *135*, 215, *215*
    parapet coping *188*, 189, 352, *352*
    piscinas 273–4, *275*
    pivot stone 126, *127*

plinth course, chamfered 181, *181*
screen 274, *276*
steps 274, *276*
string course or cornice 141, *141*
string courses 161, *161*, 215, *215*
tank 214–15, *215*
tray *351*, 352
wall coping 135, *135*, 352, *353*
water-pipe casing 161, *161*
water tank *351*, 352
water tower frags. 159, *159*
waterspout 127, *127*
window, oriel 194, *194*
window tracery 181–2, *181*, 283, *285*
windows
    church, period one 269–70, *270*, *368*
    church, period two 270–3, *271–2*
    church burial chapels *265*, 273, *273–4*, 372
windows, four-light 286, *286–7*
windows, single-light 286, *286*
stone objects
    bead, jet *213*, 214, 347
    graphite object 126
    grinding stone *139*, 140, 345
    indulgence panel 119, 124–6, *125*, 348
    mortar *126*, 127
    moulds 124, *125*, 154, *154*
    type mould 134–5, *134*, 348
Stopford, Jenny 326
stoup, holy water 266, 283
Strachey, J. 362
Strangways, Sir James (1423) 31
Strangways, Sir James (1540) 33, 36, 37, 44, 301
Strangways, James (of Westlathes) 39
Strangways, Jane 39
Strangways, Sir Thomas 39, 43
suppression **8**
    Mount Grace 23, 43–4, 100–1
    other sites 9, 12, 14, 17, 20, 21, 24
surface drainage *299*, 300
Swainson, Albert 56, 59
Swinburne, Elizabeth 39

Talbot, Edmund 38
Talman, William 10
tank rooms 196
tanks
    17th cent. kitchen area 238
    cell 2 *62*, 65
    cell 8 87, *88*, 95
    cell 14 149, *150*
    cell 20 248
    cell 21 250

east range of the inner court 265
kitchen area 196, 223, 228, 235
south-west cloister range 184
tap niches 297, *298–9*
    cell 1 62
    cell 2 65
    cell 3 69
    cell 4 73, *73*
    cell 6 80
    cell 7 83
    cell 8 95–6
    cell 9 112
    cell 10 119
    cell 11 129, 130
    cell 12 136, *137*
    cell 13 144
    cell 14 151
    cell 23 163, 282
    cell, sacrist's 61
terrace 86–7, *87*, 157
Theophilus 349
Thicket, N. Yorks. 390
Thirsk, N. Yorks. 371, 372
Thompson, Margaret 27
Thompson, Michael 56
Thornholme Priory, Lincs. 253, 391, 392
Thwaites, Edmund 39
tiles *see* ceramic floor tiles
timber buildings/structures
    pre-monastery 166–7, *167*
    period one 88–9, 172, *173*, 174, 360, 374
    cell 3 latrine 69
    cell 22 162, 281
    cell 23 162, 281
Treason Act (1535) 43
Trethewy, Robert 28
type mould 134–5, *134*

upper houses 5

Valor Ecclesiasticus 7, **34–5**, 44
Vicars Choral, Lincoln 379
Visconti, Gian Galeazzo 30
Visconti, Lucy de 29, 30
Vos, H. H. 378

wall coverings
    panelling 92, 94, 111, 385
    plaster 80, 128, 137, 148–9
wall paintings 20, 393
Ware, Herts. 28, 29, *29*, 30
Wareham, Dorset 28, 29, *29*, 30
water mill 295, 300–1, *300*
water pipes 297
    conduits 156, 190, 191
    kitchen area 224, 228
    prior's cell 183, 184, 186, 191

water supplies 399–401, 403
    Beauvale 15, 400
    London 18, 19, 295, 297, 399, 400
    Mount Grace 55, *56*, 293–8, *294–8*, 399, 400–1
water tower 156–62, *157–61*, **162**, 276, 295, 400–1
Watson, Jacqui 346
Watson, Thurstan 41
Weaver, John 57, 87
weaving equipment 42, 343, 398
Webb, Philip 304–5
Webster, Augustine, Saint 21, 43
weighing and weights 347
    coin balances 122, *123*, 139–40, *139*, 152, *152*
    coin weights 102, *102*, 154, *154*, 206, *206*
    pan weights 152, *152*, 199, 200, 236, *236*
well houses 295, *295–7*, 296–7, 401
Wells, John 40
Wenham, Peter 22
West Cowick, E. Yorks. 310, 318, 320
Westminster, London 391–2
Widrington, John 30
William, a lay brother 41
William Longespée, 3rd Earl of Salisbury 11
Williams, Rich 57, 87
Wilson, John 31, 32, 40, 42, 44, 395
Wilson, Robert 36
window glass 352–3, *354–5*, 355–6, 373–4
    cell 8 96, *97*, 99
    water tower 158, 160
windows
    cell 3 67–8, 287, *287*
    cell 4 72
    cell 5 78
    cell 7 83, 385
    cell 8 93–4, *94*
    cell 10 117, 118, 385
    cell 15 153
    cell 18 246
    cell 22 162, 281
    cells 286, *286–7*
    chapter house 283, *285*
    church
        period one 266, 269–70, *270*, 368, *368*
        period two 267, 268, 270–3, *271–2*, 370
        period three 268–9
        burial chapels *265*, 273, *273–4*, 372
    cloister arcade 276, 277–9
    granary 253–4
    oriel 190, 194, *194*, 280, 281, *282*

INDEX

prior's cell 190, 194, *194*, 280, *282*
south-west cloister range *166*, 175, 177
stables 252
water tower 160, *160*
Witham, Somerset *6*, **7–8**, 8–11, *9*
   cells 10, 374, *375*, 376
   church 361, 362, *362*, 364
   gardens, cell 383

Withen, Agnes 38
women, proscription of 38
wooden objects
   boards, oak 77, 86
   bowls 67, *67*, *70*, 71–2, 346–7, 392
   furniture frag. 86
   spoon or ladle *70*, 72, 346
Worcester, William 24
Worcester College, Oxford 380

Wyndham, Sir William 10

X-ray fluorescence spectrometry (XRF) 333, **334**, 344

Yeveley, Henry 330, 363, 368, 379, 380
York Minster, N. Yorks. 330, 368, 370

Zouch, William, 2nd Baron 19